HOLT
SOCIAL
STUDIES

United States History
Beginnings to 1877

William Deverell
Deborah Gray White

HOLT, RINEHART AND WINSTON
A Harcourt Education Company
Orlando · **Austin** · New York · San Diego · Toronto · London

Authors

William Deverell

William Deverell is Professor of History at the University of Southern California and Director of the Huntington-USC Institute on California and the West. He is the author of *Railroad Crossing: Californians and the Railroad, 1850–1910* and *Whitewashed Adobe: The Rise of Los Angeles and the Remaking of the Mexican Past.* He is the editor of the *Blackwell Companion to the American West.* With Greg Hise, he co-authored *Eden by Design: The 1930 Olmsted-Bartholomew Plan for the Los Angeles Region* and co-edited *Land of Sunshine: The Environmental History of Metropolitan Los Angeles.* He is the former chairman of the California Council for the Humanities and was the 2002–2003 Fellow of the John Randolph Haynes and Dora Haynes Foundation of Los Angeles.

Deborah Gray White

Deborah Gray White, a former New York City school teacher, is Distinguished Professor of History at Rutgers University in New Brunswick, New Jersey. A specialist in American history and the history of African Americans, she is the author of several books including: *Ar'n't I A Woman? Female Slaves in the Plantation South; Too Heavy a Load: Black Women in Defense of Themselves, 1894–1994;* and *Let My People Go, African Americans 1804–1860,* Volume 4 in the *Young Oxford History of African Americans.*

Program Consultants

Contributing Author

Kylene Beers, Ed.D.
Senior Reading Researcher
School Development Program
Yale University
New Haven, Connecticut

A former middle school teacher, Dr. Beers has turned her commitment to helping struggling readers into the major focus of her research, writing, speaking, and teaching. She is the current editor of the National Council of Teachers of English Literacy journal *Voices from the Middle* and author of *When Kids Can't Read: What Teachers Can Do* (Heinemann. 2002).

General Editor

Frances Marie Gipson, Ph.D.
Secondary Literacy
Los Angeles Unified School District
Los Angeles, California

In her current position, Dr. Gipson guides reform work for secondary instruction and supports its implementation. She has designed curriculum at the district, state, and national levels. Her leadership of a coaching collaborative with Subject Matter Projects of the University of California at Los Angeles evolved from her commitment to rigorous instruction and to meeting needs of diverse learners.

Senior Literature and Writing Specialist

Carol Jago
English Department Chairperson
Santa Monica High School
Santa Monica, California

An English teacher at the middle and high school levels for 26 years, Carol Jago also directs the reading and literature project at UCLA and writes a weekly education column for the *Los Angeles Times*. She has been published in numerous professional journals and has authored several books, including *Cohesive Writing: Why Concept Is Not Enough* (Boynton/Cook. 2002).

Consultants

Martha H. Ball, M.A.
Religion Consultant
Utah 3Rs Project Director
Utah State Office of Education
Salt Lake City, Utah

John Ferguson, M.T.S., J.D.
Senior Religion Consultant
Assistant Professor
Political Science/Criminal Justice
Howard Payne University
Brownwood, Texas

Rabbi Gary M. Bretton-Granatoor
Religion Consultant
Director of Interfaith Affairs
Anti-Defamation League
New York, New York

J. Frank Malaret
Senior Consultant
Dean, Downtown and West Sacramento Outreach Centers
Sacramento City College
Sacramento, California

Kimberly A. Plummer, M.A.
Senior Consultant
History–Social Science Educator/Advisor
Holt, Rinehart & Winston
California Consultant Manager

Andrés Reséndez, Ph.D.
Senior Consultant
Assistant Professor
Department of History
University of California at Davis
Davis, California

Academic Reviewers

Ann C. Bailey, Ph.D.
Spelman College
Atlanta, Georgia

Albert Camarillo, Ph.D.
Department of History
Stanford University

Larry Conyers, Ph.D.
Department of Anthropology
University of Denver

Willard Gatewood, Ph.D.
Emeritus Alumni Distinguished Professor
Department of History
University of Arkansas

Christopher Hendricks, Ph.D.
Department of History
Armstrong Atlantic State University
Savannah, Georgia

Skip Hyser, Ph.D.
Department of History
James Madison University
Harrisonburg, Virginia

Yasuhide Kawashima, Ph.D.
Department of History
University of Texas at El Paso

Brenda E. Stevenson, Ph.D.
Department of History
UCLA
Los Angeles, California

David Switzer, Ph.D.
Department of Social Studies
Plymouth State University

Jessica Wang, Ph.D.
Department of History
UCLA
Los Angeles, California

Nan Woodruff, Ph.D.
Department of History
Pennsylvania State University

Craig Yirush, Ph.D.
Department of History
UCLA
Los Angeles, California

Educational Reviewers

John Bilsky
Linton Middle School
Penn Hills, Pennsylvania

Michael Bloom
Ross School
Ross, California

Julie Chan, Ed.D.
Director, Literacy Instruction
Newport-Mesa Unified School District
Costa Mesa, California

Ed Felton
Coopersville Public School District
Ada, Michigan

Tim Gearhart
Daniel Lewis Middle School
Paso Robles, California

Tina Nelson
Baltimore County Public School District
Baltimore, Maryland

Vera Roberts
Lynwood Middle School
Los Angeles, California

Wendy Schanberger
Hereford Middle School
Monkton, Maryland

Teacher's Edition

Contents

Contents

UNIT 1

Connecting With the Past: Our Colonial Heritage Beginnings to 1783

History's Impact Video Series
Exploration of North America

Poor Richard, 1734.
·AN·
Almanack
For the Year of Christ
1734,
Being the second after LEAPYEAR:

Features

QUICK FACTS

Examine key facts and concepts quickly and easily with graphics.

Regions of the United States, Early 1800s **QUICK FACTS**

NORTH
- Economy base on manufacturing
- Support for tariffs—American goods could be sold at lower prices than could British goods

SOUTH
- Economy base on agriculture
- Opposition to tariffs, which increased the cost of imported goods

WEST
- Emerging economy
- Support for internal improvements and the sale of public lands

LINKING TO TODAY

Link people and events from the past to the world you live in today.

Points of View

See how different people have interpreted historical issues in different ways.

Political Cartoons

Interpret political cartoons to learn about U.S. history.

Supreme Court Decisions

Study the impact of Supreme Court decisions on U.S. history.

Social Studies Skills

Learn, practice, and apply the skills you need to study and analyze history.

Interdisciplinary Connections

Learn history through connections to other disciplines.

Writing Workshops

Learn to write about history.

Reading Social Studies

Learn and practice skills that will help you read your social studies lessons.

Literature in History

Learn about the beliefs and experiences of people who lived in other times and places in excerpts from literature.

FOCUS ON WRITING AND SPEAKING

Use writing and speaking skills to study and reflect on the events and people who made history.

Primary Sources

Relive history through eyewitness accounts, literature, and documents.

Primary Sources *continued*

Maps

Interpret maps to see where important events happened and analyze how geography has influenced history.

British Retreat from Boston

Charts, Graphics, and Time Lines

Analyze information presented visually to learn more about history.

QUICK FACTS

Causes and Effects of the Civil War

Causes
- Disagreement over the institution of slavery
- Economic differences
- Political differences

Effects
- Slavery ends
- 620,000 Americans killed
- Military districts created
- Southern economy in ruins

ANALYSIS SKILL **INTERPRETING CHARTS**

How important was slavery to the Civil War?

HOLT SOCIAL STUDIES

involves students in the study of history and helps them discover **a story well told**

Stunning visuals put students into the context of the time period, bringing people, places, and concepts to life.

History Close-up

Ranch Life

Spanish and Mexican *vaqueros*, or cowboys, were expert horseriders. They used their horses to herd cattle on the ranches of the Spanish Southwest.

Vaqueros were known for their specially designed hats.

Leather chaps protected riders from dust and scrapes.

Saddles like these were highly prized by *vaqueros*.

ANALYSIS SKILL **ANALYZING VISUALS**

What features of the *vaqueros'* life are shown in this painting?

318 CHAPTER 10

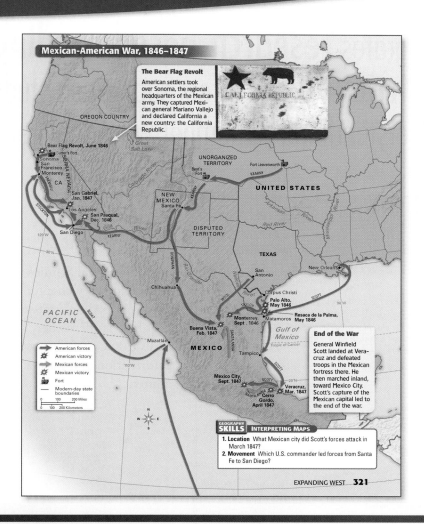

Mexican-American War, 1846–1847

The Bear Flag Revolt
American settlers took over Sonoma, the regional headquarters of the Mexican army. They captured Mexican general Mariano Vallejo and declared California a new country: the California Republic.

CALIFORNIA REPUBLIC

OREGON COUNTRY

Bear Flag Revolt, June 1846
Sutter's Fort
Sonoma
San Francisco
Monterey
SIERRA NEVADA
CA
San Gabriel, Jan. 1847
Los Angeles
San Pasqual, Dec. 1846
San Diego
120°W
30°N

Great Salt Lake

UNORGANIZED TERRITORY
Bent's Fort
Fort Leavenworth
KEARNY

Colorado River

NEW MEXICO
Santa Fe

UNITED STATES

DISPUTED TERRITORY

Gila River

Red River

Arkansas River

Missouri River

Mississippi River

TEXAS

San Antonio

Chihuahua

Corpus Christi

Palo Alto, May 1846
Resaca de la Palma, May 1846
Monterrey Sept. 1846
Matamoros

Buena Vista, Feb. 1847

PACIFIC OCEAN

Mazatlán

MEXICO

Tampico

110°W

Gulf of Mexico
Tropic of Cancer

New Orleans

90°W

End of the War
General Winfield Scott landed at Veracruz and defeated troops in the Mexican fortress there. He then marched inland, toward Mexico City. Scott's capture of the Mexican capital led to the end of the war.

Mexico City, Sept. 1847
Cerro Gordo, April 1847
Veracruz, Mar. 1847
SANTA ANNA
SCOTT

KEY
→ American forces
⚔ American victory
→ Mexican forces
⚔ Mexican victory
🏰 Fort
— Modern-day state boundaries

0   100   200 Miles
0 100 200 Kilometers

N
W E
S

GEOGRAPHY SKILLS | INTERPRETING MAPS
1. **Location** What Mexican city did Scott's forces attack in March 1847?
2. **Movement** Which U.S. commander led forces from Santa Fe to San Diego?

EXPANDING WEST **321**

Holt's unique maps offer another way to engage students, showing them the connection between history and geography. **Online Interactive Maps** provide activities that develop map skills.

The California Gold Rush

If **YOU** were there...

You are a low-paid bank clerk in New England in early 1849. Local newspaper headlines are shouting exciting news: "Gold Is Discovered in California! Thousands Are on Their Way West." You enjoy having a steady job. However, some of your friends are planning to go West, and you are being influenced by their excitement. Your friends are even buying pickaxes and other mining equipment. They urge you to go West with them.

Would you go west to seek your fortune in California? Why?

If You Were There, introducing each section, challenges students with a provocative question designed to make the history presented in that section come alive.

HOLT

History's Impact

▶ **video series**
Watch the video to understand the impact of conflict on settlement in the West.

History's Impact Video Program helps students connect history to events in the current world (available on VHS, DVD, and the *Online Textbook*).

HOLT SOCIAL STUDIES

integrates **research-based reading instruction** and offers support so students understand and remember what they learn

Reading Social Studies
by Kylene Beers

| Economics | Geography | Politics | Religion | Society and Culture | Science and Technology |

Focus on Themes In this chapter, you will read about the American people as they continued their westward expansion. You will read about the famous Oregon and Santa Fe trails, Texas's fight for independence from Mexico, and Mexico's war with the United States. Finally, you will read about the California Gold Rush that brought thousands of people west. As you read each section, you will see how **economic** issues affected the growth of different **geographic** areas.

Vocabulary in Context

FOCUS ON READING In Chapter 3 you learned how writers sometimes give you clues to a word's meaning in the same or a nearby sentence. Those clues are usually definitions, restatements in different words, or comparisons or contrasts. But what do you do if you don't know the word and the writer doesn't think to give you a direct clue?

Using Broader Context Clues If the writer doesn't give you one of those direct clues, you have to try to figure out the meaning of the word for yourself.

1. Read the whole paragraph and look for information that will help you figure out the meaning.

2. Look up the word in the dictionary to be sure of its meaning.

Notice how a student used information from the whole paragraph to learn the meaning of two unknown words.

"In 1844, the Whigs passed up Tyler and chose Senator Henry Clay of Kentucky as their presidential candidate. At first opposing *annexation*, Clay changed his mind due to pressure from southern voters. The Democratic Party chose former Tennessee governor James K. Polk to oppose Clay. Both candidates strongly favored acquiring Texas and Oregon, but Polk was perceived as the *expansionist* candidate." *(p. 317)*

I'm not sure about *annexation*. The southerners convinced Clay to be for it. Maybe if I read some more.

Oh, both presidential candidates favored *acquiring* Texas and Oregon. Maybe *annexation* means almost the same thing as *acquiring*. I'll check the dictionary.

The dictionary definition is "to add or attach." That's close. Now what about *expansionist*? I know one meaning of *expand* is similar to *add*. An *expansionist* was probably someone who wanted to add to or expand the country.

306 CHAPTER 10

Reading Social Studies lessons in every chapter focus on reading strategies that help students develop skills to successfully access information and master content.

The *Interactive Reader and Study Guide* provides **all** students with additional support to master content and standards through strategies and review.

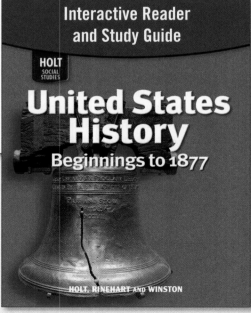

Interactive Reader and Study Guide

HOLT SOCIAL STUDIES

United States History
Beginnings to 1877

HOLT, RINEHART AND WINSTON

live ink®
a new way to read

Live Ink Online Reading Help is an online tool that displays the text of the *Holt Social Studies Online Editions* in a format that has been proven to improve comprehension and increase test scores.

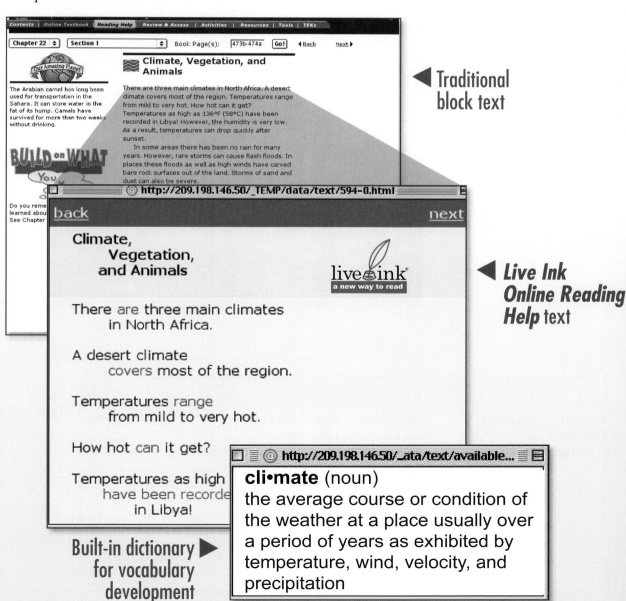

◀ Traditional block text

◀ *Live Ink Online Reading Help* text

Built-in dictionary ▶ for vocabulary development

cli•mate (noun)
the average course or condition of the weather at a place usually over a period of years as exhibited by temperature, wind, velocity, and precipitation

HOLT SOCIAL STUDIES

ensures you can **differentiate** instruction for all students

Holt's award-winning *One-Stop Planner® CD-ROM* provides easy-to-use print and technology resources that allow teachers to maximize their effectiveness and save time in planning, teaching, and assessing each lesson.

One-Stop Planner
with Test Generator

One-Stop Planner®
with ExamView® Pro Test Generator

HOLT
SOCIAL
STUDIES

United States History
Beginnings to 1877

Differentiating Instruction

English-Language Learners
Below Level
Prep Required

Materials: magazines, poster board, art supplies

California Life Collage Organize students into small groups. Have each group create a collage, in which one half of the collage shows images related to life in California under Spanish rule and the other half depicts life in California under Mexican rule. **LS** Visual/Spatial

🖎 Alternative Assessment Handbook, Rubric 8: Collages

Special Needs Learners
Below Level

Compare-and-Contrast Chart Create a chart with two columns and two rows for students to see. Title the chart *California under Spain and Mexico.* Label the columns *Similarities* and *Differences* and the rows *Spanish Rule* and *Mexican Rule.* Have students work in pairs to complete the chart. Then discuss the answers as a class. **LS** Visual/Spatial

🖎 Alternative Assessment Handbook, Rubric 7: Charts

In the *Teacher's Edition,* **Differentiating Instruction** provides additional strategies for English-Language Learners, Advanced Learners, and Special Education Students.

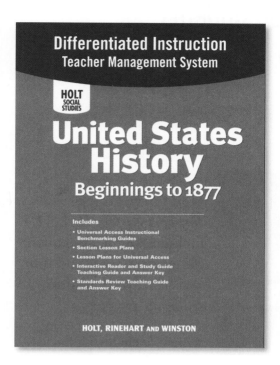

Holt's *Differentiated Instruction Teacher Management System* offers a wide variety of planning and instructional strategies all in one place.

The system includes:
• Section Lesson Plans
• Lesson Plans for Differentiated Instruction
• Instructional Benchmarking Guides
• Interactive Reader and Study Guide Teaching Guide

The *Differentiated Instruction Modified Worksheets and Tests CD-ROM* provides key resources modified to meet the specifications for students' **Individualized Education Plans (IEPs)**.

Student Edition on Audio CD Program is a direct read of the *Student Edition,* providing extra support for auditory learners, English-language learners, and reluctant readers. Also available is the *Spanish Chapter Summaries Audio CD Program.*

HOLT SOCIAL STUDIES

includes a range of **assessment options** to monitor students' progress effectively

Holt's new *Progress Assessment Support System (P.A.S.S.)* includes all the assessment for every chapter and unit and helps you monitor students' progress.

P.A.S.S. includes
• Section Quizzes
• Chapter Tests
• Diagnostic Pretest
• Unit Tests
• End-of-the-Year Test
• Assessment Rubrics

The ExamView® Pro Test Generator, on the *One-Stop Planner,* makes it easy for you to reteach and offer more support to those students who need it.

A new technology,
Holt Online Assessment,
helps you assess students'
mastery of the content.

▲ STEP 1
Create a test

▲ STEP 2
Assign a test

◀ STEP 3
View Reports

Making History–Social Science Accessible to English Learners

by Dr. Julie Chan

Dr. Julie Chan, Ed.D., is Director of Literacy Instruction in the Newport-Mesa Unified School District, located in Costa Mesa, California. She is a member of the California Reading and Literature Project (CRLP), UCI/Orange County region, and serves on the state level CRLP Secondary Academic Literacy Toolkit (SALT) development team. Dr. Chan also teaches graduate courses on "The Sociocultural Contexts of Literacy and Learning" in the Masters of Reading program at CSU Fullerton and "Linguistics in Action in the Multicultural Classroom" at Concordia University.

As increasing numbers of English Language Learners (ELLs) enter California's secondary schools each year, it is incumbent upon all of us to help each student fully access the History–Social Science curriculum.

History–Social Science instruction relies heavily on language—oral language (listening/speaking) and written language (reading/writing). Because of their limited—but developing—proficiency in the English language, ELLs have a difficult time grasping the information presented orally by the teacher, as well as struggling when reading the printed text in History–Social Science textbooks.

Chamot and O'Malley (1994) identified six areas where teachers can support ELLs: (1) conceptual understanding, (2) vocabulary, (3) language functions and discourse, (4) structures, (5) academic language skills, and (6) study skills and learning strategies. Here are some ways that teachers can make History–Social Science accessible to English Language Learners.

Conceptual Understanding While all students need to develop the concepts of time, chronology, distance, and differing ways of life, some ELLs may have never studied world history or geography and History–Social Science can be one way to learn about the United States. Teachers could approach unfamiliar concepts and content through what the *History–Social Science Framework* calls "a story well told" by reading aloud trade books to build background knowledge and/or to provide a mental model at the beginning of a unit of study.

Vocabulary Students need to learn the specialized and technical terminology of History–Social Science in order to discuss and report on the ideas studied. As students move up through the grades, the academic vocabulary of History–Social Science becomes increasingly difficult because of the complexity of the concepts it represents. Thus, knowing which words and how and when to introduce them is critical.

Language Functions and Discourse According to the California Content Standards, middle school students are expected to analyze, compare, contrast, and make judgments about social studies information. In contrast to the narrative discourse of ELD texts, social studies textbooks feature expository discourse across six text structures. By using graphic organizers that match each of the text structures, teachers can make abstract ideas, concepts, and content visible and concrete for ELLs.

Differentiating Instruction

English-Language Learners

1. Review with students important terms from this section with which they may not be familiar: *apportionment, concurrent powers, delegated powers, distinct, dual sovereignty, elastic clause, executive orders, federal system, impeach, pardons, representative democracy, reserved powers, veto.*

2. Draw a tic-tac-toe diagram (nine-square grid) for students to see. Divide the students into two groups: Xs and Os.

3. Determine which group will go first, then select one student in that group to answer a question. Given one of the vocabulary words, students are to define the term and use it in a sentence. Upon answering correctly, that group puts their mark in the square of their choosing. The first group to get three in a row wins. **LS Verbal/Linguistic**

📄 Alternative Assessment Handbook, Rubric 11: Discussions

📄 **CRF:** Vocabulary Builder Activity, Section 1

Lessons designed to support instructions for English-Language Learners can be found throughout the Teacher's Editions.

Structures Oral and written language structures present special challenges to ELLs. When teachers use research-based effective strategies to support oral and written language as well as published text structures, they can nudge their ELLs toward thinking, talking, reading, and writing like historians.

Academic Language Skills Students typically learn History–Social Science through the receptive modes of listening and reading. In contrast, they "show what they know" through the productive modes of class discussion, oral presentations and written products such as projects, reports, and expository/analytical essays. When the academic vocabulary of the content/concept to be studied is explicitly taught, ELLs can be more productive and therefore more successful at showing what they know.

Study Skills and Learning Strategies Chamot and O'Malley (1994) note that study skills, thinking skills, and social skills are also important aspects of the History–Social Science curriculum. ELLs may not have, as yet, developed the learning strategies essential to these three skill areas. Thus, teachers should help ELLs develop these skills so they can be better prepared to cope with the growing amount of new and abstract information found in grade-level History–Social Science classrooms, textbooks, and primary source documents.

Teachers who use research-based best practices in the areas of (1) conceptual understanding, (2) vocabulary, (3) language functions and discourse, (4) structures, (5) academic language skills, and (6) study skills and learning strategies will be better prepared to support growing numbers of ELLs in their History–Social Science classes, regardless of each student's proficiency level in English. Whether a teacher has regular History–Social Science classes or a sheltered section (also known in California as SDAIE, or Specially Designed Academic Instruction in English), the result will be ELLs who have greater access to the History–Social Science curriculum and who will experience greater success as learners moving into the mainstream.

Chamot, Anna Uhl and J. Michael O'Malley (1994). *The CALLA Handbook: Implementing the Cognitive Academic Language Learning Approach.* Reading, MA: Addison-Wesley Publishing Company.

The History-Social Science Framework for California Public Schools, Kindergarten through Grade Twelve (2000). Sacramento, CA: The California Department of Education.

ELL Instructional Support Services

- Use graphic organizers to teach abstract ideas.

- Teach specialized History–Social Science vocabulary and usage.

- Promote development of study skills, thinking skills, and social skills.

- Read aloud content-related materials to help students build background knowledge.

Teaching Vocabulary and Comprehension

by Dr. Kylene Beers

Dr. Kylene Beers, Ed.D., is a Senior Reading Researcher in the School Development Program of the Child Study Center at Yale University. A former middle school teacher, Dr. Beers is a respected authority on struggling readers. She is the current editor of *Voices from the Middle,* the journal of the National Council of Teachers of English; co-editor of *Into Focus: Understanding and Creating Middle School Readers;* and the author of *When Kids Can't Read—What Teachers Can Do.* Dr. Beers was the 2001 recipient of the Richard W. Halle Award given by NCTE for outstanding contributions to middle school education.

Effective Vocabulary Instruction

"Preteaching vocabulary . . . requires that the words to be taught must be key words . . . be taught in semantically and topically related sets, . . . and that only a few words be taught per lesson."

—Tierney and Cunningham

The Right Words and the Right Number The more vocabulary words we give students to learn weekly, the less chance students have of learning a word to the level needed to move it from short-term to long-term memory. Keeping the number between 5 and 10 means students have a better chance of retaining that word beyond the end of the week (Beers, 2002).

Consequently, choose wisely the words to be taught. Avid readers benefit by studying rare words—those highly unusual ones—because these students already have a solid vocabulary of the more common words. Struggling readers, however, benefit by focusing on high-utility words—those more common words that they are likely to see in other contexts. So, in the sentence, "The boys banked the canoe to the lee side of the rock," the inclination might be to teach the word *lee,* a rare word. However, if students don't know what *banked* means in this context or don't know the word *canoe,* it matters little what *lee* means. For struggling readers, a focus on high-utility words is more beneficial than a focus on rare words.

The Right Instructional Approach Tierney and Cunningham (1984) explain that offering students a list of vocabulary words with their definitions is not as effective as placing each word within a semantic context. Students learn how to use words as they read or hear them used correctly. The Reading Social Studies features in this textbook list the key terms and academic vocabulary for each chapter. Defining these terms and using them in a sentence provides students with the semantic placement that most helps them learn words. Choosing the right number of the right words and presenting words in a semantic context helps students build their vocabulary and, as a consequence, improve their comprehension.

Improving Comprehension

"Comprehension is both a product and a process, something that requires purposeful, strategic effort on the reader's part as he or she predicts, visualizes, clarifies, questions, connects, summarizes, and infers."
—Kylene Beers

When the Text is Tough

"Comprehension is only tough when you can't do it," explained the eleventh-grader. I almost dismissed his words until I realized what truth they offered. We aren't aware of all the thinking we do to comprehend a text until faced with a difficult text. Then all too clearly, we're aware of what words we don't understand, what syntax seems convoluted, and what ideas are beyond our immediate grasp. As skilled readers, we know what to do—we slow our pace, reread, ask questions, connect whatever we do understand to what we don't understand, summarize what we've read thus far, and make inferences about what the author is saying. In short, we make that invisible act of comprehension visible as we consciously push our way through the difficult text. At those times, we realize that, indeed, comprehension is tough.

Reading Strategies for Struggling Readers

It's even tougher if you lack strategies that would help you through the difficult text. Many struggling readers believe they aren't successful readers because that's just the way things are (Beers, 2002). They believe successful readers know some secret that they haven't been told (Duffy, 2002). While we don't mean to keep comprehension a secret, at times that is what we do. For example, though we tell students to "reread," we haven't shown them how to alter their reading. We tell them to "make inferences," or "make predictions," but we haven't taught them how to do such things. In other words, we tell them what to do, but don't show them how to do it, in spite of several decades of research showing the benefit of direct instruction in reading strategies to struggling readers (Baumann, 1984; Pearson, P. D., 1984; Dole, et al., 1996; Beers, 2002).

Direct Instruction

Direct instruction means telling students what you are going to teach them, modeling it for them, providing assistance as they practice it, then letting them practice it on their own. It's not saying, "visualize while you read," but, instead, explaining, "today, I'm going to read this part aloud to you. I'm going to focus on seeing some of the action in my mind as I read. I'm going to stop occasionally and tell you what I'm seeing and what in the text helped me see that." When we directly teach comprehension strategies to students by means of modeling and repeated practice, we show students that good readers don't just get it. They work hard to get it. Direct instruction takes the secret out of comprehension as it provides teachers the support they need to reach struggling readers.

Baumann, J. 1984.
"Effectiveness of a Direct Instruction Paradigm for Teaching Main Idea Comprehension." *Reading Research Quarterly, 20:* 93–108.

Beers, K. 2002.
When Kids Can't Read—What Teachers Can Do. Portsmouth: Heinemann.

Dole, J., Brown, K., and Trathen, W. 1996.
"The Effects of Strategy Instruction on the Comprehension Performance of At-Risk Students." *Reading Research Quarterly,* 31: 62–89.

Duffy, G. 2002.
"The Case for Direct Explanation of Strategies." *Comprehension Instruction: Research-Based Best Practices.* Eds. C. Block and M. Pressley. New York: Guilford Press. 28–41.

Pearson, P. D. 1984.
"Direct Explicit Teaching of Reading Comprehension." Comprehension Instruction: *Perspectives and Suggestions.* Eds. G. Duffy, L. Roehler, and J. Mason. New York: Longman. 222–233.

Tierney, R. J., and Cunningham, J. W. 1984.
"Research on Teaching Reading Comprehension." *Handbook of Reading Research.* Eds. P. D. Pearson, R. Barr, M. Kamil, P. Mosenthal. New York: Longman. 609–656.

Standard English Learners
Language Acquisition as a Scaffold to Social Studies Curricula
by Dr. Noma LeMoine

Dr. Noma LeMoine, Ph.D., is a nationally recognized expert on issues of language variation and learning in African American and other students for whom Standard English is not native. She is Director of Academic English Mastery and Closing the Achievement Gap Branch for the Los Angeles Unified School District. She is a member of the National Citizen's Commission on African American Education, an arm of the Congressional Black Caucus Education Brain Trust. Dr. LeMoine is also the author of *English for Your Success: A Language Development Program for African American Students.*

Who are Standard English Learners?

Standard English Learners (SELs) are students for whom standard English is not native or whose home language—the language acquired between infancy and five years of age—structurally does not match the language of school. Standard English Learners include African American, Hawaiian American, Mexican American, and Native American students that have in common a linguistic history grounded in languages other than English. Prior to coming in contact with English their ancestors spoke African languages, Hawaiian languages, Latin American Spanish, or Native American languages. In each case these "involuntary minorities"—people who were enslaved, colonized, conquered, or otherwise subordinated in the context of America—combined English vocabulary with their native language and fashioned new ways of communicating in their new environments. These language forms, African American Language (often referred to as Black English); Hawaiian American Language (referred

Standard English Learners arrive at school in kindergarten as competent users of the language of their home but demonstrating limited proficiency in the language of school, that is, Standard American English. They are generally classified as English Only on school language surveys even though many of the rules that govern their home language are based in languages other than English. Because of their designation as English Only, these students' need for structured programs that support their acquisition of standard and academic English is often overlooked.

SEL Administrative Support Strategies

- Provide ongoing, comprehensive professional development for teachers and paraeducators including "literature circles" centered around the literature on the culturally and linguistically responsive instruction.

- Support the development of cooperative learning communities at the school site that engage teachers in review of the research, lesson study, peer coaching, and analysis of student work as a condition necessary for effectively educating SELs.

- Infuse information on the origin and historical development of standard and non-standard languages into the instructional curriculum.

to as Hawaiian Pidgin English); Mexican American Language (referred to as Chicano English); and Native American Language (sometimes referred to as Red English) incorporate English vocabulary, but differ in structure and form from standard American English.

Language Variation and Learning in SELs

In order for culturally and linguistically diverse Standard English Learners to succeed academically they must acquire the language, culture, and literacies of school. They must become literate in the forms of English that appear in newspapers, magazines, textbooks, voting materials, and consumer contracts. How best to facilitate this learning in Standard English Learners (SELs) has proven elusive for most American public educational institutions and minimal emphasis has been placed on identifying instructional methodologies that scaffold SELs' access to core curricula. Learning is viewed as a social phenomenon and knowledge is recognized as a social construction that is influenced by the cultural and linguistic experiences, perspectives, and frames of references both students and teachers bring to the learning environment. For Standard English Learners this suggests that an instructional model, which validates and builds on prior knowledge, experiences, language and culture while supporting the acquisition of school language through content learning is an appropriate pedagogy.

The History–Social Science curriculum is perhaps the best vehicle for creating learning opportunities in both content and language acquisition areas. Opportunities to engage in critical thinking and participate in knowledge building abound in the History–Social Science curriculum. As teachers help students develop skills as historians who re-create and share knowledge, students can also be provided opportunities to develop skills as speakers, readers, and writers.

SELs must be provided opportunities to add school language and literacy to their repertoire of skills using instructional approaches that build on the culture and language they bring to the

classroom. In order for SELs to experience greater success in accessing core curricula, teachers will need to construct learning environments that are authentic, culturally responsive, support language acquisition, and build upon the experiences, learning styles, and strengths of SELs.

SEL Instructional Support Strategies

- Incorporate contrastive analysis strategies (linguistic, contextual, situational, and elicited) into the daily instruction of SELs to facilitate mastery of academic language.

- Incorporate applicable SDAIE (Specially Designed Academic Instruction in English) strategies into instruction including utilization of visuals, manipulatives, graphic organizers, media and other tools to explain concepts.

- Provide continuous and varied opportunities for students to use language to interact with each other and the content through instructional conversations.

- Provide 30 to 45 minutes per day of Mainstream English Language Development (MELD) instruction that promotes the development of listening, speaking, reading, and writing skills in standard and academic English.

- Establish classroom libraries that include culturally relevant books and provide opportunities for SELs to be read to and to engage in free voluntary reading (FVR) on a daily basis.

- Encourage student/classroom development of a personal thesaurus of conceptually coded words to support the acquisition of academic vocabulary.

- Convey knowledge on ancient Africa, Mexico, Hawaii, and North America; their cultures and history.

- Convey knowledge of the impact of diverse cultures on the modern world with an emphasis on historical and contemporary achievers.

- Make connections to students' prior knowledge, experiences, and cultural funds of knowledge to support learning and retention of learned concepts.

Professional Resources and Bibliography

Professional References

This section provides information about resources that can enrich your U.S. History class. Included are addresses of guest speakers, museum visits, electronic field trips, nonprofit organizations, and many others. Since addresses change frequently, you may want to verify them before you send your requests. You may also want to refer to the HRW Web site at http://www.hrw.com for current information.

GUEST SPEAKERS

National Council for History Education
Speakers' Bureau
26915 Westwood Rd., Suite B-2
Westlake, Ohio 44145

MUSEUM VISITS

American Association of Museums
1575 Eye Street NW. Suite 400
Washington, DC 20005

ELECTRONIC FIELD TRIPS

Library of Congress/Congressional Server
thomas.loc.gov/

NONPROFIT ORGANIZATIONS

Constitutional Rights Foundation
601 South Kingsley Drive
Los Angeles, CA 90005
213-487-5590; Fax: 213-386-0459
www.crf-usa.org

PERIODICALS

Cobblestone: The History Magazine for Young People
Cobblestone Publishing, Inc.
30 Grove St.
Peterborough, NH 03458

GOVERNMENT RESOURCES

U.S. Department of Education
400 Maryland Ave., SW
Washington, D.C. 20202-0498
800-USA-LEARN
www.ed.gov/teachers/landing.jhtml?src=fp

SUBSCRIPTION SERVICES

Magazines.com Inc.
P.O. Box 682108
Franklin, TX 37068
800-929-2691
www.magazines.com

MISCELLANEOUS

Educational Resources Information Center (ERIC)
2277 Research Blvd.
Rockville, MD 20852
800-538-3742

A Bibliography for the Social Studies Teacher

This bibliography is a select compilation of resources available for professional enrichment.

SELECTED AND ANNOTATED LIST OF READINGS

Social Studies and Language Arts

Burke, Jim. *Writing Reminders: Tools, Tips, and Techniques*
Portsmouth, NH: Heinemann, 2003

Jago, Carol. *Cohesive Writing: Why Concept Is Not Enough*
Portsmouth, NH: Heinemann, 2002

Social Studies and Standard English Mastery

LeMoine, N. and Los Angeles Unified School District. *English for Your Success: A Language Development Program for African American Students. Handbook of Successful Strategies for Educators.*
New Jersey: The Peoples Publishing Group, 1999

Ornstein-Galicia, J. *Form and Function in Chicano English*
Malabar, FL: Krieger Publishing Co., 1988

Social Studies and English Learners

Billmeyer, Rachel and Mary Lee Barton. *Teaching Reading in the Content Areas: If Not Me, Then Who?* Second Edition
Aurora, CO: Mid-Continent Regional Educational Laboratory (McREL), 1998

Buehl, Doug. *Classroom Strategies for Interactive Learning.* Second Edition.
Newark, DE: International Reading Association, 2001

Readance, John, Thomas W. Bean and R. Scott Baldwin. *Content Area Literacy: An Integrated Approach.* Eighth Edition
Dubuque, IA: Kendall/Hunt Publishing Company, 2000

Reading
like a
Historian

Historians use paintings along with many other tools to help understand the past. The famous painting on the next page, *Washington Crossing the Delaware*, captures the determination of Patriot leaders and soldiers to endure brutal conditions in the hope of winning their struggle for liberty. As you study United States history, you too will learn how to use different historical sources to **Read like a Historian.**

To find out more about reading like a historian and the historical sources that follow, visit

go.hrw.com
More Online
KEYWORD: HISTORIAN

By Frances Marie Gipson
Secondary Literacy Coordinator
Los Angeles Unified School District, Los Angeles, California

What Does It Mean to Read like a Historian?

In your history class you will be doing a lot of reading, thinking, and problem-solving. Much of your reading and thinking will center on different types of texts or materials. Since you are in a history class reading all sorts of things, a question to consider is, "What does it mean to think, read, and solve problems like a historian?"

Historians work with different types of sources to understand and learn from history. Two categories of sources are **primary** and **secondary** sources.

Primary Sources are historical documents, written accounts by a firsthand witness, or objects that have survived from the past. A study of primary sources might include letters, government documents, diaries, photographs, art objects, stamps, coins, and even clothing.

Secondary Sources are accounts of past events created by people some time after the events happened. This textbook and other books written about historical events are examples of secondary sources.

As you learn more about your work as a historian, you will begin to ask questions and analyze historical materials. You will be working as a detective, digging into history to create a richer understanding of the mysteries of the past.

How to Analyze Written Sources

Primary Sources

Common Sense

"In the following pages I offer nothing more than simple facts, plain arguments, and common sense . . .

We may as well assert that because a child has thrived upon milk, it is never to have meat, or that the first twenty years of our lives [are] to become a precedent for the next twenty.

But Britain is the parent country say some. Then the more shame upon her conduct. Even brutes do not devour their young, nor savages make war upon their families . . ."

– Thomas Paine, *Common Sense*, 1776

Asking questions can help you determine the relevance and importance of written primary sources, such as the Revolutionary War pamphlet *Common Sense*. As you analyze the primary source above and the primary and secondary sources included in this textbook, ask yourself questions like the ones below.

- Who created the source and why?

- Did the writer have firsthand knowledge of the event, or does he report what others saw or heard?

- Was the writer a neutral party, or did the author have opinions or interests that might have influenced what was recorded?

- Did the writer wish to inform or persuade others?

- Was the information recorded during the event, immediately after the event, or after some lapse of time?

The Attack on Lawrence, Kansas

"Sheriff Jones, again at the head of an army of Missourians, marched into Lawrence. In broad daylight, they threw the printing presses of two newspapers into a river. They burned down the Free State Hotel and other buildings. Antislavery Kansans seethed with rage. One eyewitness described the attack. *Sheriff Jones, after looking at the flames rising from the hotel and saying that it was 'the happiest day of his life,' dismissed the troops and they began their lawless destruction.*"

–John A. Garraty, from *The Story of America*

When reading secondary sources, such as the description of the attack on Lawrence, Kansas, historians ask additional questions to seek understanding. They try to source the text, build evidence, and interpret the message that is being conveyed. For historians, reading is a quest to find evidence to answer or challenge a historical problem. As you study secondary sources, ask questions like the ones below.

- Who is the author? What do I know about this author?
- Did the author have firsthand information? What is the author's relationship to the event?
- What might be the author's motivation in writing this piece?
- What type of evidence did the author look at?
- Are any assumptions or bias present?
- How does this document fit into the larger context of the events I am studying?
- What kind of source is it?
- Is the source an original?
- Is the content probable or reasonable?
- What does the date tell me about the event?
- What do I already know about this topic that will help me understand more of what I am reading?

How to Analyze an Artifact

Artifacts, such as this Victrola invented by Thomas Edison, take many forms. They might be coins, stone tools, pieces of clothing, or even items found in your backpack. As you study artifacts in this textbook, ask yourself questions like the ones below.

- Why was this object created?

- When and where would it have been used?

- What does the artifact tell me about the technology available at the time it was created?

- What can it tell me about the life and times of the people who used it?

- How does the artifact help to make sense of the time period?

How to Analyze a Historical Map

Maps, such as this one from 1719 of New France, are symbolic representations of places shown in relation to one another. All maps necessarily include some details and leave out others. As you study maps in this textbook, ask questions like the ones below.

- When and where was the map produced?
- What details has the mapmaker chosen to include (or exclude) on this map?
- Why was the map drawn?
- How can I determine if the map is accurate?
- How are maps used to analyze the past, present, and future?

How to Analyze a Photograph

Photographs, like the one above of African American soldiers during the Civil War, are another important source for historians. One way to study a photograph is to write down everything you think is important about it. Then divide the image into four sections and describe the important elements from each section. As you study photographs in this textbook, ask questions like the ones below.

- What is the subject of the photograph?
- What does the image reveal about its subject?
- What is the setting for the photograph?
- What other details can I observe?
- When and where in the past was the photograph created?
- How can I describe the photographer's point of view?

How to Analyze a Political Cartoon

In 1871, Thomas Nast published this cartoon—"Who Stole the People's Money"—poking fun at corruption in politics. As you study political cartoons in this textbook, use the following helpful tips and questions.

- List the parts of the political cartoon and the importance of each part.

- Describe the focus or significance of the political cartoon.

- Do the captions and call-out boxes clarify the political cartoon's purpose?

- Does the cartoon help me understand the information that I am studying in my textbook better?

Become an Active Reader

by Dr. Kylene Beers

Did you ever think you would begin reading your social studies book by reading about reading? Actually, it makes better sense than you might think. You would probably make sure you learned some soccer skills and strategies before playing in a game. Similarly, you need to learn some reading skills and strategies before reading your social studies book. In other words, you need to make sure you know whatever you need to know in order to read this book successfully.

Tip #1
Use the Reading Social Studies Pages

Take advantage of the two pages on reading at the beginning of every chapter. Those pages introduce the chapter themes; explain a reading skill or strategy; and identify key terms, people, and academic vocabulary.

Themes

Why are themes important? They help our minds organize facts and information. For example, when we talk about baseball, we may talk about types of pitches. When we talk about movies, we may discuss animation.

Historians are no different. When they discuss history or social studies, they tend to think about some common themes: Economics, Geography, Religion, Politics, Society and Culture, and Science and Technology.

Reading Skill or Strategy

Good readers use a number of skills and strategies to make sure they understand what they are reading. These lessons will give you the tools you need to read and understand social studies.

Key Terms, People, and Academic Vocabulary

Before you read the chapter, review these words and think about them. Have you heard the word before? What do you already know about the people? Then watch for these words and their meanings as you read the chapter.

Tells which theme or themes are important in the chapter

Explains a skill or strategy good readers use

Gives you practice in the reading skill or strategy

Identifies the important words in the chapter

Read like a Skilled Reader

You will never get better at reading your social studies book—or any book for that matter—unless you spend some time thinking about how to be a better reader.

Skilled readers do the following:

- They preview what they are supposed to read before they actually begin reading. They look for vocabulary words, titles of sections, information in the margin, or maps or charts they should study.

- They divide their notebook paper into two columns. They title one column "Notes from the Chapter" and the other column "Questions or Comments I Have."

- They take notes in both columns as they read.

- They read like **active readers**. The Active Reading list below shows you what that means.

- They use clues in the text to help them figure out where the text is going. The best clues are called signal words.

   Chronological Order Signal Words: *first, second, third, before, after, later, next, following that, earlier, finally*

   Cause and Effect Signal Words: *because of, due to, as a result of, the reason for, therefore, consequently*

   Comparison/Contrast Signal Words: *likewise, also, as well as, similarly, on the other hand*

Active Reading

Successful readers are **active readers**. These readers know that it is up to them to figure out what the text means. Here are some steps you can take to become an active, and successful, reader.

Predict what will happen next based on what has already happened. When your predictions don't match what happens in the text, re-read the confusing parts.

Question what is happening as you read. Constantly ask yourself why things have happened, what things mean, and what caused certain events.

Summarize what you are reading frequently. Do not try to summarize the entire chapter! Read a bit and then summarize it. Then read on.

Connect what is happening in the part you're reading to what you have already read.

Clarify your understanding. Stop occasionally to ask yourself whether you are confused by anything. You may need to re-read to clarify, or you may need to read further and collect more information before you can understand.

Visualize what is happening in the text. Try to see the events or places in your mind by drawing maps, making charts, or jotting down notes about what you are reading.

Tip #3
Pay Attention to Vocabulary

It is no fun to read something when you don't know what the words mean, but you can't learn new words if you only use or read the words you already know. In this book, we know we have probably used some words you don't know. But, we have followed a pattern as we have used more difficult words.

Key Terms and People

At the beginning of each section you will find a list of key terms or people that you will need to know. Be on the lookout for those words as you read through the section.

ACADEMIC VOCABULARY

efficient
productive and not wasteful

Academic Vocabulary

When we use a word that is important in all classes, not just social studies, we define it in the margin under the heading Academic Vocabulary. You will run into these academic words in other textbooks, so you should learn what they mean while reading this book.

Words to Know

As you read this social studies textbook, you will be more successful if you know or learn the meanings of the words on this page. There are two types of words listed here. The first list contains academic words, the words we discussed at the bottom of the previous page. These words are important in all classes, not just social studies. The second list contains words that are special to this particular topic of social studies, U.S. history.

Academic Words

abstract	expressing a quality or idea without reference to an actual thing
acquire	to get
advocate	to plead in favor of
aspects	parts
concrete	specific, real
contemporary	existing at the same time
criteria	rules for defining
distinct	separate
efficient/ efficiency	productive and not wasteful
element	part
execute	to perform, carry out
explicit	fully revealed without vagueness
facilitate	to bring about
factor	cause
implement	to put in place
implications	effects of a decision
implicit	understood though not clearly put into words
incentive	something that leads people to follow a certain course of action
innovation	a new idea or way of doing something
neutral	unbiased, not favoring either side in a conflict
principle	basic belief, rule, or law
strategy	a plan for fighting a battle or war

Social Studies Words

AD	refers to dates after Jesus's birth
BC	refers to dates before the birth of Jesus of Nazareth
BCE	refers to "Before Common Era," dates before the birth of Jesus of Nazareth
CE	refers to "Common Era," dates after Jesus's birth
century	a period of 100 years
civilization	the culture of a particular time or place
climate	the weather conditions in a certain area over a long period of time
culture	the knowledge, beliefs, customs, and values of a group of people
custom	a repeated practice; tradition
democracy	governmental rule by the people, usually on a majority rule principle
economy	the system in which people make and exchange goods and services
geography	the study of the earth's physical and cultural features
independence	freedom from forceful rule
monarchy	governmental rule by one person, a king or queen
North	the region of the United States sometimes defined by the states that did not secede from the Union during the Civil War
rebellion	an organized resistance to the established government
society	a group of people who share common traditions
South	the region of the United States sometimes defined by the states that seceded from the Union to form the Confederate States of America

Mapping the Earth

A **globe** is a scale model of the earth. It is useful for showing the entire earth or studying large areas of the earth's surface.

A pattern of lines circles the globe in east-west and north-south directions. It is called a **grid**. The intersection of these imaginary lines helps us find places on the earth.

The east-west lines in the grid are lines of **latitude**. Lines of latitude are called **parallels** because they are always parallel to each other. These imaginary lines measure distance north and south of the **equator**. The equator is an imaginary line that circles the globe halfway between the North and South Poles. Parallels measure distance from the equator in **degrees**. The symbol for degrees is °. Degrees are further divided into **minutes**. The symbol for minutes is ´. There are 60 minutes in a degree. Parallels north of the equator are labeled with an N. Those south of the equator are labeled with an S.

The north-south lines are lines of **longitude**. Lines of longitude are called **meridians**. These imaginary lines pass through the Poles. They measure distance east and west of the **prime meridian**. The prime meridian is an imaginary line that runs through Greenwich, England. It represents 0° longitude.

Lines of latitude range from 0°, for locations on the equator, to 90°N or 90°S, for locations at the Poles. Lines of longitude range from 0° on the prime meridian to 180° on a meridian in the mid-Pacific Ocean. Meridians west of the prime meridian to 180° are labeled with a W. Those east of the prime meridian to 180° are labeled with an E.

Lines of Latitude

Lines of Longitude

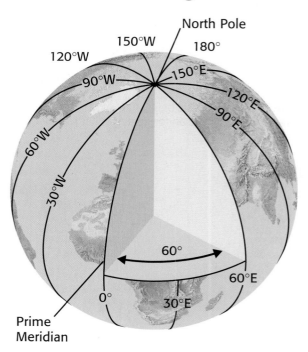

The equator divides the globe into two halves, called **hemispheres**. The half north of the equator is the Northern Hemisphere. The southern half is the Southern Hemisphere. The prime meridian and the 180° meridian divide the world into the Eastern Hemisphere and the Western Hemisphere. However, the prime meridian runs right through Europe and Africa. To avoid dividing these continents between two hemispheres, some mapmakers divide the Eastern and Western hemispheres at 20°W. This places all of Europe and Africa in the Eastern Hemisphere.

Our planet's land surface is divided into seven large landmasses, called **continents**. They are identified in the maps on this page. Landmasses smaller than continents and completely surrounded by water are called **islands**.

Geographers also organize Earth's water surface into parts. The largest is the world ocean. Geographers divide the world ocean into the Pacific Ocean, the Atlantic Ocean, the Indian Ocean, and the Arctic Ocean. Lakes and seas are smaller bodies of water.

Northern Hemisphere

Southern Hemisphere

Western Hemisphere

Eastern Hemisphere

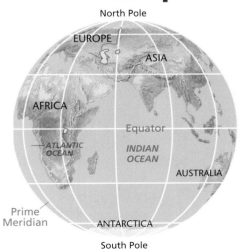

Mapmaking

A **map** is a flat diagram of all or part of the earth's surface. Mapmakers have created different ways of showing our round planet on flat maps. These different ways are called **map projections**. Because the earth is round, there is no way to show it accurately in a flat map. All flat maps are distorted in some way. Mapmakers must choose the type of map projection that is best for their purposes. Many map projections are one of three kinds: cylindrical, conic, or flat-plane.

Paper cylinder

Mercator projection

Cylindrical Projections

Cylindrical projections are based on a cylinder wrapped around the globe. The cylinder touches the globe only at the equator. The meridians are pulled apart and are parallel to each other instead of meeting at the Poles. This causes landmasses near the Poles to appear larger than they really are. The map below is a Mercator projection, one type of cylindrical projection. The Mercator projection is useful for navigators because it shows true direction and shape. However, it distorts the size of land areas near the Poles.

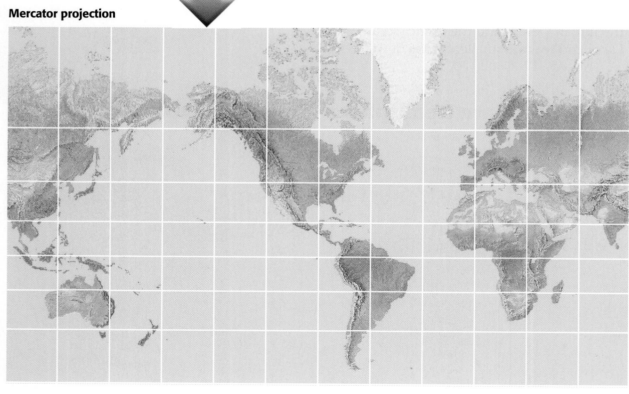

Conic Projections

Conic projections are based on a cone placed over the globe. A conic projection is most accurate along the lines of latitude where it touches the globe. It retains almost true shape and size. Conic projections are most useful for showing areas that have long east-west dimensions, such as the United States.

Paper cone

Conic projection

Flat-plane Projections

Flat-plane projections are based on a plane touching the globe at one point, such as at the North Pole or South Pole. A flat-plane projection is useful for showing true direction for airplane pilots and ship navigators. It also shows true area. However, it distorts the true shapes of land massess.

Flat plane

Flat-plane projection

Map Essentials

Maps are like messages sent out in code. Mapmakers provide certain elements that help us translate these codes. These elements help us understand the message they are presenting about a particular part of the world. Of these elements, almost all maps have titles, directional indicators, scales, and legends. The map below has all four of these elements, plus a fifth—a locator map.

❶ Title

A map's **title** shows what the subject of the map is. The map title is usually the first thing you should look at when studying a map, because it tells you what the map is trying to show.

❶ **Battles in the East** ❺

❹

	Union state
	West Virginia (Separated from Virginia in 1861 and joined the Union in 1863)
	Confederate state
➔	Union forces
✶	Union victory
➔	Confederate forces
✶	Confederate victory

0   15   30 Miles
0   15   30 Kilometers
❸

PENNSYLVANIA

Antietam
Sep. 1862

MARYLAND

WEST VIRGINIA

Shenandoah Valley

Potomac

LEE

McCLELLAN

River

POPE

Washington

Manassas Junction

Bull Run
July 1861 &
Aug. 1862

LEE

Chesapeake Bay

Fair Oaks
May – June
1862

LEE

Richmond

James River

Seven Days
June 1862

York R.

McCLELLAN

Yorktown

N
W   E
S
❷

VIRGINIA

ATLANTIC OCEAN

❷ Compass Rose

A directional indicator shows which way north, south, east, and west lie on the map. Some mapmakers use a "north arrow," which points toward the North Pole. Remember, "north" is not always at the top of a map. The way a map is drawn and the location of directions on that map depend on the perspective of the mapmaker. Most maps in this textbook indicate direction by using a compass rose. A **compass rose** has arrows that point to all four principal directions, as shown.

❸ Scale

Mapmakers use scales to represent show the distances between points on a map. Scales may appear on maps in several different forms. The maps in this textbook provide a bar **scale**. Scales give distances in miles and kilometers.

To find the distance between two points on the map, place a piece of paper so that the edge connects the two points. Mark the location of each point on the paper with a line or dot. Then, compare the distance between the two dots with the map's bar scale. The number on the top of the scale gives the distance in miles. The number on the bottom gives the distance in kilometers. Because the distances are given in large intervals, you may have to approximate the actual distance on the scale.

❹ Legend

The **legend**, or key, explains what the symbols on the map represent. Point symbols are used to specify the location of things, such as cities, that do not take up much space on the map. Some legends, such as the one shown here, show colors that represent certain elevations. Other maps might have legends with symbols or colors that represent things such as roads. Legends can also show economic resources, land use, population density, and climate.

❺ Locator Map

A locator map shows where in the world the area on the map is located. The area shown on the main map is shown in red on the locator map. The locator map also shows surrounding areas so the map reader can see how the information on the map relates to neighboring lands.

Working with Maps

The Atlas at the back of this textbook includes both physical and political maps. Physical maps, like the one you just saw, show the major physical features in a region. These features include things like mountain ranges, rivers, oceans, islands, deserts, and plains. Political maps show the major political features of a region, such as countries and their borders, capitals, and other important cities.

Historical Map

In this textbook, most of the maps you will study are historical maps. Historical maps, such as this one, are maps that show information about the past. This information might be which lands an empire controlled, where a certain group of people lived, what large cities were located in a region, or how a place changed over time. Often colors are used to indicate the different things on the map. Be sure to look at the map title and map legend first to see what the map is showing. What does this map show?

The United States, 1820

Legend:
- U.S.–Canadian border, Convention of 1818
- U.S.–Spanish territory border, Adams-Onís Treaty of 1819
- From Britain to United States, 1818
- From Spain to United States, 1819
- Disputed by United States and Great Britain, 1818

0   200   400 Miles
0   200   400 Kilometers

The Louisiana Purchase

Fort Clatsop

Bitterroot Mtns.

CASCADE RANGE

Columbia River

LEWIS'S RETURN

CLARK'S RETURN

Fort Mandan

LEWIS AND CLARK'S EXPEDITION

OREGON COUNTRY
(Claimed by Britain, Russia, Spain, and the United States)

Snake River

LOUISIANA PURCHASE
(Purchased in 1803)

GREAT PLAINS

Platte River

Missouri River

Colorado River

Pikes Peak
14,110 ft.
(4,301 m)

Santa Fe

Continental Divide

Rio Grande

SPANISH TERRITORY

PIKE'S EXPEDITION

PACIFIC OCEAN

Arkansas River

Red River

Mississippi River

Lake Superior

BRITISH TERRITORY

St. Lawrence River

Lake Michigan

Lake Huron

Lake Ontario

Lake Erie

MICHIGAN TERRITORY

INDIANA TERRITORY

OH

Ohio River

St. Charles
St. Louis

KY

TN

APPALACHIAN MOUNTAINS

MISSISSIPPI TERRITORY

New Orleans

SPANISH FLORIDA

ATLANTIC OCEAN

Gulf of Mexico

40°N

35°N

95°W   90°W   85°W   80°W

N
W   E
S

Legend:
- U.S. states and territories in 1804
- Louisiana Purchase
- Disputed by United States and Britain
- Lewis and Clark's Expedition, 1804–1806
- Pike's Expedition, 1806–1807

0   200   400 Miles
0   200   400 Kilometers

Route Map

One special type of historical map is called a route map. A route map, like the one above, shows the route, or path, that someone or something followed. Route maps can show things like trade routes, invasion routes, or the journeys and travels of people. The routes on the map are usually shown with an arrow. If more than one route is shown, several arrows of different colors may be used. What does this route map show?

The maps in this textbook will help you study and understand history. By working with these maps, you will see where important events happened, where empires rose and fell, and where people moved. In studying these maps, you will learn how geography has influenced history.

Geographic Dictionary

OCEAN
a large body of water

CORAL REEF
an ocean ridge made up of
skeletal remains of tiny sea animals

GULF
a large part of
the ocean that
extends into land

PENINSULA
an area of land that sticks
out into a lake or ocean

BAY
part of a large
body of water
that is smaller
than a gulf

ISLAND
an area of land
surrounded entirely
by water

ISTHMUS
a narrow piece of land
connecting two larger
land areas

STRAIT
a narrow body of
water connecting two
larger bodies of water

DELTA
an area where a
river deposits soil
into the ocean

SINKHOLE
a circular depression
formed when the roof
of a cave collapses

WETLAND
an area of land
covered by
shallow water

RIVER
a natural flow of
water that runs
through the land

LAKE
an inland body
of water

FOREST
an area of densely
wooded land

COAST
an area of land
near the ocean

MOUNTAIN
an area of rugged
land that generally
rises higher than
2,000 feet

VALLEY
an area of low
land between
hills or mountains

VOLCANO
an opening in Earth's crust
where lava, ash, and gases erupt

CANYON
a deep, narrow valley
with steep walls

GLACIER
a large area of
slow-moving ice

HILL
a rounded, elevated
area of land smaller
than a mountain

PLAIN
a nearly
flat area

DUNE
a hill of sand
shaped by wind

OASIS
an area in the
desert with a
water source

DESERT
an extremely dry area with
little water and few plants

PLATEAU
a large, flat,
elevated
area of land

The Five Themes of Geography

Geography is the study of the world's people and places. As you can imagine, studying the entire world is a big job. To make the job easier, geographers have created the Five Themes of Geography. They are: **Location, Place, Human-Environment Interaction, Movement,** and **Region**. You can think of the Five Themes as five windows you can look through to study a place. If you looked at the same place through five different windows, you would have five different perspectives, or viewpoints, of the place. Using the Five Themes in this way will help you better understand the world's people and places.

1 Location The first thing to study about a place is its location. Where is it? Every place has an absolute location—its exact location on Earth. A place also has a relative location—its location in relation to other places. Use the theme of location to ask questions like, "Where is this place located, and how has its location affected it?"

2 Place Every place in the world is unique and has its own personality and character. Some things that can make a place unique include its weather, plants and animals, history, and the people that live there. Use the theme of place to ask questions like, "What are the unique features of this place, and how are they important?"

3 Human-Environment Interaction
People interact with their environment in many ways. They use land to grow food and local materials to build houses. At the same time, a place's environment influences how people live. For example, if the weather is cold, people wear warm clothes. Use the theme of human-environment interaction to ask questions like, "What is this place's environment like, and how does it affect the people who live there?"

4 Movement The world is constantly changing, and places are affected by the movement of people, goods, ideas, and physical forces. For example, people come and go, new businesses begin, and rivers change their course. Use the theme of movement to ask questions like, "How is this place changing, and why?"

5 Region A region is an area that has one or more features that make it different from surrounding areas. A desert, a country, and a coastal area are all regions. Geographers use regions to break the world into smaller pieces that are easier to study. Use the theme of region to ask questions like "What common features does this area share, and how is it different from other areas?"

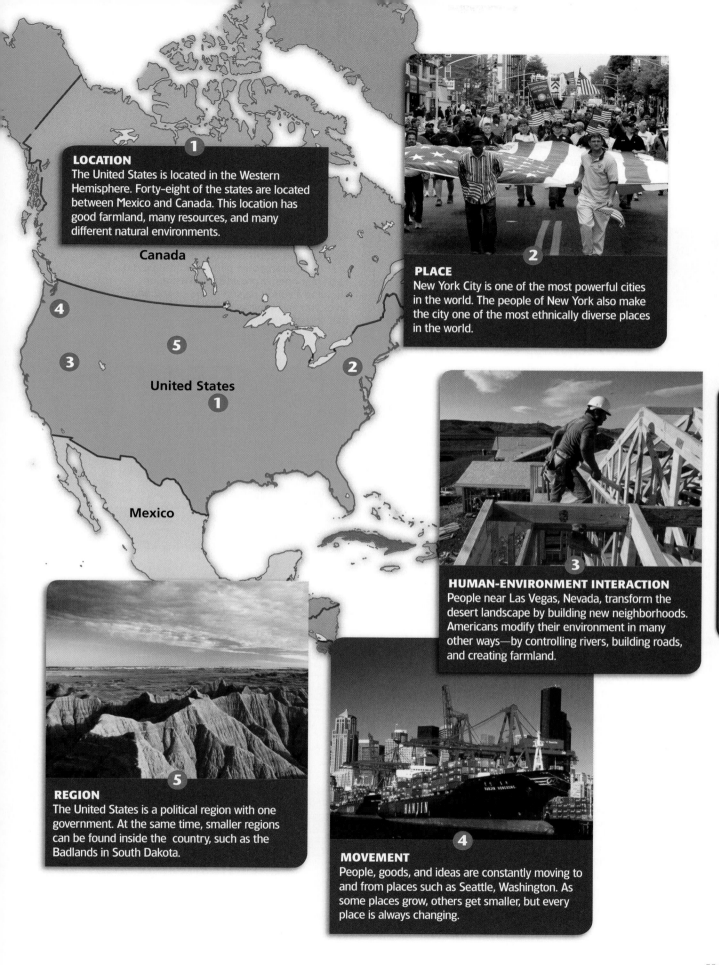

LOCATION
The United States is located in the Western Hemisphere. Forty-eight of the states are located between Mexico and Canada. This location has good farmland, many resources, and many different natural environments.

Canada

United States

Mexico

PLACE
New York City is one of the most powerful cities in the world. The people of New York also make the city one of the most ethnically diverse places in the world.

HUMAN-ENVIRONMENT INTERACTION
People near Las Vegas, Nevada, transform the desert landscape by building new neighborhoods. Americans modify their environment in many other ways—by controlling rivers, building roads, and creating farmland.

REGION
The United States is a political region with one government. At the same time, smaller regions can be found inside the country, such as the Badlands in South Dakota.

MOVEMENT
People, goods, and ideas are constantly moving to and from places such as Seattle, Washington. As some places grow, others get smaller, but every place is always changing.

How to Make This Book Work for You

Studying U.S. history will be easy for you using this textbook. Take a few minutes to become familiar with the easy-to-use structure and special features of this history book. See how this U.S. history textbook will make history come alive for you!

Unit

Each chapter of this textbook is part of a unit of study focusing on a particular time period. Each unit opener provides an illustration showing a young person of the period and gives you an overview of the exciting topics that you will study in the unit.

Chapter

Each chapter begins with a chapter-opener introduction where the sections of the chapter are listed out, and ends with Chapter Review pages and a Standardized Test Practice page.

Reading Social Studies These chapter-level reading lessons teach you skills and provide opportunities for practice to help you read the textbook more successfully. Within each chapter there is a point of reference *Focus on Reading* note in the margin to demonstrate the reading skill for the chapter. There are also questions in the Chapter Review activity to make sure that you understand the reading skill.

Social Studies Skills The Social Studies Skills lessons, that appear at the end of each chapter, give you an opportunity to learn and use a skill that you will most likely use again while in school. You will also be given a chance to make sure that you understand each skill by answering related questions in the Chapter Review activity.

Section

The Section opener pages include: Main Idea statements, an overarching Big Idea statement, and Key Terms and People. In addition, each section includes the following special features.

If You Were There . . . introductions begin each section with a situation for you to respond to, placing you in the time period and in a situation related to the content that you will be studying in the section.

Building Background sections connect what will be covered in this section with what you studied in the previous section.

Short sections of content organize the information in each section into small chunks of text that you should not find too overwhelming.

The Taking Notes feature allows you to write down the most important information from the section in a usable format.

SECTION 1

The Articles of Confederation

What You Will Learn . . .

Main Ideas
1. The American people examined many ideas about government.
2. The Articles of Confederation laid the base for the first national government of the United States.
3. The Confederation Congress established the Northwest Territory.

The Big Idea
The Articles of Confederation provided a framework for a national government.

Key Terms and People
Magna Carta, *p. 152*
English Bill of Rights, *p. 152*
constitution, *p. 153*
Virginia Statute for Religious Freedom, *p. 153*
suffrage, *p. 153*
Articles of Confederation, *p. 154*
ratification, *p. 154*
Land Ordinance of 1785, *p. 155*
Northwest Ordinance of 1787, *p. 155*
Northwest Territory, *p. 155*

TAKING NOTES As you read, take notes on the new American government in a chart like this one.

New American Government
1. Influences on new government
2. Structure of the Articles of Confederation

If YOU were there...

You live in a town in New England during the 1770s. In the town meeting, people are hotly debating about who will have the right to vote. Most think that only men who own property should be able to vote. Some think that all property owners—men and women—should have that right. A few others want all free men to have the vote. Now it is time for the meeting to decide.

How would you have voted on this issue?

BUILDING BACKGROUND At the time of the Revolution, each of the 13 states had its own government. The rights of citizens varied from state to state. In their town meetings, people often argued about exactly what those rights ought to be. Solving such issues was one step in moving toward a national government.

Ideas about Government

The American colonies had taken a bold step in declaring their independence from Great Britain in July 1776. Their next political goal was to form a new government. To do so, the American people drew from a wide range of political ideas.

English Laws and the Enlightenment
One source of inspiration was English law. England had limited the power of its kings and queens in two documents. These were Magna Carta and the English Bill of Rights. **Magna Carta**, a document signed by King John in 1215, made the king subject to law. The **English Bill of Rights**, passed in 1689, declared the supremacy of Parliament. It kept the king or queen from passing new taxes or changing laws without Parliament's consent. As a result, the people's representatives had a strong voice in England's government.

Americans were also influenced by Enlightenment—a philosophical movement that emphasized the use of reason to examine old

152 CHAPTER 5

Northwest Territory

Congress had to decide what to do with the western lands now under its control and how to raise money to pay debts. It tried to solve both problems by selling the western lands. Congress passed the **Land Ordinance of 1785**, which set up a system for surveying and dividing western lands. The land was split into townships, which were 36 square miles divided into 36 lots of 640 acres each. One lot was reserved for a public school, and four lots were given to veterans. The remaining lots were sold to the public.

To form a political system for the region, Congress passed the **Northwest Ordinance of 1787**. The ordinance established the **Northwest Territory**, which included areas that are now in Illinois, Indiana, Michigan, Ohio, Minnesota, and Wisconsin. The Northwest Ordinance created a system for bringing new states into the Union. Congress agreed that the Northwest Territory would be divided into several smaller territories with a

governor appointed by Congress. When the population of a territory reached 60,000, its settlers could draft their own constitution and ask to join the Union.

In addition, the law protected civil liberties and required that public education be provided. Finally, the ordinance stated that "there shall be neither slavery nor involuntary servitude [forced labor] in the . . . territory." This last condition banned slavery in the Territory and set the standard for future territories. However, slavery would continue to be a controversial issue.

READING CHECK Analyzing Information
How did the Northwest Ordinance of 1787 affect the United States?

SUMMARY AND PREVIEW The Northwest Ordinance settled the future of the Northwest Territory. In the next section you will read about other challenges the new government faced.

THE IMPACT TODAY
Townships remained the unit of local government after the Northwest Territory was divided into states. Many of these townships still exist today.

Section 1 Assessment

go.hrw.com
Online Quiz
KEYWORD: SR8 HP5

Reviewing Ideas, Terms, and People
1. a. **Identify** What documents influenced ideas about government in the United States?
   b. **Draw Conclusions** What impact did the **Virginia Statute for Religious Freedom** have on the U.S. government?
   c. **Elaborate** Why is the separation of government powers a requirement for a society to be free?
2. a. **Identify** What was the **Articles of Confederation**?
   b. **Summarize** What powers were granted to Congress by the Articles of Confederation?
   c. **Predict** What are some possible problems that might result from the lack of a national court system?
3. a. **Describe** How were public lands in the West divided by the **Land Ordinance of 1785**?
   b. **Evaluate** In your opinion, what was the most important element of the **Northwest Ordinance of 1787**? Why?
   c. **Elaborate** What does the assignment of township lots reveal about values of Americans at this time?

Critical Thinking
4. **Categorizing** Review your notes on the Articles of Confederation. Copy the chart below and use it to show the strengths and weaknesses of the new government.

Articles of Confederation

Strengths	Weaknesses

FOCUS ON WRITING
5. **Thinking about the Articles of Confederation** Make a list of powers the Articles of Confederation gave the national government. Which ones seem strong? Can you think of any important powers that are missing?

FORMING A GOVERNMENT **155**

Reading Check Questions end each section of content so that you can test whether or not you understand what you have just studied.

Summary and Preview statements connect what you have just studied in the section to what you will study in the next section.

Section Assessments boxes provide an opportunity for you to make sure that you understand the main ideas of the section. We also provide assessment practice online!

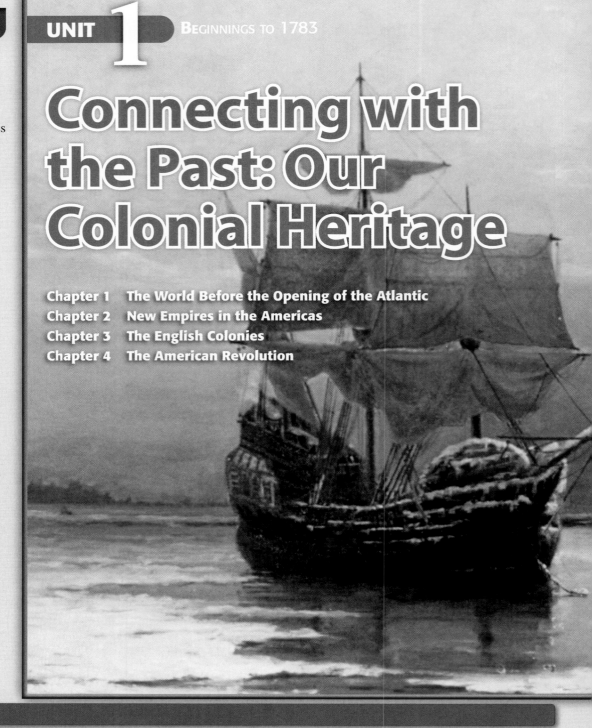

Unit Preview

Introduce the Unit

Share the information in the chapter overviews with students.

Chapter 1 Many scholars believe humans migrated to the Americas across a land bridge from Asia during the last Ice Age. Native American societies developed across Mesoamerica and South America, while diverse cultures developed across North America. Increased trade, including slave trade, helped West African kingdoms gain power. A surge in trade and new ideas also had a dramatic impact on Europe.

Chapter 2 The Portuguese ushered in an era of exploration in the 1400s. This was followed by Christopher Columbus's voyages, which paved the way for other explorers to sail to the Americas. As the Spanish established a large empire in the Americas, other European nations challenged Spain's dominance. Between the 1520s and 1860s, about 12 million enslaved Africans were shipped across the Atlantic where Europeans forced them to work in their newly formed colonies.

Chapter 3 In 1607 a group of colonists established the first permanent English settlement in North America. Hoping to gain religious freedom, English colonists began to establish settlements along the Atlantic Coast. Varied ways of life developed in these colonies as settlers adapted to different environments. English settlers *(continued on p. 1)*

Connecting with the Past: Our Colonial Heritage

Chapter 1 **The World Before the Opening of the Atlantic**
Chapter 2 **New Empires in the Americas**
Chapter 3 **The English Colonies**
Chapter 4 **The American Revolution**

Unit Resources

Planning

- Differentiated Instruction Teacher Management System: Unit Instructional Benchmarking Guides
- One-Stop Planner CD-ROM with Test Generator: Calendar Planner
- Power Presentations with Video CD-ROM
- A Teacher's Guide to Religion in the Public Schools

Differentiating Instruction

- Differentiated Instruction Teacher Management System: Lesson Plans for Differentiated Instruction
- Pre-AP Activities Guide for United States History
- Differentiated Instruction Modified Worksheets and Tests CD-ROM

Enrichment

- **CRF 2:** Economics and History Activity: Mercantilism: Government Control of Trade
- **CRF 2:** Interdisciplinary Project: What Will You Take on Your Sea Voyage?
- Civic Participation Activities
- Primary Source Library CD-ROM

Assessment

- Progress Assessment System Solution: Unit Test
- OSP ExamView Test Generator: Unit Test
- Holt Online Assessment Program, in the Premier Online Student Edition
- Alternative Assessment Handbook

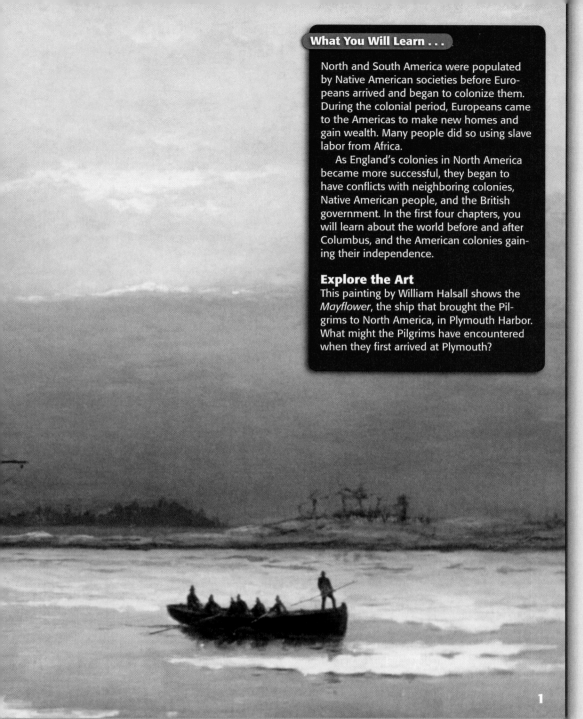

What You Will Learn . . .

North and South America were populated by Native American societies before Europeans arrived and began to colonize them. During the colonial period, Europeans came to the Americas to make new homes and gain wealth. Many people did so using slave labor from Africa.

As England's colonies in North America became more successful, they began to have conflicts with neighboring colonies, Native American people, and the British government. In the first four chapters, you will learn about the world before and after Columbus, and the American colonies gaining their independence.

Explore the Art

This painting by William Halsall shows the *Mayflower*, the ship that brought the Pilgrims to North America, in Plymouth Harbor. What might the Pilgrims have encountered when they first arrived at Plymouth?

Unit Overview *continued*

came into conflict with Native Americans and the French, causing the French and Indian War, which Great Britain won in 1763. Colonists were angered when they were expected to pay taxes to help pay for the war, and they began to protest British laws.

Chapter 4 Colonial resentment against Britain increased; shots were fired in April of 1775, starting the Revolutionary War. On July 4, 1776, the Declaration of Independence was approved. Though they received help from France and Spain, the Patriots faced obstacles in fighting the British. When the war against Britain spread to the South, Americans defeated British forces and gained their independence.

Connect to the Unit

Activity Simulation Role-Play
Provide students with the following scenario: A multinational space expedition has made contact with a non-hostile civilization on another planet. Communication has been slow but is occurring.

Ask students to predict how life on Earth might change as a result of this new contact. Have students work in pairs or in small groups to create a hypothetical conversation among people on Earth discussing the event and its possible effects. Ask for volunteers to act out their conversations for the class.
LS Interpersonal, Verbal/Linguistic

Explore the Art

The Pilgrims first landed at the tip of Cape Cod, and finally arrived in Plymouth Harbor on December 26, 1620. They crossed the Atlantic Ocean on the *Mayflower,* which archaeologists estimate was 90 feet long. The ship was loaded with over 100 settlers, who endured cramped and uncomfortable living quarters. The perilous, stormy journey lasted over two months.

Answers

Explore the Art *possible answers—unfamiliar territory, meeting Native Americans, lack of housing, limited supplies*

Democracy and Civic Education

At Level

Authority: Reasons for Government Working for Reform

1. Organize students into small groups. Have each group discuss the need for school rules. Each group should create a chart listing the costs and benefits of school rules. How well would the school function without rules? What would happen if students did not obey the school rules or authority figures? Have each group share its chart with the class.

2. Explain that societies, like schools, need governments and laws. Have each group create a second chart listing the costs and benefits of

government. The groups should then use their charts to identify what they think the purposes of government should be.

3. Have each group share its findings. Conclude by explaining that the purpose of government in the United States is to protect individual rights and to promote the common good.
LS Interpersonal, Verbal/Linguistic

📄 Alternative Assessment Handbook, Rubrics 7: Charts; and 14: Group Activity

📄 Civic Participation

Chapter 1 Planning Guide

The World before the Opening of the Atlantic

Chapter Overview	Reproducible Resources	Technology Resources
CHAPTER 1 pp. 2–33 **Overview:** In this chapter, students will learn about the first civilizations in the Americas and will examine trade in West Africa and Europe before transatlantic travel.	**Differentiated Instruction Teacher Management System:*** • Instructional Benchmarking Guides • Lesson Plans for Differentiated Instruction **Interactive Reader and Study Guide:** Chapter Graphic Organizer* **Chapter Resource File:*** • Focus on Writing Activity: A Travelogue • Social Studies Skills Activity: Interpreting Diagrams • Chapter Review Activity **A Teacher's Guide to Religion in the Public Schools***	**Power Presentations with Video CD-ROM** **Differentiated Instruction Modified Worksheets and Tests CD-ROM** **Primary Source Library CD-ROM for United States History** **Interactive Skills Tutor CD-ROM** **Student Edition on Audio CD Program** **History's Impact: United States History Video Program (VHS/DVD):** The World before the Opening of the Atlantic*
Section 1: **The Earliest Americans** **The Big Idea:** Native American societies developed across Mesoamerica and South America.	**Differentiated Instruction Teacher Management System:** Section 1 Lesson Plan* **Interactive Reader and Study Guide:** Section 1 Summary* **Chapter Resource File:*** • Vocabulary Builder Activity, Section 1	**Daily Bellringer Transparency:** Section 1* **Map Transparency:** Land Migrations of Early Peoples* **Map Transparency:** Aztec and Inca Civilizations*
Section 2: **Native American Cultures** **The Big Idea:** Many diverse Native American cultures developed across the different geographic regions of North America.	**Differentiated Instruction Teacher Management System:** Section 2 Lesson Plan* **Interactive Reader and Study Guide:** Section 2 Summary* **Chapter Resource File:*** • Vocabulary Builder Activity, Section 2	**Daily Bellringer Transparency:** Section 2* **Map Transparency:** Native American Culture Areas*
Section 3: **Trading Kingdoms of West Africa** **The Big Idea:** Using trade to gain wealth, Ghana, Mali, and Songhai were West Africa's most powerful kingdoms.	**Differentiated Instruction Teacher Management System:** Section 3 Lesson Plan* **Interactive Reader and Study Guide:** Section 3 Summary* **Chapter Resource File:*** • Vocabulary Builder Activity, Section 3	**Daily Bellringer Transparency:** Section 3* **Map Transparency:** Empires of West Africa, 800–1500*
Section 4: **Europe before Transatlantic Travel** **The Big Idea:** New ways of thinking and growth in trade changed the way people lived in Europe.	**Differentiated Instruction Teacher Management System:** Section 4 Lesson Plan* **Interactive Reader and Study Guide:** Section 4 Summary* **Chapter Resource File:*** • Vocabulary Builder Activity, Section 4	**Daily Bellringer Transparency:** Section 4* **Quick Facts Transparency:** Democracy and Republic* **Internet Activity:** Roman Contributions to Society Essay

CHAPTER 1 PLANNING GUIDE

HOLT

History's Impact
United States History Video Program (VHS/DVD)
The World before the Opening of the Atlantic
Suggested use: as a chapter introduction

Review, Assessment, Intervention

Quick Facts Transparency: The World before the Opening of the Atlantic Visual Summary*

Spanish Chapter Summaries Audio CD Program

Online Chapter Summaries in Six Languages

Quiz Game CD-ROM

Progress Assessment Support System (PASS): Chapter Test*

Differentiated Instruction Modified Worksheets and Tests CD-ROM: Modified Chapter Test

One-Stop Planner CD-ROM: ExamView Test Generator (English/Spanish)

Alternative Assessment Handbook

Holt Online Assessment Program (HOAP), in the Holt Premier Online Student Edition

PASS: Section 1 Quiz*

Online Quiz: Section 1

Alternative Assessment Handbook

PASS: Section 2 Quiz*

Online Quiz: Section 2

Alternative Assessment Handbook

PASS: Section 3 Quiz*

Online Quiz: Section 3

Alternative Assessment Handbook

PASS: Section 4 Quiz*

Online Quiz: Section 4

Alternative Assessment Handbook

Power Presentations with Video CD-ROM

Power Presentations with Video are visual presentations of each chapter's main ideas. Presentations can be customized by including Quick Facts charts, images from the text, and video clips.

Power Presentations with Video CD-ROM

HOLT
United States History
Beginnings to 1877

DIVISION FOR
PUBLIC EDUCATION
AMERICAN BAR ASSOCIATION

Developed by the Division for Public Education of the American Bar Association, these materials are part of the **Democracy and Civic Education Resources.**

- **Constitution Study Guide**
- **Supreme Court Case Studies**

Holt
Online
Learning

- Document-Based Questions
- Interactive Multimedia Activities

Teacher Resources
KEYWORD: SR8 TEACHER

Student Resources
KEYWORD: SR8 US1

- Current Events
- Chapter-based Internet Activities
- and more!

Holt Premier
Online Student Edition
Complete online support for interactivity, assessment, and reporting
- Interactive Maps and Notebook
- Standardized Test Prep
- Homework Practice and Research Activities Online

CHAPTER 1 PLANNING GUIDE

Differentiating Instruction

ENGLISH-LANGUAGE LEARNERS & STRUGGLING READERS

TARGET RESOURCE

Live Ink® Online Reading Help

Spanish Resources
Spanish Chapter Summaries Audio CD Program
One-Stop Planner CD-ROM:
- ExamView Test Generator, Spanish
- PuzzlePro, Spanish

Additional Resources
Differentiated Instruction Teacher Management System: Lesson Plans for Differentiated Instruction
Chapter Resources:
- Vocabulary Builder Activities
- Social Studies Skills Activity: Interpreting Diagrams

Quick Facts Transparencies:
- Democracy and Republic
- The World Before the Opening of the Atlantic Visual Summary

Student Edition on Audio CD Program
Online Chapter Summaries in Six Languages
Interactive Skills Tutor CD-ROM

SPECIAL NEEDS LEARNERS

TARGET RESOURCE

Differentiated Instruction Modified Worksheets and Tests CD-ROM

- Vocabulary Flash Cards
- Modified Vocabulary Builder Activities
- Modified Chapter Review Activity
- Modified Chapter Test

Additional Resources
Differentiated Instruction Teacher Management System: Lesson Plans for Differentiated Instruction
Interactive Reader and Study Guide
Social Studies Skills Activity: Interpreting Diagrams
Student Edition on Audio CD Program
Interactive Skills Tutor CD-ROM
Live Ink® Online Reading Help

ADVANCED/GIFTED AND TALENTED STUDENTS

TARGET RESOURCE

Primary Source Library CD-ROM for United States History

The Library contains longer versions of quotations in the text, extra sources, and images. Included are point-of-view articles, journals, diaries, historical fiction, and political documents.

Additional Resources
United States History Document-Based Questions Activities
Differentiated Instruction Teacher Management System: Lesson Plans for Differentiated Instruction
Chapter Resource File:
- Focus on Writing Activity: A Travelogue

Differentiated Activities in the Teacher's Edition

- First Americans Maps, p. 7
- Askia the Great's Accomplishments, p. 19
- Black Death Stories, p. 28

One-Stop Planner® CD-ROM for Differentiated Instruction

Your differentiated instruction lesson plans are available at your fingertips. Holt's Teacher Management System links teaching support tools to pages in the Interactive Teacher's Edition.

The One-Stop Planner features:

- Interactive Teacher's Edition
- Calendar Planner and pacing guides
- Editable lesson plans
- All reproducible ancillaries in Adobe Acrobat (PDF) format
- ExamView Test Generator (English and Spanish)
- Transparency and video previews

Differentiated Activities in the Teacher's Edition

- Mapping Native American Culture Groups, p. 13
- Mapping West Africa's Great Kingdoms, p. 18
- Feudalism Illustrations, p. 24

Professional Development

HOLT Professional Development

- **In-service and staff development** as part of your Holt Social Studies product purchase
- **Quick Teacher Tutorial Lesson Presentation CD-ROM**
- Intensive tuition-based **Teacher Development Institute**
- **Teaching American History Online**—2 Module Professional Development Course
- **Convenient Holt Speaker Bureau**—face-to-face workshop options
- **PRAXIS™ Test Prep** interactive Web-based content refreshers*
- **24/7 Ask A Professional Development Expert** at http://www.hrw.com/prodev/

* PRAXIS is a trademark of Educational Testing Service (ETS). This publication is not endorsed or approved by ETS.

Differentiated Activities in the Teacher's Edition

- Influence of the Olmecs, p. 8
- Anasazi Presentations, p. 11
- Joining the Iroquois League, p. 14
- Comparing and Contrasting Socrates, Plato, and Aristotle, p. 23
- Analyzing Effects of the Black Death, p. 28

• Chapter Preview •

Chapter Big Ideas

Section 1 Native American societies developed across Mesoamerica and South America.

Section 2 Many diverse Native American cultures developed across the different geographic regions of North America.

Section 3 Using trade to gain wealth, Ghana, Mali, and Songhai were West Africa's most powerful kingdoms.

Section 4 New ways of thinking and growth in trade changed the way people lived in Europe.

Focus on Writing

The **Chapter Resource File** provides a Focus on Writing worksheet to help students organize and write their travelogue.

📝 **CRF:** Focus on Writing Activity: A Travelogue

The World before the Opening of the Atlantic

FOCUS ON WRITING

A Travelogue People who make long trips often write travelogues that describe their journeys. A travelogue allows people who did not make the trip to experience some of the same sights, sounds, and thoughts that the traveler did. In this chapter, you will gather information about different regions of the world and then write a travelogue describing what a place in one of these regions might have been like.

c. 38,000–10,000 BC
Paleo-Indians migrate to the Americas.

CHAPTER EVENTS
38,000 BC

WORLD EVENTS

2 CHAPTER 1

Key to Differentiating Instruction

Below Level

Basic-level activities designed for all students encountering new material

At Level

Intermediate-level activities designed for average students

Above Level

Challenging activities designed for honors and gifted and talented students

Standard English Mastery

Activities designed to improve standard English usage

2 CHAPTER 1

Introduce the Chapter
At Level

The World before the Opening of the Atlantic

1. Tell students that in this chapter they will learn about early civilizations and cultures in the Americas before the arrival of Europeans. Students will also review the conditions in Europe that helped lead to the exploration of the Americas. 🕮 **Verbal/Linguistic**

2. Discuss with students photo albums or scrapbooks they may have created that depict or record special events and achievements in their lives.

3. Have students go through the chapter, noting maps and images, as if it were a scrapbook of the world before 1500.

4. As students look at the images, ask them to create a list of important historical events that occurred before 1500.

📝 Alternative Assessment Handbook, Rubric 11: Discussions

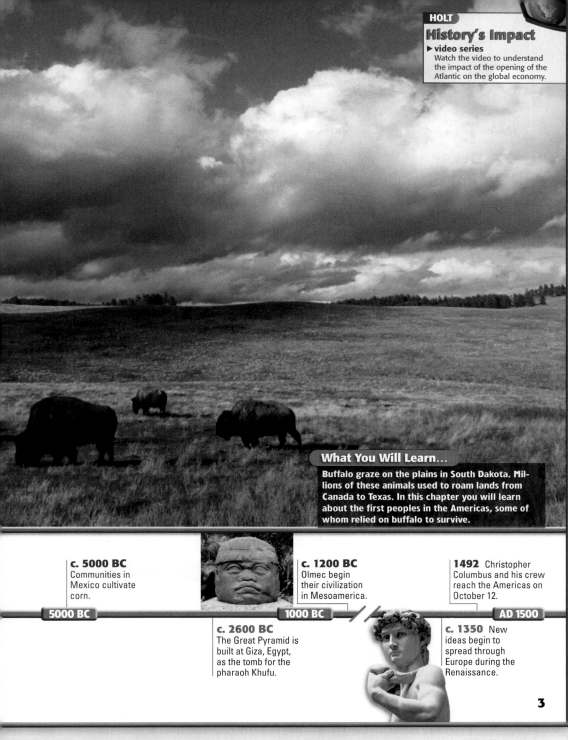

HOLT
History's Impact
► video series
Watch the video to understand the impact of the opening of the Atlantic on the global economy.

What You Will Learn...
Buffalo graze on the plains in South Dakota. Millions of these animals used to roam lands from Canada to Texas. In this chapter you will learn about the first peoples in the Americas, some of whom relied on buffalo to survive.

c. 5000 BC
Communities in Mexico cultivate corn.

c. 2600 BC
The Great Pyramid is built at Giza, Egypt, as the tomb for the pharaoh Khufu.

c. 1200 BC
Olmec begin their civilization in Mesoamerica.

c. 1350 New ideas begin to spread through Europe during the Renaissance.

1492 Christopher Columbus and his crew reach the Americas on October 12.

5000 BC   1000 BC   AD 1500

3

• Chapter Preview •

HOLT
History's Impact
► video series
See the Video Teacher's Guide for strategies for using the chapter video **The World before the Opening of the Atlantic.**

Explore the Picture

A Diverse Land Spend a minute looking at the photograph on this page. Notice how the enormous diversity of geography and climate is shown in a single landscape. When the Paleo-Indians began migrating to the Americas over 30,000 years ago, they encountered, and eventually adapted to, a land that encompassed everything from deserts to swamps and from rugged mountains to vast plains flattened by glaciers.

Analyzing Visuals How do you think these earliest Americans might have felt when they saw the landscape in this photograph? *possible answer—They might have thought the foothills and plains would provide good hunting.*

go.hrw.com
Online Resources
Chapter Resources:
KEYWORD SR8 US1
Teacher Resources:
KEYWORD: SR8 TEACHER

Explore the Time Line

1. Based on this time line, how would you describe Paleo-Indian migration to the Americas? *over a long period of time*

2. How long was it between the initial migration to the Americas and when corn was first cultivated in Mexico? *33,000 years*

3. How long had there been communities in the Americas before Christopher Columbus's arrival in 1492? *over 6,000 years*

4. How long before Columbus's voyage did new ideas spread in Europe? *142 years*

Info to Know

Development of Farming Around 5000 BC groups in what is now Mexico began growing corn. Farming changed life in the Americas. No longer were early Americans dependent on fishing, hunting, and searching for food. Farming enabled early people to settle in one place, to support larger populations, and to focus on things other than finding food. These changes helped in the development of the great Olmec, Maya, Aztec, and Inca civilizations.

Reading Social Studies

Understanding Themes

Tell students that there are many themes that are repeated throughout history. Point out to students the themes listed across this page. Ask students to explain what each theme means and how it relates to the study of history. Then introduce to students the two themes of this chapter—economics and geography. Lead students in a discussion of the roles that geography and economics played in the settlement and exploration of the Americas. Write down students' suggestions for the class to see.

Specialized Vocabulary of Social Studies

Focus on Reading Review with students the specialized social studies vocabulary terms on this page. Check to see that everyone understands the terms. Have students write a paragraph in which they use each of the terms listed. Ask volunteers to read their paragraphs to the class. Then have students brainstorm other specialized vocabulary that is used in social studies. Examples might include civilization, empire, historian, or constitution.

Reading Social Studies

| Economics | Geography | Politics | Society and Culture | Science and Technology |

Focus on Themes This chapter explains the early development of Mesoamerica and North America. You will read about early explorers from Europe, learn about early American settlements, and discover why the Spanish, the English, and the French all wanted a part of this new land. As you read the chapter, you will see how **geography** affected exploration and will learn about the **economic** issues that influenced growth and settlement.

Specialized Vocabulary of Social Studies

Focus on Reading If you flipped through the pages of this book, would you expect to see anything about square roots or formulas? How about Petri dishes or hypotheses? Of course you wouldn't. Those are terms you'd only see in math and science books.

Specialized Vocabulary Like most subjects, social studies has its own specialized vocabulary. Included in it are words and phrases you will see over and over as you read social studies materials. The charts below list some terms you may encounter as you read this book.

Terms that deal with time	
Decade	a period of 10 years
Century	a period of 100 years
Era	a long period marked by great events, developments, or figures
BC	a term used to identify dates that occurred long ago, before the birth of Jesus Christ, the founder of Christianity; it means "before Christ." BC dates get smaller as time passes, so the larger the number, the earlier the date.
AD	a term used to identify dates that occurred after Jesus's birth; it comes from a Latin phrase that means "in the year of our Lord." Unlike BC dates, AD dates get larger as time passes, so the larger the number, the later the date.
BCE	another way to refer to BC dates; it stands for "before the common era"
CE	another way to refer to AD dates; it stands for "common era"

Terms that deal with government and society	
politics	the art of creating government policies
economics	the study of the creation and use of goods and services
movement	a series of actions that bring about or try to bring about a change in society
campaign	an effort to win a political office, or a series of military actions
colony	a territory settled and controlled by a country

4 CHAPTER 1

Reading and Skills Resources

Reading Support
- Interactive Reader and Study Guide
- Student Edition on Audio CD
- Spanish Chapter Summaries Audio CD Program

Social Studies Skills Support
- Interactive Skills Tutor CD-ROM

Vocabulary Support
- **CRF:** Vocabulary Builder Activities
- **CRF:** Chapter Review Activity
- Differentiated Instruction Modified Worksheets and Tests CD-ROM:
  - Vocabulary Flash Cards
  - Vocabulary Builder Activity
  - Chapter Review Activity

OSP Holt PuzzlePro

You Try It!

The following passage shows you how some specialized vocabulary is defined in context.

Migration to the Americas

Native Americans in the Pacific Northwest carved images on **totems** —ancestor or animal spirits—on tall, wooden poles. Totem poles held great religious and historical significance for Native Americans of the Northwest. Feasts called potlatches were another unique, or unusual, aspect of these Native Americans' culture.

From Chapter 1, p. 12

Use the clues to understand meaning.

1. Find the word *totems.* The phrase after the dash is the definition. Often in this book, specialized vocabulary words are defined after a **dash**. So be on the lookout for dashes.

2. The word *potlatch* is defined in the sixth sentence. The clue to finding this definition is the word **called**. Words like **called** and **known as** can indicate that a definition is coming up. In this case, the word **feasts** is a definition of **potlatch**.

3. In the second sentence, you see a term that is in boldface print. You should recognize that word from seeing it in the section opener. The definition is **highlighted**. Why do you think some specialized vocabulary words are in boldface print while others are not?

4. The word *unique* is defined in the final sentence. The clue to finding this definition is the **comma** followed by the word **or**. So be on the lookout for commas followed by **or**.

> **As you read Chapter 1,** keep track in your notebook of the specialized vocabulary you learn.

Key Terms and People

Academic Vocabulary

Success in school is related to knowing academic vocabulary— the words that are frequently used in school assignments and discussions. In this chapter, you will learn the following academic words:

develop *(p. 8)*
classical *(p. 23)*

Reading Social Studies

Key Terms and People

Preteach these words by instructing students to create a "Double Door" FoldNote. Tell them to label the two doors History Terms and Geography Terms. Read the key terms aloud and have students write the term under the appropriate side of the FoldNote. Ask them to discuss the meanings of the words, and define any terms that the students do not understand.

LS Verbal/Linguistic, Visual/Spatial

Focus on Reading

See the **Focus on Reading** questions in this chapter for more practice on reading social studies skills.

Reading Social Studies Assessment

See the **Chapter Review** at the end of this chapter for student assessment questions related to this reading skill.

Teaching Tip

Explain to students that specialized vocabulary words can often have double meanings. The words have a different meaning when applied to a specialized field than they might to someone outside of that field. For instance, the word *check* means something completely different to a banker than it does to someone who plays hockey. Have students try to identify other words used in the study of history or geography that have double meanings.

Answers

You Try It! 3. *possible answer—Some words are in boldface print to show that they may be important words that relate to the section. Other specialized vocabulary words are not in boldface because they are used often.*

Bellringer

If YOU were there . . . Use the **Daily Bellringer Transparency** for this section to help students answer the question.

🖋️ Daily Bellringer Transparency, Section 1

Academic Vocabulary

Review with students the high-use academic term in this section.

develop the process of growing or improving (p. 8)

📖 **CRF:** Vocabulary Builder Activity, Section 1

Taking Notes

Have students copy the graphic organizer onto their own paper and then use it to take notes on the section. This activity will prepare students for the Section Assessment, in which they will complete a graphic organizer that builds on the information using a critical thinking skill.

SECTION 1

The Earliest Americans

What You Will Learn...

Main Ideas

1. Climate changes allowed Paleo-Indians to begin the first migration to the Americas.
2. Early societies existed in Mesoamerica and South America.

The Big Idea

Native American societies developed across Mesoamerica and South America.

Key Terms and People

Bering Land Bridge, *p. 6*
Paleo-Indians, *p. 6*
migration, *p. 6*
hunter-gatherers, *p. 6*
environments, *p. 7*
culture, *p. 7*

TAKING NOTES As you read, take notes on the migrations of early peoples to the Americas, as well as their earliest societies and locations.

Early Migrations to the Americas	Early Societies and Their Locations

If YOU were there...

You are living in North America about 10,000 years ago, close to the end of the Ice Age. For weeks, your group has been following a herd of elk across a marshy landscape. This trip has taken you far from your usual hunting grounds. The air is warmer here. There are thick grasses and bushes full of berries. You decide to camp here for the summer and perhaps stay a while.

How would settling here change your way of life?

BUILDING BACKGROUND The first settlers to the Americas probably came in small groups from Asia. Over thousands of years, they moved into nearly every region of North and South America. In the Americas, these people encountered, and adapted to, many different climates and types of land.

First Migration to the Americas

Many scientists believe that the first people arrived in North America during the last Ice Age. At the start of the Ice Age, Earth's climate became intensely cold. Large amounts of water froze into huge, moving sheets of ice called glaciers. As a result, ocean levels dropped more than 300 feet lower than they are today. When the sea level fell, a land bridge between northeastern Asia and present-day Alaska was exposed. Geographers call this strip of land the **Bering Land Bridge**. Although no one knows exactly when or how people crossed into North America, evidence suggests that people called **Paleo-Indians** crossed this bridge into Alaska between 38,000 and 10,000 BC.

This **migration**—a movement of people or animals from one region to another—took place over a long time. It is believed that Paleo-Indians traveled south into Canada, the United States, and Mexico following herds of animals. Over time, their descendants went as far as the southern tip of South America. These people were **hunter-gatherers**, people who hunted animals and gathered wild plants for food.

6 CHAPTER 1

Teach the Big Idea

At Level

The Earliest Americans

1. **Teach** Ask students the questions in the Main Idea boxes to teach this section.

2. **Apply** Instruct students to fold a piece of paper lengthways in the middle. Have students label the first column *The First Migration to the Americas*, and the second column *Early Mesoamerican and South American People*. Have students list the main ideas of the section under each heading. Under the second heading students

should list each group of people discussed in the text. **LS Verbal/Linguistic**

3. **Review** Have students share the main ideas they have listed under each heading.

4. **Practice/Homework** Have students create their own maps showing where each group of early Americans settled. Students should include drawings that illustrate an aspect of each group's culture. **LS Visual/Spatial**

📖 Alternative Assessment Handbook, Rubrics 13: Artwork; and 20: Map Creation

Land Migrations of Early Peoples

ASIA

180°

170°W

Bering Strait

160°W

150°W

140°W

130°W

ALASKA

Mammoth skeleton

LAURENTIDE ICE SHEET

Kernels of maize

NORTH AMERICA

120°W

30°N

Gulf of Mexico

110°W

90°W

MESOAMERICA

20°N

100°W

Maya pyramid, Chichén Itzá, Mexico

SOUTH AMERICA

About 8000 BC, Earth's climate grew warmer, and the Ice Age ended. Rising temperatures melted glaciers. Water levels in the oceans rose, and the Bering Land Bridge was covered with water.

The warmer climate at the end of the Ice Age created new **environments**, climates and landscapes that surround living things. Large herds of animals such as buffalo and deer ate new short grasses that thrived in the warm climate. As the number of these animals grew, Paleo-Indians hunted these animals for survival.

Varied environments influenced the development of different Native American societies, or groups that share a culture. **Culture** is a group's set of common values and traditions, including language, government, and family relationships.

Like all societies, Native American groups changed over time. People planted seeds, and eventually they learned to breed animals, farm, and grow plants. Maize, or corn, was one of their most important early crops. Later, they learned to grow beans and squash. Farming allowed people to stop moving around looking for food and to settle in one place. With adequate food supplies, settlements could support larger populations. As populations grew, more advanced societies began to develop.

READING CHECK Drawing Conclusions How did climate change affect early peoples' migrations?

GEOGRAPHY SKILLS **INTERPRETING MAPS**

1. **Movement** In what general direction did early peoples migrate?
2. **Human-Environment Interaction** What natural features affected the route people took from Alaska to southern North America?

Main Idea

❶ First Migration to the Americas

Climate changes allowed Paleo-Indians to begin the first migration to the Americas.

Recall What is the name of the early people who migrated to the Americas, and how did they arrive? *Paleo-Indians; crossed the Bering Land Bridge*

Identify Cause and Effect How did warmer climates at the end of the Ice Age affect the Americas? *created new environments that supported herds of smaller animals, which Paleo-Indians began hunting*

Evaluate What role does environment play in the development of a society? *food, shelter, way of life, and community development are closely related to environment*

🗺 Map Transparency: Land Migrations of Early Peoples

Linking to Today

New Theories on Migration to the Americas Scientists have dated Monte Verde, an archaeological site in Chile, as being at least 12,500 years old. Because Monte Verde is located some 10,000 miles south of the Bering Strait, some scientists think the first Americans may have come from Asia by boat and sailed south along the coast.

Interpreting Maps

Migrations of Early Peoples

Movement Why do you think the majority of people kept migrating southward? *because of harsh climate in the north; also they often followed migrating animals*

🗺 Map Transparency: Land Migrations of Early Peoples

Differentiating Instruction

Below Level

English-Language Learners

Materials: blank outline maps of the Americas and eastern Asia

1. Organize students into pairs. Have each student ask his or her partner questions about the first Americans. Questions should focus on the following:

   • where the first Americans came from (*Asia*)
   • how they came to the Americas (*by land over the Bering Land Bridge between Asia and Alaska; later in small boats*)
   • where they settled (*present-day Canada, the United States, and Mexico; descendants reached the tip of South America*)
   • how geography affected their movements, and how they lived (*traveled south to warmer areas; each group ate foods available locally*)

2. Provide outline maps of the Americas. Have pairs draw the migration of early people.
   LS **Verbal/Linguistic, Visual/Spatial**

   📋 Alternative Assessment Handbook, Rubric 20: Map Creation

Answers

Interpreting Maps 1. *south and east;* **2.** *ice sheets, mountains, rivers*

Reading Check *land bridge covered in water, different food sources*

7

❷ Early Mesoamerican and South American Societies

Early societies existed in Mesoamerica and South America.

Recall Name the civilizations that developed in Mesoamerica and South America. *Olmec, Maya, Aztec, Inca*

Compare How were the Aztecs and Incas similar? *Both had well organized governments, cities, known for building with stone. Aztecs had a writing system, Incas did not.*

Summarize What were some of the accomplishments of the Maya? *They built stone temples, palaces, bridges, large plazas, and canals to control water flow, created accurate calendars, developed a writing system.*

🗺 Map Transparency: Aztec and Inca Civilizations

Written Records
Explain to students that people who lived in southwest Asia were not the only people to have had writing systems. Remind students that writing systems mark the difference between prehistory and history.

Early Mesoamerican and South American Societies

Some of the earliest American cultures arose in Mesoamerica, a region that includes the southern part of what is now Mexico and the northern parts of Central America.

ACADEMIC VOCABULARY
develop the process of growing or improving

THE IMPACT TODAY
On the site of the Aztec capital, Tenochtitlán, workers filled the lake to build Mexico City, the modern-day capital of Mexico.

Olmec and Maya

Around 1200 BC the Olmec **developed** the earliest known civilization in Mesoamerica. The Olmec are known for their use of stone in architecture and sculpture. They built the first pyramids in the Americas, and they created sculptures of huge stone heads. When their civilization ended around 400 BC, trade had spread Olmec culture throughout the region.

Like the Olmec, the Maya grew maize and other crops and lived in small villages. These villages traded goods with each other, and by about AD 200, the Maya were building large cities.

Maya cities had pyramids, large stone temples, palaces, and bridges. The Maya also paved large plazas for public gatherings and built canals to control the flow of water through the cities.

In the 900s Maya civilization began to collapse. Historians are still not sure what caused this great civilization's decline.

Aztec

The Aztec were fierce warriors, and their superior military ability was key to their success. Around the mid-1100s AD, the Aztec migrated south to central Mexico. They conquered many towns, made alliances to build their empire, and controlled a huge trade network.

In AD 1325, the Aztec founded their capital, Tenochtitlán (tay-nawch-teet-LAHN), on an island in Lake Texcoco. It became the greatest city in the Americas and one of the world's largest cities. The city's island location made travel and trade difficult, so the Aztec built raised roads to connect the island to the shore.

Trade and tribute paid by conquered people in the form of cotton, gold, and food made the Aztec rich. By the early 1500s, they ruled the most powerful state in Mesoamerica.

Inca

The Inca began as a small tribe in the Andes Mountains of South America. They named their capital city Cuzco (KOO-skoh). In the

The ancient Maya city of Palenque was a major power on the border between the Maya highlands and lowlands. Its great temples and plazas were typical of the Classic Age of Maya civilization.

8 CHAPTER 1

Critical Thinking: Drawing Conclusions

Above Level

Influence of the Olmecs

Research Required

1. Tell students that Olmec society has been called a "mother culture" because it influenced most later civilizations in Mesoamerica.

2. Using information in the text, discuss some of the similarities between the Olmecs and the Maya and the Aztecs.

3. Have students conduct research on the Internet or use other resources to learn more about how the Olmecs influenced

later cultures. Encourage students to pay special attention to each group's agricultural methods.

4. Have students create a graphic organizer similar to the one shown that illustrates the Olmecs' influence on the Maya and Aztecs.
LS Visual/Spatial

📋 Alternative Assessment Handbook, Rubric 13: Graphic Organizers mid-1400s, the Inca began to expand their territory. By the 1500s the empire stretched along the Pacific coast from what is now northern Ecuador to central Chile. In time, the empire was home to about 12 million people. The Inca formed a strong central government with a king as ruler. The official language of the empire was Quechua. Because there was no written language, records were kept on a system of knotted strings called *quipu*.

The Inca are known for building and for art. Massive buildings and forts were made of huge stone blocks. An advanced system of highways ran the length of the empire. Paved roads and rope bridges connected all parts of Inca territory. This enabled the Inca to communicate with and control their large empire.

READING CHECK **Summarizing** What early civilizations existed in Mesoamerica and South America?

SUMMARY AND PREVIEW Early people migrated into North and South America and developed societies. In the next section you will learn about Native American cultures in North America.

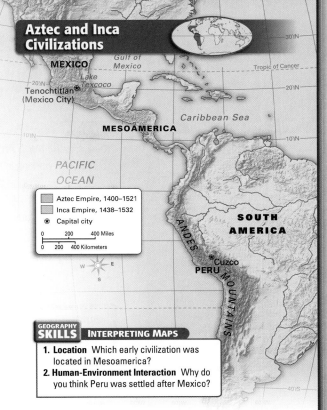

Aztec and Inca Civilizations

Aztec Empire, 1400–1521
Inca Empire, 1438–1532
⊛ Capital city

0   200   400 Miles
0   200   400 Kilometers

GEOGRAPHY SKILLS **INTERPRETING MAPS**

1. **Location** Which early civilization was located in Mesoamerica?
2. **Human-Environment Interaction** Why do you think Peru was settled after Mexico?

Section 1 Assessment

go.hrw.com
Online Quiz
KEYWORD: SR8 HP1

Reviewing Ideas, Terms, and People

1. **a. Recall** What was the Ice Age?
   b. Summarize Why were early peoples able to use the **Bering Land Bridge**?
   c. Predict Why do you think early peoples in the Americas **migrated** south?
2. **a. Identify** What is the earliest known civilization in the Americas, and where was it located?
   b. Analyze How did the Aztec build such a powerful, rich state?
   c. Draw Conclusions Which of the four civilizations discussed do you think was the most highly developed?

Critical Thinking

3. **Categorizing** Review your notes on the migration of early peoples and their societies. Then copy the table below and use it to identify the accomplishments of early American civilizations.

	Rise	Significant Accomplishments
Olmec		
Maya		
Aztec		
Inca		

FOCUS ON WRITING

4. **Understanding Ancient Peoples** Use the descriptions of the earliest Americans found in this section to list some similarities and differences between the lives of ancient peoples and your life today.

THE WORLD BEFORE THE OPENING OF THE ATLANTIC **9**

Section 1 Assessment Answers

1. **a.** Earth had freezing temperatures, large amounts of water froze into huge ice sheets
   b. The land bridge was exposed when ocean levels fell and so much water froze.
   c. warmer climate, following herds

2. **a.** Olmec; Mesoamerica
   b. fierce warriors, made alliances, collected tribute, controlled trade
   c. Maya: temples, palaces, and pyramids, structured society, writing, calendars; Aztec: large cities, written language, rich, powerful; Inca: large, well run empire

3. Olmecs—stone architecture, first pyramids, huge stone heads, number and calendar systems, method of writing used glyphs; Maya—pyramids, stone temples, jade and gold jewelry, carvings and paintings, observatories, calendars, symbol for zero; Aztecs—city of Tenochtitlán, writing system, calendar, turquoise masks and gold jewelry; Inca—kept records using cords, buildings and art

4. Students' answers should demonstrate understanding of similarities and differences between ancient life and modern life.

Bellringer

If YOU were there . . . Use the **Daily Bellringer Transparency** for this section to help students answer the question.

🖢 Daily Bellringer Transparency, Section 2

Building Vocabulary

Preteach or review the following terms:

confederation alliance (p. 14)

nomadic traveling (p. 14)

raid attack, invade (p. 14)

🖺 **CRF:** Vocabulary Builder Activity, Section 2

Taking Notes

Have students copy the graphic organizer onto their own paper and then use it to take notes on the section. This activity will prepare students for the Section Assessment, in which they will complete a graphic organizer that builds on the information using a critical thinking skill.

Native American Cultures

What You Will Learn...

Main Ideas

1. Several early societies developed in North America long before Europeans explored the continent.
2. Geographic areas influenced Native American cultures.
3. Native American cultures shared beliefs about religion and land ownership.

The Big Idea

Many diverse Native American cultures developed across the different geographic regions of North America.

Key Terms and People

pueblos, *p. 11*
kivas, *p. 11*
totems, *p. 12*
teepees, *p. 14*
matrilineal, *p. 14*
Iroquois League, *p. 14*

TAKING NOTES As you read, take notes on early societies. Write your notes in a chart like the one below.

Early Societies	
Culture Areas	
Beliefs	

If YOU were there...

You live in the North American Southwest about 1,000 years ago. You've been working in the fields for several hours today. The maize crop looks good this summer, and you are hoping for a successful harvest. After finishing your work, you walk home. The opening to your house is in a cliff wall 30 feet above a canyon floor. You must use ladders to get to the opening.

Do you like the location of your home? Why?

BUILDING BACKGROUND After crossing the land bridge from Asia during the Ice Age, hunter-gatherer groups spread into every region of North America. Many diverse cultures formed as Native Americans adapted to their different environments.

Early Societies

The earliest people in North America were hunter-gatherers. After 5000 BC some of these people learned how to farm, and they settled in villages. Although less populated than South America and Mesoamerica, North America had many complex societies long before Europeans reached the continent.

Anasazi

By 1500 BC the people who lived in the North American Southwest, like those who lived in Mesoamerica, were growing maize. One of the early farm cultures in the Southwest was the Anasazi (ah-nuh-SAH-zee). The Anasazi lived in the Four Corners region, where present-day Arizona, Colorado, New Mexico, and Utah meet. Anasazi farmers adapted to their dry environment and grew maize, beans, and squash. Over time, they began to use irrigation to increase food production. By the time the Anasazi settled in the area, they were already skilled basket makers. They wove straw, vines, and yucca to make containers for food and other items, and they eventually became skilled potters as well.

10 CHAPTER 1

Teach the Big Idea

At Level

Native American Cultures

1. **Teach** Ask students the questions in the Main Idea boxes to teach this section.

2. **Apply** Create a table with the following headings for students to see: *Arctic, Subarctic, Northwest Coast, Plateau, Great Plains, Northeast, Great Basin, California, Southwest,* and *Southeast.* Have students copy the table onto their own paper. As students read the section, have them list the Native American groups that lived in each region and explain how each group adapted to its environment.

3. **Review** Ask students to compare and contrast the information in their charts. Have students share their ideas about similarities and differences among the Native American groups.

4. **Practice/Homework** Have students create a Venn diagram that illustrates the similarities and differences among the groups discussed in this section. **LS Verbal/Linguistic**

🖺 Alternative Assessment Handbook, Rubric 11: Discussions

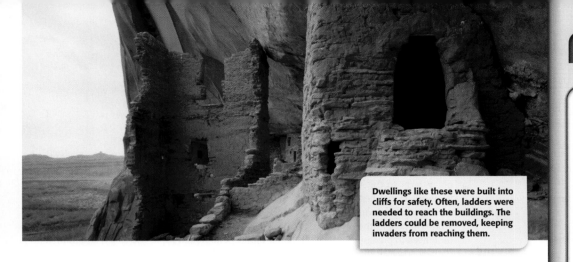

Dwellings like these were built into cliffs for safety. Often, ladders were needed to reach the buildings. The ladders could be removed, keeping invaders from reaching them.

The early Anasazi lived in pit houses dug into the ground. After about AD 750 they built **pueblos**, or aboveground houses made of a heavy clay called adobe. The Anasazi built these houses on top of each other, creating large multistoried complexes. Some pueblos had several hundred rooms and could house 1,000 people.

The Anasazi often built their houses in canyon walls and had to use ladders to enter their homes. These cliff dwellings provided a strong defense against enemies. The Anasazi also built **kivas**, underground ceremonial chambers, at the center of each community. Kivas were sacred areas used for religious ceremonies. Some of these rituals focused on the life-giving forces of rain and maize.

The Anasazi thrived for hundreds of years. After 1300 AD, however, they began to abandon their villages. Scholars believe that drought, disease, or raids by nomadic tribes from the north may have caused the Anasazi to move away from their pueblos.

Mound Builders

Several farming societies developed in the eastern part of North America after 1000 BC. The Hopewell lived along the Mississippi, Ohio, and lower Missouri river valleys. They supported their large population with agriculture and trade. They built large burial mounds to honor their dead.

The Hopewell culture had declined by AD 700. Another culture, the Mississippian, began to thrive in the same area. Skilled farmers and traders, the Mississippian built large settlements. Their largest city, Cahokia, was located near present-day Saint Louis. It had a population of 30,000.

The Mississippian built hundreds of mounds for religious ceremonies. Cahokia alone had more than 100 temple and burial mounds. These mounds had flat tops, and temples were built on top of the mounds. Many of the mounds were gigantic. Monks Mound, near Collinsville, Illinois, for example, was 100 feet high and covered 16 acres.

Several other mound-building cultures thrived in eastern North America. More than 10,000 mounds have been found in the Ohio River valley alone. Some of these mounds are shaped like birds and snakes. The mound-building cultures had declined by the time European explorers reached the Southeast. Their societies no longer existed by the early 1700s.

READING CHECK Summarizing Why did some Native American groups build mounds?

THE WORLD BEFORE THE OPENING OF THE ATLANTIC **11**

---

❷ Native American Culture Areas

Geographic areas influenced Native American cultures.

Explain How did the Inuit adapt to the harsh climate of Alaska and Canada? *built igloos, homes partially underground, fished and hunted for food, used dogs to pull sleds*

Draw Inferences Why did Subarctic peoples live in different types of shelters at different times? *When following the seasonal migrations of deer, these peoples needed shelters they could move easily. The rest of the time, they could live in more permanent dwellings.*

Summarize What different methods did Native American groups of the Southwest use to adapt to their dry climate? *learned to irrigate to grow crops, especially maize, squash, and beans; Apache and Navajo hunted small animals and foraged for food*

🗺 Map Transparency: Native American Culture Areas

Linking to Today

Potlatches In the Chinook language, the word *potlatch* means "to give." Potlatches were often associated with funerals. Even today, in some cultural groups, families may host a potlatch in honor of a deceased member on the one-year anniversary of that person's death.

Info to Know

Getting Around in the Far North In addition to dogsleds, the Inuit and Aleut used kayaks, or one-person canoes covered with skins. Kayaks enabled the Inuit to cross icy Arctic waters.

Answers

Focus on Reading *ancestor or animal spirits*

12

Native American Culture Areas

Researchers use culture areas—the geographic locations that influenced societies—to help them describe ancient Native American peoples. North America is divided into several culture areas.

North and Northwest

The far north of North America is divided into the Arctic and Subarctic culture areas. Few plants grow in the Arctic because the ground is always frozen beneath a thin top layer of soil. This harsh environment was home to two groups of people, the Inuit and the Aleut. The Inuit lived in present-day northern Alaska and Canada. Their homes were igloos, hide tents, and huts. The Aleut, whose home was in western and southern Alaska, lived in multifamily houses that were partially underground. The two groups shared many cultural features, including language. Both groups survived by fishing and hunting large mammals. The Aleut and Inuit also depended on dogs for many tasks, such as hunting and pulling sleds.

South of the Arctic lies the Subarctic, home to groups such as the Dogrib and Montagnais peoples. While they followed the seasonal migrations of deer, these peoples lived in shelters made of animal skins. At other times, they lived in villages made up of log houses. Farther south, the Kwakiutl and the Chinook thrived, thanks to the rich supply of game animals, fish, and wild plants that allowed large populations to increase without the need for farming.

FOCUS ON READING
What is the definition of **totems** according to this sentence?

Native Americans in the Pacific Northwest carved images of **totems** —ancestor or animal spirits—on tall, wooden poles. Totem poles held great religious and historical significance for Native Americans of the Northwest. Feasts called potlatches were another unique, or unusual, aspect of these Native Americans' culture. At these gatherings, hosts, usually chiefs or wealthy people, gave away most of their belongings as gifts. In this way, the hosts increased their social importance.

12 CHAPTER 1

West and Southwest

Farther south along the Pacific coast was the California region, which included the area between the Pacific and the Sierra Nevada mountain range. Food sources were plentiful, so farming was not necessary. One major plant food was acorns, which were ground into flour. People also fished and hunted deer and other game. Most Native Americans in the California region lived in groups of families of about 50 to 300. Among these groups, including the Pomo, Hupa, and Yurok, more than 100 languages were spoken.

The area east of the Sierra Nevada Mountains, the Great Basin, received little rain. To survive, Native Americans adapted to the drier climate by gathering seeds, digging roots, and trapping small animals for food. Most groups in this area, including the Paiute, Shoshone, and Ute, spoke the same language.

The Southwest culture region included the present-day states of Arizona and New Mexico, and parts of Colorado and Texas. Pueblo groups, such as the Hopi and Zuni, lived there. Like the Anasazi, these Native Americans also adapted to a dry climate. The Pueblo irrigated the land and grew maize, squash, and beans. These crops were vital to southwestern peoples. The Pueblo religion focused on two key areas of Pueblo life, rain and maize. The Pueblo performed religious rituals hoping to bring rain and a successful maize crop to their peoples.

Pueblo peoples were settled and built multistoried houses out of adobe bricks. Over time their towns grew larger, and some towns had more than 1,000 residents. Pueblo peoples made fine pottery that featured beautifully painted designs.

Bering Sea

Collaborative Learning

At Level

Early North American Societies Flash Cards

1. Have each student divide a sheet of paper into six parts, creating six note cards.

2. Ask students to label each of the cards with the name of one of the Native American societies discussed in this section.

3. On each card, have students write one question about an aspect of the Native American society they listed on the card. Encourage students to make the questions as specific as possible. Have students write the answers on the back of the cards.

4. Pair students and have partners use their cards to quiz each other.

5. When students are done, have them switch partners and repeat the process.

📊 **Verbal/Linguistic, Interpersonal**

📄 Alternative Assessment Handbook, Rubric 14: Group Activity

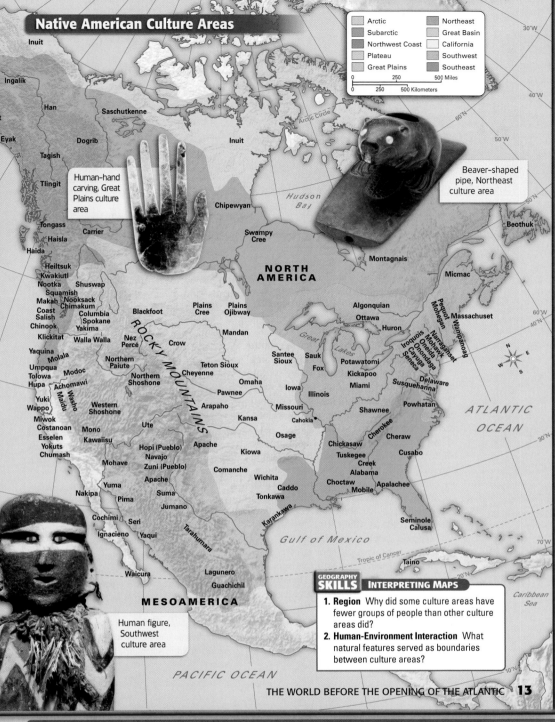

Native American Culture Areas

Legend:
- Arctic
- Subarctic
- Northwest Coast
- Plateau
- Great Plains
- Northeast
- Great Basin
- California
- Southwest
- Southeast

0 — 250 — 500 Miles
0 — 250 — 500 Kilometers

Inuit
Ingalik
uit
Eyak
Han
Tagish
Tlingit
Dogrib
Saschutkenne
Ingalik
Tongass
Haisla
Haida
Carrier
Chipewyan
Inuit
Heiltsuk
Kwakiutl
Nootka Shuswap
Squamish
Makah Nooksack
Coast Chimakum
Salish Columbia
Chinook Spokane
Klickitat Yakima
Walla Walla
Yaquina
Molala
Umpqua Modoc
Tolowa
Hupa Achomawi
Yuki Washo
Maidu
Wappo
Miwok
Costanoan Mono
Esselen Kawaiisu
Yokuts
Chumash
Mohave
Yuma
Nakipa Pima
Cochimi Seri
Ignacieno Yaqui
Waicura

Nez
Percé
Northern
Paiute
Northern
Shoshone
Western
Shoshone
Ute
Hopi (Pueblo)
Navajo
Zuni (Pueblo)
Apache
Suma
Jumano
Tarahumara
Lagunero
Guachichil

Blackfoot
Crow
Plains
Cree
Plains
Ojibway
Teton Sioux
Cheyenne
Mandan
Pawnee
Arapaho
Kansa
Osage
Apache
Kiowa
Comanche
Wichita
Caddo
Tonkawa
Karankawa

Santee
Sioux
Sauk
Fox
Omaha
Iowa
Missouri
Illinois
Cahokia
Potawatomi
Kickapoo
Miami
Shawnee

Swampy
Cree
Montagnais

Algonquian
Ottawa
Huron
Iroquois
Mohawk
Oneida
Onondaga
Cayuga
Seneca
Delaware
Susquehanna
Powhatan
Cherokee
Cheraw
Cusabo

Pequot
Mohegan
Narragansett
Massachuset
Micmac
Beothuk

NORTH
AMERICA

Hudson
Bay

Great
Lakes

ATLANTIC
OCEAN

Chickasaw
Tuskegee
Creek
Alabama
Choctaw
Mobile Apalachee

Seminole
Calusa

Gulf of Mexico

Tropic of Cancer

Taino

Caribbean
Sea

MESOAMERICA

PACIFIC OCEAN

Arctic Circle

Human-hand carving, Great Plains culture area

Beaver-shaped pipe, Northeast culture area

Human figure, Southwest culture area

GEOGRAPHY SKILLS | INTERPRETING MAPS

1. **Region** Why did some culture areas have fewer groups of people than other culture areas did?
2. **Human-Environment Interaction** What natural features served as boundaries between culture areas?

THE WORLD BEFORE THE OPENING OF THE ATLANTIC **13**

Direct Teach

Main Idea

❷ **Native American Culture Areas**

Geographic areas influenced Native American cultures.

Explain Why did the Pueblo peoples adopt a sedentary lifestyle? *They learned to grow crops and irrigate their land so they did not need to travel in search of food.*

Analyze Why do you think so many Native American groups lived along the Pacific coast of the present-day United States? *They could catch plenty of food and the climate was mild.*

🗺 Map Transparency: Native American Culture Areas

Teaching Tip

Arctic vs. Subarctic
Explain to students that arctic relates to the North Pole or the region around it. Subarctic refers to the regions immediately outside of the arctic circle or regions that have similar conditions.

Cross-Discipline Activity: Geography

At Level

Mapping Native American Culture Groups

Materials: colored pencils

1. Have students examine the map, Native American Culture Areas.

2. Have students create their own outline maps of North America. Then, have students fill in the following on their maps:
   - Native American culture areas and groups covered in this section;
   - three distinguishing features about each culture area, such as methods of obtaining

food, types of shelter, types of government, and religious rituals;
   - major geographical features, such as mountain ranges and bodies of water.

3. Maps should include a title and a legend.

4. Have students refer to their maps as you review how the environment influenced culture in North America. **LS** **Visual/Spatial**

📖 Alternative Assessment Handbook, Rubric 20: Map Creation

Answers

Interpreting Maps 1. *Geographical and climatic conditions may have limited the size of groups; ability to grow food or hunt also impacted the size of the population;* **2.** *mountains, rivers, lakes*

13

Main Idea

❷ Native American Culture Areas

Geographic areas influenced Native American cultures.

Recall Explain how the Iroquois lived. *They were farmers, hunters, and traders who lived in rectangular homes, called longhouses, that housed 8 to 10 families.*

Compare and Contrast What were some of the similarities and differences between Native American cultures in the Great Plains and the East? *While both farmed, most Plains peoples depended on buffalo for food, clothing, and shelter. Plains peoples were nomadic; Eastern groups had wood for housing, fished, and developed the Iroquois League.*

Predict What might be the differences between a matrilineal society, like the Pawnee, and a patrilineal society? *possible answers—In a matrilineal society, ties to the mother's side of the family might be stronger; women might be held in higher esteem.*

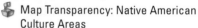 Map Transparency: Native American Culture Areas

---

MISCONCEPTION ///ALERT\\\

What about Horses? When reading about Native Americans of the Great Plains, you may picture scenes from movies or television showing Plains peoples on horses. Actually, horses did not exist in North America until European explorers brought horses to the Americas.

Answers

Analyzing Visuals *to protect their homes from intruders*

Reading Check *Different groups had to adapt to their environment; people who lived in cold climates could not farm; those who could gather food did not have to farm; those who lived near oceans fished; those on the Plains hunted. The environment affected the type of housing that was built.*

14

Iroquois Longhouse

Northeast Indians such as the Iroquois lived in longhouses made of the bark of trees. The drawing shows how the longhouses were arranged in one Iroquois village.

Why do you think a fence was placed around the longhouses?

The Apache and Navajo also lived in the Southwest. These groups were nomadic—they moved from place to place hunting small animals and foraging for food. The Apache and Navajo also supported themselves by raiding the villages of the Pueblo and others.

Great Plains

The huge Great Plains region stretches south from Canada into Texas. This culture area is bordered by the Mississippi Valley on the east and the Rocky Mountains on the west. The Plains were mainly grassland, home to millions of buffalo. Deer, elk, and other game also thrived there.

Most Great Plains peoples were nomadic hunters. Many groups hunted buffalo using bows and spears. Blackfoot and Arapaho hunters sometimes chased the animals over cliffs, drove them into corrals, or trapped them in a ring of fire. Native Americans used buffalo skins for shields, clothing, and coverings for their **teepees** — cone-shaped shelters.

Some Plains groups were farmers. The Mandan and Pawnee settled in villages and grew corn, beans, and squash. The Pawnee lived in round lodges made of dirt. Like some other Native American groups, Pawnee society was **matrilineal**. This means that people traced their ancestry through their mothers, not their fathers.

Northeast and Southeast

Eastern North America was rich in sources for food and shelter. Animals, plant foods, and fish were plentiful in the region's woodlands and river valleys. Forests provided wood for housing.

Most southeastern groups, including the Cherokee, Creek, and Seminole, lived in farming villages governed by village councils. In the Northeast, groups like the Algonquian survived by hunting and gathering plants. Those in the south farmed, hunted, gathered plants, and fished.

To the east of the Algonquian lived the Iroquois. They were farmers, hunters, and traders who lived in longhouses, or rectangular homes made from logs and bark, that housed 8 to 10 families.

The Iroquois created the **Iroquois League**. This confederation, or alliance, was established by the Cayuga, Mohawk, Oneida, Onondaga, and Seneca. The league waged war against and made peace with non-Iroquois peoples. Its goal was to strengthen the alliance against invasion. The league helped the Iroquois become one of the most powerful Native American peoples in North America.

READING CHECK **Generalizing** How did environment influence Native American cultures in North America?

Critical Thinking: Supporting a Point of View ▸ Above Level

Joining the Iroquois League

1. Review with students the significance of the Iroquois League.

2. Ask students to imagine that they are leaders in a Native American group that is considering joining the league. Each student should write a short essay explaining why the group should join the league. The essay should contain specific reasons.

3. You may wish to instruct students to conduct additional research on the Iroquois League to obtain more information to use in their essays.

4. Ask volunteers to share their essays with the class. Encourage the class to discuss the essays. **LS Verbal/Linguistic**

   📖 Alternative Assessment Handbook, Rubrics 37: Writing Assignments; and 43: Writing to Persuade

Shared Beliefs

Although they were different culturally and geographically, Native American groups of North America shared certain beliefs. The religion of most Native American peoples, for example, was linked to nature. Native Americans believed that spiritual forces were everywhere, dwelling in heavenly bodies and in sacred places on the earth. Spirits even lived within animals and plants. Native Americans tried to honor the spirits in their daily lives.

Ceremonies maintained the group's relationship with Earth and Sky, which were believed to be the sustainers of life. In addition, individuals who wanted help prayed to their spirit protector.

Native Americans also shared beliefs about property. They believed that individual ownership only applied to the crops one grew. The land itself was for the use of everyone in the village, and a person's right to use it was temporary. Native Americans also believed they should preserve the land for future generations. These beliefs contrasted sharply with those of Europeans—a difference that would cause conflict.

Despite their shared beliefs, the diverse culture groups of North America had little interest in joining together into large political units. As a result, Native Americans on the North American continent did not form large empires like the Aztec and Inca of Mesoamerica did.

READING CHECK **Identifying Points of View** What religious beliefs did Native American groups share?

SUMMARY AND PREVIEW People of North America formed many complex societies. In the next section you will read about societies in West Africa.

Section 2 Assessment

go.hrw.com
Online Quiz
KEYWORD: SR8 HP1

Reviewing Ideas, Terms, and People

1. **a. Recall** Why did the Anasazi build **kivas**?
   b. Summarize What different types of housing were built by the Anasazi?
   c. Draw Conclusions Why do you think that some mounds were built in the shape of birds and snakes?
2. **a. Identify** What are culture areas?
   b. Contrast How did food sources for Native Americans of the North and Northwest differ from those of Native Americans living in the West and Southwest?
   c. Elaborate Why was the formation of the **Iroquois League** considered to be a significant political development?
3. **a. Recall** How did Native Americans view land ownership?
   b. Analyze What role did religion play in the lives of Native Americans?
   c. Predict Why do you think most Native American groups did not form large empires like the Aztec and the Inca did?

Critical Thinking

4. **Comparing and Contrasting** Review your notes on early societies and culture areas. Then use a Venn diagram like this one to identify similarities and differences among Native American culture groups.

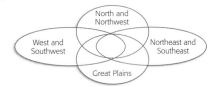

North and Northwest

West and Southwest

Northeast and Southeast

Great Plains

FOCUS ON WRITING

5. **Describing Culture** Look back through this section to discover ways in which a group's beliefs, environment, and practices can be described. Write down phrases that you think are especially useful in understanding Native American cultures.

THE WORLD BEFORE THE OPENING OF THE ATLANTIC **15**

Section 2 Assessment Answers

1. **a.** for religious ceremonies
   b. pit houses, stacked pueblos, cliff dwellings
   c. possible answer—had religious or cultural significance to the group of Native Americans
2. **a.** geographic locations that influenced societies
   b. North and Northwest—hunted large animals, fished, ate wild plants; West and Southwest—hunted, farmed, gathered plants, trapped small animals
   c. It united and strengthened politically different Native American groups among other Native American groups.

3. **a.** Individuals did not own the land, only the crops that they grew.
   b. Native Americans believed spirits were everywhere; they honored the spirits in their daily lives.
   c. possible answers—geographic barriers made uniting difficult; wanted to maintain independence; lifestyles were too diverse
4. Students' answers should show the similarities and differences of Native American cultural groups discussed in this section.
5. Students' answers should reflect an understanding of Native American cultures.

15

Trading Kingdoms of West Africa

Bellringer

If YOU were there . . . Use the **Daily Bellringer Transparency** for this section to help students answer the question.

🖋 Daily Bellringer Transparency, Section 3

Building Vocabulary

Preteach or review the following terms:

profit benefit from; gain (p. 16)

succession following in order; sequence (p. 16)

📋 **CRF:** Vocabulary Builder Activity, Section 3

Taking Notes

Have students copy the graphic organizer onto their own paper and then use it to take notes on the section. This activity will prepare students for the Section Assessment, in which they will complete a graphic organizer that builds on the information using a critical thinking skill.

What You Will Learn...

Main Ideas

1. West Africa developed three great kingdoms that grew wealthy through their control of trade.
2. Slaves became a valuable trade item in West Africa.

The Big Idea

Using trade to gain wealth, Ghana, Mali, and Songhai were West Africa's most powerful kingdoms.

Key Terms and People

Berbers, *p. 16*
Mansa Musa, *p. 18*
hajj, *p. 18*
mosques, *p. 19*
Askia the Great, *p. 19*

TAKING NOTES As you read, take notes on the rise of early African kingdoms and the role of trade in their development. Use a chart like the one below.

Kingdom	Rise	The Role of Trade
Ghana		
Mali		
Songhai		

If YOU were there...

You are a trader's assistant from the Middle East, traveling in a caravan headed for West Africa. The caravan carries many goods, but the most precious is salt. Your job is to trade the salt for gold and return the gold to your employer immediately. Your boss never meets the traders face to face.

Why is your boss so secretive?

BUILDING BACKGROUND The continent of Africa was luxuriously rich in resources. West Africa had both fertile soils and valuable minerals, especially gold and iron. Ancient trade routes had connected Africa with the Middle East and Asia for hundreds of years. Over time, trade developed between regions with different resources. Trade and abundant resources led to the growth of several great kingdoms in West Africa.

West Africa's Great Kingdoms

For hundreds of years, trade routes crisscrossed West Africa. For most of that time, West Africans did not profit much from the Saharan trade because the routes were run by **Berbers**, a group of people from northern Africa. Eventually, that situation changed. A succession of three great kingdoms came to power as their peoples gained control of valuable trade routes in West Africa. Ghana (GAH-nuh) was the first of these empires, followed by the kingdoms of Mali (MAH-lee) and Songhai (SAWNG-hy).

Kingdom of Ghana

Historians think the first people in Ghana were farmers along the Niger River. Sometime after AD 300 these farmers, the Soninke (soh-NING-kee), were threatened by nomadic herders. The herders wanted to take the farmers' water and pastures. For protection, groups of Soninke families began to band together. This banding together was the beginning of Ghana.

Teach the Big Idea

At Level

Trading Kingdoms of West Africa

1. **Teach** Ask students the questions in the Main Idea boxes to teach this section.

2. **Apply** Tell students that they will learn about three West Africa kingdoms, Ghana, Mali, and Songhai, that became rich through trade. Have each student create a chart with three columns labeled *Ghana, Mali*, and *Songhai*. The first row should be labeled *Trading Accomplishments*. Have students complete their charts by describing the accomplishments of each kingdom.

3. **Review** Using a map of the three kingdoms, discuss the importance of each country's location in relation to trade.

4. **Practice/Homework** Have students create a Venn diagram in which they show accomplishments in education and trade that were similar in the three kingdoms and those that were different. **LS** Visual/Spatial

📋 Alternative Assessment Handbook, Rubrics 7: Charts; and 13: Graphic Organizers

Ghana's rulers grew wealthy by controlling trade in salt and gold. Salt came from the north in large slabs, and gold came from the south.

What does the photo to the left suggest about the amount of salt traded in a market?

Ghana was in an ideal position to become a trading center. To the north lay the vast Sahara, the source of much of the salt. Ghana itself was rich in gold. People wanted gold for its beauty, but they needed salt in their diets to survive. Salt, which could be used to preserve food, also made bland food tasty. These qualities made salt very valuable. In fact, Africans sometimes cut up slabs of salt and used the pieces as money.

As trade in gold and salt increased, Ghana's rulers gained power. Eventually, they built up armies equipped with iron weapons that were superior to the weapons of nearby people. Over time, Ghana took control of trade from merchants. Merchants from the north and south then met to exchange goods in Ghana.

By 800 Ghana was firmly in control of West Africa's trade routes. Nearly all trade between northern and southern Africa passed through Ghana. With so many traders passing through their lands, Ghana's rulers looked for ways to make money from them. One way they raised money was by forcing traders to pay taxes. Every trader who entered Ghana had to pay a special tax

on the goods he carried. Then he had to pay another tax on any goods he took with him when he left. Ghana's rulers gained incredible wealth from trade, taxes on traders and on the people of Ghana, and their own personal stores of gold. They used their wealth to build an army and an empire.

Islam in Ghana

Extensive trade routes brought the people of Ghana into contact with people of many different cultures and beliefs. As the kingdom of Ghana extended into the Sahara, increased contact with Arab traders from the east brought the religion of Islam to Ghana.

Islam was founded in the 600s by an Arab named Muhammad. Muslims, followers of Islam, believe that God had spoken to Muhammad through an angel and had made him a prophet, someone who tells of God's messages. After Muhammad's death, his followers wrote down his teachings to form the book known as the Qur'an. Islam spread quickly through the Arabian Peninsula.

In the 1060s, a Muslim group called the Almoravids (al-muh-RAH-vuhdz) attacked Ghana in an effort to force its leaders to

THE WORLD BEFORE THE OPENING OF THE ATLANTIC **17**

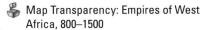

Direct Teach

Main Idea

❶ West Africa's Great Kingdoms

West Africa developed three great kingdoms that grew wealthy through their control of trade.

Recall Why is Sundiata famous? *According to legend, as Mali's ruler, he won back his country's independence and conquered nearby kingdoms.*

Explain Why did Mansa Musa travel to Mecca? *As a Muslim, it was his spiritual duty to make a hajj to Mecca.*

Summarize How did Mansa Musa's belief in Islam affect the country and people of Mali? *Mansa Musa stressed the importance of reading and writing Arabic so that people could read the Qur'an. He sent scholars to study in Morocco and these scholars later set up schools in Mali. He also brought in artists and architects to build mosques in Mali.*

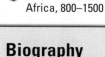 Map Transparency: Empires of West Africa, 800–1500

Biography

Sundiata (c. 1210–c. 1255) Born Mari Diata, Sundiata was the son of the king of the small kingdom of Kangaba. When his father's kingdom was overtaken by King Sumanguru of the Soso Empire, Mari Diata was forced to live in exile. Eventually he returned to defeat Sumanguru in the Battle of Kirina. After the battle, he took the name Sundiata, which means the "lion prince," and went on to establish one of the greatest empires in African history.

Answers

Interpreting Maps 1. *Niger River*
2. *Mali, Songhai*

18

Empires of West Africa, 800–1500

GEOGRAPHY SKILLS INTERPRETING MAPS

1. **Location** On what river are Timbuktu and Gao located?
2. **Region** Which empires ruled Timbuktu and Gao?

convert to Islam. The Almoravids weakened Ghana's empire and cut off many trade routes. Without its trade, Ghana could not support its empire, and the empire eventually fell. The influence of Islam, however, remained strong. By the late 1400s Islam would become the most practiced religion in the region.

Kingdom of Mali

Like Ghana, Mali lay along the upper Niger River. This area's fertile soil helped Mali grow. In addition, Mali's location on the Niger allowed its people to control trade on the river. Through this control of trade, the empire grew rich and powerful. According to legend, Mali's rise to power began under a ruler named Sundiata. Sundiata won back his country's independence and conquered nearby kingdoms, including Ghana.

Mali's most famous ruler, however, was a Muslim king named **Mansa Musa** (MAHN-sah moo-SAH). Under his leadership, Mali reached the height of its wealth, power, and fame.

Mansa Musa ruled Mali for about 25 years, from 1312 to 1337. During that time, Mali added many important trade cities, including Timbuktu (tim-buhk-TOO), Djenné (je-NAY), and Gao (GOW), to its empire. Traders came to Timbuktu from the north and the south to trade for salt, gold, metals, shells, and many other goods.

Religion was also very important to Mansa Musa. In 1324 he left Mali on a **hajj**, or pilgrimage to Mecca. Making this journey once in their lives is the spiritual duty of all Muslims. As he traveled to Mecca, Mansa Musa introduced his empire to the world. The stories of Mali's wealth and religion spread far and wide. Because of Mansa Musa's influence, Islam spread through a large part of West Africa.

Mansa Musa wanted all Muslims to be able to read the Qur'an. Therefore, he stressed the importance of learning to read and write the Arabic language. He sent scholars to study in Morocco. These scholars later set up schools in Mali for studying the Qur'an.

18 CHAPTER 1

Social Studies Skills: Using Maps

Below Level

Mapping West Africa's Great Kingdoms

Materials: blank outline maps of Africa, colored pencils or markers

1. Using the map on this page, review with students the locations and geography of the Ghana, Mali, and Songhai empires.

2. Give each student a blank outline map. Have students draw the area of each of the three empires on the blank outline map. Remind students to use a different color or pattern for each empire, and to label each empire and the approximate time period it flourished.

3. Instruct students to draw the major trade routes on their maps. They should also draw and label the major bodies of water, including the Niger River, Senegal River, Atlantic Ocean, the Gulf of Guinea, and the Mediterranean Sea. **LS** Visual/Spatial

Alternative Assessment Handbook, Rubric 20: Map Creation

To encourage the spread of Islam in West Africa, Mansa Musa brought back artists and architects from other Muslim countries to build **mosques**, or buildings for Muslim prayer, throughout his lands.

The architectural advances in cities like Timbuktu as well as an organized government, emphasis on education, and expansion of trade all combined to make Mansa Musa Mali's most successful ruler. Much of Mali's success depended on strong leaders. After Mansa Musa died, poor leadership weakened the empire. By 1500 nearly all of the lands the kingdom once ruled were lost. Only a small area of Mali remained.

Songhai Empire

In the 1300s Mansa Musa had conquered a rival kingdom of people called the Songhai, who also lived along the Niger River. As the Mali Empire weakened in the 1400s, the Songhai grew in strength. They took advantage of

Mali's decline, regained their independence, and eventually conquered most of Mali.

One of Songhai's greatest rulers was Muhammad Ture, who chose the title *askia*, a title of military rank. He became known as **Askia the Great**. Like Mansa Musa, Askia the Great was a devout Muslim who supported education and learning. Under his rule, the cities of Gao and Timbuktu flourished. They contained great mosques, universities, schools, and libraries. People came from all parts of West Africa to study mathematics, science, medicine, grammar, and law.

Askia understood that an empire needed effective government. He created a professional army, and to improve the government, he set up five provinces within Songhai. He removed local leaders and appointed new governors who were loyal to him. He also created specialized departments to oversee various tasks, much like modern-day government offices do.

THE IMPACT TODAY

Some of the mosques built by Mansa Musa can still be seen in West Africa today.

LINKING TO TODAY

Music from Senegal to Memphis

Did you know that the music you listen to today may have begun with the griots, musicians from West Africa? From the 1600s to the 1800s, many people from West Africa were brought to America as slaves. In America, these slaves continued to sing the way they had in Africa. They also continued to play traditional instruments such as the kora, shown here being played by Senegalese musician Soriba Kouyaté (far right). Over time, this music developed into a style called the blues, made popular by such artists as B. B. King (near right). In turn, the blues shaped other styles of music, including jazz and rock. So, the next time you hear a Memphis blues song or a cool jazz tune, listen for its ancient African roots.

ANALYSIS SKILL ANALYZING INFORMATION

How did West African music affect modern American music?

Main Idea

❶ West Africa's Great Kingdoms

West Africa developed three great kingdoms that grew wealthy through their control of trade.

Recall Where did the Songhai people live? *along the Niger River*

Making Inferences Do you think the fact that Askia was a Muslim affected the way that he ruled? Explain your answer. *possible answer—He might have encouraged education so that people could read the Qur'an.*

Activity Travel Brochure Have each student create a brochure promoting travel to Timbuktu during this time. Suggest to students that the brochure might feature Timbuktu's great mosques, libraries, and universities.

Map Transparency: Empires of West Africa, 800–1500

Did you know . . .

The tomb of Askia the Great was recently added to the list of World Heritage sites kept by the United Nations. The tomb is located in a complex that features two mosques.

Answers

Analyzing Information *Slaves brought to America from West Africa continued their musical traditions, which over time developed into the blues, eventually shaping jazz and rock.*

Differentiating Instruction

Below Level

Struggling Readers

1. To help students understand the contributions of Askia the Great and the significance of his rule, draw the graphic organizer for students to see. Omit the answers.

2. Explain each category to students and ask them to name an example or an accomplishment for each category.

3. Have students copy the graphic organizer and use information in their text to add details about Askia the Great's accomplishments.

4. When students have completed the graphic organizer, review the answers with the class. **LS Visual/Spatial**

Alternative Assessment Handbook Rubric 13: Graphic Organizers

Accomplishments of Askia the Great

Government	Religion	Education
• *set up five provinces*	• *was a devout Muslim*	• *opened schools and universities*
• *appointed governors loyal to him*	• *built mosques*	• *encouraged study of mathematics, medicine, science, grammar, law*
• *created departments to oversee tasks*		

Main Idea

❷ Trade and Slavery in West Africa

Slaves became a valuable trade item in West Africa.

Explain How did slave trading change over time? *At first, black Africans owned slaves who were captured in war, were criminals, or sold to pay debts; gradually Muslim traders began selling black Africans in North Africa; eventually many enslaved Africans were brought to the Americas.*

Review & Assess

Close

Organize students into small groups. Have students discuss the reasons for the rise to power of each of the three West African kingdoms and the major accomplishments of each.

Review

📖 Online Quiz, Section 3

Assess

SE Section 3 Assessment

📝 PASS: Section 3 Quiz

📝 Alternative Assessment Handbook

Reteach/Classroom Intervention

📝 Interactive Reader and Study Guide, Section 3

💿 Interactive Skills Tutor CD-ROM

Answers

Reading Check (left) *strong trading networks that brought wealth to the kingdoms*

Reading Check (right) *Slaves were valuable trade items.*

Soon after Askia the Great lost power, the empire of Songhai declined. Songhai was invaded by the Moroccans, the kingdom's northern neighbors. The Moroccans wanted to control the Saharan salt mines. They had superior military power and were able to take over Timbuktu and Gao. Changes in trade patterns completed Songhai's fall.

READING CHECK **Comparing** What did Ghana, Mali, and Songhai have in common?

West African Slave Trade

The practice of slavery had existed in Africa and in many parts of the world for centuries. Traditionally, slavery in West Africa mostly involved only black Africans, who were both slaveholders and slaves. This changed in the 600s when Arab Muslims, and later Europeans, became slave traders. Though Europeans had long traded resources with Africa, they became more interested in the growing slave trade.

People who were captured by warring groups during battle could be sold into slavery. In addition, criminals were sometimes sold as slaves. Other enslaved people were captured during raids on villages, and sometimes even the relatives of people who owed money were sold into slavery as payment for debts. Enslaved Africans were often bought to perform menial labor and domestic chores. In some cultures, having slaves raised the status of the slaveholder.

The market for West African slaves increased as Muslim traders bought or seized black Africans to sell in North Africa. West Africa was also home to many enslaved Africans brought to the Americas.

Over time, the slave trade became an important part of the West African economy. Kings traded slaves for valuable goods, such as horses from the Middle East and textiles and weapons from Europe. The trans-Saharan slave trade contributed to the power of Ghana, Mali, and Songhai.

READING CHECK **Drawing Inferences** Why did the slave trade in West Africa continue to grow?

SUMMARY AND PREVIEW Trade was important to the kingdoms of West Africa. In the next section you will learn about European trade.

Section 3 Assessment

go.hrw.com
Online Quiz
KEYWORD: SR8 HP1

Reviewing Ideas, Terms, and People

1. **a. Identify** What were the two most valuable trade items in West Africa?
   b. Describe How did **Mansa Musa** introduce his empire to the world?
   c. Elaborate Why was trade crucial to the survival of Ghana, Mali, and Songhai?
2. **a. Describe** How did some people become slaves in West Africa?
   b. Analyze What role did geography play in the development of the slave trade?
   c. Judge Why did the value of slaves as an export increase over time?

Critical Thinking

3. **Comparing and Contrasting** Review your chart on African kingdoms and trade. Then copy the diagram below and use it to show the similarities and differences in the fall of each kingdom.

Fall of Ghana, Mali, and Songhai	Similarities	Differences

FOCUS ON WRITING

4. **Gathering Information on Economies** Make a list of things that were important to the economies of the kingdoms of West Africa. Include your ideas about what seems most important to West Africans and things that you did not know about before reading this section.

20 CHAPTER 1

Section 3 Assessment Answers

1. **a.** gold and salt
   b. As a Muslim, he went on a hajj to Mecca.
   c. Trade provided wealth for each kingdom, wealth led to creation of strong governments and strong military. Without the money trade provided, empires could not stay strong.
2. **a.** captured in battle, criminals were sold as slaves, taken during a raid, sold to pay a debt
   b. Europeans and Arab Muslims became slave traders. Slaves were sold and brought to North Africa and the Americas.

   c. possible answers—Once slaves could be sold in more and more areas, the demand for them grew, causing value to rise.
3. Similarities—trade declined and kingdom lost power; Differences—Ghana's decline brought on by Almoravids; Mali's due to poor leadership; Songhai could not fight off Moroccans who wanted control over salt mines, change in trade patterns
4. Students' answers should reflect an understanding of West African economies.

Mansa Musa

How could one man's travels become a historic event?

When did he live? the late 1200s and early 1300s

Where did he live? Mali

What did he do? Mansa Musa, the ruler of Mali, was one of the Muslim kings of West Africa. He became a major figure in African and world history largely because of a pilgrimage he made to the city of Mecca.

Why is he important? Mansa Musa's spectacular journey attracted the attention of the Muslim world and of Europe. For the first time, other people's eyes turned to West Africa. During his travels, Mansa Musa gave out huge amounts of gold. His spending made people eager to find the source of such wealth. Within 200 years, European explorers would arrive on the shores of western Africa.

Identifying Points of View How do you think Mansa Musa changed people's views of West Africa?

KEY FACTS

According to chroniclers of the time, Mansa Musa was accompanied on his journey to Mecca by some 60,000 people. Of those people,

- **12,000** were servants to attend to the king.

- **500** were servants to attend to his wife.

- **14,000** were slaves wearing rich fabrics such as silk.

- **500** carried staffs heavily decorated with gold. Historians have estimated that the gold Mansa Musa gave away on his trip would be worth more than $100 million today.

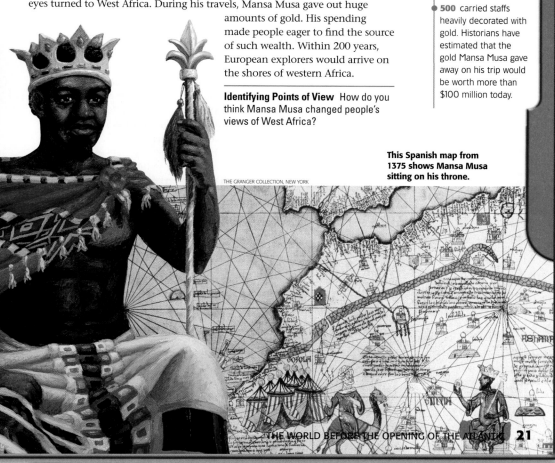

THE GRANGER COLLECTION, NEW YORK

This Spanish map from 1375 shows Mansa Musa sitting on his throne.

THE WORLD BEFORE THE OPENING OF THE ATLANTIC **21**

Reading Focus Question

Think of different historical figures and how their travels have affected history. Consider what possible effects might result from the travels of one person.

Info to Know

Mansa Musa's Journey On his famous pilgrimage to Mecca, Mansa Musa passed through several kingdoms in North Africa. From his capital of Niani, on the Upper Niger River, Mansa Musa and his entourage of thousands traveled north to Walata, to Tuat in modern-day Algeria, and then to Cairo, Egypt. From Egypt, Mansa Musa traveled to Mecca in Arabia.

Linking to Today

The Hajj The hajj is still an important ritual for Muslims today. Every year, millions of Muslims travel to Mecca for the annual hajj.

During the pilgrimage, which lasts six days, pilgrims perform special rites, including circling the Kaaba, a sacred shrine, seven times. Making the hajj is one of five duties expected of every Muslim who is physically and financially able.

About the Illustration

This illustration of Mansa Musa is an artist's conception based on available sources. However, historians are uncertain exactly what Mansa Musa looked like.

Critical Thinking: Summarizing

| At Level |

Writing a Eulogy

1. Review with students the biography of Mansa Musa. Tell students that they will write a eulogy that could have been read at Mansa Musa's funeral.

2. Ask students to include details found in this section. Encourage students to include one or two short accounts of interesting events from the life of Mansa Musa. Remind students to consider the purpose of the eulogy and their audience when writing the eulogy.

3. Ask for volunteers to deliver the eulogies to the class. Discuss with students the important contributions or accomplishments of Mansa Musa. **LS Verbal/Linguistic**

   Alternative Assessment Handbook, Rubric 41: Writing to Express

Answers

Identifying Points of View *possible answers—spread knowledge of Mali, and great wealth, sparked new trade and even more wealth for Mali*

Bellringer

If YOU were there . . . Use the **Daily Bellringer Transparency** for this section to help students answer the question.

📖 Daily Bellringer Transparency, Section 4

Academic Vocabulary

Review with students the high-use academic term in this section.

classical referring to the cultures of ancient Greece and Rome (p. 23)

📖 **CRF:** Vocabulary Builder Activity, Section 4

Taking Notes

Have students copy the graphic organizer onto their own paper and then use it to take notes on the section. This activity will prepare students for the Section Assessment, in which they will complete a graphic organizer that builds on the information using a critical thinking skill.

Europe before Transatlantic Travel

What You Will Learn...

Main Ideas

1. The Greeks and Romans established new forms of government.
2. During the Middle Ages, society eventually changed from a feudal system to the development of a middle class of artisans and merchants.
3. The Renaissance created a rebirth of arts and learning.

The Big Idea

New ways of thinking and growth in trade changed the way people lived in Europe.

Key Terms and People

Socrates, *p. 22*
Plato, *p. 22*
Aristotle, *p. 22*
reason, *p. 22*
democracy, *p. 23*
knights, *p. 24*
Black Death, *p. 25*
Michelangelo, *p. 26*
Leonardo da Vinci, *p. 26*
Johannes Gutenberg, *p. 27*
joint-stock companies, *p. 27*

TAKING NOTES As you read, take notes on the changes in society during the periods listed. Write your notes in a chart like this one.

Period of Time	Major Changes
Ancient Greece	
Roman Republic	
Middle Ages	
Renaissance	

22 CHAPTER 1

If YOU were there...

You are a peasant in the Middle Ages, living on the land of a noble. Although you and your family work very hard from sunrise to sundown, much of the food you grow goes to the noble. Your house is very small and has a dirt floor. Your parents are tired and weak, and you wish you could do something to improve their lives.

Is there any way you could change your life?

BUILDING BACKGROUND Hard work was a constant theme in the lives of peasants in the Middle Ages. Nobles were not free to live as they chose, either. As the Middle Ages ended, the Renaissance brought new ways of thinking, and the growth of cities brought big changes to the way people lived and worked.

Greek and Roman Government

During the Renaissance, European thinkers and artists rediscovered the traditions of Greece and Rome. Ancient Greek and Roman texts were translated and their ideas began to revolutionize European societies.

Greek Philosophers and Government

Ancient Greeks valued human reason and believed in the power of the human mind to think, explain, and understand life. Three of the greatest Greek thinkers, or philosophers, were **Socrates**, **Plato**, and **Aristotle**. Socrates, a great teacher, wanted to make people think and question their own beliefs. Plato, a philosopher and teacher, wrote a work called *Republic*. It describes an ideal society based on justice and fairness for everyone. Aristotle taught that people should live lives based on **reason**, or clear and ordered thinking.

Teach the Big Idea

At Level

Europe before Transatlantic Travel

1. **Teach** Ask students the questions in the Main Idea boxes to teach this section.

2. **Apply** Create a simple time line for students to see. It should begin with the Greek Classical period of the 5th and 4th centuries BC and end in the mid-1400s. Give students time to glance through Section 4 to come up with suggestions for events to add to the time line.

3. **Review** Using the time line, ask volunteers to explain the importance of various events. Remind students that the Renaissance ended in the early 1500s.

4. **Practice/Homework** Have students copy the time line developed in class on their own paper. Assign students to illustrate their time lines. **LS Verbal/Linguistic, Visual/Spatial**

📖 Alternative Assessment Handbook, Rubrics 11: Discussions; and 13: Graphic Organizers

Greek scientists and mathematicians also gained fame for their contributions to geometry and for accurately calculating the size of Earth. Doctors studied the human body to understand how it worked. One Greek engineering invention that is still used today is a water screw, which brings water to farm fields.

One of the Greeks' most lasting contributions, however, is their political system. During the time known as the **Classical** Period, around the fifth and fourth centuries BC, Greece was organized into several hundred independent city-states, which became the foundation for Greek civilization. Athens was the first Greek city-state to establish **democracy**—a form of government in which people rule themselves. All male citizens in Athens had the right to participate in the assembly, a gathering of citizens, to debate and create the city's laws. Because all male citizens in Athens participated directly in government, we call the Greek form of government a direct democracy.

Roman Law and Government

Later, Rome followed Greece's example by establishing a form of democratic government. The Roman Republic was created in 509 BC. Each year Romans elected officials to rule the city. These officials had many powers, but they only stayed in power for one year. This early republic, however, was not a democracy. Later, the Romans changed their government into one with three parts. These three parts were made up of elected representatives who protected the city and its residents.

Roman laws were written and kept on public display so all people could know them. Roman concepts of equality before the law and innocent until proven guilty protected Roman citizens' rights.

The political ideas of Greece and Rome survived to influence governments around the world, including that of the United States. In the U.S. political system, citizens vote for representatives, making the nation a democratic republic.

READING CHECK **Analyzing** How did Roman and Greek governments influence the United States?

QUICK FACTS

Democracy and Republic

Direct democracies and republics are similar forms of government in which the people rule. There are some slight differences, though.

Direct Democracy	Republic
• Every citizen votes on every issue.	• Citizens elect representatives to vote on issues.
• Ideas are debated at an assembly of all citizens.	• Ideas are debated at an assembly of representatives.

THE IMPACT TODAY

Many of the geometry rules we learn in school today come straight from the Greek mathematician Euclid. Many doctors recite the Hippocratic Oath, named after the Greek doctor Hippocrates.

ACADEMIC VOCABULARY

classical referring to the cultures of ancient Greece of Rome

---

The Roman Senate played a principal role in the Roman government.

THE WORLD BEFORE THE OPENING OF THE ATLANTIC **23**

23

❷ The Middle Ages

During the Middle Ages, society eventually changed from a feudal system to the development of a middle class of artisans and merchants.

Recall Under the feudal system, what was the relationship between lords and vassals? *Vassals gave their loyalty to their lord and promised to support the lord in battle; in exchange the lord gave vassals land.*

Explain How did the Catholic Church unify Europe during the Middle Ages? *Because nearly everyone was Christian, life revolved around the church's activities.*

Analyze How did feudalism get its start? *Frankish kings were not able to defend their empire against attacks in the 800s, so nobles began defending their own land. Nobles began to establish independent territories.*

Info to Know

Magna Carta The signing of Magna Carta by King John in 1215 (shown at lower right), was an important event. It indicated that he was no longer entirely above the law. This action inspired the English to find even more ways to limit the king's power.

History Humor

When a knight was killed in battle, what did they put on his tombstone? *Rust in peace.*

Middle Ages

As the Roman Empire fell, groups from the north and east moved into former Roman lands. By the early 500s Europe was divided into many small kingdoms. This marked the beginning of the Middle Ages, a period that lasted about a thousand years.

Feudalism

In the 480s a powerful group called the Franks conquered Gaul, the region we now call France. The Franks created a huge empire in Europe. When invaders began to attack European settlements in the 800s, the Frankish kings could not defend their empire. Because they could not depend on protection from their kings, nobles had to defend their own lands. As a result, the power of European nobles grew, and kings became less powerful. Although these nobles remained loyal to the king, they ruled their lands as independent territories.

Nobles needed soldiers to defend their lands. Nobles gave **knights**, warriors who fought on horseback, land in exchange for military service. Nobles who gave land to knights so that the knights would defend the land were called lords. A knight who promised to support the noble in battle was called a vassal. This system of promises between lords and vassals is known as feudalism.

Peasants owned no land, so they were not part of the feudal system. They did, however, need to grow food to live. As a result, a new economic system developed. Knights allowed peasants to farm land on their large estates, called manors. In return, the peasants had to give the knights food or other goods as payment.

Because of its structure, feudalism promoted the separation of territories and people. The Catholic Church, however, served as a strong unifying force among the states and people of Europe. During the Middle Ages, nearly everyone in Europe was Christian. Life revolved around the local church with markets, festivals, and religious ceremonies.

The Crusades

In the late 1000s, a long series of wars called the Crusades began between the European Christians and Muslims in Southwest Asia.

Time Line

Key Events in Europe

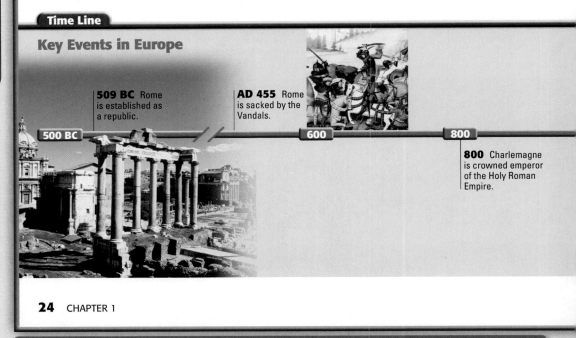

509 BC Rome is established as a republic.

AD 455 Rome is sacked by the Vandals.

500 BC   600   800

800 Charlemagne is crowned emperor of the Holy Roman Empire.

24 CHAPTER 1

Differentiating Instruction

Below Level

Special Needs Learners

1. Tell students that the term "feudalism" may sound complicated, but the society was actually organized in a straight-forward fashion. Create the following diagram for students to see:

> Nobles
> ↓
> Knights (Vassals)
> ↓
> Peasants
> ↓
> Serfs

2. Remind students of each group's role. If necessary, encourage students to reread the section titled Feudalism on this page.

3. Tell students to imagine that they are living during this time and need to explain the feudal system to someone who has just arrived in Europe. Instruct students to create an illustrated page explaining feudalism.
   LS Visual/Spatial

 Alternative Assessment Handbook, Rubric 13: Graphic Organizers

The Turks had captured Palestine, the Holy Land where Jesus had lived. Christians no longer felt safe to travel there on pilgrimages. Christians were called upon to go to war with the Turks to recapture Palestine.

Although the Crusades failed, they changed Europe forever. Trade between Europe and Asia began to grow. Europeans were introduced to new products such as apricots, rice, and cotton cloth. Returning Crusaders also brought the ideas of Muslim thinkers to Europe.

Travel, Trade, and Towns

In the Middle Ages, towns were small. After about 1000, this situation began to change. New technology helped farmers produce larger harvests. As farmers grew more food, the population increased.

Travel became safer as increased protection from knights kept larger territories secure. Adding to the security of travel were the Mongols, who took over China in the 1200s. The Mongols made routes like the Silk Road, a caravan route that started in China and ended at the Mediterranean Sea, safe for

travelers and traders. Among these traders was Marco Polo. In 1271 he journeyed from Europe to China along part of the old Silk Road. He spent 20 years living and traveling in Asia. When Marco Polo returned to Europe, he brought back stories of spices, coal, and paper money.

Trade routes spread all across Europe. Merchants brought goods from Asia and Africa to sell in European markets. Their ships also brought back rats infected with the plague. The disease, known as the **Black Death**, spread across Europe, killing an estimated 25 million people. The European economy was dramatically affected by the shortage of workers. Peasants and serfs could now demand payment for their labor. They began to move to cities, which began to grow in size.

In time, the growth of trade led to the decline of feudalism, and the manor system was weakened. A new middle class of artisans and merchants emerged, and trade cities, especially those in Italy, became commercial centers.

READING CHECK **Drawing Conclusions** How did travel and trade affect the feudal system?

1215 Nobles force King John to sign Magna Carta.

1347 The Black Death arrives in Europe, eventually killing millions.

c. 1350 The Renaissance begins.

1066 England is conquered by the Norman king William the Conqueror.

1436 Johannes Gutenberg perfects his invention of the printing press.

1000 · 1200 · 1400

ANALYSIS SKILL **READING TIME LINES**

What two factors on the time line most helped spread literacy in Europe?

THE WORLD BEFORE THE OPENING OF THE ATLANTIC **25**

Critical Thinking: Drawing Inferences

At Level

Descriptive Letters

1. Remind students that while Marco Polo was in Asia he saw paper money and coal. Europeans had never seen either of these items.

2. Have students choose one of these items and write a descriptive letter about the item to someone who has never seen it. Students should include specific ways that the item can be used. They should also include specifics about the way the item could greatly improve everyday life, and in the case of money, facilitate trade.

3. Have students illustrate their letters with a picture of the item and a picture of the item in use.

4. Ask volunteers to share their letters and their drawings with the class. **LS Verbal/Linguistic**

   Alternative Assessment Handbook, Rubric 40: Writing to Describe

---

● **Direct Teach** ●

Main Idea

❷ The Middle Ages

During the Middle Ages, society eventually changed from a feudal system to the development of a middle class of artisans and merchants.

Explain What were the Crusades? *series of wars between European Christians and Muslims in Southwest Asia*

Analyze Why were the Crusades significant to the future of Europe? *Europeans were exposed to Muslim ideas and products brought back by Crusaders.*

Predict If you grew up on a farm near the end of the Middle Ages, do you think you would stay or move to a city? *possible answer—The opportunity to make money in cities was a strong draw for many people.*

Info to Know

The Holy Land Also known as Palestine, the Holy Land is sacred to three major world religions—Judaism, Islam, and Christianity.

Teaching Tip

The Printing Press Ask students how the invention of the printing press and new ideas (such as Martin Luther's) worked together and led to major changes in Europe. *The printing press made more ideas available to people.*

Answers

Reading Time Lines *Renaissance, invention of printing press*

Reading Check *As travel became safer and trade developed, people began to move to cities. As they left farms and manors, the feudal system fell into decline.*

Trading Centers

Major cities like Venice and Florence became centers of commerce and banking during the 1300s. The trading of cloth, spices, and other goods renewed the European economy during the Renaissance.

How does this picture show a thriving economy?

Main Idea

❸ The Renaissance Expands Horizons

The Renaissance created a rebirth of arts and learning.

Describe How did classical writings that had been in the Byzantine Empire come to Italy? *Scholars fleeing from the Turkish conquest brought the works with them to Italy.*

Contrast How did the studies of Renaissance scholars differ from work done during the Middle Ages? *Renaissance scholars focused on human values, and art, literature, science, political thoughts. People worked to glorify God.*

Make Inferences What does it mean if someone is called a Renaissance man or woman? *interested in learning; have skills and knowledge in a wide range of areas*

Teaching Tip

Pronunciation Many names associated with the Renaissance, such as Leonardo da Vinci and Dante Alighieri, are hard to pronounce. Help students by having the class pronounce the names out loud together.

Biography

Michelangelo (1475–1564)

Michelangelo di Buonarroti Simoni was born in Florence, Italy, but he also worked in Rome and Bologna. He created some of the most famous statues and paintings in world history. One of these paintings is the ceiling of the Sistine Chapel in Rome. Michelangelo continually strove for perfection.

Answers

Many people are trading.

26

Renaissance

The Renaissance period brought new ways of thinking to Europe, weakening the old feudal system even more. The word *Renaissance* means "rebirth" and refers to the period that followed the Middle Ages in Europe. This movement began in Italy and eventually spread to other parts of Europe.

During the Renaissance, European rulers began to increase their power over the nobles in their countries. Fewer invasions from outside forces helped bring a period of order and stability to Europe.

Search for Knowledge

Love of art and education was a key feature of the Renaissance. As Turks conquered much of the Byzantine Empire in the East, scholars fled to Italy. They brought ancient classical writings with them. Some of the works were by Greek thinkers like Plato.

Excited by the discoveries brought by Turkish scholars, European scholars went looking for ancient texts in Latin. They discovered many Latin texts in monasteries, which had preserved works by Roman writers. As Italian scholars read these ancient texts, they rediscovered the glories of Greece and Rome.

The search for knowledge and learning spread to all fields, including art, literature, science, and political thought. The Renaissance emphasized the importance of people rather than focusing on religion. This new focus on human value and the study of humanities was called humanism. People's interest in the humanities led them to respect those who could write, create, or speak well. During the Middle Ages, most people had worked only to glorify God.

Italian artists created some of the most beautiful paintings and sculptures in the world. Their art reflected the basic Renaissance idea—the value of human beings. **Michelangelo** and **Leonardo da Vinci** are two of the greatest Renaissance artists. They are known for their work in painting, sculpture, and architecture. Da Vinci was also an inventor, engineer, and mapmaker.

Italian writers also penned great works of literature. Dante Alighieri was a politician and poet. Before Dante, most authors wrote in Latin, the language of the church. But Dante chose to write in Italian, the common language of the people. This gave ordinary people the opportunity to read Dante's work.

Many texts that Europeans rediscovered in the 1300s dealt with science. After reading these works, Renaissance scholars went on

---

Critical Thinking: Drawing Conclusions

At Level

Emergence of the Renaissance

1. Ask students to list some events that helped bring about the Renaissance. Write the students' suggestions for everyone to see. Here are a few ideas:

   • Crusaders returned with new ideas and products.
   • Power of kings increased, leading to more stability.
   • Classical writings were rediscovered.

   • The Black Death led to a large decline in population and a growth in towns and cities.
   • Trading increased along the Silk Road.

2. Organize students into small groups. Have each group rank these events in order of importance.

3. Ask a volunteer from each group to give their rankings. **LS Verbal/Linguistic**

   📄 Alternative Assessment Handbook, Rubric 11: Discussions

to make their own scientific advances. They also studied ancient math texts and built on the ideas they read about. For example, they created symbols for the square root and for positive and negative numbers. Astronomers discovered that Earth moves around the sun. Other scientists used measurements and made calculations to create better, more accurate maps.

The development of the printing press was a giant step forward in spreading new ideas. In the mid-1400s, a German man, **Johannes Gutenberg** (GOOT-uhn-berk), developed a printing press that used movable type. This allowed an entire page to be printed at once. For the first time in history, thousands of people could read the same books and share ideas about them.

Economic Changes Affect Trade

The growth in trade and services at the beginning of the Renaissance sparked a commercial revolution. This also brought a rise in mercantilism. Mercantilism is an economic system that unifies and increases the power and wealth of a nation.

Four northern Italian cities, Florence, Genoa, Milan, and Venice, developed into important trading centers. These cities played two major roles in trade. They served as ports along the Mediterranean Sea. They also served as manufacturing centers and specialized in certain crafts. This economic activity made some families in these cities very wealthy.

As trade and commerce grew, the need for banks arose. Bankers in Florence, Italy, kept money for merchants from all over Europe. The bankers also made money by charging interest on funds they loaned to merchants. The greatest bankers in Florence were from the Medici family. Although Florence was already wealthy from trade, banking increased that wealth.

During this time, merchants began to create **joint-stock companies**, or businesses in which a group of people invest together. In

a joint-stock company, the investors share in the companies' profits and losses. Forming joint-stock companies allowed investors to take fewer risks.

READING CHECK Drawing Conclusions How did the Renaissance lead to trade and a commercial revolution?

THE IMPACT TODAY

SUMMARY AND PREVIEW Greek and Roman traditions provided new ways for people to govern themselves. In the next chapter you will read about how the Renaissance paved the way for exploration of the Americas.

The demand for more books led to improvements in printing and binding that have made modern books affordable.

Reviewing Ideas, Terms, and People

1. **a. Identify** What is the difference between a direct democracy and a **republic**?
   b. Elaborate What is the importance of having a written law code?
2. **a. Describe** What is the relationship between **knights** and nobles?
   b. Elaborate How did the Crusades affect the feudal system?
3. **a. Identify** What does the term *Renaissance* mean?
   b. Analyze What is the relationship among trade, banking, and **joint-stock companies**?
   c. Elaborate What do you think was the greatest accomplishment of the Renaissance?

Critical Thinking

4. **Supporting a Point of View** Review your notes on the major changes that took place in Europe during the periods discussed in the section. In a chart like the one below, identify which period you think was most important, and explain why.

Most Important	Why

FOCUS ON WRITING

5. **Organizing a Chronology** Make a list of important events in Europe during the time discussed in this section. Reorder them from earliest to most recent.

Section 4 Assessment Answers

1. **a.** In a direct democracy, all citizens vote to decide issues and participate in government; in a republic, citizens elect representatives to govern them.
   b. When laws are written, everyone knows what they are, not just those who wrote them.
2. **a.** Knights agreed to protect a noble's lands in exchange for smaller pieces of land.
   b. Trade increased, which led to the decline of the feudal system, and the manor system was weakened.
3. **a.** rebirth

b. Merchants needed capital to fund their businesses or to expand them; banks loaned money to merchants; joint-stock companies provided ways to raise money for businesses.
c. possible answers—the art of Michelangelo and Leonardo da Vinci; the printing press

4. possible answer—The Renaissance was the most important because it led to a rebirth in society that spurred new advancements in art, literature, science, and political thought.

5. For possible answer, see time line on pages 24 and 25.

Answers

Reading Check *Trade, the growth of cities, and new crafts all created an impetus for new economic systems. Banking grew, as did joint-stock companies, which were a means to finance new business ventures.*

27

Activity Calculating Percentages

Although estimates of the death toll from the plague vary, many historians agree that Europe's population was reduced by about one third. Use almanacs or other reference works to find population figures for your city. Then calculate how many people in the city would have died from the Black Death if the disease claimed the same percentage of victims. For example, if the population of your city is 100,000, then about 33,000 people would have died.

Did you know . . .

Ships arriving from the East were often greeted at European harbors with enthusiasm—everyone wanted to see what goods they brought. In some cities, once people realized the ships might be carrying disease, ships were not allowed to enter the ports.

Linking to Today

Black Plague Today Figures from the World Health Organization show that today between 1,000 and 3,000 cases of the plague occur annually around the world. Antibiotics are effective against the disease, but treatment must begin very quickly to avoid serious illness or even death.

History and Geography

The Black Death

"And they died by the hundreds," wrote one man who saw the horror, "both day and night." The Black Death had arrived. The Black Death was a series of deadly plagues that hit Europe between 1347 and 1351, killing millions. People didn't know what caused the plague. They also didn't know that geography played a key role in its spread—as people traveled to trade, they unknowingly carried the disease with them to new places.

EUROPE

CENTRAL ASIA

CHINA

AFRICA

• Kaffa

The plague probably began in central and eastern Asia. These arrows show how it spread into and through Europe.

This ship has just arrived in Europe from the East with trade goods—and rats with fleas.

The fleas carry the plague and jump onto a man unloading the ship. Soon, he will get sick and die.

Differentiating Instruction

Struggling Readers   Below Level

Have students review the feature on these pages. Then ask students to assign names, occupations, and personalities to the people depicted in the illustration. Have students write brief stories about the roles these people are playing in the Black Death. Supply thesauri and dictionaries to help students in choosing words.
LS Visual/Spatial

Advanced/ Gifted and Talented   Above Level

Have students imagine that one third of the people in your state have died from the plague. Ask them what would be the short- and long-term economic results. Have students consider such things as loss of labor force, need for skilled workers, and impact on wages. Have students apply their ideas about the present-day results to infer the plague's effects on Europe during the Middle Ages.

The plague is so terrifying that many people think it's the end of the world. They leave town for the country, spreading the Black Death even further.

People dig mass graves to bury the dead. Often, so many people are infected that there is no one left to bury them.

The garbage and dirty conditions in the town provide food and a home for the rats, allowing disease to spread even more.

So many people die so quickly that special carts are sent through the streets to gather the bodies.

GEOGRAPHY SKILLS INTERPRETING MAPS

1. How did the Black Death reach Europe from Asia?
2. What helped spread the plague throughout Europe?

History and Geography

Did you know . . .

The Black Death was a *pandemic,* an outbreak of disease that occurs over a wide geographic area and affects an exceptionally high proportion of the population. An *epidemic,* on the other hand, is limited to a specific community or region.

Activity **Plague Cities** The map on the opposite page shows the general spread of the plague from Asia to Europe. Point out that big cities were struck especially hard by the plague. Give each student a blank outline map of Europe and Asia. Using an atlas and the map from this feature have students label the major cities from which the Black Death spread.

Info to Know

Types of Plague The different types of diseases grouped together as the Black Death spread in different ways and killed their victims at varying speeds. Doctors now call the worst form septicemic plague. With this disease, a victim's entire bloodstream was infected with bacteria. Death could come within 24 hours. Stories endure from the Black Death years of people who appeared healthy in the morning and yet were dead by nightfall. They were probably victims of the septicemic type of plague.

Critical Thinking: Evaluating Information   At Level

Just a Nursery Rhyme? Prep Required

Materials: Internet source materials

1. Explain to students that some historians think the nursery rhyme *Ring Around the Rosie* refers to symptoms of the Black Death. Some accounts, however, dispute this claim.

2. In advance, locate and duplicate Internet sources that argue both sides of the *Ring Around the Rosie* question. Make a copy for each student.

3. Have students read the articles. Then create a *For* and *Against* chart for students to see. Ask students to summarize each side's arguments. List them in the appropriate columns.

4. Call on volunteers to tell why they thought some arguments were more reliable than others. Discuss how the sources of information were related to the reliability of the information. **LS Interpersonal, Logical/Mathematical**

Alternative Assessment Handbook, Rubric 11: Discussions

Answers

Interpreting Maps 1. *carried on trading ships;* 2. *possible answers— people fleeing cities to the country, inability to bury all victims; general dirty conditions, traders spreading disease from town to town*

29

Social Studies Skills

Interpreting Diagrams

Activity Identifying Forces of Continuity and Change

Materials: photocopies of sample diagrams

Make photocopies of two to four diagrams. You might ask the librarian to suggest books that contain diagrams related to the Middle Ages. Provide each student with copies of the diagrams. Go through the diagrams as a class. Have students identify labeled items and other important features. Then have each student select one diagram and write a paragraph describing what the diagram shows. Have volunteers read their paragraphs to the class. Correct any student errors.

LS Visual/Spatial

📝 Alternative Assessment Handbook, Rubric 37: Writing Assignments

💿 Interactive Skills Tutor CD-ROM, Lesson 6: Interpret Maps, Graphs, Charts, Visuals, and Political Cartoons

---

Social Studies Skills

Analysis	Critical Thinking	Civil Participation	Study

Interpreting Diagrams

Understand the Skill

Diagrams are drawings that use lines and labels to explain or illustrate something. Different types of diagrams have different purposes. *Pictorial diagrams* show an object in simple form, much like it would look if you were viewing it. *Cutaway diagrams* show the "insides" of an object. *Component diagrams* show how an object is organized by separating it into parts. Such diagrams are sometimes also called *schematic drawings*. The ability to interpret diagrams will help you to better understand a historical object, its function, and how it worked.

Learn the Skill

Use these basic steps to interpret a diagram:

1 Determine what type of diagram it is.

2 Read the diagram's title or caption to find out what it represents.

3 Look for any labels and read them carefully. Most diagrams include text that identifies the object's parts or explains relationships between the parts.

4 If a legend is present, study it to identify and understand any symbols and colors that are used in the diagram.

5 Look for numbers or letters that might indicate a sequence of steps. Also look for any arrows that might show direction or movement.

An Early Castle

Pulley · Oven · Chapel · Fireplaces · Windows · Drawbridge · Moat · Well

Practice and Apply the Skill

Interpret the diagram of an early castle, and answer the following questions.

1. What type of diagram is this?
2. What labels in the diagram suggest how the castle was heated?
3. What was the purpose of the pulley?
4. Of what materials was the castle made?
5. What features of the castle helped make it secure against attack?

Social Studies Skills Activity: Interpreting Diagrams   `At Level`

Creating Diagrams   `Research Required`

Materials: art supplies, poster board

1. Have each student conduct research to find a diagram of a historical structure from the Middle Ages. For example, students might look for a diagram of a cathedral, a mill, or a castle (as shown in this chapter).

2. Each student should create a large copy of the diagram on poster board. Below the diagram, students should provide captions explaining the information in the diagram and provide background information about the structure.

3. Ask volunteers to share their diagrams with the class. Give other students a chance to interpret the diagrams and to ask questions. Then have volunteers explain their diagrams.

4. Display students' diagrams in a classroom exhibit. **LS Visual/Spatial**

📝 Alternative Assessment Handbook, Rubrics 3: Artwork; and 30: Research

---

Answers

Practice and Apply the Skill
1. *a cutaway diagram;* 2. *fireplaces;*
3. *to draw water from the well;* 4. *wood and some stone above the waterline and stone below the waterline;* 5. *the moat surrounding the castle, the single entrance and drawbridge, the high and narrow windows*

Chapter Review

Visual Summary

Use the visual summary below to help you review the main ideas of the chapter.

QUICK FACTS

The Americas and the Old World each had complex societies, trade routes, and economies.

Reviewing Vocabulary, Terms, and People

Complete each sentence by filling in the blank with the correct term or person.

1. During the Ice Age, a narrow strip of land called the _____ was exposed.

2. The _____ of Paleo-Indians from North to South America took thousands of years.

3. Native Americans living in the Pacific Northwest carved _____ on tall poles.

4. The first political confederation of Native Americans in North America was the _____.

5. The most famous ruler of Mali was _____.

6. While Mali's leader was on a _____, or pilgrimage, to Mecca, he introduced his empire to the world.

7. The most famous ruler of Songhai took the name _____.

8. _____ describes an ideal society based on justice in *Republic*.

Comprehension and Critical Thinking

SECTION 1 *(Pages 6–9)*

9. **a. Describe** How did early peoples in the Americas get their food?

   b. Analyze What led to the development of different culture groups in the Americas?

   c. Elaborate What features did the early civilizations of Mesoamerica and South America have in common?

SECTION 2 *(pp. 10–15)*

10. **a. Identify** Which early Native American society built cliff dwellings, and which built mounds?

   b. Analyze How did Native Americans' religious beliefs affect their lives in North America?

   c. Evaluate Do you think it was easier for Native Americans to live in the dry climates of the Southwest, where rainfall was unpredictable, or in the North, where the cold climate presented a constant challenge?

THE WORLD BEFORE THE OPENING OF THE ATLANTIC **31**

Visual Summary

Review and Inquiry Have students write at least one sentence explaining the significance of each illustration in the visual summary.

🖼 Quick Facts Transparency: The World before the Opening of the Atlantic Visual Summary

Reviewing Vocabulary, Terms, and People

1. Bering Land Bridge
2. migration
3. totems
4. Iroquois League
5. Mansa Musa
6. hajj
7. Askia the Great
8. Plato

Comprehension and Critical Thinking

9. **a.** hunter gatherers, then farmers
   b. different societies developed their own language, family relationships, and beliefs
   c. language, government, trade, system for keeping records, artisans made jewelry, known for building temples and palaces

---

Review and Assessment Resources

Review and Reinforce

SE Chapter Review

🖥 **CRF:** Chapter Review Activity

🖼 Quick Facts Transparency: The World before the Opening of the Atlantic Visual Summary

🔊 Spanish Chapter Summaries Audio CD Program

📲 Online Chapter Summaries in Six Languages

OSP Holt PuzzlePro; GameTool for ExamView

⦿ Quiz Game CD-ROM

Assess

SE Standardized Test Practice

🖥 PASS: Chapter Test

🖥 Alternative Assessment Handbook

OSP ExamView Test Generator, Chapter Test

⦿ Differentiated Instruction Modified Worksheets and Tests CD-ROM: Chapter Test

📲 Holt Online Assessment Program (in the Premier Online Edition)

Reteach/Intervene

🖥 Interactive Reader and Study Guide

🖥 Differentiated Instruction Teacher Management System: Lesson Plans for Differentiated Instruction

⦿ Differentiated Instruction Modified Worksheets and Tests CD-ROM

⦿ Interactive Skills Tutor CD-ROM

go.hrw.com

Online Resources

KEYWORD: SR8 US1

10. a. Anasazi, cliff dwellings; Hopewell and Mississippian, mounds
b. Because Native Americans believed that the spirits controlled every aspect of their beliefs, they honored the spirits every day in many activities.
c. Each group had geographic challenges, and life would not have been easy for either group.

11. a. excellent geographical location between gold and salt mines, central location for traders
b. Both were Muslim, strong, capable rulers, encouraged learning, built strong cities. Both of their empires depended on trade.
c. The trade network evolved from a relationship between black West Africans where slaves were war-captives or sold to pay off debts. Slaves became an important export for West Africans and were shipped to other parts of the world. When the Europeans arrived, the slave-trade network was already well established.

12. a. Athens, Greece had a direct democracy, in which citizens debated and then created the city's laws; Rome had a republic, in which people elected officials to represent and govern them.
b. Crusaders were introduced to new products that Europeans then wanted. Marco Polo returned with stories about goods that were largely unknown. Europeans wanted to acquire these new goods.
c. possible answers—people who did not know Latin could read texts; movable type made it possible to print books more easily and eventually more cheaply, making them more accessible to people.

Reviewing Themes

13. As climates became colder, the Bering Land Bridge was exposed; Paleo-Indians used the bridge to cross into the Americas. When the climate became warmer, the land bridge was covered with water, and people used small boats to come to the Americas.

SECTION 3 (pp. 16–20)
11. a. Describe How did geography contribute to Ghana's wealth?
b. Compare What characteristics did Mansa Musa and Askia the Great have in common?
c. Elaborate How did West Africa develop a large slave-trade network?

SECTION 4 (pp. 22–27)
12. a. Recall What role did Greek and Roman traditions play in the development of the United States?
b. Summarize How did the Crusades in Southwest Asia and the travels of Marco Polo in Asia contribute to the growth of trade in Europe?
c. Evaluate Which do you think contributed the most to the advances in learning that occurred during the Renaissance—writing in the common language of a people or inventing the printing press?

Reviewing Themes

13. Geography How did changes in climate lead to migration to the Americas?

14. Economics Describe the development of the European economy during the Middle Ages.

Using the Internet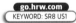

15. Activity: Compare and Contrast What causes large groups of people to migrate? Factors that influence why people migrate can be labeled as "push" and "pull." Poor climate and lack of resources "pushed" Paleo-Indians to North America. This activity will help you understand factors of migration. Enter the activity keyword, then compare and contrast push-pull factors involved in Paleo-Indian migration with the factors influencing immigration to the United States today. Create an illustrated chart to display your research.

Reading Skills

Specialized Vocabulary of Social Studies *Use the Reading Skills taught in this chapter to answer the question about the reading selection below.*

> To encourage the spread of Islam in West Africa, Mansa Musa brought back artists and architects from other Muslim countries to build **mosques**, or buildings for Muslim prayer, throughout his lands. (p. 19)

16. What is the definition of the word *mosques* in the sentence above?

Social Studies Skills

Understanding Diagrams *Use the Social Studies Skills taught in this chapter to answer the question below.*

17. Look back at the diagram on page 30. Which of the following is the main way to enter the castle?
a. well
b. moat
c. drawbridge
d. windows

FOCUS ON WRITING

18. Writing Your Travelogue. You have read about many cultures across a long span of history. Pick one area that you found the most interesting in the chapter. Organize your thoughts about the kinds of people you would have met and the kind of things you would have done if you had traveled there during the time discussed.
  Try to include information about a culture's history, customs, beliefs, practices, economies, political systems, and natural environments. Write a paragraph about what you might have liked or disliked about your trip. Be sure to include a main idea sentence and several sentences that support the main idea with evidence.

---

14. new technology helped farmers produce larger harvests, population increased, travel became safer, trade routes spread across Europe, population decline caused by Black Death led to pressure for payment to peasants and serfs for labor, cities grew, new middle class emerged, trade cities became commercial centers

Using the Internet

15. Go to the HRW Web site and enter the keyword shown to access a rubric for this activity.

KEYWORD: SR8 US1

Reading Skills

16. buildings for Muslim prayer

Social Studies Skills

17. C

Focus on Writing

18 Students' answers should include a main idea sentence, several supporting sentences, and should reflect an understanding of the chosen area and time.

Standardized Test Practice

DIRECTIONS: Read each question and write the letter of the best response.

1 Before the arrival of Europeans, the most advanced Native American societies were located in what is now
- A California.
- B the eastern United States.
- C the American Southwest.
- D Mexico.

2 The trade in gold, salt, and slaves is closely related to
- A the Inca Empire.
- B the Roman Empire.
- C West Africa.
- D the Renaissance.

3 Which of the following statements *best* describes the cause of increased trade between Europe and Asia in the late Middle Ages?
- A The interruption of trade caused by the Crusades led many merchants to travel to Asia in search of trade partners.
- B European merchants traded with Asia due to a lack of valuable natural resources in Europe.
- C The growth of towns during the Middle Ages led to an increased demand for Asian trade goods.
- D Marco Polo's stories of Asia's great wealth led many Europeans to seek out Asian goods.

4 How did the societies of North America differ from those of Central and South America?
- A Societies in North America did not create large political units like those in Central and South America.
- B North American culture groups lacked the diversity of those in Central and South America.

- C North American societies were significantly more advanced than those to the south.
- D Culture groups in North America worshipped many gods while those in Central and South America were monotheistic.

5 A result of Johannes Gutenberg's printing press was that
- A the Renaissance began.
- B more people could read the same books and share ideas.
- C European trade and commerce grew.
- D overseas trade and travel became more popular.

6 The exposure of a land bridge between Asia and present-day Alaska during the last Ice Age resulted in
- A the introduction of new plants and animals to Asia and Europe.
- B the development of farming in the Americas.
- C the migration of people into the Americas.
- D the establishment of advanced cultures in North America.

7 Examine the following passage by Marco Polo about his travels through China. Then answer the question that follows.

"Upon leaving Ta-in-fu, we traveled for seven days through a fine country in which there were many cities, where commerce and manufactures [goods] prevailed. We reached a large city named Pi-an-fu, which is very famous. Like Ta-in-fu, this city contains numerous merchants and artisans. Silk is produced here also in great quantity."

Marco Polo, from the *Travels of Marco Polo: The Venetian*

What is the main idea of this passage?

Answers

1. D
Break Down the Question: This question requires students to recall that the Aztec society in Mexico was very advanced.

2. C
Break Down the Question: This question requires students to recall factual information. Students should use a process of elimination to answer the question.

3. B
Break Down the Question: Tell students that the italicized word *best* means that more than one answer may be correct and that students are to choose the one that provides the most complete answer.

4. A
Break Down the Question: This question requires students to recall factual information. Students should use a process of elimination to answer the question.

5. B
Break Down the Question: This question requires students to recall factual information. Students should use a process of elimination to answer the question.

6. C
Break Down the Question: This question requires students to recall factual information. Students should use a process of elimination to answer the question.

7.
Break Down the Question: This question requires students to interpret information and find the main idea. Tell students to consider what Marco Polo's writing stresses about Pi-an-fu.

Intervention Resources

Reproducible
- Interactive Reader and Study Guide
- Differentiated Instruction Teacher Management System: Lesson Plans for Differentiated Instruction

Technology
- Quick Facts Transparency: The World before the Opening of the Atlantic
- Differentiated Instruction Modified Worksheets and Tests CD-ROM
- Interactive Skills Tutor CD-ROM

Tips for Test Taking

Read and Reread When answering questions about a reading selection, such as in Question 7 above, keep these suggestions in mind:

- First, read the question carefully so you know what information to look for.
- Read the selection to be sure you understand the content.
- Review the question. If you do not know the answer, reread the selection and focus on looking for the answer.

Chapter 2 Planning Guide

New Empires in the Americas

Chapter Overview	Reproducible Resources	Technology Resources
CHAPTER 2 pp. 34–67 **Overview: In this chapter, students will analyze the Age of Exploration and the effects it had on the world.**	**Differentiated Instruction Teacher Management System:*** • Instructional Benchmarking Guides **Interactive Reader and Study Guide:** Chapter Graphic Organizer* **Chapter Resource File:*** • Focus on Writing Activity: Writing a Letter • Social Studies Skills: Framing Historical Questions • Chapter Review Activity	Power Presentations with Video CD-ROM Differentiated Instruction Modified Worksheets and Tests CD-ROM Student Edition on Audio CD Program History's Impact: United States History Video Program (VHS/DVD): New Empires in the Americas*
Section 1: **Europeans Set Sail** **The Big Idea:** Europeans explored the world searching for new lands and new trade routes.	**Differentiated Instruction Teacher Management System:** Section 1 Lesson Plan* **Interactive Reader and Study Guide:** Section 1 Summary* **Chapter Resource File:*** • Vocabulary Builder Activity, Section 1	**Daily Bellringer Transparency:** Section 1* **Map Transparency:** Portuguese Routes and Exploration* **Quick Facts Transparency:** Causes and Effects of the Discovery of a Sea Route to Asia*
Section 2: **Europeans Reach the Americas** **The Big Idea:** Christopher Columbus's voyages led to new exchanges between Europe, Africa, and the Americas.	**Differentiated Instruction Teacher Management System:** Section 2 Lesson Plan* **Interactive Reader and Study Guide:** Section 2 Summary* **Chapter Resource File:*** • Vocabulary Builder Activity, Section 2 • Primary Source Activity: Columbus's letter	**Daily Bellringer Transparency:** Section 2* **Map Transparency:** Columbus's Voyages* **Map Transparency:** The Columbian Exchange*
Section 3: **Spain Builds an Empire** **The Big Idea:** Spain established a large empire in the Americas.	**Differentiated Instruction Teacher Management System:** Section 3 Lesson Plan* **Interactive Reader and Study Guide:** Section 3 Summary* **Chapter Resource File:*** • Vocabulary Builder Activity, Section 3 • Biography Activity: Explorer Malintzin • Primary Source Activities: Aztec Description of Horses; Bartolomé de Las Casas	**Daily Bellringer Transparency:** Section 3* **Map Transparency:** Spanish Explorations 1513–1542* **Map Transparency:** Spanish Viceroyalties c.1700* **Quick Facts Transparency:** Reasons for Spanish Victory*
Section 4: **The Race for Empires** **The Big Idea:** Other European nations challenged Spain in the Americas.	**Differentiated Instruction Teacher Management System:** Section 4 Lesson Plan* **Interactive Reader and Study Guide:** Section 4 Summary* **Chapter Resource File:*** • Vocabulary Builder Activity, Section 4	**Daily Bellringer Transparency:** Section 4* **Map Transparency:** Northwest Passage* **Map Transparency:** European Exploration of the Americas 1492-1682*
Section 5: **Beginnings of Slavery in the Americas** **The Big Idea:** Europeans forced millions of African slaves to work in their colonies.	**Differentiated Instruction Teacher Management System:** Section 5 Lesson Plan* **Interactive Reader and Study Guide:** Section 5 Summary* **Chapter Resource File:*** • Vocabulary Builder Activity, Section 5 • Primary Source Activity: King Afonso's letter	**Daily Bellringer Transparency:** Section 5* **Map Transparency:** African Diaspora in the United States*

Review, Assessment, Intervention

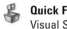 **Quick Facts Transparency:** New Empires in the Americas Visual Summary*

 Progress Assessment Support System (PASS): Chapter Test*

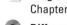 **Differentiated Instruction Modified Worksheets and Tests CD-ROM:** Modified Chapter Test

One-Stop Planner CD-ROM: ExamView Test Generator (English/Spanish)

 PASS: Section 1 Quiz*

 Online Quiz: Section 1

 Alternative Assessment Handbook

 PASS: Section 2 Quiz*

 Online Quiz: Section 2

 Alternative Assessment Handbook

 PASS: Section 3 Quiz*

 Online Quiz: Section 3

 Alternative Assessment Handbook

 PASS: Section 4 Quiz*

 Online Quiz: Section 4

 Alternative Assessment Handbook

 PASS: Section 5 Quiz*

 Online Quiz: Section 5

 Alternative Assessment Handbook

Power Presentations with Video CD-ROM

Power Presentations with Video are visual presentations of each chapter's main ideas. Presentations can be customized by including Quick Facts charts, images from the text, and video clips.

Power Presentations with Video CD-ROM

HOLT

United States History
Beginnings to 1877

MIKE, RINEHART AND WINSTON
A Harcourt Education Company

DIVISION FOR PUBLIC EDUCATION

AMERICAN BAR ASSOCIATION

Developed by the Division for Public Education of the American Bar Association, these materials are part of the **Democracy and Civic Education Resources.**

• **Constitution Study Guide**

• **Supreme Court Case Studies**

Holt Online Learning

Teacher Resources

> KEYWORD: SR8 TEACHER

Student Resources

> KEYWORD: SR8 US2

• Document-Based Questions

• Interactive Multimedia Activities

• Current Events

• Chapter-based Internet Activities

• and more!

Holt Premier
Online Student Edition

Complete online support for interactivity, assessment, and reporting

• Interactive Maps and Notebook

• Standardized Test Prep

• Homework Practice and Research Activities Online

CHAPTER 2 PLANNING GUIDE

Differentiating Instruction

ENGLISH-LANGUAGE LEARNERS & STRUGGLING READERS

TARGET RESOURCE

Live Ink® Online Reading Help

Spanish Resources

Spanish Chapter Summaries Audio CD Program

One-Stop Planner CD-ROM:
- ExamView Test Generator, Spanish
- PuzzlePro, Spanish

Additional Resources

Differentiated Instruction Teacher Management System: Lesson Plans for Differentiated Instruction

Chapter Resources:
- Vocabulary Builder Activities
- Social Studies Skills Activity: Framing Historical Questions

Quick Facts Transparencies:
- Causes and Effects of the Discovery of a Sea Route to Asia
- Reasons for Spanish Victory
- New Empires in the Americas Visual Summary

Student Edition on Audio CD Program

Online Chapter Summaries in Six Languages

Interactive Skills Tutor CD-ROM

SPECIAL NEEDS LEARNERS

TARGET RESOURCE

Differentiated Instruction Modified Worksheets and Tests CD-ROM

- Vocabulary Flash Cards
- Modified Vocabulary Builder Activities
- Modified Chapter Review Activity
- Modified Chapter Test

Additional Resources

Differentiated Instruction Teacher Management System: Lesson Plans for Differentiated Instruction

Interactive Reader and Study Guide

Social Studies Skills Activity: Framing Historical Questions

Student Edition on Audio CD Program

Interactive Skills Tutor CD-ROM

Live Ink® Online Reading Help

ADVANCED/GIFTED AND TALENTED STUDENTS

TARGET RESOURCE

Primary Source Library CD-ROM for United States History

The Library contains longer versions of quotations in the text, extra sources, and images. Included are point-of-view articles, journals, diaries, historical fiction, and political documents.

Additional Resources

United States History Document-Based Questions Activities

Differentiated Instruction Teacher Management System: Lesson Plans for Differentiated Instruction

Chapter Resource File:
- Focus on Writing Activity: Writing a Letter
- Primary Source Activity: Christopher Columbus's letter to the King and Queen of Spain, 1494
- Primary Source Activity: Primary Source Activity: Aztec Description of Horses
- Primary Source Activity: Bartolomé de Las Casas, *Brief Account of the Devastation of the Indies*
- Primary Source Activity: King Afonso of Kongo, letter to the King of Portugal, 1521

Differentiated Activities in the Teacher's Edition
- Portuguese Explorers Chart, p. 40
- North American Exploration, p. 49
- Progression of Slavery Flow Chart, p. 59
- Slavery Discussion, p. 62
- Primary Source Images, p. 63

Differentiated Activities in the Teacher's Edition
- Explorers Museum Exhibit, p. 56

Differentiated Activities in the Teacher's Edition
- Battle Journal, p. 47
- Reformation Pamphlet, p. 53
- Middle Passage Script, p. 63

One-Stop Planner® CD-ROM
for Differentiated Instruction

Your differentiated instruction lesson plans are available at your fingertips. Holt's Teacher Management System links teaching support tools to pages in the Interactive Teacher's Edition.

The One-Stop Planner features:
- Interactive Teacher's Edition
- Calendar Planner and pacing guides
- Editable lesson plans
- All reproducible ancillaries in Adobe Acrobat (PDF) format
- ExamView Test Generator (English and Spanish)
- Transparency and video previews

Professional Development

- **In-service and staff development** as part of your Holt Social Studies product purchase
- **Quick Teacher Tutorial Lesson Presentation CD-ROM**
- Intensive tuition-based **Teacher Development Institute**
- **Teaching American History Online**—2 Module Professional Development Course
- **Convenient Holt Speaker Bureau**—face-to-face workshop options
- **PRAXIS™ Test Prep** interactive Web-based content refreshers*
- **24/7 Ask A Professional Development Expert** at http://www.hrw.com/prodev/

* PRAXIS is a trademark of Educational Testing Service (ETS). This publication is not endorsed or approved by ETS.

Chapter Big Ideas

Section 1 Europeans explored the world searching for new lands and new trade routes.

Section 2 Christopher Columbus's voyages led to new exchanges between Europe, Africa, and the Americas.

Section 3 Spain established a large empire in the Americas.

Section 4 Other European nations challenged Spain in the Americas.

Section 5 Europeans forced millions of African slaves to work in their colonies.

Focus on Writing

The **Chapter Resource File** provides a Focus on Writing worksheet to help students organize and write their letters.

CRF: Focus on Writing Activity: Writing a Letter

CHAPTER **2** 1400–1750

New Empires in the Americas

FOCUS ON WRITING

Writing a Letter Long before telephones and emails, most people communicated with friends and family far away by letter. As you read this chapter, you will learn about different groups of people who came to the Americas. You will pretend to be a member of one of these groups and write a letter home to tell your friends and family about the people you meet and the experiences you have in the Americas.

WORLD

1416
Prince Henry the Navigator establishes a center for naval exploration at Sagres, Portugal.

1400

34 CHAPTER 2

Below Level

Basic-level activities designed for all students encountering new material

At Level

Intermediate-level activities designed for average students

Above Level

Challenging activities designed for honors and gifted and talented students

Standard English Mastery

Activities designed to improve standard English usage

Introduce the Chapter

At Level

Focus on Exploration

1. Tell students to imagine that space travel to other planets is accessible, affordable, and common. As a result, more people have begun to explore other planets. Tell students that they have just been offered the chance to explore another planet. Ask students to describe the plant life, animals and native peoples of the African coast and New England. Write students' responses for the class to see.

2. Ask students why they would consider going on such a trip. What would they hope to discover or gain? Discuss with students their motivations and expectations for exploring the unknown.

3. Tell students that in this chapter they will be discussing the Age of Exploration, which probably had very similar motivations and expectations to what you discussed as a class. Have students keep their ideas in mind as they read through the chapter. **LS Verbal/Linguistic**

What You Will Learn...

The ships of explorer Christopher Columbus sail again in the form of these replicas. Columbus discovered land where Europeans did not expect land to be. The news excited Europe and set off the great Age of Exploration. The Americas and Europe—and the world—would never be the same again. In this chapter you will learn more about the earliest people in North America and the Europeans who colonized it.

1492
Christopher Columbus lands in the Bahamas.

1609
Henry Hudson makes his first voyage to North America.

1619
The first Africans in North America arrive at Jamestown, Virginia.

1500

1600

1700

1533
Francisco Pizarro and his men kill Inca leader Atahualpa.

1609
Galileo Galilei becomes the first person to use a telescope to view the heavens.

1644
The Qing dynasty begins in China and will rule until 1912.

35

● **Chapter Preview** ●

HOLT
History's Impact
▶ **Video series**
See the Video Teacher's Guide for strategies for using the chapter video **New Empires in the Americas.**

Explore the Picture

Sailing into the Unknown
Christopher Columbus did not have to convince the king and queen of Spain that the world was round in order for them to sponsor his expedition. Most educated people at the time knew the world was not flat. Columbus did, however, miscalculate the circumference of the planet by about 25 percent. Columbus also assumed that Asia extended farther east than it actually did because he believed that Earth consisted mostly of land and not water.

Analyzing Visuals Ask students how sailors in these small boats might have felt as they lost sight of land and moved into the vast Atlantic Ocean. *Answers will vary, but students might consider the fear of the unknown, the thrill of an adventure, and the hard work involved in sailing across the ocean.*

go.hrw.com
Online Resources
Chapter Resources:
KEYWORD: SR8 US2
Teacher Resources:
KEYWORD: SR8 TEACHER

Explore the Time Line

1. How did Prince Henry contribute to exploration? *established a center for naval exploration*

2. How many years passed between Columbus's arrival in the Americas and Henry Hudson's arrival? *117 years*

3. In what year did Galileo use a telescope to view the heavens? *1609*

4. Which event on the time line is not related to the Age of Exploration? *Qing dynasty begins*

Linking to Today

Exploring in the 21st Century Today's explorers look toward the skies for new lands to discover. One of the more exciting adventures is on Mars, the Red Planet. NASA's Mars Exploration Rovers, Spirit and Opportunity began exploring the planet's surface in 2004 and have gathered rock samples and evidence that Mars had a wet environment long ago. Some scientists now believe that Mars possibly could have sustained life at one time.

Understanding Themes

Two themes, geography and politics, are presented in this chapter. Both are closely tied to the exploration of North and South America. Ask students how the knowledge that explorers were sailing around the world might have changed peoples' attitudes about geography. Discuss the factors that make up popular perceptions of geography, including maps. Then ask how traveling to new places and learning about new products and vast natural resources could have led to big profits for certain business people. Tell students that expanding knowledge about the world and its geography and resources are the themes for this chapter.

Outlining and History

Focus on Reading Have students bring in or provide front-page stories from a newspaper. Have them work in pairs to create an outline of the story following the format shown in the text. If possible, assign each pair a different story. When the outlines are complete, have each pair use scissors to cut the major topics, supporting ideas, and details of their outlines into separate strips of paper. Tell students to cut off the outline numbers and letters. Have pairs exchange their outlines and ask them to put the outlines back together in correct form. Have the original pair check the outline against the article to see how well the other pair completed the task.

Reading Social Studies
by Kylene Beers

| Economics | Geography | Politics | Society and Culture | Science and Technology |

Focus on Themes In this chapter you will read about European exploration of the sea and of North and South America. As you read, you will learn about how **politics** encouraged the desire to explore new trade routes and lands. You will also read to explore new trade routes and lands. You will also read about how **geography** affected the race for empires in the New World. European nations began exploring the newly discovered continents in an effort to establish colonies.

Outlining and History

Focus on Reading How can you make sense of all the facts and ideas in a chapter? One way is to take notes in the form of an outline.

Outlining a Chapter Here is an example of a partial outline for Section 4 of this chapter. Compare the outline to the information on pages 52-57. Notice how the writer looked at the heads in the chapter to determine the main and supporting ideas.

The writer picked up the first heading in the chapter (p. 52) as the first main idea. She identified it with Roman numeral I.

Section 4: The Race for Empires

I. Events in Europe
  A. The Protestant Reformation
  B. Spain and England Go to War
    1. Sea dogs
    2. Spanish Armada
II. Search for a Northwest Passage
III. Rivalry for North America
  A. English Presence in the New World
  B. French Presence in the New World
    1. Huguenots
    2. Canada
    3. Explorers
      a. Cartier
      b. Champlain
      c. Jolliet and Marquette
      d. La Salle
  C. Dutch Presence in the New World

The writer saw two smaller headings under the bigger heading on pages 52–53 and listed them as A and B.

The writer identified three facts that supported II.B. She listed them as numbers 1, 2, and 3.

The writer decided it was important to note some individual facts under B.3. That's why she added a through d.

Outlining a Few Paragraphs When you need to outline only a few paragraphs, you can use the same outline form. Just look for the main idea of each paragraph and give each one a Roman numeral. Supporting ideas withing the paragraph can be listed with A, B, and so forth. You can use Arabic numbers for specific details and facts.

36 CHAPTER 2

Reading and Skills Resources

Reading Support

- Interactive Reader and Study Guide
- Student Edition on Audio CD
- Spanish Chapter Summaries Audio CD Program

Social Studies Skills Support

- Interactive Skills Tutor CD-ROM

Vocabulary Support

- **CRF:** Vocabulary Builder Activities
- **CRF:** Chapter Review Activity
- Differentiated Instruction Modified Worksheets and Tests CD-ROM:
  - Vocabulary Flash Cards
  - Vocabulary Builder Activity
  - Chapter Review Activity

OSP Holt PuzzlePro

You Try It!

Read the following passage from this chapter. Then fill in the blanks to complete the outline below.

Conquest of the Aztec Empire

Moctezuma ruled the Aztec Empire, which was at the height of its power in the early 1500s. Moctezuma's capital, Tenochtitlán (tay-naweh-teet-LAHN), was built in the middle of Lake Texcoco, near the present-day sight of Mexico City. Tenochtitlán was a large city with temples, a palace, and buildings that were built on an island in the middle of the lake. The buildings and riches of the city impressed the conquistadors. The Spanish saw the Aztec Empire as a good source of gold and silver. They also wanted to convert the Aztec people to Christianity.

Chapter 2, (p. 46)

The Aztec had thousand of warriors. In contrast, Cortés had only 508 soldiers, around 100 sailors, 16 horses, and some guns. Cortés hoped that his superior weapons would bring him victory.

Complete this outline based on the passage you just read.

I. Moctezuma and the Aztec Empire were at the height of power in the 1500s.

   A. Tenochtitlán was the capital

      1. Built in Lake Texcoco

      2. _____

   B. The buildings and riches impressed the conquistadores

      1. _____

      2. Christianity

II. _____

   A. Cortés had fewer soldiers

   B. _____

Academic Vocabulary

Success in school is related to knowing academic vocabulary—the words that are frequently used in school assignments and discussions. In this chapter, you will learn the following academic words.

effect *(p. 40)*
structure *(p. 59)*

Key Terms and People

This chapter includes a lengthy list of explorers and terms. Organize the class into pairs. Have each pair create a table with two columns. The columns should be labeled "People" and "Things." Tell students to divide the terms and people from the Key Terms list into the appropriate categories on their charts. Discuss with students how they can tell the difference, noting how capitalization is usually, but not always, the key to distinguishing between terms and people. After students have finished their charts, have them preview the chapter and write one fact to go along with each term. Have students quiz each other on the terms in each column.

Focus on Reading

See the **Focus on Reading** questions in this chapter for more practice on reading social studies skills.

Reading Social Studies Assessment

See the **Chapter Review** at the end of this chapter for student assessment questions related to this reading skill.

Teaching Tip

Tell students that making a time line is one way to summarize in a visual manner. By organizing facts along a time line, students will be able to more clearly understand the key events in history. Remind them that a time line contains a list of single events and removes details that might confuse the student.

Answers

You Try It! **I. A. 2.** *large city with temples, palace, and buildings;* **I. B. 1.** *Aztec Empire source of gold and silver;* **II.** *Aztec had thousands of warriors;* **II.B.** *Cortés had superior weapons*

Europeans Set Sail

Bellringer

If YOU were there . . . Use the **Daily Bellringer Transparency** to help students answer the question.

📖 Daily Bellringer Transparency, Section 1

Academic Vocabulary

Review with students the high-use academic term in this section.

effect the result of an action or decision (p. 40)

📄 **CRF:** Vocabulary Builder Activity, Section 1

Taking Notes

Have students copy the graphic organizer onto their own paper and then use it to take notes on the section. This activity will prepare students for the Section Assessment, in which they will complete a graphic organizer that builds on the information using a critical thinking skill.

What You Will Learn...

Main Ideas

1. Vikings were skilled sailors, and they were the first Europeans to reach North America.
2. Prince Henry the Navigator established a school for sailors and provided financial support that enabled the Portuguese to start exploring the oceans.
3. Portuguese sailors sailed around Africa and found a sea route to Asia.

The Big Idea

Europeans explored the world searching for new lands and new trade routes.

Key Terms and People

Leif Eriksson, *p. 38*
Henry the Navigator, *p. 39*
astrolabe, *p. 40*
caravels, *p. 40*

TAKING NOTES As you read, take notes on European exploration. List the countries that explored the world and the places they explored. Write your notes in a chart like the one below.

Countries	Places Explored

If **YOU** were there...

You are a sailor living in Portugal in the mid-1400s. Several of your friends are excited about joining an expedition to sail to new lands. Although Portuguese navigators have made improvements to sailing ships and advancements in ocean travel, you have heard about the dangers other sailors have faced on the open seas.

Will you join the expedition or stay behind? Why?

BUILDING BACKGROUND Europeans were interested in the goods of Africa and Asia. In order to find new routes to these goods and to find new lands to settle, many European nations sent explorers on voyages.

Skilled Viking Sailors

The Vikings were the first Europeans to make contact with North America. They came from Scandinavia, a peninsula that includes the present-day countries of Denmark, Norway, and Sweden. The Vikings were skilled sailors who developed a new style of ship, called the longship, that curved up at both ends. Viking vessels traveled the rough North Atlantic seas better than earlier ships because their designs were more stable.

The Vikings raided countries throughout Europe, but they also developed large trading networks. Viking ships sailed to the British Isles, and the Mediterranean and Black seas. Eventually, the Vikings sailed west into the North Atlantic. There they founded a settlement on the island of Iceland in about 874. More than 100 years later, Viking Erik the Red left Iceland to settle Greenland.

Leif Eriksson, the son of Erik the Red, shared his father's love of adventure. In the year 1000, he was sailing from west Norway to Greenland when strong winds blew his ship off course and carried his ship all the way to the North American coast.

Eriksson and his crew landed on the Labrador Peninsula in present-day Canada. The Vikings then sailed farther south to the island of Newfoundland, and perhaps to what is now New England. According to their myths, Vikings saw forests, meadows, and rivers that held "larger salmon than they had ever seen."

38 CHAPTER 2

Teach the Big Idea

Europeans Set Sail

1. **Teach** Ask students the questions in the Main Idea boxes to teach this section.

2. **Apply** Have students create their own time lines that start with the Viking settlement in Iceland in about AD 874. Time lines should include the significant events involving Prince Henry the Navigator and Portuguese exploration discussed in this section.
   LS Visual/Spatial

3. **Review** Ask volunteers to share information on their time lines. Use this information to create a class time line. Have students correct and add information to their own time lines.

4. **Practice/Homework** Have students use the information in the section to write short descriptions for each event on the time line.
   📄 Alternative Assessment Handbook, Rubric 36: Time Lines

Eriksson settled in a coastal area he called Vinland, but the Vikings left after only a few years. Attacks by Native Americans posed a constant threat, and the area may have been too far from other Viking settlements to be supported.

After the Vikings left North America, Europeans did not return to the continent for centuries. In the 1400s, however, a growing interest in discovery and exploration spread across Europe.

READING CHECK **Sequencing** List the stages of Viking exploration that led to their landing in North America.

Prince Henry the Navigator

In the early 1400s Portugal became a leader in world exploration. One man in particular, Prince **Henry the Navigator**, was responsible for advances that would make exploration more successful. Although he never set out on a voyage himself, Henry greatly advanced Portugal's exploration efforts.

In the early 1400s Prince Henry built an observatory and founded a school of navigation to teach better methods of sailing. He also financed research by mapmakers and shipbuilders. Finally, he paid for expeditions to explore the west coast of Africa.

Riches in Asia

During the 1400s, Europeans had several reasons to explore the world. First, they wanted Asian spices. They hoped to bypass the merchants who had a monopoly on, or economic control of, the Asian products that reached the Mediterranean. If a sea route to Asia could be found, countries could buy spices and other items directly.

Second, religion played a role in exploration. Christians in Europe wanted to convert more people to their faith. Third, many Europeans had become interested in Asian cultures. Explorer Marco Polo's book about his travels throughout Asia remained popular in Europe long after his death in 1324. Many Europeans wanted to learn more about Asia and its culture.

History Close-up
The Caravel

A special type of ship called the caravel became the workhorse of many European explorers. Though small, caravels were sturdy. They could sail across huge oceans and up small rivers. Caravels featured important advances in sailing technology.

The smooth, rounded hull handled high seas well.

The large center rudder made quick turns possible.

Triangular sails enabled the caravel to sail into the wind.

ANALYSIS SKILL **ANALYZING VISUALS**
What features made the caravel an excellent sailing ship?

39

❸ A Sea Route to Asia

Portuguese sailors sailed around Africa and found a sea route to Asia.

Recall What was the outcome of Bartolomeu Dias's expedition along the African coast? *A storm blew his ships around the southern tip of Africa.*

Make Inferences Do you think the Indians welcomed Vasco da Gama when he reached Calicut? Explain your answer. *The Indians had been trading with Muslim and Italian merchants for many years, so they probably welcomed da Gama as another European trader.*

Evaluate What do you think life was like for enslaved Africans in Portuguese-controlled islands? *poor, because they were forced to work hard and they endured brutal living conditions*

Info to Know

Cape of Good Hope The Cape of Good Hope is a headland located near present-day Cape Town, South Africa. It rises about 840 feet above sea level and marks the turning point for ships that are traveling between the Indian and south Atlantic Oceans. Dias named it the Cape of Storms, and later on John II of Portugal renamed it the Cape of Good Hope.

Answers

Analyzing Information *wanted to gain wealth, convert people to Christianity, learn more about Asia*

Reading Check *Prince Henry built an observatory and a navigation school to teach better methods of navigation. He also financed research by mapmakers and shipbuilders and exploration of Africa's west coast.*

QUICK FACTS

Causes and Effects of the Discovery of a Sea Route to Asia

Several factors led to the discovery of a sea route from Europe to Asia.

Causes

- Financial backing from Prince Henry the Navigator
- New technology (caravel and mariner's astrolabe)
- Seeking trade with Asia and financial gain
- Converting people to Christianity
- Curiosity

Effects

- Discovery of a sea route to Asia
- Face-to-face contact with traders in distant lands
- Awareness of different cultures and ways of life

ANALYSIS SKILL ANALYZING INFORMATION

Why was trade with Asia so important to Europeans?

ACADEMIC VOCABULARY
effect the result of an action or decision

FOCUS ON READING
Make an outline for the heading "A Sea Route to Asia."

Technological Advances

New technology played a major role in advancing world exploration. Sailors began to use tools such as the magnetic compass the **astrolabe**, a device that enabled navigators to learn their ship's location by charting the position of the stars. Better instruments made it possible for sailors to travel the open seas without landmarks to guide them.

The Portuguese also made advances in shipbuilding. They began designing ships that were smaller, lighter, and easier to steer than the heavy galleons they had used before. These new ships, called **caravels** (ker-uh-velz), used triangular sails that, unlike traditional square sails, allowed ships to sail against the wind. By placing rudders at the back of the ship, the Portuguese also improved the steering of ships.

READING CHECK Analyzing How did Henry the Navigator promote exploration?

A Sea Route to Asia

By the 1400s Portugal had several motives, financial support, and the technology necessary for exploration. Portuguese explorers set out to find new lands.

Rounding Africa

Even with new technology, travel on the open seas was dangerous and difficult. One person described the **effect** on sailors of a voyage south from Portugal.

❝Those which survived could hardly be recognized as human. They had lost flesh and hair, the nails had gone from hands and feet . . . They spoke of heat so incredible that it was a marvel that ships and crews were not burnt.❞
–Sailor, quoted in *World Civilizations*, edited by Edward McNall Burns, et al.

In spite of the dangers, Portuguese explorers continued sailing south, setting up trading posts along the way.

In 1488 Portuguese navigator Bartolomeu Dias led an expedition from Portugal southward along the African coast. A storm blew his ships around the southern tip of Africa. This point became known as the Cape of Good Hope. Dias wanted to continue his voyage, but his men did not. Since supplies were very low, Dias decided to call off the voyage and return to Portugal.

Later, King Manuel of Portugal sent another explorer, Vasco da Gama, on an expedition around the Cape of Good Hope. Da Gama left Lisbon, Portugal, in July 1497 and arrived in southwestern India the next year. Portugal had won the European race for a sea route to Asia.

When da Gama reached the Indian port of Calicut, Muslim traders met him and his men. The Muslims surprised the sailors by speaking to them in Portuguese. Soon da Gama and his crew learned that the people of India had been trading with Muslim and Italian merchants who knew Portuguese. Da Gama made two more trips back to India. He even governed a small colony there.

Differentiating Instruction

Below Level

Struggling Readers

1. Organize students into pairs. Instruct pairs to create a chart of Portuguese explorers. The chart should have three columns labeled *Explorer, Discovery,* and *Outcome*.

2. Review with students the contributions of the Portuguese explorers discussed in this section and the results of their discoveries.

3. Have students work together to fill in each column. *Answers: Bartolomeu Dias, Cape of Good Hope at southern tip of Africa, first Portuguese explorer to travel to the south of Africa, future sailors to West Africa bargained with tribal leaders for gold, ivory and slaves; Vasco da Gama, traveled around the Cape of Good Hope to Calicut, India, opened direct trade between Portugal and India, governed a small colony in India and gained Portugal more wealth and power*

4. Ask students to share their charts with the class. **LS Interpersonal, Visual/Spatial**

📖 Alternative Assessment Handbook, Rubric 7: Charts

Results of Exploration

Portugal's explorations would have major results, including the start of the Atlantic slave trade. As Portuguese sailors explored the west coast of Africa, they negotiated for gold, ivory, and slaves. The slave trade devastated African communities. It led to increased warfare among kingdoms and broke up many families. The Portuguese sent many enslaved Africans to Europe and to islands in the Atlantic, where they endured brutal living conditions.

The other nations of Europe watched as new trade routes brought increased wealth and power to Portugal. They soon launched voyages of exploration to find their own water routes to Asia.

READING CHECK **Predicting** How would continued exploration affect Africans?

SUMMARY AND PREVIEW In the 1400s, the Portuguese started a new era of exploration. In the next section you will learn how Europeans reached the American continents.

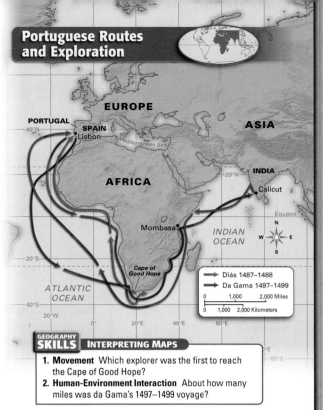

Portuguese Routes and Exploration

→ Días 1487–1488
→ Da Gama 1497–1499

0   1,000   2,000 Miles
0   1,000   2,000 Kilometers

GEOGRAPHY SKILLS **INTERPRETING MAPS**

1. **Movement** Which explorer was the first to reach the Cape of Good Hope?
2. **Human-Environment Interaction** About how many miles was da Gama's 1497–1499 voyage?

Section 1 Assessment

go.hrw.com
Online Quiz
KEYWORD: SR8 HP2

Reviewing Ideas, Terms, and People

1. **a. Identify** Who was **Leif Eriksson**?
   b. Summarize How did the Vikings eventually establish Vinland?
   c. Draw Inferences Why do you think the Vikings did not try to colonize the Americas?
2. **a. Identify** Who was Prince **Henry the Navigator**?
   b. Compare Why were **caravels** able to sail against the wind while other ships could not?
3. **a. Recall** Who was the first explorer to find a sea route from Europe to Asia?
   b. Explain How did Muslims living in India learn Portuguese?
   c. Draw Conclusions How did the slave trade affect West Africa?

Critical Thinking

4. **Summarize** Review your notes on European exploration. Then copy the chart below and use it to explain the reason for the explorations, the technology that made explorations possible, and the results of the explorations.

Reasons Technology → Results

FOCUS ON WRITING

5. **Taking Notes on Early Explorers** As you read this section, take notes on both groups of explorers you learn about. Make sure to note the differences and similarities between the two groups, where they traveled, and why.

NEW EMPIRES IN THE AMERICAS **41**

Section 1 Assessment Answers

1. **a.** first European to sail to North America
   b. sailed south to Newfoundland, settled in a coastal area
   c. discouraged by attacks, other settlements too far away
2. **a.** Portuguese ruler, started a navigation school, encouraged exploration
   b. triangular sails
3. **a.** Vasco da Gama
   b. through trade contacts with other Muslims and Italian merchants
   c. increased warfare among West African countries, broke up families

4. Reasons—desire for cheaper Asian spices, desire to convert people to Christianity, and interest in Asian culture; Technology—observatory, navigation schools, caravels, magnetic compass, astrolabe; Results—sea route to Asia, start of the Atlantic slave trade, other European countries began exploring
5. Students will note similarities and differences between Viking and Portuguese explorers

Bellringer

If YOU were there . . . Use the **Daily Bellringer Transparency** to help students answer the question.

🖋 Daily Bellringer Transparency, Section 2

Building Vocabulary

Preteach or review the following terms:

raw materials items found in nature that can be used to manufacture other products (p. 45)

uncharted not previously mapped (p. 43)

🖋 **CRF:** Vocabulary Builder Activity, Section 2

Taking Notes

Have students copy the graphic organizer onto their own paper and then use it to take notes on the section. This activity will prepare students for the Section Assessment, in which they will complete a graphic organizer that builds on the information using a critical thinking skill.

SECTION 2

Europeans Reach the Americas

What You Will Learn...

Main Ideas

1. Christopher Columbus sailed across the Atlantic Ocean and reached a continent that was previously unknown to him.
2. After Columbus's voyages, other explorers sailed to the Americas.

The Big Idea

Christopher Columbus's voyages led to new exchanges between Europe, Africa, and the Americas.

Key Terms and People

Christopher Columbus, *p. 42*
Line of Demarcation, *p. 44*
Treaty of Tordesillas, *p. 44*
Ferdinand Magellan, *p. 44*
circumnavigate, *p. 44*
Columbian Exchange, *p. 45*

TAKING NOTES As you read, take notes on the explorers, their journeys, and the effects of European voyages to the Americas. Write your notes in a chart like the one below.

Explorer	Sponsored by	Traveled to

Effects of Journeys

If **YOU** were there...

You are a European explorer who just returned to your homeland from the Americas. While you were gone, you tried new and different foods, including corn, potatoes, and cocoa. You have brought some of these foods back with you. You want your friends and family to sample these items, but they resist.

What will you say about these new foods?

BUILDING BACKGROUND Europeans, Africans, and Asians had traded with each other for centuries using land and sea routes. Native American groups knew of each other through trade routes, as well. Although sailors often explored new areas, before 1492 the two worlds had no communication with each other.

Columbus Sails across the Atlantic

Stories of fabulous kingdoms and wealth in Asia captured the imagination of **Christopher Columbus,** a sailor from Genoa, Italy. Columbus was convinced that he could reach Asia by sailing west across the Atlantic Ocean.

The Journey Begins

Columbus asked King Ferdinand and Queen Isabella of Spain to pay for an expedition across the Atlantic. He promised them great riches, new territory, and Catholic converts. It took Columbus several years to convince the king and queen, but they finally agreed to help finance the journey. Ferdinand and Isabella ordered Columbus to bring back any items of value and to claim for Spain any lands he explored.

On August 3, 1492, Columbus's three ships set sail. The *Niña* and the *Pinta* were caravels. Columbus sailed in the larger *Santa María*. The ships carried about 90 sailors and a year's worth of supplies. They made a stop in the Canary Islands, and then on September 6, they resumed their journey. Soon, they passed the limits of Columbus's

42 CHAPTER 2

Teach the Big Idea

Europeans Reach the Americas

1. **Teach** Ask students the questions in the Main Idea boxes to teach this section.
2. **Apply** Have students create a flow chart to show the impact of Columbus's voyage. Tell students to write *Columbus lands in the Caribbean* in the first block of their charts. Students should draw arrows to link the boxes that will follow. **LS Visual/Spatial**
3. **Review** Tell students to fill in their flow charts with events that occurred as a result of Columbus's voyage. *Students should*

include land claimed for Spain; conflict between Spain and Portugal; Line of Demarcation; Treaty of Tordesillas; other explorers reach Americas; discovery of the Pacific Ocean; Magellan circumnavigates the planet; Columbian Exchange; triangular trade

4. **Practice/Homework** Have students illustrate each event in their flow chart.

🖋 Alternative Assessment Handbook, Rubric 7: Charts

Columbus's Voyages 1492–1504

NORTH AMERICA

Gulf of Mexico

Tropic of Cancer

The Bahamas

San Salvador

Cuba

Jamaica

Hispaniola

Puerto Rico

MESOAMERICA

Caribbean Sea

Trinidad

SOUTH AMERICA

ATLANTIC OCEAN

Legend:
→ First voyage, 1492–1493
→ Second voyage, 1493–1496
→ Third voyage, 1498
→ Fourth voyage, 1502–1504
▨ Land seen by Columbus or crew members

0   250   500 Miles
0   250   500 Kilometers

Transatlantic Travel

NORTH AMERICA

ATLANTIC OCEAN

Azores

PORTUGAL

EUROPE

SPAIN

Canary Islands

AFRICA

SOUTH AMERICA

Equator

GEOGRAPHY SKILLS INTERPRETING MAPS

1. **Place** Where did Columbus first land?
2. **Human-Environment Interaction** Why do you think Columbus saw only the coastal area of Mesoamerica?

maps and sailed into uncharted seas. After more than a month with no sight of land, the crew grew restless.

Soon the crew saw signs of land—birds and floating tree branches. Columbus promised a reward "to him who first sang out that he saw land." On October 12, 1492, a lookout cried, "Land! Land!" ending the long journey from the Canary Islands.

The ships landed on an island in the Bahamas. Columbus thought he had found a new route to Asia. Instead, he had reached another continent that was unknown to him. Columbus called the island San Salvador, which means "Holy Savior." Columbus also visited another island he called Hispaniola. There he met the Taino (TY-noh). At that time Europeans called Asia the Indies, so Columbus, believing he was in Asia, called these Native American people Indians.

The Taino lived in small farming communities. In his journal, Columbus wrote that the Taino were "so generous . . . that

no one would believe it who has not seen it." However, Columbus and his crew were not interested in Taino culture, but in gold. After three months of exploring, looking for gold, and collecting exotic plants and animals, Columbus decided to return to Spain.

Columbus made three more journeys to the Americas during his lifetime. In 1504 he returned to Spain in poor health. Columbus died two years later, still believing that he had reached Asia.

Impact of Columbus's Voyages

The voyages of Columbus changed the way Europeans thought of the world and their place in it. A new era of interaction between Europe and the Americas had begun.

Columbus's discovery also created conflict. Both Spain and Portugal wanted to add these lands to their empires. In 1493, Pope Alexander VI, from Spain, issued a decree that set out the **Line of Demarcation**.

NEW EMPIRES IN THE AMERICAS **43**

Main Idea

❷ Other Explorers Sail to the Americas

After Columbus's voyages, other explorers sailed to the Americas.

Recall How did the Americas get their name? *A mapmaker labeled the continents America in honor of Amerigo Vespucci, who led an expedition to South America and believed that the land was not Asia, but a new continent.*

Summarize How did Magellan's fleet circumnavigate the world? How long did it take to complete the journey? *sailed from Spain down the east coast of South America, into the Pacific, west into the Indian Ocean, then back to Spain; three years*

Make Judgments Which items traded in the Columbian Exchange do you think were most valuable? Why? *possible answers—corn, potatoes, tobacco, and cocoa to Europe; horses, cattle, pigs, wheat, and barley to the Americas*

Did you know . . .

Vasco Núñez de Balboa may have been the first European to see the Pacific Ocean, but it was Ferdinand Magellan who named the body of water. He chose "Pacific" because it described the calm waters.

Answers

Analyzing Primary Sources *creating towns, controlling the collecting of gold, mayors for towns, priests and a church*

Reading Check *Columbus thought he could reach Asia by sailing west across the Atlantic Ocean from Spain.*

Primary Source

LETTER

Christopher Columbus, 1494

Two years after discovering the island of Hispaniola, Columbus wrote a letter to the Spanish king and queen outlining his ideas of its colonization.

Most High and Mighty Sovereigns,

In the first place, as regards the Island of Espanola: Inasmuch as the number of colonists who desire to go thither [there] amounts to two thousand, owing to the land being safer and better for farming and trading...

1. That in the said island there shall be founded three or four towns . . .

2. That for the better and more speedy colonization of the said island, no one shall have liberty to collect gold in it except those who have taken out colonists' papers . . .

3. That each town shall have its alcalde [Mayor] . . .

4. That there shall be a church, and parish priests or friars to administer the sacraments, to perform divine worship, and for the conversion of the Indians.

–Christopher Columbus, letter to the King and Queen of Spain, 1494

ANALYSIS SKILL **ANALYZING PRIMARY SOURCES**

What were Columbus's main concerns in founding a colony on Hispaniola?

This imaginary boundary divided the Atlantic Ocean. Spain could claim all land west of the line.

The Portuguese king believed that this arrangement favored Spain. To prevent war, the leaders of the two nations signed the **Treaty of Tordesillas**, which moved the Line of Demarcation 800 miles further west. This gave Portugal more opportunity to claim lands unexplored by other Europeans.

READING CHECK **Identifying Points of View** Why did Columbus want to sail across the Atlantic?

Other Explorers Sail to the Americas

Columbus's discoveries inspired others to sail across the Atlantic Ocean. In 1501 explorer Amerigo Vespucci (vuh-SPOO-chee) led a Spanish fleet to the coast of present-day South America. He was convinced the land he reached was not Asia. Instead, Vespucci believed he had found a "new world." A German mapmaker labeled the continents across the ocean *America* in honor of Vespucci. Europeans began using the names North America and South America for these lands.

In a Spanish settlement in present-day Panama, another explorer, Vasco Núñez de Balboa (NOON-yays day bahl-BOH-uh), heard stories from local Native Americans about another ocean farther west. Balboa set out to find it. For weeks he and his men struggled through thick jungle and deadly swamps. In 1513 they reached the top of a mountain. From this spot Balboa saw a great blue sea—the Pacific Ocean—stretching out before him.

In 1519, **Ferdinand Magellan** (muh-JEHL-uhn), a Portuguese navigator, set out with a Spanish fleet to sail down the east coast of South America. After sailing around the southern tip of the continent, Magellan continued into the Pacific even though his ships were dangerously low on food and fresh water.

Magellan's fleet sailed across the Pacific Ocean. In the Philippine Islands, Magellan was killed in a battle with native peoples. Down to three ships, the expedition continued sailing west into the Indian Ocean. In 1522 the voyage's only remaining ship returned to Spain. Only 18 members of Magellan's original crew survived. These sailors were the first people to **circumnavigate**, or go all the way around, the globe. Their entire journey was some 40,000 miles long.

European explorers and settlers took plants and animals with them to the Americas. They also brought back a variety of plants and animals to Europe, Asia, and Africa. This

---

Critical Thinking: Interpreting Maps

At Level

Mapping Voyages of Columbus

Materials: blank outline map of the world

1. Instruct students to reread the information concerning the voyages of Christopher Columbus, Amerigo Vespucci, Vasco Núñez de Balboa, and Ferdinand Magellan. Students should note years and important discoveries.

2. Have students use the blank outlines maps and colored pencils to chart the routes of these explorers and to illustrate the Columbian Exchange.

3. On their maps students should note what products traveled from Europe to the Americas, and what products were exported from the Americas to Europe. Students should also map the triangular trade between Europe, Africa, and the Americas.

4. Ask students to share their maps with the class. **LS** **Interpersonal, Visual/Spatial**

📝 Alternative Assessment Handbook, Rubric 20: Map Creation

transfer became known as the **Columbian Exchange** because it started with Columbus's explorations. The Columbian Exchange dramatically changed the world.

European explorers found many plants in the Americas that were unknown to them, including corn, potatoes, tobacco, and cocoa. They brought these items to Europe, where they were highly valued. The explorers also introduced horses, cattle, and pigs to the Americas. Native Americans came to use these animals for food and transportation. They also started to farm European grains such as wheat and barley.

Without intending to do so, the explorers also introduced deadly new diseases to the Americas. Native Americans had no natural resistance to European diseases, and often died as a result of their exposure to them.

Over time, a trading pattern involving the exchange of raw materials, manufactured products, and slaves developed among Europe, Africa, and the Americas. As part of the trade, Europeans shipped millions of enslaved Africans to work in the colonies in the New World.

READING CHECK **Evaluating** What were the negative aspects of the Columbian Exchange?

The Columbian Exchange

Items brought from the Americas
Cocoa
Corn
Potatoes
Squash
Tobacco
Turkeys

Items brought from Europe
Cattle
Citrus Fruits
Diseases
Grains
Horses
Sugarcane

ANALYSIS SKILL
Which side of the Atlantic did cattle come from? Potatoes? Sugarcane?

SUMMARY AND PREVIEW Columbus's voyages to America inspired other Europeans to explore the "New World." This led to new exchanges between both sides of the Atlantic. In the next section you will learn about Spain's empire in the Americas.

Section 2 Assessment

go.hrw.com
Online Quiz
KEYWORD: SR8 HP2

Reviewing Ideas, Terms, and People

1. a. Recall What agreement did **Christopher Columbus** make with Queen Isabella and King Ferdinand of Spain?
b. Explain Where did Columbus think he had landed when he reached the Bahamas?
c. Evaluate How did Columbus's voyage lead to a dispute between Spain and Portugal?
2. a. Identify Who was the first European explorer to see the Pacific Ocean?
b. Summarize What route did **Ferdinand Magellan**'s ships take to **circumnavigate** the globe?
c. Draw Conclusions How did the **Columbian Exchange** and the slave trade affect the economies and the people of Europe, Africa, and the Americas?

Critical Thinking

3. Supporting a Point of View Review your notes on European exploration. Then copy the graphic organizer below and use it to rank, in order, the two most important results of European voyages to the Americas. Explain your choices in the "Why" column.

Most Important	Why

FOCUS ON WRITING

4. Understanding Christopher Columbus As you read this section, pay attention to what life might have been like for Columbus and his crew as they sailed across the Atlantic. Note ways in which their voyage changed life for many Europeans.

Section 2 Assessment Answers

1. a. king and queen financed the expedition; Columbus would bring back any items of value and claim territory for Spain
b. Asia
c. Both wanted land in the Americas
2. a. Vasco Núñez de Balboa
b. from Spain, to eastern coast of South America, around the southern tip of South America, across the Pacific, west across the Indian Ocean, back to Spain

c. brought new products to Europe and the Americas, led to slave trade with Africa, introduced deadly new diseases to Native Americans, enriched European nations
3. possible answers—Christopher Columbus's explorations inspired other explorations and resulted in the Columbian Exchange; Ferdinand Magellan's crew circumnavigation of the globe showed the extent of the earth.
4. See answer to Question 2c.

45

Spain Builds an Empire

Preteach

Bellringer

Preteach

Bellringer

If YOU were there . . . Use the **Daily Bellringer Transparency** to help students answer the question.

📄 Daily Bellringer Transparency, Section 3

Building Vocabulary

Preteach or review the following terms:

convert to convince others to change to a different faith or way of thinking (p. 46)

haciendas vast Spanish estates in Central and South America (p. 50)

📄 **CRF:** Vocabulary Builder Activity, Section 3

Taking Notes

Have students copy the graphic organizer onto their own paper and then use it to take notes on the section. This activity will prepare students for the Section Assessment, in which they will complete a graphic organizer that builds on the information using a critical thinking skill.

What You Will Learn...

Main Ideas

1. Spanish conquistadors conquered the Aztec and Inca empires.
2. Spanish explorers traveled through the borderlands of New Spain, claiming more land.
3. Spanish settlers treated Native Americans harshly, forcing them to work on plantations and in mines.

The Big Idea

Spain established a large empire in the Americas.

Key Terms and People

conquistadors, p. 46
Hernán Cortés, p. 46
Moctezuma II, p. 46
Francisco Pizarro, p. 47
encomienda system, p. 50
plantations, p. 50
Bartolomé de Las Casas, p. 51

TAKING NOTES Create a chart like the one below. As you read, take notes on Spanish conquest and settlement in the Americas.

Spanish Conquest and Settlement	
Aztec Empire	
Inca Empire	
Borderlands–Southeast	
Borderlands–Southeast	

If YOU were there...

You are an Aztec warrior living in central Mexico in the 1500s. You are proud to serve your ruler, Moctezuma II. One day several hundred foreigners arrive on your shores. They are pale, bearded men, and they have strange animals and equipment.

From where do you think these strangers have come?

BUILDING BACKGROUND Spain sent many expeditions to the Americas. Like explorers from other countries, Spanish explorers claimed the land they found for their country. Much of this land was already filled with Native American communities, however.

Spanish Conquistadors

The Spanish sent **conquistadors** (kahn-kees-tuh-DAWRS), soldiers who led military expeditions in the Americas. Conquistador **Hernán Cortés** left Cuba to sail to present-day Mexico in 1519. Cortés had heard of a wealthy land to the west ruled by a king named **Moctezuma II** (mawk-tay-SOO-mah).

Conquest of the Aztec Empire

Moctezuma ruled the Aztec Empire, which was at the height of its power in the early 1500s. Moctezuma's capital, Tenochtitlán, was built in the middle of Lake Texcoco, near the present-day site of Mexico City. Tenochtitlán was a large city with temples, a palace, and buildings that were built on an island in the middle of the lake. The buildings and riches of the city impressed the Spaniards. They saw the Aztec Empire as a good source of gold and silver. They also wanted to convert the Aztec to Christianity.

The Aztec had thousands of warriors. In contrast, Cortés had only 508 soldiers, about 100 sailors, 16 horses, and some guns. Cortés hoped that his superior weapons would bring him victory. Cortés also sought help from enemies of the Aztec. An Indian woman named Malintzin (mah-LINT-suhn) helped Cortés win allies.

Teach the Big Idea

At Level

Spain Builds an Empire

1. **Teach** Ask students the questions in the Main Idea boxes to teach this section.

2. **Apply** Create a 2-column chart for students to see. Label the columns *Cause* and *Effect*. As students read this section, have them look for causes and effects and record their information in the chart. Remind students that not everything they learn in this section needs to be included in the chart, but the information they include should show a

logical progression from the conquistadors to the enslavement of Native Americans.

LS Visual/Spatial

3. **Review** Ask volunteers to share information they have included in their charts.

4. **Practice/Homework** Have students use their charts to write brief descriptions that explain the relationship between the events on their charts.

📄 Alternative Assessment Handbook, Rubric 7: Charts

At first Moctezuma believed Cortés to be a god and welcomed him. Cortés then took Moctezuma prisoner and seized control of Tenochtitlán. Eventually, Tenochtitlán was destroyed and Moctezuma was killed. Smallpox and other diseases brought by the Spanish quickened the fall of the Aztec Empire.

Conquest of the Inca Empire

Another conquistador, **Francisco Pizarro** (puh-ZAHR-oh), heard rumors of the Inca cities in the Andes of South America. The Inca ruled a large territory that stretched along the Pacific coast from present-day Chile to northern Ecuador.

Pizarro had fewer than 400 men in his army. But the Inca, like the Aztec, had no weapons to match the conquistadors' swords and guns. Though outnumbered, Pizarro's troops captured the great Inca capital at Cuzco in present-day Peru and killed the Inca leaders. By 1534 Pizarro and his Native American allies had conquered the entire Inca Empire.

In only a few years, the Spanish had conquered two great American empires. During the conquest, the Spanish and their allies killed thousands of Inca and Aztec and looted their settlements. Moreover, possibly more than three-quarters of the Aztec and Inca populations were killed by the diseases the Europeans brought.

Spanish Settlements

The Spanish began to settle their vast empire, which they called New Spain. Spain's government wanted to control migration to the Americas. Most of the emigrants were Spanish, though a few non-Spanish subjects of the king also migrated. Jews, Muslims, and non-Christians were forbidden to settle in New Spain. At first, most emigrants were men. The government then encouraged families to migrate. Eventually, women comprised one-quarter of the total emigration from Spain.

Spain ruled its large American empire through a system of royal officials. At the top was the Council of the Indies, formed in 1524 to govern the Americas from Spain. The Council appointed two viceroys, or royal governors. The Viceroyalty of Peru governed most of South America. The Viceroyalty of New Spain governed all Spanish territories in

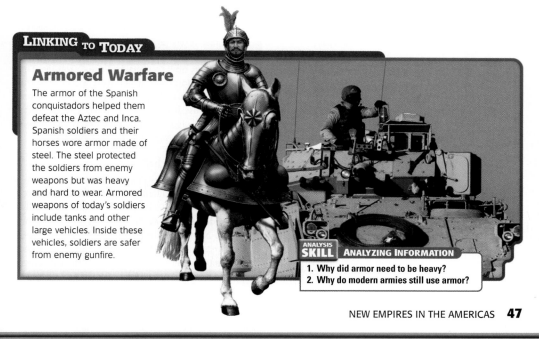

LINKING TO TODAY

Armored Warfare

The armor of the Spanish conquistadors helped them defeat the Aztec and Inca. Spanish soldiers and their horses wore armor made of steel. The steel protected the soldiers from enemy weapons but was heavy and hard to wear. Armored weapons of today's soldiers include tanks and other large vehicles. Inside these vehicles, soldiers are safer from enemy gunfire.

ANALYSIS SKILL **ANALYZING INFORMATION**

1. Why did armor need to be heavy?
2. Why do modern armies still use armor?

NEW EMPIRES IN THE AMERICAS **47**

❷ Exploring the Borderlands of New Spain

Spanish explorers traveled through the borderlands of New Spain claiming more land.

Recall What was Juan Ponce de León searching for in Florida? *the Fountain of Youth*

Analyze In what ways did de León succeed and fail in the Americas? *conquered Puerto Rico for Spain, found gold, and founded the city of San Juan; failed to colonize Florida*

Evaluate Why do you think Spain granted de Soto permission to explore such a large area of North America? *possible answers—the quest for gold, land for Spain, to spread Christianity*

Info to Know

Always be Prepared Hernando de Soto's exploration of the southern United States was one of the best-prepared expeditions in the Americas. De Soto gathered 1,000 men not including sailors, 350 horses, 13 hogs, and a number of fighting dogs.

Answers

Analyzing Information *Spanish weapons; European diseases*

Reading Check *With their superior weapons, they won battles, but diseases, such as smallpox, also killed thousands of Native Americans.*

48

Central America, Mexico, and the southern part of what is now the United States.

The Spanish established three kinds of settlements in New Spain. Pueblos served as trading posts and sometimes as centers of government. Priests started missions where they converted local Native Americans to Catholicism. The Spanish also built presidios, or military bases, to protect towns and missions.

To connect some of the scattered communities of New Spain, Spanish settlers built *El Camino Real*, or "the Royal Road." This network of roads ran for hundreds of miles from Mexico City to Santa Fe. The roads later stretched to settlements in California.

READING CHECK **Analyzing** How did the Spanish conquer the great Aztec and Inca empires?

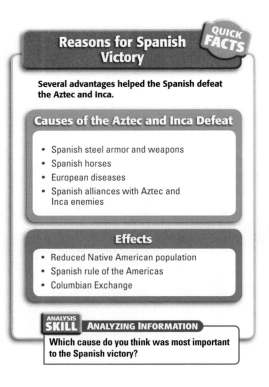

Reasons for Spanish Victory QUICK FACTS

Several advantages helped the Spanish defeat the Aztec and Inca.

Causes of the Aztec and Inca Defeat

- Spanish steel armor and weapons
- Spanish horses
- European diseases
- Spanish alliances with Aztec and Inca enemies

Effects

- Reduced Native American population
- Spanish rule of the Americas
- Columbian Exchange

ANALYSIS SKILL **ANALYZING INFORMATION**
Which cause do you think was most important to the Spanish victory?

Exploring the Borderlands of New Spain

Spain's American empire was not limited to lands taken from the conquered Aztec and the Inca empires. Many other Spanish explorers came to North America. They explored the borderlands of New Spain and claimed many new lands for the Spanish crown.

Exploring the Southeast

In 1508 explorer Juan Ponce de León landed on the Caribbean island of Puerto Rico. By 1511 he had conquered the island for Spain and founded the city of San Juan. De León also discovered gold on Puerto Rico. Spanish officials appointed him governor of the colony.

In 1512 de León discovered the coast of present-day Florida. The next year he searched Florida for a mythical Fountain of Youth. Though he never found the fabled fountain, Ponce de León acquired royal permission to colonize Florida. However, he failed in his quest to colonize the area.

Two decades later another explorer traveled through Florida. Royal officials gave Hernando de Soto permission to explore the coastal region of the Gulf of Mexico. In 1539 his expedition landed in an area near the present-day city of Tampa Bay, Florida.

De Soto then led his men north through what is now Georgia and the Carolinas. The expedition then turned west and crossed the Appalachian Mountains. De Soto discovered the Mississippi River in 1541. The explorers then traveled west into present-day Oklahoma. De Soto died in 1542 on this journey.

Exploring the Southwest

The Spanish also explored what is now the southwestern United States. In 1528 explorer Álvar Núñez Cabeza de Vaca joined conquistador Pánfilo de Narváez on an expedition to North America. Their group of 300 men first landed on the Florida coast. They faced many severe problems, including a shortage of food.

Critical Thinking: Analyzing

At Level

Settlement Life

Research Required

1. Review with students the three basic types of settlements in New Spain: pueblos, missions, and presidios. Tell students that they will be conducting research on one type of settlement.

2. Have students create a list of questions they want to answer in their research. For example, if researching pueblos, questions might include how pueblos were organized, what goods were traded, and what life was like in the pueblos.

3. Have students conduct research to answer their questions. Each student should then use the answers to create a short report or presentation about their topic. Remind students to evaluate the validity of their research sources.

4. Encourage students to include maps and illustrations in their reports. **LS Verbal/Linguistic**

📓 Alternative Assessment Handbook, Rubrics 29: Presentations; 30: Research; and 42: Writing to Inform

The group built boats, which made it possible for them to travel around the Florida panhandle. The explorers continued along the Gulf Coast and eventually reached the Mississippi River. Severe weather hit this group hard, and many members of the expedition died. De Vaca's boat shipwrecked on what is now Galveston Island in Texas. Only de Vaca and three other men survived. One survivor was a Moroccan-born slave named Estevanico. His Spanish slaveholder also survived.

Each of the four survivors was captured and enslaved by Native American groups living in the area. After six years of captivity, the men finally escaped. They journeyed on foot throughout the North American Southwest, receiving help from Native Americans they met along the way. In 1536, after turning south, the group reached Spanish settlements in Mexico.

Soon after their journey ended, Estevanico's slaveholder sold him to a Spanish viceroy. The viceroy assigned Estevanico to serve as a guide for a new expedition he was sending into the Southwest. Native Americans killed the enslaved African in 1539.

De Vaca eventually returned to Spain, where he called for better treatment of Native Americans. De Vaca later wrote about his experiences in the first European book exclusively devoted to North America. De Vaca's book increased Spanish interest in the New World. His writings fueled the rumors that riches could be found in North America.

> "For two thousand leagues did we travel, on land, and by sea in barges, besides ten months more after our rescue from captivity; untiringly did we walk across the land,... During all that time we crossed from one ocean to the other,... We heard that on the shores of the South there are pearls and great wealth, and that the richest and best is near there."
>
> –Cabeza de Vaca, *The Journey of Álvar Núñez Cabeza de Vaca*

De Vaca's account inspired other explorers to travel to North America. In 1540 Francisco Vásquez de Coronado set out to explore the North American Southwest. He wanted to find the legendary Seven Cities of Gold that were rumored to exist there. His expedition went through present-day New Mexico and Arizona, where a group of his men discovered the Grand Canyon. Coronado trekked through Texas

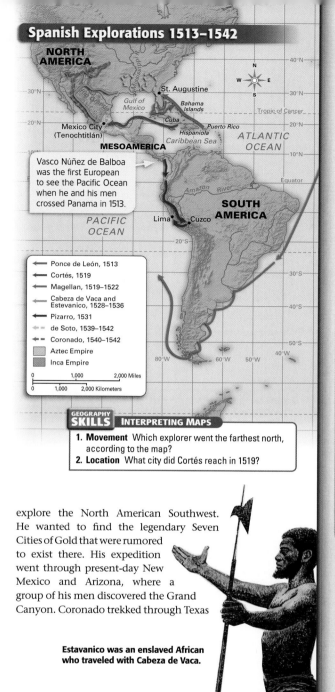

Spanish Explorations 1513–1542

Vasco Núñez de Balboa was the first European to see the Pacific Ocean when he and his men crossed Panama in 1513.

← Ponce de León, 1513
← Cortés, 1519
← Magellan, 1519–1522
← Cabeza de Vaca and Estevanico, 1528–1536
← Pizarro, 1531
← de Soto, 1539–1542
← Coronado, 1540–1542
▢ Aztec Empire
▢ Inca Empire

0   1,000   2,000 Miles
0   1,000   2,000 Kilometers

GEOGRAPHY SKILLS INTERPRETING MAPS

1. **Movement** Which explorer went the farthest north, according to the map?
2. **Location** What city did Cortés reach in 1519?

Estavanico was an enslaved African who traveled with Cabeza de Vaca.

49

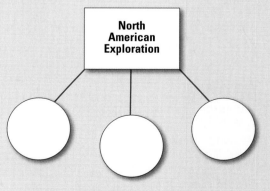

❸ Spanish Treatment of Native Americans

Spanish settlers treated Native Americans harshly, forcing them to work on plantations and in mines.

Explain What was the relationship between Spanish settlers and Native Americans under the encomienda system? *Settlers could tax Native Americans or make them work; in return settlers were supposed to protect Native Americans and convert them to Christianity.*

Identify Cause and Effect How did the growth of the Spanish Empire affect Native Americans? *Spain mined more gold and silver and needed more food to supply its empire; plantations in the Americas required lots of labor; Native Americans were treated as slaves and forced to work in the fields and mines; forced work and harsh treatment killed many Native Americans.*

Evaluate Why didn't the Spanish government enforce the laws that called for the proper treatment of Native Americans? *possible answers— The monarchy was too far away, local governors were interested only in profit, and there was a huge need for workers.*

Info to Know

More Than Just a Religion The Catholic Church assumed many functions in the Americas. The church operated as a bank, social welfare agency, and center of education. Many times priests would study the natural science and natural history of a region. They also kept records of the ways in which the Spanish culture was affecting the native societies.

Answers

Interpreting Maps 1. *Lima* **2.** *New Spain*

Reading Check *Both failed in their search for fabled locations of great promise—the Fountain of Youth and the Seven Cities of Gold.*

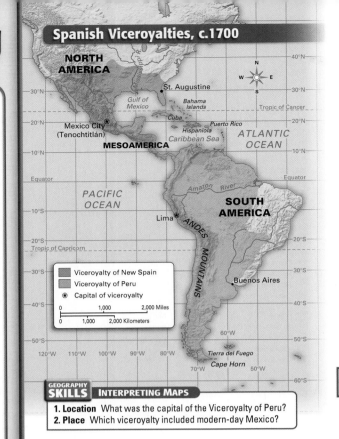

Spanish Viceroyalties, c.1700

GEOGRAPHY SKILLS **INTERPRETING MAPS**

1. Location What was the capital of the Viceroyalty of Peru?
2. Place Which viceroyalty included modern-day Mexico?

THE IMPACT TODAY

Roman Catholicism is still the most commonly practiced religion in Latin America. More than 80 percent of the population is Catholic.

and Oklahoma, going as far north as Kansas before turning around. He never found the fabled cities of gold.

READING CHECK **Comparing** How were the expeditions of Ponce de León and Coronado similar?

Spanish Treatment of Native Americans

The journeys of the Spanish explorers allowed Spain to claim a huge empire in the Americas. Spain's American colonies helped make the country very wealthy. From 1503 to 1660, Spanish fleets loaded with treasure carried 200 tons of gold and 18,600 tons of silver from the former Aztec and Inca empires to Spain. Mexico and Peru also grew food to help support Spain's growing empire. However, these gains came with a price for Native Americans. Native peoples suffered greatly at the hands of the Spanish.

Forced Labor

By 1650 the Spanish Empire in the Americas had grown to some 3 to 4 million people. Native Americans made up about 80 percent of the population. The rest were whites, Africans, and people of mixed racial background. Settlers who came from Spain were called *peninsulares* (pay-neen-soo-LAHR-ays) and usually held the highest government positions. To reward settlers for their service to the Crown, Spain established the **encomienda** (en-koh-mee-EN-duh) **system**. It gave settlers the right to tax local Native Americans or to make them work. In exchange, these settlers were supposed to protect the Native American people and convert them to Christianity. Instead, most Spanish treated the Native Americans as slaves. Native Americans were forced to work in terrible conditions. They faced cruelty and desperate situations on a daily basis.

The Spanish operated many **plantations**, large farms that grew just one kind of crop. Plantations throughout the Caribbean colonies made huge profits for their owners. It took many workers to run a plantation, however, so colonists forced thousands of Native Americans to work in the fields. Indians who were taken to work on haciendas, the vast Spanish estates in Central and South America, had to raise and herd livestock. Other Native Americans were forced to endure the backbreaking work of mining gold and silver. The forced labor and harsh treatment killed many native people in New Spain.

50 CHAPTER 2

Social Studies Skills Activity: Points of View

At Level

Debating the Treatment of Native Americans

1. Organize students into pairs. Tell the pairs they are to prepare arguments for each side of a debate about how Native Americans should be treated.

2. One student in the pair should take the point of view of Bartolomé de Las Casas, who believed the Spanish should treat Native Americans with gentleness and kindness. The other student should take the side of a plantation owner and explain why Spain established the encomienda system.

3. Instruct students to use logical reasons to support their points of view.

4. Ask students to debate the issue in front of the class. Then ask the class which side presented the most persuasive arguments and to explain why. **LS Interpersonal, Verbal/Linguistic**

📖 Alternative Assessment Handbook, Rubric 43: Writing to Persuade

The Role of the Catholic Church

The Catholic Church played a major role in the interactions of the Spanish with Native Americans. The Spanish king commanded priests to convert the local people to the Christian faith. Some Native Americans combined Spanish customs with their own. Others rejected Spanish ideas completely.

Some settlers in the Americas protested against the terrible treatment of Native Americans. A priest named **Bartolomé de Las Casas** said that the Spanish should try to convert Native Americans to Christianity by showing them love, gentleness, and kindness. The Spanish monarchs agreed, but the colonists did not always follow their laws.

READING CHECK Finding Main Ideas How did the encomienda system strengthen Spanish rule?

SUMMARY AND PREVIEW In the 1500s Spain built a vast empire in the Americas. The Spanish treated the Native Americans harshly in their new empire. In the next section you will learn about other European empires in the Americas.

Primary Source

BOOK
Brief Account of the Devastation of the Indies

Bartolomé de Las Casas, a Catholic priest in New Spain, encouraged better treatment of Native Americans.

❝When they [Spaniards] have slain all those who fought for their lives or to escape the tortures they would have to endure, that is to say, when they have slain all the native rulers and young men (since the Spaniards usually spare only the women and children, who are subjected to the hardest and bitterest servitude [slavery] ever suffered by man or beast), they enslave any survivors. With these infernal [devilish] methods of tyranny they debase and weaken countless numbers of those pitiful Indian nations.❞

–**Bartolomé de Las Casas,**
from *Brief Account of the Devastation of the Indies*

ANALYSIS SKILL **ANALYZING POINTS OF VIEW**
How did Las Casas's view of the treatment of Native American groups differ from the views of other Spaniards?

Section 3 Assessment

go.hrw.com
Online Quiz
KEYWORD: SR8 HP2

Reviewing Ideas, Terms, and People

1. **a. Identify** Who was **Moctezuma II**?
   b. Analyze How was **Hernán Cortés** able to conquer the Aztec Empire?
   c. Elaborate What advantages did the Spanish have over Native Americans?
2. **a. Recall** Which Spanish explorer received permission to colonize Florida?
   b. Analyze Why do you think Cabeza de Vaca wrote of great riches that could be found in the Americas?
   c. Evaluate Why do you think de Vaca called for better treatment of Native Americans after having been held prisoner by them?
3. **a. Identify** What was the **encomienda system**?
   b. Analyze Why do you think the king of Spain commanded Catholic priests to teach Native Americans about Christianity?

Critical Thinking

4. **Categorizing** Review your notes on Spanish conquest and settlement in the Americas. Then copy the following graphic organizer and use it to explain the impact Spain had on the Americas.

Spanish America	
government	
religion	
labor	

FOCUS ON WRITING

5. **Taking Notes on the Spanish Empire** Take notes on the Spanish conquest of the Aztec Empire and the founding of the Spanish Empire. How did this empire affect Native Americans?

NEW EMPIRES IN THE AMERICAS **51**

Direct Teach

Biography

A Change of Heart Bartolomé de Las Casas did not agree with the practices the Spanish imposed upon the Native Americans. His father was a successful merchant with close ties to the New World, where he was given land by Christopher Columbus. Young Bartolomé worked with his father and was on his way to becoming a wealthy landowner when he decided he could not treat the Native Americans so poorly. By 1514, de Las Casas freed all of his family's slaves and gave them his land.

Review & Assess

Close

Briefly review how Spain expanded its empire in the Americas and how that affected Native American societies and people.

Review

Online Quiz, Section 3

Assess

SE Section 3 Assessment
PASS: Section 3 Quiz
Alternative Assessment Handbook

Reteach/Classroom Intervention

Interactive Reader and Study Guide, Section 3
Interactive Skills Tutor CD-ROM

Section 3 Assessment Answers

1. **a.** Aztec king when Spanish arrived
   b. Moctezuma thought Cortés was a god and welcomed him; Cortés captured and killed Moctezuma and destroyed the Aztec's capital city; smallpox and other diseases weakened and killed Native American warriors.
   c. immunity to diseases, superior weaponry

2. **a.** Juan Ponce de León
   b. possible answers—to glorify his travels, encourage further exploration
   c. possible answers—Native Americans helped de Vaca escape; he recognized that

Native Americans had developed cultures and civilizations.

3. **a.** rewarded settlers, enabled them to tax Native Americans, forced them to work
   b. part of Christian duty of rulers; did not tolerate other religions

4. government—viceroyalties, increased infrastructure, bureaucracy, and taxes; religion—spread of Christianity; labor—enslavement, cruel/harsh working conditions, and influx of new diseases

5. Many died; others forced to work.

Answers

Analyzing Points of View *Unlike most Spaniards, de Las Casas was sympathetic to Native Americans. He believed that the practice of enslaving and killing Native Americans was tyrannical and was destroying Native American cultures.*

Reading Check *The encomienda system permitted settlers to tax local Native Americans or to make them work.*

Bellringer

If YOU were there . . . Use the **Daily Bellringer Transparency** to help students answer the question.

🖨 Daily Bellringer Transparency, Section 4

Building Vocabulary

Review with students the high-use term in this section.

inflation a rise in the price of goods caused by an increase in the amount of money in use (p. 53)

🖨 **CRF:** Vocabulary Builder Activity, Section 4

Taking Notes

Have students copy the graphic organizer onto their own paper and then use it to take notes on the section. This activity will prepare students for the Section Assessment, in which they will complete a graphic organizer that builds on the information using a critical thinking skill.

The Race for Empires

What You Will Learn...

Main Ideas

1. Events in Europe affected settlement of North America.
2. Several explorers searched for a Northwest Passage to the Pacific Ocean.
3. European nations raced to establish empires in North America.

The Big Idea

Other European nations challenged Spain in the Americas.

Key Terms and People

Protestant Reformation, *p. 53*
Protestants, *p. 53*
Spanish Armada, *p. 53*
Northwest Passage, *p. 54*
Jacques Cartier, *p. 54*
charter, *p. 54*

TAKING NOTES As you read, take notes on the reasons for European voyages to North America, the search for a Northwest Passage, and the development of European empires in North America.

Reasons for Voyages	Explorers' Search for a NW Passage	European Empires

If YOU were there...

The people of your village in France have always belonged to the same church. Now in the 1600s, your village is divided over religious beliefs. You have heard about the Dutch colony of New Netherland in America, where people can practice any religion freely. You would like to leave for America, but your parents are unwilling to leave their home.

> **How would you persuade your family to emigrate?**

BUILDING BACKGROUND During the 1400s, the Catholic Church was one of the most powerful institutions in Europe. Not everyone agreed with all of its teachings, however. Disagreement, and sometimes violence, led some people to search for new places to settle.

Events in Europe

Many significant events took place in Europe in the 1500s. Disagreements about religion threw Europe into turmoil. Some of these disagreements eventually led to wars. At the same time, several European nations began to compete for land and power overseas.

Key Events in European History 1450–1588

c. 1450
Johannes Gutenberg develops his movable-type printing press.

Teach the Big Idea

The Race for Empires

1. **Teach** Ask students the questions in the Main Idea boxes to teach this section.

2. **Apply** Create a chart for students to see. Label the columns *Events in Europe, Search for the Northwest Passage,* and *Rivalry for the Americas.* Have students copy the chart. As they read through this section, have students complete it with important details, noting cause-and-effect relationships.
   LS Visual/Spatial

3. **Review** Instruct students to use the chart as a study guide when reviewing this section.

4. **Practice/Homework** Have students use the information in their charts to create and illustrate a time line that shows important events discussed in the section.
   LS Visual/Spatial

   📝 Alternative Assessment Handbook, Rubrics 7: Charts; and 36: Time Lines

The Protestant Reformation

In 1517 a German priest named Martin Luther publicly criticized the Roman Catholic Church. Luther charged that the church was too wealthy and that it abused its power. Criticisms like Luther's started the **Protestant Reformation**. This religious movement began in small German towns but quickly spread to most of Europe. It became a part of many political disputes as well. The **Protestants** were reformers who protested some of the Catholic Church's practices. Many Protestants believed God meant for religion to be simple.

The printing press—a machine that produces printed copies using movable type—helped spread the ideas of the Reformation. Protestants printed large numbers of Bibles as well as short essays explaining their ideas. This let more people read and think about the Bible on their own, rather than relying solely on the teachings of a priest.

Conflicts between Catholics and Protestants took place throughout Europe, often leading to civil war. In the late 1500s French Catholics fought French Protestants, known as Huguenots (HYOO-guh-nahts). Many Huguenots eventually emigrated to the Americas in search of religious freedom.

In 1534 King Henry VIII founded the Church of England, or the Anglican Church. By making himself the head of the church, Henry challenged the authority of the pope and angered Catholics. Political issues soon became mixed with the religious struggles.

Spain and England Go to War

In the late 1500s King Philip II used Spain's great wealth to lead a Catholic Reformation against the Protestant movement. He hoped to drive the Protestants out of England. Standing in his way was the Protestant English queen Elizabeth I and her sea dogs. Sea dogs was the name given to English sailors who raided Spanish treasure ships. The most successful and daring was Sir Francis Drake.

Philip was angered by English piracy. He began gathering the **Spanish Armada**, a huge fleet of warships meant to end the English plans. The Armada had about 130 ships and some 27,000 sailors and soldiers. This mighty fleet was launched to invade England and overthrow Queen Elizabeth and the Anglican Church. But in July 1588, the much smaller, but faster, English fleet defeated the Armada in a huge battle.

The Armada's defeat shocked the Spanish. In addition to the naval defeat, Spain's economy was in trouble. The gold and silver that Spain received from the Americas caused high inflation. Inflation is a rise in the price of goods caused by an increase in the amount of money in use. Economic problems in Spain combined with the defeat of the Spanish Armada led countries such as England, France, and the Netherlands to challenge Spanish power overseas.

READING CHECK Analyzing
What led to the decline of the Spanish Empire?

1517
Martin Luther nails his ninety-five theses to the door of a church in Wittenberg, Germany.

1588
The English defeat the Spanish Armada. The loss greatly weakens Spain, allowing other European countries to claim land in North America.

53

53

❷ Search for a Northwest Passage

Several explorers searched for a Northwest Passage to the Pacific Ocean.

Identify Name the explorers sent to search for the Northwest Passage, the country he represented, and then tell how far each traveled. *John Cabot, England, believed to have reached Newfoundland, Canada; Giovanni da Verrazano, France, sailed along the coast of North America from present-day North Carolina to Maine; Jacques Cartier, France, present-day Montreal, Canada; Henry Hudson, Netherlands, present-day New York; Hudson, England, discovered a large bay in present-day northern Canada, now called Hudson Bay*

Draw Conclusions Even though none of the explorers found a Northwest Passage, why were their voyages considered successful? *Each explorer discovered new lands.*

Elaborate In your opinion, why did countries continue to send explorers in search of a Northwest Passage even though previous attempts were unsuccessful? *possible answer— Sailing from the Atlantic Ocean to the Pacific Ocean, and eventually Asia, would give a country a great deal of trading power.*

Linking to Today

A Major Seaway Although it is not a Northwest Passage, the St. Lawrence River plays a vital role in today's transportation of goods and products. The international waterway, 2,342 miles long, provides passage for large ocean-going ships into central North America. Through a series of canals, dams, and locks, vessels are able to reach cities with lake ports such as Duluth, Milwaukee, and Chicago.

Answers

Reading Check *because it would allow ships to sail from the Atlantic to the Pacific*

Search for a Northwest Passage

Europeans wanted to find a **Northwest Passage**, a water route through North America that would allow ships to sail from the Atlantic to the Pacific. The English began sending explorers to find it.

Italian sailor John Cabot knew that the king of England wanted to find such a route. Cabot offered to pay for his own expedition, asking only that the king of England grant him a royal charter to any lands he found. The king agreed, and Cabot made voyages to North America for England in 1497 and 1498.

Cabot sailed to North America, but he left very few records of his journeys. It is believed that he traveled along the coast of present-day Newfoundland in Canada. Although Cabot did not find a passage to the Pacific Ocean, his voyages were successful. They became the basis of England's claim to land in North America.

In 1524 France sent Italian captain Giovanni da Verrazano (vayr-raht-SAHN-oh) to seek a Northwest Passage. Verrazano sailed along the coast of North America from present-day North Carolina to Maine. **Jacques Cartier** (kahr-tyay), a French sailor, led France's next major exploration of North America. He made two trips to what is now Canada in 1534 and in 1535. Cartier sailed into the Saint Lawrence River and traveled all the way to present-day Montreal, claiming the areas he explored for France.

The Dutch also entered the race. They hired English captain Henry Hudson to find a Northwest Passage. Hudson first sailed to present-day New York in 1609. The following year Hudson returned to North America, sailing under the English flag. He traveled far to the north. Eventually he reached a strait that he hoped would lead to the Pacific Ocean. Instead, it led into a huge bay, later named Hudson Bay.

None of these explorers ever found a Northwest Passage. Their explorations, however, led to increased European interest in North America.

READING CHECK **Finding Main Ideas** Why did European explorers seek a Northwest Passage?

European Presence in North America

The Spanish and the Portuguese were the early leaders in overseas exploration. They dominated the colonization of the New World through the 1500s. However, Spain and Portugal focused on Central America, the Caribbean, and South America. They left much of North America unexplored. The English, French, and Dutch, however, did explore the continent. These nations then sought to expand their own empires in North America.

English Presence in the New World

In the late 1500s England decided to set up a permanent settlement in North America. This colony was to establish an English presence in the New World. Sir Walter Raleigh received a **charter**, a document giving him permission to start a colony. In 1584 he sent an expedition that landed in present-day Virginia and North Carolina. Raleigh named the entire area Virginia.

The following year, Raleigh sent another group to found a colony on Roanoke Island, off the coast of North Carolina. The English colonists at Roanoke found life hard. They fought with Native Americans and had trouble finding and growing food. After only a year, the remaining colonists returned to England.

John White, a talented artist, and 150 colonists resettled Roanoke in the spring of 1587. White's granddaughter, Virginia Dare, was the first English colonist born in North America. After a few months, White went back to England to get more supplies. War with Spain prevented White from returning for three years. When he came back, White found the colony deserted. The only clue he found to the fate of the colonists was the word *Croatoan*, the name of a nearby island, carved into a post. Did the colonists try to escape a Native American attack by fleeing to the island? White never found out. To this day, no one is certain what happened to the "lost colony" at Roanoke.

Critical Thinking: Interpreting Maps
At Level

The Rush to North America
Research Required

Materials: blank outline maps of North America, colored pencils

1. Instruct students to use the maps to chart the travels of each explorer who sought a Northwest Passage. Students should use a different color to represent each explorer. Instruct students to create a legend noting which color belongs to which explorer.

2. Have students conduct research on the natural resources of the areas covered by each explorer and to indicate natural resources on their maps. Students should create a second legend with symbols that designate these natural resources.

3. Then have students write a few paragraphs about which explorer and country they think gained the most from the expeditions of exploration and why. **LS Interpersonal, Visual/Spatial, Verbal/Linguistic**

   Alternative Assessment Handbook, Rubrics 20: Map Creation; and 37: Writing Assignments

Northwest Passage

Dutch exploration
English exploration
French exploration
Spanish exploration
New Spain, 1492–1682

NORTH AMERICA

ATLANTIC OCEAN

0   150   300 Miles
0   150   300 Kilometers

GEOGRAPHY SKILLS | **INTERPRETING MAPS**

1. **Movement** According to the map, which explorer made two voyages to find a Northwest Passage?
2. **Place** Which explorer started farthest south in searching for a Northwest Passage?

French Presence in the New World

France built its first North American settlement in Florida. French Huguenots started a few small colonies there in 1564. The Spanish soon destroyed these settlements and drove out the French. Religious wars in France slowed further French efforts to colonize North America. When the fighting ended, the French renewed efforts to settle present-day eastern Canada. The explorations of Jacques Cartier and Samuel de Champlain gave France a claim to this region.

Nearly 70 years after Cartier sailed up the Saint Lawrence, French sailor Samuel de Champlain began exploring North America. He recorded his ideas about European exploration in his journal.

"Through [exploration] we gain knowledge of different countries, regions and kingdoms; through it we attract and bring into our countries all kinds of riches; through it ...Christianity [is spread] in all parts of the earth."

–Samuel de Champlain, quoted in the *Canadian Frontier, 1534–1760,* by W. J. Eccles

Champlain followed Cartier's old paths. Over the years he made many journeys along the Saint Lawrence River. He also visited the Great Lakes, led by Native American guides.

In 1608 Champlain founded a small colony on the Saint Lawrence River. He named the colony Quebec. This trading post opened fur-trading routes for the French throughout the region. Champlain's explorations became the basis of France's claim to much of Canada.

In the late 1600s the French began spreading out from the Saint Lawrence River. Calling their North American territory New France, French fur traders, explorers, and missionaries were all on the move.

In the 1650s French missionaries reported stories about "a beautiful river, large, broad, and deep." In 1673 explorer Louis Jolliet (jahl-ee-ET) and missionary Jacques Marquette set out to find this great river, the Mississippi. (Hernando de Soto was the first European to find the Mississippi River, in 1541). They reached the river and traveled down it as far as present-day Arkansas.

Nine years later René-Robert de La Salle followed the Mississippi River to the Gulf of

NEW EMPIRES IN THE AMERICAS **55**

Direct Teach

Interpreting Maps
European Exploration of the Americas

Activity Explorers Award Ceremony Organize students into five groups and assign each group one of the countries or explorations listed in the map legend. Ask students to imagine that they are creating plaques for a European Explorers award ceremony. Have each group create a plaque acknowledging the exploration accomplishments of its assigned country or explorer. The plaque should include the explorer's name, the country he represented, and the date of the exploration. Once the plaques have been completed, students can hold a mock award ceremony.

Map Transparency: European Exploration of the Americas 1492–1682

Did you know . . .

On his last voyage, Henry Hudson sailed under the sponsorship of a group of English businessmen. Once he reached Hudson Bay, he spent several months exploring it. After a winter of suffering from extreme conditions, part of Hudson's crew mutinied. The mutineers put Hudson, his son, and seven other crew members in a small boat and cast them adrift. Some of the mutineers made it back to England and were put in prison. Hudson, his son, and the others were never heard from again.

Answers

Interpreting Maps 1. *France;*
2. *by sea into the Gulf of Mexico; overland into the southwestern and southeastern parts of North America*

56

European Exploration of the Americas, 1492–1682

Dutch exploration
English exploration
French exploration
Spanish exploration
New Spain, 1492–1682

0   150   300 Miles
0   150   300 Kilometers

Hudson's search for a Northwest Passage led him to the bay that still bears his name.

La Salle sailed down the Mississippi to its mouth and claimed for France all the land along the river and its tributaries.

Juan Ponce de León became the first European in Florida when he arrived in 1513.

Spanish explorers boldly pushed overland into North America's interior.

NORTH AMERICA

Hudson Bay
HUDSON 1610-11
CABOT 1497-98
CARTIER 1534-35
CARTIER 1534
Newfoundland
CARTIER 1535-36
HUDSON 1609
Quebec
Nova Scotia
CHAMPLAIN 1609
CHAMPLAIN 1603-1615
Great Lakes
New York
Mississippi River
LA SALLE 1679-82
Roanoke Island
ATLANTIC OCEAN
CORONADO 1540-42
DE SOTO 1539-42
CABEZA DE VACA AND ESTEVANICO 1528-36
St. Augustine
PONCE DE LEÓN 1513
Bahama Islands
Rio Grande
Gulf of Mexico
Tropic of Cancer
Cuba
Puerto Rico
CORTÉS 1519
Hispaniola
Mexico City (Tenochtitlán)
Caribbean Sea
70°W
80°W
100°W
110°W

GEOGRAPHY SKILLS   INTERPRETING MAPS

1. Region Explorers from what country explored the Great Lakes region?
2. Region In what regions did Spanish explorers travel?

56 CHAPTER 2

Collaborative Learning

At Level

Explorers Museum Exhibit

Research Required

Materials: art supplies, poster board, or butcher paper

1. Organize students into small groups and assign each group one of the following explorers: John Cabot, Jacques Cartier, Giovanni da Verrazano, or Henry Hudson.

2. Assign students to put together a museum exhibit on their assigned explorer. They should use the information in the text as a basis for further research for the explorer and his accomplishments.

3. Each group's exhibit should include a summary of the explorer's achievements, an annotated time line of his travels, and a map depicting the extent of his travels. Encourage students to include drawings, models, and additional information.

4. Have the groups display their exhibits for the class to view. **LS Interpersonal, Visual/Spatial**

Alternative Assessment Handbook, Rubrics 14: Group Activity; and 29: Presentations

Mexico. He claimed the Mississippi Valley for King Louis XIV of France. To honor the king, La Salle named the region Louisiana.

Starting in the 1700s, the French built new outposts. These included Detroit on the Great Lakes and Saint Louis and New Orleans along the Mississippi River. Most towns in the French territory were small. As late as 1688 there were only about 12,000 French settlers in New France. Its small population and the value of the fur trade led French settlers to ally and trade with local Native American groups.

Because of their close trading relationships, the French treated the Native Americans with more respect than some other European settlers had done. Many French settlers learned Native American languages, and they even adopted their ways of life.

Dutch Presence in the New World

The English and the French were not the only European powers to seek an empire in North America. The Dutch, who had merchant fleets around the world, came in search of trade. They claimed the land between the Delaware and Hudson rivers and called it New Netherland. This area included parts of what is now New York, New Jersey, Connecticut and Delaware. In 1624 the newly formed Dutch West India Company sent about 30 families to settle in New Netherland. Two years later Peter Minuit bought Manhattan Island from local Native Americans for about $24. Minuit then founded the town of New Amsterdam, today called New York City. To attract colonists, the Dutch allowed members of all religions to settle in their colony.

Minuit also helped Swedish settlers found New Sweden along the Delaware River. The first settlement, Fort Christina, was begun in 1638. The Swedish settlement was small, but the Dutch felt that it threatened Dutch lands and fur trading. The two sides fought a series of battles. Finally, the governor of New Netherland, Peter Stuyvesant (STY-vi-suhnt),

conquered New Sweden in 1655. He allowed the Swedes to continue their colony, but called it the "Swedish Nation."

READING CHECK Drawing Conclusions
Were the French explorers in North America successful? Explain.

SUMMARY AND PREVIEW The English, French, Dutch, and Swedish explored the North American continent and later established colonies there. In the next section you will learn about the establishment of slavery in the Americas.

Section 4 Assessment

go.hrw.com
Online Quiz
KEYWORD: SR8 HP2

Reviewing Ideas, Terms, and People

1. **a. Identify** What was the **Protestant Reformation**?
   b. Explain What role did the printing press play in the Protestant Reformation?
   c. Summarize What were Martin Luther's reasons for protesting the Catholic Church?
2. **a. Identify** Who was the first European to search for the **Northwest Passage**?
   b. Describe Which French and Dutch explorers tried to find the Northwest Passage?
3. **a. Recall** What happened to the first English settlements in North America?
   b. Evaluate Which European empire in North America do you think was most successful? Why?

Critical Thinking

4. **Sequencing** Review your notes on European exploration and settlement. Then create a time line like the one below and place the four events you think were most important to the development of European empires in North America on the time line. Be sure to include the date of the event, as well as a description of it and its significance.

FOCUS ON WRITING

5. **Learning about the French Empire and Other Settlements** Take notes about the French, Dutch, Swedish, and English people who settled in America. Why did they come? What did they want and need in their new home?

NEW EMPIRES IN THE AMERICAS **57**

Section 4 Assessment Answers

1. **a.** a religious movement that protested some practices of the Catholic Church
   b. helped spread the ideas of the Reformation
   c. He believed the church was too wealthy and abused its power.
2. **a.** John Cabot
   b. French: Giovanni da Verrazano, Jacques Cartier; Dutch: Henry Hudson
3. **a.** Colonists died or abandoned their settlements.
   b. possible answers: French—because of the land they claimed, their success in fur

trading, and their relationship with Native Americans; English—because of the great influence in United States law, government, and religion

4. Students' time lines will vary but should depict four significant events in the development of European empires in North America.

5. Student answers should reflect information in the text.

58   CHAPTER 2

Bellringer

If YOU were there . . . Use the **Daily Bellringer Transparency** to help students answer the question.

Daily Bellringer Transparency, Section 5

Academic Vocabulary

Review with students the high-use academic term in this section.

structure the way something is set upon or organized (p. 59)

CRF: Vocabulary Builder Activity, Section 5

Taking Notes

Have students copy the graphic organizer onto their own paper and then use it to take notes on the section. This activity will prepare students for the Section Assessment, in which they will complete a graphic organizer that builds on the information using a critical thinking skill.

SECTION 5

Beginnings of Slavery in the Americas

What You Will Learn...

Main Ideas

1. European diseases wiped out much of the Native American population, causing colonists to look for a new labor force.
2. Europeans enslaved millions of Africans and sent them to work in their colonies.
3. Slaves in the Americas created a distinct culture.

The Big Idea

Europeans forced millions of African slaves to work in their colonies.

Key Terms and People

immune, p. 58
Middle Passage, p. 59
African Diaspora, p. 60

TAKING NOTES As you read, take notes on slavery in the Americas. Use a chart like the one below.

The Slave Trade		
Need for Workers		
Slave Trade		
The Slave Culture		

If YOU were there...

You are an enslaved African living in North America. Your family is all that you have. You help each other, and your family provides some relief from the forced labor and harsh life on the plantation. Still, you long for your freedom. A fellow slave has told you of a plan to escape.

Will you stay with your family or try to flee?

BUILDING BACKGROUND European settlers in the Americas relied on support from their home countries to establish trade and provide protection. In return, the colonies were expected to produce money for the home country. Many colonies did this through plantations, mines, and other ventures that required a large labor force.

The Need for a New Labor Force

European diseases had a devastating effect on the Native American population. Measles, smallpox, and typhus were common in Europe. As a result, most adult Europeans were **immune**, or had a natural resistance, to them. Native Americans, however, had never been exposed to such diseases and had no immunity to them. As a result, many Native Americans became terribly sick after their first encounters with Europeans. Millions of them died in the years after Columbus reached the New World.

No one knows exactly how many Native Americans died from European diseases, but the loss of life was staggering. Spanish author Fernández de Oviedo reported in 1548 about the destruction of the Native Americans of Hispaniola. He reported that, of the estimated 1 million Indians who had lived on the island in 1492, "there are not now believed to be at the present time . . . five hundred persons [left]." In North America the Native American population north of Mexico was about 10 million when Columbus arrived. This

---

Teach the Big Idea

Beginnings of Slavery in the Americas

1. **Teach** Ask students the questions in the Main Idea boxes to teach this section.

2. **Apply** As students read the section, have them create flashcards that include major events or terms leading up to and involved in the growth of slavery in the Americas. Tell students the flashcards should list the event or important term on one side and an explanation or definition on the other side.
   LS Verbal/Linguistic

3. **Review** Have students work in pairs to review the section with their flashcards.

4. **Practice/Homework** Assign students to use the information on their flashcards to create cause-and-effect charts about the growth of slavery in the Americas. Have volunteers share their charts with the class.
   LS Visual/Spatial

   Alternative Assessment Handbook, Rubric 6: Cause and Effect

number would drop to less than a million. The drop in the native population played a major role in the emerging need for an alternative labor force.

Plantation agriculture was a mainstay of the colonial economic **structure**. Spain and Portugal established sugar plantations that relied on large numbers of native laborers. In the 1600s English tobacco farmers in North America also needed workers for their plantations. With a lack of Native American workers, they, too, needed another source of labor. Plantation owners in both North and South America wanted a cheap work force.

Some colonists, including Spanish priest Bartolomé de Las Casas, suggested using enslaved Africans as workers. Africans had already developed immunity to European diseases. The colonists soon agreed that slaves from West Africa could be the solution to their labor needs.

READING CHECK Analyzing How did disease contribute to the slave trade?

The Slave Trade

In 1510 the Spanish government legalized the sale of slaves in its colonies. The first full cargo ship of Africans arrived in the Americas eight years later. Over the next century, more than a million enslaved Africans were brought to the Spanish and Portuguese colonies in the New World. The Dutch and English also became active in the slave trade.

ACADEMIC VOCABULARY
structure the way something is set up or organized

Middle Passage

Enslavement was a horrible experience for the slaves. Most enslaved people had been captured in the interior of Africa, often by Africans who profited from selling slaves to Europeans. The captives were chained around the neck and then marched to the coast. This journey could be as long as 1,000 miles.

The **Middle Passage** was the voyage across the Atlantic Ocean that enslaved Africans were forced to endure. Africans were packed like cargo in the lower decks of the slave ships. The slaves were chained together and crammed

LETTER
King Afonso to King Joao III

King Afonso of the African nation of Kongo wrote a letter to the king of Portugal in 1526 asking him to do what he could to stop the practice of taking African slaves.

Sir, Your Highness should know how our Kingdom is being lost in so many ways . . . . [M]erchants are taking every day our natives, sons of the land and the sons of our noblemen and vassals and our relatives, because the thieved and men of bad conscience grab them . . . . [T]hey grab them and get them to be sold; and so great, Sir, is the corruption and licentiousness [law breaking] that our country is being completely depopulated, and Your Highness should not agree with this nor accept it as in your service. And to avoid it we need from those

(your) Kingdoms no more than some priests and a few people to teach in schools, and no other goods except wine and flour for the holy sacrament [religious service].

–King Afonso of Kongo, letter to the King of Portugal, 1526

 ANALYSIS SKILL **ANALYZING PRIMARY SOURCES**

1. Why does Afonso ask the Portuguese king to help stop the slave trade?
2. What does Afonso request from the king?

NEW EMPIRES IN THE AMERICAS **59**

Main Idea

❶ The Need for a New Labor Force

European diseases wiped out much of the Native American population, causing colonists to look for a new labor force.

Identify What three European diseases were responsible for decimating the Native American population? *measles, smallpox, and typhus*

Explain Why did colonists turn to enslaved Africans for labor on their plantations? *Africans had already developed immunity to European diseases; they were a cheap labor supply.*

Make Generalizations Why did disease take such a high toll on Native Americans? *Native Americans did not have built-in immunities like the Europeans, so diseases that were brought to the Americas by Europeans were deadly.*

Info to Know

Meaning Behind the Name The Middle Passage got its name because it was the middle leg of a three-part voyage called the triangular trade. The first segment of the journey took manufactured goods from Europe to the African "slave coast" where European sailors would exchange the cargo for captive Africans. They then sailed to the colonies where the enslaved Africans were sold to settlers. Finally the ships would take sugar, tobacco, and other products back to Europe.

Differentiating Instruction

Struggling Readers

1. Create a flow chart for students to see. Tell them to label the main box "Native Americans Die from European Diseases."

2. Have students fill in subsequent boxes with the impact this main event had on the expansion of slavery in the Americas. *Students may include a disappearing work force; Spanish government legalizes the sale of slaves; Africans are captured and enslaved; African Diaspora; growth of slavery in the Americas.*

3. Instruct students to select a topic from one box on the flow chart and write several sentences to explain that event.

4. Ask students to share their flow charts and sentences with the class. **LS Visual/Spatial, Verbal/Linguistic**

   Alternative Assessment Handbook, Rubrics 7: Charts; and 42: Writing to Inform

Answers

Analyzing Primary Sources 1. *his country is losing population* **2.** *He asks for priests and teachers.*

Reading Check *Plantations needed a large work force, and when large numbers of Native Americans died from European diseases, plantation owners turned to slaves for their labor needs.*

59

Main Idea

❷ The Slave Trade

Europeans enslaved millions of Africans and sent them to work in their colonies.

Recall Approximately how many enslaved Africans were shipped to the Americas between 1520 and 1860? *12 million*

Identify Cause and Effect Why did only one in six enslaved Africans survive the Middle Passage? *They were packed like cargo in the lower decks of the ships. They died from disease, suffocation, malnourishment, and suicide.*

Develop Explain the concept of forced migration and how it led to the African Diaspora. *Answers may vary, but should include the capturing and removing of Africans from their families and transporting them to other parts of the world.*

Checking for Understanding

True or False Answer each statement *T* if it is true or *F* if it is false. If false, explain why.

1. Colonial leaders did not see a reason to legally regulate the treatment of slaves. *F; Slave codes regulated slave treatment and behavior.*

2. Some plantation owners treated their slaves with kindness. *T*

3. Slave religion was a combination of Christianity and African religious traditions. *T*

Answers

Analyzing Information 1. *Mississippi;* **2.** *Plantations were located the South.*

60

African Diaspora in the United States

The first enslaved Africans to arrive in what is now the United States landed in Jamestown, Virginia, in August 1619. Today, descendants of enslaved Africans and other African Americans live throughout the United States.

GEOGRAPHY SKILLS | INTERPRETING MAPS

1. **Location** Which state has the highest percentage of African Americans?
2. **Human-Environment Interaction** Why might the modern African American population be centered in the South?

THE IMPACT TODAY
Almost half of Brazil's current population is of African descent.

into spaces about the size of coffins. The height between the decks was sometimes only 18 inches.

In this confinement, disease spread quickly, killing many Africans. Others suffocated or died from malnutrition. Some slaves took their own lives to end their suffering. It is estimated that one out of every six Africans died during the Middle Passage.

African Diaspora

Between the 1520s and 1860s about 12 million Africans were shipped across the Atlantic as slaves. More than 10 million of these captives survived the voyage and reached the Americas. The slave trade led to the **African Diaspora**. (A diaspora is the scattering of a people.) Enslaved Africans were sent all across the New World.

More than a third of the enslaved Africans, nearly 4 million people, were sent to Brazil. Most of those slaves were forced to work on Portuguese sugar plantations. Nearly 2 million slaves went to the colonies of New Spain. Some worked on plantations in the Caribbean, while others were taken to the mines of Peru and Mexico. Some 3 million slaves worked in British and French colonies in the Caribbean and Latin America. More than 600,000 slaves went to Britain's North American colonies that later became the United States.

Colonial leaders across the Americas developed laws that regulated slave treatment and behavior. Slaves were given few rights in the colonies. The law considered enslaved Africans to be property. In some colonies, a slaveholder was not charged with

60 CHAPTER 2

Critical Thinking: Analyzing Information   **At Level**

Abolitionists vs. the Need for Labor

1. Organize the class into small groups. Ask students to imagine that they are a group of colonists opposed to slave labor.

2. Have each group write a proposal that suggests alternatives to slave labor, including the development of other industries that would require more specialized labor.

3. Ask for members of each group to read the proposal to the class.

4. Guide students in a discussion of the ideas presented by each group. Ask students to name which ideas they believe would have been most persuasive and feasible. Have students explain and defend their choices.
LS Interpersonal Verbal/Linguistic

Alternative Assessment Handbook, Rubric 14: Group Activity

murder if he killed a slave while punishing him. Enslaved Africans, on the other hand, received harsh penalties for minor offenses, such as breaking a tool. Runaways were often tortured and sometimes killed.

The treatment of enslaved Africans varied. A few slaves reported that their masters treated them kindly. To protect their investment, some slaveholders provided adequate food and clothing for their slaves. However, severe treatment was very common. Whippings, brandings, and even worse torture were all part of American slavery.

READING CHECK **Generalizing** How were enslaved Africans treated in the Americas?

Slave Culture in the Americas

Slaves in the Americas came from many different parts of Africa. They spoke different languages and had different cultural backgrounds. But enslaved Africans also shared many customs and viewpoints. They built upon what they had in common to create a new African American culture.

Families were a vital part of slave culture. Families provided a refuge—a place not fully under the slaveholders' control. However, slave families faced many challenges. Families were often broken apart when a family member was sold to another owner. In Latin America, there were many more enslaved males than females. This made it difficult for slaves there to form stable families.

Religion was a second refuge for slaves. It gave enslaved Africans a form of expression that was partially free from their slaveholders' control. Slave religion was primarily Christian, but it included traditional elements from African religions as well. Religion gave slaves a sense of self worth and a hope for salvation in this life and the next. Spirituals were a common form of religious expression among slaves. Slaves also used songs and folktales to tell their stories of sorrow, hope, agony, and joy.

Many slaves expressed themselves through art and dance. Dances were important social events in slave communities. Like most elements of slave culture, art and dance were heavily influenced by African traditions.

READING CHECK **Identifying Points of View** Why was religion important to slaves in the Americas?

SUMMARY AND PREVIEW After disease wiped out much of the Native American population, colonists turned to slave labor. In the next chapter you will learn about English colonies in the Americas.

Section 5 Assessment

go.hrw.com
Online Quiz
KEYWORD: SR8 HP2

Reviewing Ideas, Terms, and People

1. **a. Recall** Why did so many Native Americans die after coming into contact with Europeans?
   b. Summarize Why did plantation owners turn to enslaved Africans as a labor force?
2. **a. Identify** What was the **Middle Passage**?
   b. Describe Explain how enslaved Africans were treated after they reached the colonies in the Americas.
3. **a. Explain** What are spirituals?
   b. Analyze How did religion and family provide a refuge from the harsh life enslaved Africans were forced to endure?

Critical Thinking

4. **Identifying Cause and Effect** Review your notes on the slave trade. Use a chart like the one below to explain the causes and the effects of the slave trade.

Causes → Effects

FOCUS ON WRITING

5. **Writing Your Letter** First, review your notes and decide which group you want to write about. Which details from your notes will your friends and family be most interested in? Which do you find most important? What do you want to tell them about the Americas?

NEW EMPIRES IN THE AMERICAS **61**

Activity Chain-of-Events Chart
Ask students to use the map to trace the steps and routes involved in the transatlantic slave trade. Then have students work either individually or in pairs to create chain-of-events charts showing the geographic forces that led to the growth of slavery in the English colonies. A sample chart is shown below.
LS Visual/Spatial

> The climate of the southern colonies was suited to certain crops, such as cotton, tobacco, and sugarcane.

> These crops required large amounts of labor.

> Other sources of labor, such as indentured servants, were not able to fill labor needs.

> Colonists turned to enslaved Africans to fill labor needs.

Connect to Economics

Social Classes in Colonial America

Colonial America had a variety of socio-economic classes. Large landowners, wealthy merchants, and professional workers ranked at the top of society. Free wage earners ranked below this group. They ranged from unskilled laborers to skilled workers, such as cabinetmakers or tailors. Farmers with smaller amounts of land were usually considered on the same level as these urban workers. At the bottom were people who were legally not free—white indentured servants and enslaved Africans.

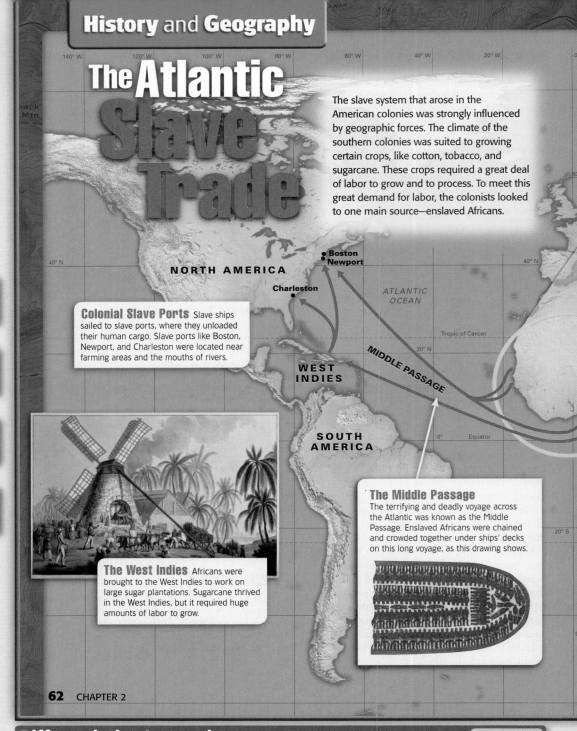

The Atlantic Slave Trade

The slave system that arose in the American colonies was strongly influenced by geographic forces. The climate of the southern colonies was suited to growing certain crops, like cotton, tobacco, and sugarcane. These crops required a great deal of labor to grow and to process. To meet this great demand for labor, the colonists looked to one main source—enslaved Africans.

Colonial Slave Ports Slave ships sailed to slave ports, where they unloaded their human cargo. Slave ports like Boston, Newport, and Charleston were located near farming areas and the mouths of rivers.

The West Indies Africans were brought to the West Indies to work on large sugar plantations. Sugarcane thrived in the West Indies, but it required huge amounts of labor to grow.

The Middle Passage The terrifying and deadly voyage across the Atlantic was known as the Middle Passage. Enslaved Africans were chained and crowded together under ships' decks on this long voyage, as this drawing shows.

62 CHAPTER 2

Differentiating Instruction

Below Level

Struggling Readers

1. Review inset maps with students. Then have students identify the region shown in the inset map above. Explain that most enslaved Africans came from West Africa. Next, have volunteers read aloud the captions by the slave forts. Then read the primary source to students and have them discuss it.

2. Have a volunteer read aloud the caption about the Middle Passage. Ask students to suggest adjectives to describe the Middle Passage.

3. Ask students to identify the destinations of the Atlantic slave trade. Next, have volunteers read aloud the Colonial Slave Ports and The West Indies captions. Ask students to identify the geographic forces that led to the slave system in the American colonies.

4. Have students interpret the bar graph. Ask students to discuss reasons for the increase in slaves over time. **LS** Visual/Spatial

   Alternative Assessment Handbook, Rubric 21: Map Reading

Slave forts began as trading posts. They where built near river mouths to provide easy access to both the sea and inland areas.

AFRICA

St. Luis de Senegal
James Fort
Accra
Elmina
Assinie
Whydah

New England traders exchanged goods for slaves on the West African coast and then transported the slaves to the American colonies or to the West Indies.

Elmina slave fort, West Africa

AFRICA

Equator 0°

20° N

20° S

Tropic of Capricorn

120° E
100° E
80° E
60° E
40° E
20° E

Slaves Brought to the Americas, 1493–1810

Number of slaves (in millions)

Years	
1493–1600	
1601–1700	
1701–1810	

Kidnapped and Taken to a Slave Ship

Mahommah G. Baquaqua was captured and sold into slavery as a young man. In this 1854 account, he recalls being taken to the African coast to board a slave ship.

"I was taken down to the river and placed on board a boat; the river was very large and branched off in two different directions, previous to emptying itself into the sea . . . We were two nights and one day on this river, when we came to a . . . place . . . [where] the slaves were all put into a pen, and placed with our backs to the fire . . . When all were ready to go aboard, we were chained together, and tied with ropes round about our necks, and were thus drawn down to the sea shore."

GEOGRAPHY SKILLS INTERPRETING MAPS

1. **Location** Why were slave forts located where they were?
2. **Human-Environment Interaction** What geographic factors influenced the development of the Atlantic slave trade?

History and Geography

Primary Source

Activity Writing a Poem Have a volunteer read aloud the primary source at left. Ask students to discuss the thoughts, feelings, and expectations of enslaved Africans sold to European slave traders and put on ships. Then have students work in pairs to write poems in which they express the thoughts and feelings of recently enslaved Africans. **LS** Verbal/Linguistic

World Events

Captives of War About half the Africans sold to traders were captives of war. African kingdoms, like those elsewhere in the world, fought each other for power and wealth. Some of these kingdoms sold war captives into slavery. These kingdoms traded slaves for European goods. As a result of the slave trade, native populations in some parts of Africa greatly decreased. These population losses had disastrous effects on Africa's development.

Info to Know

Slave Languages and Gullah Africans arriving in the Americas often spoke different languages. In time a number of pidgin, or simplified, languages developed based on English, French, Spanish, and Portuguese. One of these that has survived to this day is Gullah. This language is still spoken in parts of Georgia and the Sea Islands of South Carolina.

Differentiating Instruction

English-Language Learners
Below Level

1. Pair students and have partners take turns explaining and summarizing the information above. Students should list and define any words or phrases they do not understand.

2. Read the primary source aloud to students.

3. Then have each student create an image with a caption based on the excerpt.
LS Interpersonal, Visual/Spatial

Alternative Assessment Handbook, Rubrics 3: Artwork; and 21: Map Reading

Advanced/ Gifted and Talented
Above Level
Research Required

1. Have students conduct research on the Middle Passage. Instruct students to take notes on the conditions, perils, and death rates on slave ships.

2. Have students work in pairs to create a script for a voice-over for the opening scenes of a documentary on the Middle Passage.
LS Interpersonal, Verbal/Linguistic

Alternative Assessment Handbook, Rubrics 30: Research; and 37: Writing Assignments

Answers

Interpreting Maps 1. *Slave forts were located on the coast so that captives could be transported by ship to the Americas, and near rivers to provide easy access to inland areas.* **2.** *See the graphic organizer in the side column on the previous page.*

Social Studies Skills

Framing Historical Questions

Activity **Evaluating Questions**

Ask students to imagine that a friend of theirs has just witnessed a crime taking place. Ask students what sorts of questions they would ask their friend to learn more about the event. Then ask students to imagine that their friend just won an award. What sort of questions might they ask? Write students' suggested questions for the class to see and then evaluate each question. Point out questions that are too broad or that might be biased. Then assign students a topic from the chapter and have students practice the skill by writing five questions that would be effective in helping them conduct research on the topic.

LS Verbal/Linguistic

Alternative Assessment Handbook, Rubric 37: Writing Assignments

---

Analysis	Critical Thinking	Civic Participation	Study

Framing Historical Questions

Define the Skill

One of the most valuable ways that people gain knowledge is by asking effective questions. An effective question is one that obtains the kind of information the person asking the question desires. The ability to frame, or construct, effective questions is an important life skill as well as key to gaining a better understanding of history. Asking effective historical questions will aid you in studying history and in conducting historical research.

Learn the Skill

Effective questions are specific, straight-forward, and directly related to the topic. When we do not obtain the information we want or need, often it is because we have asked the wrong questions. Asking effective questions is not as easy as it seems. It requires thought and preparation. The following guidelines will help you in framing effective questions about history and other topics as well.

1. Determine exactly what you want to know.

2. Decide what questions to ask and write them down. Having written questions is very important. They will help guide your study or research and keep you focused on your topic and goal.

3. Review each of your questions to make sure it is specific, straight-forward, and directly related to your topic.

4. Rewrite any questions that are vague, too broad, or biased.

   Questions that are vague or too broad are likely to produce information not directly related to what you want to know. For example, if you wanted to know more about trade and the voyages of exploration that are discussed in Chapter 2, "What were the voyages of exploration?" may not be a good question to ask. This question is too broad. Its answer would not give you the information you want.

   Asking "Why was trade the most important cause of the voyages of exploration?" would not be an effective question either. This question is biased because it *assumes* trade was the main reason for the voyages, when that might not have been true. Good historical investigation assumes nothing that is not known to be fact. A more effective question, which would get the information you want, is: "Were trade and the voyages of exploration connected, and, if so, in what ways?". Do you see now why wording is so important in asking effective questions and why you should write out and review your questions beforehand?

Practice the Skill

Reread the information about Cortés and the Aztec on pages 46–47, then complete the activities below.

1. Suppose you wanted to learn more about Cortés's defeat of the Aztec. Decide whether each of the following would be an effective question to ask about this topic. Explain why or why not.

   a. What happened when the Aztec and the Spanish met?

   b. Why did other Indians betray the Aztec?

   c. What resources did Cortés have that helped him conquer the Aztec?

2. Frame five questions that would be effective in helping you to learn more about this topic.

Social Studies Skills Activity: Historical Questions   At Level

5W-How Questions

1. Write the *5W-How* questions for students to see: *Who? What? When? Where? Why?* and *How?*

2. Explain that these questions can help students frame historical questions to guide their learning and research.

3. Provide students with a topic from the chapter. Write the topic for the class to see. Have students practice as a class in using the *5W-How* questions to frame historical questions about the topic. Provide feedback.

4. Then assign a second topic and have students work independently to use the *5W-How* questions to frame five historical questions about the topic. Have volunteers share their questions with the class. Give other students a chance to evaluate each question. Correct students as needed. **LS Verbal/Linguistic**

Alternative Assessment Handbook, Rubric 37: Writing Assignments

---

Answers

Practice the Skill 1. *(a) too broad; (b) biased because of use of word betray; (c) well-framed question;* **2.** *Students' questions will vary but might include some of the following: What events led to conflict between Cortés and the Aztec? What events led up to Cortés's defeat of the Aztec? Where and when did Cortés's defeat of the Aztec take place? How did the weapons and armor of the Aztec compare to those of Cortés and his soldiers? What other resources did Cortés have that helped him defeat the Aztec?*

Chapter Review

Visual Summary

Use the visual summary below to help you review the main ideas of the chapter.

Early Exploration and Settlement

QUICK FACTS

Effects
- Destruction of Native American empires
- Columbian Exchange
- Colonies in the Americas
- Slavery in the Americas

Causes
- Competition between nations
- Desire for wealth
- Spread of Christianity

Reviewing Vocabulary, Terms, and People

1. The first Europeans to reach the East Coast of North America were the _____.

2. _____ established a navigation school and financed expeditions to the west coast of Africa.

3. One of the most important European explorers was _____, who was the first person to claim lands in the Americas for Spain.

4. The first voyage that sailed completely around the world was headed by _____.

5. Sir Walter Raleigh founded the colony of Virginia after receiving a _____, a grant to set up a colony, from the queen of England.

6. Large farms or _____, that specialize in growing one type of crop for profit, were common in Spanish America.

Comprehension and Critical Thinking

SECTION 1 *(Pages 38–41)*

7. **a. Recall** On which two islands did the Vikings establish settlements before coming to North America?

b. Analyze What factors led Europeans to begin their voyages of exploration?

c. Evaluate What do you think motivated sailors to sign on for voyages of exploration?

SECTION 2 *(pages 42–45)*

8. **a. Recall** Why was Columbus's first voyage important?

b. Summarize Explain the conflict that emerged between Spain and Portugal over their empires in the Americas and how it was resolved.

c. Evaluate Do you think the Columbian Exchange improved life or made life worse in the Americas? Explain your answer.

NEW EMPIRES IN THE AMERICAS **65**

Answers

Visual Summary

Review and Inquiry Have students use the visual summary illustration to write a summary about European exploration to the Americas.

🔲 Quick Facts Transparency: New Empires in the Americas Visual Summary

Reviewing Vocabulary, Terms, and People:

1. Vikings
2. Prince Henry the Navigator
3. Christopher Columbus
4. Ferdinand Magellan
5. charter
6. plantations

Comprehension and Critical Thinking

7. **a.** Iceland, Greenland
   b. desire to make money by finding safer, faster, and more direct trade routes to Asia and Africa, interest in Asian culture, desire to spread Christianity, advances in technology such as better ship designs, magnetic compass, and astrolabe
   c. desire to travel, adventure, riches

8. **a.** It expanded the European view of the world and began a tide of European exploration and settlement in the Americas.
   b. conflict regarding ownership over new lands in the Americas, pope established the Line of Demarcation in 1493, conflict resolved by the Treaty of Tordesillas in 1494 that moved the Demarcation Line 800 miles west

---

Review and Assessment Resources

Review and Reinforce

SE Chapter Review

📓 **CRF:** Chapter Review Activity

🔲 Quick Facts Transparency: New Empires in The Americas Visual Summary

🔊 Spanish Chapter Summaries Audio CD Program

🌐 Online Chapter Summaries in Six Languages

OSP Holt PuzzlePro, GameTool for ExamView

💿 Quiz Game CD-ROM

Assess

SE Standardized Test Practice

📓 PASS: Chapter Test

📓 Alternative Assessment Handbook

OSP ExamView Test Generator, Chapter Test

💿 Differentiated Instruction Modified Worksheets and Tests CD-ROM: Chapter Test

💿 Holt Online Assessment Program (in the Premier Online Edition)

Reteach/Intervene

📓 Interactive Reader and Study Guide

📓 Differentiated Instruction Teacher Management System: Lesson Plans for Differentiated Instruction

💿 Differentiated Instruction Modified Worksheets and Tests CD-ROM

💿 Interactive Skills Tutor CD-ROM

go hrw com
Online Resources

Chapter Resources:
KEYWORD: SR8 US2

c. Students should recognize that the Columbian Exchange brought new products to both the Americas and to Europe; brought great suffering to Native Americans and led to slavery.

9. a. southern North America, Central America, and much of South America

b. superior weapons and armor, horses, help of some Native Americans, harmful effects of European diseases on Native Americans

c. provided Spanish settlers with a tax system and free labor

10. a. It shocked Spain, weakened their power overseas, and led other countries to challenge Spain.

b. French settlements: located in many areas of North America, mainly outposts for fur trade, treated Native Americans with respect; English settlements: located along the Atlantic Coast, experienced many difficulties building colonies, had problems with Native Americans; Spanish settlements: located in the west and southwest, enslaved the Native American populations, colonies extracted valuable minerals, conversion of Native Americans important, both military outposts and village communities were established

c. Conflicts might arise among them as they vied for land, resources, and power.

11. a. cheap, available in large numbers, could be forced to work, immune to European diseases

b. religion blended Christianity and traditional religions, importance of family, music and dance

c. loss of young male population, devastation of traditional economy, disintegration of traditional culture

---

SECTION 3 *(pages 46–51)*

9. a. Identify What territories in the Americas did Spain control?

b. Analyze What factors enabled the Spanish to defeat the Aztec and the Inca?

c. Elaborate Why was the *encomienda* system important to Spanish settlers?

SECTION 4 *(pages 52–57)*

10. a. Describe What were the results of the defeat of the Spanish Armada?

b. Contrast How did French settlements in the Americas differ from the English and Spanish settlements?

c. Predict What problems might arise among the different empires with settlements in North America?

SECTION 5 *(pages 58–61)*

11. a. Explain Why did the Spanish turn to enslaved Africans as a labor force in the Americas?

b. Analyze In what ways did enslaved Africans create their own, unique culture in the Americas?

c. Evaluate What effects do you think slavery had on the populations and cultures of West African countries?

Reviewing Themes

12. Geography What geographic features in North America helped and hindered the exploration and colonization of the continent?

13. Politics In what way were the expansions of empires motivated by the politics among European nations?

Using the Internet

go.hrw.com
KEYWORD: SR8 US15

14. Activity: Illustrated Map Columbus' successful return from the New World sparked an interest in exploration that resulted in an explosion of explorers. Each explorer mapped his route and the lands that he explored. Our knowledge of the New World quickly as explorers made maps and kept detailed logs to catalog what

they found. Enter the activity keyword. Then choose a group of explorers, and research the routes they took from the country of origin to the place upon which they landed. Present your research in an annotated and illustrated map or log book. Write from the point of view of an explorer and include information about the areas they explored.

Reading Skills

Outlining and History *Use the Reading Social Studies Skill taught in this chapter to answer the following question.*

15. Make a short but complete outline of the section on pages 50–51 under the heading "Spanish Treatment of Native Americans."

Social Studies Skills

Framing Historical Questions *Use the Social Studies Skill taught in this chapter to answer the following question.*

16. Write a historial question for each of the five sections of this chapter.

FOCUS ON WRITING

17. Writing Your Letter First, review your notes and decide which group you want to write about. Which details from your notes will your friends and family be most interested in? Which do you find most important? What do you want to tell your family and friends about the Americas?

Reviewing Themes

12. mountains, deserts, wide rivers, forests

13. Many were attempts to gain wealth and power.

Using the Internet

14. Go to the HRW Web site and enter the keyword shown to access a rubric for this activity.

KEYWORD: SR8 US2

Reading Skills

15. Students will outline section.

Social Studies Skills

16. Students will write five historical questions.

Focus on Writing

17. Students will write detailed letters.

CRF: Focus on Writing Activity: Writing a Letter

Standardized Test Practice

DIRECTIONS: Read each question and write the letter of the best response.

1 Which of the following best illustrates the process known as the Columbian Exchange?

A Christopher Columbus sailed west to reach Asia and encountered the Americas.

B Corn and tomatoes were introduced to Europe from America.

C Asian goods moved long distances along the Silk Road to reach Europe.

D Advances in technology allowed sailors to better navigate on the open seas.

2 The decimation of the native population of the Americas and the need for plantation labor resulted in the

A *encomienda* system.

B establishment of religious tolerance.

C Transatlantic slave trade.

D Columbian Exchange.

3 The desire to convert people to Christianity and the demand for Asian trade goods led to

A increased interest in exploration.

B the Renaissance.

C the conquest of the Americas.

D efforts to end the slave trade.

4 Spain's empire in the Americas included all of the following *except*

A South America.

B Virginia.

C Mexico.

D Florida.

5 All of the following established colonies in North America *except*

A the Portuguese.

B the Dutch.

C the English.

D the French.

6 The voyage of enslaved Africans across the Atlantic to the Americas was known as the

A Northwest Passage.

B African Diaspora.

C Triangular Trade.

D Middle Passage.

Examine the following passage from Bernal Diaz de Castillo's account of an Aztec marketplace. Then answer the question below.

> "The bustle and noise caused by this large crowd of people was so great that it could be heard more than four miles away. Some of our men, who had traveled through Italy, said that they never had seen a marketplace that covered so large and area, which was so well regulated, and so crowded with people as this one at Mexico."
>
> —Bernal Diaz de Castillo, adapted from *The Memoirs of the Conquistador Bernal Diaz de Castillo*

7 What is the author's impression of the Aztec marketplace? How can you tell?

1. B
Break Down the Question Tell students to consider what they know about the Columbian Exchange to determine the correct answer.

2. C
Beak Down the Question This question requires students to identify cause and effect. Refer students who miss the question to the text titled "The Need for a New Labor Force" in Section 5.

3. A
Break Down the Question This question requires students to recall factual information. Refer students who miss the question to coverage of exploration in Section 1.

4. B
Break Down the Question This question requires students to recall factual information. Refer students who miss the question to coverage of Spain's empire in Section 3.

5. A
Break Down the Question Remind students to eliminate nations which they know established colonies in North America.

6. D
Break Down the Question This question requires students to recall that information from Section 5.

7.
The author is impressed with the marketplace. The author refers to the crowd of people and that the market is well regulated.

Intervention Resources

Reproducible

📋 Interactive Reader and Study Guide

📋 Differentiated Instruction Teacher Management System: Lesson Plans for Differentiated Instruction

Technology

💾 Quick Facts Transparency: New Empires in the Americas Visual Summary

💿 Differentiated Instruction Modified Worksheets and Tests CD-ROM

💿 Interactive Skills Tutor CD-ROM

Tips for Test Taking

Get a Clue! If the test item asks for vocabulary knowledge, look at the surrounding sentences for clues. Sometimes the context can help you see which definition fits. To identify the best definition of the underlined word as it is used in the **context,** consider the surrounding words and phrases.

Chapter 3 Planning Guide

The English Colonies

Chapter Overview	Reproducible Resources	Technology Resources
CHAPTER 3 pp. 68–107 **Overview: In this chapter, students will learn about the English colonies in North America and the tensions that developed there over British Tax policies.**	**Differentiated Instruction Teacher Management System:*** • Instructional Benchmarking Guides **Interactive Reader and Study Guide:** Chapter Graphic Organizer* **Chapter Resource File:*** • Focus on Writing Activity: Writing an Infomercial • Social Studies Skills Time Lines • Chapter Review Activity	**Power Presentations with Video CD-ROM** **Differentiated Instruction Modified Worksheets and Tests CD-ROM** **Student Edition on Audio CD Program** **History's Impact:** United States History Video Program (VHS/DVD): The English Colonies*
Section 1: **The Southern Colonies** **The Big Idea:** Despite a difficult beginning, the southern colonies soon flourished.	**Differentiated Instruction Teacher Management System:** Section 1 Lesson Plan* **Interactive Reader and Study Guide:** Section 1 Summary* **Chapter Resource File:*** • Vocabulary Builder Activity, Section 1 • Biography Activity: Pocahontas	**Daily Bellringer Transparency:** Section 1* **Map Transparency:** Jamestown Colony* **Map Transparency:** The Southern Colonies* **Internet Activity:** Jamestown Graph
Section 2: **The New England Colonies** **The Big Idea:** English colonists traveled to New England to gain religious freedom.	**Differentiated Instruction Teacher Management System:** Section 2 Lesson Plan* **Interactive Reader and Study Guide:** Section 2 Summary* **Chapter Resource File:*** • Vocabulary Builder Activity, Section 2 • Literature Activity: American Colonial Poetry	**Daily Bellringer Transparency:** Section 2* **Quick Facts Transparency:** Church and State*
Section 3: **The Middle Colonies** **The Big Idea:** People from many nations settled in the middle colonies.	**Differentiated Instruction Teacher Management System:** Section 3 Lesson Plan* **Interactive Reader and Study Guide:** Section 3 Summary* **Chapter Resource File:*** • Vocabulary Builder Activity, Section 3	**Daily Bellringer Transparency:** Section 3* **Quick Facts Transparency:** Characteristics of the Middle Colonies*
Section 4: **Life in the English Colonies** **The Big Idea:** The English colonies continued to grow despite many challenges.	**Differentiated Instruction Teacher Management System:** Section 4 Lesson Plan* **Interactive Reader and Study Guide:** Section 4 Summary* **Chapter Resource File:*** • Vocabulary Builder Activity, Section 4	**Daily Bellringer Transparency:** Section 4* **Map Transparencies:** The Thirteen Colonies; Triangular Trade; North American Empires before and after the Treaty of Paris **Internet Activity:** The Courts and Freedom of the Press
Section 5: **Conflict in the Colonies** **The Big Idea:** Tensions developed as the British government placed tax after tax on the colonies.	**Differentiated Instruction Teacher Management System:** Section 5 Lesson Plan* **Interactive Reader and Study Guide:** Section 5 Summary* **Chapter Resource File:*** • Vocabulary Builder Activity, Section 5 • Biography Activities: Samuel Adams; Patrick Henry; Crispus Attucks	**Daily Bellringer Transparency:** Section 5* **Quick Facts Transparency:** The Road to Revolution*

HOLT
History's Impact
United States History Video Program (VHS/DVD)
The English Colonies
Suggested use: as a chapter introduction

Review, Assessment, Intervention

 Quick Facts Transparency: The English Colonies Visual Summary*

 Progress Assessment Support System (PASS): Chapter Test*

 Differentiated Instruction Modified Worksheets and Tests CD-ROM: Modified Chapter Test

One-Stop Planner CD-ROM: ExamView Test Generator (English/Spanish)

 PASS: Section 1 Quiz*

 Online Quiz: Section 1

Alternative Assessment Handbook

PASS: Section 2 Quiz*

Online Quiz: Section 2

Alternative Assessment Handbook

 PASS: Section 3 Quiz*

 Online Quiz: Section 3

Alternative Assessment Handbook

PASS: Section 4 Quiz*

Online Quiz: Section 4

Alternative Assessment Handbook

 PASS: Section 5 Quiz*

 Online Quiz: Section 5

 Alternative Assessment Handbook

Power Presentations with Video CD-ROM

Power Presentations with Video are visual presentations of each chapter's main ideas. Presentations can be customized by including Quick Facts charts, images from the text, and video clips.

Power Presentations with Video CD-ROM
HOLT
United States History
Beginnings to 1877
HOLT, RINEHART AND WINSTON

DIVISION FOR
PUBLIC EDUCATION
AMERICAN BAR ASSOCIATION

Developed by the Division for Public Education of the American Bar Association, these materials are part of the **Democracy and Civic Education Resources.**

- **Constitution Study Guide**
- **Supreme Court Case Studies**

Holt
Online
Learning

- Document-Based Questions
- Interactive Multimedia Activities

Teacher Resources
KEYWORD: SR8 TEACHER

Student Resources
KEYWORD: SR8 US3

- Current Events
- Chapter-based Internet Activities
- and more!

Holt Premier
Online Student Edition
Complete online support for interactivity, assessment, and reporting

- Interactive Maps and Notebook
- Standardized Test Prep
- Homework Practice and Research Activities Online

CHAPTER 3 PLANNING GUIDE

Differentiating Instruction

ENGLISH-LANGUAGE LEARNERS & STRUGGLING READERS

TARGET RESOURCE

Live Ink® Online Reading Help

Spanish Resources

Spanish Chapter Summaries Audio CD Program

One-Stop Planner CD-ROM:
- ExamView Test Generator, Spanish
- PuzzlePro, Spanish

Additional Resources

Differentiated Instruction Teacher Management System: Lesson Plans for Differentiated Instruction

Chapter Resources:
- Vocabulary Builder Activities
- Social Studies Skills Activity: Interpreting Time Lines

Quick Facts Transparencies:
- Church and State
- Characteristics of the Middle Colonies
- The Road to Revolution
- The English Colonies Visual Summary

Student Edition on Audio CD Program

Online Chapter Summaries in Six Languages

Interactive Skills Tutor CD-ROM

SPECIAL NEEDS LEARNERS

TARGET RESOURCE

Differentiated Instruction Modified Worksheets and Tests CD-ROM

- Vocabulary Flash Cards
- Modified Vocabulary Builder Activities
- Modified Chapter Review Activity
- Modified Chapter Test

Additional Resources

Differentiated Instruction Teacher Management System: Lesson Plans for Differentiated Instruction

Interactive Reader and Study Guide

Social Studies Skills Activity: Interpreting Time Lines

Student Edition on Audio CD Program

Interactive Skills Tutor CD-ROM

Live Ink® Online Reading Help

ADVANCED/GIFTED AND TALENTED STUDENTS

TARGET RESOURCE

Primary Source Library CD-ROM for United States History

The Library contains longer versions of quotations in the text, extra sources, and images. Included are point-of-view articles, journals, diaries, historical fiction, and political documents.

Additional Resources

Political Cartoons Activities for United States History: Cartoon 1: The Mayflower; Cartoon 2: No Taxation without Representation

United States History Document-Based Questions Activities

Differentiated Instruction Teacher Management System: Lesson Plans for Differentiated Instruction

Pre-AP Activities Guide for United States History: Categorizing Information

Chapter Resource File:
- Focus on Writing Activity: Writing an Infomercial
- Literature Activity: American Colonial Poetry
- Primary Source Activities: Journal of Sarah Kemble Knight; Sinners in the Hands of an Angry God

Differentiated Activities in the Teacher's Edition

- Terms and Definitions, p. 73
- Labor in Virginia Venn Diagram, p. 74
- Map of the Colonies, p. 76
- Guide to Massachusetts Bay, p. 81
- Key Terms of Connecticut and Rhode Island Chart, p. 82
- Colonial Governments Chart, p. 91
- Colonial Trade Posters, p. 93
- Frontier Conflicts Time Line, p. 96

Differentiated Activities in the Teacher's Edition

- Taxation Talk, p. 99

Differentiated Activities in the Teacher's Edition

- Decision-making in the Southern Colonies, p. 75
- Mayflower Compact Simulation, p. 79
- European Influence in the Middle Colonies, p. 86
- Alternative Labor Proposals, p. 93

One-Stop Planner® CD-ROM
for Differentiated Instruction

Your differentiated instruction lesson plans are available at your fingertips. Holt's Teacher Management System links teaching support tools to pages in the Interactive Teacher's Edition.

The One-Stop Planner features:
- Interactive Teacher's Edition
- Calendar Planner and pacing guides
- Editable lesson plans
- All reproducible ancillaries in Adobe Acrobat (PDF) format
- ExamView Test Generator (English and Spanish)
- Transparency and video previews

Professional Development

- **In-service and staff development** as part of your Holt Social Studies product purchase
- **Quick Teacher Tutorial Lesson Presentation CD-ROM**
- Intensive tuition-based **Teacher Development Institute**
- **Teaching American History Online**—2 Module Professional Development Course
- **Convenient Holt Speaker Bureau**—face-to-face workshop options
- **PRAXIS™ Test Prep** interactive Web-based content refreshers*
- **24/7 Ask A Professional Development Expert** at http://www.hrw.com/prodev/

* PRAXIS is a trademark of Educational Testing Service (ETS). This publication is not endorsed or approved by ETS.

DIFFERENTIATED INSTRUCTION PLANNING GUIDE

Chapter Big Ideas

Section 1 Despite a difficult beginning, the southern colonies soon flourished.

Section 2 English colonists traveled to New England to gain religious freedom.

Section 3 People from many nations settled in the middle colonies.

Section 4 The English colonies continued to grow despite many challenges.

Section 5 Tensions developed as the British government placed tax after tax on the colonies.

CHAPTER 3 1605–1774

The English Colonies

FOCUS ON WRITING

Writing an Infomercial What if television had been invented during the time that the English colonies were being founded in North America? Instead of relying on printed flyers and word of mouth to attract settlers, the founders of colonies might have made infomercials. In this chapter you will read about life in the American colonies during different times. You will choose one time period and colony and write an infomercial encouraging English citizens to settle in the colony of your choice.

68 CHAPTER 3

Focus on Writing

The **Chapter Resource File** provides a Focus on Writing worksheet to help students write their infomercials.

> **CRF:** Focus on Writing Activity: Writing an Infomercial

UNITED STATES

1620 The Pilgrims sign the Mayflower Compact.

1620

WORLD

1648 Work is finished on India's Taj Mahal.

Mayflower Compact courtesy of the Pilgrim Society, Plymouth, Massachusetts.

Key to Differentiating Instruction

Below Level

Basic-level activities designed for all students encountering new material

At Level

Intermediate-level activities designed for average students

Above Level

Challenging activities designed for honors and gifted and talented students

Standard English Mastery

Activities designed to improve standard English usage

Introduce the Chapter

At Level

Focus on Reasons for Colonization

1. Write the following scenario for students to see. *The U.S. government has decided to found a colony on another planet. What do you think the government hopes to gain from the colony? What conditions might make you move to this distant colony? What challenges might you and other settlers face at this colony?*

2. Give students time to consider and discuss the scenario and questions. List students' answers for the class to see. Encourage students to explain their reasoning and opinions.

3. Review with students what they learned in the last chapter about European colonies in North America. *(Remind students that England, France, the Netherlands, Spain, and Sweden had all founded American colonies.)* What did these countries hope to gain from their colonies, and what challenges did colonists face?

4. Tell students that in this chapter they will learn about the thirteen colonies that England founded in North America, which would later become the United States. **LS Verbal/Linguistic**

HOLT

History's Impact
▶ video series
Watch the video to understand the impact of English settlement on North America.

What You Will Learn...

Plymouth Colony thrives again in this highly accurate re-creation. The original colonists came to North America in 1620 in search of religious freedom. By 1627, the year this scene re-creates, the colonists were well established. Their success encouraged others. In this chapter you will learn about English settlements that dotted the east coast of North America.

1670

1681
William Penn establishes the colony of Pennsylvania.

1682
Peter the Great becomes czar of Russia.

1720

1763
Pontiac, an American Indian, leads a rebellion on the western frontier.

1768
British explorer James Cook sets sail on his first trip to the South Pacific, meeting people like this Sandwich Islander.

1770

1773
Patriots stage the Boston Tea Party.

THE ENGLISH COLONIES **69**

• Chapter Preview •

HOLT

History's Impact
▶ video series
See the Video Teacher's Guide for strategies for using the chapter video **The English Colonies**.

Explore the Picture

Plymouth Colony The Pilgrims and other members of the Mayflower named their colony Plymouth after the last English port the ship stopped at on its journey. Plymouth Colony was built on the site of a former Native American town. Many of the town's inhabitants, the Wampanoag, had died from disease, most likely brought by European fishers and traders. The survivors had moved to other villages.

Analyzing Visuals What can you tell from this picture about the types of homes in the Plymouth Colony? *possible answers—built of wood with thatched roofs; had fireplaces (from chimneys); were small and set close together*

go.hrw.com
Online Resources
Chapter Resources:
KEYWORD: SR8 US3
Teacher Resources:
KEYWORD: SR8 TEACHER

Explore the Time Line

1. How long after the Pilgrims signed the Mayflower Compact was the Boston Tea Party? *153 years*
2. What colony did William Penn found, and when? *Pennsylvania, in 1681*
3. Based on the time line, what themes are addressed in this chapter? *political and economic themes of colonization and conflict*

Info to Know

English Workers In the early 1600s, English laborers were paid very little. Several able London workers reported that even though they and their families wore themselves out working long hard hours, they still only earned just enough to keep themselves alive.

Draw Conclusions Why might some English workers at the time have moved to a colony in North America? *in hopes of finding a better life for themselves*

Reading
Social Studies

Understanding Themes

The themes of economics and politics are presented in this chapter. Ask students to imagine that their families have decided to move to a foreign country to seek new opportunities. Guide students in a discussion of reasons why their families might have chosen to leave their home countries. Have students identify the difficulties they think their families might face in their new country and how they might try to overcome them. Emphasize issues related to economics and politics, such as trade and government. Write students' responses for everyone to see. Tell students that as they study this chapter, they will learn about the problems early settlers in America faced, and how they worked to overcome them.

Vocabulary Clues

Focus on Reading Organize the class into pairs. Then have each pair go through one of their textbooks. Ask students to look for sentences where a word is explained using context clues. Ask students to find five sentences that use vocabulary clues to define a term. Then have students make a list of the different ways in which the meaning of a word is given in the context of the text. Answers might include clue words or punctuation.

Reading Social Studies

by Kylene Beers

| Economics | Geography | Politics | Society and Culture | Science and Technology |

Focus on Themes In this chapter you will read about the people who settled the early colonies of North America. You will learn about the problems they faced as they felt the tug between their home-land and their new land. You will see how they settled political differences (sometimes peacefully, other times not) and learned how to trade goods and grow crops to establish a thriving economy. You will discover that the **economy** often influenced their **politics**.

Vocabulary Clues

Focus on Reading When you are reading your history textbook, you may often come across a word you do not know. If that word isn't listed as a key term, how do you find out what it means?

Using Context Clues Context means surroundings. Authors often include clues to the meaning of a difficult word in its context. You just have to know how and where to look.

Clue	How It Works	Example	Explanation
Direct Definition	Includes a definition in the same or a nearby sentence	In the late 1600s England, like most western European nations, practiced mercantilism, *the practice of creating and maintaining wealth by carefully controlling trade.*	The phrase "the practice of creating and maintaining wealth by carefully controlling trade" defines *mercantilism.*
Restatement	Uses different words to say the same thing	The British continued to keep a standing, *or permanent,* army in North America to protect the colonists against Indian attacks.	The word *permanent* is another way to say *standing.*
Comparisons or Contrasts	Compares or contrasts the unfamiliar word with a familiar one	*Unlike legal traders,* smugglers did not have permission to bring goods into the country.	The word *unlike* indicates that smugglers are different from legal traders.

70 CHAPTER 3

Reading and Skills Resources

Reading Support

📖 Interactive Reader and Study Guide

🔊 Student Edition on Audio CD Program

🔊 Spanish Chapter Summaries Audio CD Program

Social Studies Skills Support

💿 Interactive Skills Tutor CD-ROM

Vocabulary Support

📖 **CRF:** Vocabulary Builder Activities

📖 **CRF:** Chapter Review Activity

💿 Differentiated Instruction Modified Worksheets and Tests CD-ROM:
  • Vocabulary Flash Cards
  • Vocabulary Builder Activity
  • Chapter Review Activity

OSP Holt PuzzlePro

You Try It!

The following sentences are from this chapter. Each uses a definition or restatement clue to explain unfamiliar words. See if you can use the context to figure out the meaning of the words in italics.

Context Clues Up Close

From Chapter 3

1. In 1605 a company of English merchants asked King James I for the right to *found*, or establish, a settlement. *(p. 72)*

2. The majority of these workers were *indentured servants*. These servants signed a contract to work four to seven years for those who paid for their journey to America. *(p. 74)*

3. In New England, the center of politics was the *town meeting*. In town meetings people talked about and decided on issues of local interest, such as paying for schools. *(p. 91)*

Answer the questions about the sentences you read.

1. In example 1, what does the word *found* mean? What hints did you find in the sentence to figure that out?

2. In example 2, where do you find the meaning of *indentured servants*? What does this phrase mean?

3. In example 3, you learn the definition of *town meeting* in the second sentence. Can you combine these two sentences into one sentence? Try putting a dash after the word *meeting* and replacing "In town meetings" with "a place where . . ."

> **As you read Chapter 3,** look for context clues that can help you figure out the meanings of unfamiliar words or terms.

Key Terms and People

Academic Vocabulary

In this chapter, you will learn the following academic words:

authority *(p. 73)*
factors *(p. 74)*

Reading Social Studies

Key Terms and People

Challenge students to create a matching game using the key terms and people from this chapter. Organize the class into pairs, then assign each pair a term or person from the list. Have each group write a description or definition for their term on one index card and the word or name on a separate card. Collect all the index cards and place them in a basket. Have each student draw a card from the basket. Then have students try to find the person whose word or name matches the description on their card. Challenge the students even more by not allowing any talking while they match terms and descriptions!
LS Interpersonal, Verbal/Linguistic

Focus on Reading

See the **Focus on Reading** questions in this chapter for more practice on this reading social studies skill.

Reading Social Studies Assessment

See the **Chapter Review** at the end of this chapter for student assessment questions related to this reading skill.

Teaching Tip

Point out to students that there are usually hints that indicate when a word is defined in the context of the sentence. One of these hints is the use of punctuation. Commas and dashes often are used to set off phrases from the rest of the sentence. These phrases often define or restate the unfamiliar word. Another hint is the use of signal words and phrases. Phrases are often used to indicate a definition or restatement. Remind students to look for words and phrases such as *which means, which is, in other words, or, called,* and *that is.*

Answers

You Try It! 1. *establish; a restatement of the word was used;* **2.** *in the second sentence; servants who signed a contract to work a number of years for those who paid for their journey to America;* **3.** *In New England, the center of politics was the town meeting—a place where people talked about and decided issues of local interest, such as paying for school.*

Bellringer

If YOU were there . . . Use the **Daily Bellringer Transparency** to help students answer the question.

🖨 Daily Bellringer Transparency, Section 1

Academic Vocabulary

Review with students the high-use academic terms in this section.

authority power, right to rule (p. 73)

factors causes (p. 74)

🗐 **CRF:** Vocabulary Builder Activity, Section 1

Taking Notes

Have students copy the graphic organizer onto their own paper and then use it to take notes on the section. This activity will prepare students for the Section Assessment, in which they will complete a graphic organizer that builds on the information using a critical thinking skill.

The Southern Colonies

What You Will Learn...

Main Ideas

1. The settlement in Jamestown was the first permanent English settlement in America.
2. Daily life in Virginia was challenging to the colonists.
3. Religious freedom and economic opportunities were motives for founding other southern colonies, including Maryland, the Carolinas, and Georgia.
4. Farming and slavery were important to the economies of the southern colonies.

The Big Idea

Despite a difficult beginning, the southern colonies soon flourished.

Key Terms and People

Jamestown, *p. 72*
John Smith, *p. 73*
Pocahontas, *p. 73*
indentured servants, *p. 74*
Bacon's Rebellion, *p. 74*
Toleration Act of 1649, *p. 75*
Olaudah Equiano, *p. 77*
slave codes, *p. 77*

 TAKING NOTES As you read, take notes in a chart like the one below on the founding of the southern colonies.

Colony	Year	Why Founded

If YOU were there...

A year ago, in 1609, you moved to the colony of Virginia. But life here has been hard. During the winter many people died of cold or sickness. Food is always scarce. Now it is spring, and a ship has come from England bringing supplies. In a week it will sail home. Some of your neighbors are giving up and returning to England. They ask you to come, too.

Would you take the ship back to England?

BUILDING BACKGROUND Several European nations took part in the race to claim lands in the Americas. Their next step was to establish colonies in the lands that they claimed. The first English colonies were started in the late 1500s but failed. Even in successful colonies, colonists faced hardships and challenges.

Settlement in Jamestown

In 1605 a company of English merchants asked King James I for the right to found, or establish, a settlement. In 1606 the king granted the request of the company to settle in a region called Virginia.

Founding a New Colony

The investors in the new settlement formed a joint-stock company called the London Company. This allowed the group to share the cost and risk of establishing the colony. On April 26, 1607, the first 105 colonists sent by the London Company arrived in America. On May 14, about 40 miles up the James River in Virginia, the colonists founded **Jamestown**, the first permanent English settlement in North America.

A lack of preparation cost a lot of the colonists their lives. Most of the men who came to Jamestown were adventurers with no farming experience or useful skills such as carpentry. Jamestown was surrounded by marshes full of disease-carrying mosquitoes. By the time winter arrived, two-thirds of the original colonists had died.

Teach the Big Idea

The Southern Colonies

Materials: five blank index cards per student

1. **Teach** Ask students the questions in the Main Idea boxes to teach this section.
2. **Apply** Have students create colonial picture postcards. Give each student five blank index cards, one for each of the southern colonies. On the front of the postcards, have students create "I am Here" maps showing the location of the colony, the date it was founded, and its main settlements. On the backs, have students list facts about the colonies.
   LS Visual/Spatial

3. **Review** Have students share some of the facts they listed. Write the list for students to see.
4. **Practice/Homework** Have each student select one southern colony and imagine that he or she has moved there. Each student should write a letter home to England describing the colony, life there, and the challenges that he or she is facing.
   LS Verbal/Linguistic

   🗐 Alternative Assessment Handbook, Rubric 41: Writing to Express

Jamestown Colony

Williamsburg
1698

The forest could provide wood for building and for fuel.

The waters provided fish for food. But the water, so near the sea, was salty.

Jamestown
1607

Marsh

James River

Smith's Fort

Jamestown was located with defense in mind. Enemy Spanish ships would have to pass through a narrow channel to reach Jamestown, making the ships easy marks for the settlers' cannons.

GEOGRAPHY SKILLS | **INTERPRETING MAPS**

1. **Human-Environment Interaction** What were the advantages and disadvantages of locating Jamestown on a river?
2. **Human-Environment Interaction** What do you think would have been a commonly used method of transportation for people in this region?

Powhatan Confederacy

The situation in Jamestown temporarily improved after **John Smith** took control of the colony in September 1608. He forced the settlers to work harder and to build better housing by creating rules that rewarded harder workers with food. The colonists received help from the powerful Powhatan Confederacy of Native Americans after Smith made an agreement with them. The Powhatan brought food to help the colonists and taught them how to grow corn.

In 1609 some 400 more settlers arrived in Jamestown. That winter, disease and famine once again hit the colony. The colonists called this period the starving time. By the spring of 1610, only 60 colonists were still alive. Jamestown failed to make a profit until colonist John Rolfe introduced a new type of tobacco that sold well in England.

War in Virginia

John Rolfe married **Pocahontas**, daughter of the Powhatan leader, in 1614. Their marriage helped the colonists form more peaceful relations with the Powhatan. However, Pocahontas died three years later in England, which she was visiting with Rolfe.

In 1622, colonists killed a Powhatan leader. The Powhatan responded by attacking the Virginia settlers later that year. Fighting between the colonists and the Powhatan continued for the next 20 years. Because the London Company could not protect its colonists, the English Crown canceled the company's charter in 1624. Virginia became a royal colony and existed under the **authority** of a governor chosen by the king.

ACADEMIC VOCABULARY
authority power, right to rule

READING CHECK **Finding Main Ideas** What problems did the Jamestown colonists face?

THE ENGLISH COLONIES **73**

Main Idea

❷ Daily Life in Virginia

Daily life in Virginia was challenging to the colonists.

Recall What was the main cash crop in Virginia? *tobacco*

Analyze Why did the plantation system develop in Virginia? *in part because of the headright system, under which colonists who paid their way received 50 acres of land plus 50 more for each person they brought*

Contrast How were indentured servants different from slaves? *Indentured servants worked voluntarily under a contract for a specified number of years; slavery was an involuntary and permanent condition.*

Primary Source

A Note from Virginia

Interpret What does John Pory hope might become some future means of making money in Virginia? *vineyards, cattle*

Connect to Economics

The Slave Trade in the Early 1600s
Initially, farmers in Virginia did not use much slave labor, in part because England did not share in the African slave trade. In the early 1600s the Dutch, Portuguese, and Spanish controlled much of the slave trade out of West Africa.

Answers

Analyzing Primary Sources *It lists tobacco as the colony's main cash crop and means of support.*

Reading Check *Demand for labor outpaced the supply of people willing to work as indentured servants, and the cost of slaves fell.*

74

Daily Life in Virginia

In early Virginia, people lived on scattered farms rather than in towns. Tobacco farmers soon began establishing large farms called plantations.

Headright System

These plantations were made possible in part by the headright system, which was started by the London Company. Under this system, colonists who paid their own way to Virginia received 50 acres of land. A colonist could earn another 50 acres for every additional person brought from England. Rich colonists who brought servants or relatives to Virginia gained large amounts of land.

ACADEMIC VOCABULARY
factors
causes

Primary Source

LETTER
A Note from Virginia

In this 1619 letter, the secretary of the Virginia colony, John Pory, encouraged people to move to Virginia.

"As touching the quality of this country, three things there be, which in few years may bring this colony to perfection; the English plow, vineyards, & cattle ... All our riches for the present do consist in tobacco, wherein one man by his own labor has in one year, raised to himself to the value of 200 pounds sterling; and another by the means of six servants has cleared at one crop a thousand pound English. These be true, yet indeed rare examples, yet possible to be done by others."

—from *The Power of Words*, edited by T. H. Breen

ANALYSIS SKILL **ANALYZING PRIMARY SOURCES**
How does this letter indicate the importance of tobacco in Virginia?

74 CHAPTER 3

Labor in Virginia

Colonists in Virginia suffered very high death rates, which led to labor shortages. The majority of workers were **indentured servants.** These servants signed a contract to work four to seven years for those who paid for their journey to America.

Expansion of Slavery

Not all laborers in Virginia came from Europe. A Dutch ship brought the first Africans to Virginia in 1619. Some Africans were servants; others had been enslaved. Some African servants became successful farmers when their contracts ended.

The demand for workers was soon greater than the supply of people willing to work as indentured servants. Over time, the cost of slaves fell. These **factors** led some colonists to turn to slave labor. By the mid-1600s most Africans in Virginia were being kept in lifelong slavery.

Bacon's Rebellion

As plantations grew, the economy of Jamestown began to expand. Soon, colonial officials began to ask for more taxes. During the mid-1600s poor colonists protested the higher taxes. They were also upset about the governor's policies toward Native Americans. They thought the colony was not well protected against attack. In 1676 a group of former indentured servants led by Nathaniel Bacon attacked some friendly American Indians. Bacon opposed the governor's policies promoting trade with American Indians. He also thought the colonists should be able to take the Indians' land. When the governor tried to stop him, Bacon and his followers attacked and burned Jamestown in an uprising known as **Bacon's Rebellion.**

At one point, Bacon controlled much of the colony. He died of fever, however, and the rebellion soon ended.

READING CHECK **Analyzing** What factors led to the increased use of slave labor in Virginia?

Critical Thinking: Comparing and Contrasting   Below Level

Labor in Virginia Venn Diagram

1. Draw the Venn diagram for students to see. Omit the blue, italicized answers.

2. Have students copy the diagram and list words and phrases that describe each type of labor. In the overlapping area, students should list words and phrases that describe both types of labor.

3. Review students' answers as a class. Then discuss the factors that led to the increased use of slave labor in Virginia. **LS Visual/Spatial**

Indentured Servants
- *contract labor*
- *worked four to seven years*
- *worked for free passage*
- *voluntary*

Both
- *hard work*
- *worked for others*
- *farmed*

Slave Labor
- *forced labor*
- *lifelong*
- *involuntary*
- *bondage*
- *harsh*

Southern Wealth

Colonists overcame tough beginnings to create large and wealthy settlements like this one in Virginia. Churches were often the first major buildings in a growing town.

How does the large church in the picture show Virginia's wealth?

Other Southern Colonies

As Jamestown was developing in Virginia, new groups of colonists began planning their move to America. Many English Catholics came to America to escape religious persecution. English Catholics had long been against England's separation from the Roman Catholic Church. For this reason they were not allowed by the Church of England to worship freely. English leaders also feared that English Catholics would ally with Catholic countries such as France and Spain in conflicts.

Maryland

In the 1620s George Calvert, the first Lord Baltimore, asked King Charles I for a charter establishing a new colony in America for Catholics. In 1632 Charles issued the charter to Calvert's son, Cecilius, who took over the planning of the colony. Cecilius, known as the second Lord Baltimore, named the colony Maryland in honor of England's queen, Henrietta Maria. It was located just north of Virginia in the Chesapeake Bay area. Calvert intended for the colony to be a refuge for English Catholics. It would also be a proprietary colony.

This meant that the colony's proprietors, or owners, controlled the government.

In 1634 a group of 200 English Catholics came to Maryland. Included in the group were wealthy landowners, servants, craftspeople, and farmers. Settlers in Maryland benefited from the lessons learned by the Jamestown colonists. They spent their time raising corn, cattle, and hogs so that they would have enough to eat. Before long, many colonists also began growing tobacco for profit.

Although Catholics founded Maryland, a growing number of Protestants began moving there in the 1640s. Soon, religious conflicts arose between Catholics and Protestants in the colony. To reduce tensions, Lord Baltimore presented a bill to the colonial assembly that became known as the **Toleration Act of 1649**. This bill made it a crime to restrict the religious rights of Christians. This was the first law supporting religious tolerance passed in the English colonies.

The Toleration Act did not stop all religious conflict. However, it did show that the government wanted to offer some religious freedom and to protect the rights of minority groups.

THE ENGLISH COLONIES **75**

Main Idea

❸ Other Southern Colonies

Religious freedom and economic opportunities were motives for founding other southern colonies, including Maryland, the Carolinas, and Georgia.

Explain Why did English Catholics settle in the colony of Maryland? *to escape religious persecution*

Contrast How was the colony of Maryland different than Jamestown? *Jamestown—founded to make a profit; joint-stock company colony then a royal colony; faced many years of hardship and loss of life; most early settlers were adventurers; Maryland— founded to provide English Catholics with religious freedom; proprietary colony; most settlers were farmers willing to work hard.*

Info to Know

Colonial Death Rates Death rates were high for early colonists in the Chesapeake region. During the 1600s, some 40 percent of colonists died within two years of their arrival from diseases such as typhoid and malaria.

Did you know . . .

Cecilius Calvert, also known as Lord Baltimore, never visited Maryland, although he founded the colony.

Critical Thinking: Analyzing Information   `Above Level`

Decision-making in the Southern Colonies

1. Discuss with students the ways in which royal and proprietary colonies differed. Focus on who made decisions in each type of colony.

2. To start, discuss with students Maryland's Toleration Act of 1649. Mention that Lord Baltimore presented the bill to the colonial assembly. Have students discuss this process as an example of how a decision was made in a proprietary colony. To address a royal colony, discuss Georgia with students.

3. Then have students contrast how decisions were made in Virginia, Maryland, and Georgia. Have each student write a short summary of the differences among the types of colonies.
LS Verbal/Linguistic

Alternative Assessment Handbook, Rubrics 11: Discussions; and 37: Writing Assignments

Answers

Southern Wealth *The church is large enough and the architecture elaborate enough to have cost a large sum at the time it was built.*

75

Main Idea

❸ Other Southern Colonies

Religious freedom and economic opportunities were motives for founding other southern colonies, including Maryland, the Carolinas, and Georgia.

Recall Why did the Carolina colony separate into North and South Carolina? *The settlements in the colony were far apart, making them hard to govern together.*

Analyze How did James Oglethorpe hope to make Georgia different from the other colonies? *He hoped Georgia would not have large plantations owned by a few wealthy people. Instead, he wanted to give the poor and debtors a fresh start, so he originally outlawed slavery and kept land grants small.*

 Map Transparency: The Southern Colonies

Interpreting Maps
Early Slave Populations

Place What foreign territory did Georgia border? *Spanish Florida*

Identify Cause and Effect Why did South Carolina develop such a large population of enslaved Africans? *The colony's system of large land grants encouraged plantation owners to bring in large numbers of slaves.*

Answers

Interpreting Charts *1700—about 35,000; 1750—about 230,000*

Reading Check *to escape religious persecution, to farm, to get a fresh start*

The Southern Colonies

Slave Populations In the Colonies

Total Population, 1750
- 80%
- Slaves 20%

Charles Town was founded in 1670. South Carolina's large land grants encouraged plantation owners to bring in thousands of slaves.

James Oglethorpe tried to prevent slavery in Georgia. But slaves soon provided the labor for the colony's many rice plantations.

ANALYSIS SKILL INTERPRETING CHARTS
About how many slaves lived in the English colonies in 1700 and in 1750?

The Carolinas and Georgia

Colonies were also established south of Virginia. In 1663 the English king, Charles II, gave much of the land between Virginia and Spanish Florida to eight of his supporters. At first Carolina was a single colony. However, the settlements were far apart, and it was hard to govern them. In 1712 the colony separated into North and South Carolina.

Most of the colonists in North Carolina were farmers who had moved south from Virginia. Colonists primarily from Europe settled South Carolina. Those who paid their own way received large grants of land, and some brought enslaved Africans with them. By 1730 about 20,000 enslaved Africans were living in the colony, compared to some 10,000 white settlers.

South Carolina's proprietors managed the colony poorly, and the British government bought it in 1719. The Crown then purchased North Carolina in 1729, making it a royal colony as well.

In 1732 King George II granted a charter to James Oglethorpe and other trustees to found Georgia. The king hoped that Georgia would shield Britain's other colonies from Spanish Florida. Oglethorpe wanted the new colony to be a place where debtors, who had been jailed for their debts in England, could make a new start. In 1733 Oglethorpe and 120 colonists, mostly from England, founded the city of Savannah.

Oglethorpe did not want Georgia to have large plantations owned by a few wealthy individuals. He wanted many small farmers. To reach this goal, Oglethorpe outlawed slavery and limited the size of land grants. Soon, however, the settlers grew unhappy with Oglethorpe's strict rules. In 1752 the British government made Georgia a royal colony with new laws. Coastal Georgia was soon filled with large rice plantations worked by thousands of slaves.

READING CHECK Finding Main Ideas What were some of the reasons colonists came to the southern colonies?

Differentiating Instruction

Struggling Readers

Materials: outline maps of eastern United States

1. To help students learn where each colony was in relation to the others, give students blank outline maps of the eastern United States.

2. Display a master outline map as well. As you begin your discussion of each colony, draw in the basic borders of that colony on the master map.

3. Have students follow your example by adding each colony's borders to their maps in turn. Briefly discuss the location of each colony, its location in relation to the other colonies, and how its location influenced life in the colony.

4. Have students write the names of the founders of each southern colony and the date the colony was founded on the map. Continue the activity through Sections 2 and 3. (For a map of the thirteen colonies, see p. 91.)

LS Visual/Spatial

Alternative Assessment Handbook, Rubric 20: Map Creation

Economies of the Southern Colonies

The economies of the southern colonies depended on agriculture. They also exported materials for building ships, such as wood and tar. Some colonies traded with local Indians for deerskins to sell.

The colonies had many small farms and some large plantations. Farms did well because the South enjoyed a warm climate and a long growing season. Many farms grew cash crops that were sold for profit. Tobacco, rice, and indigo—a plant used to make blue dye—were the most important cash crops.

The southern colonies' cash crops required a great deal of difficult work to grow and harvest. This meant a large workforce was needed. By the 1700s enslaved Africans, rather than indentured servants, had become the main source of labor.

Slavery was a viciously brutal condition for many inhabitants of the southern colonies. One former slave named **Olaudah Equiano** recorded his experiences.

"Tortures, murder, and every other imaginable barbarity ... are practiced upon the poor slaves with impunity [no punishment]. I hope the slave-trade will be abolished."

—Olaudah Equiano, from *The Interesting Narrative of the Life of Olaudah Equiano, or Gustavus Vassa, the African*

Most of the southern colonies passed **slave codes**, or laws to control slaves. Colonies with large numbers of slaves had the strictest slave codes. For example, South Carolina's slaveholders feared that slaves would revolt. As a result, South Carolina's code said slaves could not hold meetings or own weapons. Some colonies did not allow slaveholders to free their slaves.

READING CHECK **Summarizing** What role did slavery play in the southern plantation economy? How was it regulated?

SUMMARY AND PREVIEW In this section you read about life in the southern colonies. In the next section you will learn about the New England colonies.

Section 1 Assessment

go.hrw.com
Online Quiz
KEYWORD: SR8 HP3

Reviewing Ideas, Terms, and People

1. a. Describe How did **John Smith** improve conditions in Jamestown?
b. Explain What events led to a conflict between the **Jamestown** settlers and the Powhatan Confederacy?
2. a. Recall Why were **indentured servants** necessary in Virginia?
b. Evaluate What do you think was the most serious problem faced by settlers in Virginia? Why?
3. a. Identify Which colony was the first to promote religious tolerance?
b. Analyze Why did more enslaved Africans live in South Carolina than did white settlers?
c. Predict How might the colony of Georgia have been different if Oglethorpe's plan had succeeded?
4. a. Recall What was the purpose of **slave codes**?
b. Analyze Why were slaves in high demand in the southern colonies?

Critical Thinking

5. Summarizing Review your notes on the southern colonies. Then add a new column to your chart that summarizes the successes and/or failures of each colony.

Colony	Year	Why Founded	Successes/Failures

FOCUS ON WRITING

6. Gathering Some Ideas As you read this section, take notes on the early colonies of Virginia, Maryland, the Carolinas, and Georgia. Be sure to note what advantages they offered to settlers and what difficulties settlers faced. Start to think about the people who would be most likely to settle in the southern colonies.

THE ENGLISH COLONIES **77**

Section 1 Assessment Answers

1. a. forced the colonists to work harder and improve conditions; obtained help from Powhatan
b. Some colonists killed a Powhatan leader, and in response the Powhatan attacked the settlers.
2. a. High death rates led to labor shortages.
b. Answers will vary, but problems included lack of preparation, disease, famine, and conflicts with Native Americans.
3. a. Maryland
b. Large land grants there encouraged plantation owners to bring in many enslaved Africans.

c. Students should describe Oglethorpe's plan to emphasize small farms and help debtors.
4. a. to control slaves
b. main cash crops required lots of labor
5. Virginia—profit with tobacco; Maryland—first law supporting religious toleration; Carolinas—managed poorly and bought by British government; Georgia—settlers unhappy with Oglethorpe's laws so it was bought by British government
6. Advantages—South's warm climate, long growing season; disadvantages—high death rates.

Bellringer

If YOU were there . . . Use the **Daily Bellringer Transparency** to help students answer the question.

📖 Daily Bellringer Transparency, Section 2

The English Colonies — Daily Bellringer, Section 2

Review Section 1
In each of the following pairs of sentences, choose the sentence that is TRUE.
1. **a.** The colony of Virginia was an immediate success.
   b. The colony of Virginia faced many challenges in its early years.
2. **a.** Maryland was founded by Catholics escaping religious persecution.
   b. Maryland was founded by a group hoping to make a profit.
3. **a.** By the 1700s, enslaved Africans were the main source of labor in the southern colonies.
   b. By the 1700s, indentured servants were the main source of labor in the southern colonies.

Preview Section 2
If YOU were there . . .
You live in a town near London in the early 1700s. Some of your neighbors are starting new lives in the American colonies. You would like to go with them, but you cannot afford the cost of the trip. There is one way you can go, though. You can sign a paper promising to work as a servant for five years. Then you would be free—and in a new country?
Would you sign the paper and go to America?

Consider the PROS:
• get to go for free
• free room and board
• plenty of land in America

Consider the CONS:
• may not survive the trip
• may not survive the five years
• may end up worse off

Building Vocabulary

Preteach or review the following terms:

bicameral two houses (p. 81)

congregation church members (p. 82)

covenant promise (p. 80)

dissenters people who disagree with official opinions (p. 80)

Protestant Reformation religious movement that began in the 1520s as an effort to reform the Catholic Church (p. 78)

radical extreme (p. 82)

📖 **CRF:** Vocabulary Builder Activity, Section 2

Taking Notes

Have students copy the graphic organizer onto their own paper and then use it to take notes on the section. This activity will prepare students for the Section Assessment, in which they will complete a graphic organizer that builds on the information using a critical thinking skill.

The New England Colonies

What You Will Learn...

Main Ideas

1. The Pilgrims and Puritans came to America to avoid religious persecution.
2. Religion and government were closely linked in the New England colonies.
3. The New England economy was based on trade and farming.
4. Education was important in the New England colonies.

The Big Idea

English colonists traveled to New England to gain religious freedom.

Key Terms and People

Puritans, *p. 78*
Pilgrims, *p. 78*
immigrants, *p. 78*
Mayflower Compact, *p. 79*
Squanto, *p. 79*
John Winthrop, *p. 80*
Anne Hutchinson, *p. 82*

TAKING NOTES As you read, identify the reasons English colonists came to New England. Use a chart like the one below for your notes.

Reasons for Coming to New England	
Pilgrims	
Puritans	

If YOU were there...

You live in a town near London in the early 1700s. Some of your neighbors are starting new lives in the American colonies. You would like to go with them, but you cannot afford the cost of the trip. There is one way you can go, though. You can sign a paper promising to work as a servant for five years. Then you would be free—and in a new country!

Would you sign the paper and go to America?

> **BUILDING BACKGROUND** England's first successful colonial settlements were in Virginia. They were started mainly as business ventures. Other colonists in North America had many different reasons for leaving their homes. Many, like the Pilgrims and Puritans, came to have freedom to practice their religious beliefs. Others, like the person above, simply wanted a new way of life.

Pilgrims and Puritans

Religious tensions in England remained high after the Protestant Reformation. A Protestant group called the **Puritans** wanted to purify, or reform, the Anglican Church. The Puritans thought that bishops and priests had too much power over church members.

Pilgrims on the Move

The most extreme English Protestants wanted to separate from the Church of England. These Separatists formed their own churches and cut all ties with the Church of England. In response, Anglican leaders began to punish Separatists.

The **Pilgrims** were one Separatist group that left England in the early 1600s to escape persecution. The Pilgrims moved to the Netherlands in 1608. The Pilgrims were **immigrants**—people who have left the country of their birth to live in another country.

The Pilgrims were glad to be able to practice their religion freely. They were not happy, however, that their children were learn-

---

Teach the Big Idea

The New England Colonies

1. **Teach** Ask students the questions in the Main Idea boxes to teach this section.

2. **Apply** Draw a web graphic organizer for students to see. In a central circle, write *The New England Colonies.* In circles radiating out from this central circle, write the labels *Pilgrims, Puritans, Religion and Government, Economy,* and *Education.* Have each student copy the graphic organizer and enter five or more facts in each of the circles.
    Visual/Spatial

3. **Review** As you review the section's main ideas, have volunteers share the information they listed. Enter students' answers into the version of the graphic organizer that you drew.

4. **Practice/Homework** Have each student create a map of the New England colonies, label each colony, and note when it was founded and where the Pilgrims and Puritans settled. **Visual/Spatial**

   📖 Alternative Assessment Handbook, Rubrics 13: Graphic Organizers; and 20: Map Creation ing the Dutch language and culture. The Pilgrims feared that their children would forget their English traditions. The Pilgrims decided to leave Europe altogether. They formed a joint-stock company with some merchants and then received permission from England to settle in Virginia.

On September 16, 1620, a ship called the *Mayflower* left England with more than 100 men, women, and children aboard. Not all of these colonists were Pilgrims. However, Pilgrim leaders such as William Bradford sailed with the group.

The Mayflower Compact

After two months of rough ocean travel, the Pilgrims sighted land far north of Virginia. The Pilgrims knew that they would thus be outside the authority of Virginia's colonial government when they landed. Their charter would not apply. So, they decided to establish their own basic laws and social rules to govern the colony they would found.

On November 21, 1620, 41 of the male passengers on the ship signed the **Mayflower Compact**, a legal contract in which they agreed to have fair laws to protect the general good. The Compact represents one of the first attempts at self-government in the English colonies.

In late 1620 the Pilgrims landed at Plymouth Rock in present-day Massachusetts. The colonists struggled through the winter to build the Plymouth settlement. Nearly half of the tired Pilgrims died during this first winter from sickness and the freezing weather.

Pilgrims and Native Americans

In March 1621 a Native American named Samoset walked boldly into the colonists' settlement. He spoke in broken English. Samoset had learned some English from the crews of English fishing boats. He gave the Pilgrims useful information about the peoples and places of the area. He also introduced them to a Patuxet Indian named **Squanto**. Squanto had at one time lived in Europe and spoke English as well.

From Squanto the Pilgrims learned to fertilize the soil with fish remains. Squanto also helped the Pilgrims establish relations with the local Wampanoag Indians. Conditions in the Plymouth colony began to improve.

The Pilgrims invited Wampanoag chief Massasoit and 90 other guests to celebrate their harvest. This feast became known as the first Thanksgiving. For the event, the Pilgrims killed wild turkeys. This event marked the survival of the Pilgrims in the new colony.

Primary Source

HISTORICAL DOCUMENT
The Mayflower Compact

In November 1620, Pilgrim leaders aboard the Mayflower drafted the Mayflower Compact. This excerpt from the Mayflower Compact describes the principles of the Pilgrim colony's government.

We whose names are underwritten . . . having undertaken, for the glory of God, and advancement of the Christian faith, and the honour of our King and country, a voyage to plant the first colony in the northern parts of Virginia, do by these presents solemnly and mutually in the presence of God, and one of another, covenant and combine ourselves together into a civil body politic for our better ordering and preservation and furtherance of the ends aforesaid; and by virtue hereof, to enact, constitute, and frame such just and equal laws, ordinances, acts, constitutions, and offices . . . as shall be thought most meet and convenient for the general good of the colony unto which we promise all due . . . obedience.

> The Pilgrims describe the reasons they want to form a colony in North America.

> The Pilgrims promise to obey laws that help the whole colony.

by these presents: by this document
covenant: promise
civil body politic: group organized to govern

aforesaid: mentioned above
virtue: authority
ordinances: regulations
meet: fitting

ANALYSIS SKILL **ANALYZING PRIMARY SOURCES**

1. Why do you think the colonists felt the need to establish a government for themselves?
2. How do you think the Mayflower Compact influenced later governments in America?

● **Direct Teach** ●

Main Idea

❶ Pilgrims and Puritans

The Pilgrims and Puritans came to America to avoid religious persecution.

Explain What factors led the Pilgrims to leave England and settle in America? *religious persecution in England; desire to preserve English traditions*

Elaborate What role did chance play in the aid the Pilgrims received from Native Americans? *a large one because there just happened to be friendly Native Americans living nearby who could speak English*

📖 Political Cartoons Activities for United States History, Cartoon 1: The Mayflower

Primary Source
Reading Like a Historian
The Mayflower Compact Help students practice reading the document like historians. Ask the following:

• Who wrote the Mayflower Compact? What viewpoints and beliefs did the authors hold?

• How does this document fit into a time and place in history?

Teaching Tip

Remind students of the difference between immigrants and emigrants.

Critical Thinking: Analyzing   Above Level

Mayflower Compact Simulation

1. To help students understand the importance of government, ask them to imagine what society would be like without laws. What might occur if there were no speed limits or traffic signals?

2. Then organize students into small groups. Ask them to imagine that they were planning to found a space colony on Planet Virginia. Their spaceship has gone off course, though, and they have landed on an unknown planet, which they have named Planet Plymouth. Have each group create a list of rules to

govern its colony. Students should refer to the Mayflower Compact and discuss what the "greater good" is and how to determine it.

3. Ask representatives to share some of their group's rules with the class.

4. Conclude by having students discuss why Pilgrim leaders drafted the Mayflower Compact and the significance of the document.

LS Verbal/Linguistic

📄 Alternative Assessment Handbook, Rubric 11: Discussions

Answers

Analyzing Primary Sources 1. *They were outside the authority of Virginia's colonial government and wanted to maintain a rule of law to protect the public good.* **2.** *encouraged continued support of self-government*

Main Idea

❶ Pilgrims and Puritans

The Pilgrims and Puritans came to America to avoid religious persecution.

Describe What was family life like for the Pilgrims? *Families were the center of religious life, health care, and community well-being; all family members worked; women did household duties; men worked in the fields.*

Identify Points of View How did the Pilgrims view women and children? *Evidence suggests that they valued them, because Pilgrim families traveled together to North America, children were educated, and women had more legal rights than in England.*

Identify Cause and Effect What factors led to the Great Migration, and why is it significant? *economic hardship, political crisis, and religious persecution of Puritans in England; led Puritans to found English colonies in New England*

Info to Know

How the Pilgrims Got Their Name
William Bradford gave the name Pilgrims to the group aboard the *Mayflower*. Bradford took the word from the Christian Bible. In his journal, later published under the title *Of Plymouth Plantation*, he explained that the people seeking religious freedom knew they were Pilgrims.

Activity Have students look up the word *pilgrim* in a dictionary and discuss its meaning.

Answers

Reading Check *Religious persecution contributed to the Great Migration; Puritans believed they had a covenant with God to establish an ideal Christian community.*

80

Pilgrim Community

Although the Pilgrims overcame many problems, their small settlement still struggled. Most Pilgrims became farmers, but the farmland around their settlement was poor. They had hoped to make money by trading furs and by fishing. Unfortunately, fishing and hunting conditions were not good in the area. Some colonists traded corn with American Indians for beaver furs. The Pilgrims made little money but were able to form a strong community. The colony began to grow stronger in the mid-1620s after new settlers arrived and, as in Jamestown, colonists began to have more rights to farm their own land.

The Pilgrims' settlement was different from Virginia's in that it had many families. The Pilgrims taught their children to read and offered some education to their indentured servants. Families served as centers of religious life, health care, and community well-being.

All family members worked together to survive during the early years of the colony. Women generally cooked, spun and wove wool, and sewed clothing. They also made soap and butter, carried water, dried fruit, and cared for livestock. Men spent most of their time repairing tools and working in the fields. They also chopped wood and built shelters.

Women in the Colony

In Plymouth, women had more legal rights than they did in England. In England women were not allowed to make contracts, to sue, or to own property. In America, Pilgrim women had the right to sign contracts and to bring some cases before local courts. Widows could also own property.

From time to time, local courts recognized the ways women helped the business community. Widow Naomi Silvester received a large share of her husband's estate. The court called her "a frugal [thrifty] and laborious [hardworking] woman."

Puritans Leave England

During the 1620s England's economy suffered. Many people lost their jobs. The English king, Charles I, made the situation worse by raising taxes. This unpopular act led to a political crisis. At the same time, the Church of England began to punish Puritans because they were dissenters, or people who disagree with official opinions. King Charles refused to allow Puritans to criticize church actions.

Great Migration

These economic, political, and religious problems in England led to the Great Migration. Between 1629 and 1640 many thousands of English men, women, and children left England. More than 40,000 of these people moved to English colonies in New England and the Caribbean. In 1629, Charles granted a group of Puritans and merchants a charter to settle in New England. They formed the Massachusetts Bay Company.

In 1630 a fleet of ships carrying Puritan colonists left England for Massachusetts to seek religious freedom. They were led by **John Winthrop**. The Puritans believed that they had made a covenant, or promise, with God to build an ideal Christian community.

A New Colony

The Puritans arrived in New England well prepared to start their colony. They brought large amounts of tools and livestock with them. Like the Pilgrims, the Puritans faced little resistance from local American Indians. Trade with the Plymouth colony helped them too. In addition, the region around Boston had a fairly healthful climate. Thus, few Puritans died from sickness. All of these things helped the Massachusetts Bay Colony do well. By 1691, the Massachusetts Bay Colony had expanded to include the Pilgrims' Plymouth Colony.

READING CHECK **Summarizing** What role did religion play in the establishment of the Massachusetts Bay Colony?

Collaborative Learning   At Level

First Thanksgiving News Report

1. Organize students into small groups and ask them to imagine that they are TV reporters covering the first Thanksgiving in Plymouth Colony.

2. Have each group create a script for its on-the-spot news report. Group members should assign roles for a news anchor, an on-the-spot reporter, writers, and copy editors.

3. The group's news reports should explain who the Pilgrims are, why they founded Plymouth Colony, the struggles they have faced, how Native Americans have helped them, and why they are holding a Thanksgiving feast.
LS Interpersonal, Verbal/Linguistic

4. **Extend** Have each group conduct research on what the Pilgrims ate and drank in the 1620s and then create a "menu" for the first Thanksgiving meal. **LS Verbal/Linguistic**

   Alternative Assessment Handbook, Rubrics 14: Group Activity; 30: Research; and 37: Writing Assignments

Plymouth Colony

Several years later, the second colony, Duxbury, was founded.

Plymouth Bay

The Pilgrims landed in a region of forests, streams, and rocky soil.

Plymouth Colony was surrounded by stakes that formed a wall of protection. Outside the wall were colonists' crop fields.

INDIAN TRAIL

Abandoned Indian Village

Plymouth Colony (1620)

Plymouth Colony
New England Colonies
ATLANTIC OCEAN
70°W

ANALYSIS SKILLS ANALYZING VISUALS

In what ways were Plymouth Colony and the Indian village similar and different?

Religion and Government in New England

Massachusetts Bay Colony had to obey English laws. However, its charter provided more independence than did the royal charter of Virginia. For example, it created a General Court to help run the Massachusetts colony.

The Puritan colonists turned this court into a type of self-government to represent the needs of the people. Each town sent two or three delegates to the Court. After John Winthrop served as the colony's first governor, the General Court elected the governor and his assistants. In 1644 the General Court became a two-house, or bicameral, legislature.

Politics and religion were closely linked in Puritan New England. Government leaders were also church members, and ministers often had a great deal of power in Puritan communities. Male church members were the only colonists who could vote. Colonists became full members in the church by becoming what the Puritans called God's "elect," or chosen. Reaching this status was a difficult process. Individuals had to pass a public test to prove that their faith was strong.

THE ENGLISH COLONIES **81**

Main Idea

❷ Religion and Government in New England

Religion and government were closely linked in the New England colonies.

Explain How was Connecticut's government distinctive? *Connecticut had the Fundamental Orders of Connecticut, which allowed men who were not church members to vote and made the government more democratic.*

Compare What did Roger Williams and Anne Hutchinson have in common? *both forced to leave Massachusetts because of their religious views; formed new settlements in what became the colony of Rhode Island*

Make Inferences What effect do you think the witch trials had on Puritan communities? *possible answers—harmed community trust; created fear and anxiety; led some to unite against those they distrusted*

🎞 Quick Facts Transparency: Church and State

Answers

Biography *Her ideas differed from theirs, and she undermined their religious authority.*

BIOGRAPHY

Anne Hutchinson
1591–1643

In 1634 Anne Hutchinson emigrated with her family from England to the Massachusetts Bay Colony. After settling in Boston, she worked as a nurse and midwife. She also hosted a Bible-study class that met in her home. Over time, Hutchinson began to question the teachings of the local ministers. Meanwhile, her popularity grew.

After being banished from the colony, Hutchinson settled in Rhode Island and, later, Long Island. She died in an American Indian attack. Today we remember her as a symbol of the struggle for religious freedom.

Drawing Conclusions Why do you think church leaders disliked Hutchinson's ideas?

Church and State — QUICK FACTS

Religion Affected Government
- Government leaders were church members.
- Ministers had great authority.

Government Affected Religion
- Government leaders outlawed certain religions.
- Government leaders punished dissenters.

In 1636 minister Thomas Hooker and his followers left Massachusetts to help found Connecticut, another New England colony. In 1639 Hooker wrote the Fundamental Orders of Connecticut. This set of principles made Connecticut's government more democratic. For example, the Orders allowed men who were not church members to vote. As a result, some historians call Hooker the father of American democracy. The Fundamental Orders of Connecticut also outlined the powers of the general courts.

Not all Puritans shared the same religious views. Minister Roger Williams did not agree with the leadership of Massachusetts. He called for his church to separate completely from the other New England congregations. Williams also criticized the General Court for taking land from American Indians without paying them.

Puritan leaders worried that Williams's ideas might hurt the unity of the colony. They made him leave Massachusetts. Williams took his supporters to southern New England. They formed a new settlement called Providence. This settlement later developed into the colony of Rhode Island. In Providence, Williams supported the separation of the church from the state. He also believed in religious tolerance for all members of the community.

In Boston, an outspoken woman also angered Puritan church leaders. **Anne Hutchinson** publicly discussed religious ideas that some leaders thought were radical. For example, Hutchinson believed that people's relationship with God did not need guidance from ministers.

Hutchinson's views alarmed Puritans such as John Winthrop. Puritan leaders did not believe that women should be religious leaders. Puritan leaders put Hutchinson on trial for her ideas. The court decided to force her out of the colony. With a group of followers, Hutchinson helped found the new

82 CHAPTER 3

Differentiating Instruction

Below Level

Struggling Readers

1. To help students identify the key people, events, and issues related to the colonies of Connecticut and Rhode Island, draw the graphic organizer for students to see. Omit the blue, italicized answers.

2. Have each student copy and complete the graphic organizer. Review students' answers as a class. 🅛🅢 **Visual/Spatial**

📝 Alternative Assessment Handbook, Rubric 13: Graphic Organizers

Connecticut	Rhode Island	
Thomas Hooker: *minister; left Massachusetts with followers in 1636 to found Connecticut*	**Roger Williams:** • *called for his church to separate; criticized taking land from Native Americans without payment* • *forced to leave Massachusetts* • *founded settlement of Providence*	**Anne Hutchinson:** • *Her religious views alarmed Puritan leaders.* • *put on trial; then forced out of Massachusetts* • *founded settlement of Portsmouth on Aquidneck Island*
Fundamental Orders of Connecticut, 1639: *set of principles that made colonial government more democratic*		

colony of Portsmouth, later a part of the colony of Rhode Island.

Perhaps the worst community conflicts in New England involved the witchcraft trials of the early 1690s. The largest number of trials were held in Salem, Massachusetts. In Salem a group of girls had accused people of casting spells on them. The community formed a special court to judge the witchcraft cases. The court often pressured the suspected witches to confess. Before the trials had ended, the Salem witch trials led to 19 people being put to death.

READING CHECK **Identifying Cause and Effect** What led to religious disagreements among the Puritans, and what was the result?

New England Economy

Connecticut, Massachusetts, New Hampshire, and Rhode Island were very different from the southern colonies. The often harsh climate and rocky soil meant that few New England farms could grow cash crops. Most farming families grew crops and raised animals for their own use. There was thus little demand for farm laborers. Although some people held slaves, slavery did not become as important to this region.

Merchants

Trade was vital to New England's economy. New England merchants traded goods locally, with other colonies, and overseas. Many of them traded local products such as furs, pickled beef, and pork. Many merchants grew in power and wealth, becoming leading members of the New England colonies.

Fishing

Fishing became one of the region's leading industries. The rich waters off New England's coast served as home to many fish, including cod, mackerel, and halibut. Merchants exported dried fish. Colonists also began hunting for whales that swam close to shore. Whales were captured with harpoons, or spears, and dragged to shore. Whaling provided valuable oil for lighting.

Shipbuilding

Shipbuilding became an important industry in New England for several reasons. The area had plenty of forests that provided materials for shipbuilding. As trade—particularly in slaves—in the New England seaports grew, more merchant ships were built. The fishing industry also needed ships. New England shipyards made high-quality, valuable vessels. Ship owners sometimes even told their captains to sell the ship along with the cargo when they reached their destination.

Skilled Craftspeople

The northern economy needed skilled craftspeople. Families often sent younger sons to learn skilled trades such as blacksmithing, weaving, shipbuilding, and printing. The young boys who learned skilled trades were known as apprentices.

Apprentices lived with a master craftsman and learned from him. In exchange, the boys performed simple tasks. Apprentices promised to work for a master craftsman for a set number of years. They learned trades that were essential to the survival of the colonies. Apprentices received food and often clothing from the craftsmen. Gabriel Ginings was an apprentice in Portsmouth, Rhode Island. He received "sufficient food and raiment (clothing) suitable for such an apprentice," as his 1663 contract stated.

After a certain amount of time had passed, apprentices became journeymen. They usually traveled and learned new skills in their trade. Eventually they would become a master of the trade themselves.

READING CHECK **Categorizing** What types of jobs were common in the New England colonies?

THE IMPACT TODAY

Fishing remains an important industry in New England, earning hundreds of millions of dollars each year.

THE ENGLISH COLONIES **83**

❹ Education in the Colonies

Education was important in the New England colonies.

Recall What was the first college in New England, and why was it founded? *Harvard College; to ensure educated ministers for the future*

Contrast How did education in the New England colonies differ from that in Virginia? *New England—Many communities provided public schools to ensure that children could read the Bible; Virginia—Parents or private tutors taught children, and fewer people learned to read and write.*

📑 **CRF:** Literature Activity: American Colonial Poetry

● Review & Assess ●

Close

Briefly review how and why the Plymouth, Massachusetts Bay, Connecticut, and Rhode Island colonies were formed.

Review

🔗 Online Quiz, Section 2

Assess

SE Section 2 Assessment

📑 PASS: Section 2 Quiz

📑 Alternative Assessment Handbook

Reteach/Classroom Intervention

📑 Interactive Reader and Study Guide, Section 2

💿 Interactive Skills Tutor CD-ROM

Answers

Reading Check *Parents wanted their children to be able to read the Bible and to ensure that future generations had educated ministers.*

84

Education in the Colonies

Education was important in colonial New England. Mothers and fathers wanted their children to be able to read the Bible. The Massachusetts Bay Colony passed some of the first laws requiring parents to provide instruction for their children.

Public Education

THE IMPACT TODAY

Public schools remain the primary source of education for most U.S. children. Total enrollment today is around 50 million students.

To be sure that future generations would have educated ministers, communities established town schools. In 1647 the General Court of Massachusetts issued an order that a school be founded in every township of 50 families.

Schoolchildren often used the *New England Primer,* which had characters and stories from the Bible. They learned to read at the same time that they learned about the community's religious values.

The availability of schooling varied in the colonies. There were more schools in New England than in the other colonies where most children lived far from towns. These children had to be taught by their parents or by private tutors. Most colonial children stopped their education after the elementary grades. Many went to work, either on their family farm or away from home.

Higher Education

Higher education was also important to the colonists. In 1636 John Harvard and the General Court founded Harvard College. Harvard taught ministers and met the colony's need for higher education. The second college founded in the colonies, William and Mary, was established in Virginia in 1693.

By 1700 about 70 percent of men and 45 percent of women in New England could read and write. These figures were much lower in Virginia, where Jamestown was the only major settlement.

READING CHECK **Analyzing** Why was education important to the New England colonies?

SUMMARY AND PREVIEW In this section you learned about the role that religion played in the New England colonies. In the next section you'll learn about New York, New Jersey, and Pennsylvania.

Section 2 Assessment

go.hrw.com
Online Quiz
KEYWORD: SR8 HP3

Reviewing Ideas, Terms, and People

1. **a. Recall** Why did the **Pilgrims** and **Puritans** leave Europe for the Americas?
   b. Elaborate Do you think the Pilgrims could have survived without the assistance of **Squanto** and the Massasoit? Explain your answer.
2. **a. Describe** What role did the church play in Massachusetts?
   b. Analyze Why did some colonists disagree with the leaders of Massachusetts?
3. **a. Identify** Describe the economy in the New England colonies.
   b. Analyze Why do you think New England merchants became leading members of society?
4. **a. Describe** What steps did the Massachusetts Bay Colony take to promote education?
   b. Predict What are some possible benefits that New England's emphasis on education might bring?

Critical Thinking

5. **Identifying Cause and Effect** Review your notes on the reasons English colonists came to New England. Then copy the diagram below and use it to show how the colonists' experiences caused them to build certain types of colonies.

causes → effects

FOCUS ON WRITING ✏️

6. **Comparing Colonies** Take notes on the early New England colonies. Be sure to note what advantages they offered to settlers and what difficulties settlers faced. Put a star beside the colony or colonies you might use in your infomercial.

Section 2 Assessment Answers

1. **a.** to escape religious persecution
   b. Answers should show knowledge of the ways in which Native Americans aided the Pilgrims.
2. **a.** Religion was closely tied to government, ministers had a great deal of power, and only male church members could vote.
   b. They disagreed about different aspects of religion and how to treat Native Americans.
3. **a.** little reliance on cash crops; focus on trade, fishing, shipbuilding, and skilled crafts
   b. because they became wealthy and powerful

4. **a.** required parents to educate children, established town schools and colleges
   b. possible answers—well educated colonists, well run government, attracted more settlers
5. possible answer—cause: Puritans came to practice their religion freely; effect: politics and religion were closely linked
6. Students should include notes on the Pilgrims and Puritans and the Plymouth, Massachusetts Bay, Connecticut, and Rhode Island colonies.

The Middle Colonies

If YOU were there...

You are a farmer in southern Germany in 1730. Religious wars have torn your country apart for many years. Now you hear stories about a place in America where people of all religions are welcome. But the leaders of the colony—and many of its people—are English. You would not know their language or customs. Still, you would be free to live and worship as you like.

How would you feel about moving to a country full of strangers?

BUILDING BACKGROUND The middle section of the Atlantic coast offered good land and a moderate climate. Several prominent English people established colonies that promised religious freedom. To people like the settler above, these colonies promised a new life.

New York and New Jersey

The Dutch founded New Netherland in 1613 as a trading post for exchanging furs with the Iroquois. The center of the fur trade in New Netherland was the town of New Amsterdam on Manhattan Island. Generous land grants and religious tolerance soon brought Jews, French Huguenots, Puritans, and others to the colony. Director General **Peter Stuyvesant** (STY-vuh-suhnt) led the colony beginning in 1647.

Peter Stuyvesant was forced to surrender New Amsterdam to the English in 1664.

What You Will Learn...

Main Ideas

1. The English created New York and New Jersey from former Dutch territory.
2. William Penn established the colony of Pennsylvania.
3. The economy of the middle colonies was supported by trade and staple crops.

The Big Idea

People from many nations settled in the middle colonies.

Key Terms and People

Peter Stuyvesant, *p. 85*
Quakers, *p. 86*
William Penn, *p. 86*
staple crops, *p. 87*

TAKING NOTES As you read, take notes on which nation founded each of the middle colonies. Record your notes in a chart like the one shown below.

Colony	Founding Nation
New York	
New Jersey	
Pennsylvania	

Main Idea

❶ New York and New Jersey

The English created New York and New Jersey from former Dutch territory.

Recall What was the population of New Jersey like? *diverse, with Dutch, Swedes, Finns, and Scots*

Draw Conclusions Why did New York have a Dutch influence? *The Dutch founded the settlement that later became the colony of New York.*

📄 **CRF:** Primary Source Activity: Journal of Sarah Kemble Knight

🗄 Quick Facts Transparency: Characteristics of the Middle Colonies

Main Idea

❷ Penn's Colony

William Penn established the colony of Pennsylvania.

Identify What was the capital of Pennsylvania, and what did its name mean? *Philadelphia; "the city of brotherly love"*

Summarize What beliefs did Quakers hold? *equality of men and women before God, religious tolerance, non-violence*

Answers

Biography *In keeping with his beliefs, he supported religious tolerance, immigrants, and fair dealings with Native Americans.*

Reading Check (left) *Both had diverse populations and were middle colonies; fur trade was important.*

Reading Check (right) *to provide a safe place for Quakers and religious freedom for all Christians; established an elected assembly to govern the area, which served as an example of representative self-government*

Characteristics of the Middle Colonies QUICK FACTS

Social
- New York: Dutch influence
- New Jersey: diverse population
- Pennsylvania: founded by Quakers

Economic
- successful farming of staple crops
- work force of slaves and indentured servants
- active trade with Britain and West Indies

THE IMPACT TODAY

Today New York City is the largest city in the United States, with more than 8 million people.

In 1664 an English fleet captured the undefended colony of New Amsterdam without firing a single shot. New Netherland was renamed New York, and New Amsterdam became New York City.

Soon after the English conquest in 1664, the Duke of York made Sir George Carteret and Lord John Berkeley proprietors of New Jersey. This colony occupied lands between the Hudson and Delaware rivers. It had a diverse population, including Dutch, Swedes, Finns, and Scots. The fur trade was important to the economies of New York and New Jersey through the end of the 1600s.

READING CHECK **Comparing** How were New York and New Jersey similar?

BIOGRAPHY
William Penn
1644–1718

William Penn was born in London as the son of a wealthy admiral. Penn joined the Quakers in 1666 and became an active preacher and writer of religious works. He supported toleration of dissenters.

In 1681 he received a charter to establish a new colony called Pennsylvania. There, Penn put his beliefs into practice. He insisted on fair dealings with local American Indians, welcomed immigrants, and promised religious toleration.

Making Generalizations How did Penn's ideas influence the rules of the colony?

Penn's Colony

The Society of Friends, or the **Quakers**, made up one of the largest religious groups in New Jersey. Quakers did not follow formal religious practices and dressed plainly. They believed in the equality of men and women before God. They also supported nonviolence and religious tolerance for all people. At the time, many Quaker beliefs and practices shocked most Christians. As a result, Quakers were persecuted in both England and America.

One proprietor of the New Jersey colony was a Quaker named **William Penn**. Penn wished to found a larger colony under his own control that would provide a safe home for Quakers. In 1681 King Charles II agreed to grant Penn a charter to begin a colony west of New Jersey.

Penn's colony, known as Pennsylvania, grew rapidly. Penn limited his own power and established an elected assembly. He also promised religious freedom to all Christians. His work made Pennsylvania an important example of representative self-government— a government that reflects its citizens' will— in the colonies.

Penn named the capital of his colony Philadelphia, which means "the city of brotherly love." In 1682 the Duke of York sold Penn a region to the south of Pennsylvania. This area, called Delaware, remained part of Pennsylvania until 1776.

READING CHECK **Finding Main Ideas** Why did William Penn establish Pennsylvania, and how did he influence its government?

86 CHAPTER 3

Critical Thinking: Analyzing Information
Above Level

European Influence in the Middle Colonies
Research Required

Background Many Dutch settlers remained in New York after it became an English colony. Their influence can still be seen today. For example, the Dutch contributed words such as *boss*, *cookie* (from the Dutch word *koekje*), and *stoop* to the English language.

1. Discuss with students the diversity of the people who settled the middle colonies. Ask students to identify some of the different groups who settled in the middle colonies during the early and mid-1600s.

2. Next, have students conduct research on the region of the middle colonies today to find current examples of early European influence. For example, students might look for place-names, words, or foods that show the influence of different groups of early colonists.

3. Have students make a list of their findings. Ask volunteers to share some of the items on their lists with the class.

📄 Alternate Assessment Handbook, Rubric 30: Research

Economy of the Middle Colonies

The middle colonies combined characteristics of the New England and southern colonies. With a good climate and rich land, farmers there could grow large amounts of **staple crops**—crops that are always needed. These crops included wheat, barley, and oats. Farmers also raised livestock.

Slaves were somewhat more important to the middle colonies than they were to New England. They worked in cities as skilled laborers, such as blacksmiths and carpenters. Other slaves worked on farms, onboard ships, and in the growing shipbuilding industry. However, indentured servants largely filled the middle colonies' growing labor needs. Between 1700 and 1775 about 135,000 indentured servants came to the middle colonies. About half of them moved to Pennsylvania. By 1760 Philadelphia had become the largest British colonial city. Other cities in the middle colonies, such as New York City, also grew quickly.

Trade was important to the economy of the middle colonies. Merchants in Philadelphia and New York City exported colonial goods to markets in Britain and the West Indies. These products included wheat from New York, Pennsylvania, and New Jersey.

Throughout the colonies, women made important contributions to the economy. They ran farms and businesses such as clothing and grocery stores, bakeries, and drugstores. Some women also practiced medicine and worked as nurses and midwives. However, colonial laws and customs limited women's economic opportunities.

Most colonial women worked primarily in the home. Married women managed households and raised children. Sometimes they earned money for their families by selling products like butter. They also made money through services such as washing clothes.

FOCUS ON READING
You can tell **staple crops** means "crops that are always needed" because of the dash between the vocabulary term and the definition.

READING CHECK Finding the Main Idea
On what were the economies of the middle colonies based?

SUMMARY AND PREVIEW In this section you learned about the middle colonies. In the next section you will read about colonial government, the slave trade, and conflicts that arose in the English colonies.

Main Idea

❸ Economy of the Middle Colonies

The economy of the middle colonies was supported by trade and staple crops.

Summarize How did women contribute to the middle colonies' economy? *ran farms and businesses, practiced medicine, worked as nurses and midwives*

Make Inferences Why do you think the middle colonies depended more on indentured servants than slaves for labor? *possible answers—Many colonists, such as Quakers, may have opposed slavery for religious or other reasons; indentured servants may have been easier to obtain and less expensive.*

Section 3 Assessment

go.hrw.com
Online Quiz
KEYWORD: SR8 HP3

Reviewing Ideas, Terms, and People

1. a. Describe Name the middle colonies. Where were they located?
b. Draw Inferences What led to the diverse populations of New York and New Jersey?
2. a. Identify Who are the **Quakers**?
b. Analyze How did **William Penn** attempt to create a colonial government that would be fair to all?
3. a. Describe What different types of jobs did slaves in the middle colonies hold?
b. Evaluate In what ways were women essential to the middle colonies?

Critical Thinking

4. Sequencing Review your notes about which nation founded each middle colony. Then complete the time line below by listing the event that occurred on each of the dates on the time line.

1613   1647   1664   1681

FOCUS ON WRITING

5. Comparing Colonies You've just read about early colonies in New York, New Jersey, and Pennsylvania. Think about the advantages they offered to settlers and what difficulties settlers faced. In your notes, put a star beside one of the colonies you might use in your infomercial.

THE ENGLISH COLONIES **87**

Close

Discuss why people from many nations settled in the middle colonies and how they supported themselves.

Review

Online Quiz, Section 3

Assess

SE Section 3 Assessment
PASS: Section 3 Quiz
Alternative Assessment Handbook

Reteach-Classroom Intervention

Interactive Reader and Study Guide, Section 3
Interactive Skills Tutor CD-ROM

Section 3 Assessment Answers

1. a. New York—Manhattan Island and former colony of New Netherland; New Jersey—between Hudson and Delaware rivers; Pennsylvania—west of New Jersey
b. religious tolerance, generous land grants

2. a. a religious group known as the Society of Friends, which supported religious tolerance, non-violence, and equality of men and women
b. He limited his own power, established an elected assembly that reflected the citizens' will, and provided religious freedom to all Christians.

3. a. worked as skilled laborers, farm laborers, and on board ships and in the shipbuilding industry
b. ran farms and businesses, practiced medicine, earned money for their families by selling goods

4. 1613—Dutch found New Netherland as a trading post; 1647—Peter Stuyvesant leads the colony of New Netherland; 1664—English capture the colony and rename it New York; 1681—King Charles II grants Penn charter

5. Students may note advantages such as diversity, religious freedom, good farmland, and trade.

Answers

Reading Check *trade, staple crops*

87

Activity Interpreting Maps Have students describe how physical features influenced colonial settlement patterns. *Ports, rivers, and mountains influenced the location of early colonial settlements.* Then have students examine the maps in Section 4. Have students compare the locations of early French settlements and forts to those of the English colonies and discuss reasons for the differences. *(Early French exploration, waterways, and trade shaped early French settlement along the St. Lawrence River, Great Lakes, and Mississippi River.)*
LS Visual/Spatial

Connect to Geography

The Appalachians The Appalachian Mountains extend in a series of almost continuous mountain ranges from the Canadian province of Newfoundland to central Alabama. Although long, the Appalachian chain is quite narrow, rarely exceeding 100 miles in width. The range's highest peak—Mount Mitchell in North Carolina—reaches 6,684 feet above sea level. Its lowest areas are in Massachusetts and Connecticut.

Linking to Today

The Appalachian Trail While early pioneers struggled through dense forests and over rugged land in the Appalachians, today hikers walk the Appalachian Trail for fun. This foot-path runs some 2,100 miles from Mount Katahdin in Maine to Springer Mountain in Georgia. The longest continuous footpath in North America, the Appalachian Trail runs through 14 states, seven national forests, and four national parks.

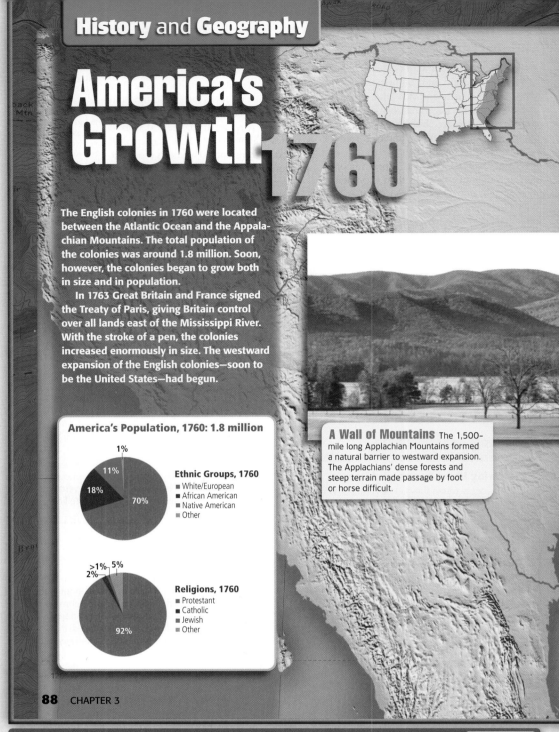

History and Geography

America's Growth 1760

The English colonies in 1760 were located between the Atlantic Ocean and the Appalachian Mountains. The total population of the colonies was around 1.8 million. Soon, however, the colonies began to grow both in size and in population.

In 1763 Great Britain and France signed the Treaty of Paris, giving Britain control over all lands east of the Mississippi River. With the stroke of a pen, the colonies increased enormously in size. The westward expansion of the English colonies—soon to be the United States—had begun.

A Wall of Mountains The 1,500-mile long Applachian Mountains formed a natural barrier to westward expansion. The Applachians' dense forests and steep terrain made passage by foot or horse difficult.

America's Population, 1760: 1.8 million

Ethnic Groups, 1760
- White/European
- African American
- Native American
- Other

1%
11%
18%
70%

Religions, 1760
- Protestant
- Catholic
- Jewish
- Other

>1%
2%
5%
92%

88 CHAPTER 3

Social Studies Skill: Interpreting Maps

At Level

Research Required

U.S. Cities Today

Materials: outline maps of the United States

1. Have students conduct research on the 10 most populous U.S. cities today.

2. Give students blank outline maps of the United States or have them draw their own. Have students mark the locations and populations of the 10 cities.

3. Then have students use their maps and the above map to answer the following questions:
   - What are the three largest U.S. cities today? *New York, Los Angeles, Chicago*

- What are some possible reasons these three cities are so populated? *possible answers— available jobs, resources, trade and business, culture and lifestyle*

- How do the locations of these cities differ from the locations of the three largest cities in 1760? *They are spread across the continent instead of all being located on the East Coast.*
LS Visual/Spatial

Alternative Assessment Handbook, Rubrics 20: Map Creation; and 21: Map Reading

Natural Harbors The largest cities in the colonies, such as Philadelphia, New York, and Boston, grew where the best natural ports were. Ships were vital to the colonies: for the growing fishing industry, for overseas trade, and to bring more settlers to the new land.

Boston Harbor provided natural protection for ships.

Boston, population 16,000

New York, population 25,000

Philadelphia, population 25,000

ME
NH
NY
MA
CT
RI
PA
NJ
MD
DE
VA
NC
SC
GA

APPALACHIAN MOUNTAINS

Mississippi River

ATLANTIC OCEAN

40° N

New England colonies
Middle colonies
Southern colonies

0   150   300 Miles
0   150   300 Kilometers

N E S W

A Flood of People The colonial population doubled between 1750 and 1770. Roughly half of the immigrants to the colonies were English. But the second-largest group of immigrants had no choice in the matter—they were enslaved people from Africa.

Tropic of Cancer

90° W   70° W

GEOGRAPHY SKILLS INTERPRETING MAPS

1. **Location** Where were the colonies' largest cities located at this time?
2. **Human-Environment Interaction** How did mountains and seas influence the location of the colonies?

THE ENGLISH COLONIES **89**

History and Geography

Info to Know

Westward Expansion As the map shows, early European colonists settled mainly along the East Coast. West of the Appalachians, fur traders and a few forts were the only signs of Europeans. By the 1750s, however, European pioneers were moving into the Ohio River valley. Pioneers found that the valley provided fertile soil for farming and plenty of wild game. After the French and Indian War, pioneers began crossing the Appalachians in greater numbers. The Proclamation of 1763, which prohibited settlement west of the Appalachians, had little effect. The Proclamation proved difficult to enforce, and pioneers ignored it. The lure of the West proved irresistible.

Linking to Today

New York City As the map shows, New York was one of the largest cities in the English colonies in 1760. Today the city is the nation's largest, with a population of more than 7 million. New York City serves as a cultural and economic center and is one of the most culturally diverse cities in the United States. The city now consists of five boroughs—the Bronx, Brooklyn, Manhattan, Staten Island, and Queens.

Making Inferences Why do you think New York City has remained a major population center? *possible answer— Its strategic location serves as a gateway for incoming immigrants and trade. It has also become a center for many major American industries.*

Critical Thinking: Analyzing Information

At Level

Pioneer Letter

1. Ask students to imagine that they live in the English colonies in 1760. Their families have recently joined a group of pioneers and settled west of the Appalachian Mountains in the Ohio River valley.

2. Have students write letters to relatives or friends in Philadelphia describing why their families have moved west and some of the hardships they faced during the trip. If time allows, have students conduct research to learn more about pioneers and westward expansion in the 1770s.

3. Have volunteers read their letters to the class.

4. **Extend** Have students conduct research on Daniel Boone and his role in westward expansion during this period. Each student should write a biographical sketch of Boone.

LS Verbal/Linguistic

Alternative Assessment Handbook, Rubrics 4: Biographies; and 25: Personal Letters

Answers

Interpreting Maps 1. *along the mid- and northern Atlantic coast;* **2.** *Immigrants arrived in North America by boat and landed on the East coast, so many colonists settled along the coast; the Appalachian Mountains formed a barrier to westward movement and settlement.*

89

Bellringer

If YOU were there . . . Use the **Daily Bellringer Transparency** to help students answer the question.

📔 Daily Bellringer Transparency, Section 4

The English Colonies — Daily Bellringer — Section 4

Review Section 3
In each pair below, select the colony or place that came first.
1. Colony of Pennsylvania OR Colony of Delaware
2. New York City OR Philadelphia
3. Colony of New Jersey OR Colony of Delaware
4. New Amsterdam OR New York City

Preview Section 4
If YOU were there ...
Your family migrated to America in the 1700s and started a small farm in western Pennsylvania. Now, more and more people are moving in. You would like to move farther west, into the Ohio River valley. But a new law says you cannot move west of the mountains because it is too dangerous. Still, you are restless and want more land and more freedom.
Why might you decide to break the law and move west?

Consider what you WANT:
• good farmland
• open space

Consider what you THINK:
• about the law
• about English government

Review Answers: 1. Colony of Pennsylvania; 2. New York City; 3. Colony of New Jersey; 4. New Amsterdam
Copyright © by Holt, Rinehart and Winston. All rights reserved.

Building Vocabulary

Preteach or review the following terms:

backcountry thinly settled rural area (p. 97)

casualties captured, injured, or killed soldiers (p. 96)

dominion an area governed by a ruler (p. 91)

Privy Council a council or group that advises a ruler (p. 90)

revivals religious gatherings where people came together to hear sermons (p. 94)

📝 **CRF:** Vocabulary Builder Activity, Section 4

Taking Notes

Have students copy the graphic organizer onto their own paper and then use it to take notes on the section. This activity will prepare students for the Section Assessment, in which they will complete a graphic organizer that builds on the information using a critical thinking skill.

Life in the English Colonies

What You Will Learn...

Main Ideas

1. Colonial governments were influenced by political changes in England.
2. English trade laws limited free trade in the colonies.
3. The Great Awakening and the Enlightenment led to ideas of political equality among many colonists.
4. The French and Indian War gave England control of more land in North America.

The Big Idea

The English colonies continued to grow despite many challenges.

Key Terms and People

town meeting, *p. 91*
English Bill of Rights, *p. 91*
triangular trade, *p. 93*
Middle Passage, *p. 94*
Jonathan Edwards, *p. 94*
Great Awakening, *p. 94*
Enlightenment, *p. 95*
Pontiac, *p. 97*

TAKING NOTES As you read, take notes on the following developments affected the growing colonies.

Development	Effects
Establishment of local government	
Political change in England	
Trade laws	
Great Awakening/ Enlightenment	
French and Indian War	

If YOU were there...

Your family migrated to America in the 1700s and started a small farm in western Pennsylvania. Now, more and more people are moving in. You would like to move farther west, into the Ohio River valley. But a new law says you cannot move west of the mountains because it is too dangerous. Still, you are restless and want more land and more freedom.

Why might you decide to break the law and move west?

BUILDING BACKGROUND When they moved to America, the English colonists brought their ideas about government. They expected to have the same rights as citizens in England. However, many officials in England wanted tight control over the colonies. As a result, some colonists, like this family, were unhappy with the policies of colonial governments.

Colonial Governments

The English colonies in North America all had their own governments. Each government was given power by a charter. The English monarch had ultimate authority over all of the colonies. A group of royal advisers called the Privy Council set English colonial policies.

Colonial Governors and Legislatures

Each colony had a governor who served as head of the government. Most governors were assisted by an advisory council. In royal colonies the English king or queen selected the governor and the council members. In proprietary colonies, the proprietors chose all of these officials. In a few colonies, such as Connecticut, the people elected the governor.

In some colonies the people also elected representatives to help make laws and set policy. These officials served on assemblies. Each colonial assembly passed laws that had to be approved first by the advisory council and then by the governor.

Teach the Big Idea

Life in the English Colonies

1. **Teach** Ask students the questions in the Main Idea boxes to teach this section.

2. **Apply** Organize students into four groups and assign each group one of this section's subsections, indicated by the blue heads. Have each group develop a detailed outline of its subsection. Then ask each group to exchange its outline with another group and write five questions and answers about the information in that outline. �LS **Verbal/Linguistic**

3. **Review** Collect students' questions and use them to review the section and quiz the class.

4. **Practice/Homework** Ask students to predict how the British colonists reacted to the Proclamation of 1763. Then have students imagine that they are colonists and write letters to the editor of a colonial newspaper expressing their views on the new law. �LS **Verbal/Linguistic**

📝 Alternative Assessment Handbook, Rubrics 37: Writing Assignments; and 41: Writing to Express

Established in 1619, Virginia's assembly was the first colonial legislature in North America. At first it met as a single body, but it was later split into two houses. The first house was known as the Council of State. The governor's advisory council and the London Company selected its members. The House of Burgesses was the assembly's second house. The members were elected by colonists.

In New England the center of politics was the **town meeting**. In town meetings people talked about and decided on issues of local interest, such as paying for schools.

In the southern colonies, people typically lived farther away from one another. Therefore, many decisions were made at the county level. The middle colonies used both county meetings and town meetings to make laws.

Political Change in England

In 1685 James II became king of England. He was determined to take more control over the English government, both in England and in the colonies.

James believed that the colonies were too independent. In 1686 he united the northern colonies under one government called the Dominion of New England. James named Sir Edmund Andros royal governor of the Dominion. The colonists disliked Andros because he used his authority to limit the powers of town meetings.

English Bill of Rights

Parliament replaced the unpopular King James and passed the **English Bill of Rights** in 1689. This act reduced the powers of the English monarch. At the same time, Parliament gained power. As time went on, the colonists valued their own right to elect representatives to decide local issues. Following these changes, the colonies in the Dominion quickly formed new assemblies and charters.

READING CHECK Finding Main Ideas How did the English Bill of Rights affect the colonists?

The Thirteen Colonies

Thirteen Colonies
ATLANTIC OCEAN

NEW FRANCE

MAINE (PART OF MASS. COLONY)

Land claimed by New York and New Hampshire

NEW HAMPSHIRE

MASSACHUSETTS

NEW YORK

RHODE ISLAND

PENNSYLVANIA

CONNECTICUT

NEW JERSEY

MARYLAND

DELAWARE

APPALACHIAN MOUNTAINS

VIRGINIA

NORTH CAROLINA

ATLANTIC OCEAN

SOUTH CAROLINA

GEORGIA

New England colonies
Middle colonies
Southern colonies

0   100   200 Miles
0   100   200 Kilometers

GEOGRAPHY SKILLS **INTERPRETING MAPS**

1. **Location** Where were the New England Colonies located in relation to the other colonies?
2. **Human-Environment Interaction** What natural feature marked the western boundary of the Southern colonies?

THE ENGLISH COLONIES **91**

• • **Direct Teach** • •

Main Idea

❶ Colonial Governments

Colonial governments were influenced by political changes in England.

Recall What served as the center of politics in New England? *town meetings, in which people decided local issues*

Analyze What forms of representative government did the English colonists begin to develop? *Some colonies had elected legislative assemblies, such as Virginia's House of Burgesses.*

Draw Conclusions What opinion do you think colonists in New England had of the Dominion of New England? *Most of them probably disliked it because the dominion limited the powers of town meetings.*

Map Transparency: The Thirteen Colonies

Answers

Interpreting Maps *1. to the north; 2. Appalachian Mountains*

Reading Check *They formed new assemblies and charters and increasingly valued their right to elect representatives to decide local issues.*

Differentiating Instruction

Below Level

Struggling Readers

1. To help students compare and contrast the different forms of colonial government, draw the graphic organizer. Omit the blue answers.

2. Have students copy and complete the graphic organizer. Review the answers as a class.

3. Then have students discuss how the English Bill of Rights affected colonial government.

LS **Verbal/Linguistic, Visual/Spatial**

Alternative Assessment Handbook, Rubric 13: Graphic Organizers

Monarch	ultimate authority over all English colonies
Privy Council	royal advisors; set English colonial policies
Governors	appointed by Crown or proprietors, or elected by people; served as head of colonial government; assisted by advisory councils
Assemblies	elected representatives; assisted in making laws and setting policies; had to get approval from advisory council and governor
Town Meetings	center of politics in New England; decided local issues
Courts	provided control over local affairs; protected individual freedoms

Colonial Courts

Colonial courts made up another important part of colonial governments. Whenever possible, colonists used the courts to control local affairs. The courts generally reflected the beliefs of their local communities. For example, many laws in Massachusetts enforced the Puritans' religious beliefs. Laws based on the Bible set the standard for the community's conduct.

Sometimes colonial courts also protected individual freedoms. For example, in 1733 officials arrested John Peter Zenger for printing a false statement that damaged the reputation of the governor of New York. Andrew Hamilton, Zenger's attorney, argued that Zenger could publish whatever he wished as long as it was true. Jury members believed that colonists had a right to voice their ideas openly and found him not guilty.

THE IMPACT TODAY
The Zenger case was the first major case establishing freedom of the press in British North America. Today this is an important right of all Americans.

READING CHECK Analyzing Information
Why were colonial assemblies and colonial courts created, and what did they do?

English Trade Laws

One of England's main reasons for founding and controlling its American colonies was to earn money from trade. In the late 1600s England, like most western European nations, practiced mercantilism, a system of creating and maintaining wealth through carefully controlled trade. A country gained wealth if it had fewer imports—goods bought from other countries—than exports—goods sold to other countries.

To support this system of mercantilism, between 1650 and 1696 Parliament passed a series of Navigation Acts limiting colonial trade. For example, the Navigation Act of 1660 forbade colonists from trading specific items such as sugar and cotton with any country other than England. The act also required colonists to use English ships to transport goods. Parliament later passed other acts that required all trade goods to pass through English ports, where duties, or import taxes, were added to the items.

Triangular Trade

Trade between Britain and its colonies took a triangular shape. Different goods were transported on the routes of the triangles and traded at ports for local goods.

manufactured goods

sugar

sugar, molasses

beef, flour

rum, iron

slaves

GEOGRAPHY SKILLS INTERPRETING MAPS
1. **Movement** Why is the movement of goods shown on the map called the triangular trade?
2. **Location** A farmer who wanted to grow sugar cane would most likely live where?

92 CHAPTER 3

Cross-Discipline Activity: Government

At Level

Reporting the Zenger Trial

Background On November 5, 1733, John Zenger published his first issue of the *New York Weekly Journal*, in which he criticized New York's colonial governor, John Cosby. As publisher, Zenger was legally responsible for the newspaper's contents. The paper's attacks on Cosby continued for a year, and in November 1734, Zenger was arrested for libel.

1. Provide students with the background of the Zenger trial.

2. Have each student write a headline and a newspaper article about the Zenger trial. In their articles, students should stress the importance of freedom of the press.

3. Have volunteers share their headlines and articles with the class. Have students discuss why freedom of the press continues to be an important right. **LS Verbal/Linguistic**

Alternative Assessment Handbook, Rubric 42: Writing to Inform

England claimed that the Navigation Acts were good for the colonies. After all, the colonies had a steady market in England for their goods. But not all colonists agreed. Many colonists wanted more freedom to buy or sell goods wherever they could get the best price. Local demand for colonial goods was small compared to foreign demand.

Despite colonial complaints, the trade restrictions continued into the 1700s. Some traders turned to smuggling, or illegal trading. They often smuggled sugar, molasses, and rum into the colonies from non-English islands in the Caribbean. Parliament responded with the Molasses Act of 1733, which placed duties on these items. British officials, however, rarely carried out this law.

By the early 1700s English merchants were trading around the world. Most American merchants traded directly with Great Britain or the West Indies. By importing and exporting goods such as sugar and tobacco, some American merchants became wealthy.

Triangular Trade

Trade between the American colonies and Great Britain was not direct. Rather, it generally took the form of **triangular trade** —a system in which goods and slaves were traded among the Americas, Britain, and Africa. There were several routes of the triangular trade. In one route colonists exchanged goods like beef and flour with plantation owners in the West Indies for sugar, some of which they shipped to Britain. The sugar was then exchanged for manufactured products to be sold in the colonies. Colonial merchants traveled great distances to find the best markets.

BIOGRAPHY

Olaudah Equiano
1745–1797

Olaudah Equiano was born in Africa in present-day Nigeria. In 1756 he was sold into slavery. Equiano survived the Middle Passage, traveling in a slave ship across the Atlantic. After arriving in the colonies, a Virginia planter purchased him and again sold him to a British naval officer. While working as a sailor, Equiano eventually earned enough money to purchase his own freedom in 1766. Equiano later settled in England and devoted himself to ending slavery.

Analyzing Information How did Equiano gain his freedom?

"I received such a salutation [smell] in my nostrils, as I had never experienced in my life; . . . I became so sick and low that I was not able to eat . . . The groans of the dying, rendered [made] the whole a scene of horror almost inconceivable [unbelievable]."

—Olaudah Equiano, from *The Interesting Narrative of the Life of Olaudah Equiano, or Gustavus Vassa, the African*

93

Main Idea

❸ Great Awakening and Enlightenment

The Great Awakening and the Enlightenment led to ideas of political equality among many colonists.

Define Describe the Great Awakening in your own words. *A religious movement that swept through the colonies in the 1730s and 1740s.*

Draw Conclusions How did John Locke's beliefs influence colonial society? *His ideas about natural rights, such as equality and liberty, began to influence colonial leaders.*

📖 **CRF:** Primary Source Activity: Sinners in the Hands of an Angry God

Biography

George Whitefield (1714–1770)

George Whitefield was born in Gloucester, England, and educated at Oxford. He experienced a strong religious awakening during his high school and college years, which he called a "new birth." He believed that every truly religious person needs to experience a rebirth in Jesus Christ, and preached this message throughout America and Great Britain.

Answers

The Great Awakening *Sermons about spiritual equality led to some demands for more political equality.*

Reading Check *As farmers began to rely less on indentured servants, they needed more slaves to work their farms. Slave traders placed as many slaves on ships as possible to increase profits, which created the terrifying and deadly conditions of the passage.*

The Great Awakening

George Whitefield gives a powerful sermon during the Great Awakening. Ministers like Whitefield emphasized personal religious experiences over official church rules. They also allowed ordinary church members—whatever their race, class, or gender—to play a role in services. The value placed on individuals of all types during the Great Awakening helped shape American political ideas about who should have a say in government.

How do you think religious freedom led to political freedom?

Middle Passage

One version of the triangular trade began with traders exchanging rum for slaves on the West African coast. The traders then sold the enslaved Africans in the West Indies for molasses or brought them to sell in the mainland American colonies.

The slave trade brought millions of Africans across the Atlantic Ocean in a voyage called the **Middle Passage**. This was a terrifying and deadly journey that could last as long as three months.

Enslaved Africans lived in a space not even three feet high. Slave traders fit as many slaves as possible on board so they could earn greater profits. Thousands of captives died on slave ships during the Middle Passage. In many cases, they died from diseases such as smallpox. As farmers began to use fewer indentured servants, slaves became even more valuable.

READING CHECK **Identifying Cause and Effect** What factors caused the slave trade to grow? How did this affect conditions on the Middle Passage?

Great Awakening and Enlightenment

In the early 1700s revolutions in both religious and nonreligious thought transformed the Western world. These movements began in Europe and affected life in the American colonies.

Great Awakening

After years of population growth, religious leaders wanted to spread religious feeling throughout the colonies. In the late 1730s these ministers began holding revivals, emotional gatherings where people came together to hear sermons.

Many American colonists experienced "a great awakening" in their religious lives. This **Great Awakening**—a religious movement that swept through the colonies in the 1730s and 1740s—changed colonial religion. It also affected social and political life. **Jonathan Edwards** of Massachusetts was one of the most important leaders of the Great Awakening. His dramatic sermons told

Critical Thinking: Finding Main Ideas
At Level

Great Awakening and Enlightenment

1. Discuss with students the significance of the Great Awakening and the Enlightenment.

2. Create a chart with two columns. Label one column *Great Awakening* and the other column *Enlightenment*. Have students copy the chart.

3. In the columns, students should write their own definitions of the movements and identify one or more of their key figures.

4. Next, have students list examples of how each movement affected political and social views in the English colonies.

5. Review students' answers as a class. Conclude by having students discuss the effects of the Great Awakening and the Enlightenment.

LS **Verbal/Linguistic**

📖 Alternative Assessment Handbook, Rubric 7: Charts

sinners to seek forgiveness for their sins or face punishment in Hell forever. In 1739 British minister George Whitefield made the second of his seven trips to America. He held revivals from Georgia to New England.

The Great Awakening drew people of different regions, classes, and races. Women, members of minority groups, and poor people often took part in services. Ministers from different colonies met and shared ideas with one another. This represented one of the few exchanges between colonies.

The Great Awakening promoted ideas that may also have affected colonial politics. Sermons about the spiritual equality of all people led some colonists to begin demanding more political equality. Revivals became popular places to talk about political and social issues. People from those colonies with less political freedom were thus introduced to more democratic systems used in other colonies.

Enlightenment

During the 1600s Europeans began to re-examine their world. Scientists began to better understand the basic laws that govern nature. Their new ideas about the universe began the Scientific Revolution. The revolution changed how people thought of the world.

Many colonists were also influenced by the **Enlightenment**. This movement, which took place during the 1700s, spread the idea that reason and logic could improve society. Enlightenment thinkers also formed ideas about how government should work.

Some Enlightenment thinkers believed that there was a social contract between government and citizens. Philosophers such as John Locke thought that people had natural rights such as equality and liberty. Eventually, ideas of the Scientific Revolution and the Enlightenment influenced colonial leaders.

READING CHECK **Summarizing** How did the Great Awakening and the Enlightenment influence colonial society?

The French and Indian War

By the 1670s tensions had arisen between New England colonists and the Wampanoag. Metacomet, a Wampanoag leader also known as King Philip, opposed the colonists' efforts to take his people's lands. In 1675 these tensions finally erupted in a conflict known as King Philip's War. The colonial militia—civilians serving as soldiers—fought American Indian warriors. Both sides attacked each other's settlements, killing men, women, and children. The fighting finally ended in 1676, but only after about 600 colonists and some 3,000 Indians had been killed, including Metacomet.

Native American Allies

Some Native Americans allied with the colonists to fight against Metacomet and his forces. These Indians had developed trade relations with colonists. They wanted tools, weapons, and other goods that Europeans could provide. In exchange, the colonists wanted furs, which they sold for large profits in Europe. As a result, each side came to depend upon the other.

French colonists traded and allied with the Algonquian and Huron. English colonists traded and allied with the Iroquois League. This powerful group united American Indians from six different groups. Many American Indians trusted the French more than they did the English. The smaller French settlements were less threatening than the rapidly growing English colonies. No matter who their allies were, many Indian leaders took care to protect their people's independence. As one leader said:

"We are born free. We neither depend upon [the governor of New France] nor [the governor of New York]. We may go where we please …and buy and sell what we please."

—Garangula, quoted in *The World Turned Upside Down*, edited by Colin G. Calloway

Main Idea

❹ The French and Indian War

The French and Indian War gave England control of more land in North America.

Describe Describe the main events of King Philip's War. *Conflict broke out in 1675 between the Wampanoag, led by Metacomet (also known as King Philip) and colonists who wanted Indian lands; ended in 1676, with the death of many colonists and Native Americans, including Metacomet.*

Identify Points of View Why did some Native Americans trust the French more than the English? *French settlements were smaller and less threatening than the rapidly growing English colonies.*

Analyze Why did some Native Americans join Europeans in wars against other Native Americans? *to protect trade alliances on which different groups of Native Americans had become dependent*

Connect to Science

The Scientific Revolution It was during the Scientific Revolution that Sir Isaac Newton developed his three laws of motion, the basic principles of modern physics.

Critical Thinking: Identifying Points of View
At Level

Native American, English, and French Relations

1. Write the following three labels for students to see: *Native Americans, English colonists,* and *French traders and settlers.*

2. Ask students to describe how these three groups interacted in North America, and write students' responses under the correct headings.

3. Then lead a discussion further exploring how Native Americans and settlers in the English colonies viewed each other.
   LS **Verbal/Linguistic**

4. **Extend** Have students conduct research on Native American groups in the region of the English colonies. Then have each student create a map showing the locations of various Native American groups and English settlements. Conclude with a class discussion on how the locations of different groups affected their viewpoints.

   Alternative Assessment Handbook, Rubrics 7: Charts; 11: Discussions; and 30: Research

Answers

Reading Check *They led to the desire for political equality and encouraged discussion about political and social issues.*

Main Idea

❹ The French and Indian War

The French and Indian War gave England control of more land in North America.

Recall Why did fighting break out in the Ohio River valley between British colonists and the French? *British colonists wanted to settle in the region, which the French opposed because such settlement might harm their valuable fur trade.*

Identify Cause and Effect What caused the French and Indian War, and how did it affect North America? *cause—France captured a British fort; effects—Britain gained Canada, all French lands east of the Mississippi, and Spanish Florida*

Elaborate How did the war change the balance of power in North America? *Great Britain and Spain controlled most of North America and vied for power there.*

Map Transparency: North American Empires before and after the Treaty of Paris

Interpreting Maps

North American Empires before and after the Treaty of Paris

Regions What happened to the amount of unclaimed land between 1754 and 1763? *decreased in size, with Spain taking some and the rest disputed by Britain, Russia, and Spain*

Place Who lived in this "unclaimed" region? *Native Americans*

Answers

Interpreting Maps 1. *Britain and Spain;* **2.** *Mississippi River*

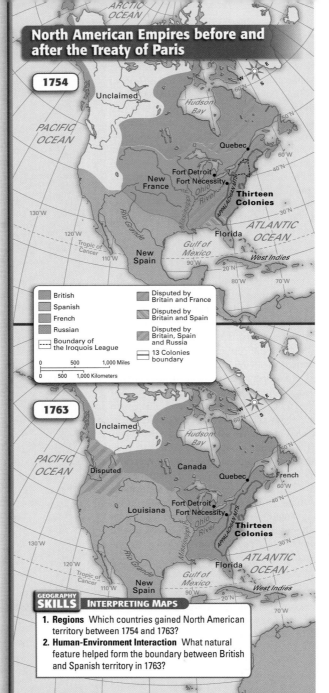

North American Empires before and after the Treaty of Paris

1754

British
Spanish
French
Russian
Boundary of the Iroquois League

Disputed by Britain and France
Disputed by Britain and Spain
Disputed by Britain, Spain and Russia
13 Colonies boundary

0   500   1,000 Miles
0   500   1,000 Kilometers

1763

GEOGRAPHY SKILLS **INTERPRETING MAPS**
1. **Regions** Which countries gained North American territory between 1754 and 1763?
2. **Human-Environment Interaction** What natural feature helped form the boundary between British and Spanish territory in 1763?

96 CHAPTER 3

War Erupts

During the late 1600s to mid-1700s, France and Great Britain struggled for control of territory in North America. British colonists wanted to settle in the Ohio River valley, where they could take advantage of the valuable fur trade and also have room for their colonies to expand. The French believed this settlement would hurt their fur trade profits. A standoff developed in the Ohio Valley where the French had built three forts. Fighting erupted in 1753 as the British military moved to take over the valley.

When a young Virginian named George Washington arrived with more soldiers, he found the area under French control. Washington and his troops built a small, simple fort that he named Fort Necessity. After his troops suffered many casualties—captured, injured, or killed soldiers—Washington finally surrendered. His defeat in 1754 was the start of the French and Indian War. Meanwhile, in 1756 fighting began in Europe, starting what became known as the Seven Years' War.

Treaty of Paris

The turning point of the war came in 1759. That year British general James Wolfe captured Quebec, gaining the advantage in the war. However, the war dragged on for four more years. Finally, in 1763 Britain and France signed the Treaty of Paris, officially ending the war.

The terms of the treaty gave Canada to Britain. Britain also gained all French lands east of the Mississippi River except the city of New Orleans and two small islands in the Gulf of St. Lawrence. From Spain, which had allied with France in 1762, Britain received Florida. In an earlier treaty, Spain had received Louisiana, the land that France had claimed west of the Mississippi River. The Treaty of Paris changed the balance of power in North America. Soon British settlers began moving west to settle new lands.

Social Studies Skills Activity: Interpreting Time Lines   `Below Level`

Frontier Conflicts Time Line

1. Have students create time lines of key dates and events related to King Philip's War, the French and Indian War, and Pontiac's Rebellion.

2. Instruct students to illustrate and annotate their time lines with related drawings and facts.

3. Have students share their time lines with the class. As they do, create a master time line for the class to see. Point out significant cause-and-effect relationships as you create the time line.

4. Lead students in a guided discussion of the significance of these frontier conflicts for the British colonists, the French, and the Native Americans in North America. Then ask students to predict how the British colonists responded to the Proclamation of 1763.

LS **Verbal/Linguistic, Visual/Spatial**

Alternative Assessment Handbook, Rubric 36: Time Lines

Western Frontier

Most colonial settlements were located along the Atlantic coast. Colonial settlers, or pioneers, slowly moved into the Virginia and Carolina backcountry and the Ohio River valley.

Indian leaders like Chief **Pontiac** opposed British settlement of this new land. Pontiac's Rebellion began in May 1763 when his forces attacked British forts on the frontier. Within one month, they had destroyed or captured seven forts. Pontiac then led an attack on Fort Detroit. The British held out for months.

British leaders feared that more fighting would take place on the frontier if colonists kept moving onto American Indian lands. To avoid more conflict, King George III issued the Proclamation of 1763. This law banned British settlement west of the Appalachian Mountains. The law also ordered settlers to leave the upper Ohio River valley.

READING CHECK **Summarizing** Why did George III issue the Proclamation of 1763?

BIOGRAPHY

Pontiac
1720–1769

Pontiac, an Ottawa chief who had fought for France, tried to resist British settlement west of the Appalachians. Calling them "dogs dressed in red who have come to rob us," he attacked the British in the Ohio country in 1763. Pontiac's rebellion was put down, and he surrendered in 1766.

Analyzing Information How did Pontiac try to stop the British?

SUMMARY AND PREVIEW In this section you read about colonial governments, the slave trade, and the conflicts with foreign countries and with Native Americans that the colonies faced as they grew. In the next section you'll learn about the increasing tension between the colonies and Great Britain that led to independence.

Section 4 Assessment

go.hrw.com
Online Quiz
KEYWORD: SR8 HP3

Reviewing Ideas, Terms, and People

1. **a. Describe** How were colonial governments organized?
   b. Analyze How did political change in England affect colonial governments?
2. **a. Explain** What is **mercantilism**?
   b. Analyze How did the Navigation Acts support the system of mercantilism?
   c. Evaluate Did the colonies benefit from mercantilism? Why or why not?
3. **a. Identify** What was the **Great Awakening**?
   b. Compare How was the **Enlightenment** similar to the Great Awakening?
4. **a. Explain** What caused the French and Indian War?
   b. Evaluate Defend the British decision to ban colonists from settling on the western frontier.

Critical Thinking

5. **Summarizing** Review your notes on the developments in the colonies during the late 1600s to mid-1700s. Then add a box to the bottom of your chart in which you briefly summarize how the colonies grew and changed during the period, as well as the challenges they faced.

Development	Effects
Establishment of local government	
Political change in England	
Trade laws	
Great Awakening/Enlightenment	
French and Indian War	

How the colonies grew and changed and challenges faced.

FOCUS ON WRITING

6. **Reviewing the Information** This section focused on what life was like in all the English colonies discussed so far. Does this information give you any new ideas about the colony you'll use in your infomercial?

THE ENGLISH COLONIES **97**

Direct Teach

Info to Know
Colonial Muskets Could you stand still while people shot at you? That is how the British and other Europeans fought during the 1600s and 1700s. The muskets soldiers used at the time were not very accurate. As a result, officers told soldiers to get close to the enemy, stand in one place, and shoot as quickly as possible. Sometimes, dozens of shots were required to hit one target!

Review & Assess

Close
Briefly review the challenges that British colonists faced during this period, and how colonists dealt with these challenges.

Review
Online Quiz, Section 4

Assess
SE Section 4 Assessment

PASS: Section 4 Quiz

Alternative Assessment Handbook

Reteach/Classroom Intervention
Interactive Reader and Study Guide, Section 4

Interactive Skills Tutor CD-ROM

Section 4 Assessment Answers

1. **a.** governor and advisory council; some also had elected assemblies or held town meetings
   b. Crowning of King James II led to loss of some political control; his removal and English Bill of Rights led to more representative government.

2. **a.** practice of creating and maintaining wealth by carefully controlling trade
   b. allowed colonists to trade only with England, giving England a guaranteed market for exports
   c. Answers will vary, but many colonists did not see mercantilism as a benefit.

3. **a.** religious movement in the 1730s and 1740s that affected colonial social and political life
   b. both raised ideas of political equality

4. **a.** British and French tensions over the Ohio River valley; French capture of a British fort
   b. possible answer—would promote peace

5. colonies started local governments and triangular trade; Great Awakening occurred; faced conflict with Native Americans

6. Students should provide notes about the colony's government, social life, and conflicts.

Answers

Biography *by leading American Indian attacks on British settlers who were invading Indian lands*

Reading Check *to stop the fighting between colonists and Native Americans*

97

Conflict in the Colonies

Bellringer

If YOU were there . . . Use the **Daily Bellringer Transparency** to help students answer the question.

🖫 Daily Bellringer Transparency, Section 5

Building Vocabulary

Preteach or review the following terms:

boycott refusal to buy a particular good or service (p. 99)

coercive forceful (p. 102)

intolerable unbearable (p. 102)

propaganda a story giving only one side in an argument (p. 101)

repeal do away with (p. 100)

resolutions something to be voted on (p. 100)

revenue money earned (p. 100)

🖫 **CRF:** Vocabulary Builder Activity, Section 5

Taking Notes

Have students copy the graphic organizer onto their own paper and then use it to take notes on the section. This activity will prepare students for the Section Assessment, in which they will complete a graphic organizer that builds on the information using a critical thinking skill.

What You Will Learn...

Main Ideas

1. British efforts to raise taxes on colonists sparked protest.
2. The Boston Massacre caused colonial resentment toward Great Britain.
3. Colonists protested the British tax on tea with the Boston Tea Party.
4. Great Britain responded to colonial actions by passing the Intolerable Acts.

The Big Idea

Tensions developed as the British government placed tax after tax on the colonies.

Key Terms and People

Samuel Adams, *p. 99*
Committees of Correspondence, *p. 99*
Stamp Act of 1765, *p. 100*
Boston Massacre, *p. 101*
Tea Act, *p. 102*
Boston Tea Party, *p. 102*
Intolerable Acts, *p. 102*

TAKING NOTES As you read, take notes in a chart like the one below on each of the new laws passed by the British government.

Law
1.
2.
3.
4.
5.

If YOU were there...

You live in the New England colonies in the 1700s. Recently, British officials have placed new taxes on tea—your favorite beverage. You've never been very interested in politics, but you're beginning to think that people far across the ocean in Britain shouldn't be able to tell you what to do. Some of your friends have joined a group that refuses to buy British tea.

Would you give up your favorite drink to join the boycott?

BUILDING BACKGROUND As the British colonies grew and became prosperous, the colonists got used to running their own lives. Britain began to seem very far away. At the same time, officials in Britain still expected the colonies to obey them and to earn money for Britain. Parliament passed new laws and imposed new taxes. But the colonists found various ways to challenge them.

Great Britain Raises Taxes

Great Britain had won the French and Indian War, but Parliament still had to pay for it. The British continued to keep a standing, or permanent, army in North America to protect the colonists against Indian attacks. To help pay for this army, Prime Minister George Grenville asked Parliament to tax the colonists. In 1764 Parliament passed the Sugar Act, which set duties on molasses and sugar imported by colonists. This was the first act passed specifically to raise money in the colonies.

British officials also tried harder to arrest smugglers. Colonial merchants were required to list all the trade goods they carried aboard their ships. These lists had to be approved before ships could leave colonial ports. This made it difficult for traders to avoid paying duties. The British navy also began to stop and search ships for smuggled goods.

Teach the Big Idea | **At Level**

Conflict in the Colonies

Materials: construction paper, art supplies

1. **Teach** Ask students the questions in the Main Idea boxes to teach this section.

2. **Apply** To help students understand why tensions increased over taxes in the colonies, have each student draw a colonial storefront. On their drawings, have students list the acts that Britain passed and draw the products it taxed, such as tea. On each product, have students draw a price tag with the word *Tax* on it. **LS Visual/Spatial**

3. **Review** As you review the section's main ideas, have students discuss the colonists' reactions to Britain's actions and taxes, and the British reactions to the colonists' protests.

4. **Practice/Homework** Have each student design a version of the stamp, or seal, the British forced colonists to buy and then a flyer listing the items that require the stamp. **LS Visual/Spatial**

🖫 Alternative Assessment Handbook, Rubric 3: Artwork

Parliament also changed the colonies' legal system by giving greater powers to the vice-admiralty courts. These courts had no juries, and the judges treated suspected smugglers as guilty until proven innocent. In regular British courts, accused persons were treated as innocent until proven guilty.

Taxation without Representation

Parliament's actions upset many colonists who had grown used to being independent. Merchants thought the taxes were unfair and hurt business. Many believed that Great Britain had no right to tax the colonies at all without their consent.

James Otis argued that the power of the Crown and Parliament was limited. Otis said they could not "take from any man any part of his property, without his consent in person or by representation." No one in Britain had asked the colonists if they wanted to be taxed. In addition, the colonists had no direct representatives in Parliament. Colonial assemblies had little influence on Parliament's decisions.

At a Boston town meeting in May 1764, local leader **Samuel Adams** agreed with Otis. He believed that Parliament could not tax the colonists without their permission. The ideas of Otis and Adams were summed up in the slogan "No Taxation without Representation," which spread throughout the colonies.

Adams helped found the **Committees of Correspondence.** Each committee got in touch with other towns and colonies. Its members shared ideas and information about the new British laws and ways to challenge them.

A popular method of protest was the boycott, in which people refused to buy British goods. The first colonial boycott started in New York in 1765. It soon spread to other colonies. Colonists hoped that their efforts would hurt the British economy and might convince Parliament to end the new taxes.

THE ENGLISH COLONIES **99**

99

Main Idea

❶ Great Britain Raises Taxes

British efforts to raise taxes on colonists sparked protest.

Identify What items were taxed under the Stamp Act? *paper items, including legal documents, licenses, newspapers, pamphlets, and playing cards*

Contrast How did the Stamp Act and the Townshend Acts differ? *The Stamp Act required colonists to pay for an official stamp to buy various paper items; the Townshend Act placed duties on imported glass, lead, paints, paper, and tea.*

Make Inferences Why do you think American colonists chose to boycott British goods as a way to protest taxes? *possible answer—because not buying British goods would hurt the British economy and perhaps persuade Parliament to change the unpopular laws or give colonists representation*

📖 **CRF:** Biography Activity: Patrick Henry

Info to Know

Taxes Taxes have existed since ancient times. Ancient Rome issued property and sales taxes. Most taxes are used either to pay for government spending, to promote economic growth, or to help spread wealth. Taxes can also be used to encourage or discourage certain activities.

Answers

Reading Check *Parliament passed the Townshend Acts; colonists boycotted many British goods; tax collectors seized the ship* Liberty *on suspicion of smuggling; Sons of Liberty attacked houses of customs officials; the governor broke up the Massachusetts legislature and asked for British troops to restore order.*

100

Stamp Act

The British government continued to search for new ways to tax the American colonies, further angering many colonists. For example, Prime Minister Grenville proposed the **Stamp Act of 1765**. This act required colonists to pay for an official stamp, or seal, when they bought paper items. The tax had to be paid on legal documents, licenses, newspapers, pamphlets, and even playing cards. Colonists who refused to buy stamps could be fined or sent to jail.

Grenville did not expect this tax to spark protest. After all, in Britain people already paid similar taxes. But colonists saw it differently. The Stamp Act was Parliament's first attempt to raise money by taxing the colonists directly, rather than by taxing imported goods.

Protests against the Stamp Act began almost immediately. Colonists formed a secret society called the Sons of Liberty. Samuel Adams helped organize the group in Boston. This group sometimes used violence to frighten tax collectors. Many colonial courts shut down because people refused to buy the stamps required for legal documents. Businesses openly ignored the law by refusing to buy stamps.

In May 1765 a Virginia lawyer named Patrick Henry presented a series of resolutions to the Virginia House of Burgesses. These resolutions stated that the Stamp Act violated colonists' rights. In addition to taxation without representation, the Stamp Act denied the accused a trial by jury. Henry's speech in support of the resolutions convinced the assembly to support some of his ideas.

Repealing the Stamp Act

In Boston the members of the Massachusetts legislature called for a Stamp Act Congress. In October 1765, delegates from nine colonies met in New York. They issued a declaration that the Stamp Act was a violation of their rights and liberties.

Pressure on Parliament to repeal, or do away with, the Stamp Act grew quickly. A group of London merchants complained that their trade suffered from the colonial boycott. Parliament repealed the Stamp Act in 1766.

Members of Parliament were upset that colonists had challenged their authority. Thus, Parliament issued the Declaratory Act, which stated that Parliament had the power to make laws for the colonies "in all cases whatsoever." The Declaratory Act further worried the colonists. The act stripped away much of their independence.

Townshend Acts

In June 1767 Parliament passed the Townshend Acts. These acts placed duties on glass, lead, paints, paper, and tea. To enforce the Townshend Acts, British officials used writs of assistance. These allowed tax collectors to search for smuggled goods. Colonists hated the new laws because they took power away from colonial governments.

The colonists responded to the Townshend Acts by once again boycotting many British goods. Women calling themselves the Daughters of Liberty supported the boycott. In February 1768 Samuel Adams wrote a letter arguing that the laws violated the legal rights of the colonists. The Massachusetts legislature sent the letter to other colonies' legislatures, who voted to join the protest.

At the same time, tax collectors in Massachusetts seized the ship *Liberty* on suspicion of smuggling. This action angered the ship's owner and the Sons of Liberty. They attacked the houses of customs officials in protest. In response, the governor broke up the Massachusetts legislature. He also asked troops to restore order. British soldiers arrived in Boston in October 1768.

READING CHECK **Sequencing** What series of events led to the arrival of British troops in Boston in 1768?

Collaborative Learning | At Level

Colonial Tax Trivia Game

1. Organize students into three teams. Assign each team either the Sugar Act, the Stamp Act, or the Townshend Acts. Have each team write five questions and answers related to its topic.

2. Review each team's questions and answers to make certain the questions are clear and relevant and the answers are correct.

3. Have the teams participate in a game of Colonial Tax Trivia. Select a team to ask the first question. The first person on either of the other teams to raise his or her hand gets to answer the question. If the answer is correct, that person's team receives a point. If the answer is incorrect, give the other team a chance to answer the question.

3. Have each team ask a question in turn. Repeat this process until all the questions have been asked. The team with the most points at the end wins. **LS Interpersonal, Verbal/Linguistic**

📖 Alternative Assessment Handbook, Rubric 14: Group Activity

NEWSPAPER ARTICLE
The Boston Massacre

An account of the Boston Massacre appeared in the Boston Gazette and Country Journal *soon after the event.*

"The People were immediately alarmed with the Report of this horrid Massacre, the Bells were set a Ringing, and great Numbers soon assembled at the Place where this tragical Scene had been acted; their Feelings may be better conceived than expressed; and while some were taking Care of the Dead and Wounded, the Rest were in Consultation what to do in these dreadful Circumstances.

But so little intimidated were they [Bostonians], notwithstanding their being within a few Yards of the Main Guard, and seeing the 29th Regiment under Arms, and drawn up in King street; that they kept their Station and appeared, as an Officer of Rank expressed it, ready to run upon the very Muzzles of their Muskets."

—*Boston Gazette and Country Journal,* March 12, 1770

ANALYSIS SKILL **ANALYZING PRIMARY SOURCES**

Why do you think the people described were not intimidated by the soldiers?

Boston Massacre

Many Bostonians saw the presence of British troops as a threat by the British government against its critics in Massachusetts. Some colonists agreed with Samuel Adams, who said, "I look upon [British soldiers] as foreign enemies." The soldiers knew that they were not welcome. Both sides resented each other, and name-calling, arguments, and fights between Bostonians and the soldiers were common.

The tension exploded on March 5, 1770. A lone British soldier standing guard had an argument with a colonist and struck him. A crowd gathered around the soldier, throwing snowballs and shouting insults. Soon a small number of troops arrived. The crowd grew louder and angrier by the moment. Some yelled, "Come on you rascals . . . Fire if you dare!" Suddenly, the soldiers fired into the crowd, instantly killing three men, including sailor Crispus Attucks. "Half Indian, half negro, and altogether rowdy," as he was called, Attucks is the best-remembered casualty of the incident. Two others died within a few days.

Samuel Adams and other protesters quickly spread the story of the shootings. They used it as propaganda—a story giving only one side in an argument—against the British. Colonists called the shootings the **Boston Massacre**. Paul Revere created an elaborate color print titled "The Bloody Massacre perpetrated in King Street" (above).

The soldiers and their officer, Thomas Preston, were charged with murder. Two Boston lawyers, Josiah Quincy and John Adams—Samuel Adams's cousin—agreed to defend the soldiers. They argued that the troops had acted in self-defense. The Boston jury agreed, finding Preston and six soldiers not guilty. Two soldiers were convicted of killing people in the crowd by accident. These men were branded on the hand and released. The trial helped calm people down, but many were still angry at the British.

READING CHECK **Analyzing** What was the significance of the Boston Massacre?

THE ENGLISH COLONIES **101**

101

Main Idea

❸ The Boston Tea Party

Colonists protested the British tax on tea with the Boston Tea Party.

Recall What was the purpose of the Tea Act? *allowed the British East India Company to sell tea directly to the colonies in hopes that cheaper tea might stop colonial smuggling of tea*

Analyze Why did colonists oppose the Tea Act? *Colonial merchants feared the British East India Company's cheap tea would put them out of business.*

Identify Cause and Effect What was the significance of the Boston Tea Party? *enraged British officials and led Parliament to punish Boston by passing the Coercive Acts, which colonists called the Intolerable Acts*

🗞 Quick Facts Transparency: The Road to Revolution

Reading Time Lines

The Road to Revolution

• What year did Great Britain begin taxing paper products in the colonies? *1765*

• When did Great Britain close Boston Harbor? *1774*

🗞 Quick Facts Transparency: The Road to Revolution

Answers

Reading Check *passage of the Tea Act in 1773; colonial merchants' fears that the act would put them out of business; colonial and British reactions to the arrival of British East India ships in Boston Harbor*

102

Colonists reacted to British laws with anger and violence. Parliament continued to pass tax after tax.

British Actions

Colonists' Reactions

1764 The Sugar Act

The Sugar Act is passed to raise money from the colonies for Britain.

Samuel Adams founds the Committees of Correspondence to improve communication among the colonies.

1765 The Stamp Act

The Stamp Act taxes newspapers, licenses, and colonial paper products.

A series of resolutions is published stating that the Stamp Act violates the rights of colonists.

The Boston Tea Party

To reduce tensions in the colonies, Parliament repealed almost all of the Townshend Acts. However, it kept the tax on tea. British officials knew that the colonial demand for tea was high despite the boycott. But colonial merchants were smuggling most of this imported tea and paying no duty on it.

The British East India Company offered Parliament a solution. The company had huge amounts of tea but was not allowed to sell it directly to the colonists. If the company could sell directly to the colonists, it could charge low prices and still make money. Cheaper tea might encourage colonists to stop smuggling. Less smuggling would result in more tax money.

Parliament agreed and passed the **Tea Act** in 1773, which allowed the British East India Company to sell tea directly to the colonists. Many colonial merchants and smugglers feared that the British East India Company's cheap tea would put them out of business. As a result, colonists united against the Tea Act.

Three ships loaded with tea from the British East India Company arrived in Boston Harbor in 1773. The Sons of Liberty demanded that the ships leave. But the governor of Massachusetts would not let the ships leave without paying the duty. Unsure of what to do, the captains waited in the harbor.

On the night of December 16, 1773, colonists disguised as Indians sneaked onto the three tea-filled ships. After dumping over 340 tea chests into Boston Harbor, the colonists headed home to remove their disguises. This event became known as the **Boston Tea Party**. Soon the streets echoed with shouts of "Boston harbour is a teapot tonight!"

READING CHECK **Summarizing** What factors led to the Boston Tea Party?

The Intolerable Acts

Lord North, the new British prime minister, was furious when he heard about the Boston Tea Party. Parliament decided to punish Boston. In the spring of 1774 it passed the Coercive Acts. Colonists called these laws the **Intolerable Acts**. The acts had several effects.

1. Boston Harbor was closed until Boston paid for the ruined tea.
2. Massachusetts's charter was canceled. The governor decided if and when the legislature could meet.
3. Royal officials accused of crimes were sent to Britain for trial. This let them face a more friendly judge and jury.

102 CHAPTER 3

Collaborative Learning

At Level

Colonial Protest Rallies

Materials: art supplies, butcher paper, poster board, sticks, string, scissors, colored markers

1. Review with students the series of events covered in this section and how the colonists and the British government responded to them.

2. Organize students into five groups and assign each group one of the following: Sugar Act, Stamp Act, Townshend Acts, Tea Act, or Intolerable Acts.

3. Ask students to imagine that their group is planning a colonial rally to protest its assigned act. Have each group create a banner, slogans, and picket signs for its rally.

4. Hold the rallies in the order in which the acts were passed. Give each group time to present its message. **LS** **Interpersonal, Kinesthetic**

📝 Alternative Assessment Handbook, Rubrics 14: Group Activity; and 34: Slogans and Banners

1770 The Boston Massacre

British soldiers fire into a crowd of colonists, killing five men.

Colonists protest and bring the soldiers to trial.

1773 The Boston Tea Party

The Tea Act is passed, making British tea cheaper than colonial tea.

Colonists protest by dumping shipments of British tea into Boston Harbor.

1774 The Intolerable Acts

Boston Harbor is closed, and British troops are quartered.

Colonists' resentment toward Britain builds.

ANALYSIS SKILL **ANALYZING VISUALS**

In what year did the conflict between Britain and the colonists turn violent?

4. General Thomas Gage became the new governor of Massachusetts.

The British hoped that these steps would bring back order in the colonies. Instead they simply increased people's anger at Britain.

READING CHECK **Analyzing** What was the purpose of the Intolerable Acts?

SUMMARY AND PREVIEW In this section you learned about the increasing dissatisfaction between the colonists and Great Britain. In the next chapter you'll learn about the result of these conflicts—the American Revolution.

Section 5 Assessment

go.hrw.com
Online Quiz
KEYWORD: SR8 HP3

Reviewing Ideas, Terms, and People

1. **a. Explain** Why did Great Britain raise taxes in its American colonies?
   b. Evaluate Which method of protesting taxes do you think was most successful for colonists? Why?
2. **a. Describe** What events led to the **Boston Massacre**?
   b. Elaborate Why do you think John Adams and Josiah Quincy agreed to defend the British soldiers that were involved in the Boson Massacre?
3. **a. Recall** What was the purpose of the **Tea Act**?
   b. Draw Conclusions What message did the **Boston Tea Party** send to the British government?
4. **a. Explain** Why did Parliament pass the Intolerable Acts?
   b. Draw Conclusions Why do you think the colonists believed that these laws were "intolerable"?

Critical Thinking

5. **Identifying Cause and Effect** Review your notes on the laws passed by the British government.

Then add a new column to your chart and identify the laws' effects.

Law	Result
1.	
2.	
3.	
4.	
5.	

FOCUS ON WRITING

6. **Gathering Information** Now you have some information about the political situation in Boston in the late 1700s. Why might someone from Britain want to immigrate to Boston at this time? Would you consider the city of Boston, rather than a whole colony, for the subject of your infomercial?

THE ENGLISH COLONIES **103**

Direct Teach

Main Idea

❹ **The Intolerable Acts**

Great Britain responded to colonial actions by passing the Intolerable Acts.

Recall What was the result of the Intolerable Acts? *They increased the colonists' anger toward Great Britain.*

Evaluate Which one of the Intolerable Acts do you think most angered colonists, and why? *Answers will vary but should reflect an understanding of how each act likely affected life in the colonies.*

Review & Assess

Close

Use the time line on these pages to review the growing tension, anger, and violence between the American colonies and the British government during the 1760s and early 1770s.

Review

Online Quiz, Section 5

Assess

SE Section 5 Assessment

PASS: Section 5 Quiz

Alternative Assessment Handbook

Reteach/Classroom Intervention

Interactive Reader and Study Guide, Section 5

Interactive Skills Tutor CD-ROM

Section 5 Assessment Answers

1. **a.** to pay for the French and Indian War and the cost of defending the colonies
   b. Answers will vary but should show a knowledge of the forms of protest the colonists used.

2. **a.** arguing, taunting, and fighting between colonists and British soldiers led to shots being fired
   b. Answers will vary but should exhibit an understanding that the trial helped calm the colonists.

3. **a.** to raise revenue and stop colonial smuggling
   b. that the colonists would act to defend their rights

4. **a.** to punish Boston for the Boston Tea Party
   b. laws were unreasonable; took power away from colonial governments

5. Sugar Act—colonial protests; boycotts; Stamp Act—boycotts; Stamp Act Congress; act repealed; Townshend Acts—boycotts; tensions increased; Boston Massacre; most repealed; Tea Act—Boston Tea Party; Intolerable Acts—Boston Harbor closed; Massachusetts charter canceled

6. Students' notes should describe the situation in Boston at the time.

Answers

Analyzing Visuals *1770*
Reading Check *to punish the citizens of Boston for the Boston Tea Party*

103

Social Studies Skills

Interpreting Time Lines

Activity Examining the Chapter Time Line Have students examine the time line at the beginning of the chapter. Ask students to identify the two categories of events that the time line shows *(U.S. events on the top and world events on the bottom)*. Next, ask students what dates the time line spans *(1620 to 1773)*. Then ask students to identify any relationships among events shown on the time line. For example, the 1620 and 1681 events both involve English colonization. The expansion of English colonization then contributed to Pontiac's Rebellion in 1763. Finally, have students skim the chapter and find three events that could be added to the chapter time line. Ask for volunteers to share their events and to indicate where they would go on the time line. Challenge students to think of other world events to add to the time line as well. **LS Visual/Spatial**

📖 Alternative Assessment Handbook, Rubric 36: Time Lines

💿 Interactive Skills Tutor CD-ROM, Lesson 3: Interpret and Create a Time Line and Sequence Events

Social Studies Skills

Interpreting Time Lines

Define the Skill

Knowing the sequence, or order, in which historical events took place is important to understanding these events. Time lines visually display the sequence of events during a particular period of time. They also let you easily see time spans between events, such as how long after one event a related event took place—and what events occurred in between. In addition, comparing time lines for different places makes relationships between distant events easier to identify and understand.

Learn the Skill

Follow these guidelines to read, interpret, and compare time lines.

1 Determine each time line's framework. Note the years it covers and the periods of time into which it is divided. Be aware that a pair of time lines may not have the same framework.

2 Study the order of events on each time line. Note the length of time between events. Compare what was taking place on different time lines around the same time period.

3 Look for relationships between events. Pay particular attention to how an event on one time line might relate to an event on another.

Practice the Skill

Interpret the time lines below to answer the following questions.

1. What is each time line's framework?
2. How long was England without a king?
3. What event in England allowed the colonists to get rid of the Dominion of New England in 1689?
4. Massachusetts' independence had troubled English officials for many years. What do the time lines suggest about why this colony was allowed to remain independent until 1686?

Events in England

1642	1649	1660	1688
Civil war breaks out between King Charles I and Parliament.	Charles I is executed; Parliament takes power.	Monarchy is restored; Charles II becomes king.	Parliament overthrows King James II and puts new king on throne.

Events in the Colonies

1641	1659	1686	1689
Massachusetts shows independence by passing own code of laws.	Virginia pledges loyalty to Charles II as king of England.	Massachusetts is united with other colonies in Dominion of New England by King James II.	Colonies disband Dominion of New England and re-establish separate governments.

104 CHAPTER 3

Social Studies Skills Activity: Interpreting Time Lines   At Level

English Colonies Time Line

Materials: art supplies, butcher paper, colored markers

1. Have students work as a class to create a large time line on butcher paper of the events covered in this chapter.

2. Organize students into groups and assign each group a specific part of the time line to complete. Start by having students copy the events from the time line that appears at the beginning of the chapter. Either tell students to leave off the world events or to keep the U.S. and world events separate, as they are on the chapter time line.

3. Have groups complete the time line by adding events from the chapter. Each group should also add photos, images, drawings, and quotes to illustrate its part of the time line. **LS Interpersonal, Visual/Spatial**

📖 Alternative Assessment Handbook, Rubric 36: Time Lines

Answers

Practice the Skill 1. *top time line—spans 1642 to 1688; bottom time line—spans 1641 to 1689;* **2.** *11 years;* **3.** *Parliament's removal of King James II in 1688;* **4.** *England was experiencing political turmoil and leaders probably did not have the time to focus on Massachusetts.*

Chapter Review

Visual Summary

Use the visual summary below to help you review the main ideas of the chapter.

QUICK FACTS

Increasing tensions between the colonies and Britain led many colonists to consider cutting ties to Britain.

• Taxation without representation
• Acts of Parliament
• Violence between colonists and British troops

Reviewing Vocabulary, Terms, and People

Match the words in the left column with the correct definition in the right column.

1. Committees of Correspondence
2. Jonathan Edwards
3. mercantilism
4. immigrants
5. indentured servants
6. William Penn
7. Pocahontas
8. Quakers
9. staple crops
10. town meeting

a. colonists who received free passage to North America in exchange for working without pay for a certain number of years

b. created in Massachusetts, these groups helped towns and colonies share information about resisting the new British laws

c. crops that are continuously in demand

d. daughter of Powhatan chief whose marriage to colonist John Rolfe eased tensions between the Powhatan and the colonists

e. one of the leaders of the Great Awakening, he urged sinners to seek forgiveness

f. Protestant sect founded in England that believed salvation was available to all people

g. people who move to another country after leaving their homeland

h. political gathering at which people make decisions on local issues

i. Quaker leader who established a colony with the goal of fair government for all

j. system of creating and maintaining wealth through controlled trade

---

Visual Summary

Review and Inquiry Have students use the visual summary to explain the factors that led the colonists to want to cut ties with Great Britain.

Quick Facts Transparency: The English Colonies Visual Summary

Reviewing Vocabulary, Terms, and People

1. b
2. e
3. j
4. g
5. a
6. i
7. d
8. f
9. c
10. h

Comprehension and Critical Thinking

11. **a.** lack of preparation, disease and starvation, conflicts with Native Americans
    b. first law in the English colonies that promoted religious tolerance
    c. Answers will vary but should indicate an understanding that a reliance on slave labor could lead to slave rebellions and an unwillingness to change the system.

Review and Assessment Resources

Review and Reinforce

SE Chapter Review

CRF: Chapter Review Activity

Quick Facts Transparency: The English Colonies Visual Summary

Spanish Chapter Summary Audio CD Program

Online Chapter Summaries in Six Languages

OSP Holt PuzzlePro; GameTool for ExamView

Quiz Game CD-ROM

Assess

SE Standardized Test Practice

PASS: Chapter Test, Forms A and B

Alternative Assessment Handbook

OSP ExamView Test Generator, Chapter Test

Differentiated Instruction Modified Worksheets and Tests CD-ROM: Chapter Test

Holt Online Assessment Program (in the Premier Online Edition)

Reteach/Intervene

Interactive Reader and Study Guide

Differentiated Instruction Teacher Management System: Lesson Plans for Differentiated Instruction

Differentiated Instruction Modified Worksheets and Tests CD-ROM

Interactive Skills Tutor CD-ROM

go.hrw.com
Online Resources
Chapter Resources:
KEYWORD: SR8 US3

12. **a.** fishing, shipbuilding, trade
  b. similar—both in New England, sought religious freedom, brought families to settle, faced little resistance from American Indians, emphasized education; different—Pilgrims: received assistance from American Indians, established the Mayflower Compact; Puritans: close link of church and state, experienced dissent
  c. Answers will vary but should indicate that those who disagreed with the church often left.

13. **a.** staple crops such as wheat, barley, and oats
  b. large land grants and religious tolerance drew a variety of settlers
  c. religious tolerance, active trade, diverse population, reliance on indentured servants

14. **a.** political shifts in England, trade restrictions, conflict with Native Americans and the French, desire to settle in the western frontier
  b. introduced political ideas of equality and liberty
  c. Answers will vary but should indicate that both events encouraged a greater demand for political equality in the colonies.

15. **a.** to pay for the French and Indian War and for keeping a standing army in North America
  b. increased tensions, violence, and anger between the colonists and the British government
  c. Answers will vary but should show an understanding that the Intolerable Acts only further angered the American colonists.

Reviewing Themes

16. influences of Magna Carta, the English Bill of Rights, and ideas from the Great Awakening and the Enlightenment

17. benefited the economy of Great Britain, but hampered the economies of the colonies

Comprehension and Critical Thinking

SECTION 1 *(Pages 72–77)*

11. **a. Explain** What problems did the settlers of Virginia face?
  b. Draw Conclusions Why was Maryland's Toleration Act of 1649 important?
  c. Predict How might the southern colonies' reliance on slave labor eventually cause problems?

SECTION 2 *(Pages 78–84)*

12. **a. Describe** On what was the economy of the New England colonies based?
  b. Compare and Contrast How were the Pilgrim and Puritan colonies similar and different?
  c. Evaluate Explain why you think the close ties between church and state in Massachusetts helped or hurt their government.

SECTION 3 *(Pages 85–89)*

13. **a. Identify** What types of crops were grown in the middle colonies?
  b. Draw Conclusions Why did the middle colonies have a more diverse population than either New England or the South?
  c. Elaborate What are some possible reasons why immigrants would have chosen to live in the middle colonies?

SECTION 4 *(Pages 90–97)*

14. **a. Identify** What challenges did the English colonies face?
  b. Analyze What effect did the Great Awakening and the Enlightenment have on the colonies?
  c. Evaluate Explain which you think had a greater impact on colonial government—the passage of the English Bill of Rights or the Great Awakening.

SECTION 5 *(Pages 98–103)*

15. **a. Recall** Why did the British believe it was necessary to raise taxes on the American colonists?
  b. Draw Conclusions How did the Boston Massacre and the Boston Tea Party affect relations between Great Britain and the colonies?
  c. Evaluate Did the British government overreact to colonial protests by issuing the Intolerable Acts? Why or why not?

Reviewing Themes

16. **Politics** What political influences shaped the governments of the British colonies?

17. **Economics** How did mercantilism affect the economies of Great Britain and the American colonies?

Reading Skills

Understanding Words through Context Clues *Use the Reading Skills taught in this chapter to answer the question about the reading selection below.*

> A popular method of protest was the boycott, in which people refused to buy British goods. (p. 99)

18. According to the reading section above, what is the best definition of *boycott*?
  a. a popular method
  b. buying British goods
  c. people refusing
  d. protest in which people refuse to buy goods

Social Studies Skills

Interpreting Time Lines *Use the Social Studies Skills taught in this chapter to answer the questions about the time lines on page 104.*

19. How many years after the English Civil War did Parliament overthrow King James II?

20. How many years did the Dominion of New England last?
  a. 41
  b. 18
  c. 3
  d. 6

�277 **FOCUS ON WRITING** ✎

21. **Writing Your Infomercial** Choose a colony and time period. Review your list of reasons why English citizens might want to live there. Then write an infomercial with at least four scenes. Each scene should have video and a voice-over telling one of the reasons for immigrating.

Reading Skills

18. d

Social Studies Skills

19. 46 years

20. c

Focus on Writing

21. **Rubric** Students' infomercials should:
  • include four scenes that clearly explain the benefits of living in the colonies
  • include voiceovers that explain the video images
  • be persuasive and enthusiastic
  • use correct grammar and spelling

Standardized Test Practice

DIRECTIONS: Read each question and write the letter of the best response.

1 Use the map below to answer the following question.

The red box on this map indicates which early colonial settlement?

A Plymouth
B Massachusetts Bay
C New Amsterdam
D Jamestown

2 Ideas about spiritual, social, and political equality arose in the colonies in the 1700s in a religious movement called

A Separatism.
B the Enlightenment.
C the Great Awakening.
D Puritanism.

3 How did Parliament's passage of the English Bill of Rights in 1689 affect England's North American colonies?

A Colonists became more interested in being governed by representatives they elected.
B Several colonies decided to unite and formed the Dominion of New England.
C The Great Awakening took place.
D A movement to end slavery developed.

4 What was the central issue in the dispute between Britain and its American colonies?

A the restrictions Parliament placed on trade
B the presence of British troops in the colonies
C the colonists' right to religious freedom
D the power to tax the colonists

5 Which side did Native Americans take in the French and Indian War?

A the British
B the French
C different groups sided with each country
D Native Americans did not fight in the French and Indian War

6 Examine the following passage from an early colonist's journal and then use it to answer the question below.

> "An Indian came to us from the chief, the great Powhatan, with the word of peace. He said that Powhatan greatly desired our friendship, and that chiefs Pasyaheigh and Tapahanagh wanted to be our friends. Powhatan said that we would be able to sow and reap our crops in peace or else he would make war upon our enemies. This message turned out to be true, for these chiefs have ever since remained in peace and continued to trade with us. We rewarded the messenger with many small gifts, which were great wonders to him."
>
> —Edward Maria Wingfield, from *A Discourse of Virginia*

Why do you think native American chiefs wanted to make peace with early English colonists?

Answers

1. D
Break Down the Question Remind students to read all the labels on the map and to identify geographic features before choosing an answer.

2. C
Break Down the Question Some students may confuse the Great Awakening and the Enlightenment. Have students look up the glossary definition for each term, if needed.

3. A
Break Down the Question This question requires students to identify cause and effect. Refer students who miss the question to the text titled "Colonial Governments" in Section 4.

4. D
Break Down the Question Point out to students that the word *central* means that they should select the main or most important issue.

5. C
Break Down the Question This question requires students to recall the trading relations between various Native American groups. Refer students who miss the question to the text titled "Native American Allies" in Section 4.

6. Students should refer to the benefits that some Native American groups received from peaceful relations with the colonists.

Break Down the Question Suggest to students that as they read through the text, they ask themselves what benefits the Native Americans received from trading with the colonists.

Intervention Resources

Reproducible

- Interactive Reader and Study Guide
- Differentiated Instruction Teacher Management System: Lesson Plans for Differentiated Instruction

Technology

- Quick Facts Transparency: The English Colonies Visual Summary
- Differentiated Instruction Modified Worksheets and Tests CD-ROM
- Interactive Skills Tutor CD-ROM

Tips for Test Taking

Track Your Time Use all the time allowed for a test to avoid making errors. Use these **checkpoints** to help monitor your time:

- How many questions should you have answered when one quarter of the time is gone?
- What should the clock read when you are halfway through the questions?
- If you find yourself behind, speed up. If you are ahead, you can—and should—slow down.

Chapter 4 Planning Guide

The American Revolution

Chapter Overview	Reproducible Resources	Technology Resources
CHAPTER 4 pp. 108–143 **Overview: In this chapter, students will learn how the American Revolution began, and will analyze its major battles and eventual outcome.**	**Differentiated Instruction Teacher Management System:*** • Instructional Benchmarking Guides **Interactive Reader and Study Guide:** Chapter Graphic Organizer* **Chapter Resource File:*** • Focus on Writing Activity: Giving an Oral Report • Social Studies Skills Activity: Determine Different Points of View • Chapter Review Activity	**Power Presentations with Video CD-ROM** **Differentiated Instruction Modified Worksheets and Tests CD-ROM** **Primary Source Library CD-ROM for United States History** **Student Edition on Audio CD Program** **History's Impact: United States History Video Program (VHS/DVD):** The American Revolution*
Section 1: **The Revolution Begins** **The Big Idea:** The tensions between the colonies and Great Britain led to armed conflict in 1775.	**Differentiated Instruction Teacher Management System:** Section 1 Lesson Plan* **Interactive Reader and Study Guide:** Section 1 Summary* **Chapter Resource File:*** • Vocabulary Builder Activity, Section 1 • Primary Source Activity: Patrick Henry • History and Geography Activity: Early Battles Around Boston	**Daily Bellringer Transparency:** Section 1* **Map Transparency:** Paul Revere's Ride* **Map Transparency:** British Retreat from Boston* **Map Transparency:** Battles for Boston 1775–76*
Section 2: **Declaring Independence** **The Big Idea:** The colonies formally declared their independence from Great Britain.	**Differentiated Instruction Teacher Management System:** Section 2 Lesson Plan* **Interactive Reader and Study Guide:** Section 2 Summary* **Chapter Resource File:*** • Vocabulary Builder Activity, Section 2 • Primary Source Activity: Choosing Sides	**Daily Bellringer Transparency:** Section 2* **Internet Activity:** Patriots vs. Loyalists Essay
Section 3: **The Struggle for Liberty** **The Big Idea:** Patriot forces faced many obstacles in the war against Britain.	**Differentiated Instruction Teacher Management System:** Section 3 Lesson Plan* **Interactive Reader and Study Guide:** Section 3 Summary* **Chapter Resource File:*** • Vocabulary Builder Activity, Section 3 • Biography Activities: Phillis Wheatley; Haym Salomon; Bernardo de Gálvez • Literature Activity: *The Crisis, No. 1* • Primary Source Activity: Albigence Waldo	**Daily Bellringer Transparency:** Section 3* **Map Transparency:** Battles in the Middle Colonies 1776–1777* **Map Transparency:** Battle of Saratoga* **Map Transparency:** War in the West 1778–79*
Section 4: **Independence!** **The Big Idea:** The war spread to the southern colonies, where the British were finally defeated.	**Differentiated Instruction Teacher Management System:** Section 4 Lesson Plan* **Interactive Reader and Study Guide:** Section 4 Summary* **Chapter Resource File:*** • Vocabulary Builder Activity, Section 4 • Primary Source Activity: General Nathanael Greene Writes to His Wife **Political Cartoons Activities for United States History,** Cartoon 3: American Independence	**Daily Bellringer Transparency:** Section 4* **Map Transparency:** Battle of Yorktown* **Map Transparency:** North America after the Treaty of Paris of 1783* **Internet Activity:** Revolutionary Battle Site Tourist Brochure

HOLT

History's Impact
United States History Video Program (VHS/DVD)

The American Revolution
Suggested use: as a chapter introduction

Review, Assessment, Intervention

🖥️ **Quick Facts Transparency:** The American Revolution Visual Summary*

🔊 **Spanish Chapter Summaries Audio CD Program**

📑 **Progress Assessment Support System (PASS):** Chapter Test*

💿 **Differentiated Instruction Modified Worksheets and Tests CD-ROM:** Modified Chapter Test

💿 **One-Stop Planner CD-ROM:** ExamView Test Generator (English/Spanish)

📑 **PASS:** Section 1 Quiz*
🖥️ **Online Quiz:** Section 1
📑 **Alternative Assessment Handbook**

📑 **PASS:** Section 2 Quiz*
🖥️ **Online Quiz:** Section 2
📑 **Alternative Assessment Handbook**

📑 **PASS:** Section 3 Quiz*
🖥️ **Online Quiz:** Section 3
📑 **Alternative Assessment Handbook**

📑 **PASS:** Section 4 Quiz*
🖥️ **Online Quiz:** Section 4
📑 **Alternative Assessment Handbook**

Power Presentations with Video CD-ROM

Power Presentations with Video are visual presentations of each chapter's main ideas. Presentations can be customized by including Quick Facts charts, images from the text, and video clips.

Power Presentations with Video CD-ROM

HOLT

United States History
Beginnings to 1877

HOLT, RINEHART AND WINSTON

DIVISION FOR
PUBLIC EDUCATION
AMERICAN BAR ASSOCIATION

Developed by the Division for Public Education of the American Bar Association, these materials are part of the **Democracy and Civic Education Resources.**

• **Constitution Study Guide**

• **Supreme Court Case Studies**

Holt ●nline Learning

Teacher Resources
KEYWORD: SR8 TEACHER

Student Resources
KEYWORD: SR8 US4

• Document-Based Questions
• Interactive Multimedia Activities

• Current Events
• Chapter-based Internet Activities
• and more!

Holt Premier
Online Student Edition
Complete online support for interactivity, assessment, and reporting

• Interactive Maps and Notebook
• Standardized Test Prep
• Homework Practice and Research Activities Online

Differentiating Instruction

ENGLISH-LANGUAGE LEARNERS & STRUGGLING READERS

TARGET RESOURCE

Live Ink® Online Reading Help

Spanish Resources

Spanish Chapter Summaries Audio CD Program

One-Stop Planner CD-ROM:
- ExamView Test Generator, Spanish
- PuzzlePro, Spanish

Additional Resources

Differentiated Instruction Teacher Management System: Lesson Plans for Differentiated Instruction

Chapter Resource File:
- Vocabulary Builder Activities
- Social Studies Skills Activity: Understanding Historical Interpretation

Quick Facts Transparency: The American Revolution Visual Summary

Student Edition on Audio CD Program

Online Chapter Summaries in Six Languages

Interactive Skills Tutor CD-ROM

SPECIAL NEEDS LEARNERS

TARGET RESOURCE

Differentiated Instruction Modified Worksheets and Tests CD-ROM

- Vocabulary Flash Cards
- Modified Vocabulary Builder Activities
- Modified Chapter Review Activity
- Modified Chapter Test

Additional Resources

Differentiated Instruction Teacher Management System: Lesson Plans for Differentiated Instruction

Interactive Reader and Study Guide

Social Studies Skills Activity: Understanding Historical Interpretation

Student Edition on Audio CD Program

Interactive Skills Tutor CD-ROM

Live Ink® Online Reading Help

ADVANCED/GIFTED AND TALENTED STUDENTS

TARGET RESOURCE

Primary Source Library CD-ROM for United States History

The Library contains longer versions of quotations in the text, extra sources, and images. Included are point-of-view articles, journals, diaries, historical fiction, and political documents.

Additional Resources

Political Cartoons Activities for United States History: Cartoon 3: American Independence

United States History Document-Based Questions Activities

Differentiated Instruction Teacher Management System: Lesson Plans for Differentiated Instruction

Chapter Resource File:
- Focus on Writing Activity: Giving an Oral Report
- Literature Activity: *The Crisis, No. 1*, by Thomas Paine
- Primary Source Activity: Patrick Henry: The Voice of Freedom
- Primary Source Activity: Choosing Sides
- Primary Source Activity: Albigence Waldo quoted in *Eyewitnesses and Others*

One-Stop Planner® CD-ROM
for Differentiated Instruction

Your differentiated instruction lesson plans are available at your fingertips. Holt's Teacher Management System links teaching support tools to pages in the Interactive Teacher's Edition.

The One-Stop Planner features:
- Interactive Teacher's Edition
- Calendar Planner and pacing guides
- Editable lesson plans
- All reproducible ancillaries in Adobe Acrobat (PDF) format
- ExamView Test Generator (English and Spanish)
- Transparency and video previews

Professional Development

- **In-service and staff development** as part of your Holt Social Studies product purchase
- **Quick Teacher Tutorial Lesson Presentation CD-ROM**
- Intensive tuition-based **Teacher Development Institute**
- **Teaching American History Online**—2 Module Professional Development Course
- **Convenient Holt Speaker Bureau**—face-to-face workshop options
- **PRAXIS™ Test Prep** interactive Web-based content refreshers*
- **24/7 Ask A Professional Development Expert** at http://www.hrw.com/prodev/

* PRAXIS is a trademark of Educational Testing Service (ETS). This publication is not endorsed or approved by ETS.

Chapter Big Ideas

Section 1 The tensions between the colonies and Great Britain led to armed conflict in 1775.

Section 2 The colonies formally declared their independence from Great Britain.

Section 3 Patriot forces faced many obstacles in the war against Britain.

Section 4 The war spread to the southern colonies, where the British were finally defeated.

Focus on Speaking

The **Chapter Resource File** provides a Focus on Speaking worksheet to help students prepare, organize, and present their oral reports.

📝 **CRF:** Focus on Speaking Activity: Giving an Oral Report

CHAPTER 4 1774–1783

The American Revolution

🎤 FOCUS ON SPEAKING

Giving an Oral Report The Revolutionary War was a very exciting time in our history, a time filled with deeds of courage and daring and ending with an amazing victory for the underdog. As you read this chapter, you will learn about the great events and heroic people of that time. Then you will prepare and give an oral report on the history of the American Revolution.

UNITED STATES

1774 The First Continental Congress meets.

1775 The Revolutionary War begins with the fighting at Lexington and Concord.

1774

WORLD

Introduce the Chapter

At Level

Considering the Pros and Cons of War

1. Guide students in a discussion about the pros and cons of a nation going to war. To start the discussion, you may wish to ask students to consider the financial and human costs of war and how war might affect a country's relations with other nations.

2. Next, remind students of the problems between the American colonies and Great Britain in the early 1770s. Ask students to imagine that they are colonial leaders debating whether to go to war against Great

Britain. Then ask students to suggest some pros and cons for the colonies if they should decide to wage war against Britain. Have students consider the size of the colonies and their lack of a unified economy or military.

3. List responses for students to see. Have students copy the list. Then, as they study the chapter, have students note how accurate their responses were. **LS** **Verbal/Linguistic**

• Chapter Preview •

HOLT
History's Impact
► video series
See the Video Teacher's Guide for strategies for using the chapter video **The American Revolution.**

Explore the Picture

A Diverse Land At the time of the American Revolution, many colonists used a gun known as a long rifle or Kentucky rifle. A rifle is a type of gun with a grooved barrel. The grooves spin the ball, or bullet, as it is shot. Compared to a musket, a long rifle can shoot a ball farther and with greater accuracy. On the other hand, soldiers could fire and reload muskets faster than rifles. Rifles also lacked bayonets for use in hand-to-hand combat.

Analyzing Visuals What can you tell about the weapons and style of fighting in the Revolutionary War from this picture? *used muskets or rifles, stood in close ranks to shoot, did not always shoot from behind cover*

go.hrw.com
Online Resources
Chapter Resources:
KEYWORD: SR8 US4
Teacher Resources:
KEYWORD: SR8 TEACHER

What You Will Learn...
Soldiers fight with single-shot muskets in this re-enactment of the Revolutionary War. The men in the colonial militias did not have regular uniforms like the British soldiers did. They wore their own clothes and often used their own supplies. In this chapter you will learn about the American War for Independece.

1776
On July 4 the thirteen colonies issue the Declaration of Independence and break away from Great Britain.

1781
The British surrender to George Washington at Yorktown.

1783 The Treaty of Paris is signed, ending the war.

1777

1780

1783

1778 France allies with the Americans and joins the war against Great Britain.

1779 Spain declares war against Great Britain.

1783 Simon Bolívar is born in present-day Venezuela.

THE AMERICAN REVOLUTION **109**

Explore the Time Line

1. What year did the American Revolution begin, and what year did it end? *1775; 1783*

2. When did colonial leaders issue the Declaration of Independence? *1776*

3. What other countries fought against Britain during the American Revolution? *France, Spain*

4. Where and when did the British surrender to George Washington? *Yorktown, 1781*

Info to Know

French Aid in the War A turning point in the American Revolution occurred when France joined the colonies in their fight against Britain. The French had remained bitter over the loss of their North American holdings after the French and Indian War. As a result, they were eager to weaken Britain's control in North America. During the American Revolution, the French proved to be a valuable ally, particularly in the colonial victory at the Battle of Yorktown, which ended the war.

Reading Social Studies

Understanding Themes

Two themes are covered in the chapter—geography and politics. These two themes played important roles in the events leading up to the independence of the United States. Ask students to predict how geography might have played a factor in the Revolutionary War. How could geography have helped or hurt the Patriots? Why? Then discuss with students the role politics played in the independence of the United States. How might political views have led the colonists to desire their freedom?

Main Ideas in Social Studies

Focus on Reading Ask students to bring in an article from a newspaper or magazine. Have students read the article and then choose two paragraphs at random. Have students use the steps listed on this page to identify the main idea of each paragraph. Remind students to identify the general topic of the paragraph, highlight important facts and details related to that topic, and then determine the author's point. Have students write out their answers to each step.

Reading Social Studies

by Kylene Beers

| Economics | Geography | Politics | Society and Culture | Science and Technology |

Focus on Themes In this chapter you will read about the events of the Revolutionary War, the war by which the United States won its independence. You will learn about some of the major battles that occurred between the American colonists and the British army and how **geography** sometimes affected their outcomes. You will also read the Declaration of Independence, one of the most important **political** documents in all of American history.

Main Ideas in Social Studies

Focus on Reading When you are reading, it is not always necessary to remember every tiny detail of the text. Instead, what you want to remember are the main ideas, the most important concepts around which the text is based.

Identifying Main Ideas Most paragraphs in history books include main ideas. Sometimes the main idea is stated clearly in a single sentence. At other times, the main idea is suggested, not stated. However, that idea still shapes the paragraph's content and the meaning of all of the facts and details in it.

News of the work spread throughout the colonies, eventually selling some 500,0000 copies. Paine reached a wide audience by writing as a common person speaking to common people. *Common Sense* changed the way many colonists viewed their king.

Topic: The paragraph is about the book *Common Sense* by Thomas Paine.

+

Facts and Details:
- Many people from different colonies read the book.
- *Common Sense* eventually sold 500,000 copies.
- Thomas Paine's writing style was easy for the common people to read.

Main Idea: The book *Common Sense* shaped the way some colonists thought about their rulers.

Steps in Identifying Main Ideas

1. Read the paragraph. Ask yourself, "What is this paragraph mostly about?" This will be the topic of the paragraph.
2. List the important facts and details that relate to that topic.
3. Ask yourself, "What seems to be the most important point the writer is making about the topic?" Or ask, "If the writer could say only one thing about this paragraph, what would it be?" This is the **main idea** of the paragraph.

110   CHAPTER 4

Reading and Skills Resources

Reading Support
- Interactive Reader and Study Guide
- Student Edition on Audio CD
- Spanish Chapter Summaries Audio CD Program

Social Studies Skills Support
- Interactive Skills Tutor CD-ROM

Vocabulary Support
- **CRF:** Vocabulary Builder Activities
- **CRF:** Chapter Review Activity
- Differentiated Instruction Modified Worksheets and Tests CD-ROM:
  - Vocabulary Flash Cards
  - Vocabulary Builder Activity
  - Chapter Review Activity
- **OSP** Holt PuzzlePro

You Try It!

The following passage is from the chapter you are about to read. Read it and then answer the questions below.

The Treaty of Paris

From Chapter 4, p. 139

After Yorktown, only a few small battles took place. Lacking the money to pay for a new army, Great Britain entered into peace talks with America. Benjamin Franklin had an influential role in the negotiations.

Delegates took more than two years to come to a peace agreement. In the Treaty of Paris of 1783, Great Britain recognized the independence of the United States. The treaty also set America's borders. A separate treaty between Britain and Spain returned Florida to the Spanish. British leaders also accepted American rights to settle and trade west of the original thirteen colonies.

After you have read the passage, answer the following questions.

1. The main idea of the second paragraph is stated in a sentence. Which sentence expresses the main idea?

2. What is the first paragraph about? What facts and details are included in the paragraph? Based on your answers to these questions, what is the main idea of the first paragraph?

As you read Chapter 4, identify the main ideas of the paragraphs you are reading.

Academic Vocabulary

Success in school is related to knowing academic vocabulary—the words that are frequently used in school assignments and discussions. In this chapter, you will learn the following academic words:

reaction *(p. 114)*
strategy *(p. 129)*

Reading Social Studies

Key Terms and People

Preteach the key terms and people for this chapter by reviewing each term with the class. Then instruct students to define or identify each term or person in the list at left. Have students select ten terms from the list and create a word search using those terms. Have students write the description of each term or person as a clue. When students have finished creating their word search, have them exchange puzzles with a partner. Then have each student complete their partner's word search by circling the key terms and people identified by the clues. **LS Verbal/Linguistic, Visual/Spatial**

Focus on Reading

See the **Focus on Reading** questions in this chapter for more practice on reading social studies skills.

Reading Social Studies Assessment

See the **Chapter Review** at the end of this chapter for student assessment questions related to this reading skill.

Teaching Tip

Finding the Main Idea Point out to students that writing a main idea statement is not the same thing as summarizing a paragraph. Help students learn how to find the main idea by asking them to identify what point the author is trying to make in a paragraph. Point out to students that not all details in a paragraph may relate to the main idea. Occasionally other facts and details are used in order to add interest.

Answers

You Try It! 1. *the second sentence;* **2.** *After the war, Great Britain began peace talks with America. Facts—only a few small battles took place, Great Britain couldn't afford new army, engaged in peace talks with America, Benjamin Franklin had influential role in negotiations; possible main idea—After the war ended, Great Britain and America began peace talks.*

Bellringer

If YOU were there . . . Use the **Daily Bellringer Transparency** for this section to help students answer the question.

Daily Bellringer Transparency, Section 1

Academic Vocabulary

Review with students the high-use academic term in this section.

reaction response (p. 114)

CRF: Vocabulary Builder Activity, Section 1

Taking Notes

Have students copy the graphic organizer onto their own paper and then use it to take notes on the section. This activity will prepare students for the Section Assessment, in which they will complete a graphic organizer that builds on the information using a critical thinking skill.

What You Will Learn...

Main Ideas

1. The First Continental Congress demanded certain rights from Great Britain.
2. Armed conflict between British soldiers and colonists broke out with the "shot heard 'round the world."
3. The Second Continental Congress created the Continental Army to fight the British.
4. In two early battles, the army lost control of Boston but then regained it.

The Big Idea

The tensions between the colonies and Great Britain led to armed conflict in 1775.

Key Terms and People

First Continental Congress, *p. 112*
Patriots, *p. 113*
minutemen, *p. 114*
Redcoats, *p. 114*
Second Continental Congress, *p. 114*
Continental Army, *p. 114*
George Washington, *p. 114*
Battle of Bunker Hill, *p. 115*

 TAKING NOTES As you read, take notes on the events that occurred in the early days of the American Revolution. Write your notes in a graphic organizer like the one below.

First Continental Congress	Battles	Second Continental Congress

The Revolution Begins

If YOU were there...

You are a member of the British Parliament in the 1770s. Some members say that the Americans are defying the king. Others point out that the colonists are British citizens who have certain rights. Now the king must decide to punish the rebellious colonists or listen to their complaints.

What advice would you give the king?

BUILDING BACKGROUND Taxes and harsh new laws led some colonists to protest against the British. In some places, the protests turned violent. The British government refused to listen, ignoring the colonists' demands for more rights. That set the stage for war.

First Continental Congress

To many colonists the closing of Boston Harbor was the final insult in a long list of abuses. In response to the mounting crisis, all the colonies except Georgia sent representatives to a meeting in October 1774. This meeting, known as the **First Continental Congress**, was a gathering of colonial leaders who were deeply troubled about the relationship between Great Britain and its colonies in America. At Carpenters' Hall in Philadelphia, the leaders remained locked in weeks of intense debate. Patrick Henry and others believed that violence was unavoidable. On the other hand, delegates from Pennsylvania and New York had strict orders to seek peace.

Wisely the delegates compromised. They encouraged colonists to continue boycotting British goods but told colonial militias to prepare for war. Meanwhile, they drafted the Declaration of Rights, a list of 10 resolutions to be presented to King George III. Included was the colonists' right to "life, liberty, and property."

The First Continental Congress did not seek a separation from Britain. Its goal was to state the colonists' concerns and ask the king to correct the problems. But before they left Philadelphia, the delegates agreed to meet in 1775 if the king refused their petition.

Patrick Henry returned from the Congress and reported to his fellow Virginians. To encourage them to support the Patriot cause,

112 CHAPTER 4

Teach the Big Idea

At Level

The Revolution Begins

1. **Teach** Ask students the questions in the Main Idea boxes to teach this section.

2. **Apply** Create a two-column chart for the students to see. Label the columns *British Action* and *American Reaction.* Have students copy the chart and list the British actions—and next to each one, the resulting American reactions—that led to the outbreak of the American Revolution.
   LS Verbal/Linguistic

3. **Review** As you review the section, have students share information from their charts. Use it to complete the master chart you created.

4. **Practice/Homework** Have students choose one of the American reactions and either write a letter to the editor or create a political cartoon in support of the action.
   LS Visual/Spatial

   Alternative Assessment Handbook, Rubrics 7: Charts; 27: Political Cartoons; and 43: Writing to Persuade

Battle of Lexington

The Battle of Lexington was the first battle of the Revolutionary War. The map shows the route that Paul Revere used to warn the minutemen of Lexington. He was captured before he could get to Concord. The photo below shows one of the actual candle lanterns used to signal Revere.

Paul Revere's Ride

Battle at Lexington

PAUL REVERE'S RIDE

Battle at Concord

Revere captured

North Church

0   2   4 Miles
0   2   4 Kilometers

Boston   Boston Harbor

Henry voiced these famous words:

" They tell us, Sir, that we are weak; unable to cope with so formidable an adversary. But when will we be stronger? Gentlemen may cry, Peace, Peace—but there is no peace. I know not what course others may take; but as for me, give me liberty or give me death. "
—Patrick Henry, quoted in *Eyewitnesses and Others*

In time many colonists came to agree with Henry. They became known as **Patriots**—colonists who chose to fight for independence from Great Britain.

READING CHECK Identifying Cause and Effect
Why did the delegates attend the First Continental Congress? What were the results?

"Shot Heard 'round the World"

The Continental Congress planned to meet again in 1775. Before it could, the situation in the colonies had changed—for the worse.

The Ride of Paul Revere

British military leaders in the colonies grew uneasy when local militias seemed to be preparing for action. The governor of Massachusetts, Thomas Gage, learned that a stockpile of weapons was stored in Concord, about 20 miles from Boston. In April 1775 he decided to seize the supplies.

THE AMERICAN REVOLUTION **113**

Critical Thinking: Identifying Points of View

At Level

Interview with Patrick Henry

1. Discuss with students Patrick Henry's role in the First Continental Congress and his belief that violence was unavoidable.

2. Ask a volunteer to read aloud the quote from Patrick Henry on this page. Have students discuss the quote. Why does Henry think "there is no peace"? Ask students if they agree with his view. What does he mean by "give me liberty or give me death"?

3. Next, ask students to imagine that they are news reporters interviewing Patrick Henry.

Have students work in pairs to write three to five questions to ask Henry about the events in this section. Each pair should then write the answers they think Henry would have given, based on the text.

4. Have volunteer pairs act out their mock interviews for the class. **LS** Verbal/Linguistic

   Alternative Assessment Handbook, Rubric 37: Writing Assignments

   CRF: Primary Source Activity: Patrick Henry: The Voice of Freedom

---

113

Main Idea

❷ "Shot Heard 'round the World"

Armed conflict between British soldiers and colonists broke out with the "shot heard 'round the world."

Identify Cause and Effect How did the minutemen respond to the battle at Lexington? *continued to attack British troops in Concord and as they retreated to Boston*

Evaluate In your opinion, which side won the fighting at Lexington and Concord, and why? *possible answer— minutemen, because the British were forced to retreat*

🗺 Map Transparency: British Retreat from Boston

Did you know . . .

After the battles at Lexington and Concord, some 10,000 colonial civilians moved out of Boston as the town became a base for British troops. By July 1775, some 13,500 British troops occupied the city.

Answers

Reading Check (top) *British concerns that militias were preparing for war; it escalated the conflict*

Reading Check (bottom) *formed the Continental Army and attempted to restore harmony with the Olive Branch Petition*

ACADEMIC VOCABULARY
reaction
response

Gage thought he had kept his plan a secret. However, Boston was full of spies for the Patriot cause. They noticed the British were preparing for action and quickly informed the Patriots. Unsure of how the British would strike, Sons of Liberty member Paul Revere enlisted the aid of Robert Newman. Newman was to climb into the steeple of the Old North Church and watch for British soldiers. If they advanced across land, Newman would display one lantern from the steeple. If they rowed across the Charles River, Newman would display two lanterns.

When Revere and fellow Patriot William Dawes saw two lights shine, they set off on horseback. Using two different routes out of Boston, they sounded the alert. As the riders advanced, drums and church bells called out the local militia, or **minutemen**—who got their name because they were ready to fight at a minute's notice.

Battles at Lexington and Concord

At dawn on April 19, the British troops arrived at the town of Lexington, near Concord, where 70 armed minutemen waited for them. Patriot captain John Parker yelled to his troops, "Don't fire unless fired upon. But if they mean to have a war, let it begin here." Suddenly a shot rang out. To this day, no one knows who fired this "shot heard 'round the world."

The battle at Lexington ended in minutes with only a few volleys fired. When the smoke cleared, 8 of the badly outnumbered minutemen lay dead, and 10 were wounded. The British, with only one soldier wounded, marched on to Concord.

Although Revere had been arrested, the citizens of Concord were warned by another rider, Samuel Prescott. Most of the weapons in Concord had already been hidden, but the few that were left were now concealed. Some of the British troops, frustrated because the stockpile had disappeared, set fire to a few buildings. In **reaction** the minutemen charged forward.

For some time the colonists had called the British soldiers **Redcoats** because they wore uniforms with bright red jackets. For the skilled colonial marksmen of Concord, the Redcoats made an easy target. The British were forced to retreat to Boston, suffering many casualties along the way. The Redcoats paid dearly for a stockpile of almost nothing.

READING CHECK Drawing Inferences Why did the Patriots need several riders? Why did they take different routes?

Second Continental Congress

King George III had refused to address the concerns listed in the Declaration of Rights. In May 1775, delegates from 12 colonies met again in Philadelphia for the **Second Continental Congress.** This second group of delegates from the colonies was still far from unified. Some called for a war, others for peace. Once again they compromised. Although the Congress did not openly revolt, delegates showed their growing dissatisfaction. They took the bold step of authorizing the Massachusetts militia to become the **Continental Army.** This force would soon include soldiers from all colonies and would carry out the fight against Britain. Congress named a Virginian, **George Washington**, to command the army.

As Washington prepared for war, the Congress pursued peace. On July 5 the delegates signed the Olive Branch Petition as a final attempt to restore harmony. King George refused to read it. Instead, he looked for new ways to punish the colonies.

READING CHECK Summarizing What did the Second Continental Congress accomplish?

Differentiating Instruction

Struggling Readers

1. Copy the graphic organizer for students to see. Omit the blue sample answers.

2. Have students copy the concept web and complete it by entering key people, dates, and events associated with Lexington and Concord.

3. Then discuss how the outbreak of fighting affected colonial relations with Great Britain.
LS Visual/Spatial

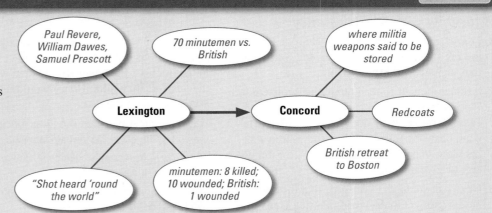

- Paul Revere, William Dawes, Samuel Prescott
- 70 minutemen vs. British
- where militia weapons said to be stored
- **Lexington** → **Concord** — Redcoats
- "Shot heard 'round the world"
- minutemen: 8 killed; 10 wounded; British: 1 wounded
- British retreat to Boston

Early Battles

While the Congress discussed peace, the Massachusetts militia began to fight. Boston was a key city in the early days of the war. Both Patriots and the British fought to hold it.

Bunker Hill

Desperate for supplies, leaders in Boston sent Benedict Arnold and a force of 400 men to New York State. Their objective was to attack the British at Fort Ticonderoga. In May 1775, Arnold captured the fort and its large supply of weapons.

Meanwhile, the poorly supplied Patriots kept the British pinned down inside Boston. Although British leaders were trying to form a battle plan, they awoke on June 17 to a stunning sight. The colonial forces had quietly dug in at Breed's Hill, a point overlooking north Boston. The Redcoats would

have to cross Boston Harbor and fight their way uphill.

As the British force of 2,400 advanced, 1,600 militia members waited. Low on gunpowder, the commander ordered his troops not to fire "until you see the whites of their eyes." As they climbed the exposed hillside with their heavy packs, the British soldiers were cut down. Twice they retreated. Stepping over the dead and wounded, they returned for a third try. The colonists were now out of ammunition, and eventually they had to retreat.

This famous conflict is now known as the Battle of Bunker Hill, although it was actually launched from Breed's Hill. While the Patriots lost, they proved they could take on the Redcoats. For the British, the battle was a tragic victory. To win, they had sacrificed about double the number of Patriot soldiers.

Battles for Boston 1775–76

The colonists were forced to retreat from Breed's Hill, but the British suffered heavy losses during the battle.

Bunker Hill
Breed's Hill
HOWE JUNE 1775

Boston

42°22'N
71°06'W
71°04'W

Boston Harbor

Nook's Hill

Dorchester Heights

General Washington arrived two weeks later and took command of 14,000 troops. In 1776 they drove the British from Boston.

Boston

THIRTEEN COLONIES

ATLANTIC OCEAN

— American advance
◄· American retreat
🪖 American troops
— British advance
·◄· British retreat
🪖 British troops
✹ British victory

0   .5   1 Mile
0   .5   1 Kilometer

71°02'W   71°00'W   70°58'W

GEOGRAPHY SKILLS INTERPRETING MAPS

1. **Place** What geographic advantage did control of Boston provide?
2. **Movement** How did British troops retreat from Boston? How can you tell?

THE AMERICAN REVOLUTION **115**

115

Connect to Economics

Funding the Revolution When the Second Continental Congress raised the Continental Army, it was reluctant to impose a new tax on the already tax-weary colonists. Thus, the Second Continental Congress printed and issued a new national currency. It was expected that individual colonies would eventually collect an equivalent amount in taxes. Because Congress had no authority to force the colonies to tax their residents, however, its demands went largely ignored. This created a significant national debt. To raise money, Congress then borrowed money from France, sold government bonds, and issued soldiers IOUs in lieu of pay.

Close

Have students review the section by discussing whether they think war was inevitable or could have been avoided if the colonists had acted differently.

Review

 Online Quiz, Section 1

Assess

SE Section 1 Assessment

📋 PASS: Section 1 Quiz

📋 Alternative Assessment Handbook

Reteach/Classroom Intervention

📋 Interactive Reader and Study Guide, Section 1

💿 Interactive Skills Tutor CD-ROM

Answers

Reading Check *possible answer— Ignoring the geography of the land could result in disaster because features, such as hills, valleys, mountains, plains, etc., can give one group an advantage in battle.*

116

Dorchester Heights

Shortly after the Battle of Bunker Hill, General Washington arrived in Boston to command the Continental Army. Washington knew that he would need heavier guns to drive the British out of Boston. And he knew where to get them—Fort Ticonderoga. Colonel Henry Knox was assigned to transport the captured cannons from Fort Ticonderoga to Boston. He successfully brought the heavy guns over 300 miles of rough terrain in the middle of winter. When Knox delivered the cannons, Washington was ready to regain control of Boston.

In March 1776 Washington moved his army to Dorchester Heights, an area that overlooked Boston from the south. He positioned the cannons on Nook's Hill, and his troops began to fire down on the British. Their guns were no match for the colonists' well-positioned artillery. "The Rebels have done more in one night than my whole army could do in months," declared British general William Howe. On March 7 Howe retreated from Boston to Canada. The birthplace of the rebellion was now in Patriot hands.

READING CHECK **Drawing Inferences** Why was the geography of the Boston area important in forming a battle plan?

SUMMARY AND PREVIEW Some colonial leaders became convinced that they could not avoid war with Great Britain. In the next section you will read about another step toward war—the writing of the Declaration of Independence.

Section 1 Assessment

Reviewing Ideas, Terms, and People

1. **a. Identify** What was the **First Continental Congress**?
   b. Make Inferences Why did the First Continental Congress send the Declaration of Rights to the king?
   c. Elaborate Why did King George III refuse to consider the colonists' declaration?
2. **a. Identify** Who warned the colonists of the British advance toward Lexington and Concord?
   b. Analyze Why did the British army march on Lexington and Concord?
   c. Elaborate What is meant by the expression "shot heard 'round the world"?
3. **a. Describe** What was the purpose of the **Second Continental Congress**?
   b. Draw Conclusions Were the delegates to the Second Continental Congress ready to revolt against George III? Explain.
   c. Evaluate Defend George III's response to the Declaration of Rights and the Olive Branch Petition.

4. **a. Identify** What leader captured Fort Ticonderoga?
   b. Draw Conclusions How was the **Continental Army** able to drive British forces out of Boston?
   c. Evaluate How would you evaluate the performance of the Continental Army in the early battles of the war? Explain.

Critical Thinking

5. **Categorizing** Review your notes on the early battles of the Revolution. Then copy the graphic organizer below and use it to categorize events in the early days of the Revolution. Some events will be attempts at peace; others will be movement toward war.

Attempts at Peace	Movement toward War

FOCUS ON SPEAKING

6. **Thinking about the Beginning** You'll have about five minutes for your report and only a minute or two to talk about the beginning of the war. What are the one or two most important things you want to say?

116 CHAPTER 4

Section 1 Assessment Answers

1. **a.** a gathering of colonial leaders
   b. to tell him what colonists wanted
   c. possible answer—angry, did not think they had a right to protest
2. **a.** Revere, Dawes, Prescott
   b. to seize militia weapons stored in Concord
   c. possible answer—The first shot of the Revolution impacted the world.
3. **a.** created a Continental Army for defense, while pursuing peace with Great Britain
   b. See answer to Question 3a.

c. possible answer—George III was trying to do what he thought was the best for Britain.

4. **a.** Benedict Arnold
   b. placed cannons overlooking Boston
   c. possible answer—did well for its size and experience, drove the British from Boston
5. Peace—*Declaration of Rights,* ask king to address problems, *Olive Branch Petition;* War—militias, boycott goods, create army
6. Despite colonial attempts at peace, fighting broke out.

BIOGRAPHY

George Washington

What would you do if you were asked to lead a new country?

When did he live? 1732–1799

Where did he live? George Washington was a true American, born in the Virginia colony. As president, he lived in New York City and Philadelphia, the nation's first two capitals. When he retired, he returned to his plantation at Mount Vernon.

What did he do? Although Washington was a wealthy farmer, he spent most of his life in the military and in politics. Leading the colonial forces to victory in the Revolutionary War, he then helped shape the new government of the United States. On April 30, 1789, he was sworn in as the first president of the United States.

Why is he so important? George Washington inspired Americans and helped to unite them. One of his great accomplishments as president was to keep the peace with Britain and France. Upon leaving the presidency, he urged Americans to avoid becoming politically divided.

Drawing Conclusions How might Washington's leadership in the Revolutionary War have prepared him for his role as president?

Mount Vernon was Washington's plantation.

KEY EVENTS

- **1775** Serves in Second Continental Congress; selected commander of the Continental Army
- **1789** Inaugurated as president
- **1793** Begins second term as president
- **1796** Publishes his Farewell Address and retires to his plantation at Mount Vernon
- **1799** Dies at Mount Vernon; his will frees his slaves

Biography

Reading Focus Question
Discuss the introductory question. Consider not only the benefits of leadership but also the challenges and disadvantages, such as being attacked in the press. Keep your answers in mind as you read the biography.

Info to Know
Washington's Early Life George Washington spent most of his early childhood on a farm near Fredericksburg, Virginia. He received irregular schooling, first with a local church leader and later with a schoolmaster. His main education came not from books but from hands-on training in outdoor occupations. He mastered tobacco growing and raising livestock, and early in his teens became familiar with surveying.

Linking to Today
Washington's Legacy George Washington may have lived more than 200 years ago, but his legacy remains apparent. He appears on both the U.S. quarter and $1 bill. He is enshrined at the Washington Monument in Washington, D.C. His image is carved in the national memorial at Mount Rushmore, South Dakota, along with those of Thomas Jefferson, Abraham Lincoln, and Theodore Roosevelt. In addition, numerous places, naval ships, and public schools have been named in Washington's honor.

Collaborative Learning
At Level

Washington Time Capsule

1. Present the following scenario: A caretaker at Mount Vernon has discovered a time capsule that George Washington buried on the grounds. Inside were 10 items and a letter from Washington. In the letter, he explains that the items symbolize the major achievements and events in his life. What are the 10 items in the time capsule?

2. Organize students into small groups. Tell each group to list the major achievements and events in Washington's life. Students should then select 10 items to represent these achievements and events. Last, each group should write Washington's letter, listing the 10 items and explaining why each was included.

3. Have each group share some of the items it listed with the class. Then lead students in a brief discussion of Washington's significance in the United States. **LS Interpersonal, Verbal/Linguistic**

📝 Alternative Assessment Handbook, Rubric 14: Group Activity

Answers

Drawing Conclusions *He gained experience directing others, managing resources, dealing with crises and challenges, overcoming obstacles, making decisions, and working with a diverse group of people under trying circumstances.*

117

Bellringer

If YOU were there... Use the **Daily Bellringer Transparency** for this section to help students answer the question.

 Daily Bellringer Transparency, Section 2

Building Vocabulary

Preteach or review the following terms:

anonymously without giving a name (p. 118)

Enlightenment movement during the 1700s that emphasized the use of reason and logic to improve society (p. 119)

ideal guiding standard or principle (p. 119)

social contract agreement between the people and the government (p. 119)

tyranny abuse of government power (p. 118)

unalienable impossible to take away (p. 119)

CRF: Vocabulary Builder Activity, Section 2

Taking Notes

Have students copy the graphic organizer onto their own paper and then use it to take notes on the section. This activity will prepare students for the Section Assessment, in which they will complete a graphic organizer that builds on the information using a critical thinking skill.

SECTION 2

Declaring Independence

What You Will Learn...

Main Ideas

1. Thomas Paine's *Common Sense* led many colonists to support independence.
2. Colonists had to choose sides when independece was declared.
3. The Declaration of Independence did not address the rights of all colonists.

The Big Idea

The colonies formally declared their independence from Great Britain.

Key Terms and People

Common Sense, p. 118
Thomas Paine, *p. 118*
Thomas Jefferson, *p. 119*
Declaration of Independence, *p. 119*
Loyalists, *p. 119*

TAKING NOTES As you read, take notes on the Declaration of Independence. Write your notes in a graphic organizer like the one below.

Influence of *Common Sense* on Declaration	Main Ideas of Declaration	People Not Included

118 CHAPTER 4

If YOU were there...

You live on a farm in New York in 1776. The conflicts with the British have torn your family apart. Your father is loyal to King George and wants to remain British. But your mother is a fierce Patriot, and your brother wants to join the Continental Army. Your father and others who feel the same way are moving to British–held Canada. Now you must decide what you will do.

Would you go to Canada or support the Patriots?

BUILDING BACKGROUND The outbreak of violence at Lexington, Concord, and Boston took some colonists by surprise. Many, like the father above, opposed independence from Britain. Those who supported freedom began to promote their cause in many ways.

Paine's *Common Sense*

"[There] is something very absurd in supporting a continent to be perpetually [forever] governed by an island." This plainspoken argument against British rule over America appeared in **Common Sense**, a 47-page pamphlet that was distributed in of Philadelphia in January 1776. *Common Sense* was published anonymously—that is, without the author's name. The author, **Thomas Paine**, argued that citizens, not kings and queens, should make laws. At a time when monarchs ruled much of the world, this was a bold idea.

News of the work spread throughout the colonies, eventually selling some 500,000 copies. Paine reached a wide audience by writing as a common person speaking to common people. *Common Sense* changed the way many colonists viewed their king. It made a strong case for economic freedom and for the right to military self-defense. It cried out against tyranny—that is, the abuse of government power. Thomas Paine's words rang out in his time, and they have echoed throughout American history.

READING CHECK **Supporting a Point of View** Would you have agreed with Thomas Paine? Explain.

Teach the Big Idea

At Level

Declaring Independence

Materials: heavy paper or poster board, colored markers

1. **Teach** Ask students the questions in the Main Idea boxes to teach this section.

2. **Apply** Have students create their own versions of the Declaration of Independence. Give each student heavy paper and colored markers. Instead of copying the text of the Declaration, have students write the main ideas stated in the document. Encourage students to illustrate the ideas.

3. **Review** As you review the section, ask for volunteers to explain the main ideas and ideals expressed in the Declaration.

4. **Practice/Homework** Have each student create a political cartoon that illustrates some of the reactions to the Declaration of Independence and its failure to recognize the rights of women and enslaved African Americans. **LS Verbal/Linguistic**

   Alternative Assessment Handbook, Rubrics 27: Political Cartoons; and 37: Writing Assignments

Independence Is Declared

Many colonial leaders agreed with Paine. In June 1776 the Second Continental Congress formed a committee to write a document declaring the colonies' independence.

A New Philosophy of Government

The committee members were John Adams, Benjamin Franklin, **Thomas Jefferson**, Robert R. Livingston, and Roger Sherman. Jefferson was the document's main author.

The **Declaration of Independence** formally announced the colonies' break from Great Britain. In doing so, it expressed three main ideas. First, Jefferson argued that all people possess unalienable rights. He stated that these rights include "life, liberty, and the pursuit of happiness."

Next, Jefferson asserted that King George III had violated the colonists' rights by taxing them without their consent. Jefferson accused the king of passing unfair laws and interfering with colonial governments. He also believed that stationing a large British army within the colonies was a burden on colonists.

Third, Jefferson stated that the colonies had the right to break from Britain. Influenced by the Enlightenment ideal of the social contract, he maintained that governments and rulers must protect the rights of citizens. In exchange, the people agree to be governed. Jefferson argued that because King George III had broken the social contract, the colonists should no longer obey him.

On July 4, 1776, the Continental Congress approved the Declaration of Independence. This act broke all ties to the British crown. The United States of America was born.

Choosing Sides

The signing of the Declaration made the rebellion a full-scale revolt against Britain. Those who supported it would be considered traitors. Colonists who chose to side with the British were known as **Loyalists**—often called Tories.

THE IMPACT TODAY

The Continental Congress voted for independence on July 2. However, because the Declaration was not approved until July 4, the fourth is celebrated today as Independence Day.

Primary Source

POINTS OF VIEW
Choosing Sides

When Ben Franklin's son William was a child, he helped his father experiment with lightning. But by the time William had grown and the Revolution started, the two men viewed the conflict differently. They exchanged letters on the subject.

"I am indeed of opinion, that the parliament has no right to make any law whatever, binding on the colonies . . . I know your sentiments differ from mine on these subjects. You are a thorough government man, which I do not wonder at, nor do I aim at converting you. I only wish you to act uprightly and steadily."

—Benjamin Franklin,
quoted in *The Writings of Benjamin Franklin Vol. III*

"I think that all laws until they are repealed ought to be obeyed and that it is the duty of those who are entrusted with the executive part of government to see that they are so."

—William Franklin,
quoted in *Benjamin and William Franklin* by Sheila L. Skemp

ANALYSIS SKILL **ANALYZING PRIMARY SOURCES**
How did the two men view the British government differently?

THE AMERICAN REVOLUTION **119**

Main Idea

❷ Independence is Declared

Colonists had to choose sides when independence was declared.

Recall What was the significance of the Declaration of Independence? *It formally broke all ties between the colonies and Great Britain and created the United States of America.*

Summarize What were the three main arguments in the Declaration of Independence? *All men possess the unalienable rights of "life, liberty, and the pursuit of happiness"; the king had violated colonists' rights by passing unfair laws; the king had broken the social contract with the colonists.*

Make Judgments How would you have reacted if you were a Patriot and your friend was a Loyalist? *Answers should indicate an understanding that differing views over independence divided the colonists.*

📰 **CRF:** Biography Activity: John Hancock

Info to Know

Reactions to the Declaration of Independence The language of the Declaration of Independence received both criticism and praise throughout the colonies. Some colonial newspapers pointed out the irony of such statements as "all men are created equal" in a slave-holding nation. One newspaper in South Carolina noted that as a clergyman read the Declaration of Independence aloud, a slave held a parasol over the clergyman's head and fanned his face.

Answers

Reading Check *possible answer— The British and the United States would have disregarded the rights of Native Americans when the colonies, or states, began growing larger.*

120

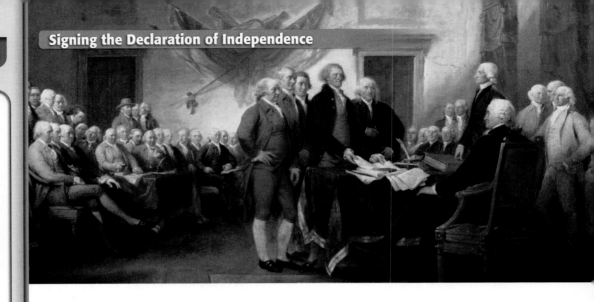

Signing the Declaration of Independence

Historians estimate that 40 to 45 percent of Americans were Patriots, while 20 to 30 percent were Loyalists. The rest were neutral.

Because of persecution by Patriots, more than 50,000 Loyalists fled the colonies during the Revolution. Most went to Canada. In doing so, they abandoned their homes and property. Divided allegiances tore apart families and friendships—even Benjamin Franklin became separated from his Loyalist son William.

Native Americans were at first encouraged by both sides to remain neutral. By the summer of 1776, however, both Patriots and the British were aggressively recruiting Indian fighters. Most sided with the British. In northern New York, four of the six Iroquois nations fought for the British. However, the Oneida and Tuscurora helped the Patriots, even delivering food to the soldiers at Valley Forge. Nevertheless, many historians agree that Native Americans would have lost out in the war, regardless of their alliance.

READING CHECK **Drawing Conclusions** Why would Native Americans have lost out no matter who won the war?

Unfinished Business

Today we recognize that the Declaration of Independence excluded many colonists. While it declared that "all men are created equal," the document failed to mention women, enslaved Africans, or Native Americans.

Women

Although many women were Patriots, the Declaration did not address their rights. At least one delegate's wife, Abigail Adams, tried to influence her husband, John, to include women's rights in the Declaration. In a letter, she expressed her concerns:

❝ Remember the Ladies, and be more generous and favorable to them than your ancestors. Do not put such unlimited power into the hands of the Husbands … If particular care and attention is not paid to the Ladies we are and will not hold ourselves bound by Laws in which we have no voice, or Representation. ❞
—Abigail Adams, quoted in *Notable American Women*

The delegates did not agree with Abigail Adams. The issue remained unresolved.

Critical Thinking: Identifying Points of View   At Level

Letters to the Editor

1. Ask students to imagine that they live in the colonies and have just heard that the Second Continental Congress has approved the Declaration of Independence.

2. Have students write a letter to the editor of a colonial newspaper explaining how they feel about the actions of the congress.

3. Suggest that students write their letters from the perspective of someone living in the

colonies such as a Loyalist, Patriot, member of militia, or British officer. Make sure that students explain why they support or do not support the actions of the Second Continental Congress.

4. Ask for volunteers to read their letters to the class. 🔲 **Verbal/Linguistic**

📰 Alternative Assessment Handbook, Rubric 17: Letters to Editors

① John Adams
② Roger Sherman
③ Robert Livingston
④ Thomas Jefferson
⑤ Benjamin Franklin
⑥ Charles Thomson
⑦ John Hancock

The Declaration of Independence was adopted on July 4, 1776. This painting shows 47 of the 56 signers of the document. The man sitting on the right is John Hancock, who was the president of the Second Continental Congress. He is accepting the Declaration from the committee that wrote it.

How realistic do you think this painting is?

African and Native Americans

The Declaration did not recognize the rights of enslaved Africans, either. In the document, its authors had compared life under British rule to living as an enslaved people. Now the obvious question arose: Why did any form of slavery exist in a land that valued personal freedom?

In July 1776 slavery was legal in all the colonies. By the 1780s the New England colonies were taking steps to end slavery. Even so, the conflict over slavery continued long after the Revolutionary War.

The Declaration of Independence also did not address the rights of Native Americans to life, liberty, or property. Despite the Proclamation of 1763, American colonists had been quietly settling on lands that belonged to Native Americans. This tendency to disregard the rights of Native Americans would develop into a pattern after the colonists won their independence from Great Britain.

READING CHECK Finding Main Ideas What groups were unrepresented in the Declaration of Independence?

SUMMARY AND PREVIEW In 1776 the colonists declared their independence. To achieve their goal, however, they would have to win a war against the British army. In the next section you will learn about some of the battles of the Revolutionary War. For a time, it seemed as if the British would defeat the colonists.

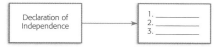

Section 2 Assessment

go.hrw.com
Online Quiz
KEYWORD: SR8 HP4

Reviewing Ideas, Terms, and People

1. **a. Identify** Who was **Thomas Paine**?
   b. Make Inferences Why do you think Thomas Paine originally published **Common Sense** anonymously?
   c. Elaborate Do you think that most colonists would have supported independence from Britain without Thomas Paine's publication of *Common Sense*? Explain.

2. **a. Identify** What two sides emerged in response to the **Declaration of Independence**? What did each side favor?
   b. Explain What arguments did the authors of the Declaration of Independence give for declaring the colonies free from British control?
   c. Predict How might some groups use the Declaration of Independence in the future to gain rights?

3. **a. Identify** Who urged her husband to "remember the ladies"?
   b. Making Inferences Why did the authors of the Declaration of Independence fail to address the rights of women, Native Americans, and African Americans in the document?

Critical Thinking

4. **Analyzing** Review your notes on the Declaration of Independence. Then copy the graphic organizer below and use it to identify three results of the Declaration of Independence.

```
┌──────────────┐          ┌──────────────┐
│ Declaration of│  ──────▶ │ 1. _____ │
│ Independence │          │ 2. _____ │
└──────────────┘          │ 3. _____ │
                          └──────────────┘
```

FOCUS ON SPEAKING

5. **Gathering Ideas about the Declaration of Independence** You are living at the time of the American Revolution. What is new and surprising about the colonists' actions? In one or two minutes, what is the most important thing you can say about the colonies' declaring independence?

THE AMERICAN REVOLUTION **121**

Main Idea

③ Unfinished Business

The Declaration of Independence did not address the rights of all colonists.

Evaluate How are Abigail Adams's concerns about representation similar to the colonists' concerns in Chapter 3? *The colonists were not represented in Parliament. Abigail Adams writes that women are not represented in the Declaration and not bound by it.*

Make Judgments Why do you think the Declaration of Independence did not address the rights of women, enslaved Africans, and Native Americans? *possible answers—Culture and tradition were against extending rights; those groups could not send delegates to the Continental Congress.*

• **Review & Assess** •

Close

Discuss whether declaring independence was justified.

Review

🖥 Online Quiz, Section 2

Assess

SE Section 2 Assessment

📝 PASS: Section 2 Quiz

📝 Alternative Assessment Handbook

Reteach/Classroom Intervention

📝 Interactive Reader and Study Guide, Section 2

💿 Interactive Skills Tutor CD-ROM

Answers

Signing the Declaration of Independence *possible answer—accurate representation of a historic event*

Reading Check *women, enslaved Africans, and Native Americans*

Section 2 Assessment Answers

1. **a.** author of *Common Sense*
   b. possible answer—fear of punishment
   c. possible answers—yes, England was unfair; no, it had a significant impact on public opinion

2. **a.** Patriots chose to fight for independence; Loyalists remained loyal to Great Britain.
   b. All men possess unalienable rights; the king had violated colonists rights by passing unfair laws; the king had broken the social contract with the colonists.

c. by citing the ideals of equality, freedom, and liberty stated in the document

3. **a.** Abigail Adams
   b. possible answer—These groups had no representation at either Continental Congress.

4. rebellion became a revolt, colonists chose sides, Loyalists fled

5. possible answer—colonial leaders said the British government had denied their rights; issued the Declaration of Independence forming the United States of America

121

Primary Source

Reading Like a Historian

Declaration of Independence

- Who wrote and signed the document? What do you know about these people?
- What basic ideas about people and government did the authors and signers hold? Did the people for whom the Declaration was being written hold the same views?
- Why did the authors write the document? What did they hope to achieve?

Activity **The Case for Independence** Discuss with students the way in which Jefferson and the other authors logically built a case for the right of the colonies to declare independence. Have students, working as a class or in small groups, create graphic organizers that show the logical progression of points in the case for independence. **LS** **Logical/Mathematical**

Exploring the Document

Top: *The Declaration shows that it is possible for people to change the government in power when it no longer reflects their will.*

Bottom: *Students might point to words such as* absolute despotism, repeated injuries and usurpations, tyranny, refused, forbidden, *and* obstructed *and mention that these words convey a sense of injustice that Jefferson and the other members of the Continental Congress thought the colonists had suffered at the hands of Great Britain.*

EXPLORING THE DOCUMENT Thomas Jefferson wrote the first draft of the Declaration in a little more than two weeks. **How is the Declaration's idea about why governments are formed still important to our country today?**

Vocabulary

impel force

endowed provided

usurpations wrongful seizures of power

evinces clearly displays

despotism unlimited power

tyranny oppressive power exerted by a government or ruler

candid fair

EXPLORING THE DOCUMENT Here the Declaration lists the charges that the colonists had against King George III. **How does the language in the list appeal to people's emotions?**

The Declaration of Independence

In Congress, July 4, 1776
The unanimous Declaration of the thirteen united States of America,

When in the Course of human events, it becomes necessary for one people to dissolve the political bands which have connected them with another, and to assume among the Powers of the earth, the separate and equal station to which the Laws of Nature and of Nature's God entitle them, a decent respect to the opinions of mankind requires that they should declare the causes which **impel** them to the separation.

We hold these truths to be self-evident, that all men are created equal, that they are **endowed** by their Creator with certain unalienable Rights, that among these are Life, Liberty, and the pursuit of Happiness. That to secure these rights, Governments are instituted among Men, deriving their just powers from the consent of the governed, That whenever any Form of Government becomes destructive of these ends, it is the Right of the People to alter or to abolish it, and to institute new Government, laying its foundation on such principles and organizing its powers in such form, as to them shall seem most likely to effect their Safety and Happiness. Prudence, indeed, will dictate that Governments long established should not be changed for light and transient causes; and accordingly all experience hath shown, that mankind are more disposed to suffer, while evils are sufferable, than to right themselves by abolishing the forms to which they are accustomed. But when a long train of abuses and **usurpations**, pursuing invariably the same Object **evinces** a design to reduce them under absolute **Despotism**, it is their right, it is their duty, to throw off such Government, and to provide new Guards for their future security.—Such has been the patient sufferance of these Colonies; and such is now the necessity which constrains them to alter their former Systems of Government. The history of the present King of Great Britain is a history of repeated injuries and usurpations, all having in direct object the establishment of an absolute **Tyranny** over these States. To prove this, let Facts be submitted to a **candid** world.

He has refused his Assent to Laws, the most wholesome and necessary for the public good.

He has forbidden his Governors to pass Laws of immediate and pressing importance, unless suspended in their operation till his Assent should be obtained; and when so suspended, he has utterly neglected to attend to them.

Differentiating Instruction

Below Level

English-Language Learners

Materials: translations of the Declaration of Independence in students' native languages (optional)

1. Help students with vocabulary and phrasing in the Declaration of Independence by writing short, simple summaries of each paragraph.

2. Once students understand the meaning of a portion of the text, help them work through the actual wording. Have students list any words they do not understand. As students

work, circulate and help students define the words they listed. If possible, pair English learners with English speakers.

3. **Extend** Provide translations of the Declaration of Independence in students' native languages. Have students use the translations to help them understand the English version. **LS** **Verbal/Linguistic**

📖 Alternative Assessment Handbook, Rubric 1: Acquiring Information

He has refused to pass other Laws for the accommodation of large districts of people, unless those people would **relinquish** the right of Representation in the Legislature, a right **inestimable** to them and **formidable** to tyrants only.

He has called together legislative bodies at places unusual, uncomfortable, and distant from the depository of their Public Records, for the sole purpose of fatiguing them into compliance with his measures.

He has dissolved Representative Houses repeatedly, for opposing with manly firmness his invasions on the rights of the people.

He has refused for a long time, after such dissolutions, to cause others to be elected; whereby the Legislative Powers, incapable of **Annihilation**, have returned to the People at large for their exercise; the State remaining in the mean time exposed to all the dangers of invasion from without, and **convulsions** within.

He has endeavored to prevent the population of these States; for that purpose obstructing the Laws of **Naturalization of Foreigners**; refusing to pass others to encourage their migration hither, and raising the conditions of new **Appropriations of Lands**.

He has obstructed the Administration of Justice, by refusing his Assent to Laws for establishing Judiciary Powers.

He has made Judges dependent on his Will alone, for the **tenure** of their offices, and the amount and payment of their salaries.

He has erected **a multitude of** New Offices, and sent hither swarms of Officers to harass our people, and eat out their substance.

He has kept among us, in times of peace, Standing Armies without the Consent of our legislature.

He has affected to render the Military independent of and superior to the Civil Power.

He has combined with others to subject us to a jurisdiction foreign to our constitution, and unacknowledged by our laws; giving his Assent to their Acts of pretended legislation:

For **quartering** large bodies of armed troops among us:

For protecting them, by a mock Trial, from Punishment for any Murders which they should commit on the Inhabitants of these States:

For cutting off our Trade with all parts of the world:

For imposing taxes on us without our Consent:

For depriving us in many cases, of the benefits of Trial by Jury:

Vocabulary

relinquish release, yield
inestimable priceless
formidable causing dread
annihilation destruction
convulsions violent disturbances
naturalization of foreigners the process by which foreign-born persons become citizens
appropriations of lands setting aside land for settlement
tenure term
a multitude of many
quartering lodging, housing

Mum Bett, a Massachusetts slave, believed that the words "all men are created equal" should apply to her and other enslaved Africans. She successfully sued for her freedom in 1781.

Historical Documents

Info to Know

Signing the Declaration On July 1, 1776, three days before the Declaration of Independence was signed, just nine of the colonies firmly supported independence. Because a vote was to be taken on July 2, supporters of independence spent the day trying to convince opposing delegates of the need for self government. One supporter, Richard Henry Lee, finally swayed South Carolina delegate Edward Rutledge, who agreed to vote for independence if the delegates from Pennsylvania and Delaware did so as well.

The following morning was spent waiting for Delaware delegate Caesar Rodney, who had been home caring for his sick wife. Rodney finally arrived, covered with mud after a frantic ride over rain-soaked roads. He cast his vote in favor of independence, and the delegates of South Carolina and Pennsylvania followed suit.

Info to Know

Celebrating Independence Day In a letter, John Adams declared that July 2, the day the Continental Congress voted for independence, should be celebrated with "poems and parade, with shows, games, sports, guns, bells, bonfires, and illuminations." However, the nation celebrates Independence Day on July 4, the day the Continental Congress approved the final draft of the Declaration. Most members did not sign the document until August 2.

The Declaration and American Soldiers After the Declaration of Independence was passed by the Continental Congress, the members requested copies be made for the commanders of the troops fighting the Revolutionary War. Official word of the Declaration of Independence reached General George Washington in New York on July 9, 1776. He then ordered that all troops be gathered for a reading of the document in order to help boost their morale.

Exploring the Document

Tyrant *means a ruler who abuses his or her right to rule by treating subjects unfairly and harshly.*

Vocabulary

arbitrary not based on law

render make

abdicated given up

foreign mercenaries soldiers hired to fight for a country not their own

perfidy violation of trust

insurrections rebellions

petitioned for redress asked formally for a correction of wrongs

unwarrantable jurisdiction unjustified authority

magnanimity generous spirit

conjured urgently called upon

consanguinity common ancestry

acquiesce consent to

EXPLORING THE DOCUMENT Here the Declaration calls the king a tyrant. **What do you think** *tyrant* **means from this passage?**

For transporting us beyond Seas to be tried for pretended offences:

For abolishing the free System of English Laws in a neighboring Province, establishing therein an **Arbitrary** government, and enlarging its Boundaries so as to **render** it at once an example and fit instrument for introducing the same absolute rule into these Colonies:

For taking away our Charters, abolishing our most valuable Laws, and altering fundamentally the Forms of our Governments:

For suspending our own Legislature, and declaring themselves invested with Power to legislate for us in all cases whatsoever.

He has **abdicated** Government here, by declaring us out of his Protection and waging War against us.

He has plundered our seas, ravaged our Coasts, burnt our towns, and destroyed the lives of our people.

He is at this time transporting large armies of **foreign mercenaries** to complete the works of death, desolation and tyranny, already begun with circumstances of Cruelty & **perfidy** scarcely paralleled in the most barbarous ages, and totally unworthy the Head of a civilized nation.

He has constrained our fellow Citizens taken Captive on the high Seas to bear Arms against their Country, to become the executioners of their friends and Brethren, or to fall themselves by their Hands.

He has excited domestic **insurrections** amongst us, and has endeavored to bring on the inhabitants of our frontiers, the merciless Indian Savages, whose known rule of warfare, is an undistinguished destruction of all ages, sexes and conditions.

In every stage of these Oppressions We have **Petitioned for Redress** in the most humble terms: Our repeated Petitions have been answered only by repeated injury. A Prince, whose character is thus marked by every act which may define a Tyrant, is unfit to be the ruler of a free People.

Nor have We been wanting in attention to our British brethren. We have warned them from time to time of attempts by their legislature to extend an **unwarrantable jurisdiction** over us. We have reminded them of the circumstances of our emigration and settlement here. We have appealed to their native justice and **magnanimity**, and we have **conjured** them by the ties of our common kindred to disavow these usurpations, which, would inevitably interrupt our connections and correspondence. They too have been deaf to the voice of justice and of **consanguinity**. We must, therefore, **acquiesce** in the necessity, which denounces our Separation, and hold them, as we hold the rest of mankind, Enemies in War, in Peace Friends.

Collaborative Learning

Celebrating the Declaration of Independence

1. Have students conduct research to find out some of the ways in which their community celebrates Independence Day. Have students share their findings. Then ask volunteers to share some of their family traditions for the holiday.

2. Next, have students discuss ways to celebrate not only independence but also the ideals expressed in the Declaration of Independence. Have students work as a class to list activities.

3. Have the class prepare to hold a celebration of the ideals in the Declaration of Independence. Have students choose activities and decorations and work in committees to prepare them.

4. Have students hold their Declaration of Independence celebration. **LS Interpersonal, Kinesthetic, Verbal/Linguistic**

   Alternative Assessment Handbook, Rubrics 14: Group Activity; and 30: Research

We, therefore, the Representatives of the united States of America, in General Congress, Assembled, appealing to the Supreme Judge of the world for the **rectitude** of our intentions, do, in the Name, and by Authority of the good People of these Colonies, solemnly publish and declare, That these United Colonies are, and of Right ought to be Free and Independent States; that they are Absolved from all Allegiance to the British Crown, and that all political connection between them and the State of Great Britain, is and ought to be totally dissolved; and that as Free and Independent States, they have full Power to levy War, conclude Peace, contract Alliances, establish Commerce, and to do all other Acts and Things which Independent States may of right do. And for the support of this Declaration, with a firm reliance on the Protection of Divine Providence, we mutually pledge to each other our Lives, our Fortunes and our sacred Honor.

John Hancock	Benjamin Harrison	Lewis Morris
Button Gwinnett	Thomas Nelson, Jr.	Richard Stockton
Lyman Hall	Francis Lightfoot Lee	John Witherspoon
George Walton	Carter Braxton	Francis Hopkinson
William Hooper	Robert Morris	John Hart
Joseph Hewes	Benjamin Rush	Abraham Clark
John Penn	Benjamin Franklin	Josiah Bartlett
Edward Rutledge	John Morton	William Whipple
Thomas Heyward, Jr.	George Clymer	Samuel Adams
Thomas Lynch, Jr.	James Smith	John Adams
Arthur Middleton	George Taylor	Robert Treat Paine
Samuel Chase	James Wilson	Elbridge Gerry
William Paca	George Ross	Stephen Hopkins
Thomas Stone	Caesar Rodney	William Ellery
Charles Carroll of Carrollton	George Read	Roger Sherman
George Wythe	Thomas McKean	Samuel Huntington
	William Floyd	William Williams
Richard Henry Lee	Philip Livingston	Oliver Wolcott
Thomas Jefferson	Francis Lewis	Matthew Thornton

Vocabulary

rectitude rightness

EXPLORING THE DOCUMENT Here is where the document declares the independence of the colonies. **Whose authority does the Congress use to declare independence?**

EXPLORING THE DOCUMENT The Congress adopted the final draft of the Declaration of Independence on July 4, 1776. A formal copy, written on parchment paper, was signed on August 2, 1776. **From whom did the Declaration's signers receive their authority to declare independence?**

EXPLORING THE DOCUMENT The following is part of a passage that the Congress removed from Jefferson's original draft: "He has waged cruel war against human nature itself, violating its most sacred rights of life and liberty in the persons of a distant people who never offended him, captivating and carrying them into slavery in another hemisphere, or to incur miserable death in their transportation thither." **Why do you think the Congress deleted this passage?**

Historical Documents

Info to Know

The Signers The 56 signers of the Declaration of Independence shared many characteristics. Almost all were Protestant white males who were fairly wealthy. In addition, 48 of the signers were born in America.

Did you know . . .

As president of the Second Continental Congress, John Hancock was the first delegate to sign the Declaration of Independence. He signed his name largely and it stands out from the other names. According to legend, Hancock wanted to make certain that King George III would see his name. As a result, the name *John Hancock* has become an informal term for a person's signature.

CRF: Biography Activity: John Hancock

Exploring the Document

Top: *"by Authority of the good People of these Colonies"*

Middle: *by authority of the colonies*

Bottom: *possible answers—Slavery was controversial, and many colonies, particularly those in the South, did not wish to abolish it; delegates from pro-slavery colonies would likely not have agreed to sign the Declaration if the passage had remained.*

Bellringer

If YOU were there. . . Use the **Daily Bellringer Transparency** for this section to help students answer the question.

📚 Daily Bellringer Transparency, Section 3

Academic Vocabulary

Review with students the high-use academic term in this section.

strategy a plan for fighting a battle or war (p. 129)

📋 **CRF:** Vocabulary Builder Activity, Section 3

Taking Notes

Have students copy the graphic organizer onto their own paper and then use it to take notes on the section. This activity will prepare students for the Section Assessment, in which they will complete a graphic organizer that builds on the information using a critical thinking skill.

SECTION 3

The Struggle for Liberty

What You Will Learn...

Main Ideas

1. Many Americans supported the war effort.
2. The Patriots both won and lost battles during the years 1775–1777.
3. France and Spain helped the Patriots fight the British.
4. The winter at Valley Forge tested the strength of Patriot troops.
5. The war continued at sea and in the West.

The Big Idea

Patriot forces faced many obstacles in the war against Britain.

Key Terms and People

mercenaries, *p. 128*
Battle of Trenton, *p. 129*
Battle of Saratoga, *p. 130*
Marquis de Lafayette, *p. 131*
Baron Friedrich von Steuben, *p. 131*
Bernardo de Gálvez, *p. 131*
John Paul Jones, *p. 133*
George Rogers Clark, *p. 133*

TAKING NOTES Create a time line like the one below. As you read, identify and describe the events occurring on each of the dates listed on your time line.

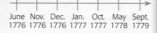

June   Nov.   Dec.   Jan.   Oct.   May   Sept.
1776   1776   1776   1777   1777   1778   1779

126 CHAPTER 4

If YOU were there...

You are a serving maid at an inn in New York City. British soldiers often stop at the inn for a meal. You sometimes overhear their conversations, though they don't notice you. Now a Patriot leader has asked you to bring him any information you hear. You want to help the Patriot cause but wonder what will happen if you are caught spying.

Would you agree to spy for the Patriots?

BUILDING BACKGROUND Many colonists struggled for the Patriot cause. Men, women, and children all made important contributions. They fought, kept farms and shops running, and provided food and supplies. In spite of their efforts, winning the war was a great challenge.

Supporting the War Effort

George Washington's chief task as the Continental Army's commander in chief was to raise troops. During the war, more than 230,000 soldiers served in the Continental Army, and another 145,000 enlisted in local militias. The typical soldier was young, often under the legal age of 16, and had little money or property. The army offered low pay, harsh conditions, and a big chance of becoming a casualty. Yet the Patriots knew they were fighting for their homes and their freedom.

Finding and keeping dedicated soldiers would be a constant challenge throughout the war. In time, the Continental Congress required states to supply soldiers. Men who could afford it often paid others, such as slaves or apprentices, to fight in their places.

One question facing General Washington was whether to recruit African Americans. Many white southerners opposed the idea, and at first Washington banned African Americans from serving. When the British promised freedom to any slave who fought on their side, however, thousands of African Americans joined the Redcoats.

Teach the Big Idea

At Level

The Struggle for Liberty

1. **Teach** Ask students the questions in the Main Idea boxes to teach this section.

2. **Apply** Create a two-column chart for students to see. Label the columns *Major Battles* and *Challenges*. Have students copy the chart and complete it by listing and describing the major battles in this section. Then have students describe the challenges the Patriots faced at various stages. **LS Verbal/Linguistic, Visual/Spatial**

3. **Review** As you review the section, have students share information from their charts.

4. **Practice/Homework** Ask students to imagine that they are a Patriot soldier at one of the battles listed in their charts. Have them write a letter home describing their impression of the battle. **LS Intrapersonal, Verbal/Linguistic**

📋 Alternative Assessment Handbook, Rubric 25: Personal Letters

Battles in the Middle Colonies 1776–77

Major Battles

- ⚔ New York, August 1776
- ⚔ Trenton, December 1776
- ⚔ Princeton, January 1777
- ⚔ Brandywine, September 1777

Colonial Forces	British Forces
Strengths	**Strengths**
• Fought for a cause they believed in	• Well-trained, well-equipped soldiers
• Got help from European nations	• Large, powerful navy
Weaknesses	**Weaknesses**
• Untrained, poorly equipped soldiers	• Had to cross Atlantic Ocean
• Small navy	• Used mercenaries as soldiers

Legend:
- ▬ British advance
- ⚔ British victory
- ▬ Colonial advance
- ⚔ Colonial victory
- ···· Proclamation Line of 1763

0   75   150 Miles
0   75   150 Kilometers

GEOGRAPHY SKILLS INTERPRETING MAPS

1. **Movement** About how far was Washington's march from Boston to New York?
2. **Human-Environment Interaction** How did geography affect the British advance on Philadelphia?

In response, the Continental Army began allowing free African Americans to serve.

While men served as soldiers, many women ran farms and businesses. Others helped the army by raising money for supplies or making clothing. Women served as messengers, nurses, and spies. A Massachusetts man noted:

❝ At every house Women and children [are] making Cartridges, running Bullets …and at the same time animating [encouraging] their Husbands and Sons to fight. ❞
—Anonymous, quoted in *Born for Liberty*, by Sara M. Evans

Perhaps the best known woman to fight in the war was Mary Ludwig Hays. She was called Molly Pitcher because she brought water to the troops. When her husband was wounded in a 1778 battle, she took his place loading cannons. Another woman, Deborah Sampson, dressed as a man and fought in several battles.

READING CHECK Summarizing How did various groups contribute to the war effort?

Defeats and Victories

As the Revolution gathered steam, it became more deadly. At first the Continental Army suffered a number of defeats. In time, though, the Patriots' patience began to pay off.

THE IMPACT TODAY

Women are still banned from ground combat. But in Operation Iraqi Freedom, women operated warships and flew combat jets and helicopters for the first time in a major air-ground conflict.

THE AMERICAN REVOLUTION **127**

Direct Teach

Main Idea

❶ Supporting the War Effort

Many Americans supported the war effort.

Explain Why did the Continental Army begin allowing free African Americans to serve? *to counter Britain's promise of freedom to any slave who joined the British*

Summarize In what ways did women help the Patriot cause? *ran farms and businesses; raised money and made clothing for army; served as messengers, nurses, and spies*

Make Judgments In your opinion, should wealthy Patriots have been allowed to pay substitutes to fight in their place? *possible answers—yes, because it wasn't illegal; no, because others were fighting for something that would benefit the wealthy*

📋 **CRF:** Biography Activity: Phillis Wheatley

🗝 **Map Transparency:** Battles in the Middle Colonies

Interpreting Charts
Colonial and British Forces
Evaluating Who do you think had the advantage at the start of the war—the British or the Patriot forces? *possible answers—the British, because they were well-trained and well-equipped; the Americans, because they were fighting in their own land for a cause in which they believed*

Critical Thinking: Finding Main Ideas

At Level

Patriot Recruitment Posters

Materials: construction paper or small poster board, colored markers and pens

1. Have students create Patriot recruitment posters to encourage enlistment in the Continental Army.

2. Students' posters should explain the benefits of enlisting, the advantages the Patriots have, and why the war is being fought. Encourage students to include one or more illustrations to enhance their posters.

3. As an option, have students create a Patriot recruitment poster directed at a specific group, such as free African Americans, Native Americans, or women. The poster should reflect the issues the group faced during the war and the ways in which the group contributed to or affected the Patriot cause.

4. Ask volunteers to share their posters with the class. 🅛🅢 **Visual/Spatial**

📋 Alternative Assessment Handbook, Rubric 28: Posters

Answers

Interpreting Maps 1. *about 200 miles;* **2.** *To get close to Philadelphia, the British had to travel far south by sea and then go north over land.*

Reading Check *Young men enlisted; some free African Americans joined the Patriots; women helped raise money and make clothes; some women served as messengers, nurses, and spies.*

127

Main Idea

❷ Defeats and Victories

The Patriots both won and lost battles during the years 1775–1777.

Recall What early defeats did the Patriots experience? *Canada— defeated at Quebec; New York— British slowly drove the Patriots out of New York and into New Jersey*

Draw Conclusions Why do you think the Patriots were defeated in New York? *possible answers—They were outnumbered; British soldiers were better trained and equipped.*

Make Judgments Do you think the Patriots should have invaded British Canada? Why or why not? *possible answers—yes, a victory there would have been worth the risk; no, the Patriots did not have enough men and supplies to risk such an endeavor*

📖 **CRF:** Biography Activity: Haym Salomon

Checking for Understanding

True or False Answer each statement *T* if it is true or *F* if it is false. If false, explain why.

1. Hessians fought for the British because they were loyal to Britain. *F, The Hessians were mercenaries who fought for money.*
2. Howe's soldiers were much better equipped than Washington's soldiers. *T*
3. George Washington's successful defense against the Hessian attack at Trenton was an important Patriot victory. *F, Washington launched the attack at Trenton.*

Answers

Crossing the Delaware *possible answer—feelings of patriotism, courage, and pride*

128

Canada

In part because the army was short on supplies, many Patriot leaders favored fighting a defensive war. Others wanted to invade British-controlled Canada and make it the "14th colony."

Patriot troops led by General Richard Montgomery captured Montreal in November 1775. The next major target was the city of Quebec. Benedict Arnold, now a general, led his troops north on a remarkable trek through the rough backcountry of Maine. He reached Quebec around the same time that Montreal fell to Montgomery. Since his first attempt to take the city failed, Arnold waited for Montgomery's troops to join his.

Taking an immense chance, the combined armies attacked during a fierce blizzard on New Year's Eve. They were quickly defeated. The Americans had suffered a crushing loss, and the Patriots' hopes of taking Canada faded.

New York

New York City became the next battleground. General Washington had moved his troops to New York, expecting the British arrival. Sure enough, in June 1776, a fleet of British ships approached New York Bay. Led by General William Howe, the British forced the Continental Army off Long Island.

Howe's 32,000 soldiers were much better equipped than Washington's 23,000 men, most of whom were militia. The Patriot general had to use all of his skills just to save his army.

In a series of battles, Howe pounded the Continental Army, forcing it to retreat farther and farther. The Redcoats captured Patriots as well as supplies. Eventually, the British pushed Washington across the Hudson River into New Jersey. Howe's revenge for his defeat at Boston was complete.

During the New York campaigns, a young Connecticut officer named Nathan Hale went behind British lines to get secret information. Seized by the British with documents hidden in the soles of his shoes, Hale was ordered to be hanged. Before his execution, he is said to

FOCUS ON READING

What is the main idea of the third paragraph under "New York"?

have declared, "I regret that I have but one life to lose for my country."

New Jersey

In November 1776 the tattered Continental Army was on the run. Washington's remaining 6,000 men were tired and discouraged. The one-year contract for many of them would end on December 31. Who would re-enlist in this losing army, and who would replace the soldiers who left? Washington's army was in danger of vanishing.

Thinking the rebellion would end soon, Howe left New Jersey in the hands of soldiers from the German state of Hesse. The Hessians were **mercenaries**—foreign soldiers who fought not out of loyalty, but for pay.

On December 7 Washington retreated across the Delaware River into Pennsylvania. Even with 2,000 fresh troops, the Patriots were near the end. "These are the times that try men's souls," wrote Thomas Paine in *The American Crisis*, a series of pamphlets he began publishing in late 1776.

Without a convincing victory, Washington knew he would lose his army. He decided to take a big chance and go on the offensive. The Americans would attack the Hessians at Trenton, New Jersey.

128 CHAPTER 4

Crossing the Delaware

George Washington and his troops crossed the partially frozen Delaware River on the night of December 25, 1776. This daring act led to a key Patriot victory at the Battle of Trenton. German American artist Emanuel Leutze created this famous painting in 1851. A version of Leutze's *Washington Crossing the Delaware* hangs in the Metropolitan Museum of Art in New York City.

What feelings do you think Leutze wanted to inspire with this painting?

Critical Thinking: Analyzing/Evaluating Information   **At Level**

Analyzing Patriot Battle Strategies

1. Organize students into small groups and have each group brainstorm different strategies that an army might use to defeat a more powerful opponent. After a brief amount of time, have each group share some of its ideas with the class.

2. Draw a chart with two columns and five rows. Label the columns *Main Strategy* and *Evaluation*. Label the rows *Quebec, New York, Trenton, Princeton,* and *Saratoga.*

3. Have each group copy the chart and describe the Patriot's main strategy at each battle. Then have the groups analyze and write an evaluation of each strategy. Was it the best strategy to use in the situation? Why or why not? Have each group share some of its evaluations.

LS Interpersonal, Verbal/Linguistic

📖 Alternative Assessment Handbook, Rubrics 7: Charts; and 16: Judging Information

On Christmas night, 1776, with a winter storm lashing about them, Washington and 2,400 soldiers silently rowed across the ice-clogged Delaware River. As morning broke, the men, short on supplies and many with no shoes, marched through the snow to reach the enemy camp.

The Hessians, having celebrated the holiday the night before, were fast asleep when the Patriots sprang upon them. The **Battle of Trenton** was an important Patriot victory. American soldiers took more than 900 prisoners.

British general Charles Cornwallis rushed to stop Washington as he marched northeast to Princeton. On the night of January 2, 1777, the Patriots left their campfires burning, then slipped into the darkness and circled behind the British troops. In the morning, Washington attacked. A local resident witnessed it:

" The battle was plainly seen from our door … and the guns went off so quick and many together that they could not be numbered …Almost as soon as the firing was over, our house was filled and surrounded with General Washington's men. "

—Anonymous, quoted in *Voices of 1776* by Richard Wheeler

As Washington watched the Redcoats flee Princeton, he cheered, "It is a fine fox chase, my boys!" Now, new soldiers joined the chase. Others re-enlisted. The army—and the Revolution—was saved.

Saratoga

The two quick defeats stung the British. In the spring of 1777, they wanted a victory.

British general John Burgoyne decided to push through New York State and cut off New England from the other colonies. The **strategy** required perfect timing. According

ACADEMIC VOCABULARY
strategy a plan for fighting a battle or war

❷ Defeats and Victories

The Patriots both won and lost battles during the years 1775–1777.

Identify Who were the Hessians? *mercenaries from the German state of Hesse who fought for the British*

Contrast How did the Patriots' actions at the Battle of Trenton differ from their actions at New York? *Patriots were on the defensive in New York, but on the offensive at Trenton.*

Evaluate Why do you think more Americans joined the Patriot efforts after the Battle of Trenton? *possible answers—They were inspired by the Patriot victory; they felt America had a chance against the British.*

📄 **CRF:** Literature Activity: The Crisis, No. 1, by Thomas Paine

Connect to Arts and the Humanities

Crossing the Delaware Artist Emanuel Leutze produced a print of his painting *Washington Crossing the Delaware.* The prints became popular additions to many American homes. Why was this a popular scene? *possible answer—The scene made Americans feel patriotic and proud because it depicted American heroism and endurance.* What color scheme did Leutze use in his painting? Why do you think he chose this scheme? *red, white, and blue; symbolizes the United States and arouses feelings of patriotism*

Differentiating Instruction

Above Level

Advanced/Gifted and Talented

Materials: butcher paper, art supplies, colored pens

1. Organize students into small groups and assign each group one of the following battles: Trenton, Princeton, or Saratoga.

2. Instruct each group to draw a map illustrating what the Patriot battle plans might have looked like. Have students refer to their texts for help. Maps should include a legend identifying troop movements and Patriot and British forces.

3. Next, have each group write a paragraph explaining one of the following: the outcome and significance of the battle; an analysis of the Patriot strategies at the battle; and, for the Battle of Saratoga, why the battle was a turning point in the war. 🆂 **Verbal/Linguistic, Visual/Spatial**

📄 Alternative Assessment Handbook, Rubrics 20: Map Creation; and 42: Writing to Inform

Main Idea

❷ Defeats and Victories

The Patriots both won and lost battles during the years 1775–1777.

Describe What was the British strategy for cutting off New England? *British general John Burgoyne's army would move south from Canada, take Fort Ticonderoga, and go on to Albany; General Howe's army would sail up the Hudson River from New York City to meet Burgoyne's army.*

Analyze What essential element of this strategy proved to be a weakness? *It required perfect timing in a day when communication was limited.*

Evaluate What role did chance play in the Patriot victory at Saratoga? *British general Howe chose not to follow the plan, which left Burgoyne's army outnumbered and alone.*

🎲 Map Transparency: Battle of Saratoga

Biography

Benedict Arnold (1741–1801) Until 1779, Benedict Arnold served the Patriots with distinction and honor, participating in the attack on Quebec and leading troops in the Battle of Saratoga. In 1778, General George Washington made Arnold the commander of Philadelphia. There, however, Arnold held secret meetings with the British, in which he made plans to surrender West Point to them. When Arnold's plan was discovered, he escaped on a British ship and later fled to Britain. Despite his service to their country, even the British looked down on Arnold as a traitor. Ever since, the name *Benedict Arnold* has been a synonym for traitor.

Answers

Reading Check *General Burgoyne surrendered his entire army, which was a much-needed victory and helped raise morale for the Patriots.*

130

---

to the plan, Burgoyne's army would invade from Canada, recapture Fort Ticonderoga, and sweep south to Albany. General Howe, in New York City, would sail up the Hudson River to meet him, strangling New England.

Indeed, Burgoyne took Ticonderoga in early July and headed toward Albany. Here, the timing went wrong for the British. Unknown to Burgoyne, Howe had left New York, sailed up the Chesapeake Bay, and captured Philadelphia. Delegates to the Continental Congress were forced to flee.

Meanwhile, Burgoyne's army bogged down in thick forests. The Patriots had chopped down large trees and dammed rivers to create obstacles. All along the route, the militia swarmed out of nowhere to attack the Redcoats. As Burgoyne neared Saratoga, New York, he found himself surrounded. On October 17, 1777, he was forced to surrender his entire army to General Horatio Gates.

The **Battle of Saratoga** in New York was the turning point of the Revolutionary War. It was the greatest victory yet for the American forces. Morale soared. Patriot James Thacher wrote, "This event will make one of the most brilliant pages of American history."

READING CHECK **Summarizing** Why was the Battle of Saratoga a turning point in the war?

Help from Europe

The French and Indian War had drastically changed the balance of power in North America. The French and Spanish had lost a large expanse of valuable land to the British. Both countries were delighted to see their powerful rival experiencing trouble in its American colonies.

The victory at Saratoga gave the Patriots something they had been desperately seeking: foreign help. Not surprisingly, it came from Britain's enemies, France and Spain. Even Britain's old ally, Holland, joined the fight on the side of the Patriots.

Battle of Saratoga

October 17, 1777 British forces under General John Burgoyne marched south, heading for Albany. They were crushed by Patriot forces under General Horatio Gates at Saratoga.

The Patriots Gain Ground

December 26, 1776 Patriots win the Battle of Trenton.

1776 | 1777

January 3, 1777 Patriots win the Battle of Princeton.

July 27, 1777 Marquis de Lafayette arrives in Philadelphia to offer his assistance to the Patriot cause.

Critical Thinking: Identifying Cause and Effect

At Level

Battle of Saratoga

1. Discuss the major events leading to the Patriot victory at the Battle of Saratoga.

2. Have students create a cause-and-effect chart illustrating how the Battle of Saratoga became a turning point in the war. Remind students to include information on how the victory at Saratoga affected the Patriots and U.S. relations with foreign nations, such as France and Spain.

3. Next, ask students to annotate their charts with notes identifying ways that foreign aid changed the course of the Revolutionary War.

4. Ask for volunteers to share information from their charts. Create a correct master chart for students to see. **LS Verbal/Linguistic, Visual/Spatial**

📝 Alternative Assessment Handbook, Rubrics 6: Cause and Effect; and 7: Charts

Two Remarkable Europeans

"The welfare of America is closely bound up with the welfare of mankind," declared a wealthy young Frenchman, the **Marquis de Lafayette**. Inspired by the ideas of the Revolution, Lafayette bought his own ship and arrived in America in 1777. He brought with him a group of well-trained soldiers and volunteered to serve in the Continental Army himself without pay.

Lafayette spoke little English and had never seen battle. However, he quickly became a skillful commander, earning the title of major general. Lafayette led 2,000 Patriots to successfully pursue 6,000 Redcoats throughout Virginia during 1780-81. He gave $200,000 of his own money to support the Revolution and wrote many letters home to powerful friends and family asking their aid for the Patriot cause.

In February 1778 another European came to serve heroically under Washington. **Baron Friedrich von Steuben**, an experienced military officer from Prussia, led with a combination of respect and fear. He started training the American troops, focusing on basic military drills. Soon he turned the Continental Army into a finely tuned fighting force. One historian has called von Steuben's feat "perhaps the most remarkable achievement in rapid military training in the history of the world."

Help from France

Benjamin Franklin, a skilled and experienced diplomat, had gone to France in 1776 to ask for support from King Louis XVI. Finally, the Battle of Saratoga in 1777 persuaded the French king that the colonists could win the war. Not until then did the king agree to an alliance with the Patriots.

In May 1778 the Continental Congress ratified the treaty of support with France. The French had been helping the Patriots all along with supplies and ammunition. After the treaty became official, the French increased the level of supplies and agreed to provide soldiers and ships. The French naval support would be a key ingredient in defeating the British.

Help from Spain

Spain, also a bitter enemy of Britain, joined the war in 1779. **Bernardo de Gálvez**, the governor of Spanish Louisiana, became a key ally to the Patriots. Gálvez gathered a small army of Spanish soldiers, French Americans, colonists, and Native Americans. Together they made their way east from Louisiana. Gálvez seized British posts all the way to Pensacola, Florida.

READING CHECK Summarizing How did France and Spain help the Patriots?

February 1778 Baron Friedrich von Steuben begins training Patriot soldiers.

June 21, 1779 Spain declares war against Britain.

1778   1779   1780

May 1778 France joins the Patriots in an alliance.

March 14, 1780 Bernardo de Gálvez, the governor of Spanish Louisiana, captures the British stronghold of Fort Charlotte at present-day Mobile, Alabama.

ANALYSIS SKILL READING TIME LINES

Which nations joined the Patriot cause?

THE AMERICAN REVOLUTION **131**

Main Idea

❹ Winter at Valley Forge

The winter at Valley Forge tested the strength of Patriot forces.

Identify What was Valley Forge? *the Continental Army's settlement during the winter of 1777–1778, located about 20 miles north of Philadelphia*

Draw Conclusions Why do you think that soldiers remained at Valley Forge despite the harsh conditions? *possible answers—out of patriotism, duty, honor, respect for Washington, belief in Patriot cause*

Contrast How did the Patriots' situation at Valley Forge that winter contrast with that of the British at Philadelphia? *While the Patriots endured harsh conditions, the British soldiers lived a life of luxury and enjoyed social events.*

Primary Source

Valley Forge

Activity Standard English Mastery

Vocabulary Building Have students list each word in the excerpt with which they are unfamiliar. Next, have students share their lists. Make a class list and help students to define each word. Then have each student write a one-to-two-sentence summary of the meaning of the passage. Remind students to use standard English. Last, ask for volunteers to share their summaries. Write them down for students to see. Critique each example. Help students see any errors in grammar or the use of standard English.

Answers

Analyzing Primary Sources
Conditions were harsh and desperate, yet the soldiers still showed readiness and contentment.

Reading Check *harsh winter weather; lack of supplies, adequate shelter, clothing, and food; illness*

JOURNAL ENTRY
Valley Forge

A surgeon at Valley Forge, Albigence Waldo kept a journal of what he saw during the winter of 1777–78.

❝The Army which has been surprisingly healthy hitherto, now begins to grow sickly from the continued fatigues they have suffered this Campaign. Yet they still show a spirit of Alacrity [cheerful readiness] and Contentment not to be expected from so young Troops. I am Sick—discontented—and out of humour. Poor food—hard lodging—Cold Weather—fatigue—Nasty Cloaths [clothes]—nasty Cookery . . . smoke and Cold—hunger and filthyness—A pox on my bad luck.❞
—Albigence Waldo, from *Diary of Surgeon Albigence Waldo of the Connecticut Line*

ANALYSIS SKILL **ANALYZING PRIMARY SOURCES**
Why did Waldo seem surprised by the soldiers' attitude?

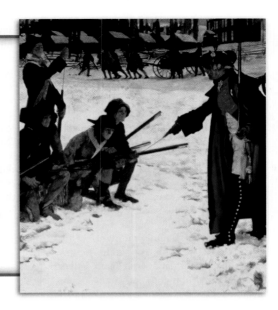

Winter at Valley Forge

The entry of France and Spain into the war came at a crucial moment. The Continental Army was running very low on supplies. In December 1777, Washington settled his 12,000 men at Valley Forge, about 20 miles north of Philadelphia. There they suffered shortages of food and clothing.

To this day, the name of Valley Forge brings to mind suffering—and courage. Yet no battles took place at this encampment. There was only one enemy: the brutal winter of 1777–78.

Washington's men lacked even the most basic protections against shin-deep snows. Over and over the general sent letters, pleading for supplies. None came.

❝To see men without clothes … without blankets to lie upon, without shoes … without a house or hut to cover them until those could be built, and submitting without a murmur, is a proof of patience and obedience which, in my opinion, can scarcely be paralleled [matched].❞
—George Washington, quoted in *George Washington: A Collection*

As winter roared in, soldiers quickly built crude shelters that offered little protection against the weather. Some soldiers had no shirts. Others had marched the shoes off their feet. At their guard posts, they stood on their hats to keep their feet from touching the freezing ground. One soldier wrote that getting food was the "business that usually employed us."

During that terrible winter, some 2,000 soldiers died of disease and malnutrition. Amazingly, the survivors not only stayed—they drilled and marched to the orders of Baron von Steuben, becoming better soldiers.

While the soldiers suffered through the winter at Valley Forge, the British lived a life of luxury in Philadelphia. Most of the Patriots had fled the city, leaving only Loyalists and British soldiers. Together they enjoyed the city's houses, taverns, and theaters, and held parties and balls.

READING CHECK Finding Main Ideas What challenges did the Continental Army face at Valley Forge?

Collaborative Learning

At Level

Valley Forge Skits

1. Organize students into small groups. Have each group create and write a script for a short skit involving three or four soldiers at Valley Forge.

2. Tell students to set the skit in the late spring of 1778 and to have soldiers discuss the hardships they faced over the winter, how they viewed the hardships, why they remained at Valley Forge, their opinions of General Washington, and how circumstances have changed in recent weeks.

3. Have the groups assign each member a role in the skit to ensure that all group members participate in the activity. Roles might include director, actor, writer, copy editor, cue-card prompter, and so on.

4. Have each group perform its skit for the class.
   LS Interpersonal, Kinesthetic, Verbal/Linguistic

   Alternative Assessment Handbook, Rubrics 14: Group Activity; and 33: Skits and Reader's Theater

War at Sea and in the West

While some Americans struggled against the British on land in the former colonies, others fought at sea and on the western frontier. Each area posed tough challenges.

War at Sea

The entry of the French navy into the war greatly aided the colonists. Many people had thought that the mighty British navy would crush the much smaller American fleet. However, the British failed to use their powerful navy effectively during the war.

In the fall of 1775, the Continental Congress made plans to build four American warships. Soon afterward the Congress formally established the marines and the Continental Navy. By adapting merchant vessels, the navy had eight fighting ships ready for combat by February 1776.

That month the tiny American navy launched a major offensive to damage the operating ability of the British fleet located off the Carolina coast. Rather than attack the fleet directly, the Patriots went after the British supply base on Nassau, in the Bahamas.

The American troops seized the main supply fort on the island. They then raised the newly created flag of the American Revolution over Nassau. After that campaign, the American navy focused on seizing British supply ships and weakening Britain's naval forces in the West Indies.

John Paul Jones

The Patriots owed much of their success on the seas to naval hero **John Paul Jones**. Jones had once been considered an outlaw. He was born John Paul in Scotland and began working on ships at a young age. After accidentally killing the leader of a mutiny, he fled to America and added Jones to his name.

When the war broke out, Jones volunteered his services to the newly created navy. He quickly established himself as a brave and clever sailor. Considered a pirate by the British, Jones captured many British supply ships. The French greatly admired Jones. When France entered the war in 1778, French leaders presented him with a small fleet of seven vessels to command. He named his flagship *Bonhomme Richard* ("Gentleman Richard") in honor of Benjamin Franklin's *Poor Richard's Almanac*.

One of Jones's most famous victories was the capture of the British warship Serapis on September 23, 1779. Early in the battle, the British knocked out the heaviest artillery on the *Bonhomme Richard*. Captain Richard Pearson of the *Serapis* then called out to Jones, "Has your ship struck [surrendered]?" Jones replied, "I have not yet begun to fight!" The battle continued for more than two hours. Finally the Americans wore down the British, who surrendered at 10:30 p.m.

The Continental Navy used fewer than 100 ships over the course of the war. Yet the British lost more than 200 ships to the small but effective American naval force.

War in the West

The lands west of the Appalachian Mountains were controlled by American Indian nations. Both the British and the Patriots tried to enlist these groups in their cause.

George Rogers Clark volunteered to lead the western campaign. Clark had been a surveyor along the Ohio and Kentucky rivers. By the time the war broke out, he knew the lands of the Midwest well. Clark created an army from the scattered settlements in the area. One of the best-known groups was the Over Mountain Men, a band of settlers from present-day Tennessee.

Determined to weaken the British support systems, Clark targeted trading villages. Following the Ohio River to the Tennessee, Clark's force set out on a 120-mile overland trek to Kaskaskia. The village's leaders learned of the attack and surrendered. A second group of Patriots took Cahokia without a fight.

In February 1779 Clark launched a surprise attack on Fort Sackville near the town

---

Main Idea

⑤ War at Sea and in the West

The war continued at sea and in the West.

Identify Cause and Effect How did the size of the Continental Navy affect its strategy against the British navy? *The Continental Navy was much smaller, so Patriot leaders chose to attack the British supply base and British supply ships.*

Make Inferences Explain how the achievements of John Paul Jones demonstrated the strategy of the Continental Navy against the British. *Jones captured many British supply ships. Despite the odds, Jones prevailed against a larger navy.*

Analyze Why do you think the British were more successful than the Americans at winning over Native Americans in the West? *possible answer—Native Americans may have been concerned that Americans would continue to move west.*

Connect to Civics

Aid from Abroad Thousands of Europeans—including French, Germans, and Irish—came to the Americans' aid during the Revolutionary War. Some 700 free black Haitians—members of what was known as the Fontages Legion—participated in the allied American and French siege of Savannah, Georgia, in 1779. Many of these fighters carried the seeds of revolution back to their homeland and were important in establishing the Haitian Republic.

Cross-Discipline Activity: English/Language Arts | At Level

A Soldier's Journal

1. Have each student assume the role of a soldier or a sailor serving with one of the following groups:
   • George Washington's army in the Northeast,
   • John Paul Jones's forces at sea, or
   • George Rogers Clark's troops in the West.

2. Have students create a journal entry describing their experience. Encourage students to use an event from their text as the focus of the entry.

3. Struggling Readers and Special Needs Learners may be paired with another student and create an illustration instead of a journal entry. **LS Intrapersonal, Verbal/Linguistic**
   Alternative Assessment Handbook, Rubric 15: Journals

Did you know . . .

The first official national flag was approved by the Continental Congress on June 14, 1777. The flag was known as the Stars and Stripes for the 13 stars and 13 stripes contained on the flag. Originally, the layout of the stars was not formalized. Several patterns are known, including stars in a circle, rows of 4-5-4, or rows of 3-2-3-2-3. In 1818, Congress passed legislation requiring that the number of stripes should remain at 13 and the number of stars should equal the number of states.

• Review & Assess •

Close

Have students review the obstacles Patriots faced during the American Revolution, and how they were able to overcome them.

Review

go.hrw.com Online Quiz, Section 3

Assess

SE   Section 3 Assessment

PASS: Section 3 Quiz

Alternative Assessment Handbook

Reteach/Classroom Intervention

Interactive Reader and Study Guide, Section 3

Interactive Skills Tutor CD-ROM

Answers

Interpreting Maps 1. *over 700 miles;* **2.** *possible answer—that land, water available for troops*

Reading Check *Jones led naval battles against the British; Clark helped contain the British in the West.*

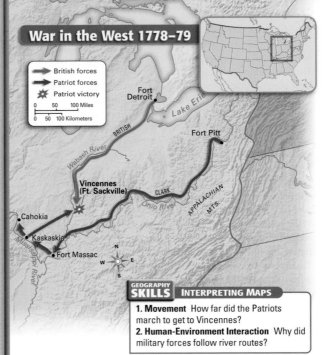

War in the West 1778–79

→ British forces
→ Patriot forces
✷ Patriot victory

0 50 100 Miles
0 50 100 Kilometers

Fort Detroit
Lake Erie
Fort Pitt
Wabash River
BRITISH
Vincennes (Ft. Sackville)
CLARK
APPALACHIAN MTS.
Cahokia
Ohio River
Kaskaskia
Fort Massac
Mississippi River

GEOGRAPHY SKILLS   INTERPRETING MAPS

1. **Movement** How far did the Patriots march to get to Vincennes?
2. **Human-Environment Interaction** Why did military forces follow river routes?

of Vincennes. The attack was unexpected because the nearby Wabash River was icy and flooded. Despite overflowing riverbanks, Clark's force of 150 men endured an 18-day march through freezing water. They also managed to bring enough Patriot flags for an army of hundreds. The flags were displayed near the fort, and the skilled pioneers sustained enough musket fire to indicate a much larger army. Falling for the ruse, the commander of Fort Sackville surrendered.

In general the British were more successful at winning over the Native Americans. But Clark's many campaigns undermined British support in the West.

READING CHECK   Finding Main Ideas How did Jones and Clark help the Patriots' war effort?

SUMMARY AND PREVIEW The Patriots faced hardships as the war continued. In the next section, you will see how they finally achieved their goal of independence.

---

go.hrw.com
Online Quiz
KEYWORD: SR8 HP4

Section 3 Assessment

Reviewing Ideas, Terms, and People

1. **a. Identify** What groups supported the Patriot war effort? How did each group contribute?
   b. Analyze Why was it difficult to find and keep soldiers in the Continental Army?
2. **a. Describe** What early defeats did the Patriots face?
   b. Elaborate Was it a mistake for the British to use **mercenaries** to help them fight the war? Why or why not?
3. **a. Elaborate** Why do you think European nations supported the colonists rather than Great Britain?
   b. Evaluate Do you think that the Patriots would have won the war without help from France and Spain? Why or why not?
4. **a. Describe** What difficulties did the Patriots face at Valley Forge?
   b. Elaborate How might weather conditions affect the outcome of a battle?
5. **a. Identify** Who was **John Paul Jones**?
   b. Compare In what ways was Jones's naval strategy like that of the Continental Army?

Critical Thinking

6. **Drawing Conclusions** Review the events on your time line. Copy the chart below and use it to identify the region in which the events took place and how the events reflected the Patriots' successes and failures.

Region	Patriot Problems	Patriot Successes

FOCUS ON SPEAKING

7. **Thinking about the Struggle for Liberty** Why was this period of the war so difficult for the Patriots? How did they struggle through? What are the one or two points that are the most important about this period of the war?

Section 3 Assessment Answers

1. **a.** young, white men—served and fought; some free Africans—served in army; women—raised money, made clothes, served as nurses, messengers, spies
   b. low pay, bad conditions, risk of death

2. **a.** Quebec, Canada; New York
   b. possible answer—yes, not as dedicated

3. **a.** enemies of Britain; hoped to weaken Britain's power
   b. possible answer—No, the British had superior numbers, supplies, and training and could outlast the weaker American forces.

4. **a.** harsh weather, illness, lack of supplies
   b. possible answer—may have made soldiers fight harder to make their suffering worthwhile

5. **a.** Patriot naval officer Jones attacked supply ships.
   b. adapted to prevail against larger force

6. Regions—at north, at sea, in the west; see the answers to Questions 1b, 2a, 4a, and 6

7. Victories boosted morale, gained help from Europe.

Independence!

If YOU were there...

You have grown up on a farm in South Carolina. You know every inch of the woods and marshes around your home. You are too young to join the Continental Army, but you have heard stories about a brave group of soldiers who carry out quick raids on the British, then disappear into the woods. These fighters get no pay and live in constant danger.

Would you consider joining the fighters? Why?

> **BUILDING BACKGROUND** As the war moved to the South, American forces encountered new problems. They suffered several major defeats. But American resistance in the southern colonies was strong. Backwoods fighters confused and frustrated the British army.

War in the South

The war across the ocean was not going the way the British government in London had planned. The northern colonies, with their ragged, scrappy fighters, proved to be tough to tame. So the British switched strategies and set their sights on the South.

The British hoped to find support from the large Loyalist populations living in Georgia, the Carolinas, and Virginia. As they moved across the South, the British also planned to free enslaved Africans and enlist them as British soldiers. Under the leadership of a new commander, General Henry Clinton, the strategy paid off—for a while.

Brutal Fighting

The southern war was particularly brutal. Much more than in the North, this phase of the war pitted Americans—Patriots versus Loyalists—against one another in direct combat. The British also destroyed crops, farm animals, and other property as they marched through the South. One British officer, Banastre Tarleton, sowed fear throughout the South by refusing to take prisoners and killing soldiers who tried to surrender.

What You Will Learn...

Main Ideas

1. Patriot forces faced many problems in the war in the South.
2. The American Patriots finally defeated the British at the Battle of Yorktown.
3. The British and the Americans officially ended the war by signing the Treaty of Paris of 1783.

The Big Idea

The war spread to the southern colonies, where the British were finally defeated.

Key Terms and People

Francis Marion, *p. 136*
Comte de Rochambeau, *p. 137*
Battle of Yorktown, *p. 137*
Treaty of Paris of 1783, *p. 139*

TAKING NOTES Review the events on your time line. Copy the chart below and use it to identify the region in which the events took place and how the events reflected the Patriots' successes and failures.

Bellringer

If YOU were there. . . Use the **Daily Bellringer Transparency** for this section to help students answer the question.

📖 Daily Bellringer Transparency, Section 4

Building Vocabulary

Preteach or review the following terms:

brigade military unit (p. 136)

devastation severe or widespread damage (p. 136)

guerrilla warfare hit-and-run attacks (p. 136)

negotiations talks held to reach an agreement or compromise (p. 139)

pitted set against (p. 135)

📝 **CRF:** Vocabulary Builder Activity, Section 4

Taking Notes

Have students copy the graphic organizer onto their own paper and then use it to take notes on the section. This activity will prepare students for the Section Assessment, in which they will complete a graphic organizer that builds on the information using a critical thinking skill.

Teach the Big Idea

At Level

Independence!

1. **Teach** Ask students the questions in the Main Idea boxes to teach this section.

2. **Apply** Ask students to identify the main events in this section. List the responses for the class to see. Next, have each student write a newspaper headline for each event. **LS Verbal/Linguistic**

3. **Review** As you review the section's main ideas, ask for volunteers to share some of their headlines with the class. List them for students to see. Then help students develop a list of details that might appear in articles accompanying the headlines.

4. **Practice/Homework** Have each student select a headline and write a brief newspaper article to go with it. **LS Visual/Spatial**

📝 Alternative Assessment Handbook, Rubric 37: Writing Assignments

❶ War in the South

Patriot forces faced many problems in the war in the South.

Explain Why did the British decide to switch strategies and focus the war in the South? *large Loyalist populations in Georgia, the Carolinas, and Virginia; planned to free slaves and have them fight*

Summarize How did guerrilla colonial fighters help the Continental Army? *by surprising the British with swift hit-and-run attacks to interfere with communication and supply lines*

Draw Conclusions How would you describe the main British strategies in the South? *use Loyalist support, free slaves to fight for British, use harsh tactics to destroy Patriot supplies and morale*

📄 **CRF:** Primary Source Activity: General Nathanael Greene Writes to His Wife

Info to Know

Native Americans and the War The Revolutionary War was costly to many Native Americans. Some Indian homelands, such as those of the Iroquois and Cherokee, suffered devastation and invasion by both armies. The war also divided some Indian groups and confederacies. For example, the Oneidas and Tuscaroras supported the Patriots. As a result they were cut off from the rest of the Iroquois League, which supported the British.

Answers

Swamp Fox *the man in front on the horse who is looking forward; appears to be leading because of his position on the boat, his mount on horseback, his uniform, and his bearing*

Reading Check *1778: British take Savannah, Georgia; 1780: British take Charleston, South Carolina; Patriots fail to retake Camden, South Carolina*

Georgia, the last colony to join the Revolution, was the first to fall to the British. A force of 3,500 Redcoats easily took Savannah in 1778 and soon put in place a new colonial government.

Britain's next major target was Charleston, South Carolina. In early 1780 General Clinton landed a force of 14,000 troops around the port city. With a minimal cost of about 250 casualties, the British scored one of their biggest victories of the war. The Patriots surrendered Charleston in May, handing over four ships and some 5,400 prisoners.

A Failed Attack

In August 1780, Patriot forces led by Horatio Gates tried to drive the British out of Camden, South Carolina. The attack was poorly executed, however. Gates had only half as many soldiers as he had planned for, and most were tired and hungry. In the heat of battle, many panicked and ran. The Patriot attack quickly fell apart. Of some 4,000 American troops, only about 700 escaped.

General Nathanael Greene arrived to reorganize the army. As he rode through the southern countryside, he was discouraged

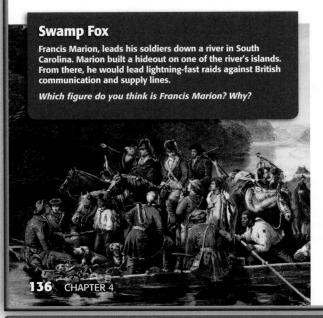

Swamp Fox

Francis Marion, leads his soldiers down a river in South Carolina. Marion built a hideout on one of the river's islands. From there, he would lead lightning-fast raids against British communication and supply lines.

Which figure do you think is Francis Marion? Why?

136 CHAPTER 4

---

by the devastation. He later wrote, "I have never witnessed such scenes."

Guerrilla Warfare

The southern Patriots switched to swift hit-and-run attacks known as guerrilla warfare. No Patriot was better at this style of fighting than **Francis Marion**. He organized Marion's Brigade, a group of guerrilla soldiers.

Marion's Brigade used surprise attacks to disrupt British communication and supply lines. Despite their great efforts, the British could not catch Marion and his men. One frustrated general claimed, "As for this . . . old fox, the devil himself could not catch him." From that point on, Marion was known as the Swamp Fox.

READING CHECK **Sequencing** List the events of the war in the South in chronological order.

Battle of Yorktown

In early 1781 the war was going badly for the Patriots. They were low on money to pay soldiers and buy supplies. The help of their foreign allies had not brought the war to a quick end as they had hoped. The British held most of the South, plus Philadelphia and New York City. The Patriots' morale took another blow when Benedict Arnold, one of America's most gifted officers, turned traitor.

Regrouped under Nathanael Greene, the Continental Army began harassing British general Charles Cornwallis in the Carolinas. Hoping to stay in communication with the British naval fleet, Cornwallis moved his force of 7,200 men to Yorktown, Virginia. It was a fatal mistake.

General Washington, in New York, saw a chance to trap Cornwallis at Yorktown. He ordered Lafayette to block Cornwallis's escape by land. Then he combined his 2,500 troops

---

Collaborative Learning

War in the South Progress Reports

1. Organize students into four groups. Ask two groups to imagine that they are military leaders stationed in the South during the latter part of the war—one with the Continental Army and the other with the British Army. Ask the other two groups to imagine that they are military leaders stationed near Yorktown in 1781—one with the Continental Army and one with the British Army.

2. Have each group create a report on the progress of the war effort in its area. Encourage

students to identify, describe, and explain factors that both hurt or benefited their efforts in the region. Have groups assign each member a role to ensure that all students participate.

3. Ask a representative from each group to present the group's progress report to the class. Then have students discuss the events that led to the war's end. 🄻🄢 **Interpersonal, Verbal/Linguistic**

📄 Alternative Assessment Handbook, Rubrics 14: Group Activity; and 42: Writing to Inform

Battle of Yorktown

The British scuttled, or purposely sank, dozens of their ships. This formed a barrier that kept the French ships from coming too close.

THIRTEEN COLONIES
Yorktown
ATLANTIC OCEAN

In October 1781, American and French troops surrounded British forces and defeated them in the Battle of Yorktown.

 American troop positions
French troop positions
British troop positions
British defensive lines

0   0.5   1 Mile
0 0.5 1 Kilometer

ANALYSIS SKILLS **ANALYZING VISUALS**

Human-Environment Interaction How did American and French forces trap the British at Yorktown?

with 4,000 French troops commanded by the **Comte de Rochambeau** (raw-shahn-BOH). Washington led the French-American force on a swift march to Virginia to cut off the other escape routes. The Patriots surrounded Cornwallis with some 16,000 soldiers. Meanwhile, a French naval fleet seized control of the Chesapeake Bay, preventing British ships from rescuing Cornwallis's stranded army.

The siege began. For weeks, the fighting steadily wore down the British defenses. In early October, Washington prepared for a major attack on the weakened British troops.

Facing near-certain defeat, on October 19, 1781, Cornwallis sent a drummer and a soldier with a white flag of surrender to Washington's camp. The Patriots took some 8,000 British prisoners—the largest British army in America.

The **Battle of Yorktown** was the last major battle of the American Revolution. Prime Minister Lord North received word of the Yorktown surrender in November. In shock he declared, "It is all over!"

READING CHECK **Drawing Conclusions** Why did the victory at Yorktown end the fighting?

THE AMERICAN REVOLUTION **137**

Direct Teach

Main Idea

❷ Battle of Yorktown

The American Patriots finally defeated the British at the Battle of Yorktown.

Recall Why did the British army move to Yorktown, Virginia? *because of harassment from the Continental Army; to maintain communications with the British naval fleet*

Finding Main Ideas How did Washington and the Patriots defeat the British at Yorktown? *With the aid of the French army and navy, they surrounded and outnumbered Cornwallis, forcing him to surrender.*

Evaluate Do you think the Patriots could have won the Revolutionary War without the help of the French? *possible answers—yes, because they would have continued to fight and eventually have worn down the British; no, because they lacked the troops and supplies needed to win the war*

📖 Map Transparency: Battle of Yorktown

go.hrw.com
Online Resources

KEYWORD: SR8 US4
ACTIVITY: Revolutionary Battle Site Tourist Brochure

Critical Thinking: Finding Main Ideas | At Level

Revolutionary War Magazine

1. Review with students the major events and people from this chapter.

2. Have each student prepare a table of contents for a historical magazine about the American Revolution. Instruct students to select key people and events to be the subjects of feature articles, spotlights, charts, and maps. Then ask students to create titles for the articles and to describe each article's content.

3. Display students' tables of contents around the classroom and have students view each other's work. **LS Verbal/Linguistic**

4. **Extend** Have students work in groups to create different sections of a historical magazine about the Revolutionary War. **LS Interpersonal, Verbal/Linguistic**

📋 Alternative Assessment Handbook, Rubric 19: Magazines

Answers

Analyzing Visuals *by surrounding them on land and by cutting off British ships so they could not rescue the British army*

Reading Check *British general Cornwallis surrendered his army, the largest British army in America to the Patriots at Yorktown.*

137

Primary Source

Sentiments of an American Woman

Info to Know

Shirts Instead of Cash Esther DeBerdt Reed wanted to donate the money collected by her campaign directly to the troops in the field. George Washington convinced her that distributing the money fairly might be difficult. At Washington's request, the money was used to purchase shirts for his army. Each shirt was embroidered with the name of the woman who made it. In gratitude, Washington awarded the members of the association "an equal place with any who have preceded them in the walk of female patriotism."

Did you know . . .

Esther DeBerdt Reed's effort to organize a large group of women to ask for contributions from women all over the country was the first example of national volunteerism. Reed, the wife of the chief executive of Pennsylvania, received contributions from about 1,645 women.

Linking to Today

Women in Military Service The role of women in military matters has changed greatly since the time *Sentiments of an American Woman* was written. Women who masqueraded as men on the battlefield, lived through the horrors of prisoner of war camps, and died in combat, now are honored at the Women in Military Service for America Memorial in Arlington, Virginia. Since its dedication in 1997, about 200,000 people annually have visited the site to learn about women's contributions to military service from the Revolutionary War to today.

Answers

Analyzing Primary Sources
1. *The writers call to mind all the acts of courage, constancy, and patriotism that they have learned about through history.*
2. *with the other women in history who have fought for justice*

138

PAMPHLET

Sentiments of an American Woman

The Continental Army received aid from female Patriots led by Esther DeBerdt Reed and Sarah Franklin Bache, the daughter of Benjamin Franklin. In 1780 these women organized a campaign that raised $300,000 for soldiers' clothing. The following pamphlet, written by the campaign's leaders, announced the campaign. In it, the authors used images of women helping with war efforts of the past to gain support for their cause.

❝On the **commencement** of actual war, the Women of America **manifested** a firm resolution to contribute . . . to the deliverance of their country. Animated by the purest patriotism they are sensible of sorrow at this day, in not offering more than barren wishes for the success of so glorious a Revolution. They aspire to **render** themselves more really useful; and this sentiment is universal from the north to the south of the Thirteen United States. Our ambition is kindled by the fame of those heroines of **antiquity** , who . . . have proved to the universe, that . . . if opinion and manners did not forbid us to march to glory by the same paths as the Men, we should at least equal, and sometimes surpass them in our love for the public good. I glory in all that which my sex has done great and **commendable**. I call to mind with enthusiasm and with admiration, all those acts of courage, of constancy and patriotism, which history has transmitted to us . . . .❞

❝So many famous sieges where the Women have been seen . . . building new walls, digging trenches with their feeble hands, furnishing arms to their defenders, they themselves darting the missile weapons on the enemy, resigning the ornaments of their apparel, and their fortune, to fill the public treasury, and to hasten the deliverance of their country; burying themselves under its ruins; throwing themselves into the flames rather than submit to the disgrace of humiliation before a proud enemy.❞

❝Born for liberty, **disdaining** to bear the irons of a **tryannic** Government, we associate ourselves . . . [with those rulers] who have extended the empire of liberty, and **contented** to reign by sweetness and justice, have broken the chains of slavery, forged by tyrants.❞

A female spy passes news to a colonial officer.

1. **commencement**: start 2. **manifested**: presented
3. **render**: make 4. **antiquity**: ancient times
5. **commendable**: praiseworthhy 6. **disdaining**: refusing
7. **tyrannic**: unjust 8. **contented**: determined

> The women declare that they would fight if they were allowed.

> The authors list ways in which women have helped fight wars in the past.

> In this phrase, the women link themselves to great women rulers of the past.

ANALYSIS SKILL · **ANALYZING PRIMARY SOURCES**

1. What do the writers "call to mind" in asking women to join the Patriots' cause?
2. With whom do the writers associate themselves?

138 CHAPTER 4

Collaborative Learning

At Level

Sentiments of an American Woman

1. Discuss with students how *Sentiments* allowed women to contribute to the war effort and why women were prohibited from participating on any other level.

2. Organize students into pairs and ask them to imagine that they are colonists who were influenced by *Sentiments of an American Woman*. Have pairs create pamphlets giving support for the ideas of Reed and Bache. Ask students to propose another idea to benefit Washington's troops.

3. Students' pamphlets should focus on the following idea: In what ways were women able to support the war effort?

4. Have students share their pamphlets with the class. Discuss how Reed's ideas influenced them and brainstorm similar volunteer ideas that might be applicable to show support for today's troops.

📖 Alternative Assessment Handbook, Rubrics 14: Group Activity; and 43: Writing to Persuade

The Treaty of Paris

After Yorktown, only a few small battles took place. Lacking the money to pay for a new army, Great Britain entered into peace talks with America. Benjamin Franklin had a key role in the negotiations.

Delegates took more than two years to come to a peace agreement. In the **Treaty of Paris of 1783**, Great Britain recognized the independence of the United States. The treaty also set America's borders. A separate treaty between Britain and Spain returned Florida to the Spanish. British leaders also accepted American rights to settle and trade west of the original thirteen colonies.

At the war's end, Patriot soldiers returned to their homes and families. The courage of soldiers and civilians had made America's victory possible. As they returned home, George Washington thanked his troops for their devotion. "I . . . wish that your latter days be as prosperous as your former ones have been glorious."

READING CHECK **Summarizing** Explain how the War for Independence finally came to an end.

North America after the Treaty of Paris of 1783

United States
British
Spanish
French
Russian

0   500   1,000 Miles
0   500   1,000 Kilometers

CANADA

NEW SPAIN

UNITED STATES

Disputed

Disputed

FLORIDA

Gulf of Mexico

ATLANTIC OCEAN

PACIFIC OCEAN

GEOGRAPHY SKILLS **INTERPRETING MAPS**

Region Which three countries disputed the area in the northwest of the continent?

SUMMARY AND PREVIEW Americans gained their independence from Great Britain in 1783. In the next chapter you will learn how the new nation formed its first government.

Section 4 Assessment

go.hrw.com
Online Quiz
KEYWORD: SR8 HP4

Reviewing Ideas, Terms, and People

1. **a. Describe** What problems did the Patriots experience in the war in the South?
   b. Analyze What advantages did the southern Patriots have over the British in the South?
2. **a. Describe** What was the Patriots' strategy for defeating the British at Yorktown?
   b. Elaborate Why do you think General Cornwallis decided to surrender at the **Battle of Yorktown**?
3. **a. Identify** Who helped to negotiate the Treaty of Paris for the Americans?
   b. Predict How might relations between Great Britain and its former colonies be affected by the war?

Critical Thinking

4. **Evaluating** Review your notes on the events that led to the end of the war. Then copy the graphic organizer below and use it to identify and describe the most important event in turning the war in the Patriots' favor.

Event	Importance to end of war

FOCUS ON SPEAKING

5. **Thinking About the Revolution's End** After reading this section, you have a picture of the whole war. In your talk, what do you want to say about how the war ended? Were there any moments that were especially trying for the colonists?

THE AMERICAN REVOLUTION **139**

Section 4 Assessment Answers

1. **a.** brutal fighting and devastation, Patriots and Loyalists pitted against each other, several important cities under British control; loss of troops at Camden, South Carolina
   b. knew the land, used guerrilla warfare
2. **a.** to use the aid of the French army and navy to surround and outnumber the British and cut off their support and retreat by sea
   b. He was surrounded, facing defeat.
3. **a.** Benjamin Franklin
   b. probably would worsen relations
4. possible answers—Cornwallis moved into Yorktown; Patriot and French troops blocked the British by land and sea; Cornwallis surrendered his army, the largest in the colonies, and Great Britain entered into peace talks with America.
5. See answer to Question 1a.

Social Studies Skills

Understanding Historical Interpretation

Social Studies Skills

| Analysis | Critical Thinking | Civic Participation | Study |

Understanding Historical Interpretation

Define the Skill

Historical interpretations are ways of explaining the past. They are based on what is known about the people, ideas, and actions that make up history. Two historians can look at the same set of facts about a person or event of the past and see things in different ways. Their explanations of the person or event, and the conclusions they reach, can be very different. The ability to recognize, understand, and evaluate historical interpretations is a valuable skill in the study of history.

Learn the Skill

When people study the past, they decide which facts are the most important in explaining why something happened. One person may believe certain facts to be important, while other people may believe other facts are more important. Therefore, their explanation of the topic, and the conclusions they draw about it, may not be the same. In addition, if new facts are uncovered about the topic, still more interpretations of it may result.

Asking the following questions will help you to understand and evaluate historical interpretations.

1 What is the main idea in the way the topic is explained? What conclusions are reached? Be aware that these may not be directly stated but only hinted at in the information provided.

2 On what facts has the writer or speaker relied? Do these facts seem to support his or her explanation and conclusions?

3 Is there important information about the topic that the writer or speaker has dismissed or ignored? If so, you should suspect that the interpretation may be inaccurate or deliberately slanted to prove a particular point of view.

Just because interpretations differ, one is not necessarily "right" and others "wrong." As long as a person considers all the evidence and draws conclusions based on a fair evaluation of that evidence, his or her interpretation is probably acceptable.

Remember, however, that trained historians let the facts *lead* them to conclusions. People who *start* with a conclusion, select only facts that support it, and ignore opposing evidence produce interpretations that have little value for understanding history.

Practice the Skill

Two widely accepted interpretations exist of the causes of the American Revolution. One holds that the Revolution was a struggle by freedom-loving Americans to be free from harsh British rule. In this view the colonists were used to self-government and resisted British efforts to take rights they claimed. The other interpretation is that a clash of economic interests caused the Revolution. In this view, the war resulted from a struggle between British and colonial merchants over control of America's economy.

Review Sections 4 and 5 of Chapter 3 and Sections 1 and 2 of Chapter 4. Then answer the following questions.

1. What facts in the textbook support the economic interpretation of the Revolution? What evidence supports the political interpretation?

2. Which interpretation seems more convincing? Explain why.

Social Studies Skills

Understanding Historical Interpretation

Activity **Chart for Practice the Skill** To support the "Practice the Skill" activity, draw a two-column chart for the class to see. Label the columns *Economic Interpretations* and *Political Interpretations*. Have students copy the chart and use it to answer Question 1. Ask for volunteers to share their answers to create a master version of the chart. Then give students time to answer Question 2. Again, ask for volunteers to share their answers with the class. Encourage student discussion and feedback. Remind students to provide reasons to support their positions.

LS Verbal/Linguistic

Alternative Assessment Handbook, Rubric 16: Judging Information

Answers

Practice and Apply the Skill
1. *economic—one of England's main reasons for founding the colonies was to earn money from trade; British attempts to tax the colonists and crack down on smuggling led to colonial protests, unrest, and eventually violence; political— amount of colonial self-government; reactions to limits on colonial self-government; ideals expressed in the Declaration of Independence;* **2.** *possible answer—the economic interpretation because money and economic power are very tempting and powerful motivators*

Social Studies Skills Activity: Understanding Historical Interpretation

Interpretation of the Battle of Saratoga   At Level

1. Have students review the material in Section 3 under the heading "Saratoga." Based on expert historical interpretation, this passage describes the Battle of Saratoga as "the greatest victory yet for the American forces."

2. Review with students the Revolutionary battles up to and including the Battle of Saratoga. Then have students discuss whether or not they agree with the historical interpretation that the Battle of Saratoga was the greatest American victory up to that point.

3. Then have each student write one to two paragraphs either supporting or refuting this historical interpretation. Students who disagree should indicate which battle they think was "the greatest victory yet." Remind students to provide reasons and evidence from the textbook to support their positions.

LS Verbal/Linguistic

Alternative Assessment Handbook, Rubric 43: Writing to Persuade

Chapter Review

Visual Summary

Use the visual summary below to help you review the main ideas of the chapter.

QUICK FACTS

Speeches and protests ignited revolutionary feelings.

Patriots fought Loyalists in the Revolutionary War.

The American colonies gained independence and became the United States.

Reviewing Vocabulary, Terms, and People

1. What were American colonists who remained loyal to Great Britain called?
   a. Whigs
   b. Loyalists
   c. Royalists
   d. Democrats

2. What was the name of the battle in which the Patriots finally defeated the British?
   a. Battle of Saratoga
   b. Battle of New Jersey
   c. Battle of Yorktown
   d. Battle of Valley Forge

3. What was the name for the colonial military force created to fight the British?
   a. mercenaries
   b. Redcoats
   c. Hessians
   d. Continental Army

4. Who was the French nobleman who helped the Patriots fight the British?
   a. Bernardo de Gálvez
   b. Marquis de Lafayette
   c. Baron von Steuben
   d. Lord Dunmore

Comprehension and Critical Thinking

SECTION 1 *(Pages 112–117)*

5. a. **Recall** What actions did the First and Second Continental congresses take?
   b. **Analyze** How did the events at Lexington and Concord change the conflict between Great Britain and the colonies?
   c. **Elaborate** Why do you think that control of Boston early in the Revolutionary War was important?

SECTION 2 *(Pages 118–121)*

6. a. **Identify** Why is July 4, 1776, a significant date?
   b. **Draw Conclusions** What effect did *Common Sense* have on colonial attitudes toward Great Britain?
   c. **Predict** How might the content of the Declaration of Independence lead to questions over the issue of slavery?

THE AMERICAN REVOLUTION **141**

Review and Assessment Resources

Review and Reinforce

SE Chapter Review

📑 **CRF:** Chapter Review Activity

📑 Quick Facts Transparency: The American Revolution Visual Summary

🔊 Spanish Chapter Summaries Audio CD Program

🌐 Online Chapter Summaries in Six Languages

OSP Holt PuzzlePro, GameTool for ExamView

💿 Quiz Game CD-ROM

Assess

SE Standardized Test Practice

📑 PASS: Chapter Test, Forms A and B

📑 Alternative Assessment Handbook

OSP ExamView Test Generator, Chapter Test

💿 Differentiated Instruction Modified Worksheets and Tests CD-ROM: Chapter Test

🌐 Holt Online Assessment Program (in the Premier Online Edition)

Reteach/Intervene

📑 Interactive Reader and Study Guide

📑 Differentiated Instruction Teacher Management System: Lesson Plans for Differentiated Instruction

💿 Differentiated Instruction Modified Worksheets and Tests CD-ROM

💿 Interactive Skills Tutor CD-ROM

go.hrw.com
Online Resources

Chapter Resources:
KEYWORD: SR8 US4

6. a. date on which the Continental Congress approved the Declaration of Independence

b. changed the way many colonists viewed the king, made a strong case for economic freedom and military self-defense

c. It states that "all men are created equal" and have unalienable rights, but at the same time many colonists were slave holders.

7. a. defeats in Canada, New York

b. with victories at the Battles of Trenton and Saratoga

c. possible answers: No—Foreign aid provided training, money, and military help on sea and land; Yes—the tide had already begun to turn in favor of the Patriots, who would have worn down the British eventually.

8. a. knew there was a large Loyalist population in Georgia, the Carolinas, and Virginia; planned to free enslaved Africans and have them fight

b. possible answer—because of debates over borders, the roles of France and Spain, and whether Americans could settle and trade west of the original thirteen colonies

c. possible answers—victory at Yorktown, because the Patriots captured Britain's largest army in America; French aid, because it enabled the Patriots to surround the British army at Yorktown

Social Studies Skills

9. c

10. possible answer—The Continental Army was no match against the Redcoats.

Reviewing Themes

11. rights to life, liberty, and the pursuit of happiness

12. settlements were scattered, troops had to travel long distances

---

SECTION 3 (Pages 126–134)

7. a. Describe What difficulties did the Patriots experience in the early years of the war?

b. Analyze How did the Patriots turn the tide of the war?

c. Elaborate Could the Patriots have succeeded in the war without foreign help? Explain.

SECTION 4 (Pages 135–139)

8. a. Recall Why did the British think they might find support in the southern colonies?

b. Make Inferences Why did it take more than two years for the British and the Americans to agree to the terms of the Treaty of Paris?

c. Evaluate In your opinion, what was the most important reason for the Patriots' defeat of the British?

Social Studies Skills

Understanding Historical Interpretation *Use the Social Studies Skills taught in this chapter to answer the questions about the reading selection below.*

> In a series of battles, Howe pounded the Continental Army, forcing it to retreat farther and farther. The Redcoats captured Patriots as well as supplies. Eventually, the British pushed Washington across the Hudson River into New Jersey. Howe's revenge for his defeat at Boston was complete. (p. 128)

9. Which statement from the passage is an interpretation of historical facts?

a. The Redcoats captured Patriots as well as supplies.

b. Eventually, the British pushed Washington across the Hudson River into New Jersey.

c. Howe's revenge for his defeat at Boston was complete.

10. What might a different interpretation of the facts be?

Reviewing Themes

11. Politics What are three important rights listed in the Declaration of Independence?

12. Geography What role did geography play in the fighting that took place in the West?

Reading Skills

Main Ideas in Social Studies *Use the Reading Skills taught at the beginning of the chapter to answer the question about the reading selection below.*

> (1) Native Americans were at first encouraged by both sides to remain neutral. (2) By the summer of 1776, however, both Patriots and the British were aggressively recruiting Indian fighters. (3) Most sided with the British. (4) In northern New York, four of the six Iroquois nations fought for the British. (p. 120)

13. Which sentence contains the main idea of the paragraph?

a. Sentence 1

b. Sentence 2

c. Sentence 3

d. Sentence 4

Using the Internet KEYWORD: SR8 US4

14. Activity: Researching The Battle of Saratoga showed the world that the Patriots were capable of defeating the British. This victory gave Benjamin Franklin the chance to use his fame as a scientist and diplomat to convince France to aid the Patriots. Enter the activity keyword and explain how these factors led to a Patriot victory and how the American Revolution affected France.

FOCUS ON SPEAKING

15. Prepare Your Oral Report Review your notes and be sure you've identified one or two important ideas, events, or people for each period of the war. Now, start to prepare your oral report by writing a one-sentence introduction to your talk. Then write a sentence or two about each period of the war. Write a concluding sentence that makes a quick connection between the Revolutionary War and our lives today. Practice your talk until you can give it with only a glance or two at your notes.

Reading Skills

13. Sentence 3

Using the Internet

14. Go to the HRW Web site and enter the keyword shown to access a rubric for this activity.

> KEYWORD: SR8 US4

Focus on Speaking

15. Rubric Students' oral reports should:
- include an introduction, two sentences on each period of the war, and a conclusion.
- discuss the war in chronological order.
- provide vivid descriptions to engage the audience.
- use standard English and proper grammar.

CRF: Focus on Speaking Activity: Giving an Oral Report

Standardized Test Practice

DIRECTIONS: Read each question and write the letter of the best response.

1 What action would a Loyalist have been *least* likely to take during the Revolution?

A flee the colonies for England

B support the *Olive Branch Petition*

C oppose the Declaration of Independence

D join the Continental Army

2 Which of the following events took place *last*?

A The Declaration of Independence was issued.

B The Second Continental Congress met.

C The battles at Lexington and Concord occurred.

D The Battle of Bunker Hill took place.

3 Why was the victory at the Battle of Saratoga so important to the Patriot cause?

A It allowed the Declaration of Independence to be issued.

B It forced the British army to retreat from Boston.

C It convinced France to aid the colonies in their fight.

D It caused the British government to give up the war.

4 The most brutal and destructive fighting of the war probably occurred

A in the southern colonies.

B at Valley Forge.

C in New England.

D at Lexington and Concord.

5 The Declaration of Independence's claim that people have a right to "life, liberty, and the pursuit of happiness" shows the influence of what Enlightenment thinker from Europe?

A Jonathan Edwards

B John Locke

C King George III

D Thomas Paine

6 In what way was Clark's battle strategy the same as John Paul Jone's strategy?

A They both were badly outnumbered by the British.

B They both knew the colonial Midwest region well.

C They both aimed to weaken the British by attacking their supply lines.

D They both survived the winter at Valley Forge.

7

> "These are the times that try men's souls. The summer soldier and the sunshine patriot will, in this crisis, shrink from the service of his country, but he that stands it now, deserves the love and thanks of man and woman. Tyranny . . . is not easily conquered, yet we have this consolation with us, that the harder the conflict, the more glorious the triumph."
>
> —Thomas Paine, *The Crisis,* 1776

What point is Paine trying to make in this passage?

A Although war is glorious, many people are unwilling to take part in it.

B The price of independence may be too high for what will be gained by obtaining it.

C Most colonists do not understand what sacrifices some are making for their freedom.

D Despite the difficulties, the colonists' cause is worthy and they should not give up.

Intervention Resources

Reproducible

- Interactive Reader and Study Guide
- Differentiated Instruction Teacher Management System: Lesson Plans for Differentiated Instruction

Technology

- Quick Facts Transparency: The American Revolution Visual Summary
- Differentiated Instruction Modified Worksheets and Tests CD-ROM
- Interactive Skills Tutor CD-ROM

Tips for Test Taking

Study the Directions Read the following to students: To follow directions correctly you have to know what the directions are. Read all test directions as if they contain the key to lifetime happiness and several years' of allowance. Then read them again. Next, study the answer sheet. How is it laid out? How are the choices arranged—vertically, horizontally? Be very sure you know exactly what to do and how to do it before you make your first mark.

Answers

1. D

Break Down the Question This question asks what a Loyalist would likely not have done. Tell students to start by eliminating any actions that Loyalists likely would have taken, which leaves only answer D.

2. A

Break Down the Question This question requires students to sequence a series of events. Suggest that students first order the events they are certain about and then try to fill in other events.

3. C

Break Down the Question This question requires students to identify cause and effect. Tell students in such cases to think about what they know about the event in question and what happened after or as a result of the event.

4. A

Break Down the Question Suggest that students first eliminate any choices where fighting did not occur (Valley Forge) and then recall what they know about the remaining options.

5. B

Break Down the Question This question requires students to recall information covered in Grade 7.

6. C

Break Down the Question Suggest that students eliminate any choices that do not involve battle strategy and then recall what they know about the remaining options.

7. D

Break Down the Question Suggest that students go through the reading phrase by phrase and interpret each one in turn. Then have them review the reading to get its full meaning. Here, focus on the phrases "but he that stands it now, deserves the love and thanks of man and woman" and "the harder the conflict, the more glorious the triumph."

A Biographical Narrative

Bellringer

Motivate Ask students to name some of the people they have read about in this unit. Then ask them which of these people's lives would make the most interesting stories. Lead students to discuss what makes a narrative interesting. Tell students they will write a biographical narrative in this workshop.

Adding Details

Move Beyond Plot Remind students that just telling what happened does not make events come alive. In addition to describing an event, students should tell what the subject thought and felt about what happened. Tell students they want to help their readers experience the events through the subject's eyes.

Using Transitions

Link It Up Model the use of transitions for students. Choose a series of events from the unit. Next, write the events for students to see. Then ask students to help you link each event with an appropriate transition word. When all events are linked, erase the transitions and challenge students to think of a new set of appropriate transition words.

Assignment

Write a biographical narrative about a person who lived in the early Americas before or during the colonial period.

TIP **Asking Questions** Try using the *5W-How?* questions (*Who? What? When? Where? Why? How?*) to help you think of descriptive details. Ask questions such as, **Who** was this person? **What** was he or she doing? Exactly **where** and **when** did the event occur? **How** did the person or other people react to the event?

You have been listening to and telling narratives all your life. A biographical narrative, a form of historical writing, is a true story about an event or brief period in a person's life.

1. Prewrite

Getting Started

- Think of all the people you read about in this unit. Which ones interested you most?
- What particular events and situations in these people's lives seem most exciting or significant?

Pick one of these events or situations as the subject of your narrative.

Creating an Interesting Narrative

Make your narrative lively and interesting by including

- **Physical descriptions** of people, places, and things, using details that appeal to the five senses (sight, hearing, touch, smell, taste)
- **Specific actions** that relate directly to the story you are telling
- **Dialogue** between the people involved or direct **quotations**
- **Background information** about the place, customs, and setting
- **All relevant details and information** needed to relate the events of the story and how they affected the person (and perhaps history)

Organize the events in your narrative in chronological order, the order in which they occurred.

2. Write

You can use this framework to help you draft your narrative.

A Writer's Framework

Introduction	Body	Conclusion
■ Grab your reader's attention with a striking detail or bit of dialogue. ■ Introduce the historical person and setting, using specific details. ■ Set the scene by telling how the event or situation began.	■ Present actions and details in the order in which they occurred. ■ Connect actions with transition words like *first, then, next,* and *finally*. ■ Provide specific details to make the person and the situation come alive.	■ Wrap up the action of the narrative. ■ Tell how the person was affected by what happened. ■ Explain how the event or situation was important in the person's life and how it affected history.

Differentiating Instruction

Advanced/ Gifted and Talented | Above Level

1. Challenge students to present their narrative as a historian might by incorporating primary and secondary source quotes.

2. Instruct students to provide a footnote giving the citation, or source, for each quotation. Last, students should create a bibliography of their sources to go with their biographical narrative. **LS** **Verbal/Linguistic**

English-Language Learners | Below Level

1. Write the sequence words listed in the Tip on the next page for students to see.

2. Have students write each sequence word on a note card and then write the equivalent in their primary language on the card's back.

3. Pair students and have them use the cards to quiz each other. **LS** **Interpersonal, Verbal/Linguistic**

3. Evaluate and Revise

Evaluating

Read through your completed draft to make sure your narrative is complete, coherent, and clear. Then look for ways to improve it.

Evaluation Questions for a Biographical Narrative

- Does your introduction grab the reader's attention? Do you introduce the historical person and tell how the event or situation began?
- Do you include details to make the person, place, and event seem real?
- Are the actions in the story in the order they occurred?

- Have you included all of the actions and details a reader would need to understand what happened?
- Does the conclusion tell how the event or situation affected the person and history?

Revising

When you revise your narrative, you may need to add transition words. Transition words help you link ideas between sentences and paragraphs. Notice the words in bold in the following sentences.

> **After** Cabeza de Vaca and the other adventurers left the beach and started inland, they separated into different groups. **Later**, Cabeza de Vaca heard that many of the others had died. **Still**, he never lost faith that he would reach his fellow Spaniards in Mexico.

4. Proofread and Publish

Proofreading

Throughout your narrative, you used transition words to link events. Make sure that you have spelled the words correctly and have not confused them with other words. For example, be sure to use two *l*'s in *finally* and not to mistake the transition word *then* for the comparative word *than*.

Publishing

One good way to share your biographical narrative is to exchange it with one or more classmates who have written about the same person you have. After reading each other's narratives, you can compare and contrast them. How are your stories similar? How do they differ?

5. Practice and Apply

Use the steps and strategies outlined in this workshop to write your biographical narrative.

TIP **Showing Sequence** A clear sense of the sequence of events is important in any narrative. Here is a list of words that show those relationships.

after	next
before	now
finally	soon
first	still
(second, etc.)	then
last	when
later	while

Acting Workshop

Play It Out Encourage students who are having trouble adding thoughts and feelings to their narratives to form small groups and act out each narrative as a play. Then have the student playing the subject describe his or her thoughts and feelings while the other students take notes.

Teaching Tip

Person and Tense Remind students to use the third person and the past tense throughout their biographical narratives. When students proofread their papers, suggest that they circle all pronouns and underline all verbs to make sure they match.

Practice & Apply

Rubric

Students' biographical narratives should

- start with a striking detail or interesting bit of dialogue.
- clearly identify the subject and the historical setting.
- present actions and details in the order in which they occurred.
- correctly and effectively use transitions to link events.
- provide vivid details and dialogue to bring the person and the story alive.
- wrap up the story and explain how the situation affected the subject.
- use correct grammar, punctuation, spelling, and capitalization.

Special Needs Learners [Below Level]

1. Have special needs learners draw the person and events they have selected as the subject of their biographical narratives.

2. Have a classroom aide or fellow student listen and take notes while the student describes what is happening in the picture.

3. Then have the aide or fellow student use the notes to guide the special needs learners in writing his or her biographical narrative.

4. If the student gets stuck, direct the aide or fellow student to prompt him or her by asking questions about the picture. Questions might include: Who are the people in the picture? What are they doing? Why are they doing these things? What happened next? How do you think the person felt during these events? What sights and sounds did the person see and hear during the events? **LS** **Visual/Spatial**

Introduce the Unit

Share the information in the chapter overviews with students.

Chapter 4 American colonists formed state and federal governments based on English laws, Enlightenment ideas, and American models of government. The federal government established by the Articles of Confederation lacked the power to rule effectively, however. To remedy this problem, American leaders wrote a new constitution that created a stronger central government. Eventually, the required nine states ratified the U.S. Constitution.

Chapter 5 The framers of the U.S. Constitution developed a federal system, dividing power between the federal and state governments. A system of checks and balances divides federal power among the legislative, executive, and judicial branches of government. To address concerns about individual rights, the first Congress added 10 amendments, known as the Bill of Rights, to the Constitution. In addition to these rights, all U.S. citizens have certain responsibilities to society.

Chapter 6 With the Constitution ratified, U.S. leaders set about creating a new federal government. These leaders faced numerous challenges, including how to pay off the national debt, how to respond to foreign threats, and how to *(continued on p. 147)*

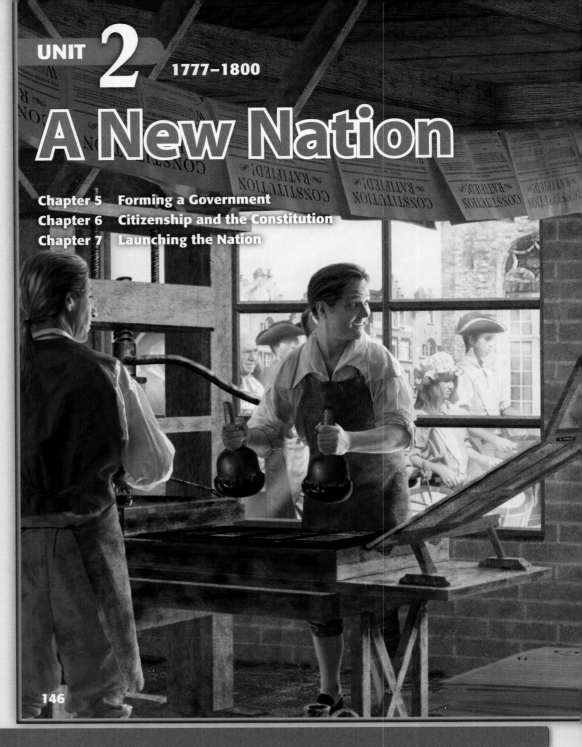

UNIT 2
1777–1800

A New Nation

Chapter 5 Forming a Government
Chapter 6 Citizenship and the Constitution
Chapter 7 Launching the Nation

146

Unit Resources

Planning

- Differentiated Instruction Teacher Management System: Unit Instructional Benchmarking Guides
- One-Stop Planner CD-ROM with Test Generator: Calendar Planner
- Power Presentations with Video CD-ROM
- A Teacher's Guide to Religion in the Public Schools

Differentiating Instruction

- Differentiated Instruction Teacher Management System: Lesson Plans for Differentiated Instruction
- Pre-AP Activities Guide for United States History
- Differentiated Instruction Modified Worksheets and Tests CD-ROM

Enrichment

- **CRF 6:** Economics and History: The National Debt
- **CRF 6:** Interdisciplinary Projects: Planning the New Capital: Drama Script; Student Almanac
- Civic Participation Activities
- Primary Source Library CD-ROM

Assessment

- Progress Assessment System Solution: Unit Test
- OSP ExamView Test Generator: Unit Test
- Holt Online Assessment Program, in the Premier Online Student Edition
- Alternative Assessment Handbook

The **Differentiated Instruction Teacher Management System** provides a planning and instructional benchmarking guide for this unit.

After the Revolutionary War, much needed to be done in the new United States. The ideas of the Revolution had to be preserved in its new government.

During the first years of the United States, political leaders met and discussed the form that the government should take. Often, people disagreed about how the new nation should be organized. Debates still take place about the framework of the U.S. government, which is written in the Constitution.

In the next three chapters you will learn about the creation of the Constitution and how that document affects us today.

Explore the Art

In this scene, a teenaged printer's devil, or apprentice, is shown reading about the recent approval of the Constitution. How does the art show citizens' ideas about the Constitution?

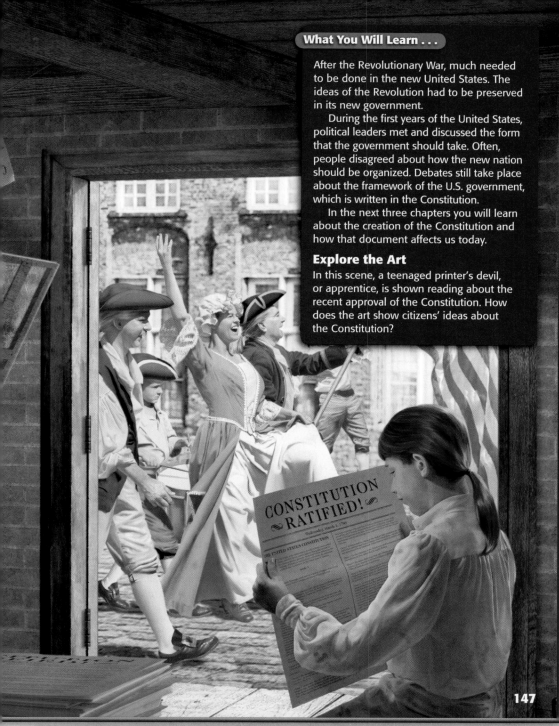

CONSTITUTION RATIFIED!

147

Unit Overview *continued*

resolve domestic conflicts. President George Washington and his administration set many precedents. Not all Americans agreed on the best course of government, however. As a result, political parties developed, although Washington warned against them.

Connect to the Unit

Activity **Solving Challenges Facing New Governments** Ask students to brainstorm a list of challenges that any new government might face. Have students rank the answers they suggested in order of importance. Organize students into groups and give each group one of the problems that the class decided was among the most important. Have each group come up with three solutions a government might use to meet this challenge. At the end of the unit, have students compare their solutions to the actions U.S. leaders took. **LS** **Interpersonal, Logical/Mathematical**

Explore the Art

Ratification celebrations for the U.S. Constitution were particularly festive in Baltimore, Maryland. After the state ratified the Constitution, the city of Baltimore held a large parade and picnic. The centerpiece of the parade was a 15-foot ship named *Federalist,* which represented the ship of state.

Today the nation celebrates the U.S. Constitution on September 17, known as Constitution Day.

About the Illustration

This illustration is an artist's conception based on available sources. However, historians are uncertain exactly what this scene looked like.

Democracy and Civic Education

At Level

Responsibility: Civic Virtue

Research Required

Background Explain to students that part of citizenship is civic virtue, or working to promote the common good. Students can help to promote the common good in a number of ways, such as being informed citizens, promoting issues they feel strongly about, or doing volunteer work or community service.

1. Have students discuss what they think is meant by the term *common good*.

2. Lead a discussion about the ways that students can help promote the common good.

3. Then have students work as a class to create brochures or pamphlets that explain the need for civic virtue and list area volunteer and community-service opportunities for students. Have students create and set up an information booth in their school to hand out the information to other students. **LS** **Interpersonal, Verbal/Linguistic**

Alternative Assessment Handbook, Rubrics 14: Group Activity; and 37: Writing Assignments

Civic Participation

Answers

Explore the Art *The parade, people's expressions, and the newspaper coverage indicate that many Americans considered the ratification of the Constitution to be a wonderful event to be celebrated and reported.*

Chapter 5 Planning Guide

Forming a Government

Chapter Overview	Reproducible Resources	Technology Resources
CHAPTER 5 pp. 148–177 **Overview:** In this chapter, students will learn about the founding fathers and their role in the formation of the U.S. government.	**Differentiated Instruction Teacher Management System:*** • Instructional Benchmarking Guides • Lesson Plans for Differentiated Instruction **Interactive Reader and Study Guide:** Chapter Graphic Organizer* **Chapter Resource File*** • Focus on Writing Activity: A Newspaper Editorial • Social Studies Skills Activity: Determine Different Points of View • Chapter Review Activity	Power Presentations With Video CD-ROM Differentiated Instruction Modified Worksheets and Tests CD-ROM Primary Source Library CD-ROM for United States History Student Edition on Audio CD Program History's Impact: United States History Video Program (VHS/DVD): Forming a Government*
Section 1: **The Articles of Confederation** **The Big Idea:** The Articles of Confederation provided a framework for a national government.	**Differentiated Instruction Teacher Management System:** Section 1 Lesson Plan* **Interactive Reader and Study Guide:** Section 1 Summary* **Chapter Resource File*** • Vocabulary Builder Activity, Section 1 • Primary Source Activity: Iroquois Great Law of Peace • History and Geography Activity: The Northwest Territory	Daily Bellringer Transparency: Section 1* Map Transparency: The Land Ordinances of 1785 and 1787*
Section 2: **The New Nation Faces Challenges** **The Big Idea:** Problems faced by the young nation made it clear that a new constitution was needed.	**Differentiated Instruction Teacher Management System:** Section 2 Lesson Plan* **Interactive Reader and Study Guide:** Section 2 Summary* **Chapter Resource File*** • Vocabulary Builder Activity, Section 2	Daily Bellringer Transparency: Section 2* Map Transparency: The United States Faces Trade Barriers* Quick Facts Transparency: Weaknesses of the Articles of Confederation*
Section 3: **Creating the Constitution** **The Big Idea:** A new constitution provided a framework for a stronger national government.	**Differentiated Instruction Teacher Management System:** Section 3 Lesson Plan* **Interactive Reader and Study Guide:** Section 3 Summary* **Chapter Resource File*** • Vocabulary Builder Activity, Section 3 • Biography Activity: Signers of the Constitution • Primary Source Activity: Benjamin Franklin Addresses the Constitutional Convention	Daily Bellringer Transparency: Section 3* Quick Facts Transparency: Great Compromise* Quick Facts Transparency: The Constitution Strengthens the National Government* Internet Activity: Biographies of Constitutional Convention Leaders
Section 4: **Ratifying the Constitution** **The Big Idea:** Americans carried on a vigorous debate before ratifying the Constitution.	**Differentiated Instruction Teacher Management System:** Section 4 Lesson Plan* **Interactive Reader and Study Guide:** Section 4 Summary* **Chapter Resource File*** • Vocabulary Builder Activity, Section 4 • Biography Activity: George Mason • History and Geography Activity: Ratifying the Constitution • Literature Activity: *Federalist Paper* "No. 15" • Biography Activity: Mercy Otis Warren	Daily Bellringer Transparency: Section 4* Quick Facts Transparency: Federalists v. Antifederalists* Internet Activity: Hamilton and Madison Articles

HOLT
History's Impact
United States History Video Program (VHS/DVD)
Forming a Government
Suggested use: as a chapter introduction

Review, Assessment, Intervention

 Quick Facts Transparency: Forming a Government Visual Summary*

 Progress Assessment Support System (PASS): Chapter Test*

 Differentiated Instruction Modified Worksheets and Tests CD-ROM: Modified Chapter Test

 One-Stop Planner CD-ROM: ExamView Test Generator (English/Spanish)

 Alternative Assessment Handbook

 PASS: Section 1 Quiz*
 Online Quiz: Section 1
 Alternative Assessment Handbook

 PASS: Section 2 Quiz*
 Online Quiz: Section 2
 Alternative Assessment Handbook

 PASS: Section 3 Quiz*
 Online Quiz: Section 3
 Alternative Assessment Handbook

 PASS: Section 4 Quiz*
 Online Quiz: Section 4
 Alternative Assessment Handbook

Power Presentations with Video CD-ROM

Power Presentations with Video are visual presentations of each chapter's main ideas. Presentations can be customized by including Quick Facts charts, images from the text, and video clips.

Developed by the Division for Public Education of the American Bar Association, these materials are part of the **Democracy and Civic Education Resources.**

• **Constitution Study Guide**

• **Supreme Court Case Studies**

Holt Online Learning

Teacher Resources
KEYWORD: SR8 TEACHER

Student Resources
KEYWORD: SR8 US5

• Document-Based Questions
• Interactive Multimedia Activities

• Current Events
• Chapter-based Internet Activities
• and more!

Holt Premier
Online Student Edition
Complete online support for interactivity, assessment, and reporting

• Interactive Maps and Notebook
• Standardized Test Prep
• Homework Practice and Research Activities Online

CHAPTER 5 PLANNING GUIDE

Differentiating Instruction

ENGLISH-LANGUAGE LEARNERS & STRUGGLING READERS

Live Ink® Online Reading Help

Spanish Resources
Spanish Chapter Summaries Audio CD Program
One-Stop Planner CD-ROM:
- ExamView Test Generator, Spanish
- PuzzlePro, Spanish

Additional Resources
Differented Instruction Teacher Management System: Lesson Plans for Differentiated Instruction
Chapter Resources:
- Vocabulary Builder Activities
- Social Studies Skills Activity: Determine Different Points of View

Quick Facts Transparencies:
- Weaknesses of the Articles of Confederation
- Great Compromise
- The Constitution Strengthens the National Government
- Federalists v. Antifederalists
- Forming a Government Visual Summary

Student Edition on Audio CD Program
Online Chapter Summaries in Six Languages
Interactive Skills Tutor CD-ROM

SPECIAL NEEDS LEARNERS

Differentiated Instruction Modified Worksheets and Tests CD-ROM
- Vocabulary Flash Cards
- Modified Vocabulary Builder Activities
- Modified Chapter Review Activity
- Modified Chapter Test

Additional Resources
Differentiated Instruction Teacher Management System: Lesson Plans for Differentiated Instruction
Interactive Reader and Study Guide
Social Studies Skills Activity: Determine Different Points of View
Student Edition on Audio CD Program
Interactive Skills Tutor CD-ROM
Live Ink® Online Reading Help

ADVANCED/GIFTED AND TALENTED STUDENTS

Primary Source Library CD-ROM for United States History

The Library contains longer versions of quotations in the text, extra sources, and images. Included are point-of-view articles, journals, diaries, historical fiction, and political documents.

Additional Resources
Political Cartoons Activities for United States History: Cartoon 4: Ratifying the Constitution
United States History Document-Based Questions Activities
Differentiated Instruction Teacher Management System: Lesson Plans for Differentiated Instruction
Chapter Resource File:
- Focus on Writing Activity: A Newspaper Editorial
- Literature Activity: *Federalist Paper* "No. 15"
- Primary Source Activity: Iroquois Great Law of Peace
- Primary Source Activity: Benjamin Franklin Addresses the Constitutional Convention

Differentiated Activities in the Teacher's Edition

- Constitution Flash Cards, p. 156
- International Relations Dialogues, p. 159
- Writing Newspaper Headlines, p. 160
- Constitutional Convention Invitations, p. 164
- Visualizing Balanced Government, p. 166

Differentiated Activities in the Teacher's Edition

- Accomplishments of Franklin, p. 169

Differentiated Activities in the Teacher's Edition

- Influences on American Government Debates, p. 153
- Origins of the Constitution Restaurant Menu, p. 157
- Recipe for Government, p. 166
- Federalists v. Antifederalists Essay, p. 171

One-Stop Planner® CD-ROM
for Differentiated Instruction

Your differentiated instruction lesson plans are available at your fingertips. Holt's Teacher Management System links teaching support tools to pages in the Interactive Teacher's Edition.

The One-Stop Planner features:
- Interactive Teacher's Edition
- Calendar Planner and pacing guides
- Editable lesson plans
- All reproducible ancillaries in Adobe Acrobat (PDF) format
- ExamView Test Generator (English and Spanish)
- Transparency and video previews

Professional Development

- **In-service and staff development** as part of your Holt Social Studies product purchase
- **Quick Teacher Tutorial Lesson Presentation CD-ROM**
- Intensive tuition-based **Teacher Development Institute**
- **Teaching American History Online**—2 Module Professional Development Course
- **Convenient Holt Speaker Bureau**—face-to-face workshop options
- **PRAXIS™ Test Prep** interactive Web-based content refreshers*
- **24/7 Ask A Professional Development Expert** at http://www.hrw.com/prodev/

* PRAXIS is a trademark of Educational Testing Service (ETS). This publication is not endorsed or approved by ETS.

• Chapter Preview •

Chapter Big Ideas

Section 1 The Articles of Confederation provided a framework for a national government.

Section 2 Problems faced by the young nation made it clear that a new constitution was needed.

Section 3 A new constitution provided a framework for a stronger national government.

Section 4 Americans carried on a vigorous debate before ratifying the Constitution.

Focus on Writing

The **Chapter Resource File** provides a Focus on Writing worksheet to help students organize and write their newspaper editorials.

CRF: Focus on Writing Activity: A Newspaper Editorial

Key to Differentiating Instruction

Below Level

Basic-level activities designed for all students encountering new material

At Level

Intermediate-level activities designed for average students

Above Level

Challenging activities designed for honors and gifted and talented students

Standard English Mastery

Activities designed to improve standard English usage

CHAPTER 5   **1777–1791**

Forming a Government

FOCUS ON WRITING

A Newspaper Editorial It is 1788 and you're writing an editorial for a local newspaper. You want to convince your readers that the new Constitution will be much better than the old Articles of Confederation. In this chapter you'll find the information you need to support your opinion.

UNITED STATES

1777 The Continental Congress approves the Articles of Confederation on November 15.

1775

WORLD

1778 The United States and France become allies.

Introduce the Chapter

At Level

Focus on Forming a New Government

1. Explain to students that once the Revolutionary War began and the Declaration of Independence was signed, it was left to Americans to decide how to form a new government. Then ask students what kind of government they might want to form if they had just gained independence from a monarchy.

2. Explain to students that they are going to learn about the form of government that the Americans formed after the Revolutionary War.

Have students predict some of the issues that arose as the new government was being established. Write students' predictions for them to see and save the list.

3. Have students make a copy of the predictions. Tell them to note how accurate or inaccurate each of their predictions was as they read the chapter. **LS** Logical/Mathematical

What You Will Learn . . .

This photo shows Speaker of the House Dennis Hastert swearing in the 108ᵗʰ Congress, the legislative branch of the U.S. government. In this chapter, you will learn about the nation's earliest government, the Articles of Confederation, and its failures to achieve national unity. You will also read about the writing of the Constitution and how it attempted to solve the problems of the Articles by creating a new system of government with three branches.

1781
On March 1 the Articles of Confederation go into effect after being ratified by all 13 states.

Collection of the American Numismatic Society, New York

1785
The United States begins using the dollar currency.

1786
Shays's Rebellion breaks out in Massachusetts.

1787
On May 14, state delegates begin to arrive at the Constitutional Convention in Philadelphia.

1791
The Bill of Rights is ratified by the states in December.

1780

1785

1790

1782
Spain completes its conquest of British Florida.

1787
The Ottoman Empire declares war on Russia.

1791
The *Lady Washington* becomes the first U.S. ship to reach Japan.

FORMING A GOVERNMENT **149**

• Chapter Preview •

HOLT
History's Impact
▶ video series
See the Video Teacher's Guide for strategies for using the chapter video **Forming a Government**.

Explore the Picture

Congress in Session Every year on January 3, unless otherwise specified, members of Congress take their places in the Capitol Building in Washington, D.C., for the start of a new session. Members gather to fulfill their constitutional responsibility of making the nation's laws. Congress decides issues such as how large the U.S. armed forces will be and whether federal taxes will increase. Each session, lawmakers make decisions that affect not only national and world affairs but also your life, school, and community.

Analyzing Visuals Why might the Speaker of the House formally swear in members at the start of a new session of Congress? *to emphasize the seriousness of representatives' responsibility to make the nation's laws*

go.hrw.com
Online Resources
Chapter Resources:
KEYWORD: SR8 US5
Teacher Resources:
KEYWORD: SR8 TEACHER

Explore the Time Line

1. How many years after the Continental Congress approved the Articles of Confederation were they ratified by all 13 states? *a little under 4 years*

2. When did the United States begin using the dollar currency? *1785*

3. What happened the same year that the Bill of Rights was ratified? *The* Lady Washington *became the first U.S. ship to reach Japan.*

Connect to Economics

United States Currency The U.S. Constitution gives Congress sole power to coin money and regulate its value. Congress established the dollar as the basic unit of money and created a national mint in Philadelphia. In 1794 Philadelphia minted the first U.S. silver dollar. It featured a liberty head on the front and an eagle on the back. The mint also produced $10 gold coins called eagles.

Reading
Social Studies

Understanding Themes

Ask students what might have been some areas of concern for the United States following the Revolutionary War. Help students to see that an immediate concern of U.S. leaders was the creation of a new government. Ask students how they might go about choosing a government to rule a nation. What might be some important powers of that new government? What might happen if the people do not fully support the new government? Point out to students that American society and culture was greatly affected by the new government of the United States. Remind students to focus on the key themes of politics, and society and culture as they read this chapter.

Chronological Order

Focus on Reading Ask each student to write one or two paragraphs that detail a typical school day. Have students write their descriptions in chronological order, from the time they wake up in the morning until they go to sleep. Ask students to exchange descriptions with a partner. Have each student circle words or phrases that signal chronological order. Then have students use those words to create a sequence chain that tracks the events of a typical day for that person.

Reading Social Studies

by Kylene Beers

| Economics | Geography | Politics | Society and Culture | Science and Technology |

Focus on Themes Visualize a row of dominoes, lined up one after the other. Push over the first one, and—one after the other—all eventually fall. In this way, the events in this chapter are like dominoes that cause each other to occur. These events, one after another, finally led to the formation of a new government and a new **society**. If you read closely, you will see that **political** disagreements started the entire process.

Understanding Chronological Order

Focus on Reading Like falling dominoes, historical events can create huge chains of results, often stretching over many years. To understand history and events, therefore, we often need to see how they are related in time.

Understanding Chronological Order The word **chronological** means "related to time." Events discussed in this history book are discussed in **sequence**, in the order in which they happened. To understand history better, you can use a sequence chain to take notes about events in the order they happened.

Sequence Chain

1620
The Pilgrims sign the Mayflower Compact.

↓

1639
Connecticut creates the first constitution in the English colonies.

↓

1689
The English Bill of Rights is passed.

↓

1776
The American colonies declare their independence from Great Britain.

Tip: Writers sometimes signal chronological order, or sequence, by using words or phrases like these:

first, before, then, later, soon, after, before long, next, eventually, finally

150 CHAPTER 5

Reading and Skills Resources

Reading Support

📖 Interactive Reader and Study Guide

🔊 Student Edition on Audio CD Program

🔊 Spanish Chapter Summaries Audio CD Program

Social Studies Skills Support

💿 Interactive Skills Tutor CD-ROM

Vocabulary Support

📑 **CRF:** Vocabulary Builder Activities

📑 **CRF:** Chapter Review Activity

💿 Differentiated Instruction Modified Worksheets and Tests CD-ROM:
  • Vocabulary Flash Cards
  • Vocabulary Builder Activity
  • Chapter Review Activity

OSP Holt PuzzlePro

You Try It!

Read the following passage and answer the questions that follow.

Farmers Rebel

From Chapter 5, p. 161

In August 1786, farmers in three western counties began a revolt. Bands of angry citizens closed down courts in western Massachusetts. Their reasoning was simple—with the courts shut down, no one's property could be taken. In September, a poor farmer and Revolutionary War Veteran, Daniel Shays, led hundreds of men in a forced shutdown of the Supreme Court in Springfield, Massachusetts. The state government ordered the farmers to stop the revolt under threat of capture and death. These threats only made Shays and his followers more determined. The uprising of farmers to protest high taxes and heavy debt became known as Shays's Rebellion.

Shays's forces were defeated by state troops in January 1787. By February many of the rebels were in prison. During their trials, 14 leaders were sentenced to death. However, the state soon freed most of the rebels, including Shays.

After you have read the passage, answer the following questions.

1. Which happened first—citizens closing courts in western Massachusetts or Shays shutting down the Supreme Court? How can you tell?

2. What happened after Shays's forces were defeated by state troops?

3. Draw a sequence chain that shows the effects of Shays's Rebellion in the order they occurred.

> **Before you read Chapter 5,** look for clues that signal the order in which events occurred.

Reading Social Studies

Key Terms and People

To help students identify and study the key terms and people, have students create a Key-Term FoldNote. Have students fold a sheet of paper in half vertically. Then have students cut along every third or fourth line from the right edge of the paper to the center fold. Students will write the term or person on the outside of each tab. As students learn each key term, have them write a description or definition on the inside. Encourage students to study these people and terms regularly.

LS Verbal/Linguistic, Kinesthetic

Focus on Reading

See the **Focus on Reading** questions in this chapter for more practice on this reading social studies skill.

Reading Social Studies Assessment

See the **Chapter Review** at the end of this chapter for student assessment questions related to this reading skill.

Teaching Tip

Time lines are excellent tools for showing chronological order. Time lines can be created for all sorts of situations. Students could create a time line of their own lives by noting their date of birth, when certain major events occurred, such as starting school or moving to a new home. Students could also create a time line showing the history and development of their community or city. Students can even create a time line to keep track during the year of important events in U.S. history.

Answers

You Try It! 1. *citizens closed down the courts; because the passage uses dates to show order;* **2.** *the rebels were imprisoned and its leaders were sentenced to death;* **3.** *Sequence chain—Shays's forces were defeated; rebels were imprisoned and leaders sentenced to death; most rebels were freed.*

Bellringer

If YOU were there . . . Use the **Daily Bellringer Transparency** to help students answer the question.

🔖 Daily Bellringer Transparency, Section 1

Forming a Government

Daily Bellringer
Section 1

Review the Previous Chapter

Read the list of events below and put them in the correct order.

a. George Washington and his troops cross the Delaware River and launch a surprise attack to win the Battle of Trenton.

b. France joins the Patriots in the war against Great Britain.

c. British general Charles Cornwallis surrenders to General George Washington in the Battle of Yorktown.

d. Minutemen and Redcoats clash at Lexington and Concord.

e. The thirteen colonies formally declare independence from Britain.

Preview Section 1

If YOU were there ...

You live in a town in New England during the 1770s. In the town meeting, people are hotly debating about who will have the right to vote. Most think that only men who own property should be able to vote. Some think that all property owners—men and women—should have that right. A few others want all free men to have the vote. Now it is time for the meeting to decide. **How would you have voted on this issue?**

Consider reasons to LIMIT voting:
• Voters should be taxpayers.
• Voters should be educated.
• Voters should be eligible to hold political office.
• Voters should be adult citizens.

Consider reasons to WIDEN voting:
• Government applies to all people, so all people should have a voice.
• All people have rights.
• All people are equal under the law.

Review Answers: d, e, a, b, c

Copyright © by Holt, Rinehart and Winston. All rights reserved.

Building Vocabulary

Preteach or review the following terms:

controversial subject to debate (p. 155)

ordinance official law or rule (p. 155)

📋 **CRF:** Vocabulary Builder Activity, Section 1

Taking Notes

Have students copy the graphic organizer onto their own paper and then use it to take notes on the section. This activity will prepare students for the Section Assessment, in which they will complete a graphic organizer that builds on the information using a critical thinking skill.

The Articles of Confederation

What You Will Learn . . .

Main Ideas

1. The American people examined many ideas about government.
2. The Articles of Confederation laid the base for the first national government of the United States.
3. The Confederation Congress established the Northwest Territory.

The Big Idea

The Articles of Confederation provided a framework for a national government.

Key Terms and People

Magna Carta, *p. 152*
English Bill of Rights, *p. 152*
constitution, *p. 153*
Virginia Statute for Religious Freedom, *p. 153*
suffrage, *p. 153*
Articles of Confederation, *p. 154*
ratification, *p. 154*
Land Ordinance of 1785, *p. 155*
Northwest Ordinance of 1787, *p. 155*
Northwest Territory, *p. 155*

 TAKING NOTES As you read, take notes on the new American government in a chart like this one.

New American Government
1. Influences on new government
2. Structure of the Articles of Confederation

If YOU were there...

You live in a town in New England during the 1770s. In the town meeting, people are hotly debating about who will have the right to vote. Most think that only men who own property should be able to vote. Some think that all property owners—men and women—should have that right. A few others want all free men to have the vote. Now it is time for the meeting to decide.

How would you have voted on this issue?

BUILDING BACKGROUND At the time of the Revolution, each of the 13 states had its own government. The rights of citizens varied from state to state. In their town meetings, people often argued about exactly what those rights ought to be. Solving such issues was one step in moving toward a national government.

Ideas about Government

The American colonies had taken a bold step in declaring their independence from Great Britain in July 1776. Their next political goal was to form a new government. To do so, the American people drew from a wide range of political ideas.

English Laws and the Enlightenment

One source of inspiration was English law. England had limited the power of its kings and queens in two documents. These were Magna Carta and the English Bill of Rights. **Magna Carta**, a document signed by King John in 1215, made the king subject to law. The **English Bill of Rights**, passed in 1689, declared the supremacy of Parliament. It kept the king or queen from passing new taxes or changing laws without Parliament's consent. As a result, the people's representatives had a strong voice in England's government.

Americans were also influenced by Enlightenment—a philosophical movement that emphasized the use of reason to examine old

---

Teach the Big Idea

At Level

The Articles of Confederation

1. **Teach** Ask students the questions in the Main Idea boxes to teach this section.

2. **Apply** Organize students into groups of three. Assign each group one of the following topics: *Ideas about Government, Articles of Confederation*, or *Northwest Territory*. Ask students to imagine that it is the late 1700s. Have each group member create a flyer informing the American public about the group's assigned topic. **LS Verbal/Linguistic, Visual/Spatial**

3. **Review** Regroup students so that each new group includes members who worked on each topic. Have each student explain his or her flyer to the other group members.

4. **Practice/Homework** Have each student write a letter to the editor either for or against the Articles of Confederation. Students should provide support for their positions. **LS Verbal/Linguistic**

📋 Alternative Assessment Handbook, Rubrics 14: Group Activity; and 17: Letters to Editors ideas and traditions. Philosopher John Locke believed that a social contract existed between political rulers and the people they ruled. Baron de Montesquieu argued that the only way people could achieve liberty was through the separation of governmental powers.

American Models of Government

Americans had their own models of self-government to follow, like town meetings, the Virginia House of Burgesses, and the Mayflower Compact. In 1639 the people of Connecticut drew up the English colonies' first written **constitution**. A constitution is a set of basic principles and laws that states the powers and duties of the government. In addition, the Declaration of Independence clearly set forth the beliefs on which Americans thought government should be based.

State Constitutions

To keep individual leaders from gaining too much power, the new state constitutions created limited governments, or governments in which all leaders have to obey the laws.

Most state constitutions had rules to protect the rights of citizens. Some banned slavery. Some protected the rights of those accused of a crime. Thomas Jefferson's ideas about religious freedom were included in the **Virginia Statute for Religious Freedom**. This document declared that no person could be forced to attend a particular church or be required to pay for a church with tax money.

Right to Vote

Under British rule, only free, white men that owned land could vote. Many states' constitutions expanded **suffrage**, or the right to vote, by allowing any white man who paid taxes to vote. In every state, however, only landowners could hold public office. Some states originally allowed women and free African Americans to vote, but these rights were soon taken away. Suffrage would not be restored to these groups for decades to come.

READING CHECK **Comparing** What two principles were common to state constitutions written during the Revolutionary War?

Women's Suffrage
New Jersey allowed women to vote when it first joined the United States. This right was taken away by 1807.

Why do you think women were not allowed to vote in the early United States?

FORMING A GOVERNMENT **153**

Differentiating Instruction

Above Level

Advanced/Gifted and Talented

1. Organize the class into three groups. Have students discuss within their groups which ideas and documents shaped American beliefs about government.

2. Next, have each group decide which document had the greatest influence and was the most important in the development of American representative government.

3. Each group should build a debate around that premise by developing arguments showing the merits and influence of the document as well as arguments showing the flaws and weaknesses of the document.

4. Have each group perform its debate for the class. **LS Interpersonal, Verbal/Linguistic**

   Alternative Assessment Handbook, Rubric 10: Debates

• **Direct Teach** •

Main Idea

❶ Ideas about Government

The American people examined many ideas about government.

Recall What documents did Americans look to when creating a new government? *Magna Carta, English Bill of Rights, Mayflower Compact, Fundamental Orders of Connecticut, Declaration of Independence, state constitutions, Virginia Statute of Religious Freedom*

Analyze Describe three key ideas from these documents that influenced U.S. government. *possible answers— rule of law, people hold the power, limited government, constitutional protection of rights, separation of powers, representative government, separation of church and state*

Make Generalizations In what ways was suffrage expanded and limited in state constitutions? *Constitutions in general expanded voting rights for white men, while limiting suffrage for African Americans and women.*

CRF: Primary Source Activity: Iroquois Great Law of Peace

Linking to Today

Separation of Church and State Public debate over religious freedom and the separation of church and state continues today. Current examples include school prayer, the presence of religious organizations in public schools, and the words to the Pledge of Allegiance.

Answers

Women's Suffrage *possible answer—At the time, many people thought women's place was in the home and that women did not have the ability to vote intelligently.*

Reading Check *the people hold the power of government , limited government*

2 Articles of Confederation

The Articles of Confederation laid the base for the first national government of the United States.

Recall What was the ratification process for the Articles of Confederation? *It was sent to the state legislatures for official approval.*

Draw Conclusions Why do you think that the Committee of Thirteen did not provide for a president in the Articles of Confederation? *possible answer—feared a president might become as powerful as a monarch*

Contrast Under the Articles of Confederation, how did the power of the national government compare to that of the state governments? *possible answer—The state governments held most of the power, even being able to refuse requests from Congress.*

Info to Know

The Limits of the Articles of Confederation Under the Articles of Confederation, the states did not always respond to the requests of Congress. The legislative body did not even meet on a regular basis. Members also did not attend every meeting. A great deal of effort was required to get enough members gathered to ratify the Treaty of Paris, which ended the American Revolution.

The Land Ordinances of 1785 and 1787

Surveying the West
In 1785 the Northwest Territory was organized into lots that could be sold, and in 1787 a government was organized.

One section = 1 square mile

Half section 320 acres

Quarter section 160 acres

Each township contained 36 sections. Each section was one square mile.

6	5	4	3	2	1
7	8	9	10	11	12
18	17	16	15	14	13
19	20	21	22	23	24
30	29	28	27	26	25
31	32	33	34	35	36

One township = 6 square miles

CANADA

WISCONSIN 1848

MICHIGAN 1837

NORTHWEST TERRITORY

ILLINOIS 1818

INDIANA 1816

OHIO 1803 Area of first survey

0   100   200 Miles
0   100   200 Kilometers

GEOGRAPHY SKILLS INTERPRETING MAPS
1. **Location** Which states were formed out of the Northwest Territory?
2. **Region** Into how many sections was a township divided?

Articles of Confederation

The Second Continental Congress was organized to create a national government. The Continental Congress appointed a Committee of Thirteen, with one member from each colony. This group was assigned to discuss and draft the Articles of Confederation, the new national constitution.

Under the **Articles of Confederation**, Congress would become the national government, but it would have limited powers in order to protect the liberties of the people. Each state had one vote in the Congress. Congress could settle conflicts among the states, make coins, borrow money, and make treaties with other countries and with Native Americans. Congress could also ask the states for money and soldiers. However, states had the power to refuse these requests. In addition, the government did not have a president or a national court system.

The Second Continental Congress passed the Articles of Confederation on November 15, 1777. Then it sent the Articles to each state legislature for **ratification**, or official approval, before the new national government could take effect.

Conflicts over claims to western lands slowed the process, but by 1779 every state except Maryland had ratified the Articles. Maryland's leaders refused to ratify until other states gave up their western land claims. Thomas Jefferson assured Maryland that western lands would be made into new states, rather than increasing territory for existing states. Satisfied with this condition, in March 1781 Maryland ratified the Articles. This put the first national government of the United States into effect.

READING CHECK Summarizing What were two weaknesses in the new national government?

Collaborative Learning

At Level

Forming a School Government

1. Organize students into groups. Tell each group to create a set of rules for the school. The rules must apply fairly to everyone and promote student rights. In addition, each group member must agree to the set of rules.

2. When the groups have finished, write each group's rules for students to see. Then have the class work to create one set of three to five rules. Each class member must approve all the rules.

3. Have students discuss the difficulties they encountered during the exercise. Then have them compare their experience to that of creating the Articles of Confederation. What issues and challenges did the Committee of Thirteen face?
LS Interpersonal, Verbal/Linguistic

4. **Extend** Have each student draw a large picture of a parchment document and in it outline the powers of Congress and the states under the Articles of Confederation.
LS Verbal/Linguistic

📖 Alternative Assessment Handbook, Rubrics 11: Discussions; and 42: Writing to Inform

Answers

Interpreting Maps 1. *Illinois, Indiana, Michigan, Ohio, Wisconsin* **2.** *36 sections*
Reading Check *The states had the right to refuse requests from Congress; there was not a president or a national court system.*

Northwest Territory

Congress had to decide what to do with the western lands now under its control and how to raise money to pay debts. It tried to solve both problems by selling the western lands. Congress passed the **Land Ordinance of 1785**, which set up a system for surveying and dividing western lands. The land was split into townships, which were 36 square miles divided into 36 lots of 640 acres each. One lot was reserved for a public school, and four lots were given to veterans. The remaining lots were sold to the public.

To form a political system for the region, Congress passed the **Northwest Ordinance of 1787**. The ordinance established the **Northwest Territory**, which included areas that are now in Illinois, Indiana, Michigan, Ohio, Minnesota, and Wisconsin. The Northwest Ordinance created a system for bringing new states into the Union. Congress agreed that the Northwest Territory would be divided into several smaller territories with a governor appointed by Congress. When the population of a territory reached 60,000, its settlers could draft their own constitution and ask to join the Union.

In addition, the law protected civil liberties and required that public education be provided. Finally, the ordinance stated that "there shall be neither slavery nor involuntary servitude [forced labor] in the . . . territory." This last condition banned slavery in the Territory and set the standard for future territories. However, slavery would continue to be a controversial issue.

THE IMPACT TODAY

Townships remained the unit of local government after the Northwest Territory was divided into states. Many of these townships still exist today.

READING CHECK Analyzing Information
How did the Northwest Ordinance of 1787 affect the United States?

SUMMARY AND PREVIEW The Northwest Ordinance settled the future of the Northwest Territory. In the next section you will read about other challenges the new government faced.

Section 1 Assessment

go.hrw.com
Online Quiz
KEYWORD: SR8 HP5

Reviewing Ideas, Terms, and People

1. **a. Identify** What documents influenced ideas about government in the United States?
   b. Draw Conclusions What impact did the **Virginia Statute for Religious Freedom** have on the U.S. government?
   c. Elaborate Why is the separation of government powers a requirement for a society to be free?
2. **a. Identify** What was the **Articles of Confederation**?
   b. Summarize What powers were granted to Congress by the Articles of Confederation?
   c. Predict What are some possible problems that might result from the lack of a national court system?
3. **a. Describe** How were public lands in the West divided by the **Land Ordinance of 1785**?
   b. Evaluate In your opinion, what was the most important element of the **Northwest Ordinance of 1787**? Why?
   c. Elaborate What does the assignment of township lots reveal about values of Americans at this time?

Critical Thinking

4. **Categorizing** Review your notes on the Articles of Confederation. Copy the chart below and use it to show the strengths and weaknesses of the new government.

Articles of Confederation

Strengths	Weaknesses

FOCUS ON WRITING

5. **Thinking about the Articles of Confederation** Make a list of powers the Articles of Confederation gave the national government. Which ones seem strong? Can you think of any important powers that are missing?

FORMING A GOVERNMENT **155**

Section 1 Assessment Answers

1. **a.** Magna Carta, English Bill of Rights, Mayflower Compact, Fundamental Orders of Connecticut, Declaration of Independence, state constitutions, Virginia Statute of Religious Freedom
   b. established precedent of freedom of religion
   c. limits power, gives citizens a voice
2. **a.** national constitution for first U.S. government
   b. settle conflicts between states, make coins, borrow money, make treaties, ask states for money and soldiers
   c. possible answers—state courts might interpret laws differently; no federal system of appeal
3. **a.** into townships; four lots reserved for veterans and one for a public school
   b. established territorial representation and public education; prohibited slavery
   c. valued education and veterans
4. strengths—limited government, Congress could settle conflicts, mint coins, borrow money, negotiate treaties; weaknesses—states could refuse requests from Congress; no president or national court system
5. Answers will vary but should reflect an understanding of the Articles of Confederation.

● **Direct Teach** ●

Main Idea

❸ **Northwest Territory**

The Confederation Congress established the Northwest Territory.

Recall What was the purpose of the Land Ordinance of 1785? *to set up a system for surveying and dividing western public lands*

Summarize What important rights did the Northwest Ordinance of 1787 provide? *civil liberties, public education; freedom from slavery*

📰 **CRF:** History and Geography Activity: The Northwest Territory

🖨 Map Transparency: The Land Ordinances of 1785 and 1787

● **Review & Assess** ●

Close

Have students summarize some of the early actions of the new nation of the United States.

Review

📘 Online Quiz, Section 1

Assess

📄 **SE** Section 1 Assessment
📄 **PASS:** Section 1 Quiz
📄 Alternative Assessment Handbook

Reteach/Classroom Intervention

📄 Interactive Reader and Study Guide, Section 1
💿 Interactive Skills Tutor CD-ROM

Answers

Reading Check *created a way to incorporate new states, ban slavery, protect civil liberties, and provide public education in the Northwest Territory*

155

Activity Ship of State Graphic Organizer Draw a simple sailing ship for students to see. Have each student make a large copy of the ship and name it the *US Constitution: The Ship of State*. Then have students label different parts of the ship with the six items listed here that influenced the U.S. Constitution. Each student should write a phrase or sentence explaining the significance of each idea. In addition, encourage students to select parts of the ship that they think represent the idea in some way. Have volunteers share their work with the class. **LS Verbal/Linguistic, Visual/Spatial**

Linking to Today

Parliament Today Parliament, the lawmaking body of Great Britain, is bicameral. That is, it consists of two parts, or houses. Parliament is made up of the House of Lords, appointed by the monarch, and the House of Commons, elected by the people. This system enables each house to check and improve the work of the other house. Today, however, the House of Lords holds little power. The House of Commons is now the only real lawmaking body in Britain. It has complete control of all money bills and most other public legislation.

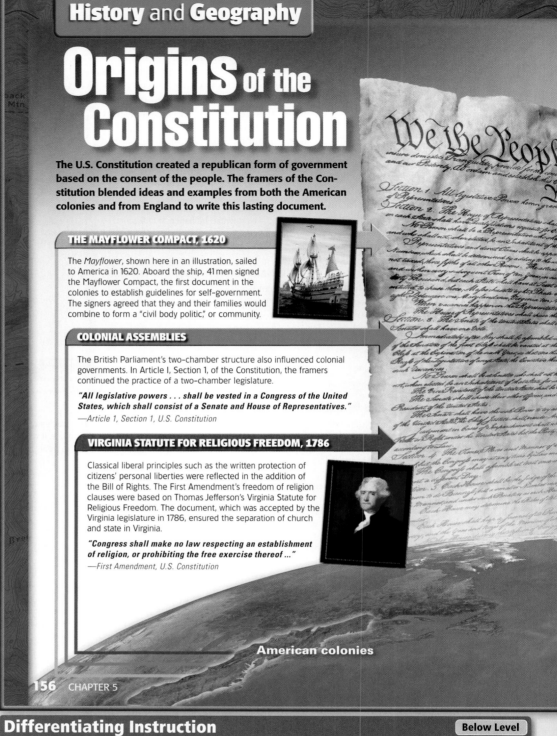

History and Geography

Origins of the Constitution

The U.S. Constitution created a republican form of government based on the consent of the people. The framers of the Constitution blended ideas and examples from both the American colonies and from England to write this lasting document.

THE MAYFLOWER COMPACT, 1620

The *Mayflower*, shown here in an illustration, sailed to America in 1620. Aboard the ship, 41 men signed the Mayflower Compact, the first document in the colonies to establish guidelines for self-government. The signers agreed that they and their families would combine to form a "civil body politic," or community.

COLONIAL ASSEMBLIES

The British Parliament's two-chamber structure also influenced colonial governments. In Article I, Section 1, of the Constitution, the framers continued the practice of a two-chamber legislature.

"All legislative powers . . . shall be vested in a Congress of the United States, which shall consist of a Senate and House of Representatives."
—Article 1, Section 1, U.S. Constitution

VIRGINIA STATUTE FOR RELIGIOUS FREEDOM, 1786

Classical liberal principles such as the written protection of citizens' personal liberties were reflected in the addition of the Bill of Rights. The First Amendment's freedom of religion clauses were based on Thomas Jefferson's Virginia Statute for Religious Freedom. The document, which was accepted by the Virginia legislature in 1786, ensured the separation of church and state in Virginia.

"Congress shall make no law respecting an establishment of religion, or prohibiting the free exercise thereof ..."
—First Amendment, U.S. Constitution

American colonies

156 CHAPTER 5

Differentiating Instruction

Below Level

Struggling Readers

Research Required

Materials: blank note cards

1. Organize the class into six groups. Assign each group one of the influences listed above.

2. Have each group use this feature as well as the text in the previous chapter to prepare flash cards that explain the significance of the group's assigned topic and how it influenced the U.S. Constitution.

3. Have volunteers from each group present some of the group's cards to the class. Correct any student misconceptions or errors.

4. Reorganize students into groups that contain one member from each of the previous groups. In these new groups, have each member in turn use his or her flash cards to quiz the other members. **LS Interpersonal, Verbal/Linguistic**

📖 Alternative Assessment Handbook, Rubric 14: Group Activity

MAGNA CARTA, 1215

In this painting King John of England is signing Magna Carta, or the Great Charter, which established that the king was subject to the law just like everyone else. It also declared that people could not be deprived of their lives, liberty, or property *"except by the lawful judgment of [their] peers, or by the law of the land."* Compare this language to that of the Fifth Amendment to the Constitution.

"No person shall be . . . deprived of life, liberty, or property, without due process of law . . ."
—Fifth Amendment, U.S. Constitution

THE ENGLISH BILL OF RIGHTS, 1689

This painting shows King William and Queen Mary of England. Before taking the throne, William and Mary had to accept the English Bill of Rights. The English Bill of Rights took even more power away from the monarch than did Magna Carta. It also protected the rights of English citizens. These ideas would later influence the U.S. Constitution.

"Excessive bail ought not be required, nor excessive fines imposed; nor cruel and unusual punishments inflicted."
—English Bill of Rights

THE ENLIGHTENMENT, 1700s

Enlightenment thinkers such as English philosopher John Locke supported the movement toward self-government. Locke argued in his writings that government could exist only with *"the consent of the governed."* The framers of the Constitution looked to Locke for inspiration when writing the Constitution, as you can see from its very first words.

"We the people of the United States . . . "
—Preamble, U.S. Constitution

England

ANALYSIS SKILL ANALYZING INFORMATION

1. What documents did the framers look to when writing the Constitution?
2. How did the English Parliamentary system affect the kind of government the framers created?

World Events

Magna Carta Although Magna Carta became a cornerstone of constitutional government and rule by law, its original purpose was to limit the king's powers and protect the nobles' feudal rights. It included such concepts as church freedom, trial by jury, freedom from taxation without cause and consent, and due process of law. The document's final article empowered English barons to take up arms against the king if he violated its conditions.

Connect to Government

The British Constitution The British Constitution is not a single document. Instead, it consists partly of several great documents. Among them are Magna Carta, the Petition of Rights, the Habeas Corpus Act, the English Bill of Rights, and the Act of Settlement. It also includes acts of Parliament, which can be changed by later Parliaments. Some features of the British government have never even been written down but are based largely on tradition.

Did You Know?

The College of William and Mary was the second university established in the colonies. Chartered in 1693 and named after King William III and Queen Mary II, it is located in Williamsburg, Virginia.

Differentiating Instruction

Above Level

Advanced/Gifted and Talented

Research Required

Materials: colored markers and pencils

1. Have students discuss the ideas listed above that influenced the U.S. Constitution.

2. Ask students to imagine that they have just opened a new restaurant called Constitutional Cuisine. Have each student create a menu for the restaurant. The menu should list the ideas above as dishes and provide a description of each dish that explains the idea's significance. Encourage students to be creative in their names and descriptions.

3. Students should base the price of each dish on that idea's importance to the Constitution.

4. In addition, students might organize the dishes into categories based on ideas such as rule of law, limited government, consent of the governed, separation of powers, and individual rights. **LS Verbal/Linguistic**

   Alternative Assessment Handbook, Rubric 37: Writing Assignments

Answers

Analyzing Information 1. *Mayflower Compact, Virginia Statute for Religious Freedom, Magna Carta, English Bill of Rights;* **2.** *The framers used the same two-chamber structure for Congress that the British Parliament used.*

157

Building Vocabulary

Preteach or review the following terms:

creditors people who lend money (p. 161)

debtors people who owe money (p. 161)

inflation a rise in prices combined with the reduced value of money (p. 160)

📝 **CRF:** Vocabulary Builder Activity, Section 2

Taking Notes

Have students copy the graphic organizer onto their own paper and then use it to take notes on the section. This activity will prepare students for the Section Assessment, in which they will complete a graphic organizer that builds on the information using a critical thinking skill.

The New Nation Faces Challenges

If YOU were there...

You own an orchard in Maryland in the 1780s. When you sell apples and apple pies in the market, people pay you with paper money. But now the tax collector says you must pay your taxes in gold or silver coins, not paper money. You and the other farmers are furious. Is this the liberty you fought a war for?

What would you do to protest against these taxes?

BUILDING BACKGROUND Americans surprised the world by winning their independence from Great Britain. But the 13 new states were far from being a strong nation. Internal problems, especially with taxes and the economy, led to protests and rebellion. The government also had trouble with foreign trade and treaties.

Relations with Other Countries

Under the Articles of Confederation, Congress could not force states to provide soldiers for an army. The Continental Army had disbanded, or dissolved, soon after the signing of the Treaty of Paris of 1783. Without an army, the national government found it difficult to protect its citizens against foreign threats.

Trouble with Britain

It was also difficult to enforce international treaties such as the Treaty of Paris of 1783. The United States found it especially hard to force the British to turn over "with all convenient speed" their forts on the American side of the Great Lakes. The United States wanted to gain control of these forts because they protected valuable land and fur-trade routes. Still, Britain was slow to withdraw from the area. A British official warned against the United States trying to seize the forts by force. He said that any attempt to do so would be opposed by the thousands of British soldiers who had settled in Canada after the Revolution "who are ready to fly to arms at a moment's warning."

The United States Faces Trade Barriers

0   150   300 Miles
0   150   300 Kilometers

AMERICAN TRADE ROUTE
Spain closed the lower Mississippi River to U.S. shipping, hurting western trade with eastern markets.

EXPORTS TO BRITAIN
High British tariffs discouraged American exports to Britain.

BLOCKADE

ATLANTIC OCEAN

WEST INDIES TRADE
Britain closed many ports to American ships.

BLOCKADE
New Orleans

Gulf of Mexico

BLOCKADE
WEST INDIES

30°N
Tropic of Cancer
80°W   70°W   20°N

GEOGRAPHY SKILLS INTERPRETING MAPS
1. **Movement** Along what river did trade goods reach the port of New Orleans?
2. **Location** Along what three routes did U.S. trade face foreign barriers?

Trade with Britain

The United States also faced problems trading with Great Britain. After the signing of the Treaty of Paris, Britain closed many of its ports to American ships. Before the Revolutionary War, colonial ships had traded a great deal with the British West Indies and stopped there on their way to other destinations. This travel and trading stopped after 1783.

In addition, Britain forced American merchants to pay high **tariffs**—taxes on imports or exports. The tariffs applied to goods such as rice, tobacco, tar, and oil that were grown or mined in the United States and then sold in Britain. Merchants had to raise prices to cover the tariffs. Ultimately, the costs would be passed on to customers, who had to pay higher prices for the goods. The economic condition of the country was getting worse by the day.

Trade with Spain

In 1784 Spanish officials closed the lower Mississippi River to U.S. shipping. Western farmers and merchants were furious because they used the Mississippi to send goods to eastern and foreign markets. Congress tried to work out an agreement with Spain, but the plan did not receive a majority vote in Congress. The plan could not be passed. As a result, Spain broke off the negotiations.

Many state leaders began to criticize the national government. Rhode Island's representatives wrote, "Our federal government is but a name; a mere shadow without substance [power]." Critics believed that Spain might have continued to negotiate if the United States had possessed a strong military. These leaders believed that the national government needed to be more powerful.

FORMING A GOVERNMENT **159**

Direct Teach

Main Idea

❶ Relations with Other Countries

The United States had difficulties with other nations.

Identify Cause and Effect How did closed trade markets affect the U.S. economy? *Exports fell, imports from Britain rose, and British merchants could undersell American merchants, which further hurt the economy.*

Main Idea

❷ Economic Problems

Internal economic problems plagued the new nation.

Recall What domestic economic problems did the states experience? *problems with interstate commerce, war debts, and a weak economy*

Analyze How did inflation hurt the economy? *decreased trade and business, which contributed to a depression*

Info to Know

Trade with China In 1785 the ship *Empress of China* returned to New York from China. The ship's owners had traded more than 40 tons of ginseng for tea and other Chinese products. Many Americans hoped that this success at opening trade with China would mean the United States would not have to rely so much on trade with Great Britain.

Answers

A Farmer Leads a Revolt *The state militia defeated the rebellion and arrested many of those involved, who were later freed. The rebellion convinced many Americans that the Articles of Confederation were too weak.*

Reading Check *The Confederation Congress did not have the authority to pass tariffs or to order the states to do so.*

160

Impact of Closed Markets

The closing of markets in the British West Indies seriously affected the U.S. economy. James Madison of Virginia wrote about the crisis.

> ❝The Revolution has robbed us of our trade with the West Indies . . . without opening any other channels to compensate [make up for] it. In every point of view, indeed, the trade of this country is in a deplorable [terrible] condition.❞
> —James Madison, quoted in *Independence on Trial* by Frederick W. Marks III

Farmers could no longer export their goods to the British West Indies. They also had to hire British ships to carry their goods to British markets, which was very expensive. American exports dropped while British goods flowed freely into the United States.

This unequal trade caused serious economic problems for the new nation. British merchants could sell manufactured products in the United States at much lower prices than locally made goods. This difference in prices hurt American businesses.

The Confederation Congress could not correct the problem because it did not have the authority either to pass tariffs or to order the states to pass tariffs. The states could offer little help. If one state passed a tariff, the British could simply sell their goods in another state. Most states did not cooperate in trade matters. Instead, states worked only to increase their own trade rather than working to improve the trade situation for the whole country.

In 1785 the situation led a British magazine to call the new nation the Dis-United States. As a result of the trade problems with Britain, American merchants began looking for other markets such as China, France, and the Netherlands. Despite such attempts, Britain remained the most important trading partner of the United States.

READING CHECK **Analyzing** Why was the Confederation Congress unable to solve America's economic problems?

Economic Problems

In addition to international trade issues, other challenges soon appeared. Trade problems among the states, war debts, and a weak economy plagued the states.

Trade among States

Because the Confederation Congress had no power to regulate **interstate commerce** — trade between two or more states—states followed their own trade interests. As a result, trade laws differed from state to state. This situation made trade difficult for merchants whose businesses crossed state lines.

Inflation

After the Revolutionary War, most states had a hard time paying off war debts and struggled to collect overdue taxes. To ease this hardship, some states began printing large amounts of paper money. The result was inflation. This money had

A Farmer Leads a Revolt

Daniel Shays, at the top of the steps, stands firm in the face of demands that he leave the courthouse in Springfield, Massachusetts. By shutting down the courts, farmers hoped to stop the government from selling their land.

What was the outcome of Shays's Rebellion?

Struggling Readers

Materials: poster board, glue or tape

1. Organize the class into small, mixed-level groups. Ask students to imagine that they are newspaper publishers who must determine the headlines for the next issue of their papers.

2. Have each group write a headline and several subheadlines for each of the following topics: problems with Great Britain and Spain; problems associated with tariffs; economic problems that arose under the Articles of

Confederation; and the consequences of Shays's Rebellion.

3. Then have each group arrange its headline and subheadlines on a poster board in the way they would appear in a newspaper.

LS **Interpersonal, Verbal/Linguistic**

📄 Alternative Assessment Handbook, Rubrics 14: Group Activity; and 37: Writing Assignments or no real value, because states did not have gold or silver reserves to back it up. **Inflation** occurs when there are increased prices for goods and services combined with the reduced value of money. Congress had no power to stop states from issuing more paper money and thus stop inflation.

Weak Economy

In Rhode Island the state legislature printed large amounts of paper money worth very little. This made debtors—people who owe money—quite happy. They could pay back their debts with paper money worth less than the coins they had borrowed. However, creditors—people who lend money—were upset. Hundreds of creditors fled Rhode Island to avoid being paid back with worthless money.

The loss of trade with Britain combined with inflation created a **depression**. A depression is a period of low economic activity combined with a rise in unemployment.

READING CHECK **Summarizing** What economic problems did the new nation face?

Shays's Rebellion

Each state handled its economic problems differently. Massachusetts refused to print worthless paper money. It tried to pay its war debts by collecting taxes on land.

Heavy Debts for Farmers

Massachusetts's tax policy hit farmers hard. As landowners, they had to pay the new taxes. However, farmers had trouble paying their debts. The courts began forcing them to sell their property. Some farmers had to serve terms in debtors' prison; others had to sell their labor.

Many government leaders in the state did not care about the problems of poor farmers, however. In some cases, farmers actually owed these leaders money.

Farmers Rebel

In August 1786, farmers in three western counties began a revolt. Bands of angry citizens closed down courts in western Massachusetts. Their reasoning was simple—with the courts shut down, no one's property could be taken. In September a poor farmer and Revolutionary War veteran, **Daniel Shays**, led hundreds of men in a forced shutdown of the Supreme Court in Springfield, Massachusetts. The state government ordered the farmers to stop the revolt under threat of capture and death. These threats only made Shays and his followers more determined. The uprising of farmers to protest high taxes and heavy debt became known as **Shays's Rebellion**.

Shays's Defeat

Shays's forces were defeated by state troops in January 1787. By February many of the rebels were in prison. During their trials, 14 leaders were sentenced to death. However, the state soon freed most of the rebels, including Shays. State officials knew that many citizens of the state agreed with the rebels and their cause.

READING CHECK **Finding Main Ideas** What led to Shays's Rebellion?

FORMING A GOVERNMENT **161**

Direct Teach

Main Idea

❸ Shays's Rebellion

Shays's Rebellion pointed out weaknesses in the Articles of Confederation.

Recall What was Shays's Rebellion, and why was it significant? *uprising of Massachusetts farmers in 1786; convinced many that the Articles of Confederation were too weak*

Identify Points of View Why do you think Daniel Shays and the other rebels took the actions that they did? *pushed to the breaking point; felt they had nothing to lose*

Make Judgments Do you think the actions of Daniel Shays and the other rebels were justified? Explain your answer. *possible answers—Yes, they were fighting to save their farms; no, they had a right to protest taxes but not in the way that they did.*

Primary Source

Two Views of Shays's Rebellion

Shays's Rebellion greatly upset many American leaders. George Washington exclaimed, "I am mortified [embarrassed] beyond expression." Washington feared that the United States must look "ridiculous in the eyes of all Europe." Not everyone saw the rebellion this way, though. Thomas Jefferson, serving as ambassador to France, responded to the event differently. "A little rebellion, now and then, is a good thing," he said. "The tree of liberty must be refreshed from time to time with the blood of patriots and tyrants."

Critical Thinking: Identifying Points of View   At Level

Economic Problems Journals

1. Assign each student one of the following roles: western merchant who sends items back East, eastern farmer who exports goods to British markets, North Carolina tobacco planter, Rhode Island creditor, or Massachusetts farmer.

2. Have each student write one or more journal entries about the economic problems that he or she faces. Have students refer to the text and to the United States Faces Trade Barriers map.

3. Encourage students to propose solutions to the economic problems they face.

4. **Extend** Have students think about possible solutions to the economic problems caused by the weakness of the Articles of Confederation. Then have each student write a petition to the Confederation Congress asking for specific changes to the Articles and explaining how the changes would improve the economy.

LS **Logical/Mathematical, Verbal/Linguistic**

Alternative Assessment Handbook, Rubrics 15: Journals; and 35: Solving Problems

Answers

Reading Check (left) *trade problems among the states, war debts, weak economy*

Reading Check (right) *growing anger among Massachusetts farmers over the state's economic policies, which led to rising debts and the risk of losing their farms, having to serve time in debtors' prison, or having to sell their labor*

161

❹ Calls for Change

Many Americans called for changes in the national government.

Describe How did some states address the problems of the weak national government? *Some states sent delegates to the Annapolis Convention; some delegates called for a Constitutional Convention.*

Evaluate Why do you think some states chose not to send delegates to the Annapolis Convention? *possible answers—fear of losing state power; experienced fewer problems*

⬛ Quick Facts Transparency: Weaknesses of the Articles of Confederation

● Review & Assess ●

Close

Have students review the strengths and weaknesses of the Articles of Confederation.

Review

📲 Online Quiz, Section 2

Assess

SE Section 2 Assessment

📓 PASS: Section 2 Quiz

📓 Alternative Assessment Handbook

Reteach/Classroom Intervention

📓 Interactive Reader and Study Guide, Section 2

💿 Interactive Skills Tutor CD-ROM

Answers

Reading Check *because the weaknesses of the Articles of Confederation caused problems with foreign nations, international trade issues, domestic economic problems, and Shays's Rebellion*

Calls for Change

In the end, Shays's Rebellion showed the weakness of the Confederation government. It led some Americans to admit that the Articles of Confederation had failed to protect the ideals of liberty set forth in the Declaration of Independence.

When Massachusetts had asked the national government to help put down Shays's Rebellion, Congress could offer little help. More Americans began calling for a stronger central government. They wanted leaders who would be able to protect the nation in times of crisis.

Earlier in 1786 the Virginia legislature had called for a national conference. It wanted to talk about economic problems and ways to change the Articles of Confederation. The meeting took place in Annapolis, Maryland, in September 1786.

> **Weaknesses of the Articles of Confederation** QUICK FACTS
> - Most power held by states
> - One branch of government
> - Legislative branch has few powers
> - No executive branch
> - No judicial system
> - No system of checks and balances

Nine states decided to send delegates to the Annapolis Convention but some of their delegates were late and missed the meeting. Connecticut, Georgia, Maryland, and South Carolina did not respond to the request at all and sent no delegates.

Because of the poor attendance, the participants, including James Madison and Alexander Hamilton, called on all 13 states to send delegates to a Constitutional Convention in Philadelphia in May 1787. They planned to revise the Articles of Confederation to better meet the needs of the nation.

READING CHECK Finding Main Ideas
Why did some people believe the national government needed to change?

SUMMARY AND PREVIEW Many Americans believed that Shays's Rebellion was final proof that the national government needed to be changed. In the next section you will read about the Constitutional Convention.

Section 2 Assessment

go.hrw.com
Online Quiz
KEYWORD: SR8 HP5

Reviewing Ideas, Terms, and People

1. **a. Summarize** What problems did the United States experience with Spain and Great Britain?
   b. Predict What are some possible results of the growing problems between the United States and Great Britain? Why?
2. **a. Describe** What difficulties were involved with **interstate commerce**?
   b. Analyze What was the cause of inflation in the new nation, and how could it have been prevented?
3. **a. Explain** How did Massachusetts's tax policy affect farmers?
   b. Evaluate Defend the actions of **Daniel Shays** and the other rebels.
4. **a. Recall** Why did Madison and Hamilton call for a Constitutional Convention?
   b. Analyze How did Shay's Rebellion lead to a call for change in the United States?

Critical Thinking

5. **Categorizing** Review your notes on the problems faced by the new nation. Then identify those problems as either domestic or international in a graphic organizer like the one shown below.

Domestic Problems	International Problems

FOCUS ON WRITING ✏️

6. **Identifying Problems** In this section you learned about several problems of the young United States. Were any of those problems made worse by the powers that the Articles of Confederation did or did not give the national government?

Section 2 Assessment Answers

1. **a.** Great Britain—refused to hand over forts, closed ports to U.S. ships, set high tariffs; Spain—closed Mississippi to U.S. shipping
   b. possible answer—could go to war because of problems stated in previous answer
2. **a.** Lack of regulation and lack of cooperation between states made trade difficult for some merchants.
   b. Some states began printing large amounts of paper money; little could be done.
3. **a.** Heavy taxes forced farmers to sell their land or else go into debt and risk imprisonment.

b. Answers should show an understanding of the rebels' anger over high taxes.

4. **a.** weaknesses in Articles of Confederation, poor attendance at Annapolis Convention
   b. convinced many Americans that the Articles of Confederation were too weak

5. Domestic—no power to regulate interstate commerce, could not help states keep order, could not stop inflation; International—could not pass tariffs, enforce treaties

6. See answer to Question 5.

Creating the Constitution

If YOU were there...

You are a merchant in Connecticut in 1787. You have been a member of your state legislature for several years. This spring, the legislature is choosing delegates to a convention to revise the Articles of Confederation. Delegates will meet in Philadelphia. It means leaving your business in others' hands for most of the summer. Still, you hope to be chosen.

Why would you want to go to the Constitutional Convention?

BUILDING BACKGROUND It didn't take long for people to realize that the Articles of Confederation had many weaknesses. By the mid-1780s most political leaders agreed that changes were needed. To make those changes, they called on people with experience in government.

Constitutional Convention

In February 1787 the Confederation Congress invited each state to send delegates to a convention in Philadelphia. The goal of the meeting was to improve the Articles of Confederation.

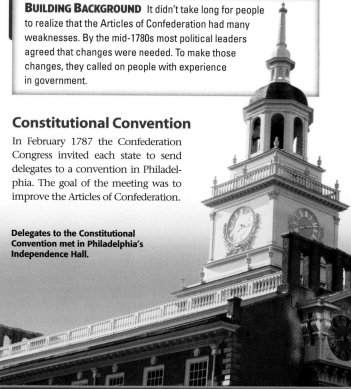

Delegates to the Constitutional Convention met in Philadelphia's Independence Hall.

What You Will Learn . . .

Main Ideas

1. The Constitutional Convention met to improve the government of the United States.
2. The issue of representation led to the Great Compromise.
3. Regional debate over slavery led to the Three-Fifths Compromise.
4. The U.S. Constitution created federalism and a balance of power.

The Big Idea

A new constitution provided a framework for a stronger national government.

Key Terms and People

Constitutional Convention, p. 164
James Madison, p. 164
Virginia Plan, p. 164
New Jersey Plan, p. 165
Great Compromise, p. 165
Three-Fifths Compromise, p. 166
popular sovereignty, p. 167
federalism, p. 167
legislative branch, p. 167
executive branch, p. 167
judicial branch, p. 167
checks and balances, p. 167

TAKING NOTES As you read, take notes on the conflicts that arose during the Constitutional Convention and the compromises reached.

Conflicts	→	Compromises

FORMING A GOVERNMENT **163**

---

❶ Constitutional Convention

The Constitutional Convention met to improve the government of the United States.

Identify Who were some key delegates to the convention, and who served as its president? *Benjamin Franklin, James Madison, George Washington (president)*

Analyze How might the Constitution have been different if African Americans, Native Americans, and women had been able to attend the convention? *possible answer—Issues such as slavery and suffrage might have been addressed differently.*

📝 **CRF:** Biography Activity: Signers of the Constitution

📝 **CRF:** Primary Source Activity: Benjamin Franklin Addresses the Constitutional Convention

Info to Know

A Well Prepared Man James Madison began preparing for the Constitutional Convention in the fall of 1786 by reading works of political history, classical republicanism, and modern political theory. With Thomas Jefferson's help, Madison had acquired a small library of the social and economic philosophies of the Enlightenment, including the 37-volume set of Denis Diderot's *Encyclopédie.*

Answers

Reading Check *to discuss ways to improve the Articles of Confederation*

164

Roger Sherman   James Madison   James Wilson

Meeting in Philadelphia

The **Constitutional Convention** was held in May 1787 in Philadelphia's Independence Hall to improve the Articles of Confederation. However, delegates would leave with an entirely new U.S. Constitution.

Most delegates were well educated, and many had served in state legislatures or Congress. Benjamin Franklin and **James Madison** were there. Revolutionary War hero George Washington was elected president of the Convention.

Several important voices were absent. John Adams and Thomas Jefferson could not attend. Patrick Henry chose not to attend because he did not want a stronger central government. Women, African Americans, and Native Americans did not take part because they did not yet have the rights of citizens.

READING CHECK **Summarizing** What was the purpose of the Constitutional Convention?

Great Compromise

Several issues divided the delegates to the Constitutional Convention. Some members wanted only small changes to the Articles of Confederation, while others wanted to rewrite the Articles completely.

Those delegates who wanted major changes to the Articles had different goals. For example, small and large states had different ideas about representation, economic concerns such as tariffs, and slavery. In addition, delegates disagreed over how strong to make the national government.

Virginia Plan

After the delegates had met for four days, Edmund Randolph of Virginia presented the **Virginia Plan**. He proposed a new federal constitution that would give sovereignty, or supreme power, to the central government. The legislature would be

164 CHAPTER 5

Differentiating Instruction

Struggling Readers

Materials: paper, art supplies, invitations (optional)

1. Have students identify the purpose of the Constitutional Convention *(to discuss ways to improve the Articles of Confederation).*

2. Then ask students to identify some characteristics that delegates would need for the convention to succeed *(government experience, education, knowledge of Enlightenment thinkers, charisma, diplomacy, patience, good listening and speaking skills).* List students' ideas for the class to see.

3. Ask students to imagine that they are creating invitations for the convention. Have each student write a persuasive invitation to send to proposed delegates. (Provide models of invitations, if possible.) The invitations should include the convention's date and location, notable individuals who will attend, and why attendance is vital. **LS Verbal/Linguistic**

📝 Alternative Assessment Handbook, Rubric 43: Writing to Persuade

1 Roger Sherman **4** James Madison
2 Alexander Hamilton **5** George Washington
3 Benjamin Franklin **6** James Wilson

This painting shows the signing of the Constitution on September 17, 1787. James Madison, number 4 on the diagram, became known as the "Father of the Constitution" for his ideas about government and his ability to lead the delegates to agreement. *Which person did the artist choose to make the focus of this painting? Why do you think that is?*

bicameral—made up of two houses, or groups of representatives—and chosen on the basis of state populations. Larger states would thus have more representatives than would smaller states. Delegates from the smaller states believed that it would give too much power to the larger states.

New Jersey Plan

The smaller states came up with a plan to stop the larger states from getting too much power. New Jersey delegate William Paterson presented the small-state or **New Jersey Plan**, which called for a unicameral, or one-house, legislature. The plan gave each state an equal number of votes, thus an equal voice, in the federal government. The plan gave the federal government the power to tax citizens in all states, and it allowed the government to regulate commerce.

Compromise is Reached

After a month of debate, the delegates were unable to agree on how states should be represented. The convention reached a deadlock.

Finally, Roger Sherman of Connecticut proposed a compromise plan. The legislative branch would have two houses. Each state, regardless of its size, would have two representatives in the Senate, or upper house. This would give each state an equal voice, pleasing the smaller states. In the House of Representatives, or lower house, the number of representatives for each state would be determined by the state's population. This pleased the larger states. The agreement to create a two-house legislature became known as the **Great Compromise**. James Wilson, a great speaker, saw his dream of a strong national government come true.

READING CHECK Contrasting How did the Virginia Plan and New Jersey Plan differ?

THE IMPACT TODAY

All U.S. states but one modeled their legislative branches on the federal one, with a House of Representatives and a Senate. Nebraska has a unicameral legislature.

QUICK FACTS

Virginia Plan	Great Compromise	New Jersey Plan
• Gave more power to national government • Bicameral legislature • Number in both houses based on population	• Bicameral legislature • Number of representatives based on state populations in lower house • Number of representatives equal from each state in upper house	• Gave more power to state governments • Unicameral legislature • Number of representatives equal from each state

FORMING A GOVERNMENT **165**

---

❸ Three-Fifths Compromise

Regional debate over slavery led to the Three-Fifths Compromise.

Explain How did regional differences and the issue of slavery divide the Constitutional Convention? *Southern delegates wanted slaves to be counted as part of state populations, which would give southern states more power; Northerners disagreed, because northern states had fewer slaves.*

Analyze How did the Three-Fifths Compromise resolve the debate? *Delegates agreed to count each slave as three-fifths of a person when determining representation.*

Draw Conclusions Why did the delegates agree to allow the international slave trade to continue for another 20 years? *to appease southern delegates and to give southern economies, which were dependent on the international slave trade, time to adjust to its end*

Primary Source

Reading Like a Historian
Compromise and the Slave Trade
To help students read the excerpts like historians, ask the following questions:

- What states and regions of the country do Rutledge and Morris represent?

- What regional concerns and biases may have influenced each man's point of view?

- In what context was each statement made? What issues or concerns was each man addressing?

Answers

Analyzing Primary Sources
Rutledge is pro-slavery, and Morris is anti-slavery.

Reading Check *Delegates agreed to end the international slave trade in 20 years rather than immediately.*

166

POINTS OF VIEW
Compromise and the Slave Trade

The issue of slavery highlighted the growing division between the North and the South. Gouverneur Morris of New York spoke with much emotion against the Three-Fifths Compromise. Also, the idea of banning the foreign slave trade prompted southerners such as John Rutledge of South Carolina to defend the practice.

❝If the Convention thinks that North Carolina, South Carolina, and Georgia will ever agree to the plan [to prohibit slave trade], unless their right to import slaves be untouched, the expectation is vain [useless].❞

—John Rutledge,
quoted in *The Atlantic Monthly,* February 1891,
by Frank Gaylord Cook

❝The admission of slaves into the Representation . . . comes to this: that the inhabitant of [a state] who goes to the coast of Africa and . . . tears away his fellow creatures from their dearest connections and damns them to the most cruel bondage [slavery], shall have more votes in a Government [established] for protection of the rights of mankind.❞

—Gouverneur Morris,
quoted in *Founding the Republic,* edited by John J. Patrick

ANALYSIS SKILL **ANALYZING PRIMARY SOURCES**

Finding Main Ideas How did these two views of slavery differ?

Three-Fifths Compromise

The debate over representation also involved regional differences. Southern delegates wanted enslaved Africans to be counted as part of their state populations. This way they would have more representatives, and more power, in Congress. Northerners disagreed. They wanted the number of slaves to determine taxes but not representation.

To resolve this problem, some delegates thought of a compromise. They wanted to count three-fifths of the slaves in each state as part of that state's population to decide how many representatives a state would have. After much debate, the delegates voted to accept the proposal, called the **Three-Fifths Compromise**. Under this agreement each slave would be counted as three-fifths of a person when determining representation.

Another major issue was the foreign slave trade. Some of the delegates believed slavery was wrong and wanted the federal government to ban the slave trade. Others said that the southern states' economies needed the slave trade. Many southern delegates said they would leave the Union if the Constitution immediately ended the slave trade.

Worried delegates reached another compromise, agreeing to end the slave trade in 20 years. The delegates omitted, or left out, the words *slavery* and *slave* in the Constitution. They referred instead to "free Persons" and "all other Persons." Oliver Ellsworth summed up the view of many delegates. He said, "The morality or wisdom of slavery . . . are considerations belonging to the states themselves."

READING CHECK **Summarizing** What compromise was reached over the issue of the slave trade?

Differentiating Instruction

Advanced/ Gifted and Talented [Above Level]

Recipe for Government Have students write a recipe for creating the U.S. government. Tell them that the framers of the Constitution chose political ideas from many sources (the ingredients) to draft the Constitution. Then they decided how to balance these ideas (the measurements) and put them into practice (the directions). **LS Verbal/Linguistic**

📝 Alternative Assessment Handbook, Rubric 39: Writing to Create

English-Language Learners [Below Level]

Visualizing Balanced Government Have each student create a political cartoon or visual diagram illustrating how the U.S. government is balanced under the U.S. Constitution. Students might focus on one aspect, such as federalism or checks and balances, or on the topic in general. **LS Visual/Spatial**

📝 Alternative Assessment Handbook, Rubrics 3: Artwork; and 27: Political Cartoons

The Living Constitution

Most Convention delegates wanted a strong national government. At the same time, they hoped to protect **popular sovereignty**, the idea that political authority belongs to the people. Americans had boldly declared this idea in the Declaration of Independence.

Federalist Government

The delegates also wanted to balance the power of the national government with the powers of the states. Therefore, the delegates created **federalism**. Federalism is the sharing of power between a central government and the states that make up a country.

Under the Constitution, each state must obey the authority of the federal, or national, government. States have control over government functions not specifically assigned to the federal government. This includes control of local government, education, the chartering of corporations, and the supervision of religious bodies. States also have the power to create and oversee civil and criminal law. States, however, must protect the welfare of their citizens.

Checks and Balances

The Constitution also balances the power among three branches, each responsible for separate tasks. The first is the **legislative branch**, or Congress. Congress is responsible for proposing and passing laws. It is made up of two houses, as created in the Great Compromise. The Senate has two members from each state. In the House of Representatives each state is represented according to its population.

The second branch, the **executive branch**, includes the president and the departments that help run the government. The executive branch makes sure the law is carried out. The third branch is the **judicial branch**. The judicial branch is made up of all the national courts. This branch is responsible for interpreting laws, punishing criminals, and settling disputes between states.

The framers of the Constitution created a system of **checks and balances**, which keeps any branch of government from becoming too powerful. For example, Congress has the power to pass bills into law. The president has the power to veto, or reject, laws that Congress passes. However, Congress can override the president's veto with a two-thirds

LINKING TO TODAY

Legislative Branch

When it first met in 1789, the U.S. House of Representatives had just 65 members. As the nation's population grew, more members were added. Today, the number has been set at 435, to prevent the size of the House from growing unmanageable. Though the numbers of women and minorities in Congress are still unrepresentative of the population as a whole, Congress has become more diverse. Linda and Loretta Sanchez, pictured here, are the first sisters to serve in Congress at the same time.

ANALYSIS SKILL ANALYZING INFORMATION

How is the change in makeup of the legislative branch shown through Linda and Loretta Sanchez?

FORMING A GOVERNMENT **167**

The Constitution Strengthens the National Government

Strengths of the Constitution	Weaknesses of the Articles of Confederation
✔ most power held by national government	• most power held by states
✔ three branches of government	• one branch of government
✔ legislative branch has many powers	• legislative branch has few powers
✔ executive branch led by president	• no executive branch
✔ judicial branch to review the laws	• no judicial system
✔ firm system of checks and balances	• no system of checks and balances

majority vote. The Supreme Court has the power to review laws passed by Congress and strike down any law that violates the Constitution by declaring it *unconstitutional*.

The final draft of the Constitution was completed in September 1787. Only 3 of the 42 delegates who remained refused to sign. The signed Constitution was sent first to Congress and then to the states for ratification. The delegates knew that the Constitution was not a perfect document but they believed they had protected the ideas of republicanism.

READING CHECK Summarizing Explain how the system of checks and balances works in the United States.

SUMMARY AND PREVIEW The Constitution balanced power among three branches of the federal government but was only written after many compromises. In the next section you will read about Antifederalist and Federalist views of the Constitution, and the struggle to get it approved by the States.

Section 3 Assessment

go.hrw.com
Online Quiz
KEYWORD: SR8 HP5

Reviewing Ideas, Terms, and People

1. **a. Recall** Why did the Confederation Congress call for a **Constitutional Convention**?
   b. Elaborate Why do you think it was important that most delegates had served in state legislatures?
2. **a. Identify** What was the **Great Compromise**?
   b. Draw Conclusions How did state issues lead to debate over structure of the central government?
3. **a Explain** What was the debate between North and South over counting slave populations?
   b. Contrast How did delegates' views differ on the issue of the foreign slave trade?
4. **a. Recall** Why did the framers of the Constitution create a system of **checks and balances**?
   b. Evaluate Did the Constitution resolve the weaknesses in the Articles of Confederation? Explain your answer.

Critical Thinking

5. **Identifying Cause and Effect** Review your notes on the Constitutional Convention compromises. Then copy the graphic organizer below and use it to show how the compromises affected the framework of the new government.

Compromise	→	Effect

FOCUS ON WRITING

6. **Thinking about the Constitution** Look back through what you've just read and make a list of important features of the Constitution. Be sure to note important compromises.

168 CHAPTER 5

Info to Know

Hamilton on Government In the midst of the debates at the Constitutional Convention, Alexander Hamilton gave one of the longest speeches of the proceedings. He was a strong supporter of the British government and urged delegates to create one like it. He suggested that the presidency be a lifetime job and even offered his own plan for the government—one modeled on Britain's. The rest of the delegates appear to have politely listened to Hamilton's suggestions and then ignored them and returned to the discussion at hand.

Review & Assess

Close

Have students summarize how the U.S. Constitution resolved the weaknesses in the Articles of Confederation.

Review

🖥 Online Quiz, Section 3

Assess

SE Section 3 Assessment

📋 PASS: Section 3 Quiz

📋 Alternative Assessment Handbook

Reteach/Classroom Intervention

📋 Interactive Reader and Study Guide, Section 3

💿 Interactive Skills Tutor CD-ROM

Answers

Reading Check *The system of checks and balances keeps any one branch of government from becoming too powerful.*

Section 3 Assessment Answers

1. **a.** to improve the Articles of Confederation
   b. needed government experience
2. **a.** resolved opposing views in the Virginia and New Jersey Plans on how to allot state representation
   b. possible answer—Concerns over state representation led to a bicameral legislature with an upper house based on equal state votes and a lower house based on state population.
3. **a.** Southern delegates wanted slaves to be counted as part of state populations; Northerners disagreed.

   b. along South-North regional lines
4. **a.** to limit each branch's power
   b. See Quick Facts chart above.
5. Great Compromise—See the answers to Questions 2a and 2b; Three-fifths Compromise—resolved opposing southern and northern views on how to count slaves when determining state representation by counting each slave as three-fifths of a person
6. Students should describe the key issues, debates, and solutions in this section.

Benjamin Franklin

How did one man accomplish so much?

When did he live? 1706–1790

Where did he live? Benjamin Franklin was born in Boston but ran away to Philadelphia at age 17 and made it his home. He also crossed the Atlantic Ocean eight times and visited 10 countries.

What did he do? What *didn't* he do! He was a printer, publisher, creator of the first circulating library, the first president of the University of Pennsylvania, inventor, scientist, philosopher, musician, economist, and the first U.S. Postmaster General. In politics he was a leading revolutionary, signer of the Declaration of Independence, head of an antislavery organization, delegate to the Constitutional Convention, and diplomat.

Why is he important? Benjamin Franklin, son of a candlemaker, became a celebrity in his own time, both in America and in Europe. Few people have mastered so many fields of knowledge and accomplished so much. He invented many useful objects, from bifocal glasses to the lightning rod. One of the oldest founding fathers, Franklin inspired younger revolutionaries such as Thomas Jefferson. Franklin believed strongly that people should volunteer and be in public service.

Finding Main Ideas How did Benjamin Franklin's life reflect his belief in public service?

KEY EVENTS

1729 Becomes owner and publisher of the *Pennsylvania Gazette*

1732–1758 Publishes *Poor Richard: An Almanack*

1752 Performs famous experiment using a kite to show that electricity exists in storm clouds

1775 Submits the Articles of Confederation

1779 Appointed minister to France

1782 Helps negotiate the Treaty of Paris with Britain

Poor Richard, 1734. AN Almanack For the Year of Christ 1734, Being the second after LEAP

169

Critical Thinking: Categorizing   **Below Level**

Accomplishments of Benjamin Franklin

1. Create a chart titled *Accomplishments of Benjamin Franklin.* Ask students to identify Franklin's many accomplishments, based on the biography and time line above. List students' answers for the class to see.

2. Then help students create categories by which to organize Franklin's accomplishments. Categories might include Government Service, Inventions, Community Service, and so on. Add the category labels to your chart.

3. Have students copy the chart and complete it by listing each of Franklin's accomplishments in the correct category.

4. Review the answers as a class. Then summarize for students Franklin's significance in American history.

Alternative Assessment Handbook, Rubric 7: Charts

Reading Focus Question
Read aloud the introductory question to students. Next, have students read the information under "What did he do?" to see how much Franklin accomplished. Ask students if they can think of any people today who are as accomplished as Franklin was. Then ask students how they think Franklin was able to accomplish so much.

Linking to Today
Daylight Savings Benjamin Franklin is well known for his many inventions that made life better for people. In addition, Franklin also invented daylight savings time. In an essay written in 1784, he first suggested the practice of advancing clocks forward in the summer. During World War I many nations adopted this system to conserve fuel. Today many nations, including the United States, continue the practice of daylight savings time each spring.

Did you know . . .
During the Constitutional Convention, Ben Franklin had an aisle seat. According to some accounts, he enjoyed occasionally tripping delegates as they walked by.

Primary Sources
Poor Richard: An Almanack Benjamin Franklin published *Poor Richard: An Almanack* over a period of many decades. Write the following sayings for students to see.

• "He that lies down with dogs, shall rise up with fleas."
• "Great talkers, little doers."
• "Haste makes waste."

Ask students to choose one of the sayings, rewrite it in their own words, and then explain its meaning.

Answers
Finding Main Ideas *Most of his accomplishments and actions benefited others, from his service in government to his many inventions to his support of education and social causes.*

Bellringer

If YOU were there . . . Use the **Daily Bellringer Transparency** to help students answer the question.

🖨 Daily Bellringer Transparency, Section 4

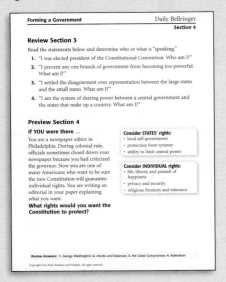

Academic Vocabulary

Review with students the high-use academic term in this section.

advocate to plead in favor of (p. 171)

📃 **CRF:** Vocabulary Builder Activity, Section 4

Taking Notes

Have students copy the graphic organizer onto their own paper and then use it to take notes on the section. This activity will prepare students for the Section Assessment, in which they will complete a graphic organizer that builds on the information using a critical thinking skill.

Ratifying the Constitution

What You Will Learn . . .

Main Ideas

1. Federalists and Antifederalists engaged in debate over the new Constitution.
2. The *Federalist Papers* played an important role in the fight for ratification of the Constitution.
3. Ten amendments were added to the Constitution to provide a Bill of Rights to protect citizens.

The Big Idea

Americans carried on a vigorous debate before ratifying the Constitution.

Key Terms and People

Antifederalists, *p. 170*
George Mason, *p. 170*
Federalists, *p. 170*
Federalist Papers, p. 171
amendments, *p. 173*
Bill of Rights, *p. 173*

TAKING NOTES As you read, take notes on the differing views of the U.S. Constitution.

Federalists		Antifederalists
	vs.	

If YOU were there...

You are a newspaper editor in Philadelphia. During colonial rule, officials sometimes closed down your newspaper because you had criticized the governor. Now you are one of many Americans who want to be sure the new Constitution will guarantee individual rights. You are writing an editorial in your paper explaining what you want.

What rights would you want the Constitution to protect?

> **BUILDING BACKGROUND** The new Constitution did not make everyone happy. Even its framers knew they had not made a perfect document. Many people still did not want a strong national government. They were afraid it would become as tyrannical as the British government had been. Before approving the Constitution, they wanted to be sure that their rights would be protected.

Federalists and Antifederalists

When the Constitution was made public, a huge debate began among many Americans. **Antifederalists** — people who opposed the Constitution—thought that the Constitutional Convention should not have created a new government. Others thought the Constitution gave too much power to the central government. For some Antifederalists, the main problem was that the Constitution did not have a section that guaranteed individual rights. Delegate **George Mason** became an Antifederalist for this reason.

Many Antifederalists were small farmers and debtors. However, some were wealthy. Some Revolutionary War heroes were also strong Antifederalists, including Richard Henry Lee, Samuel Adams, and Patrick Henry. Antifederalists were challenged by many Americans who believed that the United States needed a stronger central government.

Federalists, supporters of the Constitution, included James Madison, George Washington, Benjamin Franklin, Alexander Hamilton, and John Jay. Most Federalists believed that the

---

Teach the Big Idea

Ratifying the Constitution

1. **Teach** Ask students the questions in the Main Idea boxes to teach this section.

2. **Apply** Have each student create a flow chart for the ratification of the Constitution. Tell students to use the following as the first and last entries.
   - **September 17, 1787:** The Constitutional Convention approves the Constitution.
   - **December 1791:** States ratify the Bill of Rights.
   LS Visual/Spatial

3. **Review** As you review the section, have students share information in their flow charts.

4. **Practice/Homework** Have each student write a newspaper article about one of the events in his or her flow chart.
   LS Verbal/Linguistic

   📃 Alternative Assessment Handbook, Rubrics 13: Graphic Organizers; and 37: Writing Assignment

Federalists v. Antifederalists QUICK FACTS

Alexander Hamilton
Federalist
- Supported the Constitution as an excellent plan for government
- Defended his views in the *Federalist Papers*

George Mason
Antifederalist
- Opposed the Constitution
- Believed the Constitution needed a section guaranteeing individual rights

Constitution offered a good balance of power. They thought it was a careful compromise between various political views. Many Federalists were wealthy planters, farmers, and lawyers. However, many others were poor workers and craftspeople. Merchants also supported the Constitution.

Federalists and Antifederalists debated whether the new Constitution should be approved by the state legislatures. They made speeches and printed pamphlets **advocating** their views. The Federalists had to convince people a change in the structure of government was needed. To do this, they had to overcome people's fears that the Constitution would make the government too powerful.

READING CHECK Comparing and Contrasting
Explain the similarities and differences between the Antifederalists and the Federalists.

Federalist Papers

One of the most important defenses of the Constitution appeared in a series of essays that became known as the **Federalist Papers**. These essays supporting the Constitution were written anonymously under the name Publius. They were actually written by Hamilton, Madison, and Jay.

The authors of the *Federalist Papers* tried to reassure Americans that the new federal government would not overpower the states. In *Federalist Paper* No. 10, Madison argued that the diversity of the United States would prevent any single group from dominating the government.

The *Federalist Papers* were widely reprinted in newspapers around the country as the debate over the Constitution continued. Finally, they were collected and published in book form in 1788.

FOCUS ON READING
Take notes on the chronological order of this section. Which was written first, the *Federalist Papers* or the Bill of Rights?

ACADEMIC VOCABULARY
advocate
to plead in favor of

FORMING A GOVERNMENT **171**

Direct Teach

Main Idea

❶ Federalists and Antifederalists

Federalists and Antifederalists engaged in debate over the new Constitution.

Describe What were the Federalists' main arguments in favor of the Constitution? *that the Constitution offered a good balance of power and was a careful compromise between various political views*

Analyze What were the Antifederalists' main fears regarding the Constitution? *that it would create a government as tyrannical as that of Britain's and fail to protect Americans' individual rights*

CRF: Biography Activity: George Mason

Quick Facts Transparency: Federalists v. Antifederalists

Activity Federalists v. Antifederalists Have students write a short statement expressing what they think Hamilton and Mason might have said to each other regarding the debate over ratification of the U.S. Constitution.

go.hrw.com
Online Resources

KEYWORD: SR8 US5
ACTIVITY: Hamilton and Madison Articles

Differentiating Instruction

Above Level

Advanced/Gifted and Talented

1. Organize the class into two groups: one group representing the views of the Federalists, and the other group representing the views of the Antifederalists.

2. Have each student make a list of points that support his or her group's assigned position. Ask students to share their lists of points as two students write the lists for the class to see. Correct any student errors or misconceptions.

3. Have each student write a short persuasive essay explaining his or her position and urging other Americans to adopt it. Encourage students to create at least one visual aid, such as a chart or a graph, to support their essays.

4. Ask for volunteers to read their essays to the class. **LS** Verbal/Linguistic, Visual/Spatial

Alternative Assessment Handbook, Rubric 43: Writing to Persuade

Answers

Focus on Reading *the* Federalist Papers

Reading Check *similarities—Many were farmers; most wanted to see the Articles revised in some way; differences—Federalists supported the Constitution and a stronger central government, tended to be wealthier; Antifederalists opposed the Constitution for various reasons; tended to be less affluent.*

171

Main Idea

❷ Federalist Papers

The *Federalist Papers* played an important role in the fight for ratification of the Constitution.

Identify Who were the main authors of the *Federalist Papers*? *Alexander Hamilton, James Madison, John Jay*

Identify Points of View What fears did the *Federalist Papers* address? *that the federal government would overpower the states; that one group would dominate the government*

📖 Political Cartoons Activities for United States History, Cartoon 4: Ratifying the Constitution

📖 **CRF:** History and Geography Activity: Ratifying the Constitution

📖 **CRF:** Literature Activity: *Federalist Paper* "No. 15"

Teaching Tip

Reading Historical Documents To help students read difficult historical documents, tell students to scan the material and note any terms or phrases they do not understand. Help students define these terms and phrases. Then have students read the document carefully for its meaning.

Primary Source

HISTORIC DOCUMENT
Federalist Paper No. 10

In November 1787, Number 10 in the series called the Federalist Papers *was written in support of the Constitution. In it, James Madison describes the way federalism will overcome disagreements within society.*

❝A landed interest, a manufacturing interest, a mercantile [trading] interest, a moneyed interest, with many lesser interests, grow up of necessity in civilized nations, and divide them into different classes, actuated [moved] by different sentiments and views. The regulation of these various and interfering interests [opinions] forms the principal task of modern legislation, and involves the spirit of party and faction [group] in the necessary and ordinary operations of the government . . .

The federal Constitution forms a happy combination . . . the great . . . interests being referred to the national [legislature]; the local and particular to the state legislatures . . . The influence of factious leaders may kindle [start] a flame within their particular states, but will be unable to spread a general conflagration [large fire] through the other states.❞

—James Madison, quoted in *Living American Documents*, edited by Isidore Starr, et al.

Madison believes that lawmakers are responsible for regulating the many competing concerns that make up society.

The federal government will handle issues affecting the nation as a whole; state and local governments will handle those concerning local issues.

ANALYSIS SKILL **ANALYZING PRIMARY SOURCES**
Why does Madison think federalism will prevent disagreement?

The Constitution needed only 9 states to pass it. However, to establish and preserve national unity, each state needed to ratify it. Every state except Rhode Island held special state conventions that gave citizens the chance to discuss and vote on the Constitution.

Paul Revere served on a committee supporting ratification. He wrote of the Constitution, "The proposed . . . government, is well calculated [planned] to secure the liberties, protect the property, and guard the rights of the citizens of America."

Antifederalists also spoke out in state conventions. In New York, one citizen said, "It appears that the government will fall into the hands of the few and the great."

On December 7, 1787, Delaware became the first state to ratify the Constitution. Throughout the rest of 1787 and the first half of 1788, eight other states approved it. The Constitution went into effect in June 1788 after New Hampshire became the ninth state to ratify it.

Political leaders across America knew the new government needed the support of Virginia and New York, where debate still raged. Virginia had the largest population in the nation. New York was an important center for business and trade.

Finally, Madison and other Virginia Federalists convinced Virginia to ratify it in mid-1788. In New York, Jay and Hamilton said that New York City would break away and join the new government. New York State ratified the Constitution in July. Rhode Island was the last state to ratify it in May 1790.

READING CHECK **Drawing Conclusions**
Why were Virginia and New York important to the ratification of the Constitution?

Answers

Analyzing Primary Sources
Madison thinks that federalism forms a happy combination, where the great interests belong to the national government, and the local interests belong to the state governments.

Reading Check *Virginia had the largest population in the nation, and New York was an important center for business and trade; political leaders needed the two states' support to maintain national unity and support for the Constitution.*

Collaborative Learning

At Level

Commemorative Stamps

Materials: art supplies

1. Explain to students that the U.S. Post Office occasionally issues special stamps to commemorate an individual or event. Organize students into groups and have each group design and create a series of commemorative stamps celebrating the Constitution and the Bill of Rights.

2. Encourage students to design stamps that represent the following: the Constitutional Convention, the debate over ratification, the *Federalist Papers*, inclusion of a Bill of Rights, and the celebration over ratification.

3. Groups should assign members specific roles or topics to ensure that all students participate.

4. Display the groups' stamps around the classroom. **LS Interpersonal, Visual/Spatial**

📖 Alternative Assessment Handbook, Rubrics 3: Artwork; and 14: Group Activity

Bill of Rights

Several states ratified the Constitution only after they were promised that a bill protecting individual rights would be added to it. Many Antifederalists did not think that the Constitution would protect personal freedoms.

Some Federalists said that the nation did not need a federal bill of rights because the Constitution itself was a bill of rights. It was, they argued, written to protect the liberty of all U.S. citizens.

James Madison wanted to make a bill of rights one of the new government's first priorities. In Congress's first session, Madison encouraged the legislators to put together a bill of rights. The rights would then be added to the Constitution as **amendments**, or official changes. In Article V of the Constitution, the founders had provided a way to change the document when necessary in order to reflect the will of the people. The process requires that proposed amendments must be approved by a two-thirds majority of both houses of Congress and then ratified by three-fourths of the states before taking effect.

Legislators took ideas from the state ratifying conventions, the Virginia Declaration of Rights, the English Bill of Rights, and the Declaration of Independence to make sure that the abuses listed in the Declaration of Independence would be illegal under the new government. In September 1789 Congress proposed 12 amendments and sent them to the states for ratification. By December 1791 the states had ratified the **Bill of Rights**—10 of the proposed amendments intended to protect citizens' rights.

These 10 amendments set a clear example of how to amend the Constitution to fit the needs of a changing nation. The flexibility of the U.S. Constitution has allowed it to survive for more than 200 years.

READING CHECK **Summarizing** Why is being able to amend the Constitution important?

THE IMPACT TODAY

In 1789, Madison suggested an amendment limiting Congress's power over its own salary. This amendment was not passed until 1992.

SUMMARY AND PREVIEW Early disagreements over individual rights resulted in the Bill of Rights. In the next chapter you will learn about the structure of the Constitution.

Section 4 Assessment

go.hrw.com
Online Quiz
KEYWORD: SR8 HP5

Reviewing Ideas, Terms, and People

1. **a. Identify** Who were the **Federalists** and the **Antifederalists**?
   b. Draw Conclusions What was the main argument of the Antifederalists against the Constitution?
   c. Elaborate Do you agree with the Antifederalists or the Federalists? Explain your position.
2. **a. Recall** When did the Constitution go into effect?
   b. Draw Conclusions Why was it important that all 13 states ratify the Constitution?
   c. Elaborate Do you think that the *Federalist Papers* played an essential role in the ratification of the Constitution? Explain your answer.
3. **a. Recall** Why did Congress add the **Bill of Rights**?
   b. Explain From where did legislators' ideas for the Bill of Rights come?
   c. Elaborate Do you agree with the Antifederalists or the Federalists? Explain your position.

Critical Thinking

4. **Analyzing** Review your notes on Federalist and Antifederalist views. Then identify the outcome of the debate in a graphic organizer like the one below. Be sure to mention the Bill of Rights.

| Federalist Views | → | Outcome |
| Antifederalist Views | → | |

FOCUS ON WRITING

5. **Organizing Your Evidence** In this section you learned how the Bill of Rights was an important addition to the Constitution. You now have all your evidence about the difference between the Articles of Confederation and the Constitution. Choose two or three of the most important points and prepare to defend the Constitution, just like Alexander Hamilton and James Madison did in the *Federalist Papers*.

FORMING A GOVERNMENT **173**

Social Studies Skills

Determine Different Points of View

Activity Analyzing Points of View

Ask students to imagine that they attended a basketball game at which their school team lost by a wide margin to a rival school's team. How might their points of view of the game differ from those of the winning team's fans? How might the players' points of view differ from those of the fans, even on the same team? Have students discuss the answers and the factors that might influence each point of view. Then have each student consider a viewpoint that he or she holds about school. Have students free-write for 10 minutes about what factors might shape their points of view. Ask for volunteers to share their answers with the class.

LS Verbal/Linguistic

- Alternative Assessment Handbook, Rubrics 11: Discussions; and 37: Writing Assignments

- Interactive Skills Tutor CD-ROM, Lesson 18: Identify Point of View and Frame of Reference

---

Analysis | Critical Thinking | Civic Participation | Study

Determine Different Points of View

Define the Skill

A *point of view* is a person's outlook or attitude. It is the way that he or she looks at a topic or thing. Each person's point of view is shaped by his or her background. Because people's backgrounds are different, their points of view are too. Since a person's point of view shapes his or her opinions, knowing that point of view helps you understand and evaluate those opinions. Being able to detect differences in point of view is important to understanding differences in people's opinions and actions in history.

Learn the Skill

When you encounter someone's beliefs, opinions, or actions in your study of history, use the following guidelines to determine his or her point of view.

1. Look for information about the person's background.

2. Ask yourself what factors in the person's background might have influenced his or her opinion or action concerning the topic or event.

3. Be aware that sometimes the person's opinion or actions themselves will provide clues to his or her point of view.

Benjamin Lincoln led the troops that put down Shays's Rebellion in Massachusetts. He was also a state politician and a general during the Revolution. Lincoln offered this explanation of Shays's uprising.

" Among [the main causes] I rank the ease with which … credit was obtained …in the time of [the Revolution] …. The moment the day arrived when all discovered that things were fast returning [to normal], …and that the

indolent [lazy persons] and improvident [unwise persons] would soon experience the evils of their idleness and sloth, many startled [panicked] …and …complained … of the weight of public taxes … and at the cruelty of … creditors [those to whom money is owed] to call for their just dues [rightful payment]… The disaffected [unhappy people] … attempted … to stop the courts of law, and to suspend the operations of government. This they hoped to do until … an end should thereby be put to public and private debts. "

Lincoln's background as a general, state official, and leader against the rebels likely gave him a negative point of view on the revolt. His reference to the rebels as lazy and unwise also provides clues to his attitude. You should weigh such factors when evaluating the accuracy of his statement.

Practice the Skill

The following statement about Shays's Rebellion came from a Massachusetts farmer. Read it and apply the guidelines to answer the questions.

" I have labored hard …all my days. I have been … obliged to do more than my part in the [Revolution], been loaded with …rates [taxes], …have been …[abused] by sheriffs …and [debt] collectors …I have lost a great deal …[T]he great men are going to get all we have, and I think it is time for us to …put a stop to it. "

1. From what point of view is this person commenting on the revolt? What is his opinion of it?

2. How does his view of himself differ from Lincoln's view of people like him?

3. Is this view of the revolt likely to be more accurate than Lincoln's view? Why or why not?

Social Studies Skills Activity: Determine Different Points of View

Federalists Versus Antifederalists **At Level**

1. Have students review the material in Section 4 under "Federalists and Antifederalists."

2. Then have each student create a chart contrasting the points of view of the Federalists and Antifederalists. The chart should also list the factors that might have influenced each group's viewpoint.

3. Have students share their answers as you create a master chart. Then have students discuss the factors that contributed to each group's point of view. **LS** Verbal/Linguistic, Visual/Spatial

4. **Extend** Have each student write a short speech that James Madison might have given to explain his point of view on the Bill of Rights. Have volunteers deliver their speeches to the class. **LS** Verbal/Linguistic

- Alternative Assessment Handbook, Rubrics 7: Charts; and 37: Writing Assignments

---

Answers

Practice the Skill 1. *from the point of view of a farmer who is struggling to pay debts; supports the revolt;* **2.** *sees himself as hard working, deserving of reward for his part in the Revolution, and abused by officials and used by "great men";* **3.** *The two views are probably equally biased. Together they provide a more complete picture of the perspectives and issues involved in the rebellion.*

174

Chapter Review

Visual Summary

Use the visual summary below to help you review the main ideas of the chapter.

QUICK FACTS

The Articles of Confederation
• first government of United States
• weak union of states
• weaknesses led to Shays's Rebellion

The Constitution
• framework of today's govern- ment
• strengthened national government
• three branches
• checks and balances

Bill of Rights
• first 10 amendments
• ensures basic rights

Reviewing Vocabulary, Terms, and People

Match the numbered person or term with the correct lettered definition.

1. Bill of Rights
2. checks and balances
3. constitution
4. Constitutional Convention
5. *Federalist Papers*
6. inflation
7. Northwest Territory
8. William Paterson
9. tariffs
10. Three-Fifths Compromise

a. agreement that stated that each slave would be counted as three-fifths of a person when deter- mining representation

b. delegate to the Constitutional Convention who proposed the New Jersey Plan

c. increased prices for goods and services com- bined with the reduced value of money

d. area including present-day Illinois, Indiana, Michigan, Ohio, Wisconsin, and part of Minnesota

e. meetings held in Philadelphia at which del- egates from the states attempted to improve the existing government

f. series of essays in support of the Constitution

g. set of basic principles that determines the powers and duties of a government

h. system that prevents any branch of government from becoming too powerful

i. taxes on imports or exports

j. the first 10 amendments to the Constitution

Answers

Visual Summary

Review and Inquiry Have students examine the visual summary.

🖳 Quick Facts Transparency: Forming a Government Visual Summary

Reviewing Vocabulary, Terms and People

1. j	**6.** c
2. h	**7.** d
3. g	**8.** b
4. e	**9.** i
5. f	**10.** a

Comprehension and Critical Thinking

11. a. could settle conflicts among the states, make coins, borrow money, make treaties with other countries and with Native Americans, and ask the states for money and soldiers
b. passed the Land Ordinance of 1785, which helped systematize the division of territory; passed the Northwest Ordinance of 1787, which established the Northwest Territory
c. Answers will vary, but students should show an understanding of the documents and institutions that influenced the development of the nation.

Review and Assessment Resources

Review and Reinforce

SE Chapter Review

📄 **CRF:** Chapter Review Activity

🖳 Quick Facts Transparency: Forming a Government Visual Summary

📼 Spanish Chapter Summaries Audio CD Program

🔲 Online Chapter Summaries in Six Languages

OSP Holt PuzzlePro; GameTool for ExamView

💿 Quiz Game CD-ROM

Assess

SE Standardized Test Practice

📄 PASS: Chapter Test, Forms A and B

📄 Alternative Assessment Handbook

OSP ExamView Test Generator, Chapter Test

💿 Differentiated Instruction Modified Worksheets and Tests CD-ROM: Chapter Test

🔲 Holt Online Assessment Program (in the Premier Online Edition)

Reteach/Intervene

📄 Interactive Reader and Study Guide

📄 Differentiated Instruction Teacher Management System: Lesson Plans for Differentiated Instruction

💿 Differentiated Instruction Modified Worksheets and Tests CD-ROM

💿 Interactive Skills Tutor CD-ROM

go.hrw.com
Online Resources

Chapter Resources: KEYWORD: SR8 US5

12. a. a revolt by farmers in response to Massachusetts's tax policy

b. Answers may include that foreign nations viewed the United States as weak because its national government had few powers and the nation experienced economic problems.

c. Answers will vary, but students should be familiar with the various trade, economic, domestic, and international problems the nation faced.

13. a. established a system of federalism, created a powerful bicameral legislature, created an executive branch led by a president, created a judicial branch headed by a Supreme Court, balanced power among these three branches, created a system of checks and balances

b. Great Compromise—satisfied small states by creating an upper house with equal state representation, satisfied large states by creating a lower house with representation based on population; Three-Fifths Compromise—satisfied northern and southern states by counting each slave as three-fifths of a person to determine state representation

c. Answers will vary, but students should be aware of the unresolved issues in the Constitution, such as slavery and the lack of a bill of rights.

14. a. to protect individual rights

b. thought it should not have been created, that it gave too much power to the central government, that it needed a bill of rights

c. Answers will vary but should reflect an understanding of each group's views.

Reviewing Themes

15. problems enforcing treaties with foreign nations, limited political authority over the states

16. Political disagreements over state representation, the powers of the national government, how the government should be separated, and slavery led to compromises.

Comprehension and Critical Thinking

SECTION 1 *(Pages 152–155)*

11. a. Describe What powers did the Articles of Confederation give the national government?

b. Summarize What did the Confederation Congress do to strengthen the United States?

c. Evaluate Which document or institution do you think had the greatest influence on the development of the United States? Why?

SECTION 2 *(Pages 158–162)*

12. a. Recall What was Shays's Rebellion?

b. Draw Conclusions What was the general attitude of foreign nations toward the new government of the United States? Why?

c. Evaluate Of the problems experienced by the Confederation Congress, which do you think was the most harmful? Why?

SECTION 3 *(Pages 163–168)*

13. a. Describe In what ways did the Constitution strengthen the central government?

b. Explain How did the two compromises reached during the Constitutional Convention satisfy competing groups?

c. Elaborate In your opinion were there any weaknesses in the Constitution? Explain your answer.

SECTION 4 *(Pages 170–173)*

14. a. Recall Why was the Bill of Rights added to the Constitution?

b. Draw Conclusions Why were some Americans opposed to the Constitution?

c. Evaluate Would you have supported the Federalists or the Antifederalists? Explain your answer.

Reviewing Themes

15. Politics What political problems resulted from a weak central government under the Articles of Confederation?

16. Politics How did political disagreements lead to important compromises in the creation of the Constitution?

Reading Skills

Understanding Chronological Order *Use the Reading Skills taught in this chapter to answer the question below.*

17. Organize the following events chronologically according to the chapter.

a. The *Federalist Papers* are published.

b. The Constitution is ratified.

c. The Articles of Confederation are ratified.

d. Shays's Rebellion occurs.

e. The Constitutional Convention meets in Philadelphia.

Social Studies Skills

Determine Different Points of View *Use the Social Studies Skills taught in this chapter to answer the question below.*

18. List three differences between the Virginia Plan and the New Jersey Plan.

FOCUS ON WRITING

19. Writing Your Editorial You should start your editorial with a strong statement of your opinion about the Constitution. Then write two sentences about each of your main points of support—a weakness of the Articles of Confederation and/or a strength of the Constitution. End your editorial with a call to action: Ask the delegates to the Constitutional Convention to ratify the Constitution. Remember that you are trying to convince people to make a very important decision for our country—be persuasive.

Reading Skills

17. c, d, e, a, b

Social Studies Skills

18. Virginia Plan—proposed by Edmund Randolph, bicameral legislature based on population, larger states had a greater voice in the federal government; New Jersey Plan—proposed by William Paterson, unicameral legislature with equal representation per state, states had an equal voice in the federal government

Focus on Writing

19. Rubric Students' editorials should:

- strongly and clearly express the opinion.
- include at least two pieces of evidence to support the opinion.
- end with a call to action.
- be persuasive.
- use correct grammar, punctuation, spelling, and capitalization.

CRF: Focus on Writing Activity: A Newspaper Editorial

Standardized Test Practice

DIRECTIONS: *Read each question and write the letter of the best response.*

1 Which term would *best* describe the newly independent nation in the 1780s?

A strong

B united

C troubled

D confident

2 Under the Articles of Confederation, the greatest amount of power was in the hands of the

A Congress.

B American people.

C national government.

D states.

3 The structure of the U.S. Congress was created at the Constitutional Convention by the

A Virginia Plan.

B Great Compromise.

C New Jersey Plan.

D Three-Fifths Compromise.

4 The nation's most widespread problems under the Articles of Confederation involved

A trade.

B suffrage.

C slavery.

D rebellion.

5 The main objective of the Northwest Ordinance of 1787 was to

A establish a national government with limited powers.

B create a system for bringing new states into the Union.

C settle border disputes between the United States and Canada.

D regulate interstate commerce and curb inflation.

6 All of the following documents influenced the system of government established by the U.S. Constitution *except*

A the English Bill of Rights.

B the Mayflower Compact.

C Magna Carta.

D the Olive Branch Petition.

7

> *"*The powers delegated by the proposed Constitution to the federal government are few and defined. Those which are to remain in the State governments are numerous and . . . will extend to all objects which . . . concern the lives, liberties, and properties of the people . . . The operations of the federal government will be most extensive and important in times of war and danger; those of the State governments in times of peace and security.*"*
>
> —James Madison, *Federalist Paper No. 45*

What point was Madison making about the system of government created by the proposed Constitution?

A The states will continue to be in charge of day-to-day government of the people.

B The federal government's main function will be to keep peace among the states.

C The state governments will have greater power than the new federal government.

D The most important governing powers will be held by the new federal government.

Intervention Resources

Reproducible

- Interactive Reader and Study Guide
- Differentiated Instruction Teacher Management System: Lesson Plans for Differentiated Instruction

Technology

- Quick Facts Transparency: Forming a Government Visual Summary
- Differentiated Instruction Modified Worksheets and Tests CD-ROM
- Interactive Skills Tutor CD-ROM

Tips for Test Taking

Take It All In When students first start a test, encourage them to briefly preview the test to get a mental map of their tasks:

- Know how many questions they have to complete.
- Know where to stop.
- Set time checkpoints.
- Do the easy sections first; easy questions can be worth just as many points as hard ones.

Answers

1. C
Break Down the Question: This question requires students to synthesize information in Section 1. Have students think about what they know about the nation under the Articles of Confederation.

2. D
Break Down the Question: This question requires students to recall factual information. Students should use a process of elimination to answer the question.

3. B
Break Down the Question: This question requires students to recall factual information. Students should use a process of elimination to answer the question.

4. A
Break Down the Question: This question requires students to evaluate information. Tell students to consider the types of problems the United States experienced and what most of these problems had in common.

5. B
Break Down the Question: This question requires students to recall factual information. Refer students who have trouble to the text "Northwest Territory" in Section 1.

6. D
Break Down the Question: This question requires students to recall factual information. Encourage students to use process of elimination to answer this question.

7. A
Break Down the Question: This questions requires students to interpret information and find the main idea. Suggest that students focus on the phrases, "Those which are to remain in the State governments . . . concern the lives, liberties, and properties of the people," and "those of the States governments in times of peace and security."

Citizenship and the Constitution

Chapter Overview	Reproducible Resources	Technology Resources
CHAPTER 6 pp. 178–229 **Overview:** In this chapter, students will learn about the Constitution, the Bill of Rights, and what it means to be a U.S. citizen.	**Differentiated Instruction Teacher Management System:*** • Instructional Benchmarking Guides • Lesson Plans for Differentiated Instruction **Interactive Reader and Study Guide:** Chapter Graphic Organizer* **Chapter Resource File:*** • Focus on Writing Activity: A Pamphlet • Social Studies Skills Activity: Determining the Context of Statements • Chapter Review Activity **Pre-AP Activities Guide for United States History:** Note Taking* **A Teacher's Guide to Religion in the Public Schools***	**Power Presentations with Video CD-ROM** **Differentiated Instruction Modified Worksheets and Tests CD-ROM** **Primary Source Library CD-ROM for United States History** **Interactive Skills Tutor CD-ROM** **Student Edition on Audio CD Program** **History's Impact: United States History Video Program (VHS/DVD):** Citizenship and the Constitution*
Section 1: **Understanding the Constitution** **The Big Idea:** The U.S. Constitution balances the powers of the federal government among the legislative, executive, and judicial branches.	**Differentiated Instruction Teacher Management System:** Section 1 Lesson Plan* **Interactive Reader and Study Guide:** Section 1 Summary* **Chapter Resource File:*** • Vocabulary Builder Activity, Section 1 • Biography Activity: Daniel K. Inouye • History and Geography Activity: House Membership, 1990-2000 • Biography Activity: John Jay • Biography Activity: Sandra Day O'Connor	**Daily Bellringer Transparency:** Section 1* **Quick Facts Transparency:** Separation of Powers* **Quick Facts Transparency:** Checks and Balances* **Internet Activity:** Supreme Court Case Summaries
Section 2: **The Bill of Rights** **The Big Idea:** The Bill of Rights was added to the Constitution to define clearly the rights and freedoms of citizens.	**Differentiated Instruction Teacher Management System:** Section 2 Lesson Plan* **Interactive Reader and Study Guide:** Section 2 Summary* **Chapter Resource File:*** • Vocabulary Builder Activity, Section 2 • Primary Source Activity: Hortensius, "An Essay on the Liberty of the Press" **Political Cartoons Activities for United States History,** Cartoon 6: Bill of Rights: "Liberty vs. Order"*	**Daily Bellringer Transparency:** Section 2*
Section 3: **Rights and Responsibilities of Citizenship** **The Big Idea:** American citizenship involves great privileges and serious responsibilities.	**Differentiated Instruction Teacher Management System:** Section 3 Lesson Plan* **Interactive Reader and Study Guide:** Section 3 Summary* **Chapter Resource File:*** • Vocabulary Builder Activity, Section 3 • Primary Source Activity: What It Means to Be an American: Two Views • Literature Activity: *The Free Citizen,* by Theodore Roosevelt **Political Cartoons Activities for United States History, Cartoon 5:** Duties of Citizenship*	**Daily Bellringer Transparency:** Section 3* **Internet Activity:** Tracking U.S. Immigration

SE Student Edition	Print Resource	Audio CD
TE Teacher's Edition	Transparency	CD-ROM
go.hrw.com	**LS** Learning Styles	Video
OSP One-Stop Planner CD-ROM	* also on One-Stop Planner CD	

HOLT
History's Impact
United States History Video Program (VHS/DVD)

Citizenship and the Constitution
Suggested use: as a chapter introduction

Review, Assessment, Intervention

- **Quick Facts Transparency:** Citizenship and the Constitution Visual Summary*
- **Spanish Chapter Summaries Audio CD Program**
- **Online Chapter Summaries in Six Languages**
- **Progress Assessment Support System (PASS):** Chapter Test*
- **Differentiated Instruction Modified Worksheets and Tests CD-ROM:** Modified Chapter Test
- **One-Stop Planner CD-ROM:** ExamView Test Generator (English/Spanish)
- **Holt Online Assessment Program (HOAP),** in the Holt Premier Online Student Edition

- **PASS:** Section 1 Quiz*
- **Online Quiz:** Section 1
- **Alternative Assessment Handbook**

- **PASS:** Section 2 Quiz*
- **Online Quiz:** Section 2
- **Alternative Assessment Handbook**

- **PASS:** Section 3 Quiz*
- **Online Quiz:** Section 3
- **Alternative Assessment Handbook**

Power Presentations with Video CD-ROM

Power Presentations with Video are visual presentations of each chapter's main ideas. Presentations can be customized by including Quick Facts charts, images from the text, and video clips.

Power Presentations with Video CD-ROM
HOLT
United States History
Beginnings to 1877

DIVISION FOR PUBLIC EDUCATION
AMERICAN BAR ASSOCIATION

Developed by the Division for Public Education of the American Bar Association, these materials are part of the **Democracy and Civic Education Resources.**

- **Constitution Study Guide**
- **Supreme Court Case Studies**

Holt Online Learning

- Document-Based Questions
- Interactive Multimedia Activities

Teacher Resources
KEYWORD: SR8 TEACHER

Student Resources
KEYWORD: SR8 US6

- Current Events
- Chapter-based Internet Activities
- and more!

Holt Premier
Online Student Edition
Complete online support for interactivity, assessment, and reporting
- Interactive Maps and Notebook
- Standardized Test Prep
- Homework Practice and Research Activities Online

CHAPTER 6 PLANNING GUIDE

Differentiating Instruction

ENGLISH-LANGUAGE LEARNERS & STRUGGLING READERS

TARGET RESOURCE

live ink®
a new way to read

Live Ink® Online Reading Help

Spanish Resources

Spanish Chapter Summaries Audio CD Program

One-Stop Planner CD-ROM:
- ExamView Test Generator, Spanish
- PuzzlePro, Spanish

Additional Resources

Differentiated Instruction Teacher Management System: Lesson Plans for Differentiated Instruction

Chapter Resources:
- Vocabulary Builder Activities
- Social Studies Skills Activity: Determining the Context of Statements

Quick Facts Transparencies:
- Separation of Powers
- Checks and Balances
- Citizenship and the Constitution Visual Summary

Student Edition on Audio CD Program

Online Chapter Summaries in Six Languages

Interactive Skills Tutor CD-ROM

SPECIAL NEEDS LEARNERS

TARGET RESOURCE

Differentiated Instruction Modified Worksheets and Tests CD-ROM

- Vocabulary Flash Cards
- Modified Vocabulary Builder Activities
- Modified Chapter Review Activity
- Modified Chapter Test

Additional Resources

Differentiated Instruction Teacher Management System: Lesson Plans for Differentiated Instruction

Interactive Reader and Study Guide

Social Studies Skills Activity: Determining the Context of Statements

Student Edition on Audio CD Program

Interactive Skills Tutor CD-ROM

Live Ink® Online Reading Help

ADVANCED/GIFTED AND TALENTED STUDENTS

TARGET RESOURCE

Primary Source Library CD-ROM for United States History

The Library contains longer versions of quotations in the text, extra sources, and images. Included are point-of-view articles, journals, diaries, historical fiction, and political documents.

Additional Resources

Political Cartoons Activities for United States History: Cartoon 6: Bill of Rights: "Liberty vs. Order"; Cartoon 5: Duties of Citizenship

United States History Document-Based Questions Activities

Differentiated Instruction Teacher Management System: Lesson Plans for Differentiated Instruction

Chapter Resource File:
- Focus on Writing Activity: A Pamphlet
- Literature Activity: *The Free Citizen,* by Theodore Roosevelt
- Primary Source Activities: Hortensius, "An Essay on the Liberty of the Press"; What It Means to Be an American: Two Views

One-Stop Planner® CD-ROM
for Differentiated Instruction

Your differentiated instruction lesson plans are available at your fingertips. Holt's Teacher Management System links teaching support tools to pages in the Interactive Teacher's Edition.

The One-Stop Planner features:
- Interactive Teacher's Edition
- Calendar Planner and pacing guides
- Editable lesson plans
- All reproducible ancillaries in Adobe Acrobat (PDF) format
- ExamView Test Generator (English and Spanish)
- Transparency and video previews

Professional Development

- **In-service and staff development** as part of your Holt Social Studies product purchase
- **Quick Teacher Tutorial Lesson Presentation CD-ROM**
- Intensive tuition-based **Teacher Development Institute**
- **Teaching American History Online**—2 Module Professional Development Course
- **Convenient Holt Speaker Bureau**—face-to-face workshop options
- **PRAXIS™ Test Prep** interactive Web-based content refreshers*
- **24/7 Ask A Professional Development Expert** at http://www.hrw.com/prodev/

* PRAXIS is a trademark of Educational Testing Service (ETS). This publication is not endorsed or approved by ETS.

DIFFERENTIATED INSTRUCTION PLANNING GUIDE

Chapter Preview

Chapter Big Ideas

Section 1 The U.S. Constitution balances the powers of the federal government among the legislative, executive, and judicial branches.

Section 2 The Bill of Rights was added to the Constitution to define clearly the rights and freedoms of citizens.

Section 3 American citizenship involves great privileges and serious responsibilities.

Citizenship and the Constitution

Focus on Writing

The **Chapter Resource File** provides a Focus on Writing worksheet to help students organize and write their pamphlets.

CRF: Focus on Writing Activity: A Pamphlet

FOCUS ON WRITING

A Pamphlet Everyone in the United States benefits from our Constitution. However, many people don't know the Constitution as well as they should. In this chapter you will read about the Constitution and the rights and responsibilities it grants to citizens. Then you'll create a four-page pamphlet to share this information with your fellow citizens.

UNITED STATES

1788
The Constitution goes into effect after New Hampshire becomes the ninth state to ratify it.

1787 · 1800

1791 The Bill of Rights becomes part of the Constitution on December 15.

178 CHAPTER 6

Key to Differentiating Instruction

Below Level

Basic-level activities designed for all students encountering new material

At Level

Intermediate-level activities designed for average students

Above Level

Challenging activities designed for honors and gifted and talented students

Standard English Mastery

Activities designed to improve standard English usage

Introduce the Chapter

At Level

Focus on Citizenship

1. Ask students to discuss the concept of citizenship and what it means to them.

2. Ask students if they can identify any rights and responsibilities associated with American citizenship.

3. To help students get started, write some rights and responsibilities for the class to see. Rights might include freedom of speech, freedom of religion, freedom of assembly, and the right to trial by jury. Responsibilities might include

obeying laws and authority figures, paying taxes, and serving on juries.

4. Explain to students that in this chapter they will learn about two important documents—the United States Constitution and the Bill of Rights. Point out that these documents outline many of the rights and responsibilities of American citizens and affect students' lives on a daily basis. **LS Verbal/Linguistic**

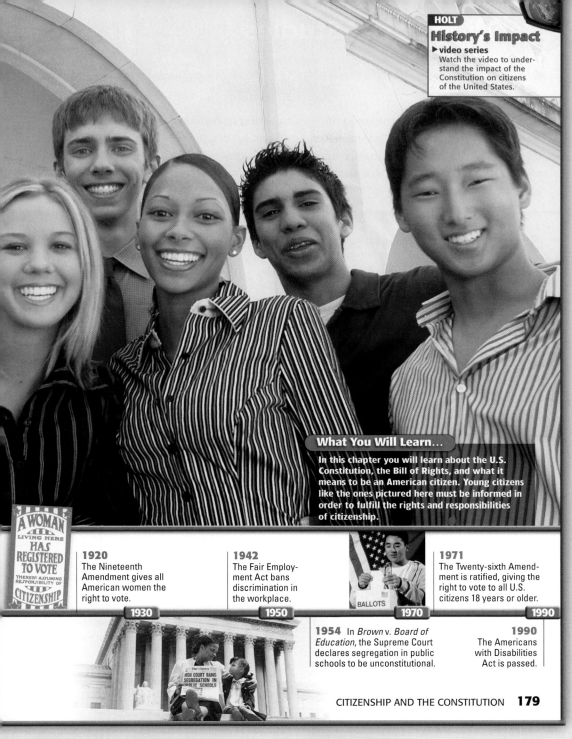

HOLT

History's Impact

▶ video series

Watch the video to understand the impact of the Constitution on citizens of the United States.

What You Will Learn...

In this chapter you will learn about the U.S. Constitution, the Bill of Rights, and what it means to be an American citizen. Young citizens like the ones pictured here must be informed in order to fulfill the rights and responsibilities of citizenship.

1920
The Nineteenth Amendment gives all American women the right to vote.

1942
The Fair Employment Act bans discrimination in the workplace.

1971
The Twenty-sixth Amendment is ratified, giving the right to vote to all U.S. citizens 18 years or older.

1930 **1950** **1970** **1990**

1954 In *Brown* v. *Board of Education*, the Supreme Court declares segregation in public schools to be unconstitutional.

1990
The Americans with Disabilities Act is passed.

BALLOTS

A WOMAN LIVING HERE HAS REGISTERED TO VOTE THEREBY ASSUMING RESPONSIBILITY OF CITIZENSHIP

CITIZENSHIP AND THE CONSTITUTION **179**

• Chapter Preview •

HOLT

History's Impact

▶ video series

See the Video Teacher's Guide for strategies for using the chapter video **Citizenship and the Constitution**.

Explore the Picture

Becoming a U.S. Citizen The process by which foreign citizens become U.S. citizens is called naturalization. Congress established the requirements for naturalization in the Immigration and Nationality Act (INA). Among these requirements are the ability to read, write, and speak English; knowledge and understanding of U.S. history and government; belief in the principles of the U.S. Constitution; and good moral character.

Analyzing Visuals How do you think the young people in the photo feel about becoming old enough to enjoy the full rights and responsibilities of American citizenship? *possible answer—proud, happy, and excited*

go.hrw.com

Online Resources

Chapter Resources:
KEYWORD: SR8 US6

Teacher Resources:
KEYWORD: SR8 TEACHER

Explore the Time Line

1. What year did the U.S. Constitution go into effect? *1788*

2. What became part of the U.S. Constitution on December 15, 1791? *the Bill of Rights*

3. How and when did the Nineteenth Amendment change voting rights? *1920; gave women the right to vote*

4. How and when did the Twenty-sixth Amendment change voting rights? *1971; gave all U.S. citizens 18 years or older the right to vote*

Info to Know

Freedom of Speech Seven years after the Bill of Rights was added to the Constitution, the U.S. Congress passed the Sedition Act of 1798. This act seemed to restrict freedom of speech by making it a crime for a person to say or write anything "false, scandalous and malicious against the government." The U.S. Supreme Court upheld the law's constitutionality, however. Ten people were imprisoned under this law.

Understanding Themes

Introduce the key theme of this chapter—politics—to the class by asking them to briefly explain what they know about our political system in the United States. Write students' ideas for the class to see. Help students to see which ideas are correct and which are incorrect. Have students create a collage that reflects the political ideas that were instituted by the U.S. Constitution.

Summarizing Historical Texts

Focus on Reading Organize the class into pairs. Then assign each pair of students a different amendment from the U.S. Constitution. Have groups use the steps explained at right to create a summary of their amendment. You might want to assign another amendment to groups that finish early. After students have finished, have each group present its summary to the class. Encourage students to write down the key points in each summary.

Reading Social Studies
by Kylene Beers

| Economics | Geography | Politics | Society and Culture | Science and Technology |

Focus on Themes In this chapter you will read about the three branches of government, the Bill of Rights, and the duties and responsibilities of a United States citizen. As you read about each of these topics, you will see the American **political system** at work—not only in the Bill of Rights, but through the responsibilities U.S. citizens have as they vote for leaders and work to help their communities and nation.

Summarizing Historical Texts

Focus on Reading History books are full of information. Sometimes the sheer amount of information they contain can make processing what you read difficult. In those cases, it may be helpful to stop for a moment and summarize what you've read.

Writing a Summary A summary is a short restatement of the most important ideas in a text. The example below shows three steps used in writing a summary. First underline important details. Then write a short summary of each paragraph. Finally, combine these paragraph summaries into a short summary of the whole passage.

The Constitution
Article II, Section 1
1. The <u>executive Power</u> shall be vested in a <u>President of the United States of America</u>. He shall hold his Office during the Term of <u>four Years</u>, and, together with the <u>Vice President</u>, chosen for the same Term, be <u>elected</u>, as follows:
2. <u>Each State shall appoint</u>, in such Manner as the Legislature thereof may direct, a Number of <u>Electors</u>, equal to the whole <u>Number of Senators and Representatives</u> to which the State may be entitled in the Congress; but no Senator or Representative, or Person holding an Office of Trust or Profit under the United States, shall be appointed an Elector.

Summary of Paragraph 1
The executive branch is headed by a president and vice president, each elected for four-year terms.

Summary of Paragraph 2
The electors who choose the president and vice president are appointed. Each state has the same number of electors as it has members of Congress.

Combined Summary
The president and vice president who run the executive branch are elected every four years by state-appointed electors.

180 CHAPTER 6

Reading and Skills Resources

Reading Support
- Interactive Reader and Study Guide
- Student Edition on Audio CD Program
- Spanish Chapter Summaries Audio CD Program

Social Studies Skills Support
- Interactive Skills Tutor CD-ROM

Vocabulary Support
- **CRF:** Vocabulary Builder Activities
- **CRF:** Chapter Review Activity
- Differentiated Instruction Modified Worksheets and Tests CD-ROM:
  - Vocabulary Flash Cards
  - Vocabulary Builder Activity
  - Chapter Review Activity

OSP Holt PuzzlePro

You Try It!

The following passage is from the U.S. Constitution. As you read it, decide which facts you would include in a summary of the passage.

The Constitution

Article I, Section 2

1. The House of Representatives shall be composed of Members chosen every second Year by the People of the several States, and the Electors in each State shall have the Qualifications requisite for Electors of the most numerous branch of the State Legislature.

2. No person shall be a Representative who shall not have attained to the Age of twenty five years, and been seven Years a Citizen of the United States, and who shall not, when elected, be an Inhabitant of the State in which he shall be chosen.

After you read the passage, answer the following questions.

1. Which of the following statements best summarizes the first paragraph of this passage?

   a. Congress has a House of Representatives.

   b. Members of the House of Representatives are elected every two years by state electors.

2. Using the steps described on the previous page, write a summary of the second paragraph of this passage.

3. Combine the summary statement you chose in Question 1 with the summary statement you wrote in Question 2 to create a single summary of this entire passage.

As you read Chapter 6, think about what details you would include in a summary of each paragraph.

Key Terms and People

Chapter 6

Section 1
federal system *(p. 184)*
impeach *(p. 184)*
veto *(p. 184)*
executive orders *(p. 185)*
pardons *(p. 185)*
Thurgood Marshall *(p. 186)*
Sandra Day O'Connor *(p. 186)*

Section 2
James Madison *(p. 216)*
majority rule *(p. 216)*
petition *(p. 217)*
search warrant *(p. 218)*
due process *(p. 218)*
indict *(p. 218)*
double jeopardy *(p. 218)*
eminent domain *(p. 218)*

Section 3
naturalized citizens *(p. 222)*
deport *(p. 222)*
draft *(p. 223)*
political action committees *(p. 224)*
interest groups *(p. 224)*

Academic Vocabulary

Success in school is related to knowing academic vocabulary—the words that are frequently used in school assignments and discussions. In this chapter, you will learn the following academic words:

distinct *(p. 183)*
influence *(p. 224)*

Reading Social Studies

Key Terms and People

Read the terms and people to students. Then ask students to choose five to eight terms with which they are unfamiliar. Have students define the terms they selected. Then have each student create a crossword puzzle using the definitions he or she wrote as clues. If time permits, have students exchange their puzzles with a partner and complete the other person's crossword. Then have students check their answers. **LS Verbal/Linguistic, Visual/Spatial**

Focus on Reading

See the **Focus on Reading** questions in this chapter for more practice on this reading social studies skill.

Reading Social Studies Assessment

See the **Chapter Review** at the end of this chapter for student assessment questions related to this reading skill.

Teaching Tip

Summarizing may be a difficult concept for students to grasp. Students may think that every fact is an important detail. Remind students that not every fact is important when writing a summary. One way to help students keep to the important details is to have them identify the main idea of each paragraph in a few words. Then instruct students to identify only those details that support that main idea. Model this strategy for students by summarizing a paragraph or two as a class.

Answers

You Try It! 1. *b;* **2.** *possible answer—Members of the House of Representatives must meet certain age and residency requirements.* **3.** *Members of the House of Representatives are elected every two years and must meet certain age and residency requirements.*

Bellringer

If YOU were there . . . Use the **Daily Bellringer Transparency** to help students answer the question.

🖫 Daily Bellringer Transparency, Section 1

Academic Vocabulary

Review with students the high-use academic term in this section.

distinct separate (p. 183)

Building Vocabulary

Preteach or review the following term:

apportionment system that keeps total House membership at 435 members (p. 183)

📰 **CRF:** Vocabulary Builder Activity, Section 1

Taking Notes

Have students copy the graphic organizer onto their own paper and then use it to take notes on the section. This activity will prepare students for the Section Assessment, in which they will complete a graphic organizer that builds on the information using a critical thinking skill.

SECTION 1

Understanding the Constitution

What You Will Learn...

Main Ideas

1. The framers of the Constitution devised the federal system.
2. The legislative branch makes the nation's laws.
3. The executive branch enforces the nation's laws.
4. The judicial branch determines whether or not laws are constitutional.

The Big Idea

The U.S. Constitution balances the powers of the federal government among the legislative, executive, and judicial branches.

Key Terms and People

federal system, p. 182
impeach, p. 184
veto, p. 184
executive orders, p. 185
pardons, p. 185
Thurgood Marshall, p. 186
Sandra Day O'Connor, p. 186

TAKING NOTES As you read, take notes on the structure of each of the branches of government in a chart like the one below.

Branch	Structure
Legislative	
Executive	
Judicial	

If YOU were there...

You have just been elected to the U.S. House of Representatives. You know that committees do much of the work in Congress. They deal with many different fields such as foreign policy, agriculture, national security, science, and education. You would like to ask for a spot on a committee whose work interests you.

Which committee would you ask to serve on?

> **BUILDING BACKGROUND** When the framers of the Constitution met in Philadelphia in 1787, they created a national government with three branches that balance one another's powers.

The Federal System

The framers of the Constitution wanted to create a government powerful enough to protect the rights of citizens and defend the country against its enemies. To do so, they set up a **federal system** of government, a system that divided powers between the states and the federal government.

The framers used the federal system, also known as federalism, to structure the Constitution. The Constitution assigns certain powers to the national government. These are called delegated powers. Among them are the rights to coin money and to regulate trade. Reserved powers are those kept by the states. These powers include creating local governments and holding elections. Concurrent powers are those shared by the federal and state governments. They include taxing, borrowing money, and enforcing laws.

Sometimes, Congress has had to stretch its delegated powers to deal with new or unexpected issues. A clause in the Constitution states that Congress may "make all Laws which shall be necessary and proper" for carrying out its duties. This clause, called the elastic clause—because it can be stretched (like elastic)—provides flexibility for the government.

READING CHECK Summarizing How is power divided between the federal and state governments?

Teach the Big Idea

At Level

Understanding the Constitution

1. **Teach** Ask students the questions in the Main Idea boxes to teach this section.

2. **Apply** Have students scan the section and the Quick Facts diagrams. Tell students to close their books. List the three branches of government for students to see. Then call out a power of one of the branches. Have students determine to which branch the power belongs. Continue until students have assigned all the powers. **LS Visual/Spatial**

3. **Review** As you review the section's main ideas, have students summarize how the Constitution divides government power.

4. **Practice/Homework** Have each student create a mobile illustrating the division of power between the federal government and state governments and among the three branches of the federal government. **LS Visual/Spatial**

   📰 Alternative Assessment Handbook, Rubrics 3: Artwork; and 7: Charts

U.S. Constitution

Legislative Branch (Congress)	Executive Branch (President)	Judicial Branch (Supreme Court)
• Writes the laws • Confirms presidential appointments • Approves treaties • Grants money • Declares war	• Proposes laws • Administers the laws • Commands armed forces • Appoints ambassadors and other officials • Conducts foreign policy • Makes treaties	• Interprets the Constitution and other laws • Reviews lower-court decisions

Legislative Branch

The federal government has three branches, each with **distinct** responsibilities and powers. This separation balances the branches and keeps any one of them from growing too powerful. The first branch of government is the legislative branch, or Congress. It makes the nation's laws. Article I of the Constitution divides Congress into the House of Representatives and the Senate.

With 435 members, the House of Representatives is the larger congressional house. The U.S. Census, a population count made every 10 years, determines how many members represent each state. A system called apportionment keeps total membership at 435. If one state gains a member, another state loses one. Members must be at least 25 years old, live in the state where they were elected, and have been U.S. citizens for seven years. They serve two-year terms.

The Senate has two members, or senators, per state. Senators represent the interests of the whole state, not just a district. They must be at least 30 years old, have been U.S. citizens for nine years, and live in the state they represent. They serve six-year terms. The senior senator of a state is the one who has served

the longer of the two. Members of Congress can serve an unlimited number of terms.

The political party with more members in each house is the majority party. The one with fewer members is the minority party. The leader of the House of Representatives, or Speaker of the House, is elected by House members from the majority party.

The U.S. vice president serves as president of the Senate. He takes no part in Senate debates but can vote to break ties. If he is absent, the president pro tempore (pro tem for short) leads the Senate. There is no law for how the Senate must choose this position, but it traditionally goes to the majority party's senator who has served the longest.

Congress begins sessions, or meetings, each year in the first week of January. Both houses do most of their work in committees. Each committee studies certain types of bills, or suggested laws. For example, all bills about taxes begin in the House Ways and Means Committee.

ACADEMIC VOCABULARY
distinct separate

READING CHECK Comparing and Contrasting
What are the similarities in requirements for members of the House of Representatives and the Senate? What are the differences?

CITIZENSHIP AND THE CONSTITUTION **183**

● Direct Teach ●

Main Idea

❶ The Federal System

The framers of the Constitution devised the federal system

Define What is federalism? *a government system that divides powers between the states and the federal government*

Contrast How do delegated, reserved, and concurrent powers differs? *delegated—powers granted to the federal government; reserved—powers kept by the states; concurrent—powers shared by state and federal governments*

📓 **CRF:** Biography Activity: Daniel K. Inouye

Main Idea

❷ Legislative Branch

The legislative branch makes the nation's laws.

Recall Which article of the Constitution defines the legislative branch? *Article I*

Draw Conclusions Why do you think the legislature performs most of its work in committees? *Legislators cannot study every bill, and committees enable legislators to share the work among groups.*

📓 **CRF:** History and Geography Activity: House Membership, 1990–2000

📦 Quick Facts Transparency: Separation of Powers

Collaborative Learning

Above Level

Analyzing Federalism Skits

1. Explain that one reason the framers of the Constitution delegated some powers to the federal government—rather than reserving them for state governments—was to avoid difficult situations between the states.

2. Organize the class into five small groups. Assign each group one of the following delegated powers: the coining of money, regulating interstate and international trade, providing for national defense, declaring war, and conducting diplomacy.

3. Have each group create a skit highlighting the confusion that might occur if state governments held the delegated power. Each member of the group should participate in the skit in some way.

4. Have each group present its skit. Then lead a class discussion about the importance of the division of powers in the Constitution.
LS Interpersonal, Kinesthetic

📓 Alternative Assessment Handbook, Rubric 33: Skits and Reader's Theater

Answers

Reading Check (left page) *some powers are delegated to the federal government, some reserved to state governments, and others are shared*

Reading Check *similarities—must live in the state they represent and where elected; differences—Representatives must be at least 25 years old and have been U.S. citizens for seven years; senators must be at least 30 and have been U.S. citizens for nine years.*

❸ Executive Branch

The executive branch enforces the nation's laws.

Describe What are the requirements to serve as president? *native-born U.S. citizen at least 35 years old and a U.S. resident for at least 14 years*

Analyze How does the system of checks and balances make it difficult for Congress to pass a law that the president opposes? *Congress must achieve a two-thirds majority vote to override a presidential veto.*

📖 Quick Facts Transparency: Checks and Balances

Connect to Government

Exercising the Veto The president's ability to veto legislation is an important check on Congress's power. Between 1789 and 1990, presidents vetoed 2,492 bills, with 2,433 of these vetoes taking place after 1865. Congress overrode these vetoes only 103 times.

Info to Know

The Nixon Pardon Perhaps the most famous pardon in presidential history took place on September 8, 1974, when President Gerald R. Ford pardoned Richard Nixon, the former president. Nixon had resigned from office after being accused of involvement in illegal actions while president. Ford explained that he granted the pardon because prosecuting a former president would be too disturbing for the nation.

Checks and Balances QUICK FACTS

Executive Branch (President)
Checks on:
Legislative Branch
• May adjourn Congress in certain situations
• May veto bills
Judicial Branch
• Appoints judges

Legislative Branch (Congress)
Checks on:
Executive Branch
• May reject appointments
• May reject treaties
• May withhold funding for presidential initiatives
• May impeach president
• May override a veto
Judicial Branch
• May propose constitutional amendments to overrule judicial decisions
• May impeach Supreme Court justices

Judicial Branch (Supreme Court)
Checks on:
Executive Branch
• May declare executive actions unconstitutional
Legislative Branch
• May declare laws unconstitutional

Executive Branch

Article II of the Constitution lists the powers of the executive branch. This branch enforces the laws passed by Congress.

President and Vice President

As head of the executive branch, the president is the most powerful elected leader in the United States. To qualify for the presidency or vice presidency, one must be a native-born U.S. citizen at least 35 years old. The president must also have been a U.S. resident for 14 years.

Americans elect a president and vice president every four years. Franklin D. Roosevelt, who won four times, was the only president to serve more than two terms. Now, the Twenty-second Amendment limits presidents to two terms. If a president dies, resigns, or is removed from office, the vice president becomes president for the rest of the term.

The House of Representatives can **impeach**, or vote to bring charges of serious crimes against, a president. Impeachment cases are tried in the Senate. If a president is found guilty, Congress can remove him from office. In 1868 Andrew Johnson was the first president to be impeached. President Bill Clinton was impeached in 1998. However, the Senate found each man not guilty.

Working with Congress

The president and Congress are often on different sides of an issue. However, they must still work together.

Congress passes laws. The president, however, can ask Congress to pass or reject bills. The president also can **veto**, or cancel, laws Congress has passed. Congress can try to override, or undo, the veto. However, this is difficult since it takes a two-thirds

184 CHAPTER 6

Critical Thinking: Comparing and Contrasting   [Below Level]

Separation of Powers Trifold

Materials: white construction paper or small poster board

1. Have students fold large pieces of paper into three equal, horizontal sections to create trifolds.

2. Have students label the sections *Legislative Branch*, *Executive Branch*, and *Judicial Branch*.

3. Ask volunteers to use the Separation of Powers Quick Facts diagram and the text to identify the powers and duties of each branch.

In addition, ask students to identify some government positions in each branch (such as representative, senator, president, and justice) and some requirements and duties of those positions. As volunteers provide information, have students fill in their trifolds.

🖎 **Verbal/Linguistic, Visual/Spatial**

📝 Alternative Assessment Handbook, Rubric 7: Charts

📖 Quick Facts Transparency: Separation of Powers

majority vote. To carry out laws affecting the Constitution, treaties, and statutes, the president issues **executive orders**. These commands have the power of law. The president also may grant **pardons**, or freedom from punishment, to persons convicted of federal crimes or facing criminal charges.

The president also commands the armed forces. In emergencies, the president can call on U.S. troops. Only Congress, however, can declare war. Other executive duties include conducting foreign relations and creating treaties. Executive departments do most of the executive branch work. As of 2004 there were 15 such departments. The president chooses department heads, who are called secretaries, and the Senate approves them. The heads make up the cabinet, which advises the president.

READING CHECK Drawing Conclusions
What is the president's most important power?

Judicial Branch

The third branch of government, the judicial branch, is made up of a system of federal courts headed by the U.S. Supreme Court. The Constitution created the Supreme Court, but the Judiciary Act of 1789 created the system of lower district and circuit courts.

Article III generally outlines the courts' duties. Federal courts can strike down a state or federal law if the court finds a law unconstitutional. Congress can then try to revise the law to make it constitutional.

District Courts

The president makes appointments to federal courts. In an effort to keep federal judges free of party influence, the judges are given life appointments. The lower federal courts are divided according to cases over which they have jurisdiction, or authority. Each state has at least one of the 94 district courts.

THE IMPACT TODAY

In 2002 the new Department of Homeland Security was given cabinet-level status to protect against terrorism.

SUPREME COURT DECISIONS

Background of the Court
The rest of the Supreme Court Decisions you see in this book will highlight important cases of the Court. But in this first one, we'll discuss the history of the Court.

The first Supreme Court met in 1790 at the Royal Exchange in New York City. The ground floor of this building was an open-air market. When the national government moved to Philadelphia, the Court met in basement rooms in Independence Hall. Once in Washington, the Court heard cases in the Capitol building until the present Supreme Court building was completed in 1932.

Circuit Riding
Today the Supreme Court holds court only in Washington, D.C. In the past, however, the justices had to travel through assigned circuits, hearing cases together with a district judge in a practice known as riding circuit.

The justices complained bitterly about the inconvenience of travel, which was often over unpaved roads and in bad weather. This system was not just inconvenient to the justices, however. Some people worried about the fairness of a system that required justices who had heard cases at trial to rule on them again on appeal. Other people, however, thought that the practice helped keep the justices in touch with the needs and feelings of the average citizen. Eventually,

circuit riding interfered so much with the increased amount of business of the Supreme Court that Congress passed a law ending the practice in the late 1800s.

Path to the Supreme Court
When a case is decided by a state or federal court, the losing side may have a chance to appeal the decision to a higher court. Under the federal system, this higher court is called the court of appeals. A person who loses in that court may then appeal to the Supreme Court to review the case. But the Supreme Court does not have to accept all appeals. It usually chooses to hear only cases in which there is an important legal principle to be decided or if two federal courts of appeals disagree on how an issue should be decided.

ANALYSIS SKILL ANALYZING INFORMATION
1. What are two reasons why the practice of circuit riding ended?
2. Why do you think the Supreme Court does not hear every case that is appealed to it?

CITIZENSHIP AND THE CONSTITUTION **185**

Biography

Sandra Day O'Connor (b. 1930) Supreme Court justice Sandra Day O'Connor has achieved several firsts in her career. By 1965 she was the first female assistant attorney general in Arizona. In the Arizona Senate, she held the position of majority leader for two years—the first woman to hold such a position in the nation. When President Ronald Reagan appointed O'Connor to the Supreme Court, she was yet again the first woman to hold the position.

🗐 **CRF:** Biography Activity: Sandra Day O'Connor

Close

Have students discuss whether the three branches of government share power equally and, if not, which branch has the most power and why.

Review

🗐 Online Quiz, Section 1

Assess

SE Section 1 Assessment

🗐 PASS: Section 1 Quiz

🗐 Alternative Assessment Handbook

Reteach/Classroom Intervention

🗐 Interactive Reader and Study Guide, Section 1

◉ Interactive Skills Tutor CD-ROM

Answers

Focus on Reading *A person convicted of a crime may take the case to the courts of appeal, which decides if the lower court heard the case appropriately and, if not, the lower court might retry the case.*

Reading Check *federal court system headed by the Supreme Court and including district courts and courts of appeal; interpret the Constitution; review decisions of lower courts*

186

FOCUS ON READING Jot down a short summary of the appeals process after reading this paragraph.

Courts of Appeals

If someone convicted of a crime believes the trial was unfair, he or she may take the case to the court of appeals. There are 13 courts of appeals. Each has a panel of judges to decide if cases heard in the lower courts were tried appropriately. If the judges uphold, or accept, the original decision, the original outcome stands. Otherwise, the case may be retried in the lower court.

Supreme Court

THE IMPACT TODAY
Supreme Court rulings can have dramatic effects on the nation, as in *Bush* v. *Gore*, which decided the outcome of the 2000 presidential election.

After a case is decided by the court of appeals, the losing side may appeal the decision to the Supreme Court. Thousands of cases go to the Supreme Court yearly in the hope of a hearing, but the Court has time to hear only about 100. Generally, the cases heard involve important constitutional or public-interest issues. If the Court declines to hear a case, the court of appeals decision is final.

Nine justices sit on the Supreme Court. The chief justice of the United States leads the Court. Unlike the president and members of Congress, there are no specific constitutional requirements to become a justice.

In recent decades, the Supreme Court has become more diverse. In 1967 **Thurgood Marshall** became the first African American justice. **Sandra Day O'Connor** became the first female Court justice after her 1981 appointment by President Ronald Reagan.

READING CHECK **Summarizing** Describe the structure and responsibilities of the judicial branch.

SUMMARY AND PREVIEW In this section you learned about the balance between the different branches of the federal government. In the next section you will learn about the Bill of Rights.

---

go.hrw.com
Online Quiz
KEYWORD: SR8 HP6

Section 1 Assessment

Reviewing Ideas, Terms, and People

1. **a. Describe** What type of government did the Constitution establish for the United States?
   b. Contrast What is the difference between delegated, reserved, and concurrent powers?
2. **a. Recall** What role does the vice president serve in the legislative branch?
   b. Compare and Contrast In what ways are the Senate and the House of Representatives similar and different?
   c. Elaborate Why do you think the requirements for serving in the Senate are stricter than those for serving in the House of Representatives?
3. **a. Describe** What powers are granted to the president?
   b. Make Generalizations Why is it important that the president and Congress work together?
   c. Evaluate What do you think is the most important power granted to the president? Why?
4. **a. Explain** What is the main power of the judicial branch?
   b. Evaluate Which branch of government do you feel is most important? Explain your answer.

Critical Thinking

5. **Categorizing** Review your notes on the branches of government. Then copy the web diagram below and use it to show two powers of each branch of government.

Legislative

Separation of Powers

Executive

Judicial

FOCUS ON WRITING ✎

6. **Gathering Information about the Constitution** Look back through what you've just read about the Constitution. Make a list of four or five of the most important features of the Constitution. You'll put that list on the second page of your pamphlet.

186 CHAPTER 6

Section 1 Assessment Answers

1. **a.** federal system
   b. delegated—powers granted to federal government; reserved—powers kept by states; concurrent—shared powers
2. **a.** serves as president of Senate; can break ties
   b. similar—legislative branch, make laws, meet at same time; different—requirements, size, length of terms, who they represent, leaders
   c. possible answer—because senators serve longer terms, represent a larger area, and are fewer in number than Representatives

3. **a.** powers to propose, enforce, and veto laws; command armed forces; appoint ambassadors; conduct foreign policy; make treaties; issue executive orders; grant pardons
   b. to keep the country running smoothly
   c. See answer to Question 3a.
4. **a.** to interpret the U.S. Constitution
   b. Students should support their opinions.
5. See the Quick Facts diagram on p. 183.
6. Students might mention federalism, separation of powers, and checks and balances.

James Madison

What would you do to create a brand-new government?

When did he live? 1751–1836

Where did he live? Like several of the founding fathers, James Madison was a Virginian. He grew up in the town of Montpelier, and he kept a home there for his whole life.

What did he do? Through the persuasive power of his writing, Madison helped create the foundations of the U.S. government.

Why is he important? Madison is known as the Father of the Constitution. A brilliant thinker, he provided many of the basic ideas in the Constitution. He argued tirelessly for a strong national government, for separate branches of government, and for rights such as freedom of religion. He then rallied support for adoption of the Constitution and the Bill of Rights. In 1809 Madison became the fourth president of the United States. As president, he led the country through another war with Britain, the War of 1812. He and his wife, Dolley, were forced to flee Washington temporarily when the British invaded the capital and set fire to the White House.

Summarizing Why is Madison known as the Father of the Constitution?

KEY EVENTS

1780
Madison serves in the Continental Congress.

1787
Madison keeps a written record of the Constitutional Convention.

1787–1788
Madison helps write the *Federalist Papers*, urging support for the Constitution.

1801–1809
Madison serves as secretary of state under President Thomas Jefferson.

1809–1817
Madison serves two terms as president.

James Madison was an important force in the writing of the Constitution.

CITIZENSHIP AND THE CONSTITUTION **187**

Biography

Reading Focus Question

Have students discuss the introductory question. Ask them to consider the actions the founding fathers took to create a new government for the United States. What did the founding fathers think the purpose of government was? *(such as, to serve the people and to promote the common good)* What did they create to serve as the foundation of the government? *(U.S. Constitution)* Tell students to consider Madison's role in creating the U.S. government as they read his biography.

Info to Know

Madison: Supporter for Independence
James Madison was an early supporter of colonial independence from Great Britain. While a student at the College of New Jersey (now Princeton University), he participated in demonstrations against British control of the colonies. He was later elected to Virginia's 1776 Revolutionary convention.

Madison: Father of the Constitution
During Madison's lifetime, people began calling him the Father of the Constitution. He disliked the nickname, though, and thought it inappropriate. The Constitution was not "the off-spring of a single brain," he explained, but rather "the work of many heads and many hands."

Critical Thinking: Summarizing

At Level

Tribute to Madison

1. Ask students to imagine that they are hosting a tribute to James Madison in his later years.

2. Have each student write a short speech to introduce Madison before he speaks to the audience. The speech should summarize Madison's many accomplishments and explain his significance in the formation of the U.S. government.

3. Ask volunteers to present their Madison introductions to the class. **LS Verbal/Linguistic**

4. **Extend** Have students create the design for a plaque to award to Madison at the tribute. The plaque should focus on Madison's contributions to the writing of the Constitution and as a U.S. president. **LS Verbal/Linguistic, Visual/Spatial**

Alternative Assessment Handbook, Rubrics 3: Artwork; and 37: Writing Assignments

Answers

Summarizing *He provided many of the basic ideas in the Constitution and rallied support for its adoption.*

187

Info to Know

The Preamble Although short, the Preamble was hotly debated in the state ratifying conventions. The delegates objected to the Preamble's opening phrase "We the People," because they had been appointed by the states, rather than elected by the people. Patrick Henry challenged this phrase during the ratifying process in Virginia, saying "The people gave them [the delegates to the Constitutional Convention] no power to use their name. That they exceeded their power is perfectly clear."

Interpret What do you think the three opening words of the Preamble to the Constitution mean? *Students might suggest that the words are stating that the American people have the power to create a Constitution and to establish a government.*

CRF: Primary Source Activity: Thomas Paine, *The Rights of Man*

Teaching Tip

Reading Roman Numerals Some students may have trouble reading the Roman numerals that appear in the Constitution. Before starting the document, spend a few minutes going over the Roman numeral system with the class. If possible, provide students with a chart defining Roman numerals through 30.

The Constitution of the United States

Preamble
The short and dignified preamble explains the goals of the new government under the Constitution.

We the People of the United States, in Order to form a more perfect Union, establish Justice, insure domestic Tranquility, provide for the common defense, promote the general Welfare, and secure the Blessings of Liberty to ourselves and our Posterity, do ordain and establish this Constitution for the United States of America.

Note: The parts of the Constitution that have been lined through are no longer in force or no longer apply because of later amendments. The titles of the sections and articles are added for easier reference.

Article I   The Legislature

Section 1.   Congress

All legislative Powers herein granted shall be vested in a Congress of the United States, which shall consist of a Senate and House of Representatives.

Section 2.   The House of Representatives

1. Elections   The House of Representatives shall be composed of Members chosen every second Year by the People of the several States, and the Electors in each State shall have the Qualifications requisite for Electors of the most numerous Branch of the State Legislature.

2. Qualifications   No Person shall be a Representative who shall not have attained to the Age of twenty five Years, and been seven Years a Citizen of the United States, and who shall not, when elected, be an Inhabitant of that State in which he shall be chosen.

3. Number of Representatives   Representatives and direct Taxes shall be apportioned among the several States which may be included within this Union, according to their respective Numbers, which shall be determined by adding to the whole Number of free Persons, including **those bound to Service**[1] for a Term of Years, and excluding Indians not taxed, three fifths of **all other Persons**.[2] The actual **Enumeration**[3] shall be made within three Years after the first Meeting of the Congress of the United States, and within every subsequent Term of ten Years, in such Manner as they shall by Law direct. The Number of Representatives shall not exceed one for every thirty Thousand, but each State shall have at Least one Representative; and until such enumeration shall be made, the State of New Hampshire shall be entitled to choose three, Massachoosetts eight, Rhode-Island and Providence Plantations one, Connecticut five, New-York six, New Jersey four, Pennsylvania eight, Delaware one, Maryland six, Virginia ten, North Carolina five, South Carolina five, and Georgia three.

4. Vacancies   When vacancies happen in the Representation from any State, the Executive Authority thereof shall issue Writs of Election to fill such Vacancies.

5. Officers and Impeachment   The House of Representatives shall choose their Speaker and other Officers; and shall have the sole Power of impeachment.

Legislative Branch

Article I explains how the legislative branch, called Congress, is organized. The chief purpose of the legislative branch is to make laws. Congress is made up of the Senate and the House of Representatives.

The House of Representatives

The number of members each state has in the House is based on the population of the individual state. In 1929 Congress permanently fixed the size of the House at 435 members.

Vocabulary

[1] **those bound to Service** indentured servants

[2] **all other Persons** slaves

[3] **Enumeration** census or official population count

Main Idea

Recall What two groups make up Congress? *the House of Representatives and the Senate*

Identify What information about the House of Representatives is outlined in Article I, Section 2 of the Constitution? *elections, qualifications, number of representatives, vacancies, officers, and impeachment*

Summarize What powers are granted to the House of Representatives? *to make laws, to choose the Speaker of the House and other officers, and to impeach*

Connect to Civics: Justice

The House as a Court The House of Representatives helps make the nation's laws. Sometimes, however, the House becomes a court of law. This situation may occur if a high-ranking federal official disobeys the law. The Constitution gives the House the authority to bring charges against the individual. If the House does so, the Senate conducts the trial.

Did you know . . .

The Union passed the first income tax during the Civil War to pay for maintaining the army.

Main Idea

Recall How many senators are elected from each state? *two*

Summarize What privileges are outlined in Article I, Section 6? *Senators and representatives are paid for their services out of the U.S. Treasury, and they have a number of other privileges, including immunity from arrest except in cases of treason, felony, and breach of peace.*

📦 Quick Facts Transparency: Federal Office Terms and Requirements

Connect to Civics: Responsibility

The Seventeenth Amendment Senators are no longer "chosen by the Legislature thereof," but rather are elected by the people of their state. The Seventeenth Amendment made this change to the Constitution. Before voting, all citizens have the responsibility to learn about the candidates, such as senators and other officials.

Exploring the Document

allows one branch of government to exert power over another branch of government

---

The Vice President

The only duty that the Constitution assigns to the vice president is to preside over meetings of the Senate. Modern presidents have usually given their vice presidents more responsibilities.

EXPLORING THE DOCUMENT If the House of Representatives charges a government official with wrongdoing, the Senate acts as a court to decide if the official is guilty. **How does the power of impeachment represent part of the system of checks and balances?**

Vocabulary

[4] **pro tempore** temporarily

[5] **Impeachments** official accusations of federal wrongdoing

---

Section 3. The Senate

1. Number of Senators The Senate of the United States shall be composed of two Senators from each State, ~~chosen by the Legislature thereof,~~ for six Years; and each Senator shall have one Vote.

2. Classifying Terms Immediately after they shall be assembled in Consequence of the first Election, they shall be divided as equally as may be into three Classes. The Seats of the Senators of the first Class shall be vacated at the Expiration of the second Year, of the second Class at the Expiration of the fourth Year, and of the third Class at the Expiration of the sixth Year, so that one third may be chosen every second Year; ~~and if Vacancies happen by Resignation, or otherwise, during the Recess of the Legislature of any State, the Executive thereof may make temporary Appointments until the next Meeting of the Legislature, which shall then fill such Vacancies.~~

3. Qualifications No Person shall be a Senator who shall not have attained to the Age of thirty Years, and been nine Years a Citizen of the United States, and who shall not, when elected, be an Inhabitant of that State for which he shall be chosen.

4. Role of Vice-President The Vice President of the United States shall be President of the Senate, but shall have no Vote, unless they be equally divided.

5. Officers The Senate shall choose their other Officers, and also a President **pro tempore**,[4] in the Absence of the Vice President, or when he shall exercise the Office of President of the United States.

6. Impeachment Trials The Senate shall have the sole Power to try all **Impeachments**.[5] When sitting for that Purpose, they shall be on Oath or Affirmation. When the President of the United States is tried, the Chief Justice shall preside: And no Person shall be convicted without the Concurrence of two thirds of the Members present.

7. Punishment for Impeachment Judgment in Cases of Impeachment shall not extend further than to removal from Office, and disqualification to hold and enjoy any Office of honor, Trust or Profit under the United States: but the Party convicted shall nevertheless be liable and subject to Indictment, Trial, Judgment and Punishment, according to Law.

Federal Office Terms and Requirements — QUICK FACTS

Position	Term	Minimum Age	Residency	Citizenship
President	4 years	35	14 years in the U.S.	natural-born
Vice President	4 years	35	14 years in the U.S.	natural-born
Supreme Court Justice	unlimited	none	none	none
Senator	6 years	30	state in which elected	9 years
Representative	2 years	25	state in which elected	7 years

Section 4. Congressional Elections

1. Regulations The Times, Places and Manner of holding Elections for Senators and Representatives, shall be prescribed in each State by the Legislature thereof; but the Congress may at any time by Law make or alter such Regulations, except as to the Places of choosing Senators.

2. Sessions ~~The Congress shall assemble at least once in every Year, and such Meeting shall be on the first Monday in December, unless they shall by Law appoint a different Day.~~

Section 5. Rules/Procedures

1. Quorum Each House shall be the Judge of the Elections, Returns and Qualifications of its own Members, and a Majority of each shall constitute a **Quorum**[6] to do Business; but a smaller Number may **adjourn**[7] from day to day, and may be authorized to compel the Attendance of absent Members, in such Manner, and under such Penalties as each House may provide.

2. Rules and Conduct Each House may determine the Rules of its Proceedings, punish its Members for disorderly Behaviour, and, with the Concurrence of two thirds, expel a Member.

3. Records Each House shall keep a Journal of its Proceedings, and from time to time publish the same, excepting such Parts as may in their Judgment require Secrecy; and the Yeas and Nays of the Members of either House on any question shall, at the Desire of one fifth of those Present, be entered on the Journal.

4. Adjournment Neither House, during the Session of Congress, shall, without the Consent of the other, adjourn for more than three days, nor to any other Place than that in which the two Houses shall be sitting.

Section 6. Payment

1. Salary The Senators and Representatives shall receive a Compensation for their Services, to be ascertained by Law, and paid out of the Treasury of the United States. They shall in all Cases, except Treason, Felony and Breach of the Peace, be privileged from Arrest during their Attendance at the Session of their respective Houses, and in going to and returning from the same; and for any Speech or Debate in either House, they shall not be questioned in any other Place.

2. Restrictions No Senator or Representative shall, during the Time for which he was elected, be appointed to any civil Office under the Authority of the United States, which shall have been created, or the **Emoluments**[8] whereof shall have been increased during such time; and no Person holding any Office under the United States, shall be a Member of either House during his **Continuance**[9] in Office.

Vocabulary

[6] **Quorum** the minimum number of people needed to conduct business

[7] **adjourn** to stop indefinitely

[8] **Emoluments** salary

[9] **Continuance** term

Historical Documents

Info to Know

Senate Firsts Since the Senate's first session in New York City on March 4, 1789, a number of other firsts have taken place in the U.S. Senate.

- September 30, 1788—first two senators elected: Robert Morris and William Maclay, both from Pennsylvania

- November 1816—first former senator to be elected president: James Monroe

- February 1870—first African American to take the oath as U.S. Senator: Hiram R. Revels

- November 1922—first female senator appointed: Rebecca Felton

- January 2001—first presidential First Lady to be elected senator: Hillary Rodham Clinton

Connect to Science and Technology

Availability of Information For many years, the best way for the public to learn about congressional proceedings was to consult the *Congressional Record*, a bulky set of printed volumes. With the increased availability of the Internet, tracking a congressperson's votes has become much easier. The Library of Congress publishes a Web site that covers many aspects of the government. In addition, independent organizations, such as Project Vote Smart, provide links to track congressional votes.

go.hrw.com

Online Resources

KEYWORD: SR8 US6
ACTIVITY: Library of Congress: Checking on Your Legislators

Vocabulary

[10] **Bills** proposed laws

EXPLORING THE DOCUMENT The framers felt that because members of the House are elected every two years, representatives would listen to the public and seek its approval before passing taxes. **How does Section 7 address the colonial demand of "no taxation without representation"?**

EXPLORING THE DOCUMENT The veto power of the president is one of the important checks and balances in the Constitution. **Why do you think the framers included the ability of Congress to override a veto?**

Section 7. How a Bill Becomes a Law

1. Tax Bills All **Bills**[10] for raising Revenue shall originate in the House of Representatives; but the Senate may propose or concur with Amendments as on other Bills.

2. Lawmaking Every Bill which shall have passed the House of Representatives and the Senate, shall, before it become a Law, be presented to the President of the United States: If he approve he shall sign it, but if not he shall return it, with his Objections to that House in which it shall have originated, who shall enter the Objections at large on their Journal, and proceed to reconsider it. If after such Reconsideration two thirds of that House shall agree to pass the Bill, it shall be sent, together with the Objections, to the other House, by which it shall likewise be reconsidered, and if approved by two thirds of that House, it shall become a Law. But in all such Cases the Votes of both Houses shall be determined by yeas and Nays, and the Names of the Persons voting for and against the Bill shall be entered on the Journal of each House respectively. If any Bill shall not be returned by the President within ten Days (Sundays excepted) after it shall have been presented to him, the Same shall be a Law, in like Manner as if he had signed it, unless the Congress by their Adjournment prevent its Return, in which Case it shall not be a Law.

3. Role of the President Every Order, Resolution, or Vote to which the Concurrence of the Senate and House of Representatives may be necessary (except on a question of Adjournment) shall be presented to the President of the United States; and before the Same shall take Effect, shall be approved by him, or being disapproved by him, shall be repassed by two thirds of the Senate and House of Representatives, according to the Rules and Limitations prescribed in the Case of a Bill.

How a Bill Becomes a Law

❶ A member of the House or the Senate introduces a bill and refers it to a committee.

❷ The House or Senate Committee may approve, rewrite, or kill the bill.

❸ The House or the Senate debates and votes on its version of the bill.

❹ House and Senate conference committee members work out the differences between the two versions.

❺ Both houses of Congress pass the revised bill.

Section 8.

Powers Granted to Congress

1. Taxation The Congress shall have Power To lay and collect Taxes, **Duties,**[11] **Imposts**[12] and **Excises,**[13] to pay the Debts and provide for the common Defense and general Welfare of the United States; but all Duties, Imposts and Excises shall be uniform throughout the United States;

2. Credit To borrow Money on the credit of the United States;

3. Commerce To regulate Commerce with foreign Nations, and among the several States, and with the Indian Tribes;

4. Naturalization and Bankruptcy To establish an uniform **Rule of Naturalization,**[14] and uniform Laws on the subject of Bankruptcies throughout the United States;

5. Money To coin Money, regulate the Value thereof, and of foreign Coin, and fix the Standard of Weights and Measures;

6. Counterfeiting To provide for the Punishment of counterfeiting the **Securities**[15] and current Coin of the United States;

7. Post Office To establish Post Offices and post Roads;

8. Patents and Copyrights To promote the Progress of Science and useful Arts, by securing for limited Times to Authors and Inventors the exclusive Right to their respective Writings and Discoveries;

9. Courts To constitute Tribunals inferior to the supreme Court;

10. International Law To define and punish Piracies and Felonies committed on the high Seas, and Offences against the Law of Nations;

Vocabulary

[11] **Duties** tariffs

[12] **Imposts** taxes

[13] **Excises** internal taxes on the manufacture, sale, or consumption of a commodity

[14] **Rule of Naturalization** a law by which a foreign-born person becomes a citizen

[15] **Securities** bonds

6 The president signs or vetoes the bill.

7 Two-thirds majority vote of Congress is needed to approve a vetoed bill. Bill becomes a law.

ANALYSIS SKILL **ANALYZING INFORMATION**
Why do you think the framers created this complex system for adopting laws?

CITIZENSHIP AND THE CONSTITUTION **193**

Answers

Linking to Today *individual states or smaller nations under the umbrella of the U.S. government*

Analyzing Information *to make certain the laws passed represent the will of the people and the good of the nation*

Main Idea

Describe What do Clauses 11–16 ensure and regulate? *control of the military*

Summarize What Congressional powers are explained in Clause 17? *Congress has the power to make laws for the District of Columbia, the nation's capital. Congress also has the power to regulate use of other property belonging to the national government, such as forts and arsenals.*

Make Inferences Why do you think the framers of the Constitution included a clause prohibiting titles of nobility? *Students might respond that the framers wanted to make sure that no class system or aristocracy would exist in the United States as it did in Great Britain.*

Connect to Civics: Authority

Activity Ask students to conduct research on the minimum wage law or on the creation of military academies as examples of when the elastic clause was used to meet the changing needs of American society. Then have each student write a letter to the framers of the Constitution. In their letters, students should use their research to explain how future government officials have used the elastic clause and their authority responsibly.

Vocabulary

[16] **Letters of Marque and Reprisal** documents issued by governments allowing merchant ships to arm themselves and attack ships of an enemy nation

The Elastic Clause

The framers of the Constitution wanted a national government that was strong enough to be effective. This section lists the powers given to Congress. The last portion of Section 8 contains the so-called elastic clause.

11. War To declare War, grant **Letters of Marque and Reprisal**,[16] and make Rules concerning Captures on Land and Water;

12. Army To raise and support Armies, but no Appropriation of Money to that Use shall be for a longer Term than two Years;

13. Navy To provide and maintain a Navy;

14. Regulation of the Military To make Rules for the Government and Regulation of the land and naval Forces;

15. Militia To provide for calling forth the Militia to execute the Laws of the Union, suppress Insurrections and repel Invasions;

16. Regulation of the Militia To provide for organizing, arming, and disciplining, the Militia, and for governing such Part of them as may be employed in the Service of the United States, reserving to the States respectively, the Appointment of the Officers, and the Authority of training the Militia according to the discipline prescribed by Congress;

17. District of Columbia To exercise exclusive Legislation in all Cases whatsoever, over such District (not exceeding ten Miles square) as may, by Cession of particular States, and the Acceptance of Congress, become the Seat of the Government of the United States, and to exercise like Authority over all Places purchased by the Consent of the Legislature of the State in which the Same shall be, for the Erection of Forts, Magazines, Arsenals, dock-Yards, and other needful Buildings;—And

18. Necessary and Proper Clause To make all Laws which shall be necessary and proper for carrying into Execution the foregoing Powers, and all other Powers vested by this Constitution in the Government of the United States, or in any Department or Officer thereof.

The Elastic Clause

The elastic clause has been stretched (like elastic) to allow Congress to meet changing circumstances.

Section 9. Powers Denied Congress

1. Slave Trade ~~The Migration or Importation of such Persons as any of the States now existing shall think proper to admit, shall not be prohibited by the Congress prior to the Year one thousand eight hundred and eight, but a Tax or duty may be imposed on such Importation, not exceeding ten dollars for each Person.~~

2. Habeas Corpus The Privilege of the **Writ of Habeas Corpus**[17] shall not be suspended, unless when in Cases of Rebellion or Invasion the public Safety may require it.

3. Illegal Punishment No **Bill of Attainder**[18] or **ex post facto Law**[19] shall be passed.

4. Direct Taxes No **Capitation**,[20] or other direct, Tax shall be laid, unless in Proportion to the Census or enumeration herein before directed to be taken.

5. Export Taxes No Tax or Duty shall be laid on Articles exported from any State.

6. No Favorites No Preference shall be given by any Regulation of Commerce or Revenue to the Ports of one State over those of another; nor shall Vessels bound to, or from, one State, be obliged to enter, clear, or pay Duties in another.

7. Public Money No Money shall be drawn from the Treasury, but in Consequence of Appropriations made by Law; and a regular Statement and Account of the Receipts and Expenditures of all public Money shall be published from time to time.

8. Titles of Nobility No Title of Nobility shall be granted by the United States: And no Person holding any Office of Profit or Trust under them, shall, without the Consent of the Congress, accept of any present, Emolument, Office, or Title, of any kind whatever, from any King, Prince, or foreign State.

Section 10. | Powers Denied the States

1. Restrictions No State shall enter into any Treaty, Alliance, or Confederation; grant Letters of Marque and Reprisal; coin Money; emit Bills of Credit; make any Thing but gold and silver Coin a Tender in Payment of Debts; pass any Bill of Attainder, ex post facto Law, or Law impairing the Obligation of Contracts, or grant any Title of Nobility.

2. Import and Export Taxes No State shall, without the Consent of the Congress, lay any Imposts or Duties on Imports or Exports, except what may be absolutely necessary for executing it's inspection Laws: and the net Produce of all Duties and Imposts, laid by any State on Imports or Exports, shall be for the Use of the Treasury of the United States; and all such Laws shall be subject to the Revision and Control of the Congress.

3. Peacetime and War Restraints No State shall, without the Consent of Congress, lay any Duty of Tonnage, keep Troops, or Ships of War in time of Peace, enter into any Agreement or Compact with another State, or with a foreign Power, or engage in War, unless actually invaded, or in such imminent Danger as will not admit of delay.

EXPLORING THE DOCUMENT Although Congress has implied powers, there are also limits to its powers. Section 9 lists powers that are denied to the federal government. Several of the clauses protect the people of the United States from unjust treatment. **In what ways does the Constitution limit the powers of the federal government?**

Vocabulary

[17] **Writ of Habeas Corpus** a court order that requires the government to bring a prisoner to court and explain why he or she is being held

[18] **Bill of Attainder** a law declaring that a person is guilty of a particular crime

[19] **ex post facto Law** a law that is made effective prior to the date that it was passed and therefore punishes people for acts that were not illegal at the time

[20] **Capitation** a direct uniform tax imposed on each head, or person

Info to Know

Writ of Habeas Corpus The term *habeas corpus* derives from Medieval Latin and means "you shall have the body." This protection against unlawful imprisonment is the only civil liberty that the framers included in the original text of the Constitution. All other basic rights and liberties guaranteed to American citizens are outlined in the Bill of Rights.

Exploring the Document

The government cannot suspend the writ of habeas corpus or pass bills of attainder or ex post facto laws.

Main Idea

Identify Which branch of the government is outlined in Article II? *the executive branch*

Make Inferences Why might many of the delegates to the Constitutional Convention have opposed a one-person executive? *Students might suggest that the delegates feared that they might create another monarchy, as in Great Britain.*

Summarize How are the president and vice president elected? *They are chosen by the electoral college—electors chosen by the states according to rules established by the legislatures.*

Map Transparency: The Electoral College

Info to Know

The U.S. President Initially, the writers of the Constitution agreed that the president would be chosen by the national legislature for a single, seven-year term. Many delegates opposed a strong executive branch. However, when the Constitution was turned over to the Committee on Style, Gouverneur Morris, who wanted a stronger executive, reworded the article outlining the role of the president. He shortened the length of the president's term, allowed the president to run for more than one term, and altered the method by which the president would be elected. These changes passed with little debate. For one, the delegates were ready to go home. For another, many members thought that George Washington would be the first president and believed that he would not abuse the power of the executive branch.

Executive Branch

The president is the chief of the executive branch. It is the job of the president to enforce the laws. The framers wanted the president's and vice president's terms of office and manner of selection to be different from those of members of Congress. They decided on four-year terms, but they had a difficult time agreeing on how to select the president and vice president. The framers finally set up an electoral system, which varies greatly from our electoral process today.

Presidential Elections

In 1845 Congress set the Tuesday following the first Monday in November of every fourth year as the general election date for selecting presidential electors.

Article II The Executive

Section 1. The Presidency

1. Terms of Office The executive Power shall be vested in a President of the United States of America. He shall hold his Office during the Term of four Years, and, together with the Vice President, chosen for the same Term, be elected, as follows:

2. Electoral College Each State shall appoint, in such Manner as the Legislature thereof may direct, a Number of Electors, equal to the whole Number of Senators and Representatives to which the State may be entitled in the Congress: but no Senator or Representative, or Person holding an Office of Trust or Profit under the United States, shall be appointed an Elector.

3. Former Method of Electing President ~~The Electors shall meet in their respective States, and vote by Ballot for two Persons, of whom one at least shall not be an Inhabitant of the same State with themselves. And they shall make a List of all the Persons voted for, and of the Number of Votes for each; which List they shall sign and certify, and transmit sealed to the Seat of the Government of the United States, directed to the President of the Senate. The President of the Senate shall, in the Presence of the Senate and House of Representatives, open all the Certificates, and the Votes shall~~

The Electoral College

11 Number of Electors

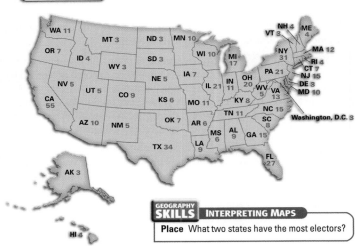

GEOGRAPHY **SKILLS** INTERPRETING MAPS

Place What two states have the most electors?

Answers

Interpreting Maps *California (55) and Texas (34)*

then be counted. The Person having the greatest Number of Votes shall be the President, if such Number be a Majority of the whole Number of Electors appointed; and if there be more than one who have such Majority, and have an equal Number of Votes, then the House of Representatives shall immediately choose by Ballot one of them for President; and if no Person have a Majority, then from the five highest on the List the said House shall in like Manner choose the President. But in choosing the President, the Votes shall be taken by States, the Representation from each State having one Vote; A quorum for this purpose shall consist of a Member or Members from two thirds of the States, and a Majority of all the States shall be necessary to a Choice. In every Case, after the Choice of the President, the Person having the greatest Number of Votes of the Electors shall be the Vice President. But if there should remain two or more who have equal Votes, the Senate shall choose from them by Ballot the Vice President.

4. Election Day The Congress may determine the Time of choosing the Electors, and the Day on which they shall give their Votes; which Day shall be the same throughout the United States.

5. Qualifications No Person except a natural born Citizen, or a Citizen of the United States, at the time of the Adoption of this Constitution, shall be eligible to the Office of President; neither shall any Person be eligible to that Office who shall not have attained to the Age of thirty five Years, and been fourteen Years a Resident within the United States.

6. Succession In Case of the Removal of the President from Office, or of his Death, Resignation, or Inability to discharge the Powers and Duties of the said Office, the Same shall devolve on the Vice President, and the Congress may by Law provide for the Case of Removal, Death, Resignation or Inability, both of the President and Vice President, declaring what Officer shall then act as President, and such Officer shall act accordingly, until the Disability be removed, or a President shall be elected.

7. Salary The President shall, at stated Times, receive for his Services, a Compensation, which shall neither be increased nor diminished during the Period for which he shall have been elected, and he shall not receive within that Period any other Emolument from the United States, or any of them.

8. Oath of Office Before he enter on the Execution of his Office, he shall take the following Oath or Affirmation:—"I do solemnly swear (or affirm) that I will faithfully execute the Office of President of the United States, and will to the best of my Ability, preserve, protect and defend the Constitution of the United States."

EXPLORING THE DOCUMENT The youngest elected president was John F. Kennedy; he was 43 years old when he was inaugurated. (Theodore Roosevelt was 42 when he assumed office after the assassination of McKinley.) **What is the minimum required age for the office of president?**

Presidential Salary

In 1999 Congress voted to set future presidents' salaries at $400,000 per year. The president also receives an annual expense account. The president must pay taxes only on the salary.

Historical Documents

Info to Know

Presidential Qualifications Political concerns of the time determined many of the qualifications for the presidency included in the U.S. Constitution. For example, during the Constitutional Convention, a rumor spread that the delegates intended to invite a foreign king to rule the country. To squelch this rumor, the delegates included a constitutional provision requiring the president to be a natural-born citizen. In addition, the delegates added a 14-year residency requirement for the president to disqualify any Loyalists who had left during the American Revolution and then returned to the United States.

Exploring the Document
35 years old

Historical Documents

Did you know . . .

The term *first lady* became common after the Civil War. Before that time, presidents' wives were referred to as Mrs. President or presidentress. Although first ladies are not mentioned in the Constitution, almost all presidents—even unmarried ones—have found someone to fill that role. For example, Dolley Madison served as first lady for widower Thomas Jefferson, before assuming that role for her own husband. Recent first ladies have done more than serve as their husbands' hostesses, however. Some first ladies—such as Eleanor Roosevelt, Betty Ford, Rosalynn Carter, and Hillary Rodham Clinton—have had highly visible roles.

go.hrw.com

Online Resources

KEYWORD: SR8 US6
ACTIVITY: First Ladies Biographies

Commander in Chief

Today the president is in charge of the army, navy, air force, marines, and coast guard. Only Congress, however, can decide if the United States will declare war.

Appointments

Most of the president's appointments to office must be approved by the Senate.

Vocabulary

[21] **Reprieves** delays of punishment

[22] **Pardons** releases from the legal penalties associated with a crime

The State of the Union

Every year the president presents to Congress a State of the Union message. In this message, the president introduces and explains a legislative plan for the coming year.

Section 2. | Powers of Presidency |

1. Military Powers The President shall be Commander in Chief of the Army and Navy of the United States, and of the Militia of the several States, when called into the actual Service of the United States; he may require the Opinion, in writing, of the principal Officer in each of the executive Departments, upon any Subject relating to the Duties of their respective Offices, and he shall have Power to grant **Reprieves**[21] and **Pardons**[22] for Offences against the United States, except in Cases of Impeachment.

2. Treaties and Appointments He shall have Power, by and with the Advice and Consent of the Senate, to make Treaties, provided two thirds of the Senators present concur; and he shall nominate, and by and with the Advice and Consent of the Senate, shall appoint Ambassadors, other public Ministers and Consuls, Judges of the supreme Court, and all other Officers of the United States, whose Appointments are not herein otherwise provided for, and which shall be established by Law: but the Congress may by Law vest the Appointment of such inferior Officers, as they think proper, in the President alone, in the Courts of Law, or in the Heads of Departments.

3. Vacancies The President shall have Power to fill up all Vacancies that may happen during the Recess of the Senate, by granting Commissions which shall expire at the End of their next Session.

Section 3. | Presidential Duties |

He shall from time to time give to the Congress Information of the State of the Union, and recommend to their Consideration such Measures as he shall judge necessary and expedient; he may, on extraordinary Occasions, convene both Houses, or either of them, and in Case of Disagreement between them, with Respect to the Time of Adjournment, he may adjourn them to such Time as he shall think proper; he shall receive Ambassadors and other public Ministers; he shall take Care that the Laws be faithfully executed, and shall Commission all the Officers of the United States.

Section 4. | Impeachment |

The President, Vice President and all civil Officers of the United States, shall be removed from Office on Impeachment for, and Conviction of, Treason, Bribery, or other high Crimes and Misdemeanors.

Article III — The Judiciary

Section 1. — Federal Courts and Judges

The judicial Power of the United States shall be vested in one supreme Court, and in such inferior Courts as the Congress may from time to time ordain and establish. The Judges, both of the supreme and inferior Courts, shall hold their Offices during good Behavior, and shall, at stated Times, receive for their Services a Compensation, which shall not be diminished during their Continuance in Office.

Section 2. — Authority of the Courts

1. General Authority The judicial Power shall extend to all Cases, in Law and Equity, arising under this Constitution, the Laws of the United States, and Treaties made, or which shall be made, under their Authority;—to all Cases affecting Ambassadors, other public Ministers and Consuls;—to all Cases of admiralty and maritime Jurisdiction;—to Controversies to which the United States shall be a Party;—to Controversies between two or more States —between a State and Citizens of another State; —between Citizens of different States;—between Citizens of the same State claiming Lands under Grants of different States, and between a State, or the Citizens thereof, and foreign States, Citizens or Subjects.

2. Supreme Authority In all Cases affecting Ambassadors, other public Ministers and Consuls, and those in which a State shall be Party, the supreme Court shall have original Jurisdiction. In all the other Cases before mentioned, the supreme Court shall have appellate Jurisdiction, both as to Law and Fact, with such Exceptions, and under such Regulations as the Congress shall make.

Federal Judicial System QUICK FACTS

Supreme Court
Reviews cases appealed from lower federal courts and highest state courts

Courts of Appeals
Review appeals from district courts

District Courts
Hold trials

Judicial Branch

The Articles of Confederation did not set up a federal court system. One of the first points that the framers of the Constitution agreed upon was to set up a national judiciary. In the Judiciary Act of 1789, Congress provided for the establishment of lower courts, such as district courts, circuit courts of appeals, and various other federal courts. The judicial system provides a check on the legislative branch: it can declare a law unconstitutional.

Biography

John Marshall (1755–1835) The U.S. Supreme Court was considered a fairly unimportant institution in its early years. When John Marshall was appointed chief justice in 1801, the Supreme Court did not even have its own building. As chief justice, Marshall established the Supreme Court as the final interpreter of the Constitution and made the Court into an important check on the president and Congress.

Identify What is the primary subject of Article IV? *relations among states*

Explain What rights are citizens entitled to if they move to or visit another state? *the same privileges and immunities of citizens of that state*

📦 Quick Facts Transparency: Federalism

Exploring the Document

allows the people rather than the federal government to determine the laws of each state

Vocabulary

[23] **Corruption of Blood** punishing the family of a person convicted of treason

The States

States must honor the laws, records, and court decisions of other states. A person cannot escape a legal obligation by moving from one state to another.

EXPLORING THE DOCUMENT The framers wanted to ensure that citizens could determine how state governments would operate. **How does the need to respect the laws of each state support the principle of popular sovereignty?**

3. Trial by Jury The Trial of all Crimes, except in Cases of Impeachment, shall be by Jury; and such Trial shall be held in the State where the said Crimes shall have been committed; but when not committed within any State, the Trial shall be at such Place or Places as the Congress may by Law have directed.

Section 3. Treason

1. Definition Treason against the United States, shall consist only in levying War against them, or in adhering to their Enemies, giving them Aid and Comfort. No Person shall be convicted of Treason unless on the Testimony of two Witnesses to the same overt Act, or on Confession in open Court.

2. Punishment The Congress shall have Power to declare the Punishment of Treason, but no Attainder of Treason shall work **Corruption of Blood**,[23] or Forfeiture except during the Life of the Person attainted.

Article IV Relations among States

Section 1. State Acts and Records

Full Faith and Credit shall be given in each State to the public Acts, Records, and judicial Proceedings of every other State. And the Congress may by general Laws prescribe the Manner in which such Acts, Records and Proceedings shall be proved, and the Effect thereof.

Section 2. Rights of Citizens

1. Citizenship The Citizens of each State shall be entitled to all Privileges and Immunities of Citizens in the several States.

2. Extradition A Person charged in any State with Treason, Felony, or other Crime, who shall flee from Justice, and be found in another State, shall on Demand of the executive Authority of the State from which he fled, be delivered up, to be removed to the State having Jurisdiction of the Crime.

3. Fugitive Slaves No Person held to Service or Labour in one State, under the Laws thereof, escaping into another, shall, in Consequence of any Law or Regulation therein, be discharged from such Service or Labour, but shall be delivered up on Claim of the Party to whom such Service or Labour may be due.

Federalism QUICK FACTS

National
- Declare war
- Maintain armed forces
- Regulate interstate and foreign trade
- Admit new states
- Establish post offices
- Set standard weights and measures
- Coin money
- Establish foreign policy
- Make all laws necessary and proper for carrying out delegated powers

Shared
- Maintain law and order
- Levy taxes
- Borrow money
- Charter banks
- Establish courts
- Provide for public welfare

State
- Establish and maintain schools
- Establish local governments
- Regulate business within the state
- Make marriage laws
- Provide for public safety
- Assume other powers not delegated to the national government or prohibited to the states

ANALYSIS SKILL | **ANALYZING INFORMATION**

Why does the power to declare war belong only to the national government?

Section 3. | New States

1. Admission New States may be admitted by the Congress into this Union; but no new State shall be formed or erected within the Jurisdiction of any other State; nor any State be formed by the Junction of two or more States, or Parts of States, without the Consent of the Legislatures of the States concerned as well as of the Congress.

2. Congressional Authority The Congress shall have Power to dispose of and make all needful Rules and Regulations respecting the Territory or other Property belonging to the United States; and nothing in this Constitution shall be so construed as to Prejudice any Claims of the United States, or of any particular State.

Section 4. | Guarantees to the States

The United States shall guarantee to every State in this Union a Republican Form of Government, and shall protect each of them against Invasion; and on Application of the Legislature, or of the Executive (when the Legislature cannot be convened), against domestic Violence.

EXPLORING THE DOCUMENT In a republic, voters elect representatives to act in their best interest. **How does Article IV protect the practice of republicanism in the United States?**

Linking to Today

Admission of New States Although the framers of the Constitution wanted to allow new states to be admitted, many also wanted to preserve the power of the original states. One delegate suggested that the new states' total number of House representatives should never exceed the original states' total number of representatives.

Draw Conclusions If this suggestion had become part of the Constitution, how might it have affected the current U.S. government? *States along the Atlantic coast would have a disproportionate amount of political power.*

Exploring the Document
guarantees that every state will have a representative government

---

Answers

Analyzing Information *to prevent states from declaring war on one another or on a foreign nation*

201

Historical Documents

Linking to Today

Amendments to the Constitution Of the thousands of proposals for amendments to the Constitution, only 33 have obtained the required two-thirds vote in Congress. One historic amendment, the Equal Rights Amendment, was first proposed in 1923, but is still not part of the U.S. Constitution.

Activity **Researching the ERA**
Organize the class into small groups to conduct research on the Equal Rights Amendment. Assign each group one of the following research topics: the text of the Equal Rights Amendment (ERA); Alice Paul, the author of the ERA; the history of the ERA; the current political status of the amendment; and arguments for and against making the ERA part of the Constitution. Have each group present its findings to the class.
LS Interpersonal, Verbal/Linguistic

Exploring the Document

See the chart, Amending the U.S. Constitution, at right; possible answer—changes in American society or culture

EXPLORING THE DOCUMENT America's founders may not have realized how long the Constitution would last, but they did set up a system for changing or adding to it. They did not want to make it easy to change the Constitution. **By what methods may the Constitution be amended? Under what sorts of circumstances do you think an amendment might be necessary?**

National Supremacy

One of the biggest problems facing the delegates to the Constitutional Convention was the question of what would happen if a state law and a federal law conflicted. Which law would be followed? Who would decide? The second clause of Article VI answers those questions. When a federal law and a state law disagree, the federal law overrides the state law. The Constitution and other federal laws are the "supreme Law of the Land." This clause is often called the supremacy clause.

Article V | Amending the Constitution

The Congress, whenever two thirds of both Houses shall deem it necessary, shall propose Amendments to this Constitution, or, on the Application of the Legislatures of two thirds of the several States, shall call a Convention for proposing Amendments, which, in either Case, shall be valid to all Intents and Purposes, as Part of this Constitution, when ratified by the Legislatures of three fourths of the several States, or by Conventions in three fourths thereof, as the one or the other Mode of Ratification may be proposed by the Congress; Provided that ~~no Amendment which may be made prior to the Year One thousand eight hundred and eight shall in any Manner affect the first and fourth Clauses in the Ninth Section of the first Article; and that no State, without its Consent, shall be deprived of its equal Suffrage in the Senate.~~

Article VI | Supremacy of National Government

All Debts contracted and Engagements entered into, before the Adoption of this Constitution, shall be as valid against the United States under this Constitution, as under the Confederation.

This Constitution, and the Laws of the United States which shall be made in Pursuance thereof; and all Treaties made, or which shall be made, under the Authority of the United States, shall be the supreme Law of the Land; and the Judges in every State shall be bound thereby, any Thing in the Constitution or Laws of any State to the Contrary notwithstanding.

The Senators and Representatives before mentioned, and the Members of the several State Legislatures, and all executive and judicial Officers, both of the United States and of the several States, shall be bound by Oath or Affirmation, to support this Constitution; but no religious Test shall ever be required as a Qualification to any Office or public Trust under the United States.

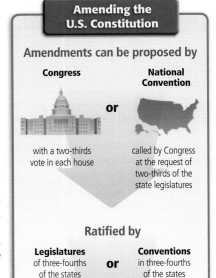

Amending the U.S. Constitution

Amendments can be proposed by

Congress
with a two-thirds vote in each house

or

National Convention
called by Congress at the request of two-thirds of the state legislatures

Ratified by

Legislatures
of three-fourths of the states

or

Conventions
in three-fourths of the states

Amendment is added to the Constitution.

Article VII | Ratification

The Ratification of the Conventions of nine States, shall be sufficient for the Establishment of this Constitution between the States so ratifying the Same.

Done in Convention by the Unanimous Consent of the States present the Seventeenth Day of September in the Year of our Lord one thousand seven hundred and Eighty seven and of the Independence of the United States of America the Twelfth In witness whereof We have hereunto subscribed our Names,

George Washington—
President and deputy from Virginia

Delaware
George Read
Gunning Bedford Jr.
John Dickinson
Richard Bassett
Jacob Broom

Maryland
James McHenry
Daniel of
  St. Thomas Jenifer
Daniel Carroll

Virginia
John Blair
James Madison Jr.

North Carolina
William Blount
Richard Dobbs Spaight
Hugh Williamson

South Carolina
John Rutledge
Charles Cotesworth
  Pinckney
Charles Pinckney
Pierce Butler

Georgia
William Few
Abraham Baldwin

New Hampshire
John Langdon
Nicholas Gilman

Massachusetts
Nathaniel Gorham
Rufus King

Connecticut
William Samuel Johnson
Roger Sherman

New York
Alexander Hamilton

New Jersey
William Livingston
David Brearley
William Paterson
Jonathan Dayton

Pennsylvania
Benjamin Franklin
Thomas Mifflin
Robert Morris
George Clymer
Thomas FitzSimons
Jared Ingersoll
James Wilson
Gouverneur Morris

Attest:
William Jackson,
Secretary

Ratification

The Articles of Confederation called for all 13 states to approve any revision to the Articles. The Constitution required that 9 out of the 13 states would be needed to ratify the Constitution. The first state to ratify was Delaware, on December 7, 1787. Almost two-and-a-half years later, on May 29, 1790, Rhode Island became the last state to ratify the Constitution.

Historical Documents

Info to Know
Signers of the Constitution At 27 years old, Jonathan Dayton was the youngest person to sign the Constitution. At 81, Benjamin Franklin was the oldest. Franklin's signature was particularly important. As one of the most renowned men in America, he lent respectability to the new document.

History Humor
Franklin's Epitaph Benjamin Franklin, well-known for his many expressions of wit and wisdom, composed his own tongue-in-cheek epitaph at the age of 22: "The body of Benjamin Franklin, Printer (like the cover of an old book, its contents torn out and stripped of its lettering and gilding), lies here, food for worms; but the work shall not be lost, for it will (as he believed) appear once more in a new and more elegant edition, revised and corrected by the Author."

Main Idea

Recall What are the first 10 amendments to the Constitution called? *Bill of Rights*

Summarize What fundamental liberties are guaranteed by the First Amendment in the Bill of Rights? *freedom of religion, freedom of speech, freedom of the press, freedom of assembly*

World Events

Jefferson in Paris At the time of the Constitutional Convention, Thomas Jefferson was in Paris as part of a diplomatic mission to France. Jefferson became increasingly convinced of the evils of monarchy as he saw the violations of civil liberties that the French people had to tolerate. For example, the king could issue a *lettre du cachet*, which could order someone exiled or imprisoned without recourse. In addition, the aristocracy could destroy land without having to pay the owner for the damage. In his letters to delegates to the Constitutional Convention, Jefferson strongly urged the inclusion of a bill of rights.

Exploring the Document

possible answer—It is a right on which the United States was founded.

Bill of Rights

One of the conditions set by several states for ratifying the Constitution was the inclusion of a bill of rights. Many people feared that a stronger central government might take away basic rights of the people that had been guaranteed in state constitutions.

EXPLORING THE DOCUMENT The First Amendment forbids Congress from making any "law respecting an establishment of religion" or restraining the freedom to practice religion as one chooses. **Why is freedom of religion an important right?**

Rights of the Accused

The Fifth, Sixth, and Seventh Amendments describe the procedures that courts must follow when trying people accused of crimes.

Vocabulary

[24] **quartered** housed

[25] **Warrants** written orders authorizing a person to make an arrest, a seizure, or a search

[26] **infamous** disgraceful

[27] **indictment** the act of charging with a crime

Constitutional Amendments

Note: The first 10 amendments to the Constitution were ratified on December 15, 1791, and form what is known as the Bill of Rights.

Amendments 1–10. The Bill of Rights

Amendment I

Congress shall make no law respecting an establishment of religion, or prohibiting the free exercise thereof; or abridging the freedom of speech, or of the press; or the right of the people peaceably to assemble, and to petition the Government for a redress of grievances.

Amendment II

A well regulated Militia, being necessary to the security of a free State, the right of the people to keep and bear Arms, shall not be infringed.

Amendment III

No Soldier shall, in time of peace be **quartered**[24] in any house, without the consent of the Owner, nor in time of war, but in a manner to be prescribed by law.

Amendment IV

The right of the people to be secure in their persons, houses, papers, and effects, against unreasonable searches and seizures, shall not be violated, and no **Warrants**[25] shall issue, but upon probable cause, supported by Oath or affirmation, and particularly describing the place to be searched, and the persons or things to be seized.

Amendment V

No person shall be held to answer for a capital, or otherwise **infamous**[26] crime, unless on a presentment or **indictment**[27] of a Grand Jury, except in

Fundamental Liberties

Freedom of Religion   Freedom of Speech

cases arising in the land or naval forces, or in the Militia, when in actual service in time of War or public danger; nor shall any person be subject for the same offence to be twice put in jeopardy of life or limb; nor shall be compelled in any criminal case to be a witness against himself, nor be deprived of life, liberty, or property, without due process of law; nor shall private property be taken for public use, without just compensation.

Amendment VI

In all criminal prosecutions, the accused shall enjoy the right to a speedy and public trial, by an impartial jury of the State and district wherein the crime shall have been committed, which district shall have been previously **ascertained**[28] by law, and to be informed of the nature and cause of the accusation; to be confronted with the witnesses against him; to have compulsory process for obtaining witnesses in his favor, and to have the Assistance of Counsel for his defence.

Amendment VII

In suits at common law, where the value in controversy shall exceed twenty dollars, the right of trial by jury shall be preserved, and no fact tried by a jury, shall be otherwise reexamined in any Court of the United States, than according to the rules of the common law.

Amendment VIII

Excessive bail shall not be required, nor excessive fines imposed, nor cruel and unusual punishments inflicted.

Amendment IX

The enumeration in the Constitution, of certain rights, shall not be construed to deny or disparage others retained by the people.

Amendment X

The powers not delegated to the United States by the Constitution, nor prohibited by it to the States, are reserved to the States respectively, or to the people.

Trials

The Sixth Amendment makes several guarantees, including a prompt trial and a trial by a jury chosen from the state and district in which the crime was committed.

Vocabulary

[28] **ascertained** found out

EXPLORING THE DOCUMENT The Ninth and Tenth Amendments were added because not every right of the people or of the states could be listed in the Constitution. **How do the Ninth and Tenth Amendments limit the power of the federal government?**

Freedom of Assembly

Freedom to Petition the Government

Freedom of the Press

ANALYSIS SKILL **ANALYZING INFORMATION**

Which amendment guarantees these fundamental freedoms?

CITIZENSHIP AND THE CONSTITUTION **205**

Historical Documents

Explain What does the Eleventh Amendment confirm? *No federal court may try a case in which a state is being sued by a citizen of another state or of a foreign country.*

Summarize How did the Twelfth Amendment change the electoral college? *It changed the procedure for choosing a president. The presidential electors would vote for president and vice president on separate ballots.*

Identify Cause and Effect Which three amendments do you think were a consequence of the Civil War? *Thirteenth, Fourteenth, and Fifteenth Amendments*

Reading Time Lines
Amendments to the U.S. Constitution

Activity Have each student select one amendment on the time line that is of particular interest to him or her. Ask students to conduct research on the amendment's passage and place the amendment in a matrix of events, people, time, and place. Have students use the information to create a collage of words and images that evokes the era in which the amendment was added to the Constitution. **LS** **Verbal/Linguistic, Visual/Spatial**

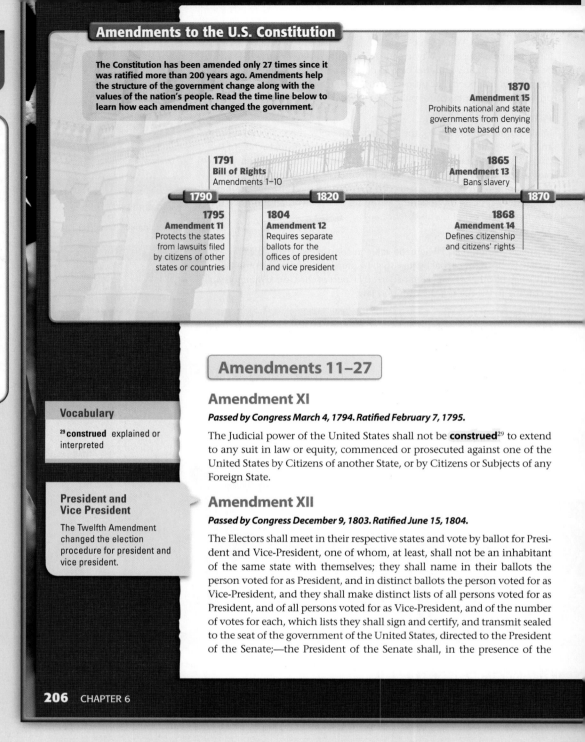

Amendments to the U.S. Constitution

The Constitution has been amended only 27 times since it was ratified more than 200 years ago. Amendments help the structure of the government change along with the values of the nation's people. Read the time line below to learn how each amendment changed the government.

1791
Bill of Rights
Amendments 1–10

1795
Amendment 11
Protects the states from lawsuits filed by citizens of other states or countries

1804
Amendment 12
Requires separate ballots for the offices of president and vice president

1865
Amendment 13
Bans slavery

1868
Amendment 14
Defines citizenship and citizens' rights

1870
Amendment 15
Prohibits national and state governments from denying the vote based on race

1790   1820   1870

Amendments 11–27

Vocabulary

[29] **construed** explained or interpreted

President and Vice President

The Twelfth Amendment changed the election procedure for president and vice president.

Amendment XI

Passed by Congress March 4, 1794. Ratified February 7, 1795.

The Judicial power of the United States shall not be **construed**[29] to extend to any suit in law or equity, commenced or prosecuted against one of the United States by Citizens of another State, or by Citizens or Subjects of any Foreign State.

Amendment XII

Passed by Congress December 9, 1803. Ratified June 15, 1804.

The Electors shall meet in their respective states and vote by ballot for President and Vice-President, one of whom, at least, shall not be an inhabitant of the same state with themselves; they shall name in their ballots the person voted for as President, and in distinct ballots the person voted for as Vice-President, and they shall make distinct lists of all persons voted for as President, and of all persons voted for as Vice-President, and of the number of votes for each, which lists they shall sign and certify, and transmit sealed to the seat of the government of the United States, directed to the President of the Senate;—the President of the Senate shall, in the presence of the

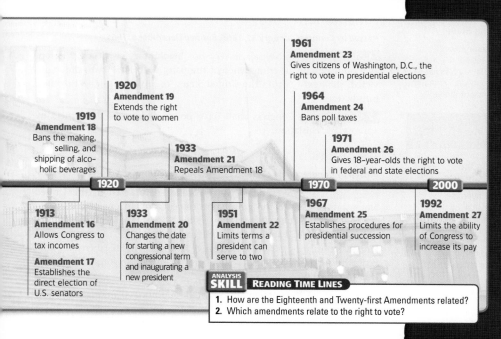

1919
Amendment 18
Bans the making, selling, and shipping of alcoholic beverages

1920
Amendment 19
Extends the right to vote to women

1933
Amendment 21
Repeals Amendment 18

1961
Amendment 23
Gives citizens of Washington, D.C., the right to vote in presidential elections

1964
Amendment 24
Bans poll taxes

1971
Amendment 26
Gives 18-year-olds the right to vote in federal and state elections

1913
Amendment 16
Allows Congress to tax incomes

Amendment 17
Establishes the direct election of U.S. senators

1933
Amendment 20
Changes the date for starting a new congressional term and inaugurating a new president

1951
Amendment 22
Limits terms a president can serve to two

1967
Amendment 25
Establishes procedures for presidential succession

1992
Amendment 27
Limits the ability of Congress to increase its pay

1920   **1970**   **2000**

ANALYSIS SKILL   READING TIME LINES

1. How are the Eighteenth and Twenty-first Amendments related?
2. Which amendments relate to the right to vote?

Senate and House of Representatives, open all the certificates and the votes shall then be counted;—The person having the greatest number of votes for President, shall be the President, if such number be a majority of the whole number of Electors appointed; and if no person have such majority, then from the persons having the highest numbers not exceeding three on the list of those voted for as President, the House of Representatives shall choose immediately, by ballot, the President. But in choosing the President, the votes shall be taken by states, the representation from each state having one vote; a quorum for this purpose shall consist of a member or members from two-thirds of the states, and a majority of all the states shall be necessary to a choice. ~~And if the House of Representatives shall not choose a President whenever the right of choice shall devolve upon them, before the fourth day of March next following, then the Vice-President shall act as President, as in case of the death or other constitutional disability of the President.~~—The person having the greatest number of votes as Vice-President, shall be the Vice-President, if such number be a majority of the whole number of Electors appointed, and if no person have a majority, then from the two highest numbers on the list, the Senate shall choose the Vice-President; a quorum for the purpose shall consist of two-thirds of the whole number of Senators, and a majority of the whole number shall be necessary to a choice. But no person constitutionally ineligible to the office of President shall be eligible to that of Vice-President of the United States.

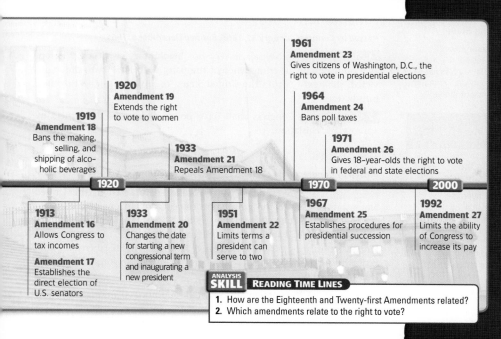

Historical Documents

Info to Know

Postwar Amendments Three amendments—the Thirteenth, Fourteenth, and Fifteenth—were meant initially to respond to changes demanded by the northern victory in the Civil War. When the Fourteenth Amendment was passed, many southerners interpreted it as punishing the South by extending civil rights to African Americans. Scholars have argued that the Fourteenth Amendment remains the most important addition to the Constitution since the Bill of Rights because of its inclusion of due process and equal protection clauses.

Evaluate Why do you think that scholars consider the Fourteenth Amendment so important? *Students might suggest that it redefined citizenship and guaranteed African Americans civil rights. It also made the Bill of Rights apply to state law.*

Answers

Reading Time Lines 1. *Eighteenth Amendment established the ban on alcohol (Prohibition); the Twenty-first Amendment repealed Prohibition.* **2.** *Fifteenth, Nineteenth, Twenty-third, Twenty-fourth and Twenty-sixth Amendments*

Historical Documents

Linking to Today

Civil Liberties Throughout the 1900s, the U.S. Supreme Court extended the coverage of the civil liberties provided in the Bill of Rights. In earlier times, justices had ruled that the Bill of Rights did not override state laws. Although the Fourteenth Amendment stated that the states could not deprive citizens of their constitutional rights, few justices changed their opinions. In the mid-1900s, Justice Hugo Black began to reinterpret the Fourteenth Amendment. He believed that the guarantees in the Bill of Rights were absolute. The Civil Rights Act, passed in 1964, was the most far-reaching civil rights bill in the nation's history. This act forbids discrimination in public accommodations.

Activity **Collaborative Learning**
Have students bring to class newspaper articles related to the exercise of civil liberties. Using these articles as discussion prompts, have students describe what they think are proper and improper limitations of civil liberties.

Abolishing Slavery

Although some slaves had been freed during the Civil War, slavery was not abolished until the Thirteenth Amendment took effect.

Protecting the Rights of Citizens

In 1833 the Supreme Court ruled that the Bill of Rights limited the federal government but not the state governments. This ruling was interpreted to mean that states were able to keep African Americans from becoming state citizens and keep the Bill of Rights from protecting them. The Fourteenth Amendment defines citizenship and prevents states from interfering in the rights of citizens of the United States.

Vocabulary

[30] **involuntary servitude** being forced to work against one's will

---

Amendment XIII

Passed by Congress January 31, 1865. Ratified December 6, 1865.

1. Slavery Banned Neither slavery nor **involuntary servitude,**[30] except as a punishment for crime whereof the party shall have been duly convicted, shall exist within the United States, or any place subject to their jurisdiction.

2. Enforcement Congress shall have power to enforce this article by appropriate legislation.

Amendment XIV

Passed by Congress June 13, 1866. Ratified July 9, 1868.

1. Citizenship Defined All persons born or naturalized in the United States, and subject to the jurisdiction thereof, are citizens of the United States and of the State wherein they reside. No State shall make or enforce any law which shall abridge the privileges or immunities of citizens of the United States; nor shall any State deprive any person of life, liberty, or property, without due process of law; nor deny to any person within its jurisdiction the equal protection of the laws.

2. Voting Rights Representatives shall be apportioned among the several States according to their respective numbers, counting the whole number of persons in each State, ~~excluding Indians not taxed~~. But when the right to vote at any election for the choice of electors for President and Vice-President of the United States, Representatives in Congress, the Executive and Judicial officers of a State, or the members of the Legislature thereof, is denied to any of the ~~male~~ inhabitants of such State, ~~being twenty-one years of age~~, and citizens of the United States, or in any way abridged, except for participation in rebellion, or other crime, the basis of representation therein shall be reduced in the proportion which the number of such ~~male~~ citizens shall bear to the whole number of ~~male~~ citizens ~~twenty-one years of age~~ in such State.

3. Rebels Banned from Government No person shall be a Senator or Representative in Congress, or elector of President and Vice-President, or hold any office, civil or military, under the United States, or under any State, who, having previously taken an oath, as a member of Congress, or as an officer of the United States, or as a member of any State legislature, or as an executive or judicial officer of any State, to support the Constitution of the United States, shall have engaged in insurrection or rebellion against the same, or given aid or comfort to the enemies thereof. But Congress may by a vote of two-thirds of each House, remove such disability.

4. Payment of Debts The validity of the public debt of the United States, authorized by law, including debts incurred for payment of pensions and

The Reconstruction Amendments

The Thirteenth, Fourteenth, and Fifteenth Amendments are often called the Reconstruction Amendments. This is because they arose during Reconstruction, the period of American history following the Civil War. The country was reconstructing itself after that terrible conflict. A key aspect of Reconstruction was extending the rights of citizenship to former slaves.

The Thirteenth Amendment banned slavery. The Fourteenth Amendment required states to respect the freedoms listed in the Bill of Rights, thus preventing states from denying rights to African Americans. The Fifteenth Amendment gave African American men the right to vote.

African Americans participate in an election.

 ANALYSIS SKILL **ANALYZING INFORMATION**

Why was the Thirteenth Amendment needed?

---

bounties for services in suppressing insurrection or rebellion, shall not be questioned. But neither the United States nor any State shall assume or pay any debt or obligation incurred in aid of insurrection or rebellion against the United States, ~~or any claim for the loss or emancipation of any slave~~; but all such debts, obligations and claims shall be held illegal and void.

5. Enforcement The Congress shall have the power to enforce, by appropriate legislation, the provisions of this article.

Amendment XV

Passed by Congress February 26, 1869. Ratified February 3, 1870.

1. Voting Rights The right of citizens of the United States to vote shall not be denied or abridged by the United States or by any State on account of race, color, or previous condition of servitude.

2. Enforcement The Congress shall have the power to enforce this article by appropriate legislation.

Main Idea

Explain What did the Eighteenth Amendment ban? *the making, sale, and transport of alcohol*

Make Inferences Why do you think the Eighteenth Amendment was repealed? *Students might suggest its impracticality and enormous unpopularity.*

Elaborate What factors do you think contributed to the passage of the Nineteenth Amendment? *Students might suggest the strong leadership and determination of women as well as organized, grassroots suffrage campaigns throughout the country.*

Info to Know

Effects of Prohibition The Eighteenth Amendment may have banned the manufacture, sale and transportation of liquor, but it also created an underground culture of bootlegging, smuggling, and organized crime. Speakeasies—illegal bars that sold alcoholic beverages—sprang up in large cities. These bars devised elaborate gadgets to hide the illegal evidence in case of police raids. New York City alone had over 30,000 speakeasies, twice the city's number of bars before Prohibition.

Exploring the Document

the principle of direct representation

EXPLORING THE DOCUMENT The Seventeenth Amendment requires that senators be elected directly by the people instead of by the state legislatures. **What principle of our government does the Seventeenth Amendment protect?**

Prohibition

Although many people believed that the Eighteenth Amendment was good for the health and welfare of the American people, it was repealed 14 years later.

Amendment XVI

Passed by Congress July 2, 1909. Ratified February 3, 1913.

The Congress shall have power to lay and collect taxes on incomes, from whatever source derived, without apportionment among the several States, and without regard to any census or enumeration.

Amendment XVII

Passed by Congress May 13, 1912. Ratified April 8, 1913.

1. Senators Elected by Citizens The Senate of the United States shall be composed of two Senators from each State, elected by the people thereof, for six years; and each Senator shall have one vote. The electors in each State shall have the qualifications requisite for electors of the most numerous branch of the State legislatures.

2. Vacancies When vacancies happen in the representation of any State in the Senate, the executive authority of such State shall issue writs of election to fill such vacancies: *Provided,* That the legislature of any State may empower the executive thereof to make temporary appointments until the people fill the vacancies by election as the legislature may direct.

3. Future Elections This amendment shall not be so construed as to affect the election or term of any Senator chosen before it becomes valid as part of the Constitution.

Amendment XVIII

Passed by Congress December 18, 1917. Ratified January 16, 1919. Repealed by Amendment XXI.

1. Liquor Banned After one year from the ratification of this article the manufacture, sale, or transportation of intoxicating liquors within, the importation thereof into, or the exportation thereof from the United States and all territory subject to the jurisdiction thereof for beverage purposes is hereby prohibited.

2. Enforcement The Congress and the several States shall have concurrent power to enforce this article by appropriate legislation.

3. Ratification This article shall be inoperative unless it shall have been ratified as an amendment to the Constitution by the legislatures of the several States, as provided in the Constitution, within seven years from the date of the submission hereof to the States by the Congress.

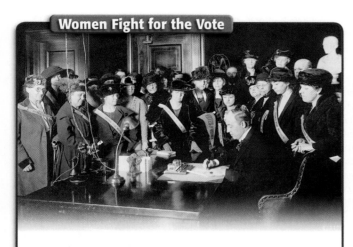

Women Fight for the Vote

To become part of the Constitution, a proposed amendment must be ratified by three-fourths of the states. Here, suffragists witness Kentucky governor Edwin P. Morrow signing the Nineteenth Amendment in January 1920. By June of that year, enough states had ratified the amendment to make it part of the Constitution. American women, after generations of struggle, had finally won the right to vote.

ANALYSIS SKILL | **ANALYZING INFORMATION**

What right did the Nineteenth Amendment grant?

Amendment XIX

Passed by Congress June 4, 1919. Ratified August 18, 1920.

1. Voting Rights The right of citizens of the United States to vote shall not be denied or abridged by the United States or by any State on account of sex.

2. Enforcement Congress shall have power to enforce this article by appropriate legislation.

Amendment XX

Passed by Congress March 2, 1932. Ratified January 23, 1933.

1. Presidential Terms The terms of the President and the Vice President shall end at noon on the 20th day of January, and the terms of Senators and Representatives at noon on the 3d day of January, of the years in which such terms would have ended if this article had not been ratified; and the terms of their successors shall then begin.

Women's Suffrage

Abigail Adams and others were disappointed that the Declaration of Independence and the Constitution did not specifically include women. It took many years and much campaigning before suffrage for women was finally achieved.

Historical Documents

Biography

Elizabeth Cady Stanton The efforts of Elizabeth Cady Stanton, a tireless crusader for women's rights, contributed to the passage of the Nineteenth Amendment in 1920. At her urging, in 1878 Senator Aaron A. Sargent of California introduced a women's suffrage amendment to the Constitution. This amendment was introduced and defeated repeatedly throughout Stanton's lifetime. She died in 1902, eighteen years before the passage of the amendment for which she had worked so hard.

Primary Source

Abigail Adams, "Remember the Ladies" In 1776, Abigail Adams wrote a letter to John Adams, in which she describes women's determination to be heard and represented. "In the new code of laws which I suppose it will be necessary for you to make I desire you would remember the ladies, and be more generous and favorable to them than your ancestors. Do not put such unlimited power into the hands of the husbands. Remember all men would be tyrants if they could. If particular care and attention is not paid to the ladies we are determined to foment a rebellion, and will not hold ourselves bound by any laws in which we have no voice, or representation."

Answers

Analyzing Information *granted women the right to vote*

Historical Documents

Biography

George W. Norris (1861–1944) During his long congressional career, George W. Norris not only created and worked to pass the Twentieth Amendment but also worked for the introduction of presidential primaries and for the direct election of senators. Though a Republican, Norris rarely voted along party lines. In defense of his independence, he claimed he "would rather be right than regular."

Connect to the Arts and Humanities

Inaugural Poems At the 1961 inauguration of John F. Kennedy, Robert Frost recited his poem "The Gift Outright." To honor Kennedy, Bill Clinton revived the tradition at his 1993 inauguration, during which Maya Angelou read her poem "On the Pulse of Morning."

Activity **Interpreting and Reciting Poetry** Have students use the library or Internet sources to locate poems read at presidential inaugurations. Ask for volunteers to read the poems aloud. Discuss what these poems convey or evoke about the significance of the moment and the promise of a new presidency.

Taking Office

In the original Constitution, a newly elected president and Congress did not take office until March 4, which was four months after the November election. The officials who were leaving office were called lame ducks because they had little influence during those four months. The Twentieth Amendment changed the date that the new president and Congress take office. Members of Congress now take office during the first week of January, and the president takes office on January 20.

2. Meeting of Congress The Congress shall assemble at least once in every year, and such meeting shall begin at noon on the 3d day of January, unless they shall by law appoint a different day.

3. Succession of Vice President If, at the time fixed for the beginning of the term of the President, the President elect shall have died, the Vice President elect shall become President. If a President shall not have been chosen before the time fixed for the beginning of his term, or if the President elect shall have failed to qualify, then the Vice President elect shall act as President until a President shall have qualified; and the Congress may by law provide for the case wherein neither a President elect nor a Vice President shall have qualified, declaring who shall then act as President, or the manner in which one who is to act shall be selected, and such person shall act accordingly until a President or Vice President shall have qualified.

4. Succession by Vote of Congress The Congress may by law provide for the case of the death of any of the persons from whom the House of Representatives may choose a President whenever the right of choice shall have devolved upon them, and for the case of the death of any of the persons from whom the Senate may choose a Vice President whenever the right of choice shall have devolved upon them.

5. Ratification ~~Sections 1 and 2 shall take effect on the 15th day of October following the ratification of this article.~~

6. Ratification ~~This article shall be inoperative unless it shall have been ratified as an amendment to the Constitution by the legislatures of three-fourths of the several States within seven years from the date of its submission.~~

Amendment XXI

Passed by Congress February 20, 1933. Ratified December 5, 1933.

1. 18th Amendment Repealed The eighteenth article of amendment to the Constitution of the United States is hereby repealed.

2. Liquor Allowed by Law The transportation or importation into any State, Territory, or Possession of the United States for delivery or use therein of intoxicating liquors, in violation of the laws thereof, is hereby prohibited.

3. Ratification ~~This article shall be inoperative unless it shall have been ratified as an amendment to the Constitution by conventions in the several States, as provided in the Constitution, within seven years from the date of the submission hereof to the States by the Congress.~~

Amendment XXII

Passed by Congress March 21, 1947. Ratified February 27, 1951.

1. Term Limits No person shall be elected to the office of the President more than twice, and no person who has held the office of President, or acted as President, for more than two years of a term to which some other person was elected President shall be elected to the office of President more than once. ~~But this Article shall not apply to any person holding the office of President when this Article was proposed by Congress, and shall not prevent any person who may be holding the office of President, or acting as President, during the term within which this Article becomes operative from holding the office of President or acting as President during the remainder of such term.~~

2. Ratification ~~This article shall be inoperative unless it shall have been ratified as an amendment to the Constitution by the legislatures of three-fourths of the several States within seven years from the date of its submission to the States by the Congress.~~

After Franklin D. Roosevelt was elected to four consecutive terms, limits were placed on the number of terms a president could serve.

Amendment XXIII

Passed by Congress June 16, 1960. Ratified March 29, 1961.

1. District of Columbia Represented The District constituting the seat of Government of the United States shall appoint in such manner as Congress may direct:

A number of electors of President and Vice President equal to the whole number of Senators and Representatives in Congress to which the District would be entitled if it were a State, but in no event more than the least populous State; they shall be in addition to those appointed by the States, but they shall be considered, for the purposes of the election of President and Vice President, to be electors appointed by a State; and they shall meet in the District and perform such duties as provided by the twelfth article of amendment.

2. Enforcement The Congress shall have power to enforce this article by appropriate legislation.

EXPLORING THE DOCUMENT From the time of President George Washington's administration, it was a custom for presidents to serve no more than two terms in office. Franklin D. Roosevelt, however, was elected to four terms. The Twenty-second Amendment restricted presidents to no more than two terms in office. **Why do you think citizens chose to limit the power of the president in this way?**

Voting Rights

Until the ratification of the Twenty-third Amendment, the people of Washington, D.C., could not vote in presidential elections.

CITIZENSHIP AND THE CONSTITUTION **213**

Historical Documents

Info to Know

Poll Taxes Congress started trying to eliminate poll taxes in 1939. These taxes had been instituted in some southern states after Reconstruction and were still in effect in five of those states in 1964. The poll tax was often explicitly adopted to discriminate against African American voters. For example, when a poll tax was passed in Virginia in 1902, one representative said, "Discrimination! Why, that is precisely what we propose."

Twenty-sixth Amendment As of 1970, four states had established a minimum voting age lower than 21. That year, Congress passed a law allowing citizens 18 and older to vote in federal elections. The U.S. Supreme Court found the law constitutional but noted that Congress did not have the power to set the voting age in state elections. To remedy any conflicts between federal and state voting standards, Congress passed the Twenty-sixth Amendment, which established 18 as the minimum voting age in all elections in the United States. The amendment was quickly ratified.

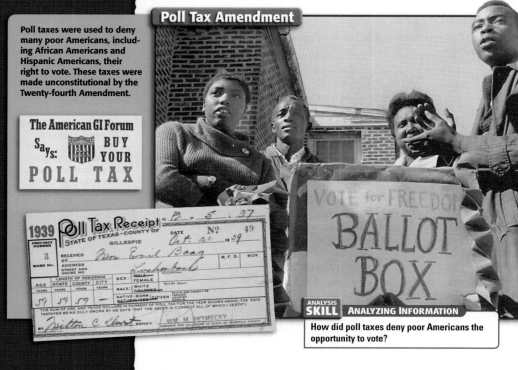

Poll Tax Amendment

Poll taxes were used to deny many poor Americans, including African Americans and Hispanic Americans, their right to vote. These taxes were made unconstitutional by the Twenty-fourth Amendment.

ANALYSIS SKILL ANALYZING INFORMATION

How did poll taxes deny poor Americans the opportunity to vote?

Presidential Disability

The illness of President Eisenhower in the 1950s and the assassination of President Kennedy in 1963 were the events behind the Twenty-fifth Amendment. The Constitution did not provide a clear-cut method for a vice president to take over for a disabled president or upon the death of a president. This amendment provides for filling the office of the vice president if a vacancy occurs, and it provides a way for the vice president—or someone else in the line of succession—to take over if the president is unable to perform the duties of that office.

Amendment XXIV

Passed by Congress August 27, 1962. Ratified January 23, 1964.

1. Voting Rights The right of citizens of the United States to vote in any primary or other election for President or Vice President, for electors for President or Vice President, or for Senator or Representative in Congress, shall not be denied or abridged by the United States or any State by reason of failure to pay poll tax or other tax.

2. Enforcement The Congress shall have power to enforce this article by appropriate legislation.

Amendment XXV

Passed by Congress July 6, 1965. Ratified February 10, 1967.

1. Sucession of Vice President In case of the removal of the President from office or of his death or resignation, the Vice President shall become President.

2. Vacancy of Vice President Whenever there is a vacancy in the office of the Vice President, the President shall nominate a Vice President who shall take office upon confirmation by a majority vote of both Houses of Congress.

Answers

Analyzing Information *by requiring people to pay a tax to vote, which many poor people could not afford*

3. Written Declaratrion Whenever the President transmits to the President pro tempore of the Senate and the Speaker of the House of Representatives his written declaration that he is unable to discharge the powers and duties of his office, and until he transmits to them a written declaration to the contrary, such powers and duties shall be discharged by the Vice President as Acting President.

4. Removing the President Whenever the Vice President and a majority of either the principal officers of the executive departments or of such other body as Congress may by law provide, transmit to the President pro tempore of the Senate and the Speaker of the House of Representatives their written declaration that the President is unable to discharge the powers and duties of his office, the Vice President shall immediately assume the powers and duties of the office as Acting President.

Thereafter, when the President transmits to the President pro tempore of the Senate and the Speaker of the House of Representatives his written declaration that no inability exists, he shall resume the powers and duties of his office unless the Vice President and a majority of either the principal officers of the executive department or of such other body as Congress may by law provide, transmit within four days to the President pro tempore of the Senate and the Speaker of the House of Representatives their written declaration that the President is unable to discharge the powers and duties of his office. Thereupon Congress shall decide the issue, assembling within forty-eight hours for that purpose if not in session. If the Congress, within twenty-one days after receipt of the latter written declaration, or, if Congress is not in session, within twenty-one days after Congress is required to assemble, determines by two-thirds vote of both Houses that the President is unable to discharge the powers and duties of his office, the Vice President shall continue to discharge the same as Acting President; otherwise, the President shall resume the powers and duties of his office.

Amendment XXVI

Passed by Congress March 23, 1971. Ratified July 1, 1971.

1. Voting Rights The right of citizens of the United States, who are eighteen years of age or older, to vote shall not be denied or abridged by the United States or by any State on account of age.

2. Enforcement The Congress shall have power to enforce this article by appropriate legislation.

Amendment XXVII

Originally proposed September 25, 1789. Ratified May 7, 1992.

No law, varying the compensation for the services of the Senators and Representatives, shall take effect, until an election of representatives shall have intervened.

Expanded Suffrage

The Voting Rights Act of 1970 tried to set the voting age at 18. However, the Supreme Court ruled that the act set the voting age for national elections only, not for state or local elections. The Twenty-sixth Amendment gave 18-year-old citizens the right to vote in all elections.

Historical Documents

Info to Know

Congressional Pay Raises Ironically, one of the latest constitutional amendments to pass was proposed by one of the Constitution's framers, James Madison. Although amendments that have been proposed in recent decades have included a deadline for passage, Madison never included one for what became the Twenty-seventh Amendment. The amendment states that congressional pay raises cannot take effect until a new Congress meets. Madison had suggested the amendment in 1789, along with the other amendments that eventually formed the Bill of Rights. However, just six states ratified the amendment—out of the 11 needed to pass it at the time—and it was largely forgotten. Then in the 1980s, an aide to a Texas legislator began a crusade to get the amendment passed. After more than 200 years, Michigan became the required 38th state to approve the Twenty-seventh Amendment.

Bellringer

If YOU were there . . . Use the **Daily Bellringer Transparency** to help students answer the question.

🖨 Daily Bellringer Transparency, Section 2

Building Vocabulary

Preteach or review the following terms:

ascertained found out (p. 219)

assembly holding meetings or demonstrating (p. 217)

infringed taken away (p. 218)

prescribed authorized (p. 218)

quartered housed (p. 218)

warrants written orders authorizing a person to make an arrest, a seizure, or a search (p. 218)

📄 CRF: Vocabulary Builder Activity, Section 2

Taking Notes

Have students copy the graphic organizer onto their own paper and then use it to take notes on the section. This activity will prepare students for the Section Assessment, in which they will complete a graphic organizer that builds on the information using a critical thinking skill.

The Bill of Rights

If YOU were there...

Your father runs a bookshop in colonial Boston in 1770. Your family lives in a very small, brick house. You and your sisters must share one small room. One day, a red-coated British officer knocks on your door and strides into the parlor. He says that your family will have to provide a room and meals for two British soldiers. "We're already crowded!" you protest, but he insists.

Would you support the British government's requirement that colonists provide food and shelter for troops? Why?

BUILDING BACKGROUND People in the American colonies resented the British soldiers stationed in their towns. They objected to sudden searches and to soldiers being housed in private homes. They disliked censorship of their newspapers. When the Constitution was written, Americans remembered those wrongs. They insisted on adding a bill of rights to the document.

First Amendment

Federalist **James Madison** promised that a bill of rights would be added to the Constitution. This promise allowed the Constitution to pass. In 1789 Madison began writing down a huge list of proposed amendments. He then presented a shorter list to the House of Representatives. Of those, the House approved 12. The states ratified 10, which took effect December 15, 1791. Those 10 amendments, called the Bill of Rights, protect U.S. citizens' individual liberties.

The protection of individual liberties is important in a representative democracy. Without safeguards, people's rights would not always be protected because of **majority rule**. This is the idea that the greatest number of people in society can make policies for everyone. While this means that most people agree on what the law should be, it also means that smaller groups might lose their rights. The Bill of Rights ensures that the rights of all citizens are protected.

The ideas spelled out in the First Amendment form the most basic rights of all U.S. citizens. These rights include freedom of religion,

What You Will Learn...

Main Ideas

1. The First Amendment guarantees basic freedoms to individuals.
2. Other amendments focus on protecting citizens from certain abuses.
3. The rights of the accused are an important part of the Bill of Rights.
4. The rights of states and citizens are protected by the Bill of Rights.

The Big Idea

The Bill of Rights was added to the Constitution to define clearly the rights and freedoms of citizens.

Key Terms and People

James Madison, *p. 216*
majority rule, *p. 216*
petition, *p. 217*
search warrant, *p. 218*
due process, *p. 218*
indict, *p. 218*
double jeopardy, *p. 218*
eminent domain, *p. 218*

TAKING NOTES As you read, take notes on the freedoms protected by the Bill of Rights and which amendment protects each. The first right has been filled in for you as an example.

Rights/Freedoms	Amendment
1. Freedom of religion	

Teach the Big Idea

At Level

The Bill of Rights

Materials: slips of paper listing either a specific right found in the Bill of Rights or a number from 1 to 10

Prep Required

1. **Teach** Ask students the questions in the Main Idea boxes to teach this section.
2. **Apply** Discuss with students the meaning and importance of each amendment in the Bill of Rights. Make a chart of the information for students to see. **LS** **Verbal/Linguistic**
3. **Review** Hand each student one of the prepared slips of paper. Have students circulate to match specific rights to the correct amendment number.
4. **Practice/Homework** Have students draw political cartoons illustrating what could happen without the protections provided by the Bill of Rights. **LS** **Visual/Spatial**

📄 Alternative Assessment Handbook, Rubrics 7: Charts; and 27: Political Cartoons freedom of the press, freedom of speech, freedom of assembly, and the right to petition.

In the spirit of Thomas Jefferson's Virginia Statute for Religious Freedom, the First Amendment begins, "Congress shall make no law respecting an establishment of religion, or prohibiting the free exercise thereof." In other words, the government cannot support or interfere with the practice of a religion. This amendment keeps the government from favoring one religion over any other or establishing an official religion.

The First Amendment also guarantees freedom of speech and of the press. This means that Americans have the right to express their own ideas and views. They also have the right to hear the ideas and views of others. Former senator Margaret Chase Smith discussed why these freedoms are important. "The key to security," she once said, "is public information."

Freedom of speech does not mean that people can say anything they want to, however. The Constitution does not protect slander—false statements meant to damage someone's reputation. Libel, or intentionally writing a lie that harms another person, is not protected, either. The Supreme Court has also ruled that speech that endangers public safety is not protected. For example, Justice Oliver Wendell Holmes declared in 1919 that falsely shouting "Fire" in a crowded theater is not protected as free speech.

Americans also have freedom of assembly, or of holding meetings. Any group may gather to discuss issues or conduct business. If people gather peacefully and do not engage in illegal activities, the government cannot interfere. The right to **petition**, or make a request of the government, is another right of the American people. Any American can present a petition to a government official. This right lets Americans show dissatisfaction with a law. They can also suggest new laws.

THE IMPACT TODAY

Free-speech protection has also been applied to "symbolic" speech—nonverbal communication that expresses an idea, such as wearing a protest button.

READING CHECK **Summarizing** What rights does the First Amendment guarantee to Americans?

Amendment I
Congress shall make no law respecting an establishment of religion, or prohibiting the free exercise thereof; or abridging the freedom of speech, or of the press; or the right of the people peaceably to assemble, and to petition the Government for a redress of grievances.

Workers use the right of assembly to protest a proposed budget in New York City.

217

217

❷ Protecting Citizens

Other amendments focus on protecting citizens from certain abuses.

Identify What basic right does the Second Amendment protect? *the right to bear arms*

Analyze How does a search warrant protect Americans and their property? *It prevents authorities from searching someone's home or property without permission.*

Linking to Today

The National Guard Over time, the National Guard's federal mission has broadened. After the terrorist attacks of September 11, 2001, state and federal governments called upon the National Guard to provide security at home and assist the nation's military in combating terrorism abroad.

Info to Know

Quartering Troops In 1689, Parliament passed an act that protected British citizens from having to house or quarter troops in their homes. The British law did not apply to the colonies in America, though. During the French and Indian War (1754–63), colonists discovered that they had no legal protection against the British practice of quartering troops.

Answers

Reading Check *They related to disputes that American colonists had with Great Britain over quartering troops and forced search and seizure.*

218

Amendment II
A well regulated Militia, being necessary to the security of a free State, the right of the people to keep and bear Arms, shall not be infringed.

Amendment III
No Soldier shall, in time of peace be quartered in any house, without the consent of the Owner, nor in time of war, but in a manner to be prescribed by law.

Amendment IV
The right of the people to be secure in their persons, houses, papers, and effects, against unreasonable searches and seizures, shall not be violated, and no Warrants shall issue, but upon probable cause, supported by Oath or affirmation, and particularly describing the place to be searched, and the persons or things to be seized.

Protecting Citizens

The Second, Third, and Fourth Amendments relate to colonial disputes with Britain and reflect many of the ideals outlined in the Declaration of Independence. The Second Amendment deals with state militias and the right to bear arms. Colonial militias played a big role in the Revolutionary War. The framers of the Constitution thought that the states needed their militias for emergencies. Today the National Guard has largely replaced organized state militias.

Supporters of gun-control laws have generally argued that the Second Amendment was intended to protect the collective right of states to maintain well-regulated militia units. Opponents hold that the amendment was meant to protect an individual's right of self-defense. The meaning of the amendment continues to be debated.

The Third Amendment prevents the military from forcing citizens to house soldiers. Before the Revolution, the British pressured colonists to shelter and feed British soldiers. British leaders also forced colonists to submit to having their property searched for illegal goods. Anger over such actions led to the

218 CHAPTER 6

Fourth Amendment rule against "unreasonable searches and seizures." Before a citizen's property can be searched, authorities must now get a **search warrant**. This order gives authorities permission to search someone's property. A judge issues this order only when it seems likely that a search might uncover evidence relating to a crime. In emergencies, however, police can make an emergency search. This may preserve evidence needed to prove possible illegal activity.

READING CHECK Finding Main Ideas
Why were the Third and Fourth Amendments matters of great importance to Americans when the Bill of Rights was written?

Rights of the Accused

The Fifth, Sixth, Seventh, and Eighth Amendments provide guidelines for protecting the rights of the accused. According to the Fifth Amendment, the government cannot punish anyone without **due process** of law. This means that the law must be fairly applied. A grand jury decides if there is enough evidence to **indict** (en-DYT), or formally accuse, a person. Without an indictment, the court cannot try anyone for a serious crime. The Fifth Amendment also protects people from having to testify at their own criminal trial. To keep from testifying, a person need only "take the Fifth." In addition, anyone found not guilty in a criminal trial cannot face **double jeopardy**. In other words, he or she cannot be tried again for the same crime.

The final clause of the Fifth Amendment states that no one can have property taken without due process of law. There is one exception: the government's power of **eminent domain**. This is the power to take personal property to benefit the public. One example would be taking private land to build a public road. However, the government must pay the owners a fair price for the property. If the property was gained illegally, then the owners are not paid.

Collaborative Learning
At Level

Class Bill of Rights

1. Organize the class into groups. Have each group develop a list of 10 rights they would like to include in a "Class Bill of Rights." Tell students that the document must clearly protect students' rights while focusing on creating an effective classroom.

2. After all groups have completed their lists, ask a representative from each group to present that group's ideas to the class.

3. Make a list of the ideas for students to see. Have students discuss the ideas that appear on several lists. What concerns do they reflect? Then have students compare their lists with the Bill of Rights.

4. Have students vote to determine which 10 rights to include in their official "Class Bill of Rights." Post the list in the classroom. **LS** Interpersonal, Verbal/Linguistic

📄 Alternative Assessment Handbook, Rubric 14: Group Activity

The Sixth Amendment protects the rights of a person who has been indicted. It guarantees that person a speedy public trial. Public trials ensure that laws are being followed by allowing the public to witness the proceedings. Accused people have the right to know the charges against them and can hear and question witnesses testifying against them. Accused people have the right to an attorney. If they cannot pay for legal service, the government must provide it. Sometimes accused persons refuse their Sixth Amendment rights. For example, some defendants refuse the services of an attorney, while others choose to have a trial in front of a judge alone instead of before a jury. In many cases, defendants can forgo trial and agree to a plea bargain. This means that a defendant pleads guilty to a lesser charge and avoids risking conviction for a crime with a greater sentence.

The Seventh Amendment states that juries can decide civil cases. It is possible to harm another person without committing a crime. In such cases, the injured party may sue, or seek justice, in a civil court. Civil cases usually involve disputes over money or property. For example, someone might bring a civil suit against a person who refuses to repay a debt.

Amendment V
No person shall be held to answer for a capital, or otherwise infamous crime, unless on a presentment or indictment of a Grand Jury, except in cases arising in the land or naval forces, or in the Militia, when in actual service in time of War or public danger; nor shall any person be subject for the same offence to be twice put in jeopardy of life or limb; nor shall be compelled in any criminal case to be a witness against himself, nor be deprived of life, liberty, or property, without due process of law; nor shall private property be taken for public use, without just compensation.

Amendment VI
In all criminal prosecutions, the accused shall enjoy the right to a speedy and public trial, by an impartial jury of the State and district wherein the crime shall have been committed, which district shall have been previously ascertained by law, and to be informed of the nature and cause of the accusation; to be confronted with the witnesses against him; to have compulsory process for obtaining witnesses in his favor, and to have the Assistance of Counsel for his defence.

Amendment VII
In suits at common law, where the value in controversy shall exceed twenty dollars, the right of trial by jury shall be preserved, and no fact tried by a jury, shall be otherwise reexamined in any Court of the United States, than according to the rules of the common law.

A judge and jury listen to a witness in a courtroom in Orange County, California.

CITIZENSHIP AND THE CONSTITUTION **219**

❸ Rights of the Accused

The rights of the accused are an important part of the Bill of Rights.

Recall What is the purpose of bail? *It allows people to avoid staying in jail during a trial.*

Make Inferences Why do you think the Bill of Rights provides for bail? *because defendants have not yet been proven guilty*

Make Generalizations In what ways has the Supreme Court influenced the way states carry out the death penalty? *The Court ruled that although execution itself is not cruel and unusual, some methods of carrying out the death penalty are either cruel and unusual or unfair.*

MISCONCEPTION ///ALERT\\\

Free Education? Children and young adults who attend public schools do not pay for their education. However, that does not mean that their education is free. American citizens, whether they have children in the public school system or not, share the responsibility of funding public education in their state through the payment of different kinds of taxes, such as state or property taxes.

Answers

Reading Check *allows for bail, prevents courts from setting unfairly high bail, and bans "cruel and unusual punishment"*

A Right to Bail

The Eighth Amendment allows for bail. Bail is a set amount of money that defendants promise to pay the court if they fail to appear in court at the proper time.

By posting, or paying, bail, a defendant can avoid staying in jail before and during a trial. If a defendant does not show up in court for trial, the court demands the bail money be paid and issues a warrant for arrest.

The Eighth Amendment keeps courts from setting unfairly high bail. However, in cases of very serious crimes, a judge may refuse to set bail altogether. This can be the case, for example, if the court regards a defendant as being potentially dangerous to the public by being left free. A judge can also deny bail if he or she thinks the defendant will not show up for trial. In such cases the defendant must remain in jail through the trial.

> **Amendment VIII**
> Excessive bail shall not be required, nor excessive fines imposed, nor cruel and unusual punishments inflicted.

"Cruel and Unusual Punishments"

The Eighth Amendment also bans "cruel and unusual punishments" against a person convicted of a crime. For many years, Americans have debated the question of what exactly constitutes cruel and unusual punishment. The debate has often centered on the issue of capital punishment. In 1972 the Supreme Court ruled that the way in which most states carried out the death penalty was cruel and unusual. The Court also found that the ways in which many states sentenced people to death were unfair. However, a few years later, the Court ruled that not all executions were in themselves cruel and unusual.

Most states still allow the death penalty. Those that do must follow the Supreme Court's rules. To do so, many states have changed the ways in which they carry out the death penalty.

> **READING CHECK** **Summarizing** What is the purpose of the Eighth Amendment?

Rights of States and Citizens

The final two amendments in the Bill of Rights give a general protection for other rights not addressed by the first eight amendments. These amendments also reserve some governmental powers for the states and the people.

Ninth Amendment

The Ninth Amendment says that the rights listed in the Constitution are not the only rights that citizens have. This amendment has allowed the courts and Congress to decide other basic rights of citizens.

The Constitution does not address the question of education. However, most Americans believe that it is a basic and essential right. This seems especially true in view of the fact that American citizens must be able to vote for the people who represent them in government. "Education is not just another

> **Amendment IX**
> The enumeration in the Constitution, of certain rights, shall not be construed to deny or disparage others retained by the people.
>
> **Amendment X**
> The powers not delegated to the United States by the Constitution, nor prohibited by it to the States, are reserved to the States respectively, or to the people.

Differentiating Instruction

Advanced/ Gifted and Talented [Above Level]

Ninth Amendment Have students discuss the rights they think should be included under the Ninth Amendment. List the ideas for students to see. Have the class discuss and vote on which rights to include. Discuss why the framers of the Constitution included the Ninth Amendment.

LS **Interpersonal, Verbal/Linguistic**

Alternative Assessment Handbook, Rubric 11: Discussions

English-Language Learners [Below Level]

Illustrated Bill of Rights Go through each amendment in the Bill of Rights with students. Define unfamiliar terms as needed. Then have students work as a class or in small groups to create an illustrated Bill of Rights. Students should provide at least one illustration and a short caption for each amendment. Display students' work in the classroom. **LS** **Interpersonal, Visual/Spatial**

Alternative Assessment Handbook, Rubric 3: Artwork

consumer item. It is the bedrock [foundation] of our democracy," explained educational leader Mary Hatwood Futrell. Today state governments offer free education from elementary to high school—to all citizens.

Tenth Amendment

The Tenth Amendment recognizes that the states and the people have additional powers. These powers are any ones that the Constitution does not specifically give to Congress—the delegated powers. The Tenth Amendment makes it clear that any powers not either delegated to the federal government or prohibited to the states belong to the states and the people. Thus, the last amendment in the Bill of Rights protects citizens' rights. It helps to keep the balance of power between the federal and state governments.

READING CHECK **Summarizing** How does the Tenth Amendment protect the rights of citizens?

SUMMARY AND PREVIEW In this section you learned about the Bill of Rights. In the next section you will learn about the responsibilities of citizenship.

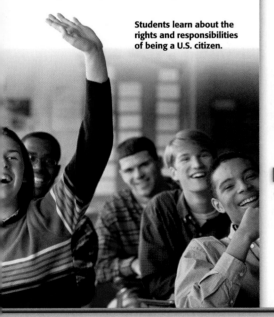
Students learn about the rights and responsibilities of being a U.S. citizen.

go.hrw.com
Online Quiz
KEYWORD: SR8 HP6

Section 2 Assessment

Reviewing Ideas, Terms, and People

1. **a. Identify** What basic rights are protected by the First Amendment?
   b. Explain What does the right to **petition** the government mean?
   c. Elaborate Why is freedom of the press an important right?
2. **a. Describe** How are citizens protected under the Third and Fourth Amendments?
   b. Draw Conclusions In what ways did British actions before the Revolution lead to the Second, Third, and Fourth Amendments?
3. **a. Identify** What protections does the Eighth Amendment provide for people accused of crimes?
   b. Elaborate Why is it important that the Bill of Rights protects people accused of crimes?
4. **a. Recall** What is the purpose of the final two amendments in the Bill of Rights?
   b. Analyze How does the Tenth Amendment balance power between national and state governments?

Critical Thinking

5. **Summarizing** Copy the chart below. Use it to summarize the rights guaranteed to citizens by each amendment in the Bill of Rights.

Amendment	Right
1	
2	
3	
4	
5	
6	
7	
8	
9	
10	

FOCUS ON WRITING

6. **Gathering Information about the Bill of Rights** What freedoms are guaranteed by the Bill of Rights? Make a list of the most important freedoms. You'll list those freedoms on the third page of your pamphlet.

CITIZENSHIP AND THE CONSTITUTION **221**

Bellringer

If YOU were there . . . Use the **Daily Bellringer Transparency** to help students answer the question.

🔖 Daily Bellringer Transparency, Section 3

Academic Vocabulary

Review with students the high-use academic term in this section.

influence change or have an effect on (p. 224)

📓 **CRF:** Vocabulary Builder Activity, Section 3

go.hrw.com
Online Resources

KEYWORD: SR8 US6
ACTIVITY: Tracking U.S. Immigration

Taking Notes

Have students copy the graphic organizer onto their own paper and then use it to take notes on the section. This activity will prepare students for the Section Assessment, in which they will complete a graphic organizer that builds on the information using a critical thinking skill.

SECTION 3

Rights and Responsibilities of Citizenship

What You Will Learn...

Main Ideas

1. Citizenship in the United States is determined in several ways.
2. Citizens are expected to fulfill a number of important duties.
3. Active citizen involvement in government and the community is encouraged.

The Big Idea

American citizenship involves great privileges and serious responsibilities.

Key Terms

naturalized citizens, *p. 222*
deport, *p. 222*
draft, *p. 223*
political action committees, *p. 224*
interest groups, *p. 224*

 TAKING NOTES As you read, look for information on three ways a person can become a U.S. citizen. Take notes in a graphic organizer like the one below.

If YOU were there...

Your older brother and his friends have just turned 18. That means they must register with selective service. But it also means that they are old enough to vote in national elections. You are interested in the upcoming elections and think it would be exciting to have a real voice in politics. But your brother and his friends don't even plan to register to vote.

How would you persuade your brother that voting is important?

> **BUILDING BACKGROUND** Whether you are born an American citizen or become one later, citizenship brings many rights and privileges. But it also brings duties and responsibilities. Voting is both a right and a responsibility.

Gaining U.S. Citizenship

People become U.S. citizens in several ways. First, anyone born in the United States or a territory it controls is a citizen. People born in a foreign country are U.S. citizens if at least one parent is a U.S. citizen. Foreign-born people whose parents are not citizens must move to the United States to become **naturalized citizens**. Once in the United States, they go through a long process before applying for citizenship. If they succeed, they become naturalized citizens, giving them most of the rights and responsibilities of other citizens.

In the United States, legal immigrants have many of the rights and responsibilities of citizens but cannot vote or hold public office. The U.S. government can **deport**, or return to the country of origin, immigrants who break the law.

Legal immigrants over age 18 may request naturalization after living in the United States for five years. All legal immigrants have to

---

Teach the Big Idea

At Level

Rights and Responsibilities of Citizenship

1. **Teach** Ask students the questions in the Main Idea boxes to teach this section.

2. **Apply** Ask students to imagine that they work for the immigration department. Have each student create a two-page Citizenship Guide. The guide should provide information on how to become a naturalized citizen, the duties of citizenship, participating in the political process, and serving the community. **LS** **Verbal/Linguistic**

3. **Review** As you review the section, have students identify and explain the duties and responsibilities of citizenship.

4. **Practice/Homework** Have each student create a collage illustrating the rights and responsibilities of citizenship. Collages might include drawings, quotations, newspaper and magazine clippings, photographs, cloth, stickers, and so on. **LS** **Visual/Spatial**

   📓 Alternative Assessment Handbook, Rubrics 8: Collages; and 37: Writing Assignments support themselves financially. If not, someone must assume financial responsibility for them. Immigrants must be law-abiding and support the U.S. Constitution. They must demonstrate understanding of written and spoken English. They also must show basic knowledge of U.S. history and government.

When this is done, candidates go before a naturalization court and take an oath of allegiance to the United States. They then get certificates of naturalization.

Only two differences between naturalized and native-born citizens exist. Naturalized citizens can lose their citizenship, and they cannot become president or vice president. Many famous Americans have been naturalized citizens, including scientist Albert Einstein and former secretary of state Madeleine Albright.

READING CHECK Drawing Conclusions Why does U.S. law have such demanding requirements for people to become naturalized citizens?

Duties of Citizenship

For a representative democracy to work, Americans need to fulfill their civic duties. "The stakes...are too high for government to be a spectator sport," former Texas congresswoman Barbara Jordan once said.

Citizens elect officials to make laws for them. In turn, citizens must obey those laws and respect the authorities who enforce them. Obeying laws includes knowing what they are and staying informed about changes. Ignorance of a law will not prevent a person from being punished for breaking it.

Another duty is paying taxes for services such as public roads, police, and public schools. People pay sales taxes, property taxes, and tariffs. Many Americans also pay a tax on their income to the federal, and sometimes state, government.

Citizens have the duty to defend the nation. Men 18 years or older must register with selective service. In the event of a **draft**, or required military service, those able

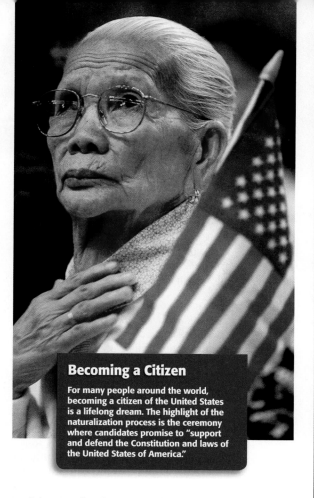

Becoming a Citizen

For many people around the world, becoming a citizen of the United States is a lifelong dream. The highlight of the naturalization process is the ceremony where candidates promise to "support and defend the Constitution and laws of the United States of America."

to fight are already registered. Although women do not register, many serve in the armed forces.

Americans have the right to a trial by jury under the Sixth Amendment. To protect this right, citizens should be willing to serve on a jury when they are called. Otherwise, fulfilling each person's Sixth Amendment rights would be difficult.

READING CHECK Making Inferences Why does citizenship carry with it certain responsibilities?

CITIZENSHIP AND THE CONSTITUTION **223**

Main Idea

❸ Citizens and Government

Active citizen involvement in government and the community is encouraged.

Describe What steps can citizens take to vote intelligently? *study information about the issues and candidates from a variety of sources*

Analyze What do you think are some positive and negative issues related to political action committees and interest groups? *positive—can help raise public and political interest in important issues; negative—can bog down the political process as groups compete to promote their issues; money raised can be used to influence politicians*

📄 **CRF:** Literature Activity: *The Free Citizen,* by Theodore Roosevelt

Connect to Civics: Responsibility

Voter Participation Political scientists compiled information regarding voter participation in several nations during the 1980s and discovered that the United States ranked among the lowest in voter turnout. In a survey of 20 democracies, the United States ranked 19th in voter participation.

Activity **Get Out the Vote Speech**
Have students write a speech in which they encourage Americans to cast their votes in an upcoming election.
LS Verbal/Linguistic

Responsibilities of Citizens

For representative democracy to work, citizens must do their part. Each activity pictured here serves an important role in the community.

Jury Duty

Military Service

Citizens and Government

Taking part in the elections process by voting may be a citizen's most vital duty. Through free elections, U.S. citizens choose who will lead their government.

Function of Elections

It is essential for citizens to learn as much as they can about the issues and candidates before voting. Information is available from many sources: the Internet, newspapers, television, and other media. However, voters should also be aware that some material may be propaganda or material that is biased deliberately to help or harm a cause.

In addition to voting, many Americans choose to campaign for candidates or issues. Anyone can help campaign, even if he or she is not eligible to vote. Many people also help campaigns by giving money directly or through **political action committees** (PACs), groups that collect money for candidates who support certain issues.

Influencing Government

ACADEMIC VOCABULARY
influence
change or have an effect on

Even after an election, people can **influence** officials. Political participation is part of our nation's identity and tradition. When colonists protested British rule in the 1700s, they formed committees and presented their views to political leaders.

As the new American nation grew, so did political participation. French diplomat

Alexis de Tocqueville visited the United States in 1831 to study American democracy. He was amazed at the large number of political groups Americans participated in. He wrote about them:

❝ What political power could ever carry on the vast multitude [large number] of lesser undertakings which the American citizens perform every day, with the assistance of the principle of association [joining a group]? Nothing, in my opinion, is more deserving of our attention than the intellectual and moral associations of America. ❞
—Alexis de Tocqueville, *Democracy in America*

U.S. citizens sometimes work with **interest groups**. These groups of people share a common interest that motivates them to take political action. Interest groups organize speeches and rallies to support their cause. However, citizens need not join a group to influence government. They can write letters to leaders of government or attend city council meetings. Active political participation is an important duty for U.S. citizens and immigrants alike.

Helping the Community

Commitment to others moves many Americans to volunteer in community service groups. Some small communities rely on volunteers for services such as fire protection and law enforcement.

Other volunteer groups help government-sponsored agencies. For example, Citizens on

Collaborative Learning

At Level

Helping the Community

1. Guide students in a short discussion about how volunteer groups help your local community. Ask for students to share some of their volunteer experiences.

2. Ask students to identify some specific problems or needs in the local community that would benefit from volunteer efforts.

3. Organize the class into groups of five or six. Have each group select one of the problems or needs identified in the discussion.

4. Have group members work together to develop a volunteer project to help address the local problem or need. Each group should also develop a plan for carrying out its project.
LS Interpersonal, Verbal/Linguistic

Community Service

Voting

Obey the Law

ANALYSIS SKILL **ANALYZING VISUALS**

Which responsibilities can you fulfill now, without waiting until you turn 18 years old?

Patrol and Neighborhood Watch groups ask volunteers to walk their neighborhoods and tell police if they observe possible criminal activity in the area. The American Red Cross helps citizens in times of natural disasters or other emergencies. The Boy Scouts and Girl Scouts plan many projects such as planting trees to improve the environment. Even simple acts such as picking up trash in parks or serving food in shelters help a community.

READING CHECK **Summarizing** In what ways do volunteer groups benefit the community?

SUMMARY AND PREVIEW In this section you learned about citizens' duties toward their nation and their communities. In the next chapter you will learn about the first government formed under the Constitution.

Section 3 Assessment

go.hrw.com
Online Quiz
KEYWORD: SR8 HP6

Reviewing Ideas, Terms, and People

1. **a. Identify** What are the different ways in which a person can become a U.S. citizen?
   b. Make Inferences Why do you think the law requires an immigrant to live in the United States at least five years before he or she can apply to become a **naturalized citizen**?
2. **a. Describe** What are three duties expected of U.S. citizens?
   b. Evaluate In your opinion, which duty expected of citizens is the most important? Why?
3. **a. Identify** In what ways can citizens participate in the election process?
   b. Draw Conclusions Why is it important that citizens participate in the political process?

Critical Thinking

4. **Categorizing** Review your notes on U.S. citizen-

ship. Then add the responsibilities of citizenship to your graphic organizer.

U.S. Citizenship → Responsibilities

FOCUS ON WRITING

5. **Thinking about Citizenship** The last page of your pamphlet will have two parts—one part on requirements for citizenship and one part on the responsibilities of citizens. Look back through this section and make two lists, one on requirements and one on responsibilities.

CITIZENSHIP AND THE CONSTITUTION **225**

Section 3 Assessment Answers

1. **a.** born in the United States or a U.S. territory, have at least one parent who is a citizen, or become a naturalized citizen
   b. to make sure people understand and fully accept the rights and responsibilities of being a U.S. citizen

2. **a.** possible answers—pay taxes, obey laws, register for military draft, serve on juries, vote
   b. Answers will vary but should reflect an understanding of the duties of citizenship, as listed in previous answer.

3. **a.** vote, campaign for candidates, work with interest groups
   b. possible answer—To work effectively, a representative democracy needs an informed and politically active citizenry.

4. become a citizen—see answer to Question 1a; responsibilities—see answer to Question 2a.

5. Students should note the information in the answers to Questions 1a and 2a.

225

Determining the Context of Statements

Activity Historical Context Chart

To extend the "Practice the Skill" activity, create a chart with four rows. Have students help you complete the chart by providing responses for each of the four points listed under "Learn the Skill." Then have students consider how well Henry's statement reflects the values, attitudes, and practices of Americans today. Encourage discussion and feedback. **LS** Verbal/Linguistic, Visual/Spatial

📖 Alternative Assessment Handbook, Rubrics 7: Charts; and 11: Discussions

Social Studies Skills

| Analysis | Critical Thinking | Civic Participation | Study |

Determining the Context of Statements

Define the Skill

A *context* is the circumstances under which something happens. *Historical context* includes values, beliefs, conditions, and practices that were common in the past. At times, some of these were quite different from what they are today. To truly understand a historical statement or event, you have to take its context into account. It is not right to judge what people in history did or said based on present-day values alone. To be fair, you must also consider the historical context of the statement or event.

Learn the Skill

To better understand something a historical figure said or wrote, use the following guidelines to determine the context of the statement.

1. Identify the speaker or writer, the date, and the topic and main idea of the statement.

2. Determine the speaker's or writer's attitude and point of view about the topic.

3. Review what you know about beliefs, conditions, or practices related to the topic that were common at the time. Find out more about the times in which the statement was made if you need to.

4. Decide how well the statement reflects the values, attitudes, and practices of people living at that time. Then, determine how well it reflects values, attitudes, and practices related to the topic today.

Applying these guidelines will give you a better understanding of statements made by the

Constitution's framers. You read in Chapter 6 that the Constitution created a representative democracy. However, the original Constitution gave most Americans little voice in choosing their leaders. Only the House of Representatives was elected by the voters. Alexander Hamilton, one of Constitutional Convention's leaders, told the delegates:

"The people are turbulent and changing; they seldom judge or determine right. Give therefore to the first [upper] class a distinct, permanent share in government. They will check the unsteadiness of the second [the masses]."

By modern standards, Hamilton's remark is undemocratic. But think about the times in which it was made. Shays's Rebellion had recently occurred. In addition, in those days most Americans had little or no education. Many could not even read or write. When its historical context is considered, the statement seems less harsh and extreme.

Practice the Skill

Read the following statement made by Patrick Henry in 1788. Then answer the questions to determine its context and better understand it.

"The Constitution is said to have beautiful features, but … they appear to me horribly frightful.…Your dearest rights may be sacrificed by what may be a small minority … [that] … may continue forever unchangeably this government, although horribly defective."

1. What was Henry's opinion of the Constitution?
2. How might Americans' recent experience in the Revolution have caused him to feel that way?

Social Studies Skills Activity: Determining the Context of Statements

Alexis de Tocqueville Statement `At Level`

1. Have students review the statement by Alexis de Tocqueville, located under the heading "Citizens and Government" in Section 3. Ask for a volunteer to read the quote aloud to the class. Discuss the statement's meaning.

2. Then have students use the steps listed under "Learn the Skill" to determine the context of the statement. Have students consider the following questions:

   • Why might de Tocqueville have been so impressed by this aspect of American life?

Perhaps people were not so involved in political groups in France at the time.

• Do you think someone touring America today would have this same impression? *Answers will vary, but students should exhibit an understanding of how times have changed and how these changes will affect peoples' impressions.* **LS** Verbal/Linguistic

📖 Alternative Assessment Handbook, Rubric 11: Discussions

Answers

Practice the Skill 1. *He disliked it and thought it would enable a minority to rule the majority and deny people their rights.* **2.** *Americans had recently fought to win their freedom from a monarchy they considered abusive. Many Americans at the time feared a strong central government and thought it would trample on people's rights.*

Chapter Review

Visual Summary

Use the visual summary below to help you review the main ideas of the chapter.

QUICK FACTS

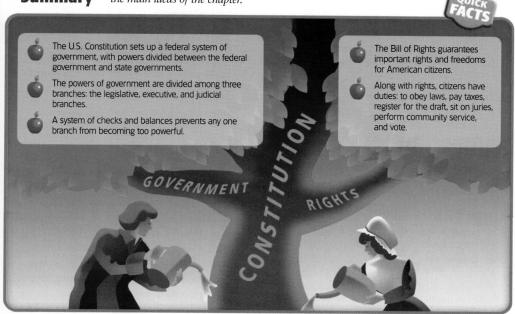

- The U.S. Constitution sets up a federal system of government, with powers divided between the federal government and state governments.
- The powers of government are divided among three branches: the legislative, executive, and judicial branches.
- A system of checks and balances prevents any one branch from becoming too powerful.

- The Bill of Rights guarantees important rights and freedoms for American citizens.
- Along with rights, citizens have duties: to obey laws, pay taxes, register for the draft, sit on juries, perform community service, and vote.

GOVERNMENT · CONSTITUTION · RIGHTS

Reviewing Vocabulary, Terms, and People

1. Who promised to add a bill of rights to the U.S. Constitution?
   a. Benjamin Franklin   **c.** Alexander Hamilton
   b. Thomas Jefferson   **d.** James Madison

2. What is the term for a person born in another country who becomes a citizen of the United States?
   a. immigrant   **c.** naturalized citizen
   b. partial citizen   **d.** separatist

3. What are powers granted to the states called?
   a. reserved powers   **c.** stately powers
   b. concurrent powers   **d.** delegated powers

4. What is the permission to look for evidence of a crime in a particular location called?
   a. petition   **c.** indictment
   b. impeachment   **d.** search warrant

5. Who was the first female Supreme Court justice?
   a. Abigail Adams   **c.** Barbara Jordan
   b. Susan B. Anthony   **d.** Sandra Day O'Connor

CITIZENSHIP AND THE CONSTITUTION **227**

7. a. first 10 amendments to the Constitution; to protect citizens rights and freedoms against majority rule

b. guarantees citizens' basic freedoms and prevents the government from taking certain actions such as quartering troops and using "unreasonable searches and seizures"; recognizes that states and citizens have all powers not delegated to the federal government or prohibited to the states

c. Answers will vary, but students should exhibit an understanding of each amendment of the Bill of Rights.

8. a. born in United States or in a U.S. territory, at least one parent is a U.S. citizen, or become a naturalized citizen

b. through voting, campaigning for candidates, political action committees, interest groups, writing letters to government representatives

c. possible answer—The government would cease to function well, if at all, if citizens stopped performing duties such as voting and paying taxes.

Reading Skills

9. a

Reviewing Themes

10. possible answers—federalism, checks and balances, separation of powers, presidential powers, Bill of Rights

11. Answers will vary, but students should show an understanding that U.S. representative democracy requires that Americans vote intelligently, stay politically informed, and express their political opinions.

Comprehension and Critical Thinking

SECTION 1 *(Pages 182–186)*

6. a. Describe Name each branch of government and explain the duties of each.

b. Analyze What checks and balances exist between the branches of government?

c. Evaluate Do you think the three branches of government share their power equally? Explain your answer.

SECTION 2 *(Pages 216–221)*

7. a. Identify What is the Bill of Rights, and why was it added to the Constitution?

b. Analyze In what ways does the Bill of Rights protect individuals from the power of government?

c. Elaborate Which of the amendments in the Bill of Rights do you think is the most important? Why?

SECTION 3 *(Pages 222–225)*

8. a. Describe What are the ways in which a person can gain U.S. citizenship?

b. Analyze How are citizens able to influence their government?

c. Predict What might result if individuals failed to fulfill their duties as citizens?

Reading Skills

Summarizing Historical Texts *Use the Reading Skills taught in this chapter to answer the question about the reading selection below.*

> "The judicial power of the United States shall be vested in one supreme Court, and in such inferior Courts as the Congress may from time to time … establish. The Judges, both of the supreme and inferior Courts, shall hold their Offices during good Behavior, and … receive for their Services a Compensation…"

9. Which of the following is the best summary of the selection?

a. The U.S. judiciary consists of the Supreme Court and lower courts, and judges are paid.

b. Congress creates lower courts.

Reviewing Themes

10. Politics What important ideas has the U.S. Constitution contributed to government?

11. Politics Why is active political participation an important responsibility for people in the United States?

Social Studies Skills

Determining the Context of Statements *Use the Social Studies Skills taught in this chapter to answer the questions about the quotation below.*

> "What political power could ever carry on the vast multitude [large number] of lesser undertakings which the American citizens perform every day, with the assistance of the principle of association [joining a group]? Nothing, in my opinion, is more deserving of our attention than the intellectual and moral associations of America."
>
> —Alexis de Tocqueville, *Democracy in America*

12. De Tocqueville wrote this about his trip to the United States in 1831. What is his main idea?

a. Governments can fill every need of citizens.

b. American organizations cannot accomplish much.

c. American organizations get too much attention.

d. American organizations fill important needs of citizens that government cannot.

13. Do you think that de Tocqueville's statement accurately describes modern America? Why or why not?

FOCUS ON WRITING

14. Creating a Pamphlet You have gathered information about the Constitution, Bill of Rights, and citizenship. Use that information to create your pamphlet. On the first page, write a title and a phrase that will get your audience's attention. On each of the following pages, you can use this format: (1) a heading and sentence at the top of the page identifying the topic of the page, and (2) the list of the most important points for that topic. Remember that page 2 is on the Constitution, page 3 is on the Bill of Rights, and page 4 is on citizenship.

Social Studies Skills

12. d

13. possible answers—Yes, Americans continue to form and attend groups to sway political opinion and promote issues; no, intellectual and moral groups are not as fashionable or powerful now as they were in the 1830s.

Focus on Writing

14. Rubric Students' pamphlets should:
- provide one page each on the Constitution, the Bill of Rights, and citizenship
- have engaging titles
- include a final summary of the importance of the Constitution and citizenship
- use correct grammar, punctuation, spelling, and capitalization.

📰 **CRF:** Focus on Writing: A Pamphlet

Standardized Test Practice

DIRECTIONS: Read each question and write the letter of the best response.

1 Which of the following rights is *not* protected in the Bill of Rights?

A the right to bear arms

B the right to public education

C the right to jury trials

D the right to free speech

2 The right of every American to be a member of a political party is an example of

A the principle of dual sovereignty.

B the First Amendment right to freedom of assembly.

C the principle of majority rule.

D the Fifth Amendment right to due process of law.

3 Obeying laws, paying taxes, and willingness to serve on a jury are all

A methods of gaining U.S. citizenship.

B duties of U.S. citizens.

C ways in which citizens can influence their government.

D protected by the Second Amendment.

4 The First Amendment would protect

A a reporter that knowingly spreads lies about someone.

B an individual who peacefully protests a government policy.

C an individual who falsely shouts, "Fire" in a crowded theater.

D a hunter who keeps a rifle at home.

5 Which of the following is an example of a check that the executive branch has on the legislative branch?

A The president may declare laws unconstitutional.

B The vice president serves as president of the Senate.

C The president may veto bills passed by Congress.

D The president may appoint members of Congress.

6 Which of the following protects the rights of the accused?

A the guarantee of a speedy trial

B the right to vote cannot be denied because of sex

C the right to sign a petition

D the right to keep and bear arms

7

"What a president says and thinks is not worth five cents unless he has the people and Congress behind him. Without Congress, I'm just a six-feet-four Texan. With Congress, I'm President of the United States in the fullest sense."

— President Lyndon Johnson

What point about government was President Johnson making in this remark?

A The president should be directly elected by the people.

B Congress should not have any ability to control the president.

C The president needs the support of Congress to be effective.

D Congress and the president should share some powers.

Intervention Resources

Technology

Quick Facts Transparency: Citizenship and the Constitution Visual Summary

Differentiated Instruction Modified Worksheets and Tests CD-ROM

Interactive Skills Tutor CD-ROM

Tips for Test Taking

Negative Does Not Fit Tell students to watch for negative words in questions such as *never, unless, not,* and *except.* When a question contains one of these negative words, students should look for the answer that does not fit with the other answers. Have students practice this tip on Questions 2 above.

Chapter 7 Planning Guide

Launching the Nation

Chapter Overview	Reproducible Resources	Technology Resources
CHAPTER 7 pp. 230–257 **Overview:** In this chapter, students will learn how the nation's leaders organized their new government by paying off the national debt, dealing with foreign and domestic conflicts, and forming political parties.	**Differentiated Instruction Teacher Management System:*** • Instructional Benchmarking Guides • Lesson Plans for Differentiated Instruction **Interactive Reader and Study Guide:** Chapter Graphic Organizer* **Chapter Resource File:*** • Focus on Writing Activity: A Nobel Nomination • Social Studies Skills Activity: Making Group Decisions • Chapter Review Activity	**Power Presentations with Video CD-ROM** **Differentiated Instruction Modified Worksheets and Tests CD-ROM** **Primary Source Library CD-ROM for United States History** **Interactive Skills Tutor CD-ROM** **Student Edition on Audio CD Program** **History's Impact: United States History Video Program (VHS/DVD):** Launching the Nation*
Section 1: **Washington Leads a New Nation** **The Big Idea:** President Washington and members of Congress established a new national government.	**Differentiated Instruction Teacher Management System:** Section 1 Lesson Plan* **Interactive Reader and Study Guide:** Section 1 Summary* **Chapter Resource File:*** • Vocabulary Builder Activity, Section 1 • Biography Activity: Martha Washington • Biography Activity: Alexander Hamilton	**Daily Bellringer Transparency:** Section 1*
Section 2: **Hamilton and National Finances** **The Big Idea:** Treasury secretary Alexander Hamilton developed a financial plan for the national government.	**Differentiated Instruction Teacher Management System:** Section 2 Lesson Plan* **Interactive Reader and Study Guide:** Section 2 Summary* **Chapter Resource File:*** • Vocabulary Builder Activity, Section 2 • Economics and History Activity: The National Debt • History and Geography Activity: The Nation's Capital • Interdisciplinary Projects: Planning the Nation's Capital Drama Skit; Student Almanac • Primary Source Activity: Jefferson and Hamilton Disagree about Government	**Daily Bellringer Transparency:** Section 2* **Quick Facts Transparency:** Hamilton's Economic Plan* **Internet Activity:** Washington, D.C.: Then and Now
Section 3: **Challenges for the New Nation** **The Big Idea:** The United States faced significant foreign and domestic challenges under Washington.	**Differentiated Instruction Teacher Management System:** Section 3 Lesson Plan* **Interactive Reader and Study Guide:** Section 3 Summary* **Chapter Resource File:*** • Vocabulary Builder Activity, Section 3 • Primary Source Activity: President George Washington's Farewell Address **Political Cartoons Activities for United States History, Cartoon 7:** The French Revolution	**Daily Bellringer Transparency:** Section 3* **Map Transparency:** Pinckney's Treaty* **Map Transparency:** Fighting in the Northwest Territory* **Internet Activity:** French Revolution Chart
Section 4: **John Adams's Presidency** **The Big Idea:** The development of political parties in the United States contributed to differing ideas about the role of the federal government.	**Differentiated Instruction Teacher Management System:** Section 4 Lesson Plan* **Interactive Reader and Study Guide:** Section 4 Summary* **Chapter Resource File:*** • Vocabulary Builder Activity, Section 4 • Biography Activity: Abigail Adams	**Daily Bellringer Transparency:** Section 4* **Map Transparency:** The First Political Parties*

HOLT

History's Impact
United States History Video Program (VHS/DVD)

Launching the Nation
Suggested use: as a chapter introduction

Review, Assessment, Intervention

 Quick Facts Transparency: Launching the Nation Visual Summary*

Spanish Chapter Summaries Audio CD Program

 Progress Assessment Support System (PASS): Chapter Test*

Differentiated Instruction Modified Worksheets and Tests CD-ROM: Modified Chapter Test

One-Stop Planner CD-ROM: ExamView Test Generator (English/Spanish)

Holt Online Assessment Program (HOAP), in the Holt Premier Online Student Edition

---

 PASS: Section 1 Quiz*

 Online Quiz: Section 1

Alternative Assessment Handbook

 PASS: Section 2 Quiz*

Online Quiz: Section 2

Alternative Assessment Handbook

 PASS: Section 3 Quiz*

 Online Quiz: Section 3

Alternative Assessment Handbook

 PASS: Section 4 Quiz*

 Online Quiz: Section 4

Alternative Assessment Handbook

Power Presentations with Video CD-ROM

Power Presentations with Video are visual presentations of each chapter's main ideas. Presentations can be customized by including Quick Facts charts, images from the text, and video clips.

Power Presentations with Video CD-ROM

United States History
Beginnings to 1877

HOLT, RINEHART AND WINSTON

DIVISION FOR PUBLIC EDUCATION
AMERICAN BAR ASSOCIATION

Developed by the Division for Public Education of the American Bar Association, these materials are part of the **Democracy and Civic Education Resources.**

- **Constitution Study Guide**
- **Supreme Court Case Studies**

Holt Online Learning

Teacher Resources
KEYWORD: SR8 TEACHER

Student Resources
KEYWORD: SR8 US7

- Document-Based Questions
- Interactive Multimedia Activities

- Current Events
- Chapter-based Internet Activities
- and more!

Holt Premier
Online Student Edition

Complete online support for interactivity, assessment, and reporting

- Interactive Maps and Notebook
- Standardized Test Prep
- Homework Practice and Research Activities Online

Differentiating Instruction

ENGLISH-LANGUAGE LEARNERS & STRUGGLING READERS

TARGET RESOURCE

Live Ink® Online Reading Help

Spanish Resources

Spanish Chapter Summaries Audio CD Program

One-Stop Planner CD-ROM:
- ExamView Test Generator, Spanish
- PuzzlePro, Spanish

Additional Resources

Differentiated Instruction Teacher Management System: Lesson Plans for Differentiated Instruction

Chapter Resources:
- Vocabulary Builder Activities
- Social Studies Skills Activity: Making Group Decisions

Quick Facts Transparencies:
- Hamilton's Economic Plan
- Launching the Nation Visual Summary

Student Edition on Audio CD Program

Online Chapter Summaries in Six Languages

Interactive Skills Tutor CD-ROM

SPECIAL NEEDS LEARNERS

TARGET RESOURCE

Differentiated Instruction Modified Worksheets and Tests CD-ROM

- Vocabulary Flash Cards
- Modified Vocabulary Builder Activities
- Modified Chapter Review Activity
- Modified Chapter Test

Additional Resources

Differentiated Instruction Teacher Management System: Lesson Plans for Differentiated Instruction

Interactive Reader and Study Guide

Social Studies Skills Activity: Making Group Decisions

Student Edition on Audio CD Program

Interactive Skills Tutor CD-ROM

Live Ink® Online Reading Help

ADVANCED/GIFTED AND TALENTED STUDENTS

TARGET RESOURCE

Primary Source Library CD-ROM for United States History

The Library contains longer versions of quotations in the text, extra sources, and images. Included are point-of-view articles, journals, diaries, historical fiction, and political documents.

Additional Resources

Political Cartoons Activities for United States History: Cartoon 7: The French Revolution

United States History Document-Based Questions Activities

Differentiated Instruction Teacher Management System: Lesson Plans for Differentiated Instruction

Pre-AP Activities Guide for United States History: Identifying Main Ideas and Supporting Details

Chapter Resource File:
- Focus on Writing Activity: A Nobel Nomination
- Primary Source Activity: Jefferson and Hamilton Disagree about Government
- Primary Source Activity: President George Washington's Farewell Address

Differentiated Activities in the Teacher's Edition

- Explaining Hamilton's Economic Plan, p. 239
- Native American Conflict Time Lines, 246

One-Stop Planner® CD-ROM
for Differentiated Instruction

Your differentiated instruction lesson plans are available at your fingertips. Holt's Teacher Management System links teaching support tools to pages in the Interactive Teacher's Edition.

The One-Stop Planner features:
- Interactive Teacher's Edition
- Calendar Planner and pacing guides
- Editable lesson plans
- All reproducible ancillaries in Adobe Acrobat (PDF) format
- ExamView Test Generator (English and Spanish)
- Transparency and video previews

Differentiated Activities in the Teacher's Edition

- Late 1700s Domestic Conflicts Chart, p. 247

Professional Development

- **In-service and staff development** as part of your Holt Social Studies product purchase
- **Quick Teacher Tutorial Lesson Presentation CD-ROM**
- Intensive tuition-based **Teacher Development Institute**
- **Teaching American History Online**—2 Module Professional Development Course
- **Convenient Holt Speaker Bureau**—face-to-face workshop options
- **PRAXIS™ Test Prep** interactive Web-based content refreshers*
- **24/7 Ask A Professional Development Expert** at http://www.hrw.com/prodev/

* PRAXIS is a trademark of Educational Testing Service (ETS). This publication is not endorsed or approved by ETS.

Differentiated Activities in the Teacher's Edition

- Résumé for Washington, p. 235
- Presidential Farewell Addresses, p. 248
- Record of the XYZ Affair, p. 251

Chapter Big Ideas

Section 1 President Washington and members of Congress established a new national government.

Section 2 Treasury secretary Alexander Hamilton developed a financial plan for the national government.

Section 3 The United States faced significant foreign and domestic challenges under Washington.

Section 4 The development of political parties in the United States contributed to differing ideas about the role of the federal government.

Focus on Writing

The **Chapter Resource File** provides a Focus on Writing worksheet to help students write their Nobel nomination.

CRF: Focus on Writing Activity: A Nobel Nomination

Key to Differentiating Instruction

Below Level

Basic-level activities designed for all students encountering new material

At Level

Intermediate-level activities designed for average students

Above Level

Challenging activities designed for honors and gifted and talented students

Standard English Mastery

Activities designed to improve standard English usage

230 CHAPTER 7

Launching the Nation

FOCUS ON WRITING

A Nobel Nomination Every year a few people are nominated for a Nobel Prize for their work to improve the world. In this chapter you will read about four great Americans—Washington, Hamilton, Jefferson, and Adams. Then you'll choose one of these great leaders and write a Nobel Prize nomination for him.

UNITED STATES

1789
George Washington becomes the first president.

1785

WORLD

1789
The French Revolution begins.

230 CHAPTER 7

Introduce the Chapter

At Level

Organizing the New Government

1. Remind students that the U.S. Constitution created a new system of government for the United States. However, the work was not yet done. The nation's leaders still needed to establish and organize this new government.

2. Write the following question for students to see: *What might your first actions be as part of the nation's new government?* Give students a few minutes to predict some of the new government's first actions. Write students' predictions for the class to see.

3. Then ask students what they think some of the challenges facing the nation's new government might be. Make a list of students' predictions.

4. Tell students to determine the accuracy of their predictions as they read the chapter.
   LS **Verbal/Linguistic**

   Alternative Assessment Handbook, Rubric 11: Discussions

230 CHAPTER 7

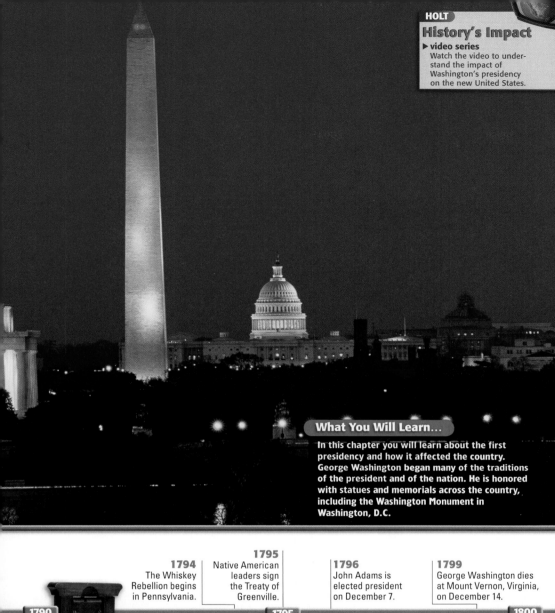

What You Will Learn...

In this chapter you will learn about the first presidency and how it affected the country. George Washington began many of the traditions of the president and of the nation. He is honored with statues and memorials across the country, including the Washington Monument in Washington, D.C.

● **Chapter Preview** ●

HOLT
History's Impact
▶ video series
See the Video Teacher's Guide for strategies for using the chapter video **Launching the Nation**.

Explore the Picture

The Washington Monument Of the many statues and monuments dedicated to George Washington, the Washington Monument is perhaps the most famous. The monument was designed by architect Robert Mills, who also designed the U.S. Treasury Building and the Patent Office. Construction began in 1848, but was halted for various reasons in the mid-1850s. Building finally resumed in 1880, and the monument was officially opened to the public in 1888. Built of granite covered with marble, the monument rises more than 555 feet and is topped by an aluminum pyramid. It remains the world's tallest masonry structure.

Analyzing Visuals The Washington Monument symbolizes Washington and his leadership. What adjectives might describe the monument? *possible answers—impressive, towering, influential, powerful, dignified, elegant*

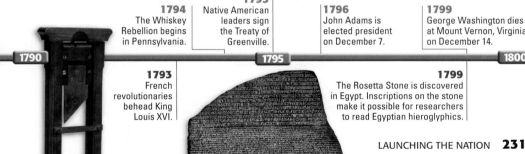

1794
The Whiskey Rebellion begins in Pennsylvania.

1795
Native American leaders sign the Treaty of Greenville.

1796
John Adams is elected president on December 7.

1799
George Washington dies at Mount Vernon, Virginia, on December 14.

1790

1795

1800

1793
French revolutionaries behead King Louis XVI.

1799
The Rosetta Stone is discovered in Egypt. Inscriptions on the stone make it possible for researchers to read Egyptian hieroglyphics.

LAUNCHING THE NATION **231**

Explore the Time Line

1. When did Washington become the first U.S. president? *1789*

2. What other event began that same year? *French Revolution*

3. What did Native American leaders sign in 1795? *Treaty of Greenville*

4. Who was elected as the second president of the United States in 1796? *John Adams*

Connect to the Arts and Humanities

The Nation's Capital During Washington's presidency, the nation's capital was moved to a site along the Potomac River. This site became the city of Washington, D.C. French engineer Pierre Charles L'Enfant designed the layout of the new capital. L'Enfant envisioned a city with fountains, gardens, and public parks and a system of boulevards radiating out from the city center. Today, Washington, D.C. is a cultural center as well as the seat of the nation's government.

Reading
Social Studies

Understanding Themes

Introduce students to the two main themes of this chapter—politics and economics—by asking students to make a list of different items that might need to be addressed by the new government created by the U.S. Constitution. Remind students that the previous government was weak at the national level. Point out to students that although the Constitution formed the new government, many political and economic decisions still had to be made by the new government.

Inferences about History

Focus on Reading Have students write two inferences about daily life, current events in the news, or pop culture. Tell them to make one of the inferences an educated guess and the other one a weak guess. After several minutes, have students hand in their inferences. Read several inferences aloud and allow students to guess which inferences are based on an educated guess and which are not. Discuss with the class what makes a good inference, noting the importance of reliable facts and sound judgment.

Reading Social Studies

by Kylene Beers

| Economics | Geography | Politics | Society and Culture | Science and Technology |

Focus on Themes This chapter, titled "Launching the Nation," describes how the early leaders established this nation's **political** and **economic** systems. You will read about Washington's presidency, Hamiliton's plan for financial security for the nation, the establishment of two parties to elect the president, and Jefferson's struggles with both Washington and Hamilton. Throughout the chapter, you will see that disagreement often defined these early days.

Inferences about History

Focus on Reading What's the difference between a good guess and a weak guess? A good guess is an *educated* guess. In other words, the guess is based on some knowledge or information. That's what an **inference** is, an educated guess.

Making Inferences About What You Read To make an inference, combine information from your reading with what you already know, and make an educated guess about what it all means. Once you have made several inferences, you may be able to draw a conclusion that ties them all together.

Question What kind of person was Alexander Hamilton?

Inside the Text
- Hamilton ran a company when he was just a teenager.
- He had a career as a lawyer.
- He became the Secretary of the Treasury under Washington.

Outside the Text
- Running a company takes intelligence and cleverness.
- Becoming a lawyer takes dedication.
- Washington probably wanted someone clever and capable.

Inference Alexander Hamilton was an intelligent, clever, and dedicated man.

Steps for Making Inferences
1. Ask a question.
2. Note information "Inside the Text."
3. Note information "Outside the Text."
4. **Use both sets of information to make an educated guess, or inference.**

232 CHAPTER 7

Reading and Skills Resources

Reading Support
- Interactive Reader and Study Guide
- Student Edition on Audio CD Program
- Spanish Chapter Summaries Audio CD Program

Social Studies Skills Support
- Interactive Skills Tutor CD-ROM

Vocabulary Support
- **CRF:** Vocabulary Builder Activities
- **CRF:** Chapter Review Activity
- Differentiated Instruction Modified Worksheets and Tests CD-ROM:
  - Vocabulary Flash Cards
  - Vocabulary Builder Activity
  - Chapter Review Activity

OSP Holt PuzzlePro

You Try It!

Read the following passage and answer the questions that follow.

Economic Differences

Hamilton wanted new forms of economic growth. He wanted to promote manufacturing and business. He even suggested that the government award a prize to companies that made excellent products.

In addition, Hamilton wanted to pass higher tariffs. Known as protective tariffs, these taxes would raise the prices of foreign products. Hamilton hoped this would cause Americans to buy U.S. goods. As a result, American manufacturing would be protected from foreign competition.

Jefferson worried about depending too much on business and manufacturing. He believed that farmers were the most independent voters . . . Jefferson wanted to help farmers by keeping the costs of the goods they bought low. Lower tariffs would help keep prices low.

From Chapter 7, p. 240–241

After you read the passage, answer the following questions.

1. Which two questions can be answered directly from the text above and which one requires that you make an inference?

   a. Who wanted higher tariffs, Hamilton or Jefferson?
   b. Why do you think Hamilton and Jefferson had different views on the importance of manufacturing?
   c. Which man wanted to help the farmers?

2. To answer question b, it might help to know that Hamilton lived in New York City and Jefferson was from the more rural area of Virginia. Use that information and information in the passage to explain why one man valued manufacturing more than the other.

Key Terms and People

Chapter 7

Section 1
George Washington *(p. 234)*
electoral college *(p. 234)*
Martha Washington *(p. 234)*
precedent *(p. 235)*
Judiciary Act of 1789 *(p. 236)*

Section 2
Alexander Hamilton *(p. 238)*
national debt *(p. 238)*
bonds *(p. 238)*
speculators *(p. 239)*
Thomas Jefferson *(p. 239)*
loose construction *(p. 242)*
strict construction *(p. 242)*
Bank of the United States *(p. 242)*

Section 3
French Revolution *(p. 243)*
Neutrality Proclamation *(p. 244)*
privateers *(p. 244)*
Jay's Treaty *(p. 245)*
Pinckney's Treaty *(p. 245)*
Little Turtle *(p. 246)*
Battle of Fallen Timbers *(p. 247)*
Treaty of Greenville *(p. 247)*
Whiskey Rebellion *(p. 247)*

Section 4
political parties *(p. 250)*
Federalist Party *(p. 250)*
Democratic-Republican Party *(p. 250)*
XYZ affair *(p. 252)*
Alien and Sedition Acts *(p. 253)*
Kentucky and Virginia Resolutions
(p. 253)

Academic Vocabulary

In this chapter, you will learn the following academic words:

agreement *(p. 237)*
neutral *(p. 244)*

As you read Chapter 7, remember that you need to combine what you already know with the information in the chapter to make inferences.

Reading Social Studies

Key Terms and People

Introduce the key terms and people for this chapter by having students define or describe each term or person. Then have students write a paragraph in which they use at least seven key terms or people. Remind students to use each term correctly. **LS** Verbal/Linguistic

Focus on Reading

See the **Focus on Reading** questions in this chapter for more practice on this reading social studies skill.

Reading Social Studies Assessment

See the **Chapter Review** at the end of this chapter for student assessment questions related to this reading skill.

Teaching Tip

To help students learn how to make inferences, have students create a T-chart. Ask students to label one column of the chart *Inside the Text,* and the other column *Outside the Text.* Then have students pay attention to the details in the passage above to complete the first column, and use their own outside knowledge on the subject to complete the second column. Students should then use the information in each column to make an inference.

Answers

You Try It! 1. *answered directly—a and c; inference—b;* **2.** *Because Hamilton was from an urban area that relied on manufacturing, he supported laws that favored manufacturing. Jefferson on the other hand did not feel strongly about manufacturing because he was from a region that relied economically on farming.*

Bellringer

If YOU were there . . . Use the **Daily Bellringer Transparency** to help students answer the question.

📦 Daily Bellringer Transparency, Section 1

Academic Vocabulary

Review with students the high-use academic term in this section.

agreement a decision reached by two or more people or groups (p. 237)

📄 **CRF:** Vocabulary Builder Activity, Section 1

Taking Notes

Have students copy the graphic organizer onto their own paper and then use it to take notes on the section. This activity will prepare students for the Section Assessment, in which they will complete a graphic organizer that builds on the information using a critical thinking skill.

What You Will Learn...

Main Ideas

1. In 1789 George Washington became the first president of the United States.
2. Congress and the president organized the executive and judicial branches of government.
3. Americans had high expectations of their new government.

The Big Idea

President Washington and members of Congress established a new national government.

Key Terms and People

George Washington, *p. 234*
electoral college, *p. 234*
Martha Washington, *p. 234*
precedent, *p. 235*
Judiciary Act of 1789, *p. 236*

TAKING NOTES As you read, take notes in a graphic organizer like the one below on why and how George Washington was chosen as president.

234 CHAPTER 7

Washington Leads a New Nation

If YOU were there...

You are a seamstress in New York City in 1789. You've joined the excited crowd in the streets for inauguration day. Church bells are ringing, and people are cheering. Even though you were just a young child during the Revolution, Washington is your hero. Now you watch as he takes the oath of office. You are proud to see that he is wearing a suit of American-made cloth.

What would you think America's future would be like under President Washington?

> **BUILDING BACKGROUND** George Washington was more than just a popular war hero. People naturally looked to him as a national leader. He had taken part in the Continental Congresses and in creating the Constitution. He helped establish and strengthen the new national government.

The First President

Americans believed in **George Washington**. They saw him as an honest leader and a hero of the Revolution. Many believed he should be the first U.S. president. Washington had been looking forward to retirement and a quiet life on his Virginia farm. When he hesitated at becoming a candidate for the presidency, his friends convinced him to run. Fellow politician Gouverneur Morris told him, "Should the idea prevail [win] that you would not accept the presidency, it should prove fatal . . . to the new government." Morris concluded confidently, "Of all men, you are the best fitted to fill that office."

In January 1789 each of the 11 states that had passed the Constitution sent electors to choose the first president. These delegates formed a group called the **electoral college**—a body of electors who represent the people's vote in choosing the president. The electoral college selected Washington unanimously, and John Adams became his vice president.

Washington's wife, First Lady **Martha Washington**, entertained guests and attended social events with her husband. She described the

---

Teach the Big Idea

Washington Leads a New Nation

Materials: blank note cards

1. **Teach** Ask students the questions in the Main Idea boxes to teach this section.
2. **Apply** Give each student three note cards. Have students write one of the section's blue heads on each card. On the back of the first two cards, have students record the actions that Washington and Congress took and the precedents they set to organize the national government. On the back of the third card,

have students record Americans' expectations for the new government. 🔵 **Verbal/Linguistic**

3. **Review** As you review, have students share the information on their note cards.
4. **Practice/Homework** Have each student take on the role of an American in 1790, and write a journal entry describing his or her emotions about Washington's election.

📄 Alternative Assessment Handbook, Rubrics 1: Acquiring Information; and 15: Journals scene to her niece: "I have not had one half-hour to myself since the day of my arrival." She ran the presidential household with style.

Other women, such as author Judith Sargent Murray, believed that women needed to play a greater role in the new nation than Martha Washington did. Murray, Abigail Adams, and others believed in Republican Motherhood, the idea that women played an important role in teaching their children to be good citizens.

Some promoters of Republican Motherhood did not expect women to participate in politics or business. Other people, however, hoped that Republican Motherhood would lead to greater opportunities for women. They hoped more women would receive an education. Only a few families were willing to provide much education for their daughters, and adult women rarely had the time or money to get an education later in life. Most women in the early republic faced long days managing their households and working hard inside or outside the home to support their families.

READING CHECK Analyzing Why was Washington selected to be president?

Organizing the Government

Hard work also lay ahead for members of the new government. The new federal government had to create policies and procedures that would determine the future of the country. As President Washington noted in a letter to James Madison, "The first of everything in our situation will serve to establish a precedent." A **precedent** is an action or decision that later serves as an example.

Congress created departments in the executive branch for different areas of national policy. Washington met with the department heads, or cabinet members, who advised him. For two of his most important cabinet positions, Washington chose carefully. He picked Alexander Hamilton as secretary of the treasury and Thomas Jefferson as secretary of state. Henry Knox served as secretary of war, and Samuel Osgood was chosen as postmaster general. Hamilton was a gifted economic planner, and Jefferson had served as ambassador to France. Knox had helped Washington run the Continental Army, and Osgood had government experience.

The First Cabinet

Washington's cabinet members kept him informed on political matters and debated important issues with one another. Each of the men chosen had experience that made him a wise choice to advise the nation's first president. By 1792 cabinet meetings were a common practice.

ANALYSIS SKILL ANALYZING VISUALS

How do you think a modern cabinet meeting might look different from the one shown here?

① Henry Knox, secretary of war
② Thomas Jefferson, secretary of state
③ Edmund Randolph, attorney general
④ Alexander Hamilton, secretary of the treasury
⑤ George Washington, president

LAUNCHING THE NATION **235**

Differentiating Instruction

Above Level

Advanced/Gifted and Talented

Materials: photocopies of a model résumé

1. Tell students that a résumé is a record of a person's qualifications and experience, which a person submits to apply for a job. Instruct students to create a résumé for George Washington as if he were applying for the job of U.S. president.

2. Provide students with photocopies of a proper résumé to use as a model.

3. Students' résumés should provide information about Washington's leadership experience and communicate why he would be good for the job of president.

4. Conclude by discussing with the class why Americans elected Washington as their first president. **LS** Verbal/Linguistic

📋 Alternative Assessment Handbook, Rubric 31: Résumés

235

❷ Organizing the Government

Congress and the president organized the executive and judicial branches of government.

Explain What was the purpose of the Judiciary Act of 1789? *set up three levels of federal courts and defined their powers and relationships to the state courts*

Summarize How were federal judges selected? *The president nominated them, and Congress either approved or rejected candidates.*

Info to Know

A Rough Start When George Washington became president, there was no White House to live in. Instead, the president and First Lady Martha Washington lived in a house on 3 Cherry Street in New York City. Although nicknamed the Palace, the house was not tremendously glamorous. For example, the ceilings were so low that one woman's hat caught fire when she brushed against the chandelier.

A Rural Nation

Urban vs. Rural Population, 1790

Urban 5%
Rural 95%

Today we know that presidents have cabinet meetings with their top advisers. This practice started during Washington's presidency and were common by 1792.

To set up the federal court system and the courts' location, Congress passed the **Judiciary Act of 1789**. This act created three levels of federal courts and defined their powers and relationship to the state courts. It set up federal district courts and circuit courts of appeals. The president nominated candidates for federal judgeships. Those candidates then had to be approved or rejected by the Senate. Washington wrote about the importance of these duties:

> "I have always been persuaded that the stability and success of the national government … would depend in a considerable degree on the interpretation and execution of its laws. In my opinion, therefore, it is important that the judiciary system should not only be independent in its operations, but as perfect as possible in its formation."
> —George Washington, quoted in *The Real George Washington*, edited by Parry et al.

The basic parts of the federal government were now in place. Leaders began to face the challenges of the new nation. Hard work lay ahead.

READING CHECK Finding Main Ideas
What two important precedents were established for the federal government?

Americans' Expectations of Government

Most Americans had high expectations for their government. They wanted improved trade, free from too many restrictions. But they also expected the government to protect them and to keep the economy stable. However, the idea of belonging to one united nation was new to them.

In 1790 the United States was home to almost 4 million people. Most Americans lived in the countryside and worked on farms. Farmers wanted fair tax laws and the right to settle western lands. They did not want the government to interfere with their daily lives.

Other Americans worked in towns as craftspeople, laborers, or merchants. These people looked to the government to help their businesses. Most merchants wanted simpler trade laws established. Manufacturers wanted laws to protect them from foreign competitors.

Critical Thinking: Identifying Points of View
At Level

Letters to President Washington

1. Have students discuss the expectations that Americans had for their new national government. Remind students of the problems that Americans had been facing under the Articles of Confederation.

2. Divide the class in half. Assign one half the role of American farmers in 1790. Assign the other half the role of merchants or manufacturers in New York City in 1790.

3. Have each student write a letter to President Washington from the point of view of his or her assigned role. In their letters, students should congratulate Washington on his election and share their hopes and concerns for the new national government.

4. Ask for volunteers to read their letters aloud. Conclude by having students compare and contrast America in 1790 with America today.

LS **Verbal/Linguistic**

Alternative Assessment Handbook, Rubric 41: Writing to Express

Answers

Reading Check *established executive departments and cabinet; established the federal court system by passing the Judiciary Act of 1789*

Some Americans lived in growing cities like New York, shown above. However, the new republic was overwhelmingly rural. Most Americans lived and worked on farms.

Why might rural Americans and urban Americans want different things from their new government?

Most cities were small. Only New York City and Philadelphia had populations larger than 25,000. New York City was the first capital of the United States, and it represented the spirit of the new nation. Although badly damaged during the Revolution, the city had already begun to recover. Citizens got rid of many signs of British rule.

New York City had a bustling economy. International trade and business became more active. A French visitor to New York City noted the city's energy.

"Everything in the city is in motion; everywhere the shops resound [ring out] with the noise of workers ...one sees vessels arriving from every part of the world."
—A French visitor to New York, quoted in *New York in the American Revolution* by Wilbur Abbott

In 1792 some 24 stockbrokers signed an **agreement** under a buttonwood tree on Wall Street. This agreement was the foundation for what later became the New York Stock Exchange. It cemented Wall Street's image as the economic hub of the United States.

By 1790 the city's population had topped 33,000 and was growing rapidly. To many officials, this vibrant city reflected the potential future of the new nation. It was thus a fitting place for the capital.

ACADEMIC VOCABULARY
agreement a decision reached by two or more people or groups

THE IMPACT TODAY
Today the New York Stock Exchange is the largest market for securities, or stocks, in the world.

READING CHECK **Analyzing** Why was New York City chosen as the first capital of the United States?

SUMMARY AND PREVIEW Americans, led by President George Washington, set up their new government. In the next section you will read about Alexander Hamilton's economic plan.

Section 1 Assessment

Online Quiz
KEYWORD: SR8 HP7

Reviewing Ideas, Terms, and People
1. **a. Describe** What role did the electoral college play in **George Washington's** election to the presidency?
   b. Summarize What were some of **Martha Washington's** duties as First Lady?
2. **a. Describe** What **precedent** did President Washington and Congress establish regarding the executive branch?
   b. Explain What was the purpose of the **Judiciary Act of 1789**?
   c. Evaluate What do you think was the most important element of the Judiciary Act of 1789? Why?
3. **a. Recall** What city served as the first capital of the United States? Why?
   b. Draw Conclusions What expectations did most Americans have of their government?
   c. Make Judgments Do you think New York City should still be the capital city of the United States? Explain.

Critical Thinking
4. **Comparing** Review your notes on George Washington. Then copy the chart below and use it to compare how Washington and Congress organized the new government.

Washington's Decisions	Acts of Congress

   First U.S. Government

FOCUS ON WRITING

5. **Thinking about Washington's Contributions** In this section you learned some things about George Washington as president. Jot down one or two things you could use to support his nomination for a Nobel Prize.

LAUNCHING THE NATION **237**

Section 1 Assessment Answers

1. **a.** represented the people's vote; voted to elect George Washington as the first president
   b. entertained guests, attended social events with her husband, ran presidential household
2. **a.** created executive departments, the heads of which served as a cabinet to the president
   b. created three levels of federal courts, defined their powers and relationships to state courts
   c. possible answers—creation of courts of appeals, because Americans could appeal rulings; creation of federal district courts, because provided justice across the country

3. **a.** New York City; was one of the largest U.S. cities and a center of economic activity
   b. wanted improved trade free from too many restrictions, protection, and a stable economy
4. Sample answer—Washington's Decisions: chose cabinet members; Acts of Congress: organized executive and judicial branches of government, passed the Judiciary Act of 1789
5. possible answers—first U.S. president; set many precedents, established practice of cabinet meetings

237

Hamilton and National Finances

Bellringer

If YOU were there . . . Use the **Daily Bellringer Transparency** to help students answer the question.

🔖 Daily Bellringer Transparency, Section 2

Building Vocabulary

Preteach or review the following terms:

mint a place to make coins (p. 241)

monopoly sole or exclusive control (p. 241)

tariff an extra charge on goods (p. 241)

📋 **CRF:** Vocabulary Builder Activity, Section 2

Taking Notes

Have students copy the graphic organizer onto their own paper and then use it to take notes on the section. This activity will prepare students for the Section Assessment, in which they will complete a graphic organizer that builds on the information using a critical thinking skill.

What You Will Learn...

Main Ideas

1. Hamilton tackled the problem of settling national and state debt.
2. Thomas Jefferson opposed Hamilton's views on government and the economy.
3. Hamilton created a national bank to strengthen the U.S. economy.

The Big Idea

Treasury secretary Alexander Hamilton developed a financial plan for the national government.

Key Terms and People

Alexander Hamilton, *p. 238*
national debt, *p. 238*
bonds, *p. 238*
speculators, *p. 239*
Thomas Jefferson, *p. 239*
loose construction, *p. 242*
strict construction, *p. 242*
Bank of the United States, *p. 242*

TAKING NOTES As you read, take notes on the economic problems facing the nation when Alexander Hamilton became secretary of the treasury, as well as Hamilton's solutions to the problems.

If YOU were there...

You live on a plantation in North Carolina in the 1790s. You have just heard that the federal government plans to pay most of the northern states' debts from the war. Now your neighbors are outraged about this idea. It means more taxes and tariffs! New York and Massachusetts are far away, they say. Why should North Carolina farmers have to pay northern debts?

Would you pay other states' war debts? Why?

BUILDING BACKGROUND Some of the new nation's biggest problems were economic. The national and state governments had run up huge debts during the war. But the proposed solutions to these problems revealed differences in regional viewpoints. Southern planters and northern businesspeople had very different views of how the national economy should develop.

Settling the Debt

Alexander Hamilton seemed born with a head for economics. While still in his teens, he helped run a shipping company in his native British West Indies. Family friends then sent him to the American colonies for an education. Hamilton eventually married into a wealthy New York family and began practicing law. He served as Washington's aide and as a delegate to four Continental Congresses.

National Debt

As secretary of the treasury, Hamilton's biggest challenge was paying off the **national debt**—money owed by the United States—from the Revolutionary War. The United States owed about $11.7 million to foreign countries and about $40.4 million to U.S. citizens. During the war the government raised money with bonds. **Bonds** are certificates of debt that carry a promise to buy back the bonds at a higher price. But the government could not afford to keep this promise. Bondholders who needed money sold

---

Hamilton and National Finances

1. **Teach** Ask students the questions in the Main Idea boxes to teach this section.

2. **Apply** Have students, working either individually or in pairs, use the blue and red headings in this section to create an outline of the information. Tell students to write at least two supporting details under each heading. Encourage students to write their supporting details in sentence form. **LS Verbal/Linguistic**

3. **Review** Have students share information from their outlines with the class. Create a master outline for the class to see and use it to correct any student errors.

4. **Practice/Homework** Have each student use the information in his or her outline to create a five-question quiz about the section content. **LS Verbal/Linguistic**

📋 Alternative Assessment Handbook, Rubric 37: Writing Assignments

Alexander Hamilton developed a three-point plan to solve the nation's financial problems.

1 Deal with the Debt
- Take on the foreign and domestic debt by replacing creditors' old, low-value bonds with new, interest-bearing bonds

  would build investor confidence in the stability of the new nation

- Take over most of the states' $25 million Revolutionary War debts

  would free up state money for business and trade

2 Gain Revenue
- Pass a tariff to both bring in money and help American manufacturers

3 Stabilize the Banking System
- Create a national bank
- Create a national mint

Total Debt

Domestic debt $40.4 million
State debt $25 million
Foreign debt $11.7 million

---

their bonds for less than the original value to **speculators**, or people who buy items at low prices in the hope that the value will rise and they can sell the items for a profit.

Hamilton wanted to pay the foreign debt immediately and gradually repay the total value of all bonds. The second part of his plan caused disagreements because paying full value would allow speculators to make a profit. Hamilton thought this was fair. He said, "He [the speculator] paid what the commodity [bond] was worth . . . and took the risks."

Thomas Jefferson disagreed. He thought the idea cheated bondholders who had sold their bonds at low prices. Jefferson wrote, "Immense sums were thus filched [stolen] from the poor and ignorant." But more politicians agreed with Hamilton. In 1790 the government exchanged old bonds for new, more reliable ones that were guaranteed.

States' Debts

The states owed $25 million for Revolutionary War expenses. Hamilton wanted the federal government to pay for $21.5 million of this debt. Hamilton believed that this action would help the federal government. He

thought that paying the states' debts would help the national economy. Debtor states would not have to spend so much on repayment and would have money to develop business and trade. Increased business and trade would put more money back into the national economy.

The South, however, did not want to help the federal government pay the debts of other states. States such as Virginia and North Carolina did not have many war debts. They thought Hamilton's idea was unfair. Patrick Henry said he did not believe that the Constitution gave Congress the power to pay state debts. Hamilton knew that he needed the help of southern representatives to get his plan approved.

Moving the Capital

Hamilton also knew that he had something to bargain with. Southern officials wanted to change the location of the nation's capital. Many southerners thought that having the capital in New York gave the northern states too much influence over national policy. Hamilton, Jefferson, and James Madison met in June 1790. Hamilton

---

Differentiating Instruction

Below Level

Struggling Readers

1. Have students examine the above Quick Facts: Hamilton's Economic Plan. Go over the various elements of Hamilton's economic plan as a class.

2. To help students better understand the nation's economic problems and Hamilton's financial plan, compare them to aspects of an individual's personal finances, such as credit card debt, IOUs, balancing a checkbook, checking and savings accounts, and so on.

3. Have students go through the Quick Facts chart and explain Hamilton's economic plan in their own words point by point.
   LS Verbal/Linguistic, Visual/Spatial

   Alternative Assessment Handbook, Rubric 11: Discussions

   CRF: Economics and History Activity: The National Debt

   Quick Facts Transparency: Hamilton's Economic Plan

Direct Teach

Main Idea

1 Settling the Debt

Hamilton tackled the problem of settling national and state debt.

Explain What economic problem did the young nation face, and how did Alexander Hamilton propose to solve it? *high national debt; pay the foreign debt immediately; gradually pay back the full value of bonds*

Identify Points of View Why did Jefferson oppose paying the full value of bonds? *would reward speculators and cheat the original bondholders who sold at low prices*

Make Judgments Do you think Hamilton's plan for the federal government to take over state war debts was fair to southern states? *possible answers—yes, all the states benefited from the Revolutionary War and should help pay for it; no, southern states had few war debts and should not pay.*

CRF: Economics and History Activity: The National Debt

CRF: History and Geography Activity: The Nation's Capital

CRF: Interdisciplinary Projects: Planning the Nation's Capital Drama Skit; Student Almanac

Quick Facts Transparency: Hamilton's Economic Plan

Info to Know

The Confusing National Debt When he accepted the position of treasury secretary, Alexander Hamilton faced a large and confusing national debt with several different creditors. The debt included IOUs written by the quartermaster, the officer in charge of army supplies; winning tickets from lotteries that the government had held to raise money and could not repay; and certificates that soldiers had received when the government had been unable to pay them for their military service. It was Hamilton's task to sort through this paperwork in an attempt to reduce the national debt.

Main Idea

❷ Jefferson Opposes Hamilton

Thomas Jefferson opposed Hamilton's views on government and the economy.

Recall What did Hamilton think a strong central government should do? *balance power between the masses and the wealthy*

Contrast How did Jefferson's and Hamilton's views on how to promote economic growth differ? *Hamilton— promote manufacturing and business and pass higher tariffs; Jefferson— promote agriculture and keep tariffs low*

Develop Defend either Hamilton's or Jefferson's view of democracy. *Answers should reflect an understanding of each point of view.*

📄 **CRF:** Primary Source Activity: Jefferson and Hamilton Disagree about Government

Info to Know

Sectional Tensions The debate over Hamilton's economic plans revealed tensions between northern and southern states. Most speculators lived in the North. In the South, Virginians in particular hated Hamilton's programs. Virginia senator George Mason expressed his dismay, saying that Hamilton has "done us more injury than Great Britain."

Answers

Biography *He was free, highly educated, and had a paying job.*

Reading Check *Southerners thought the plan was unfair because southern states had few war debts; Hamilton agreed to get the national capital moved farther south.*

240

---

promised to convince northern members of Congress to move the capital. Jefferson and Madison then agreed to gather support in the South for Hamilton's debt plan.

The compromise worked. The national capital was moved to Philadelphia in 1791 for 10 years. For the capital's permanent location, Washington chose a place on the Potomac River that included part of both Maryland and Virginia. The land was made up of swamps and farms. This site would eventually become the city of Washington, D.C.

THE IMPACT TODAY
Washington, D.C., and the surrounding areas are home to more than 7 million people today. The city is not only the nation's capital but also a major tourist attraction.

READING CHECK **Identifying Points of View** How did southerners feel about the federal government paying state war debts, and how did Hamilton change their minds?

BIOGRAPHY

Benjamin Banneker (1731–1806)

Benjamin Banneker was born to a free African American family in rural Maryland. He attended a Quaker school but was largely self-educated. He was a skilled mathematician and scientist. His mathematical skills prompted Thomas Jefferson to give him a job surveying the land for the new national capital.

Draw Conclusions How was Benjamin Banneker's life different from most African Americans' of the time?

Jefferson Opposes Hamilton

Hamilton and Jefferson did not cooperate for long. Instead, they began to disagree about how to define the authority of the central government. Hamilton believed in a strong federal government. Jefferson wanted to protect the powers of the states. Their conflict reflected basic differences in their opinions about democracy. Hamilton had little faith in the average individual. He once said that "the people . . . seldom judge or determine [decide] right."

Differing Views

Hamilton wanted a strong central government that balanced power between the "mass of the people" and wealthier citizens. He believed that his approach would protect everyone's liberties while keeping the people from having too much power.

Jefferson disagreed strongly with Hamilton's views of the average citizen's ability to make decisions for the country. He admitted that "the people can not be all, and always, well informed." However, Jefferson believed that it was the right of the people to rule the country.

Economic Differences

Hamilton and Jefferson also fought over how the country's economy should grow. Hamilton wanted new forms of economic growth. He wanted to promote manufacturing and business. He even suggested that the

U.S. Capitol in Washington, D.C.

240 CHAPTER 7

Critical Thinking: Contrasting

At Level

Hamilton vs. Jefferson

1. Lead students in a discussion contrasting Hamilton's and Jefferson's views.

2. Copy the graphic organizer for students to see. Omit the blue answers. Have each student copy the organizer and complete it by listing Hamilton's arguments for and Jefferson's arguments against Hamilton's economic plan.
   LS Verbal/Linguistic, Visual/Spatial

📄 Alternative Assessment Handbook, Rubric 13: Graphic Organizers

Hamilton	Jefferson
pay full value of bonds	
• *builds investor confidence; speculators took the risks, so fair*	• *rewards speculators; cheats bondholders who sold bonds at low prices*
pass higher tariffs	
• *protects American manufacturing from foreign competition*	• *hurts farmers by raising costs of imports*
create a national bank	
• *"necessary and proper"; gives central government a place to deposit money*	• *elastic clause refers to necessity, not convenience*

POINT OF VIEW
Role of a Citizen

Alexander Hamilton thought that the average citizen had no interest in public affairs.

❝We must take man as we find him, and if we expect him to serve the public, [we] must interest his passions in doing so. A reliance on pure patriotism has been the source of many of our errors.**❞**

—Alexander Hamilton,
quoted in *Odd Destiny: The Life of Alexander Hamilton* by Marie B. Hecht

Thomas Jefferson believed that each citizen could work to better society.

❝It is my principle that the will of the Majority should always prevail [win] . . . Above all things I hope the education of the common people will be attended to; [I am] convinced that on their good sense we may rely with the most security for the preservation of a due degree of liberty.**❞**

—Thomas Jefferson,
from *Thomas Jefferson: A Biography in His Own Words*

ANALYSIS SKILL **ANALYZING POINTS OF VIEW**

How did the views of Hamilton and Jefferson differ?

government award a prize to companies that made excellent products.

In addition, Hamilton wanted to pass higher tariffs. Known as protective tariffs, these taxes would raise the prices of foreign products. Hamilton hoped this would cause Americans to buy U.S. goods. As a result, American manufacturing would be protected from foreign competition.

Jefferson worried about depending too much on business and manufacturing. He believed that farmers were the most independent voters. They did not depend on other people's work to make a living.

Jefferson wrote, "Our governments will remain virtuous [pure] for many centuries; as long as they are chiefly agricultural." Jefferson wanted to help farmers by keeping the costs of the goods they bought low. Lower tariffs would help keep prices low.

READING CHECK **Summarizing** What were the main differences between Hamilton and Jefferson concerning the power of the nation's government?

National Debate

Hamilton's and Jefferson's differences became more and more public in early 1791. The two men had very different opinions about how the government should approach its economic problems.

Hamilton's Plan for a National Bank

Hamilton wanted to start a national bank where the government could safely deposit its money. The bank would also make loans to the government and businesses. Hamilton also thought that the United States should build a national mint, a place to make coins. Then the country could begin issuing its own money.

Hamilton knew that people who wanted to protect states' rights might have a strong reaction to the idea of a national bank, so he suggested limiting it to a 20-year charter. After that time Congress could decide whether to extend the charter. Hamilton also asked each state to start its own bank so the national bank would not have a monopoly.

THE IMPACT TODAY

The U.S. Mint was established in 1792 and now produces between 11 billion and 20 billion coins each year.

Cooperative Learning
At Level

Strict and Loose Construction

1. Write the definitions of loose construction and strict construction for students to see. Ask students if they can think of examples of loose and strict construction at the school or in their community.

2. Organize the class into pairs. Have one partner from each pair create a brief description of his or her interpretation of loose construction. Have the other partner create a description of his or her interpretation of strict construction.

3. Then have each pair write one to two paragraphs explaining how loose and strict construction affected debates over Hamilton's financial plan. **LS** **Interpersonal, Verbal/Linguistic**

📝 Alternative Assessment Handbook, Rubrics 9: Comparing and Contrasting; and 37: Writing Assignments

---

Main Idea

❸ National Debate

Hamilton created a national bank to strengthen the U.S. economy.

Identify What was the function of the Bank of the United States? *to provide a safe place for the federal government's money; to make loans to the government and businesses; to stabilize the economy*

Summarize How did Hamilton's plan for a national bank address states' rights? *proposed limiting the bank's charter to 20 years; encouraged states to start their own banks to prevent a monopoly*

Evaluate Do you agree with loose construction or strict construction of the Constitution? *Answers will vary but should reflect an understanding of each term.*

Connect to Economics

Tariffs Nations usually establish tariffs for two reasons—to provide a source of income for the government and to promote the development of domestic industries by raising the price of imports. Economic planners hope that making foreign goods more expensive will lead people to buy goods made in their own country.

Answers

Analyzing Points of View *Hamilton thought the average citizen was not interested in public affairs; Jefferson thought that educated citizens would act to preserve liberty.*

Reading Check *Hamilton—wanted a strong central government; did not trust the judgment of the masses; Jefferson—wanted to protect the power of the states; believed in the average citizen's ability to make good decisions for the nation*

Linking to Today

The Federal Reserve The Federal Reserve, commonly called the "Fed," serves as the nation's central bank today. The national government created the Federal Reserve system in 1913 to stabilize the nation's monetary and banking systems. The Fed supervises member banks, holds cash reserves, and moves money into or out of circulation. The Fed is organized into two levels—national and district. At the national level, a 7-member Board of Governors makes the key decisions. At the district level, 12 Federal Reserve banks serve different regions of the nation.

● **Review & Assess** ●

Close

Have students discuss Hamilton's and Jefferson's differing views of democracy. Which view do students think most Americans hold today?

Review

Online Quiz, Section 2

Assess

SE Section 2 Assessment

PASS: Section 2 Quiz

Alternative Assessment Handbook

Reteach/Classroom Intervention

Interactive Reader and Study Guide, Section 2

Interactive Skills Tutor CD-ROM

Answer

Reading Check *They thought a national bank would strengthen and stabilize the nation's economy.*

242

Jefferson's Opposes the Bank

Both Jefferson and Madison believed that Hamilton's plans for the economy gave too much power to the federal government. They also thought the U.S. Constitution did not give Congress the power to create a bank. But Hamilton quoted the elastic clause, which states that Congress can "make all laws which shall be necessary and proper" to govern the nation.

Hamilton declared that the clause allowed the government to create a national bank. Hamilton believed in loose construction of the Constitution. **Loose construction** means that the federal government can take reasonable actions that the Constitution does not specifically forbid.

Jefferson thought that the elastic clause should be used only in special cases. He wrote to President Washington, "The Constitution allows only the means which are 'necessary,' not those which are merely 'convenient.'"

Jefferson believed in strict construction of the Constitution. People who favor **strict construction** think that the federal government should do only what the Constitution specifically says it can do.

President Washington and Congress agreed with Hamilton. They hoped a bank would offer stability for the U.S. economy. In February 1791 Congress enacted the charter for the **Bank of the United States**—the country's first national bank. The bank played an important role in making the U.S. economy more stable.

READING CHECK **Drawing Conclusions** Why did Congress and the president agree to create a national bank?

SUMMARY AND PREVIEW Washington and Hamilton developed plans for paying the national debt. In the next section you will read about the U.S. neutrality policy.

Section 2 Assessment

go.hrw.com
Online Quiz
KEYWORD: SR8 HP7

Reviewing Ideas, Terms, and People

1. **a. Describe** What economic problems did the new government face?
   b. Summarize What compromise did **Alexander Hamilton**, **Thomas Jefferson**, and James Madison reach regarding repayment of state debts?
2. **a. Identify** What disagreement did Jefferson and Hamilton have over the central government?
   b. Draw Conclusions Hamilton was a New Yorker, while Jefferson was from Virginia. How do you think that affected their views on the economy?
   c. Elaborate Do you agree with Hamilton or Jefferson regarding the average citizen's ability to make decisions for the country? Explain your answer.
3. **a. Recall** Why did Jefferson oppose the creation of the **Bank of the United States**?
   b. Contrast What is the difference between **loose construction** and **strict construction** of the Constitution?
   c. Elaborate Defend Alexander Hamilton's stance in favor of the creation of a national bank.

Critical Thinking

4. **Identifying Solutions** Review your notes on U.S. economic problems and Hamilton's solutions. Then copy the chart below and use it to show how Hamilton's views on the economy differed from those of Thomas Jefferson.

	Hamilton	Jefferson
Bonds		
Economy		
Tariffs		
National Bank		

FOCUS ON WRITING

5. **Gathering Information about Hamilton and Jefferson** Both Hamilton and Jefferson were strong leaders who helped shape the government of the young United States. What could you say about either of them to support a nomination for a Nobel Prize?

Section 2 Assessment Answers

1. **a.** high national debt from Revolutionary War
   b. support for Hamilton's plan for state debts in exchange for national capital farther south

2. **a.** Jefferson—protect states' powers; Hamilton—strong central government
   b. Hamilton favored manufacturing and trade, more common in the North; Jefferson favored farming, important to the southern economy.
   c. Answers should reflect an understanding of each man's viewpoint.

3. **a.** thought it gave the federal government too much power and that it was unconstitutional

   b. loose—federal government can take necessary actions not prohibited; strict—can do only what Constitution says
   c. possible answers—safe place to deposit federal money; will stabilize the economy

4. Hamilton—pay full value; wanted to promote manufacturing and business; higher tariffs; supported; Jefferson—paying full price cheats bondholders; farming; lower tariffs to protect farmers and keep prices low; against

5. possible answer—served in Cabinet positions

Challenges for the New Nation

If YOU were there...

You are the captain of an American merchant ship in the 1790s. Your ship has just picked up cargo in the French West Indies. You are headed back to your home port of Philadelphia. Suddenly, a British warship pulls alongside your ship. Marines swarm aboard. They order you into the nearest harbor and seize your goods.

How would this incident affect your views of Great Britain?

BUILDING BACKGROUND As the new nation tried to get organized, it faced economic problems and internal divisions. Even more difficult challenges came from conflicts in Europe. The United States could not avoid being caught up in fighting between France and Great Britain.

Remaining Neutral

Tensions between France and Britain began to build after the French people rebelled against their king. On July 14, 1789, citizens of Paris attacked and captured the Bastille, a hated fortress and prison that stood as a mighty symbol of royal power.

The storming of the Bastille was one of the first acts of the **French Revolution** —a rebellion of French people against their king in 1789. The French people overthrew their king and created a republican government.

French revolutionaries storm the Bastille.

What You Will Learn...

Main Ideas

1. The United States tried to remain neutral regarding events in Europe.
2. The United States and Native Americans came into conflict in the Northwest Territory.
3. The Whiskey Rebellion tested Washington's administration.
4. In his Farewell Address, Washington advised the nation.

The Big Idea

The United States faced significant foreign and domestic challenges under Washington.

Key Terms and People

French Revolution, p. 243
Neutrality Proclamation, p. 244
privateers, p. 244
Jay's Treaty, p. 245
Pinckney's Treaty, p. 245
Little Turtle, p. 246
Battle of Fallen Timbers, p. 247
Treaty of Greenville, p. 247
Whiskey Rebellion, p. 247

TAKING NOTES As you read, take notes on the challenges faced by the new nation during Washington's administration.

Challenges

LAUNCHING THE NATION **243**

Main Idea

❶ Remaining Neutral

The United States tried to remain neutral regarding events in Europe.

Recall What significant American event helped inspire the French Revolution? *American Revolution*

Identify Cause and Effect How did Washington respond to conflicts between France and Great Britain? *issued the Neutrality Proclamation, stating that the United States would not take sides in European conflicts*

Elaborate How did Edmond Genet and American privateers threaten U.S. neutrality? *Their actions could have led Great Britain to attack the United States and draw it into war.*

📓 Political Cartoons Activities for United States History, Cartoon 7: The French Revolution

World Events

American Influence In August 1789, French revolutionaries issued the Declaration of the Rights of Man and of the Citizen, a document modeled after the Declaration of Independence. The Marquis de Lafayette—a Frenchman who had fought in the Revolutionary War alongside Washington—helped write this document. Lafayette sent the key to the Bastille to President Washington, saying, "It is a tribute which I owe to you, as a son to my adoptive father, as an aide-de-camp to my General, as a Missionary of Liberty to its Patriarch."

Answers

Focus on Reading *The French revolted against their monarchy and put in place a republican government based on democratic principles.*

244

FOCUS ON READING
What can you tell about France before 1793 using this paragraph and what you already know about democracies?

ACADEMIC VOCABULARY
neutral unbiased, not favoring either side in a conflict

Many French citizens had been inspired to take action by the American Revolution. Many Americans, in turn, supported the French Revolution. They thought that France was creating the same kind of democracy as the United States.

Some Americans worried about the French Revolution's violent riots and attacks on traditional authority. Revolutionaries shocked many Americans by beheading King Louis XVI in January 1793 and Queen Marie-Antoinette later that year.

A few years after the French Revolution started, France and Great Britain went to war. Some Americans supported the French, while others backed the British. Some wanted to remain **neutral**.

The Neutrality Proclamation

The debate divided Congress and Washington's cabinet. Washington presented his opinion to Congress on April 22, 1793:

> "The duty and interest of the United States require that they should with sincerity and good faith adopt and pursue a conduct friendly and impartial [unbiased] towards the belligerent [fighting] powers."
>
> —George Washington, quoted in *The Real George Washington* by Parry et al.

This **Neutrality Proclamation** stated that the United States would not take sides with any European countries that were at war. Washington believed his plan was the safest for the long run, but not everyone agreed.

Some members of Congress criticized Washington's ideas. James Madison believed that the president had gone beyond his authority. He questioned Washington's right to issue the proclamation without the approval of Congress.

The French Question

France's new representative to the United States, Edmond Genet (zhuh-NAY), asked American sailors to help France fight England by commanding **privateers**. Privateers were private ships hired by a country to attack its enemies. Washington told Genet that using American privateers violated U.S. neutrality. Jefferson wanted the French revolutionaries to succeed, but even he agreed that allowing France to use American privateers against England was a bad idea.

Jefferson was still upset by U.S. policy toward France. He believed that the United States should back France because France had supported the United States during the Revolutionary War. Hamilton, on the other hand, was pro-British. He hoped to strengthen trading ties with Britain—the most powerful trading nation in the world at the time. Jefferson thought that Hamilton had too much influence on the president's foreign policy and that Hamilton consequently interfered with Jefferson's role as secretary of state. Jefferson decided to resign from Washington's cabinet in 1793.

Time Line

The Struggle for Neutrality

April 1789 George Washington becomes president.

1789

July 1789 French citizens storm the Bastille.

October 1790 British-backed Little Turtle defeats U.S. forces under General Josiah Harmar.

April 1793 President Washington issues the Neutrality Proclamation.

1793

November 1794 Jay's Treaty sparks protest throughout the United States.

244

Critical Thinking: Finding Main Ideas

At Level

Neutrality Proclamation Press Release

Materials: current White House press release (optional)

1. Ask students to imagine that they are press secretaries to President Washington. Have each student create a press release announcing the Neutrality Proclamation. If possible, provide a sample press release as a model.

2. The press release should summarize the contents of the proclamation and explain Washington's reasons for making it.

3. Ask for a volunteer to role play the press secretary and to read aloud his or her press release to the class. Have other students play the role of reporters and ask questions.

4. Conclude by having students evaluate Washington's decision to have the nation remain neutral and whether they agree with it. Students should provide support for their points of view. 🖽 **Verbal/Linguistic**

📓 Alternative Assessment Handbook, Rubric 42: Writing to Inform

Jay's Treaty

There were other threats to U.S. neutrality. In late 1793 the British seized ships carrying food to the French West Indies. Hundreds of the ships were neutral American merchant ships. Also, British officers were helping Native Americans fight settlers.

Washington wanted to prevent another war with the British. He sent Chief Justice John Jay to London to work out a compromise. The British knew the United States lacked a strong navy and that U.S. businesses relied heavily on British trade. However, the British did not want to fight another war in America.

In November 1794 the two sides signed Jay's Treaty. **Jay's Treaty** settled the disputes that had arisen between the United States and Great Britain in the early 1790s. The British would pay damages on seized American ships and abandon their forts on the northwestern frontier. The United States agreed to pay debts it owed the British.

The treaty was unpopular and sparked violent protests. Citizens and congressional leaders thought the treaty hurt trade and did not punish Britain enough for some of its actions. Southerners were especially angry that the treaty did not ask Britain to repay them for slaves that Britain had set free during the Revolutionary War. Washington did not like the treaty but believed it was the most that could be done. At his urging the Senate approved the treaty.

Pinckney's Treaty

American businesses faced problems as well. The Spanish disputed the border between the United States and Florida. Spain closed the port of New Orleans to U.S. trade in 1784. This hurt the American economy because all goods moving down the Mississippi to places in the East or overseas had to pass through New Orleans.

Washington asked Ambassador Thomas Pinckney to meet with Spanish officials to discuss the problem. He asked the Spaniards to reopen New Orleans to U.S. trade. Pinckney also asked for the right of deposit in New Orleans. This right would allow American boats to transfer goods in New Orleans without paying cargo fees.

Spanish minister Manuel de Godoy (goh-THOY) tried to delay reaching an agreement, hoping Pinckney would become desperate and sign a treaty that favored the Spanish. He was worried that the United States and Great Britain might join against Spain after signing Jay's Treaty. Pinckney was patient, however, and his patience was rewarded.

In October 1795, Godoy agreed to **Pinckney's Treaty**, which settled the border and trade disputes with Spain. Under the treaty Spain agreed to recognize the U.S. southern boundary as 31°N latitude. Spain's government also reopened the port at

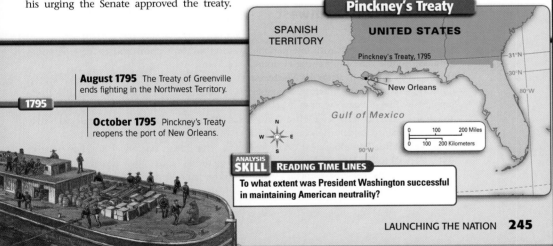

August 1795 The Treaty of Greenville ends fighting in the Northwest Territory.

1795

October 1795 Pinckney's Treaty reopens the port of New Orleans.

Pinckney's Treaty

SPANISH TERRITORY

UNITED STATES

Pinckney's Treaty, 1795

31°N
30°N
80°W

New Orleans

Gulf of Mexico

N W E S

90°W

0   100   200 Miles
0   100   200 Kilometers

ANALYSIS SKILL | **READING TIME LINES**

To what extent was President Washington successful in maintaining American neutrality?

LAUNCHING THE NATION **245**

Main Idea

❷ Conflict in the Northwest Territory

The United States and Native Americans came into conflict in the Northwest Territory.

Recall Why did Native Americans in the northwest go to war in the early 1790s, and who led them? *because Americans continued to settle the Northwest Territory; Miami chief Little Turtle*

Identify Cause and Effect What were the results of the Battle of Fallen Timbers? *U.S. victory broke the strength of Indian forces in the region; led to Treaty of Greenville, under which Native Americans gave up much of their land for $20,000 and a guarantee of their safety*

Interpret What did Little Turtle mean when he said "The trail has been long and bloody; it has no end"? *He knew that the U.S. Army would not stop fighting his people and that settlers would not stop coming.*

🖳 Map Transparency: Fighting in the Northwest Territory

Interpreting Maps

Fighting in the Northwest Territory

Place What victories did Native Americans achieve against U.S. forces in the early 1790s? *Harmar's Battle, St. Clair's Battle*

🖳 Map Transparency: Fighting in the Northwest Territory

Answers

Analyzing Visuals *swords or sabers, shotguns or rifles*

Reading Check *thought neutrality was the safest and most reasonable plan for the long run*

246

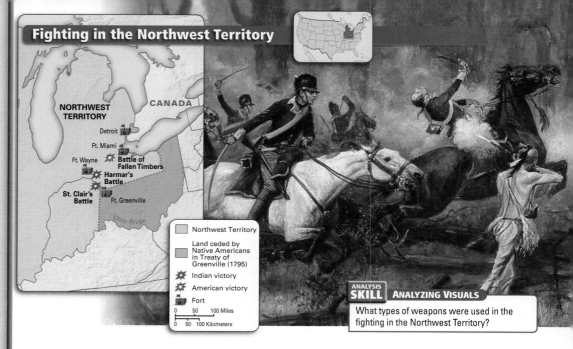

Fighting in the Northwest Territory

- ▨ Northwest Territory
- ▨ Land ceded by Native Americans in Treaty of Greenville (1795)
- ✸ Indian victory
- ✸ American victory
- 🏰 Fort

0   50   100 Miles
0   50 100 Kilometers

ANALYSIS SKILL   ANALYZING VISUALS
What types of weapons were used in the fighting in the Northwest Territory?

New Orleans to American ships and gave them the right of deposit. Because it opened the frontier to more expansion, Washington and most other Americans believed that Pinckney's Treaty was a successful compromise.

READING CHECK Summarizing Why did President Washington want the United States to remain neutral?

Conflict in the Northwest Territory

As the United States dealt with international conflicts, trouble was also brewing at home. Americans continued to settle the Northwest Territory despite Native Americans' protests. Supplied by British traders with guns, Native Americans went to war. In 1790 a Native American alliance under the command of Miami chief **Little Turtle** defeated U.S. forces under General Josiah Harmar. Then in 1791, Native Americans defeated General Arthur St. Clair's troops.

General Wayne Takes Command

In 1792 President Washington gave command of the army in the West to General Anthony Wayne. Wayne's task was to bring troops to the frontier to fight against the Indians. In 1793 General Wayne arrived in Ohio. Many of his men were ill from smallpox and influenza, so they were unable to fight well.

Wayne's troops moved north and built Fort Greenville, where they remained during the winter. They built additional forts for protection and to have supplies at hand.

As the summer of 1794 neared, several Native American groups led by Little Turtle attacked a supply train near the fort. Wayne and his men responded. They attacked Native American towns and burned crops.

The British no longer aided the Native Americans after this defeat, and Little Turtle realized that they were outmatched. He urged his people to seek peace.

246   CHAPTER 7

Differentiating Instruction

At Level

English-Language Learners

1. Organize the class into small groups and have each group create a time line of the conflicts that took place with Native Americans in the Northwest Territory in the early 1790s.

2. Time lines should include at least six key dates and entries for events from 1790 to 1795. Encourage the groups to provide annotations and illustrations to enhance their time lines.

3. Display the groups' time lines in the classroom. Use them to lead a class review of the cause-and-effect relationships among the events.
   LS Interpersonal, Visual/Spatial

📃 Alternative Assessment Handbook, Rubrics 14: Group Activity; and 36: Time Lines

"The trail has been long and bloody; it has no end. The [whites] ... are many. They are like the leaves of the trees. When the frost comes they fall and are blown away. But when the sunshine comes again they come back more plentiful than ever before."

—Little Turtle, quoted in *The Ohio Frontier* by Douglas Hurt

The End of Conflict

On August 20, 1794, Native Americans fought Wayne's troops in the **Battle of Fallen Timbers** and were defeated. The battle was named for an area where many trees had been destroyed by a tornado. Wayne's forces burned Indians' villages and fields. The strength of Indian forces in the region was broken.

The frontier war soon ended. In August 1795, Native American leaders signed the **Treaty of Greenville**, which gave the United States claim to most Indian lands in the Northwest Territory. The treaty also guaranteed the safety of citizens there. In exchange, Native Americans received $20,000 worth of goods and an acknowledgment of their claim to the lands they still held.

READING CHECK Finding Main Ideas What conflicts did the United States face in the late 1700s?

The Whiskey Rebellion

Other conflicts occurred on the frontier. Congress passed a tax on American-made whiskey in March 1791. The tax was part of Hamilton's plan to raise money to help pay the federal debt. He was also testing the power of the federal government to control the states' actions.

Reaction in the West

People in areas such as western Pennsylvania were bitter about the tax. They were already angry with the federal government, which they believed did not protect settlers from Native American attacks and did not allow settlers enough opportunities for trade. The farmers' corn crops were often made into whiskey, which was easier to transport than

the corn. Because cash was rare, whiskey became like money in their region. The farmers believed that the tax was aimed specifically at them.

Farmers who produced small amounts of whiskey for trade argued that they could not afford the tax. They believed they should be able to keep the money they had made from a product they created themselves. Protests in 1792 led President Washington to issue a proclamation saying that people had to obey the law.

Westerners also disliked the fact that cases about the law were to be tried in a district court. These courts were usually far away from the people they affected and were a great inconvenience to them.

Whiskey Rebellion Is Crushed

The complaints of western Pennsylvanians were at first expressed peacefully. But by 1794 fighting had broken out. In what became known as the **Whiskey Rebellion**, farmers lashed out against the tax on whiskey. Protesters refused to pay the tax. They even tarred and feathered tax collectors. Some called themselves the new Sons of Liberty.

Incidents of violence spread to other states. President Washington feared that the rebels threatened the federal government's authority. He believed he needed to make people understand that the Constitution gave Congress the right to pass and enforce the tax.

Washington declared that he could "no longer remain a passive [inactive] spectator" in the event. He personally led the army in military action against the rebellion—the first and only time an American president has done so. The army of about 13,000 men approached western Pennsylvania in November 1794. By this time most of the rebels had fled. The Whiskey Rebellion ended without a battle.

READING CHECK Supporting a Point of View Defend the viewpoint of the Pennsylvania farmers who did not want to pay the whiskey tax.

Direct Teach

Main Idea

❸ The Whiskey Rebellion

The Whiskey Rebellion tested Washington's administration.

Recall Why did Congress pass a tax on American-made whisky? *to raise money to pay off the federal debt; to test the power of the federal government to control states' actions*

Summarize What occurred during the Whiskey Rebellion? *Western Pennsylvania farmers' protests against the whiskey tax turned violent; Washington led forces against the rebels, who mostly fled.*

Evaluate What was the significance of the Whiskey Rebellion? *helped emphasize the authority of the federal government to pass taxes and to put down domestic rebellions*

Answers

Reading Check (left) *They faced a border dispute with Spanish-controlled Florida and conflicts with Native Americans in the Northwest.*

Reading Check (right) *possible answers—They had made the whiskey and should have been able to keep the profits from its sale; they could not afford the tax and had to travel long distances to plead their case.*

Differentiating Instruction

Below Level

Struggling Readers

1. To help students explain the domestic conflicts the United States faced in the late 1700s, draw the graphic organizer for students to see. Omit the blue sample answers.

2. Have students copy the organizer and complete it by listing the key people, events, and issues in each conflict. **LS** Visual/Spatial

📝 Alternative Assessment Handbook, Rubric 13: Graphic Organizers

Domestic Conflicts, Late 1700s

Northwest Territory
- *Native Americans went to war over American settlement in the region.*
- *Miami chief Little Turtle*
- *General Anthony Wayne*
- *Battle of Fallen Timbers*
- *U.S. victory broke Indian strength in region.*
- *Treaty of Greenville*

Whiskey Rebellion
- *Congress passed a whiskey tax.*
- *Western Pennsylvania farmers protested tax.*
- *Fighting broke out.*
- *President Washington led army against the rebellion; rebels fled.*
- *showed authority of the federal government*

Primary Source

Washington's Farewell Address

Activity A Farewell Address

Have students discuss if they think Washington's advice on political parties and foreign nations is applicable today. Then ask students to imagine that they are the current president of the United States. What advice would they give the nation if they were retiring today? Have each student make a bulleted list of topics that he or she would address.

LS Verbal/Linguistic

📓 Alternative Assessment Handbook, Rubric 11: Discussions

Connect to Science and Technology

Getting the Word Out President Washington sent the draft of his Farewell Address to the publisher of the Philadelphia newspaper *American Daily Advertiser*. The *Advertiser* printed the address, and other newspapers soon picked it up. In this way, Americans slowly learned about the president's Farewell Address. Today, modern communications devices enable Americans to hear or read presidential messages immediately instead of waiting weeks or months.

HISTORICAL DOCUMENT
Washington's Farewell Address

On September 19, 1796, President George Washington's Farewell Address first appeared in a Philadelphia newspaper. In it, Washington wrote about the nation's economy, political parties, and foreign policy.

While, then, every part of our country . . . feels an immediate and particular interest in union, all the parts combined cannot fail to find in the united mass . . . greater strength, greater resource, proportionally greater security from external danger, [and] a less frequent interruption of their peace by foreign nations; . . .

I have already **intimated**[1] to you the danger of [political] parties in the state, with particular reference to the founding of them on geographical **discriminations**[2]. Let me now take a more **comprehensive**[3] view, and warn you in the most solemn manner against the **baneful**[4] effects of the spirit of party, generally.

If, in the opinion of the people, the distribution or **modification**[5] of the constitutional powers be in any particular wrong, let it be corrected by an amendment . . .

Promote, then, as an object of primary importance, institutions for the general **diffusion**[6] of knowledge . . . As the structure of a government gives force to public opinion, it is essential that public opinion should be enlightened . . .

[Avoid] likewise the accumulation of debt, . . . not ungenerously throwing upon **posterity**[7] the burden, which we ourselves ought to bear . . .

Observe good faith and justice towards all nations; **cultivate**[8] peace and harmony with all . . .

The great rule of conduct for us, in regard to foreign nations, is . . . to have with them as little political connection as possible.

It is our true policy to steer clear of permanent alliances with any portion of the foreign world . . . There can be no greater error than to expect, or **calculate**[9] upon real favors from nation to nation. It is an illusion, which experience must cure, which a just pride ought to discard.

The duty of holding a neutral conduct may be inferred . . . from the obligation which justice and humanity impose on every nation . . . to maintain **inviolate**[10] the relations of peace and **amity**[11] towards other nations.

> Washington lists the benefits of uniting the states under one government.

> In this phrase, Washington emphasizes his warning against the dangers of political parties.

> Washington points out the need for education.

> This is Washington's advice to the new nation about foreign policy.

[1] **intimated**: told
[2] **discriminations**: differences
[3] **comprehensive**: complete
[4] **baneful**: destructive
[5] **modification**: change
[6] **diffusion**: spreading
[7] **posterity**: future generations
[8] **cultivate**: seek
[9] **calculate**: plan
[10] **inviolate**: unchanging
[11] **amity**: friendship

ANALYSIS SKILL ▶ **ANALYZING PRIMARY SOURCES**

1. What events happened before Washington left office that might have led to his warning against political parties?
2. Why did Washington suggest neutrality as a foreign policy?

Critical Thinking: Comparing Primary Sources   **Above Level**

Presidential Farewell Addresses

Research Required

1. Have students conduct research to find a farewell address from a recent U.S. president. Tell students to read the address and note the key points.

2. Next, have students complete **Primary Source Activity: President George Washington's Farewell Address, in the Chapter Resource File.**

3. Then have each student write an essay comparing the recent Farewell Address to Washington's. The essay should compare tone, major points, and issues. Encourage students to include quotes from each document to support the points in their essays.

4. Ask for volunteers to read their essays to the class. **LS Verbal/Linguistic**

📓 Alternative Assessment Handbook, Rubric 42: Writing to Inform

📓 **CRF:** Primary Source Activity: President George Washington's Farewell Address

Answers

Analyzing Primary Sources
1. *disagreements between Jefferson and Hamilton; Jefferson's resignation*
2. *thought that alliances with other nations were illusions; that alliances could draw the nation into war*

Washington Says Farewell

In 1796 Washington decided not to run for a third presidential term. He wrote that he was "tired of public life" and "devoutly [strongly] wished for retirement." He also wanted to remind Americans that the people were the country's true leaders.

With the help of Alexander Hamilton and James Madison, Washington wrote his Farewell Address. In it he spoke about what he believed were the greatest dangers to the American republic. Among these were the dangers of foreign ties and political conflicts at home. Washington warned against forming permanent ties with other countries because choosing sides could draw the United States into war.

He also worried about growing political conflicts within the nation. Washington believed that disagreements between political groups weakened government. Political unity, he said, was a key to national success.

Washington left office warning the nation to work out its differences and protect its independence. Washington also warned against too much public debt. He thought the government should try not to borrow money. He wanted future generations to be protected from debt.

He concluded his speech by looking forward to his retirement and praising his country. "I anticipate . . . the sweet enjoyment . . . of good laws under a free government, the ever favorite object of my heart."

READING CHECK Finding Main Ideas
What issues did Washington believe were most dangerous to the future of the new nation?

SUMMARY AND PREVIEW Americans responded to foreign and domestic conflict during Washington's presidency. In the next section you will read about the formation of political parties in the United States and the presidency of John Adams.

Section 3 Assessment

go.hrw.com
Online Quiz
KEYWORD: SR8 HP7

Reviewing Ideas, Terms, and People

1. **a. Describe** What did Washington's **Neutrality Proclamation** state?
   b. Compare and Contrast In what ways were **Jay's Treaty** and **Pinckney's Treaty** similar and different?
2. **a. Identify** Who were the leaders of American Indian and U.S. forces in the conflict in the Northwest Territory?
   b. Predict What are some possible consequences of the **Treaty of Greenville** for American Indians in the Northwest Territory?
3. **a. Recall** Why did Congress tax American-made whiskey?
   b. Explain How did the tax lead to the **Whiskey Rebellion**?
   c. Elaborate Why do you think that President Washington personally led the army against westerners in the Whiskey Rebellion?
4. **a. Describe** What warnings did Washington give the nation in his Farewell Address?
   b. Draw Conclusions Why did Washington not run for a third term as president?

Critical Thinking

5. **Categorizing** Review your notes on the challenges the young United States faced. Then categorize those challenges as either foreign or domestic in a graphic organizer like this one.

Challenges	
Foreign	
Domestic	

FOCUS ON WRITING

6. **Thinking about Washington, Hamilton, and Jefferson** In this section you read about the activities of these three men during a difficult time for our country. What did you learn that you could add to a Nobel Prize nomination for any of these leaders?

Bellringer

If YOU were there . . . Use the **Daily Bellringer Transparency** to help students answer the question.

📖 Daily Bellringer Transparency, Section 4

Building Vocabulary

Preteach or review the following terms:

dignity seriousness, impressiveness (p. 251)

resolution formal decision (p. 253)

rivalry competition (p. 250)

tribute payment by one ruler or state to another (p. 252)

📄 **CRF:** Vocabulary Builder Activity, Section 4

Taking Notes

Have students copy the graphic organizer onto their own paper and then use it to take notes on the section. This activity will prepare students for the Section Assessment, in which they will complete a graphic organizer that builds on the information using a critical thinking skill.

SECTION 4

What You Will Learn...

Main Ideas

1. The rise of political parties created competition in the election of 1796.
2. The XYZ affair caused problems for President John Adams.
3. Controversy broke out over the Alien and Sedition Acts.

The Big Idea

The development of political parties in the United States contributed to differing ideas about the role of the federal government.

Key Terms

political parties, *p. 250*
Federalist Party, *p. 250*
Democratic-Republican Party, *p. 250*
XYZ affair, *p. 252*
Alien and Sedition Acts, *p. 253*
Kentucky and Virginia Resolutions, *p. 253*

TAKING NOTES As you read, take notes on the two political parties that emerged during the election of 1796, their views on government, their candidates in the 1796 election, and the outcome of the election. Use a graphic organizer like the one below for your notes.

Election of 1796	
Political Parties	
Views on Government	
Candidates	
Outcome	

John Adams's Presidency

If YOU were there...

You are a newspaper editor in Virginia in 1798. You've joined Jefferson's political party, which opposes the new president. In fact, your paper has printed many articles that criticize him, calling him greedy and foolish. You believe that's your right in a free country. But now Congress has passed a law that makes it illegal to criticize the government. You could be arrested for your articles!

Would you stop criticizing the government? Why?

BUILDING BACKGROUND People within the new United States had differing viewpoints on many issues. Personal rivalries among political leaders also created divisions in the new nation. Trying to limit dissent in the country, the federal government passed several unpopular laws.

The Election of 1796

The election of 1796 began a new era in U.S. politics. For the first time, more than one candidate ran for president. **Political parties**, groups that help elect people and shape policies, had begun to form during Washington's presidency. Despite Washington's warnings about political parties, the rivalry between two parties dominated the 1796 election.

Alexander Hamilton helped found the **Federalist Party**, which wanted a strong federal government and supported industry and trade. The Federalists chose John Adams and Thomas Pinckney as candidates. Adams knew he was not well liked in the South or the West, but he hoped people would support him after they thought about his years of loyal public service.

Thomas Jefferson and James Madison founded the **Democratic-Republican Party**. Its members, called Republicans, wanted to limit the federal government's power. (This party is not related to today's Republican Party.) They chose Thomas Jefferson and Aaron Burr as their candidates.

Teach the Big Idea

At Level

John Adams's Presidency

1. **Teach** Ask students the questions in the Main Idea boxes to teach this section.

2. **Apply** Have each student draw a box on a piece of paper and label the box *Presidency of John Adams*. Students should then connect the box to three, large empty boxes below it. In each box, tell students to describe an event in this section that divided Federalists and Republicans. Tell students to use the section headings as clues.
   LS Visual/Spatial

3. **Review** As you review the section, have students share the information they listed.

4. **Practice/Homework** Have each student create two bumper stickers, one expressing the view of the Federalist Party and one expressing the view of the Democratic-Republican Party on a major event or issue in this section. **LS** Verbal/Linguistic

   📄 Alternative Assessment Handbook, Rubrics 13: Graphic Organizers; and 34: Slogans and Banners

The First Political Parties, 1796

Federalists/North

Alexander Hamilton

John Adams

John Jay

Republicans/South

Thomas Jefferson

James Madison

Albert Gallatin

TERRITORY NORTHWEST OF OHIO RIVER

SOUTHWEST TERRITORY

VT 4
NH 6
MA 16
NY 12
RI 4
CT 9
PA DR-14 F-1
NJ 7
DE 3
MD DR-4 F-7
VA DR-20 F-1
KY 4
NC DR-11 F-1
TN 3
SC 8
GA 4

70°W
90°W

Federalist (Adams)

Democratic-Republican (Jefferson)

11   Number of electoral votes

0   150   300 Miles
0   150   300 Kilometers

GEOGRAPHY SKILLS   **INTERPRETING MAPS**

Region Which political party had more electoral votes in 1796?

Party differences were based partly on where and how people lived. Businesspeople in the cities tended to support the Federalists. Farmers in more isolated areas generally favored the Democratic-Republicans. Both sides attacked each other. Republicans called Adams a royalist—an insult to a man so involved in the Revolution. The Federalists accused the Republicans of favoring the French.

In the end, Adams defeated Jefferson. At the time, the person who came in second in a presidential election became vice president. So, after months of campaigning against one another, Adams and Jefferson took office together.

READING CHECK   Finding Main Ideas
How did the election of 1796 change the nature of politics in the United States?

President Adams and the XYZ Affair

John Adams had the challenging task of following Washington as president. The people had adored Washington. Adams would have to work hard to win the people's trust.

A New President

At first glance, John Adams did not appear well suited for the presidency. Although Adams had been a leading Patriot during the American Revolution and had later served as a foreign diplomat, he lacked Washington's dignity, and most people saw him as a cold and distant person. Still, many people—even his opponents—respected Adams. They recognized his hard work, honesty, and intelligence.

LAUNCHING THE NATION   **251**

Direct Teach

Main Idea

❶ The Election of 1796

The rise of political parties created competition in the election of 1796.

Recall Why was the election of 1796 different from the previous election? *Political parties began to form and, as a result, more than one candidate ran for president.*

Make Generalizations What role did geography play in the two political parties? *Federalists—cities, North; Republicans—farms, more isolated areas, South and West*

📦 Map Transparency: The First Political Parties

Biography

John Adams (1735–1826) Adams was well prepared for the presidency. In addition to serving as Washington's vice president, Adams had served in the Massachusetts state legislatures and attended the First Continental Congress. In 1779 he had been elected to the Massachusetts Constitutional Convention, where he wrote the first draft of the state constitution.

📝 CRF: Biography Activity: Abigail Adams

Differentiating Instruction

Advanced/Gifted and Talented

Above Level

1. Discuss the significance of the XYZ affair with the class. Then ask students to imagine that they are official record keepers for Congress and are taking notes on the congressional debates about the XYZ affair.

2. Have students write out the "official" record of the debates, including a time line of the actual events of the XYZ affair.

3. Students should include Americans' reaction to the affair as well as reasons for and against declaring war on France.

4. Ask volunteers to present their work to the class. 🄻🅂 **Verbal/Linguistic**

📝 Alternative Assessment Handbook, Rubric 36: Time Lines

Answers

Interpreting Maps *Federalist Party*

Reading Check *It saw the rise of political parties and more than one candidate for president for the first time.*

Main Idea

❷ President Adams and the XYZ Affair

The XYZ affair caused problems for President John Adams.

Explain Why was following Washington a challenge for President Adams? *Americans adored Washington but saw Adams as less dignified and somewhat cold.*

Recall What did Adams hope to accomplish by sending diplomats to France? *improve French relations*

Summarize How did Adams react to the XYZ affair? *informed Congress, asked it to expand the navy and create a peacetime army in case of war, and worked to reopen peace talks with France*

Make Judgments Do you think Adams should have pushed for war? Why or why not? *Answers will vary but should reflect an understanding of the reasons for and against war at the time.*

📝 **CRF: Biography Activity: Abigail Adams**

Checking for Understanding

True or False Answer each statement *T* if it is True or *F* if it is false. If false, explain why.

1. In the presidential election of 1796, political parties played a role for the first time. *T*

2. The XYZ affair almost led to war between France and the United States. *T*

3. The Democratic-Republican Party strongly supported the Alien and Sedition Acts. *F, the Federalists supported the acts.*

Answers

Interpreting Political Cartoons
the woman is being robbed

Reading Check *Americans, angry about the French request for a bribe (tribute), were willing to fund the military to fight the French.*

252

THE XYZ AFFAIR POLITICAL CARTOON

After the XYZ affair, French ships continued to attack American merchant ships. In this cartoon, the United States is represented by the woman. The men, symbolizing the French, are taking valuables from her. The people in the distance are other European nations.

Why do you think this man is encouraging the woman to look away?

These people aren't helping the woman. What do you think the cartoon is suggesting by this?

ANALYSIS SKILL **INTERPRETING POLITICAL CARTOONS**
How does the cartoon show that America is being preyed upon by the French?

The United States and France

One of Adams's first goals as president was to improve the relationship between the United States and France. You may remember that the French had once tried to hire American privateers to help them fight Great Britain, a practice Washington frowned upon. Adams sent U.S. diplomats to Paris to smooth over the conflict and to negotiate a treaty to protect U.S. shipping.

When the diplomats arrived in France, they learned that French foreign minister Talleyrand would not speak with them. Instead, they had a strange and secret visit from three French agents. Shockingly, the agents said that Talleyrand would discuss a treaty only in

exchange for a $250,000 bribe. The French government also wanted a loan of $12 million. The amazed diplomats refused these demands.

In March 1798 President Adams told Congress that the peace-seeking mission had failed. He described the French terms, substituting the letters X, Y, and Z for the names of the French agents. Upon hearing the disgraceful news, Federalists in Congress called for war with France.

The **XYZ affair**, as the French demand for a bribe came to be called, outraged the American public. "Millions for defense, but not one cent for tribute!" became the rallying cry of the American people.

Preparations for War

Fearing war, Adams asked Congress to expand the navy to a fleet of more than 30 ships. He thought war with France might be unavoidable. He also decided the United States should keep a peacetime army. Congress approved both measures.

Although Adams had asked Congress for military support, he did not want to go to war with France. He was worried about its cost. So he did not ask Congress to declare war. Instead, he tried to reopen peace talks with France.

Peace Efforts

Adams's decision not to declare war stunned Federalists. Despite intense pressure from members of his own party, Adams refused to change his mind.

American and French ships, however, began fighting each other in the Caribbean. Adams sent a representative to France to engage in talks to try to end the fighting. The United States and France eventually signed a treaty. Adams then forced two members of his cabinet to resign for trying to block his peace efforts.

READING CHECK **Identifying Points of View**
What did Americans mean when they said "Millions for defense, but not one cent for tribute"?

Collaborative Learning
At Level

Talk-Radio History

1. Have students use a talk-radio format to hold a panel discussion on John Adams's presidency. Organize the class into three groups and assign each group one of the following topics: (a) the XYZ affair; (b) the Alien and Sedition Acts; and (c) the Virginia and Kentucky Resolutions.

2. Select two students in each group to sit on a panel and answer questions from "callers." The other students will serve as callers. All

group members should help prepare questions and answers about the group's assigned topic.

3. Have each group conduct its talk-radio show for the class. Students should "call in" to the talk-radio show and ask questions. Panel members should respond. Then give students in other groups a chance to ask questions.

LS **Interpersonal, Verbal/Linguistic**

📝 Alternative Assessment Handbook, Rubric 14: Group Activity

The Alien and Sedition Acts

Many Democratic-Republicans continued to sympathize with France. Federalists, angered by their stand, called them "democrats, mobocrats, and all other kinds of rats."

In 1798, the Federalist-controlled Congress passed four laws known together as the **Alien and Sedition Acts**. These laws were said to protect the United States, but the Federalists intended them to crush opposition to war. The most controversial was the Sedition Act, which forbade anyone from publishing or voicing criticism of the federal government. In effect, this cancelled basic protections of freedom of speech and freedom of the press.

The two main Democratic-Republican leaders, Thomas Jefferson and James Madison, viewed these acts as a misuse of the government's power. Attacking the problem at the state level, they wrote resolutions passed by the Kentucky legislature in 1798 and in Virginia in 1799. Known as the **Kentucky and Virginia Resolutions**, these documents argued that the Alien and Sedition Acts were unconstitutional. They stated that the federal government could not pass these acts because they interfered with state government. Madison and Jefferson pressured Congress to repeal the Alien and Sedition Acts. Congress did not, although it allowed the acts to expire within a few years.

The Kentucky and Virginia Resolutions did not have the force of national law, but they supported the idea that states could challenge the federal government. This idea would grow to have a tremendous impact on American history later in the 1800s.

READING CHECK **Analyzing** How did the Kentucky and Virginia Resolutions support the rights of states?

SUMMARY AND PREVIEW Political parties formed to reflect different viewpoints. In the next chapter you will read about Thomas Jefferson's presidency.

---

go.hrw.com
Online Quiz
KEYWORD: SR8 HP7

Section 4 Assessment

Reviewing Ideas, Terms, and People

1. **a. Recall** What two **political parties** emerged before the election of 1796? Who were the founders of each party?
   b. Analyze What effect did political parties have on the election of 1796?
   c. Elaborate Do you think it was difficult for Adams and Jefferson to serve together as president and vice president? Explain your answer.
2. **a. Recall** What was one of Adams's first goals as president?
   b. Make Inferences Why were Federalists shocked by Adams's decision to resume peace talks with the French?
3. **a. Identify** What did the **Alien and Sedition Acts** state?
   b. Explain What idea regarding states' rights did the **Kentucky and Virginia Resolutions** support?
   c. Elaborate Would you have supported the Alien and Sedition Acts? Explain your answer.

Critical Thinking

4. **Contrasting** Review your notes on the election of 1796 and the formation of political parties. Then create a chart like this one identifying how each of the terms listed below reflected party disagreements.

XYZ Affair	
Alien and Sedition Acts	
Kentucky and Virginia Resolutions	

FOCUS ON WRITING

5. **Gathering Information about John Adams** Take some notes about John Adams's contributions that would support his nomination for the Nobel Prize. Then begin to compare and contrast all four leaders you have studied in this chapter. Which one will you nominate?

LAUNCHING THE NATION **253**

Section 4 Assessment Answers

1. **a.** Federalist Party, Hamilton; Democratic-Republican Party, Jefferson and Madison
   b. resulted in more than one candidate running for president for the first time
   c. possible answers—yes, the bitter campaign would have made it difficult for them to get along; no, they were professionals and would have worked together for the good of the nation
2. **a.** to improve U.S. relations with France
   b. They had expected him to call for war.
3. **a.** forbade anyone from publishing or voicing criticism of the federal government

   b. States could challenge the federal government.
   c. possible answers—yes, kept the nation unified; no, violated free speech
4. Federalist—many called for war; passed Alien and Sedition Acts; opposed the resolutions; Democratic-Republican—many supported France; viewed acts as misuse of power; wrote resolutions to repeal Alien and Sedition Acts
5. possible answer—kept the nation out of war despite conflicts

---

Making Group Decisions

Social Studies Skills

Analysis	Critical Thinking	Civic Participation	Study

Making Group Decisions

Define the Skill

Democracy is one of the most valued principles of American society. It is based on the idea that the members of society, or representatives they choose, make the decisions that affect society. Decision-making would be much more efficient if just one person decided what to do and how to do it. However, that method is not at all democratic.

Making decisions as a group is a complicated and difficult skill. However, it is an important one at all levels of society—from governing the nation to making group decisions at school, in the community, and with your friends. At every level, the skill is based on the ability of the group's members to interact in effective and cooperative ways.

Learn the Skill

Think about the job the first Congress faced after the Constitution was ratified. The nation was still millions of dollars in debt from the Revolutionary War. Congress had to find a way to pay these debts as well as raise money to run the government.

Leaders like Jefferson and Hamilton had ideas about how to accomplish these goals. However, neither man could act alone. In a democracy the group—in this case Congress—must make the decisions and take the actions.

This task was complicated by the fact that Jefferson and Hamilton disagreed on what to do. Each man's supporters in Congress pushed his point of view. Fortunately, its members were able to overcome their differences, compromise on goals and actions, and accept group decisions they might not have agreed with personally. Had they not possessed

this ability and skill, the nation's early years might have been even more difficult than they were.

Like that first Congress, being part of an effective group requires that you behave in certain ways.

❶ **Be an active member.** Take part in setting the group's goals and in making its decisions. Participate in planning and taking group action.

❷ **Take a position.** State your views and work to persuade other members to accept them. However, also be open to negotiating and compromising to settle differences within the group.

❸ **Be willing to take charge if leadership is needed.** But also be willing to follow the leadership of other members.

Practice the Skill

Suppose that you are a member of the first Congress. With a group of classmates, you must decide what and who should be taxed to raise the money the government needs. Remember that you are an elected official. If you do something to upset the people, you could lose your job. When your group has finished, answer the following questions.

1. Did your group have a plan for completing its task? Did it discuss what taxes to pass? Compared to other members, how much did you take part in those activities?

2. How well did your group work together? What role did you play in that? Was it a positive contribution or a negative one? Explain.

3. Was your group able to make a decision? If not, why? If so, was compromise involved? Do you support the decision? Explain why or why not.

Chapter Review

Visual Summary

Use the visual summary below to help you review the main ideas of the chapter.

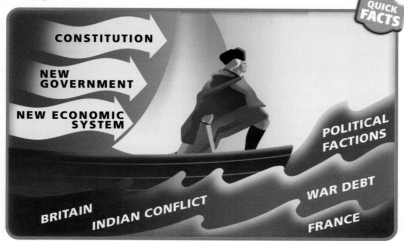

QUICK FACTS

CONSTITUTION

NEW GOVERNMENT

NEW ECONOMIC SYSTEM

POLITICAL FACTIONS

BRITAIN   INDIAN CONFLICT

WAR DEBT

FRANCE

Reviewing Vocabulary, Terms, and People

Complete each sentence by filling in the blank with the correct term or person.

1. The _____ established the structure of the federal court system and its relationship to state courts.

2. Federalists angered many Republicans when they passed the _____ to protect the United States from traitors.

3. As president, Washington was able to establish several _____, or decisions that serve as examples for later action.

4. Farmers in western Pennsylvania protested taxes in the _____.

5. The _____ was created in order to strengthen the U.S. economy.

Comprehension and Critical Thinking

SECTION 1 *(Pages 234–237)*

6. **a. Recall** What precedents did President Washington and Congress establish for the executive and judicial branches?

   b. Draw Conclusions Why did Americans select George Washington as their first president?

   c. Evaluate Do you think the newly established government met the expectations of its citizens? Why or why not?

SECTION 2 *(Pages 238–242)*

7. **a. Identify** What changes did Alexander Hamilton make to the national economy?

   b. Contrast In what ways did Hamilton and Jefferson disagree on the economy?

   c. Evaluate Which of Hamilton's economic plans do you think was the most important to the new nation? Why?

LAUNCHING THE NATION **255**

Visual Summary

Review and Inquiry Have volunteers create a cluster diagram of the information in the visual summary for the class to see. Then ask students what the visual summary communicates that a cluster diagram cannot. *Students should focus on the visual elements: image of Washington implies his dignity, strength, and influence in leading the country; the sail implies progress; the waves imply danger.*

🗄 Quick Facts Transparency: Launching the Nation Visual Summary

Reviewing Vocabulary, Terms, and People

1. Judiciary Act of 1789
2. Alien and Sedition Acts
3. precedents
4. Whiskey Rebellion
5. Bank of the United States

Comprehension and Critical Thinking

6. **a.** departments and cabinet in the executive branch; Judiciary Act of 1789 to create three levels of federal courts
   b. thought he was honest, patriotic, and a good leader
   c. possible answers—Yes, the citizens re-elected Washington so their expectations must have been met; no, the new government had too many problems.

Review and Assessment Resources

Review and Reinforce

SE Chapter Review

📋 **CRF:** Chapter Review Activity

🗄 Quick Facts Transparency: Launching the Nation Visual Summary

📻 Spanish Chapter Summaries Audio CD Program

💻 Online Chapter Summaries in Six Languages

OSP Holt PuzzlePro; GameTool for ExamView

💿 Quiz Game CD-ROM

Assess

SE Standardized Test Practice

📋 PASS: Chapter Test, Forms A and B

📋 Alternative Assessment Handbook

OSP ExamView Test Generator, Chapter Test

💿 Differentiated Instruction Modified Worksheets and Tests CD-ROM: Chapter Test

💻 Holt Online Assessment Program (in the Premier Online Edition)

Reteach/Intervene

📋 Interactive Reader and Study Guide

📋 Differentiated Instruction Teacher Management System: Lesson Plans for Differentiated Instruction

💿 Differentiated Instruction Modified Worksheets and Tests CD-ROM

💿 Interactive Skills Tutor CD-ROM

go.hrw.com

Online Resources

Chapter Resources:
KEYWORD: SR8 US7

7. a. had the federal government repay bonds at full value and take on much of the states' war debts, increased tariffs, proposed a national bank and national mint

b. Hamilton—focused on business and manufacturing, wanted higher tariffs and a national bank; Jefferson—focused on farmers, wanted lower tariffs; opposed a national bank

c. possible answers—raising tariffs, protected American manufacturing; National Bank, stabilized the economy

8. a. remaining neutral, conflicts with Britain on the high seas and on the frontier, conflict with Spain over access to New Orleans, conflicts with Native Americans in the northwest, Whiskey Rebellion

b. thought neutrality was the safest and most reasonable plan

c. possible answer—successful, nation overcame several challenges and avoided war with Britain

9. a. Rivalry between the parties dominated the election and resulted in more than one candidate running for president for the first time.

b. Some Americans supported the acts, while other Americans strongly opposed them, saying they were unconstitutional.

c. possible answers—The two parties would continue to oppose each other and not work together; Congress would be divided; leaders would focus on party goals and not the common good.

Reviewing Themes

10. national debt, including money owed to foreign nations, money owed on Revolutionary War bonds, and states' war debts; Hamilton developed a plan to pay the foreign debt immediately, gradually repay the full value of bonds, raise tariffs to increase revenue, take on much of the states' war debts, and create a national bank and mint.

11. Politics became more divisive and sectionalized, but at the same time offered Americans more of a choice in candidates and views.

SECTION 3 (Pages 243–249)

8. a. Describe What challenges did the nation face during Washington's presidency?

b. Make Inferences Why did Washington believe that it was important for the United States to remain neutral in foreign conflicts?

c. Evaluate Rate the success of Washington's presidency. Explain the reasons for your rating.

SECTION 4 (Pages 250–253)

9. a. Describe What role did political parties play in the election of 1796?

b. Analyze How did the Alien and Sedition Acts create division among some Americans?

c. Predict How might the political attacks between the Federalist and Democratic-Republican parties lead to problems in the future?

Reviewing Themes

10. Economics What economic problems troubled the nation at the beginning of Washington's presidency? How were they solved?

11. Politics How did the creation of political parties change politics in the United States?

Using the Internet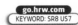

12. Activity: Creating a Poster In 1798 war with France seemed on the horizon. The Federalist-controlled Congress passed a law that made it a crime to criticize the government in print. In 1971 war raged in Vietnam and the president used a court order to stop publication of information critical of the government's actions in Vietnam. What do these events have in common? Enter the activity keyword. Then research the Alien and Sedition Acts and the Pentagon Papers case during the Vietnam War. Create a poster to display your information and to illustrate the connection between a free press and a democratic society.

Reading Skills

Inferences about History *Use the Reading Skills taught in this chapter to answer the question about the reading selection below.*

> Party differences were based partly on where and how people lived. Businesspeople in the cities tended to support the Federalists. Farmers in more isolated areas generally favored the Democratic-Republicans. (p. 251)

13. Which of the following statements can be inferred from the section?

a. Farmers wanted a large federal government.

b. Urban Americans were usually Republicans.

c. Merchants supported John Adams.

d. People in the cities had different concerns than did the rural population.

Social Studies Skills

Making Group Decisions *Use the Social Studies Skills taught in this chapter to answer the questions below.*

Get together with a group of three or four students and discuss the Alien and Sedition Acts. Answer the following questions individually and as a group.

14. Do you think that limits were needed on Americans' speeches and printed articles at the time?

15. What other ideas might Congress have considered to solve the problem of disagreement?

FOCUS ON WRITING

16. Writing a Nobel Nomination Now that you've chosen your nominee for the Nobel Prize, you can start to write your nomination. Begin with a sentence that identifies the person you are nominating. Then give at least three reasons for your nomination. Each reason should include a specific achievement or contribution of this person. End your nomination with a sentence that sums up your reasons for nominating this person for the Nobel Prize. Be persuasive. You need to convince the Nobel Prize committee that this person deserves the prize more than anyone else in the world!

Using the Internet

12. Go to the HRW Web site and enter the keyword shown to access a rubric for this activity.

KEYWORD: SR8 US7

Reading Skills

13. d

Social Studies Skills

14. Answers will vary but students should present their views within the context of the period.

15. possible answers—suggested compromises to address some of each party's concerns; found ways to resolve the issues that were dividing the nation

Focus on Writing

16. Rubric Students' Nobel nominations should:

- clearly identify the person being nominated
- provide at least three specific reasons for the nomination
- be persuasive
- use correct grammar, punctuation, spelling, and capitalization.

CRF: Focus on Writing: A Nobel Nomination

Standardized Test Practice

DIRECTIONS: Read each question and write the letter of the best response.

1 In the 1790s, most Americans

A lived in the countryside and worked on family farms.

B lived in small towns and worked as laborers or craftspeople.

C lived in cities and worked as laborers, crafts-people, or merchants.

D lived west of the Appalachian Mountains or wanted to move West.

2 In his Farewell Address in 1796, President Washington advised Americans of

A the nation's need for a national bank.

B his fear of a British invasion to end American independence.

C his wish that the office of president be given more power.

D the dangers of ties with foreign nations.

3 President Washington demonstrated the government's power under the new Constitution to enforce federal law in the way he handled the

A Whiskey Rebellion.

B Alien and Sedition Acts.

C XYZ affair.

D Judiciary Act of 1789.

4 The two-party system that exists in American politics today first arose during the election of which president?

A George Washington

B John Adams

C Thomas Jefferson

D James Madison

5 Why did George Washington issue the Neutrality Proclamation?

A He feared that involvement in the war between France and Britain was dangerous.

B He hoped to show the world that the United States was a peaceful nation.

C He wanted to concentrate on internal problems that faced the nation.

D Jefferson persuaded Washington to stay neutral toward France.

6 Which of the following was an issue on which Alexander Hamilton and Thomas Jefferson had differing views?

A protective tariffs

B national bank

C role of the central government

D all of the above

7 Examine the following passage from a description of the Alien Act and then use it to answer the question below.

> "The Alien Law has been bitterly criticized as a direct attack upon our liberties. In fact, it affects only foreigners who are plotting against us, and has nothing to do with American citizens. It gives authority to the President to order out of the country all aliens he judges dangerous to the peace and safety of the United States, or whom he suspects of treason or secret plots against the government."
>
> — Timothy Pickering, adapted from *Life of Timothy Pickering, Vol. III*

What is the author's point of view toward the Alien Law?

Answers

1. **A**
Break Down the Question This question requires students to recall factual information. Have students consider where most Americans lived at the time.

2. **D**
Break Down the Question Tell students who are unsure about the answer to try to think of Washington's various actions in office, such as the Neutrality Proclamation. Students should then look for the option that best aligns with those actions.

3. **A**
Break Down the Question Tell students first to eliminate any events that did not take place during Washington's administration (B and C). Then have students consider what they know about the remaining two choices.

4. **B**
Break Down the Question Tell students to consider what they know about Washington's election. *(It was unanimous.)* Students should then eliminate Jefferson and Madison because students have not yet studied their administrations.

5. **A**
Break Down the Question This question requires students to recall factual information. Refer students to the text titled "The Neutrality Proclamation" in Section 3.

6. **D**
Break Down the Question This question requires students to recall factual information. Refer students to the text titled "Jefferson Opposes Hamilton" in Section 2.

7. The author believes the law is reasonable and does not infringe on the rights of American citizens.

Intervention Resources

Reproducible

- Interactive Reader and Study Guide
- Differentiated Instruction Teacher Management System: Lesson Plans for Differentiated Instruction

Technology

- Quick Facts Transparency: Launching the Nation Visual Summary
- Differentiated Instruction Modified Worksheets and Tests CD-ROM
- Interactive Skills Tutor CD-ROM

Tips for Test Taking

Jot It Down Quickly Read the following to students: You might have made a special effort to memorize some information for a test. If you are worried you will forget, use this strategy. As soon as the testing period begins, jot the information down on the back of your test or on a piece of scratch paper. You can then stop worrying about forgetting and focus on the test.

258 UNIT 2

Preteach

Bellringer

Motivate Ask volunteers to explain a political process, such as the division of power in Congress. Next, discuss as a class why clear explanations of political processes are important. Lead students to conclude that explanations are important because political participation and awareness is essential in a democracy. Tell students that in this workshop they will write a paper explaining a political process.

Direct Teach

Considering Audience

Adjusting Readability Tell students that when they write something, they should consider whether their audience will understand it. One way to increase comprehension is to adjust readability. Explain that three main factors contribute to a text's readability: difficulty of vocabulary, sentence length, and paragraph length. Select a paragraph from the textbook and have students work as a class to rewrite it at a lower readability level. Help students simplify vocabulary, shorten sentences, and, if appropriate, break up the paragraph. Then have students practice the skill independently on a second paragraph. Remind students to make certain the new version makes sense, is grammatically and factually correct, and includes all the main points in the original.

Assignment

Write a paper explaining how the federal system balances power among the legislative, executive, and judicial branches of government.

TIP Using a Graphic Organizer
A chart like the following can help you organize the body of your explanation.

Legislative	Executive	Judicial

Explaining a Political Process

How do you register to vote? What is the difference between a civil court and a federal court? When we want to know about a process or system of our government, we often turn to written explanations.

1. Prewrite

Considering Purpose and Audience

In this assignment, you will be writing for an audience of middle school students. You'll need to
- identify questions they might have about the process or system
- identify factors or details that might confuse them

As you plan your paper, keep your audience in mind.

Collecting and Organizing the Information

The big idea, or thesis, of your explanation will be that the federal system balances the power among the three branches of government. To collect information about each branch and its powers, you can use a chart like the one on the left. Be sure to note the relationships among the parts. Also, note the important characteristics of each part. When you have completed the chart, you will have the basic organization of your paper.

2. Write

You can use this framework to help you write your first draft.

A Writer's Framework

Introduction	Body	Conclusion
■ State the big idea of your paper. ■ Explain briefly why this topic is important to the reader.	■ Identify the important characteristics of each part of the process or system. ■ Explain any relationships between or among the parts. ■ Define terms your readers might not know. ■ Where appropriate, include graphics to illustrate your explanation.	■ Restate your big idea in different words. ■ Summarize your main points.

Differentiating Instruction

Stuggling Readers [Below Level]

1. As students gather information, have them list any terms they do not understand.

2. Tell students to look up each of the terms in a thesaurus to find more familiar synonyms.

3. Then have students replace the difficult terms with the synonyms they found and reread the information. **LS Verbal/Linguistic**

Special Needs Learners [Below Level]

1. Have a group of three students role play the three branches of government.

2. Have the student playing the legislative branch write a bill/law on two pieces of paper and give them to the other two students. Each of these students should then explain what his or her branch will do with the bill/law. **LS Interpersonal, Kinesthetic**

3. Evaluate and Revise

Evaluating
Clear, straightforward language is important when explaining how things work. Use the following questions to discover ways to improve your paper.

Evaluation Questions for an Explanation of a Process or System

- Does your big-idea statement accurately reflect your explanation of the process or system?
- Do you discuss each part of the process or system in logical order?
- Do you include details and information to explain each part of the process or system?

- If you used bulleted or numbered lists, are the items parallel—that is, do they have the same grammatical forms or structures?
- Does your conclusion restate your big idea and explain the importance of your topic?

Revising
Sometimes a complex explanation sounds even more complex when you try to explain it in a paragraph. In those cases, a bulleted list of facts or examples may make it easier for your readers to understand the information you are presenting. As you revise your paper, consider whether you have any information you should put in a bulleted list.

4. Proofread and Publish

Proofreading
If you use special formatting in your paper, it is important to make sure that it is consistent. Here are some things to check:

- If you have used boldface or italic type, have you always used it in the same way—for important information, for a heading, for a technical term?
- If you have used a list of items, have you consistently used numbers or bullets?

Publishing
Since you are writing this paper for students, you might find a student in the sixth or seventh grade to read it. Find out whether your explanation seems clear and interesting.

5. Practice and Apply
Use the steps and strategies outlined in this workshop to write your explanation of a process or system.

A NEW NATION **259**

TIP **Using Bulleted Lists** The items in a bulleted list should be in the **same** grammatical forms or structures.
Not the same:
Duties of the legislative branch include
- interpret laws
- overseeing lower courts

The same:
Duties of the legislative branch include
- interpreting laws
- overseeing lower courts

Introduce the Unit

Share the information in the chapter overviews with students.

Chapter 8 Thomas Jefferson's presidency was marked by expansion and conflict. The nation almost doubled in size, and exploration led to new knowledge of the West. Expansionism and impressment caused conflict with Native Americans as well as a war with Britain.

Chapter 9 James Monroe's presidency was marked by the Era of Good Feelings, a time of relative peace, economic growth, and increasing nationalism. The United States asserted itself in foreign affairs and was developing a national identity, but disputes over slavery began to divide the nation.

Chapter 10 The expansion of political rights and Andrew Jackson's election indicated the increased power of the American people. Jackson's presidency was marked by political conflicts, growing sectional differences, economic problems, and the removal of Native Americans from the Southeast.

Chapter 11 Settlers braved difficult trails to reach Oregon and California. In the 1830s, Texas rebelled against Mexican rule and gained independence. In 1846, conflicts with Mexico led to war. Manifest Destiny and land gained from the U.S victory in the war with Mexico resulted in expansion to California, where gold was discovered.

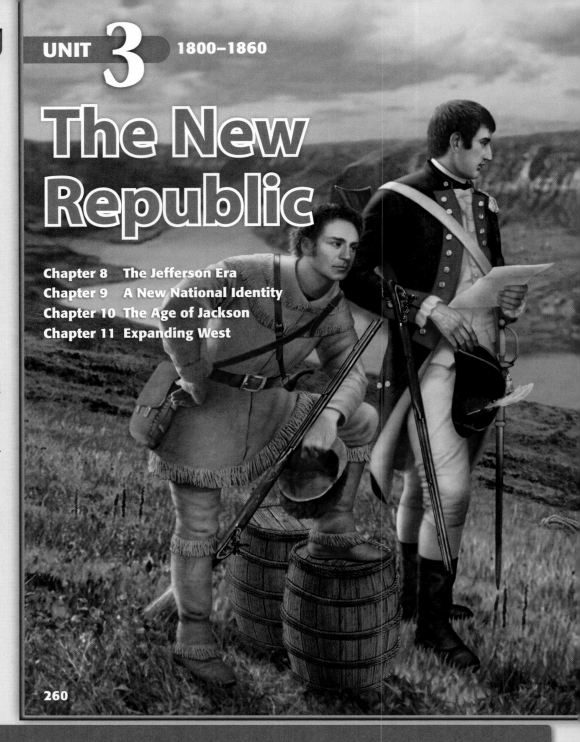

UNIT 3 1800–1860

The New Republic

260

Unit Resources

Planning

- Differentiated Instruction Teacher Management System: Unit Instructional Benchmarking Guides
- One-Stop Planner CD-ROM with Test Generator: Calendar Planner
- Power Presentations with Video CD-ROM
- A Teacher's Guide to Religion in the Public Schools

Differentiating Instruction

- Differentiated Instruction Teacher Management System: Lesson Plans for Differentiated Instruction
- Pre-AP Activities Guide for United States History
- Differentiated Instruction Modified Worksheets and Tests CD-ROM

Enrichment

- **CRF 8:** Economics and History: Embargoes—Economic Diplomacy
- **CRF 10:** Economics and History: The Panic of 1837
- **CRF 11:** Interdisciplinary Project: Share the Westward Adventure
- Civic Participation Activities
- Primary Source Library CD-ROM

Assessment

- Progress Assessment System Solution: Unit Test
- OSP ExamView Test Generator: Unit Test
- Holt Online Assessment Program, in the Premier Online Student Edition
- Alternative Assessment Handbook

What You Will Learn...

By the time the country had experienced two presidential terms, people had begun to think of themselves as Americans. A new sense of pride and unity influenced all areas of American society, from politics to art, from economics to religion. Settlers began moving deeper into the continent and the Untied States began to grow. In the next four chapters, you will learn about the first expansion of the young nation.

Explore the Art

In this picture, Lewis and Clark are shown asking advice from Sacagawea, a teenaged Shoshone Indian who helped them on their exploration of the continent. How does this picture show the challenges facing the explorers?

261

Connect to the Unit

Materials: butcher paper, drawing supplies

Activity **A Time Collage** Briefly discuss with students what the idea of national identity means. Begin by having students describe what it means to be an American. Explain to students that during the early 1800s people were just beginning to develop a sense of what it meant to be an American.

Tell students that during this unit they are going to create a linear time collage. Hang a large strip of butcher paper on the wall of the classroom. Divide the paper into seven sections and label them from 1800 to 1860. After each chapter, have students create and draw images, such as a map showing settlers' travels to the west, that apply to the topics in that chapter in appropriate places on the time line. At the end of the unit, have students discuss how their images reflect a sense of American identity.

Explore the Art

Have students examine the painting at left. Ask students to predict how the three individuals—Lewis, Clark, and Sacagawea—might have played a role in building the new nation. Then ask students to discuss how the painting expresses the optimism of the young nation.

About the Illustration

This illustration is an artist's conception based on available sources. However, historians are uncertain exactly what this scene looked like.

Democracy and Civic Education

At Level

Responsibility: Participating in the Political Process

Research Required

Background Explain that democracy expanded in the mid-1800s. More Americans gained the right to vote and the ways in which citizens could participate in the political process expanded.

1. Discuss with students why it is important in a republic to have informed citizens who actively participate in the political process. Then discuss with students the ways in which they can participate in politics.

2. Have students choose an issue facing their school or community. During the study of this unit, have students work as a class to gather information about the issue.

3. Help students decide upon a course of action for addressing the issue. Students might write to a local or state official, organize a community awareness campaign, or form an organization to address the issue. **LS** **Interpersonal, Verbal/Linguistic**

Answers

Explore the Art *illustrates the rugged landscape over which they will have to travel and the limited transportation available*

Chapter 8 Planning Guide

The Jefferson Era

Chapter Overview	Reproducible Resources	Technology Resources
CHAPTER 8 pp. 262–293 **Overview:** In this chapter, students will study the presidency of Thomas Jefferson, the Louisiana Purchase, the War of 1812, and other challenges the nation faced as it grew.	**Differentiated Instruction Teacher Management System:*** • Instructional Benchmarking Guides • Lesson Plans for Differentiated Instruction **Interactive Reader and Study Guide:** Chapter Graphic Organizer* **Chapter Resource File:*** • Focus on Writing Activity: A Letter of Recommendation • Social Studies Skills Activity: Working in Groups to Solve Issues • Chapter Review Activity	**Power Presentations with Video CD-ROM** **Differentiated Instruction Modified Worksheets and Tests CD-ROM** **Primary Source Library CD-ROM for United States History** **Interactive Skills Tutor CD-ROM** **Student Edition on Audio CD Program** **History's Impact: United States History Video Program (VHS/DVD):** The Jefferson Era*
Section 1: **Jefferson Becomes President** **The Big Idea:** Thomas Jefferson's election began a new era in American government.	**Differentiated Instruction Teacher Management System:** Section 1 Lesson Plan* **Interactive Reader and Study Guide:** Section 1 Summary* **Chapter Resource File:*** • Vocabulary Builder Activity, Section 1 • Biography Activities: Aaron Burr; John Marshall • Primary Source: Jefferson's 1801 Inaugural Address	**Daily Bellringer Transparency:** Section 1* **Quick Facts Transparency:** The Election of 1800* **Internet Activity:** Thomas Jefferson and Politics Essay
Section 2: **The Louisiana Purchase** **The Big Idea:** Under President Jefferson's leadership, the United States added the Louisiana Territory.	**Differentiated Instruction Teacher Management System:** Section 2 Lesson Plan* **Interactive Reader and Study Guide:** Section 2 Summary* **Chapter Resource File:*** • Vocabulary Builder Activity, Section 2 • Biography Activity: Sacagawea • History and Geography Activity: Pike Explores the Southwest	**Daily Bellringer Transparency:** Section 2* **Map Transparency:** The Louisiana Purchase and Western Expeditions*
Section 3: **The Coming of War** **The Big Idea:** Challenges at home and abroad led the United States to declare war on Great Britain.	**Differentiated Instruction Teacher Management System:** Section 3 Lesson Plan* **Interactive Reader and Study Guide:** Section 3 Summary* **Chapter Resource File:*** • Vocabulary Builder Activity, Section 3 • Biography Activity: Tecumseh • Literature Activity: *A Warrior's Speech* • Primary Source Activity: A Shawnee Leader Seeks Allies	**Daily Bellringer Transparency:** Section 3*
Section 4: **The War of 1812** **The Big Idea:** Great Britain and the United States went to battle in the War of 1812.	**Differentiated Instruction Teacher Management System:** Section 4 Lesson Plan* **Interactive Reader and Study Guide:** Section 4 Summary* **Chapter Resource File:*** • Vocabulary Builder Activity, Section 4	**Daily Bellringer Transparency:** Section 4* **Map Transparency:** The War of 1812* **Quick Facts Transparency:** Analyzing the War of 1812* **Internet Activity:** "The Star-Spangled Banner" Poster

SE Student Edition   Print Resource   Audio CD

TE Teacher's Edition   Transparency   CD-ROM

 go.hrw.com   **LS** Learning Styles   Video

OSP One-Stop Planner CD-ROM   * also on One-Stop Planner CD

HOLT
History's Impact
United States History Video Program (VHS/DVD)

The Jefferson Era
Suggested use: as a chapter introduction

Review, Assessment, Intervention

 Quick Facts Transparency: The Jefferson Era Visual Summary*

 Spanish Chapter Summaries Audio CD Program

 Progress Assessment Support System (PASS): Chapter Test*

 Differentiated Instruction Modified Worksheets and Tests CD-ROM: Modified Chapter Test

 One-Stop Planner CD-ROM: ExamView Test Generator (English/Spanish)

 Holt Online Assessment Program (HOAP), in the Holt Premier Online Student Edition

 PASS: Section 1 Quiz*
 Online Quiz: Section 1
 Alternative Assessment Handbook

 PASS: Section 2 Quiz*
 Online Quiz: Section 2
 Alternative Assessment Handbook

 PASS: Section 3 Quiz*
 Online Quiz: Section 3
 Alternative Assessment Handbook

 PASS: Section 4 Quiz*
 Online Quiz: Section 4
 Alternative Assessment Handbook

Power Presentations with Video CD-ROM

Power Presentations with Video are visual presentations of each chapter's main ideas. Presentations can be customized by including Quick Facts charts, images from the text, and video clips.

Power Presentations with Video CD-ROM

HOLT
United States History
Beginnings to 1877

HOLT, RINEHART and WINSTON
A Harcourt Education Company

DIVISION FOR
PUBLIC EDUCATION
AMERICAN BAR ASSOCIATION

Developed by the Division for Public Education of the American Bar Association, these materials are part of the **Democracy and Civic Education Resources.**

- **Constitution Study Guide**
- **Supreme Court Case Studies**

Holt Online Learning

Teacher Resources
KEYWORD: SR8 TEACHER

Student Resources
KEYWORD: SR8 US8

- Document-Based Questions
- Interactive Multimedia Activities

- Current Events
- Chapter-based Internet Activities
- and more!

Holt Premier
Online Student Edition
Complete online support for interactivity, assessment, and reporting

- Interactive Maps and Notebook
- Standardized Test Prep
- Homework Practice and Research Activities Online

CHAPTER 8 PLANNING GUIDE

Differentiating Instruction

ENGLISH-LANGUAGE LEARNERS & STRUGGLING READERS

TARGET RESOURCE

Live Ink® Online Reading Help

Spanish Resources

Spanish Chapter Summaries Audio CD Program

One-Stop Planner CD-ROM:
- ExamView Test Generator, Spanish
- PuzzlePro, Spanish

Additional Resources

Differentiated Instruction Teacher Management System: Lesson Plans for Differentiated Instruction

Chapter Resources:
- Vocabulary Builder Activities
- Social Studies Skills Activity: Working in Groups to Solve Issues

Quick Facts Transparencies:
- The Election of 1800
- Analyzing the War of 1812
- The Jefferson Era Visual Summary

Student Edition on Audio CD Program

Online Chapter Summaries in Six Languages

Interactive Skills Tutor CD-ROM

SPECIAL NEEDS LEARNERS

TARGET RESOURCE

Differentiated Instruction Modified Worksheets and Tests CD-ROM

- Vocabulary Flash Cards
- Modified Vocabulary Builder Activities
- Modified Chapter Review Activity
- Modified Chapter Test

Additional Resources

Differentiated Instruction Teacher Management System: Lesson Plans for Differentiated Instruction

Interactive Reader and Study Guide

Social Studies Skills Activity: Working in Groups to Solve Issues

Student Edition on Audio CD Program

Interactive Skills Tutor CD-ROM

Live Ink® Online Reading Help

ADVANCED/GIFTED AND TALENTED STUDENTS

TARGET RESOURCE

Primary Source Library CD-ROM for United States History

The Library contains longer versions of quotations in the text, extra sources, and images. Included are point-of-view articles, journals, diaries, historical fiction, and political documents.

Additional Resources

Political Cartoons Activities for United States History: Cartoon 9: The Louisiana Purchase; Cartoon 8: Party Politics in the Jefferson Era

United States History Document-Based Questions Activities

Differentiated Instruction Teacher Management System: Lesson Plans for Differentiated Instruction

Chapter Resource File:
- Focus on Writing Activity: A Letter of Recommendation
- Literature Activity: *A Warrior's Speech* by Chief Tecumseh
- Primary Source Activity: Jefferson's 1801 Inaugural Address
- Primary Source Activity: A Shawnee Leader Seeks Allies

One-Stop Planner® CD-ROM

for Differentiated Instruction

Your differentiated instruction lesson plans are available at your fingertips. Holt's Teacher Management System links teaching support tools to pages in the Interactive Teacher's Edition.

The One-Stop Planner features:

- Interactive Teacher's Edition
- Calendar Planner and pacing guides
- Editable lesson plans
- All reproducible ancillaries in Adobe Acrobat (PDF) format
- ExamView Test Generator (English and Spanish)
- Transparency and video previews

Professional Development

- **In-service and staff development** as part of your Holt Social Studies product purchase
- **Quick Teacher Tutorial Lesson Presentation CD-ROM**
- Intensive tuition-based **Teacher Development Institute**
- **Teaching American History Online**—2 Module Professional Development Course
- **Convenient Holt Speaker Bureau**—face-to-face workshop options
- **PRAXIS™ Test Prep** interactive Web-based content refreshers*
- **24/7 Ask A Professional Development Expert** at http://www.hrw.com/prodev/

* PRAXIS is a trademark of Educational Testing Service (ETS). This publication is not endorsed or approved by ETS.

Chapter Big Ideas

Section 1 Thomas Jefferson's election began a new era in American government.

Section 2 Under President Jefferson's leadership, the United States added the Louisiana Territory.

Section 3 Challenges at home and abroad led the United States to declare war on Great Britain.

Section 4 Great Britain and the United States went to battle in the War of 1812.

Focus on Writing

The **Chapter Resource File** provides a Focus on Writing worksheet to help students organize and write their letters of recommendation.

📋 **CRF:** Focus on Writing Activity: A Letter of Recommendation

CHAPTER 8 1800–1815

The Jefferson Era

FOCUS ON WRITING

A Letter of Recommendation Americans love lists—the five best books of the year, the 10 best video games, the three best soccer players. As you read this chapter you will gather some information about Thomas Jefferson. Then you will write a letter to your newspaper telling why Jefferson should be on the newspaper's "Top Ten American Presidents" list.

| UNITED STATES | 1801 Thomas Jefferson takes office. | 1803 U.S. Senate approves the Louisiana Purchase. |

1800

WORLD **1802** An army of former slaves led by Toussaint-Louverture defeats a French army in Haiti.

Introduce the Chapter

At Level

Focus on the Jefferson Administration

1. Explain to students that the presidential election of 1800 was very close. Have students use what they learned in the last chapter to predict what some of the main issues in the election might have been. (*Students might suggest the extent of the federal government's power, the Bank of the United States, relations with France, and the Alien and Sedition Acts.*)

2. Next, have students preview the chapter by reading the section titles and the blue headings and by looking at the images.

3. Then ask students if they can tell from this quick preview what some of the important events of the Jefferson era were. List students' responses for the class to see.

4. Conclude by having students discuss which of the events they listed would have been most significant to the development of the United States. Tell students to keep the discussion in mind as they study the chapter.
🔲 **Verbal/Linguistic, Visual/Spatial**

What You Will Learn...

In this chapter you will learn about the presidency of Thomas Jefferson. A man of many talents, Jefferson looked back to classical architecture to design his Virginia home, Monticello.

1804
Lewis and Clark begin their westward journey.

1807
Congress passes the Embargo Act.

1812
Congress declares war against Great Britain.

1815
The Battle of New Orleans is fought.

1805   1810   1815

1807
The slave trade is abolished in the British Empire.

1814
Kurozumi Munetada founds an influential Shinto religious sect that stresses patriotism in Japan.

THE JEFFERSON ERA **263**

• **Chapter Preview** •

HOLT
History's Impact
► video series
See the Video Teacher's Guide for strategies for using the chapter video **The Jefferson Era**.

Explore the Picture

Monticello Thomas Jefferson designed and built Monticello, his plantation home near Charlottesville, Virginia. Inside, the house provided a library for Jefferson's large collection of books as well as space for his many inventions. Outside, the grounds featured gardens where Jefferson experimented with growing new types of plants, flowers, and vegetables.

Analyzing Visuals The portion of Monticello covered by the white dome is called the Dome Room. How might Jefferson have used this room? *possible answers—for weather or astronomical observations; for observing his plantation*

go.hrw.com
Online Resources
Chapter Resources:
KEYWORD: SR8 US8
Teacher Resources:
KEYWORD: SR8 TEACHER

Explore the Time Line

1. Who led a slave rebellion in Haiti in 1802 that defeated a French army? *Toussaint-Louverture*

2. When did the British Empire abolish the slave trade? *1807*

3. Whom did the United States go to war against during this period, and when did the war begin? *Great Britain; 1812*

4. Which event do you think led to the expansion of the United States? *U.S. Senate's approval of the Louisiana Purchase in 1803.*

Info to Know

Jefferson Thomas Jefferson had a good-humored nature. A brilliant conversationalist, he could talk just as easily about chemistry or horse racing as politics or philosophy. He loved architecture, art, and geography. He not only knew French, Greek, Italian, Latin, and Spanish but also studied some 40 Native American languages. At the same time, Jefferson struggled with a deep sense of loneliness. The death of his wife, Martha Wayles Skelton, and of five of his six children caused him untold grief.

Reading
Social Studies

Understanding Themes

Two themes—geography and politics—are the focus of this chapter. Students will learn about the Louisiana Purchase and the expedition of Lewis and Clark. Help students understand the challenges that the geography of the West presented to the exploration of these lands. As students read the chapter, help them see the relationship between geography and politics during this time in American history.

Public Documents in History

Focus on Reading Have students consider the types of public documents that they have already seen or studied. The Declaration of Independence and the U.S. Constitution are two examples that students should know. They may also be familiar with state laws concerning driving or voter information bulletins that are published before an election. Point out to students that these are all examples of public documents. Guide students in a discussion of the language used in public documents. Ask students why public documents might be of use to historians.

Reading Social Studies

| Economics | Geography | Politics | Society and Culture | Science and Technology |

Focus on Themes In this chapter you will learn about Thomas Jefferson's presidency. You will read what happened when Jefferson's first run to be president ended in a tie. After that, you will learn about his decision to buy Louisiana from the French, see how he encouraged the exploration of the West, and discover why, during his second term, America found herself at war with Great Britain. You will see how America's expanding **geography** and **politics** were intertwined.

Public Documents in History

Focus on Reading Historians use many types of documents to learn about the past. These documents can often be divided into two types—private and public. Private documents are those written for a person's own use, such as letters, journals, or notebooks. Public documents, on the other hand, are available for everyone to read and examine. They include such things as laws, tax codes, and treaties.

Studying Public Documents Studying public documents from the past can tell us a great deal about the politics and society of the time. However, public documents can often be confusing or difficult to understand. When you read such a document, you may want to use a list of questions like the one below to be sure you understand what you're reading.

You can often figure out the topic of a public document from the title and introduction.

Public documents often use unfamiliar words or use familiar words in unfamiliar ways. For example, the document on the next page uses the word *augmented*. Do you know what the word means in this context? If not, you should look it up.

Many public documents deal with several issues and will therefore have several main ideas.

Question Sheet for Public Documents

1. What is the topic of the document?
2. Do I understand what I'm reading?
3. Is there any vocabulary in the document that I do not understand?
4. What parts of the document should I re-read?
5. What are the main ideas and details of the document?
6. What have I learned from reading this document?

264 CHAPTER 8

Reading and Skills Resources

Reading Support

- Interactive Reader and Study Guide
- Student Edition on Audio CD Program
- Spanish Chapter Summaries Audio CD Program

Social Studies Skills Support

- Interactive Skills Tutor CD-ROM

Vocabulary Support

- **CRF:** Vocabulary Builder Activities
- **CRF:** Chapter Review Activity
- Differentiated Instruction Modified Worksheets and Tests CD-ROM:
  - Vocabulary Flash Cards
  - Vocabulary Builder Activity
  - Chapter Review Activity

OSP Holt PuzzlePro

You Try It!

The passage below was taken from a Post Office notice from 1815. Read the passage and then answer the questions that follow.

Rates of Postage

Postmasters will take notice, that by an act of Congress, passed on the 23d instant, the several rates of postage are augmented fifty per cent; and that after the first of February next, the Rates of Postage for single Letters will be,
For any distance not exceeding 40 miles, 12 cents
  Over 40 miles and not exceeding 90 miles, 15 cents
  Over 90 miles and not exceeding 150 miles, 18 1/2 cents
  Over 150 miles and not exceeding 300 miles, 25 1/2 cents
  Over 300 miles and not exceeding 500 miles, 30 cents
  Over 500 miles, 37 1/2 cents
  Double letters, or those composed of two pieces of paper, double those rates.
  Triple letters, or those composed of three pieces of paper, triple those rates.
  Packets, or letters composed of four or more pieces of paper, and weighing one ounce or more, avoirdupois, are to be rated equal to one single letter for each quarter ounce.

After reading the document above, answer the following questions.

1. What is this document about?

2. What was the main idea or ideas of this document? What supporting details were included?

3. Look at the word *packets* in the last paragraph of the document. The word is not used here in the same way we usually use *packets* today. What does the word mean in this case? How can you tell?

4. Are there any other words in this passage with which you are unfamiliar? How might not knowing those words hinder your understanding of the passage?

Key Terms and People

As you read Chapter 8, look for passages from other public documents. What can these documents teach you about the past?

Reading Social Studies

Key Terms and People

Preteach the key terms and people for this chapter by hosting a vocabulary game for students. Write the key terms and people for students to see. Then organize the class into teams. Read aloud definitions or descriptions, and have teams take turns guessing which term identifies the description. If one team guesses incorrectly, allow the next team an opportunity to guess the answer. Assign points for each correct answer. You might want to have students keep a list of correct descriptions for each term. **LS** Interpersonal, Verbal/Linguistic

Focus on Reading

See the **Focus on Reading** questions in this chapter for more practice on this reading social studies skill.

Reading Social Studies Assessment

See the **Chapter Review** at the end of this chapter for student assessment questions related to this reading skill.

Teaching Tip

Students will often be called upon to interpret public documents. Point out to students that they should use the same techniques to analyze a public document as they do with any type of document. Have students practice reading public documents by showing them some examples, such as laws, deeds, and government proclamations. Libraries and the Internet are good places to find public documents. Encourage students to use these documents in their research.

Answers

You Try It! **1.** *postage rates;* **2.** *main idea—Congress has raised postage rate; details—postage rates depend on the distance a letter will travel, letters with more than one piece of paper cost more to send, packets over one ounce are charged by the quarter ounce;* **3.** *large envelopes; they hold more than four pieces of paper and weigh more than one ounce.* **4.** *possible answers— augmented, avoirdupois; it might lead to a misinterpretation of the document.*

Bellringer

If YOU were there . . . Use the **Daily Bellringer Transparency** to help students answer the question.

📖 Daily Bellringer Transparency, Section 1

Academic Vocabulary

Review with students the high-use academic term in this section.

functions uses or purposes (p. 269)

📄 **CRF:** Vocabulary Builder Activity, Section 1

Taking Notes

Have students copy the graphic organizer onto their own paper and then use it to take notes on the section. This activity will prepare students for the Section Assessment, in which they will complete a graphic organizer that builds on the information using a critical thinking skill.

What You Will Learn...

Main Ideas

1. The election of 1800 marked the first peaceful transition in power from one political party to another.
2. President Jefferson's beliefs about the federal government were reflected in his policies.
3. *Marbury* v. *Madison* increased the power of the judicial branch of government.

The Big Idea

Thomas Jefferson's election began a new era in American government.

Key Terms and People

John Adams, *p. 266*
Thomas Jefferson, *p. 266*
John Marshall, *p. 270*
Marbury v. *Madison*, *p. 270*
judicial review, *p. 270*

TAKING NOTES As you read, take notes in a graphic organizer like this one. List the details of the election of 1800, Jefferson's beliefs and policies, and how the power of the judicial branch changed during his time in office.

Election of 1800	
Jefferson's Beliefs and Policies	
Power of the Judical Branch	

Jefferson Becomes President

If YOU were there...

You are a member of the Virginia electoral college from a frontier district—and you are tired! For days, the college has been wrangling over the presidential election. You've had almost no sleep. Who shall it be—John Adams or Thomas Jefferson? Your vote depends on your personal judgment.

Which candidate would you choose for president?

BUILDING BACKGROUND John Adams had not been a popular president, but many still admired his ability and high principles. Both he and Thomas Jefferson had played major roles in winning independence and shaping the new government. Now, political differences sharply divided the two men and their supporters. In the election of 1800, voters were also divided.

The Election of 1800

In the presidential election of 1800, Federalists **John Adams** and Charles C. Pinckney ran against Democratic-Republicans **Thomas Jefferson** and Aaron Burr. Each party believed that the American republic's survival depended upon the success of their candidates. With so much at stake, the election was hotly contested.

Unlike today, candidates did not travel around giving speeches. Instead, the candidates' supporters made their arguments in letters and newspaper editorials. Adams's supporters claimed that Jefferson was a pro-French radical. Put Jefferson in office, they warned, and the violence and chaos of the French Revolution would surely follow. Plus, Federalists argued, Jefferson's interest in science and philosophy proved that he wanted to destroy organized religion.

Democratic-Republican newspapers responded that Adams wanted to crown himself king. What else, they asked, could be the purpose of the Alien and Sedition Acts? Republicans also hinted that Adams would use the newly created permanent army to limit Americans' rights.

Teach the Big Idea

Jefferson Becomes President

1. **Teach** Ask students the questions in the Main Idea boxes to teach this section.

2. **Apply** Have students list the section's key people, events, and issues. Write the list for students to see. Then ask students to imagine that they are news reporters. Have each student write a headline for each main event and issue. Model the activity by doing the first headline for students. **LS Verbal/Linguistic**

3. **Review** As you review the section, have students share their related headlines with the class.

4. **Practice/Homework** Select one headline and have each student write an article or draw a political cartoon to accompany the headline. **LS Verbal/Linguistic, Visual/Spatial**

📄 Alternative Assessment Handbook, Rubrics 27: Political Cartoons; and 42: Writing to Inform

The Election of 1800
QUICK FACTS

John Adams and the Federalists
- Rule by wealthy class
- Strong federal government
- Emphasis on manufacturing
- Loose interpretation of the Constitution
- British alliance

Thomas Jefferson and the Democratic-Republicans
- Rule by the people
- Strong state governments
- Emphasis on agriculture
- Strict interpretation of the Constitution
- French alliance

Election Results

Adams receives 65 votes, and Pinckney receives 64 votes.

Jefferson and running mate Burr receive 73 votes each.

- Peaceful change of political power from one party to another
- The tied race led to the Twelfth Amendment (1804), which created a separate ballot for president and vice president.

When the election results came in, Jefferson and Burr had won 73 electoral votes each to 65 for Adams and 64 for Pinckney. The Democratic-Republicans had won the election, but the tie between Jefferson and Burr caused a problem. Under the Constitution at that time, the two candidates with the most votes became president and vice president. The decision went to the House of Representatives as called for in the Constitution.

The House, like the electoral college, also deadlocked. Days went by as vote after vote was called, each ending in ties. Exhausted lawmakers put their heads on their desks and slept between votes. Some napped on the floor.

Jefferson finally won on the thirty-sixth vote. The election marked the first time that one party had replaced another in power in the United States.

The problems with the voting system led Congress to propose the Twelfth Amendment. This amendment created a separate ballot for president and vice president.

READING CHECK **Analyzing Information**
What was significant about Jefferson's victory?

Direct Teach

Main Idea

❶ The Election of 1800

The election of 1800 marked the first peaceful transition in power from one political party to another.

Identify Who were the candidates in the election, and what party did each represent? *See chart at left.*

Contrast How did the two parties' positions in the election differ? *See chart at left.*

Identify Cause and Effect Why did the election lead to the Twelfth Amendment? *because Jefferson and Burr tied; showed the need to have separate tickets for president and vice president*

Activity **Campaign Slogans** Have each student create a campaign slogan for each political party in the election of 1800.

- Alternative Assessment Handbook, Rubric 34: Slogans and Banners
- **CRF:** Biography Activity: Aaron Burr
- Quick Facts Transparency: The Election of 1800

The Election of 1800 Have students find the Twelfth Amendment to the U.S. Constitution in their textbooks and rewrite it in their own words.

go.hrw.com
Online Resources
KEYWORD: SR8 US8
ACTIVITY: Thomas Jefferson and Politics Essay

Differentiating Instruction

Below Level

English-Language Learners

1. Help students go through the Quick Facts chart above. Define any words or terms with which students are unfamiliar.

2. Then have each student create a large copy of the chart and add symbols or drawings to represent each party characteristic and election result. Model the activity to help students get started. Draw a hammer to show Federalists' emphasis on manufacturing and a sheaf of wheat to show Democratic-Republicans' emphasis on agriculture.

3. As students work, check that each one accurately understands the chart.

4. Have volunteers share some of the symbols they created with the class. **LS Visual/Spatial**

- Alternative Assessment Handbook, Rubrics 3: Artwork; and 7: Charts
- Quick Facts Transparency: The Election of 1800

Answers

Reading Check *The election was the first time that one party had replaced another in power in the United States.*

267

Main Idea

❷ Jefferson's Policies

President Jefferson's beliefs about the federal government were reflected in his policies.

Recall In his 1801 inaugural address, what political ideas does Jefferson express? *support for the will of the majority, limited government, and protection of civil liberties*

Analyze How did Jefferson and Congress put these Democratic-Republican ideas into practice? *will of the majority—did away with unpopular taxes; limited government—cut military funds and size, kept government small; civil liberties—let Alien and Sedition Acts expire*

Make Generalizations In what ways did Jefferson try to make his inauguration a reflection of Democratic-Republican ideals? *walked to the Capitol rather than ride in a carriage or on horseback; stressed need for limited government and protection of civil liberties in his inaugural address*

📃 **CRF:** Primary Source Activity: Jefferson's 1801 Inaugural Address

Primary Source

Jefferson's Inaugural Address

Draw Conclusions Based on his phrase "shall not take from the mouth of labor the bread it has earned," what do you think was Jefferson's position on taxation? Explain your answer. *He did not support taxing the money that people earned from their work.*

Primary Source

SPEECH
Jefferson's Inaugural Address

On March 4, 1801, Thomas Jefferson gave his first inaugural address. In the following excerpt, Jefferson describes his thoughts on the nation's future.

By using phrases like these, Jefferson tries to reassure his political opponents.

Here Jefferson states his opinion of what is essential to good government.

This phrase shows Jefferson's determination to keep government small.

❝Let us, then, fellow citizens, unite with one heart and one mind ... [E]very difference of opinion is not a difference of principle. We have called by different names brethren[1] of the same principle. We are all republicans; we are all federalists.❞

❝Still one thing more, fellow citizens, a wise and frugal[2] Government, which shall restrain men from injuring one another, shall leave them otherwise free to regulate their own pursuits of industry and improvement, and shall not take from the mouth of labor the bread it has earned. This is the sum of good government ... ❞

1. **brethren:** brothers 2. **frugal:** thrifty

ANALYSIS SKILL **ANALYZING PRIMARY SOURCES**

What words and phrases indicate Jefferson's support for a small national government?

Jefferson's Policies

When Jefferson took office, he brought with him a style and political ideas different from those of Adams and Washington. Jefferson was less formal than his predecessors, and he wanted to limit the powers of government.

Jefferson Is Inaugurated

Americans looked forward with excitement to Jefferson's first speech as president. People from across the nation gathered in the new capital, Washington, D.C., to hear him. Curious travelers looked with pride at the partially completed Capitol building and at the executive mansion (not yet called the White House). The two buildings dominated the surrounding homes and forests.

Small businesses dotted the landscape. At one of these, a modest boardinghouse, the president-elect was putting the finishing touches on his speech. On the morning of March 4, 1801, he left the boardinghouse and walked to the Capitol. The leader of a republic, Jefferson believed, should not ride in fancy carriages.

Jefferson read his speech in a quiet voice. He wanted to make it clear that he supported the will of the majority. He also stressed the need for a limited government and the protection of civil liberties.

From these humble surroundings in which Jefferson delivered his speech, Washington eventually grew into a large and impressive city. Over the years, the Capitol and the executive mansion were joined by other state buildings and monuments. Jefferson, who had long dreamed of a new national capital that would be independent of the interests of any one state, was pleased to be a part of this process of building a federal city.

Jefferson in Office

President Jefferson faced the task of putting his republican ideas into practice. One of his first actions was to select the members of his cabinet. His choices included James Madison as secretary of state and Albert Gallatin as secretary of the treasury.

Jefferson would also benefit from the Democratic-Republican Party's newly won control of both houses of Congress. At Jefferson's urging, Congress allowed the hated Alien and Sedition Acts to expire. Jefferson

THE IMPACT TODAY

A monument to Thomas Jefferson was completed in 1943 and is one of the most frequently visited sites in Washington, D.C.

Critical Thinking: Evaluating Information

Above Level

Thomas Jefferson Report Card

1. Discuss with students Jefferson's main actions in office. As you do, list for students the Democratic-Republican ideas Jefferson supported and the Federalist ideas he kept.

2. Next, have students explain how Jefferson's actions in office reflected the Democratic-Republican views that he expressed in his 1801 inaugural address.

3. Have each student use the information in this section to create a report card for Jefferson's first presidential administration.

4. Students' report cards should list Jefferson's main goals, as expressed in his inaugural address, and then provide a grade for each goal based on Jefferson's actions in office. Students should also explain each grade.

LS **Verbal/Linguistic**

📃 Alternative Assessment Handbook, Rubric 16: Judging Information

📃 **CRF:** Primary Source Activity: Jefferson's 1801 Inaugural Address

Answers

Analyzing Primary Sources *"frugal Government," "free to regulate their own pursuits of industry and improvement"*

lowered military spending and reduced the size of the army. The navy was cut to seven active ships. Jefferson and Gallatin hoped that saving this money would allow the government to repay the national debt. Jefferson also asked Gallatin to find ways to get rid of domestic taxes, like the tax on whiskey. The Democratic-Republican-led Congress passed the laws needed to carry out these policies.

The entire national government in 1801 consisted only of several hundred people. Jefferson preferred to keep it that way. He believed that the primary **functions** of the federal government were to protect the nation from foreign threats, deliver the mail, and collect customs duties.

Jefferson did recognize that some of the Federalist policies—such as the creation of the Bank of the United States—should be kept. Although Jefferson had battled Hamilton over the Bank, as president he agreed to leave it in place.

READING CHECK **Summarizing** What policy changes did Democratic-Republicans introduce, and which Federalist policies did Jefferson keep?

Marbury v. Madison

Although Republicans controlled the presidency and Congress, Federalists dominated the federal judiciary. In an effort to continue their control over the judiciary, Federalist legislators passed the Judiciary Act of 1801 shortly before their terms of office ended. This act created 16 new federal judgeships that President Adams filled with Federalists before leaving office. The Republican press called these people midnight judges, arguing that Adams had packed the judiciary with Federalists the night before he left office.

Some of these appointments were made so late that the documents that authorized them had not been delivered by the time Adams left office. This led to controversy once Jefferson took office. William Marbury, named as a justice of the peace by President Adams, did not receive his documents before Adams left office. When Jefferson took office, Marbury demanded the documents. On Jefferson's advice, however, the new secretary of state, James Madison, refused to deliver them. Jefferson argued that the appointment of the midnight judges was not valid.

ACADEMIC VOCABULARY

functions
uses or purposes

SUPREME COURT DECISIONS

Marbury v. Madison (1803)

Background of the Case Shortly before Thomas Jefferson took office, John Adams had appointed William Marbury to be a justice of the peace. Adams had signed Marbury's commission, but it was never delivered. Marbury sued to force Madison to give him the commission.

The Court's Ruling
The Court ruled that the law Marbury based his claim on was unconstitutional.

The Court's Reasoning
The Judiciary Act of 1789 gave the Supreme Court the authority to hear a wide variety of cases, including those like Marbury's. But the Supreme Court ruled that Congress did not have the power to make such a law. Why? Because the Constitution limits the types of cases the Supreme Court can hear. Thus, the law was in conflict with the Constitution and had to be struck down.

Why It Matters
Marbury v. Madison was important for several reasons. It confirmed the Supreme Court's power to declare acts of Congress unconstitutional. By doing so, it established the Court as the final authority on the Constitution. This helped make the judicial branch of government equal to the other two branches. Chief Justice John Marshall and later federal judges would use this power of judicial review as a check on the legislative and executive branches.

ANALYSIS SKILL **ANALYZING INFORMATION**
1. What do you think it means to be the final authority on the Constitution?
2. How did Marbury v. Madison affect the Constitution's system of checks and balances?

THE JEFFERSON ERA **269**

---

❸ Marbury v. Madison

Marbury v. *Madison* increased the power of the judicial branch of government.

Summarize Explain the Supreme Court's ruling in *Marbury* v. *Madison*. *The Court ruled that it did not have the authority to hear cases such as Marbury's and, thus, that the law upon which the case was based was unconstitutional.*

Analyze How does the power of judicial review strengthen the role of the judicial branch? *gives it a check on the other branches of government*

📓 **CRF:** Biography Activity: John Marshall

Close

Have students work as a class to write a summary of Jefferson's first term in office as president.

Review

🖥 Online Quiz, Section 1

Assess

SE Section 1 Assessment

📓 PASS: Section 1 Quiz

📓 Alternative Assessment Handbook

Reteach/Classroom Intervention

📓 Interactive Reader and Study Guide, Section 1

💿 Interactive Skills Tutor CD-ROM

Answers

Reading Check *established the U.S. Supreme Court's power of judicial review, which strengthened the judicial branch's power in relation to the other two branches of government*

Marbury brought suit, asking the Supreme Court to order Madison to deliver the appointment papers. Marbury claimed that the Judiciary Act of 1789 gave the Supreme Court the power to do so.

John Marshall, a Federalist appointed by John Adams, was the chief justice of the United States. Chief Justice Marshall and President Jefferson disagreed about many political issues. When Marshall agreed to hear Marbury's case, Jefferson protested, saying that the Federalists "have retired into the judiciary as a stronghold." Marshall wrote the Court's opinion in *Marbury* v. *Madison*, a case that helped establish the Supreme Court's power to check the power of the other branches of government. The Constitution, Chief Justice Marshall noted, gave the Supreme Court authority to hear only certain types of cases. A request like Marbury's was not one of them. The law that Marbury's case depended upon was, therefore, unconstitutional.

John Marshall served as chief justice of the United States for 34 years.

In denying Marbury's request in this way, the Court avoided a direct confrontation with Jefferson's administration. But more importantly, it established the Court's power of **judicial review**, the power to declare an act of Congress unconstitutional. Marshall and later federal judges would use this power of judicial review to make the judiciary a much stronger part of the national government.

READING CHECK Analyzing Information
Why was *Marbury* v. *Madison* an important ruling?

┌ **SUMMARY AND PREVIEW** A peaceful transfer of power took place in Washington after the election of 1800. In the next section you will read about the Louisiana Purchase.

---

go.hrw.com
Online Quiz
KEYWORD: SR8 HP8

Section 1 Assessment

Reviewing Ideas, Terms, and People

1. **a. Identify** What were the political parties and who were their candidates in the election of 1800?
   b. Analyze Why was the election of 1800 significant?
2. **a. Describe** What ideas for government did **Thomas Jefferson** stress in his inaugural address?
   b. Compare and Contrast What similarities and differences did Jefferson's Republican government have with the previous Federalist one?
   c. Elaborate Defend Jefferson's preference for keeping the national government small.
3. **a. Identify** Who was **John Marshall**?
   b. Draw Conclusions Why is the power of **judicial review** important?
   c. Predict How might the *Marbury* v. *Madison* ruling affect future actions by Congress?

Critical Thinking

4. **Categorizing** Review your notes on Jefferson's beliefs and policies as president. Then copy the graphic organizer below and show how he brought change through his policies.

Jefferson as President

Federalist Policies	Republican Policies

FOCUS ON WRITING ✏

5. **Gathering Ideas about a Person's Accomplishments** Look back through what you have just read to see what you have learned about Jefferson's decisions in office. Make a list of the traits you think each decision shows in Jefferson.

270 CHAPTER 8

Section 1 Assessment Answers

1. **a.** Federalists—John Adams, Charles C. Pinckney; Republicans—Thomas Jefferson, Aaron Burr
   b. first peaceful transfer of power from one U.S. political party to another
2. **a.** the will of the majority, limited government, and the protection of civil liberties
   b. similarities—national bank, small federal government; differences—Jefferson cut military spending and taxes, let Alien and Sedition Acts expire.
   c. Jefferson believed that limiting government would protect civil liberties.

3. **a.** Chief justice of the United States who wrote the opinion in *Marbury* v. *Madison*
   b. It gave the Supreme Court the power to declare an act of Congress unconstitutional, which strengthened the judicial branch's power.
   c. Congress would be more aware of whether proposed laws are constitutional.
4. cut military spending and taxes to limit powers of government; kept Bank of the United States; let Alien and Sedition Acts expire
5. Students might list characteristics such as intelligence, humility, leadership, and so on.

Thomas Jefferson

How would you inspire people to seek freedom?

When did he live? He was born on April 13, 1743. He died on July 4, 1826, within hours of the death of President John Adams, his rival and friend. The date was also the fiftieth anniversary of the Declaration of Independence.

Where did he live? He was born in Albemarle County, Virginia, where he inherited a large estate from his father. At age 26 he began building his elegant lifetime home, Monticello, which he designed himself. He spent much of his life away from home, in Philadelphia; Washington, D.C.; and Europe. Yet he always longed to return to his peaceful home.

What did he do? Jefferson wanted only three of his accomplishments listed on his tomb: author of the Declaration of American Independence, author of the Virginia Statute for Religious Freedom, and Father of the University of Virginia. What did he *not* mention? Governor of Virginia, lawyer, revolutionary leader, writer, philosopher, inventor, architect, plant scientist, book collector, musician, astronomer, ambassador, secretary of state—and, of course, president of the United States.

Why is he important? Jefferson's powerful words in the Declaration of Independence have inspired people throughout the world to seek freedom, equality, and self-rule. His most celebrated achievement as president (1801–1809) was the purchase of the Louisiana Territory from France. The Louisiana Purchase of 1803 nearly doubled the size of the United States. Jefferson then sponsored the Lewis and Clark expedition to explore this new territory.

Evaluating Why has Thomas Jefferson been a hero to generations of Americans?

Thomas Jefferson wrote the Declaration of Independence and later served as president of the United States.

KEY EVENTS

1767 Begins practicing law in Virginia

1769–1776 Serves in Virginia House of Burgesses

1776 Drafts the first version of the Declaration of Independence

1789 Appointed secretary of state by George Washington

1801 Inaugurated as president

1803 Authorizes the purchase of Louisiana from France

1809 Retires to Monticello

THE JEFFERSON ERA **271**

Biography

Reading Focus Question
Have students discuss the introductory question. Ask them to consider the actions that the American colonists took to seek freedom as well as actions people take today. Tell students to keep their answers in mind as they read the biography.

Info to Know

Jefferson: The Renaissance Man
Thomas Jefferson was a man of many talents. He was knowledgeable in architecture, agriculture, law, philosophy, and science. He wrote, however, that science was his "supreme delight." Jefferson enjoyed observing and recording nature and corresponded with scientists around the world. He also enjoyed putting his knowledge to practical use. His inventions range from an improved plow design, to a two-faced clock, to a device that attached to his hand and made copies of whatever he wrote.

Jefferson: The Bibliophile Jefferson's passion for science was matched by his passion for books. He preferred the classics and could read in seven languages. In 1815 his personal library totaled more than 6,500 volumes. His library later became the basis of what is now the Library of Congress.

Jefferson: The Real Man Although multitalented, Jefferson lacked some qualities expected of leaders. He was not a good public speaker. He was shy, spoke quietly, and often mumbled.

Critical Thinking: Analyzing Information

At Level

Analyzing Jefferson's Epitaph

1. Ask students to discuss why Jefferson chose to list only three of his many accomplishments on his tomb. Have students review some of the accomplishments he left out (listed above under "What did he do?").

2. Explain to students that Jefferson wanted his tomb to list the ways in which he gave to the American people, not his achievements.

3. Have students, working either individually or in small groups, write their own epitaphs for Thomas Jefferson. Tell students their epitaphs should list what they think are Jefferson's most important contributions and accomplishments.

   Alternative Assessment Handbook, Rubric 14: Group Activity; and 37: Writing Assignments

Answers

Evaluating *because his words and actions have inspired people throughout the world to seek freedom, equality, and self-rule*

Bellringer

If YOU were there . . . Use the **Daily Bellringer Transparency** to help students answer the question.

🖨 Daily Bellringer Transparency, Section 2

The Jefferson Era   Daily Bellringer
                                         Section 2

Review Section 1
Indicate whether each sentence below is **TRUE** or **FALSE**. If the sentence is false, change the underlined word to make the sentence true.

1. The <u>Federalist</u> candidates for the presidency in the election of 1800 were Thomas Jefferson and Aaron Burr.
2. Having tied at 73 electoral votes apiece, it was left to the <u>U.S. Senate</u> to decide between Jefferson and Burr.
3. The tie in the election of 1800 led to the <u>Twelfth Amendment</u>, which created a separate ballot for president and vice president.
4. President Jefferson chose <u>Albert Gallatin</u> as secretary of state.

Preview Section 2
If YOU were there . . .
You and your family live on a small farm in Kentucky in about 1800. Raised on the frontier, you are a skillful hunter and trapper. One day at the trading post, you see a poster calling for volunteers to join the Corps of Discovery. This expedition will explore the vast region west of the Mississippi River. You think it would be exciting—but dangerous. You might never come home.
Would you volunteer to join the Corps of Discovery?

Consider reasons FOR volunteering:
• chance to explore a nearly uninhabited territory
• would be performing an invaluable service to the country
• would be honored upon your return

Consider reasons AGAINST volunteering:
• would leave the family short staffed on the farm
• very real possibility of never seeing your home again
• unknown dangers might lie ahead

Review Answers: 1. F, Republican; 2. F, House of Representatives; 3. T; 4. F, James Madison

Copyright © by Holt, Rinehart and Winston. All rights reserved.

Building Vocabulary

Preteach or review the following terms:

strict constructionist one who thinks the federal government may do only what the U.S. Constitution specifically says it may do (p. 274)

surveying mapping out (p. 275)

📝 **CRF:** Vocabulary Builder Activity, Section 2

Taking Notes

Have students copy the graphic organizer onto their own paper and then use it to take notes on the section. This activity will prepare students for the Section Assessment, in which they will complete a graphic organizer that builds on the information using a critical thinking skill.

The Louisiana Purchase

What You Will Learn...

Main Ideas

1. As American settlers moved West, control of the Mississippi River became more important to the United States.
2. The Louisiana Purchase almost doubled the size of the United States.
3. Expeditions led by Lewis, Clark, and Pike increased Americans' understanding of the West.

The Big Idea

Under President Jefferson's leadership, the United States added the Louisiana Territory.

Key Terms and People

Louisiana Purchase, *p. 274*
Meriwether Lewis, *p. 275*
William Clark, *p. 275*
Lewis and Clark expedition, *p. 275*
Sacagawea, *p. 276*
Zebulon Pike, *p. 276*

TAKING NOTES As you read, take notes in a graphic organizer like the one below on the events leading up to the Louisiana Purchase and the exploration that followed.

Events Leading to Louisiana Purchase	Exploration that Followed Louisiana Purchase

If **YOU** were there...

You and your family live on a small farm in Kentucky in about 1800. Raised on the frontier, you are a skillful hunter and trapper. One day at the trading post, you see a poster calling for volunteers to join the Corps of Discovery. This expedition will explore the vast region west of the Mississippi River. You think it would be exciting—but dangerous. You might never come home.

Would you volunteer to join the Corps of Discovery?

BUILDING BACKGROUND As the 1800s began, the United States was expanding steadily westward. More lands were opened, and settlers moved in to occupy them. Americans were also curious about the vast lands that lay farther West. Adventurous explorers organized expeditions to find out more about those lands.

American Settlers Move West

By the early 1800s, thousands of Americans settled in the area between the Appalachians and the Mississippi River. As the region's population grew, Kentucky, Tennessee, and Ohio were admitted to the Union. Settlers in these states depended upon the Mississippi and Ohio rivers to move their products to eastern markets.

New Orleans, located at the mouth of the Mississippi, was a very important port. Its busy docks were filled with settlers' farm products and valuable furs bought from American Indians. Many of these cargoes were then sent to Europe. At the same time, manufactured goods passed through the port on their way upriver. As American dependence on the river grew, Jefferson began to worry that a foreign power might shut down access to New Orleans.

"There is on the globe one single spot, the possessor of which is our natural and habitual enemy. It is New Orleans, through which the produce of three-eighths of our territory must pass to market."
—Thomas Jefferson, quoted in *Annals of America, Volume 4, 1797–1820*

Teach the Big Idea

The Louisiana Purchase

1. **Teach** Ask students the questions in the Main Idea boxes to teach this section.

2. **Apply** Have each student create a time line of key events related to the Louisiana Purchase. 🄻🄢 **Visual/Spatial**

3. **Review** Review students' time lines as a class. Have students discuss the ways in which the United States benefited from the purchase of Louisiana.

4. **Practice/Homework** Have each student create a Louisiana Purchase fact sheet. The fact sheet should include information such as a summary of how and why the purchase took place, the date and cost, the size and location of the Louisiana Territory, and so on. 🄻🄢 **Verbal/Linguistic**

📝 Alternative Assessment Handbook, Rubrics 36: Time Lines; and 42: Writing to Inform

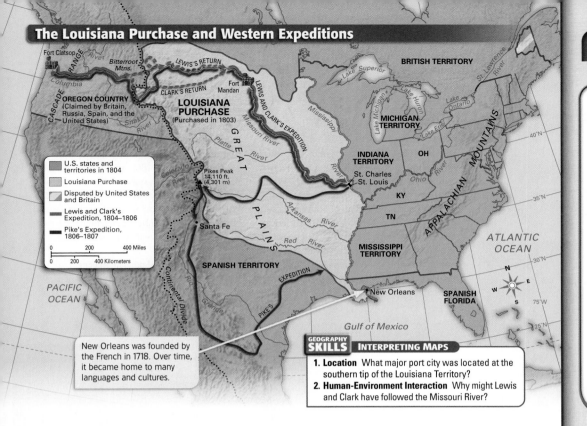

The Louisiana Purchase and Western Expeditions

MAP KEY
- U.S. states and territories in 1804
- Louisiana Purchase
- Disputed by United States and Britain
- Lewis and Clark's Expedition, 1804–1806
- Pike's Expedition, 1806–1807

0   200   400 Miles
0   200   400 Kilometers

New Orleans was founded by the French in 1718. Over time, it became home to many languages and cultures.

GEOGRAPHY SKILLS **INTERPRETING MAPS**

1. **Location** What major port city was located at the southern tip of the Louisiana Territory?
2. **Human-Environment Interaction** Why might Lewis and Clark have followed the Missouri River?

Spain controlled both New Orleans and Louisiana. This region stretched west from the mighty Mississippi River to the great Rocky Mountains. Although Spain owned Louisiana, Spanish officials found it impossible to keep Americans out of the territory. "You can't put doors on open country," the foreign minister said in despair.

Years of effort failed to improve Spain's position. Under a secret treaty, Spain agreed to trade Louisiana to France, passing the problem on to someone else. One Spanish officer expressed his relief. "I can hardly wait to leave them [the Americans] behind me," he said.

READING CHECK Analyzing Information
Why was New Orleans important to settlers in the western regions of the United States?

Louisiana

In 1802, just before handing over Louisiana to France, Spain closed New Orleans to American shipping. Angry farmers worried about what this would do to the economy. President Jefferson asked the U.S. ambassador to France, Robert R. Livingston, to try to buy New Orleans. Jefferson sent James Monroe to help Livingston.

Napoléon and Louisiana

France was led by Napoléon (nuh-POH-lee-uhn), a powerful ruler who had conquered most of Europe. He dreamed of rebuilding France's empire in North America.

Napoléon's strategy was to use the French colony of Haiti, in the Caribbean, as a supply

THE JEFFERSON ERA **273**

Main Idea

2 Louisiana

The Louisiana Purchase almost doubled the size of the United States.

Explain Why did Jefferson want to buy New Orleans from France? *Before handing over Louisiana to France, Spain had closed New Orleans to American shipping, which hurt American farmers.*

Sequence What chain of events led to the Louisiana Purchase? *See the time line in the Differentiating Instruction activity below.*

Analyze What role did chance play in the Louisiana Purchase? *Students should describe the various setbacks that led France to sell Louisiana.*

📓 Political Cartoons Activities for United States History, Cartoon 9: The Louisiana Purchase

📦 Map Transparency: The Louisiana Purchase and Western Expeditions

base. From there he could send troops to Louisiana. However, enslaved Africans had revolted and freed themselves from French rule. Napoléon sent troops to try to regain control of the island, but they were defeated in 1802. This defeat ended his hopes of rebuilding a North American empire.

Jefferson Buys Louisiana

The American ambassador got a surprising offer during his negotiations with French foreign minister Charles Talleyrand. When the Americans tried to buy New Orleans, Talleyrand offered to sell all of Louisiana.

With his hopes for a North American empire dashed, Napoléon had turned his attention back to Europe. France was at war with Great Britain, and Napoléon needed money for military supplies. He also hoped that a larger United States would challenge British power.

Livingston and Monroe knew a bargain when they saw one. They quickly accepted the French offer to sell Louisiana for $15 million.

The news pleased Jefferson. But as a strict constructionist, he was troubled. The Constitution did not mention the purchase of foreign lands. He also did not like spending large amounts of public money. Nevertheless, Jefferson agreed to the purchase in the belief that doing so was best for the country.

On October 20, 1803, the Senate approved the agreement of the **Louisiana Purchase**, which roughly doubled the size of the United States. With the $15 million in the French treasury, Napoléon boasted, "I have given England a rival who, sooner or later, will humble her pride."

READING CHECK Making Inferences
Why was the Louisiana Purchase important to the future of the United States?

The Journey West

The time line and photographs you see here show some of the key events and places of the Lewis and Clark expedition. Read the journal entries to get an idea of what the explorers faced.

A large keelboat and two smaller boats were needed to get the supply-heavy expedition moving west.

Small boats helped the travelers move supplies across the Great Plains.

May 14, 1804	August 3, 1804	October 1804 – April 1805
The expedition begins near St. Louis.	The first official council between representatives of the United States and Plains Indians is held.	The expedition establishes Fort Mandan to spend the winter. There, the explorers meet a French fur trader and his wife, Sacagawea.

April 7, 1805 We are about to penetrate a country at least 2,000 miles in width, on which the foot of civilized man had never trodden (walked upon).
—Meriwether Lewis

274 CHAPTER 8

Answers

Reading Check *It roughly doubled the size of the United States, which would benefit future western settlement and economic growth.*

Differentiating Instruction

Struggling Readers

1. To help students understand the sequence of events that led to the Louisiana Purchase, copy the time line for students to see. Omit the blue answers.

2. Have students copy the time line. Then help students complete it as you discuss each event. **LS** Visual/Spatial

LOUISIANA PURCHASE

1800 → **1802** → **1803** → **The Louisiana**

1800
Spain trades Louisiana to France.

1802
• **Spain** *closes New Orleans to the United States.*
• **Jefferson instructs** *Livingston and Monroe to try to buy New Orleans from France.*
• **France** *offers to sell all of Louisiana because of setbacks in Haiti and a war against Great Britain.*

1803
The United States buys *Louisiana for $15 million.*

The Louisiana Purchase roughly doubles *the size of the United States.*

Explorers Head West

Americans knew little about western Native Americans or the land they lived on. President Jefferson wanted to learn more about the people and land of the West. He also wanted to see if there was a river route that could be taken to the Pacific Ocean.

Lewis and Clark Expedition

In 1803 the president asked Congress to fund an expedition to explore the West. To lead it, he chose former army captain **Meriwether Lewis**. Lewis then chose his friend Lieutenant **William Clark** to be the co-leader of the expedition.

To prepare for the journey, Lewis spent weeks studying with experts about plants, surveying, and other subjects. This knowledge would allow him to take careful notes on what he saw. With Clark, Lewis carefully selected about 50 skilled frontiersmen to join the Corps of Discovery, as they called their group.

In May 1804 the **Lewis and Clark expedition** began its long journey to explore the Louisiana Purchase. The Corps of Discovery traveled up the Missouri River to the village of St. Charles. Once past this village the men would receive no more letters, fresh supplies, or reinforcements.

Lewis and Clark used the Missouri River as their highway through the unknown lands. As they moved upstream, a lookout on the boats kept a sharp eye out for sandbars and for tree stumps hidden underwater. When darkness fell, the weary explorers would pull their boats ashore. They cooked, wrote in their journals, and slept. Swarms of gnats, flies, and mosquitoes often interrupted their sleep.

The explorers paddled down the Columbia River toward the Pacific in five canoes.

The expedition relied on 24 horses to cross the Rocky Mountains.

August 12, 1805
Lewis climbs the first ridge to the Continental Divide.

September 1805
The expedition nearly starves. Local peoples help the explorers.

November 7, 1805
The expedition reaches a bay of the Pacific Ocean.

August 23, 1805 The hills or mountains were not like those I had seen, but like the side of a tree straight up.
–William Clark

ANALYSIS SKILL | **READING TIME LINES**
On what date did the explorers reach the western most point of their journey?

THE JEFFERSON ERA **275**

Main Idea

❸ Explorers Head West

Expeditions led by Lewis, Clark, and Pike increased Americans' understanding of the West.

Identify Who was Sacagawea? *She was a Shoshone woman who helped the Lewis and Clark expedition along with her husband, a French fur trader.*

Summarize What did the Lewis and Clark expedition achieve? *learned about western lands and paths, made contact with many Native American groups, collected data about western plants and animals*

Identify Points of View How do you think Native Americans viewed the Lewis and Clark expedition? *possible answer—with a mix of curiosity, interest, uncertainty, fear*

📓 **CRF:** Biography Activity: Sacagawea

Checking for Understanding

True or False Answer each statement *T* if it is true and *F* if it is false. If false, explain why.

1. The Nez Percé provided food for the Lewis and Clark expedition. *T*
2. Lewis and Clark succeeded in finding a river route across the West to the Pacific Ocean. *F; They did not find a river route.*
3. Zebulon Pike's report of his expedition offered many Americans their first description of the Pacific Northwest. *F; the Southwest*

Answers

Analyzing Primary Sources *its lush grass and huge herds of buffalo, elk, and antelope*

Primary Source

JOURNAL ENTRY
September 17, 1804, Great Plains

While traveling across the Great Plains, Meriwether Lewis marveled at the richness of the land.

"The shortness . . . of grass gave the plain the appearance throughout its whole extent of beautiful bowling-green in fine order . . . this scenery, already rich, pleasing, and beautiful was still farther heightened by immense herds of Buffaloe, deer Elk and Antelopes which we saw in every direction feeding on the hills and plains. I do not think I exaggerate when I estimate the number of Buffalo which could be compre[hend]ed at one view to amount to 3000."

—Meriwether Lewis, quoted in *Original Journals of the Lewis and Clark Expedition,* edited by Reuben Bold Theraites

ANALYSIS SKILL **ANALYZING PRIMARY SOURCES**

What did Lewis find so impressive about the Great Plains?

Insects were not the only cause of sleeplessness for the Corps of Discovery. As weeks passed without seeing any Native Americans, the explorers wondered what their first encounter would be like.

Contact with Native Americans

During the summer of 1804 the Corps of Discovery had pushed more than 600 miles upriver without seeing any Native Americans. But when the men spotted huge buffalo herds in the distance, they guessed that Indian groups would be nearby. Many Indian groups depended on the buffalo for food, clothing, and tools.

Lewis used interpreters to talk to the leaders of each of the peoples they met. He told them that the United States now owned the land on which the Native Americans lived. Yet the explorers relied on the goodwill of the people they met. **Sacagawea** (sak-uh-juh-WEE-uh),

a Shoshone from the Rocky Mountains, accompanied the group with her husband, a French fur trader who lived with the Mandan Indians and served as a guide and interpreter. Sacagawea helped the expedition by naming plants and by gathering edible fruits and vegetables for the group. At one point, the group met with Sacagawea's brother, who provided horses and a guide to lead the expedition across the mountains.

After crossing the Rocky Mountains, Lewis and Clark followed the Columbia River. Along the way they met the powerful Nez Percé. Like the Shoshone, the Nez Percé provided the expedition with food. At last, in November 1805, Lewis and Clark reached the Pacific Ocean. The explorers stayed in the Pacific Northwest during the rough winter. In March 1806 Lewis and Clark set out on the long trip home.

Lewis and Clark had not found a river route across the West to the Pacific Ocean. But they had learned much about western lands and paths across the Rockies. The explorers also established contact with many Native American groups and collected much valuable information about western plants and animals.

Pike's Exploration

In 1806 a young army officer named **Zebulon Pike** was sent on another mission to the West. He was ordered to find the starting point of the Red River. This was important because the United States considered the Red River to be a part of the Louisiana Territory's western border with New Spain.

Heading into the Rocky Mountains, in present-day Colorado, Pike tried to reach the summit of the mountain now known as Pike's Peak. In 1807 he traveled into Spanish-held lands until Spanish cavalry arrested him. They suspected Pike of being a spy. When he was finally released, he returned to the United States and reported on his trip. Despite his imprisonment, he praised the opportunities for doing business with the Spanish in the Southwest. Pike's

---

Collaborative Learning
At Level

Expedition Murals

Materials: butcher paper, art supplies

1. Organize the class into two groups and assign one group the Lewis and Clark expedition and the other group Pike's exploration.

2. Have each group create a mural of its assigned expedition. The mural should illustrate the goal of the expedition, the route traveled, geographic landmarks spotted, Native American groups encountered, and other significant achievements.

3. Each group should also write a paragraph identifying and explaining the images in its mural. Before students start, have each group submit a small drawing of its mural for approval.

4. Display the murals in the classroom and have each group explain its mural to the class.

LS Interpersonal, Visual/Spatial

📓 Alternative Assessment Handbook, Rubrics 3: Artwork; and 14: Group Activity

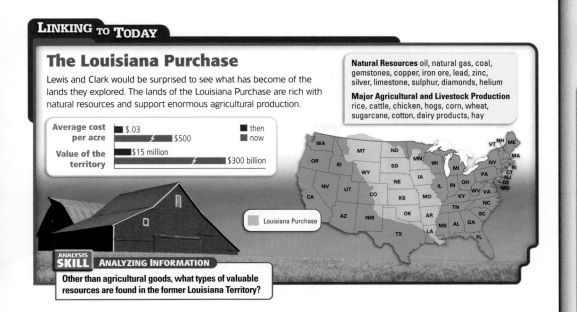

The Louisiana Purchase

Lewis and Clark would be surprised to see what has become of the lands they explored. The lands of the Louisiana Purchase are rich with natural resources and support enormous agricultural production.

Natural Resources oil, natural gas, coal, gemstones, copper, iron ore, lead, zinc, silver, limestone, sulphur, diamonds, helium

Major Agricultural and Livestock Production rice, cattle, chicken, hogs, corn, wheat, sugarcane, cotton, dairy products, hay

	then	now
Average cost per acre	$.03	$500
Value of the territory	$15 million	$300 billion

Louisiana Purchase

ANALYSIS SKILL ANALYZING INFORMATION
Other than agricultural goods, what types of valuable resources are found in the former Louisiana Territory?

report offered many Americans their first description of the Southwest.

READING CHECK Supporting a Point of View What would you do if you were Pike and found yourself in Spanish territory?

SUMMARY AND PREVIEW The Louisiana Purchase nearly doubled the size of the United States. In the next section you will learn about increasing tensions between the United States and Great Britain.

Section 2 Assessment

go.hrw.com
Online Quiz
KEYWORD: SR8 HP8

Reviewing Ideas, Terms, and People

1. **a. Identify** What new states were added to the Union by the early 1800s?
   b. Explain Why were New Orleans and the Mississippi River important to setters in the West?
2. **a. Recall** What two reasons did Napoléon have for selling Louisiana to the United States?
   b. Summarize Why was the **Louisiana Purchase** important to the United States?
   c. Predict What are some possible results of expansion into the Louisiana Purchase?
3. **a. Describe** What areas did the Lewis and Clark expedition and the Pike expedition explore?
   b. Draw Conclusions Why were **Meriwether Lewis** and **William Clark** chosen to lead the exploration of the Louisiana Purchase?

Critical Thinking

4. **Sequencing** Review your notes on the Louisiana Purchase. Then copy the graphic organizer below and use it to rank the three most important effects of the Louisiana Purchase, from most important to least important, and explain why you chose that order.

Importance	Why
1.	
2.	
3.	

FOCUS ON WRITING

5. **Gathering Information about a Person's Actions** Make a list of Jefferson's actions—the ones that would put him on that top-ten list. Add any new character traits you have discovered.

THE JEFFERSON ERA **277**

Section 2 Assessment Answers

1. **a.** Kentucky, Tennessee, and Ohio
   b. Settlers used the river and the port at New Orleans to transport products to and from markets.

2. **a.** needed money for a war against Britain; hoped that a larger United States would challenge Britain's power in North America
   b. It roughly doubled the size of the nation.
   c. possible answers—addition of new states; conflict with Native Americans; westward settlement; U.S. population growth

3. **a.** present-day western United States
   b. Lewis—Jefferson's assistant, former army captain, outdoorsman; Clark—served with Lewis in the military, drew maps, could lead

4. (1) doubled size of United States—more land for settlers; (2) natural resources—helped support enormous agricultural production; (3) Lewis and Clark expedition—discovered much information about plants and animals in the west

5. Actions might include the Louisiana Purchase and the Lewis and Clark expedition.

Direct Teach

Main Idea

❸ Explorers Head West

Expeditions led by Lewis, Clark, and Pike increased Americans' understanding of the West.

Recall What was the purpose of Pike's expedition? *to find the origin of the Red River, which the United States claimed formed Louisiana's western border with New Spain*

Describe Where did Pike go, and what famous landmark did he see? *to the Southwest, Spanish-held lands, Pike's Peak*

CRF: History and Geography Activity: Pike Explores the Southwest

Review & Assess

Close

Have students discuss the ways in which the United States benefited from the Louisiana Purchase.

Review

Online Quiz, Section 2

Assess

SE Section 2 Assessment

PASS: Section 2 Quiz

Alternative Assessment Handbook

Reteach/Classroom Intervention

Interactive Reader and Study Guide, Section 2

Interactive Skills Tutor CD-ROM

Answers

Linking to Today *oil, natural gas, coal, gemstones, copper, iron ore, lead, zinc, silver, limestone, sulphur, diamonds, helium*

Reading Check *possible answers— consider the opportunities, weigh the benefits and costs of staying, try to establish friendly ties, try to trade, leave*

277

Bellringer

If YOU were there . . . Use the **Daily Bellringer Transparency** to help students answer the question.

🖨 Daily Bellringer Transparency, Section 3

Building Vocabulary

Preteach or review the following terms:

brazen bold and without shame (p. 279)

neutrality not taking part or supporting either side in a war (p. 279)

Northwest Territory lands including present-day Illinois, Indiana, Michigan, Ohio, Wisconsin, and part of Minnesota (p. 280)

petitions formal written requests (p. 280)

repeal cancellation (p. 280)

🖨 **CRF:** Vocabulary Builder Activity, Section 3

Taking Notes

Have students copy the graphic organizer onto their own paper and then use it to take notes on the section. This activity will prepare students for the Section Assessment, in which they will complete a graphic organizer that builds on the information using a critical thinking skill.

The Coming of War

What You Will Learn...

Main Ideas

1. Violations of U.S. neutrality led Congress to enact a ban on trade.
2. Native Americans, Great Britain, and the United States came into conflict in the West.
3. The War Hawks led a growing call for war with Great Britain.

The Big Idea

Challenges at home and abroad led the United States to declare war on Great Britain.

Key Terms and People

USS *Constitution*, p. 278
impressment, p. 279
embargo, p. 279
Embargo Act, p. 279
Non-Intercourse Act, p. 280
Tecumseh, p. 280
Battle of Tippecanoe, p. 282
War Hawks, p. 282
James Madison, p. 283

TAKING NOTES Create a graphic organizer like the one below. As you read, take notes on the challenges that led to the United States to declare war on Great Britain.

If YOU were there...

You are a tea merchant in Boston in 1807, but right now your business is at a standstill. A new law forbids trading with European nations. Now, Boston Harbor is full of empty ships. It seems to you that the law is hurting American merchants more than European ones! You know that some merchants are breaking the law and smuggling goods, just to stay in business.

Would you obey the law or turn to smuggling?

BUILDING BACKGROUND The United States tried to stay neutral in the conflicts between France and Great Britain, but it was impossible to avoid getting involved. French and British ships interfered with American trade across the Atlantic. The British also caused trouble along the western frontier. Many Americans began to urge war with Great Britain.

Violations of Neutrality

During the late 1700s and early 1800s, American merchant ships fanned out across the oceans. The overseas trade, while profitable, was also risky. Ships had to travel vast distances, often through violent storms. Merchant ships sailing in the Mediterranean risked capture by pirates from the Barbary States of North Africa, who would steal cargo and hold ships' crews for ransom. Attacks continued until the United States sent the **USS *Constitution***, a large warship, and other ships to end them.

The Barbary pirates were a serious problem, but an even larger threat soon loomed. When Great Britain and France went to war in 1803, each country wanted to stop the United States from supplying goods to the other. Each government passed laws designed to prevent American merchants from trading with the other. In addition, the British and French navies captured many American merchant ships searching for war supplies.

The real trouble, however, started when Britain began stopping and searching American ships for sailors who had run away from the British navy, forcing the sailors to return to British ships.

The Coming of War

1. **Teach** Ask students the questions in the Main Idea boxes to teach this section.

2. **Apply** Have each student use the section and the time line in it to create his or her own drawing of the Road to the War of 1812. Students should draw a winding road and alongside it provide annotations and illustrations depicting the main events and issues covered in this section.
LS Verbal/Linguistic, Visual/Spatial

3. **Review** Have students use their drawings to review the causes of the War of 1812.

4. **Practice/Homework** Have each student create a recruitment poster urging Americans to enlist in the fight against the British. Students should include at least two reasons for the war. **LS Verbal/Linguistic, Visual/Spatial**

🖨 Alternative Assessment Handbook, Rubrics 28: Posters; and 36: Time Lines

The USS *Constitution*

CONNECTING TO SCIENCE AND TECHNOLOGY

In the early years of the republic, foreign trade was critical to the nation's survival. In 1797 Congress decided to create a navy to protect American merchant ships. The powerful warship USS *Constitution* was a key part of the new navy and was undefeated in battle. It is the oldest commissioned warship in the world.

The main mast is 220 feet high.

Copper sheathing supplied by Paul Revere protected the hull.

People on the spar, or top, deck were exposed to enemy fire.

ANALYSIS SKILL ANALYZING DIAGRAMS

1. Why do you think gunpowder was stored on the bottom deck?
2. What was the purpose of the copper sheathing?

The crew slept and ate on the berth deck.

Most of the ship's cannons were located on the gun deck.

Boys called "powder monkeys" carried gunpowder from the orlop, or lowest, deck up to the gunners.

Sometimes U.S. citizens were captured by accident. This **impressment**, or the practice of forcing people to serve in the army or navy, continued despite American protests.

Soon Britain was even targeting American navy ships. In June 1807, for example, the British ship *Leopard* stopped the U.S. Navy ship *Chesapeake* and tried to remove sailors. When the captain of the *Chesapeake* refused, the British took the sailors by force. The brazen attack on the *Chesapeake* stunned Americans.

The Embargo Act

Great Britain's violations of U.S. neutrality sparked intense debate in America about how to respond. Some people wanted to go to war. Others favored an **embargo**, or the banning of trade, against Britain.

Jefferson, who had easily won re-election in 1804, supported an embargo. At his urging, in late 1807 Congress passed the **Embargo Act**. The law essentially banned trade with all foreign countries. American ships could not sail to foreign ports. American ports were also

THE JEFFERSON ERA **279**

Main Idea

❶ Violations of Neutrality

Violations of U.S. neutrality led Congress to enact a ban on trade.

Recall Why did Congress pass the Embargo Act? *to punish Britain and France and to protect American merchant ships from capture*

Identify Cause and Effect How did the Embargo Act affect Jefferson's popularity? *damaged it and helped revive the Federalist Party*

Evaluate How successful was the Embargo Act? *not very—had little effect on Britain and France; financially hurt American merchants*

📰 Political Cartoons Activities for United States History, Cartoon: 8: Party Politics in the Jefferson Era

📄 **CRF:** Economics and History Activity: Embargoes—Economic Diplomacy

Reading Time Lines
America's Road to War

(Activity) News Bulletins Have students transform each entry on the time line into a "live" news bulletin, such as students might see on TV or hear on the radio. Ask volunteers to deliver their news bulletins to the class.

Answers

Reading Check *similar—banned foreign trade, hurt the American economy; different—The Non-Intercourse Act banned American trade only with Britain and France and their colonies.*

280

---

closed to British ships. Congress hoped that the embargo would punish Britain and France and protect American merchant ships from capture.

The effect of the law was devastating to American merchants. Without foreign trade, they lost enormous amounts of money. Northern states that relied heavily on trade were especially hard hit by the embargo. Congressman Josiah Quincy of Massachusetts, in a speech before Congress, described the situation. "All the business of the nation is in disorder. All the nation's industry is at a standstill," he said.

The embargo damaged Jefferson's popularity and strengthened the Federalist Party. Angry merchants sent Jefferson hundreds of petitions demanding the repeal of the Embargo Act. One New Englander said the embargo was like "cutting one's throat to stop the nosebleed." Even worse, the embargo had little effect on Britain and France.

Non-Intercourse Act

In 1809 Congress tried to revive the nation's trade by replacing the unpopular act with the **Non-Intercourse Act**. This new law banned trade only with Britain, France, and their colonies. It also stated that the United States would resume trading with the first side that stopped violating U.S. neutrality. In time, however, the law was no more successful than the Embargo Act.

READING CHECK **Comparing and Contrasting** In what ways were the Embargo Act and the Non-Intercourse Act similar and different?

Conflict in the West

Disagreements between Great Britain and the United States went beyond the neutrality issue. In the West, the British and Native Americans again clashed with American settlers over land.

The Conflict over Land

In the early 1800s, Native Americans in the old Northwest Territory continued to lose land as thousands of settlers poured into the region. The United States had gained this land in the Treaty of Greenville, but Indian leaders who had not agreed to the treaty protested the settlers' arrival. Frustrated Indian groups considered what to do. In the meantime, Britain saw an opportunity to slow America's westward growth. British agents from Canada began to arm Native Americans who were living along the western frontier. Rumors of British activity in the old Northwest Territory quickly spread, filling American settlers with fear and anger.

Tecumseh Resists U.S. Settlers

Soon an Indian leader emerged who seemed more than capable of halting the American settlers. **Tecumseh** (tuh-KUHM-suh), a Shawnee chief, had watched angrily as Native Americans were pushed off their land. A brilliant speaker, he warned other Indians about the dangers they faced from settlers. He believed that the Native Americans had to do what white Americans had done: unite.

Time Line

America's Road to War

June 22, 1807 The British navy takes sailors from the U.S. Navy ship *Chesapeake*.

1807

December 22, 1807 The United States responds to impressment by passing the Embargo Act.

1809

January 9, 1809 Congress passes the Non-Intercourse Act.

280 CHAPTER 8

Differentiating Instruction

Below Level

Struggling Readers

1. To help students understand the effects of the Embargo Act of 1807, copy the graphic organizer for students to see. Omit the blue answers.

2. Have students copy the graphic organizer by providing the information requested.

3. Review the answers as a class. **LS** Visual/Spatial

📄 Alternative Assessment Handbook, Rubric 13: Graphic Organizers

Embargo Act of 1807
- **What it did:** *essentially banned trade with all foreign countries*
- **Why it was passed:** *to punish Britain and France; to protect American merchant ships from capture*

Political Effects
hurt Jefferson's popularity; revived the Federalist Party

Economic Effects
was devastating to American merchants

POLITICAL CARTOON
The Embargo Act
The unpopularity of the Embargo Act prompted political cartoonists to show visually how the act was hurting American trade.

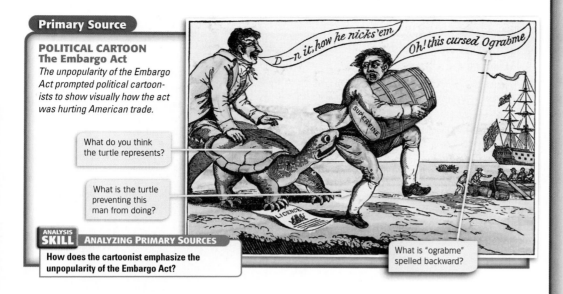

What do you think the turtle represents?

What is the turtle preventing this man from doing?

D—n it, how he nicks 'em

Oh! this cursed Ograbme

SUPERFINE

LICENCE

What is "ograbme" spelled backward?

ANALYSIS SKILL **ANALYZING PRIMARY SOURCES**

How does the cartoonist emphasize the unpopularity of the Embargo Act?

Tecumseh hoped to unite the Native Americans of the northwestern frontier, the South, and the eastern Mississippi Valley. He was helped by his brother, a religious leader called the Prophet. They founded a village called Prophetstown for their followers near the Wabash and Tippecanoe rivers.

The Battle of Tippecanoe

The governor of the Indiana Territory, William Henry Harrison, watched Tecumseh's activities with alarm. Harrison called him "one of those uncommon geniuses which spring up occasionally to . . . overturn the established order." The governor was convinced that Tecumseh had British backing. If true, Tecumseh could be a serious threat to American power in the West.

In 1810 Tecumseh met face to face with Harrison. The governor urged him to follow the Treaty of Greenville that had been signed in 1795. Tecumseh replied, "The white people have no right to take the land from the Indians, because the Indians had it first." No single chief, he insisted, could sell land belonging to all American Indians who used it. In response, Harrison warned Tecumseh not to resist the power of the United States.

June 18, 1812
The United States declares war against Britain.

1810

November 4, 1811
When the twelfth Congress convenes, Kentucky representative Henry Clay leads the call for war against Britain.

1812

ANALYSIS SKILL **READING TIME LINES**

What events led to war against Great Britain?

THE JEFFERSON ERA **281**

Critical Thinking: Finding Main Ideas   At Level

Frontier Interviews

1. Ask students to imagine that they are roving reporters assigned to the old Northwest Territory in the early 1800s.

2. Have each student write a series of short interviews with Tecumseh, a British agent, and Governor William Henry Harrison. In their interviews, students should ask the individuals to explain their goals, current activities, and future plans.

3. Then have each student combine his or her interviews into a newspaper article on the frontier situation.

4. Ask volunteers to read their articles aloud to the class. Then lead a class discussion on the effects of the Battle of Tippecanoe on Native Americans and on U.S.-British relations.

Alternative Assessment Handbook, Rubric 37: Writing Assignments

---

Main Idea

❷ Conflict in the West

Native Americans, Great Britain, and the United States came into conflict in the West.

Identify Who was Tecumseh, and what did he want to accomplish? *Shawnee chief and influential Native American leader; wanted to unite Native Americans against U.S. settlers pushing them off their lands*

Explain Why did Great Britain want to help Native Americans along the western frontier? *hoped to slow the westward growth of the United States*

Identify Points of View How did William Henry Harrison view Tecumseh? *possible answer—with respect for his intelligence and abilities and with fear for the threat he felt Tecumseh posed*

📰 **CRF:** Biography Activity: Tecumseh

Connect to Economics

U.S. Exports From 1807 to 1809, the total value of all U.S. exports dropped from $108 million to $22 million. During the same period, the total value of U.S. exports to Great Britain dropped from $23 million to $3 million.

Draw Conclusions What does this data say about the trade relationship between Great Britain and the United States? *The United States was dependent on trade with Britain, which made up a significant portion of total U.S. trade before the Embargo Act.*

Answers

Analyzing Primary Sources *by showing Americans trying to load goods illegally onto a British ship as a turtle holds them back and one man curses the embargo in frustration*

Reading Time Lines *British impressment, such as the* Chesapeake *incident; Embargo Act; Non-Intercourse Act; calls for war*

281

Main Idea

❸ Call for War

The War Hawks led a growing call for war with Great Britain.

Identify Who were the War Hawks? *several young members of Congress who took the lead in calling for war*

Contrast Describe the views of the opposing sides in the war debate. *War Hawks—stop British influence among frontier Indians, invade Canada, end British trade restrictions; opponents to war—renew friendly business ties with Britain, foolish to fight Britain's larger and better equipped military*

Evaluate What did the United States risk by declaring war against Britain in 1812? *human and economic losses; being defeated; losing independence*

📃 **CRF:** Literature Activity: *A Warrior's Speech* by Chief Tecumseh

📃 **CRF:** Primary Source Activity: A Shawnee Leader Seeks Allies

Primary Source

Views of War

Activity Ask volunteers to read each excerpt aloud. Have students discuss each man's point of view. Then have students suggest how they think each man would have responded to the other's statement. **LS** **Verbal/Linguistic**

Answers

Analyzing Points of View *Tecumseh thought the land belonged to Native Americans and that white settlement was evil; Harrison wanted the land for U.S. settlers.*

Focus on Reading *"independence . . . is lost"*

Reading Check *Tecumseh was trying to unite all Native Americans in the northwestern frontier, the South, and the eastern Mississippi Valley against settlers and the expansion of settlement.*

282

Primary Source

POINTS OF VIEW
Views of War

Tecumseh urged Native Americans to unite to oppose what he called the "evil" of white settlement.

❝The only way to stop this evil is for all the red men to unite in claiming a common and equal right to the land, as it was at first, and should be yet. Before, the land never was divided, but belonged to all, for the use of each person. No group had a right to sell, not even to each other, much less to strangers who want all and will not do with less.❞

—**Tecumseh**

William Henry Harrison was proud of his efforts to obtain land for settlers.

❝By my own exertions in securing the friendship of the chiefs . . . by admitting them at all times to my house and table, my propositions for the purchase of their lands were successful beyond my . . . hopes . . . In the course of seven years the Indian title was extinguished to the amount of fifty millions of acres.❞

—**William Henry Harrison**

ANALYSIS SKILL **ANALYZING POINTS OF VIEW**
How did Harrison's and Tecumseh's views on western settlement differ?

Tecumseh traveled south to ask the Creek nation to join his forces. In his absence, Harrison attacked. Harrison raised an army and marched his troops close to Prophetstown. Fighting broke out when the Prophet ordered an attack on Harrison's camp on November 7, 1811.

The Indians broke through army lines, but Harrison maintained a "calm, cool, and collected" manner, according to one observer. During the all-day battle, Harrison's soldiers forced the Indian warriors to retreat and then destroyed Tecumseh's village. Said Chief Shabbona, "With the smoke of that town and loss of that battle, I lost all hope." Although Tecumseh was safe, U.S. forces defeated Tecumseh and his followers in the **Battle of Tippecanoe**. The defeat destroyed Tecumseh's dream of a great Indian confederation. He fled to Canada.

FOCUS ON READING
What words did Calhoun use that had strong emotions tied to them for Americans? (See "The War Hawks" section.)

READING CHECK Finding Main Ideas
Why were U.S. officials worried about Tecumseh's actions?

282 CHAPTER 8

Call for War

The evidence of British support for Tecumseh further inflamed Americans. A Democratic-Republican newspaper declared, "The war on the Wabash [River] is purely BRITISH." Many Americans felt that Britain had encouraged Tecumseh to attack settlers in the West.

The War Hawks

Several young members of Congress—called **War Hawks** by their opponents—took the lead in calling for war against Britain. These legislators, most of whom were from the South and West, were led by Henry Clay of Kentucky, John C. Calhoun of South Carolina, and Felix Grundy of Tennessee. They saw war as the only answer to British insults. "If we submit," Calhoun warned, "the independence of this nation is lost." Calls for war grew. Leaders wanted to put a stop to British influence among Native Americans. They also wanted to invade

---

Collaborative Learning

At Level

War Rally

Materials: poster board, art supplies

1. Ask students to imagine that they are going to a war rally in Washington in 1812. Organize the class into four groups and assign each group to be War Hawks, New England Federalists, others opposed to war, or journalists.

2. Have the first three groups prepare speeches, signs, and banners supporting their positions. Have the journalists write questions to ask each group. In addition, assign some students specific people to portray, such as Henry Clay.

3. Assign students in each group specific tasks to perform based on their ability levels and learning styles.

4. Hold the class rally. You might want to reserve a large space, such as the school's gym, for the activity.

📃 Alternative Assessment Handbook, Rubric 14: Group Activity

Canada and gain more land for settlement. Others were angered by British trade restrictions that hurt southern planters and western farmers. War Hawks gave emotional speeches urging Americans to stand up to Great Britain.

The Opposition

The strongest opponents of the War Hawks were New England Federalists. British trade restrictions and impressment had hurt New England's economy. People there wanted to renew friendly business ties with Britain instead of fighting another war.

Other politicians argued that war with Great Britain would be foolish. They feared that the United States was not yet ready to fight powerful Britain. America's army and navy were small and poorly equipped compared to Britain's military. In addition, Americans could produce only a fraction of the military supplies Britain could. Senator Obadiah German of New York pleaded with the War Hawks to be patient: "Prior to any declaration of war . . . my plan would be, and my first wish is, to prepare for it—to put the country in complete armor."

Declaring War

Republican **James Madison** was elected president in 1808. He faced the difficulty of continuing an unpopular trade war begun by Jefferson. He also felt growing pressure from the War Hawks. By 1812 he decided that Congress must vote on war. Speaking to Congress, Madison blasted Great Britain's conduct. He asked Congress to decide how the nation should respond.

When Congress voted a few days later, the War Hawks won. For the first time in the nation's brief history, Congress had declared war. Months later, Americans elected Madison to a second term. He would serve as commander in chief during the War of 1812.

READING CHECK **Summarizing** Why did the United States declare war in 1812?

SUMMARY AND PREVIEW Conflicts on the frontier and with Great Britain dominated U.S. foreign policy under Jefferson and Madison. In the next section you will read about the War of 1812.

---

go.hrw.com
Online Quiz
KEYWORD: SR8 HP8

Section 3 Assessment

Reviewing Ideas, Terms, and People

1. **a. Describe** In what ways did the war between France and Britain cause problems for the United States?
   b. Make Inferences What were the reasons for the failure of the **Embargo Act**?
   c. Elaborate Why do you think embargoes against Britain and France failed?
2. **a. Describe** What was **Tecumseh's** goal?
   b. Explain What role did Great Britain play in the conflict between the United States and American Indians on the western frontier?
3. **a. Identify** Who were the **War Hawks**? Why did they support war with Britain?
   b. Elaborate Would you have supported going to war against Great Britain? Explain your answer.

Critical Thinking

4. **Categorizing** Review your notes on the challenges that led to the War of 1812. Were most challenges foreign or domestic? Categorize them in a chart like the one below.

Foreign	Domestic

FOCUS ON WRITING

5. **Taking Notes** Take notes about any of Jefferson's actions and character traits you can identify during the buildup to war with Britain. Save this information for the top-ten list you will create at the end of the chapter.

THE JEFFERSON ERA **283**

Section 3 Assessment Answers

1. **a.** Both nations began stopping and searching American ships.
   b. ineffective, hurt American economy
   c. possible answer—Britain and France were able to trade elsewhere.

2. **a.** to unite Native Americans and stop the spread of American settlement
   b. Britain supplied military aid to Indians.

3. **a.** Congress members who called for war; wanted to stop British influence among frontier Indians, invade Canada, and end trade restrictions

   b. Answers will vary, but students should exhibit an understanding of the causes that led the United States to declare war.

4. Foreign—Great Britain's impressments and violations of U.S. neutrality; Britain's military aid to frontier Native Americans; Domestic—Embargo and Non-Intercourse Acts; battles with Native Americans; War Hawks calls for war

5. Students should take notes on Jefferson's foreign relations policies and problems.

Info to Know

Madison Becomes President In 1808, Thomas Jefferson declined to run for a third term as president. Instead, he supported his secretary of state, James Madison, as the Democratic-Republican candidate. Although criticism of the Embargo Act had hurt the Republicans, Madison easily won over Federalist candidate Charles C. Pinckney. Madison went on to serve two terms as the nation's fourth president.

• Review & Assess •

Close

Have students review in order the series of events that led to the U.S. declaration of war against Great Britain, starting with the war between Britain and France.

Review

Online Quiz, Section 3

Assess

SE Section 3 Assessment

PASS: Section 3 Quiz

Alternative Assessment Handbook

Reteach/Classroom Intervention

Interactive Reader and Study Guide, Section 3

Interactive Skills Tutor CD-ROM

Answers

Reading Check *British impressment of American sailors, British influence of American Indians on the frontier; unpopular trade war not working; growing pressure from War Hawks*

Bellringer

If YOU were there . . . Use the **Daily Bellringer Transparency** to help students answer the question.

📇 Daily Bellringer Transparency, Section 4

Academic Vocabulary

Review with students the high-use academic term in this section.

consequences the effects of a particular event or events (p. 287)

📇 **CRF:** Vocabulary Builder Activity, Section 4

Taking Notes

Have students copy the graphic organizer onto their own paper and then use it to take notes on the section. This activity will prepare students for the Section Assessment, in which they will complete a graphic organizer that builds on the information using a critical thinking skill.

The War of 1812

What You Will Learn...

Main Ideas

1. American forces held their own against the British in the early battles of the war.
2. U.S. forces stopped British offensives in the East and South.
3. The effects of the war included prosperity and national pride.

The Big Idea

Great Britain and the United States went to battle in the War of 1812.

Key Terms and People

Oliver Hazard Perry, *p. 285*
Battle of Lake Erie, *p. 285*
Andrew Jackson, *p. 286*
Treaty of Fort Jackson, *p. 286*
Battle of New Orleans, *p. 286*
Hartford Convention, *p. 287*
Treaty of Ghent, *p. 287*

 TAKING NOTES Create a graphic organizer like the one below. As you read, take notes on the sequence of events in the War of 1812, from beginning to end.

Sequence of Events
1.
2.
3.
4.
5.
6.
7.

If **YOU** were there...

It's 1812, and the United States and Great Britain are at war. You are a sailor on an American merchant ship that has been licensed as a privateer. Your ship's mission will be to chase and capture ships of the mighty British navy. Even with the help of merchant ships like yours, the American navy is badly outnumbered. You know you face danger and may not survive.

Do you think your mission will succeed?

BUILDING BACKGROUND Anger against Great Britain's actions finally provoked the United States into the War of 1812. Britain's great navy gave it a clear advantage at sea, but the war was also fought on several other fronts. Victories in major battles along the frontier gave Americans a new sense of unity.

Early Battles

In the summer of 1812 the United States found itself in a war with one of the world's most powerful nations. Despite the claims by the War Hawks, the War of 1812 would not be a quick and easy fight.

War at Sea

When the war began, the British navy had hundreds of ships. In contrast, the U.S. Navy had fewer than 20 ships. None of them was as powerful as the greatest British warships.

Most of the British navy's ships, however, were scattered around the globe. Although small, the U.S. Navy had well-trained sailors and powerful new warships such as the USS *Constitution*. American vessels defeated British ships several times in one-on-one duels. Such victories embarrassed the British and raised American morale. Eventually, the British ships blockaded America's seaports.

Battles Along the Canadian Border

American leaders hoped to follow up victories at sea with an overland invasion of Canada. Three attacks were planned—from Detroit, from Niagara Falls, and from up the Hudson River valley toward Montreal.

Teach the Big Idea

The War of 1812

1. **Teach** Ask students the questions in the Main Idea boxes to teach this section.

2. **Apply** Have each student divide a sheet of paper into six window panes and label the panes *War at Sea, Battles Along the Canadian Border, The Creek War, British Attacks in the East, The Battle of New Orleans,* and *Effects of the War.* (The titles match headings in the section.) Tell students to use words, phrases, headlines, and drawings to record the key ideas, events, and people for each topic. **LS Verbal/Linguistic, Visual/Spatial**

3. **Review** Have students share some of their entries from each window pane.

4. **Practice/Homework** Have each student create a commemorative stamp depicting a significant event of the war. **LS Visual/Spatial**

📇 Alternative Assessment Handbook, Rubric 3: Artwork

The War of 1812

Disputed

BRITISH TERRITORY

Disputed

ME (PART OF MA)

Montreal

Plattsburg VT

ILLINOIS TERRITORY

York Thames Fort Niagara NY NH Boston

MA

MICHIGAN TERR.

Fort Detroit

PERRY HARRISON

Lake Erie

CT RI

New York City 40°N

Fort Dearborn

INDIANA TERRITORY

OH

PA

NJ Philadelphia

Baltimore DE

Washington, D.C. MD

MISSOURI TERRITORY

VA

KY

35°N

TN

NC

JACKSON

SC

MISSISSIPPI TERRITORY

Tallapoosa River

Horseshoe Bend

Alabama River

GA

30°N

SPANISH TERRITORY

LA

Fort Mims

SPANISH TERRITORY

ATLANTIC OCEAN

Disputed

New Orleans

Gulf of Mexico 85°W 75°W

90°W 80°W 25°N

Map Legend:
- ▬ American forces
- ✸ American victories
- ▬ British forces
- ✸ British victories
- ⫼ British blockades
- ✸ Creek victory

0   150   300 Miles
0   150   300 Kilometers

GEOGRAPHY SKILLS INTERPRETING MAPS

1. **Location** According to the map, what major southern port was affected by the British blockade?
2. **Region** Which battles took place in the Great Lakes region?

The attack from Detroit failed when British soldiers and Indians led by Tecumseh captured Fort Detroit. The other American attacks failed when state militia troops refused to cross the Canadian border, arguing that they did not have to fight in a foreign country.

In 1813 the United States went on the attack again. A key goal was to break Britain's control of Lake Erie. The navy gave the task to Commodore **Oliver Hazard Perry**. After building a small fleet, Perry sailed out to meet the British on September 10, beginning the **Battle of Lake Erie**. The battle ended

when the British surrendered. Perry sent a message to General William Henry Harrison: "We have met the enemy and they are ours." Perry's brilliant victory forced the British to withdraw, giving the U.S. Army control of the lake and new hope.

With American control of Lake Erie established, General Harrison marched his army into Canada. At the Battle of the Thames River in October 1813, he defeated a combined force of British troops and Native Americans. Harrison's victory ended British power in the Northwest. Tecumseh's death

THE JEFFERSON ERA **285**

Main Idea

❶ Early Battles

American forces held their own against the British in the early battles of the war.

Describe What were the U.S. Navy's strengths and weaknesses early in the war? *strengths—powerful new warships, well-trained sailors, British navy scattered; weaknesses—smaller and weaker than British navy*

Summarize Trace the early battles along the Canadian border. *After a failed invasion of Canada, the United States won the Battle of Lake Erie, forcing the British off the lake, and the Battle of the Thames River, ending British power in the Northwest.*

Draw Conclusions Why do you think many of the war's early battles took place along the Canadian border? *Canada was British territory.*

📦 Map Transparency: The War of 1812

Interpreting Maps
The War of 1812

Drawing Conclusions Why do you think the British attacked New Orleans? *to try to gain control of the city's port and the Mississippi River*

📦 Map Transparency: The War of 1812

Collaborative Learning

At Level

War of 1812 Trading Cards

Prep Required

Materials: blank index cards, art supplies

1. Organize students into small groups. Have the members of each group discuss and list the main events, people, and issues of the War of 1812.

2. Have each group rank the list by order of significance. Give each group 10 index cards. Have the groups create trading cards for the 10 most significant people, events, battles, and issues of the war. On the front of each card, students should provide a name and an

image for a person or event. On the back of each card, students should provide facts about the person or event on the front of the card.

3. Have each group share its cards with the class. Lead a class discussion of the activity. Which events and people did all the groups include? Which did only one group include?

LS Interpersonal, Verbal/Linguistic

📝 Alternative Assessment Handbook, Rubric 14: Group Activity

Answers

Interpreting Maps 1. *New Orleans;* **2.** *Battles of Fort Detroit, Lake Erie, and Thames*

285

❷ Great Britain on the Offensive

U.S. forces stopped British offensives in the East and South.

Summarize How did the war progress in the East? *The British took Washington, D.C., but U.S. forces at Fort McHenry stopped the British invasion of Baltimore, and the British retreated.*

Analyze What was unusual about the Battle of New Orleans? *took place after the war had ended*

📄 **CRF:** Biography Activity: Dolley Madison

Info to Know

"The Star-Spangled Banner" A young American named Francis Scott Key watched anxiously as British forces shelled Fort McHenry. As night fell, he wondered whether the American flag would still be flying over the fort in the morning. Early the next day, through the mist and smoke, Key saw with joy that the flag still flew. The British attack had failed. To celebrate, he wrote "The Star-Spangled Banner." It became the national anthem in 1931.

go.hrw.com
Online Resources

KEYWORD: SR8 US8
ACTIVITY: "The Star-Spangled Banner" Poster

Answers

Reading Check (left) *Great Britain—most powerful nation in the world, hundreds of warships; U.S.—defeated some British warships in one-on-one battles, war on home territory*

Reading Check (right) *major American victory; Andrew Jackson became a hero.*

---

during the fighting also dealt a blow to the British alliance with Native Americans in the region.

The Creek War

Meanwhile, war with American Indians erupted in the South. Creek Indians, angry at American settlers for pushing into their lands, took up arms in 1813. A large force attacked Fort Mims on the Alabama River, destroying the fort and killing close to 250 of its defenders. In response, the commander of the Tennessee militia, **Andrew Jackson**, gathered about 2,000 volunteers to move against the Creek nation.

In the spring of 1814 Jackson attacked the Creek along the Tallapoosa River in Alabama. Jackson's troops won this battle, the Battle of Horseshoe Bend. The **Treaty of Fort Jackson**, signed late in 1814, ended the Creek War and forced the Creek to give up millions of acres of their land.

THE IMPACT TODAY
Inspired by the Americans' strength at Fort McHenry, Francis Scott Key wrote the national anthem, "The Star-Spangled Banner."

READING CHECK **Comparing** What advantages did Great Britain and the United States have at the start of the war?

First Lady Saves Washington's Portrait

Dolley Madison refused to leave Washington, D.C., until a famous portrait of the first president was saved from the executive mansion.

286 CHAPTER 8

Great Britain on the Offensive

Despite U.S. success on the western and southern frontiers, the situation in the East grew worse. After defeating France in April 1814, the British sent more troops to America.

British Attacks in the East

Now reinforced, the British attacked Washington, D.C. President Madison was forced to flee when the British broke through U.S. defenses. The British set fire to the White House, the Capitol, and other government buildings.

The British sailed on to Baltimore, Maryland, which was guarded by Fort McHenry. They shelled the fort for 25 hours. The Americans refused to surrender Fort McHenry. The British chose to retreat instead of continuing to fight.

The Battle of New Orleans

After the attack on Washington, the British moved against New Orleans. British commanders hoped to capture the city and thus take control of the Mississippi River.

Andrew Jackson commanded the U.S. forces around New Orleans. His troops were a mix of regular soldiers, including two battalions of free African Americans, a group of Choctaw Indians, state militia, and pirates led by Jean Lafitte.

The battle began on the morning of January 8, 1815. Some 5,300 British troops attacked Jackson's force of about 4,500. The British began marching toward the U.S. defenses, but they were caught on an open field. The British were cut down with frightening speed. More than 2,000 British soldiers were killed or wounded. The Americans, for their part, had suffered about 70 casualties. The **Battle of New Orleans** made Andrew Jackson a hero and was the last major conflict of the War of 1812.

READING CHECK **Finding Main Ideas** What happened at the Battle of New Orleans?

Cross-Discipline Activity: Music

Above Level

"The Star-Spangled Banner"

Prep Required

Materials: Lyrics and a recording of "The Star-Spangled Banner"

1. Play for students a recording of "The Star-Spangled Banner." Have students share what they feel when they hear the national anthem.

2. Provide students with the song's lyrics. Instruct students to write new lyrics to the tune of "The Star-Spangled Banner" that describe another significant battle or event of the War of 1812. Alternatively, have students

compile a series of images depicting key events of the war and create a slide show that could be accompanied by "The Star-Spangled Banner."

3. Close by having students discuss how "The Star-Spangled Banner" exemplifies the mood of Americans following the War of 1812.

LS **Auditory/Musical, Verbal/Linguistic**

📄 Alternative Assessment Handbook, Rubrics 26: Poems and Songs; and 29: Presentations

Causes of the War
- Impressment of American sailors
- Interference with American shipping
- British military aid to Native Americans

Effects of the War
- Increased sense of national pride
- American manufacturing boosted
- Native American resistance weakened

Effects of the War

Before the battle of New Orleans, a group of New England Federalists gathered secretly at Hartford, Connecticut. At the **Hartford Convention**, Federalists agreed to oppose the war and send delegates to meet with Congress. Before the delegates reached Washington, however, news arrived that the war had ended. Some critics now laughed at the Federalists, and the party lost much of its political power.

Slow communications at the time meant that neither the Federalists nor Jackson knew about the **Treaty of Ghent**. The treaty, which had been signed in Belgium on December 24, 1814, ended the War of 1812.

Though each nation returned the territory it had conquered, the fighting did have several **consequences**. The War of 1812 produced intense feelings of patriotism among many Americans for having stood up to the mighty British. The war also broke the power of many Native American groups. Finally, a lack of goods caused by the interruption in trade boosted American manufacturing.

ACADEMIC VOCABULARY
consequences the effects of a particular event or events

READING CHECK Analyzing Information
What were the main effects of the War of 1812?

SUMMARY AND PREVIEW The War of 1812 convinced Americans that the young nation would survive. In the next chapter you will see how the United States continued to grow.

Section 4 Assessment

go.hrw.com
Online Quiz
KEYWORD: SR8 HP8

Reviewing Ideas, Terms, and People
1. **a. Identify** What losses did American forces face in the early battles of the War of 1812? What victories did they win?
   b. Make Generalizations What role did American Indians play in the war?
2. **a. Describe** What attacks did the British lead against American forces?
   b. Evaluate What do you think were the two most important battles of the war? Why?
3. **a. Identify** What was the purpose of the **Hartford Convention**?
   b. Draw Conclusions How did the United States benefit from the War of 1812?

Critical Thinking
4. **Comparing and Contrasting** Review your notes on the battle dates. Then compare and contrast the details of the major battles during the War of 1812 in a chart like this one.

Battle	Details (Winner, Location, Importance)

FOCUS ON WRITING
5. **Organizing Your Ideas** Reorder the items on your lists from least important to most important.

THE JEFFERSON ERA **287**

Section 4 Assessment Answers

1. **a.** losses—Fort Detroit, failed invasions of Canada; victories—Battles of Lake Erie, Thames River, Horseshoe Bend
   b. often sided with British; Creek War
2. **a.** attacks at Washington, D.C., Fort McHenry and Baltimore, and New Orleans
   b. possible answer—Fort McHenry, Americans stopped the British invasion; Lake Erie, Americans regained control of Lake Erie
3. **a.** to organize Federalist opposition to the war
   b. increased national pride; boosted manufacturing

4. Fort Detroit—British, Detroit, Britain gained control of Lake Erie; Lake Erie—U.S., Lake Erie, Americans regained control of Lake Erie; Thames River—U.S., Thames River, broke British and Native American Indian in the Northwest; Washington D.C.—Britain, Washington D.C., Britain took the capitol; Fort McHenry—U.S., Baltimore, Americans stopped British invasion; New Orleans—U.S., New Orleans, last major conflict
5. Students should reorder and rank their lists.

History and Geography

Activity **Illustrating the Growing America** Ask students if they have ever heard the United States referred to as a young country. Point out that the United States is about 230 years old, a comparatively young nation by historical standards. Ask students to think of the United States as a developing child. In its first years, it was like an infant—13 states born along the Atlantic coast. Over time, the child began to have growth spurts—growing larger and more self-sufficient with each addition of territory. Have each student create a political cartoon or drawing that illustrates this idea of the expansion of the United States up to 1820. Have volunteers explain their cartoons or drawings to the class. **LS Visual/Spatial**

Info to Know

Population Boom The U.S. population more than doubled between 1790 and 1820, increasing from about 3.9 million to 10.1 million. The number of Americans in the West grew particularly fast during this period. In 1790 about 4 percent of the U.S. population lived west of the Appalachians. By 1820 this figure had grown significantly.

America's Growth 1820

In 1803, the United States made the biggest land purchase in its history—the Louisiana Purchase. With this purchase, the country stretched west all the way to the Rocky Mountains. In 1819, the United States acquired Florida from Spain, gaining even more new territory. By 1820, the young American republic had roughly doubled in size, as you can see on the map. Explorers, traders, and settlers began to pour into the new lands in search of wealth, land, and a place to call home.

Claimed by U.S., ceded to Great Britain in 1818

49th Parallel

42nd Parallel

Oregon Country

ROCKY MOUNTAINS

The Oregon Country Both the United States and Great Britain claimed the Oregon Country.

America's Population, 1820: 10.1 million

Ethnic Groups, 1820
- White/European
- African American
- Native American
- Other

4% 1% 18% 77%

Religions, 1820
- Protestant
- Catholic
- Jewish
- Other

1% <1% 4% 94%

PACIFIC OCEAN

Spanish Territory

- Louisiana Purchase, 1803
- Claimed by United States and Great Britain, 1818
- Convention of 1818
- From Britain to United States, 1818
- Adams-Onís Treaty of 1819
- From Spain to United States, 1819

0   150   300 Miles
0   150   300 Kilometers

288 CHAPTER 8

120° W   110° W

Critical Thinking: Summarizing

At Level

The Nation in 1820

1. Have volunteers read aloud the introduction and captions above. Then have students discuss the information in the feature.

2. Ask students to write a description of the United States in 1820 for someone who has never been there. Students should answer some or all of the following questions in their descriptions: What states and territories make up the United States? What major physical features does the United States include? What bodies of water form natural boundaries for the United States? What other nations have claims to lands near the United States? What is the distance from the northernmost point to the southernmost point of the United States? What is the distance from the easternmost point to the westernmost point?

3. Have volunteers present their descriptions to the class. **LS Verbal/Linguistic**

   Alternative Assessment Handbook, Rubric 40: Writing to Describe

Early Traders Soon after Lewis and Clark explored the Louisiana Territory, American fur trappers and traders began setting up trading posts there. Many of these posts became towns later as settlers arrived.

Unorganized Territory

Missouri River

Through the Gaps Settlers crossed the Appalachians through valleys called gaps. In time, roads were built through the gaps, making it easier for Americans to head west.

Delaware Gap

ATLANTIC OCEAN

40° N

Missouri Territory

APPALACHIAN MTS

Cumberland Gap

Arkansas Territory

Red River

Mississippi River

The Mighty Mississippi The Mississippi River was the great highway of the central United States. Americans west of the Appalachians shipped farm goods and supplies up and down the Mississippi and its major port, New Orleans.

Louisiana

• New Orleans

Gulf of Mexico **Unorganized Territory (Florida)**

GEOGRAPHY SKILLS INTERPRETING MAPS

1. **Movement** In which main directions did the United States expand before 1820?
2. **Region** Based on the map, why do you think the United States was interested in claiming the Oregon Country?

70° W

N W E S

THE JEFFERSON ERA **289**

Connect to Geography

Cumberland Gap The Cumberland Gap provided a route west for many American settlers. This gap is located near the point where the states of Kentucky, Virginia, and Tennessee now meet. Daniel Boone, who led pioneers west, blazed the Wilderness Trail through the Cumberland Gap. The main migration of settlers through the Cumberland Gap occurred between 1775 and 1810. During this period, between 200,000 and 300,000 people passed through the gap heading west. The Cumberland Gap National Historical Park now preserves part of the valley.

Connect to Math

Calculating Growth In 1790 the United States and its territories totaled 888,811 square miles. The Louisiana Purchase of 1803 added an additional 827,192 square miles of land. After the 1819 treaty negotiations with Spain, the United States gained Florida, which added another 58,560 square miles. In addition, the United States received other territories totaling 13,443 square miles.

Activity Have students determine the size of the United States at the end of 1803 and 1819. *(1803–1,716,003 square miles; 1819—1,788,006 square miles)* Then have students determine the percentage of the 1819 total that came from the Louisiana Purchase and from land acquired from Spain *(Louisiana Purchase—46.3 percent; from Spain— 4 percent).*

Critical Thinking: Summarizing

At Level

Daniel Boone Biography

Research Required

Materials: *The Adventures of Colonel Daniel Boone* (optional)

1. Explain to students that Daniel Boone is one of our nation's most legendary frontiersmen and is best known for his exploration of Kentucky.

2. Have each student conduct research on Daniel Boone's life, contributions, and achievements.

3. Have students use their research to write biographical sketches of Boone, with a focus on his contributions to westward expansion and settlement.

4. **Extend** Have students locate and read part or all of *The Adventures of Colonel Daniel Boone.* Students should summarize what they read in a paragraph or short essay.
LS Verbal/Linguistic

Alternative Assessment Handbook, Rubrics 4: Biographies; and 37: Writing Assignments

Answers

Interpreting Maps 1. *mainly northwest and west; some south;* **2.** *possible answer—continued the United States westward to the Pacific Ocean and provided additional ports*

Social Studies Skills

Working in Groups to Solve Issues

Activity Discussing the Banning of Cell Phones on Campus

Ask students to imagine that they are members of the student council. The school board wants to ban the use of cell phones on campus. The student council opposes this action. Organize students into groups and assign half the members each position. Have students role play a discussion between the student council and the school board. Group members should try to find one solution to the issue and be prepared to compromise and negotiate if needed. Remind students to respect and listen to differing views and to give each member a chance to participate. Groups should select one member on each side to take notes. Each group should then write down its final solution. After students have completed the activity, have each group share its solution with the class and describe the decision-making process. Students should discuss any problems the group had and how well the group was able to compromise and listen to opposing views. **LS Interpersonal**

Alternative Assessment Handbook, Rubric 14: Group Activity

Social Studies Skills

Working in Groups to Solve Issues

Define the Skill

You already know that the decision-making process is more difficult in a group than it is if just one person makes the decisions. However, group decision-making becomes an even greater challenge when controversial issues are involved.

Group members must have additional skills for the group to function effectively when conflict exists within it. These include respect for differing views, the arts of persuasion and negotiation, and an ability to compromise. A group may not be able to find solutions to controversial problems unless its members have these skills.

Learn the Skill

Some of the biggest challenges Congress faced in the early 1800s were related to the war between Great Britain and France. Some Americans supported the British, while others favored the French. Both countries hoped for American help. When the United States would not take sides, they each began interfering with U.S. ships on the open seas.

As you read in this chapter, Congress tried to solve this problem by passing the Embargo Act. That solution was controversial, however. The northern states were hard hit by the law's ban on overseas trade. Their representatives in Congress demanded a less extreme action. The result was the Non-Intercourse Act. This law was a compromise between members who wanted to lift the trade ban and those who wanted to continue it. Congress was able to solve this problem because its members were able to work around their differences.

The skills Congress needed to reach its solution are valuable ones for any group that must make decisions involving controversial issues. They include the following attitudes and behaviors.

❶ **Willingness to take a position.** If an issue is controversial, it is likely that group members will have differing opinions about it. You have a right to state your views and try to persuade others that you are correct.

❷ **Willingness to listen to differing views.** Every other member has the same right you do. You have a duty to listen to their views, even if you do not agree. Disrespect for those whose views differ from yours makes it more difficult for the group to reach a solution.

❸ **Willingness to debate.** Debate is a form of "healthy" argument because it defends and attacks ideas instead of the people who hold them. Debating the group's differences of opinion is an important step in reaching a solution.

❹ **Willingness to negotiate and compromise.** If debate does not produce agreement, a compromise may be needed. Often it is better to have a solution that members may not like, but can accept, than to have no agreement at all.

Practice the Skill

Check your understanding of the skill by answering the following questions.

1. Why would refusing to listen to other members make group decision-making more difficult?
2. Why is compromise often a better solution than forcing a decision on members who disagree?

Social Studies Skills Activity: Working in Groups to Solve Issues

Posters about How to Work in Groups

At Level

1. Ask students to imagine that they are members of a student government council. The council's discussions often lead to disagreements and arguments that seem to go nowhere and rarely result in decisions.

2. Have each student create a poster to display at council meetings. The poster should provide advice for working in groups to solve issues. Students' posters should address and elaborate upon each of the four points listed under

"Learn the Skill." In addition, students' posters should explain the importance of being able to work in groups to solve issues.

3. Have volunteers share their work with the class. Select the best student posters to display in public areas of the school.
   LS Verbal/Linguistic, Visual/Spatial

Alternative Assessment Handbook, Rubric 28: Posters

Answers

Practice the Skill 1. *This refusal might lead to antagonism between members and further prevent any ability to compromise. In addition, one cannot fully present one's position without understanding others' points of view.*
2. *because a compromise gives all members something they want, instead of only certain members getting their way; leads to more group support for the final decision*

Chapter Review

Visual Summary

Use the visual summary below to help you review the main ideas of the chapter.

QUICK FACTS

The Nation at War and Peace

1803
Marbury v. Madison gives the Supreme Court the power of judicial review.

1803
The United States doubles its size by making the Louisiana Purchase.

1807–09
Congress passes the Embargo and Non-Intercourse Acts.

1811
William Henry Harrison defeats Tecumseh's forces at the Battle of Tippecanoe.

1814
Federalists hold the Hartford Convention to protest the War of 1812.

1812
The War of 1812 begins between Great Britain and the United States.

1814
The Treaty of Ghent ends the War of 1812.

1815
Andrew Jackson wins the Battle of New Orleans.

Reviewing Vocabulary, Terms, and People

Complete each sentence by filling in the blank with the correct term or person.

1. The War of 1812 ended soon after the U.S. victory over the British at the _____.

2. After winning the election of 1800, _____ became the third president of the United States.

3. The power of the Supreme Court to declare acts of Congress unconstitutional is known as _____.

4. After U.S. neutrality was violated, the United States issued an _____ against trade with foreign nations.

5. In 1803 Congress approved the _____ , which added former French territory in the West to the United States.

Comprehension and Critical Thinking

SECTION 1 *(Pages 266–270)*

6. **a. Recall** What were the key issues in the election of 1800?

   b. Analyze In what ways did *Marbury* v. *Madison* affect the power of the judicial branch?

   c. Evaluate Which of Jefferson's new policies do you think was most important? Why?

SECTION 2 *(Pages 272–277)*

7. **a. Describe** What was the purpose of the Lewis and Clark expedition?

   b. Draw Conclusions What are three ways in which the United States benefited from the Louisiana Purchase.

   c. Evaluate Do you think that Napoléon made a wise decision when he sold Louisiana to the United States? Explain your answer.

Visual Summary

Review and Inquiry Have students examine the visual summary. Ask students to create flash cards for the events. Students should put the date on one side and the event on the other. Have students find five other significant dates and events to make additional flash cards. Students can quiz each other using the flash cards.

   Quick Facts Transparency: The Jefferson Era Visual Summary

Reviewing Vocabulary, Terms, and People

1. Battle of Fort McHenry
2. Thomas Jefferson
3. judicial review
4. embargo
5. Louisiana Purchase

Comprehension and Critical Thinking

6. **a.** size of the national government; relations with France, civil liberties
   b. increased the power of the judicial branch in relation to the other two branches
   c. Answers will vary, but students should identify one of Jefferson's new policies and provide reasons to support the choice.

Review and Assessment Resources

Review and Reinforce

SE Chapter Review

📰 **CRF:** Chapter Review Activity

🖳 Quick Facts Transparency: The Jefferson Era Visual Summary

🔊 Spanish Chapter Summaries Audio CD Program

🖳 Online Chapter Summaries in Six Languages

OSP Holt PuzzlePro; GameTool for ExamView

💿 Quiz Game CD-ROM

Assess

SE Standardized Test Practice

📰 PASS: Chapter Test, Forms A and B

📰 Alternative Assessment Handbook

OSP ExamView Test Generator, Chapter Test

💿 Differentiated Instruction Modified Worksheets and Tests CD-ROM: Chapter Test

🖳 Holt Online Assessment Program (in the Premier Online Edition)

Reteach/Intervene

📰 Interactive Reader and Study Guide

📰 Differentiated Instruction Teacher Management System: Lesson Plans for Differentiated Instruction

💿 Differentiated Instruction Modified Worksheets and Tests CD-ROM

💿 Interactive Skills Tutor CD-ROM

go.hrw.com
Online Resources

Chapter Resources:
KEYWORD: SR8 US8

Answers

7. a. to learn more about the people and land of the west; to see if there was a river route to the Pacific Ocean

b. gained a large increase in territory, new resources, land for farming and livestock, and control of New Orleans

c. possible answers—yes, he needed to focus on Europe; no, New Orleans was a major port city, and Louisiana held potential resources.

8. a. War Hawks

b. for—British impressment and violation of neutrality, British influence over frontier Indians, trade restrictions ineffective and hurting the economy; against—should renew friendly ties with Britain, cannot compete against Britain's powerful military

c. possible answer—Britain and France could trade elsewhere.

9. a. led troops to victory against the Creek at Battle of Horseshoe Bend and against the British at Battle of New Orleans

b. Washington, D.C. was the capitol, and New Orleans was a major port.

c. might be seen as more of a military power; might convince others that the American experiment in democracy will survive

Reviewing Themes

10. Great Plains, Rocky Mountains, Pacific coastal region

11. The Federalist Party lost much of its political power.

Using the Internet

12. Go to the HRW Web site and enter the keyword shown to access

> KEYWORD: SR8 TEACHER

SECTION 3 *(Pages 278–283)*

8. a. Identify What group led the call for war with Great Britain?

b. Contrast What arguments were given in favor of war with Great Britain? What arguments were given against war with Britain?

c. Elaborate In your opinion, why were the Embargo Act and the Non-Intercourse Act unsuccessful?

SECTION 4 *(Pages 284–287)*

9. a. Identify What role did Andrew Jackson play in the War of 1812?

b. Make Inferences Why did the British want to capture the cities of Washington and New Orleans?

c. Predict In what ways might the U.S. victory over Great Britain in the war affect the status of the United States in the world?

Reviewing Themes

10. Geography Through what geographic regions did the Lewis and Clark expedition travel?

11. Politics What impact did the Hartford Convention have on American politics?

Using the Internet

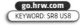
go.hrw.com
KEYWORD: SR8 US8

12. Activity: Journal Entry Prior to Lewis and Clark's expedition, some thought that woolly mammoths, unicorns, and seven-foot-tall beavers lived in the uncharted West. The Corps of Discovery set off to find out the truth about this uncharted land. They also wanted to search for a Northwest Passage that would speed commerce and bring wealth to the young nation. Enter the activity keyword. Research the Web sites and take the point of view of one of the explorers. Write a series of journal entries outlining the thoughts, feelings, discoveries, and events surrounding the journey. Include drawings of what you might have seen in the West in your journal entries.

Reading Skills

Public Documents in History *Use the Reading Skills taught in this chapter to answer the question below.*

13. Which of the following are examples of public documents?

a. the Constitution

b. Meriwether Lewis's journal

c. list of rules for a swimming pool

d. a Harry Potter book

Social Studies Skills

Working in Groups to Solve Issues *Use the Social Studies Skills taught in this chapter to answer the questions below.*

14. Organize into groups of two or three students. Decide which of the following reasons for the War of 1812 you think might have been most important in Congress's decision to declare war.

a. impressment of American sailors

b. trade barriers with Britain and France

c. battles with Native Americans on the frontier

d. gaining land in Canada

FOCUS ON WRITING

15. Writing Your Letter of Recommendation You already have a main idea and an opinion statement for your letter: Thomas Jefferson deserves to be on the list of the top-ten American presidents. Now, look at all your information and pick out three or four points—actions or character traits—that you think are the most important. Write a sentence on each of those points to add to your letter. Put the sentences in order, from the least important to the most important. Finally, conclude with one or two sentences that sum up why you think Thomas Jefferson was such an important president.

Reading Skills

13. a

Social Studies Skills

14. Group members should work together to select an answer and to supply reasons to support it.

Focus on Writing

15. Rubric Students' letters of recommendation should:

- include at least three supporting points.
- present the points from least to most important.
- end with a summary.
- use correct grammar, punctuation, spelling, and capitalization.

CRF: Focus on Writing Activity: A Letter of Recommendation

Standardized Test Practice

DIRECTIONS: Read each question and write the letter of the best response.

1 The Supreme Court's decision in the 1803 case *Marbury* v. *Madison* is an example of

A checks and balances.

B reserved powers.

C delegated powers.

D dual sovereignty.

2 Most of the fighting in the War of 1812 took place

A in Europe.

B in Canada.

C in the United States.

D at sea.

3 Why did President Jefferson agree to buy Louisiana from France?

A He wanted to learn more about the lands and peoples east of the Mississippi River.

B He believed that the United States would benefit from the purchase.

C He wanted to end the French threat in North America.

D He hoped to increase the president's constitutional powers.

4 The United States went to war with Britain in 1812 for all of the following reasons *except*

A to weaken the alliance between Britain and France.

B to protect the rights of U.S. ships on the high seas.

C to end British influence among Indian groups on the frontier.

D to stop trade restrictions against American merchants.

5 The Lewis and Clark expedition was significant because it

A introduced the United States to valuable raw materials such as coal.

B improved America's knowledge of the West.

C led to U.S. settlement of the Southwest.

D opened trade between the United States and Native Americans in the West.

6 During the War of 1812, trade interruptions resulted in

A the repeal the Embargo Act.

B a rise in unemployment.

C an increase in the production of cotton in the South.

D a boost to U.S. manufacturing.

7

> "Though the will of the majority is in all cases to prevail, that will, to be rightful, must be reasonable . . . [T]he minority possess their equal rights, which equal laws must protect . . . Let us then, fellow citizens, unite with one heart and one mind . . . We have been called by different names brethren of the same principle. We are all republicans; we are all federalists."
>
> —President Thomas Jefferson, Inaugural Address, 1801

What did Jefferson mean in making this statement?

A that the Federalists should not run a candidate in 1804

B that citizens should support the nation despite their political differences

C that the Republicans should not be punished for their views

D that all Americans should join a political party

THE JEFFERSON ERA **293**

Intervention Resources

Reproducible

- Interactive Reader and Study Guide
- Differentiated Instruction Teacher Management System: Lesson Plans for Differentiated Instruction

Technology

- Quick Facts Transparency: The Jefferson Era Visual Summary
- Differentiated Instruction Modified Worksheets and Tests CD-ROM
- Interactive Skills Tutor CD-ROM

Tips for Test Taking

Anticipate the Answers Read the following to students: Before you read the answer choices, answer the question yourself. Then read the choices. If the answer you gave is among the choices listed, it is probably correct!

Answers

1. A

Break Down the Question Suggest that students first eliminate any places where fighting did not occur (in Europe) and then recall what they know about the remaining options.

2. D

Break Down the Question Suggest that students first eliminate any places where fighting did not occur (in Europe) and then recall what they know about the remaining options.

3. B

Break Down the Question Point out that this question is looking for reasons for the Purchase. Students should first eliminate any options that are not reasons (D) and then rank the remaining options.

4. C

Break Down the Question Point out that this question assumes that all of the reasons except one are correct. Students might test each answer by asking if it is really true.

5. B

Break Down the Question Suggest that students first reject patently untrue statements (A), and then concentrate on exactly what the expedition did, not on effects that came later.

6. D

Break Down the Question Point out to students that the words *resulted in* in the question means that they need to identify an effect. Tell students that in such cases they should think about what happened after the events.

7. B

Break Down the Question Point out to students that the phrase "Let us then" indicates that Jefferson is about to make his main point—"unite with one heart and one mind." He then ends by restating the idea of unity: "We are all republicans; we are all federalists."

Chapter 9 Planning Guide

A New National Identity

Chapter Overview	Reproducible Resources	Technology Resources
CHAPTER 9 pp. 294–317 **Overview:** In this chapter, students will analyze the development of both American foreign policy and culture.	**Differentiated Instruction Teacher Management System:*** • Instructional Benchmarking Guides • Lesson Plans for Differentiated Instruction **Interactive Reader and Study Guide:** Chapter Graphic Organizer* **Chapter Resource File:*** • Focus on Writing Activity: A Character Sketch • Social Studies Skills Activity: Identifying Central Issues • Chapter Review Activity **A Teacher's Guide to Religion in the Public Schools***	**Power Presentations with Video CD-ROM** **Differentiated Instruction Modified Worksheets and Tests CD-ROM** **Primary Source Library CD-ROM for United States History** **Interactive Skills Tutor CD-ROM** **Student Edition on Audio CD Program** **History's Impact: United States History Video Program (VHS/DVD):** A New National Identity*
Section 1: **American Foreign Policy** **The Big Idea:** The United States peacefully settled disputes with foreign powers.	**Differentiated Instruction Teacher Management System:** Section 1 Lesson Plan* **Interactive Reader and Study Guide:** Section 1 Summary* **Chapter Resource File:*** • Vocabulary Builder Activity, Section 1 • Primary Source Activity: Alexis de Tocqueville's Democracy in America • Primary Source Activity: John Quincy Adams's Fourth of July 1821 Address **Political Cartoons Activities for United States History,** Cartoon 10: The Monroe Doctrine*	**Daily Bellringer Transparency:** Section 1* **Map Transparency:** U.S. Boundary Changes, 1818–1819* **Internet Activity:** Revolutions in Latin America
Section 2: **Nationalism and Sectionalism** **The Big Idea:** A rising sense of national unity allowed some regional differences to be set aside and national interests to be served.	**Differentiated Instruction Teacher Management System:** Section 2 Lesson Plan* **Interactive Reader and Study Guide:** Section 2 Summary* **Chapter Resource File:*** • Vocabulary Builder Activity, Section 2 • History and Geography Activity: The National Road	**Daily Bellringer Transparency:** Section 2* **Map Transparency:** U.S. Roads and Canals, 1850* **Map Transparency:** The Missouri Compromise, 1820* **Internet Activity:** Erie Canal and National Road Map or Brochure
Section 3: **American Culture** **The Big Idea:** As the United States grew, developments in many cultural areas contributed to the creation of a new American identity.	**Differentiated Instruction Teacher Management System:** Section 3 Lesson Plan* **Interactive Reader and Study Guide:** Section 3 Summary* **Chapter Resource File:*** • Vocabulary Builder Activity, Section 3 • Biography Activity: Catherine Maria Sedgwick • Biography Activity: Noah Webster • Literature Activity: *The Prairie,* by James Fenimore Cooper • Biography Activity: Thomas Cole	**Daily Bellringer Transparency:** Section 3* **Internet Activity:** American Culture Display

HOLT
History's Impact
United States History Video Program (VHS/DVD)
A New National Identity
Suggested use: as a chapter introduction

Review, Assessment, Intervention

Quick Facts Transparency: A New National Identity Visual Summary*

Spanish Chapter Summaries Audio CD Program

Progress Assessment Support System (PASS): Chapter Test*

Differentiated Instruction Modified Worksheets and Tests CD-ROM: Modified Chapter Test

One-Stop Planner CD-ROM: ExamView Test Generator (English/Spanish)

Alternative Assessment Handbook

Holt Online Assessment Program (HOAP), in the Holt Premier Online Student Edition

PASS: Section 1 Quiz*

Online Quiz: Section 1

Alternative Assessment Handbook

PASS: Section 2 Quiz*

Online Quiz: Section 2

Alternative Assessment Handbook

PASS: Section 3 Quiz*

Online Quiz: Section 3

Alternative Assessment Handbook

Power Presentations with Video CD-ROM

Power Presentations with Video are visual presentations of each chapter's main ideas. Presentations can be customized by including Quick Facts charts, images from the text, and video clips.

Power Presentations with Video CD-ROM

HOLT

United States History
Beginnings to 1877

HOLT, RINEHART AND WINSTON
A Harcourt Education Company

DIVISION FOR
PUBLIC EDUCATION
AMERICAN BAR ASSOCIATION

Developed by the Division for Public Education of the American Bar Association, these materials are part of the **Democracy and Civic Education Resources.**

• **Constitution Study Guide**

• **Supreme Court Case Studies**

Holt Online Learning

Teacher Resources
KEYWORD: SR8 TEACHER

Student Resources
KEYWORD: SR8 US9

• Document-Based Questions

• Interactive Multimedia Activities

• Current Events

• Chapter-based Internet Activities

• and more!

Holt Premier
Online Student Edition
Complete online support for interactivity, assessment, and reporting

• Interactive Maps and Notebook

• Standardized Test Prep

• Homework Practice and Research Activities Online

CHAPTER 9 PLANNING GUIDE

Differentiating Instruction

ENGLISH-LANGUAGE LEARNERS & STRUGGLING READERS

TARGET RESOURCE

Live Ink® Online Reading Help

Spanish Resources
Spanish Chapter Summaries Audio CD Program

One-Stop Planner CD-ROM:
- ExamView Test Generator, Spanish
- PuzzlePro, Spanish

Additional Resources

Differentiated Instruction Teacher Management System: Lesson Plans for Differentiated Instruction

Chapter Resources:
- Vocabulary Builder Activities
- Social Studies Skills Activity: Identifying Central Issues

Quick Facts Transparency: A New National Identity Visual Summary

Student Edition on Audio CD Program

Online Chapter Summaries in Six Languages

Interactive Skills Tutor CD-ROM

SPECIAL NEEDS LEARNERS

TARGET RESOURCE

Differentiated Instruction Modified Worksheets and Tests CD-ROM

- Vocabulary Flash Cards
- Modified Vocabulary Builder Activities
- Modified Chapter Review Activity
- Modified Chapter Test

Additional Resources

Differentiated Instruction Teacher Management System: Lesson Plans for Differentiated Instruction

Interactive Reader and Study Guide

Social Studies Skills Activity: Identifying Central Issues

Student Edition on Audio CD Program

Interactive Skills Tutor CD-ROM

Live Ink® Online Reading Help

ADVANCED/GIFTED AND TALENTED STUDENTS

TARGET RESOURCE

Primary Source Library CD-ROM for United States History

The Library contains longer versions of quotations in the text, extra sources, and images. Included are point-of-view articles, journals, diaries, historical fiction, and political documents.

Additional Resources

Political Cartoons Activities for United States History: Cartoon 10: The Monroe Doctrine

United States History Document-Based Questions Activities

Differentiated Instruction Teacher Management System: Lesson Plans for Differentiated Instruction

Chapter Resource File:
- Focus on Writing Activity: A Character Sketch
- Literature Activity: *The Prairie,* by James Fenimore Cooper
- Primary Source Activity: Alexis de Tocqueville's Democracy in America
- Primary Source Activity: John Quincy Adams's Fourth of July 1821 Address

One-Stop Planner® CD-ROM
for Differentiated Instruction

Your differentiated instruction lesson plans are available at your fingertips. Holt's Teacher Management System links teaching support tools to pages in the Interactive Teacher's Edition.

The One-Stop Planner features:
- Interactive Teacher's Edition
- Calendar Planner and pacing guides
- Editable lesson plans
- All reproducible ancillaries in Adobe Acrobat (PDF) format
- ExamView Test Generator (English and Spanish)
- Transparency and video previews

Professional Development

- **In-service and staff development** as part of your Holt Social Studies product purchase
- **Quick Teacher Tutorial Lesson Presentation CD-ROM**
- Intensive tuition-based **Teacher Development Institute**
- **Teaching American History Online**—2 Module Professional Development Course
- **Convenient Holt Speaker Bureau**—face-to-face workshop options
- **PRAXIS™ Test Prep** interactive Web-based content refreshers*
- **24/7 Ask A Professional Development Expert** at http://www.hrw.com/prodev/

* PRAXIS is a trademark of Educational Testing Service (ETS). This publication is not endorsed or approved by ETS.

CHAPTER 9 1812–1830

A New National Identity

FOCUS ON WRITING

A Character Sketch Nations, like people, have characters. For example, a nation might be described as peaceful or aggressive, prosperous or struggling. In this chapter you'll read about the United States as a new nation with a new identity, or character. Then you'll write a paragraph describing that character.

UNITED STATES
1816
James Monroe is elected president.

1815

WORLD
1815
Napoléon returns to power in France but is defeated at the Battle of Waterloo.

294 CHAPTER 9

Introduce the Chapter

At Level

The Character of a Country

1. Ask students to think about the character of the early United States as they have learned from their studies. Have students imagine the country as a person. How would they describe this person—young, feisty, aggressive, soft-spoken, opinionated? Write their descriptions for students to see and save the list.

2. Explain to students that they are going to learn how the United States began to be considered a major power in the North American continent. They will learn about the beginnings of U.S. foreign policy and the continued growth of the nation as it began to struggle internally with issues of slavery.

3. Have students copy the list of descriptions. At the chapter's close, discuss with students how the nation has matured. Ask students what additional qualities they would add to their list describing the nation.
   LS Logical/Mathematical

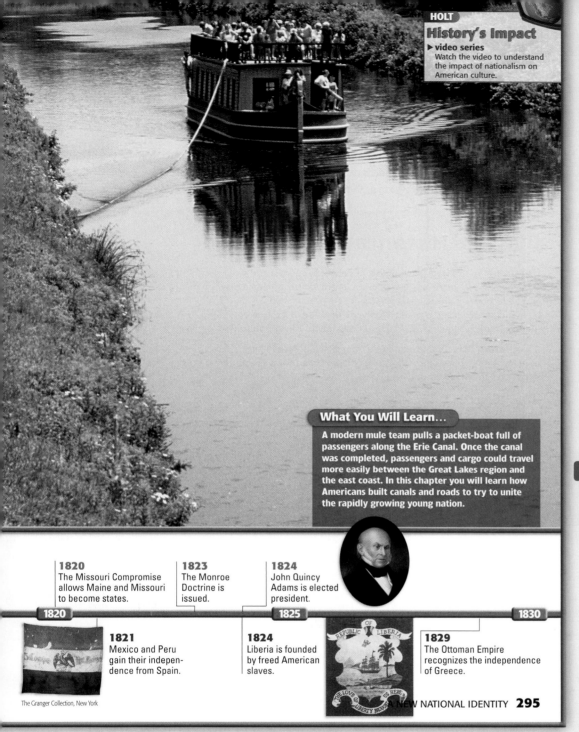

What You Will Learn...

A modern mule team pulls a packet-boat full of passengers along the Erie Canal. Once the canal was completed, passengers and cargo could travel more easily between the Great Lakes region and the east coast. In this chapter you will learn how Americans built canals and roads to try to unite the rapidly growing young nation.

1820
The Missouri Compromise allows Maine and Missouri to become states.

1823
The Monroe Doctrine is issued.

1824
John Quincy Adams is elected president.

1820

1825

1830

1821
Mexico and Peru gain their independence from Spain.

1824
Liberia is founded by freed American slaves.

1829
The Ottoman Empire recognizes the independence of Greece.

The Granger Collection, New York

A NEW NATIONAL IDENTITY **295**

• Chapter Preview •

HOLT
History's Impact
▶ video series
See the Video Teacher's Guide for strategies for using the chapter video **A New National Identity**

Explore the Picture

The Erie Canal The Erie Canal was one of the largest projects in a boom period for canal building in the early 1800s. Canal transportation was cheaper and easier than overland transportation, but building canals was also very expensive.

Analyzing Visuals What can you tell from the photo about transporting goods by canal? *possible answers—transport larger quantities than by horse; many boats can use the same waterway; a more direct route than by land*

go.hrw.com
Online Resources
Chapter Resources:
KEYWORD: SR8 US9
Teacher Resources:
KEYWORD: SR8 TEACHER

Explore the Time Line

1. In what year did James Monroe become president of the United States? *1816*

2. What two major U.S. events happened during Monroe's presidency? *the Missouri Compromise, the Monroe Doctrine*

3. When did Mexico and Peru gain their independence from Spain? *1821*

4. Which country was founded by freed American slaves? When? *Liberia; 1824*

Info to Know

Transportation Americans' experiences during the War of 1812 contributed to a push for better transportation following the war. When the British blockaded the U.S. coastline, American merchants and farmers were forced to rely on overland transportation to get goods to market. They found that the roads were terrible. A four-horse team pulling a wagon full of goods took 75 days to make the journey from Worcester, Massachusetts, to Charleston, South Carolina!

Reading Social Studies
by Kylene Beers

| Economics | Geography | Politics | Society and Culture | Science and Technology |

Understanding Themes

Introduce the key themes of this chapter—politics and culture—by asking students to read the Focus on Themes section on this page. Have students pay attention to the specific issues that affected politics and society and culture in the United States. Preview for students the important political and cultural events mentioned in this chapter, such as the Missouri Compromise and the rise of Hudson River School. Then have each student draw a picture that represents one event and its related theme.

Bias and Historical Events

Focus on Reading Point out to students that letters to the editor and political cartoons commonly display bias. Provide students with a copy of a recent letter to the editor or political cartoon from a local newspaper. Have each student follow the steps listed on this page to analyze the document for bias. You may even want to provide an example of an unbiased letter so that students can compare the two. Discuss with students why recognizing bias might be important in evaluating sources for research.

Focus on Themes This chapter is titled "A New National Identity" because it explains how the United States government established relations with European powers and how Americans developed a strong sense of national pride even as they struggled with important state issues. You will learn about the Monroe Doctrine, the Missouri Compromise, the Cumberland Road project, and the rise of music, literature, and public schools—events that changed the country's **culture** and **politics**.

Bias and Historical Events

Focus on Reading As you read this chapter, you will find that some people supported the idea of using federal dollars to create new and better roads. Others, however, did not think federal dollars should be used that way. People who can only see one side of an issue or situation may become biased, or prejudiced against the opposite view.

Recognizing Bias To understand the events and people in history, you have to be able to recognize a speaker or writer's bias. Here are some steps you can take to do that.

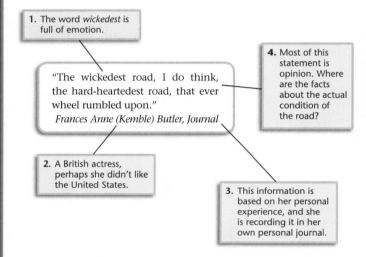

1. The word *wickedest* is full of emotion.

"The wickedest road, I do think, the hard-heartedest road, that ever wheel rumbled upon."
Frances Anne (Kemble) Butler, Journal

2. A British actress, perhaps she didn't like the United States.

3. This information is based on her personal experience, and she is recording it in her own personal journal.

4. Most of this statement is opinion. Where are the facts about the actual condition of the road?

Steps to Recognize Bias

1. **Look at the words and images.** Are they emotionally charged? Do they present only one side or one point of view?

2. **Look at the writer.** What's the writer's background and what does that tell you about the writer's point of view?

3. **Look at the writer's sources.** Where does the writer get his or her information? Does the writer rely on sources who only support one point of view?

4. **Look at the information.** How much is fact and how much is opinion? Remember, facts can be proven. Opinions are personal beliefs—they can easily be biased.

296 CHAPTER 9

Reading and Skills Resources

Reading Support
- Interactive Reader and Study Guide
- Student Edition on Audio CD Program
- Spanish Chapter Summaries Audio CD Program

Social Studies Skills Support
- Interactive Skills Tutor CD-ROM

Vocabulary Support
- **CRF:** Vocabulary Builder Activities
- **CRF:** Chapter Review Activity
- Differentiated Instruction Modified Worksheets and Tests CD-ROM:
  - Vocabulary Flash Cards
  - Vocabulary Builder Activity
  - Chapter Review Activity

OSP Holt PuzzlePro

You Try It!

The following passage is from the chapter you are getting ready to read. As you read the passage, think about living during the early to mid-1800s when there were no public schools.

Architecture and Education

Americans also embraced educational progress. Several early American political leaders expressed a belief that democracy would only succeed in a country of educated and enlightened people. But there was no general agreement on who should provide that education.

Eventually, the idea of a state-funded public school gathered support. In 1837 Massachusetts lawmakers created a state board of education. Other states followed this example, and the number of public schools slowly grew.

From Chapter 9, p. 311

After you read the passage, answer the following questions.

1. You are the editor of your town's newspaper in the year 1835. You think schools should be financed by the state government rather than the federal government. You decide to write an editorial to express your opinion. Which of the phrases below would reveal your personal bias to your readers? Why? What words in each statement create bias?
   a. Overbearing federal government
   b. Protecting state interests
   c. Powerful federal government
   d. Concerned state citizens

2. If you were going to write the editorial described in question 1, how could you avoid biased statements? How do you think this might affect people's reactions to your writing?

Key Terms and People

Chapter 9

Section 1
Rush-Bagot Agreement *(p. 298)*
Convention of 1818 *(p. 298)*
James Monroe *(p. 299)*
Adams-Onís Treaty *(p. 299)*
Simon Bolívar *(p. 300)*
Monroe Doctrine *(p. 300)*

Section 2
nationalism *(p. 302)*
Henry Clay *(p. 302)*
American System *(p. 302)*
Cumberland Road *(p. 303)*
Erie Canal *(p. 303)*
Era of Good Feelings *(p. 303)*
sectionalism *(p. 304)*
Missouri Compromise *(p. 305)*
John Quincy Adams *(p. 305)*

Section 3
Washington Irving *(p. 308)*
James Fenimore Cooper *(p. 309)*
Hudson River school *(p. 310)*
Thomas Cole *(p. 310)*
George Caleb Bingham *(p. 310)*

Academic Vocabulary

Success in school is related to knowing academic vocabulary— the words that are frequently used in school assignments and discussions. In this chapter, you will learn the following academic words:

circumstances *(p. 300)*
incentive *(p. 303)*

As you read Chapter 9, study the primary source documents carefully. Do you see any examples of bias?

Reading Social Studies

Key Terms and People

Preteach the key terms and people from this chapter by having students create a three-panel flip chart FoldNote like the one below. Have students fold a piece of paper in half from top to bottom. Then have them fold the paper into thirds from side to side. Have students cut along each of the vertical fold lines to the fold in the middle of the paper. Have students label the flaps *Section 1, 2,* and *3,* then have them write the key terms or people for that section on the outside of the flap. On the inside of the chart, have students define or describe each term. Encourage students to review these terms and people regularly.

LS Verbal/Linguistic

Focus on Reading

See the **Focus on Reading** questions in this chapter for more practice on this reading social studies skill.

Reading Social Studies Assessment

See the **Chapter Review** at the end of this chapter for student assessment questions related to this reading skill.

Teaching Tip

Point out to students that oftentimes bias is used in order to persuade readers to the author's point of view. Remind students to look for words that express emotion, the writer's background, and statements that express opinion rather than fact.

Answers

You Try It! 1. *a; because it slants people's opinion away from federal government; words that create bias— overbearing, protecting, powerful, and concerned;* **2.** *Student editorials should explain the negative results of federal control of public education.*

American Foreign Policy

What You Will Learn...

Main Ideas

1. The United States and Great Britain settled their disputes over boundaries and control of waterways.
2. The United States gained Florida in an agreement with Spain.
3. With the Monroe Doctrine, the United States strengthened its relationship with Latin America.

The Big Idea

The United States peacefully settled disputes with foreign powers.

Key Terms and People

Rush-Bagot Agreement, *p. 298*
Convention of 1818, *p. 298*
James Monroe, *p. 299*
Adams-Onís Treaty, *p. 299*
Simon Bolívar, *p. 300*
Monroe Doctrine, *p. 300*

 TAKING NOTES Create a chart like the one below. As you read, take notes on the foreign policy issues the United States had to deal with between 1817 and 1823.

Foreign Policy Issues

If YOU were there...

You are a Spanish settler living in West Florida in 1820. Your family has lived in Florida for many years. Only a few years ago, people in Spanish Florida were furious when American soldiers occupied the town of Pensacola. Now you hear that Spain has signed a treaty with the United States—Florida is no longer Spanish territory but rather part of the United States.

How would you feel about living under a new government?

BUILDING BACKGROUND The War of 1812 left the United States stronger and more self-confident. The new nation had remained strong against a great European power. The United States then turned to diplomacy as a way to settle international issues.

Settling Disputes with Great Britain

The Treaty of Ghent ended the War of 1812, yet there were issues left unresolved. The United States and British Canada both wanted to keep their navies and fishing rights on the Great Lakes. In the spring of 1817, the two sides compromised with the **Rush-Bagot Agreement**, which limited naval power on the Great Lakes for both the United States and British Canada.

Another treaty with Britain gave the United States fishing rights off parts of the Newfoundland and Labrador coasts. This treaty, known as the **Convention of 1818**, also set the border between the United States and Canada at 49°N latitude as far west as the Rocky Mountains. Interest in the valuable fur trade in the Oregon Country was another issue resolved by this treaty. Both countries agreed to occupy the Pacific Northwest together, an agreement that would be tested in the years to come.

READING CHECK Summarizing What were the main disputes between the United States and Britain?

Teach the Big Idea

At Level

American Foreign Policy

1. **Teach** Ask students the questions in the Main Idea boxes to teach this section.

2. **Apply** Explain to students that foreign policy develops as nations try to solve international problems. Create a chart with two columns and four rows for students to see. Label the columns *Dispute and How Resolved*, and *U.S. Benefits or Costs*. Label the rows *Britain, Spain,* and *Latin America*. Have each student copy and complete the chart. **LS** Visual/Spatial

3. **Review** As you review the section's main ideas, have students help you complete a master copy of the chart.

4. **Practice/Homework** Have students read, listen to, or view the daily news and take notes on current international disputes. Then have students discuss some of the disputes they listed and how countries might try to resolve them. **LS** Logical/Mathematical

🗐 Alternative Assessment Handbook, Rubric 7: Charts

U.S. Boundary Changes, 1818–1819

Map Legend:
- U.S.–Canadian border, Convention of 1818
- U.S.–Spanish territory border, Adams-Onís Treaty of 1819
- From Britain to United States, 1818
- From Spain to United States, 1819
- Disputed by United States and Great Britain, 1818

0   200   400 Miles
0   200   400 Kilometers

GEOGRAPHY SKILLS **INTERPRETING MAPS**

1. **Place** What territory did the United States acquire from Spain in 1819?
2. **Region** What western region was claimed by both the United States and Great Britain?

United States Gains Florida

The United States also had a dispute over its southern border with Spanish Florida. In 1818 Secretary of State John Quincy Adams, son of John and Abigail Adams, held talks with Spanish diplomat Luis de Onís about letting Americans settle in Florida. Meanwhile, President **James Monroe**, elected in 1816, had sent U.S. troops to secure the U.S.–Florida border. General Andrew Jackson led these soldiers.

At the same time, conflicts arose between the United States and the Seminole Indians of Florida. The Seminole often helped runaway slaves and sometimes raided U.S. settlements. In April 1818 Jackson's troops invaded Florida to capture Seminole raiders. This act began the First Seminole War. During the war Jackson took over most of Spain's

important military posts. Then he overthrew the governor of Florida. He carried out these acts against Spain without receiving direct orders from President Monroe. Jackson's actions upset Spanish leaders. Most Americans, however, supported Jackson.

Jackson's presence in Florida convinced Spanish leaders to negotiate. In 1819 the two countries signed the **Adams-Onís Treaty**, which settled all border disputes between Spain and the United States. Under this treaty, Spain gave East Florida to the United States. In return, the United States gave up its claims to what is now Texas. U.S. leaders also agreed to pay up to $5 million of U.S. citizens' claims against Spain.

THE IMPACT TODAY

Florida was admitted as a U.S. state in 1845 and is now home to about 16 million people.

READING CHECK **Summarizing** How were the disagreements between the United States and Spanish Florida settled?

A NEW NATIONAL IDENTITY **299**

Main Idea

❸ Monroe Doctrine

With the Monroe Doctrine, the United States strengthened its relationship with Latin America.

Identify Cause and Effect What events in Latin America led to the Monroe Doctrine? *struggles for independence in Latin America*

Draw Conclusions Why do you think the United States chose not to issue a joint statement with Great Britain to keep European influence out of Latin America? *did not want British influence in the area, either; United States and Britain were competing for trade in the Americas.*

Make Judgments Do you think the Monroe Doctrine was a good or bad idea for U.S. foreign policy? *possible answers: good—made the United States strong in the eyes of world; bad—may have hurt the nation's relationships with European countries*

📄 **CRF:** Primary Source Activity: John Quincy Adams's Fourth of July 1821 Address

📄 Political Cartoons Activities for United States History: Cartoon 10: The Monroe Doctrine

Primary Source

The Monroe Doctrine

The Monroe Doctrine became an important U.S. policy statement. Later presidents invoked the Monroe Doctrine to build the Panama Canal and to confront the Soviet Union over missiles it had built in Cuba.

Answers

Analyzing Primary Sources
1. *European interference in Latin America would be seen as hostile to the United States.* **2.** *The United States would not interfere with existing colonies.*

300

Primary Source

HISTORIC DOCUMENT
The Monroe Doctrine

President James Monroe established the foundation for U.S. foreign policy in Latin America in the Monroe Doctrine of 1823.

In this phrase, Monroe warns European nations against trying to influence events in the Western Hemisphere.

Monroe notes here the difference between existing colonies and newly independent countries.

The occasion has been judged proper for asserting . . . that the American continents . . . are henceforth not to be considered as subjects for future colonization by any European powers . . .

The political system of the allied powers is essentially different . . . from that of America. We . . . declare that <u>we should consider any attempt on their part to extend their system to any portion of this hemisphere as dangerous to our peace and safety</u> . . .

With the existing colonies . . . we have not interfered and shall not interfere. But with the governments who have declared <u>their independence and maintained it, and whose independence we have . . . acknowledged, we could not view any interposition[1] for the purpose of oppressing them . . . by any European power in any other light than as the manifestation[2] of an unfriendly disposition[3] toward the United States.</u>

ANALYSIS SKILL **ANALYZING PRIMARY SOURCES**
1. What warning did President Monroe give to European powers in the Monroe Doctrine?
2. How does Monroe say the United States will treat existing European colonies?

[1] **interposition:** interference
[2] **manifestation:** evidence
[3] **disposition:** attitude

Monroe Doctrine

ACADEMIC VOCABULARY
circumstances surrounding situation

Meanwhile, Spain had other problems. By the early 1820s most of the Spanish colonies in the Americas had declared independence. Revolutionary fighter **Simon Bolívar**, called the Liberator, led many of these struggles for independence. The political **circumstances** surrounding the revolutions reminded most American leaders of the American Revolution. As a result, they supported these struggles.

After Mexico broke free from Spain in 1821, President Monroe grew worried. He feared that rival European powers might try to take control of newly independent Latin American countries. He was also concerned about Russia's interest in the northwest coast of North America.

Secretary of State Adams shared President Monroe's concerns. In a Fourth of July speech before Congress, Adams said that the United States had always been friendly with European powers, and that the country did not want to be involved in wars with them. He implied that he supported the newly independent countries, but said the United States would not fight their battles.

Great Britain was also interested in restraining the influence of other European nations in the Americas. This was because Britain had formed close trading ties with most of the independent Latin American countries. Britain wanted to issue a joint statement with the United States to warn the rest of Europe not to interfere in Latin America.

Instead, Secretary of State Adams and President Monroe decided to put together a document protecting American interests. The **Monroe Doctrine**, was an exclusive statement of American policy warning European powers not to interfere with the Americas.

300 CHAPTER 9

Critical Thinking: Identifying Points of View   **At Level**

Monroe Doctrine News Articles

1. Have students write a newspaper article about the Monroe Doctrine.

2. Students should choose whether they would like to be a reporter for a U.S. newspaper or a reporter from a country in Europe.

3. Encourage students to come up with a headline and a political cartoon, illustration, or other visual aid to accompany their newspaper articles.

4. Ask volunteers to share their articles with the class. Encourage feedback.

5. Conclude by leading a class discussion on the various points of view that Americans and others had toward the Monroe Doctrine.
LS Verbal/Linguistic, Visual/Spatial

📄 Alternative Assessment Handbook, Rubric 23: Newspapers

The doctrine was issued by the president on December 2, 1823, during his annual message to Congress.

The Monroe Doctrine had four basic points.

1. The United States would not interfere in the affairs of European nations.
2. The United States would recognize, and not interfere with, colonies that already existed in North and South America.
3. The Western Hemisphere was to be off-limits to future colonization by any foreign power.
4. The United States government would consider any European power's attempt to colonize or interfere with nations in the Western Hemisphere to be a hostile act.

Some Europeans strongly criticized the Monroe Doctrine, but few European countries challenged it. The doctrine has remained important to U.S. foreign policy. The United States has continued to consider Latin America within its sphere of influence—the area a nation claims some control over. At times, it has intervened in Latin American affairs when its own interests, such as national security, were at risk.

READING CHECK **Analyzing** What effect did the revolutions in Latin America have on U.S. foreign policy?

SUMMARY AND PREVIEW In this section you learned that U.S. foreign policy was characterized by both compromise and strong leadership in the years following the War of 1812. In the next section you will learn about the rising sense of national pride that developed as the United States grew and expanded.

Section 1 Assessment

go.hrw.com
Online Quiz
KEYWORD: SR8 HP9

Reviewing Ideas, Terms, and People

1. **a. Identify** What issues were settled between the United States and Great Britain in 1817 and 1818?
   b. Make Inferences Why would the United States and Britain agree to occupy the Pacific Northwest together?
   c. Elaborate Why were the **Rush-Bagat Agreement** and the **Convention of 1818** compromises?
2. **a. Recall** What problems existed between Spain and the United States?
   b. Analyze Why was the **Adams-Onís Treaty** important?
   c. Evaluate Do you think that Andrew Jackson was right to act without orders? Explain your answer.
3. **a. Describe** What did the **Monroe Doctrine** state?
   b. Contrast How did the Monroe Doctrine differ from Adams's Fourth of July Address?
   c. Elaborate What do you think the newly independent Latin American countries thought of the Monroe Doctrine?

Critical Thinking

4. **Identifying Cause and Effect** Review your notes regarding U.S. foreign policy issues. Create a new chart and, for each issue, identify the nations involved, the agreement or doctrine, and the effects.

Nations	Agreement/Doctrine	Issue	Effects

FOCUS ON WRITING

5. **Determining Relationships** One of the main ways you can tell about someone's character is by how he or she treats others. As you read this section, start a list of words and phrases that describe how the United States acted in relationships with other nations. For example, lists might include words and phrases like "willing to compromise" and "firm."

A NEW NATIONAL IDENTITY **301**

Direct Teach

Info to Know

Politics and the Monroe Doctrine The Monroe Doctrine played a role in the presidential ambitions of John Quincy Adams, who hoped to succeed Monroe in the White House. Adams knew that many Americans were suspicious of him because he desired close relations with Great Britain. When the British wanted to issue a joint declaration opposing European influence in the Americas, Adams persuaded Monroe to issue the doctrine without British involvement. Americans approved of this decision, and Adams avoided being attacked as pro-British in the 1824 election.

go.hrw.com
Online Resources
KEYWORD: SR8 US9
ACTIVITY: Revolutions in Latin America

Review & Assess

Close

Have students work individually to write a brief summary of the major agreements and doctrines discussed in this section.

Review
Online Quiz, Section 1

Assess
SE Section 1 Assessment
PASS: Section 1 Quiz
Alternative Assessment Handbook

Reteach-Classroom Intervention
Interactive Reader and Study Guide, Section 1
Interactive Skills Tutor CD-ROM

Section 1 Assessment Answers

1. **a.** naval and fishing rights, U.S.-Canadian border dispute, Northwest fur trade
   b. interest in the fur trade
   c. In order to gain rights, both nations accepted limits.
2. **a.** disputes over Texas and Spanish Florida
   b. settled border disputes with Spain
   c. possible answers: no—military leaders should not attack other countries without orders; yes—it forced Spain to negotiate.
3. **a.** Europe should stay out of Western Hemisphere; U.S. will not interfere in European affairs.

   b. Adams said the United States would not fight the battles of Latin American countries; Monroe Doctrine threatened force against European intervention.
   c. possible answers: good—kept Europeans from interfering; bad—gave the United States control over Latin America

4. sample answer: U.S. and British Canada; Rush-Bagot Agreement; limited both sides' naval power on Great Lakes

5. possible answers—forceful, strong, rude, protective, possessive, diplomatic

Answers

Reading Check *The United States wanted to keep European influence out of newly independent countries; created Monroe Doctrine, warning European nations not to interfere in the Western Hemisphere.*

Bellringer

If YOU were there . . . Use the **Daily Bellringer Transparency** to help students answer the questions.

🖵 Daily Bellringer Transparency, Section 2

Academic Vocabulary

Review with students the high-use academic term in this section.

incentive something that leads people to follow a certain course of action (p. 303)

📰 **CRF:** Vocabulary Builder Activity, Section 2

Taking Notes

Have students copy the graphic organizer onto their own paper and then use it to take notes on the section. This activity will prepare students for the Section Assessment, in which they will complete a graphic organizer that builds on the information using a critical thinking skill.

Nationalism and Sectionalism

What You Will Learn...

Main Ideas

1. Growing nationalism led to improvements in the nation's transportation systems.
2. The Missouri Compromise settled an important regional conflict.
3. The outcome of the election of 1824 led to controversy.

The Big Idea

A rising sense of national unity allowed some regional differences to be set aside and national interests to be served.

Key Terms and People

nationalism, *p. 302*
Henry Clay, *p. 302*
American System, *p. 302*
Cumberland Road, *p. 303*
Erie Canal, *p. 303*
Era of Good Feelings, *p. 303*
sectionalism, *p. 304*
Missouri Compromise, *p. 305*
John Quincy Adams, *p. 305*

TAKING NOTES As you read, take notes on how each of the following contributed to national unity.

302 CHAPTER 9

If YOU were there...

You live near the western end of the newly completed Erie Canal in New York State in 1831. In fact, your older brothers helped build the canal. Every day you watch as mules pull the canal boats along the still water of the canal. Sometimes the boats carry passengers traveling from city to city. You have never been far from your home, and you are curious about their journey.

What would you like to ask the travelers on the canal boat?

BUILDING BACKGROUND Peace, prosperity, and a growing country gave Americans a sense of national unity. In practical terms, building roads and canals also helped unify the nation. They made travel easier, linking people from different regions of the country. Nevertheless, some regional conflicts continued.

Growing Nationalism

Pleased by successful negotiations with foreign powers, Americans enjoyed a rising sense of nationalism. **Nationalism** is feelings of pride and loyalty to a nation. This new national unity found a strong supporter in U.S. Representative **Henry Clay** from Kentucky.

Clay believed that a strong national economy would promote national feeling and reduce regional conflicts. He developed a plan that came to be known as the **American System**—a series of measures intended to make the United States economically self-sufficient. To build the economy, he pushed for a national bank that would provide a single currency, making interstate trade easier. Clay wanted the money from a protective tariff to be used to improve roads and canals. These internal improvements would unite the country.

Some members of Congress believed that the Constitution did not permit the federal government to spend money on internal improvements. Clay argued that the possible gains for the country justified federal action.

Teach the Big Idea

Nationalism and Sectionalism

1. **Teach** Ask students the questions in the Main Idea boxes to teach this section.

2. **Apply** Organize students into three groups. Assign each group a main idea from the section. Have each group create a 10-question quiz on its topic as well as a separate answer key. Have groups exchange quizzes, complete the ones they receive, and then return the completed quizzes to their authors for grading. **LS Interpersonal, Verbal/Linguistic**

3. **Review** As you review the section, have the groups share questions and answers from their quizzes.

4. **Practice/Homework** Have each student select one quiz question to explore in a paragraph. Students should address the questions who, what, where, when, why, and how, as applicable, in their paragraphs. **LS Verbal/Linguistic**

   📰 Alternative Assessment Handbook, Rubrics 1: Acquiring Information; and 37: Writing Assignments

Roads and Canals

In the early 1800s most roads in the United States were made of dirt, making travel difficult. British actress Frances Kemble described one New York road she had struggled along during a visit in the 1830s.

"The wickedest road, I do think, the cruellest, hard-heartedest road, that ever [a] wheel rumbled upon."

—Frances Anne (Kemble) Butler, *Journal*

To improve the nation's roads, Congress agreed with Clay and invested in road building. The **Cumberland Road** was the first road built by the federal government. It ran from Cumberland, Maryland, to Wheeling, a town on the Ohio River in present-day West Virginia. Construction began in 1815. Workers had to cut a 66-foot-wide band, sometimes through forest, to make way for the road. Then they had to use shovels and pickaxes to dig a 12- to 18-inch roadbed, which they filled with crushed stone. All of the work had to be done without the benefit of today's bulldozers and steamrollers.

By 1818 the road reached Wheeling. By 1833 the National Road, as the expansion was called, stretched to Columbus, Ohio. By 1850 it reached all the way to Illinois.

Meanwhile, Americans tried to make water transportation easier by building canals. One of the largest projects was the **Erie Canal**, which ran from Albany to Buffalo, New York.

Construction of the canal began in 1817 and was completed in 1825. Using shovels, British, German, and Irish immigrants dug the entire canal by hand. The canal cost millions of dollars, but it proved to be worth the expense. The Erie Canal allowed goods and people to move between towns on Lake Erie and New York City and the east coast. Its success served as an **incentive** for a canal-building boom across the country.

Era of Good Feelings

From 1815 to 1825 the United States enjoyed the **Era of Good Feelings**, an era of peace, pride, and progress. The phrase was coined

ACADEMIC VOCABULARY

incentive
something that leads people to follow a certain course of action

U.S. Roads and Canals, 1850

Roads
Canals

Americans used flatboats, like this one, to travel the country's canals.

Travelers on the National Road stopped at inns to eat and rest from a long day's journey.

GEOGRAPHY SKILLS INTERPRETING MAPS

1. **Region** In what region of the United States were most canals located?
2. **Movement** About how long was the National Road?

A NEW NATIONAL IDENTITY **303**

Main Idea

❷ Missouri Compromise

The Missouri Compromise settled an important regional conflict.

Explain What problem did Missouri's request for statehood cause? *threatened to upset the balance of power between the free states and the slave states in the Senate*

Analyze How did the Missouri Compromise satisfy both the North and the South? *kept the number of free states and slave states equal and maintained the balance of power*

Make Judgments If you were a senator in 1820, would you have voted for or against the Missouri Compromise? Why? *possible answers: against—to prevent the spread of slavery; for—to preserve the peace between the states*

 Map Transparency: The Missouri Compromise, 1820

History Humor

What are the three rules of diplomacy?

1. Compromise
2. Compromise
3. Compromise

Answers

Interpreting Maps 1. *South;* **2.** *It was Missouri's southern border, leaders may have hoped this line would maintain balance in the future.*

Biography *wanted to preserve the Union*

Reading Check *easier to transport goods across the nation*

The Missouri Compromise, 1820

The Missouri Compromise banned slavery in the region north of 36°30'N.

- Free state
- Free territory
- Slave state
- Slave territory

Missouri Compromise line (36°30'N)

BIOGRAPHY

Henry Clay
1777–1852

Known as the silver-tongued Kentuckian, Henry Clay was a gifted speaker. He became involved in local politics early in his life, and by age 29 he was appointed to the U.S. Senate. Throughout his career in the Senate, he was dedicated to preserving the Union. The Missouri Compromise and a later agreement, the Compromise of 1850, helped to ease sectional tensions, at least temporarily.

Analyzing Why did Henry Clay work for compromises between regions?

by a Boston editor in 1817 during James Monroe's visit to New England early in his presidency.

The emphasis on national unity was strengthened by two Supreme Court case decisions that reinforced the power of the federal government. In the 1819 case *McCulloch* v. *Maryland*, the Court asserted the implied powers of Congress in allowing for the creation of a national bank. In the 1824 case *Gibbons* v. *Ogden*, the Court said that the states could not interfere with the power of Congress to regulate interstate commerce.

READING CHECK **Drawing Inferences** How did new roads and canals affect the economy?

Missouri Compromise

Even during the Era of Good Feelings, disagreements between the different regions—known as **sectionalism**—threatened the Union. One such disagreement arose in 1819 when Congress considered Missouri's application to enter the Union as a slave state. At the time, the Union had 11 free states and 11 slave states. Adding a new slave state would have tipped the balance in the Senate in favor of the South.

To protect the power of the free states, the House passed a special amendment. It declared that the United States would accept Missouri as a slave state, but importing enslaved Africans into Missouri would be illegal. The amendment also set free the children of Missouri slaves. Southern politicians angrily opposed this plan.

North Carolina senator Nathaniel Macon wanted to continue adding slave states. "Why depart from the good old way, which has kept us in quiet, peace, and harmony?" he asked. Eventually, the Senate rejected the amendment. Missouri was still not a state.

Critical Thinking: Identifying Points of View | At Level

The Missouri Compromise

1. Write the following for students to see:
   North—100   South—76

2. Explain to students that these numbers show the North/South split in the House of Representatives at the time of the Missouri Compromise. While all 76 southern representatives voted to allow Missouri to enter the Union as a slave state, only 14 northerners voted for the measure.

3. Ask students how many votes were needed for a House majority *(88)* and how many the measure received *(90)*.

4. Have each student draw a copy of the map shown above. Then have students annotate the map by listing the political, economic, and social points of view in the free states and the slave states that were dividing the nation and which the Missouri Compromise addressed.

5. Ask volunteers to share the information they listed. **LS Visual/Spatial**

   Alternative Assessment Handbook, Rubrics 11: Discussions; and 20: Map Creation

Henry Clay convinced Congress to agree to the **Missouri Compromise**, which settled the conflict that had arisen from Missouri's application for statehood. This compromise had three main conditions:

1. Missouri would enter the Union as a slave state.
2. Maine would join the Union as a free state, keeping the number of slave and free states equal.
3. Slavery would be prohibited in any new territories or states formed north of 36°30' latitude—Missouri's southern border.

Congress passed the Missouri Compromise in 1820. Despite the success of the compromise, there were still strong disagreements between the North and South over the expansion of slavery.

READING CHECK **Drawing Conclusions** Why did Henry Clay propose the Missouri Compromise to resolve the issue of Missouri statehood?

The Election of 1824

Soon, a presidential election also brought controversy. Andrew Jackson won the most popular votes in 1824. However, he did not have enough electoral votes to win office. Under the Constitution, the House of Representatives had to choose the winner. When the House chose **John Quincy Adams** as president, Jackson's supporters claimed that Adams had made a **corrupt bargain** with Henry Clay. These accusations grew after Adams chose Clay to be secretary of state. The controversy weakened Adams's support.

FOCUS ON READING
How is the term **corrupt bargain** an example of semantic slanting?

READING CHECK **Drawing Inferences** Why did Adams have weak support during his presidency?

SUMMARY AND PREVIEW Strong nationalistic feeling contributed to the development of America's politics and economy. In the next section you will read about the development of a new national culture.

go.hrw.com
Online Quiz
KEYWORD: SR8 HP9

Section 2 Assessment

Reviewing Ideas, Terms, and People

1. **a. Describe** What was the **Era of Good Feelings**?
   b. Analyze Explain the impact the *McCulloch* v. *Maryland* and *Gibbons* v. *Ogden* decisions had on the federal government.
   c. Predict How would transportation improvements eventually aid the economy of the United States?
2. **a. Recall** What role did **Henry Clay** play in the debate over Missouri's statehood?
   b. Explain What problem did Missouri's request for statehood cause?
   c. Elaborate Was the **Missouri Compromise** a good solution to the debate between free states and slave states? Explain your answer.
3. **a. Identify** Who were the candidates in the presidential election of 1824? How was the winner determined?
   b. Draw Conclusions Why did **John Quincy Adams** lose popular support following the election of 1824?

Critical Thinking

4. **Evaluating** Review your notes on nationalism during the Era of Good Feelings. Then copy the following graphic organizer, and use it to identify how threats to nationalism were resolved by the Missouri Compromise.

Sectional differences → Missouri Compromise → Outcome 1. 2. 3.

FOCUS ON WRITING

5. **Judging Self-Esteem** Another way you can tell about people's characters is by how they view themselves. Are they self-confident? Do they make healthy choices? As you read this section, think of the United States as a person and jot down notes about the view the United States had of itself. Is the new nation pleased with itself? Does it feel confident or confused?

A NEW NATIONAL IDENTITY **305**

History and Geography

History and Geography

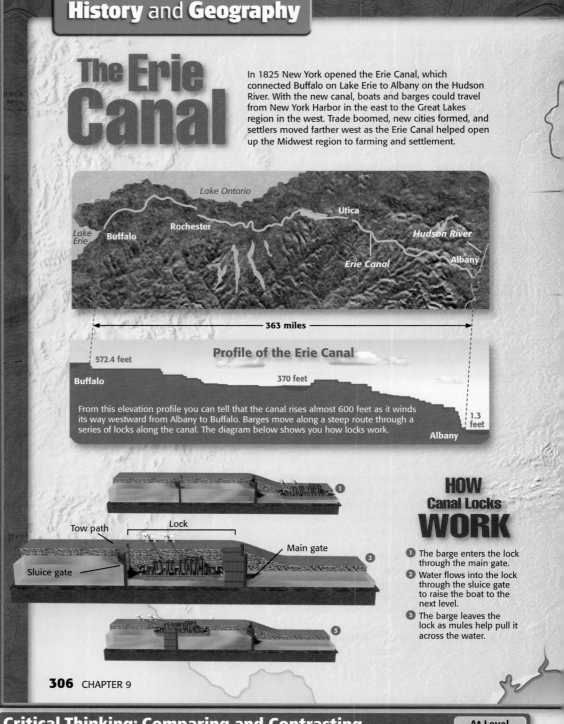

The Erie Canal

In 1825 New York opened the Erie Canal, which connected Buffalo on Lake Erie to Albany on the Hudson River. With the new canal, boats and barges could travel from New York Harbor in the east to the Great Lakes region in the west. Trade boomed, new cities formed, and settlers moved farther west as the Erie Canal helped open up the Midwest region to farming and settlement.

Lake Ontario

Lake Erie
Buffalo
Rochester
Utica
Hudson River
Erie Canal
Albany

363 miles

Profile of the Erie Canal

572.4 feet
Buffalo
370 feet
1.3 feet
Albany

From this elevation profile you can tell that the canal rises almost 600 feet as it winds its way westward from Albany to Buffalo. Barges move along a steep route through a series of locks along the canal. The diagram below shows you how locks work.

Tow path
Lock
Main gate
Sluice gate

HOW Canal Locks WORK

❶ The barge enters the lock through the main gate.
❷ Water flows into the lock through the sluice gate to raise the boat to the next level.
❸ The barge leaves the lock as mules help pull it across the water.

306 CHAPTER 9

Activity Erie Canal Grand Opening Flyer
Lead a discussion on the Erie Canal. Have each student create a flyer advertising the opening of the canal that provides information about why canal transportation is better than other available options. Students should consider both people traveling west as well as those shipping goods.
LS Verbal/Linguistic, Visual/Spatial

Connect to Geography
The Canal Route The Erie Canal was built through the Mohawk Valley, a natural pass through the Appalachian Mountains in eastern New York. Colonists had learned this route from Native Americans. This location was chosen because no locks or aqueducts would be needed for some 80 miles.

Teaching Tip

Relate to the Familiar Relate the height of the Erie Canal to objects with which students are familiar. Tell students to use 10 feet as the average height of a one-story building. Have students use this figure to estimate how many stories a building would need to be to equal the rise of the Erie Canal. *(60 stories)*

Critical Thinking: Comparing and Contrasting
At Level

Modern Canals
Research Required

1. Have each student conduct research on a canal in use today, such as the Panama Canal, the Suez Canal, the New York Canal System, the Sault Sainte Marie canals, the Intracoastal Waterway, or the Illinois Waterway.

2. Have each student create a chart comparing and contrasting the modern canal to the Erie Canal. Assign students specific points of comparison (such as the information listed in the Erie Canal Fast Facts on the next page) and

have students provide the same information for each canal. Then have students write a summary explaining the significance of each canal.

3. Have volunteers share their charts with the class. **LS** Verbal/Linguistic, Visual/Spatial

Alternative Assessment Handbook, Rubrics 7, Charts; 9: Comparing and Contrasting; and 30: Research

The Erie Canal

Later canals extended west into Ohio and Indiana.

Settlers and goods moved west.

Agricultural products moved east.

Trade through New York Harbor boomed as goods flowed along the Erie Canal to overseas markets and back to settlers and cities in the West.

EFFECTS OF THE CANAL

Thanks to the canal, the cost of shipping dropped. Lower costs led to increases in shipping and in city populations.

Cost of Shipping

1824: $100 per ton by road

1825: $10 per ton by canal

Population Growth

Population (Thousands) — Albany, Buffalo, Chicago, Cleveland — Year 1820, 1830, 1840

GEOGRAPHY SKILLS — INTERPRETING MAPS

1. **Region** How did the Erie Canal affect western lands?
2. **Location** What effect do you think the Erie Canal had on New York City?

ATLANTIC OCEAN

A NEW NATIONAL IDENTITY **307**

Info to Know

Erie Canal Fast Facts
opened: October 25, 1825
cost: about $7 million
endpoints: Buffalo and Albany, New York
length: 363 miles (584 km)
width: 40 feet (12 m)
towpath width: 14 feet
depth: 4 feet (1.2 m)
total number of locks: 83
total number of aqueducts: 18
nicknames: "Clinton's Folly," "Clinton's Big Ditch"

Linking to Today

Erie Canal Today Many of the Erie Canal's original 83 locks are still in use today, although the locks' sizes have been changed to accommodate larger vessels. People also use the canal towpaths for recreation, such as walking, bicycling, and even cross-country skiing.

Did you know . . .

When work began on the Erie Canal, the United States did not have a single school of engineering.

Connect to Economics

A Sound Investment Profits from the Erie Canal paid for the cost of the project within nine years of the canal's opening. The canal soon made New York the busiest port in the United States.

Did You Know . . .

New York Governor DeWitt Clinton was a major supporter of the Erie Canal project. Clinton's image was featured on the U.S. $1,000 bill, printed between 1869 and 1880.

Cross-Discipline Activity: Music

Above Level

Erie Canal Song

Prep Required

Materials: lyrics and recording of the song "The Erie Canal," by Thomas S. Allen, 1905

1. Distribute to students copies of the lyrics for the song "The Erie Canal." Next, play a recording of the song. Have students discuss the song's meaning and why the Erie Canal was chosen as a topic for a popular song.

2. Organize students into small groups and have each group write new lyrics to the tune of "The Erie Canal" that describe the effects and significance of the canal as described above.

3. Have each group perform its new version of "The Erie Canal" for the class.

LS Auditory/Musical, Interpersonal

📖 Alternative Assessment Handbook, Rubrics 14: Group Activity; and 26: Poems and Songs

Answers

Interpreting Maps 1. *It enabled trade goods to be shipped farther west, so trade boomed, new cities formed and others grew, and settlers moved farther west.* **2.** *possible answer—greatly increased the amount of goods traded through New York City and helped the city grow and prosper*

Bellringer

If YOU were there . . . Use the Daily Bellringer Transparency to help students answer the question.

🖎 Daily Bellringer Transparency, Section 3

Building Vocabulary

Preteach or review the following terms:

revival renewed faith (p. 310)

satire writing that uses ridicule (p. 309)

🗐 **CRF:** Vocabulary Builder Activity, Section 3

go.hrw.com
Online Resources
KEYWORD: SR8 US9
ACTIVITY: American Culture Display

Taking Notes

Have students copy the graphic organizer onto their own paper and then use it to take notes on the section. This activity will prepare students for the Section Assessment, in which they will complete a graphic organizer that builds on the information using a critical thinking skill.

American Culture

What You Will Learn...

Main Ideas

1. American writers created a new style of literature.
2. A new style of art showcased the beauty of America and its people.
3. American ideals influenced other aspects of culture, including religion and music.
4. Architecture and education were affected by cultural ideals.

The Big Idea

As the United States grew, developments in many cultural areas contributed to the creation of a new American identity.

Key Terms and People

Washington Irving, *p. 308*
James Fenimore Cooper, *p. 309*
Hudson River school, *p. 310*
Thomas Cole, *p. 310*
George Caleb Bingham, *p. 310*

TAKING NOTES As you read, take notes on the new developments in American culture in the 1820s and 1830s. Write your notes in a chart like the one below.

	Characteristics
Literature	
Visual arts	
Religious music	
Architecture	
Education	

If **YOU** were there...

You live in Philadelphia in 1830. Though you've lived in the city all your life, you dream about the West and the frontier. Now you've discovered a wonderful writer whose stories tell about frontier life and events in American history. You can't wait to read his next exciting adventure. You think that perhaps someday you could be a frontier hero, too.

Why would the frontier seem so exciting?

BUILDING BACKGROUND Until the early 1800s, Americans took most of their cultural ideas from Great Britain and Europe. But as American politics and the economy developed, so too did a new national culture. Writers and artists were inspired by American history and the American landscape.

American Writers

Like many people the world over, Americans expressed their thoughts and feelings in literature and art and sought spiritual comfort in religion and music. Developments in education and architecture also reflected the growing national identity.

One of the first American writers to gain international fame was **Washington Irving**. Born in 1783, he was named after George Washington. Irving's works often told about American

American Arts

Early to mid-1800s
American architects are inspired by ancient Greece and Rome.

Teach the Big Idea

American Culture

Materials: blank note cards

1. **Teach** Ask students the questions in the Main Idea boxes to teach this section.

2. **Apply** Have each student create flash cards for two to three of the key people or ideas covered in the text under each of the blue headings. On the front of each card, students should label a person or idea. On the back of each card, students should provide a bulleted list of details and a one-sentence summary of how the person or idea contributed to a developing American identity. **LS Verbal/Linguistic**

3. **Review** Have students share information from their flash cards.

4. **Practice/Homework** Have students use their flash cards to create annotated time lines for the section. **LS Visual/Spatial**

🗐 Alternative Assessment Handbook, Rubric 36: Time Lines

history. Through a humorous form of writing called satire, Irving warned that Americans should learn from the past and be cautious about the future.

Irving shared this idea in one of his best-known short stories, "Rip Van Winkle." This story describes a man who falls asleep during the time of the American Revolution. He wakes up 20 years later to a society he does not recognize. Irving published this and another well-known tale, "The Legend of Sleepy Hollow," in an 1819–20 collection.

In some of his most popular works, Irving combined European influences with American settings and characters. His work served as a bridge between European literary traditions and a new type of writer who focused on authentically American characters and society.

Perhaps the best known of these new writers was **James Fenimore Cooper**. Cooper was born to a wealthy New Jersey family in 1789. Stories about the West and the Native Americans who lived on the frontier fascinated him. These subjects became the focus of his best-known works.

Cooper's first book was not very successful, but his next novel, *The Spy*, was a huge success. Published in 1821, it was an adventure story set during the American Revolution. It appealed to American readers' patriotism and desire for an exciting, action-filled story.

In 1823 Cooper published *The Pioneers*, the first of five novels featuring the heroic character Natty Bumppo. Cooper's novels told of settling the western frontier and included historical events. For example, his novel *The Last of the Mohicans* takes place during the French and Indian War. By placing fictional characters in a real historical setting, Cooper popularized a type of writing called historical fiction.

Some critics said that Cooper's characters were not interesting. They particularly criticized the women in his stories; one writer labeled them "flat as a prairie." Other authors of historical fiction, such as Catharine Maria Sedgwick, wrote about interesting heroines. Sedgwick's characters were inspired by the people of the Berkshire Hills region of Massachusetts, where she lived. Her works include *A New-England Tale* and *Hope Leslie*.

READING CHECK **Analyzing** How did American writers such as Irving and Cooper help create a new cultural identity in the United States?

A New Style of Art

The writings of Irving and Cooper inspired painters. These artists began to paint landscapes that showed the history of America and the beauty of the land. Earlier American painters had mainly painted portraits. By the

1827
John Audubon begins publishing *The Birds of America*, which is highly admired in England.

A NEW NATIONAL IDENTITY **309**

309

❷ A New Style of Art

A new style of art showcased the beauty of America and its people.

Recall Who was one of the founders of the Hudson River school?
Thomas Cole

Summarize How had the style of American painting changed by the 1840s? *More artists were combining scenes of American landscapes with scenes from daily life.*

📖 **CRF:** Biography Activity: Thomas Cole

❸ Religion and Music

American ideals influenced other aspects of culture, including religion and music.

Explain What was the purpose of revival meetings? *reawakening religious faith*

Evaluate Why was a song about the Battle of New Orleans a good campaign song for Andrew Jackson? *Jackson had led American forces to a convincing victory over a larger British force at the battle.*

Answers

Reading Check (left) *movement away from portraiture toward landscape painting, reflected Americans' new nationalism and pride in their country*

Reading Check (right) *spirituals—reflected emphasis on religion and revivalism; folk music—reflected spirit of nationalism*

310

1830s the Hudson River school had emerged. The artists of the **Hudson River school** created paintings that reflected national pride and an appreciation of the American landscape. They took their name from the subject of many of their paintings—the Hudson River valley.

Landscape painter **Thomas Cole** was a founder of the Hudson River school. He had moved to the United States from Britain in 1819. He soon recognized the unique qualities of the American landscape. As his work gained fame, he encouraged other American artists to show the beauty of nature. "To walk with nature as a poet is the necessary condition of a perfect artist," Cole once said.

By the 1840s the style of American painting was changing. More artists were trying to combine images of the American landscape with scenes from people's daily lives. An important example of this style is *Fur Traders Descending the Missouri* by **George Caleb Bingham**. This painting shows the rugged, lonely lives of traders in the West.

READING CHECK **Finding Main Ideas** How did the style of American art change to reflect the American way of life in the early 1800s?

Religion and Music

Through the early and mid-1800s, several waves of religious revivalism swept the United States. During periods of revivalism, meetings were held for the purpose of reawakening religious faith. These meetings sometimes lasted for days and included large sing-alongs.

At many revival meetings people sang songs called spirituals. Spirituals are a type of folk hymn found in both white and African American folk-music traditions. This type of song developed from the practice of calling out text from the Bible. A leader would call out the text one line at a time, and the congregation would sing the words using a familiar tune. Each singer added his or her own style to the tune. The congregation of singers sang freely as inspiration led them.

While spirituals reflected the religious nature of some Americans, popular folk music of the period reflected the unique views of the growing nation in a different way. One of the most popular songs of the era was "Hunters of Kentucky," which celebrated the Battle of New Orleans. It became an anthem for the spirit of nationalism in the United States and was used successfully in Andrew Jackson's campaign for the presidency in 1828.

READING CHECK **Summarizing** How did music reflect American interests in the early and mid-1800s?

Architecture and Education

American creativity extended to the way in which people designed buildings. Before the American Revolution, most architects followed the style used in Great Britain. After the

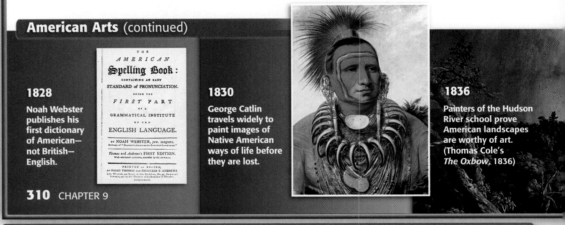

American Arts (continued)

1828 Noah Webster publishes his first dictionary of American—not British—English.

1830 George Catlin travels widely to paint images of Native American ways of life before they are lost.

1836 Painters of the Hudson River school prove American landscapes are worthy of art. (Thomas Cole's *The Oxbow*, 1836)

310 CHAPTER 9

Critical Thinking: Identifying Points of View | At Level

Landscape Art and Poetry

1. Write the words *wild grandeur* for students to see. Ask students what they think the phrase means. Define *grandeur* if needed.

2. Explain that nature poet William Bryant admired painter Thomas Cole's "scenes of wild grandeur peculiar to our country." Write the quote for students to see. Ask students, based on the quotation and the paintings in this section, what qualities Bryant and Cole admired in America (*ruggedness, wild spaces, untamed nature*).

3. Discuss with students how the American landscape has changed and how modern Americans view nature.

4. Have each student either write a poem or create a drawing or painting that conveys the student's feelings about American wilderness and nature.

5. Ask volunteers to present their works to the class. **LS** **Verbal/Linguistic, Visual/Spatial**

📖 Alternative Assessment Handbook: Rubrics 3: Artwork; and 41: Writing to Express

Revolution, leaders such as Thomas Jefferson called for Americans to model their architecture after the styles used in ancient Greece and Rome. Many Americans admired the ancient civilization of Greece and the Roman Republic because they contained some of the same democratic and republican ideals as the new American nation did.

As time went by, more architects followed Jefferson's ideas. Growing American cities soon had distinctive new buildings designed in the Greek and Roman styles. These buildings were usually made of marble or other stone and featured large, stately columns.

Americans also embraced educational progress. Several early American political leaders expressed a belief that democracy would only succeed in a country of educated and enlightened people. But there was no general agreement on who should provide that education.

Eventually, the idea of a state-funded public school gathered support. In 1837 Massachusetts lawmakers created a state board of education. Other states followed this example, and the number of public schools slowly grew.

READING CHECK Identifying Points of View
Why did some Americans call for new architectural styles and more education after the American Revolution?

ANALYSIS SKILL **ANALYZING INFORMATION**
How do these artistic developments show Americans' increasing sense of identity?

SUMMARY AND PREVIEW As the United States grew, so did a unique national identity. In Chapter 10 you will read about the changing face of American democracy.

Section 3 Assessment

go.hrw.com
Online Quiz
KEYWORD: SR8 HP9

Reviewing Ideas, Terms, and People
1. **a. Describe** What topics interested American writers in the early 1800s?
   b. Draw Conclusions Why is **Washington Irving** considered an important American writer?
2. **a. Identify** What influence did **Thomas Cole** have on American painters?
   b. Describe How did American painting styles change from the early period to the mid-1800s?
3. **a. Describe** What effect did religious revivalism have on American music?
   b. Elaborate Why do you think folk songs like "Hunters of Kentucky" were popular?
4. **a. Identify** On what historical examples did many American architects model their buildings?
   b. Predict What might be some possible results of the growing interest in education in the United States?

Critical Thinking
5. **Categorizing** Review your notes about new developments in American culture. Copy the graphic organizer below and use it to show how these cultural developments reflected a new American identity.

Cultural Development	⟶	New Identity
Cultural Development	⟶	New Identity
Cultural Development	⟶	New Identity
Cultural Development	⟶	New Identity
Cultural Development	⟶	New Identity

FOCUS ON WRITING

6. **Identifying Values** You can tell much about someone's values by what that person makes. For instance, you could guess that a person who creates a collage of personal mementos for a friend's birthday is creative and values personal relationships. As you read this section, make note of what the United States created and what it valued.

A NEW NATIONAL IDENTITY **311**

Section 3 Assessment Answers

1. **a.** American history, the frontier
   b. bridge between European traditions and the new American style
2. **a.** founder of the Hudson River school; encouraged artists to concentrate on the beauty of nature
   b. from portraits, to landscapes, to landscape with scenes from daily life
3. **a.** led to the development of the spiritual form
   b. celebrated national pride
4. **a.** to show the link between American democracy and the ideals of Greece and Rome
   b. more colleges, equal rights movements
5. literature—American characteristics/settings; visual arts—pride in American landscape; religious music—faith, national pride; architecture—imitated Greece/Rome; education—growth of public schools
6. possible answers—historical fiction, landscape art, spiritual and nationalist music, Roman and Greek architecture; valued self, religion, classical ideals

Literature in History

The Last of the Mohicans

As You Read As students read, have them take notes on descriptive words and phrases they find that might describe Natty Bumppo, such as *sunburnt and long-faded complexion.* Then have students draw a picture or write a summary of Bumppo's characteristics based on the words they listed. Discuss with students why Bumppo's image appealed to American readers of the period.

Meet the Writer

James Fenimore Cooper Cooper's action-packed stories illustrated two distinct ways of life. He portrayed Native American life as free and respectful of nature. On the other hand, many Europeans in his stories were rule-driven and disrespectful of the environment. Cooper's works also showed concern for individual freedoms and property rights.

Did You Know . . .

Cooper's *Leather-Stocking Tales* follow Natty Bumppo from a young man to old age. In the order of the hero's life, they are: *The Deerslayer* (1841), *The Last of the Mohicans* (1826), *The Pathfinder* (1840), *The Pioneers* (1823), and *The Prairie* (1827).

Answers

Guided Reading 1. *has at least one Native American friend; likes spending time in nature; is of European descent;* **2.** *green hunting shirt (he hunts); cap of skins (he traps); a knife, a rifle, and a pouch and horn (he is resourceful and can protect himself); a girdle of wampums and moccasins (he trades or interacts with Native Americans); buckskin leggings (he travels through rough terrain)*

Literature of the American Frontier

from *The Last of the Mohicans*
by James Fenimore Cooper (1789–1851)

About the Reading The Last of the Mohicans *is one of five novels known as the* Leatherstocking Tales. *These novels follow the life and adventures of American pioneer Natty Bumppo (also known as Leatherstocking, Hawkeye, and the Deerslayer). Bumppo is the perfect woodsman: resourceful, honest, kind to both his friends and his enemies, but always a loner at heart.*

AS YOU READ Try to imagine what Natty Bumppo looks like.

On that day, two men were lingering on the banks of a small but rapid stream . . . While one of these loiterers showed the red skin and wild accoutrements of a native of the woods, the other exhibited, through the mask of his rude and nearly savage equipments, the brighter though sunburnt and long-faded complexion of one who might claim descent from a European parentage. ❶

The frame of the white man, judging by such parts as were not concealed by his clothes, was like that of one who had known hardships and exertion from his earliest youth. His person, though muscular, was rather attenuated than full; but every nerve and muscle appeared strung and indurated by unremitted exposure and toil. He wore a hunting shirt of forest green, fringed with faded yellow, and a summer cap of skins which had been shorn of their fur. He also bore a knife in a girdle of wampum, ❷ like that which confined the scanty garments of the Indian, but no tomahawk. His moccasins were ornamented after the . . . fashion of the natives, while the only part of his underdress which appeared below the hunting frock was a pair of buckskin leggings that laced at the sides, and which were gartered above the knees with the sinews of a deer. A pouch and horn completed his personal accoutrements, though a rifle of great length, which the theory of the more ingenious whites had taught them was the most dangerous of all firearms, leaned against a neighboring sapling.

GUIDED READING

WORD HELP

accoutrements dress and gear
rude crude, rough
attenuated made thin
indurated hardened
unremitted ongoing
gartered fastened
ingenious clever

❶ **What do you learn about Natty Bumppo in the first paragraph?**

❷ A "girdle of wampum" is a belt strung with beads. Wampum were used by Native Americans for both money and decoration.

Make a list of the items Bumppo wears and carries. What does each item suggest about him?

Differentiating Instruction

Struggling Readers | Below Level

Group Interpretation Organize the class into small groups and assign each group one of the selections to interpret in the students' own words. One member of each group should record the group's descriptions and organize them into a coherent summary. Have a volunteer from each group read the summary aloud. Discuss the differences in each group's interpretation.
LS Interpersonal, Verbal/Linguistic

Advanced/ Gifted and Talented | At Level

Writing Historical Fiction Ask students to imagine that they are historical fiction writers like Cooper. Have students use a historical event in this chapter as the basis for a short story with fictional characters. Have students either briefly describe their story ideas or write their stories. Ask for volunteers to share their ideas or stories. Then discuss how historical fiction is a useful tool in studying history. **LS** Verbal/Linguistic

from *The Legend of Sleepy Hollow*

by Washington Irving (1783–1859)

About the Reading *"The Legend of Sleepy Hollow" has been called one of the first American short stories. Even though it is based on an old German folktale, its setting, a small village in the Hudson River valley, is American through and through. Irving's knack for capturing the look and the feel of the region made the story instantly popular—as did the tale's eerie central character, a horseman without a head.*

AS YOU READ Try to picture both the ghost and the setting.

The dominant spirit, however, that haunts this enchanted region, and seems to be commander in chief of all the powers of the air, is the apparition of a figure on horseback without a head. It is said by some to be the ghost of a Hessian trooper, ❶ whose head had been carried away by a cannon ball, in some nameless battle during the revolutionary war, and who is ever and anon seen by the country folk, hurrying along in the gloom of night, as if on the wings of the wind. His haunts are not confined to the valley, but extend at times to the adjacent roads, and especially to the vicinity of a church at no great distance. Indeed, certain of the most authentic historians of those parts, who have been careful in collecting and collating the floating facts concerning this spectre, allege, that the body of the trooper having been buried in the church yard, the ghost rides forth to the scene of battle in nightly quest of his head, ❷ and that the rushing speed with which he sometimes passes along the hollow, like a midnight blast, is owing to his being belated, and in a hurry to get back to the church yard before day break.

Such is the general purport of this legendary superstition, which has furnished materials for many a wild story in that region of shadows; and the spectre is known, at all the country firesides, by the name of The Headless Horseman of Sleepy Hollow. ❸

GUIDED READING

WORD HELP

dominant prevailing; ruling
apparition a ghostlike form that appears suddenly
collating comparing
spectre ghost
allege to firmly state
purport sense; gist

❶ A Hessian trooper is a German mercenary soldier from the American Revolution.

How and when is the horseman said to have died?

❷ *Why does the horseman ride forth each night?*

❸ *What is happening "at all the country firesides"? What does this suggest about how early Americans entertained themselves?*

CONNECTING LITERATURE TO HISTORY

1. **Drawing Inferences** The writing of the period reflects a new national culture and identity. What do these passages suggest about the thoughts, feelings, or lives of early Americans?

2. **Making Predictions** *The Last of the Mohicans* takes place during the French and Indian War. Whose side do you think Natty Bumppo would most likely take—that of the French and Indians, that of the English, or neither? Explain.

3. **Drawing Conclusions** Both of these stories were very popular in their time. Why do you think these stories were so popular? What is it about the stories that makes them entertaining?

A NEW NATIONAL IDENTITY **313**

Critical Thinking: Evaluating Information

At Level

Literary Biographical Posters

Research Required

1. Have students use the library or the Internet to conduct research on Cooper, Irving, or another writer covered in this chapter.

2. Students should write three to four questions about the selected author that they would like to answer through their research. Students should then use the questions to guide their research.

3. Have each student use the information to create a poster that shows an image of the writer, gives a short biographical description, and provides a listing of the writer's most well-known works. **LS Verbal/Linguistic**

📖 Alternative Assessment Handbook, Rubric 28: Posters; and 30: Research

Literature in History

The Legend of Sleepy Hollow

As You Read As students read, have them copy down words from the excerpt that set a spooky atmosphere, such as *spirit, haunts,* and *enchanted.* Inform students that legends and superstitions feed on common fears or traditional beliefs. Ask students for examples of superstitions they know. Then lead a discussion on why superstitions helped make *The Legend of Sleepy Hollow* so popular.

Meet the Writer

Washington Irving During his lifetime, Irving was also a lawyer, businessman, and a U.S. diplomat to England and Spain. His true passion was writing, however. He devoted himself entirely to writing in 1817. Unfavorable reviews of his *Tales of a Traveller* (1824) led him to give up writing fiction, though. He instead wrote histories and biographies until his death. His grave, fittingly, is in the Sleepy Hollow Cemetery and is now a national historic landmark.

Answers

Guided Reading 1. *A cannon ball knocked off his head during the Revolutionary War;* **2.** *to look for his head;* **3.** *People tell stories about the headless horseman; Early Americans shared stories around their fireplaces as a means of entertainment.*

Connecting Literature to History
1. *possible answer—*Mohicans *suggests that Americans viewed the frontier and those who lived there as wild and untamed.* Sleepy Hollow *suggests that Americans loved to hear and to tell imaginative stories with a basis in history;* **2.** *possible answer—French and Indian side, because he seems to have a strong relationship with the Native Americans;* **3.** *possible answers— popular because early Americans could see themselves in the stories, helped shape their national image; entertaining because stories showed the exciting and sometimes mysterious side of the New World*

313

Social Studies Skills

Identifying Central Issues

Activity Central Issues in the Community Write the following statement for students to see: *The school district's budget will be cut $300,000 next year.* Tell students this statement is hypothetical. Ask students to identify the most important questions and concerns that people might have in response to this news. Responses might include the following: What will the schools have to cut to lower their budgets—such as teachers, textbooks, art classes, and so on? Will classes be bigger? Will extracurricular activities be cut? Will free lunches be cut? After a brief period of discussion, ask students to identify what all these concerns have in common. Lead students to realize that the central issue involved is how will budget cuts affect educational quality and school life. To extend the activity, have students practice the skill on an article from their school or local newspaper. **LS** Logical/Mathematical

📝 Alternative Assessment Handbook, Rubric 11: Discussions

💿 Interactive Skills Tutor CD-ROM: Lesson 12: Identify Issues and Problems

Analysis	Critical Thinking	Civic Participation	Study

Identifying Central Issues

Define the Skill

The reasons for historical events are often complex and difficult to determine. An accurate understanding of them requires the ability to identify the central issues involved. A *central issue* is the main topic of concern in a discussion or dispute. In history, these issues are usually matters of public debate or concern. They generally involve political, social, moral, economic, or territorial matters.

Being able to identify central issues lets you go beyond what the participants in an event said and gain a more accurate understanding of it. The skill also useful for understanding issues today, and for the evaluating statements of those involved.

Learn the Skill

In this chapter you learned about dispute that arose over Missouri's admission to the Union. Yet that was not what this controversy was really about. Recognizing the central issue in this dispute helps you understand why each side fought so hard over just one state.

Use the following steps to identify central issues when you read about historical events.

① Identify the main subject of the information.

② Determine the nature and purpose of what you are reading. Is it a primary source or a secondary one? Why has the information been provided?

③ Find the strongest or most forceful phrases or statements in the material. These are often clues to the issues or ideas the speaker or writer thinks most central or important.

④ Determine how the information might be connected to the major events or controversies that were concerning the nation at the time.

Practice the Skill

Soon after the Missouri Compromise passed, Secretary of State John Quincy Adams wrote:

"The impression produced upon my mind by the progress of this discussion [the dispute over Missouri] is that the bargain between freedom and slavery contained in the Constitution …is morally and politically vicious, …cruel and oppressive.…I have favored this Missouri Compromise, believing it to be all that can be effected [accomplished] under the present Constitution, and from an extreme unwillingness to put the Union at hazard [risk]. But perhaps it would have been a …bolder course to have persisted in the restriction upon Missouri till it should have terminated [ended] in a convention of the states to …amend the Constitution. This would have produced a new Union of thirteen or fourteen states unpolluted with slavery.…If the Union must be dissolved, slavery is precisely the question upon which it ought to break. For the present, however, this contest [issue] is laid to sleep."

Apply the steps to identifying central issues to analyze Adams's statement and answer the following questions

1. About what subject was Adams writing? What was his reason for making these remarks?

2. What did Adams believe was the most important issue in the dispute? What strong language does he use to indicate this?

3. What evidence suggests Adams did not think the breakup of the Union the central issue?

Answers

Practice the Skill 1. *Missouri Compromise; to discuss why he supported the Missouri Compromise and to explain his views on the issues involved;* **2.** *the issue of slavery; "that the bargain between freedom and slavery contained in the Constitution . . . is morally and politically vicious, . . . cruel and oppressive. . . ." and "if the Union must be dissolved, slavery is precisely the question upon which it ought to break."* **3.** *his comment about what might have been a bolder course of action, which might have produced a new Union of fewer states in which slavery was banned*

Social Studies Skills Activity: Identifying Central Issues   At Level

Guided and Independent Practice

1. Have volunteers read aloud the Section 1 text titled "United States Gains Florida."

2. Have students work as a class to go through the four steps listed under "Learn the Skill" to identify the central issues in this text. (*In this text, the central issues were the disagreements between the United States and Spain over American settlement and actions in Florida.*)

3. Then assign students the text in Section 1 titled "Monroe Doctrine." Have students work

independently to identify the central foreign policy issue dealt with by the doctrine. Discuss the answer as a class. (*President Monroe wanted to prevent European nations from gaining control of newly independent Latin American countries, protect American interests, and avoid wars with Europe.*)

LS Verbal/Linguistic

📝 Alternative Assessment Handbook, Rubric 1: Acquiring Information

Chapter Review

Visual Summary

Use the visual summary below to help you review the main ideas of the chapter.

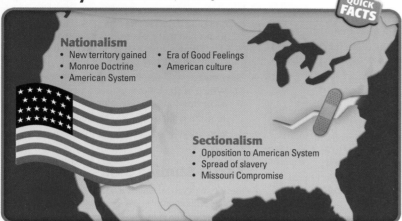

QUICK FACTS

Nationalism
- New territory gained
- Monroe Doctrine
- American System
- Era of Good Feelings
- American culture

Sectionalism
- Opposition to American System
- Spread of slavery
- Missouri Compromise

Reviewing Vocabulary, Terms, and People

Match the word in the left column with the correct definition in the right column.

1. American System
2. George Caleb Bingham
3. Simon Bolívar
4. Henry Clay
5. Erie Canal
6. Hudson River school
7. James Monroe
8. Monroe Doctrine
9. nationalism
10. Rush-Bagot Agreement

a. an agreement that limited naval power on the Great Lakes for both the United States and British Canada

b. American artist known for his focus on the American landscape and people

c. sense of pride and devotion to a nation

d. a group of American artists in the mid-1800s who focused on the American landscape

e. a leader of independence movements in Latin America, known as the Liberator

f. the plan to raise tariffs in order to finance internal improvements such as roads and canals

g. president who promoted the acquisition of Florida, closer ties to Latin America, and presided during the Era of Good Feelings

h. project that connected the Hudson River to Lake Erie and improved trade and transportation

i. representative from Kentucky who promoted improvements in transportation and the Missouri Compromise

j. U.S. declaration that any attempt by a foreign nation to establish colonies in the Americas would be viewed as a hostile act

---

Answers

Visual Summary

Review and Inquiry Have students use the Visual Summary to review the chapter's key terms and ideas. Be sure students understand the symbolism of both the flag and the bandage in the image.

🖳 Quick Facts Transparency: A New National Identity Visual Summary

Reviewing Vocabulary, Terms, and People

1. f
2. b
3. e
4. i
5. h
6. d
7. g
8. j
9. c
10. a

Review and Assessment Resources

Review and Reinforce

SE Chapter Review

🖳 **CRF:** Chapter Review Activity

🖳 Quick Facts Transparency: A New National Identity Visual Summary

🔊 Spanish Chapter Summaries Audio CD Program

🌐 Online Chapter Summaries in Six Languages

OSP Holt PuzzlePro; GameTool for ExamView

💿 Quiz Game CD-ROM

Assess

SE Standardized Test Practice

🖳 PASS: Chapter Test, Forms A and B

🖳 Alternative Assessment Handbook

OSP ExamView Test Generator, Chapter Test

💿 Differentiated Instruction Modified Worksheets and Tests CD-ROM: Chapter Test

🌐 Holt Online Assessment Program (in the Premier Online Edition)

Reteach/Intervene

🖳 Interactive Reader and Study Guide

🖳 Differentiated Instruction Teacher Management System: Lesson Plans for Differentiated Instruction

💿 Differentiated Instruction Modified Worksheets and Tests CD-ROM

💿 Interactive Skills Tutor CD-ROM

go.hrw.com
Online Resources

Chapter Resources:
KEYWORD: SR8 US9

Comprehension and Critical Thinking

11. a. (1) United States would not interfere in European affairs or wars; (2) United States would recognize existing colonies in Americas; (3) Americas were off limits to future colonization; (4) United States would treat interference in Latin American countries as a threat and respond accordingly.

b. agreed to Rush-Bagot Agreement, which limited naval power on the Great Lakes, set the boundary at the 49th parallel, and shared the fur trade in the Northwest

c. possible answer: Monroe Doctrine—established the United States as the main power in the Western Hemisphere

12. a. territories gained; roads and canals built

b. northern and southern members of Congress disagreed about whether to admit Missouri to the Union as a slave state; agreed to the Missouri Compromise, which brought in Missouri as a slave state and Maine as a free state.

c. possible answer—might have weakened national unity and faith in democracy

13. a. Spirituals reflected the emphasis on religion; folk music reflected an interest in American heroes.

b. American artists and writers wanted cultural independence and a separate identity from Europe.

c. possible answer: art—prefer landscapes to portraits

Reviewing Themes

14. Success made Americans proud of their country and its leadership.

15. desire to show the country's uniqueness, rising nationalism, and improvements in education

Using the Internet

16. Go to the HRW Web site and enter the keyword shown to access a rubric for this activity.

> KEYWORD: SR8 US9

Comprehension and Critical Thinking

SECTION 1 *(Pages 298–301)*

11. a. Identify What were the four main points of the Monroe Doctrine?

b. Draw Conclusions How did the United States compromise in its disputes with British Canada?

c. Evaluate Which of the issues that the United States faced with foreign nations do you think was most important? Why?

SECTION 2 *(Pages 302–305)*

12. a. Recall What developments helped strengthen national unity in this period?

b. Analyze How was the disagreement over Missouri's statehood an example of sectionalism? How was the disagreement resolved?

c. Predict What effect might the election of 1824 have on national unity? Why?

SECTION 3 *(Pages 308–311)*

13. a. Describe How did popular music show the interests of Americans in the early 1800s?

b. Make Inferences Why do you think new American styles of art and literature emerged?

c. Elaborate Which element of American culture of the early 1800s do you find most appealing? Why?

Reviewing Themes

14. Politics How did the relations of the United States with foreign nations lead to a rise in nationalism?

15. Society and Culture What led to the creation of a uniquely American culture?

Using the Internet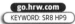

16. Activity: Researching In this chapter, you learned about the development of a new, creative spirit in American arts. Artists created works that featured American scenes and characters. Enter the activity keyword and research the development of American culture in art and literature. Then create a visual display.

Reading Skills

Bias and Historical Events *Use the Reading Skills taught in this chapter to answer the question about the reading selection below.*

> When the House chose John Quincy Adams as president, Jackson's supporters claimed that Adams had made a corrupt bargain with Henry Clay. These accusations grew after Adams chose Clay to be secretary of state. *(p. 305)*

17. Which of the following used a biased definition, according to the above selection?

a. Andrew Jackson   **c.** Henry Clay

b. supporters of Jackson   **d.** John Quincy Adams

Social Studies Skills

Identifying Central Issues *Use the Social Studies Skills taught in this chapter to answer the question about the reading selection below.*

> [Henry Clay] developed a plan that came to be known as the American System—a series of measures intended to make the United States economically self-sufficient. To build the economy, he pushed for a national bank that would provide a single currency, making interstate trade easier. Clay wanted the money from a protective tariff to be used to improve roads and canals. *(p. 302)*

18. Which of the following is the central issue addressed by the American System?

a. economic unity

b. protective tariff

c. national bank

d. improving roads and canals

FOCUS ON WRITING

19. Writing a Character Sketch Write a paragraph describing your overall impression of the nation's character. Write one sentence describing each of these aspects of the United States: its relationships with others, its feelings about itself, and its values.

Reading Skills

17. b

Social Studies Skills

18. a

Focus on Writing

19. Rubric Students' character sketches should:
- start with an overall impression of the nation.
- describe the nation's relationships with others, feelings about itself, and values.
- use proper grammar, punctuation, spelling, and capitalization.

CRF: Focus on Writing Activity: A Character Sketch

Standardized Test Practice

DIRECTIONS: Read each question and write the letter of the best response.

1 Use the map below to answer the following question.

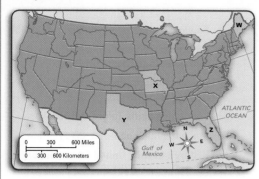

The present-day state that became part of the United States in the Adams-Onís Treaty of 1819 is shown on the map by the letter

A W.

B X.

C Y.

D Z.

2 The principle that European nations could establish no more colonies in North and South America was set forth in the

A Missouri Compromise.

B Rush-Bagot Agreement.

C Monroe Doctrine.

D Convention of 1818.

3 The Missouri Compromise had a significant effect on the United States because it

A established the present border with Canada.

B prohibited slavery north of Missouri's southern border.

C led to the expansion of roads and canals.

D settled conflicts between Native Americans in the West and the federal government.

4 Greek- and Roman-style architecture became common in the United States in the early 1800s because of

A the popularity of President George Washington, who liked the building style.

B Americans' admiration for the ideals of Greek democracy and republicanism.

C the nation's desire to build as strong a military as the Greeks and Romans had.

D Americans' great feeling of nationalism after the War of 1812.

5 Which painting would have been typical of an artist of the Hudson River school in the 1830s and 1840s?

A a portrait of a famous American

B a Native American hunting game

C a portrait of an ancient Greek or Roman lawmaker

D a scene showing America's natural beauty

6 Examine the following passage from a letter about American education and then use it to answer the question below.

> "A lady asked me one day, 'What state is Virginia in?' Another asked, 'Is Canada in Kentucky?' Another supposed that 'Joe Graphy [geography] was very hard to learn.' Such is the cause of all our mistakes in religion, morals, and politics. When we are educated we can cast off prejudice and superstition. Education improves our judgments and restrains our passions. In short, it enables us to discover what is best for our welfare."
>
> — Anne Newport Royall, adapted from *Letters from Alabama, 1817-1822*

Why might Royall and others try to make education available to more Americans? Explain.

Answers

1. D

Break Down the Question Students need to recall information and recognize Florida on a map. Refer students who miss the question to the material "United States Gains Florida" and the map "U.S. Boundary Changes, 1818–1819" in Section 1.

2. C

Break Down the Question This question requires students to recall factual information. Students should use a process of elimination to answer the question. Refer students who miss the question to the material "Monroe Doctrine" in Section 1.

3. B

Break Down the Question This question requires students to recall cause and effect. Refer students who miss the question to the material "Missouri Compromise" in Section 2.

4. B

Break Down the Question Although A, C, and D may *seem* correct to students who do not recall the material completely, these distracters are incorrect. Refer students who miss the question to the material "Architecture and Education" in Section 3.

5. D

Break Down the Question This question requires students to recall factual information. Refer students who miss the question to the material "A New Style of Art" in Section 3.

6. possible answer—Education keeps us from making religious, moral, and political mistakes. Education helps the country.

Intervention Resources

Reproducible

- Interactive Reader and Study Guide
- Differentiated Instruction Teacher Management System: Lesson Plans for Differentiated Instruction

Technology

- Quick Facts Transparency: A New National Identity Visual Summary
- Differentiated Instruction Modified Worksheets and Tests CD-ROM
- Interactive Skills Tutor CD-ROM

Tips for Test Taking

How Much Do I Write? If an open-ended question contains one of the following terms, then students will probably need to write several sentences to provide a complete answer.

- defend
- describe
- explain
- justify
- why
- write

Remind students that they can also provide drawings or sketches to enhance what they write.

Chapter 10 Planning Guide

The Age of Jackson

Chapter Overview	Reproducible Resources	Technology Resources
CHAPTER 10 pp. 318–341 **Overview:** In this chapter, students will study the presidency of Andrew Jackson, the increased conflict between the northern and southern states that marked his administration, and Jackson's policies toward Native Americans.	**Differentiated Instruction Teacher Management System:*** • Instructional Benchmarking Guides • Lesson Plans for Differentiated Instruction **Interactive Reader and Study Guide:** Chapter Graphic Organizer* **Chapter Resource File:*** • Focus on Writing Activity: An Interview • Social Studies Skills Activity: Solving Problems • Chapter Review Activity **A Teacher's Guide to Religion in the Public Schools***	Power Presentations with Video CD-ROM Differentiated Instruction Modified Worksheets and Tests CD-ROM Primary Source Library CD-ROM for United States History Interactive Skills Tutor CD-ROM Student Edition on Audio CD Program History's Impact: United States History Video Program (VHS/DVD): The Age of Jackson*
Section 1: **Jacksonian Democracy** **The Big Idea:** The expansion of voting rights and the election of Andrew Jackson signaled the growing power of the American people.	**Differentiated Instruction Teacher Management System:** Section 1 Lesson Plan* **Interactive Reader and Study Guide:** Section 1 Summary* **Chapter Resource File:*** • Vocabulary Builder Activity, Section 1	Daily Bellringer Transparency: Section 1*
Section 2: **Jackson's Administration** **The Big Idea:** Andrew Jackson's presidency was marked by political conflicts.	**Differentiated Instruction Teacher Management System:** Section 2 Lesson Plan* **Interactive Reader and Study Guide:** Section 2 Summary* **Chapter Resource File:*** • Vocabulary Builder Activity, Section 2 • Biography Activity: John C. Calhoun • Biography Activity: Daniel Webster • Primary Source Activity: President Jackson's Proclamation Regarding Nullification • Primary Source Activity: The Bank War of 1832—Two Views • Economics and History Activity: The Panic of 1837 **Political Cartoons Activities for United States History,** Cartoon 11: Jackson and the Bank* **U.S. Supreme Court Case Studies:** *McCulloch* v. *Maryland**	Daily Bellringer Transparency: Section 2* Quick Facts Transparency: Regions of the United States, Early 1800s* Internet Activity: Calhoun and Webster Debate Nullification
Section 3: **Indian Removal** **The Big Idea:** President Jackson supported a policy of Indian removal.	**Differentiated Instruction Teacher Management System:** Section 3 Lesson Plan* **Interactive Reader and Study Guide:** Section 3 Summary* **Chapter Resource File:*** • Vocabulary Builder Activity, Section 3 • Biography Activities: Sequoya; Black Hawk • History and Geography Activity: The Seminole Wars • Literature Activity: *Surrender Speech* by Chief Black Hawk **U.S. Supreme Court Case Studies:** *Worchester* v. *Georgia* (1832)*	Daily Bellringer Transparency: Section 3* Map Transparency: Second Seminole War* Internet Activity: Indian Removal

CHAPTER 10 PLANNING GUIDE

Legend

SE Student Edition
TE Teacher's Edition
go.hrw.com go.hrw.com
OSP One-Stop Planner CD-ROM
Print Resource
Transparency
Learning Styles
Audio CD
CD-ROM
Video

* also on One-Stop Planner CD

Review, Assessment, Intervention

- **Quick Facts Transparency:** The Age of Jackson Visual Summary*
- **Spanish Chapter Summaries Audio CD Program**
- **Progress Assessment Support System (PASS):** Chapter Test*
- **Differentiated Instruction Modified Worksheets and Tests CD-ROM:** Modified Chapter Test
- **One-Stop Planner CD-ROM:** ExamView Test Generator (English/Spanish)
- **Holt Online Assessment Program (HOAP),** in the Holt Premier Online Student Edition

- **PASS:** Section 1 Quiz*
- **Online Quiz:** Section 1
- **Alternative Assessment Handbook**

- **PASS:** Section 2 Quiz*
- **Online Quiz:** Section 2
- **Alternative Assessment Handbook**

- **PASS:** Section 3 Quiz*
- **Online Quiz:** Section 3
- **Alternative Assessment Handbook**

HOLT
History's Impact
United States History Video Program (VHS/DVD)
The Age of Jackson
Suggested use: as a chapter introduction

Power Presentations with Video CD-ROM

Power Presentations with Video are visual presentations of each chapter's main ideas. Presentations can be customized by including Quick Facts charts, images from the text, and video clips.

Power Presentations with Video CD-ROM
HOLT
United States History
Beginnings to 1877
HOLT, RINEHART and WINSTON
A Harcourt Education Company

DIVISION FOR
PUBLIC EDUCATION
AMERICAN BAR ASSOCIATION

Developed by the Division for Public Education of the American Bar Association, these materials are part of the **Democracy and Civic Education Resources.**

- **Constitution Study Guide**
- **Supreme Court Case Studies**

Holt Online Learning

Teacher Resources
KEYWORD: SR8 TEACHER

Student Resources
KEYWORD: SR8 US10

- Document-Based Questions
- Interactive Multimedia Activities

- Current Events
- Chapter-based Internet Activities
- and more!

Holt Premier
Online Student Edition
Complete online support for interactivity, assessment, and reporting

- Interactive Maps and Notebook
- Standardized Test Prep
- Homework Practice and Research Activities Online

Differentiating Instruction

ENGLISH-LANGUAGE LEARNERS & STRUGGLING READERS

TARGET RESOURCE

Live Ink® Online Reading Help

Spanish Resources

Spanish Chapter Summaries Audio CD Program

One-Stop Planner CD-ROM:
- ExamView Test Generator, Spanish
- PuzzlePro, Spanish

Additional Resources

Differentiated Instruction Teacher Management System: Lesson Plans for Differentiated Instruction

Chapter Resources:
- Vocabulary Builder Activities
- Social Studies Skills Activity: Solving Problems

Quick Facts Transparencies:
- Regions of the United States, Early 1800s
- The Age of Jackson Visual Summary

Student Edition on Audio CD Program

Online Chapter Summaries in Six Languages

Interactive Skills Tutor CD-ROM

SPECIAL NEEDS LEARNERS

TARGET RESOURCE

Differentiated Instruction Modified Worksheets and Tests CD-ROM

- Vocabulary Flash Cards
- Modified Vocabulary Builder Activities
- Modified Chapter Review Activity
- Modified Chapter Test

Additional Resources

Differentiated Instruction Teacher Management System: Lesson Plans for Differentiated Instruction

Interactive Reader and Study Guide

Social Studies Skills Activity: Solving Problems

Student Edition on Audio CD Program

Interactive Skills Tutor CD-ROM

Live Ink® Online Reading Help

ADVANCED/GIFTED AND TALENTED STUDENTS

TARGET RESOURCE

Primary Source Library CD-ROM for United States History

The Library contains longer versions of quotations in the text, extra sources, and images. Included are point-of-view articles, journals, diaries, historical fiction, and political documents.

Additional Resources

Political Cartoons Activities for United States History: Cartoon 11: Jackson and the Bank

United States History Document-Based Questions Activities

Differentiated Instruction Teacher Management System: Lesson Plans for Differentiated Instruction

Chapter Resource File:
- Focus on Writing Activity: An Interview
- Literature Activity: *Surrender Speech* by Chief Black Hawk
- Primary Source Activity: President Jackson's Proclamation Regarding Nullification
- Primary Source Activity: The Bank War of 1832—Two Views

Differentiated Activities in the Teacher's Edition
- Regions of the United States Map, p. 327

Differentiated Activities in the Teacher's Edition
- Indian Removal Memorial, p. 334

Differentiated Activities in the Teacher's Edition
- Election of 1828 Political Advertisements, p. 323
- Book outline of Jackson's bank policies, p. 329
- Speech Opposing Indian Removal Act, p. 333

One-Stop Planner® CD-ROM
for Differentiated Instruction

Your differentiated instruction lesson plans are available at your fingertips. Holt's Teacher Management System links teaching support tools to pages in the Interactive Teacher's Edition.

The One-Stop Planner features:
- Interactive Teacher's Edition
- Calendar Planner and pacing guides
- Editable lesson plans
- All reproducible ancillaries in Adobe Acrobat (PDF) format
- ExamView Test Generator (English and Spanish)
- Transparency and video previews

Professional Development

HOLT Professional Development

- **In-service and staff development** as part of your Holt Social Studies product purchase
- **Quick Teacher Tutorial Lesson Presentation CD-ROM**
- Intensive tuition-based **Teacher Development Institute**
- **Teaching American History Online**—2 Module Professional Development Course
- **Convenient Holt Speaker Bureau**—face-to-face workshop options
- **PRAXIS™ Test Prep** interactive Web-based content refreshers*
- **24/7 Ask A Professional Development Expert** at http://www.hrw.com/prodev/

* PRAXIS is a trademark of Educational Testing Service (ETS). This publication is not endorsed or approved by ETS.

Chapter Big Ideas

Section 1 The expansion of voting rights and the election of Andrew Jackson signaled the growing power of the American people.

Section 2 Andrew Jackson's presidency was marked by political conflicts.

Section 3 President Jackson supported a policy of Indian removal.

Focus on Writing

The **Chapter Resource File** provides a Focus on Writing worksheet to help students organize and write their interviews.

CRF: Focus on Writing Activity: An Interview

CHAPTER **10** 1828–1840

The Age of Jackson

FOCUS ON WRITING

An Interview You are a reporter for a large city newspaper in the year 1837. Andrew Jackson has just left office, and you have been given the assignment of interviewing him about his presidency and his role in American politics. As you read this chapter, you will write interview questions for your interview with Jackson.

1828
UNITED STATES Andrew Jackson is elected president.
Sequoya finishes a written language for the Cherokee.

183

1829
WORLD Louis Braille publishes a reading system for the blind.

Key to Differentiating Instruction

Below Level

Basic-level activities designed for all students encountering new material

At Level

Intermediate-level activities designed for average students

Above Level

Challenging activities designed for honors and gifted and talented students

Standard English Mastery

Activities designed to improve standard English usage

Introduce the Chapter

At Level

A Controversial Character

1. Tell students that they are going to learn about the presidency of Andrew Jackson, a strong man who often found himself in disagreements with others on national issues.

2. Ask students to scan the chapter and examine the section titles, major headings, photographs, maps, and charts. Have students identify some of the controversial actions taken by Jackson. Make a list of students' responses for the class to see.

3. Explain to students that previewing a text can help them familiarize themselves with what they are about to read and make it easier to learn. Have students copy the list of topics they suggested and then jot down anything they learned about them based on their preview of the chapter. Next, have students write any questions they have about the text.

4. Tell students to add information to their lists and to answer their questions as they read the chapter. **LS Verbal/Linguistic, Visual/Spatial**

HOLT
History's Impact
▶ **video series**
See the Video Teacher's Guide for strategies for using the chapter video **The Age of Jackson**.

Explore the Picture

Statue of Andrew Jackson The statue of Andrew Jackson pictured at left stands in the center of Lafayette Park in Washington, D.C. The statue honors Jackson's leadership in the Battle of New Orleans during the War of 1812. Cast by sculptor Clark Mills, the statue was made from a bronze cannon captured during Jackson's last campaign against the Spanish in Florida. As the first equestrian statue in the United States, it is remarkable for its perfect balance, with the center of gravity based in the horse's hind feet.

Analyzing Visuals What details in the statue symbolize Jackson's drive and spirit? *possible answers—the way in which he is tipping his hat in salute; his upright mount on the rearing horse, which suggests strength and determination*

go.hrw.com
Online Resources
Chapter Resources:
KEYWORD: SR8 US10
Teacher Resources:
KEYWORD: SR8 TEACHER

What You Will Learn...

In this chapter you will learn about how President Andrew Jackson helped shape the United States. He was so influential that historians refer to his presidency as the Age of Jackson. This statue of Jackson has stood in Washington, D.C., for more than 150 years and captures the drive and spirit of the seventh president of the United States.

1832
Andrew Jackson vetoes the charter renewal of the national Bank of the United States.

1836
Martin Van Buren is elected president.

1838
The Trail of Tears begins when U.S. troops remove the Cherokee from Georgia.

1835

1832 A British reform bill doubles the number of British men who can vote.

1833
Slavery is abolished in the British Empire.

1838
Dutch colonists known as Boers clash with the Zulu in southern Africa.

1839
The Opium War breaks out between Great Britain and China.

THE AGE OF JACKSON **319**

Explore the Time Line

1. In what year was Andrew Jackson elected president? *1828*

2. What did Andrew Jackson veto in 1832? *charter of the Bank of the United States*

3. What is the Trail of Tears, and when did it begin? *U.S. troops' removal of Cherokee from Georgia, which began in 1838*

4. What major contribution did Sequoya make, and when? *developed a written language for the Cherokee in 1828*

Info to Know

Jackson's Veto Power Andrew Jackson referred to the Second Bank of the United States as the "monster bank" and viewed it as a pawn of the rich and powerful in the eastern states. Jackson's 1832 veto of the charter of the Bank was only one among many vetoes he made in his quest to be a president for the poor rather than the rich.

Reading
Social Studies

Understanding Themes

Introduce the main themes from this chapter—economics and politics—by asking students to explain how politics and economics might be intertwined. Help students to see that political decisions are sometimes based on economic factors. For example Northerners felt that tariffs would benefit manufacturing, therefore the federal government passed the so-called Tariff of Abominations. Ask students to think of situations in which political decisions might have an effect on economic conditions.

Drawing Conclusions about the Past

Focus on Reading Have students practice the skill of drawing conclusions. Ask students to bring in a newspaper or magazine article on a subject of interest to them. Then have each student read his or her article and select one or two paragraphs over which to make inferences. Have students write down several facts from their articles. Then have students write down two or three inferences based on those facts. Lastly, have students draw sound conclusions from their facts and inferences. Ask students to exchange papers and analyze their partner's conclusions.

Reading Social Studies

by Kylene Beers

Economics	Geography	Politics	Society and Culture	Science and Technology

Focus on Themes In this chapter you will read about the events that shaped the United States from 1828–1838. You will see how **political** and **economic** decisions were intertwined. For instance, you will read about the tensions between southern and northern states over tariff regulations. You will also read about the forced relocation of many Native Americans to the West. Understanding how economic issues led to political decisions will help you understand this time.

Drawing Conclusions about the Past

Focus on Reading Writers don't always tell you everything you need to know about a subject. Sometimes you need to think critically about what they have said and see what it all adds up to.

Drawing Conclusions Earlier in this book you learned how to make inferences. Sometimes when you read, you will need to make several inferences and put them together. The result is a **conclusion**, an informed judgment that you make by combining information.

Election of 1828

The 1828 campaign focused a great deal on the candidates' personalities. Jackson's campaigners described him as a war hero who had been born poor and rose to success through his own hard work.

Adams was a Harvard graduate whose father had been the second U.S. president. Jackson's supporters described Adams as being out of touch with everyday people . . . When the ballots were counted, Jackson had defeated Adams, winning a record number of popular votes. *(pp. 323–324)*

Inference: Jackson shared many qualities with American voters.

+

Inference: Adams enjoyed many privileges that most Americans did not.

+

Inference: Jackson easily won the election by a huge majority.

Conclusion: In 1828, Americans chose a president to whom they could relate.

320 CHAPTER 10

Reading and Skills Resources

Reading Support

- Interactive Reader and Study Guide
- Student Edition on Audio CD Program
- Spanish Chapter Summaries Audio CD Program

Social Studies Skills Support

- Interactive Skills Tutor CD-ROM

Vocabulary Support

- **CRF:** Vocabulary Builder Activities
- **CRF:** Chapter Review Activity
- Differentiated Instruction Modified Worksheets and Tests CD-ROM:
  - Vocabulary Flash Cards
  - Vocabulary Builder Activity
  - Chapter Review Activity

OSP Holt PuzzlePro

You Try It!

The following passage is from the chapter you are getting ready to read. As you read the passage, look for the facts of the situation.

The Election of 1834

In 1834 a new political party formed to oppose Jackson. Its members called themselves Whigs, after an English political party that opposed the monarchy to make the point that Jackson was using his power like a king. The Whig Party favored the idea of a weak president and a strong Congress. Unable to agree on a presidential candidate, the Whigs nominated four men to run against Vice President Martin Van Buren. With strong backing from Jackson, Van Buren won the election.

From Chapter 10, p. 330

After you read the passage, answer the following questions.

1. From this passage, what can you infer about President Jackson's popularity with the Whig Party?

2. The Whigs could not choose a single presidential candidate, so they nominated four men. Based on what you know about elections from your studies and your past experiences, how do you think this affected the votes each man received?

3. Jackson's backing helped Van Buren win the presidency. From this, what can you infer about Jackson's popularity with the American people as a whole?

4. Using the inferences you made answering questions 1 through 3, draw a conclusion about why Van Buren won the election of 1834.

> **As you read Chapter 10,** use your personal background knowledge and experience to draw conclusions about what you are reading.

Key Terms and People

Academic Vocabulary

Success in school is related to knowing academic vocabulary—the words that are frequently used in school assignments and discussions. In this chapter, you will learn the following academic words:

criteria *(p. 328)*
contemporary *(p. 333)*

Reading Social Studies

Key Terms and People

Preteach the key terms and people from this chapter to the class. Then have each student write a sentence for each key term. Remind students to use each term correctly. Have students rewrite their sentences, leaving blanks where the key term or person belongs. Have students exchange papers with a partner and complete the fill-in-the-blank activity.
LS Verbal/Linguistic

Focus on Reading

See the **Focus on Reading** questions in this chapter for more practice on this reading social studies skill.

Reading Social Studies Assessment

See the **Chapter Review** at the end of this chapter for student assessment questions related to this reading skill.

Teaching Tip

Remind students that there will be times when they have to draw conclusions to fill in small gaps in the text. Tell students to look carefully at the labels of questions in the textbook. When they see a label that reads *Draw Conclusions*, students should use facts from the text and their own knowledge of similar situations to draw a logical conclusion. Help students practice this skill by asking them questions that require them to draw on their own knowledge.

Answers

You Try It! 1. *Jackson was very unpopular with the Whigs because they felt he had too much power.* **2.** *It lowered the number of votes each man received.* **3.** *Jackson remained very popular and the people supported the candidate that he endorsed.* **4.** *Van Buren won the election of 1834 because the Whig Party disliked Jackson, they had too many candidates in the election, and the people supported Jackson's choice for president.*

Bellringer

If YOU were there . . . Use the **Daily Bellringer Transparency** to help students answer the question.

🖨 Daily Bellringer Transparency, Section 1

Building Vocabulary

Preteach or review the following terms:

cabinet presidential advisors (p. 324)

inauguration a formal ceremony to place someone in office (p. 324)

spoils as used here, valued goods (p. 324)

📝 CRF: Vocabulary Builder Activity, Section 1

Taking Notes

Have students copy the graphic organizer onto their own paper and then use it to take notes on the section. This activity will prepare students for the Section Assessment, in which they will complete a graphic organizer that builds on the information using a critical thinking skill.

Jacksonian Democracy

What You Will Learn...

Main Ideas

1. Democracy expanded in the 1820s as more Americans held the right to vote.
2. Jackson's victory in the election of 1828 marked a change in American politics.

The Big Idea

The expansion of voting rights and the election of Andrew Jackson signaled the growing power of the American people.

Key Terms and People

nominating conventions, *p. 323*
Jacksonian Democracy, *p. 323*
Democratic Party, *p. 323*
John C. Calhoun, *p. 323*
spoils system, *p. 324*
Martin Van Buren, *p. 324*
Kitchen Cabinet, *p. 324*

TAKING NOTES As you read, take notes on how an expansion of voting rights led to Andrew Jackson's election to the presidency. Write your notes in a flowchart like the one below.

If YOU were there...

It's 1829, and you live in Washington, D.C. You've come with a friend to the party for Andrew Jackson's inauguration as president. Your friend admires Jackson as a man of the people. You are less sure about his ability. Jackson's inauguration soon turns into a rowdy party, as mobs crowd into the White House. They break glasses and overturn the furniture.

How would you feel about having Jackson as your president?

BUILDING BACKGROUND In the early years of the United States, the right to vote belonged mainly to a few—free white men who owned property. As the country grew, more men were given the right to vote. This expansion of democracy led to the election of Andrew Jackson, a war hero. But not everyone approved of Jackson.

Expansion of Democracy

America in the early 1800s was changing fast. In the North, workshops run by the craftspeople who owned them were being replaced by large-scale factories owned by businesspeople and staffed by hired workers. In the South, small family farms began to give way to large cotton plantations, owned by wealthy white people and worked by enslaved African Americans. Wealth seemed to be concentrating into fewer hands. Many ordinary Americans felt left behind.

These same people also began to believe they were losing power in their government. In the late 1700s some Americans thought that government was best managed by a small group of wealthy, property-owning men. Government policies seemed targeted to help build the power of these people. The result was a growing belief that the wealthy were tightening their grip on power in the United States.

Hoping for change, small farmers, frontier settlers, and slaveholders rallied behind reform-minded Andrew Jackson, the popular hero of the War of 1812 and presidential candidate in the 1824 election. They believed Jackson would defend the rights of the common

---

Teach the Big Idea

Jacksonian Democracy

1. **Teach** Ask students the questions in the Main Idea boxes to teach this section.

2. **Apply** Pair students and have each pair use the term *Jacksonian Democracy* to create an acrostic. For each letter in *Jacksonian Democracy*, students should find a key term, figure, event, or issue from the section that includes that letter. Students should then write the terms horizontally so that the letters in *Jacksonian Democracy* align vertically.
   LS Interpersonal, Verbal/Linguistic

3. **Review** To review the section, have students share terms from their acrostics.

4. **Practice/Homework** Have students imagine they have just attended a Jackson inauguration party. Have each student write a journal entry about the election, the party, and the expansion of democracy.
   LS Intrapersonal, Verbal/Linguistic
   📝 Alternative Assessment Handbook, Rubric 15: Journals

Democracy in Action

Democracy spread in the early 1800s as more people became active in politics. Many of these people lived in the new western states. In these mostly rural areas, a political rally could be as simple as neighboring farmers meeting to talk about the issues of the day, as the farmers in the painting on the right are doing.

During the early 1800s democracy and demonstrations blossomed in the United States. The demonstrators of today owe much to the Americans of Andrew Jackson's time. Today, political rallies are a familiar sight in communities all over the country.

ANALYSIS SKILL ANALYZING INFORMATION

How are the people in both pictures practicing democracy?

---

people and the slave states. And they had been bitterly disappointed in the way Jackson had lost the 1824 election because of the decision in the House of Representatives.

During the time of Jackson's popularity, a number of democratic reforms were made. Many states changed their qualifications for voters. They lowered or even eliminated the requirement that men own a certain amount of property in order to vote or hold office. Political parties began holding public **nominating conventions**, where party members choose the party's candidates. Previously, candidates were selected by party leaders. This period of expanding democracy in the 1820s and 1830s later became known as **Jacksonian democracy**.

READING CHECK Finding Main Ideas
How did voting rights change in the early 1800s?

Election of 1828

Jackson supporters were determined that their candidate would win the 1828 election. The **Democratic Party** arose from these supporters of Jackson. Many people who backed President Adams began calling themselves National Republicans.

The 1828 presidential contest was a rematch of the 1824 election. Once again, John Quincy Adams faced Andrew Jackson. Jackson chose **John C. Calhoun** as his vice presidential running mate.

The Campaign

The 1828 campaign focused a great deal on the candidates' personalities. Jackson's campaigners described him as a war hero who had been born poor and rose to success through his own hard work.

THE IMPACT TODAY

Just as they did in the 1820s, presidential campaigns today frequently focus on personal image—strong versus weak or government-insider versus newcomer, for example.

THE AGE OF JACKSON **323**

323

❷ Election of 1828

Jackson's victory in the election of 1828 marked a change in American politics.

Identify Who were the candidates in the election of 1828, and what party did each represent? *John Quincy Adams, National Republican party; Andrew Jackson, Democratic Party*

Draw Conclusions Why did Jackson's supporters view his victory as a win for the common people? *because most of his supporters were farmers and settlers, as opposed to members of the eastern elite*

Make Judgments What is your opinion of the spoils system? *possible answers: approve—an appropriate reward for hard work; disapprove—could lead to corruption*

● Review & Assess ●

Close

Have students summarize Jacksonian Democracy.

Review

📕 Online Quiz, Section 1

Assess

SE Section 1 Assessment

📝 PASS: Section 1 Quiz

📝 Alternative Assessment Handbook

Reteach/Classroom Intervention

📝 Interactive Reader and Study Guide, Section 1

🔘 Interactive Skills Tutor CD-ROM

Answers

Analyzing Primary Sources
as "a rabble, a mob"

Reading Check *People who were not rewarded might cause discord.*

LETTER

People's President

Washington resident Margaret Bayard Smith was surprised by the chaos surrounding Jackson's inauguration.

❝What a scene did we witness! . . . a rabble, a mob, of boys, . . . women, children, scrambling, fighting, romping . . . Cut glass and china to the amount of several thousand dollars had been broken. . . . But it was the people's day, and the people's President, and the people would rule.❞

—Margaret Bayard Smith, quoted in *Eyewitness to America*, edited by David Colbert

ANALYSIS SKILL **ANALYZING PRIMARY SOURCES**

How does the author view the people that support Jackson?

Adams was a Harvard graduate whose father had been the second U.S. president. Jackson's supporters described Adams as being out of touch with everyday people. Even a fan of Adams agreed that he was "as cold as a lump of ice." In turn, Adams's supporters said Jackson was hot tempered, crude, and ill-equipped to be president of the United States. When the ballots were counted, Jackson had defeated Adams, winning a record number of popular votes.

Jackson's Inauguration

Jackson's supporters saw his victory as a win for the common people. A crowd cheered outside the Capitol as he took his oath of office. The massive crowd followed Jackson to a huge party on the White House lawn. The few police officers on hand had difficulty controlling the partygoers.

As president, Jackson rewarded some of his supporters with government jobs. This **spoils system**—the practice of giving government jobs to political backers—comes from the saying "to the victor belong the spoils [valued goods] of the enemy."

Secretary of State **Martin Van Buren** was one of Jackson's strongest allies in his official cabinet. President Jackson also relied a great deal on his **Kitchen Cabinet**, an informal group of trusted advisers who sometimes met in the White House kitchen.

READING CHECK **Analyzing** How might the spoils system cause disputes?

SUMMARY AND PREVIEW The expansion of democracy swept Andrew Jackson into office. In the next section you will read about the increasing regional tensions that occurred during Jackson's presidency.

Section 1 Assessment

go.hrw.com
Online Quiz
KEYWORD: SR8 HP10

Reviewing Ideas, Terms, and People

1. **a. Recall** What changes did the new western states make that allowed more people to vote?
   b. Draw Conclusions How did **nominating conventions** allow the people more say in politics?
   c. Predict How might changes to the voting process brought about by **Jacksonian Democracy** affect politics in the future?
2. **a. Recall** What two new political parties faced off in the election of 1828? Which candidate did each party support?
   b. Make Inferences Why did **Andrew Jackson** have more popular support than did Adams?
   c. Evaluate Do you think the spoils system was an acceptable practice? Explain your answer.

Critical Thinking

3. **Identifying Effect** Review your notes on the election of Andrew Jackson to the presidency. Then use a cause-and-effect chart like this one to show the ways in which Jacksonian Democracy increased Americans' political power.

| Jacksonian Democracy | → | increased Americans' political power | → | |

FOCUS ON WRITING

4. **Noting Significance** As you read this section, note things that made Jackson's political campaign and election significant in the history of American politics.

Section 1 Assessment Answers

1. **a.** loosened voting requirements to let more white men vote; gave the people the right to nominate their electors
   b. by giving people more of a say in deciding a political party's candidates
   c. possible answer—expansion in voting might lead to elected officials who represent a broader range of the common people's views
2. **a.** Democrats—Andrew Jackson; National Republicans—John Quincy Adams
   b. Jackson was a popular war hero and seen as a self-made man; Adams was seen as elite

and out of touch with everyday people.
   c. possible answers—yes, just reward for hard work; no, could lead to corruption
3. Students' charts might include the following: expansion of voting rights; involvement of people in nominating conventions; formation of Democratic Party
4. Students should note how the expansion of voting rights and political involvement and the election of Jackson signaled the growing political power of the American people.

Andrew Jackson

If you were president, how would you use your powers?

When did he live? 1767–1845

Where did he live? Jackson was born in Waxhaw, a region along the border of the North and South Carolina colonies. In 1788 he moved to Nashville, Tennessee, which was still a part of North Carolina. There he built a mansion called the Hermitage. He lived in Washington as president, then retired to the Hermitage, where he died.

What did he do? Jackson had no formal education, but he taught himself law and became a successful lawyer. He became Tennessee's first representative to the U.S. Congress and also served in the Senate. Jackson became a national hero when his forces defeated the Creek and Seminole Indians. He went on to battle the British in the Battle of New Orleans during the War of 1812. Jackson was elected as the nation's seventh president in 1828 and served until 1837.

Why is he so important? Jackson's belief in a strong presidency made him both loved and hated. He vetoed as many bills as the six previous presidents together. Jackson also believed in a strong Union. When South Carolina tried to nullify, or reject, a federal tariff, he threatened to send troops into the state to force it to obey.

Identifying Cause and Effect Why did Jackson gain loyal friends and fierce enemies?

KEY EVENTS

1796–1797
Served in the U.S. House of Representatives

1797–1798
Served in the U.S. Senate

1798–1804
Served on the Tennessee Supreme Court

1821
Governor of Florida Territory

1823–1825
Served in the U.S. Senate

1829–1837
Served as president of the United States

1832
Vetoed rechartering the Second Bank of the United States. Threatened to send troops to South Carolina when it tried to nullify a federal tariff

Jackson received a scar from a British officer as a boy.

THE AGE OF JACKSON **325**

325

Bellringer

If YOU were there . . . Use the **Daily Bellringer Transparency** to help students answer the question.

📖 Daily Bellringer Transparency, Section 2

The Age of Jackson — Daily Bellringer, Section 2

Review Section 1

Match the sets of letters to the correct vocabulary term.

1. ANDREW _ _ _ KSON   CHE
2. DEM _ _ _ ATIC PARTY   JAC
3. SP _ _ _ S SYSTEM   OCR
4. KIT _ _ _ N CABINET   OIL

Preview Section 2

If you were there ...
You live on a small farm in South Carolina in 1829. Your family grows corn and cotton to sell, as well as vegetables for your own table. Although you grow your own food, you also depend on imported wool, flax, iron, and hemp to make ropes. But the government has just put new taxes on these products from Europe. Now they're too expensive for you to buy! **How would you feel about the new taxes on imports?**

Consider reasons to SUPPORT the new taxes:
- helping American manufacturers compete with foreign companies
- bringing in money for government
- helping the North's economy

Consider reasons to OPPOSE the new taxes:
- making goods you need too costly
- causing you hardship
- hurting the South's economy

Review Answers: 1. JAC, Andrew Jackson; 2. OCR, Democratic Party; 3. OIL, spoils system; 4. CHE, kitchen cabinet

Copyright © by Holt, Rinehart and Winston. All rights reserved.

Academic Vocabulary

Review with students the high-use academic term in this section.

criteria basic requirements (p. 328)

📝 **CRF:** Vocabulary Builder Activity, Section 2

Taking Notes

Have students copy the graphic organizer onto their own paper and then use it to take notes on the section. This activity will prepare students for the Section Assessment, in which they will complete a graphic organizer that builds on the information using a critical thinking skill.

Jackson's Administration

What You Will Learn...

Main Ideas

1. Regional differences grew during Jackson's presidency.
2. The rights of the states were debated amid arguments about a national tariff.
3. Jackson's attack on the Bank sparked controversy.
4. Jackson's policies led to the Panic of 1837.

The Big Idea

Andrew Jackson's presidency was marked by political conflicts.

Key Terms and People

Tariff of Abominations, *p. 327*
states' rights doctrine, *p. 328*
nullification crisis, *p. 328*
Daniel Webster, *p. 328*
McCulloch v. *Maryland, p. 330*
Whig Party, *p. 330*
Panic of 1837, *p. 331*
William Henry Harrison, *p. 331*

TAKING NOTES As you read, use a diagram like the one below to show the conflicts facing Andrew Jackson during his administration. Add more ovals to your organizer as necessary.

Three distinct regions emerge.

↓

Congress passes Tariff of Abominations.

↓

(blank)

If YOU were there...

You live on a small farm in South Carolina in 1829. Your family grows corn and cotton to sell, as well as vegetables for your own table. Although you grow your own food, you also depend on imported wool, flax, iron, and hemp to make ropes. But the government has just put new taxes on these products from Europe. Now they're too expensive for you to buy!

How would you feel about the new taxes on imports?

> **BUILDING BACKGROUND** Even though Americans had a new feeling of national unity, different sections of the country still had very different interests. The industrial North competed with the agricultural South and the western frontier. As Congress favored one section over another, political differences also grew.

Sectional Differences Increase

Regional differences had a major effect on Andrew Jackson's presidency. Americans' views of Jackson's policies were based on where they lived and the economy of those regions.

Three Regions Emerge

There were three main U.S. regions in the early 1800s. The North, first of all, had an economy based on trade and on manufacturing. Northerners supported tariffs because tariffs helped them compete with British factories. Northerners also opposed the federal government's sale of public land at cheap prices. Cheap land encouraged potential laborers to move from northern factory towns to the West.

The second region was the South. Its economy was based on farming. Southern farmers raised all types of crops, but the most popular were the cash crops of cotton and tobacco. Southerners sold a large portion of their crops to foreign nations.

Teach the Big Idea

Jackson's Administration

1. **Teach** Ask students the questions in the Main Idea boxes to teach this section.

2. **Apply** For each of the section key terms and people, have students write a sentence explaining how that term or person relates to the sectional and/or political conflicts that took place during Jackson's presidency. Then have each student create a flowchart that links all the key terms and people. **LS Verbal/Linguistic, Visual/Spatial**

3. **Review** As you review the section's main ideas, have volunteers share the information they listed about each key term or person.

4. **Practice/Homework** Have each student select one of the key terms or people and write a news article about that event, issue, or person. **LS Verbal/Linguistic**

📝 Alternative Assessment Handbook, Rubrics 7: Charts; and 42: Writing to Inform

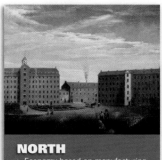

NORTH
- Economy based on manufacturing
- Support for tariffs—American goods could be sold at lower prices than could British goods

SOUTH
- Economy based on agriculture
- Opposition to tariffs, which increased the cost of imported goods

WEST
- Emerging economy
- Support for internal improvements and the sale of public lands

Southerners imported their manufactured goods. Tariffs made imported goods more expensive for southern farmers. In addition, high tariffs angered some of the South's European trading partners. These trading partners would likely raise their own tariffs in retaliation. To avoid this situation, southerners called for low tariffs.

Southerners also relied on enslaved African Americans to work the plantations. The issue of slavery would become increasingly controversial between the North and South.

In the third region, the West, the frontier economy was just emerging. Settlers supported policies that boosted their farming economy and encouraged further settlement. Western farmers grew a wide variety of crops. Their biggest priority was cheap land and internal improvements such as better roads and water transportation.

Tariff of Abominations

Tariffs became one of the first issues that President Jackson faced. In 1827, the year before Jackson's election, northern manufacturers began to demand a tariff on imported woolen goods. Northerners wanted the tariff

to protect their industries from foreign competition, especially from Great Britain.

British companies were driving American ones out of business because they could manufacture goods more cheaply than American businesses could. The tariff northerners wanted, however, was so high that importing wool would be impossible. Southerners opposed the tariff, claiming it would hurt their economy.

Before Andrew Jackson took office, Congress placed a high tariff on imports, causing angry southerners to call it the **Tariff of Abominations**. (An abomination is a hateful thing.) Southern voters were outraged.

President John Quincy Adams signed the tariff legislation, even though he did not fully support it. In early U.S. history, presidents tended to reserve veto power for legislation that they believed violated the Constitution. Signing the tariff bill meant Adams would surely be defeated in his re-election bid. The new tariff added fuel to the growing sectional differences plaguing the young nation.

READING CHECK Summarizing Describe the sectional economic differences in the United States during the early 1800s.

THE AGE OF JACKSON **327**

Main Idea

❷ States' Rights Debate

The rights of the states were debated amid arguments about a national tariff.

Explain How did southerners use the states' rights doctrine to support the idea of nullification? *stated that states had the greater power and, thus, had the right to reject any federal law with which they disagreed*

Identify Points of View How did Webster and Jackson view the nullification crisis? *both opposed nullification; Webster—thought national unity was more important that states' rights; Jackson—threatened to use federal troops to enforce federal laws*

📄 **CRF:** Biography Activities: John C. Calhoun; Daniel Webster

📄 **CRF:** Primary Source Activity: President Jackson's Proclamation Regarding Nullification

go.hrw.com
Online Resources

KEYWORD: SR8 US10
ACTIVITY: Calhoun and Webster Debate Nullification

Answers

Focus on Reading *that the debate further increased sectional tensions that would continue to divide the nation*

States' Rights Debate

When Andrew Jackson took office in 1829, he was forced to respond to the growing conflict over tariffs. At the core of the dispute was the question of an individual state's right to disregard a law that had been passed by the U.S. Congress.

Nullification Crisis

ACADEMIC VOCABULARY
criteria
basic requirements

Early in his political career, Vice President John C. Calhoun had supported the **criteria** needed for a strong central government. But in 1828 when Congress passed the Tariff of Abominations, Calhoun joined his fellow southerners in protest. Economic depression and previous tariffs had severely damaged the economy of his home state, South Carolina. It was only beginning to recover in 1828. Some leaders in the state even spoke of leaving the Union over the issue of tariffs.

In response to the tariff, Calhoun drafted the *South Carolina Exposition and Protest*. It stated that Congress should not favor one state or region over another. Calhoun also used the Protest to advance the **states' rights doctrine**. He argued that, because the states had formed the national government, state power should be greater than federal power. He believed states had the right to nullify, or reject, any federal law they judged to be unconstitutional.

FOCUS ON READING
What conclusions can you draw about the importance of the states' rights debate after reading this section?

Calhoun's theory was controversial, and it drew some fierce challengers. Many of them were from the northern states that had benefited from increased tariffs. These opponents believed that the American people, not the individual states, made up the Union. Conflict between the supporters and the opponents of nullification deepened. The dispute became known as the **nullification crisis**.

Although he chose not to put his name on his *Exposition and Protest*, Calhoun did resign from the vice presidency. Martin Van Buren replaced him as vice president when Jackson was re-elected to a second term. John C. Calhoun is the only vice president in our history to resign his office.

The Hayne-Webster Debate

The debate about states' rights began early in our nation's history. Thomas Jefferson and James Madison supported the states' power to disagree with the federal government in the Virginia and Kentucky Resolutions of 1798–99. Some of the delegates at the Hartford Convention supported states' rights. But Calhoun's theory went further. He believed that states could judge whether a law was or was not constitutional. This position put the power of the Supreme Court in question.

The issue of nullification was intensely debated on the floor of the Senate in 1830. Robert Y. Hayne, senator from South Carolina, defended states' rights. He argued that nullification gave states a way to lawfully protest against federal legislation. **Daniel Webster** of Massachusetts argued that the United States was one nation, not a pact among independent states. He believed that the welfare of the nation should override that of individual states.

Jackson Responds

Although deeply opposed to nullification, Jackson was also concerned about economic problems in the southern states. In 1832 Jackson urged Congress to pass another tariff that lowered the previous rate. South Carolina thought the slight change was inadequate. The state legislature took a monumental step; it decided to test the doctrine of states' rights.

South Carolina's first action was to pass the Nullification Act. It declared that the 1828 and 1832 tariffs were "null, void…[and not] binding upon this State, its officers or citizens." South Carolina threatened to withdraw from the Union if federal troops were used to collect duties. The legislature also voted to form its own army. Jackson was enraged.

The president sternly condemned nullification. Jackson declared that he would enforce the law in South Carolina. At his request, Congress passed the Force Bill

---

Critical Thinking: Finding Main Ideas

Nullification Crisis Graphic Organizer

1. To help students understand the issues involved in the Nullification Crisis, draw the graphic organizer for students to see. Omit the blue, italicized answers.

2. Have each student copy the organizer and complete it by explaining the key figures, events, and issues on each side.

LS Verbal/Linguistic, Visual/Spatial

📄 Alternative Assessment Handbook, Rubric 13: Graphic Organizers

States' Rights
- **Southern opinion of tariffs:** *abominable*
- **States' Rights:** *state power should be greater than federal power*
- **Nullification:** *States' have the right to nullify federal laws with which they disagree.*
- **John C. Calhoun:** *major proponent*

Nullification Crisis

Federal Authority
- **Daniel Webster:** *promoted national unity over states' rights*
- **President Jackson:** *opposed nullification*
- **Actions/Results:** *Jackson wanted to send troops to enforce tariffs; Congress and South Carolina compromised to lower tariffs gradually.*

approving use of the army if necessary. In light of Jackson's determined position, no other state chose to support South Carolina.

Early in 1833, Henry Clay of Kentucky had proposed a compromise that would lower the tariff little by little over several years.

As Jackson's intentions became clear, both the U.S. Congress and South Carolina moved quickly to approve the compromise. The Congress would decrease the tariff, and South Carolina's leaders would enforce the law.

Despite the compromise, neither side changed its beliefs about states' rights. The argument would continue for years, ending in the huge conflict known as the Civil War.

READING CHECK **Summarizing** What led to the nullification crisis, and why was it important?

Jackson Attacks the Bank

President Jackson upheld federal authority in the nullification crisis. He did not, however, always support greater federal power. For example, he opposed the Second Bank of the United States, founded by Congress in 1816.

The Second Bank of the United States was given a 20-year charter. This charter gave it the power to act exclusively as the federal government's financial agent. The Bank held federal deposits, made transfers of federal funds between states, and dealt with any payments or receipts involving the federal government. It also issued bank notes, or paper currency. Some 80 percent of the Bank was privately owned, but its operations were supervised by Congress and the president.

Many states, particularly in the South, had opposed the Bank. Small farmers believed that the Bank only helped wealthy businesspeople. Jackson also questioned the legality of the Bank. He believed it was an unconstitutional extension of the power of Congress. The states, he thought, should have the power to control the banking system.

Some states decided to take action. Maryland tried to pass a tax that would limit the

Main Idea

3 Jackson Attacks the Bank

Jackson's attack of the bank sparked controversy.

Describe How did the state of Maryland try to take action against the Second Bank of the United States? *It passed a tax to limit the operations of the Bank's state branch, and took the branch cashier, James McCulloch, to court when he refused to pay the tax.*

Identify Cause and Effect What occurred as a result of this action? *The case went to the U.S. Supreme Court, which ruled in* McCulloch v. Maryland *that the Bank was constitutional.*

Evaluate Were Jackson's actions to weaken the Bank's power effective? *His actions weakened the bank's power and helped western expansion but also led to inflation, which hurt the economy.*

📖 Political Cartoons Activities for United States History, Cartoon 11: Jackson and the Bank

📖 **CRF:** Primary Source Activity: The Bank War of 1832—Two Views

📖 U.S. Supreme Court Case Studies: *McCulloch* v. *Maryland*

Primary Source

POINTS OF VIEW

States' Rights vs. the Union

The framers of the Constitution created a document that was remarkable in its scope. But a few issues were unresolved. One of the most controversial was the matter of states' rights versus the authority of the federal government. Daniel Webster insisted that the interests of the Union should prevail. John C. Calhoun believed that the powers of the states were greater.

❝While the Union lasts we have high, exciting, gratifying prospects spread out before us, for us and our children. God grant that in my day . . . my eyes shall be turned to behold the gorgeous ensign of the republic . . . bearing for its motto . . . Liberty and Union, now and forever one and inseparable.❞

—Daniel Webster

from the Hayne–Webster debate, 1830

❝If there be no protective power in the reserved rights of the states, they must in the end be forced to rebel . . .❞

—John C. Calhoun

from a letter to Virgil Maxcy, September 11, 1830

ANALYSIS SKILL **ANALYZING PRIMARY SOURCES**

Finding Main Ideas How did the views of Calhoun and Webster differ?

THE AGE OF JACKSON **329**

Differentiating Instruction

Above Level

Advanced/Gifted and Talented

1. Have each student write an outline of a chapter that might have appeared in Jackson's memoirs. The chapter should address Jackson's thoughts about the U.S. Supreme Court case *McCulloch* v. *Maryland* and the Second Bank of the United States, his actions to defeat the Bank, and how his actions affected the U.S. economy.

2. Pair students and have partners exchange outlines. Each student should then evaluate his or her partner's outline from the point of view of Jackson's publisher. Students should consider the clarity and order of the material and its publication value. Then have students revise their outlines based on the reviews.

LS Interpersonal, Verbal/Linguistic

📖 Alternative Assessment Handbook, Rubric 42: Writing to Inform

Answers

Analyzing Primary Sources
Webster strongly supported federal power, whereas Calhoun supported the rights of the states.

Reading Check *Southern states asserted their power to nullify tariffs, which most Southerners opposed; it demonstrated the nation's growing sectionalism and division over the issue of federal versus state power.*

❹ Panic of 1837

Jackson's policies led to the Panic of 1837.

Define What was the Whig Party? *political party formed by a group of Jackson's opponents*

Explain What helped Van Buren win the election in 1836? *strong support from Jackson; division of Whig support among four candidates*

Analyze What role did the economy play in the presidential election of 1840? *The Panic of 1837 decreased support for the incumbent Van Buren, which helped Whig candidate William Henry Harrison win the election.*

📑 **CRF:** Economics and History Activity: The Panic of 1837

Teaching Tip

Modernize the Symbol
The symbol of the hydra in the political cartoon at right may be unfamiliar to students. To help students understand the cartoon better, ask them to suggest images that political cartoonists today might use to portray either a difficult political problem for a president to solve or a president who is in a conflict with several political opponents.

Answers

Analyzing Primary Sources *It shows that many politicians opposed Jackson's policies*

Reading Check *Small farmers, particularly in the South, thought the Bank benefited only wealthy businesspeople; Jackson questioned the Bank's legality.*

POLITICAL CARTOON
Jackson against the Bank

Andrew Jackson's fight with the Bank was the subject of many political cartoons, like this one.

In this scene, Jackson is shown fighting a hydra that represents the national bank. The hydra is a mythological monster whose heads grow back when cut off. The heads of the hydra are portraits of politicians who opposed Jackson's policies.

Nicholas Biddle is at the center of the hydra. Why?

Andrew Jackson fights the hydra with a cane labeled "veto."

Why do you think the cartoonist chose this monster to represent the Bank?

ANALYSIS SKILL **ANALYZING PRIMARY SOURCES**

How does this image show the difficulty Jackson had politically?

Bank's operations. James McCulloch, cashier of the Bank's branch in Maryland, refused to pay this tax. The state took him to court, and the resulting case went all the way to the U.S. Supreme Court. In **McCulloch v. Maryland**, the Court ruled that the national bank was constitutional.

Nicholas Biddle, the Bank's director, decided to push for a bill to renew the Bank's charter in 1832. Jackson campaigned strongly for the bill's defeat. "I will kill it," he promised. True to his word, Jackson vetoed the legislation when Congess sent it to him.

Congress could not get the two-thirds majority needed to override Jackson's veto. Jackson also weakened the Bank's power by moving most of its funds to state banks. In many cases, these banks used the funds to offer easy credit terms to people buying land. While this practice helped expansion in the West, it also led to inflation.

In the summer of 1836 Jackson tried to slow this inflation. He ordered Americans to use only gold or silver—instead of paper bank notes—to buy government-owned land. This

policy did not help the national economy as Jackson had hoped. Jackson did improve the economy by lowering the national debt. However, his policies opened the door for approaching economic troubles.

READING CHECK **Analyzing** Why did critics of the Second Bank of the United States oppose it?

Panic of 1837

Jackson was still very popular with voters in 1836. Jackson chose not to run in 1836, and the Democrats nominated Vice President Martin Van Buren.

In 1834 a new political party formed to oppose Jackson. Its members called themselves Whigs, after an English political party that opposed the monarchy, to make the point that Jackson was using his power like a king. The **Whig Party** favored the idea of a weak president and a strong Congress. Unable to agree on a presidential candidate, the Whigs nominated four men to run against Vice President Martin Van Buren. With strong backing from Jackson, Van Buren won the election.

Critical Thinking: Identifying Cause and Effect
At Level

1840 Whig Campaign Flyer

Materials: paper, colored markers, current political campaign flyer (optional)

1. Have each student create a campaign flyer supporting Whig candidate William Henry Harrison in the election of 1840.

2. Students' fliers should address the Panic of 1837, public views of Van Buren's presidency, and Harrison's background and character versus that of Van Buren. If possible, provide students with a copy of a current political campaign advertisement to use as a model.

3. Ask for volunteers to explain their fliers to the class. Use the activity to launch a guided discussion of the causes and effects of the Panic of 1837 and the outcome of the election of 1840. **LS** **Intrapersonal, Visual/Spatial**

📑 Alternative Assessment Handbook, Rubric 37: Writing Assignments

Supreme Court and Capitalism

CONNECT TO ECONOMICS

During the early 1800s, the Supreme Court made several rulings that helped define federal power over contracts and commerce. These rulings reinforced capitalism as the ruling economic system in the United States.

What effect did the Supreme Court have on economic development?

1810		1819	1824
Fletcher v. Peck State legislatures could not pass laws violating existing contracts.	**Dartmouth College v. Woodward** State legislatures could not pass laws to change the charters of institutions or businesses.	**McCulloch v. Maryland** States do not have right to tax federal institutions	**Gibbons v. Ogden** Only federal government has the right to regulate interstate and foreign commerce

Shortly after Van Buren took office, the country experienced the **Panic of 1837**, a severe economic depression. Jackson's banking policies and his unsuccessful plan to curb inflation contributed to the panic. But people blamed Van Buren.

In 1840 the Whigs united against the weakened Van Buren to stand behind one candidate, **William Henry Harrison**, an army general. Harrison won in an electoral landslide. The Whigs had achieved their goal of winning the presidency.

READING CHECK Identifying Cause and Effect
What contributed to the Panic of 1837, and how did it affect the 1840 election?

SUMMARY AND PREVIEW The states' rights debate dominated much of Jackson's presidency. In the next section you will learn about the removal of American Indians from the southeastern United States.

go.hrw.com
Online Quiz
KEYWORD: SR8 HP10

Section 2 Assessment

Reviewing Ideas, Terms, and People

1. **a. Recall** On what were the economies of the northern, southern, and western states based?
   b. Predict How might the sectional issues involved in the dispute over the **Tariff of Abominations** lead to future problems between North and South?
2. **a. Describe** What roles did **Daniel Webster** and John C. Calhoun play in the **nullification crisis**?
   b. Summarize What idea did supporters of the **states' rights doctrine** promote?
3. **a. Describe** What problems resulted from weakening the Bank?
   b. Draw Conclusions Why did Jackson veto the bill to renew the Second Bank of the United States?
4. **a. Recall** What caused the **Panic of 1837**?
   b. Summarize How did the **Whig Party** win the election of 1840?
   c. Elaborate Why do you think Jackson chose not to run for the presidency in 1836? Do you think he made the right decision? Why?

Critical Thinking

5. **Identifying Cause and Effect** Review your notes on the political conflicts during Jackson's administration. Then use a graphic organizer like the one below to show how some of Jackson's policies dealing with conflicts led to the Panic of 1837.

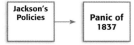

Jackson's Policies → Panic of 1837

FOCUS ON WRITING

6. **Identifying Important Conflicts** Stories about conflict sell newspapers. As you read this section, list important conflicts that occurred during Jackson's presidency and note the role Jackson played in creating or resolving the conflicts.

THE AGE OF JACKSON **331**

Direct Teach

Interpreting Charts

Supreme Court and Capitalism

Compare What do all four of these cases have in common? *issues of federal versus state authority*

Review & Assess

Close
Have students summarize how political and economic policies during Jackson's presidency contributed to sectional divisions in the nation.

Review
Online Quiz, Section 2

Assess
SE Section 2 Assessment
PASS: Section 2 Quiz
Alternative Assessment Handbook

Reteach/Classroom Intervention
Interactive Reader and Study Guide, Section 2
Interactive Skills Tutor CD-ROM

Section 2 Assessment Answers

1. **a.** North—trade and manufacturing, South—agriculture, West—farming and settlement
   b. possible answer—might have contributed to increased sectional divisions in Congress
2. **a.** Calhoun supported nullification and states' rights; Webster opposed nullification and supported national unity over states' rights.
   b. state power should be greater than federal
3. **a.** Smaller banks began offering easy credit terms for buying land, which led to inflation.
   b. did not think the bank was constitutional

4. **a.** Jackson's banking policies; inflation
   b. united behind one candidate, Harrison, and emphasized his war record, log-cabin roots
   c. Students should note that Jackson's actions had angered many.
5. Sectional Differences—people divided over political policies by region; Nullification Crisis—states' rights versus federal authority over tariffs; National Bank—Jackson opposed Bank, led to economic problems
6. Notes should address conflicts listed above.

Answers

Connect to Economics *helped define federal power over contracts and commerce; reinforced capitalism*

Reading Check *cause—Jackson's banking policies and unsuccessful plan to curb inflation; effect—Whig Party candidate, William Henry Harrison, won the election of 1840*

331

Preteach

Bellringer

If YOU were there . . . Use the **Daily Bellringer Transparency** to help students answer the question.

📖 Daily Bellringer Transparency, Section 3

Academic Vocabulary

Review with students the high-use academic term in this section.

contemporary existing at the same time (p. 333)

📝 **CRF:** Vocabulary Builder Activity, Section 3

Taking Notes

Have students copy the graphic organizer onto their own paper and then use it to take notes on the section. This activity will prepare students for the Section Assessment, in which they will complete a graphic organizer that builds on the information using a critical thinking skill.

Indian Removal

What You Will Learn...

Main Ideas

1. The Indian Removal Act authorized the relocation of Native Americans to the West.
2. Cherokee resistance to removal led to disagreement between Jackson and the Supreme Court.
3. Other Native Americans resisted removal with force.

The Big Idea

President Jackson supported a policy of Indian removal.

Key Terms and People

Indian Removal Act, *p. 332*
Indian Territory, *p. 332*
Bureau of Indian Affairs, *p. 332*
Sequoya, *p. 333*
Worcester v. *Georgia, p. 334*
Trail of Tears, *p. 334*
Black Hawk, *p. 335*
Osceola, *p. 335*

 TAKING NOTES As you read, use a graphic organizer like the one below to show the steps Andrew Jackson and the U.S. government took toward Indian removal.

Indian removal

If YOU were there...

You belong to the Cherokee nation. Your family has farmed rich lands in Georgia for as long as anyone can remember. You've learned some new ways from white settlers, too. At school you've learned to read both English and Cherokee. But now that doesn't seem important. The U.S. government is sending you and your people far away to unknown places in the West.

How would you feel about being taken away from your home?

> **BUILDING BACKGROUND** President Andrew Jackson had become famous as an Indian fighter. He had no sympathy with Native Americans' claim to the lands where they had always lived. With public support, he reversed the government's pledge to respect Indian land claims. The result was the brutal removal of the southeastern peoples to empty lands in the West.

Indian Removal Act

Native Americans had long lived in settlements stretching from Georgia to Mississippi. However, President Jackson and other political leaders wanted to open this land to settlement by American farmers. Under pressure from Jackson, Congress passed the **Indian Removal Act** in 1830, authorizing the removal of Native American who lived east of the Mississippi River to lands in the West.

Congress then established **Indian Territory**—U.S. land in what is now Oklahoma where Native Americans were moved to. Some supporters of this plan, like John C. Calhoun, argued that removal to Indian Territory would protect Indians from further conflicts with American settlers. "One of the greatest evils to which they are subject is that incessant [constant] pressure of our population," he noted. "To guard against this evil . . . there ought to be the strongest . . . assurance that the country given [to] them should be theirs." To manage Indian removal to western lands, Congress approved the creation of a new government agency, the **Bureau of Indian Affairs**.

Teach the Big Idea

At Level

Indian Removal

1. **Teach** Ask students the questions in the Main Idea boxes to teach this section.

2. **Apply** Organize students into small groups. Assign each group one of the following: (1) Choctaw, Creek, and Chickasaw; (2) Cherokee; (3) Fox, Sauk, and Seminole. Have each group create a storyboard that uses images and captions to narrate how the policy of Indian removal affected its assigned Native American group(s).
LS Interpersonal, Visual/Spatial

3. **Review** As you review the section, have each group explain its storyboard to the class.

4. **Practice/Homework** Have each student write a poem from the point of view of a Native American in response to the U.S. government's policy of Indian removal during this period. **LS Verbal/Linguistic**

📝 Alternative Assessment Handbook, Rubrics 26: Poems and Songs; and 29: Presentations

Indian Removal

During the Trail of Tears, thousands of Cherokee died from disease, starvation, and harsh weather. They were forced to walk hundreds of miles to their new land in the West. Other Native Americans were also moved, with similar results.

What can you see in this painting that indicates this was a difficult journey?

The Choctaw were the first Indians sent to Indian Territory. The Mississippi legislature abolished the Choctaw government and then forced the Choctaw leaders to sign the Treaty of Dancing Rabbit Creek. This treaty gave more than 7.5 million acres of their land to the state. The Choctaw moved to Indian Territory during a disastrous winter trip. Federal officials in charge of the move did not provide enough food or supplies to the Choctaw, most of whom were on foot. About one-fourth of the Choctaw died of cold, disease, or starvation.

News of the Choctaw's hardships caused other Indians to resist removal. When the Creek resisted in 1836, federal troops moved in and captured some 14,500 of them. They led the Creek, many in chains, to Indian Territory. One Creek woman remembered the trip being filled with "the awful silence that showed the heartaches and sorrow at being taken from the homes and even separation from loved ones." The Chickasaw, who lived in upper Mississippi, negotiated a treaty for better supplies on their trip to Indian Territory. Nevertheless, many Chickasaw lives were also lost during removal.

READING CHECK Finding Main Ideas What major changes did President Jackson make to U.S. policy regarding Native Americans?

Cherokee Resistance

Many Cherokee had believed that they could prevent conflicts and avoid removal by adopting the **contemporary** culture of white people. In the early 1800s they invited missionaries to set up schools where Cherokee children learned how to read and write in English. The Cherokee developed their own government modeled after the U.S. Constitution with an election system, a bicameral council, and a court system. All of these were headed by a principal chief.

A Cherokee named **Sequoya** used 86 characters to represent Cherokee syllables to create a writing system for their own complex language. In 1828 the Cherokee began publishing a newspaper printed in both English and Cherokee.

The adoption of white culture did not protect the Cherokee. After gold was discovered on their land in Georgia, their treaty rights

ACADEMIC VOCABULARY
contemporary existing at the same time

THE AGE OF JACKSON **333**

Main Idea

❷ Cherokee Resistance

Cherokee resistance to removal led to disagreement between Jackson and the Supreme Court.

Explain Why did the adoption of white culture not protect the Cherokee from removal? *because gold was discovered on their land*

Summarize What steps did the Cherokee take to try to resist removal, and what was the result? *They sued the state, and their case went to the Supreme Court, which ruled in their favor; the state of Georgia ignored the ruling and removed them anyway; during the Trail of Tears, many Cherokee died.*

📑 **CRF:** Biography Activity: Sequoya

📑 U.S. Supreme Court Case Studies: *Worchester* v. *Georgia* (1832)

Connect to Government

Worcester* v. *Georgia The status of Indian nations in the courts remained undefined until the Supreme Court case *Worcester* v. *Georgia*. In his decision, Chief Justice John Marshall wrote that the "acts of Georgia are repugnant to the Constitution . . . [and] in direct hostility with treaties [that] . . . solemnly pledge the faith of the United States to restrain their citizens from trespassing on [Cherokee land]."

Answers

Analyzing Points of View
1. *before—author is concerned about rights, tone is angry; after—author concerned about the tragedy of the Trail of Tears.* **2.** *possible answers— exhausted, sad, angry, relieved*

Reading Check *The Supreme Court ruled that the laws of Georgia did not apply to the Cherokee nation; Jackson did not take any action to enforce the Court's ruling.*

334

---

were ignored. Georgia leaders began preparing for the Cherokee's removal. When they refused to move, the Georgia militia began attacking Cherokee towns. In response, the Cherokee sued the state. They said that they were an independent nation and claimed that the government of Georgia had no legal power over their lands.

In 1832 the Supreme Court, under the leadership of Chief Justice John Marshall, agreed. In **Worcester v. Georgia** the Court ruled that the Cherokee nation was a distinct community in which the laws of Georgia had no force. The Court also stated that only the federal government, not the states, had authority over Native Americans.

Georgia, however, ignored the Court's ruling, and President Jackson took no action to make Georgia follow the ruling. "John Marshall has made his decision; now let him enforce it," Jackson supposedly said. By not enforcing the Court's decision, Jackson violated his presidential oath to uphold the laws of the land. However, most members of Congress and American citizens did not protest the ways Jackson removed Native Americans.

In the spring of 1838, U.S. troops began to remove all Cherokee to Indian Territory. A few were able to escape and hide in the mountains of North Carolina. After the Cherokee were removed, Georgia took their businesses, farms, and property.

The Cherokee's 800-mile forced march became known as the **Trail of Tears**. During the march, the Cherokee suffered from disease, hunger, and harsh weather. Almost one-fourth of the 18,000 Cherokee died on the march.

THE IMPACT TODAY
Today more than 60,000 Cherokee or Cherokee descendants live in present-day Oklahoma.

READING CHECK Finding Main Ideas
What was the *Worcester* v. *Georgia* ruling, and what was Jackson's response?

Primary Source

PERSONAL ACCOUNTS
Trail of Tears

The Cherokee knew that they would be forced to march West, but they did not know that so many of their people would die on the way. Here are two accounts of the Trail of Tears, one written before it started and one written after, both by Cherokee who made the trip.

March 10, 1838
Beloved Martha, I have delayed writing to you so long. . . . If we Cherokees are to be driven to the west by the cruel hand of oppression to seek a new home in the west, it will be impossible. . . . It is thus all our rights are invaded."

—Letter from Jenny, a Cherokee girl, just before her removal

"Long time we travel on way to new land. People feel bad when they leave Old Nation. Women cry and make sad wails, Children cry and many men cry . . . but they say nothing and just put heads down and keep on go towards West. Many days pass and people die very much."

—Recollections of a survivor of the Trail of Tears

ANALYSIS SKILL **ANALYZING POINTS OF VIEW**

1. What is different about the concerns of the Cherokee before and after the Trail of Tears?
2. How do you think the survivors of the Trail of Tears felt when they reached their new homeland?

334 CHAPTER 10

Cross-Discipline Activity: Art
Below Level

Indian Removal Memorial

Materials: art supplies; images of memorials, such as Vietnam Veterans Memorial (optional)

1. Have students describe the main actions and events that led to the removal of Native American groups in the Southeast.

2. Then have students, working either individually or in small groups, design memorials for the many Native Americans in the Southeast who died either resisting removal or being forcibly removed. Give students choices for their memorials, such as a statue, a plaque, or a marker to set along the route of the Trail of Tears. Each student or group should write a paragraph explaining the memorial.

3. Display the memorials in the classroom.
LS **Verbal/Linguistic, Visual/Spatial**

📑 Alternative Assessment Handbook, Rubric 3: Artwork

Other Native Americans Resist

Other Native Americans decided to fight U.S. troops to avoid removal. Chief **Black Hawk**, a leader of Fox and Sauk Indians, decided to fight rather than leave Illinois. By 1832, however, the Sauk forces were running out of food and supplies, and by 1850 they had been forced to leave.

In Florida, Seminole leaders were forced to sign a removal treaty that their followers decided to ignore. A leader named **Osceola** called upon his followers to resist with force, and the Second Seminole War began. Osceola was captured and soon died in prison. His followers, however, continued to fight. Some 4,000 Seminole were removed and hundreds of others killed. Eventually, U.S. officials decided to give up the fight. Small groups of Seminole had resisted removal, and their descendants live in Florida today.

READING CHECK **Evaluating** How effective was Native American resistance to removal?

Second Seminole War

GEOGRAPHY SKILLS **INTERPRETING MAPS**

1. **Location** In what parts of Florida was the Second Seminole War fought?
2. **Place** Where was the last battle of the Second Seminole War fought?

SUMMARY AND PREVIEW President Jackson supported the removal of thousands of Native Americans from their traditional lands to the federal territory in the West. In the next chapter you will learn about the westward growth of the nation as farmers, ranchers, and other settlers moved West.

go.hrw.com
Online Quiz
KEYWORD: SR8 HP10

Section 3 Assessment

Reviewing Ideas, Terms, and People

1. **a. Identify** What Native American groups were affected by the **Indian Removal Act**? Where were they relocated?
   b. Explain Why did government officials want to relocate Native Americans to the West?
   c. Predict What are some possible effects that the Indian Removal Act might have on Native Americans already living in the West?
2. **a. Identify** What was the **Trail of Tears**?
   b. Analyze Why did the state of Georgia want to relocate the Cherokee, and what did the Cherokee do in response?
   c. Elaborate What do you think of President Jackson's refusal to enforce the **Worcester v. Georgia** ruling?
3. **a. Describe** What led to the Second Seminole War?
   b. Compare and Contrast How were the Seminole and the Sauk resistance efforts similar and different?

Critical Thinking

4. **Comparing and Contrasting** Review your notes on Indian removal. Then copy the chart below and use it to identify the Native American groups and their responses to the removal.

Native American Group	Response to Removal

FOCUS ON WRITING

5. **Understanding Causes and Effects** As you read, identify the causes and effects of the Jackson administration's policy of Indian relocation.

THE AGE OF JACKSON **335**

Main Idea

❸ Other Native Americans Resist

Other Native Americans resisted removal with force.

Identify and Compare Who were Chief Black Hawk and Osceola, and what did they have in common? *Black Hawk—leader of Fox and Sauk Indians; Osceola—Seminole leader; both called on followers to resist removal with force*

- **CRF:** Biography Activity: Black Hawk
- **CRF:** History and Geography Activity: The Seminole Wars
- **CRF:** Literature Activity: *Surrender Speech* by Chief Black Hawk
- Map Transparency: Second Seminole War

● **Review & Assess** ●

Close
Have students summarize the effects of Jackson's Indian removal policy.

Review
Online Quiz, Section 3

Assess
SE Section 3 Assessment
- PASS: Section 3 Quiz
- Alternative Assessment Handbook

Reteach/Classroom Intervention
- Interactive Reader and Study Guide, Section 3
- Interactive Skills Tutor CD-ROM

Section 3 Assessment Answers

1. **a.** Choctaw, Creek, Chickasaw, Cherokee, Fox, Sauk, Seminole; Indian Territory
   b. to open up more lands for settlement
   c. possible answer—conflict with newcomers, competition for resources
2. **a.** 800-mile forced march of the Cherokee from their lands in Georgia to Indian Territory, during which many Cherokee died
   b. why—gold had been found on their lands; Cherokee response—sued state of Georgia
   c. possible answers—His decision was unfair and possibly unconstitutional

3. **a.** When Seminole leaders were forced to sign a removal treaty, other Seminole fought.
   b. similar—both resisted; different—Sauk were removed, many of the Seminole resisted
4. Choctaw and Chickasaw—sent to Indian Territory; Cherokee—adopted white culture then sued state, sent to Indian Territory; Sauk—fought, removed; Seminole—fought, ultimately successful in resistance
5. Students should indicate that the Indian removal policy led to the removal and death of many Native Americans in the Southeast.

Answers

Interpreting Maps 1. *East coast and north central;* **2.** *Fort Lauderdale*

Reading Check *Overall, not effective, although some Native Americans successfully resisted removal.*

335

Activity Analyzing Trends and Patterns Read aloud to students the information in the feature and then lead a discussion about Indian removal and its effects. Next, have students examine the table and the map and look for trends and patterns in U.S.–Native American relations. Have volunteers identify trends and patterns. (trends— *Over time the U.S. government offered Native Americans a decreasing amount of money and then land in exchange for Indian land in treaties. The land offered amounted to removal. patterns—pattern of conflict, treaties, and removal*) To extend the activity, have each student write a short essay summarizing trends and patterns in Indian Removal Treaties and the effects of the treaties.

LS Verbal/Linguistic

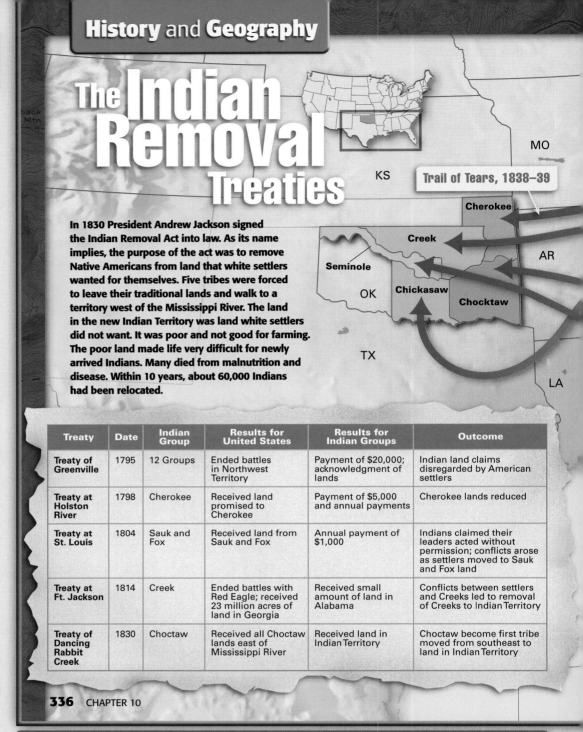

History and Geography

The Indian Removal Treaties

Trail of Tears, 1838–39

In 1830 President Andrew Jackson signed the Indian Removal Act into law. As its name implies, the purpose of the act was to remove Native Americans from land that white settlers wanted for themselves. Five tribes were forced to leave their traditional lands and walk to a territory west of the Mississippi River. The land in the new Indian Territory was land white settlers did not want. It was poor and not good for farming. The poor land made life very difficult for newly arrived Indians. Many died from malnutrition and disease. Within 10 years, about 60,000 Indians had been relocated.

Treaty	Date	Indian Group	Results for United States	Results for Indian Groups	Outcome
Treaty of Greenville	1795	12 Groups	Ended battles in Northwest Territory	Payment of $20,000; acknowledgment of lands	Indian land claims disregarded by American settlers
Treaty at Holston River	1798	Cherokee	Received land promised to Cherokee	Payment of $5,000 and annual payments	Cherokee lands reduced
Treaty at St. Louis	1804	Sauk and Fox	Received land from Sauk and Fox	Annual payment of $1,000	Indians claimed their leaders acted without permission; conflicts arose as settlers moved to Sauk and Fox land
Treaty at Ft. Jackson	1814	Creek	Ended battles with Red Eagle; received 23 million acres of land in Georgia	Received small amount of land in Alabama	Conflicts between settlers and Creeks led to removal of Creeks to Indian Territory
Treaty of Dancing Rabbit Creek	1830	Choctaw	Received all Choctaw lands east of Mississippi River	Received land in Indian Territory	Choctaw become first tribe moved from southeast to land in Indian Territory

336 CHAPTER 10

Critical Thinking: Analyzing Information

At Level

Effects of Indian Removal

Materials: 18" × 12" sheets of light-colored construction paper

1. Organize students into groups of three. Have each group select one sign maker. The other two members will serve as writers.

2. Distribute one sheet of construction paper to each group. Have the sign maker fold the paper to make two sections that are 9" × 12" and then open the sheet. Instruct students to write Indian Relocation across the top of the page and label the two columns

Effects on Native Americans' Lives and *Effects on Settlers' Lives.*

3. Instruct the groups to discuss the ways that lives were changed by Indian removal and treaties and have writers record the group's observations in the appropriate columns.

4. Have group volunteers share some of their observations with the class. **LS** Interpersonal, Verbal/Linguistic

📖 Alternative Assessment Handbook, Rubrics 7: Charts; and 14: Group Activity

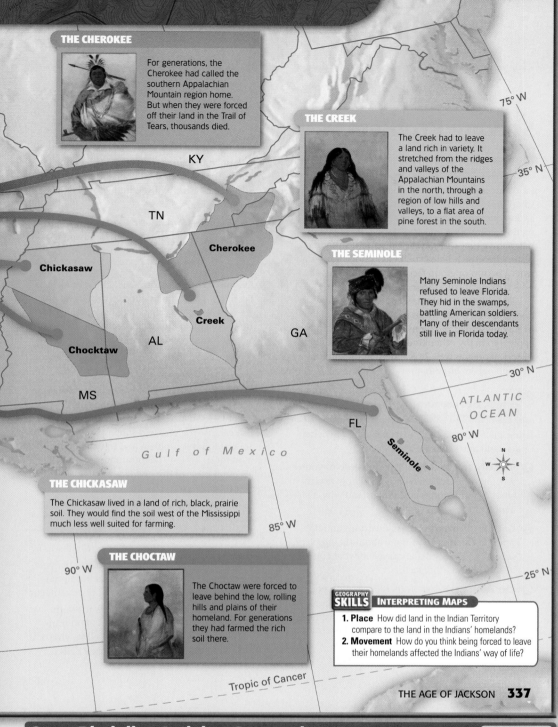

THE CHEROKEE

For generations, the Cherokee had called the southern Appalachian Mountain region home. But when they were forced off their land in the Trail of Tears, thousands died.

THE CREEK

The Creek had to leave a land rich in variety. It stretched from the ridges and valleys of the Appalachian Mountains in the north, through a region of low hills and valleys, to a flat area of pine forest in the south.

THE SEMINOLE

Many Seminole Indians refused to leave Florida. They hid in the swamps, battling American soldiers. Many of their descendants still live in Florida today.

THE CHICKASAW

The Chickasaw lived in a land of rich, black, prairie soil. They would find the soil west of the Mississippi much less well suited for farming.

THE CHOCTAW

The Choctaw were forced to leave behind the low, rolling hills and plains of their homeland. For generations they had farmed the rich soil there.

KY

TN

Cherokee

Chickasaw

Creek

Chocktaw

AL

GA

MS

FL

Seminole

Gulf of Mexico

ATLANTIC OCEAN

75° W

35° N

30° N

80° W

25° N

85° W

90° W

Tropic of Cancer

GEOGRAPHY SKILLS INTERPRETING MAPS

1. **Place** How did land in the Indian Territory compare to the land in the Indians' homelands?
2. **Movement** How do you think being forced to leave their homelands affected the Indians' way of life?

THE AGE OF JACKSON **337**

337

History and Geography

Linking to Today

Native American Populations A little less than half of the 2 million Native Americans in the United States today live on or near the nation's more than 250 Indian reservations. Each year the Native American population continues to grow. Of the total number of Native Americans, the majority live west of the Mississippi River, particularly in Arizona, California, Oklahoma, New Mexico, and South Dakota.

Info to Know

Native American Literacy While in the Cherokee Regiment of the U.S. Army, in the early 1800s, Sequoya recognized the need for Native American literacy. Many Native Americans were unable to read military orders, send letters home, record events, or even read the treaties they signed. The creation of Talking Leaves, the Cherokee written language, had begun.

Linking to Today

The Cherokee Historians estimate that when Europeans arrived in North America, about 22,000 Cherokee lived in the present-day southeastern United States. Today the largest concentrations of Cherokee are the Eastern Band in North Carolina and the Cherokee Nation of Oklahoma. The federal government also recognizes one other Cherokee group, the United Bank of Keetoowahs, in Oklahoma. More than 50 other groups that are not recognized by the federal government also claim Cherokee heritage.

Cross-Discipline Activity: Geography

At Level

Comparing and Contrasting Regions

Research Required

1. Organize students into five groups and assign each group one of the Native American groups labeled on the map.

2. Have each group conduct research on the climate and physical geography of the assigned group's traditional homelands as well as the climate and physical geography of the area to which the group was relocated.

3. Instruct each group to create a large table comparing and contrasting the two regions. Encourage students to include images or

photographs of the regions to enhance their tables. Groups should then write a summary of the differences between the two regions.

4. Have each group present its work to the class.

5. Have students discuss how geographic differences contributed to the hardships Native Americans faced when forced to relocate.

LS Interpersonal, Verbal/Linguistic

Alternative Assessment Handbook, Rubrics 7: Charts; 14: Group Activity; and 30: Research

Answers

Interpreting Maps 1. *The land in Indian Territory was poor and not good for farming, whereas many of the relocated Indians came from areas with fertile soils, plains, and rolling hills.*
2. *possible answer—They had to adjust to a new climate and learn how to hunt differently, grow food differently, and rely on different materials for their homes and clothing.*

Solving Problems

Social Studies Skills

| Analysis | Critical Thinking | Civic Participation | Study |

Solving Problems

Define the Skill

Problem solving is a process for finding workable solutions to difficult situations. The process involves asking questions, identifying and evaluating information, comparing and contrasting, and making judgments. Problem solving is useful in studying history because it helps you better understand problems a person or group faced at a point in time and how they dealt with those difficulties.

The ability to understand and evaluate how people solved problems in the past also can help in solving similar problems today. The skill can be applied to many other kinds of difficulties besides historical ones as well. It is a method for thinking through almost any situation.

Learn the Skill

Using the following steps will enable you to better understand and solve problems.

1 **Identify the problem.** Ask questions of yourself and others to make sure you know exactly what the situation is and understand why it is a problem.

2 **Gather information.** Ask questions and do other research to learn more about the problem, such as its history, what caused it, what contributes to it, and other factors.

3 **List options.** Based on the information you have gathered, identify possible options for solving the problem that you might consider. Be aware that your final solution will probably be better and easier to reach if you have as many options as possible to consider.

4 **Evaluate the options.** Weigh each option you are considering. Think of and list the advantages it has as a solution, as well as its potential disadvantages.

5 **Choose and implement a solution.** After comparing the advantages and disadvantages of each possible solution, choose the one that seems best and apply it.

6 **Evaluate the solution.** Once the solution has been tried, evaluate its effectiveness in solving the problem. This step will tell you if the solution was a good one, or if another of the possible solutions should be tried instead.

Practice the Skill

One of the most challenging situations that President Jackson faced was the nullification crisis. You can use the problem-solving skills to better understand this problem and to evaluate his solution for it. Review the information about the nullification crisis in this chapter. Then answer the questions below.

1. What was the specific problem that Jackson faced? Why was it a problem?

2. What event led to the problem? What earlier circumstances and conditions contributed to it?

3. List possible solutions to the problem that you would have considered if you had been president, along with advantages and disadvantages.

4. Jackson threatened to send troops to South Carolina to enforce federal law. Do you think his solution was the best one? Explain why, or if not, what solution would have been better.

Social Studies Skills

Solving Problems

Activity Problem-Solving Role Play Organize students into groups to practice their problem-solving skills. Assign each group a current or hypothetical issue or problem within the school or community. Then have each group address this issue by writing an outline incorporating the steps included on this page. Groups should begin by identifying the problem and should conclude by suggesting a solution. Have a volunteer from each group present his or her group's outline to the class. Encourage other students to evaluate each group's solution. **LS** **Interpersonal, Logical/Mathematical**

- Alternative Assessment Handbook, Rubric 35: Solving Problems

- Interactive Skills Tutor CD-ROM: Lessons 12: Identify Issues and Problems; and 16: Identify Possible Solutions and Predict Consequences

Answers

Practice the Skill 1. *The South Carolina legislature passed a resolution nullifying the tariffs of 1828 and 1832 and threatened to secede if the federal government used force to try to collect the duties. This situation posed a problem because it threatened federal authority and the Union.* **2.** *passage of the 1832 tariff; passage of the 1828 tariffs and the states' rights doctrine;* **3.** *Answers will vary, but students should provide logical advantages and disadvantages for each proposed solution.* **4.** *Answers will vary, but students should exhibit an understanding of the advantages and disadvantages of using troops and provide reasons to support why another solution, if offered, would have been better.*

338

Social Studies Skills Activity: Solving Problems | At Level

Alternate Solutions to Indian Removal

1. Have students review the text in Section 3 under the headings "Indian Removal Act" and "Cherokee Resistance."

2. Organize students into groups and ask the groups to imagine that they are members of the U.S. Congress at that time. Have each group consider a solution to the problem of American settlers wanting to move into Native American lands that does not require forcing Native Americans to move and that respects their right to their lands.

3. Each group should create a flow chart showing its responses for each of the steps listed under "Learn the Skill."

4. Have a representative from each group present his or her group's flow chart to the class. Have students evaluate each group's proposed solution and discuss possible advantages and disadvantages. **LS** **Interpersonal, Logical/Mathematical**

- Alternative Assessment Handbook, Rubrics 14: Group Activity; and 35: Solving Problems

Visual Summary

Use the visual summary below to help you review the main ideas of the chapter.

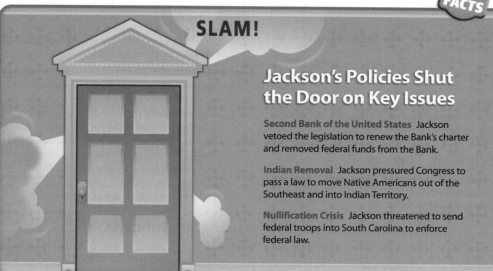

SLAM!

Jackson's Policies Shut the Door on Key Issues

Second Bank of the United States Jackson vetoed the legislation to renew the Bank's charter and removed federal funds from the Bank.

Indian Removal Jackson pressured Congress to pass a law to move Native Americans out of the Southeast and into Indian Territory.

Nullification Crisis Jackson threatened to send federal troops into South Carolina to enforce federal law.

Reviewing Vocabulary, Terms, and People

Complete each sentence by filling in the blank with the correct term or person.

1. In the Supreme Court case of _____, the Court ruled that the federal government, not the states, had authority over the Cherokee.

2. President Jackson's group of advisers was known as the _____ because of where its members met in the White House.

3. _____ served as Andrew Jackson's vice president until he resigned due to the dispute over nullification.

4. The _____ supported the power of the states over the federal government.

5. The practice of rewarding supporters with positions in government is known as the _____.

Comprehension and Critical Thinking

SECTION 1 *(Pages 322–324)*

6. **a. Identify** What changes took place in the early 1800s that broadened democracy in the United States?

   b. Analyze How was Jackson's victory in the election of 1828 a reflection of a change in American politics?

   c. Evaluate Do you think the changes brought about by Jacksonian Democracy went far enough in expanding democracy? Why or why not?

SECTION 2 *(Pages 326–331)*

7. **a. Describe** What conflicts troubled the Jackson administration?

Answers

Visual Summary

Review and Inquiry Ask students how the images in the Visual Summary relate to the chapter content. For instance, what is the significance of the door slammed shut? Could any of Jackson's policies be represented by an open door? Which ones? What other symbols could be used to represent some of the policies of the Jackson administration?

 Quick Facts Transparency: The Age of Jackson Visual Summary

Reviewing Vocabulary, Terms, and People

1. *Worcester* v. *Georgia*
2. kitchen cabinet
3. John C. Calhoun
4. states' rights doctrine
5. spoils system

Comprehension and Critical Thinking

6. **a.** Many states expanded voting rights to enable more white men to vote; some states allowed voters to nominate their electors; political parties began holding nominating conventions.

   b. More people had the vote, and Jackson and Calhoun received a record number of popular votes.

   c. Students should note that voting rights expanded but still excluded groups such as African Americans, Native Americans, and women.

Review and Assessment Resources

Review and Reinforce

SE Chapter Review

CRF: Chapter Review Activity

 Quick Facts Transparency: The Age of Jackson Visual Summary

 Spanish Chapter Summaries Audio CD Program

 Online Chapter Summaries in Six Languages

OSP Holt PuzzlePro; GameTool for ExamView

 Quiz Game CD-ROM

Assess

SE Standardized Test Practice

 PASS: Chapter Test, Forms A and B

 Alternative Assessment Handbook

OSP ExamView Test Generator, Chapter Test

 Differentiated Instruction Modified Worksheets and Tests CD-ROM: Chapter Test

 Holt Online Assessment Program (in the Premier Online Edition)

Reteach/Intervene

 Interactive Reader and Study Guide

 Differentiated Instruction Teacher Management System: Lesson Plans for Differentiated Instruction

 Differentiated Instruction Modified Worksheets and Tests CD-ROM

 Interactive Skills Tutor CD-ROM

go.hrw.com
Online Resources

Chapter Resources:
KEYWORD: SR8 US10

7. a. Tariff of Abominations, Nullification Crisis, issues connected to the Second Bank of the United States, inflation
b. led to Jackson's veto, inflation of the economy, and angered members of Congress
c. possible answer—might lead to increasing sectional divisions in the nation that could possibly threaten the unity of the nation

8. a. Cherokee who created a writing system for the Cherokee language
b. Cherokee—adopted white culture, appealed to the U.S. courts; Seminole—fought
c. possible answers—Yes, he did not personally agree with the decision; no, Jackson failed to fulfill his duties as president and to respect the power of the judiciary.

Reviewing Themes

9. Whig Party; favored a weak president

10. desire for land and wealth— Farmers wanted land, and gold was discovered on Cherokee land.

Social Studies Skills

11. a

Reading Skills

12. a

---

b. Draw Conclusions What were the results of the conflict over the Second Bank of the United States?

c. Predict How might sectional differences and the debate over states' rights lead to future problems for the United States?

SECTION 3 (Pages 332–335)

8. a. Identify Who was Sequoya? What important contribution did he make?

b. Contrast In what different ways did the Cherokee and the Seminole attempt to resist removal to Indian Territory?

c. Elaborate Do you agree with Jackson's refusal to enforce the *Worcester* v. *Georgia* ruling? Why or why not?

Reviewing Themes

9. Politics What new political party rose in opposition to President Andrew Jackson? What was the party's attitude toward the power of the president?

10. Economics What economic factors influenced the policy of Indian removal?

Social Studies Skills

Solving Problems Use the Social Studies Skills taught in this chapter to answer the question about the reading selection below.

> Northerners wanted the tariff to protect their industries from foreign competition, especially from Great Britain. British companies were driving smaller American companies out of business by selling factory goods more cheaply than Americans could afford to make them . . . Southerners opposed the tariff, claiming it would hurt their economy. *(p. 327)*

11. Which of the following might be a reasonable solution to the problem discussed above?
a. passing a low tariff
b. passing a high tariff only in the South
c. Britain passing a tariff
d. selling northern and British goods for a higher price

Reading Skills

Drawing Conclusions about the Past Use the Reading Skills taught in this chapter to answer the question about the reading selection below.

> Native Americans had long lived in settlements stretching from Georgia to Mississippi. However, President Jackson and other political leaders wanted to open this land to settlement by American farmers. *(p. 332)*

12. Which statement below can you conclude from the passage above?
a. Farmers moved onto the Native Americans' land after they were removed.
b. Native Americans wanted to move from their lands.
c. Native Americans resisted removal.
d. Government officials had to use force to remove Native Americans from their land.

Using the Internet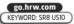

13. Activity: Writing a newspaper Enter the activity keyword and research Jackson's presidency. Then create a party newspaper, using the template provided, that supports or criticizes his policies. Use evidence to support your articles either in favor or against his policies. Write from the point of view of a supporter or from the point of view of a political enemy.

FOCUS ON WRITING

14. Writing Interview Questions Review the notes you have taken about Jackson's political significance, the conflicts he was involved in, and the causes and effects of his policies toward Indians. Then, based on your notes, begin writing questions for your interview with Jackson. What will the readers of your newspaper want to learn more about? Write at least 10 interview questions that your readers will want to know the answer to.

Using the Internet

13. Go to the HRW Web site and enter the keyword shown to access a rubric for this activity.

KEYWORD: SR8 US10

Focus on Writing

14. Rubric Students' interview questions should:
- require more than a yes or no answer.
- address Jackson's campaign and election, the conflicts he was involved in, and the causes and effects of his Indian policies.
- use correct grammar, punctuation, spelling, and capitalizations.

📰 **CRF:** Focus on Writing Activity: An Interview

Standardized Test Practice

DIRECTIONS: Read each question and write the letter of the best response.

1 The era surrounding the presidency of Andrew Jackson is *best* known for an expansion in
A freedom of speech.
B religious toleration.
C states' rights.
D voting rights.

2 Which of the following was *least important* to the South's economy in the 1830s?
A small farming
B manufacturing
C plantation agriculture
D trade

3 What action did the Cherokee take to resist their removal from Georgia and North Carolina to the West?
A sued the state of Georgia in the courts
B destroyed neighbors' farms and businesses
C went to war against the U.S. government
D staged a protest called the Trail of Tears

4 The debate between John C. Calhoun and Daniel Webster over states' rights was *most like* the debate between
A the Patriots and the Loyalists.
B the Antifederalists and the Federalists.
C England and France during the French and Indian War.
D the large states and the small states during the Constitutional Convention.

5 President Jackson's weakening of the Second Bank of the United States resulted in
A inflation and other economic problems.
B the nullification crisis.
C the rise of the Democratic Party.
D increasing sectionalism.

6 Which of the following was *not* a difference between the North and the South?
A conflicting views on the issue of slavery
B disagreement over the Indian removal policy
C different economic interests
D disagreement over protective tariffs

7

> "The people have preserved . . . their . . . Constitution, for forty years, and have seen their happiness, prosperity, and renown grow with its growth, and strengthen with its strength. . . I have not coolly weighed the chances of preserving liberty when the bonds that unite us together shall be broken . . . [Let us not have] 'Liberty first and Union afterwards,' but . . . that other sentiment, dear to every true American heart,—Liberty and Union, now and for-ever, one and inseparable!"
>
> –Daniel Webster

From the content of this passage, one could conclude that the writer would have been opposed to
A a protective tariff.
B nationalism.
C nullification.
D internal improvements.

1. D
Break Down the Question: If students have a hard time choosing between options *C* and *D*, point out that the question asks for the issue for which the era is *best* known.

2. B
Break Down the Question: Remind students to pay attention to italicized words. Here, the phrase *least important* means that more than one answer may be partially correct.

3. A
Break Down the Question: This question requires students to recall factual information. Refer students who have trouble to the text titled "Cherokee Resistance" in Section 3.

4. B
Break Down the Question: This question connects to information covered in Chapter 4.

5. A
Break Down the Question: This question requires students to recall factual information. Refer students who have trouble to the text titled "Jackson Attacks the bank" in Section 2.

6. B
Break down the Question This question requires students to recall factual information. Refer students who have trouble to the text titled "Sectional Differences Increase" in Section 2.

7. C
Break Down the Question: To help students identify the overall meaning of a passage, tell them to look for key repeated words or phrases. Here, point out the repetition of the idea of unity expressed through the words *unity, Union,* and *one and inseparable.* Then tell students to identify which answer is most *opposed* to unity or Union?

Intervention Resources

Reproducible
- Interactive Reader and Study Guide
- Differentiated Instruction Teacher Management System: Lesson Plans for Differentiated Instruction

Technology
- Quick Facts Transparency: The Age of Jackson Visual Summary
- Differentiated Instruction Modified Worksheets and Tests CD-ROM
- Interactive Skills Tutor CD-ROM

Tips for Test Taking

Significant Details Students will often be asked to recall details from a reading passage. Tell students in such situations to read the question before they read the passage. Then, as they read the passage, students should underline key details. Remind students that the correct answer will not always precisely match the wording of the passage, however.

Chapter 11 Planning Guide

Expanding West

Chapter Overview	Reproducible Resources	Technology Resources
CHAPTER 11 pp. 342–375 **Overview: In this chapter, students will examine the movement of Americans to the West and the expansion of U.S. influence in Texas and California.**	**Differentiated Instruction Teacher Management System:*** • Instructional Benchmarking Guides • Lesson Plans for Differentiated Instruction **Interactive Reader and Study Guide:** Chapter Graphic Organizer* **Chapter Resource File:*** • Focus on Writing Activity: Outline for a Documentary Film • Social Studies Skills Activity: Interpreting Maps: Expansion • Chapter Review Activity	**Power Presentations with Video CD-ROM** **Differentiated Instruction Modified Worksheets and Tests CD-ROM** **Primary Source Library CD-ROM for United States History** **Interactive Skills Tutor CD-ROM** **Student Edition on Audio CD Program** **History's Impact: United States History Video Program (VHS/DVD):** Expanding West*
Section 1: **Trails to the West** **The Big Idea:** The American West attracted a variety of settlers.	**Differentiated Instruction Teacher Management System:** Section 1 Lesson Plan* **Interactive Reader and Study Guide:** Section 1 Summary* **Chapter Resource File:*** • Vocabulary Builder Activity, Section 1 • Biography Activity: James P. Beckwourth	**Daily Bellringer Transparency:** Section 1* **Map Transparency:** Trails Leading West*
Section 2: **The Texas Revolution** **The Big Idea:** In 1836, Texas gained its independence from Mexico.	**Differentiated Instruction Teacher Management System:** Section 2 Lesson Plan* **Interactive Reader and Study Guide:** Section 2 Summary* **Chapter Resource File:*** • Vocabulary Builder Activity, Section 2 • Interdisciplinary Project: Share the Westward Adventure • Biography Activity: Lorenzo de Zavala	**Daily Bellringer Transparency:** Section 2* **Map Transparency:** The Texas Revolution* **Internet Activity:** Texas Revolution Ballad
Section 3: **The Mexican-American War** **The Big Idea:** The ideals of manifest destiny and the outcome of the Mexican-American War led to U.S. expansion to the Pacific Ocean.	**Differentiated Instruction Teacher Management System:** Section 3 Lesson Plan* **Interactive Reader and Study Guide:** Section 3 Summary* **Chapter Resource File:*** • Vocabulary Builder Activity, Section 3 • History and Geography Activity: Spanish Missions in California • Primary Source Activities: From the Journal of Junípero Serra; A Mexican Views the War	**Daily Bellringer Transparency:** Section 3* **Map Transparency:** Mexican-American War, 1846–1847* **Internet Activity:** Spanish Missions Model
Section 4: **The California Gold Rush** **The Big Idea:** The California gold rush changed the future of the West.	**Differentiated Instruction Teacher Management System:** Section 4 Lesson Plan* **Interactive Reader and Study Guide:** Section 4 Summary* **Chapter Resource File:*** • Vocabulary Builder Activity, Section 4 • Literature: *New Orleans to San Francisco in '49* • Biography Activities: Biddy Mason; Levi Strauss • Primary Source Activity: Family Letters During the California Gold Rush	**Daily Bellringer Transparency:** Section 4* **Quick Facts Transparency:** Westward Movement in the United States*

Review, Assessment, Intervention

Quick Facts Transparency: Expanding West Visual Summary*

Spanish Chapter Summaries Audio CD Program

Progress Assessment Support System (PASS): Chapter Test*

Differentiated Instruction Modified Worksheets and Tests CD-ROM: Modified Chapter Test

One-Stop Planner CD-ROM: ExamView Test Generator (English/Spanish)

Alternative Assessment Handbook

PASS: Section 1 Quiz*

Online Quiz: Section 1

Alternative Assessment Handbook

PASS: Section 2 Quiz*

Online Quiz: Section 2

Alternative Assessment Handbook

PASS: Section 3 Quiz*

Online Quiz: Section 3

Alternative Assessment Handbook

PASS: Section 4 Quiz*

Online Quiz: Section 4

Alternative Assessment Handbook

Power Presentations with Video CD-ROM

Power Presentations with Video are visual presentations of each chapter's main ideas. Presentations can be customized by including Quick Facts charts, images from the text, and video clips.

Power Presentations with Video CD-ROM

HOLT
SOCIAL STUDIES
United States History
Beginnings to 1877

HOLT, RINEHART AND WINSTON
A Harcourt Education Company

DIVISION FOR
PUBLIC
EDUCATION
AMERICAN BAR ASSOCIATION

Developed by the Division for Public Education of the American Bar Association, these materials are part of the **Democracy and Civic Education Resources.**

• **Constitution Study Guide**

• **Supreme Court Case Studies**

Holt Online Learning

Teacher Resources
KEYWORD: SR8 TEACHER

Student Resources
KEYWORD: SR8 US11

• Document-Based Questions
• Interactive Multimedia Activities

• Current Events
• Chapter-based Internet Activities
• and more!

Holt Premier
Online Student Edition

Complete online support for interactivity, assessment, and reporting

• Interactive Maps and Notebook
• Standardized Test Prep
• Homework Practice and Research Activities Online

Differentiating Instruction

ENGLISH-LANGUAGE LEARNERS & STRUGGLING READERS

TARGET RESOURCE

Live Ink® Online Reading Help

Spanish Resources

Spanish Chapter Summaries Audio CD Program

One-Stop Planner CD-ROM:
- ExamView Test Generator, Spanish
- PuzzlePro, Spanish

Additional Resources

Differentiated Instruction Teacher Management System: Lesson Plans for Differentiated Instruction

Chapter Resources:
- Vocabulary Builder Activities
- Social Studies Skills Activity: Interpreting Maps: Expansion

Quick Facts Transparencies:
- Westward Movement in the United States
- Expanding West Visual Summary

Student Edition on Audio CD Program

Online Chapter Summaries in Six Languages

Interactive Skills Tutor CD-ROM

SPECIAL NEEDS LEARNERS

TARGET RESOURCE

Differentiated Instruction Modified Worksheets and Tests CD-ROM

- Vocabulary Flash Cards
- Modified Vocabulary Builder Activities
- Modified Chapter Review Activity
- Modified Chapter Test

Additional Resources

Differentiated Instruction Teacher Management System: Lesson Plans for Differentiated Instruction

Interactive Reader and Study Guide

Social Studies Skills Activity: Interpreting Maps: Expansion

Student Edition on Audio CD Program

Interactive Skills Tutor CD-ROM

Live Ink® Online Reading Help

ADVANCED/GIFTED AND TALENTED STUDENTS

TARGET RESOURCE

Primary Source Library CD-ROM for United States History

The Library contains longer versions of quotations in the text, extra sources, and images. Included are point-of-view articles, journals, diaries, historical fiction, and political documents.

Additional Resources

Political Cartoons Activities for United States History: Cartoon 12: James Polk and Foreign Policy; Cartoon 13: The California Gold Rush

United States History Document-Based Questions Activities

Differentiated Instruction Teacher Management System: Lesson Plans for Differentiated Instruction

Pre-AP Activities Guide for United States History: Document-Based Questions

Chapter Resource File:
- Focus on Writing Activity: Outline for a Documentary Film
- Primary Source Activities: From the Journal of Junípero Serra; A Mexican Views the War

One-Stop Planner® CD-ROM
for Differentiated Instruction

Your differentiated instruction lesson plans are available at your fingertips. Holt's Teacher Management System links teaching support tools to pages in the Interactive Teacher's Edition.

The One-Stop Planner features:
· Interactive Teacher's Edition
· Calendar Planner and pacing guides
· Editable lesson plans
· All reproducible ancillaries in Adobe Acrobat (PDF) format
· ExamView Test Generator (English and Spanish)
· Transparency and video previews

Professional Development

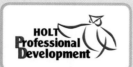

· **In-service and staff development** as part of your Holt Social Studies product purchase
· **Quick Teacher Tutorial Lesson Presentation CD-ROM**
· Intensive tuition-based **Teacher Development Institute**
· **Teaching American History Online**—2 Module Professional Development Course
· **Convenient Holt Speaker Bureau**—face-to-face workshop options
· **PRAXIS™ Test Prep** interactive Web-based content refreshers*
· **24/7 Ask A Professional Development Expert** at http://www.hrw.com/prodev/

* PRAXIS is a trademark of Educational Testing Service (ETS). This publication is not endorsed or approved by ETS.

Chapter Big Ideas

Section 1 The American West attracted a variety of settlers.

Section 2 In 1836, Texas gained its independence from Mexico.

Section 3 The United States expanded to the Pacific Ocean due to manifest destiny and the Mexican-American War.

Section 4 The California gold rush changed the future of the West.

Focus on Writing

The **Chapter Resource File** provides a Focus on Writing worksheet to help students create the outlines for their documentary films.

📖 **CRF:** Focus on Writing Activity: Outline for a Documentary Film

---

CHAPTER 11 1800–1855

Expanding West

✏️ **FOCUS ON WRITING**

Outline for a Documentary Film Many documentary films have been made about the history of the United States, but there is always room for one more. In this chapter you will read about the westward expansion of the United States, a period filled with excitement and challenge. Then you will create an outline for a documentary film to be used in middle-school history classes.

UNITED STATES

1811
John Jacob Astor founds the fur-trading post Astoria on the Columbia River.

1810

WORLD

Key to Differentiating Instruction

Below Level

Basic-level activities designed for all students encountering new material

At Level

Intermediate-level activities designed for average students

Above Level

Challenging activities designed for honors and gifted and talented students

Standard English Mastery

Activities designed to improve standard English usage

Introduce the Chapter

At Level

Focus on Westward Expansion

1. Ask students why people in the eastern United States might have wanted to move West during the mid-1800s. What factors were pulling or pushing Americans to go West? Write the labels *Push Factors* and *Pull Factors* for students to see. Have students predict what some of these factors were. Write students' responses under the applicable headings and save the list.

2. Next, have students discuss what challenges settlers might have faced while traveling West and then while building new settlements.

3. Then have students identify the groups who already lived in the West where Americans were going. Ask students to predict how Native Americans and Mexican settlers in the West might have viewed the newly arriving U.S. settlers.

4. Explain to students that they are going to learn about the westward expansion of the United States during the mid-1800s. Tell students that the idea of westward expansion would become an important part of American culture. **LS Verbal/Linguistic**

What You Will Learn...

In this chapter you will learn about how the United States expanded west. The country acquired vast amounts of territory in a short time. Lured by land and gold, hundreds of thousands of Americans followed trails west in search of a better life. However, many Californio families, like the one pictured here, had already lived in California for generations.

● **Chapter Preview** ●

HOLT
History's Impact
▶ video series
See the Video Teacher's Guide for strategies for using the chapter video **Expanding West**.

Explore the Picture

The Lugo Family Spanish and Mexican families, such as the Lugo family pictured at left, had been living in the West for generations when U.S. settlers began coming to the region. The Lugo family were major land-owners in Spanish California. The family's clothing reflects the region's Spanish heritage.

Analyzing Visuals How many generations can you identify in the photograph? *Answers will vary, but the photo shows around four generations of the family.*

1827
The United States and Great Britain agree to continue joint occupation of Oregon Country.

1846
The United States declares war against Mexico.

1848
Gold is discovered in California on January 24.

1820 — **1830** — **1840** — **1850**

1821
Mexico wins its independence from Spain.

1838
Californios revolt unsuccessfully against the Mexican government.

1842
China gives Great Britain control of the island of Hong Kong.

1854
Commodore Matthew Perry negotiates a trade treaty with Japan.

EXPANDING WEST **343**

Explore the Time Line

1. When did the United States declare war against Mexico? *1846*

2. With what nation did the United States agree to joint occupation of Oregon Country in 1827? *Great Britain*

3. How long after John Jacob Astor founded the fur-trading post Astoria was gold discovered in California? *37 years*

4. Based on the time line, what are some major themes in this chapter? *geography (expansion), politics (war, conflict, and foreign relations)*

Info to Know

The West and the American Character
American movement West affected not only the physical size of the United States but also American culture. According to historian Frederick Jackson Turner, Americans are proud of their frontier history and the qualities it took to survive and thrive in the harsh conditions of the West. These qualities included individualism, self-reliance, mobility, and optimism. To this day, Americans celebrate these qualities as part of the national character.

Reading
Social Studies

Understanding Themes

Introduce this chapter to students by telling them that the chapter deals with westward expansion. Ask students to suggest ways in which geography might have affected the settlement of the West. Have students examine a map to help them formulate their answers. Then ask students to predict what economic issues might have led to or resulted from westward expansion. Have each student create an illustration that shows how the two themes of economics and geography might have affected the settlement of the West.

Vocabulary in Context

Focus on Reading Choose a paragraph or two that contain words with which students are likely to be unfamiliar. Write the unfamiliar words for the class to see. Have students read the entire paragraph looking for clues as to the meaning of each word. Then have students write out their definitions of the terms. When students are finished, have them look the words up in a dictionary and write down the definition given there. Ask students if their definition came close to the one in the dictionary. What clues did they use to arrive at their definition?

Reading Social Studies
by Kylene Beers

| Economics | Geography | Politics | Society and Culture | Science and Technology |

Focus on Themes In this chapter you will read about the American people as they continued to move west. You will read about the famous Oregon and Santa Fe trails, Texas's fight for independence from Mexico, and Mexico's war with the United States. Finally, you will read about the California Gold Rush that brought thousands of people west. As you read each section, you will see how **economic** issues affected the growth of different **geographic** areas.

Vocabulary in Context

Focus on Reading In Chapter 3 you learned how writers sometimes give you clues to a word's meaning in the same or a nearby sentence. Those clues are usually definitions, restatements in different words, or comparisons or contrasts. But what do you do if you don't know the word and the writer doesn't think to give you a direct clue?

Using Broader Context Clues If the writer doesn't give you one of those direct clues, you have to try to figure out the meaning of the word for yourself.

1. Read the whole paragraph and look for information that will help you figure out the meaning.

2. Look up the word in the dictionary to be sure of its meaning.

Notice how a student used information from the whole paragraph to learn the meaning of two unknown words.

In 1844, the Whigs passed up Tyler and chose Senator Henry Clay of Kentucky as their presidential candidate. At first opposing *annexation*, Clay changed his mind due to pressure from southern politicians. The Democratic Party chose former Tennessee governor James K. Polk to oppose Clay. Both candidates strongly favored *acquiring* Texas and Oregon, but Polk was perceived as the *expansionist* candidate. *(p. 355)*

> I'm not sure about *annexation*. The southerners convinced Clay to be for it. Maybe I'll understand if I read some more.

> Oh, both presidential candidates favored *acquiring* Texas and Oregon. Maybe *annexation* means almost the same thing as *acquiring*. I'll check the dictionary.

> The dictionary definition is "to add or attach." That's close. Now what about *expansionist*? I know one meaning of *expand* is similar to *add*. An *expansionist* was probably someone who wanted to add to or expand the country.

344 CHAPTER 11

Reading and Skills Resources

Reading Support
- Interactive Reader and Study Guide
- Student Edition on Audio CD Program
- Spanish Chapter Summaries Audio CD Program

Social Studies Skills Support
- Interactive Skills Tutor CD-ROM

Vocabulary Support
- **CRF:** Vocabulary Builder Activities
- **CRF:** Chapter Review Activity
- Differentiated Instruction Modified Worksheets and Tests CD-ROM:
  - Vocabulary Flash Cards
  - Vocabulary Builder Activity
  - Chapter Review Activity

OSP Holt PuzzlePro

You Try It!

The following passage is from the chapter you are about to read. Read the passage and then answer the questions.

American Settlement in the Mexican Cession

From Chapter 11, p. 361

The war ended after Scott took Mexico City. In February 1848, the United States and Mexico signed the Treaty of Guadalupe Hidalgo, which officially ended the war and forced Mexico to turn over much of its northern territory to the United States. Known as the Mexican Cession, this land included the present-day states of California, Nevada, and Utah . . .

In exchange for this vast territory, the United States agreed to pay Mexico $15 million. In addition, the United States agreed to assume claims of more than $3 million held by American citizens against the Mexican government.

Refer to the passage to answer the following questions.

1. Do you know what the word *cession* means? What clues in the first paragraph can help you figure out what the word might mean? Use those clues to write a definition of cession.

2. Look *cession* up in a dictionary. How does your definition compare to the dictionary definition?

3. In your experience, what does the word *assume* usually mean? Do you think that meaning is the one used in the second paragraph? If not, what do you think *assume* means in this case?

4. Look *assume* up in a dictionary. Does one of its meanings match the one you came up with?

> **As you read Chapter 11,** use context clues to figure out the meanings of unfamiliar words. Check yourself by looking the words up in a dictionary.

Key Terms and People

Academic Vocabulary

Success in school is related to knowing academic vocabulary— the words that are frequently used in school assignments and discussions. In this chapter, you will learn the following academic words:

explicit *(p. 351)*
elements *(p. 357)*

Reading Social Studies

Key Terms and People

To preview the key terms and people from this chapter, have the class create an illustrated children's book about the West. Each page in the book will be dedicated to a separate term or person and will define or identify that word, as well as include an illustration. Assign each student a term or person from the list at left. Have students look up the importance of their term. Then have students create a page for the children's book. Combine all the pages together to complete the book.

LS **Visual/Spatial, Verbal/Linguistic**

Focus on Reading

See the **Focus on Reading** questions in this chapter for more practice on this reading social studies skill.

Reading Social Studies Assessment

See the **Chapter Review** at the end of this chapter for student assessment questions related to this reading skill.

Teaching Tip

Many times primary sources contain words with which students will be unfamiliar. In these instances, remind students to first attempt to figure out the meaning of the word based on the content of the whole paragraph. Encourage students to use a dictionary to define words about which they are unsure. Help students practice defining words based on context by asking them to read primary source documents on a regular basis.

Answers

You Try It! 1. *clues*—Mexico turned over much of its northern territory, this land included; *possible definition—a cession is an area of land that one country gives to another;* **2.** *dictionary definition— the act of yielding property to another;* **3.** *to guess or suppose; no; to take over;* **4.** *yes; to take on or adopt*

Trails to the West

Bellringer

If YOU were there . . . Use the **Daily Bellringer Transparency** to help students answer the question.

🖨 Daily Bellringer Transparency, Section 1

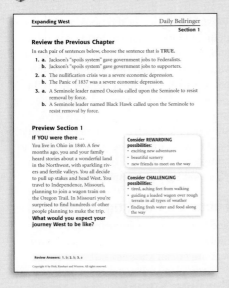

Building Vocabulary

Preteach or review the following terms:

Oregon Country early to mid-1800s name for the Pacific Northwest (p. 347)

persecuted to be treated unfairly or cruelly because of religious beliefs, race, ethnicity, or gender (p. 349)

🖨 **CRF:** Vocabulary Builder Activity, Section 1

Taking Notes

Have students copy the graphic organizer onto their own paper and then use it to take notes on the section. This activity will prepare students for the Section Assessment, in which they will complete a graphic organizer that builds on the information using a critical thinking skill.

What You Will Learn...

Main Ideas

1. During the early 1800s, Americans moved west of the Rocky Mountains to settle and trade.
2. The Mormons traveled west in search of religious freedom.

The Big Idea

The American West attracted a variety of settlers.

Key Terms and People

John Jacob Astor, *p. 346*
mountain men, *p. 346*
Oregon Trail, *p. 348*
Santa Fe Trail, *p. 349*
Mormons, *p. 349*
Brigham Young, *p. 349*

TAKING NOTES Create a diagram like the one below. As you read, take notes on the different groups that settled in the American West, the trails they took, and their motives for moving West.

Trails	Travelers	Motives

If YOU were there...

You live in Ohio in 1840. A few months ago, you and your family heard stories about a wonderful land in the Northwest, with sparkling rivers and fertile valleys. You all decide to pull up stakes and head West. You travel to Independence, Missouri, planning to join a wagon train on the Oregon Trail. In Missouri, you're surprised to find hundreds of other people planning to make the trip.

What would you expect your journey West to be like?

BUILDING BACKGROUND Many Americans in the Jacksonian Era were restless, curious, and eager to be on the move. The American West drew a variety of settlers. Some looked for wealth and adventure. Others, like this family on its way to the Northwest, dreamed of rich farmland and new homes.

Americans Move West

In the early 1800s, Americans pushed steadily westward, moving even beyond the territory of the United States. They traveled by canoe and flatboat, on horseback, and by wagon train. Some even walked much of the way.

The rush to the West occurred, in part, because of a hat. The "high hat," made of water-repellent beaver fur, was popular in the United States and Europe. While acquiring fur for the hats, French, British, and American companies gradually killed off the beaver population in the East. Companies moved west in search of more beavers. Most of the first non-Native Americans who traveled to the Rocky Mountains and the Pacific Northwest were fur traders and trappers.

American merchant **John Jacob Astor** created one of the largest fur businesses, the American Fur Company. His company bought skins from western fur traders and trappers who became known as **mountain men**. These adventurers were some of the first easterners to explore and map the Rocky Mountains and lands west of them. Mountain men lived lonely and often dangerous lives. They trapped animals on their own, far from towns and settlements. Mountain men such as Jedediah Smith, Manuel Lisa, Jim Bridger, and Jim

---

Teach the Big Idea

At Level

Trails to the West

1. **Teach** Ask students the questions in the Main Idea boxes to teach this section.

2. **Apply** Create a four-column chart for students to see. Title the chart *Americans Move West* and label the columns *Why, How, Where,* and *When*. Have students use the information in the section to complete the chart. Students should list the reasons why Americans went West, the ways in which they traveled, the trails they took, and when they went. **LS Verbal/Linguistic**

3. **Review** To review the section's main ideas, have students help you complete a master copy of the chart.

4. **Practice/Homework** Have each student create an advertisement for a wagon train heading West. The ad should persuade people to join the wagon train and provide information about the trip.
   LS Verbal/Linguistic, Visual/Spatial

   🖨 Alternative Assessment Handbook, Rubrics 2: Advertisements; and 7: Charts

Trails Leading West

Trails, Distances, and Travel Times

California	2,000 miles, 6 months
Santa Fe	1,200 miles, 2 months
Mormon	1,300 miles, 4 months
Old Spanish	700 miles, 7 weeks
Oregon	2,000 miles, 6 months
Fort or trading post	

Jim Beckwourth was an African American fur trapper and explorer of the West in the early 1800s.

GEOGRAPHY SKILLS · INTERPRETING MAPS

1. **Movement** Which trails took the longest to travel?
2. **Human-Environment Interaction** What difficulties do you think travelers on the trails faced?

Beckwourth survived many hardships during their search for wealth and adventure. To survive on the frontier, mountain men adopted Native American customs and clothing. In addition, they often married Native American women. The Indian wives of trappers often worked hard to contribute to their success.

Pioneer William Ashley saw that frequently bringing furs out of the Rocky Mountains was expensive. He asked his traders to stay in the mountains and meet once a year to trade and socialize. This practice helped make the fur trade more profitable. The yearly meeting was known as the rendezvous. At the rendezvous, mountain men and Native American trappers sold their fur to fur-company agents. It was thus important to bring as many furs as possible. One trapper described the people at a typical rendezvous in 1837. He saw Americans, Canadian French, some Europeans, and "Indians, of nearly every tribe in the Rocky Mountains."

The rendezvous was filled with celebrating and storytelling. At the same time, the meeting was also about conducting business. Western artist Alfred Jacob Miller described how trade was begun in the rendezvous camp.

"The Fur Company's great tent is raised; the Indians erect their picturesque [beautiful] white lodges; the accumulated [collected] furs of the hunting season are brought forth and the Company's tent is a …busy place."

—Alfred Jacob Miller, quoted in *The Fur Trade of the American West*, by David J. Wishart

In 1811, John Jacob Astor founded a fur-trading post called Astoria at the mouth of the Columbia River. Astoria was one of the first American settlements in what became known as Oregon Country. American Indians occupied the region, which was rich in forests, rivers, and wildlife. However, Britain, Russia, Spain, and the United States all claimed the land. The United States based its claim on

EXPANDING WEST **347**

---

❷ Mormons Travel West

The Mormons traveled west in search of religious freedom.

Identify Who established the Church of Jesus Christ of Latter-day Saints?
Joseph Smith

Make Generalizations Why did the Mormon settlement in Utah succeed?
It was well-planned, with broad roads and surrounding farms, and Mormon leaders maintained discipline and order.

Did you know. . .

European demand for hats made from beaver pelts fueled the fur trade in America. The soft fur was removed from the skin, fashioned into felt, and molded into hats. Gentlemen wore beaver hats to be fashionable, and some armies made them part of their uniforms. At the height of the fad, an estimated 100,000 beavers a year were trapped and killed for hats.

Info to Know

The California Trail An average day on the California Trail usually began at 4 A.M. After organizing livestock and yoking the oxen to the wagons, settlers began the day's journey. Travel ended at nightfall, when settlers circled their wagons. Although Native American attacks were rare, the trip was unpleasant and dangerous. In 1849 some 1,500 people died on the California Trail.

Answers

Mormon Pioneers *nine*

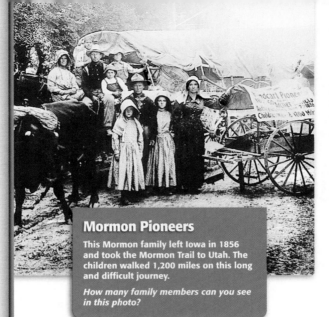

Mormon Pioneers

This Mormon family left Iowa in 1856 and took the Mormon Trail to Utah. The children walked 1,200 miles on this long and difficult journey.

How many family members can you see in this photo?

the exploration of merchant captain Robert Gray, who had reached the mouth of the Columbia River in 1792.

Recognizing the huge economic value of the Pacific Northwest, the United States made treaties in which Spain and Russia gave up their claims to various areas. The United States also signed treaties with Britain allowing both countries to occupy Oregon Country, the Columbia River, and its surrounding lands.

By the 1840s, the era of American fur trading in the Pacific Northwest was drawing to a close. The demand for beaver furs had fallen because fashions changed. Too much trapping had also greatly reduced the number of beavers. Some mountain men gave up their work and moved back east. Their daring stories, however, along with the treaties made by the U.S. government, inspired other Americans to move West. Lured by rich resources and a mild climate, easterners poured into Oregon Country in the 1840s. These new settlers soon replaced the mountain men on the frontier.

The Oregon Trail

Many settlers moving to Oregon Country and other western areas followed the 2,000-mile-long **Oregon Trail**, which stretched from places such as Independence, Missouri, or Council Bluffs, Iowa, west into Oregon Country. The trail followed the Platte and Sweetwater Rivers over the Plains. After it crossed the Rocky Mountains, the trail forked. The northern branch led to the Willamette Valley in Oregon. The other branch went to California and became known as the California Trail.

Traveling the trail challenged the strength and determination of pioneer families. The journey usually began after the rainy season ended in late spring and lasted about six months. The cost, about $600 for a family of four, was high at a time when a typical worker usually made about $1.50 per day. Young families made up most groups of settlers. They gathered in wagon trains for the trip. There could be as few as 10 wagons or as many as several dozen in a wagon train.

The wagons were pulled by oxen, mules, or horses. Pioneers often walked to save their animals' strength. They kept up a tiring pace, traveling from dawn until dusk. Settler Jesse Applegate recalled the advice he received from an experienced Oregon pioneer: "Travel, *travel*, TRAVEL . . . Nothing is good that causes a moment's delay."

Some pioneers brought small herds of cattle with them on the trail. They faced severe hardships, including shortages of food, supplies, and water. Rough weather and geographic barriers, such as rivers and mountains, sometimes forced large numbers of pioneers to abandon their wagons. In the early days of the Oregon Trail, many Native Americans helped the pioneers, acting as guides and messengers. They also traded goods for food. Although newspapers reported Native American "massacres" of pioneers, few settlers died during Indian attacks.

The settlers who arrived safely in Oregon and California found generally healthy

Collaborative Learning

Above Level

Western Trails Scrapbook

Research Required

1. Organize students into groups. Have each group use the library or other resources to locate letters, diaries, journals, and images about life on the Oregon, California, and Santa Fe trails.

2. Have group members list recurring themes, problems, attitudes, and moods found in the entries as well as factors that varied along the trails.

3. Have each group create a scrapbook that combines primary source accounts and images to illustrate recurring themes as well

as unique aspects of life on the western trails. Groups might want to assign a topic or focus to each page or spread of their scrapbook.

4. Display the scrapbooks in the classroom and give students time to view them.

LS Interpersonal, Verbal/Linguistic, Visual/Spatial

Alternative Assessment Handbook, Rubrics 30: Research; and 32: Scrapbooks and pleasant climates. By 1845 some 5,000 settlers occupied the Willamette Valley.

The Santa Fe Trail

The **Santa Fe Trail** was another important path west. It led from Independence, Missouri, to Santa Fe, New Mexico. It followed an ancient trading route first used by Native Americans. American traders loaded their wagon trains with cloth and other manufactured goods to exchange for horses, mules, and silver from Mexican traders in Santa Fe.

The long trip across blazing deserts and rough mountains was dangerous. But the lure of high profits encouraged traders to take to the trail. One trader reported a 2,000 percent profit on his cargo. The U.S. government helped protect traders by sending troops to ensure that Native Americans were not a threat.

READING CHECK Contrasting How were the Oregon and Santa Fe trails different?

Mormons Travel West

One large group of settlers traveled to the West in search of religious freedom. In 1830 a young man named Joseph Smith founded the Church of Jesus Christ of Latter-day Saints in western New York. The members of Joseph Smith's church became known as **Mormons**. Smith told his followers that he had found and translated a set of golden tablets containing religious teachings. The writings were called the *Book of Mormon*.

Church membership grew rapidly. However, certain beliefs and practices caused Mormons to be persecuted. For example, beginning in the 1850s some Mormon men practiced polygamy—a practice in which one man is married to several women at the same time. This practice was outlawed by the church in 1890.

In the early 1830s Smith and his growing number of converts left New York. They formed new communities, first in Ohio, then in Missouri, and finally in Illinois. All

three communities eventually failed, and an anti-Mormon mob murdered Smith in 1844. Following Smith's murder, **Brigham Young** became head of the Mormon Church. Young chose what is now Utah as the group's new home, and thousands of Mormons took the Mormon Trail to the area near the Great Salt Lake, where they prospered. By 1860 there were about 40,000 Mormons in Utah.

READING CHECK Finding Main Ideas
Why did Mormons move west?

> **SUMMARY AND PREVIEW** Some of the first Americans to move West were fur traders and trappers. Settlers soon followed. In the next section you will learn about the Texas Revolution.

go.hrw.com
Online Quiz
KEYWORD: SR8 HP11

Section 1 Assessment

Reviewing Ideas, Terms, and People

1. **a. Identify** What was the **Oregon Trail**?
   b. Elaborate Would you have chosen to leave your home to travel west? Why?
2. **a. Identify** Who are the **Mormons**?
   b. Summarize What difficulties led Mormons to move to Utah?

Critical Thinking

3. **Drawing Conclusions** Review your notes on early American settlement in the West. Then copy the chart below and use it to identify challenges of the trip that western travelers faced.

Travelers	Challenges Faced

FOCUS ON WRITING

4. **Describing Trails West** As you read this section, note important topics that you might want to cover in your documentary film. In addition, write down ideas about how you might present information about each topic. For example, will you use a narrator to tell the life story of Joseph Smith, or will you have actors present it dramatically?

EXPANDING WEST **349**

Section 1 Assessment Answers

1. **a.** a trail that led more than 2,000 miles West across the Rocky Mountains to Oregon Country; one of the main routes of western settlement
   b. Answers will vary but should reflect an understanding of the difficulties of traveling west, such as shortages of food and water, rough weather, and geographic barriers.

2. **a.** members of the Church of Jesus Christ of Latter-day Saints, founded by Joseph Smith
   b. religious persecution and failed communities elsewhere

3. Oregon/California Trail—long, expensive, harsh geography; Santa Fe Trail—mountains, deserts; Santa Fe, Mexico; Mormon Trail—long trip, harsh geography

4. Students should take notes on topics related to the fur trade in the Northwest and to the Oregon, Santa Fe, and Mormon trails.

Close

Have students revisit and discuss the predictions they made in the Chapter Introduction activity. How accurate were students' predictions?

Review

Online Quiz, Section 1

Assess

SE Section 1 Assessment

PASS: Section 1 Quiz

Alternative Assessment Handbook

Reteach/Classroom Intervention

Interactive Reader and Study Guide, Section 1

Interactive Skills Tutor CD-ROM

Answers

Reading Check (left) *Oregon Trail—longer and more expensive to travel, used by settlers moving West; Santa Fe Trail—shorter, used as a trade route*

Reading Check (right) *to build a community and escape religious persecution*

Bellringer

If YOU were there . . . Use the **Daily Bellringer Transparency** to help students answer the question.

📄 Daily Bellringer Transparency, Section 2

Academic Vocabulary

Review with students the high-use academic term in this section.

explicitly fully revealed without vagueness (p. 351)

📄 **CRF:** Vocabulary Builder Activity, Section 2

Taking Notes

Have students copy the graphic organizer onto their own paper and then use it to take notes on the section. This activity will prepare students for the Section Assessment, in which they will complete a graphic organizer that builds on the information using a critical thinking skill.

The Texas Revolution

What You Will Learn...

Main Ideas

1. Many American settlers moved to Texas after Mexico achieved independence from Spain.
2. Texans revolted against Mexican rule and established an independent nation.

The Big Idea

In 1836, Texas gained its independence from Mexico.

Key Terms and People

Father Miguel Hidalgo y Costilla, *p. 350*

empresarios, *p. 350*

Stephen F. Austin, *p. 351*

Antonio López de Santa Anna, *p. 351*

Alamo, *p. 352*

Battle of San Jacinto, *p. 352*

TAKING NOTES As you read, take notes on the events that led to the independence of Texas. Write your notes in steps, as shown below.

1. Mexican government hires empresarios.
2. _____
3. _____
4. _____

If YOU were there...

You are the father of a large farm family in Missouri. There is not enough land for everyone, so you're looking for another opportunity. One day, a Mexican government official comes to town. He is looking for people to settle in Texas. The Mexican government is offering generous tracts of land to colonists. However, you have to become a citizen of Mexico and follow Mexican laws.

Would you decide to move your family to Texas? Why?

BUILDING BACKGROUND Spain controlled a vast amount of territory in what would later become the American Southwest. The Spanish built missions and forts in Texas to establish control of that region. But the settlements were far apart, and conflicts with Native Americans discouraged Spanish settlers from moving to Texas. When Mexico became an independent republic, it actively looked for more settlers.

American Settlers Move to Texas

Mexico had a long, unprotected border that stretched from Texas to California. Mexico's Spanish rulers worried constantly about attacks from neighbors. They also were concerned about threats from within Mexico.

Their fears were justified. Mexicans moved to overthrow Spanish rule in the early 1800s. In September 1810 **Father Miguel Hidalgo y Costilla,** a Mexican priest, led a rebellion of about 80,000 poor Indians and mestizos, or people of Indian and Spanish ancestry. They hoped that if Mexico became independent from the Spanish monarchy, their lives would improve.

Hidalgo's revolt failed, but the rebellion he started grew. In 1821 Mexico became independent. In 1824 it adopted a republican constitution that declared rights for all Mexicans. The new Mexican government hired **empresarios**, or agents, to bring settlers to Texas. They paid the agents in land.

Teach the Big Idea

The Texas Revolution

1. **Teach** Ask students the questions in the Main Idea boxes to teach this section.

2. **Apply** Discuss the main events in this section related to Mexican independence from Spain, the Texas War for Independence, and the aftermath of these events. Then have students create annotated time lines covering these events. Students' time lines should provide brief captions explaining the significance of each entry. **LS Visual/Spatial**

3. **Review** As you review the section's main ideas, have students check their time lines to see if they accurately traced the main events in the section.

4. **Practice/Homework** Have students copy their time lines onto a larger piece of paper and then add drawings to illustrate at least four of the events on their time lines. **LS Visual/Spatial**

📄 Alternative Assessment Handbook, Rubrics 3: Artwork; and 36: Time Lines

Settling Texas

Stephen F. Austin, shown at left, and other settlers were empresarios—they received land from the Mexican government for the purpose of bringing settlers to Texas. Their holdings were guaranteed with a contract like the one below.

Why do you think the Mexican government wanted to attract settlers to Texas?

In 1822 one young agent, **Stephen F. Austin**, started a colony on the lower Colorado River. The first 300 families became known as the Old Three Hundred. Austin's successful colony attracted other agents, and American settlers flocked to the region.

In exchange for free land, settlers had to obey Mexican laws. But some settlers often **explicitly** ignored these laws. For example, despite the ban on slavery, many brought slaves. Concerned that it was losing control to the growing American population, Mexico responded. In 1830, it banned further settlement by Americans. Angry about the new law, many Texans began to think of gaining independence from Mexico.

Meanwhile, Mexico had come under the rule of General **Antonio López de Santa Anna**. He soon suspended Mexico's republican constitution and turned his attention to the growing unrest in Texas.

READING CHECK Finding Main Ideas Why did settlers move to Texas?

Texans Revolt against Mexico

In October 1835 the Mexican army tried to remove a cannon from the town of Gonzales, Texas. Rebels stood next to the cannon. Their flag read, "Come and take it." In the following battle, the rebels won. The Texas Revolution, also known as the Texas War for Independence, had begun.

Texas Independence

On March 2, 1836, Texans declared their independence from Mexico. The new Republic of Texas was born. Both the declaration and the constitution that shortly followed were modeled after the U.S. documents. The Texas constitution, however, made slavery legal.

Delegates to the new Texas government chose politician David Burnet as president and Lorenzo de Zavala as vice president. Another revolutionary, Sam Houston, was named to head the Texas army. Austin went to the United States to seek money and troops.

ACADEMIC VOCABULARY
explicit fully revealed without vagueness

EXPANDING WEST **351**

• **Direct Teach** •

Main Idea

❶ **American Settlers Move to Texas**

Many American settlers moved to Texas after Mexico achieved independence from Spain.

Identify When did Mexico achieve independence from Spain? *1821*

Analyze Why is Stephen F. Austin an important figure in Texas history? *In 1822 he started a colony of American settlers in Mexican Texas, which thrived and attracted more American settlers to Texas.*

Make Judgments Do you agree with the decision of Mexican officials to ban further American settlement in Texas in 1830? *Answers will vary but should reflect an understanding that Mexico banned U.S. settlement because American settlers were not following Mexican laws, and Mexico was concerned about losing control.*

CRF: Interdisciplinary Project: Share the Westward Adventure

go.hrw.com
Online Resources

KEYWORD: SR8 US11
ACTIVITY:
Texas Revolution Ballad

Critical Thinking: Finding Main Ideas
At Level

Texas Issues Broadsides

Materials: poster board, art supplies

1. Discuss with students the reasons why Mexico opened Texas up to American settlement, why American settlers went to Texas, why tensions developed between Texas settlers and the Mexican government, and the main events that led to the Texas War for Independence.

2. Organize the class into three groups and assign each group one of the following broadsides: one promoting American settlement in Texas, one urging the Mexican government to close Texas to American settlement, and one urging Texas settlers to declare independence from Mexico. Have each student create the broadside assigned to his or her part of the class.

3. Have volunteers from each group share their broadsides with the class.
   LS Verbal/Linguistic, Visual/Spatial

   Alternative Assessment Handbook, Rubric 28: Posters

Answers

Settling Texas *possible answers—to settle the land; to protect northern Mexico from attack*

Reading Check *lure of the promise of free land*

Main Idea

2 Texans Revolt against Mexico

Texans revolted against Mexican rule and established an independent nation.

Recall When did Texas declare independence from Mexico? *March 2, 1836*

Evaluate How did Santa Anna's decision to execute the Texas prisoners at Goliad hurt the Mexican war effort? *The prisoners' deaths rallied the Texas forces and motivated them to avenge the deaths.*

Draw Conclusions Why do you think most Texans hoped the United States would annex Texas? *possible answer—Many Texans had originally lived in the United States and still saw themselves as part of that nation.*

📖 **CRF:** Biography Activity: Lorenzo de Zavala

🖨 Map Transparency: The Texas Revolution

Biography

Juan Seguín (1806–1890) Born in San Antonio, Texas, in 1806, Juan Seguín became a well-known Tejano politician. Seguín led a troop of Tejano cavalry in the Texas victory at San Jacinto. After the Texas Revolution, he served in the Texas Senate and later as mayor of San Antonio. In 1842, however, he moved his family to Mexico because of rising tensions between Anglos and Tejanos in Texas.

Battle at the Alamo

FOCUS ON READING Use this section to summarize the events of the battle at the Alamo.

The Texans' actions angered Santa Anna. He began assembling a force of thousands to stop the rebellion.

A hastily created army of Texas volunteers had been clashing with Mexican troops for months. Under Colonel Jim Travis, a small force took the town of San Antonio. It then occupied the **Alamo**, an abandoned mission near San Antonio that became an important battle site in the Texas Revolution. Volunteers from the United States, including frontiersman Davy Crockett and Colonel Jim Bowie, joined the Alamo's defense.

The rebels, numbering fewer than 200, hoped to stall the huge Mexican force while a larger Texas army assembled. For almost two weeks, from February 23 to March 6, 1836, the Texans held out. Travis managed to get a message to other Texans through enemy lines:

❝ I call on you in the name of Liberty, of patriotism, and everything dear to the American character, to come to our aid with all dispatch [speed] …VICTORY OR DEATH. ❞
—William Travis, from a letter written at the Alamo, 1836

Before dawn on March 6, the Mexican army attacked. Despite heavy losses, the army overcame the Texans. All the defenders of the Alamo were killed, though some civilians survived. Following a later battle, at Goliad, Santa Anna ordered the execution of 350 prisoners who had surrendered. Texans were enraged by the massacres.

Battle of San Jacinto

Santa Anna now chased the untrained forces of Sam Houston. Outnumbered, the Texans fled east. Finally, they reorganized at the San Jacinto River, near Galveston Bay. There, the Texans took a stand.

Santa Anna was confident of victory, but he was careless in choosing the site for his camp. On the afternoon of April 21, 1836, while Mexican troops were resting, Houston's forces swarmed the camp, shouting, "Remember the Alamo! Remember Goliad!"

The fighting ended swiftly. Santa Anna's army was destroyed. In the **Battle of San Jacinto**, the Texans captured Santa Anna and forced him to sign a treaty giving Texas its independence.

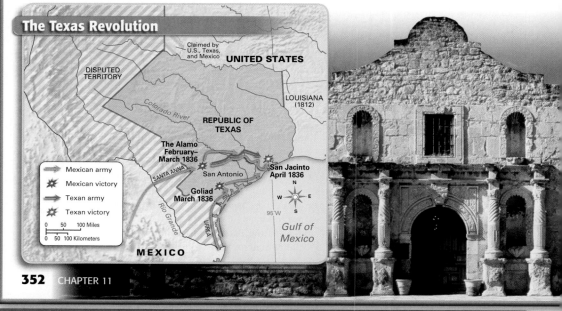

The Texas Revolution

- Claimed by U.S., Texas, and Mexico
- UNITED STATES
- DISPUTED TERRITORY
- Colorado River
- LOUISIANA (1812)
- REPUBLIC OF TEXAS
- The Alamo February–March 1836
- SANTA ANNA
- San Antonio
- San Jacinto April 1836
- Goliad March 1836
- Rio Grande
- URREA
- Gulf of Mexico
- MEXICO

Legend:
- Mexican army
- Mexican victory
- Texan army
- Texan victory

0 50 100 Miles
0 50 100 Kilometers

Critical Thinking: Comparing and Contrasting   At Level

Rebellions Comparison Chart

1. Create a chart with four rows and two columns for students to see. Title the chart *Rebellions* and label each row as follows: *Reasons for Rebellion, Major Figures, Major Battles,* and *Main Effects of the Rebellion.* Label the columns *Mexico* and *Texas.*

2. Have students work either independently or as a class to complete the chart. If time allows, have students conduct research to find additional information beyond that provided in the textbook.

3. Discuss with students the similarities and differences between the Mexican rebellion for independence from Spain and the Texas rebellion for independence from Mexico. **LS Visual/Spatial**

4. **Extend** Have students create a similar chart comparing and contrasting the Texas and American revolutions. **LS Visual/Spatial**

📝 Alternative Assessment Handbook, Rubric 7: Charts

An Independent Nation

Sam Houston was the hero of the new independent nation of Texas. The republic created a new town named Houston and made it the capital. Voters elected Sam Houston as president. Stephen F. Austin became secretary of state.

To increase the population, Texas offered land grants. American settlers came from nearby southern states, often bringing slaves with them to help grow and harvest cotton.

Most Texans hoped that the United States would annex, or take control of, Texas, making it a state. The U.S. Congress also wanted to annex Texas. But President Andrew Jackson refused. He was concerned that admitting Texas as a slave state would upset the fragile balance of free and slave states. The president also did not want to have a war with Mexico over Texas.

Finally, Jackson did recognize Texas as an independent nation. France did so in 1839. Britain, which wanted to halt U.S. expansion, recognized Texas in 1840.

The Mexican government, however, did not recognize Santa Anna's forced handover of Texas. In 1837 the republic organized

the Texas Rangers to guard its long frontier from Mexican and Native American attacks. Finally, in 1844 Texas and Mexico signed a peace treaty.

READING CHECK **Finding Main Ideas** What issues did the new nation of Texas face?

SUMMARY AND PREVIEW American settlers in Texas challenged the Mexican government and won their independence. In the next section you will learn about the war between Mexico and the United States.

On March 6, 1836, Texans fought and lost the Battle of the Alamo. A rallying cry for the Texans at the Battle of San Jacinto was "Remember the Alamo!" The single star of the flag represents the Republic of Texas, also called the Lone Star Republic.

Why do you think "Remember the Alamo!" was a rallying cry for Texas troops at San Jacinto?

Section 2 Assessment

Reviewing Ideas, Terms, and People

1. **a. Identify** What role did **Stephen F. Austin** play in the settlement of Texas?
   b. Make Inferences Why did Mexican officials want to bring more settlers to Texas?
   c. Evaluate Do you think Mexico's requirements for foreign immigrants were reasonable or unreasonable? Explain.
2. **a. Describe** What were the important battles in the War for Texas Independence? Why was each important?
   b. Make Inferences Why did Texas offer land grants to settlers?
   c. Predict What problems might the Republic of Texas face?

Critical Thinking

3. **Sequencing** Review your notes on American settlement in Texas. Then copy the graphic organizer below and use it to show the significant events in the history of the Republic of Texas.

Significant Events
1. Houston is founded and made the capital.
2.
3.
4.
5.
6.
7.

FOCUS ON WRITING

4. **Explaining the Texas Revolution** As you read this section, make note of the most important players and events in the story of how Texas gained independence from Mexico. Consider also how you will present information about these people and events to your film's audience. What words, images, and sounds will make the story of the revolution come alive for them?

EXPANDING WEST **353**

Section 2 Assessment Answers

1. **a.** started a colony on the lower Colorado River
   b. Few Mexicans lived in Texas, and the Mexican government wanted to attract more settlers to protect and control the region better.
   c. possible answers: yes—because Mexico controlled the region and had the right to demand settlers follow its laws; no—because the Mexican government had no right to tell settlers what religion to practice
2. **a.** Gonzales—began the revolution; Alamo—inspired Texans to resist; San Jacinto—Santa Anna was defeated

   b. increase population; control the region
   c. possible answers—economic problems, such as issuing currency, defending borders, establishing and enforcing laws, and diplomatic relations with other nations
3. October 1835—Battle at Gonzales; March 1836—declaration of independence from Mexico, formation of Republic of Texas; Battle of the Alamo; April 1836—Battle of San Jacinto
4. Images and sounds might include the Gonzales cannon, the Alamo, and rallying cries such as "Remember the Alamo! Remember Goliad!"

353

Bellringer

If YOU were there . . . Use the **Daily Bellringer Transparency** to help students answer the question.

🗄 Daily Bellringer Transparency, Section 3

Academic Vocabulary

Review with students the high-use academic term in this section.

elements the basic parts of an individual's surroundings (p. 357)

📄 **CRF:** Vocabulary Builder Activity, Section 3

Taking Notes

Have students copy the graphic organizer onto their own paper and then use it to take notes on the section. This activity will prepare students for the Section Assessment, in which they will complete a graphic organizer that builds on the information using a critical thinking skill.

The Mexican-American War

What You Will Learn...

Main Ideas

1. Many Americans believed that the nation had a manifest destiny to claim new lands in the West.
2. As a result of the Mexican-American War, the United States added territory in the Southwest.
3. American settlement in the Mexican Cession produced conflict and a blending of cultures.

The Big Idea

The ideals of manifest destiny and the outcome of the Mexican-American War led to U.S. expansion to the Pacific Ocean.

Key Terms and People

manifest destiny, *p. 354*
James K. Polk, *p. 355*
vaqueros, p. 357
Californios, *p. 357*
Bear Flag Revolt, *p. 358*
Treaty of Guadalupe Hidalgo, *p. 361*
Gadsden Purchase, *p. 361*

TAKING NOTES Create a graphic organizer like the one below. Use it to define *manifest destiny* and then list the events in the expansion of the United States.

354 CHAPTER 11

If YOU were there...

Your family are Californios, Spanish settlers who have lived in California for many years. You raise horses on your ranch. So far, you have gotten along with American settlers. But it has become clear that the American government wants to take over California. You hear that fighting has already started between American and Mexican troops.

How might life change under American rule?

> **BUILDING BACKGROUND** Mexican independence set the stage for conflict and change in the West and Southwest. At the same time, American settlers continued to move westward, settling in the Mexican territories of Texas and California. American ambitions led to clashes with Mexico and the people who already lived in Mexico's territories.

Manifest Destiny

"We have it in our power to start the world over again."
—Thomas Paine, from his pamphlet *Common Sense*

Americans had always believed they could build a new, better society founded on democratic principles. In 1839 writer John O'Sullivan noted, "We are the nation of human progress, and who will, what can, set limits to our onward march?"

Actually, there was one limit: land. By the 1840s the United States had a booming economy and population. Barely 70 years old, the nation already needed more room for farms, ranches, businesses, and ever-growing families. Americans looked West to what they saw as a vast wilderness, ready to be taken.

Some people believed it was America's **manifest destiny**, or obvious fate, to settle land all the way to the Pacific Ocean in order to spread democracy. O'Sullivan coined the term in 1845. He wrote that it was America's "manifest destiny to overspread and to possess the whole continent which Providence [God] has given us for the development of the great experiment of liberty . . ."

Teach the Big Idea

The Mexican-American War

1. **Teach** Ask students the questions in the Main Idea boxes to teach this section.

2. **Apply** Have students work as a class to help you list the main events and issues in this section. Then have students write a news headline for each event or issue.
   LS Verbal/Linguistic

3. **Review** As you review the section's main ideas, have students share their headlines. Encourage feedback and discussion of headlines.

4. **Practice/Homework** Have each student select one of their headlines—or assign students a headline or topic—and create a political cartoon to go with it. Students should provide short captions explaining their political cartoons. Have volunteers share their cartoons with the class.
   LS Visual/Spatial

📄 Alternative Assessment Handbook, Rubrics 27: Political Cartoons; and 42: Writing to Inform

Manifest Destiny

John Gast's 1872 painting *American Progress* shows the spirit of manifest destiny leading settlers westward.

What in this painting shows how settlers traveled west?

The Mississippi River is in the background as settlers push farther west.

The woman represents America, moving west and bringing sunlight, settlers, and telegraph wires to the new lands.

Native Americans and buffalo are pushed away by the approaching settlers.

In the 1840s and 1850s, manifest destiny was tied up with the slavery issue. If America expanded, would slavery be allowed in the new territories? Several presidents became involved in the difficult issue. Among them was President John Tyler. A pro-slavery Whig, Tyler wanted to increase the power of the southern slave states by annexing Texas. His fellow Whigs disagreed.

In 1844, the Whig Party passed up Tyler and chose Senator Henry Clay of Kentucky as its presidential candidate. At first opposing annexation, Clay changed his mind due to pressure from southern politicians. The Democratic Party chose former Tennessee governor **James K. Polk** to oppose Clay. Both candidates strongly favored acquiring Texas and Oregon.

Southerners feared the loss of Texas, a possible new slave state. Others worried that Texas might become an ally of Britain. These concerns helped Polk narrowly defeat Clay.

Acquiring New Territory

President Polk quickly set out to fulfill his campaign promise to annex Oregon and

Texas. By the 1820s, Russia and Spain had given up their claims to Oregon Country. Britain and the United States had agreed to occupy the territory together.

As more Americans settled there, they began to ask that Oregon become part of the United States. Polk wanted to protect these settlers' interests. Some politicians noted that Oregon Country would provide a Pacific port for the growing U.S. trade with China.

Meanwhile, Britain and the United States disagreed over how to draw the United States–Canadian border. American expansionists cried, "Fifty-four forty or fight!" This slogan referred to 54°40' north latitude, the line to which Americans wanted their northern territory to extend.

Neither side really wanted a war, though. In 1846 Great Britain and the United States signed a treaty that gave the United States all Oregon land south of the forty-ninth parallel. This treaty drew the border that still exists today. Oregon became an organized U.S. territory in February 1848.

Texas came next. By March 1845, Congress had approved annexation and

Main Idea

❶ Manifest Destiny

Many Americans believed that the nation had a manifest destiny to claim new lands in the West.

Identify Who won the presidential election in 1844, and why? *James K. Polk, because many voters supported expansion and he was perceived as the expansionist candidate*

Explain What did "Fifty-four forty or fight!" mean? *slogan used by American expansionists who wanted the U.S.-Canadian border at that parallel*

Identify Points of View How do you think people of other cultures and nations viewed the idea of manifest destiny? *possible answer—Some may have viewed it as an arrogant position, whereas others with similar views might have supported the idea.*

📄 Political Cartoons Activities for United States History, Cartoon 12: James Polk and Foreign Policy

Critical Thinking: Identifying Points of View　　　　At Level

Illustrating Manifest Destiny

1. Write the two John O' Sullivan quotations (found on the previous page) for students to see. Have students paraphrase the quotations in modern English.

2. Have students discuss the quotations and the idea of manifest destiny. Students should consider the various reasons that Americans supported and opposed manifest destiny.

3. Then have each student create a political cartoon or drawing that captures the idea of

manifest destiny in the United States in the 1840s. Display the cartoons or drawings for students to view.

4. Close with a class discussion about how the idea of manifest destiny led Americans to expand the borders of the United States.
LS Visual/Spatial

📄 Alternative Assessment Handbook, Rubrics 3: Artwork; and 27: Political Cartoons

Answers

Manifest Destiny *on foot, on horseback, in trains, wagons, and stagecoaches*

355

❶ Manifest Destiny

Many Americans believed that the nation had a manifest destiny to claim new lands in the West.

Sequence List in order the events leading to U.S. acquisition of Texas and Oregon. *March 1845: U.S. Congress approves Texas annexation; June 1845: Texas Congress approves annexation; 1846: treaty with Britain establishes U.S.-Canadian border; 1848: Oregon a U.S. territory*

Recall What served as the focus of everyday life in California during Spanish rule? *the missions*

Summarize What happened to the missions after Mexico gained independence from Spain? *Mexico ended the mission system, and the mission lands went to the wealthiest Californios, who created vast ranchos.*

Compare How was life for California Indians similar under Spain and Mexico? *Either willingly or by force, Indians adopted Spanish and Mexican ways of life and performed much of the hard labor.*

📄 **CRF:** History and Geography Activity: Spanish Missions in California

📄 **CRF:** Primary Source Activity: From the Journal of Junipero Serra

Answers

Analyzing Visuals *activities, clothing, tools of their trade, environment*

needed only the support of the Republic of Texas. Americans continued to pour into Texas. Texas politicians hoped that joining the United States would help solve the republic's financial and military problems. The Texas Congress approved annexation in June 1845. Texas became part of the United States in December. This action angered the Mexican government, which considered Texas to be a "stolen province."

California under Mexico

Although the annexation of Texas angered Mexico, it still had settlements in other areas of the present-day Southwest to govern. New Mexico was the oldest settled area, with its capital at Santa Fe. Mexico also controlled present-day Arizona, Nevada, and California.

During early Spanish rule, the mission system had dominated much of the present-day Southwest. Over time, it had become less important there, especially in New Mexico, where settlers lived in small villages. In California, however, missions remained the focus of everyday life. Missions under later Spanish rule carried out huge farming and ranching operations using the labor of Native Americans. Some of the Indians came willingly to the missions. Others were brought by force. Usually, they were not allowed to leave the mission once they had arrived. They had to adopt the clothing, food, and religion of the Spanish priests.

Missions often sold their goods to local pueblos, or towns, that arose near the missions and presidios. One wealthy California settler, Mariano Guadalupe Vallejo, remembered the early days.

❝We were the pioneers of the Pacific coast, building towns and missions while General [George] Washington was carrying on the war of the Revolution.❞

—Mariano Guadalupe Vallejo, quoted in *Eyewitnesses and Others*

After winning independence from Spain in 1821, Mexico began to change old Spanish

History Close-up
Ranch Life

Spanish and Mexican *vaqueros*, or cowboys, were expert horseriders. They used their horses to herd cattle on the ranches of the Spanish Southwest.

Vaqueros were known for their specially designed hats.

Leather chaps protected riders from dust and scrapes.

Saddles like these were highly prized by *vaqueros*.

ANALYSIS SKILL **ANALYZING VISUALS**
What features of the *vaqueros'* life are shown in this painting?

356 CHAPTER 11

Differentiating Instruction

English-Language Learners
Below Level
Prep Required

Materials: magazines, poster board, art supplies

California Life Collage Organize students into small groups. Have each group create a collage, in which one half of the collage shows images related to life in California under Spanish rule and the other half depicts life in California under Mexican rule. **LS Visual/Spatial**

📄 Alternative Assessment Handbook, Rubric 8: Collages

Special Needs Learners
Below Level

Compare-and-Contrast Chart Create a chart with two columns and two rows for students to see. Title the chart *California under Spain and Mexico.* Label the columns *Similarities* and *Differences* and the rows *Spanish Rule* and *Mexican Rule.* Have students work in pairs to complete the chart. Then discuss the answers as a class. **LS Visual/Spatial**

📄 Alternative Assessment Handbook, Rubric 7: Charts

policies toward California and Texas. In 1833, for example, Mexico ended the mission system in California. Mission lands were broken up, and huge grants were given to some of the wealthiest California settlers, including Vallejo. They created vast ranchos, or ranches, with tens of thousands of acres of land. **Vaqueros**, or cowboys, managed the large herds of cattle and sheep. Cowhides were so valuable that they were called "California banknotes." Hides were traded for household items and luxury goods with ship captains from the eastern United States. Some settlers also made wine and grew citrus fruits.

Although they had been freed from the missions, for most California Indians the <u>elements</u> of life changed very little. They continued to herd animals and do much of the hard physical labor on ranches and farms. Some, however, ran away into the wilderness or to the nearby towns of San Diego and Los Angeles.

The Californios

Because of the great distance between California and the center of Mexico's government, by the early 1820s California had only around 3,200 colonists. These colonists, called **Californios**, felt little connection to their faraway government.

Californios developed a lasting reputation for hospitality and skilled horse riding. In *Two Years Before the Mast*, American novelist Richard Henry Dana Jr. wrote about his encounters with Californio culture. He described, for example, what happened after a Californio served a feast to Dana and a friend.

"We took out some money and asked him how much we were to pay. He shook his head and crossed himself, saying that it was charity—that the Lord gave it to us."

—Richard Henry Dana Jr. from *Two Years Before the Mast*

In addition to traders and travelers, a small number of settlers also arrived from the United States. They were called Anglos by the Californios. Although there were few

Anglo settlers in California, their calls for independence increased tensions between Mexico and the United States.

READING CHECK **Drawing Inferences** How did manifest destiny affect Spanish and Mexican rule in California?

Mexican-American War

Diplomatic relations between Mexico and the United States became increasingly strained. U.S. involvement in California and Texas contributed to this tension.

Conflict Breaks Out

Mexico had long insisted that its northern border lay along the Nueces River. The United States said the border was farther south, along the Rio Grande. In June 1845 President Polk ordered General Zachary Taylor to lead an army into the disputed region.

Polk sent diplomat John Slidell to Mexico City to try to settle the border dispute. Slidell

ACADEMIC VOCABULARY
elements the basic parts of an individual's surroundings

❷ Mexican-American War

As a result of the Mexican-American War, the United States added territory in the Southwest.

Recall Why did the United States declare war against Mexico? *disagreement over the U.S.-Mexico border; Mexican attack on U.S. soldiers stationed in disputed area*

Summarize Briefly describe the Bear Flag Revolt. *In 1846 a small group of American settlers seized Sonoma and declared California an independent nation, but U.S. forces soon arrived and claimed the region.*

Make Generalizations What did the American public think of the war with Mexico? *Many Americans supported the war, and many men signed up to fight, but many Whigs and abolitionists opposed the war.*

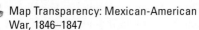 Map Transparency: Mexican-American War, 1846–1847

Info to Know

Opposition to the War Henry David Thoreau, a writer and philosopher, opposed the Mexican-American War. He spent a night in jail rather than pay taxes that might support the war effort. Thoreau described his views on peaceful resistance to the government in an essay titled "Civil Disobedience." His ideas later inspired the civil rights leader Martin Luther King Jr.

---

came with an offer to buy New Mexico and California for $30 million. Mexican officials refused to speak to him.

In March 1846, General Taylor led his troops to the Rio Grande. He camped across from Mexican forces stationed near the town of Matamoros, Mexico. In April, the Mexican commander told Taylor to withdraw from Mexican territory. Taylor refused. The two sides clashed, and several U.S. soldiers were killed.

President Polk delivered the news to Congress.

❝ Mexico has passed the boundary of the United States, has invaded our territory, and shed American blood upon the American soil …The two nations are now at war. ❞
—James K. Polk, from his address to Congress, May 11, 1846

Polk's war message was persuasive. Two days later, Congress declared war on Mexico.

War Begins

At the beginning of the war with Mexico, the U.S. Army had better weapons and equipment. Yet it was greatly outnumbered and poorly prepared. The government put out a call for 50,000 volunteers. About 200,000 responded. Many were young men who thought the war would be a grand adventure in a foreign land.

On the home front, many Americans supported the war. However, many Whigs thought the war was unjustified and avoidable. Northern abolitionists also opposed the conflict. They feared the spread of slavery into southwestern lands.

While Americans debated the war, fighting proceeded. General Taylor's soldiers won battles south of the Nueces River. Taylor then crossed the Rio Grande and occupied Matamoros, Mexico. While Taylor waited for more men, Polk ordered General Stephen Kearny to attack New Mexico. On August 18, 1846, Kearny took Santa Fe, the capital city, without a fight. He claimed the entire province of New Mexico for the United States and marched west to California, where another conflict with Mexico was already under way.

The Bear Flag Revolt

In 1846, only about 500 Americans lived in the huge province of California, in contrast to about 12,000 Californios. Yet, in the spirit of manifest destiny, a small group of American settlers seized the town of Sonoma, north of San Francisco, on June 14. Hostilities began between the two sides when the Americans took some horses that were intended for the Mexican militia. In what became known as the **Bear Flag Revolt**, the Americans declared California to be an independent nation. Above the town, the rebels hoisted a hastily made flag of a grizzly bear facing a red star. Californios laughed at the roughly-made bear, thinking it "looked more like a pig than a bear."

John C. Frémont, a U.S. Army captain, was leading a mapping expedition across the Sierra Nevadas when he heard of the possible war with Mexico. Frémont went to Sonoma and quickly joined the American settlers in their revolt against the Californios. Because war had already broken out between the United States and Mexico, Frémont's actions were seen as beneficial to the American cause in the region. His stated goal, however, was Californian independence, not to annex California to the United States. During the revolt, several important Californios were taken prisoner, including Mariano Vallejo. Vallejo and his brother were held at an Anglo settlement for two months without any formal charges being brought against them. Long after his release, Vallejo wrote a history of California that included an account of his time as a bear flag prisoner.

But the bear flag was quick to fall. In July, U.S. naval forces came ashore in California and raised the stars and stripes. Kearny's army arrived from the East. The towns of San Diego, Los Angeles, and San Francisco fell rapidly. In August, U.S. Navy Commodore Robert Stockton claimed California for the United States. Some Californios continued to resist until early 1847, when they surrendered.

Collaborative Learning

Above Level

Songs for the Road to War

1. Write the following events for students to see:
   • U.S. annexation of Texas
   • U.S.-Mexico border disputes
   • conflicts between Mexican and U.S. troops
   • declaration of war against Mexico by the U.S. Congress

2. Organize students into small groups. Ask the groups to imagine that they are songwriters at the time of the Mexican-American War. They have been hired to write a song describing the events leading to the war. The song should either increase patriotism or serve as an anthem for those opposing the war.

3. Select and play a tune for students to use or have each group choose an existing tune they like. Students should write catchy lyrics to go with the tune.

4. Have each group sing its song to the class.
   LS Auditory/Musical, Interpersonal

   📁 Alternative Assessment Handbook, Rubric 26: Poems and Songs

Mexican-American War, 1846–1847

The Bear Flag Revolt
American settlers took over Sonoma, the regional headquarters of the Mexican army. They captured Mexican general Mariano Vallejo and declared California a new country: the California Republic.

CALIFORNIA REPUBLIC

OREGON COUNTRY

Bear Flag Revolt, June 1846
Sutter's Fort
Sonoma
San Francisco
Monterey
CA
San Gabriel, Jan. 1847
Los Angeles
San Pasqual, Dec. 1846
San Diego
KEARNY

Great Salt Lake

SIERRA NEVADA

FREMONT

STOCKTON

Colorado River

Gila River

UNORGANIZED TERRITORY

Fort Leavenworth
KEARNY

Bent's Fort

KEARNY

NEW MEXICO
Santa Fe

UNITED STATES

Arkansas River

Red River

Mississippi River

DISPUTED TERRITORY

DONIPHAN

Rio Grande

TEXAS

San Antonio

New Orleans

Chihuahua

WOOL

Nueces River

Corpus Christi

TAYLOR

Palo Alto, May 1846

SCOTT

PACIFIC OCEAN

SLOAT

Buena Vista, Feb. 1847

Mazatlán

SANTA ANNA

Monterrey, Sept. 1846
Matamoros
Resaca de la Palma, May 1846

Gulf of Mexico

Tropic of Cancer

Tampico

MEXICO

Mexico City, Sept. 1847
SCOTT
Cerro Gordo, April 1847
SANTA ANNA

Veracruz, Mar. 1847
SCOTT

End of the War
General Winfield Scott landed at Veracruz and defeated troops in the Mexican fortress there. He then marched inland, toward Mexico City. Scott's capture of the Mexican capital led to the end of the war.

Legend:
- → American forces
- ✳ American victory
- → Mexican forces
- ✳ Mexican victory
- ⌂ Fort
- — Modern-day state boundaries

0   100   200 Miles
0   100   200 Kilometers

N W E S

GEOGRAPHY SKILLS | INTERPRETING MAPS
1. **Location** What Mexican city did Scott's forces attack in March 1847?
2. **Movement** Which U.S. commander led forces from Santa Fe to San Diego?

EXPANDING WEST **359**

Direct Teach

Interpreting Maps
Mexican-American War 1846–1847
Within months of the war's start, U.S. forces had captured all the major cities and towns along the coast of California and controlled much of the territory north of Mexico City.

Locate Where did most of the fighting in the war take place? *in disputed parts of Texas and in Mexico along the Gulf Coast, inland, and in California*

Map Transparency: Mexican-American War 1846–1847

Connect to Journalism
A War of Many Firsts The Mexican-American War was the first U.S. war fought mainly on foreign soil. It was also the first time that many newspapers sent reporters to cover a U.S. conflict. Reporters used horses to send news articles back to their papers in the East. The war was also one of the first to be photographed.

Did you know . . .
The standard U.S. Army uniform in the war was sky blue, but many soldiers disliked the color. As a result, some regiments created their own uniforms, complete with frills such as feathers, fringe, and silk. One Indiana soldier whose uniform was dark blue with silver lace said, "Let 'em go to . . . with their sky blue. I'll be blowed if they make a Regular out of me."

Critical Thinking: Analyzing Information

At Level

Reporting the War

1. Ask students to imagine that they are newspaper reporters covering the Mexican-American War. Have each student write an article about one of the major events or battles shown on the map above as if they were present.

2. The article should include a headline, date, byline, and a clear and chronological account of events. Articles should also address the questions "who, when, where, what, and how."

3. Tell students that newspapers of the time often sensationalized stories to sell more papers. Encourage students to use this same approach when writing their headlines and articles. Students might also include on-the-spot "interviews."

4. Ask volunteers to read their articles aloud to the class. **LS Verbal/Linguistic**

   Alternative Assessment Handbook, Rubrics 23: Newspapers; and 42: Writing to Inform

Answers

Interpreting Maps 1. *Veracruz;*
2. *General Stephen Kearny*

359

Main Idea

❷ Mexican-American War

As a result of the Mexican-American War, the United States added territory in the Southwest.

Identify Who led the U.S. forces to victory at the Battle of Buena Vista? *U.S. general Zachary Taylor*

Analyze Why do you think General Scott attacked Veracruz before Mexico City? *Veracruz was located on the coast, it was the strongest fortress in Mexico, and its defeat was needed to break Mexican resistance.*

Make Judgments Do you agree with President Polk's decision to replace Taylor with Scott? Explain. *Answers will vary, but students should exhibit an understanding of why Polk replaced Taylor and of the accomplishments of both Taylor and Scott.*

📋 **CRF:** Primary Source Activity: A Mexican Views the War

Answers

Reading Check *Santa Fe, Aug. 18, 1846; Buena Vista, Feb. 1847; Veracruz, Mar. 29, 1847; Cerro Gordo, April 1847; Mexico City, Sept.14, 1847*

American soldier

War's End

In Mexico General Taylor finally got the reinforcements he needed. He drove his forces deep into enemy lands. Santa Anna, thrown from office after losing Texas, returned to power in Mexico in September 1846. Quickly, he came after Taylor.

The two armies clashed at Buena Vista in February 1847. After a close battle with heavy casualties on both sides, the Mexican Army retreated. The next morning, the cry went up: "The enemy has fled! The field is ours!"

Taylor's success made him a war hero back home. The general's popularity troubled President Polk, and when Taylor's progress stalled, Polk gave the command to General Winfield Scott. A beloved leader, he was known by his troops as "Old Fuss and Feathers" because of his strict military discipline.

Scott sailed to the port of Veracruz, the strongest fortress in Mexico. On March 29, after an 88-hour artillery attack, Veracruz fell.

Scott moved on to the final goal, Mexico City, the capital. Taking a route similar to one followed by Spanish conquistador Hernán Cortés in 1519, the Americans pushed 200 or so miles inland. Santa Anna tried to stop the U.S. forces at Cerro Gordo in mid-April, but failed. By August 1847, U.S. troops were at the edge of Mexico City.

After a truce failed, Scott ordered a massive attack on Mexico City. Mexican soldiers and civilians fought fierce battles in and around the capital. At a military school atop the steep, fortified hill of Chapultepec, young Mexican cadets bravely defended their hopeless position. At least one soldier jumped to his death rather than surrender to the invading forces. Finally, on September 14, 1847, Mexico City fell. Santa Anna soon fled the country.

READING CHECK **Sequencing** In chronological order, list the key battles of the Mexican-American War.

Critical Thinking: Sequencing

Below Level

Mexican-American War Time Line

1. To help students understand the sequence of events in the Mexican War, copy the graphic organizer here for students to see. Omit the blue, italicized answers.

2. Have students copy the time line and complete it by describing the key events of the war. Review the answers as a class.
   LS Visual/Spatial

📋 Alternative Assessment Handbook, Rubric 36: Time Lines

March 1846
U.S. and Mexican troops clash.

August 1846
California is controlled by American forces.

September 1847
U.S. troops under Scott capture Mexico City.

August 1846
U.S. troops under Kearny take Santa Fe, New Mexico

February 1847
Santa Anna and Taylor battle at Buena Vista.

Battle of Buena Vista

After the two-day Battle of Buena Vista, the American army gained control of northern Mexico. At the beginning of the battle, Mexican forces outnumbered the Americans. But the Mexicans suffered more than twice as many casualties.

Why was the Battle of Buena Vista a turning point in the Mexican-American War?

Mexican soldier

American Settlement in the Mexican Cession

The war ended after Scott took Mexico City. In February 1848, the United States and Mexico signed the **Treaty of Guadalupe Hidalgo**, which officially ended the war and forced Mexico to turn over much of its northern territory to the United States. Known as the Mexican Cession, this land included the present-day states of California, Nevada, and Utah. In addition, it included most of Arizona and New Mexico and parts of Colorado and Wyoming. The United States also won the area claimed by Texas north of the Rio Grande. The Mexican Cession totaled more than 500,000 square miles and increased the size of the United States by almost 25 percent.

Agreements and Payments

In exchange for this vast territory, the United States agreed to pay Mexico $15 million. In addition, the United States assumed claims of more than $3 million held by American citizens against the Mexican government. The treaty also addressed the status of Mexicans in the Mexican Cession. The treaty provided that they would be "protected in the free enjoyment of their liberty and property, and secured in the free exercise of their religion." The Senate passed the treaty in March 1848.

After the war with Mexico, some Americans wanted to guarantee that any southern railroad to California would be built completely on American soil. James Gadsden, U.S. minister to Mexico, negotiated an important agreement with Mexico in December 1853. Under the terms of the **Gadsden Purchase**, the U.S. government paid Mexico $10 million. In exchange, the United States received the southern parts of what are now Arizona and New Mexico. With this purchase, the existing boundary with Mexico was finally fixed.

Surge of American Settlers

After the Mexican-American War, a flood of Americans moved to the Southwest. American newcomers struggled against longtime residents to control the land and other valuable resources, such as water and minerals. Most Mexicans, Mexican Americans, and Native Americans faced legal, economic, and social discrimination. As a result, they found it difficult to protect their rights.

The Treaty of Guadalupe Hidalgo promised to protect Mexican American residents' property rights. Yet differences between Mexican and U.S. land laws led to great confusion. The U.S. government often made Mexican American landowners go to court to prove that they had titles to their land. Landowners had to pay their own travel costs as well as those of witnesses and interpreters. They also had to pay attorneys' and interpreters' fees. These legal battles often bankrupted landowners. New settlers also tended to ignore Mexican legal concepts, such as community property or community water rights.

Main Idea

❸ American Settlement in the Mexican Cession

American settlement in the Mexican Cession produced conflict and a blending of cultures.

Analyze Why did conflicts occur between the different groups living in the American Southwest? *because of a desire to control valuable resources; different laws and views regarding property and water rights, lack of respect for Native American lands and holy places*

Summarize How did different cultures shape one another in the American Southwest? *use of English and Spanish; mix of heritage of place-names; celebration of Mexican and American holidays; cultural sharing of skills, knowledge, traditions*

Make Judgments Do you agree with Brigham Young's view of water use and water rights? Why or why not? *Answers will vary, but students should exhibit an understanding of the importance of water rights and access in the dry climate of the West.*

Linking to Today

Mexican Americans Today

Region Outside of the Southwest, what regions of the United States have large percentages of Mexican Americans? *Southeast, particularly Florida and North Carolina; Great Lakes region*

Answers

Interpreting Maps 1. *Southwest, particularly the region of the U.S.-Mexican border;* **2.** *California and New Mexico*

362

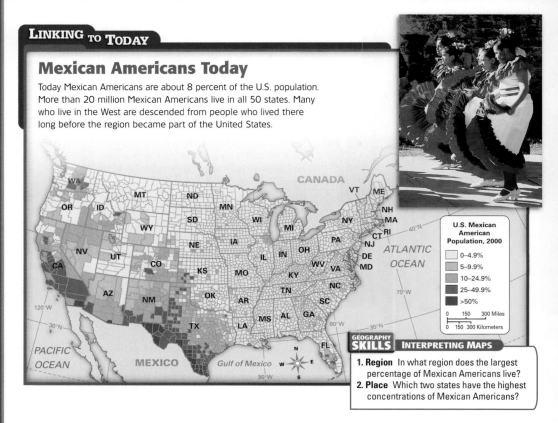

LINKING TO TODAY

Mexican Americans Today

Today Mexican Americans are about 8 percent of the U.S. population. More than 20 million Mexican Americans live in all 50 states. Many who live in the West are descended from people who lived there long before the region became part of the United States.

U.S. Mexican American Population, 2000

- 0–4.9%
- 5–9.9%
- 10–24.9%
- 25–49.9%
- >50%

0   150   300 Miles
0 150 300 Kilometers

GEOGRAPHY SKILLS | **INTERPRETING MAPS**

1. **Region** In what region does the largest percentage of Mexican Americans live?
2. **Place** Which two states have the highest concentrations of Mexican Americans?

THE IMPACT TODAY

Mexican holidays like Cinco de Mayo and Día de los Muertos are still popular holidays in the Southwest.

White settlers also battled with American Indians over property rights. In some areas, for example, new white settlers soon outnumbered southwestern Native Americans. The Anglo settlers often tried to take control of valuable water resources and grazing lands. In addition, settlers rarely respected Indian holy places. Native American peoples such as the Navajo and the Apache tried to protect their land and livestock from the settlers. Indians and settlers alike attacked one another to protect their interests.

Cultural Encounters

Despite conflicts, different cultures shaped one another in the Southwest. In settlements with large Mexican populations, laws were often printed in both English and Spanish.

Names of places—such as San Antonio, San Diego, and Santa Barbara—show Hispanic heritage. Other place-names, such as Taos and Tesuque, are derived from Native American words. Communities throughout the Southwest regularly celebrated both Mexican and American holidays.

Mexican and Native American knowledge and traditions also shaped many local economies. Mexican Americans taught Anglo settlers about mining in the mountains. Many ranching communities were first started by Mexican settlers. In addition, Mexican Americans introduced new types of saddles and other equipment to American ranchers. Adobe, developed by the Anasazi Indians, was adopted from the Pueblo people by the Spanish. It is still commonly

362 CHAPTER 11

Cross-Discipline Activity: Geography

At Level

Water Rights

1. Have students use the library and other resources to conduct research on water-rights laws in one or more states in the Southwest today.

2. If students have difficulty, suggest they investigate water issues related to California, the Colorado River, or the Rio Grande.

3. Tell students to write three questions to guide and focus their research. Then have students take notes on the information they find.

4. Give students several options for presenting their information, such as creating a computer or multimedia presentation, a triptych, or a report.

5. Have volunteers present quick summaries of what they learned to the class.
   LS Verbal/Linguistic, Visual/Spatial

Alternative Assessment Handbook, Rubrics 22: Multimedia Presentations; 29: Presentations; and 30: Research used by American residents in New Mexico, Arizona, and California.

Trade also changed the Southwest. For example, the Navajo created handwoven woolen blankets to sell to Americans. Americans in turn brought manufactured goods and money to the Southwest. Due to exchanges like these, the economies of many Mexican American and Native American communities in the Southwest began to change.

Water Rights

Eastern water-use laws commonly required owners whose land bordered streams or rivers to maintain a free flow of water. These restrictions generally prevented landowners from constructing dams because doing so would infringe upon the water rights of neighbors downstream.

In the typically dry climate of the West, large-scale agriculture was not possible without irrigation. Dams and canals were required

to direct scarce water to fields. This need conflicted with the accepted eastern tradition of equal access to water.

Brigham Young established a strict code regulating water rights for the Mormon community. In any dispute over water use, the good of the community would outweigh the interests of individuals. Young's approach stood as an example for modern water laws throughout the West.

READING CHECK **Summarizing** What were some of the early important agreements between the United States and Mexico, and why were they significant?

SUMMARY AND PREVIEW America's westward expansion continued rapidly after the Mexican-American War. In the next section you will learn about the California gold rush.

Section 3 Assessment

go.hrw.com
Online Quiz
KEYWORD: SR8 HP11

Reviewing Ideas, Terms, and People

1. **a. Define** What was **manifest destiny**?
   b. Make Inferences Why was westward expansion such an important issue in the election of 1844?
   c. Evaluate Do you think California benefited from Mexican independence? Why or why not?

2. **a. Recall** Why did the United States declare war on Mexico?
   b. Summarize What was General Winfield Scott's strategy for winning the war with Mexico?
   c. Elaborate Would you have sided with those who opposed the war with Mexico or with those who supported it? Why?

3. **a. Describe** What conflicts did American settlers, Native Americans, and Mexican Americans in the Mexican Cession experience?
   b. Draw Conclusions Why were water rights so important in the American Southwest?
   c. Evaluate In your opinion, what was the most important effect of the annexation of the Mexican Cession?

Critical Thinking

4. **Identifying Cause and Effect** Review your notes on manifest destiny and U.S. territorial expansion. Then use the graphic organizer below to show how Americans' expansion into California caused war, as well as the effects of the war.

FOCUS ON WRITING

5. **Explaining the Mexican-American War** How will you convey ideas, such as manifest destiny, in a film? How will you explain to your audience the Mexican-American War's role in expansion of the United States? Consider these questions as you read this section.

EXPANDING WEST **363**

Direct Teach

Linking to Today

Water Usage in the West In 1902 the federal government created the Bureau of Reclamation. The Bureau built dams, reservoirs, and canals to bring additional water to dry western regions. Today the Bureau manages all the water in 17 states west of the Mississippi River.

Review & Assess

Close

Ask students to review how the idea of manifest destiny led to the Mexican-American War and affected life in what is now the American Southwest.

Review

Online Quiz, Section 3

Assess

SE Section 3 Assessment

PASS: Section 3 Quiz

Alternative Assessment Handbook

Reteach/Classroom Intervention

Interactive Reader and Study Guide, Section 3

Interactive Skills Tutor CD-ROM

Section 3 Assessment Answers

1. **a.** belief that U.S. territory should extend to the Pacific Ocean
   b. because of the related slavery issues and because both candidates supported expansion
   c. Possible answers—yes, gained statehood; no, led to discrimination against many Californios and Native Americans

2. **a.** border disputes; Mexican attack on U.S. forces in disputed territory; Polk's call for war
   b. to take the Mexican capital, Mexico City

   c. Answers will vary but should reflect an understanding of Americans' different views about the war.

3. **a.** conflicts over control of land and water
   b. because of the West's generally dry climate
   c. Answers will vary but should reflect an understanding of the effects, listed in next answer.

4. causes—see answer to Question 2a; effects—expansion of United States, cultural blending and conflicts among groups in the Southwest

5. Students should consider various aspects of U.S. western expansion.

Answers

Reading Check *Treaty of Guadalupe Hidalgo; Gadsden Purchase; greatly increased the size of the United States; set the current border between Mexico and the United States; affected life of Mexican and Native Americans living in what is now the American Southwest*

363

Bellringer

If YOU were there . . . Use the **Daily Bellringer Transparency** to help students answer the question.

📖 Daily Bellringer Transparency, Section 4

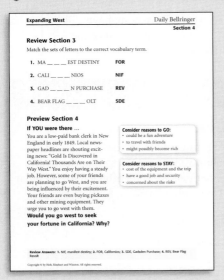

Building Vocabulary

Preteach or review the following terms:

famine severe food shortage (p. 368)

hospitality kind, friendly treatment of visitors (p. 365)

nugget as used here, a lump of metal in its natural state (p. 365)

📝 **CRF:** Vocabulary Builder Activity, Section 4

Taking Notes

Have students copy the graphic organizer onto their own paper and then use it to take notes on the section. This activity will prepare students for the Section Assessment, in which they will complete a graphic organizer that builds on the information using a critical thinking skill.

SECTION 4

The California Gold Rush

Main Ideas

1. The discovery of gold brought settlers to California.
2. The gold rush had a lasting impact on California's population and economy.

The Big Idea

The California gold rush changed the future of the West.

Key Terms and People

John Sutter, *p. 365*
Donner party, *p. 365*
forty-niners, *p. 365*
prospect, *p. 366*
placer miners, *p. 366*

TAKING NOTES As you read, take notes on the California gold rush in a chart like the one below.

Gold Rush	
How was gold first discovered?	
How was a stake claimed?	
What was life like in camps?	
Who came to California for gold?	

If YOU were there...

You are a low-paid bank clerk in New England in early 1849. Local newspaper headlines are shouting exciting news: "Gold Is Discovered in California! Thousands Are on Their Way West." You enjoy having a steady job. However, some of your friends are planning to go west, and you are being influenced by their excitement. Your friends are even buying pickaxes and other mining equipment. They urge you to go west with them.

> **Would you go west to seek your fortune in California? Why?**

BUILDING BACKGROUND At the end of the Mexican-American War, the United States gained control of Mexican territories in the West, including all of the present-day state of California. American settlements in California increased slowly at first. Then, the discovery of gold brought quick population growth and an economic boom.

Discovery of Gold Brings Settlers

In the 1830s and 1840s, Americans who wanted to move to California started up the Oregon Trail. At the Snake River in present-day Idaho, the trail split. People bound for California took the southern route, which became known as the California Trail. This path ran through the Sierra Nevada mountain range. American emigrants and traders on the California Trail tried to cross these mountains before the season's first snows.

Although many Americans traveled along the California Trail, few actually settled in California. American merchants were usually more interested in trading goods made in factories than in establishing settlements. They traded for gold and silver coins, hides, and tallow (animal fat used to make soap and candles) from Mexico. California became a meeting ground for traders from Mexico and the United States.

Before the Mexican-American War, California's population consisted mostly of Mexicans and Native Americans. When Mexico

---

Teach the Big Idea

At Level

The California Gold Rush

1. **Teach** Ask students the questions in the Main Idea boxes to teach this section.

2. **Apply** Ask students to imagine that gold has just been discovered on the grounds of their school. Have students predict some short- and long-term consequences of the find. Write the predictions for students to see. Then have students compare and contrast their predictions to the effects of the California gold rush. **LS Verbal/Linguistic**

3. **Review** To review the section's main ideas, have students explain the causes and effects of the California gold rush.

4. **Practice/Homework** Have each student write one to three paragraphs summarizing the historical significance of the California gold rush. **LS Verbal/Linguistic**

📝 Alternative Assessment Handbook, Rubrics 11: Discussions; and 42: Writing to Inform controlled California, Mexican officials did not want many Americans to settle there. However, in 1839 they did give Swiss immigrant **John Sutter** permission to start a colony. Sutter's Fort, located near the Sacramento River, soon became a popular rest stop for many American emigrants. These new arrivals praised Sutter's hospitality and helpfulness. By the mid-1840s some Anglo Californians were publishing newspaper advertisements and guidebooks encouraging other settlers to move West.

The **Donner party** was a group of western travelers who went to California but were stranded in the Sierra Nevada Mountains during winter. The party began its journey West in the spring of 1846. Trying to find a shortcut, the group left the main trail and got lost. When the Donner party reached the Sierra Nevada Mountains, they became trapped by heavy snows. They were stuck and had almost no food.

A rescue party found the starving and freezing group in February 1847. Of the original 87 travelers, 42 had died.

Gold in California

In January 1848, Sutter sent a carpenter named James Marshall to build a sawmill beside a nearby river. While working near Sutter's Mill, Marshall glanced at the ground. "I reached my hand down and picked it up; it made my heart thump, for I was certain it was gold."

Sutter and Marshall agreed to keep the discovery a secret. However, when they examined the work site the next day, they met a Spanish-speaking Native American worker holding a nugget and shouting, "Oro [gold]! Oro! Oro!"

Sutter's workers soon quit to search for gold. Stories of the discovery rapidly spread across the country. President Polk added to the national excitement by confirming the California gold strike in his farewell message to Congress in December 1848. In 1849 about 80,000 gold-seekers came to California, hoping to strike it rich. These gold-seeking migrants to California were called **forty-niners**. As one Iowa woman who

"Gold Fever"

"Gold fever" brought 80,000 people, like this miner, to California in 1849 alone. One California newspaper captured the excitement: "The whole country, from San Francisco to Los Angeles, and from the sea shore to the base of the Sierra Nevadas, resounds with the cry of 'gold, GOLD, GOLD!' while the field is left half planted, the house half built, and everything neglected but the manufacture of shovels and pickaxes." Below is a piece of jewelry made from nuggets found in California.

Why was everything neglected except for "the manufacture of shovels and pickaxes"?

EXPANDING WEST **365**

Direct Teach

Main Idea

❶ **Discovery of Gold Brings Settlers**

The discovery of gold brought settlers to California.

Identify Who made up the majority of travelers on the California Trail before the gold rush? *American merchants trading manufactured goods to Mexican merchants for gold, silver, hides, and tallow*

Sequence What sequence of events led to the California gold rush? *John Sutter began building a sawmill. His carpenter, James Marshall, discovered gold while working. Word of the discovery soon spread.*

Elaborate Why was the United States lucky in the timing of the California gold rush? *If gold had been found a few years earlier, California would have still been Mexican land.*

Biography

John Sutter (1803–1880) You might think that John Sutter became wealthy from the discovery of gold. Just the opposite occurred, though. As word of the gold discovery spread, Sutter's workers left him, and gold seekers overran his land. What's more, Sutter had received his land from the Mexican government and was unable to defend his title in the U.S. courts. By 1852—just four years after the discovery of gold—he was bankrupt.

Collaborative Learning

At Level

Gold Rush Guide

Prep Required

Materials: heavy white paper, art supplies

1. Organize students into small groups and ask group members to imagine that they are heading to California during the gold rush.

2. Have group members brainstorm and list items they might need for the long trip West as well as supplies they might need once they arrive out West.

3. After a set period, have each group share some of the items it listed with the class.

4. Then give each group two sheets of heavy white paper and have students fold and staple the sheets to make a four-page booklet.

5. Have each group create a Gold Rush Guide for forty-niners. The guide should include ways to get to California, supplies to obtain, and tips for success. **LS Interpersonal, Verbal/Linguistic**

 Alternate Assessment Handbook, Rubrics 14: Group Activity; and 37: Writing Assignment

Answers

"Gold Fever" *The lure of instant wealth mining gold led people to rush off, forgetting everything else except the tools needed for mining—shovels and pickaxes.*

❶ Discovery of Gold Brings Settlers

The discovery of gold brought settlers to California.

Define Who was able to "stake a claim"? *the first person on a site*

Analyze Why was the lack of a court system a problem in the early days of the gold rush? *In the case of competing claims, no court system was available to decide the claim, and violence sometimes erupted.*

Make Inferences What effects do you think gold mining had on the California environment? *possible answer—Gold mining harmed the environment because of the need to move large amounts of earth and dig tunnels.*

📑 **CRF:** Literature Activity: *New Orleans to San Francisco in '49*

📑 Political Cartoons Activities for United States History, Cartoon 13: The California Gold Rush

Info to Know

The Daily Drudgery of Mining Few of the thousands of prospectors who flocked to California realized how difficult mining would be. Panning for gold was the simplest mining technique but also the most labor-intensive. First, a miner dug a load of dirt to fill the pan. The miner then submerged the pan in water and shook it until any gold deposits settled on the bottom. Most gold miners worked 50 pans during a 10-hour day. One forty-niner said that prospecting combined "the various arts of canal-digging, ditching, laying stone walls, ploughing, and hoeing potatoes."

Staking a Claim

left to find gold recalled, "At that time the 'gold fever' was contagious, and few, old or young, escaped the malady [sickness]." Nearly 80 percent of the forty-niners were Americans, while the rest came from all over the world.

Most forty-niners braved long and often dangerous journeys to reach California. Many easterners and Europeans arrived via sea routes. Midwestern gold-seekers usually traveled West in wagon trains. Most forty-niners first arrived in San Francisco. This port town became a convenient trade center and stopping point for travelers. As a result, its population increased from around 800 in March 1848 to more than 25,000 by 1850.

Staking a Claim

Few of the forty-niners had any previous gold-mining experience. The work was difficult and time-consuming. The forty-niners would **prospect**, or search for gold, along the banks of streams or in shallow surface mines. The early forty-niners worked an area that ran for 70 miles along rivers in northern California.

The first person to arrive at a site would "stake a claim." Early miners frequently banded together to prospect for gold. The miners agreed that each would keep a share of whatever gold was discovered. When one group abandoned a claim, more recent arrivals often took it over, hoping for success. Sometimes, two or more groups arrived in an area at the same time. In the early gold-rush days, before courts were established, this competition often led to conflict. Occasionally, violent disputes arose over competing claims.

Mining methods varied according to the location. The most popular method, placer (PLA-suhr) mining, and was done along rivers and streams. **Placer miners** used pans or other devices to wash gold nuggets out of loose rock and gravel. To reach gold deposits buried in

366 CHAPTER 11

Differentiating Instruction

Struggling Readers   Below Level

1. Ask students to imagine that it is 1849 and a wagon train firm has hired them to create an advertisement urging people to go to California.

2. Copy the graphic organizer here for students to see. Omit the blue, italicized answers.

3. Have students copy the organizer and complete it by listing the reasons people went to California in 1849. 🅛 **Visual/Spatial**

Catch the Fever!
HEAD TO CALIFORNIA!!!!
IT OFFERS ALL THE FOLLOWING:

- *Get rich mining for gold.*
- *Open your own business in a booming mining town.*
- *Work in farming or ranching.*

COME TO CALIFORNIA TODAY!!

Miners came to California from around the world to make their fortune. In the photo on the left, Anglo and Chinese miners work together in Auburn Ravine in 1852. Above, a woman joins men to look for gold. Fewer women than men moved west to search for gold, but the ones that did often found greater social and economic opportunity than they had in the east.

Why might people leave their homes and travel long distances in search of gold?

the hills, miners had to dig shafts and tunnels. These tasks were usually pursued by mining companies, rather than by individuals.

In 1853 California's yearly gold production peaked at more than $60 million. Individual success stories inspired many miners. One lucky man found two and a half pounds of gold after only 15 minutes of work. Two African American miners found a rich gold deposit that became known as Negro Hill in honor of their discovery. The vast majority of miners, however, did not become rich. Forty-niner Alonzo Delano commented that the "lean, meager [thin], worn-out and woebegone [sorrowful] miner…might daily be seen at almost every point in the upper mines."

Life in the Mining Camps

Mining camps sprang up wherever enough people gathered to look for gold. These camps had colorful names, such as Hangtown or Poker Flat.

Miners in the camps came from many cultures and backgrounds. Most miners were young, unmarried men in search of adventure. Only around 5 percent of gold-rush immigrants were women or children. The hardworking women generally made good money by cooking meals, washing clothes, and operating boardinghouses. One such woman, Catherine Haun, recalled her first home in California.

"We were glad to settle down and go housekeeping in a shed that was built in a day of lumber purchased with the first fee …For neighbors, we had a real live saloon. I never have received more respectful attention than I did from these neighbors."

—Catherine Haun, quoted in *Ordinary Americans,* edited by Linda R. Monk

Haun's husband was a lawyer. He concluded that he could make more money practicing law than he could panning for gold. He was one of many people who made a good living supplying miners with food, clothing, equipment, and other services. Miners paid high prices for basic necessities because the large amounts of gold in circulation caused severe inflation in California. A loaf of bread, for example, might cost 5 cents in the East, but it would sell for 50 to 75 cents in San Francisco. Eggs sometimes sold for $1 a piece.

Some settlers took full advantage of these conditions for free enterprise. Biddy Mason and her family, for instance, had arrived in California as slaves. A Georgia slaveholder had brought them during the gold-rush years. Mason quickly discovered that most Californians opposed slavery, particularly in the gold mines. She and her family gained their freedom and moved to the small village of Los Angeles. There she saved money until she could purchase some land. Over time, Mason's property increased in value from $250 to $200,000. She became one of the wealthiest landowners in California, a community leader, and a well-known supporter of charities.

Main Idea

❶ Discovery of Gold Brings Settlers

The discovery of gold brought settlers to California.

Explain Why did many Chinese immigrants go to California during the gold rush? *lure of gold and to escape economic hardship and famine in southeastern China*

Summarize What challenges did immigrant miners face in California? *lack of welcome by Americans, monthly tax, discrimination, violence, limited legal redress*

Draw Conclusions Why do you think the courts favored Americans over immigrants? *possible answer—because judges thought immigrants shouldn't take away opportunities from Americans*

📄 **CRF:** Biography Activity: Levi Strauss

World Events

China and the Gold Rush In the mid-1800s China was in political and economic chaos. A tiny minority of wealthy people owned much of the land, while the vast majority of people were peasants who owned little. Such conditions encouraged hundreds of thousands of Chinese to seek their fortunes in the American West between 1850 and 1882.

Westward Movement in the United States

QUICK FACTS

Causes
- Americans believe in the idea of manifest destiny.
- The United States acquires vast new lands in the West.
- Pathfinders open trails to new territories.
- Gold is discovered in California.

Effects
- Native Americans are forced off lands.
- Americans travel west to settle new areas.
- The United States stretches to the Pacific Ocean.
- California experiences a population boom.

Immigrants to California

THE IMPACT TODAY

Today California is the nation's most populous state.

The lure of gold in California attracted miners from around the world. Many were from countries that had seen few immigrants to the United States in the past. They were drawn to California by the lure of wealth. For example, famine and economic hardship in southeastern China caused many Chinese men to leave China for America. Most hoped to find great wealth, and then return home to China. These immigrants were known in Chinese as *gam saan haak,* or "travelers to Gold Mountain." Between 1849 and 1853 about 24,000 Chinese men moved to California. "From far and near we came and were pleased," wrote merchant Lai Chun-chuen in 1855.

Chinese immigrants soon discovered that many Americans did not welcome them, however. In 1852, California placed a high monthly tax on all foreign miners. Chinese miners had no choice but to pay this tax if they wanted to prospect for gold in California. Some Chinese workers were the targets of violent attacks. If the Chinese

miners dared to protest the attacks, the legal system favored Americans over immigrants.

Despite such treatment, many Chinese immigrants still worked in the gold mines. Some looked for other jobs. Others opened their own businesses. A newspaper reported Chinese working as "ploughmen, laundry-men, placer miners, woolen spinners and weavers, domestic servants, cigar makers, [and] shoemakers."

In 1849 alone, about 20,000 immigrants arrived in California not only from China but also from Europe, Mexico, and South America. Like most American gold-seekers, these new arrivals intended to return home after they had made their fortunes. However, many decided to stay. Some began businesses. For example, Levi Strauss, a German immigrant, earned a fortune by making tough denim pants for miners.

READING CHECK **Categorizing** What types of people came to California hoping to benefit from the gold rush?

Impact on California

During the Spanish and Mexican periods of settlement, California's population grew slowly. The arrival of the forty-niners changed this dramatically.

Population Boom

California's population explosion made it eligible for statehood only two years after being acquired by the United States. In 1850 California became the 31st state.

However, fast population growth had negative consequences for many Californios and California Native Americans. One early observer of the gold rush described why.

❝The Yankee regarded every man but [his own kind] as an interloper [trespasser], who had no right to come to California and pick up the gold of 'free and enlightened citizens.'❞

—W. Kelly, quoted in *The Other Californians,* by Robert F. Heizer and Alan F. Almquist

---

Critical Thinking: Identifying Points of View
At Level

Chinese Immigrant Letters

1. Discuss with students the experiences of Chinese immigrants who came to California during the gold rush.

2. Have students use the information to write a series of letters from a male Chinese immigrant to family and friends back in China. The letters should provide detailed descriptions of prospecting, life in mining towns, and other experiences. In addition, letters should either encourage the immigrant's family or friends to make the trip or discourage them from

coming. Students should consider why Chinese immigrants came to California and the challenges they faced.

3. Have volunteers read some of their letters to the class. Encourage feedback and discussion.

LS Verbal/Linguistic

📄 Alternative Assessment Handbook, Rubric 40: Writing to Describe

Answers

Reading Check *U.S. easterners and midwesterners, including enslaved African Americans, and immigrants from China, Europe, Mexico, and South America*

San Francisco Grows

San Francisco boomed in the early years of the Gold Rush.

What factors led to San Francisco's population growth?

San Francisco Population, 1847–1850

Economic Growth

In addition to rapid population growth, a flood of new businesses and industries transformed California's economy. Gold mining remained an important part of the state's early economy. But Californians soon discovered other ways to make a living. Farming and ranching, for example, became industries for those willing to do the necessary hard labor.

California faced an obstacle to growth, though. The state was isolated from the rest of the country. It was difficult to bring in and ship out goods. The answer to the isolation problem was to bring the railroad all the way to California. Californians would have to wait almost 20 years for that. Completion of the transcontinental railroad in 1869 at last gave Californians the means to grow a stronger economy.

READING CHECK Analyzing Information
What political effect resulted from California's rapid population growth?

SUMMARY AND PREVIEW Americans moved west to create new lives and seize new opportunities. In the next chapter you will learn about the Industrial Revolution in America.

go.hrw.com
Online Quiz
KEYWORD: SR8 HP11

Section 4 Assessment

Reviewing Ideas, Terms, and People

1. **a. Recall** Why was Sutter's Mill important?
   b. Summarize What types of people participated in the California gold rush, and how did they take part in it?
   c. Elaborate What are some possible problems caused by the arrival of so many new settlers to California?
2. **a. Describe** How did some people hope to solve the problem of California's isolation from the rest of the country?
   b. Draw Inferences What effect did California's rapid population growth have on Californios and Native Americans?
   c. Evaluate Overall, do you think that the gold rush had a positive or negative effect on California? Explain.

Critical Thinking

3. **Evaluating** Review your notes on the gold rush. Then copy the graphic organizer below. Use it to show how the discovery of gold changed California.

Discovery of Gold

FOCUS ON WRITING

4. **Describing the California Gold Rush** As you read this section, take note of significant events and effects of the gold rush. Consider also how your film can convey the excitement of that time in American history.

EXPANDING WEST **369**

369

Activity **America's Growth Time Line** Have students examine the feature and describe how the nation expanded between 1820 and 1853. Then have each student create a large time line that shows how the United States expanded during that time. Instruct students to divide their time lines into five-year periods. Students should also write a short description for each entry.

Then ask students to discuss how they think people already living in California and Oregon felt as thousands more people poured into the areas during the 1840s and 1850s. Conclude by having students identify and discuss the costs and benefits of U.S. westward expansion during this period. **LS** **Verbal/Linguistic, Visual/Spatial**

Linking to Today

California Today During the 1840s California's population was comprised of only a few thousand people. Now, almost 34 million people live in California, the third largest state in land area. The "Golden State," as it is officially nicknamed, also has an enormous economy. If California were an independent country, it would have one of the ten strongest economies in the world.

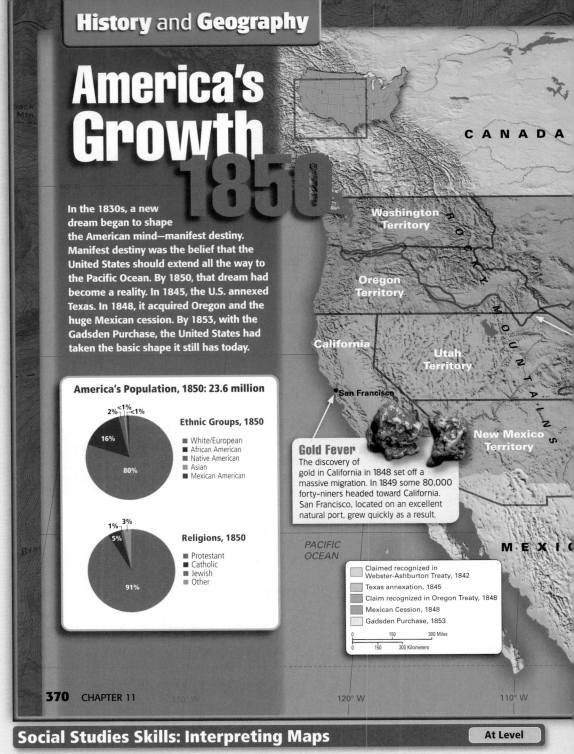

History and Geography

America's Growth 1850

In the 1830s, a new dream began to shape the American mind—manifest destiny. Manifest destiny was the belief that the United States should extend all the way to the Pacific Ocean. By 1850, that dream had become a reality. In 1845, the U.S. annexed Texas. In 1848, it acquired Oregon and the huge Mexican cession. By 1853, with the Gadsden Purchase, the United States had taken the basic shape it still has today.

America's Population, 1850: 23.6 million

Ethnic Groups, 1850
- 80% White/European
- 16% African American
- 2% Native American
- <1% Asian
- <1% Mexican American

Religions, 1850
- 91% Protestant
- 5% Catholic
- 3% Jewish
- 1% Other

Gold Fever
The discovery of gold in California in 1848 set off a massive migration. In 1849 some 80,000 forty-niners headed toward California. San Francisco, located on an excellent natural port, grew quickly as a result.

Claimed recognized in Webster-Ashburton Treaty, 1842
Texas annexation, 1845
Claim recognized in Oregon Treaty, 1848
Mexican Cession, 1848
Gadsden Purchase, 1853

0 150 300 Miles
0 150 300 Kilometers

370 CHAPTER 11

Social Studies Skills: Interpreting Maps

At Level

The West: Then and Now

1. Display a current map of the United States for students to see. Cover up the western region of the map. Ask students to discuss ways in which the United States might be different had these western states not become part of the Union. *possible answers—Other nations would control the area, the U.S. population would be much smaller, and the nation would lose the area's resources.*

2. Then ask students to compare the map above to the current U.S. map (now uncovered).

Ask students to identify the states eventually created from the land that the United States gained between 1842 and 1853.

3. Conclude by reviewing the significant historical events (e.g., the Texas War for Independence and the Mexican-American War) that had a major effect on the boundaries of the United States. **LS** **Visual/Spatial**

Alternative Assessment Handbook, Rubric 21: Map Reading

Water Rights Water was critical in the dry West. Bitter disputes arose over who had the water rights to streams. Gold Rush miners developed a simple system: whoever used the water first owned the rights to it. In other parts of the West, the community as a whole had a right to use the water source.

Manifest Destiny With the belief that the United States was destined to spread across the continent, called manifest destiny, settlers headed West to tame new lands. Supporters of manifest destiny believed it was God's will that the United States should expand and spread democracy across North America.

GREAT PLAINS

Oregon Trail

Missouri River

Mississippi River

Unorganized Territory

Indian Territory

The Rocky Mountains The Rocky Mountains were a gigantic obstacle to settlers on their way West. Pathfinders like Lt. John C. Frémont traveled widely in the region, making maps and noting possible trails. The South Pass, through which the Oregon Trail ran, was one of the few easy ways through the great chain of mountains.

ATLANTIC OCEAN

Claimed by Texas

Texas

Gulf of Mexico

30°

GEOGRAPHY SKILLS INTERPRETING MAPS

1. **Movement** Why did San Francisco grow so rapidly?
2. **Human-Environment Interaction** Why was water so important in the West?

N S E W

70° W

Tropic of Cancer

90° W

EXPANDING WEST **371**

History and Geography

MISCONCEPTION ALERT

A Salty River? A desalination plant—or a facility that takes the salt out of water—has been built near the Colorado River in Arizona. But wait, isn't the water in the Colorado River fresh water? Yes and no. Farmers spray water from the river onto fields for irrigation. Because the desert soil contains so much salt, the runoff water is salty. The desalination plant purifies the runoff water so it can be sent back into the Colorado River and reused.

Info to Know

The Mexican Cession The territory granted to the United States by the Mexican Cession had long belonged to Spain and then Mexico. By 1850, however, the Hispanic population in the region was outnumbered by settlers from the United States.

Connect to Geography

Hispanics in the Southwest According to the 2000 census, about 19.7 million Hispanic or Latino Americans lived in Arizona, California, New Mexico, and Texas. This figure is more than half the total Hispanic population of the entire United States. Nearly 3.7 million Asian Americans and some 2.25 million African Americans also lived in California, making it the most diverse state in the nation.

Cross-Discipline Activity: Math

Above Level

Graphing Hispanic Populations

1. Have students use information from the U.S. Census Bureau to obtain data about the current Hispanic population in each of the states in the Southwest.

2. Have each student use the data to create a bar graph showing the percentage of each state's population that is Hispanic. Then have each student create a circle graph that shows the

percentage of the nation's total Hispanic population that lives in each of the states of the Southwest. Remind students to provide a title, a legend, and a caption for each graph.

3. Ask volunteers to share their graphs with the class. **LS Visual/Spatial**

Alternative Assessment Handbook, Rubrics 7: Charts; and 30: Research

Answers

Interpreting Maps 1. *The city was located on an excellent natural port for arriving ships and during the Gold Rush thousands of people went there.* **2.** *The West is arid, and water is needed for people, crops, and livestock.*

371

Social Studies Skills

Social Studies Skills

Analysis	Critical Thinking	Civic Participation	Study

Interpreting Maps: Expansion

Activity Expansion Maps Scavenger Hunt Have students go on an expansion map scavenger hunt. Give students a set amount of time to find three examples of expansion maps in their textbooks. Have students mark the pages of each map. Award the first student to find three maps a prize of some kind. Have the winning student identify the pages on which the maps are located. Then guide students in interpreting each of the three maps. Conclude by having each student write a few sentences describing in his or her own words what an expansion map is.

LS Visual/Spatial

📖 Alternative Assessment Handbook, Rubric 21: Map Reading

💿 Interactive Skills Tutor CD-ROM, Lesson 6: Interpret Maps, Graphs, Charts, Visuals, and Political Cartoons

Interpreting Maps: Expansion

Define the Skill

Maps show features on Earth's surface. These can be physical features, such as mountains and rivers, or human features, such as roads and settlements. Historical maps show an area as it was in the past. Some show how a nation's boundaries changed over time. Interpreting maps can answer questions about history as well as geography.

Learn the Skill

Follow these steps to gain information from a map.

❶ Read the title to determine what the map is about and the time period it covers.

❷ Study the legend or key to understand what the colors or symbols on the map mean. Note the map scale, which is used to measure distances.

❸ Note the map's other features. Maps often contain labels and other information in addition to what is explained in the legend or key.

Practice the Skill

Interpret the map below to answer the following questions about the expansion of the United States.

1. The addition of which territory almost doubled the size of the United States.

2. What was the smallest expansion of U.S. borders, and when did it take place?

3. According to the map, when did California become part of the United States?

4. What choice of overland routes did a traveler have for getting to California?

5. What physical obstacles does the map show such a traveler would face?

Growth of the United States to 1853

- United States, 1783
- Louisiana Purchase, 1803
- Red River Basin, 1818
- Spanish Cession, 1819
- Texas Annexation, 1845
- Oregon Country, 1846
- Mexican Cession, 1848
- Gadsden Purchase, 1853
- Disputed Territory

0 300 600 Miles
0 300 600 Kilometers

Social Studies Skills Activity: Interpreting Maps: Expansion

Interpreting Expansion Maps   **At Level**

1. Display a modern political map of the United States for students to see. (One is available in the Atlas in the back of the textbook.)

2. Have students compare the map to the one shown above. Ask students to identify the states that are now located in each of the areas of expansion labeled on the map above. Use the activity to make certain students understand how to read the expansion map.

3. Then have each student write a paragraph describing the information in the map above. Tell students to be as thorough as possible.

4. Next, ask for a volunteer to read his or her description to the class. Then ask students which is easier to understand, the written description or the map. Use the question to help students understand the use of expansion maps in the study of history. **LS Visual/Spatial**

📖 Alternative Assessment Handbook, Rubrics 21: Map Reading

Answers

Practice the Skill *(refer to map key on p. 374)* **1.** *Louisiana Territory;* **2.** *Gadsden Purchase in 1853;* **3.** *1848;* **4.** *California Trail, Old Spanish Trail;* **5.** *Rocky Mountains*

Visual Summary

Use the visual summary below to help you review the main ideas of the chapter.

QUICK FACTS

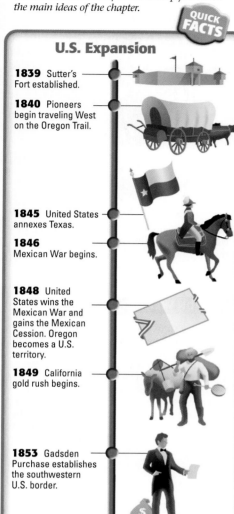

U.S. Expansion

1839 Sutter's Fort established.

1840 Pioneers begin traveling West on the Oregon Trail.

1845 United States annexes Texas.

1846 Mexican War begins.

1848 United States wins the Mexican War and gains the Mexican Cession. Oregon becomes a U.S. territory.

1849 California gold rush begins.

1853 Gadsden Purchase establishes the southwestern U.S. border.

Reviewing Vocabulary, Terms, and People

Identify the correct term or person from the chapter that best fits each of the following descriptions.

1. Mexican priest who led a rebellion for independence from Spain
2. Spanish colonists in California
3. A group of pioneers who were stranded in the Sierra Nevada Mountains and struggled to survive the winter
4. Agents hired by the Mexican government to attract settlers to Texas
5. The belief that the United States was meant to expand across the continent to the Pacific Ocean
6. Members of the Church of Jesus Christ of Latter-day Saints
7. Fur traders and trappers who lived west of the Rocky Mountains and in the Pacific Northwest
8. Mexican ruler who fought to keep Texas from gaining independence
9. Swiss immigrant who received permission from Mexico to start a colony in California
10. Western trail from Missouri to New Mexico that was an important route for trade between American and Mexican merchants

Comprehension and Critical Thinking

SECTION 1 *(Pages 346–349)*

11. a. Identify What different groups of people traveled West?

   b. Draw Conclusions Why did Brigham Young move the Mormon community to Utah?

   c. Predict What are some possible problems that might result from American settlement in the West?

12. a. Austin—empresario who founded an American colony in Mexican Texas; Santa Anna—leader of Mexico, who led forces against the Texans in the Texas War for Independence

b. anger over some Mexican actions, such as banning of further American settlement and the importation of slaves; Santa Anna's suspension of Mexico's republican constitution

c. in both, the people in a colonial region fought against their mother country for protection of what they saw as their rights and liberties

13. a. concerns over the spread of slavery, balance of power between slave and free states

b. Mining, ranching, saddles, and adobe are examples of Mexican and Native American influence on American settlers.

c. problems related to governing and protecting such a large area

14. a. Both provided goods and services to miners, some opened and ran their own businesses; some immigrants mined.

b. possible answers—difficult to support and care for a family while prospecting; had few attachments to prevent them from going to California

c. continued population and economic growth, continued discrimination against Hispanics and Native Americans

---

SECTION 2 *(Pages 350–353)*

12. a. Identify Who were Stephen F. Austin and Antonio López de Santa Anna?

b. Draw Conclusions Why did settlers in Texas rebel against Mexican rule?

c. Elaborate In what ways was the Texas struggle for independence similar to that of the United States?

SECTION 3 *(Pages 354–363)*

13. a. Recall Why were some Americans opposed to the annexation of new territories?

b. Draw Conclusions What economic and cultural influences did Native Americans and Mexican Americans have on American settlers in the Mexican Cession?

c. Predict What are some possible problems the acquisition of so much territory might cause the United States?

SECTION 4 *(Pages 364–369)*

14. a. Identify What roles did women and immigrants play in the California gold rush?

b. Make Inferences Why were most gold-rush settlers young, unmarried men?

c. Predict What long-term effects might the gold rush have on California's future?

Reviewing Themes

15. Economics What role did economics play in the desire of Americans to go west?

16. Geography What were the main trails to the West, and what areas did they pass through?

Reading Skills

Vocabulary in Context *Use the Reading Skills taught in this chapter to answer the question about the reading selection below.*

> Texas politicians hoped that joining the United States would help solve the republic's financial and military problems. The Texas Congress approved annexation in June 1845. Texas became part of the United States in December. *(p. 356)*

---

17. Determine the definition of *annexation* using context clues.

Social Studies Skills

Interpreting Maps: Expansion *Use the Social Studies Skills taught in this chapter to answer the question about the map below.*

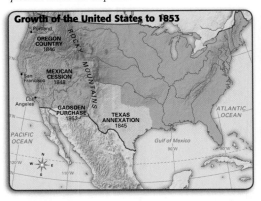

Growth of the United States to 1853

18. Place the expansions in the order of which they were acquired by the United States, according to the map.

FOCUS ON WRITING

19. Writing an Outline for a Documentary Film Look back through all your notes, and choose one topic from this chapter that you think would make a good 10-minute documentary. Your outline should be organized by scene (no more than 3 scenes), in chronological order. For each scene, give the following information: main idea of scene, costumes and images to be used, audio to be used, and length of scene. As you plan, remember that the audience will be students your own age.

Reviewing Themes

15. possible answer—Many Americans went West in hopes of improving their lives economically.

16. See the map on p. 385.

Reading Skills

17. joining the United States; became part of

Social Studies Skills

18. Texas, Oregon, Mexican Cession, Gadsden Purchase

Focus on Writing

19. Rubric Students' outlines for documentary films should:

- clearly introduce the main idea
- include images
- include narration that explains the images
- be informative and appealing

CRF: Focus on Writing: Outline for a Documentary Film

Standardized Test Practice

DIRECTIONS: Read each question and write the letter of the best response.

1 Use the map below to answer the following question.

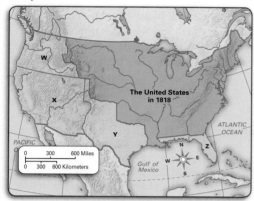

The United States in 1818

The part of the present-day United States that was once claimed by Britain, Spain, and Russia is shown on the map by the letter

- A W.
- B X.
- C Y.
- D Z.

2 In general, what position did Californios take toward the Mexican War?

- A They supported the war because they wanted independence from Mexico.
- B They supported the war because they wanted to become U.S. citizens.
- C They opposed the war because they feared it might bring an end to slavery.
- D They opposed the war because they did not want to lose control of California.

3 What was the *main* reason John Jacob Astor founded Astoria at the mouth of the Columbia River in 1811?

- A Plenty of freshwater and salt-water fish were available for residents to eat.
- B The soil there was rich and good for farming.
- C Trappers could use the river to bring furs from the mountains to trade.
- D The location offered easy protection from attacks by Native Americans or the French.

4 The *main* attraction of Texas for many Americans in the 1820s and 1830s was the

- A freedom to practice the Catholic faith.
- B availability of cheap or free land.
- C desire to become citizens of Mexico.
- D Mexican rebellion against Spain.

5 Which of the following was *not* due to the Mexican-American War?

- A Mexican foods and festivals became more important to American culture.
- B Prosperity of Mexican landowners in the Southwest increased under U.S. rule.
- C Mexican Americans introduced new ideas to the United States.
- D The size of the United States increased by about 25 percent.

6 Examine the following flier about cheap land available in the Dakota Territory and then use it to answer the question below.

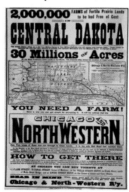

Who might have been attracted by this description of Dakota? Why?

Tips for Test Taking

In Your Own Words Sometimes the wording of a question might be a bit different than the language students are used to using. Tell students to read the question and then restate it in their own words to make sure they understand what is being asked.

Bellringer

Motivate Write the following for students to see: "Lissa was excited when she received her first driver's license." Ask students to brainstorm causes and effects of the event. Then have students consider the effects they listed as causes and list further effects. Help students build a cause-and-effect chain. Explain that in this workshop students will write a paper explaining causes or effects of a historical event.

SE Social Studies Skills 19: Short- and Long-term Causal Patterns

CRF 19: Social Studies Skills Activity: Short- and Long-term Causal Patterns

Interactive Skills Tutor CD-ROM, Lesson 7: Identify Cause and Effect

Determining Causes

Get Your Reasons Straight Remind students that not all the details they will read about as they study the War of 1812 will be causes or effects. Have students double-check the causes or effects they identified by asking one of the following questions:

- **Causes:** How did this action or situation contribute to the war?
- **Effects:** How did the war lead to this event or situation?

Organizing

How Important Is It? Explain to students that they have two choices when organizing information by importance—from least to most important, and from most to least important. Suggest that students who are organizing by order of importance make two outlines, one using each option. Then have students choose the option that works best.

Assignment

Write a paper explaining the causes or the effects of the War of 1812.

TIP Using a Graphic Organizer
Use a graphic organizer like this to organize your research.

Cause 1
↓
Cause 2
↓
Event or Situation
↓
Effect
↓
Effect

Cause and Effect in History

Historians try to make sense of an event by considering why the event happened and what resulted from it. Exploring causes and effects can provide a deeper understanding of historical events and how they are connected to one another.

1. Prewrite

Identifying Causes and Effects

A **cause** is an action or a situation that makes something else happen. What happens is called an **effect**. For example, if you stay up too late watching TV (cause), you might find yourself nodding off in class (effect). Often an event or situation will have several causes as well as several effects. In those cases, we may look at the order in which the causes or effects occurred, or we may look at their relative importance.

Researching and Organizing

For this paper, you will write about the causes or the effects of the event—the War of 1812. Gather information from the chapter in this textbook, an encyclopedia, or another source recommended by your teacher.

- Look for two or three reasons (causes) why the War of 1812 (the event or situation) occurred.
- At the same time, consider the war as a cause. Look for two or three effects of the war.

Then choose whether to write about the causes or the effects.

2. Write

You can use this framework to help you write your first draft.

A Writer's Framework

Introduction	Body	Conclusion
■ Begin with a quote or interesting fact about the event. ■ Identify the event you will discuss. [The War of 1812] ■ Identify whether you will be discussing the causes or the effects.	■ Present the causes or effects in chronological (time) order or order of importance. ■ Explain each cause or effect in its own paragraph, providing support with facts and examples.	■ Summarize your ideas about the causes or the effects of the event [the war].

Differentiating Instruction

English-Language Learners   Below Level   Standard English Mastery

1. Students may not be familiar with the transitional cause-and-effect words and phrases listed in the second Tip on the next page.

2. List the words and phrases and help students define each one. Then have the class use each word or phrase in a sentence.

3. Some students may be confused by the way that placement of transitions within a sentence can vary in English. Some appear before the ideas to which they connect, and some after. Illustrate this point by having students identify the idea to which each cause-and-effect transition connects.

4. Last, have students scan the text on the War of 1812 and look for cause-and-effect transitions. Help students identify the ideas to which each one connects. **LS Verbal/Linguistic**

3. Evaluate and Revise

Evaluating

Drawing clear, logical connections is the key to writing about causes and effects. Use these questions to evaluate and revise your paper.

Evaluation Questions for an Explanation of Causes or Effects

- Does the introduction begin with an interesting quotation or fact?
- Does the introduction identify the event [the war] and the causes or events to be discussed?
- Is each cause or effect explained in its own paragraph?
- Do facts and examples help to explain each cause or effect and connect it to the event [the war]?
- Are the causes or effects organized clearly—by chronological order or order of importance?
- Does the conclusion summarize the causes or effects and their importance?

TIP Recognizing False Cause-and-Effect In planning your essay, be careful to avoid false cause-and-effect relationships. The fact that one thing happened before or after another doesn't mean one caused the other. For example, the fact that James Madison was elected in 1808, just four years before the War of 1812, does not mean his election caused the War of 1812.

Revising

Make sure the connections between the war and its causes or effects are clear by sharing your paper with a classmate. If your classmate is confused, add background information. If he or she disagrees with your conclusions, add evidence or rethink your reasoning.

TIP Using Transitions Here are some transitional words and phrases that show cause or effect relationships: *because, as a result, therefore, for, since, so, consequently, for this reason.*

4. Proofread and Publish

Proofreading

Some transitional words and phrases need to be set off from the sentence with commas. Here are two examples:

- The Louisiana Territory was a huge region of land. *As a result,* the size of the United States almost doubled when the land was purchased.
- Jefferson wanted to know more about the land he had purchased. *Therefore,* he asked Congress to fund an expedition.

Check your paper to see if you need to add commas after or around any transitional words or phrases.

Publishing

Get together with a classmate and share causes and/or effects. Compare your lists to see whether you have identified different causes or effects. Share your findings with your class.

5. Practice and Apply

Use the steps and strategies outlined in this workshop to write your explanation of the causes or effects of the War of 1812.

THE NEW REPUBLIC **377**

Advanced/ Gifted and Talented   `Above Level`

1. Have students prepare their papers as if they are making a presentation to Congress either during or after the War of 1812.

2. Students writing a paper on the war's causes should present an analysis of the causes and recommend ways that war might have been avoided. Students writing a paper on the war's effects should provide solutions for addressing the negative effects. **LS** **Verbal/Linguistic**

Stuggling Readers   `Below Level`

1. If students have trouble identifying cause and effect, have them practice the skill on an easier selection. Choose an applicable selection from a fifth or sixth grade history text.

2. Have students work in pairs to create a cause-and-effect chart for the selection. Tell students to look for the cause-and-effect transitions listed above to help them. Correct any student errors. **LS** **Logical/Mathematical**

Reteach

Check Organization

Sort It Out Have students trade papers. In the margin next to each paragraph have students write a word or a phrase identifying the cause or effect discussed. Have them write "divide paragraph" next to any paragraph with more than one cause or effect. Have them write "combine paragraphs" next to any paragraphs that discuss the same cause or effect and then draw an arrow linking the two paragraphs to combine.

Teaching Tip

Stay on Topic Remind students that each paragraph must have a topic sentence. In most cases, it should be the first sentence of the paragraph. Check students' papers as they write and point out any paragraphs without topic sentences.

Practice & Apply

Rubric

Students' explanations of causes or effects should

- begin with an interesting quote or fact about the War of 1812.
- clearly identify the topic.
- accurately explain the causes or effects of the War of 1812.
- provide a paragraph and support for each cause or effect.
- follow either chronological order or order of importance.
- end with a summary.
- use correct grammar, punctuation, spelling, and capitalization.

Introduce the Unit

Share the information in the chapter overviews with students.

Chapter 12 During the early 1800s the Industrial Revolution dramatically changed the way in which goods were made. Americans' lives changed as well, as many people began working in factories. These changes were coupled with dramatic advances in transportation and technology.

Chapter 13 The invention of the cotton gin created a new cash crop for the South—cotton. This crop soon dominated the southern economy. Cotton production depended heavily on slave labor. Enslaved Africans were forced to perform hard labor and suffered terrible conditions. Nonetheless, slaves developed a rich culture and a deep religious sense.

Chapter 14 In the mid 1800s, waves of immigrants led to rapid growth of cities and a rise in urban problems. Meanwhile, a number of Americans began working to reform society, improve women's rights, and end slavery. Many Americans began to look for more intense meaning in their lives through deeper religious commitment, philosophy, and Romantic art and literature.

Chapter 15 In the mid-1800s tensions between the North and the South heightened over slavery. These tensions were increased by political divisions that culminated in 1860 with the election of Abraham Lincoln. As a result, several southern states seceded from the Union.

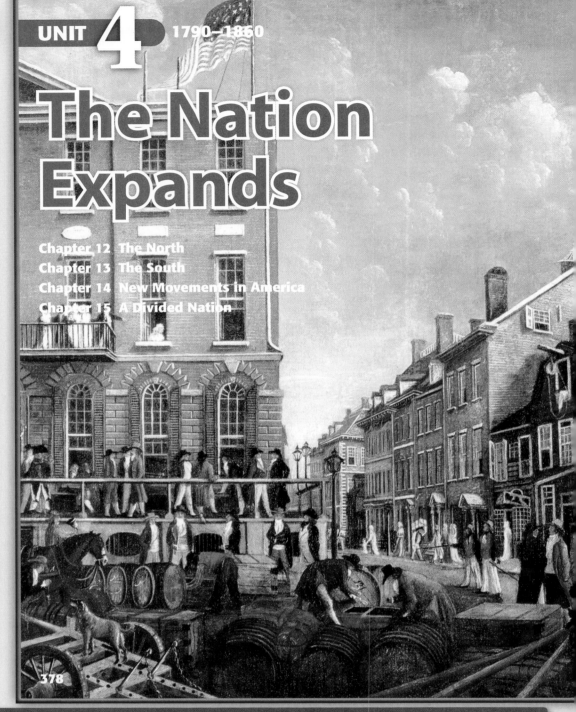

UNIT 4 1790–1860

The Nation Expands

Chapter 12 The North
Chapter 13 The South
Chapter 14 New Movements in America
Chapter 15 A Divided Nation

378

Unit Resources

Planning

- Differentiated Instruction Teacher Management System: Unit Instructional Benchmarking Guides
- One-Stop Planner CD-ROM with Test Generator: Calendar Planner
- Power Presentations with Video CD-ROM
- A Teacher's Guide to Religion in the Public Schools

Differentiating Instruction

- Differentiated Instruction Teacher Management System: Lesson Plans for Differentiated Instruction
- Pre-AP Activities Guide for United States History
- Differentiated Instruction Modified Worksheets and Tests CD-ROM

Enrichment

- **CRF 12**: Interdisciplinary Project: Using Measurements
- **CRF 15**: Economics and History: Economic Rivalry
- Civic Participation Activities
- Primary Source Library CD-ROM

Assessment

- Progress Assessment System Solution: Unit Test
- **OSP** ExamView Test Generator: Unit Test
- Holt Online Assessment Program, in the Premier Online Student Edition
- Alternative Assessment Handbook

The United States continued to grow in size and wealth, experiencing a new revolution of technology and business as did other parts of the world. During the earliest phases of expansion, regions of the United States developed differently from each other. Citizens differed in their ideas of progress, government, and religion. For the success of the nation, they tried to compromise on their disagreements. In the next four chapters, you will learn about two regions in the United States, and how they were alike and different.

Explore the Art

This painting shows a bustling street scene in New York City around 1797. What does the scene indicate about business in the city during this period?

379

Unit Preview

Connect to the Unit

Activity Focus on Regional **Differences** Ask students to discuss the differences between regions of the United States today. How is the East Coast different from the West Coast? How is the Midwest different from the Southwest? After a brief discussion, point out that differences between the North and the South led to growing tensions during the first part of the 1800s.

Create a Venn diagram for students to see. Label the circles North and South. Have students use what they have learned so far to predict what some of the similarities and differences might be. **LS** Verbal/Linguistic, Visual/Spatial

Explore the Art

During the early 1800s America grew at a rapid pace, and cities such as New York were a strong example of this expansion. New inventions, cheaper transportation, and more labor caused the city's economy to prosper. New York became so big that by the mid-1800s it processed more products than all other American ports combined. One result of this growth in the country's cities was slave labor, which became a bitter topic that later divided the nation.

About the Illustration

This illustration is an artist's conception based on available sources. However, historians are uncertain exactly what this scene looked like.

Democracy and Civic Education

At Level

Justice: Opposing Unjust Laws

Research Required

Background Explain that in the 1830s, some Americans began taking more organized action to try to achieve abolition, or a complete end to slavery. These Americans felt the laws that allowed slavery to exist were unjust.

1. Have students discuss what citizens should do when they think a law is unjust. What makes a law unjust? What actions can citizens take to try to change unjust laws? How can citizens work to promote justice in their local communities?

2. Organize students into groups. Have each group conduct research on actions citizens can take to oppose unjust laws.

3. Have each group use its research to create a storyboard for a televised public service announcement to educate Americans on what they can do to change unjust laws. **LS** Interpersonal, Verbal/Linguistic

📑 Alternative Assessment Handbook, Rubrics 14: Group Activity; and 29: Presentations

📑 Civic Participation

Answers

Explore the Art *The scene shows large, impressive buildings, transportation vehicles, paved streets, street lights, and large amounts of trade goods.*

Chapter 12 Planning Guide

The North

Chapter Overview	Reproducible Resources	Technology Resources
CHAPTER 12 pp. 380–409 **Overview: In this chapter, students will analyze the economic, cultural, physical, and social effects of technological improvements on the Northern states.**	**Differentiated Instruction Teacher Management System:*** • Instructional Benchmarking Guides • Lesson Plans for Differentiated Instruction **Interactive Reader and Study Guide:** Chapter Graphic Organizer* **Chapter Resource File:*** • Focus on Writing Activity: Newspaper Advertisement • Social Studies Skills Activity: Personal Conviction and Bias • Chapter Review Activity	**Power Presentations with Video CD-ROM** **Differentiated Instruction Modified Worksheets and Tests CD-ROM** **Primary Source Library CD-ROM for United States History** **Interactive Skills Tutor CD-ROM** **Student Edition on Audio CD Program** **History's Impact: United States History Video Program (VHS/DVD):** The North*
Section 1: **The Industrial Revolution in America** **The Big Idea:** The Industrial Revolution transformed the way goods were produced in the United States.	**Differentiated Instruction Teacher Management System:** Section 1 Lesson Plan* **Interactive Reader and Study Guide:** Section 1 Summary* **Chapter Resource File:*** • Vocabulary Builder Activity, Section 1 • Biography Activity: Samuel Slater	**Daily Bellringer Transparency:** Section 1* **Internet Activity:** Samuel Slater Plaque
Section 2: **Changes in Working Life** **The Big Idea:** The introduction of factories changed working life for many Americans.	**Differentiated Instruction Teacher Management System:** Section 2 Lesson Plan* **Interactive Reader and Study Guide:** Section 2 Summary* **Chapter Resource File:*** • Vocabulary Builder Activity, Section 2 • Biography Activity: Sarah Bagley	**Daily Bellringer Transparency:** Section 2* **Internet Activity:** Lowell Girls Scrapbook
Section 3: **The Transportation Revolution** **The Big Idea:** New forms of transportation improved business, travel, and communication in the United States.	**Differentiated Instruction Teacher Management System:** Section 3 Lesson Plan* **Interactive Reader and Study Guide:** Section 3 Summary* **Chapter Resource File:*** • Vocabulary Builder Activity, Section 3 • Literature Activity: Mark Twain Pilots a Steamboat • History and Geography Activity: The Transportation Revolution **Political Cartoons Activities for United States History,** Cartoon 14: Fears of the Railroad* **U.S. Supreme Court Case Studies:** *Gibbons* v. *Ogden* (1824)*	**Daily Bellringer Transparency:** Section 3* **Map Transparency:** Transportation Routes, 1850*
Section 4: **More Technological Advances** **The Big Idea:** Advances in technology led to new inventions that continued to change daily life and work.	**Differentiated Instruction Teacher Management System:** Section 4 Lesson Plan* **Interactive Reader and Study Guide:** Section 4 Summary* **Chapter Resource File:*** • Vocabulary Builder Activity, Section 4 • Biography Activity: John Deere • Interdisciplinary Project: Using Measurements	**Daily Bellringer Transparency:** Section 4*

SE Student Edition   Print Resource   Audio CD

TE Teacher's Edition   Transparency   CD-ROM

go. hrw.com   go.hrw.com   **LS** Learning Styles   Video

OSP One-Stop Planner CD-ROM   * also on One-Stop Planner CD

HOLT
History's Impact
United States History Video Program (VHS/DVD)
The North
Suggested use: as a chapter introduction

Review, Assessment, Intervention

- **Quick Facts Transparency:** The North Visual Summary*
- **Spanish Chapter Summaries Audio CD Program**
- **Online Chapter Summaries in Six Languages**
- **Progress Assessment Support System (PASS):** Chapter Test*
- **Differentiated Instruction Modified Worksheets and Tests CD-ROM:** Modified Chapter Test
- **One-Stop Planner CD-ROM:** ExamView Test Generator (English/Spanish)
- **GO Holt Online Assessment Program (HOAP),** in the Holt Premier Online Student Edition

- **PASS:** Section 1 Quiz*
- **Online Quiz:** Section 1
- **Alternative Assessment Handbook**

- **PASS:** Section 2 Quiz*
- **Online Quiz:** Section 2
- **Alternative Assessment Handbook**

- **PASS:** Section 3 Quiz*
- **Online Quiz:** Section 3
- **Alternative Assessment Handbook**

- **PASS:** Section 4 Quiz*
- **Online Quiz:** Section 4
- **Alternative Assessment Handbook**

Power Presentations with Video CD-ROM

Power Presentations with Video are visual presentations of each chapter's main ideas. Presentations can be customized by including Quick Facts charts, images from the text, and video clips.

Power Presentations with Video CD-ROM
HOLT
United States History
Beginnings to 1877
HOLT, RINEHART AND WINSTON

DIVISION FOR
PUBLIC EDUCATION
AMERICAN BAR ASSOCIATION

Developed by the Division for Public Education of the American Bar Association, these materials are part of the **Democracy and Civic Education Resources.**

- **Constitution Study Guide**
- **Supreme Court Case Studies**

Holt Online Learning

- Document-Based Questions
- Interactive Multimedia Activities

Teacher Resources
KEYWORD: SR8 TEACHER

Student Resources
KEYWORD: SR8 US12

- Current Events
- Chapter-based Internet Activities
- and more!

Holt Premier
Online Student Edition
Complete online support for interactivity, assessment, and reporting
- Interactive Maps and Notebook
- Standardized Test Prep
- Homework Practice and Research Activities Online

Differentiating Instruction

ENGLISH-LANGUAGE LEARNERS & STRUGGLING READERS

TARGET RESOURCE

live ink®
a new way to read

Live Ink® Online Reading Help

Spanish Resources

Spanish Chapter Summaries Audio CD Program

One-Stop Planner CD-ROM:
- ExamView Test Generator, Spanish
- PuzzlePro, Spanish

Additional Resources

Differentiated Instruction Teacher Management System: Lesson Plans for Differentiated Instruction

Chapter Resources:
- Vocabulary Builder Activities
- Social Studies Skills Activity: Personal Conviction and Bias

Quick Facts Transparency: The North Visual Summary

Student Edition on Audio CD Program

Online Chapter Summaries in Six Languages

Interactive Skills Tutor CD-ROM

SPECIAL NEEDS LEARNERS

TARGET RESOURCE

Differentiated Instruction Modified Worksheets and Tests CD-ROM

- Vocabulary Flash Cards
- Modified Vocabulary Builder Activities
- Modified Chapter Review Activity
- Modified Chapter Test

Additional Resources

Differentiated Instruction Teacher Management System: Lesson Plans for Differentiated Instruction

Interactive Reader and Study Guide

Social Studies Skills Activity: Personal Conviction and Bias

Student Edition on Audio CD Program

Interactive Skills Tutor CD-ROM

Live Ink® Online Reading Help

ADVANCED/GIFTED AND TALENTED STUDENTS

TARGET RESOURCE

Primary Source Library CD-ROM for United States History

The Library contains longer versions of quotations in the text, extra sources, and images. Included are point-of-view articles, journals, diaries, historical fiction, and political documents.

Additional Resources

Political Cartoons Activities for United States History: Cartoon 14: Fears of the Railroad

United States History Document-Based Questions Activities

Differentiated Instruction Teacher Management System: Lesson Plans for Differentiated Instruction

Chapter Resource File:
- Focus on Writing Activity: Newspaper Advertisement
- Literature Activity: Mark Twain Pilots a Steamboat

One-Stop Planner® CD-ROM
for Differentiated Instruction

Your differentiated instruction lesson plans are available at your fingertips. Holt's Teacher Management System links teaching support tools to pages in the Interactive Teacher's Edition.

The One-Stop Planner features:
- Interactive Teacher's Edition
- Calendar Planner and pacing guides
- Editable lesson plans
- All reproducible ancillaries in Adobe Acrobat (PDF) format
- ExamView Test Generator (English and Spanish)
- Transparency and video previews

Professional Development

- **In-service and staff development** as part of your Holt Social Studies product purchase
- **Quick Teacher Tutorial Lesson Presentation CD-ROM**
- Intensive tuition-based **Teacher Development Institute**
- **Teaching American History Online**—2 Module Professional Development Course
- **Convenient Holt Speaker Bureau**—face-to-face workshop options
- **PRAXIS™ Test Prep** interactive Web-based content refreshers*
- **24/7 Ask A Professional Development Expert** at http://www.hrw.com/prodev/

*PRAXIS is a trademark of Educational Testing Service (ETS). This publication is not endorsed or approved by ETS.

Chapter Big Ideas

Section 1 The Industrial Revolution transformed the way goods were produced in the United States.

Section 2 The introduction of factories changed working life for many Americans.

Section 3 New forms of transportation improved business, travel, and communication in the United States.

Section 4 Advances in technology led to new inventions that continued to change daily life and work.

Focus on Writing

The **Chapter Resource File** provides a Focus on Writing worksheet to help students organize and write their newspaper advertisements.

CRF: Focus on Writing Activity: A Newspaper Advertisement

380 CHAPTER 12

CHAPTER 12 1790–1860

The North

FOCUS ON WRITING

Newspaper Advertisement The Industrial Revolution was a time when a great many new inventions were introduced. You work for an advertising agency, and your job is to design an advertisement for one of the inventions mentioned in this chapter. As you read, take notes on the inventions, their inventors, and how they changed life in the United States. Then choose one invention and design a newspaper advertisement to persuade readers to buy or use the invention.

UNITED STATES

1807
Robert Fulton's *Clermont* becomes the first commercially successful steamboat.

1790

WORLD

1790
The first steam-powered mill opens in Great Britain.

380 CHAPTER 12

Introduce the Chapter

At Level

Farm Versus Factory

1. Organize the students into two groups: those who work on farms and those who work in factories. You might want to show students pictures of modern-day farms and factories to get them thinking about daily activities, how hard they might have to work, where they would live, and how life differs in rural and urban areas.

2. Start a classroom discussion by asking students to complete these sentences:

(a) "Working on a farm is better than working in a factory because . . . ," and (b) "Working in a factory is better than working on a farm because . . ."

3. List responses for students to see. Tell students to keep these responses in mind as they read the chapter and learn about how the Industrial Revolution changed life for Americans at home and at work.
LS Verbal/Linguistic

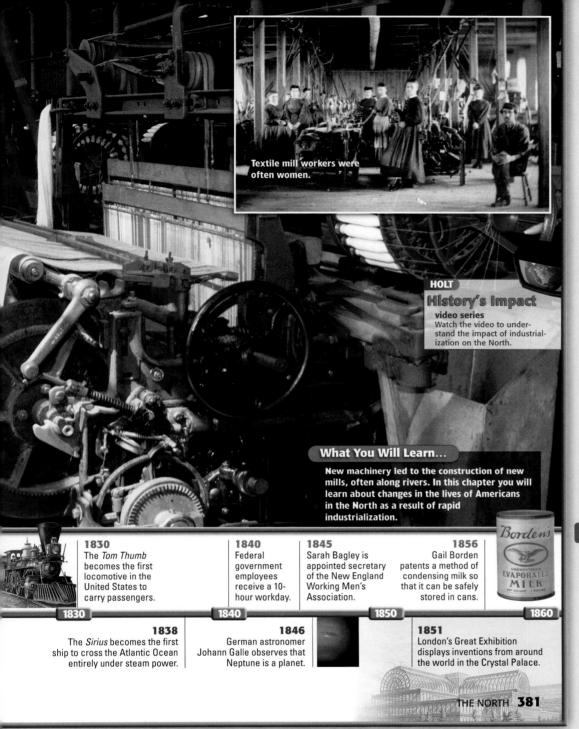

Textile mill workers were often women.

HOLT
History's Impact
video series
Watch the video to understand the impact of industrialization on the North.

What You Will Learn...

New machinery led to the construction of new mills, often along rivers. In this chapter you will learn about changes in the lives of Americans in the North as a result of rapid industrialization.

1830
The *Tom Thumb* becomes the first locomotive in the United States to carry passengers.

1838
The *Sirius* becomes the first ship to cross the Atlantic Ocean entirely under steam power.

1840
Federal government employees receive a 10-hour workday.

1846
German astronomer Johann Galle observes that Neptune is a planet.

1845
Sarah Bagley is appointed secretary of the New England Working Men's Association.

1851
London's Great Exhibition displays inventions from around the world in the Crystal Palace.

1856
Gail Borden patents a method of condensing milk so that it can be safely stored in cans.

Borden's
UNSWEETENED
EVAPORATED
MILK
NET WEIGHT 1 POUND

1830 1840 1850 1860

HOLT
History's Impact
▶ video series
See the Video Teacher's Guide for strategies for using the chapter video **The North**.

Explore the Picture

Water-Powered Mills Textile mills built in the early 1800s relied on water for power. Flowing rivers or waterfalls turned waterwheels that powered the mill machinery inside. With developments in steam-powered machinery, factories began to shift to steam power. As a result, factories were no longer necessarily built along rivers and streams. Today, however, old mills can still be found along many streams and rivers, particularly in the Northeast.

Analyzing Visuals How do you think a textile mill, like the one shown in the picture, might change a town? Students might suggest that it provided employment for many but also affected the environment.

go.hrw.com
Online Resources

Chapter Resources:
KEYWORD: SR8 US12
Teacher Resources:
KEYWORD: SR8 TEACHER

Explore the Time Line

1. When did the first steam-powered mill open in Great Britain? *1790*

2. How long after the first commercially successful steamboat in the United States was the nation's first passenger locomotive? *23 years*

3. How and when did working conditions change for government employees during this period? *Employees received a 10-hour workday in 1840.*

Info to Know

The *Sirius* Two ships competed to be the first to cross the Atlantic Ocean under steam power. The *Sirius* left England a few days before the *Great Western*, but arrived in New York just a few hours before her competitor. The *Sirius* actually ran out of coal near the end of the race. The captain refused to hoist the sails and instead fed cabin doors, a spare mast, and even furniture into the furnace.

Understanding Themes

Introduce this chapter by asking students how goods were produced in the United States prior to the 1800s. Point out to students that goods were made by hand before the Industrial Revolution introduced machines and factories to manufacturing. Ask students what types of technology would have been necessary to do this. Then ask students what sort of economic effects this faster method of producing goods might have had. Remind students to pay attention to the two themes of the chapter—science and technology, and economics.

Causes and Effects in History

Focus on Reading Point out to students that causes and effects can be seen in everyday life, not just in historical events. Ask students to think of events in their lives or in their community that have a clear cause-and-effect sequence. Have each student create a cause and effect chain that has at least four links. Then have students cut their chain into separate events so that each event is on a separate piece of paper. Have students exchange papers with a partner. Then have each student try to piece together the events in the cause and effect chain. Ask students to go over the proper sequence with their partners.

Reading Social Studies
by Kylene Beers

| Economics | Geography | Politics | Society and Culture | Science and Technology |

Focus on Themes As you read this chapter, you will learn about how increased **science and technology** brought about what is called the Industrial Revolution. As a result of the Industrial Revolution, you will see how American **economic** patterns changed. Next, you will read about how family life changed as more and more people went to work in factories. Finally, you will see how new methods of transportation changed where people lived and how new inventions affected daily life and work.

Causes and Effects in History

Focus on Reading Have you heard the saying, "We have to understand the past to avoid repeating it."? That is one reason we look for causes and effects in history.

Cause and Effect Chains You might say that all of history is one long chain of causes and effects. It may help you to understand the course of history better if you draw out such a chain as you read.

Since the 1790s, <u>wars between European powers</u> had interfered with U.S. trade. <u>American customers were no longer able to get all the manufactured goods</u> they were used to buying from British and European manufacturers . . . <u>Americans began to buy the items they needed from American manufacturers</u> instead of from foreign suppliers. As <u>profits for American factories grew</u>, <u>manufacturers began to spend more money expanding their factories</u> . . .

At the same time, many <u>Americans began to realize that the United States had been relying too heavily on foreign goods</u>. *(p. 389)*

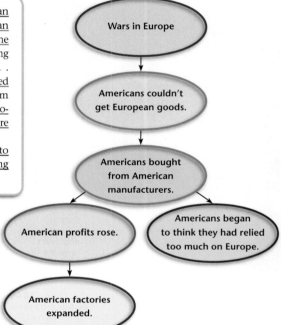

Wars in Europe

↓

Americans couldn't get European goods.

↓

Americans bought from American manufacturers.

↓

American profits rose.   Americans began to think they had relied too much on Europe.

↓

American factories expanded.

Reading and Skills Resources

Reading Support
- Interactive Reader and Study Guide
- Student Edition on Audio CD Program
- Spanish Chapter Summaries Audio CD Program

Social Studies Skills Support
- Interactive Skills Tutor CD-ROM

Vocabulary Support
- **CRF:** Vocabulary Builder Activities
- **CRF:** Chapter Review Activity
- Differentiated Instruction Modified Worksheets and Tests CD-ROM:
  - Vocabulary Flash Cards
  - Vocabulary Builder Activity
  - Chapter Review Activity

OSP Holt PuzzlePro

You Try It!

The following passage is from the chapter you about to read. As you read each paragraph, ask yourself what is the cause and what is the effect of what is being discussed.

Workers Organize

From Chapter 12, p. 394

Factories continued to spread in the 1800s. Craftspeople, who made goods by hand, felt threatened. Factories quickly produced low-priced goods. To compete with factories, shop owners had to hire more workers and pay them less . . .

The wages of factory workers also went down as people competed for jobs. A wave of immigration in the 1840s brought people from other, poorer countries. They were willing to work for low pay. More immigrants came to the Northeast, where the mills were located, than to the South. Competition for jobs also came from people unemployed during the Panic of 1837.

After you have read the passage, answer the following questions.

1. What cause is being discussed in the first paragraph? What were its effects?

2. Draw a cause and effect chain that shows the events described in the first paragraph.

3. What main effect is discussed in the second paragraph? How many causes are given for it?

4. Draw a cause and effect chain that shows the events described in the second paragraph.

As you read Chapter 12, look for words that signal causes or effects. Picture these causes and effects as the links in a cause and effect chain.

Key Terms and People

Chapter 12

Section 1
Industrial Revolution *(p. 385)*
textiles *(p. 385)*
Richard Arkwright *(p. 385)*
Samuel Slater *(p. 386)*
technology *(p. 387)*
Eli Whitney *(p. 387)*
interchangeable parts *(p. 387)*
mass production *(p. 387)*

Section 2
Rhode Island system *(p. 391)*
Francis Cabot Lowell *(p. 392)*
Lowell system *(p. 392)*
trade unions *(p. 394)*
strikes *(p. 394)*
Sarah G. Bagley *(p. 395)*

Section 3
Transportation Revolution *(p. 396)*
Robert Fulton *(p. 397)*
Clermont (p. 397)
Gibbons v. Ogden (p. 397)
Peter Cooper *(p. 398)*

Section 4
Samuel F. B. Morse *(p. 402)*
telegraph *(p. 402)*
Morse code *(p. 403)*
John Deere *(p. 404)*
Cyrus McCormick *(p. 404)*
Isaac Singer *(p. 405)*

Academic Vocabulary

Success in school is related to knowing academic vocabulary— the words that are frequently used in school assignments and discussions. In this chapter, you will learn the following academic words:

efficient *(p. 385)*
concrete *(p. 395)*

Reading Social Studies

Key Terms and People

Read the list aloud so that students will know how to pronounce each term or name. Then organize the students into pairs and assign each pair a person or term from the list. Have each pair identify the importance of the person or term. Then have each group draw a picture that represents the significance of that term or person. Have each student present the term, description or definition, and illustration to the class. Encourage students to take notes on the presentations. **LS Verbal/Linguistic, Visual/Spatial, Interpersonal**

Focus on Reading

See the **Focus on Reading** questions in this chapter for more practice on this reading social studies skill.

Reading Social Studies Assessment

See the **Chapter Review** at the end of this chapter for student assessment questions related to this reading skill.

Teaching Tip

Students may occasionally have difficulty identifying causes and effects as they read. Point out to students that causes and effects are often signaled by certain words. Ask students what words might signal causes and effects. Help them see that words like *as, since, because,* and *motivated by* all indicate causes. Some words that signal effect are: *led to, resulted in, as a result, began to, therefore,* and *then*.

Answers

You Try It! 1. *cause—factories continued to spread; effects— craftspeople felt threatened, shop owners had to compete with factories by hiring more workers, workers were paid less;* **2.** *Factories spread; craftspeople felt threatened; more workers were hired; each shop worker was paid less;* **3.** *effect—wages went down; three causes—a wave of immigration, immigrants willing to work for lower wages, and competition for jobs due to unemployment;* **4.** *causes— immigration and unemployment; effects—wages went down, immigrants willing to work for low pay, immigrants move to northeast.*

Bellringer

If YOU were there . . . Use the **Daily Bellringer Transparency** to help students answer the question.

📽 Daily Bellringer Transparency, Section 1

The North   Daily Bellringer
                                    Section 1

Review the Previous Chapter
Read the list of events below and put them in the correct order.
a. Gold is discovered at Sutter's Mill in California.
b. The forces of Santa Anna are defeated, securing Texan independence.
c. The Donner party gets snowed in when they reach the Sierra Nevada mountains in California.
d. John Jacob Astor opens a fur trading post in Oregon Country.
e. The Mexican-American War ends with the signing of the Treaty of Guadalupe-Hidalgo.

Preview Section 1
If YOU were there ...
You live in a small Pennsylvania town in the 1780s. Your father is a blacksmith, but you earn money for the family, too. You raise sheep and spin their wool into yarn. Your sisters knit the yarn into warm wool gloves and mittens. You sell your products to merchants in the city. But now you hear that someone has invented machines that can spin thread and make cloth. **Would you still be able to earn the same amount of money for your family? Why?**

Consider feeling ENCOURAGED:
• Greater efficiency could increase profit.
• Machines could free up your time.
• Technology is often inspiring.

Consider feeling APPREHENSIVE:
• The machines may be too expensive.
• Quality standards might decrease.
• You would be giving up control.

Review Answers: d, b, c, e, a
Copyright © by Holt, Rinehart and Winston. All rights reserved.

Academic Vocabulary

Review with students the high-use academic term in this section.

efficient productive and not wasteful (p. 385)

📋 **CRF:** Vocabulary Builder Activity, Section 1

Taking Notes

Have students copy the graphic organizer onto their own paper and then use it to take notes on the section. This activity will prepare students for the Section Assessment, in which they will complete a graphic organizer that builds on the information using a critical thinking skill.

Main Ideas

1. The invention of new machines in Great Britain led to the beginning of the Industrial Revolution.
2. The development of new machines and processes brought the Industrial Revolution to the United States.
3. Despite a slow start in manufacturing, the United States made rapid improvements during the War of 1812.

The Big Idea

The Industrial Revolution transformed the way goods were produced in the United States.

Key Terms and People

Industrial Revolution, *p. 385*
textiles, *p. 385*
Richard Arkwright, *p. 385*
Samuel Slater, *p. 386*
technology, *p. 387*
Eli Whitney, *p. 387*
interchangeable parts, *p. 387*
mass production, *p. 387*

 TAKING NOTES As you read, make a list of the key contributions of the Industrial Revolution and who initiated them. Write your notes in a chart like the one below.

Contributor	Invention/improvement

The Industrial Revolution in America

If YOU were there...

You live in a small Pennsylvania town in the 1780s. Your father is a blacksmith, but you earn money for the family, too. You raise sheep and spin their wool into yarn. Your sisters knit the yarn into warm wool gloves and mittens. You sell your products to merchants in the city. But now you hear that someone has invented machines that can spin thread and make cloth.

Would you still be able to earn the same amount of money for your family? Why?

BUILDING BACKGROUND In the early 1700s making goods depended on the hard work of humans and animals. It had been that way for hundreds of years. Then new technology brought a change so radical that it is called a revolution. It began in Great Britain and soon spread to the United States.

Beginning of the Industrial Revolution

At the beginning of the 1700s, the majority of people in Europe and the United States were farmers. They made most of what they needed by hand. For example, female family members usually made clothing. First, they used a spinning wheel to spin raw materials, such as cotton or wool, into thread. Then they used a hand loom to weave the thread into cloth.

Some families produced extra cloth to sell to merchants, who sold it for a profit. In towns, a few skilled workers made goods by hand in their own shops. These workers included blacksmiths, carpenters, and shoemakers. Their ways of life had stayed the same for generations.

A Need for Change

By the mid-1700s, however, changes in Great Britain led to a greater demand for manufactured goods. As agriculture and roads

---

Teach the Big Idea

The Industrial Revolution in America

1. **Teach** Ask students the questions in the Main Idea boxes to teach this section.

2. **Apply** Create a flow chart by writing the section's main ideas in large, vertically stacked boxes. Have students copy the flow chart and complete it by entering supporting details about the main ideas into the boxes. **LS Visual/Spatial**

3. **Review** As you review the section, have students share the information in their flow charts and discuss the cause-and-effect connections among events. Ask students to explain how the section's main ideas relate.

4. **Practice/Homework** Have students create poster-sized, illustrated versions of their flow charts. **LS Visual/Spatial**

📋 Alternative Assessment Handbook, Rubrics 13: Graphic Organizers; and 28: Posters

Textile Mill and Water Frame

SCIENCE AND TECHNOLOGY

A water frame adapts the power of flowing water into energy that moves wheels and gears through a system of belts. These wheels and gears then move parts of machines such as looms and spinning wheels.

1 Flowing water from a river turned the waterwheel. The giant wheel turned smaller gears connected to belts. **2** These belts moved parts of the machinery in the mill.

5 After the thread was spun, it moved to the loom to be woven into cloth. Workers called spoolers watched the looms and made sure that the spools of thread were kept straight.

4 Then the raw cotton was spun into thread on a spinning frame.

3 A machine for cleaning the raw cotton was the first step.

ANALYSIS SKILL **ANALYZING VISUALS**

What provided the power for the machines in the mill?

---

improved, cities and populations grew. Overseas trade also expanded. Traditional manufacturing methods did not produce enough goods to meet everyone's needs.

People began creating ways to use machines to make things more **efficient**. These changes led to the **Industrial Revolution**, a period of rapid growth in using machines for manufacturing and production that began in the mid-1700s.

Textile Industry

The first important breakthrough of the Industrial Revolution took place in how **textiles**, or cloth items, were made. Before the Industrial Revolution, spinning thread took much more time than making cloth. Several workers were needed to spin enough thread to supply a single weaver.

In 1769 Englishman **Richard Arkwright** invented a large spinning machine called a water frame. The water frame could produce dozens of cotton threads at the same time. It lowered the cost of cotton cloth and increased the speed of textile production.

The water frame used flowing water as its source of power. Merchants began to build large textile mills, or factories, near rivers and streams. The mills were filled with spinning machines. Merchants began hiring people to work in the mills.

Additional improvements also speeded up the spinning process. Britain soon had the world's most productive textile manufacturing industry.

ACADEMIC VOCABULARY
efficient
productive and not wasteful

READING CHECK Drawing Conclusions
How did machines speed up textile manufacturing?

THE NORTH **385**

Differentiating Instruction

English-Language Learners   At Level   Standard English Mastery

1. Lead a discussion on the beginning of the Industrial Revolution. Have students develop four key points about the topic. Write the points for students to see.

2. Ask students to write four newspaper headlines based on the points. Have volunteers present their headlines to the class.

3. Then have students select one of the four headlines and write a five-sentence article to go with it. Circulate to help students with their grammar and use of standard English. **LS** Verbal/Linguistic

Alternative Assessment Handbook, Rubric 42: Writing to Inform

Differentiated Instruction Resources
See p. 379c of the Chapter Planner for additional resources for differentiating instruction.

---

❷ New Machines and Processes

The development of new machines and processes brought the Industrial Revolution to the United States.

Recall Who was Samuel Slater, and how did he contribute to the textile industry in the United States? *skilled British mechanic who brought the knowledge of British textile machines to the United States, which led to the development of American textile mills*

Analyze Why were most American mills located in New England? *The region had many rivers and streams to power the mills, and the region's merchants were willing to invest.*

📋 **CRF:** Biography Activity: Samuel Slater

Info to Know

Opposition to Mills Not all Americans welcomed industrial innovations from Great Britain. Some Americans thought the import of British industry threatened American self-sufficiency. Others argued that mill owners violated people's water rights by building dams. In one case, some people sabotaged the dam that fed a Slater mill.

Analyzing Visuals

Elements of Mass Production
Mass production often requires financial resources beyond the means of an individual owner. Have students discuss how mass production may have led to corporate ownership of the large manufacturing firms of today.

Answers

Connect to Economics
interchangeable parts, machine tools, division of labor

386

New Machines and Processes

New machines encouraged the rise of new processes in business and manufacturing. As the machines used to make products became more efficient, the processes involved changed dramatically.

Slater and His Secrets

The new textile machines allowed Great Britain to produce cloth faster and cheaper than other countries could. To protect British industry, the British Parliament had made it illegal for skilled mechanics or machine plans to leave the country. Disguised as a farmer, **Samuel Slater**, a skilled British mechanic, immigrated to the United States after carefully memorizing the designs of textile mill machines. Soon after arriving, he sent a letter to Moses Brown, who owned a textile business in New England. Slater claimed he could improve the way textiles were manufactured in the United States.

Brown had one of his workers test Slater's knowledge of machinery. Slater passed. Brown's son, Smith Brown, and son-in-law, William Almy, formed a partnership with Slater. In 1793 they opened their first mill in Pawtucket, Rhode Island. The production of cotton thread by American machines had begun. Slater ran the mill and the machinery. He was confident that his new machines would work well.

❝ If I do not make as good yarn as they do in England, I will have nothing for my services, but will throw the whole of what I have attempted over the bridge. ❞
—Samuel Slater, quoted in *The Ingenious Yankees*, by Joseph and Francis Gies

Slater's machines worked, and the Pawtucket mill became a success. Slater's wife also invented a new cotton thread for sewing. In 1798 Slater formed his own company to build a mill. By the time he died in 1835, he owned all or part of 13 textile mills.

Other Americans began building textile mills. Most were located in the Northeast. In New England in particular, merchants had the money to invest in new mills. More importantly, this region had many rivers and streams that provided a reliable supply of power. Fewer mills were built in the South, partly because investors in the South concentrated on expanding agriculture. There, agriculture was seen as an easier way to make money.

Elements of Mass Production

CONNECT TO ECONOMICS
Mass-production techniques allow manufacturers to efficiently create more goods for the marketplace. Mass production requires the use of interchangeable parts, machine tools, and the division of labor.

What are the three elements of mass production?

Interchangeable Parts
Eli Whitney developed the idea of using interchangeable parts. Interchangeable, or identical, parts are needed so each part does not have to be custom-made by hand.

Machine Tools
Machine tools like this one make parts that are identical and therefore interchangeable.

386 CHAPTER 12

Differentiating Instruction

Below Level

Struggling Readers

1. Draw the following graphic organizer for students to see. Omit the blue answers.
2. Have each student copy the organizer and complete it by describing the innovations of Slater and Whitney and the effects of those innovations. **LS** Visual/Spatial

📋 Alternative Assessment Handbook, Rubric 13: Graphic Organizers

Samuel Slater		**Effects**
Innovation: *machine production of cotton thread in mills*	→	• *spread of textile mills, many in New England* • *increased productivity of American textiles*

Eli Whitney		**Effects**
Innovation: *idea of interchangeable parts*	→	• *easy to assemble and replace parts* • *mass production*

A Manufacturing Breakthrough

Despite these great changes, most manufacturing was still done by hand. In the late 1790s the U.S. government worried about a possible war with France, so it wanted more muskets for the army. Skilled workers made the parts for each weapon by hand. No two parts were exactly alike, and carefully fitting all the pieces together took much time and skill.

As a result, American gun makers could not produce the muskets quickly enough to satisfy the government's demand. Factories needed better **technology**, the tools used to produce items or to do work.

In 1798 inventor **Eli Whitney** tried to address some of these problems. Whitney gave officials a proposal for mass-producing guns for the U.S. government using water-powered machinery. Whitney explained the benefits of his ideas.

" I am persuaded that machinery moved by water [and] adapted to this business would greatly reduce the labor and facilitate [ease] the manufacture of this article. "

—Eli Whitney, quoted in *Technology in America*, edited by Carroll W. Pursell

Whitney also came up with the idea of using **interchangeable parts** —parts of a machine that are identical. Using interchangeable parts made machines easier to assemble and broken parts easier to replace. Whitney promised to build 10,000 muskets in two years. The federal government gave him money to build his factory, and in 1801 Whitney was called to Washington, D.C., to give a demonstration.

Whitney stood before President John Adams and his secetary of war. He had an assortment of parts for 10 guns. He then randomly chose parts and quickly assembled them into muskets. To the audience's amazement, he repeated the process several times.

Whitney's Influence

Whitney had proven that American inventors could improve upon the new British technology. Machines that produced matching parts soon became standard in industry. Interchangeable parts sped up **mass production**, the efficient production of large numbers of identical goods.

READING CHECK Summarizing How did Eli Whitney influence American manufacturing?

Division of Labor
Mass production uses a division of labor in which the work is divided among several people, each doing a specific task, like the worker shown here.

Mass-Produced Goods
The end result are goods that have been mass-produced. Eli Whitney used mass-production techniques to manufacture firearms.

THE NORTH **387**

387

Main Idea

❸ Slow Start in Manufacturing

Despite a slow start in manufacturing, the United States made rapid improvements during the War of 1812.

Explain According to Albert Gallatin, why were so few factories being built in the United States? *attractiveness of farming, abundance of cheap land, high price of labor, lack of capital to invest in factories*

Identify Cause and Effect How did the War of 1812 affect American manufacturing? *The war prevented the import of many foreign goods, which led Americans to buy American-made goods, which in turn led to increased manufacturing.*

Make Inferences Do you think all Americans supported higher tariffs? *possible answer—People who bought foreign goods, such as farmers, likely would have opposed higher tariffs.*

Linking to Today
Modern Manufacturing

Activity Have students find articles, with pictures if possible, about manufacturing in the United States today. Post students' articles on a class bulletin board. Then review a few of the articles each day during the study of this chapter.
LS Verbal/Linguistic

Answers

Linking to Today *Complex products made of multiple parts can be assembled quickly.*

388

LINKING TO TODAY

Modern Manufacturing

The word *manufacture* comes from Latin words that mean "to make by hand." Yet in modern manufacturing, machines—not human hands—do most of the work.

A key feature of modern manufacturing is the assembly line. An assembly line is a long conveyer belt. As the product moves along the belt, or "down the line," workers assemble it. Often, the workers use machines to help them. On a growing number of assembly lines, there are no workers at all: the product is assembled by computer-controlled robots.

Although a far cry from Eli Whitney's factory, modern factories use the same elements of mass production that Whitney did more than 200 years ago.

ANALYSIS SKILL | **ANALYZING INFORMATION**

How do interchangeable parts help the modern assembly line work?

Slow Start in Manufacturing

Despite the hard work of people such as Samuel Slater and Eli Whitney, manufacturing in the United States grew slowly. In 1810 Secretary of the Treasury Albert Gallatin suggested some reasons why there were so few factories in the United States.

❝ [The reasons include] ... the superior attractions of agricultural pursuits [farming], ... the abundance of land compared with the population, the high price of labor, and the want [lack] of sufficient capital [investment]. ❞
—Albert Gallatin, quoted in *Who Built America*, edited by Bruce C. Levine et al.

Gallatin and others believed that few people would choose to work in a factory if they could own their own farm instead. In Great Britain, on the other hand, land was more scarce and more expensive than in the United States. As a result, fewer people were able to own farms. British factory workers generally were willing to work for lower wages than factory workers in the United States were.

Because British manufacturers had plenty of factory workers with technical skills, they could produce large amounts of goods less expensively than most American businesses could. Consequently, they could charge lower prices for the goods. Lower British prices made it difficult for many American manufacturers to compete with British companies. This situation in turn discouraged American investors from spending the money needed to build new factories and machinery. As a result, only a few industries had found a place in the American economy. These included cotton goods, flour milling, weapons, and iron production.

388 CHAPTER 12

Critical Thinking: Analyzing Information
At Level

Factory Owner Letter Requesting a Loan

1. Ask students to imagine that they are American manufacturers in 1814 seeking bank loans to expand their factories.

2. Have each student write a letter to convince a bank to give him or her a loan.

3. In their letters, students should address the benefits of mass production, the need to

promote American manufacturing, the goods they are producing at their factories, and the factories' profit potential.

4. Have volunteers read their letters to the class.
LS Logical/Mathematical, Verbal/Linguistic

Alternative Assessment Handbook, Rubric 43: Writing to Persuade

These circumstances began to change around the time of the War of 1812. Since the 1790s, wars between European powers had interfered with U.S. trade. American customers were no longer able to get all the manufactured goods they were used to buying from British and European manufacturers. Then, during the War of 1812, British ships blockaded eastern seaports, preventing foreign ships from delivering goods. Americans began to buy the items they needed from American manufacturers instead of from foreign suppliers. As profits for American factories grew, manufacturers began to spend more money expanding their factories. State banks and private investors began to lend money to manufacturers for their businesses.

At the same time, many Americans began to realize that the United States had been relying too heavily on foreign goods. If the United States could not meet its own needs, it might be weak and open to attack. Former president Thomas Jefferson, who had once opposed manufacturing, changed his mind. He, too, realized that the United States was too dependent on imports.

"To be independent for the comforts of life we must fabricate [make] them ourselves. We must now place the manufacturer by the side of the agriculturalist [farmer]."

—Thomas Jefferson, from *The Writings of Thomas Jefferson*, edited by P. L. Ford

In February 1815, New Yorkers celebrated the end of the War of 1812 and the return of free trade. The streets were decorated and filled with merchants whose ships were loaded with goods. "With Peace and Commerce, America Prospers," declared one display. Eager businesspeople prepared to lead the United States into a period of industrial growth. They urged northern politicians to pass higher tariffs on foreign goods to protect American companies.

READING CHECK **Analyzing** How did the War of 1812 aid the growth of American manufacturing?

SUMMARY AND PREVIEW The Industrial Revolution started with the textile industry in England but soon spread to the United States. In the next section you will learn about how the spread of factories changed the working lives of many Americans.

THE IMPACT TODAY
American dependence on some foreign goods, such as oil, is still being debated today.

Section 1 Assessment

go.hrw.com
Online Quiz
KEYWORD: SR8 HP12

Reviewing Ideas, Terms, and People

1. a. Identify What was the first industry to begin to use machines to manufacture goods?
b. Predict In what ways might life for workers change as a result of the **Industrial Revolution**?

2. a. Recall In what part of the United States were most mills located? Why?
b. Draw Conclusions How did the ideas of **Samuel Slater** and **Eli Whitney** affect manufacturing in the United States?
c. Evaluate Whose contributions do you think were more important—Slater's textile machines or Whitney's **interchangeable parts**? Why?

3. a. Identify What event encouraged the growth of American manufacturing? Why?
b. Contrast Why was manufacturing in Great Britain in the early years more successful than that in the United States?

Critical Thinking

4. Drawing Conclusions Review your notes on key inventions and improvements during the Industrial Revolution. Then copy the chart below and use it to show how each contribution affected manufacturing.

Invention/improvement	Effect on Manufacturing

FOCUS ON WRITING

5. Noting Inventions In your notebook, create a three-column chart. In the first column, list any inventions mentioned in this section. In the second column, identify the inventor. In the third column, describe the invention and its benefits.

THE NORTH **389**

Section 1 Assessment Answers

1. a. textile industry
b. move from working on farms or in homes to working in factories; loss of work for some skilled laborers; poorer working conditions

2. a. Northeast; had many rivers and streams to provide a reliable supply of water power
b. led to spread of mills, the growth of the American textile industry, mass production, and the cheaper manufacture of goods
c. Answers will vary but should reflect an understanding of each man's contributions.

3. a. War of 1812; with the loss of many foreign imports, Americans bought more American goods, which increased manufacturing
b. Britain had less available, cheap land; and thus more workers and lower wages.

4. Arkwright's water frame—lowered costs, increased speed, led to textile mills; Slater's export of British textile machine designs—led to American textile mills; Whitney's interchangeable parts—led to mass production; War of 1812; see answer to 3a.

5. See the previous answer.

• Review & Assess •

Close
Briefly review the ways in which the Industrial Revolution came to the United States.

Review
Online Quiz, Section 1

Assess
SE Section 1 Assessment
PASS: Section 1 Quiz
Alternative Assessment Handbook

Reteach/Classroom Intervention
Interactive Reader and Study Guide, Section 1
Interactive Skills Tutor CD-ROM

Answers

Reading Check *The war prevented the import of many foreign goods, which led Americans to buy American-made goods, which in turn led to increased manufacturing.*

389

Changes in Working Life

Bellringer

If YOU were there . . . Use the **Daily Bellringer Transparency** to help students answer the question.

📖 Daily Bellringer Transparency, Section 2

The North   Daily Bellringer
                                   Section 2

Review Section 1
Indicate whether each sentence below is **TRUE** or **FALSE**. If the sentence is false, change the underlined word to make the sentence true.
1. <u>Samuel Slater</u> invented the large spinning machine called a water frame.
2. <u>Richard Arkwright</u> came up with the idea of using interchangeable parts.
3. The efficient production of large numbers of identical goods is known as <u>major production</u>.
4. Items made from cloth are called <u>textiles</u>.

Preview Section 2
If YOU were there . . .
You live on a dairy farm in Massachusetts in about 1820. On the farm, you get up at dawn to milk the cows, and your work goes on until night. But now you have a chance at a different life. A nearby textile mill is hiring young people. You would leave the farm and live with other workers. You could go to classes. Most important, you could earn money of your own.
Would you go to work in the textile mill? Why?

Consider reasons TO WORK in the mill:
• to satisfy your restlessness
• to assert your independence
• opportunity to make new friends

Consider reasons NOT TO WORK in the mill:
• obligations to family
• fear of the unknown
• rumors of harsh working conditions

Review Answers: 1. F, Richard Arkwright; 2. F, Eli Whitney; 3. F, mass production; 4. T

Copyright © by Holt, Rinehart and Winston. All rights reserved.

Academic Vocabulary

Review with students the high-use academic term in this section.

concrete specific, real (p. 395)

📑 **CRF:** Vocabulary Builder Activity, Section 2

Taking Notes

Have students copy the graphic organizer onto their own paper and then use it to take notes on the section. This activity will prepare students for the Section Assessment, in which they will complete a graphic organizer that builds on the information using a critical thinking skill.

What You Will Learn...

Main Ideas

1. The spread of mills in the Northeast changed workers' lives.
2. The Lowell System revolutionized the textile industry in the Northeast.
3. Workers organized to reform working conditions.

The Big Idea

The introduction of factories changed working life for many Americans.

Key Terms and People

Rhode Island system, *p. 391*
Francis Cabot Lowell, *p. 392*
Lowell system, *p. 392*
trade unions, *p. 394*
strikes, *p. 394*
Sarah G. Bagley, *p. 395*

TAKING NOTES As you read, take notes on how mills changed workers' lives, and how workers organized to fight many of these changes.

Changes to workers' lives → Workers' reaction

If YOU were there...

You live on a dairy farm in Massachusetts in about 1820. On the farm, you get up at dawn to milk the cows, and your work goes on until night. But now you have a chance at a different life. A nearby textile mill is hiring young people. You would leave the farm and live with other workers. You could go to classes. Most important, you could earn money of your own.

Would you go to work in the textile mill? Why?

BUILDING BACKGROUND As factories and mills were established, the way people worked changed drastically. One dramatic change was the opportunity that factory work gave to young women. For young women in farm families, it was almost the only chance they had to earn their own money and a measure of independence.

Mills Change Workers' Lives

Workers no longer needed the specific skills of craftspeople to run the machines of the new mills. The lives of workers changed along with their jobs. Resistance to these changes sometimes sparked protests.

Many mill owners in the United States could not find enough people to work in factories because other jobs were available. At first, Samuel Slater and his two partners used apprentices—young men who worked for several years to learn the trade. However, they often were given only simple work. For example, their jobs included feeding cotton into the machines and cleaning the mill equipment. They grew tired of this work and frequently left. Apprentice James Horton, for example, ran away from Slater's mill. "Mr. Slater . . . keep me always at one thing . . . ," Horton complained. "I might have stayed there until this time and never knew nothing."

Eventually, Slater began to hire entire families who moved to Pawtucket to work in the mills. This practice allowed Slater to fill his labor needs at a low cost. Children as well as adults worked in the mills.

Teach the Big Idea

At Level

Changes in Working Life

1. **Teach** Ask students the questions in the Main Idea boxes to teach this section.

2. **Apply** Ask students to imagine that they are factory workers who also write for a workers' magazine. Have each student write an article titled "Factory Life" describing how factories have changed workers' lives in the Northeast. Students should address the effects of factories on farm families and craftspeople, the type of factory systems that developed, the advantages and disadvantages of mill work, and the role of labor unions.

3. **Review** Ask volunteers to read their articles aloud. Discuss them to review the section.

4. **Practice/Homework** Have each student create a political cartoon for the magazine that contrasts the reality of mill work with the image owners promoted. **LS Visual/Spatial**

📑 Alternative Assessment Handbook, Rubrics 27: Political Cartoons; and 42: Writing to Inform

NEWSPAPER ADVERTISEMENT
Family Wanted

This advertisement appeared in a Rhode Island, newspaper in 1823. In it, a company requests that families come to work at a factory. The practice of hiring entire families was common at the time, especially in Britain. In America, it became known as the Rhode Island system.

The advertisement requests more than one family.

Why do you think Blackstone wants large families?

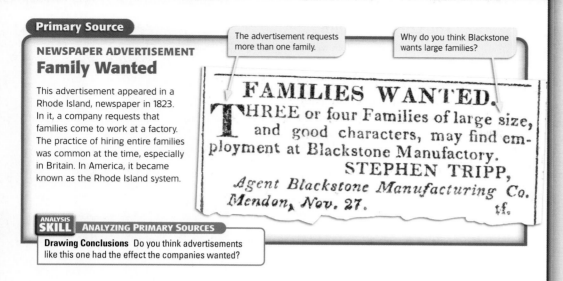

FAMILIES WANTED.

THREE or four Families of large size, and good characters, may find employment at Blackstone Manufactory.
STEPHEN TRIPP,
Agent Blackstone Manufacturing Co.
Mendon, Nov. 27.
tf.

ANALYSIS SKILL **ANALYZING PRIMARY SOURCES**

Drawing Conclusions Do you think advertisements like this one had the effect the companies wanted?

On most farms children worked to help their families. Therefore, few people complained about the hiring of children to work in factories. H. Humphrey, an author of books on raising children, told parents that children needed to be useful. Humphrey wrote, "If he [a child] will not study, put him on to a farm, or send him into the shop, or in some other way provide regular employment for him." The machines made many tasks in the mill simple enough for children to do. Mill owners profited because they paid children low wages. Adults usually earned as much in a day as most children did in a week.

To attract families to his mill, Slater built housing for the workers. He also provided them with a company store where they could buy necessities. In addition, he started the practice of paying workers with credit at the company store. Instead of paying the full price for an item all at once, small payments could be made over a period of time. This practice allowed Slater to reinvest his money in his business.

Slater's strategy of hiring families and dividing factory work into simple tasks became known as the **Rhode Island system**. Mill owners throughout the Northeast copied Slater's methods. Owners advertised with "Men with growing families wanted." They also sent recruiters to poor communities to find new workers. For many people, the chance to work in a factory was a welcome opportunity to earn money and to learn a new skill.

One of the earliest of the mill towns, Slatersville, was named after Samuel Slater. The town was built by Slater and his brother John. It included two houses for workers and their families, the owner's house, the company store, and the Slatersville Mill. The mill was the largest and most modern industrial building of its time.

The mills employed not only the textile workers who operated the machinery but also machine part makers and dam builders. Although the company store sold food and necessary items to workers, mill towns supported the same variety of businesses any other town needed to thrive. These included tailors and dressmakers, butchers, and other small workshops.

READING CHECK **Summarizing** What problem did Slater have in his mills, and how did he solve it?

Direct Teach

Main Idea

❶ Mills Change Workers' Lives

The spread of mills in the Northeast changed workers' lives.

Recall What was the Rhode Island system, and why did Samuel Slater decide to adopt it? *what—practice of hiring families and dividing factory work into simple tasks; why—because apprentices grew tired of the work and often left, and families provided several workers at low cost*

Identify Cause and Effect What were some effects of Slater's use of the Rhode Island system? *Other mill owners began using the system; mill towns developed to provide mill families with a place to live and shop.*

Compare In what ways was a mill town similar to other small towns in the United States at the time? *Mill towns provided a variety of businesses, just as in other towns.*

Primary Source

Family Wanted

Draw Conclusions Why does the advertisement request large families? *The larger the family, the more low-paid workers a factory owner gained, because factory owners paid children less.*

Critical Thinking: Finding Main Ideas   At Level

Slater's Mill Want Ad

1. Have each student create an advertisement seeking employees for Slater's mills. Students should address the following questions in their advertisements:

   • What types of workers does Slater want to attract?

   • What segments of society might want to work in a mill?

   • What incentives might appeal to and attract possible employees?

   • Why would a person want to work in one of Slater's mills as opposed to another mill?

2. Have volunteers share their advertisements with the class.

3. Then lead a discussion on working conditions in mills during this period. **L5 Verbal/Linguistic**

   📖 Alternative Assessment Handbook, Rubric 2: Advertisements

Answers

Analyzing Primary Sources *possible answer—yes, because people were looking for work and farm families were used to their children working.*

Reading Check *He had trouble finding enough people to work in his mills. He began hiring entire families to work at low wages and divided factory work into simple tasks; also built housing for workers and provided a company store.*

Main Idea

❶ The Lowell System

The Lowell system revolutionized the textile industry in the Northeast.

Recall What system did Francis Cabot Lowell use in his mills, and who did he hire under this system? *Lowell system; young, unmarried women from local farms*

Explain Why did young women want to work in the Lowell mills? *ability to make own money; higher wages than they could earn elsewhere*

Summarize What were working and living conditions like for Lowell girls? *worked hard for 12 to 14 hours a day; bells provided a rigid schedule, lived in clean boardinghouses, encouraged to use free time to take classes and form clubs*

Predict How do you think mill workers felt as owners kept increasing the size and speed of their machines? *possible answers—angry at having to work harder, tired from overwork, wanted higher wages*

Info to Know

Working Women In addition to the mills, women in the Northeast had other opportunities for work in the early 1800s. One historical study found that the jobs available to women depended upon their race and ethnicity. Native-born women in New England could find clerical and sales jobs. Immigrant women often found semiskilled factory work. Newer immigrant women and free African American women were largely limited to domestic service.

go.hrw.com

Online Resources

KEYWORD: SR8 US12
ACTIVITY: Lowell Girls Scrapbook

The Lowell System

Not all mill owners followed this system. **Francis Cabot Lowell**, a businessman from New England, developed a very different approach. His ideas completely changed the textile industry in the Northeast.

The **Lowell system** was based on water-powered textile mills that employed young, unmarried women from local farms. The system included a loom that could both spin thread and weave cloth in the same mill. Lowell constructed boardinghouses for the women. Boardinghouse residents were given a room and meals along with their jobs.

With financial support from investors of the Boston Manufacturing Company, Lowell's first textile mill opened in Waltham, Massachusetts, in 1814. "From the first starting of the first power loom there was not . . . doubt about the success," wrote one investor. In 1822, the company built a larger mill in a Massachusetts town later named Lowell. Visitors to Lowell were amazed by the clean factories and neatly kept boardinghouses as well as the new machinery.

The young millworkers soon became known as Lowell girls. The mills paid them between $2 and $4 each week. The workers paid $1.25 for room and board. These wages were much better than those women could earn per week in other available jobs, such as domestic work.

Many young women came to Lowell from across New England. They wanted the chance to earn money instead of working on the family farm. "I must of course have something of my own before many more years have passed over my head," wrote one young woman. The typical Lowell girl worked at the mills for about four years.

Unlike other factory workers, the Lowell girls were encouraged to use their free time to take classes and form women's clubs. They even wrote their own magazine, the *Lowell Offering*. Lucy Larcom, who started working at Lowell at age 11, later praised her fellow workers.

No record exists today of the name of this girl, who worked in a mill around 1850. Judging from the photograph, if she were in school today, she would probably be in the seventh or eighth grade. Although hard to see in this photograph, her hands and arms are scratched and swollen—telltale signs of the hard labor required of young girls who worked up to 14 hours per day.

TIME TABLE OF THE LOWELL MILLS

Morning Bells

First bell . . . . 4:30 AM

Second bell . . . . 5:30 AM

Third bell . . . . 6:20 AM

Dinner (Lunch) Bells

Ring out . . . . 12:00 PM

Ring in . . . . 12:35 PM

Evening Bells

Ring out . . . . 6:30 PM

Except on Saturday Evenings

—*The Table of the Lowell Mills, October 21, 1851*

Social Studies Skills: Assessing the Credibility of Primary Sources

A *Lowell Offering* Excerpt   Above Level

Background Some people criticized the *Lowell Offering* for providing an unrealistic view of mill life. For example, one cover made the mill look more like a garden than a factory. In 1845 Harriet Farley, the editor, defended the magazine.

1. Read aloud the following: "We have never published anything which our own experience had convinced us was unfair. But, if in our sketches, there is too much light, and too little shade, let our excuse be . . .

We have not thought it necessary to state . . . that our life was a toilsome one—for we supposed that would be universally understood."

2. Have students discuss how Farley defends the magazine's image of mill life and whether her argument is valid. What factors might have influenced her viewpoint? Why might the editors have chosen to ignore the harsh realities of mill life? **LS Verbal/Linguistic**

Alternative Assessment Handbook: Rubric 16: Judging Information

History Close-up

Life of a Mill Girl

Girls had to keep their hair pulled back so it did not get caught in the machines, resulting in serious injury—or death.

Windows were rarely opened, to prevent air from blowing the threads. The result is a hot, stuffy room.

The air is dirty and causes breathing problems. One visitor remarked, "The atmosphere . . . is charged with cotton filaments and dust, which . . . are very injurious to the lungs."

This girl is straightening threads as they enter the power loom, a job that cut her hands.

Girls must shout to be heard above the noise of the power looms. Visitors to the mill routinely referred to the sound of the machines as "deafening."

ANALYSIS SKILL **ANALYZING VISUALS**

Judging from the photograph on page 392, what might be the condition of the girl's hands in this illustration? Why?

THE NORTH **393**

Direct Teach

History Close-up
Life of a Mill Girl

Activity **Lowell Girl Journal Entry**
Ask students to imagine that they have found an old journal written by a Lowell girl. Have students use the information in the images and captions at left to write one journal entry describing a day in the life of a Lowell girl.
LS Intrapersonal, Verbal/Linguistic

📑 Alternative Assessment Handbook, Rubric 15: Journals

Biography

Lucy Larcom (1826–1893) Lucy Larcom provides an example of one Lowell girl's life. Larcom was 1 of 10 children, several of whom worked in the Lowell mills. The Larcom family moved to Lowell, Massachusetts, after the father died. Together, Lucy and her sisters Abigail, Emeline, and Lydia earned almost $230 in factory wages in 1836. Besides supporting their mother and family, two of the Larcom sisters became accomplished writers. Emeline played a central role in founding *Operatives' Magazine*, a literary journal. Lucy became a noted poet and editor, and the author of *A New England Girlhood*.

Did You Know . . .

The minor league baseball team in Lowell, Massachusetts is named the Lowell Spinners in honor of the region's history of textile mills.

Collaborative Learning

At Level

Lowell Offering Magazine

Materials: heavy white paper, art supplies

1. Organize students into small groups. Ask the groups to imagine that they are contributors to the *Lowell Offering* magazine.

2. Have each group fold and staple together two pieces of paper to create a "magazine." Students should design a cover for the magazine and fill the inside pages with articles and other items related to life and working conditions in the Lowell mills. In addition to articles, students might include artwork, poetry, an advice column, stories, editorials, club listings, schedules and menus, and so on. Groups might also create a slogan or mill song to print on the inside or back cover.

3. If time allows, have students conduct research on the Lowell girls to enhance the contents of their magazines. **LS Verbal/Linguistic**

📑 Alternative Assessment Handbook, Rubrics 14: Group Activity; and 19: Magazines

Answers

Analyzing Visuals *scratched and swollen; Straightening threads as they entered the power loom would have cut her hands.*

393

Main Idea

❸ Workers Organize

Workers organized to reform working conditions.

Explain What had happened to the wages of craftspeople and factory workers by the 1840s? *craftspeople—to compete with factories, shop owners hired more workers and paid them less; factory workers—wages went down as competition for jobs increased*

Make Inferences Why did employers think that union workers prevented them from competing? *Employers thought they would have to pay union workers higher wages, which would make it harder for them to sell finished goods at lower prices than their competitors.*

Checking for Understanding

True or False Answer each statement *T* if it is true or *F* if it is false. If false, explain why.
1. Samuel Slater's system of hiring families and dividing factory work into simple tasks became known as the Lowell system. *F; Rhode Island system*
2. Many young women did not want to work in the mills because they could earn more working at home. *F; Many did want to work in the mills because they could earn more than at other jobs.*
3. Trade unions worked to improve pay and working conditions. *T*

Answers

Analyzing Primary Sources
Bagley viewed it as similar to slavery.

Reading Check *Lowell system—employed young, unmarried women from local farms; Rhode Island system—employed entire families*

MAGAZINE ARTICLE
Sarah G. Bagley and Workers' Rights

Lowell girl Sarah G. Bagley wrote magazine articles and made speeches about working in the mills. She organized workers to help change conditions.

Bagley says that mill girls work to help their family members.

Bagley believes that most mill girls would leave their jobs if they could.

"Is anyone such a fool as to suppose that out of six thousand factory girls in Lowell, sixty would be there if they could help it? Whenever I raise the point that it is immoral to shut us up in a close room twelve hours a day in the most monotonous and tedious of employment I am told that we have come to the mills voluntarily and we can leave when we will. Voluntarily! . . . the whip which brings us to Lowell is necessity. We must have money; a father's debts are to be paid, an aged mother to be supported, a brother's ambition to be aided and so the factories are supplied. Is this to act from free will?. . . Is this freedom? To my mind it is slavery."

—Sarah G. Bagley, quoted in *The Belles of New England: The Women of the Textile Mills and the Families Whose Wealth They Wove*, by William Moran

ANALYSIS SKILL **ANALYZING PRIMARY SOURCES**
How did Bagley view the idea that workers must endure poor conditions?

"I regard it as one of the privileges [advantages] of my youth that I . . . [grew] up among those active, interesting girls, whose lives . . . had principle [ideals] and purpose distinctly their own."
—Lucy Larcom, from *A New England Girlhood*

Mill life was hard, however. The workday was between 12 and 14 hours long, and daily life was carefully controlled. Ringing bells ordered workers to breakfast or lunch. Employees had to work harder and faster to keep up with new equipment. Cotton dust also began to cause health problems, such as chronic cough, for workers.

THE IMPACT TODAY
In the 1950s, labor union membership reached its peak; about 40 percent of the workforce belonged to unions. Today only about 14 percent of the working population belongs to a labor union.

READING CHECK **Contrasting** How was the Lowell system different from the Rhode Island system?

Workers Organize

Factories continued to spread in the 1800s. Craftspeople, who made goods by hand, felt threatened. Factories quickly produced low-priced goods. To compete with factories, shop owners had to hire more workers and pay them less. Shoemaker William Frazier complained about the situation in the mid-1840s. "We have to sit on our seats from twelve to sixteen hours per day, to earn one dollar."

The wages of factory workers also went down as people competed for jobs. A wave of immigration in the 1840s brought people from other, poorer countries. They were willing to work for low pay. More immigrants came to the Northeast, where the mills were located, than to the South. Competition for jobs also came from people unemployed during the financial Panic of 1837. For example, about 50,000 workers in New York City alone had lost their jobs.

The Beginning of Trade Unions

Facing low wages and the fear of losing their jobs, skilled workers formed **trade unions**, groups that tried to improve pay and working conditions. Eventually, unskilled factory workers also formed trade unions. Most employers did not want to hire union workers. Employers believed that the higher cost of union employees prevented competition with other manufacturers.

Sometimes labor unions staged protests called **strikes**. Workers on strike refuse to work until employers meet their demands. Most early strikes were not successful, however. Courts and police usually supported companies, not striking union members.

394 CHAPTER 12

Differentiating Instruction

Above Level

Advanced/Gifted and Talented

1. Ask students to imagine that they work for the New England Working Men's Association. Have each student write a speech for Sarah G. Bagley to raise money for the association's efforts to improve working conditions in the mills.

2. Students' speeches should summarize the following issues: working conditions, increased competition for jobs, decreasing wages, the 10-hour workday, child labor, and union organization.

3. Have volunteers present their speeches to the class. Conclude by having students describe how Bagley and others contributed to the early labor-union movement. **LS Verbal/Linguistic**

📝 Alternative Assessment Handbook, Rubric 43: Writing to Persuade

Labor Reform Efforts

A strong voice in the union movement was that of millworker **Sarah G. Bagley**. She founded the Lowell Female Labor Reform Association in 1844 and publicized the struggles of factory laborers. The association's two main goals were to influence an investigation of working conditions by the Massachusetts state legislature and to obtain a 10-hour workday. Members of the association passed out pamphlets and circulated petitions.

President Martin Van Buren had granted a 10-hour workday in 1840 for many federal employees. Bagley wanted this rule to apply to employees of private businesses. These men and women often worked 12 to 14 hours per day, six days per week.

Many working men and women supported the 10-hour-workday campaign, despite the opposition of business owners. In 1845 Sarah Bagley was elected vice president of the New England Working Men's Association. She was the first woman to hold such a high-ranking position in the American labor movement.

Over time, the unions achieved some **concrete** legal victories. Connecticut, Maine, New Hampshire, Ohio, Pennsylvania, and a few other states passed 10-hour-workday laws.

ACADEMIC VOCABULARY
concrete
specific, real

For factory workers in other states, long hours remained common. One witness described how children were "summoned by the factory bell before daylight" and worked until eight o'clock at night "with nothing but [a] recess of forty-five minutes to get their dinner." Union supporters continued to fight for work reforms such as an end to child labor in factories during the 1800s.

READING CHECK Finding Main Ideas

Why did workers form unions, and what were the main goals of union reformers?

SUMMARY AND PREVIEW With the growth of factories, workers faced new opportunities and challenges. In the next section you will learn about how the Transportation Revolution brought changes to commerce and the daily lives of Americans.

Section 2 Assessment

go.hrw.com
Online Quiz
KEYWORD: SR8 HP12

Reviewing Ideas, Terms, and People

1. **a. Identify** What problems did many mill owners have in finding workers?
   b. Analyze How did Samuel Slater's **Rhode Island system** change employment practices in mills?
2. **a. Describe** What was life like for mill workers in the **Lowell system**?
   b. Make Inferences Why would young women have wanted to go to work in the Lowell mills?
3. **a. Recall** Why did workers form **trade unions**?
   b. Predict What are some possible problems that might arise between factory owners and trade unions?

Critical Thinking

4. **Drawing Conclusions** Review your notes on mills and workers' reactions to them. Then copy the graphic organizer to the right and use it to show how Slater, Lowell, and Sarah G. Bagley affected workers' lives.

- Samuel Slater →
- Francis Cabot Lowell →
- Sarah G. Bagley →

Effect on Workers

FOCUS ON WRITING

5. **Examining Working Conditions** This section tells about mill life and conditions for workers. In the chart you started for the first section, list the two labor systems used by mills, the person who developed each, and the benefits of each system.

THE NORTH **395**

Direct Teach

Main Idea

❸ **Workers Organize**

Workers organized to reform working conditions.

Identify Who was Sarah G. Bagley, and why was she important? *a key player in the labor union movement; first woman to hold a high position in labor movement, played a leading role in reforming working conditions*

Summarize How did labor unions improve working conditions in the mid-1800s? *some states passed 10-hour workday laws*

📄 **CRF:** Biography Activity: Sarah Bagley

Review & Assess

Close

Have students summarize how life for workers in the Northeast changed during the early and mid-1800s.

Review

📕 Online Quiz, Section 2

Assess

SE Section 2 Assessment

📄 PASS: Section 2 Quiz

📄 Alternative Assessment Handbook

Reteach/Classroom Intervention

📄 Interactive Reader and Study Guide, Section 2

💿 Interactive Skills Tutor CD-ROM

Section 2 Assessment Answers

1. **a.** difficulty finding and keeping enough workers willing to do simple work all day
   b. Entire families, including children, began working in the mills; mill towns developed.

2. **a.** Workers, mostly young women, worked hard for 12 to 14 hours per day, lived in boardinghouses, and were encouraged to use their free time to take classes and form clubs.
   b. wanted the chance to earn money; preferable to life on a farm or as a servant; could earn more than in other jobs

3. **a.** concerns about low wages, job competition, and working conditions
   b. Strikes could lead to conflict and possible violence as owners tried to end them.

4. Slater—hired entire families to work in mills, divided work into simple tasks; Lowell—hired young women to work in mills, encouraged education and women's clubs; Bagley—worked for labor reform; founded the Lowell Female Labor Reform Association

5. Students should describe Slater's Rhode Island system and Lowell's Lowell system.

Answers

Reading Check *Workers formed unions in an attempt to increase wages and improve working conditions. The main goals of unions were to improve working conditions and wages and to obtain a 10-hour workday.*

395

Building Vocabulary

Preteach or review the following terms:

deposits concentrations of minerals lying in an underground pocket (p. 401)

monopolistic when one company controls an industry or market (p. 397)

📝 **CRF:** Vocabulary Builder Activity, Section 3

Taking Notes

Have students copy the graphic organizer onto their own paper and then use it to take notes on the section. This activity will prepare students for the Section Assessment, in which they will complete a graphic organizer that builds on the information using a critical thinking skill.

SECTION 3

The Transportation Revolution

What You Will Learn...

Main Ideas

1. The Transportation Revolution affected trade and daily life.
2. The steamboat was one of the first developments of the Transportation Revolution.
3. Railroads were a vital part of the Transportation Revolution.
4. The Transportation Revolution brought many changes to American life and industry.

The Big Idea

New forms of transportation improved business, travel, and communication in the United States.

Key Terms and People

Transportation Revolution, *p. 396*
Robert Fulton, *p. 397*
Clermont, *p. 397*
Gibbons v. *Ogden*, *p. 397*
Peter Cooper, *p. 398*

TAKING NOTES Create a time line like the one below. As you read, fill in the time line with the key events in the development of the steamboat and the locomotive as vital forms of transportation.

1824	1840
1807	1830	1860

396 CHAPTER 12

If YOU were there...

You live in a small town in Iowa in the 1860s. You've never been more than 30 miles from home and have always traveled by wagon or on horseback. Now there are plans to build a railroad westward from Chicago, 200 miles to the east. The tracks will come through your town! Twice a week, trains will bring goods from the city and take people farther west.

How would the coming of the railroad change your life?

BUILDING BACKGROUND The Industrial Revolution changed how goods were made. It brought great changes in the ways that many Americans lived. But changes in technology led to major changes in other areas of life, too. Changes in transportation would bring remote parts of America closer together.

Trade and Daily Life

During the 1800s the United States experienced a **Transportation Revolution**—a period of rapid growth in the speed and convenience of travel because of new methods of transportation. The Transportation Revolution created a boom in business across the country, particularly by reducing shipping time and costs. As one foreign observer declared in 1835, "The Americans . . . have joined the Hudson to the Mississippi, and made the Atlantic Ocean communicate with the Gulf of Mexico."

These improvements were made possible largely by the invention of two new forms of transportation: the steamboat and steam-powered trains. They enabled goods, people, and information to travel rapidly and efficiently across the United States.

READING CHECK **Finding Main Ideas** What benefits did the Transportation Revolution bring to trade and daily life?

Teach the Big Idea

At Level

The Transportation Revolution

1. **Teach** Ask students the questions in the Main Idea boxes to teach this section.

2. **Apply** Have each student write the Big Idea, listed above, in the middle of a piece of paper. Above the Big Idea, have students draw a box and label it *Causes*. Below the Big Idea, have students draw a box and label it *Effects*. Have students list the factors that led to new forms of transportation and identify what those new forms were. Then

have students describe the effects of the Transportation Revolution. **LS Visual/Spatial**

3. **Review** Have the class review the causes and effects of the Transportation Revolution.

4. **Practice/Homework** Have each student write a paragraph summarizing the significance of the Transportation Revolution. **LS Verbal/Linguistic**

📋 Alternative Assessment Handbook, Rubrics 13: Graphic Organizers; and 37: Writing Assignments

Steamboats

American and European inventors had developed steam-powered boats in the late 1700s. However, they were not in wide use until the early 1800s.

Steamboat Era

In 1803 American **Robert Fulton** tested his first steamboat design in France. Several years later, he tested the first full-sized commercial steamboat, called the ***Clermont***, in the United States. On August 9, 1807, the *Clermont* traveled against the current up the Hudson River without trouble. Demand for steamboat ferry service soon arose.

The steamboat was well suited for river travel. It could move upriver and did not rely on wind power. Steamboats increased trade and profits because goods could be moved quickly and thus more cheaply. More than 500 steamboats were in use in the United States by 1840. By the 1850s, steamboats were also being used to carry people and goods across the Atlantic Ocean.

Mississippi River Steamboats

Deckhands load a Mississippi River steamboat in Memphis, Tennessee. By the mid-1800s, hundreds of steamboats traveled up and down American rivers. Steamboats enabled Americans to ship more goods farther, faster, and for less money than ever before.

Upstream River Rates

(line graph: y-axis "Dollars (per 100 pounds)" from 0 to 10; x-axis "Year" 1800, 1810, 1820, 1830, showing a declining line from about 9 in 1800 to near 0 in 1830)

Gibbons v. Ogden

Increased steamboat shipping led to conflict over waterway rights. In 1819 Aaron Ogden sued Thomas Gibbons for operating steamboats in New York waters that Ogden said he owned. Gibbons did not have a license to operate in New York, but argued that his federal license gave him the right to use New York waterways.

In the case of ***Gibbons v. Ogden***, which reached the Supreme Court in 1824, the Court reinforced the federal government's authority to regulatee trade between the states by ending monopolistic control over waterways in several states. The ruling freed up waters to even greater trade and shipping.

READING CHECK **Summarizing** Explain the effects of the *Gibbons* v. *Ogden* ruling.

Main Idea

❶ Trade and Daily Life

The Transportation Revolution affected trade and daily life.

Define What was the Transportation Revolution? *a period of rapid growth in the speed and convenience of travel because of new forms of transportation*

Identify What two new modes of transportation largely contributed to the Transportation Revolution? *steamboats; steam-powered trains*

Main Idea

❷ Steamboats

The steamboat was one of the first developments of the Transportation Revolution.

Recall Who was Robert Fulton? *American steamboat designer who produced the first full-sized commercial steamboat, the* Clermont

Explain Why were steamboats well suited for river travel? *could travel upriver; did not rely on wind power*

Make Inferences Why do you think Ogden did not want Gibbons to operate a steamboat service in New York? *because Ogden had a monopoly; he wanted to keep all the business and profits for himself*

📃 **CRF:** Literature Activity: Mark Twain Pilots a Steamboat

📃 Supreme Court Case Studies: *Gibbons v. Ogden* (1824)

Differentiating Instruction

Below Level

English-Language Learners

1. Have students examine the image on this page. Ask them to explain what the various people in the image are doing. Next, have students examine the way the people are dressed. What two categories of people can students identify based on dress? *(passengers and workers loading cargo)* Based on these groups, what services did steamboats provide? *(passenger and freight services)*

2. Guide students in a discussion about the development of the steamboat and how it affected trade and daily life.

3. Then have each student write at least three newspaper headlines about steamboat development and its effects.

4. Have volunteers present their headlines to the class. **LS** **Verbal/Linguistic, Visual/Spatial**

📝 Alternative Assessment Handbook, Rubric 42: Writing to Inform

Answers

Reading Check (previous page) *connected people and improved communication across the nation by making travel faster and more convenient; reduced shipping time and costs, which led to a boom in business*

Reading Check *reinforced federal government's authority to regulate trade between states*

❸ American Railroads

Railroads were a vital part of the Transportation Revolution.

Identify Where and when were steam-powered trains first developed? *in Great Britain in the early 1800s*

Analyze What was the significance of the 1830 race involving the *Tom Thumb* locomotive? *Although the locomotive lost, the race showed the power and speed of even a small locomotive and helped lead to railroad fever in the United States.*

Summarize In what ways did railroads affect daily life? *reduced travel time, linked many major cities, helped tie communities together, sped up communication and the pace of life*

Make Inferences Why do you think railroad companies became some of the nation's most powerful businesses? *possible answers—controlled passenger and freight transportation; profited from the growth of trade*

📖 Political Cartoons Activities for United States History, Cartoon 14: Fears of the Railroad

Analyzing Visuals

The Steam Train

Activity Riding in a Steam Engine
Ask students to imagine that it is the mid-1800s and they are riding on a steam locomotive for the first time. The engineer invites them to join him in the engine car. Have students describe what it is like there based on the images and information at right. *(Students might suggest that it is loud, hot, steamy, and rough travel but exciting.)*

Answers

Science and Technology *to heat the water in order to produce steam, which powers the train's pistons*

American Railroads

What the steamboat did for water travel, the train did for overland travel. Steam-powered trains had first been developed in Great Britain in the early 1800s. However, they did not become popular in the United States until the 1830s. In 1830 **Peter Cooper** built a small but powerful locomotive called the *Tom Thumb*. He raced the locomotive against a horse-drawn railcar. Eyewitness John Latrobe later described the race, in which *Tom Thumb* had a slow start and fell behind. Latrobe wrote, "The pace increased, the passengers shouted, the engine gained on the horse . . . then the engine passes the horse, and a great hurrah hailed the victory." Unfortunately for Cooper, victory was spoiled when *Tom Thumb* broke down and lost the race near the end.

Despite the defeat, the contest showed the power and speed of even a small locomotive. Railroad fever soon spread. By 1840 railroad companies had laid about 2,800 miles of track—more than existed in all of Europe. French economist Michel Chevalier described Americans as having "a perfect passion for railroads."

As more railroads were built, engineers and mechanics overcame many tough challenges. Most British railroads, for example, ran on straight tracks across flat ground. In the United States, however, many railroads had to run up and down steep mountains, around tight curves, and over swift rivers. Railroad companies also built the tracks quickly and often with the least expensive materials available. As time went on, engineers and mechanics built heavier, faster, and more powerful steam locomotives.

By 1860 about 30,000 miles of railroad linked almost every major city in the eastern United States. As a result, the economy surged forward. For example, American locomotives hauled more freight than those in any other country. The railroad companies quickly became some of the most powerful businesses in the nation. As the railroad

The Steam Train

SCIENCE AND TECHNOLOGY

Boiling water produces steam, which pushes pistons back and forth in a steam engine. These pistons are connected to rods that rotate the wheels of the locomotive.

Why does the train have a firebox?

Piston

① As steam follows the path of the white arrows in to the cylinder, the pressure pushes the piston in the direction of the large blue arrow. Connecting rods turn the wheel half a turn.

② When the small valve rod moves, the other valve is blocked, pushing steam into the other side of the cylinder. The pressure moves the piston in the direction of the large blue arrow and the wheel completes a turn.

398 CHAPTER 12

Differentiating Instruction

Below Level

Struggling Readers

Materials: art supplies

1. Lead a discussion on the innovations of the Transportation Revolution and the effects of those innovations on the economy and daily life in the United States.

2. Have each student create a drawing illustrating innovations of the Transportation Revolution.

3. Then have each student write a caption for his or her drawing explaining how transportation innovations changed life in the United States.
LS Visual/Spatial

📖 Alternative Assessment Handbook, Rubric 3: Artwork

system grew, manufacturers and farmers could send their goods to distant markets.

In addition to their tremendous economic impact, the railroads made a powerful impression on the senses of passengers and observers. Trains were the fastest form of transportation most people had ever experienced. While wagons often traveled less than 2 miles per hour, locomotives averaged about 20 miles per hour. Writer George Templeton Strong of New York City described the thrill of a steam train passing by in the night:

"Whizzing and rattling and panting, with its fiery furnace gleaming in front, its chimney vomiting fiery smoke above, and its long train of cars rushing along behind like the body and tail of a gigantic dragon— . . . and all darting forward at the rate of twenty miles an hour. Whew!"

—George Templeton Strong, quoted in *The Market Revolution* by Charles Sellers

Riding on the early trains was often an adventure, but it could also be quite dangerous. Engineers trying to stay on time sometimes traveled too fast. English citizen Charles Richard Weld was on a railroad car that flew off the tracks. To his amazement, the other passengers did not complain about the accident. Instead, they praised the engineer for trying to keep on schedule!

Passengers accepted such risks because the railroads reduced travel time dramatically. Railroads also helped tie communities together. In 1847 Senator Daniel Webster spoke for many people in the United States when he declared that the railroad "towers above all other inventions of this or the preceding age."

THE IMPACT TODAY

In 1883 four standard time zones were introduced in the United States to help railroads offer uniform train schedules. Today travelers might cross one or more time zones in a single airplane flight.

READING CHECK Drawing Inferences
In what ways did railroads affect the economy of the United States?

Chimney · Regulator · Boiler · Firebox · Fire doors · Water · Smoke box · Piston

THE NORTH **399**

Critical Thinking: Acquiring Information

Above Level

Baltimore and Ohio Railroad

Research Required

1. Have students work in groups to conduct research on the Baltimore and Ohio Railroad, the first steam-operated railway in the United States to provide both freight and passenger service.

2. Organize students into small groups to investigate different aspects of the railroad. Topics for research might include locomotives and cars, routes of tracks, formation of the company, history of the company's growth, and leaders of the company. Each group

should write one or more questions to guide its research.

3. Have each group create a display combining articles, captions, drawings, diagrams, and maps about its topic.

4. Display students' work in the classroom.
LS Interpersonal, Verbal/Linguistic

Alternative Assessment Handbook, Rubrics 29: Presentations; and 30: Research

Main Idea

❹ Transportation Revolution Brings Changes

The Transportation Revolution brought many changes to American life and industry.

Recall How did the railroads affect settlement patterns in the United States? *Towns and cities along rail lines grew, while those not near railroads suffered; some cities developed into transportation hubs.*

Identify Cause and Effect How did the coal industry change the landscape? *New coal mining towns developed, and coal mines created deep gashes in the earth.*

Analyze How were the railroad and steel industries interrelated? *Railroads transported steel to build factories and machines; steel was used to make the rails for trains.*

📋 **CRF:** History and Geography Activity: The Transportation Revolution

🗄 Map Transparency: Transportation Routes, 1850

Info to Know

The Railroad in the Midwest In 1850, Illinois was still a frontier state, with 8 of its 10 cities located on Lake Michigan or along the Mississippi or Illinois rivers. Railroads brought a population explosion to formerly small Illinois towns. Between 1850 and 1855, Cairo, Illinois, grew from 300 to 1,300 inhabitants; Vandalia, Illinois, grew from 360 to 1,000; and Freeport, Illinois, grew from 1,400 to 5,000 residents.

Answers

Interpreting Maps 1. *in the northeast;* **2.** *Americans laid tracks and built tunnels and bridges for railroads, cut down trees and cleared forests for timber, and dug mines in the earth for coal.*

400

Transportation Routes, 1850

By 1850 the United States already had about 9,000 miles of railroad track. Timber was needed for railroad ties, cars, and bridges and as fuel for steam locomotives.

Railroad
Coal   Timber

0   150   300 Miles
0   150   300 Kilometers

GEOGRAPHY SKILLS   INTERPRETING MAPS

1. Region Where were most railroads located in 1850?

2. Human-Environment Interaction How does this map suggest that people modified the landscape?

Transportation Revolution Brings Changes

The Transportation Revolution brought many changes to America. Steamboats and railroads made getting goods to distant markets much easier and less costly. People in all areas of the nation now had access to products made and grown far away. More than ever before, there was a national economy. The wealth, however, was centered in the North.

Railroads contributed to the expansion of the borders of the nation and guided population growth. Towns sprang up at railroad junctions. Those towns that did not have railroads nearby suffered. Cities grew as trains brought new residents and raw materials for industry and construction. The growing prosperity of the nation, especially in the North, encouraged Americans to take pride in their country.

A New Fuel

The Transportation Revolution also increased the use of certain natural resources that had not been important until then. Throughout the early Transportation Revolution, wood was the primary source of fuel for trains and steamboats, as well as for cooking, light, and heat. As faster locomotives were built, coal replaced wood as the main source of power. A half ton of coal produces as much energy as two tons of wood but at half the cost. Coal also became popular for heating homes. Railroads transported the coal from mines to towns and cities.

As the demand for coal increased, a coal-mining industry developed in many states, including Pennsylvania, western Virginia, and Illinois. Coal mining changed the landscape in a number of ways. New towns, such as Coal City and Carbondale in Illinois,

400 CHAPTER 12

Critical Thinking: Analyzing Information   **At Level**

Railroads, Coal, and Steel Diagram

1. Guide students in a discussion of the relationships among wood, coal, iron, steel, and the railroad industry.

2. Have students refer to their texts to understand how and why coal replaced timber as a fuel source, and why steel replaced iron. Make a class list of the uses of coal and steel.

3. Then have each student create a diagram showing the relationship among the railroad industry and the coal and steel industries.

4. Have volunteers explain their diagrams with the class. Correct any student errors.
LS Visual/Spatial

📋 Alternative Assessment Handbook, Rubric 7: Charts

sprang up in places where coal deposits existed. Miners made deep gashes in the earth removing the coal.

Later, in the 1870s, the demand for coal increased as the demand for steel grew. Steel is made through a smelting process—heating iron ore to very high temperatures. Coal was used to fire the furnaces. Steel, which is much stronger than iron, was increasingly used to build factories and the machines they produced. Steel was also used to make the rails that trains ride on.

The growing market for steel helped fuel the need for more railroads. Railroads transported steel to places where new factories were being built. Railroads also brought new steel farming tools and machines to farmers in the Midwest. Using the new equipment, farmers produced more crops. Railroads then transported their harvests to markets.

Effects of Railroads

The railroads played a role in the growth of other businesses as well. The logging indus-try expanded as people in the growing towns and cities needed wood for houses and furniture. As newspaper publishing increased, demand for paper grew. Lumber items became the primary product of New England. Settlers spreading out across the Midwest cut down trees and plowed up prairies to make farmland. Deforestation, or cutting down and removing trees, took place on a large scale.

Railroads also caused cities to grow. Some cities became transportation hubs. Chicago was one such city. Its location on Lake Michigan made it an ideal transportation hub, linking the Midwest to the East and South.

READING CHECK Analyzing Information
What role did railroads play in the growth of the coal industry?

SUMMARY AND PREVIEW The Transportation Revolution changed the way business was done. In the next section you will learn about more technological advances.

FOCUS ON READING
What causes and effects do you see in this section?

• **Review & Assess** •

Close

Briefly review the ways in which the Transportation Revolution changed American trade, industry, and life.

Review

Online Quiz, Section 3

Assess

SE Section 3 Assessment

PASS: Section 3 Quiz

Alternative Assessment Handbook

Reteach/Classroom Intervention

Interactive Reader and Study Guide, Section 3

Interactive Skills Tutor CD-ROM

Section 3 Assessment

go.hrw.com
Online Quiz
KEYWORD: SR8 HP12

Reviewing Ideas, Terms, and People

1. a. Identify What forms of transportation were improved or invented at this time?
b. Explain What effect did the **Transportation Revolution** have on the United States?
2. a. Describe What were the benefits of steamboat travel?
b. Analyze What effect did the ruling in the **Gibbons** v. **Ogden** case have on federal government?
3. a. Describe What event showed the power and speed of locomotives?
b. Draw Conclusions How did railroads affect trade and business in the United States?
c. Elaborate Why do you think Americans were fascinated by railroads?
4. a. Describe What physical obstacles did railroad construction in the United States face?
b. Analyze What effects did the Transportation Revolution have on the U.S. economy?
c. Elaborate Do you think the Transportation Revolution played a role in deforestation? Explain.

Critical Thinking

5. Identifying Effects Review your time line on the steamboat and the locomotive. Then copy the chart below and use it to show how they affected business, travel, and communication in the United States.

Steamboat / Locomotive → Effects

FOCUS ON WRITING

6. Describing Travel Inventions Add the steamboat and locomotive to your list. Note the individuals involved in their development as well as how these new methods of travel changed life for people in the United States.

THE NORTH **401**

Section 3 Assessment Answers

1. a. steamboats, steam-powered trains
b. made travel faster, more convenient; reduced shipping time and costs

2. a. could go upriver; did not need wind power
b. reinforced its authority over the states

3. a. 1830 race that pitted the locomotive Tom Thumb against a horse-drawn railcar
b. economy grew, became easier and faster to get goods to distant markets, railroad companies became powerful businesses
c. possible answer—At the time, locomotives were the fastest, most powerful machines.

4. a. steep mountains, uneven land, swift rivers
b. created a national economy; led to new industries and the growth of other industries
c. yes, wood for tracks and growing cities

5. enabled goods, people, and information to travel rapidly and efficiently; affected business and population growth; increased prosperity

6. Students should identify the key people and effects of the Transportation Revolution.

Answers

Focus on Reading *changes in environment because of logging and mining; rising demand for coal as a result of rising demand for steel; rising demand for steel because of new factories, machines, and rails; rising demand for railroads to transport steel and harvests; rising demand for wood as a result of growing towns and newspaper publishing; deforestation as a result of rising demand for wood; city growth as a result of access to railroads*

Reading Check *As faster trains were built, coal replaced wood as the main source of power.*

401

Building Vocabulary

Preteach or review the following terms:

magnetism force of attraction for iron exerted by magnets or by electrical charges or currents (p. 402)

reaper harvesting machine (p. 404)

transcontinental crossing the continent (p. 403)

📖 **CRF:** Vocabulary Builder Activity, Section 4

Taking Notes

Have students copy the graphic organizer onto their own paper and then use it to take notes on the section. This activity will prepare students for the Section Assessment, in which they will complete a graphic organizer that builds on the information using a critical thinking skill.

What You Will Learn…

Main Ideas

1. The telegraph made swift communication possible from coast to coast.
2. With the shift to steam power, businesses built new factories closer to cities and transportation centers.
3. Improved farm equipment and other labor-saving devices made life easier for many Americans.
4. New inventions changed lives in American homes.

The Big Idea

Advances in technology led to new inventions that continued to change daily life and work.

Key Terms and People

Samuel F. B. Morse, *p. 402*
telegraph, *p. 402*
Morse code, *p. 403*
John Deere, *p. 404*
Cyrus McCormick, *p. 404*
Isaac Singer, *p. 405*

TAKING NOTES As you read, take notes on the new advances in technology listed in the section. Create a graphic organizer like the one shown below that identifies the effects of each.

Inventions	Effects
Telegraph	
Steam Power	
Mass Production	
Home Inventions	

More Technological Advances

If YOU were there...

You own a small shop in Chicago, Illinois, in the 1850s. You sell ladies' hats and gowns. When you need more hats, you send a letter to the manufacturer in New York. Sometimes it takes weeks for the letter to get there. One day, the owner of the shop next door tells you about a wonderful new machine. It can send orders from Chicago to New York in just minutes!

How would a machine like this change your business?

BUILDING BACKGROUND The Industrial and Transportation revolutions had far-reaching effects on Americans' lives. They led to still more innovations in technology. Some of the new machines and devices speeded up processes for business owners. Others made life easier for people at home.

Telegraph Speeds Communication

In 1832 **Samuel F. B. Morse** perfected the **telegraph**—a device that could send information over wires across great distances. To develop the telegraph, Morse studied electricity and magnetism.

Time Line

American Inventions

1798 Eli Whitney proposed the idea of mass producing guns. Machines like this one made it possible for workers to make interchangeable parts efficiently.

1831 Cyrus McCormick invents the mechanical reaper. Harvesting grain becomes eight times more efficient.

Teach the Big Idea

At Level

More Technological Advances

1. **Teach** Ask students the questions in the Main Idea boxes to teach this section.

2. **Apply** Ask students to imagine that they are writers for an 1800s magazine called "New Technology Today." Have each student write an article describing the new inventions covered in this section and explaining how they are improving life for Americans at home and at work. **LS Verbal/Linguistic**

3. **Review** To review, have volunteers read their articles aloud. Correct any student errors or misconceptions.

4. **Practice/Homework** Have each student, working for the same magazine, write a fictional interview with one of the key people in this section. **LS Verbal/Linguistic**

📖 Alternative Assessment Handbook, Rubric 42: Writing to Inform

Morse put the work of other scientists together in a practical machine.

The telegraph sent pulses, or surges, of electric current through a wire. The telegraph operator tapped a bar, called a telegraph key, that controlled the length of each pulse. At the other end of the wire, these pulses were changed into clicking sounds. A short click was called a dot. A long click was called a dash. Morse's partner, Alfred Lewis Vail, developed a system known as **Morse code**—different combinations of dots and dashes that represent each letter of the alphabet. For example, *dot dot dot, dash dash dash, dot dot dot* is the distress signal called SOS. Skilled telegraph operators could send and receive many words per minute.

Several years passed before Morse was able to connect two locations with telegraph wires. Despite that achievement, people doubted his machine. Some people did not think that he was reading messages sent from miles away. They claimed that he was making lucky guesses.

Morse's break came during the 1844 Democratic National Convention in Baltimore, Maryland. A telegraph wired news of the presidential candidate's nomination to politicians in Washington. The waiting politicians responded, "Three cheers for the telegraph!" Telegraphs were soon sending and receiving information for businesses, the government, newspapers, and private citizens.

The telegraph grew with the railroad. Telegraph companies strung their wires on poles along railroads across the country. They established telegraph offices in many train stations. Thousands of miles of telegraph line were added every year in the 1850s. The first transcontinental line was finished in 1861. By the time he died in 1872, Morse was famous across the United States.

READING CHECK Identifying Cause and Effect
What event led to the widespread use of the telegraph, and what effect did the telegraph have on cross-country communications?

1832 Samuel F. B. Morse invents the telegraph. Long-distance communication becomes almost instantaneous.

1837 John Deere invents the steel plow. The tough prairie sod can be cut and the thick soil ploughed without having to constantly clean the plow.

THE NORTH **403**

Main Idea

❷ Steam Power and New Factories

With the shift to steam power, businesses built new factories closer to cities and transportation centers.

Recall What began to replace water power in factories? *steam power*

Identify Cause and Effect How did the use of steam power change where factories were located? *Factories no longer had to be located on streams or waterfalls, so owners began to build factories near cities for better access to workers and markets.*

Main Idea

❸ Improved Farm Equipment

Improved farm equipment and other labor-saving devices made life easier for many Americans.

Recall What problem was John Deere trying to solve with his steel plow? *existing iron plows were not strong enough to plow thick soil*

Identify Cause and Effect How did Cyrus McCormick's mechanical reaper change agriculture? *enabled farmers to harvest huge fields*

📑 **CRF:** Biography Activity: John Deere

Answers

Reading Check (left) *Factories were built closer to cities, which led to lower wages and shipping costs, made cities industrial centers, drew immigrants and rural people, and led to urban growth.*

Reading Check (right) *advertisements, demonstrations, provided repair and spare parts departments, offered credit*

Steam Power and New Factories

At the start of the Industrial Revolution, most factories ran on waterpower. In time, however, factory owners began using steam power. This shift brought major changes to the nation's industries. Water-powered factories had to be built near streams or waterfalls. In contrast, steam power allowed business owners to build factories almost anywhere. Yet the Northeast was still home to most of the nation's industry. By 1860 New England alone had as many factories as the entire South did.

Some companies decided to build their factories closer to cities and transportation centers. This provided easier access to workers, allowing businesses to lower wages. Being closer to cities also reduced shipping costs. Cities soon became the center of industrial growth. People from rural areas as well as foreign countries flocked to the cities for factory jobs.

Factory workers improved the designs of many kinds of machines. Mechanics invented tools that could cut and shape metal, stone, and wood with great precision. By the 1840s this new machinery was able to produce interchangeable parts. Within a short period of time, the growing machine-tool industry was even making customized equipment.

READING CHECK Finding Main Ideas
What changes resulted from the shift to steam power?

Improved Farm Equipment

During the 1830s, technology began transforming the farm as well as the factory. In 1837 blacksmith **John Deere** saw that friends in Illinois had difficulty plowing thick soil with iron plows. He thought a steel blade might work better. His design for a steel plow was a success. By 1846 Deere was selling 1,000 plows per year.

In 1831 **Cyrus McCormick** developed a new harvesting machine, the mechanical reaper, which quickly and efficiently cut down wheat. He began mass producing his reapers in a Chicago factory. McCormick used new methods to encourage sales. His company advertised, gave demonstrations, and provided a repair and spare parts department. He also let customers buy on credit.

The combination of Deere's plow and McCormick's reaper allowed Midwestern farmers to plant and harvest huge crop fields. By 1860, U.S. farmers were producing more than 170 million bushels of wheat and more than 800 million bushels of corn per year.

READING CHECK Summarizing What marketing methods did McCormick use to help sell his farm equipment?

American Inventions (continued)

1849 Walter Hunt invents the safety pin.

W. Hunt.
Pin.
Nº 6,281. *Patented Apr. 10. 1849.*
Fig. 1. Fig. 2.

UNITED STATES PATENT OFFICE.

WALTER HUNT, OF NEW YORK, N. Y., ASSIGNOR TO WM. RICHARDSON AND JNO. RICHARDSON.

DRESS-PIN.

Specification of Letters Patent No. 6,281, dated April 10, 1849.

To all whom it may concern:
Be it known that I, WALTER HUNT, of the city, county, and State of New York, have invented a new and useful Improvement in the Make or Form of Dress-Pins, of which ... to the bar C, (see Figs. 6, 7 and 8,) which combined with the advantages of the spring and catch, renders it equally ornamental, and at the same time more secure and durable than any other plan of a clasp pin, heretofore in use, there being no joint to break or ...

404

1851 Isaac Singer improves the sewing machine. The production and repair of clothing becomes much easier.

Changing Life at Home

Many inventions of the Industrial Revolution simply made life easier. When Alexis de Tocqueville of France visited the United States in the early 1830s, he identified what he called a very American quality.

> "[Americans want] to be always making life more comfortable and convenient, to avoid trouble, and to satisfy the smallest wants [desires] without effort and almost without cost."
> —Alexis de Tocqueville, from *Democracy in America*

The sewing machine was one of these conveniences. Elias Howe, a factory apprentice in Lowell, Massachusetts, first invented it. **Isaac Singer** then made improvements to Howe's design. Like McCormick, Singer allowed customers to buy his machines on credit and provided service. By 1860 Singer's company was the world's largest maker of sewing machines.

Other advances improved on everyday items. In the 1830s, iceboxes cooled by large blocks of ice became available. Iceboxes stored fresh food safely for longer periods. Iron cookstoves began replacing cooking fires and stone hearths.

Companies also began to mass produce earlier inventions. This allowed many families to buy household items, such as clocks, that they could not afford in the past. For example, a clock that cost $50 in 1800 was selling for only $1.50 by the 1850s. Additional useful items created during this period include matches introduced in the 1830s, and the safety pin, invented in 1849. All of these inventions helped make life at home more convenient for an increasing number of Americans.

READING CHECK **Analyzing** How did labor-saving inventions affect daily life?

SUMMARY AND PREVIEW New machines and inventions changed the way Americans lived and did business in the early 1800s. In the next section you will learn how agricultural changes affected the South.

THE IMPACT TODAY
New inventions, such as cell phones, laptop computers, and microwave ovens, continue to make life easier and more convenient for people today.

1859 Manufactured goods become more valuable than agricultural goods in the country's economy for the first time. The United States is becoming a modern industrial nation.

ANALYSIS SKILL **READING TIME LINES**
Which two inventions improved American agriculture?

Section 4 Assessment

go.hrw.com
Online Quiz
KEYWORD: SR8 HP12

Reviewing Ideas, Terms, and People
1. **a. Describe** How did the **telegraph** work?
   b. Predict What impact might the telegraph have on the future of the United States?
2. **a. Describe** How did waterpowered factories differ from steam-powered factories?
   b. Explain How did the shift to steam power lead to the growth of cities?
3. **a. Identify** What contributions did **Cyrus McCormick** and **John Deere** make to farming?
   b. Analyze What effect did new inventions have on agriculture in the United States?
4. **a. Identify** What inventions improved life at home?
   b. Evaluate Which invention do you think had the greatest effect on the daily lives of Americans? Why?

Critical Thinking
5. **Supporting a Point of View** Review your notes on technological advances and their effects. Then create a graphic organizer like the one below that shows the top three advances you think are most important and why.

Most Important	Why

FOCUS ON WRITING

6. **Describing Technological Advances** Add notes about the inventions mentioned in this section to your chart. Think about which invention you will use for your newspaper advertisement.

THE NORTH **405**

405

Social Studies Skills

Social Studies Skills

| Analysis | Critical Thinking | Civic Participation | Study |

Personal Conviction and Bias

Materials: copies of newspaper front and editorial pages

1. Pass out photocopies of the editorial page and the front page from a local newspaper. Have students contrast the articles that appear on each page. Guide students in determining that the front-page news coverage is mainly objective reporting of facts. The editorial page likely contains many opinionated items.

2. Next, have students examine the editorials and letters to the editor. Ask students to identify any biases the writers might hold. How are these biases shaping the writers' viewpoints and opinions? See if students can find examples of stereotyping or prejudice.

3. Then assign students one editorial or letter to the editor. Have each student create a three-column chart listing the verifiable statements, or facts; the unverifiable statements, or opinions; and any examples of bias. Review students' charts as a class.
   LS Verbal/Linguistic

- Alternative Assessment Handbook, Rubric 7: Charts

- Interactive Skills Tutor CD-ROM, Lesson 20: Evaluate Sources of Information for Authenticity, Reliability, and Bias

Personal Conviction and Bias

Define the Skill

Everyone has *convictions,* or firmly-held beliefs. However, when we let our beliefs automatically slant or shape our point of view on topics, we may be showing bias. *Bias* is a fixed idea or opinion about someone or something. Some bias is based on a set of ideas about a group to which the person or thing belongs. This type of bias is called a *stereotype*. If the group is defined by race, religion, age, gender, or similar characteristics, the bias is known as *prejudice*.

Bias, stereotypes, and prejudice are not always negative in nature. They include favorable opinions too. For example, the belief a student is good at math because that person is male is a bias that shows both stereotyping and prejudice.

We should always be on guard for the presence of personal bias. Eliminating stereotyping and prejudice is particularly important. However, even "good" biases can slant how we view, judge, and communicate information. Honest and accurate communication requires that the information and ideas we express be as free of bias as possible.

Learn the Skill

Not all beliefs are biases, even if those beliefs are strongly held. Biases are beliefs that have little or no evidence to support them. The more unreasonable a person's view is in light of facts and evidence, the more likely it is that the belief is a bias.

Another characteristic of bias is the person's reluctance to question his or her belief if it is challenged by evidence. Sometimes people stubbornly cling to views that overwhelming evidence proves wrong. This is why bias is defined as a "fixed" idea or opinion. One of the most damaging effects of bias, and a good reason for trying to avoid it, is that it can prevent us from learning new things.

The following precautions can help you to reduce the amount of bias you hold and express.

❶ When discussing a topic, keep in mind beliefs and experiences in your own background that might affect how you feel about the topic.

❷ Try to not mix statements of fact with statements of opinion. Clearly separate and indicate what you *know* to be true from what you *believe* to be true.

❸ Avoid using emotional, positive, or negative words when communicating factual information.

Practice the Skill

In 1834 Tennessee congressman Davy Crockett visited the textile mills at Lowell, Massachusetts. Read his account of the "Lowell girls" who worked in the factory and complete the activity below.

"Here are thousands [of young women], useful to others, …with the prospect before them of future comfort and respectability …There are more than five thousand females employed in Lowell; and when you come to see the amount of labour performed by them, in superintending [operating] the different machinery, you will be astonished."

Suppose that you were a "Lowell girl" who has just read this account of Crockett's visit. Write a letter to the editor of the *Lowell Offering* reacting to the biases and stereotypes about women that Crockett shows in his account.

Answers

Practice the Skill *Answers will vary, but students should note that Crockett assumes that the work the women are doing makes them useful and will help ensure their respectability. He also thinks everyone will be astonished to see the amount and type of work the women are doing.*

Social Studies Skills Activity: Personal Conviction and Bias

Identifying Bias in Primary Sources   At Level

1. Have students review "Primary Source: Sarah G. Bagley and Workers' Rights" in Section 2 of this chapter.

2. Write the following questions for students to see. Have students work in pairs or in small groups to answer the questions.

- What beliefs and experiences in Bagley's background might have shaped her views?

- What opinions does she present?

- What emotional or negative language does she use?

- What biases and stereotypes does the passage reveal?

3. Discuss students' answers as a class. If time allows, have students compare and contrast the biases of Crockett to those of Bagley.
   LS Interpersonal, Verbal/Linguistic

- Alternative Assessment Handbook, Rubric 16: Judging Information

Chapter Review

Visual Summary

Use the visual summary below to help you review the main ideas of the chapter.

INDUSTRIAL REVOLUTION
• Mass production
• Interchangeable parts
• The Lowell and Rhode Island systems

Telegraph

TRANSPORTATION REVOLUTION

Water and Steam Power

Factories

Railroad and Steamboat

New Farm Machinery

To Growing Cities

QUICK FACTS

Reviewing Vocabulary, Terms, and People

Complete each sentence below by filling in the blank with the correct term or person from the chapter.

1. The system of _____ was developed to represent letters of the alphabet when sending telegraph messages.

2. The first American woman to hold a high-ranking position in the labor movement was _____.

3. The _____ was a period of rapid growth in the use of machines and manufacturing.

4. The first locomotive in the United States was built by _____.

5. Workers would sometimes go on _____ to force factory owners to meet their demands for better pay and working conditions.

6. The _____ industry, which produced cloth items, was the first to use machines for manufacturing.

Comprehension and Critical Thinking

SECTION 1 *(Pages 384–389)*

7. **a. Identify** What ideas did Eli Whitney want to apply to the manufacture of guns?

b. Analyze How did the War of 1812 lead to a boom in manufacturing in the United States?

c. Elaborate Why do you think the Industrial Revolution began in Great Britain rather than in the United States?

SECTION 2 *(Pages 390–395)*

8. **a. Describe** What was mill life like?

b. Draw Conclusions How did the Rhode Island system and the Lowell system change the lives of American workers?

c. Evaluate Were reformers such as Sarah G. Bagley effective in improving labor conditions? Why?

Visual Summary

Review and Inquiry Each of the inventions shown in the picture can be seen as in some way contributing to the growth of cities. Have students list the key events and people connected to each invention shown. Then have each student write a paragraph describing how the visual summary illustrates the overall effects of the Industrial Revolution.

Quick Facts Transparency: The North Visual Summary

Reviewing Vocabulary, Terms, and People

1. Morse code

2. Sarah G. Bagley

3. Industrial Revolution

4. Peter Cooper

5. strike

6. textile

Comprehension and Critical Thinking

7. **a.** interchangeable parts and the use of machines powered by water

b. The War of 1812 stopped the export of many foreign goods, which led Americans to buy American goods, which in turn increased manufacturing.

c. possible answer—Great Britain had more trouble meeting the demand for goods, which led to the development of machines to improve efficiency.

Review and Assessment Resources

Review and Reinforce

SE Chapter Review

CRF: Chapter Review Activity

Quick Facts Transparency: The North Visual Summary

Spanish Chapter Summaries Audio CD Program

Online Chapter Summaries in Six Languages

OSP Holt PuzzlePro; GameTool for ExamView

Quiz Game CD-ROM

Assess

SE Standardized Test Practice

PASS: Chapter Test, Forms A and B

Alternative Assessment Handbook

OSP ExamView Test Generator, Chapter Test

Differentiated Instruction Modified Worksheets and Tests CD-ROM: Chapter Test

Holt Online Assessment Program (in the Premier Online Edition)

Reteach/Intervene

Interactive Reader and Study Guide

Differentiated Instruction Teacher Management System: Lesson Plans for Differentiated Instruction

Differentiated Instruction Modified Worksheets and Tests CD-ROM

Interactive Skills Tutor CD-ROM

go.hrw.com
Online Resources

Chapter Resources:
KEYWORD: SR8 US12

8. a. monotonous work for long hours; sometimes dangerous
b. Many people, including women and children, moved to towns or cities and began working in factories instead of on farms or at home.
c. possible answers—Yes, several states passed 10-hour workday laws; no, success was limited because the courts and police supported the owners.

9. a. business and trade grew; improved travel for people
b. possible answers—They had a successful business that the country depended upon, owned lots of land, and were a huge employer.
c. Students' answers will vary, but should reflect an understanding of the ways in which the Transportation Revolution changed the economy and life in the United States.

10. a. shifted to using steam power, which enabled factories to be built almost anywhere
b. People could communicate quickly over long distances.
c. Answers will vary, but students should consider working conditions in factories and how factories affected the local environment, such as through increased pollution.

Reviewing Themes

11. Students might mention the water frame, the steam engine, the steamboat, the railroad, the telegraph, the mechanical reaper, the sewing machine, the icebox, or even matches or safety pins. Students should provide reasons to support their selections.

12. The Industrial Revolution created a boom in business and led to economic growth and expansion. With advances in manufacturing, agriculture, transportation, and communication, farms and businesses were able to produce more goods faster and at lower prices, and trade increased.

SECTION 3 (Pages 396–401)
9. a. Describe How were Americans affected by the introduction of steamboats?
b. Make Inferences How did railroad companies become some of the most powerful businesses in the country?
c. Elaborate In your opinion, what was the most important result of the Transportation Revolution?

SECTION 4 (Pages 402–405)
10. a. Recall What important change took place in how factories were powered?
b. Draw Conclusions How did the telegraph affect communication in the United States?
c. Evaluate Do you think moving factories close to cities helped or hurt working life? Explain.

Reviewing Themes

11. Science and Technology Rank what you think are the three most important inventions of the Industrial Revolution. Explain your choices.

12. Economics What was the overall effect of the Industrial Revolution on the U.S. economy?

Using the Internet

go.hrw.com
KEYWORD: SS8 US12

13. Activity: Advertisement The Industrial Revolution changed the way goods were produced. New inventions created easier, faster, or completely new ways of doing things. Enter the activity keyword and research inventions made between 1790 and 1860. Then create an advertisement for one of the inventions that might have appeared in a magazine during that time in history.

408 CHAPTER 12

Reading Skills

Causes and Effects in History Use the Reading Skills taught in this chapter to answer the question about the reading selection below.

> Many young women came to Lowell from across New England. They wanted the chance to earn money instead of working on the family farm. (p. 392)

14. According to the passage above, what was a cause for moving to Lowell?
a. working long hours
b. earning money
c. meeting people
d. working on a farm

Social Studies Skills

Personal Conviction and Bias Use the Social Studies Skills taught in this chapter to answer the question about the reading selection below.

> "Is anyone such a fool as to suppose that out of six thousand factory girls in Lowell, sixty would be there if they could help it?"
> —Sarah G. Bagley, quoted in The Belles of New England by William Moran

15. Do you think that Bagley's opposition to the Lowell system was unfairly biased? Why or why not?

FOCUS ON WRITING

16. Writing Your Newspaper Advertisement Look over your chart, and choose one invention for your advertisement. Then answer these questions to help you plan your advertisement: Who is your audience? Who will buy this invention? How will the invention benefit this audience? What words or phrases will best persuade this audience? Once you have answered these questions, design your advertisement. To draw readers' attention to your ad, include an illustration, a catchy heading, and a few lines of text.

Using the Internet

13. Go to the HRW Web site and enter the keyword shown to access a rubric for this activity.

KEYWORD: SR8 TEACHER

Reading Skills

14. b

Social Studies Skills

15. Answers will vary, but students should exhibit an understanding of bias and provide examples from the reading selection to support their positions.

Focus on Writing

16. Rubric Students' newspaper advertisements should
- briefly describe the invention
- explain the benefits of the invention and who can use it
- be persuasive
- include an illustration and catchy heading that grabs readers' attention

CRF: Focus on Writing: Newspaper Advertisement

Standardized Test Practice

DIRECTIONS: Read each question and write the letter of the best response.

1 The first machines of the Industrial Revolution were powered by

A electricity.

B water.

C animals.

D coal.

2 The earliest important evidence of the Industrial Revolution in America was found in

A the way cotton was processed for market.

B the production of tobacco products.

C the manufacture of cloth and thread.

D the construction of the first steam railroads.

3 The Transportation Revolution of the mid-1800s had all of the following effects *except*

A reducing the time and cost of shipping products.

B helping to create a boom in business and agriculture across the nation.

C making travel upstream on rivers faster and easier.

D limiting the federal government's ability to control trade among states.

4 What change in technology allowed business owners to sell their goods in markets across the country?

A the Lowell system

B the growth of railroads

C the invention of the telegraph

D the Arkwright system

5 Eli Whitney's idea of interchangeable parts resulted in

A the dominance of American manufacturing.

B the beginning of the Industrial Revolution.

C a rapid expansion of railroads.

D the mass production of goods.

6 The inventions of John Deere and Cyrus McCormick

A improved communication.

B introduced two new factory labor systems.

C helped increase agricultural production in the United States.

D led to manufacturing breakthroughs in the textile industry.

7

> "The little money I could earn—one dollar a week, besides the price of my board—was needed in the family, and I must return [from home] to the mill . . . I began to reflect on life rather seriously for a girl of twelve or thirteen. What was I here for? What would I make of myself? . . . We did not forget that we were working girls . . . clearing away a few weeds from the overgrown track of independent labor for other women . . . [so that] no real odium [disrespect] could be attached to any honest toil that any self-respecting woman might undertake."
>
> —from *A New England Girlhood* by Lucy Larcom (1824–1893)

From the content of this passage, you can determine that the writer was commenting about

A the mass-production system.

B the Lowell system.

C the Rhode Island system.

D the trade union system.

1. B
Break Down the Question: This question requires students to place events in their correct sequence. Point out that the question focuses on the Industrial Revolution, which eliminates options A and C.

2. C
Break Down the Question: This question requires students to recall factual information. Refer students who have trouble to Section 1.

3. D
Break Down the Question: This question requires students to identify cause and effect. Remind students that the word *except* means they should choose the answer that is *not* an effect of the Industrial Revolution.

4. B
Break Down the Question: This question requires students to identify cause and effect. Refer students who have trouble to Section 3.

5. D
Break Down the Question: This question requires students to recall factual information. Refer students who have trouble to Section 1.

6. C
Break Down the Question: This question requires students to recall factual information. Refer students who have trouble to Section 4.

7. B
Break Down the Question: Point out to students that the source and author of a reading selection often provide a clue to what the selection is about. For example, the name of the source here reveals that the author was a New England girl, and thus she was likely to be a Lowell girl.

Intervention Resources

Reproducible

- Interactive Reader and Study Guide
- Differentiated Instruction Teacher Management System: Lesson Plans for Differentiated Instruction

Technology

- Quick Facts Transparency: The North Visual Summary
- Differentiated Instruction Modified Worksheets and Tests CD-ROM
- Interactive Skills Tutor CD-ROM

Tips for Test Taking

Go With Your Gut When taking tests, a person's first impulse about an answer is many times correct. Tell students to consider carefully before changing their answers to multiple choice or true-false questions. If students do decide to change an answer, they should do so because they are confident about the change.

Chapter 13 Planning Guide

The South

Chapter Overview	Reproducible Resources	Technology Resources
CHAPTER 13 pp. 410–433 **Overview:** In this chapter, students will study the development of the South's social structure during the early 1800s.	**Differentiated Instruction Teacher Management System:*** • Instructional Benchmarking Guides • Lesson Plans for Differentiated Instruction **Interactive Reader and Study Guide:** Chapter Graphic Organizer* **Chapter Resource File:*** • Focus on Writing Activity: Biographical Sketch • Social Studies Skills Activity: Interpreting Graphs • Chapter Review Activity **A Teacher's Guide to Religion in the Public Schools***	Power Presentations with Video CD-ROM Differentiated Instruction Modified Worksheets and Tests CD-ROM Primary Source Library CD-ROM for United States History Interactive Skills Tutor CD-ROM Student Edition on Audio CD Program History's Impact: United States History Video Program (VHS/DVD): The South*
Section 1: **Growth of the Cotton Industry** **The Big Idea:** The invention of the cotton gin made the South a one-crop economy and increased the need for slave labor.	**Differentiated Instruction Teacher Management System:** Section 1 Lesson Plan* **Interactive Reader and Study Guide:** Section 1 Summary* **Chapter Resource File:*** • Vocabulary Builder Activity, Section 1 • Biography Activity: Eli Whitney • History and Geography Activity: Cotton in the South	Daily Bellringer Transparency: Section 1* Map Transparency: The Cotton Kingdom* Internet Activity: Tredegar Iron Works Report
Section 2: **Free Southern Society** **The Big Idea:** Southern society centered around agriculture.	**Differentiated Instruction Teacher Management System:** Section 2 Lesson Plan* **Interactive Reader and Study Guide:** Section 2 Summary* **Chapter Resource File:*** • Vocabulary Builder Activity, Section 2 • Biography Activity: Mary Boykin Chesnut • Literature Activity: Plantation Life before Emancipation • Primary Source Activity: Frances Anne Kemble, *Journal of a Residence on a Georgian Plantation*	Daily Bellringer Transparency: Section 2*
Section 3: **The Slave System** **The Big Idea:** The slave system in the South produced harsh living conditions and occasional rebellions.	**Differentiated Instruction Teacher Management System:** Section 3 Lesson Plan* **Interactive Reader and Study Guide:** Section 3 Summary* **Chapter Resource File:*** • Vocabulary Builder Activity, Section 3 • Primary Source Activity: Jacob Stroyer, *My Life in the South* • Biography Activity: Nat Turner • Biography Activity: Denmark Vesey • Primary Source Activity: The Denmark Vesey Conspiracy	Daily Bellringer Transparency: Section 3* Map Transparency: Nat Turner's Rebellion* Internet Activity: Slave Cabin Drawings

HOLT

History's Impact

United States History Video Program (VHS/DVD)

The South

Suggested use: as a chapter introduction

Review, Assessment, Intervention

Quick Facts Transparency: The South Visual Summary*

Spanish Chapter Summaries Audio CD Program

Progress Assessment Support System (PASS): Chapter Test*

Differentiated Instruction Modified Worksheets and Tests CD-ROM: Modified Chapter Test

Online Chapter Summaries in Six Languages

One-Stop Planner CD-ROM: ExamView Test Generator (English/Spanish)

Alternative Assessment Handbook

Holt Online Assessment Program (HOAP), in the Holt Premier Online Student Edition

---

PASS: Section 1 Quiz*

Online Quiz: Section 1

Alternative Assessment Handbook

PASS: Section 2 Quiz*

Online Quiz: Section 2

Alternative Assessment Handbook

PASS: Section 3 Quiz*

Online Quiz: Section 3

Alternative Assessment Handbook

Power Presentations with Video CD-ROM

Power Presentations with Video are visual presentations of each chapter's main ideas. Presentations can be customized by including Quick Facts charts, images from the text, and video clips.

Power Presentations with Video CD-ROM

HOLT

United States History

Beginnings to 1877

HOLT, RINEHART and WINSTON
A Harcourt Education Company

DIVISION FOR PUBLIC EDUCATION

AMERICAN BAR ASSOCIATION

Developed by the Division for Public Education of the American Bar Association, these materials are part of the **Democracy and Civic Education Resources.**

- **Constitution Study Guide**
- **Supreme Court Case Studies**

Holt Online Learning

- Document-Based Questions
- Interactive Multimedia Activities

Teacher Resources

KEYWORD: SR8 TEACHER

Student Resources

KEYWORD: SR8 US13

- Current Events
- Chapter-based Internet Activities
- and more!

Holt Premier
Online Student Edition

Complete online support for interactivity, assessment, and reporting

- Interactive Maps and Notebook
- Standardized Test Prep
- Homework Practice and Research Activities Online

CHAPTER 13 PLANNING GUIDE

Differentiating Instruction

ENGLISH-LANGUAGE LEARNERS & STRUGGLING READERS

TARGET RESOURCE

Live Ink® Online Reading Help

Spanish Resources
Spanish Chapter Summaries Audio CD Program
One-Stop Planner CD-ROM:
- ExamView Test Generator, Spanish
- PuzzlePro, Spanish

Additional Resources
Differentiated Instruction Teacher Management System: Lesson Plans for Differentiated Instruction
Chapter Resources:
- Vocabulary Builder Activities
- Social Studies Skills Activity: Interpreting Graphs

Quick Facts Transparency: The South Visual Summary
Student Edition on Audio CD Program
Online Chapter Summaries in Six Languages
Interactive Skills Tutor CD-ROM

SPECIAL NEEDS LEARNERS

TARGET RESOURCE

Differentiated Instruction Modified Worksheets and Tests CD-ROM

- Vocabulary Flash Cards
- Modified Vocabulary Builder Activities
- Modified Chapter Review Activity
- Modified Chapter Test

Additional Resources
Differentiated Instruction Teacher Management System: Lesson Plans for Differentiated Instruction
Interactive Reader and Study Guide
Social Studies Skills Activity: Interpreting Graphs
Student Edition on Audio CD Program
Interactive Skills Tutor CD-ROM
Live Ink® Online Reading Help

ADVANCED/GIFTED AND TALENTED STUDENTS

TARGET RESOURCE

Primary Source Library CD-ROM for United States History

The Library contains longer versions of quotations in the text, extra sources, and images. Included are point-of-view articles, journals, diaries, historical fiction, and political documents.

Additional Resources
United States History Document-Based Questions Activities
Differentiated Instruction Teacher Management System: Lesson Plans for Differentiated Instruction
Chapter Resource File:
- Focus on Writing Activity: Biographical Sketch
- Literature Activity: Plantation Life before Emancipation
- Primary Source Activity: Frances Anne Kemble, *Journal of a Residence on a Georgian Plantation*
- Primary Source Activity: Jacob Stroyer, *My Life in the South*
- Primary Source Activity: The Denmark Vesey Conspiracy

One-Stop Planner® CD-ROM
for Differentiated Instruction

Your differentiated instruction lesson plans are available at your fingertips. Holt's Teacher Management System links teaching support tools to pages in the Interactive Teacher's Edition.

The One-Stop Planner features:
- Interactive Teacher's Edition
- Calendar Planner and pacing guides
- Editable lesson plans
- All reproducible ancillaries in Adobe Acrobat (PDF) format
- ExamView Test Generator (English and Spanish)
- Transparency and video previews

Professional Development

- **In-service and staff development** as part of your Holt Social Studies product purchase
- **Quick Teacher Tutorial Lesson Presentation CD-ROM**
- Intensive tuition-based **Teacher Development Institute**
- **Teaching American History Online**—2 Module Professional Development Course
- **Convenient Holt Speaker Bureau**—face-to-face workshop options
- **PRAXIS™ Test Prep** interactive Web-based content refreshers*
- **24/7 Ask A Professional Development Expert** at http://www.hrw.com/prodev/

* PRAXIS is a trademark of Educational Testing Service (ETS). This publication is not endorsed or approved by ETS.

Chapter Big Ideas

Section 1 The invention of the cotton gin made the South a one-crop economy and increased the need for slave labor.

Section 2 Southern society centered around agriculture.

Section 3 The slave system in the South produced harsh living conditions and occasional rebellions.

Focus on Writing

The **Chapter Resource File** provides a Focus on Writing worksheet to help students organize and write their biographical sketches.

📓 **CRF:** Focus on Writing Activity: Biographical Sketch

CHAPTER 13   **1790–1860**

The South

FOCUS ON WRITING

Biographical Sketch In this chapter you will learn about life in the South during the first half of the nineteenth century. Read the chapter, and then write a two-paragraph biographical sketch about a day in the life of a person living on a large cotton farm in the South. You might choose to write about a wealthy male landowner, his wife, or an enslaved man or woman working on the farm. As you read, think about what life would have been like for the different people who lived and worked on the farm. Take notes about farm life in your notebook.

UNITED STATES   **1793** Eli Whitney invents the cotton gin.

1800

1794 France ends slavery in its colonies.

 WORLD

Key to Differentiating Instruction

Below Level

Basic-level activities designed for all students encountering new material

At Level

Intermediate-level activities designed for average students

Above Level

Challenging activities designed for honors and gifted and talented students

Standard English Mastery

Activities designed to improve standard English usage

Introduce the Chapter

At Level

Impact of Technology

1. Tell students that in this chapter they will learn how a single invention revived the economy the South.

2. Have students think of new technology and inventions that they have seen in their lifetime *(e.g., cell phone, DVD, GPS)*. Write the answers for students to see.

3. Then ask students how life has changed because of each new piece of technology or invention. What impact has there been on jobs, communication, and leisure, for example? Are there health or safety issues related to the new invention or technology? Can students predict other changes that might occur in their lifetime? **LS Verbal/Linguistic**

What You Will Learn...

These enslaved people were photographed on a South Carolina plantation in the year 1861. The issue of slavery would have a serious and dramatic impact on the history of the entire United States. In this chapter you will learn how the South developed an agricultural economy, and how that economy was dependent on the labor of enslaved people.

● **Chapter Preview** ●

HOLT
History's Impact
► video series
See the Video Teacher's Guide for strategies for using the chapter video **The South**.

Explore the Picture

Life on a Southern Plantation
From sunrise to sunset, enslaved Africans' lives were controlled. A ringing bell or blowing horn called workers to the fields before dawn. On cotton plantations, June was a particularly hard month because the fields had to be broken up by hand with tools. Under the glare of the hot sun, each adult slave was expected to break up a half acre of ground per day.

Analyzing Visuals What evidence can you see in the photo that life for enslaved Africans on a southern plantation was harsh? *possible answer—The people shown have no shoes; they carry hand tools; they are not smiling.*

go.hrw.com
Online Resources
Chapter Resources:
KEYWORD: SR8 US13
Teacher Resources:
KEYWORD: SR8 TEACHER

1808 A congressional ban on importing slaves into the United States takes effect.

1831 Nat Turner's Rebellion leads to fears of further slave revolts in the South.

1848 Joseph R. Anderson becomes the owner of the Tredegar Iron Works, the South's only large iron factory.

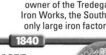

1820   1840   1860

1807 Parliament bans the slave trade in the British Empire.

1835 Alexis de Tocqueville publishes *Democracy in America*.

1837 Victoria is crowned queen of Great Britain.

1858 A treaty at Tianjin, China, gives Hong Kong to the United Kingdom.

THE SOUTH **411**

Explore the Time Line

1. What did Eli Whitney invent in 1793? *the cotton gin*

2. In what year did the U.S. Congress ban the import of slaves into the country? *1808*

3. Which two countries limited aspects of slavery and the slave trade prior to the 1808 U.S. ban? *France and Great Britain*

4. What effect did Nat Turner's Rebellion in 1831 have? *fears of further slave revolts in the South*

Info to Know

Congressional Ban on Importing Slaves Even though the United States banned the importation of enslaved Africans in 1808, the ban did not undermine or end slavery. Planters in need of labor in Georgia and South Carolina hurried to beat the ban by importing tens of thousands of enslaved Africans before the ban took effect. The illegal smuggling of slaves continued, and the slave population increased as children— the next generation of slaves—were born into slavery.

Reading Social Studies

Understanding Themes

Two themes, economics and culture, are presented in this chapter about the South. Ask students to recall ways in which the economy of the South was different than that of the rest of the United States. Remind students that the South depended economically on agriculture. Then ask students to predict how the society and culture of the South might have been affected by this reliance on agriculture. Ask students to write down their predictions and to see which ones are correct as they read the chapter.

Online Research

Focus on Reading Organize the class into small groups. Have students in each group discuss their Internet use and Web sites that they find useful for conducting research. Ask groups to list what they find most valuable about those sites, such as quality of information, layout, and ease of use. Remind students that not all Web sites contain verifiable information. Ask students to list how they determine the quality of information when they are using the Internet. Have each group report its opinions to the class. Discuss the qualities of a Web site that are most important to consider when conducting research.

Reading Social Studies
by Kylene Beers

| Economics | Geography | Politics | Society and Culture | Science and Technology |

Focus on Themes This chapter takes you into the heart of the South from 1800 through the mid-1800s. As you read, you will discover that the South depended on cotton as its **economic** backbone, especially after the invention of the cotton gin. You will also read about the slave system in the South during this time and about the harsh living conditions slaves endured. As you will see, the South was home to a variety of **societies and cultures**.

Online Research

Focus on Reading Researching history topics on the Web can give you access to valuable information. However, just because the information is on the Web doesn't mean it is automatically valuable!

Evaluating Web Sites Before you use information you find online, you need to evaluate the site it comes from. The checklist below can help you determine if the site is worth your time.

Evaluating Web Sites

Site: _____ URL: _____ Date of access: _____

Rate each item on this 1–3 scale. Then add up the total score.

	No	Some	Yes
I. Authority			
a. Authors are clearly identified by name.	1	2	3
b. Contact information is provided for authors.	1	2	3
c. Author's qualifications are clearly stated.	1	2	3
d. Site has been updated recently.	1	2	3
II. Content			
a. Site's information is useful to your project.	1	2	3
b. Information is clear and well-organized.	1	2	3
c. Information appears to be at the right level.	1	2	3
d. Links to additional important information are provided.	1	2	3
e. Information can be verified in other sources.	1	2	3
f. Graphics are helpful, not just decorative.	1	2	3
III. Design and Technical Elements			
a. Pages are readable and easy to navigate.	1	2	3
b. Links to other sites work.	1	2	3

Total Score _____

36–28 = very good site   27–20 = average site   below 20 = poor site

---

412 CHAPTER 13

Reading and Skills Resources

Reading Support

- Interactive Reader and Study Guide
- Student Edition on Audio CD Program
- Spanish Chapter Summaries Audio CD Program

Social Studies Skills Support

- Interactive Skills Tutor CD-ROM

Vocabulary Support

- **CRF:** Vocabulary Builder Activities
- **CRF:** Chapter Review Activity
- Differentiated Instruction Modified Worksheets and Tests CD-ROM:
  - Vocabulary Flash Cards
  - Vocabulary Builder Activity
  - Chapter Review Activity

OSP Holt PuzzlePro

You Try It!

The passage below is from the chapter you are about to read.

Cotton Becomes Profitable

Cotton had been grown in the New World for centuries, but it had not been a very profitable crop. Before cotton could be spun into thread for weaving into cloth, the seeds had to be removed from the cotton fibers.

From Chapter 13, p. 414

Long-staple cotton, also called black-seed cotton, was fairly easy to process. Workers could pick the seeds from the cotton with relative ease. But long-staple cotton grew well in only a few places in the South. More common was short-staple cotton, also known as green-seed cotton. Removing the seeds from this cotton was difficult and time consuming. A worker could spend an entire day picking the seeds from the single pound of short-staple cotton.

After you read the passage, complete the following activity.

Suppose that after reading this passage you decide to do some research on cotton growing. You use a search engine that directs you to a site. At that site, you find the information described below. Using the evaluation criteria listed on the previous page, decide if this is a site you would recommend to others.

a. The authors of the site are listed as "Bob and Mack, good friends who enjoy working together."

b. The site was last updated on "the last time we got together."

c. The title of the site is "Cotton Pickin'." There are few headings.

d. This ten-page site includes nine pages about the authors' childhood on a cotton farm. No illustrations are included.

e. Pages are very long; but, they load quickly as there are no graphics. There is one link to a site selling cotton clothing.

Chapter 13

Section 1
cotton gin *(p. 415)*
planters *(p. 416)*
cotton belt *(p. 416)*
factors *(p. 417)*
Tredegar Iron Works *(p. 419)*

Section 2
yeomen *(p. 422)*

Section 3
folktales *(p. 427)*
spirituals *(p. 427)*
Nat Turner's Rebellion *(p. 428)*
Nat Turner *(p. 428)*

Academic Vocabulary

Success in school is related to knowing academic vocabulary— the words that are frequently used in school assignments and discussions. In this chapter, you will learn the following academic words:

primary *(p. 418)*
aspect *(p. 426)*

As you read Chapter 13, think about what topics would be interesting to research on the Web. If you do some research on the Web, remember to use the evaluation list to analyze the Web site.

Reading Social Studies

Key Terms and People

Preteach the key terms and people from this chapter by asking students what they think each term means or who each person was. Ask the class to identify the terms or people about which they know the least. Write the list of terms for the class to see. Have each student define or identify the terms or people. Then have each student draw an illustration to represent each term or person.
LS Verbal/Linguistic, Visual/Spatial

Focus on Reading

See the **Focus on Reading** questions in this chapter for more practice on this reading social studies skill.

Reading Social Studies Assessment

See the **Chapter Review** at the end of this chapter for student assessment questions related to this reading skill.

Teaching Tip

Remind students of the importance of citing their sources correctly. Stress to students that as they evaluate a Web site, they should write down important information about that site. Among the items students should include in their documentation are the author or authors of a Web site, the exact URL, or address, of the site, the date they accessed the Web site, the date the site was last revised, and the name of the Web site.

Answers

You Try It! *Students should conclude that they would not want to recommend this site to others. Students should note that, among other things, the Web site was not written by qualified authors, nor does it provide useful information about growing cotton.*

413

Bellringer

If YOU were there . . . Use the **Daily Bellringer Transparency** to help students answer the question.

📇 Daily Bellringer Transparency, Section 1

Academic Vocabulary

Review with students the high-use academic term in this section.

primary main, most important (p. 418)

📰 **CRF:** Vocabulary Builder Activity, Section 1

Taking Notes

Have students copy the graphic organizer onto their own paper and then use it to take notes on the section. This activity will prepare students for the Section Assessment, in which they will complete a graphic organizer that builds on the information using a critical thinking skill.

SECTION 1

Growth of the Cotton Industry

What You Will Learn...

Main Ideas

1. The invention of the cotton gin revived the economy of the South.
2. The cotton gin created a cotton boom in which farmers grew little else.
3. Some people encouraged southerners to focus on other crops and industries.

The Big Idea

The invention of the cotton gin made the South a one-crop economy and increased the need for slave labor.

Key Terms and People

cotton gin, *p. 415*
planters, *p. 416*
cotton belt, *p. 416*
factors, *p. 417*
Tredegar Iron Works, *p. 419*

TAKING NOTES As you read, take notes on the causes of the cotton boom in the South. Record your notes in a graphic organizer like the one shown below.

414 CHAPTER 13

If YOU were there...

You are a field-worker on a cotton farm in the South in about 1800. Your job is to separate the seeds from the cotton fibers. It is dull, tiring work because the tiny seeds are tangled in the fibers. Sometimes it takes you a whole day just to clean one pound of cotton! Now you hear that someone has invented a machine that can clean cotton 50 times faster than by hand.

How might this machine change your life?

> **BUILDING BACKGROUND** Sectional differences had always existed between different regions of the United States. The revolutionary changes in industry and transportation deepened the differences between North and South. The South remained mainly agricultural. New technology helped the region become the Cotton Kingdom.

Reviving the South's Economy

Before the American Revolution, three crops dominated southern agriculture—tobacco, rice, and indigo. These crops, produced mostly by enslaved African Americans, played a central role in the southern economy and culture.

After the American Revolution, however, prices for tobacco, rice, and indigo dropped. When crop prices fell, the demand for and the price of slaves also went down. In an effort to protect their incomes, many farmers tried, with little success, to grow other crops that needed less labor. Soon, however, cotton would transform the southern economy and greatly increase the demand for slave labor.

Cotton Becomes Profitable

Cotton had been grown in the New World for centuries, but it had not been a very profitable crop. Before cotton could be spun into thread for weaving into cloth, the seeds had to be removed from the cotton fibers.

Teach the Big Idea

Growth of the Cotton Industry

1. **Teach** Ask students the questions in the Main Idea boxes to teach this section.

2. **Apply** Help students understand the significance of the cotton gin to southern agriculture and the South's economy. Have students use information in the section to write a brief encyclopedia entry about the cotton gin. In their entries, have students answer the questions who, what, when, where, how, and why. **LS Verbal/Linguistic**

3. **Review** As you review the section, invite volunteers to read aloud portions of their encyclopedia entries.

4. **Practice/Homework** Ask students to imagine they are southern farm workers who spent all day removing seeds from just one pound of cotton. Have them write journal entries reacting to news of the invention of the cotton gin. **LS Verbal/Linguistic**

📰 Alternative Assessment Handbook, Rubric 15: Journals

Cotton Gin

Eli Whitney's cotton gin enabled workers to easily remove seeds from cotton fibers. The result was a dramatic increase in cotton production in the South.

How did the cotton gin remove seeds from cotton fibers?

❶ The operator turned the crank.

❷ The crank turned a roller with teeth that stripped the seeds away from the cotton fiber.

❸ Brushes on a second roller lifted the seed-less cotton off the teeth of the first cylinder and dropped it out of the machine.

❹ A belt connected the rollers so that they would both turn when the crank was turned.

Long-staple cotton, also called black-seed cotton, was fairly easy to process. Workers could pick the seeds from the cotton with relative ease. But long-staple cotton grew well in only a few places in the South. More common was short-staple cotton, which was also known as green-seed cotton. Removing the seeds from this cotton was difficult and time consuming. A worker could spend an entire day picking the seeds from a single pound of short-staple cotton.

By the early 1790s the demand for American cotton began increasing rapidly. For instance, in Great Britain, new textile factories needed raw cotton that could be used for making cloth, and American cotton producers could not keep up with the high demand for their cotton. These producers of cotton needed a machine that could remove the seeds from the cotton more rapidly.

Eli Whitney's Cotton Gin

Northerner Eli Whitney finally patented such a machine in 1793. The year before, Whitney had visited a Georgia plantation owned by Catherine Greene where workers were using a machine to remove seeds from long-staple cotton. This machine did not work well on short-staple cotton, and Greene asked Whitney if he could improve it. By the next spring, Whitney had perfected his design for the **cotton gin**, a machine that removes seeds from short-staple cotton. ("Gin" is short for engine.) The cotton gin used a hand-cranked cylinder with wire teeth to pull cotton fibers from the seeds.

Whitney hoped to keep the design of the gin a secret, but the machine was so useful that his patent was often ignored by other manufacturers. Whitney described how his invention would improve the cotton business.

THE IMPACT TODAY

The same patent law that protected Whitney's invention of the the cotton gin protects the rights of inventors today.

THE SOUTH **415**

415

❷ The Cotton Boom

The cotton gin created a cotton boom in which farmers grew little else.

Recall How did the cotton gin affect cotton production in the South? *made cotton so profitable that many southern farmers began growing cotton, and cotton production spread and increased rapidly*

Identify Cause and Effect Increased cotton production led to an economic boom in the South. What were the effects of this economic boom on the region? *attracted new settlers, built up wealth among wealthy white southerners, firmly embedded slavery in the South*

📑 **CRF:** History and Geography Activity: Cotton in the South

🗺 Map Transparency: The Cotton Kingdom

Interpreting Maps
The Cotton Kingdom

Before and After Which states (or future states) produced cotton before 1820? *Virginia, North Carolina, South Carolina, Georgia, Alabama, Tennessee, Mississippi, Louisiana* Which grew cotton after 1820? *Missouri, Arkansas, Texas, Florida, Oklahoma (Indian Territory)*

🗺 Map Transparency: The Cotton Kingdom

Info to Know

Cotton Gin Patent After perfecting the cotton gin, Eli Whitney was given the sole right to make the machine in 1794. But other people were easily able to make cotton gins, and began doing so. Whitney sued planters for violating his rights, but he gained next to nothing from his legal battles.

Answers

Interpreting Charts 1. *the South;* **2.** *2.1 million bales*

Reading Check *made processing cotton easier and quicker; increased production of cotton as a cash crop; led to an economic boom*

416

"One man will clean ten times as much cotton as he can in any other way before known and also clean it much better than in the usual mode [method]. This machine may be turned by water or with a horse, with the greatest ease, and one man and a horse will do more than fifty men with the old machines."

—Eli Whitney, quoted in *Eli Whitney and the Birth of American Technology* by Constance McLaughlin Green

Whitney's gin revolutionized the cotton industry. **Planters**—large-scale farmers who held more than 20 slaves—built cotton gins that could process tons of cotton much faster than hand processing. A healthy crop almost guaranteed financial success because of high demand from the textile industry.

READING CHECK **Drawing Conclusions** What effects did the cotton gin have on the southern economy?

The Cotton Boom

Whitney's invention of the cotton gin made cotton so profitable that southern farmers abandoned other crops in favor of growing cotton. The removal of Native Americans opened up more land, while the development of new types of cotton plants helped spread cotton production throughout the South as far west as Texas. This area of high cotton production became known as the **cotton belt.**

Production increased rapidly—from about 2 million pounds in 1791 to roughly a billion pounds by 1860. As early as 1840, the United States was producing more than half of the cotton grown in the entire world. The economic boom attracted new settlers, built up wealth among wealthy white southerners, and firmly put in place the institution of slavery in the South.

The Cotton Kingdom

After the invention of the cotton gin, the amount of cotton produced each year in the United States soared, as the chart below shows. The area of land devoted to growing cotton also increased dramatically between 1820 and 1860, as shown on the map.

U.S. Cotton Production, 1800–1860

Cotton (in 100,000 bales) — Year

ANALYSIS SKILL INTERPRETING CHARTS
1. In what region of the United States was the cotton belt?
2. How many bales of cotton were produced in 1860?

Extent of cotton growing by 1820
Extent of cotton growing by 1860

0 150 300 Miles
0 150 300 Kilometers

416 CHAPTER 13

Differentiating Instruction

Below Level

Struggling Readers

1. Review with students the positive and negative effects of the cotton boom.
2. Draw the chart on the right for students to see. Omit the blue, italicized answers.
3. Have students copy the chart and complete it by listing the positive and negative effects of the cotton boom on the South's economy.
LS Visual/Spatial

Effects of Cotton Boom

Positive	Negative
• *Growth of economy*	• *increased reliance on one crop—cotton*
• *Build-up of wealth*	• *firmly embedded the institution of slavery in the South*
• *The South became a major player in world trade.*	• *increased internal slave trade*
• *Development of cotton trade*	
• *Growth of cotton-related industries*	

Cotton Belt

Cotton had many advantages as a cash crop. It cost little to market. Unlike food staples, harvested cotton could be stored for a long time. Because cotton was lighter than other staple crops, it also cost less to transport long distances.

Farmers eager to profit from growing cotton headed west to find land. Farmers also began to apply scientific methods to improve crop production. Cotton had one disadvantage as a crop—it rapidly used up the nutrients in the soil. After a few years, cotton could make the land useless for growing anything. Some agricultural scientists recommended crop rotation—changing the crop grown on a particular plot of land every few years. Different crops needed different nutrients, so crop rotation would keep the land fertile longer. Other agricultural scientists began to study soil chemistry, in an effort to keep the land rich and productive.

As the cotton belt grew, farmers continued trying to improve the crop. Agricultural scientists worked at crossbreeding short-staple cotton with other varieties. As a result, new, stronger types of cotton were soon growing throughout the cotton belt. This led to expansion of the cotton industry through the 1860s.

The cotton boom involved much more than growing and harvesting cotton. Harvested cotton had to be ginned, pressed into bales, and then shipped to market or to warehouses. Special agents helped do everything from marketing cotton to customers to insuring crops against loss or damage. Factories were built to produce items needed by cotton farmers, such as ropes to bale cotton.

Growing and harvesting cotton required many field hands. Rather than pay wages to free workers, planters began to use more slave labor. Congress had made bringing slaves into the United States illegal in 1808. However, the growing demand for slaves led to an increase in the slave trade within the United States.

Cotton Trade

In an 1858 speech before the U.S. Senate, South Carolina politician James Henry Hammond declared, "Cotton is King!" Without cotton, Hammond claimed, the world economy would fail. He believed that southern cotton was one of the most valuable resources in the world. Southern cotton was used to make cloth in England and the North. Many southerners shared Hammond's viewpoints about cotton. Southerner David Christy declared, "King cotton is a profound [learned] statesman, and knows what measures will best sustain [protect] his throne."

The cotton boom made the South a major player in world trade. Great Britain became the South's most valued foreign trading partner. Southerners also sold tons of cotton to the growing textile industry in the northeastern United States. This increased trade led to the growth of major port cities in the South, including Charleston, South Carolina; Savannah, Georgia; and New Orleans, Louisiana.

In these cities, crop brokers called **factors** managed the cotton trade. Farmers sold their cotton to merchants, who then made deals with the factors. Merchants and factors also arranged loans for farmers who needed to buy supplies. They often advised farmers on how to invest profits. Once farmers got their cotton to the port cities factors arranged for transportation aboard trading ships.

However, shipping cotton by land to port cities was very difficult in the South. The few major road projects at the time were limited to the Southeast. Most southern farmers had to ship their goods on the region's rivers. On the Ohio and Mississippi rivers, flatboats and steamboats carried cotton and other products to port. Eventually, hundreds of steamboats traveled up and down the mighty Mississippi River each day.

READING CHECK Identifying Cause and Effect
What effect did the cotton boom have on the slave trade within the United States?

THE IMPACT TODAY
The Port of New Orleans remains a major seaport. It handles about 85 million tons of cargo annually.

THE SOUTH **417**

417

Main Idea

❸ Other Crops and Industries

Some people encouraged southerners to focus on other crops and industries.

Recall What were some other important crops in the South? *corn, rice, sweet potatoes, wheat, sugarcane, tobacco, hemp, and flax*

Explain Why were most southern factories built to serve the needs of farmers? *The South's economy centered on agriculture.*

Analyze Why did some people encourage southerners to try a variety of crops and investments? *reliance on one crop was risky; wanted to modernize and promote industry; to keep the soil healthy*

Analyzing Visuals

The South's Cotton Economy

Have students examine the image at right to answer the following:

• Where was most cotton processed? *in the South*

• Where were most of the textile mills to which sailing ships carried cotton? *northeastern United States, Great Britain*

Connect to Geography

Tobacco and the South Farmers found that healthy tobacco plants needed nutrient-rich soils. Tobacco so badly bleached the land of nutrients that after just three years, the soil required 20 years of rest before it was usable for farming again. Before farmers learned to rotate crops, they instead rotated fields, planting tobacco on fresh land until the soil's nutrients were exhausted.

The South's Cotton Economy

Eli Whitney's cotton gin began the cotton boom. Soon, the Cotton Kingdom stretched across the South. For the cotton planters to succeed, they had to get their cotton to market.

Enslaved African Americans did most of the planting, harvesting, and processing of cotton.

Cotton was shipped on river steamboats to major ports such as Charleston.

From southern ports, sailing ships carried the cotton to distant textile mills.

Other Crops and Industries

Some leaders worried that the South was depending too much on cotton. They wanted southerners to try a variety of cash crops and investments.

ACADEMIC VOCABULARY
primary
main, most important

Food and Cash Crops

One such crop was corn, the **primary** southern food crop. By the late 1830s the top three corn-growing states in the nation were all in the South. The South's other successful food crops included rice, sweet potatoes, wheat, and sugarcane.

Production of tobacco, the South's first major cash crop, was very time consuming because tobacco leaves had to be cured, or dried, before they could be shipped to market. In 1839 a slave discovered a way to improve the drying process by using heat from burning charcoal. This new, faster curing process increased tobacco production.

Partly as a result of the cotton boom, hemp and flax also became major cash crops. Their fibers were used to make rope and sackcloth. Farmers used the rope and sackcloth to bundle cotton into bales.

Industry

Many of the first factories in the South were built to serve farmers' needs by processing crops such as sugarcane. In 1803 the nation's first steam-powered sawmill was built in Donaldsonville, Louisiana. This new technology enabled lumber companies to cut, sort, and clean wood quickly.

By the 1840s, entrepreneurs in Georgia began investing in cotton mills. In 1840, there were 14 cotton mills; by the mid-1850s, there were more than 50. A few mill owners followed the model established by Francis Cabot Lowell. However, most built small-scale factories on the falls of a river for water power. A few steam-powered mills were built in towns without enough water power.

Southerners such as Hinton Rowan Helper encouraged industrial growth in the South.

"We should . . . keep pace with the progress of the age. We must expand our energies, and acquire habits of enterprise and industry; we should rouse ourselves from the couch of lassitude [laziness] and inure [set] our minds to thought and our bodies to action."

— Hinton Rowan Helper, *The Impending Crisis of the South: How to Meet It*

418 CHAPTER 13

Critical Thinking: Identifying Points of View

Above Level

Dependence on Cotton Editorial

1. Ask students to imagine themselves as one of the southern leaders who worried about over-reliance on cotton. Have each student write an editorial to support his or her position.

2. Editorials should include a position statement, present at least two strong reasons to support the position, and provide evidence (such as examples or statistics) to support each reason.

3. Remind students that some of the readers of their editorials will have different points of view on the issue. Students should try to address these people's concerns and convince them to change their positions.

4. Ask for volunteers to read their editorials aloud.
   LS Verbal/Linguistic

   Alternative Assessment Handbook, Rubric 43: Writing to Persuade

A large amount of cotton was sold to textile mills in the northeastern United States.

Textile mills in Great Britain were the largest foreign buyers of southern cotton.

ANALYSIS SKILL **DRAWING CONCLUSIONS**

Why do you think cotton was so important to the South's economy?

Joseph R. Anderson followed Helper's advice. In 1848 he became the owner of the **Tredegar Iron Works** in Richmond, Virginia—one of the most productive iron works in the nation. It was the only factory to produce bridge materials, cannons, steam engines, and other products.

Industry, however, remained a small part of the southern economy. Southern industry faced stiff competition from the North and from England, both of which could produce many goods more cheaply. And as long as agricultural profits remained high, southern investors preferred to invest in land.

READING CHECK **Making Inferences** Why were there fewer industries in the South?

SUMMARY AND PREVIEW You have read about how southern farmers worked to improve farming methods. In the next section you will read about the structure of southern society.

FOCUS ON READING

What kind of Web site would you look for to learn more about the Tredegar Iron Works?

Section 1 Assessment

go.hrw.com
Online Quiz
KEYWORD: SR8 HP13

Reviewing Ideas, Terms, and People

1. **a. Describe** How did the **cotton gin** make processing cotton easier?
   b. Draw Conclusions Why had slavery been on the decline before the invention of the cotton gin? How did slavery change as a result of the cotton gin?
   c. Predict How might the rise of cotton production and slavery affect Southern society?
2. **a. Identify** What areas made up the **cotton belt**?
   b. Evaluate Do you think the South should have paid more attention to its industrial growth? Why?
3. **a. Describe** What other crops and industries were encouraged in the South?
   b. Make Inferences Why were some southern leaders worried about the South's reliance on cotton?

Critical Thinking

4. **Identifying Cause and Effect** Review your notes on the causes of the cotton boom. Then add to your graphic organizer by identifying the effects of the cotton boom on the South.

FOCUS ON WRITING

5. **Noting Life on the Cotton Farm** In your notebook, note how Whitney's gin changed life on the farm. Also note other details about cotton farming you could include in your sketch.

Section 1 Assessment Answers

1. **a.** much faster way to remove seeds from cotton fibers than by hand
   b. Crop prices had fallen and the demand for farm workers had declined; cotton gin led to an increase in the production of cotton, which created more demand for slave labor.
   c. possible answer—since slavery became more common, southern society would become a focal point in the fight against slavery
2. **a.** land stretching from Virginia to Texas
   b. possible answer—Yes, it was dangerous for the South's economy to be totally dependent on agriculture and one crop.

3. **a.** corn, rice, sweet potatoes, wheat, sugarcane, mills, iron works
   b. reliance on one crop was risky
4. Slavery—demand for slave labor, increase in slave trade; Economy—build up of wealth, dependence on cotton; Population—attracted new settlers; Trade—growth of port cities
5. possible answers—more growing and harvesting of cotton; more slave labor; trade became important part of southern economy; South reliant on one crop

Direct Teach

Connect to Economics

Reliance on Cotton Have students think about some of the problems that might occur for an economy dependent on one crop. *Bad weather, labor shortages, or plague could ruin the crop and lead to a downturn in the economy.*

go.hrw.com
Online Resources

KEYWORD: SR8 US13
ACTIVITY: Tredegar Iron Works Report

Review & Assess

Close

Have students describe the South's economy before and after the development of the cotton gin.

Review

Online Quiz, Section 1

Assess

SE Section 1 Assessment

PASS: Section 1 Quiz

Alternative Assessment Handbook

Reteach/Classroom Intervention

Interactive Reader and Study Guide, Section 1

Interactive Skills Tutor CD-ROM

Answers

Drawing Conclusions *because cotton was highly profitable and was in high demand*

Focus on Reading *Internet search engines; encyclopedia sites; Richmond, Virginia historical society sites*

Reading Check *People thought cash crops were a better investment than industry.*

419

Bellringer

If YOU were there . . . Use the **Daily Bellringer Transparency** to help students answer the question.

🖨 Daily Bellringer Transparency, Section 2

| The South | Daily Bellringer |
| | Section 2 |

Review Section 1

Read the statements below and determine who or what is "speaking."

1. "In 1793 I invented a machine that pulls cotton seeds away from the plant's fibers. Who am I?"
2. "I was the owner of the Tredegar Iron Works in Richmond, Virginia. Who am I?"
3. "We were farmers who held more than 20 slaves. Who are we?"
4. "I was the South's primary food crop. What am I?"

Preview Section 2

If YOU were there . . .
Your family owns a small farm in Georgia in the 1840s. Sometimes you work in the fields, but more often you tend the vegetable garden and peach orchard. Since you have no close neighbors, you look forward to Sundays. Going to church gives you a chance to socialize with other young people. Sometimes you wonder what it would be like to live in a city like Savannah.

How would life be different if you left the farm for the city?

Consider POSITIVE differences:
• You would be introduced to different cultures.
• There would be opportunities to partake in cultural events.
• Employment options would be greater and more varied.

Consider NEGATIVE differences:
• You could become confused about what you believe.
• There would be greater opportunity to stray from your ideals.
• Living conditions could be cramped and unpleasant.

Review Answers: 1. Eli Whitney; 2. Joseph R. Anderson; 3. planters; 4. corn

Copyright © by Holt, Rinehart and Winston. All rights reserved.

Building Vocabulary

Preteach or review the following terms:

descendant a person related to an individual in the past (p. 423)

discrimination unfair treatment of a person or group (p. 423)

🖹 **CRF:** Vocabulary Builder Activity, Section 2

Taking Notes

Have students copy the graphic organizer onto their own paper and then use it to take notes on the section. This activity will prepare students for the Section Assessment, in which they will complete a graphic organizer that builds on the information using a critical thinking skill.

What You Will Learn...

Main Ideas

1. Southern society and culture consisted of four main groups.
2. Free African Americans in the South faced a great deal of discrimination.

The Big Idea

Southern society centered around agriculture.

Key Term

yeomen, *p. 422*

TAKING NOTES As you read, take notes on the different segments of southern society. Record the information you find in a graphic organizer like the one below.

Group	Life
Planters	
Yeomen	
Poor Whites	
Free African Americans	

Southern Society

If YOU were there...

Your family owns a small farm in Georgia in the 1840s. Sometimes you work in the fields, but more often you tend the vegetable garden and peach orchard. Since you have no close neighbors, you look forward to Sundays. Going to church gives you a chance to socialize with other young people. Sometimes you wonder what it would be like to live in a city like Savannah.

How would life be different if you left the farm for the city?

BUILDING BACKGROUND Although the South had some industry, agriculture was the heart of the southern economy. Cotton was king. As a result, wealthy plantation families were the most prominent social class in southern society. Small farmers, however, made up the largest part of the population.

Southern Society and Culture

Popular fiction often made it seem that all white southerners had many slaves and lived on large plantations. Many fiction writers wrote about wealthy southern families who had frequent, grand parties. The ideal image of the South included hospitality and well-treated slaves on beautiful plantations that almost ran themselves.

This romantic view was far from the reality. During the first half of the 1800s, only about one-third of white southern families had slaves. Fewer families had plantations. Despite their small numbers, these planters had a powerful influence over the South. Many served as political leaders. They led a society made up of many different kinds of people, including yeomen farmers, poor whites, slaves, and free African Americans. Each of these segments of society contributed to the economic success of the South.

Teach the Big Idea

Southern Society

1. **Teach** Ask students the questions in the Main Idea boxes to teach this section.

2. **Apply** Ask students to fold a piece of paper into four quarters. Label each quarter with one of the following social groups in free southern society: *planters, yeomen, poor whites,* and *free African Americans.* Have students use the information in this section to fill in each section of their papers. **LS Verbal/Linguistic**

3. **Review** To review the section's main ideas, have students help you complete a master copy of the chart.

4. **Practice/Homework** Have each student write a one-sentence summary for each part of the chart. Then have students combine their sentences to create a one-paragraph summary of the chart. **LS Verbal/Linguistic**

🖹 Alternative Assessment Handbook, Rubric 7: Charts

Planters

As the wealthiest members of southern society, planters also greatly influenced the economy. Some showed off their wealth by living in beautiful mansions. Many others chose to live more simply. A visitor described wealthy planter Alexander Stephens's estate as "an old wooden house" surrounded by weeds. Some planters saved all of their money to buy more land and slaves.

Male planters were primarily concerned with raising crops and supervising slave laborers. They left the running of the plantation household to their wives. The planter's wife oversaw the raising of the children and supervised the work of all slaves within the household. Slave women typically cooked, cleaned, and helped care for the planter's children. Wives also took on the important social duties of the family. For example, many southern leaders discussed political issues at the dances and dinners hosted by their wives.

Planters often arranged their children's marriages based on business interests. Lucy Breckinridge, the daughter of a wealthy Virginia planter, was married by arrangement in 1865. Three years earlier, she had described in her journal how she dreaded the very thought of marriage. "A woman's life after she is married, unless there is an immense amount of love, is nothing but suffering and hard work." How Breckinridge's life in her own arranged marriage would have turned out cannot be known. She died of typhoid fever just months after her wedding.

❶ Southern Society and Culture

Southern society and culture consisted of four main groups.

Recall About how many white southern families had slaves in the first half of the 1800s? *one-third*

Contrast How did the social status of planters and yeomen differ? *Planters had more power and wealth than yeomen.*

Evaluate Why might some wealthy planters prefer to live simply? *possible answers—did not enjoy society life; preferred to use money to buy more land or slaves*

- **CRF:** Biography Activity: Mary Boykin Chesnut
- **CRF:** Literature Activity: Plantation Life before Emancipation
- **CRF:** Primary Source Activity: Frances Anne Kemble, *Journal of a Residence on a Georgian Plantation*

History Close-up

A Southern Plantation

Antebellum (Latin for "before the war") refers to the style of plantation houses such as the one shown here. This Classical Revival style was popular in the South in the 30 years prior to the Civil War. Features include a symmetrical design, pillars, gabled roofs, wrap-around balconies, and evenly spaced windows.

A Southern Plantation

A typical plantation had fields as well as many buildings where different work was done. This picture shows some of the more important buildings that were a part of the plantation system.

Slave Cabins
Slaves lived crowded together in small cabins. Cabins are crude, wooden structures with dirt floors.

Fields

Barn

Warehouse

Smokehouse

Cotton-Ginning Shed
This sizable plantation had several large cotton gins. The vital machines were housed in a shed to protect them from the weather.

Overseer's House

Plantation House
The planter and his family lived in the plantation house. The planter's wife was in charge of running the household.

Stable

Fields

ANALYSIS SKILL **ANALYZING VISUALS**
How can you tell that the owner of this plantation was wealthy?

THE SOUTH **421**

Collaborative Learning

At Level

The Southern News

1. Organize the class into small groups. Have each group create the front page of a southern newspaper, including a masthead, headlines, articles, advertisements, and illustrations.

2. Encourage students to direct their newspapers towards a target audience of one of the four main groups in southern society in the first half of the 1800s.

3. Have each group present its front page to the class. Then discuss with students the topics and issues of importance to southern society.

LS Interpersonal, Verbal/Linguistic

Alternative Assessment Handbook, Rubrics 14: Group Activity; and 23: Newspapers

Answers

Analyzing Visuals *plantation house is huge, beautiful mansion; has large stable, two cotton gin sheds, many slave cabins*

Main Idea

❶ Southern Society and Culture

Southern society and culture consisted of four main groups.

Recall How big was the typical yeoman farm? *100 acres*

Summarize How was religion an important part of southern society? *Most white southerners shared similar religious beliefs; neighbors often visited only at church events; slaveholders used religion to defend slavery.*

Info to Know

Free African Americans in the South
Free African Americans in the South were more likely to live in cities than in rural areas. By 1860, free African Americans outnumbered slaves 10 to 1 in Baltimore and 5 to 1 in Washington. On the eve of the Civil War, New Orleans was home to 10,000 free African Americans. In the cities, the discrimination that free African Americans faced could be harsh. For example, an 1832 Baltimore law stated that free African Americans were subject to the same treatment and punishment as enslaved Africans.

Free African Americans in the South

In 1860 about 1 out of 50 African Americans in the South was free. Many worked in skilled trades, like this barber in Richmond, Virginia. In Charleston, South Carolina, a system of badges was set up to distinguish between free African Americans and slaves.

How would the work of the free African American in this picture be different from that of slaves in the South?

Yeomen and Poor Whites

Most white southerners were **yeomen**, owners of small farms. Yeomen owned few slaves or none at all. The typical farm averaged 100 acres. Yeomen took great pride in their work. In 1849 a young Georgia man wrote, "I desire above all things to be a 'Farmer.' It is the most honest, upright, and sure way of securing all the comforts of life."

Yeoman families, including women and children, typically worked long days at a variety of tasks. Some yeomen held a few slaves, but worked along side them.

The poorest of white southerners lived on land that could not grow cash crops. They survived by hunting, fishing, raising small gardens, and doing odd jobs for money.

Religion and Society

Most white southerners shared similar religious beliefs. Because of the long distances between farms, families often saw their neighbors only at church events, such as revivals or socials. Rural women often played volunteer roles in their churches. Wealthy white southerners thought that their religion justified their position in society and the institution of slavery. They argued that God created some people, like themselves, to rule others. This belief opposed many northern Christians' belief that God was against slavery.

Urban Life

Many of the largest and most important cities in the South were strung along the Atlantic coast and had begun as shipping centers. Although fewer in number, the southern cities were similar to northern cities. City governments built public water systems and provided well-maintained streets. Public education was available in some places. Wealthy residents occasionally gave large sums of money to charities, such as orphanages and public libraries. Southern urban leaders wanted their cities to appear as modern as possible.

As on plantations, slaves did much of the work in southern cities. Slaves worked as domestic servants, in mills, in shipyards, and at skilled jobs. Many business leaders held slaves or hired them from nearby plantations.

READING CHECK **Summarizing** What different groups made up southern society?

Differentiating Instruction

Below Level

Struggling Readers

1. Draw the graphic organizer for students to see. Omit the blue, italicized answers.

2. Have each student copy the graphic organizer and complete it by identifying as many details as possible that describe southern city life.

3. Have students use their organizers to make a general statement about life in the urban South. **LS** Visual/Spatial

Alternative Assessment Handbook, Rubric 13: Graphic Organizers

Life in the Urban South

Public Services	Role of Slavery
• *Water systems*	• *Manual labor*
• *Well-maintained streets*	• *Domestic servants*
• *Some public education*	• *Hired from nearby plantations*

Answers

Free African Americans in the South *has a skilled job; earns a wage*
Reading Check *wealthy planters, yeomen, poor whites, enslaved Africans, and free African Americans*

Free African Americans and Discrimination

Although the vast majority of African Americans in the South were enslaved, more than 250,000 free African Americans lived in the region by 1860. Some were descendants of slaves who were freed after the American Revolution. Others were descendants of refugees from Toussaint L'Ouverture's Haitian Revolution in the late 1790s. Still others were former slaves who had run away, been freed by their slaveholder, or earned enough money to buy their freedom.

Free African Americans lived in both rural and urban areas. Most lived in the countryside and worked as paid laborers on plantations or farms. Free African Americans in cities often worked a variety of jobs, mostly as skilled artisans. Some, like barber William Johnson of Natchez, Mississippi, became quite successful in their businesses. Some free African Americans, especially those in the cities, formed social and economic ties with one another. Churches often served as the center of their social lives.

Free African Americans faced constant discrimination from white southerners. Many governments passed laws limiting the rights of free African Americans. Most free African Americans could not vote, travel freely, or hold certain jobs. In some places, free African Americans had to have a white person represent them in any business transaction. In others, laws restricted where they were allowed to live or conduct business.

Many white southerners argued that free African Americans did not have the ability to take care of themselves, and they used this belief to justify the institution of slavery. "The status of slavery is the only one for which the African is adapted," wrote one white Mississippian. To many white southerners, the very existence of free African Americans threatened the institution of slavery.

READING CHECK Finding Main Ideas What challenges did free African Americans face in the South?

SUMMARY AND PREVIEW Southern society was led by rich planters but included groups of small farmers, slaves, and free African Americans as well. These groups each had their own cultures. In the next section you will read about life under slavery.

Section 2 Assessment

go.hrw.com
Online Quiz
KEYWORD: SR8 HP13

Reviewing Ideas, Terms, and People

1. **a. Identify** What was the largest social group in the South? How did its members make a living?
   b. Compare In what ways were southern cities similar to northern cities?
   c. Elaborate Which southern social class do you think had the most difficult life? Why?
2. **a. Describe** What jobs were available to free African Americans in the South?
   b. Analyze Why did many white southerners fear free African Americans?
   c. Elaborate Why do you think that discrimination against free African Americans was harsher in the South than in the North?

Critical Thinking

3. **Comparing and Contrasting** Review your notes on the different kinds of people who lived in the South. Then use a graphic organizer like the one below to identify the similarities and differences of the lives of planters, yeomen, and free African Americans.

Similarities
Planters | Free African Americans | Yeomen

FOCUS ON WRITING

4. **Describing the Life of Cotton Farmers** In your notebook, describe the different roles played by male planters and their wives. What challenges would female planters have faced? When would the planters have had a chance to socialize?

THE SOUTH **423**

Section 2 Assessment Answers

1. **a.** yeomen; owned and operated small farms
   b. both provided public services, such as water systems, streets, education
   c. possible answer—enslaved Africans; no rights and long days of hard, physical labor
2. **a.** (cities) skilled artisans or craftspeople, (rural) plantation or farm workers
   b. feared that they would start rebellions and viewed them as a threat to slavery
   c. Some southerners feared the influence free African Americans might have on slaves.

3. Planters—large plantations, wealthy, more than 20 slaves, influential; Yeomen—small farms, few or no slaves, worked long days; Free African Americans—paid laborers, artisans; Similarities—free, agriculture important

4. Planters supervised growing of crops; wives ran plantation household. Answers will vary, but female planters might have faced challenges such as social pressure and a lack of legal rights. Planters socialized at dances and dinners organized by wives.

Direct Teach

Main Idea

2 Free African Americans and Discrimination

Free African Americans in the South faced a great deal of discrimination.

Recall What were the main types of jobs that free African Americans held in the South? *worked as paid laborers on plantations or farms, worked as skilled artisans in cities*

Summarize How had free African Americans often gained their freedom? *ancestors were freed after American Revolution, were descendants of refugees from the Haitian Revolution, bought their freedom*

Review & Assess

Close

Summarize the five main groups that made up southern society and describe the role of each group in the South's agricultural economy.

Review

Online Quiz, Section 2

Assess

SE Section 2 Assessment
PASS: Section 2 Quiz
Alternative Assessment Handbook

Reteach/Classroom Intervention

Interactive Reader and Study Guide, Section 2
Interactive Skills Tutor CD-ROM

Answers

Reading Check *discrimination and harsh laws that limited where they could live, what work they could do, and with whom they could meet*

423

The Slave System

Preteach

Bellringer

If YOU were there . . . Use the **Daily Bellringer Transparency** to help students answer the question.

📠 Daily Bellringer Transparency, Section 3

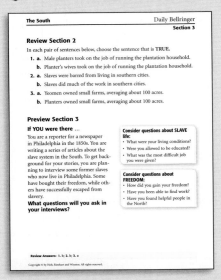

Academic Vocabulary

Review with students the high-use academic term in this section.

aspect part (p. 426)

📝 **CRF:** Vocabulary Builder, Section 3

Taking Notes

Have students copy the graphic organizer onto their own paper and then use it to take notes on the section. This activity will prepare students for the Section Assessment, in which they will complete a graphic organizer that builds on the information using a critical thinking skill.

Main Ideas

1. Slaves worked at a variety of jobs on plantations.
2. Life under slavery was difficult and dehumanizing.
3. Slave culture centered around family, community, and religion.
4. Slave uprisings led to stricter slave codes in many states.

The Big Idea

The slave system in the South produced harsh living conditions and occasional rebellions.

Key Terms and People

folktales, *p. 427*
spirituals, *p. 427*
Nat Turner's Rebellion, *p. 428*
Nat Turner, *p. 428*

TAKING NOTES As you read, take notes on the slavery system in a graphic organizer like the one shown below.

	Life as an Enslaved Person
Work	
Life	
Culture	

If YOU were there...

You are a reporter for a newspaper in Philadelphia in the 1850s. You are writing a series of articles about the slave system in the South. To get background for your stories, you are planning to interview some former slaves who now live in Philadelphia. Some have bought their freedom, while others have successfully escaped from slavery.

What questions will you ask in your interviews?

> **BUILDING BACKGROUND** While most white southern families were not slaveholders, the southern economy depended on the work of slaves. This was true not only on large plantations but also on smaller farms and in the cities. Few chances existed for enslaved African Americans to escape their hard lives.

Slaves and Work

Most enslaved African Americans lived in rural areas where they worked on farms and plantations. Enslaved people on small farms usually did a variety of jobs. On large plantations, most slaves were assigned to specific jobs, and most worked in the fields. Most slaveholders demanded that slaves work as much as possible. Supervisors known as drivers, who were sometimes slaves themselves, made sure that slaves followed orders and carried out punishments.

Working in the Field

Most plantation owners used the gang-labor system. In this system, all field hands worked on the same task at the same time. They usually worked from sunup to sundown. Former slave Harry McMillan had worked on a plantation in South Carolina. He recalled that the field hands usually did not even get a break to eat lunch. "You had to get your victuals [food] standing at your hoe," he remembered.

Men, women, and even children older than about 10 usually did the same tasks. Sickness and poor weather rarely stopped the work. "The times I hated most was picking cotton when the frost was on the bolls [seed pods]," recalled former Louisiana slave Mary Reynolds. "My hands git sore and crack open and bleed."

Teach the Big Idea

The Slave System

1. **Teach** Ask students the questions in the Main Idea boxes to teach this section.

2. **Apply** Write the Big Idea for students to see. Below it, write the following headings from the section: *Slaves and Work, Life Under Slavery, Slave Culture,* and *Slave Uprisings.*

3. **Review** As you review the section, have volunteers share important points from the text that support the Big Idea. Write the information under the appropriate headings.

4. **Practice/Homework** Ask students to imagine that they are northerners visiting the South. Have each student write a letter home describing his or her observations about the slave system. **LS Verbal/Linguistic, Visual/Spatial**

📋 Alternative Assessment Handbook, Rubrics 7: Charts; and 25: Personal Letters

Working in the Planter's Home

Some slaves worked as butlers, cooks, or nurses in the planter's home. These slaves often had better food, clothing, and shelter than field hands did, but they often worked longer hours. They had to serve the planter's family 24 hours a day.

Working at Skilled Jobs

On larger plantations, some enslaved African Americans worked at skilled jobs, such as blacksmithing or carpentry. Sometimes planters let these slaves sell their services to other people. Often planters collected a portion of what was earned but allowed slaves to keep the rest. In this way, some skilled slaves earned enough money to buy their freedom from their slaveholders. For example, William Ellison earned his freedom in South Carolina by working for wages as a cotton gin maker. For years, he worked late at night and on Sundays. He bought his freedom with the money he earned. Eventually, he was also able to buy the freedom of his wife and daughter.

READING CHECK **Summarizing** What were some types of work done by enslaved people on plantations?

Life Under Slavery

Generally, slaveholders viewed slaves as property, not as people. Slaveholders bought and sold slaves to make a profit. The most common method of sale was at an auction. The auction itself determined whether families would be kept together or separated. Sometimes a buyer wanted a slave to fill a specific job, such as heavy laborer, carpenter, or blacksmith. The buyer might be willing to pay for the slave who could do the work, but not for that slave's family. Families would then be separated with little hope of ever getting back together.

Slave traders sometimes even kidnapped free African Americans and then sold them into slavery. For example, Solomon Northup,

a free African American, was kidnapped in Washington, D.C. He spent 12 years as a slave until he finally proved his identity and gained his release.

Living Conditions

Enslaved people often endured poor living conditions. Planters housed them in dirt-floor cabins with few furnishings and often leaky roofs. The clothing given to them was usually simple and made of cheap, coarse fabric. Some slaves tried to brighten up their

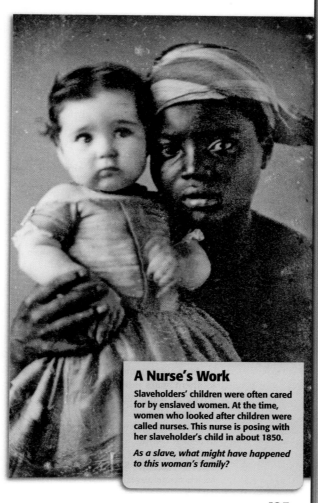

A Nurse's Work

Slaveholders' children were often cared for by enslaved women. At the time, women who looked after children were called nurses. This nurse is posing with her slaveholder's child in about 1850.

As a slave, what might have happened to this woman's family?

THE SOUTH **425**

425

❷ Life Under Slavery

Life under slavery was difficult and dehumanizing.

Recall How did planters encourage obedience? *more food or better living conditions; harsh punishments*

Draw Conclusions What effects do you think states' strict slave codes had on enslaved Africans' lives? *possible answer—kept slaves isolated, illiterate, and powerless*

Connect to Science

Health of Slaves Poor diet, exhaustion, unsanitary living conditions, and exposure to the outdoor elements made slaves vulnerable to many health problems and diseases, including blindness, rickets, scurvy, leprosy, tuberculosis, and pneumonia. Outbreaks of cholera and yellow fever frequently occurred as well. Poor diet and health contributed to a low life expectancy for enslaved Africans. For example, in Louisiana in 1850, an enslaved man could expect to live only 29 years, an enslaved woman only 34 years.

clothing by sewing on designs from discarded scraps of material. In this way, they expressed their individuality and personalized the clothing assigned to them by the planters.

Likewise, many slaves did what they could to improve their small food rations. Some planters allowed slaves to keep their own gardens for vegetables, and chickens for eggs. Other slaves were able to add a little variety to their diet by fishing or picking wild berries.

Punishment and Slave Codes

Some planters offered more food or better living conditions to encourage slaves' obedience. However, most slaveholders used punishment instead. Some would punish one slave in front of others as a warning to them all. Harry McMillan recalled some of the punishments he had witnessed.

> "The punishments were whipping, putting you in the stocks [wooden frames to lock people in] and making you wear irons and a chain at work. Then they had a collar to put round your neck with two horns, like cows' horns, so that you could not lie down ... Sometimes they dug a hole like a well with a door on top. This they called a dungeon keeping you in it two or three weeks or a month, or sometimes till you died in there."

—Harry McMillan, quoted in *Major Problems in the History of the American South, Volume I*, edited by Paul D. Escott and David R. Goldfield

ACADEMIC VOCABULARY
aspect part

To further control slaves' actions, many states passed strict laws called slave codes. Some laws prohibited slaves from traveling far from their homes. Literacy laws in most southern states prohibited the education of slaves. Alabama, Virginia, and Georgia had laws that allowed the fining and whipping of anyone caught teaching enslaved people to read and write.

READING CHECK **Summarizing** How did slaveholders control slaves?

426 CHAPTER 13

Typical Daily schedule:

3:00 a.m.	*Out of bed, tend animals*
6:00 a.m.	*Prayers*
7:00 a.m.	*Start work*
12:00 p.m.	*Lunch*
1:00 p.m.	*Return to work*
7:00 p.m.	*Dinner*
8:00 p.m.	*Return to work*
11:00 p.m.	*Lights out*

Slave Culture

Many enslaved Africans found comfort in their community and culture. They made time for social activity, even after exhausting workdays, in order to relieve the hardship of their lives.

Family and Community

Family was the most important **aspect** of slave communities, and slaves feared separation more than they feared punishment. Josiah Henson never forgot the day that he and his family were auctioned. His mother begged the slaveholder who bought her to buy Josiah, too. The slaveholder refused, and Henson's entire family was separated. "I must have been then between five or six years old," he recalled years later. "I seem to see and hear my poor weeping mother now."

Critical Thinking: Analyzing Primary Sources

Slavery: An Oral History

Research Required

Background: Explain to students that during the 1930s, more than 2,300 first-person narratives of former slaves were recorded and collected in *Born in Slavery: Slave Narratives from the Federal Writers' Project, 1936–1938*. This seventeen-volume collection is available online through the Library of Congress.

1. Ask students to conduct research on the oral histories of former slaves recorded in the slave narratives from the Federal Writers' Project.

2. Ask each student to identify one primary source that he or she finds particularly descriptive or moving in its portrayal of the slavery experience.

3. Have students take turns reading aloud their selections and invite them to share their responses. **LS Verbal/Linguistic**

📖 Alternative Assessment Handbook, Rubric 30: Research

Answers

Reading Check *harsh punishments and strict slave codes*

426

The lives of slaves revolved around the work that was required of them. For many, this meant doing the backbreaking work of harvesting and loading tons of cotton. Most slaves found hope and a short escape from their daily misery in Sunday church services. Others sought to escape permanently and ran away, hoping to reach the freedom of the North. A failed escape attempt, however, could result in a cruel whipping—or worse.

What different aspects of slavery are shown in these pictures?

Hauling the Whole Week's Pickings by William Henry Brown, The Historic New Orleans Collection

Enslaved parents kept their heritage alive by passing down family histories as well as African customs and traditions. They also told **folktales**, or stories with a moral, to teach lessons about how to survive under slavery. Folktales often included a clever animal character called a trickster. The trickster—which often represented slaves—defeated a stronger animal by outwitting it. Folktales reassured slaves that they could survive by outsmarting more powerful slaveholders.

Religion

Religion also played an important part in slave culture. By the early 1800s many slaves were Christians. They came to see themselves, like the slaves in the Old Testament, as God's chosen people, much like the Hebrew slaves in ancient Egypt who had faith that they would someday live in freedom.

Some slaves sang **spirituals**, emotional Christian songs that blended African and European music, to express their religious beliefs. For example, "The Heavenly Road" reflected slaves' belief in their equality in the eyes of God.

" Come, my brother, if you never did pray,
I hope you pray tonight;
For I really believe I am a child of God
As I walk on the heavenly road. "

—Anonymous, quoted in *Afro-American Religious History*, edited by Milton C. Sernett

Slaves blended aspects of traditional African religions with those of Christianity. They worshipped in secret, out of sight of slaveholders. Some historians have called slave religion the invisible institution.

THE IMPACT TODAY
The musical influence of these inspirational slave songs can be heard today in gospel music.

THE SOUTH **427**

427

Main Idea

❹ Slave Uprisings

Slave uprisings led to stricter slave codes in many states.

Identify What was the most violent U.S. slave revolt? When did it occur? *Nat Turner's Rebellion; August 1831*

Elaborate How do you think slaves responded to stronger slave codes? *possible answer—increased desire to run away or revolt*

📋 **CRF:** Biography Activities: Nat Turner; Denmark Vesey

📋 **CRF:** Primary Source Activity: The Denmark Vesey Conspiracy

📦 Map Transparency: Nat Turner's Rebellion

Answers

Analyzing Visuals 1. *Southampton County, Virginia;* **2.** *about 71 days*

Reading Check *helped them believe that one day they would be free; helped them endure slavery; helped them see themselves as equal*

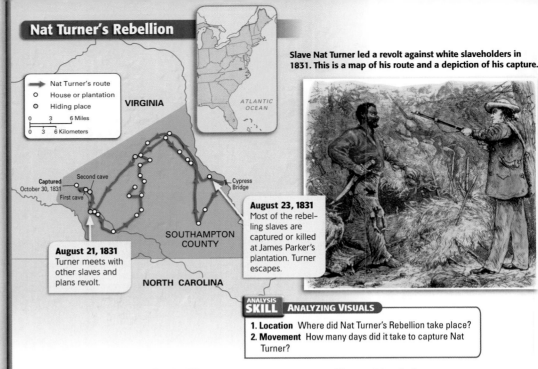

Nat Turner's Rebellion

→ Nat Turner's route
○ House or plantation
◉ Hiding place

VIRGINIA

0   3   6 Miles
0   3   6 Kilometers

ATLANTIC OCEAN

Captured October 30, 1831
First cave
Second cave

Cypress Bridge

SOUTHAMPTON COUNTY

August 21, 1831 Turner meets with other slaves and plans revolt.

NORTH CAROLINA

August 23, 1831 Most of the rebelling slaves are captured or killed at James Parker's plantation. Turner escapes.

Slave Nat Turner led a revolt against white slaveholders in 1831. This is a map of his route and a depiction of his capture.

ANALYSIS SKILL **ANALYZING VISUALS**

1. **Location** Where did Nat Turner's Rebellion take place?
2. **Movement** How many days did it take to capture Nat Turner?

Seeds of Rebellion

Maintaining their own religious beliefs and practices was only one way in which enslaved people resisted slaveholders' attempts to control them completely. In small ways, slaves rebelled against the system daily. Sometimes they worked slower to protest long hours in the fields. Other times they ran away for a few days to avoid an angry slaveholder. Some slaves tried to escape permanently, but most left only for short periods, often to go and visit relatives.

Gaining freedom by escaping to the North was hard. If discovered, slaves were captured and sent back to their slaveholders, where they faced certain punishment or death. However, thousands of enslaved people succeeded in escaping.

READING CHECK **Summarizing** How did slaves' religious beliefs affect their attitudes toward slavery?

428 CHAPTER 13

Slave Uprisings

Although violent slave revolts were relatively rare, white southerners lived in fear of them. Two planned rebellions were stopped before they began. Gabriel Prosser planned a rebellion near Richmond, Virginia, in 1800. Denmark Vesey planned one in Charleston, South Carolina, in 1822. Authorities executed most of those involved in planning these rebellions. Though Vesey was executed as the leader of the Charleston conspiracy, several accounts written after his death by antislavery writers claimed he was a hero.

The most violent slave revolt in the United States occurred in 1831 and is known as **Nat Turner's Rebellion.** **Nat Turner**, a slave from Southampton County, Virginia, believed that God had told him to end slavery. On an August night in 1831, Turner led a group of slaves in a plan to kill all of the slaveholders and their families in the county. First, they

Differentiating Instruction

English-Language Learners Below Level

1. Copy the graphic organizer for students to see. Omit the blue, italicized answers.

2. Have each student copy the graphic organizer and complete it by listing the ways in which enslaved Africans challenged the slavery system.

3. Review the answers then lead a discussion about why these tactics failed to end the system of slavery. ⓛ **Visual/Spatial**

working slower

Challenging the Slavery System

running away

violent revolts

Advanced Learners/ Gifted and Talented Above Level

Nat Turner Dialogue Have students write an imagined dialogue between Nat Turner and a fellow enslaved African. In the dialogue, Turner should persuade his fellow worker to join his rebellion. ⓛ **Verbal/Linguistic**

📋 Alternative Assessment Handbook, Rubric 43: Writing to Persuade attacked the family that held Turner as a slave. Soon they had killed about 60 white people in the community.

More than 100 innocent slaves who were not part of Turner's group were killed in an attempt to stop the rebellion. Turner himself led authorities on a chase around the countryside for six weeks. He hid in caves and in the woods before he was caught and brought to trial. Before his trial, Turner made a confession. He expressed his belief that the revolt was justified and worth his death: "I am willing to suffer the fate that awaits me." He was executed on November 11, 1831. After the rebellion, many states strengthened their slave codes. The new codes placed stricter control on the slave population. Despite the resistance of enslaved people, slavery continued to spread.

READING CHECK Finding Main Ideas
What was Nat Turner's Rebellion, and what happened as a result?

SUMMARY AND PREVIEW Several groups of African Americans attempted to end slavery by rebellion. All of the attempts failed. In the next chapter you will read about efforts to reform American society.

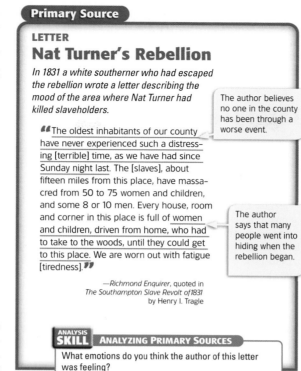

Primary Source

LETTER
Nat Turner's Rebellion

In 1831 a white southerner who had escaped the rebellion wrote a letter describing the mood of the area where Nat Turner had killed slaveholders.

The author believes no one in the county has been through a worse event.

"The oldest inhabitants of our county have never experienced such a distressing [terrible] time, as we have had since Sunday night last. The [slaves], about fifteen miles from this place, have massacred from 50 to 75 women and children, and some 8 or 10 men. Every house, room and corner in this place is full of women and children, driven from home, who had to take to the woods, until they could get to this place. We are worn out with fatigue [tiredness]."

The author says that many people went into hiding when the rebellion began.

—*Richmond Enquirer*, quoted in
The Southampton Slave Revolt of 1831
by Henry I. Tragle

ANALYSIS SKILL **ANALYZING PRIMARY SOURCES**

What emotions do you think the author of this letter was feeling?

Section 3 Assessment

go.hrw.com
Online Quiz
KEYWORD: SR8 HP13

Reviewing Ideas, Terms, and People

1. **a. Identify** What different types of work were done by slaves on plantations?
   b. Elaborate Do you think that skilled slaves had advantages over other slaves? Why or why not?
2. **a. Describe** What were living conditions like for most slaves?
   b. Summarize In what different ways did slaveholders encourage obedience from their slaves?
3. **a. Recall** What was the purpose of **folktales**?
   b. Explain How did slaves try to maintain a sense of community?
4. **a. Describe** What was the outcome of **Nat Turner's Rebellion**?
   b. Elaborate What do you think were some reasons why slaves rebelled?

Critical Thinking

5. **Evaluating** Review your notes on the slavery system. Then use a graphic organizer like the one shown below to identify the two most important reasons enslaved people challenged the system as well as how they did so.

Reasons for Challenging Slavery	→	Ways of Challenging Slavery

FOCUS ON WRITING

6. **Describing the Life of Slaves** Add notes about the life of slaves to your notebook. What would it have been like to be a slave? How would it have felt to have been separated from your family?

THE SOUTH **429**

Section 3 Assessment Answers

1. **a.** agricultural, domestic, and skilled
   b. possible answer—yes, skilled work possibly more interesting, could have chance to buy freedom

2. **a.** severe work schedules and working conditions; harsh punishments; poor clothing, food, and shelter
   b. more food or improved working conditions, punishment, slave codes

3. **a.** to teach how to survive under slavery
   b. through religion and folktales

4. **a.** About 60 white people and more than 100 innocent slaves killed; Turner executed; many states strengthened slave codes
   b. hardship, injustice, lack of freedom

5. Reasons—treated as property, punishment, slave codes; Ways—work slower, try to escape, rebellion

6. possible answers: life as a slave—hard work, strict punishment, discrimination, religious faith and folktales help to cope; separated from family—anger and sadness, community becomes like family

Social Studies Skills

Interpreting Graphs

Activity Graphs in the Media

Materials: copies of various graphs from magazines and newspapers

Before class, find at least one example of a bar graph, a line graph, and a circle graph in magazines or newspapers. Display each graph in turn for the class to see. Have students identify each type of graph. Then ask students to describe the information shown in the graph legend. Have students identify what each color in the graph represents. Next, ask students to identify the labels in the graph and use them to explain what information the graph is showing. To test students' understanding, ask one to two questions about each graph that require students to interpret the information in the graph and to identify relationships or trends shown.

LS **Visual/Spatial**

✎ Alternative Assessment Handbook, Rubric 7: Charts

💿 Interactive Skills Tutor CD-ROM, Lesson 6: Interpret Maps, Graphs, Charts, Visuals, and Political Cartoons

---

Social Studies Skills

| Analysis | Critical Thinking | Civic Participation | Study |

Interpreting Graphs

Define the Skill

Graphs are drawings that classify and display data in a clear, visual format. There are three basic types of graphs. *Line graphs* and *bar graphs* plot changes in quantities over time. Bar graphs are also used to compare quantities within a category at a particular time. *Circle graphs*, also called *pie graphs*, have a similar use. The circle represents the whole of something, and the slices show what proportion of the whole is made by each part.

Being able to interpret graphs accurately lets you see and understand relationships more easily than in tables or in written explanations. This is especially true if the information is detailed or the relationships are complicated.

Learn the Skill

The following guidelines will help you interpret data that is presented as a graph.

❶ Read the title to identify the subject and purpose of the graph. Note the kind of graph, remembering what each type is designed to indicate. Also note how the graph's subject relates to any printed material that accompanies it

❷ Study the graph's parts. Place close attention to the labels that define each axis. Note the units of measure. Identify the categories used. If there are different colors on bars or lines in the graph, determine what those differences mean.

❸ Analyze the data in the graph. Note any increases or decreases in quantities. Look for trends, changes, and other relationships in the data.

❹ Apply the information in the graph. Use the results of your analysis to draw conclusions. Ask yourself what generalizations can be made about the trends, changes, or relationships shown in the graph.

Practice the Skill

The graph below is a double-line graph. It shows both changes and relationships over time. This type of graph allows you to see how changes in one thing compare with changes in something else. Apply the guidelines to interpret the graph and answer the questions that follow.

1. What is shown on each axis of this graph? What are the units of measure on each axis?

2. What do each of the lines represent?

3. What was the total population of the South in 1810? in 1850? By how much did the African American population grow during that period?

4. Was the white population or the black population growing faster? Explain how you know.

Social Studies Skills Activity: Interpreting Graphs | At Level |

Graph Quiz

1. Have students examine the graph "U.S. Cotton Production, 1800–1860" on p. 416. Have each student create a three-question quiz about the graph. Assign students the type of quiz to create, such as multiple choice, short answer, or true-false.

2. Have each student create a separate answer key for his or her quiz.

3. Then have students exchange quizzes with partners. Students should answer the quizzes

they receive and return them to their authors for grading.

4. Then have each student write a few sentences summarizing the information shown in the graph. Ask for volunteers to read their summaries to the class. **LS** **Interpersonal, Verbal/Linguistic**

✎ Alternative Assessment Handbook, Rubrics 7: Charts; and 37: Writing Assignments

---

Answers

Practice the Skill **1.** *vertical axis—Population (in millions), in units of one million; horizontal axis—year, in ten-year increments;* **2.** *blue—African American population in the South, 1810–1850; green—total population in the South, 1810–1850;* **3.** *1810—about 3.25 million; 1850—about 8.9 million; almost 2 million;* **4.** *white population, calculated by subtracting growth of African American population from growth of total population*

Visual Summary

Use the visual summary below to help you review the main ideas of the chapter.

QUICK FACTS

Southern Society Planters were at the top of southern society.

Cotton Economy In addition to cotton, southern farmers grew other cash crops and staple crops.

Slavery The strength of the southern economy depended on slave labor.

Reviewing Vocabulary, Terms, and People

Match the definition on the left with the correct term on the right.

1. A region of cotton-producing areas that stretched from South Carolina to Texas
2. Emotional songs that mixed African and European music and expressed religious beliefs
3. Owners of small farms who made up the largest social class in the South
4. Crop brokers who often managed the cotton trade in the South
5. Wealthy farmers and plantation owners

a. cotton belt

b. factors

c. planters

d. spirituals

e. yeomen

Comprehension and Critical Thinking

SECTION 1 *(Pages 414–419)*

6. a. **Describe** How did the cotton gin lead to a cotton boom in the South?

   b. **Analyze** What were the positive and negative results of the cotton boom?

   c. **Evaluate** Do you think that the South suffered as a result of its reliance on cotton? Why or why not?

SECTION 2 *(Pages 420–423)*

7. a. **Describe** What three groups made up white southern society?

   b. **Compare and Contrast** In what ways were the lives of free African Americans and white southerners similar and different?

   c. **Predict** What might have been the attitude of yeomen and poor white southerners toward slavery? Why?

THE SOUTH **431**

Answers

Visual Summary

Review and Inquiry Ask students how the images in the Visual Summary relate to the chapter content. Have students describe what important ideas in the chapter are not part of the visual.

🖳 Quick Facts Transparency: The South Visual Summary

Reviewing Vocabulary, Terms, and People

1. a
2. d
3. e
4. b
5. c

Comprehension and Critical Thinking

6. a. made cotton easier to process, more cotton was planted

   b. positive—created wealth, boosted southern economy; negative—increased demand for slaves, led to an economy that was overly dependent on cotton

   c. possible answer—yes, had nothing else to depend upon during times when cotton prices fell

---

Review and Assessment Resources

Review and Reinforce

SE Chapter Review

🖳 CRF: Chapter Review Activity

🖳 Quick Facts Transparency: The South Visual Summary

🔊 Spanish Chapter Summaries Audio CD Program

Online Chapter Summary in Six Languages

OSP Holt PuzzlePro; GameTool for ExamView

💿 Quiz Game CD-ROM

Assess

SE Standardized Test Practice

🖳 PASS: Chapter Test, Forms A and B

🖳 Alternative Assessment Handbook

OSP ExamView Test Generator, Chapter Test

💿 Differentiated Instruction Modified Worksheets and Tests CD-ROM: Chapter Test

Holt Online Assessment Program (in the Premier Online Edition)

Reteach/Intervene

🖳 Interactive Reader and Study Guide

🖳 Differentiated Instruction Teacher Management System: Lesson Plans for Differentiated Instruction

💿 Differentiated Instruction Modified Worksheets and Tests CD-ROM

💿 Interactive Skills Tutor CD-ROM

go.hrw.com

Online Resources

Chapter Resources:
KEYWORD: SR8 US13

7. a. planters, yeomen, and poor white southerners

b. similar—both had a degree of freedom; different—African Americans suffered harsh discrimination and legal restrictions.

c. possible answers—might have felt no connection to slavery since they generally did not own slaves; might have liked it because the slaves did most of the difficult physical labor and menial tasks

8. a. work slower, run away, revolts

b. By passing down their family heritage, telling stories, and holding onto their religious beliefs, slaves could find meaning in their lives despite the arduous conditions under which they lived. Religion helped slaves hope for freedom, even if it meant waiting for the next life.

c. possible answers—greater control of slaves; more widespread encouragement of slavery; harsher life for enslaved Africans

Reading Skills

9. b

Using the Internet

10. Go to the HRW Web site and enter the keyword shown to access a rubric for this activity.

> KEYWORD: SR8 TEACHER

Reviewing Themes

11. Planters grew wealthy, some yeomen were able to own their own land, slaves worked even harder under harsh conditions.

12. The southern economy grew, wealth built up among wealthy white southerners, the South became a major player in the world trade of cotton, a cotton trade developed, and cotton-related industries grew.

SECTION 3 *(Pages 424–429)*

8. a. Identify What are some small ways in which slaves tried to challenge the slave system?

b. Make Inferences How did religion and family help slaves cope with their lives?

c. Predict What could be some possible results of stronger strengthening of slave codes in the South?

Reading Skills

Online Research *Use the Reading Skills taught in this chapter to answer the question below.*

9. Which of the following would be the best Web site to find information about life in the South before the Civil War?

 a. a Civil War historian's homepage

 b. a collection of autobiographies written by slaves

 c. a site with information about how to grow cotton

 d. a collection of biographies of inventors

Using the Internet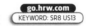

> go.hrw.com
> KEYWORD: SR8 US13

10. Activity: Writing Diary Entries Enslaved African Americans faced harsh working and living conditions. Many tried to escape the slave system. Enter the activity keyword and research the attempts by enslaved African Americans to reach the North and the people who assisted them. Imagine you were trying to help slaves travel to freedom. Write four entries into a diary. In each entry, describe your experiences. Include thumbnail maps to trace their trip.

Social Studies Skills

13. b

14. c

Reviewing Themes

11. Society and Culture How were the different social classes in the South affected by the cotton boom?

12. Economics How did the cotton boom affect the economy of the South?

Social Studies Skills

Interpreting Graphs *Use the Social Studies Skills taught in this chapter to answer the questions about the graph below.*

13. What span of time saw the largest increase in cotton production?

 a. 1800 to 1820   **c.** 1840 to 1860

 b. 1820 to 1840   **d.** after 1860

14. About what year did cotton production reach 1.2 million bales per year?

 a. 1800   **c.** 1840

 b. 1820   **d.** 1860

> **FOCUS ON WRITING**

15. Writing Your Biographical Sketch Look over your notes about life on a cotton farm. Then choose an imaginary person to write about. Think about what life would have been like for this person. What might he or she have looked like? How might he or she have spoken? What might a typical day have been like? Once you have answered these questions, write two paragraphs about a day in the life of this person.

Focus on Writing

15. Rubric Students' biographical sketches should:

- identify the imaginary person and his or her social class.
- describe what the person does and how he or she looks.
- accurately describe a typical day in the life of a person from the selected social class.
- use precise nouns and adjectives.
- provide two paragraphs.

  CRF: Focus on Writing Activity: Biographical Sketch

Standardized Test Practice

DIRECTIONS: Read each question and write the letter of the best response.

1

U.S. Cotton Production, 1795–1805

The *main* reason for the changes shown in the graph was

A the invention and use of the cotton gin.

B a decline in the number of slaves.

C the end of the international slave trade.

D a switch from food crops to cash crops.

2 All of the following helped enslaved African Americans to endure and survive slavery *except*

A religion.

B slave codes.

C spirituals.

D folktales.

3 Because some southerners feared farmers had become too reliant on cotton, they encouraged farmers to

A stop using the cotton gin.

B try growing a variety of cash crops.

C demand higher tariffs.

D introduce cotton and slavery to the West.

4 Which statement accurately describes southern society in the mid-1800s?

A Very few white southerners owned slaves.

B Few white southerners owned the land they farmed.

C Many African Americans in the South owned land.

D Most white southerners were small farmers.

5 Free African Americans in the South in the early and mid-1800s

A had the same rights and freedoms as white southerners.

B had few rights and freedoms.

C usually had escaped from slavery.

D could travel freely in their home states.

6 Examine the following passage from a northern woman's journal of her stay in Georgia and then use it to answer the question below.

> "On my return from the river I had a long and painful talk with Mr. Butler on the subject of the whipping of Teresa [a slave worn out from childbearing and field work, who asked the author to try to get her work load reduced]. Those discussions are terrible. They throw me into great distress [worry] for the slaves, whose position is completely hopeless; for myself, whose efforts on their behalf sometimes seem to me worse than useless; and for Mr. Butler, whose part in this horrible system fills me by turns with anger and pity."
>
> –Frances Anne Kemble, adapted from *Journal of a Residence on a Georgian Plantation in 1838–1839*

What might be the differences between Kemble and Butler on the question of slavery?

Intervention Resources

Reproducible

📖 Interactive Reader and Study Guide

📑 Differentiated Instruction Teacher Management System: Lesson Plans for Differentiated Instruction

Technology

💾 Quick Facts Transparency: The South Visual Summary

💿 Differentiated Instruction Modified Worksheets and Tests CD-ROM

💿 Interactive Skills Tutor CD-ROM

Tips for Test Taking

Master the Question #2 To help students answer questions testing reading comprehension, have them do the following:

• First, read the selection.

• Next, master the questions.

• Then reread the selection. The answers will be clearer with a second reading.

Remind students that tests are not meant to trick them but to test their knowledge and ability to think clearly.

Chapter 14 Planning Guide

New Movements in America

Chapter Overview	Reproducible Resources	Technology Resources
CHAPTER 14 pp. 434–471 **Overview: In this chapter, students will learn about the changing American society of the early 1800s.**	**Differentiated Instruction Teacher Management System:*** • Instructional Benchmarking Guides • Lesson Plans for Differentiated Instruction **Interactive Reader and Study Guide:** Chapter Graphic Organizer* **Chapter Resource File:*** • Focus on Writing Activity: Persuasive Letter • Social Studies Skills Activity: Accepting Social Responsibility • Chapter Review Activity	**Power Presentations with Video CD-ROM** **Differentiated Instruction Modified Worksheets and Tests CD-ROM** **Primary Source Library CD-ROM for United States History** **Student Edition on Audio CD Program** **History's Impact: United States History Video Program (VHS/DVD):** New Movements in America*
Section 1: **Immigrants and Urban Challenges** **The Big Idea:** The population of the United States grew rapidly in the early 1800s with the arrival of millions of immigrants.	**Differentiated Instruction Teacher Management System:** Section 1 Lesson Plan* **Interactive Reader and Study Guide:** Section 1 Summary* **Chapter Resource File:*** • Vocabulary Builder Activity, Section 1	**Daily Bellringer Transparency:** Section 1* **Quick Facts Transparency:** Push-Pull Factors of Immigration*
Section 2: **American Arts** **The Big Idea:** New movements in art and literature influenced many Americans in the early 1800s.	**Differentiated Instruction Teacher Management System:** Section 2 Lesson Plan* **Interactive Reader and Study Guide:** Section 2 Summary* **Chapter Resource File:*** • Vocabulary Builder Activity, Section 2 • Literature Activity: *Jack and Jill,* by Louisa May Alcott	**Daily Bellringer Transparency:** Section 2* **Internet Activity:** Who's Who of Transcendentalism
Section 3: **Reforming Society** **The Big Idea:** Reform movements in the early 1800s affected religion, education, and society.	**Differentiated Instruction Teacher Management System:** Section 3 Lesson Plan* **Interactive Reader and Study Guide:** Section 3 Summary* **Chapter Resource File:*** • Vocabulary Builder Activity, Section 3 • Biography Activities: Charles Finney; Dorothea Dix; Mary Lyon and Emma Willard	**Daily Bellringer Transparency:** Section 3* **Internet Activity:** Education Reformers Interview
Section 4: **The Movement to End Slavery** **The Big Idea:** In the mid-1800s, debate over slavery increased as abolitionists organized to challenge slavery in the United States.	**Differentiated Instruction Teacher Management System:** Section 4 Lesson Plan* **Interactive Reader and Study Guide:** Section 4 Summary* **Chapter Resource File:*** • Vocabulary Builder Activity, Section 4 • Biography Activity: Abolitionists • Primary Source Activities: David Walker; Frederick Douglass • History and Geography: The Underground Railroad	**Daily Bellringer Transparency:** Section 4* **Map Transparency:** The Underground Railroad*
Section 5: **Women's Rights** **The Big Idea:** Reformers sought to improve women's rights in American society.	**Differentiated Instruction Teacher Management System:** Section 5 Lesson Plan* **Interactive Reader and Study Guide:** Section 5 Summary* **Chapter Resource File:*** • Vocabulary Builder Activity, Section 5 • Biography Activity: Suffragettes • Primary Source Activity: Elizabeth Cady Stanton	**Daily Bellringer Transparency:** Section 5*

Key

SE Student Edition		📑 Print Resource	▶ Audio CD
TE Teacher's Edition		🖥 Transparency	💿 CD-ROM
go.hrw.com		**LS** Learning Styles	📹 Video
OSP One-Stop Planner CD-ROM		* also on One-Stop Planner CD	

Review, Assessment, Intervention

🖥 **Quick Facts Transparency:** New Movements in America Visual Summary*

▶ **Spanish Chapter Summaries Audio CD Program**

📑 **Progress Assessment Support System (PASS):** Chapter Test*

💿 **Differentiated Instruction Modified Worksheets and Tests CD-ROM:** Modified Chapter Test

💿 **One-Stop Planner CD-ROM:** ExamView Test Generator (English/Spanish)

📑 **Alternative Assessment Handbook**

📑 **PASS:** Section 1 Quiz*
Online Quiz: Section 1
📑 **Alternative Assessment Handbook**

📑 **PASS:** Section 2 Quiz*
Online Quiz: Section 2
📑 **Alternative Assessment Handbook**

📑 **PASS:** Section 3 Quiz*
Online Quiz: Section 3
📑 **Alternative Assessment Handbook**

📑 **PASS:** Section 4 Quiz*
Online Quiz: Section 4
📑 **Alternative Assessment Handbook**

📑 **PASS:** Section 5 Quiz*
Online Quiz: Section 5
📑 **Alternative Assessment Handbook**

Power Presentations with Video CD-ROM

Power Presentations with Video are visual presentations of each chapter's main ideas. Presentations can be customized by including Quick Facts charts, images from the text, and video clips.

Power Presentations with Video CD-ROM
HOLT SOCIAL STUDIES
United States History
Beginnings to 1877
Includes
• PowerPoint® Presentations
• Videos
• Quick Facts Charts
• Image Bank
HOLT, RINEHART AND WINSTON
A Harcourt Education Company

DIVISION FOR **PUBLIC EDUCATION**
AMERICAN BAR ASSOCIATION

Developed by the Division for Public Education of the American Bar Association, these materials are part of the **Democracy and Civic Education Resources.**

• **Constitution Study Guide**
• **Supreme Court Case Studies**

Holt Online Learning

Teacher Resources
KEYWORD: SR8 TEACHER

Student Resources
KEYWORD: SR8 US14

• Document-Based Questions
• Interactive Multimedia Activities

• Current Events
• Chapter-based Internet Activities
• and more!

Holt Premier
Online Student Edition
Complete online support for interactivity, assessment, and reporting
• Interactive Maps and Notebook
• Standardized Test Prep
• Homework Practice and Research Activities Online

CHAPTER 14 PLANNING GUIDE

Differentiating Instruction

ENGLISH-LANGUAGE LEARNERS & STRUGGLING READERS

TARGET RESOURCE

Live Ink® Online Reading Help

Spanish Resources

Spanish Chapter Summaries Audio CD Program

One-Stop Planner CD-ROM:
- ExamView Test Generator, Spanish
- PuzzlePro, Spanish

Additional Resources

Differentiated Instruction Teacher Management System: Lesson Plans for Differentiated Instruction

Chapter Resource File:
- Vocabulary Builder Activities
- Social Studies Skills Activity: Accepting Social Responsibility

Quick Facts Transparencies:
- Push-Pull Factors of Immigration
- New Movements in America Visual Summary

Student Edition on Audio CD Program

Online Chapter Summaries in Six Languages

Interactive Skills Tutor CD-ROM

SPECIAL NEEDS LEARNERS

TARGET RESOURCE

Differentiated Instruction Modified Worksheets and Tests CD-ROM

- Vocabulary Flash Cards
- Modified Vocabulary Builder Activities
- Modified Chapter Review Activity
- Modified Chapter Test

Additional Resources

Differentiated Instruction Teacher Management System: Lesson Plans for Differentiated Instruction

Interactive Reader and Study Guide

Social Studies Skills Activity: Accepting Social Responsibility

Student Edition on Audio CD Program

Interactive Skills Tutor CD-ROM

Live Ink® Online Reading Help

ADVANCED/GIFTED AND TALENTED STUDENTS

TARGET RESOURCE

Primary Source Library CD-ROM for United States History

The Library contains longer versions of quotations in the text, extra sources, and images. Included are point-of-view articles, journals, diaries, historical fiction, and political documents.

Additional Resources

Political Cartoons Activities for United States History: Cartoon 15: Temperance Reform

United States History Document-Based Questions Activities

Differentiated Instruction Teacher Management System: Lesson Plans for Differentiated Instruction

Chapter Resource File:
- Focus on Writing Activity: Persuasive Letter
- Literature Activity: *Jack and Jill*
- Primary Source Activity: David Walker, "An Appeal to the Colored Citizens of the World"
- Primary Source Activity: Frederick Douglass, "What the Black Man Wants"
- Primary Source Activity: Elizabeth Cady Stanton, Letter to Lucretia Mott, 1876

One-Stop Planner® CD-ROM
for Differentiated Instruction

Your differentiated instruction lesson plans are available at your fingertips. Holt's Teacher Management System links teaching support tools to pages in the Interactive Teacher's Edition.

The One-Stop Planner features:
- Interactive Teacher's Edition
- Calendar Planner and pacing guides
- Editable lesson plans
- All reproducible ancillaries in Adobe Acrobat (PDF) format
- ExamView Test Generator (English and Spanish)
- Transparency and video previews

Professional Development

- **In-service and staff development** as part of your Holt Social Studies product purchase
- **Quick Teacher Tutorial Lesson Presentation CD-ROM**
- Intensive tuition-based **Teacher Development Institute**
- **Teaching American History Online**—2 Module Professional Development Course
- **Convenient Holt Speaker Bureau**—face-to-face workshop options
- **PRAXIS™ Test Prep** interactive Web-based content refreshers*
- **24/7 Ask A Professional Development Expert** at http://www.hrw.com/prodev/

* PRAXIS is a trademark of Educational Testing Service (ETS).
This publication is not endorsed or approved by ETS.

DIFFERENTIATED INSTRUCTION PLANNING GUIDE

Chapter Big Ideas

Section 1 The population of the United States grew rapidly in the early 1800s with the arrival of millions of immigrants.

Section 2 New movements in art and literature influenced many Americans in the early 1800s.

Section 3 Reform movements in the early 1800s affected religion, education, and society.

Section 4 In the mid-1800s, debate over slavery increased as abolitionists organized to challenge slavery in the United States.

Section 5 Reformers sought to improve women's rights in American society.

Focus on Writing

The **Chapter Resource File** provides a Focus on Writing worksheet to help students organize and write their persuasive letters.

📝 **CRF:** Focus on Writing Activity: Persuasive Letter

CHAPTER 14 1815–1850

New Movements in America

FOCUS ON WRITING 📝

Persuasive Letter Your local newspaper is running a competition for students to answer the question, "What event or movement in history had the greatest impact on life in the United States?" This chapter tells about many important events and movements in the United States. As you read, take notes on each. Then decide which you believe has most affected life for people in the United States. Write a letter to the newspaper arguing your position.

UNITED STATES

1817
Thomas Gallaudet founds a school for people who have hearing impairments.

1820

WORLD

1824
British laws making trade unions illegal are repealed.

Key to Differentiating Instruction

Below Level

Basic-level activities designed for all students encountering new material

At Level

Intermediate-level activities designed for average students

Above Level

Challenging activities designed for honors and gifted and talented students

Standard English Mastery

Activities designed to improve standard English usage

Introduce the Chapter | At Level

Focus on Activism

1. Explain to students that Americans have developed a strong tradition of identifying social problems and creating groups and strategies to solve those problems.

2. Lead a guided discussion about activism in the United States today. Ask students to identify some activist organizations, such as Mothers Against Drunk Driving (MADD) or Habitat for Humanity. What methods do these groups use to effect change and promote their cause?

What other social problems or issues exist today? What actions might students take?

3. Explain that activism, or reform, became a major trend in the United States in the early and mid-1800s. As students read the chapter, ask them to compare the issues reformers addressed in the 1800s to those activists address today. **LS Verbal/Linguistic**

📝 Alternative Assessment Handbook, Rubric 11: Discussions

What You Will Learn...

In this chapter you will learn about dramatic changes in the United States in the early to mid-1800s. Ships filled with goods sailed back and forth across the Atlantic Ocean between Europe and the United States, as this painting of a busy port city shows. Many of these ships also brought people. The United States experienced a dramatic increase in immigration during this time period, particularly from Europe. Irish immigrants, forced from their homes by the potato famine, moved to the United States and built thriving communities. The photograph above shows a modern parade on Saint Patrick's Day, an Irish celebration day.

1831
William Lloyd Garrison begins publishing the abolitionist newspaper the *Liberator*.

1848
A major meeting for women's rights—the Seneca Falls Convention—is held in New York.

1850 Nathaniel Hawthorne publishes *The Scarlet Letter*.

1830

1840

1850

1829 French educator Louis Braille creates a writing system of raised dots for people who are blind.

1845 A potato famine in Ireland increases Irish immigration to the United States.

1848 Revolutionaries attempt to unify German-speaking peoples in central Europe.

NEW MOVEMENTS IN AMERICA **435**

Explore the Picture

Growing Immigration Between 1840 and 1860, more than 4 million immigrants came to the United States to begin new lives. The largest groups came from Ireland and Germany. Many of these immigrants entered the United States at New York Harbor. Beginning in 1855, immigrants passed through a central processing center on arrival. There, officials took down immigrants' names and provided information to try to help new immigrants.

Analyzing Visuals Based on the image, what might be some initial hardships that immigrants faced? *moving their belongings, finding their way around in a large, strange city*

go.hrw.com
Online Resources

Chapter Resources:
KEYWORD: SR8 US14
Teacher Resources:
KEYWORD: SR8 TEACHER

Explore the Time Line

1. Who founded a school for the hearing impaired, and when? *Thomas Gallaudet, 1817*

2. In what year was a major meeting for women's rights held, and what was it called? *1848; Seneca Falls Convention*

3. What event caused an increase in Irish immigration to the United States? *potato famine in 1845*

Info to Know

Braille Writing System The Braille system of writing for the blind consists of one to six dots arranged in 63 different combinations. Over time, additional versions of Braille have been developed for math, scientific writing, and computers. More recently, the use of Braille has begun decreasing with developments in computer-voice technology.

Reading Social Studies

by Kylene Beers

Understanding Themes

Introduce the main themes of this chapter to the class. Discuss with students several movements that affected society and culture in the United States at this time, such as abolition, immigration, and the Second Great Awakening. Ask students how some of these issues might have been affected by the religious beliefs of some Americans. Help students to understand what effects religion and society and culture had on these new movements in America.

Information and Propaganda

Focus on Reading Locate examples of each type of propaganda discussed on this page. Share those examples with the class. Then ask students to identify each type of propaganda and what information they used to determine that. Ask students to locate their own examples of propaganda by looking at magazines, Web sites, and other resources. Encourage students to share their examples with the class.

Focus on Themes The mid-1800s was a time of change in America. **Society and culture** changed for several reasons: thousands of immigrants arrived in America; women began to work hard for equal rights; and the North and South debated more and more over the slavery issue. Religious beliefs helped shape people's views toward abolition—the move to end slavery—and women's suffrage—the move to give women the right to vote. This chapter discusses all these issues.

Information and Propaganda

Focus on Reading Where do you get information about historical events and people? One source is this textbook and others like it. You can expect the authors of your textbook to do their best to present the facts objectively and fairly. But some sources of historical information may have a totally different purpose in mind. For example, ads in political campaigns may contain information, but their main purpose is to persuade people to act or think in a certain way.

Recognizing Propaganda Techniques Propaganda is created to change people's opinions or get them to act in a certain way. Learn to recognize propaganda techniques, and you will be able to separate propaganda from the facts.

"People who don't support public education are greedy monsters who don't care about children!"

→ **Name Calling** Using loaded words, words that create strong positive or negative emotions, to make someone else's ideas seem inappropriate or wrong

"People all around the country are opening free public schools. It's obviously the right thing to do."

→ **Bandwagon** Encouraging people to do something because "everyone else is doing it"

"If we provide free education for all children, everyone will be able to get jobs. Poverty and unemployment will disappear."

→ **Oversimplification** Making a complex situation seem simple, a complex problem seem easy to solve

436 CHAPTER 14

Reading and Skills Resources

Reading Support

- Interactive Reader and Study Guide
- Student Edition on Audio CD Program
- Spanish Chapter Summaries Audio CD Program

Social Studies Skills Support

- Interactive Skills Tutor CD-ROM

Vocabulary Support

- **CRF:** Vocabulary Builder Activities
- **CRF:** Chapter Review Activity
- Differentiated Instruction Modified Worksheets and Tests CD-ROM:
  - Vocabulary Flash Cards
  - Vocabulary Builder Activity
  - Chapter Review Activity

OSP Holt PuzzlePro

You Try It!

The flyer below was published in the year 1837. Read it and then answer the questions that follow.

Flyer from 1837

OUTRAGE.

Fellow Citizens,

AN ABOLITIONIST,

of the most revolting character is among you, exciting the feelings of the North against the South. A seditious Lecture is to be delivered THIS EVENING, at 7 o'clock, at the Presbyterian Church in Cannon-street. You are requested to attend and unite in putting down and silencing by peaceable means this tool of evil and fanaticism. Let the rights of the States guaranteed by the Constitution be protected.

Feb. 27, 1837. The Union forever!

After studying the flyer, answer the following questions.

1. What is the purpose of this flyer?

2. Who do you think distributed this flyer?

3. Do you think this flyer is an example of propaganda? Why or why not? If you think it is propaganda, what kind is it?

4. If you were the subject of this flyer, how would you feel? How might you respond to it?

> **As you read Chapter 14**, look carefully at all the primary sources. Do any of them include examples of propaganda?

Reading Social Studies

Key Terms and People

Have students look over the list of key terms and people. Review with students each term that relates to a social, cultural, or reform movement (*nativism, transcendentalism, temperance, common-school movement, abolition, women's rights*). Then have students preview the chapter and write a sentence about each movement and why it was important. You might wish to have students use related key terms in the same sentence. Ask for volunteers to share these sentences with the class.

Focus on Reading

See the **Focus on Reading** questions in this chapter for more practice on this reading social studies skill.

Reading Social Studies Assessment

See the **Chapter Review** at the end of this chapter for student assessment questions related to this reading skill.

Teaching Tip

Students may come across propaganda from time to time when doing research on the Internet. Ask students to carefully evaluate the Web sites they come across. Remind students of the important questions to ask to evaluate a Web site, which they learned in the previous chapter. Point out to students that occasionally they may visit a site that uses the propaganda techniques mentioned here. Ask students how propaganda Web sites might affect the validity of their research.

Answers

You Try It! 1. *possible answers—to inform supporters of slavery that an abolitionist would be delivering a lecture in their community; to encourage supporters of slavery to stop the meeting;* **2.** *possible answers—a slave holder or opponent of abolition;* **3.** *yes, because it uses name calling to make abolition seem wrong;* **4.** *Students' answers will vary, but should indicate that the flyer is trying to appeal to people's emotions.*

Immigrants and Urban Challenges

If YOU were there...

It is 1850, and you are a German immigrant standing on the deck of a steamboat, crossing Lake Erie. Other immigrants are on board, but they are strangers to you. Soon, you will arrive at your new home in Cleveland, Ohio. You've been told that other Germans have settled there. You hope to find friends and work as a baker. Right now, America seems very big and very strange.

What would you expect from your new life in America?

BUILDING BACKGROUND The revolutions in industry, transportation, and technology were not the only major changes in the United States in the mid-1800s. Millions of immigrants, mostly from Europe, swelled the population. Some settled in the rich farmland of the Midwest, while others moved to cities.

Millions of Immigrants Arrive

In the mid-1800s, large numbers of immigrants crossed the Atlantic Ocean to begin new lives in the United States. More than 4 million of them settled in the United States between 1840 and 1860, most from Europe. More than 3 million of these immigrants arrived from Ireland and Germany. Many of them were fleeing economic or political troubles in their native countries.

Fleeing the Irish Potato Famine

Most immigrants from the British Isles during that period were Irish. In the mid-1840s, potato blight, a disease that causes rot in potatoes, left many families in Ireland with little food. More than a million Irish people died of starvation and disease. Even more fled to the United States.

Most Irish immigrants were very poor. Many settled in cities in Massachusetts, New Jersey, New York, and Pennsylvania. They worked at unskilled jobs in the cities or on building canals and

Push-Pull Factors of Immigration — QUICK FACTS

Pull Factors
- Jobs
- Greater freedom and equality
- Abundant land

Push Factors
- Starvation
- Poverty
- Lack of political freedom

Starvation and poverty pushed many Irish families such as this one from their homes, while economic opportunities pulled them toward the United States.

ANALYSIS SKILL — ANALYZING VISUALS
How was freedom a push factor and a pull factor?

railroads. Irish women often worked as domestic servants for wealthy families, laboring 16 or more hours per day. In 1849 a Boston health committee reported that low wages forced most Irish immigrants to live in poor housing.

Still, many immigrants enjoyed a new feeling of equality. Patrick Dunny wrote home to his family about this situation.

"People that cuts a great dash [style] at home … think it strange [in the United States] for the humble class of people to get as much respect as themselves."
—Patrick Dunny, quoted in *Who Built America?* by Bruce Levine et al.

A Failed German Revolution

Many Germans also came to the United States during this time. In 1848 some Germans had staged a revolution against harsh rule. Some educated Germans fled to the United States to escape persecution caused by their political activities. Most German immigrants, however, were working class, and they came for economic reasons. The United States seemed to offer both greater economic opportunity and more freedom from government control. While most Irish immigrants were Catholics, German immigrant groups included Catholics, Jews, and Protestants.

German immigrants were more likely than the Irish to become farmers and live in rural areas. They moved to midwestern states where more land was available. Unlike the Irish, a high percentage of German immigrants arrived in the United States with money. Despite their funds and skills, German immigrants often were forced to take low-paying jobs. Many German immigrants worked as tailors, seamstresses, bricklayers,

THE IMPACT TODAY
Many immigrants still come to the United States today. More than 16.4 million entered the United States between 1980 and 2000.

NEW MOVEMENTS IN AMERICA **439**

① Millions of Immigrants Arrive

Millions of immigrants, mostly German and Irish, arrived in the United States despite anti-immigrant movements.

Summarize How did immigration change the American labor force in the mid-1800s? *Many immigrants went to the Midwest to farm; others filled the need for cheap labor in towns and cities, especially in the Northeast.*

Identify Cause and Effect How did anti-Catholicism contribute to the creation of the Know-Nothing Party? *Nativists formed the Know-Nothing Party in part to keep Catholics out of public office.*

② Rapid Growth of Cities

Industrialization led to the growth of cities.

Recall In which regions did U.S. cities grow the most during the mid-1800s? Why? *Northeast and mid-Atlantic states; contained three quarters of the country's manufacturing jobs*

Categorize What types of jobs did the new middle class hold? *skilled workers such as master craftspeople and business owners such as merchants, manufacturers, and professionals*

Answers

Focus on Reading *yes, presents a highly biased view of immigrants*

Reading Check (left) *felt threatened by immigrants' different cultures and worried that they might lose jobs to immigrants who would work for lower wages*

Reading Check (right) *Improvements in transportation and the rise of new jobs in industry led many people to move to urban areas.*

---

servants, clerks, cabinetmakers, bakers, and food merchants.

Anti-Immigration Movements

Industrialization and the waves of people from Europe greatly changed the American labor force. While many immigrants went to the Midwest to get farmland, other immigrants filled the need for cheap labor in towns and cities. Industrial jobs in the Northeast attracted many people.

Yet a great deal of native-born Americans feared losing their jobs to immigrants who might work for lower wages. Some felt **implicitly** threatened by the new immigrants' cultures and religions. For example, before Catholic immigrants arrived, most Americans were Protestants. Conflicts between Catholics and Protestants in Europe caused American Protestants to mistrust Catholic immigrants. Those Americans and others who opposed immigration were called **nativists**.

In the 1840s and 1850s some nativists became politically active. An 1844 election flyer gave Americans this warning.

> "Look at the . . . thieves and vagabonds [tramps] roaming our streets . . . monopolizing [taking] the business which properly belongs to our own native and true-born citizens."
> —Election flyer, quoted in *Who Built America?* by Bruce Levine et al.

In 1849 nativists founded a political organization, the **Know-Nothing Party**, that supported measures making it difficult for foreigners to become citizens or hold office. Its members wanted to keep Catholics and immigrants out of public office. They also wanted to require immigrants to live in the United States for 21 years before becoming citizens. Know-Nothing politicians had some success getting elected during the 1850s. Later, disagreements over the issue of slavery caused the party to fall apart.

READING CHECK Understanding Cause and Effect Why did the Know-Nothing Party try to limit the rights of immigrants?

ACADEMIC VOCABULARY

implicit understood though not clearly put into words

FOCUS ON READING

Look carefully at the quotation to the right from an election flyer. Does it include any examples of propaganda?

Rapid Growth of Cities

The Industrial Revolution led to the creation of many new jobs in American cities. These city jobs drew immigrants from many nations as well as migrants from rural parts of the United States. The Transportation Revolution helped connect cities and made it easier for people to move to them. As a result of these two trends, American cities grew rapidly during the mid-1800s. Cities in the northeastern and Middle Atlantic states grew the most. By the mid-1800s, three-quarters of the country's manufacturing jobs were in these areas.

The rise of industry and the growth of cities changed American life. Those who owned their own businesses or worked in skilled jobs benefited most from those changes. The families of these merchants, manufacturers, professionals, and master craftspeople made up a growing social class. This new **middle class** was a social and economic level between the wealthy and the poor. Those in this new middle class built large, dignified homes that demonstrated their place in society.

In the growing cities, people found entertainment and an enriched cultural life. Many living in these cities enjoyed visiting places such as libraries and clubs, or attending concerts or lectures. In the mid-1800s people also attended urban theaters. Favorite pastimes, such as bowling and playing cards, also provided recreation for urban residents.

Cities during this time were compact and crowded. Many people lived close enough to their jobs that they could walk to work. Wagons carried goods down streets paved with stones, making a noisy, busy scene. One observer noted that the professionals in New York City always had a "hurried walk."

READING CHECK Summarizing How did the Industrial Revolution affect life in American cities?

Collaborative Learning

Above Level

Mid-1850s Classified Newspaper

Materials: poster board, art supplies, word processing software (optional)

1. Organize students into small groups. Ask them to imagine that they work at a classified weekly in New York City in the mid-1800s.

2. Have each group create a classified-ad page that includes ads for jobs directed at immigrants, ads for farmland for sale in the Midwest, notices for meetings of immigrant aid societies, and notices for meetings of nativist groups and the Know-Nothing Party.

3. Groups can write their ads and then arrange them on poster board, or students might use computers to create their classified ad pages. Display students' work around the classroom.

LS Interpersonal, Verbal/Linguistic

Alternative Assessment Handbook, Rubrics 14: Group Activity; and 23: Newspapers

History Close-up

New York City, mid-1800s

In the mid-1800s, cities such as New York City lured thousands of people in search of jobs and a better life. Many city dwellers found life difficult in the crowded urban conditions.

Many city residents, particularly immigrants, lived in crowded, unsafe conditions.

Many immigrants and other poor city dwellers worked long hours in factories at dangerous jobs.

Women—and frequently children—labored all day in small rooms making clothing to be sold to the wealthy.

City streets were crowded with people buying, selling, and transporting goods.

The first floor of the building served many purposes—living quarters, kitchen, and work space. Here, garments were finished for sale.

ANALYSIS SKILL **ANALYZING VISUALS**

How is this scene similar to one you might see in a large American city today? How is it different?

NEW MOVEMENTS IN AMERICA **441**

Differentiating Instruction

Struggling Readers

1. Discuss with students the reasons for the rapid growth of U.S. cities and the problems that developed as a result of this growth.

2. Draw the graphic organizer onto the chalkboard. Omit the blue, italicized answers.

3. Have each student copy and complete the organizer. **LS** Visual/Spatial

📋 Alternative Assessment Handbook, Rubric 13: Graphic Organizers

Growth of U.S. Cities	
Reasons for Growth	**Problems of Growth**
• increased immigration from Europe	• overcrowding
• *Transportation Revolution connected cities.*	• *poor, unsafe, dirty housing conditions*
• *Industrial Revolution created new jobs.*	• *lack of public services*
• *People moved to cities seeking work.*	• *poor sanitation*
	• *diseases and epidemics*
	• *no permanent police force or firefighters*

History Close-up

New York City, mid-1800s
Have students examine the image and then ask them the following:

• What types of work are visible in the image? *dressmaking, market trade, hauling goods*

• What were dwellings like for many city residents? *crowded, limited furnishings, drab and unsanitary*

• Based on the image, what might be some problems that people experienced in cities in the mid-1800s? *possible answers—crowding, dirty streets from horses, poor housing and working conditions, disease as a result of crowding*

Activity **Step into the Picture** Ask students to imagine that they are one of the people in the image. Have them write a letter from that person's perspective to a friend who lives elsewhere describing an average day in New York City. **LS** Verbal/Linguistic, Visual/Spatial

📋 Alternative Assessment Handbook, Rubric 40: Writing to Describe

Info to Know

Nativism Turns Violent In some cases, nativism in the mid-1800s turned violent, particularly in eastern U.S. cities. For example, in 1834 a mob burned down the Ursuline Convent outside Boston, Massachusetts. In 1844 a protest by a nativist group led to a riot in Philadelphia, Pennsylvania. Similar riots and attacks on Catholic churches occurred elsewhere.

Answers

Analyzing Visuals *similar—crowded street with people going about their work, open-air marketplace where people are buying and selling goods, people living and working in close quarters, factories; different—horses and buggies, technology, clothing*

441

442

Direct Teach

Main Idea

❸ Urban Problems

American cities experienced urban problems due to rapid growth.

Recall What urban problems developed as a result of rapid growth of cities in the mid-1800s? *overcrowding, poor and unsafe housing, lack of public services, unhealthy conditions, disease and epidemics, crime, fire danger, no permanent police force or fire protection*

Make Judgments Despite urban problems, do you think immigrants preferred life in America to that in their home countries? Why? *possible answer—yes, because life in America was still better than the conditions they left behind*

Review & Assess

Close

Have students review the causes and effects of increased U.S. immigration in the mid-1800s.

Review

Online Quiz, Section 1

Assess

SE Section 1 Assessment

PASS: Section 1 Quiz

Alternative Assessment Handbook

Reteach/Classroom Intervention

Interactive Reader and Study Guide, Section 1

Interactive Skills Tutor CD-ROM

Answers

Reading Check *Cities did not have the necessary plans, public services, or regulations to deal with the rapid growth that was occurring.*

Urban Problems

American cities in the mid-1800s faced many challenges due to rapid growth. Because public and private transportation was limited, city residents had to live near their workplaces. In addition, there was a lack of safe housing. Many city dwellers, particularly immigrants, could afford to live only in **tenements**— poorly designed apartment buildings that housed large numbers of people. These structures were often dirty, overcrowded, and unsafe.

Public services were also poor. The majority of cities did not have clean water, public health regulations, or healthful ways to get rid of garbage and human waste. Under these conditions, diseases spread easily, and epidemics were common. In 1832 and 1849, for example, New York City suffered cholera epidemics that killed thousands.

City life held other dangers. As urban areas grew, they became centers of criminal activity. Most cities—including New York, Boston, and Philadelphia—had no permanent or organized force to fight crime.

Instead, they relied on volunteer night watches, which offered little protection.

Fire was another constant and serious danger in crowded cities. There was little organized fire protection. Most cities were served by volunteer fire companies. Firefighters used hand pumps and buckets to put out fires. In addition, there were not enough sanitation workers and road maintenance crews. These shortages and flaws caused health and safety problems for many city residents.

READING CHECK Analyzing Why did so many American cities have problems in the mid-1800s?

SUMMARY AND PREVIEW Immigrants expected a better life in America, but not all Americans welcomed newcomers. The rapid growth of cities caused many problems. In the next section you will read about how America developed its own style of art and literature.

Section 1 Assessment

go.hrw.com
Online Quiz
KEYWORD: SR8 HP14

Reviewing Ideas, Terms, and People

1. **a. Identify** Who were the **nativists**?
   b. Compare and Contrast In what ways were Irish and German immigrants to the United States similar and different?
   c. Predict How might the rise of anti-immigrant groups lead to problems in the United States?
2. **a. Describe** What led to the growth of cities?
   b. Analyze How did the rise of industrialization and the growth of cities change American society?
3. **a. Describe** What were **tenements**?
   b. Summarize What problems affected American cities in the mid-1800s?
   c. Evaluate What do you think was the biggest problem facing cities in the United States? Why?

Critical Thinking

4. **Identifying Cause and Effect** Review your notes on the causes of immigration and urban growth. Then add the effects of each to your graphic organizer.

   Immigration → [Effects]

   Urban Growth → [Effects]

FOCUS ON WRITING

5. **Identifying Important Events** In your notebook, create a two-column chart. In the first column, list events described in this section. In the second column, write a description of each event and a note about how it changed life in the United States.

442 CHAPTER 14

Section 1 Assessment Answers

1. **a.** Americans who opposed immigration
   b. similar—sought economic opportunity, forced to take low-paying jobs; different— reasons for coming, religions, economic status, where settled, jobs they held
   c. could lead to violence against immigrants

2. **a.** Better transportation and the Industrial Revolution led people to move to cities.
   b. A new social class, the middle class, developed; urban problems increased.

3. **a.** poorly designed apartment buildings that housed large numbers of people
   b. overcrowding, unsafe housing, lack of public services, epidemics, crime, fire danger
   c. Students should discuss one of the problems listed in the previous answer.

4. immigration—effects: rapid population and city growth, anti-immigration movements; urban growth—effects: more urban problems

5. Students should list events related to the causes and effects of increased immigration.

American Arts

If YOU were there...

You are a teacher living in Massachusetts in the 1840s. Some of your neighbors have started an experimental community. They want to live more simply than present-day society allows. They hope to have time to write and think, while still sharing the work. Some people will teach, others will raise food. You think this might be an interesting place to live.

What would you ask the leaders of the community?

BUILDING BACKGROUND Great changes were taking place in American culture. The early 1800s brought a revolution in American thought. Artists, writers, and philosophers pursued their ideals and developed truly American styles.

Transcendentalists

Some New England writers and philosophers found spiritual wisdom in **transcendentalism**, the belief that people could transcend, or rise above, material things in life. Transcendentalists also believed that people should depend on themselves and their own insights, rather than on outside authorities. Important transcendentalists included **Ralph Waldo Emerson**, **Margaret Fuller**, and **Henry David Thoreau**.

Walden Pond, where Thoreau lived for two years

What You Will Learn...

Main Ideas

1. Transcendentalists and utopian communities withdrew from American society.
2. American Romantic painters and writers made important contributions to art and literature.

The Big Idea

New movements in art and literature influenced many Americans in the early 1800s.

Key Terms and People

transcendentalism, *p. 443*
Ralph Waldo Emerson, *p. 443*
Margaret Fuller, *p. 443*
Henry David Thoreau, *p. 443*
utopian communities, *p. 444*
Nathaniel Hawthorne, *p. 444*
Edgar Allan Poe, *p. 445*
Emily Dickinson, *p. 445*
Henry Wadsworth Longfellow, *p. 445*
Walt Whitman, *p. 445*

TAKING NOTES Create a graphic organizer like the one shown below. Use it to take notes on the new movements in art and literature.

	Transcendentalism	Romanticism
What		
Who		

NEW MOVEMENTS IN AMERICA **443**

Teach the Big Idea

At Level

American Arts

1. **Teach** Ask students the questions in the Main Idea boxes to teach this section.
2. **Apply** Have students write each of the blue headings in the section on a piece of paper. Tell students to leave space below each heading. Have students read the material under each heading and create an outline for the content under that heading. **LS Verbal/Linguistic**
3. **Review** To review the section, have volunteers share with the class the information they provided in their outlines.
4. **Practice/Homework** Have each student write an imaginary interview with one of the key figures covered in the section. The interview should include at least five questions and answers. **LS Verbal/Linguistic**

   Alternative Assessment Handbook, Rubric 37: Writing Assignments

---

Asher Durand's *The First Harvest in the Wilderness*

Direct Teach

Main Idea

❶ Transcendentalists

Transcendentalists and utopian communities withdrew from American society.

Define In your own words, explain transcendentalism. *possible answer— belief that people should rise above material things, depend on themselves and their own insights, and live simply in tune with nature*

Identify Who were some key transcendentalists? *Ralph Waldo Emerson, Margaret Fuller, Henry David Thoreau*

Make Judgments Do you think utopian communities are possible? Why or why not? *possible answers— yes, if people agree to work for the good of the group; no, because inherent human weaknesses will cause all attempts to fail*

Biography

Emily Dickinson (1830–1886) Emily Dickinson did not achieve fame during her lifetime. Of the more than 1,775 poems that she wrote, only 10 were published while she was alive. Not until 1955—nearly 80 years after her death—were all of her poems collected and published.

go.hrw.com
Online Resources

KEYWORD: SR8 US14
ACTIVITY:
Who's Who of
Transcendentalism

Answers

Reading Check *because members did not work together well enough for the groups to survive*

444

Emerson was a popular writer and thinker who argued that Americans should disregard institutions and follow their own beliefs. "What I must do is all that concerns me, not what the people think," he wrote in an essay called "Self-Reliance." Fuller edited the famous transcendentalist publication *The Dial*. Thoreau advised self-reliance and simple living away from society in natural settings. He wrote his book *Walden* after living for two years at Walden Pond.

Some transcendentalists formed a community at Brook Farm, Massachusetts, in the 1840s. It was one of many experiments with **utopian communities**, groups of people who tried to form a perfect society. People in utopian communities pursued **abstract** spirituality and cooperative lifestyles. However, few communities lasted for long. In most, members did not work together well.

ACADEMIC VOCABULARY
abstract
expressing a quality or idea without reference to an actual thing

READING CHECK Drawing Inferences
Why did most utopian communities last for only a short time?

444 CHAPTER 14

American Romanticism

Ideas about the simple life and nature also inspired painters and writers in the early and mid-1800s. Some joined the Romantic movement that had begun in Europe. Romanticism involved a great interest in nature, an emphasis on individual expression, and a rejection of many established rules. These painters and writers felt that each person brings a unique view to the world. They believed in using emotion to guide their creative output. Some Romantic artists, like Thomas Cole, painted the American landscape. Their works celebrated the beauty and wonder of nature in the United States. Their images contrasted with the huge cities and corruption of nature that many Americans saw as typical of Europe.

Many female writers, like Ann Sophia Stephens, wrote historical fiction that was popular in the mid-1800s. New England writer **Nathaniel Hawthorne** wrote *The Scarlet Letter* during that period. One of the greatest classics of Romantic literature, it explored Puritan

---

Differentiating Instruction

Below Level

Struggling Readers

1. Draw the graphic organizer for students to see. Omit the blue, italicized answers.

2. Have each student copy the organizer and complete it by listing the main influences of the key people and ideas related to the American Romantic movement.
   LS Visual/Spatial

   Alternative Assessment Handbook, Rubric 13: Graphic Organizers

American Romantic Movement

↓

Ideas
simple life, nature, emotion, individualism, democracy and American history

↓

Artists and Writers
artists: Thomas Cole (Hudson River school); writers: Stephens, Hawthorne, Melville, Poe, Dickinson, Longfellow, Whitman

American Romantic authors also wrote a great deal of poetry. The poet **Edgar Allan Poe**, also a short story writer, became famous for a haunting poem called "The Raven." Other gifted American poets included **Emily Dickinson**, **Henry Wadsworth Longfellow**, and **Walt Whitman**. Most of Dickinson's short, thoughtful poems were not published until after her death. Longfellow, the best-known poet of the mid-1800s, wrote popular story-poems, like *The Song of Hiawatha*. Whitman praised American individualism and democracy in his simple, unrhymed poetry. In his poetry collection *Leaves of Grass*, he wrote, "The United States themselves are essentially the greatest poem."

READING CHECK **Summarizing** Who were some American Romantic authors, and why were they important?

life in the 1600s. Hawthorne's friend Herman Melville, a writer and former sailor, wrote novels about the sea, such as *Moby-Dick* and *Billy Budd*. Many people believe that *Moby-Dick* is one of the finest American novels ever written.

SUMMARY AND PREVIEW American Romantic artists and authors were inspired by ideas about the simple life, nature, and spirituality. In the next section you will learn about ideas that changed American society.

Section 2 Assessment

go.hrw.com
Online Quiz
KEYWORD: SR8 HP14

Reviewing Ideas, Terms, and People

1. **a. Identify** What were the main teachings of **transcendentalism**?
   b. Summarize What **utopian community** was established in the United States, and what was its goal?
   c. Elaborate Do you agree with transcendentalists that Americans put too much emphasis on institutions and traditions? Explain your answer.
2. **a. Recall** Who were some important American authors and poets at this time?
   b. Explain What ideas did artists in the Romantic movement express?
   c. Evaluate Do you think the Romantic movement was important to American culture? Explain.

Critical Thinking

3. **Comparing and Contrasting** Review your notes on new movements in art and literature. Then copy the graphic organizer below and use it to show the similarities and differences between the two movements.

Transcendentalism　Similarities　Romanticism

FOCUS ON WRITING

4. **Describing Artistic Movements** Two artistic movements are described in this section, transcendentalism and romanticism. Write these two movements in the first column of your chart. Then in the second column, write a brief description of each and explain how writings from each either described or influenced life in the United States.

NEW MOVEMENTS IN AMERICA **445**

Section 2 Assessment Answers

1. **a.** the belief that people could transcend, or rise above, material things in life
   b. Brook Farm; tried to form a perfect society
   c. possible answers—Yes, America needed to focus on the individual ruggedness and natural wilderness that made it great; no, these institutions and traditions worked.
2. **a.** Ann Sophia Stephens, Nathaniel Hawthorne, Herman Melville, Edgar Allan Poe, Emily Dickinson, Henry Wadsworth Longfellow, and Walt Whitman

   b. beauty and wonder of nature, emotion, individualism, democracy and history
   c. possible answers—Yes, the movement helped America develop an independent culture; no, the movement just copied Europe.
3. similar—focus on nature and simple life, individualism, personal insight; different—transcendentalism: philosophy; Romantics: focused more on emotion and American history
4. Students should address the ideas of each movement, described in the previous answer.

445

Literature in History

"The Midnight Ride of Paul Revere"

As You Read Before students read the poem, have them each write a few sentences describing what they think a hero is. Next, as students read the poem, have them list the ways in which Longfellow describes Revere as a hero. Then ask students to discuss how their descriptions of a hero compare to Longfellow's.

Connect to Literature

The Fireside Poets Henry Wadsworth Longfellow was among a group of Boston poets known as the Fireside Poets. In addition to Longfellow, the group included Oliver Wendell Holmes, James Russell Lowell, and John Greenleaf Whittier. They were called Fireside Poets because people often read their poems aloud at the fireside as family entertainment.

Meet the Writer

Henry Wadsworth Longfellow (1807–1882) A prolific poet as well as a translator of many languages, Longfellow was the most popular American poet of his time. For many Americans, he became the symbolic figure of the Poet: wise, graybearded, and living in a world of romance. His most popular poems include *The Song of Hiawatha* (1855) and *The Courtship of Miles Standish* (1858).

GUIDED READING

WORD HELP

belfry bell tower
muster gathering
barrack building where soldiers meet
grenadiers a soldier that throws grenades

❶ When the poem was written, there were still a few people alive who had lived during the Revolution.

❷ Longfellow uses poetic language to make Revere's story more dramatic.

❸ The sounds of the night are described to help the reader feel the excitement.

Literature of the Young Nation: Romanticism and Realism

from "The Midnight Ride of Paul Revere"
by Henry Wadsworth Longfellow (1807–1882)

About the Reading *"The Midnight Ride of Paul Revere" was published in a book called* Tales of a Wayside Inn. *The book is a collection of poems that tell well-known stories from history and mythology. By including the story of Paul Revere with other famous stories, Longfellow helped increase the importance of Paul Revere's ride.*

AS YOU READ Notice how Longfellow describes Revere as a hero.

Listen my children and you shall hear
Of the midnight ride of Paul Revere,
On the eighteenth of April, in Seventy-five;
Hardly a man is now alive
Who remembers that famous day and year. ❶

He said to his friend, "If the British march
By land or sea from the town to-night,
Hang a lantern aloft in the belfry arch
Of the North Church tower as a signal light,—
One if by land, and two if by sea;
And I on the opposite shore will be,
Ready to ride and spread the alarm
Through every . . . village and farm,
For the country folk to be up and to arm." ❷
. . . .
Meanwhile, his friend, through alley and street
Wanders and watches with eager ears,
Till in the silence around him he hears
The muster of men at the barrack door,
The sound of arms, and the tramp of feet,
And the measured tread of the grenadiers,
Marching down to their boats on the shore. ❸

Differentiating Instruction

Below Level

Special Needs Learners

Materials: blank paper, colored pens or pencils, old magazines and newspapers

1. Read "The Midnight Ride of Paul Revere" aloud to the class. Discuss the meaning of the passage with students. If necessary, review the historical background. Then help students list the key events that occur in the passage.

2. Have each student create a piece of artwork that illustrates the passage. Students might choose to create a drawing, a comic strip, or a collage.

3. Instruct students to incorporate several of the key events from the passage into their artwork. In addition, each student should write a caption describing his or her artwork.

4. Display students' artwork in the classroom.
LS Visual/Spatial

Alternative Assessment Handbook, Rubric 3: Artwork

from *Little Women*

by Louisa May Alcott (1832–1888)

About the Reading Little Women *is a novel about four sisters living in a small New England town before the Civil War. Still popular with young people today,* Little Women *describes a family much like the one Louisa May Alcott grew up in. Alcott based the main character, Jo March, on herself. Like Alcott, Jo was different from most women of her time. She was outspoken, eager for adventure, and in conflict with the role her society expected her to play.*

AS YOU READ Try to understand how Jo is different from Aunt March.

Jo happened to suit Aunt March, who was lame and needed an active person to wait upon her. The childless old lady had offered to adopt one of the girls when the troubles came, and was much offended because her offer was declined . . .

The old lady wouldn't speak to them for a time, but happening to meet Jo at a friend's, . . . she proposed to take her for a companion. ❶ This did not suit Jo at all, but she accepted the place since nothing better appeared, and to everyone's surprise, got on remarkably well with her irascible relative . . .

I suspect that the real attraction was a large library of fine books, which was left to dust and spiders since Uncle March died . . . The dim, dusty room, with the busts staring down from the tall bookcases, the cozy chairs, the globes, and, best of all, the wilderness of books, in which she could wander where she liked, made the library a region of bliss to her . . . ❷

Jo's ambition was to do something very splendid. What it was she had no idea, as yet, but left it for time to tell her, and, meanwhile, found her greatest affliction in the fact that she couldn't read, run, and ride as much as she liked. ❸ A quick temper, sharp tongue, and restless spirit were always getting her into scrapes, and her life was a series of ups and downs, which were both comic and pathetic. But the training she received at Aunt March's was just what she needed, and the thought that she was doing something to support herself made her happy in spite of the perpetual "Josy-phine!"

GUIDED READING

WORD HELP

lame disabled
irascible angry
bliss happiness
ambition hope for the future
affliction problem
pathetic very sad
perpetual constant

❶ *Some women kept companions to help entertain them and perform small chores. Why might Jo not want to be a companion?*

❷ *How does Jo differ from ideas about women in the 1880s?*

❸ *What might Jo be able to do for work in the 1800s?*

CONNECTING LITERATURE TO HISTORY

1. **Drawing Conclusions** Henry Wadsworth Longfellow was the most popular American poet of his time. How does his version of Paul Revere's ride increase the importance of the story?

2. **Comparing and Contrasting** The lives of women in the 1800s were very different from the lives of women today. How does this excerpt of *Little Women* show some similarities and differences between now and then?

NEW MOVEMENTS IN AMERICA **447**

Literature in History

Little Women

As You Read Tell students as they read the passage to list adjectives and phrases that describe Jo and Aunt March. Ask volunteers to share some of the items they listed. Then have students use the lists to contrast Jo and Aunt March.

Meet the Writer

Louisa May Alcott (1832–1888)

The daughter of an impractical Massachusetts philosopher, Louisa May Alcott had to work hard from childhood to support her mother and three sisters. She tried sewing, teaching in country schools, working as a domestic, and serving as a Civil War nurse before finding fame as a writer. The success of *Little Women* enabled Alcott to write in her journal, "Paid up all the debts . . . !"

Cross-Discipline Activity: Literature

At Level

Character Analysis Chart

1. Have students read the passage from *Little Women*. Then have each student create a three-column chart and label the columns *Jo*, *Interactions*, and *Aunt March*.

2. In the middle column, have students list each interaction between Jo and Aunt March in the passage, including inferred interactions. In the other columns, have students describe what each interaction reveals about each character.

3. Ask volunteers to share the information they listed in their charts. Have students discuss each character and how Alcott reveals their personalities.

4. Then have students discuss how the two women's characters and interactions reflect aspects of American society in the mid-1800s.
LS Verbal/Linguistic

Alternative Assessment Handbook, Rubrics 7: Charts; and 11: Discussions

Answers

Guided Reading **1.** *possible answer—She is active and the job will prevent her from running, riding, and reading as much as she would like.*
2. *Jo is outspoken, active, and ambitious at a time when women were expected to be focused on domestic concerns.*
3. *possible answers—seamstress, mill worker, writer, teacher, reformer, companion, domestic*

Connecting Literature to History
1. *Longfellow's version presents Paul Revere as the lone, heroic rider who spread the news of the approaching British.*
2. *reveals that women's personalities may be much the same but that opportunities for women in the 1800s were more limited*

447

Bellringer

If YOU were there . . . Use the **Daily Bellringer Transparency** to help students answer the question.

🖨 Daily Bellringer Transparency, Section 3

Building Vocabulary

Preteach or review the following terms:

conversion moving to faith or belief (p. 448)

offenders people who break a law (p. 450)

revivals emotional religious meetings (p. 448)

segregated separate (p. 452)

temperance avoidance of alcohol (p. 449)

📰 **CRF:** Vocabulary Builder Activity, Section 3

Taking Notes

Have students copy the graphic organizer onto their own paper and then use it to take notes on the section. This activity will prepare students for the Section Assessment, in which they will complete a graphic organizer that builds on the information using a critical thinking skill.

SECTION 3

Reforming Society

What You Will Learn...

Main Ideas

1. The Second Great Awakening sparked interest in religion.
2. Social reformers began to speak out about temperance and prison reform.
3. Improvements in education reform affected many segments of the population.
4. Northern African American communities became involved in reform efforts.

The Big Idea

Reform movements in the early 1800s affected religion, education, and society.

Key Terms and People

Second Great Awakening, *p. 448*
Charles Grandison Finney, *p. 448*
Lyman Beecher, *p. 448*
temperance movement, *p. 449*
Dorothea Dix, *p. 450*
common-school movement, *p. 450*
Horace Mann, *p. 450*
Catharine Beecher, *p. 451*
Thomas Gallaudet, *p. 451*

TAKING NOTES Create a time line like the one shown below. As you read, list the important events of the reform movements next to the appropriate date on the time line. Some dates might have more than one event.

1817   1821   1835   1837   1841

If YOU were there...

You live in New York State in the 1850s. You are the oldest daughter in your family. Since childhood you have loved mathematics, which puzzles your family. Your sisters are happy learning to sew and cook and run a household. You want more. You know that there is a female seminary nearby, where you could study and learn much more. But your parents are undecided.

> **How might you persuade your parents to send you to the school?**

BUILDING BACKGROUND Along with changes in American culture, changes were also taking place in American society. A religious revival swept the country. Reform-minded men and women tried to improve all aspects of society, from schools to taverns. Reforms in education opened up new opportunities for young women.

Second Great Awakening

During the 1790s and early 1800s, some Americans took part in a Christian renewal movement called the **Second Great Awakening**. It swept through towns across upstate New York and through the frontier regions of Kentucky, Ohio, Tennessee, and South Carolina. By the 1820s and 1830s, this new interest in religion had spread to New England and the South.

Charles Grandison Finney was one of the most important leaders of the Second Great Awakening. After experiencing a dramatic religious conversion in 1821, Finney left his career as a lawyer and began preaching. He challenged some traditional Protestant beliefs, telling congregations that each individual was responsible for his or her own salvation. He also believed that sin was avoidable. Finney held revivals, emotional prayer meetings that lasted for days. Many people converted to Christianity during these revivals. Finney told new converts to prove their faith by doing good deeds.

Finney's style of preaching and his ideas angered some traditional ministers, like Boston's **Lyman Beecher**. Beecher wanted to prevent Finney from holding revivals in his city. "You mean to

---

Teach the Big Idea

At Level

Reforming Society

1. **Teach** Ask students the questions in the Main Idea boxes to teach this section.

2. **Apply** Create a four-column chart for students to see. Title the chart *Reforming Society* and label the columns *Why, Who, What,* and *When.* Have each student copy the chart and use the information in the section to complete it. Students should list why reform was needed, key reformers, the reform efforts they made, and when these reforms occurred. **LS** **Verbal/Linguistic, Visual/Spatial**

3. **Review** To review, have students help you complete a master copy of the chart.

4. **Practice/Homework** Ask students to conduct research on one reformer in the section who interests them. Each student should find one fact about the reformer to share with the class. **LS** **Verbal/Linguistic**

📰 Alternative Assessment Handbook, Rubrics 7: Charts; and 30: Research carry a streak of fire to Boston. If you attempt it, as the Lord liveth, I'll meet you . . . and fight every inch of the way." Despite the opposition of Beecher and other traditional ministers, Finney's appeal remained powerful. Also, the First Amendment guarantee of freedom of religion prevented the government from passing laws banning the new religious practices. Ministers were therefore free to spread their message of faith and salvation to whomever wished to listen.

Due to the efforts of Finney and his followers, church membership across the country grew a great deal during the Second Great Awakening. Many new church members were women and African Americans. The African Methodist Episcopal Church spread across the Middle Atlantic states. Although the movement had begun in the Northeast and on the frontier, the Second Great Awakening renewed some people's religious faith throughout America.

READING CHECK Drawing Conclusions
What impact did the Second Great Awakening have on religion in America?

Social Reformers Speak Out

Renewed religious faith often led to involvement in movements to reform society. Urban growth had caused problems that reformers wanted to fix. Members of the growing middle class, especially women, often led the efforts. Many of the women did not work outside the home and hired servants to care for their households. This gave them time to work in reform groups. Social reformers tackled alcohol abuse, prison and education reform, and slavery.

Temperance Movement

Many social reformers worked to prevent alcohol abuse. They believed that Americans drank too much. In the 1830s, on average, an American consumed seven gallons of alcohol per year. Countless Americans thought that alcohol abuse caused social problems, such as family violence, poverty, and criminal behavior.

Americans' worries about the effects of alcohol led to the growth of a **temperance movement**. This reform effort urged people to use self-discipline to stop drinking hard liquor.

❶ Second Great Awakening

The Second Great Awakening sparked interest in religion.

Identify What areas of the United States were affected by the Second Great Awakening? *upstate New York, frontier regions of Kentucky, Ohio, Tennessee, South Carolina, New England, and the South*

Evaluate Why do you think many people were drawn to Finney's preaching? *possible answer—He was a charismatic preacher, willing to challenge traditional beliefs.*

CRF: Biography Activity: Charles Finney

❷ Social Reformers Speak Out

Social reformers began to speak out about temperance and prison reform.

Explain How did the Second Great Awakening contribute to social reform? *Renewed religious faith led people to want to improve society.*

Analyze What social problems did people think were caused by alcohol abuse, and what movement formed to address these problems? *family violence, poverty, and criminal behavior; temperance movement*

Political Cartoons Activities for United States History, Cartoon 15: Temperance Reform

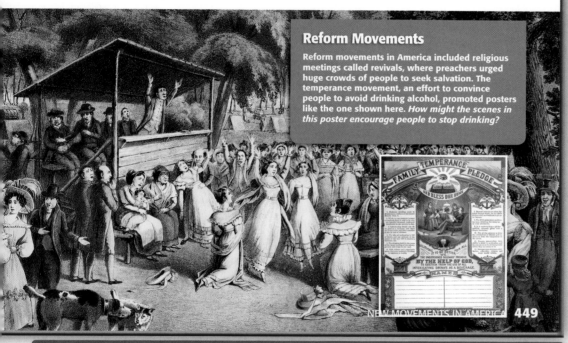

Reform Movements

Reform movements in America included religious meetings called revivals, where preachers urged huge crowds of people to seek salvation. The temperance movement, an effort to convince people to avoid drinking alcohol, promoted posters like the one shown here. *How might the scenes in this poster encourage people to stop drinking?*

NEW MOVEMENTS IN AMERICA **449**

Critical Thinking: Finding Main Ideas

At Level

Second Great Awakening Magazine Cover

Materials: art supplies, heavy-stock paper

1. Lead a discussion on the Second Great Awakening and its effects on society.

2. Then ask students to imagine that they work at an early 1800s magazine that covers trends in society. Have students, working either individually or in small groups, create a cover for an edition of the magazine on the Second Great Awakening.

3. The cover should provide the name of the magazine, titles and tag lines for articles in the magazine, and one or more images. The article titles and tag lines should cover all aspects of the Second Great Awakening as well as some other issues of the day.

4. Display the covers around the classroom.
   LS Verbal/Linguistic, Visual/Spatial

Alternative Assessment Handbook, Rubric 19: Magazines

Answers

Reform Movements *by showing how temperance promotes a strong, happy family life*

Reading Check *Church membership increased, particularly among women and African Americans, and some people's religious faith increased across the nation.*

Main Idea

❷ Social Reformers Speak Out

Social reformers began to speak out about temperance and prison reform.

Identify How did Dorothea Dix contribute to the improvement of American society? *Dix pushed for better conditions and facilities for the mentally ill, which led to the creation of many state hospitals.*

Draw Conclusions How were reform schools an improvement over prisons? *Children were not treated as adult offenders and learned useful skills.*

Activity Civics: Responsibility
Have students write short essays in response to the following question: *Do you think individuals can still make a difference in society, such as Dorothea Dix and Josiah Quincy did?* Ask volunteers to read their essays aloud to the class. **LS Verbal/Linguistic**

📖 Alternative Assessment Handbook, Rubric 37: Writing Assignment

📖 **CRF:** Biography Activity: Dorothea Dix

Connect to Science and Technology

Access to Textbooks Technological developments in the early 1800s also helped improved education. New printing techniques made producing textbooks less expensive. Textbooks became more widely distributed, and more students had access to them.

Answers

Reading Check *worked to reform prisons by building state hospitals for the mentally ill, providing reform schools for young offenders, and creating houses of correction for adult offenders*

450

Reformers asked people to limit themselves to beer and wine in small amounts. Groups like the American Temperance Society and the American Temperance Union helped to spread this message. Minister Lyman Beecher spoke widely about the evils of alcohol. He claimed that people who drank alcohol were "neglecting the education of their families—and corrupting their morals."

Prison Reform

Another target of reform was the prison system. **Dorothea Dix** was a middle-class reformer who visited prisons throughout Massachusetts beginning in 1841. Dix reported that mentally ill people frequently were jailed with criminals. They were sometimes left in dark cells without clothes or heat and were chained to the walls and beaten. Dix spoke of what she saw to the state legislature.

In response, the Massachusetts government built facilities for the mentally ill. Dix's work had a nationwide effect. Eventually, more than 100 state hospitals were built to give mentally ill people professional care.

Prisons also held runaway children and orphans. Some had survived only by begging or stealing, and they got the same punishment as adult criminals. Boston mayor Josiah Quincy asked that young offenders receive different punishments than adults. In the 1820s, several state and local governments founded reform schools for children who had been housed in prisons. There, children lived under strict rules and learned useful skills.

Some reformers also tried to end the overcrowding and cruel conditions in prisons. Their efforts led to the creation of houses of correction. These institutions did not use punishment alone to change behavior. They also offered prisoners education.

THE IMPACT TODAY

McGuffey's Readers were among the first "graded" textbooks. Organizing classes by grades was a new idea that is standard practice today.

READING CHECK **Summarizing** How did reformers change the punishment of criminals?

Improvements in Education

Another challenge facing America in the early 1800s was poor public education. Most American families believed that some schooling was useful. However, many children worked in factories or on farms to help support their families. If children could read the Bible, write, and do simple math, that was often considered to be enough.

Education in the Early 1800s

The availability of education varied widely. New England had the most schools, while the South and West had the fewest. Few teachers were trained. Schoolhouses were small, and students of all ages and levels worked in one room.

McGuffey's Readers were the most popular textbooks. William Holmes McGuffey, an educator and minister, put selections from British and American literature in them as well as reading lessons and instruction in moral and social values.

Social background and wealth affected the quality of education. Rich families sent children to private schools or hired tutors. However, poor children had only public schools. Girls could go to school, but parents usually thought that girls needed little education and kept them home. Therefore, few girls learned to read.

Common-School Movement

Reformers thought that education made children responsible citizens. People in the **common-school movement** wanted all children taught in a common place, regardless of background. **Horace Mann** was a leader of this movement.

In 1837 Mann became Massachusetts's first secretary of education. He convinced the state to double its school budget and raise teachers' salaries. He lengthened the school year and began the first school for teacher training. Mann's success set a standard for education reform throughout the country.

Critical Thinking: Solving Problems

At Level

Prisoners' Bill of Rights

1. Describe the conditions in prisons during the early 1800s. Then organize students into small groups and ask the groups to imagine that they are members of an organization involved in prison reform in the early 1800s.

2. Have each group's members discuss what they hope to achieve through reform. Students should consider living conditions in prisons, who should be placed in prisons, the privileges prisoners should be allowed, and how to deal with juvenile offenders.

3. Have each group provide its suggestions for reform in the form of a prisoners' bill of rights.

4. Write some of the suggested reforms for the class to see. Then have students compare their ideas to the actual reform efforts made in the early 1800s. **LS Verbal/Linguistic**

📖 Alternative Assessment Handbook, Rubrics 14: Group Activity; and 37: Writing Assignment

Women's Education

Education reform created greater opportunities for women. **Catharine Beecher** started an all-female academy in Hartford, Connecticut. The first college-level educational institution available to women was the Troy Female Seminary, opened by Emma Willard in 1821. Several other women's colleges opened during the 1830s, including Mount Holyoke College. Mary Lyon began Mount Holyoke in 1837 as a place for women to develop skills to be of service to society.

Teaching People with Special Needs

Efforts to improve education also helped people with special needs. In 1831 Samuel Gridley Howe opened the Perkins School for the Blind in Massachusetts. Howe traveled widely, talking about teaching people with visual impairment. **Thomas Gallaudet** improved the education and lives of people with hearing impairments. He founded the first free American school for hearing-impaired people in 1817.

READING CHECK **Summarizing** What were Horace Mann's achievements?

BIOGRAPHY

Horace Mann
1796–1859

Born in Franklin, Massachusetts, Mann had little schooling, but he educated himself well enough at the local library to get into Brown University and attend law school. Despite a busy law practice, he served in the Massachusetts legislature for 10 years. He was also an outspoken advocate for public education. In 1837 the state created the post of secretary of education for him. His achievements in that office made him famous. He later served in the U.S. House of Representatives and as president of Antioch College in Ohio. His influence on education is reflected by the fact that many American schools are named for him.

Analyzing Information How do you think Mann's own education influenced his desire for public schools?

Primary Source

SPEECH
Horace Mann to the Board of Education

In a speech to the newly created Massachusetts Board of Education, Horace Mann, the board's first secretary, described the purpose of the public school system.

"[T]here should be a free district school, sufficiently safe, and sufficiently good, for all of the children... where they may be well instructed in the rudiments [basics] of knowledge, formed to propriety of demeanor [good behavior], and imbued [filled] with the principles of duty... It is on this common platform, that a general acquaintanceship [friendship] should be formed between the children of the same neighborhood. It is here, that the affinities [qualities] of a common nature should unite them together."

—Horace Mann, quoted in *The Republic and the School*, edited by Lawrence A. Cremin

> Mann believed all students should receive free education.

> Neighborhood children should attend school together to form a common bond.

ANALYSIS SKILL **ANALYZING PRIMARY SOURCES**

Besides knowledge, what purpose did Mann believe the public schools had?

NEW MOVEMENTS IN AMERICA **451**

Direct Teach

Main Idea

❸ Improvements in Education

Improvements in education reform affected many segments of the population.

Recall What factors affected access to education in the early 1800s? *social background and wealth*

Summarize How did Horace Mann work to reform education? *He led the common-school movement, which called for all children to be taught in a common place and worked to improve educational funding, training, and pay for teachers.*

Analyze Why do you think reformers wanted all children taught in a common school? *So that all students would receive the same educational experience.*

Identify Cause and Effect How did reform efforts improve access to education? *Efforts led to academies and colleges for women and schools for the blind and hearing-impaired.*

CRF: Biography Activity: Mary Lyon and Emma Willard

go.hrw.com
Online Resources

KEYWORD: SR8 US14
ACTIVITY: Education Reformers Interview

Collaborative Learning

At Level

Education in Early 1800s America

Materials: butcher paper, colored markers, art supplies

1. Organize students into small groups. Have each group create an annotated time line of educational reform from 1800 to 1860.

2. The groups' time lines should cover the significant people, events, and ideas connected with the common-school movement and the expansion of educational opportunities for African Americans, women, and people with special needs.

3. Each group should provide a title for its time line and a brief caption summarizing each time line entry. Encourage students to illustrate their time lines with drawings or photographs.
LS **Interpersonal, Visual/Spatial**

Alternative Assessment Handbook, Rubrics 14: Group Activity; and 36: Time Lines

Answers

Biography *He did not receive much schooling, but had a desire to be educated, which may have given him a desire to help other people who felt the same way.*

Analyzing Primary Sources *to provide a safe environment, teach good behavior and morals, and to form neighborhood bonds among children*

Reading Check *set a national standard for education reform; leader of common-school movement; first Massachusetts Secretary of Education; convinced state to increase school budget and teachers' salaries, lengthen school year; began first school for teacher training*

451

Direct Teach

Main Idea

❹ African American Communities

Northern African American communities became involved in reform efforts.

Describe How did Quakers in Philadelphia influence opportunities for African Americans? *Quakers believed in equality and supported education for African Americans.*

Contrast How did educational opportunities for African Americans differ across the nation? *Free African Americans in the North and Midwest had some chances to attend school, but in the South laws barred most enslaved Africans from getting an education.*

Draw Conclusions How might attending college have improved African Americans' opportunities? *possible answer—They could get better jobs and learn the skills to serve as community leaders.*

Connect to Civics: Justice

School Segregation More than 100 years before the Supreme Court case *Brown v. the Board of Education of Topeka* (1954), another court case addressed segregation in America's schools. In 1848, Benjamin Roberts, an African American printer, sued the Boston School Committee for making his five-year-old daughter Sarah attend an all-black school. Charles Sumner and black attorney Robert Morris provided the defense in the case, but without success. In 1850 the Massachusetts Supreme Judicial Court ruled in *Sarah C. Roberts v. The City of Boston* that segregated schools were constitutional. The case served as a precedent, or standard, in later cases involving racial segregation, including *Plessy v. Ferguson* (1896).

African American Communities

Free African Americans usually lived in segregated, or separate, communities in the North. Most of them lived in cities such as New York, Boston, and Philadelphia. Community leaders were often influenced by the Second Great Awakening and its spirit of reform.

Founded by former slave Richard Allen, the Free African Religious Society became a model for other groups that pressed for racial equality and the education of blacks. In 1816, Allen became the first bishop of the African Methodist Episcopal Church, or AME Church. This church broke away from white Methodist churches after African Americans were treated poorly in some white congregations.

Other influential African Americans of the time, such as Alexander Crummel, pushed for the creation of schools for black Americans. The New York African Free School in New York City educated hundreds of children, many of whom became brilliant scholars and important African American leaders. Philadelphia also had a long history of educating African Americans. This was largely because Philadelphia was a center of Quaker influence, and the Quakers believed strongly in equality. The city ran seven schools for African American students by the year 1800. In 1820 Boston followed Philadelphia's lead and opened a separate elementary school for African American children. The city began allowing them to attend school with whites in 1855.

African Americans rarely attended college because few colleges would accept them. In 1835 Oberlin College became the first to do so. Harvard University soon admitted African Americans, too. African American colleges were founded beginning in the 1840s. In 1842 the Institute for Colored Youth opened in Philadelphia. Avery College, also in Pennsylvania, was founded in 1849.

452 CHAPTER 14

Differentiating Instruction

Below Level

Struggling Readers

Prep Required

Materials: art supplies, sample certificates of commendation or awards (optional)

1. If available, show students sample certificates of commendation or awards. Explain that such items are often given to people in appreciation for their efforts or contributions.

2. Ask students to select one of the reformers mentioned in this section and to create a certificate of commendation for that person. The commendation should include the person's name, a description of the reform or problem he or she is associated with, and a summary of the person's efforts or contributions.

3. Then hold a mock award ceremony at which volunteers read aloud their certificates of commendation. **LS** Verbal/Linguistic

📖 Alternative Assessment Handbook, Rubric 37: Writing Assignment

While free African Americans had some opportunities to attend school in the North and Midwest, few had this chance in the South. Laws in the South barred most enslaved people from getting any education, even at the primary school level. While some slaves learned to read on their own, they almost always did so in secret. Slaveholders were fearful that education and knowledge in general might encourage a spirit of revolt among enslaved African Americans.

READING CHECK **Drawing Conclusions** Why was it difficult for African Americans to get an education in the South in the early 1800s?

SUMMARY AND PREVIEW The efforts of reformers led to improvements in many aspects of American life in the early to mid-1800s. In the next section you will learn about reform-minded people who opposed the practice of slavery.

This photograph (left) of the 1855 class at Oberlin College shows the slow integration of African Americans into previously white colleges. Some churches also became more integrated, and preachers like the one pictured above began calling for equality between races.
Why might preachers have been particularly influential in calls for more integration?

Section 3 Assessment

go.hrw.com
Online Quiz
KEYWORD: SR8 HP14

Reviewing Ideas, Terms, and People

1. **a. Identify** What was the **Second Great Awakening**, and who was one of its leaders?
   b. Summarize What effects did the Second Great Awakening have on religion in the United States?
2. **a. Identify** What role did **Dorothea Dix** play in social reforms of the early 1800s?
   b. Summarize What different reforms helped improve the U.S. prison system?
   c. Elaborate How might the Second Great Awakening have led to the growth of social reform movements?
3. **a. Identify** What was the **common-school movement**, and who was one of its leaders?
   b. Analyze Why did reformers set out to improve education in the United States?
   c. Evaluate Do you think **Horace Mann's** ideas for educational reform were good ones? Explain.
4. **a. Recall** In what cities were the first public schools for African Americans located?
   b. Draw Conclusions How did free African Americans benefit from educational reforms?

Critical Thinking

5. **Categorizing** Review the reform-movement events on the time line in your notes. Then use a chart like the one below to identify the leaders and accomplishments of each reform movement.

Movement	Leaders	Accomplishments
Prison and Mental Health Reform		
Temperance		
Education		

FOCUS ON WRITING

6. **Choosing Important Events** This section covers the reform of social issues such as religion, prisons, and education. Write the reforms described in your chart. Write a note about the reform and about the important people involved in it. Think about how each one influenced life in the United States.

NEW MOVEMENTS IN AMERICA **453**

Direct Teach

Biography

Harriet Jacobs (1813–1897) Harriet Jacobs was born into slavery and orphaned at a young age. She learned to read from her first mistress. After Jacobs escaped slavery and fled North, she wrote *Incidents in the Life of a Slave Girl*. Jacobs' emotionally charged account was a fierce indictment of slavery. On the title page, Jacobs writes, "Northerners know nothing at all about Slavery. They think it is perpetual bondage only. They have no conception of the depth of *degradation* involved in that word, *Slavery*; if they had, they would never cease their efforts until so horrible a system was overthrown." Jacobs' narrative was rediscovered during the civil rights movement of the 1960s. Many experts considered the account to be a work of fiction until scholars authenticated it in 1981.

Review & Assess

Close

Have students review the major reform movements and leading reformers covered in this section.

Review

Online Quiz, Section 3

Assess

SE Section 3 Assessment
PASS: Section 3 Quiz
Alternative Assessment Handbook

Reteach/Classroom Intervention

Interactive Reader and Study Guide, Section 3
Interactive Skills Tutor CD-ROM

Answers

New Opportunities *because they were community leaders, and many people heard them speak*

Reading Check *Southern laws barred educating most enslaved people because slaveholders feared education would lead to slave revolts.*

453

Section 3 Assessment Answers

1. **a.** Christian renewal movement; Charles Grandison Finney
   b. Church membership grew, and religious faith was renewed nationwide.
2. **a.** Dix pushed for facilities for the mentally ill.
   b. reform schools, houses of correction
   c. Renewed religious faith led people to want to help others and improve society.
3. **a.** movement to educate all children in a common place; Horace Mann
   b. poor, limited public education

   c. possible answer—yes, because they increased access to and funding for education
4. **a.** New York, Philadelphia, and Boston
   b. More African Americans had the chance to attend public schools and colleges.
5. Prison/Mental Health—Dix, Quincy; state hospitals, reform schools; Temperance—Beecher; alcohol abuse; Education—Mann, common-school; Beecher, all-female academy; Howe and Gallaudet, special needs; Crummel, African Americans
6. See previous answer.

The Movement to End Slavery

454 CHAPTER 14

Preteach

Bellringer

If YOU were there . . . Use the **Daily Bellringer Transparency** to help students answer the question.

🖥 Daily Bellringer Transparency, Section 4

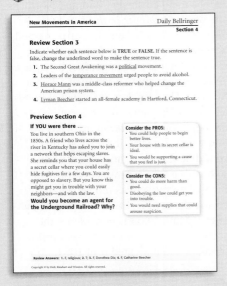

New Movements in America — Daily Bellringer Section 4

Review Section 3
Indicate whether each sentence below is **TRUE** or **FALSE**. If the sentence is false, change the underlined word to make the sentence true.
1. The Second Great Awakening was a <u>political</u> movement.
2. Leaders of the <u>temperance movement</u> urged people to avoid alcohol.
3. <u>Horace Mann</u> was a middle-class reformer who helped change the American prison system.
4. <u>Lyman Beecher</u> started an all-female academy in Hartford, Connecticut.

Preview Section 4

If YOU were there …
You live in southern Ohio in the 1850s. A friend who lives across the river in Kentucky has asked you to join a network that helps escaping slaves. She reminds you that your house has a secret cellar where you could easily hide fugitives for a few days. You are opposed to slavery. But you know this might get you in trouble with your neighbors—and with the law. **Would you become an agent for the Underground Railroad? Why?**

Consider the PROS:
• You could help people to begin better lives.
• Your house with its secret cellar is ideal.
• You would be supporting a cause that you feel is just.

Consider the CONS:
• You could do more harm than good.
• Disobeying the law could get you into trouble.
• You would need supplies that could arouse suspicion.

Review Answers: 1. F, religious; 2. T; 3. F, Dorothea Dix; 4. F, Catherine Beecher

Copyright © by Holt, Rinehart and Winston. All rights reserved.

Building Vocabulary

Preteach or review the following terms:

emancipation freedom from slavery (p. 455)

narrative a story or account (p. 456)

obstructed blocked or hindered (p. 458)

📰 **CRF:** Vocabulary Builder Activity, Section 4

Taking Notes

Have students copy the graphic organizer onto their own paper and then use it to take notes on the section. This activity will prepare students for the Section Assessment, in which they will complete a graphic organizer that builds on the information using a critical thinking skill.

What You Will Learn...

Main Ideas

1. Americans from a variety of backgrounds actively opposed slavery.
2. Abolitionists organized the Underground Railroad to help enslaved Africans escape.
3. Despite efforts of abolitionists, many Americans remained opposed to ending slavery.

The Big Idea

In the mid-1800s, debate over slavery increased as abolitionists organized to challenge slavery in the United States.

Key Terms and People

abolition, *p. 454*
William Lloyd Garrison, *p. 455*
American Anti-Slavery Society, *p. 455*
Angelina and Sarah Grimké, *p. 455*
Frederick Douglass, *p. 456*
Sojourner Truth, *p. 456*
Underground Railroad, *p. 456*
Harriet Tubman, *p. 458*

TAKING NOTES As you read, take notes on the different abolitionist movements that existed, the leaders of each movement, and the methods used by each group to oppose slavery. Write your notes in a chart like the one below.

Movement	Members	Methods

If YOU were there...

You live in southern Ohio in the 1850s. A friend who lives across the river in Kentucky has asked you to join a network that helps escaping slaves. She reminds you that your house has a secret cellar where you could easily hide fugitives for a few days. You are opposed to slavery. But you know this might get you in trouble with your neighbors—and with the law.

Would you become an agent for the Underground Railroad? Why?

BUILDING BACKGROUND The early 1800s brought many movements for social reform in the United States. Perhaps the most important and far-reaching was the movement for the abolition of slavery. While reformers worked to end slavery, many also took risks to help slaves to escape.

Americans Oppose Slavery

Some Americans had opposed slavery since before the country was founded. Benjamin Franklin was the president of the first anti-slavery society in America, the Pennsylvania Society for Promoting the Abolition of Slavery. In the 1830s, Americans took more organized action supporting **abolition**, or a complete end to slavery.

Differences among Abolitionists

Abolitionists came from many different backgrounds and opposed slavery for various reasons. The Quakers were among the first groups to challenge slavery on religious grounds. Other religious leaders gave speeches and published pamphlets that moved many Americans to support abolition. In one of these, abolitionist Theodore Weld wrote that "everyman knows that slavery is a curse." Other abolitionists referred to the Declaration of Independence. They reminded people that the American Revolution had been fought in the name of liberty.

Teach the Big Idea

At Level

The Movement to End Slavery

1. **Teach** Ask students the questions in the Main Idea boxes to teach this section.

2. **Apply** Have each student, working individually or in pairs, write a summary of each part of the section, indicated by the blue headings. 🖎 **Verbal/Linguistic**

3. **Review** As you review the section, have volunteers share their summaries. Write them for the class to see and ask students to provide supporting details for each one.

4. **Practice/Homework** Ask students to imagine that they belong to an antislavery society. Have them create fliers announcing the group's next meeting, at which Harriet Tubman will be speaking. The fliers should explain the group's goals, why Americans should support abolition, and what Tubman will be talking about. 🖎 **Verbal/Linguistic**

📰 Alternative Assessment Handbook, Rubric 37: Writing Assignments

Antislavery reformers did not always agree on the details, however. They differed over how much equality they thought African Americans should have. Some believed that African Americans should receive the same treatment as white Americans. In contrast, other abolitionists were against full political and social equality.

Some abolitionists wanted to send freed African Americans to Africa to start new colonies. They thought that this would prevent conflicts between the races in the United States. In 1817 a minister named Robert Finley started the American Colonization Society, an organization dedicated to establishing colonies of freed slaves in Africa. Five years later, the society founded the colony of Liberia on the west coast of Africa. About 12,000 African Americans eventually settled in Liberia. However, many abolitionists who once favored colonization later opposed it. Some African Americans also opposed it. David Walker was one such person. In his 1829 essay, *Appeal to the Colored Citizens of the World*, Walker explained his opposition to colonization.

> "The greatest riches in all America have arisen from our blood and tears: and they [whites] will drive us from our property and homes, which we have earned with our blood."
>
> —David Walker, quoted in *From Slavery to Freedom* by John Hope Franklin and Alfred A. Moss Jr.

Spreading the Abolitionist Message

Abolitionists found many ways to further their cause. Some went on speaking tours or wrote pamphlets and newspaper articles. John Greenleaf Whittier wrote abolitionist poetry and literature. **William Lloyd Garrison** published an abolitionist newspaper, the *Liberator*, beginning in 1831. In 1833 Garrison also helped found the **American Anti-Slavery Society**. Its members wanted immediate emancipation and racial equality for African Americans. Garrison later became its president.

Both the *Liberator* and the Anti-Slavery Society relied on support from free African Americans. Society members spread

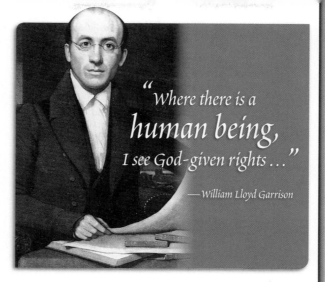

> "Where there is a *human being*, I see God-given rights ..."
>
> —William Lloyd Garrison

antislavery literature and petitioned Congress to end federal support of slavery. In 1840 the American Anti-Slavery Society split. One group wanted immediate freedom for enslaved African Americans and a bigger role for women. The others wanted gradual emancipation and for women to play only minor roles in the movement.

Angelina and Sarah Grimké, two white southern women, were antislavery activists of the 1830s. They came from a South Carolina slaveholding family but disagreed with their parents' support of slavery. Angelina Grimké tried to recruit other white southern women in a pamphlet called *Appeal to the Christian Women of the South* in 1836.

> "I know you do not make the laws, but ... if you really suppose you can do nothing to overthrow slavery you are greatly mistaken ... Try to persuade your husband, father, brothers, and sons that slavery is a crime against God and man."
>
> —Angelina Grimké, quoted in *The Grimké Sisters from South Carolina*, edited by Gerda Lerner

This essay was very popular in the North. In 1839 the Grimké sisters wrote *American Slavery As It Is*. The book was one of the most important antislavery works of its time.

NEW MOVEMENTS IN AMERICA **455**

Main Idea

❶ Americans Oppose Slavery

Americans from a variety of backgrounds actively opposed slavery.

Recall What were some reasons that abolitionists opposed slavery? *for religious reasons, was morally wrong, because it went against the right to liberty for which the American Revolution had been fought*

Contrast How did some abolitionists differ in their views toward African Americans? *differed over how much equality they thought African Americans should have and whether to support colonization*

Draw Conclusions How did Angelina Grimké believe women could help bring an end to slavery? *by persuading the men in their lives that slavery was wrong*

📋 **CRF:** Biography Activity: Abolitionists

📋 **CRF:** Primary Source Activity: David Walker, "An Appeal to the Colored Citizens of the World"

World Events

British Abolitionists Many American abolitionists looked to Great Britain for examples of how to oppose slavery. The British abolitionist movement began in the 1780s, and achieved success in 1807 when Britain outlawed the slave trade. In 1834 a law abolishing slavery throughout the British Empire went into effect. British antislavery efforts did not stop, however. In 1840 the British and Foreign Anti-Slavery Society held the Worlds's Anti-Slavery Convention in London. Convention members asked the British government to pressure other countries to end slavery. In the mid-1800s, British warships began stopping slave ships and freeing any enslaved Africans they found.

Abolitionist Movement
movement to end slavery completely

Leaders	Methods
• Frederick Douglass	• lectures, speeches
• William Lloyd Garrison	• pamphlets
• Angelina and Sarah Grimké	• newspapers, articles
• Sojourner Truth	• antislavery societies
• Harriet Tubman	• nonfiction books, plays, poetry, novels
• and others	• petitions to Congress

❶ Americans Oppose Slavery

Americans from a variety of backgrounds actively opposed slavery.

Identify Who were some leading abolitionists? *Theodore Weld, David Walker, William Lloyd Garrison, Robert Finley, Angelina and Sarah Grimké, Frederick Douglass, Sojourner Truth, Harriet Jacobs, William Wells Brown, (discussed later, John Quincy Adams and Harriet Tubman)*

Interpret In the quotation on this page, what does Frederick Douglass mean when he says the Fourth of July is not his? *possible answer—that the freedom enjoyed and celebrated by some Americans was not available to enslaved African Americans or even fully to free African Americans*

Elaborate How did the words of former enslaved Africans, such as Frederick Douglass, serve as powerful weapons in the abolitionist movement? *provided firsthand accounts of the cruel and harsh reality of slavery*

Connect to Science

The North Star Fugitive slaves traveling by night often used the North Star to determine their route, because this star marks the general location of the North Pole.

Make Inferences Why do you think Frederick Douglass named his newspaper *North Star? possible answer—to refer to his own escape from slavery; to express that he hoped the paper would guide people in their quest to end slavery*

Answers

Reading Check *gave public lectures and wrote narratives, plays, and novels describing their experiences and the harsh reality of slavery*

African American Abolitionists

Many former slaves were active in the anti-slavery cause. **Frederick Douglass** escaped from slavery when he was 20 and went on to become one of the most important African American leaders of the 1800s. Douglass secretly learned to read and write as a boy, despite a law against it. His public-speaking skills impressed members of the Anti-Slavery Society. In 1841 they asked him to give regular lectures.

At a Fourth of July celebration in 1852, he captured the audience's attention with his powerful voice.

❝The blessings in which you, this day, rejoice, are not enjoyed in common …This Fourth of July is *yours*, not *mine*. You may rejoice, I must mourn.❞
—Frederick Douglass, quoted in *From Slavery to Freedom* by John Hope Franklin and Alfred A. Moss Jr.

In addition to his many speaking tours in the United States and Europe, Douglass published a newspaper called the *North Star* and wrote several autobiographies. His autobiographies were intended to show the injustices of slavery.

Another former slave, **Sojourner Truth**, also contributed to the abolitionist cause. She claimed God had called her to travel through the United States and preach the truth about slavery and women's rights. With her deep voice and quick wit, Truth became legendary in the antislavery movement for her fiery and dramatic speeches.

Other African Americans wrote narratives about their experiences as slaves to expose the cruelties that many slaves faced. In 1861, Harriet Jacobs published *Incidents in the Life of a Slave Girl*, one of the few slave narratives by a woman. William Wells Brown wrote an antislavery play as well as a personal narrative in the form of a novel called *Clotel*.

READING CHECK **Finding Main Ideas** In what ways did African Americans participate in the abolition movement?

The Underground Railroad

By the 1830s, a loosely organized group had begun helping slaves escape from the South. Free African Americans, former slaves, and a few white abolitionists worked together. They created what became known as the **Underground Railroad**. The organization was not an actual railroad but was a network of people who arranged transportation and hiding places for fugitives, or escaped slaves.

Fugitives would travel along routes that led them to northern states or sometimes into Canada. At no time did the Railroad have a central leadership. No one person, or group of people, was ever officially in charge. Despite the lack of any real structure, the Underground Railroad managed to achieve dramatic results.

Often wearing disguises, fugitives moved along the "railroad" at night, led by people known as conductors. Many times, the fugitives had no other guideposts but the stars. They stopped to rest during the day at "stations," often barns, attics, or other places on property owned by abolitionists known as station masters. The station masters hid and fed the fugitives.

Harriet Tubman was a courageous conductor on the Underground Railroad.

Collaborative Learning

"Who Am I?" Game

Materials: small box from which students can draw slips of paper

1. Assign each student one of the individuals mentioned in the section. Have each student use the information in the text to write a description of the individual's contributions to the fight against slavery—without mentioning the individual's name.

2. Have students place their descriptions in a box. Then ask volunteers to pick descriptions from the box and read them aloud to the class.

3. Have other students try to identify the individuals described. Students should not answer their own descriptions.

LS Verbal/Linguistic

📄 Alternative Assessment Handbook, Rubric 40: Writing to Describe

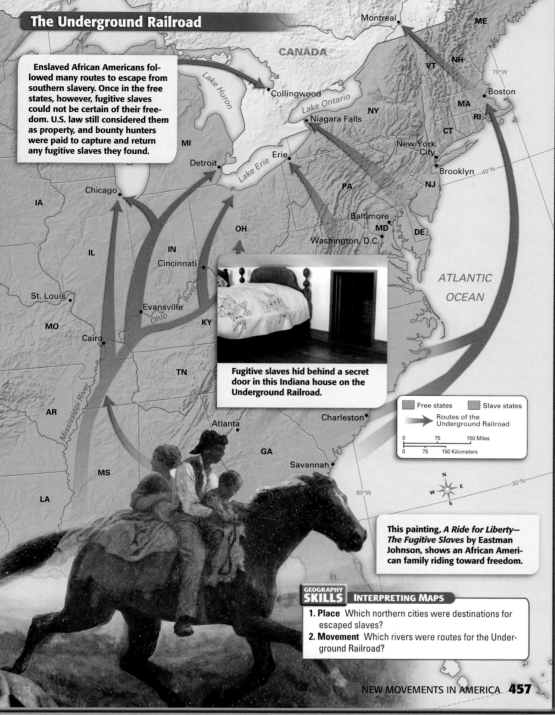

The Underground Railroad

Enslaved African Americans followed many routes to escape from southern slavery. Once in the free states, however, fugitive slaves could not be certain of their freedom. U.S. law still considered them as property, and bounty hunters were paid to capture and return any fugitive slaves they found.

Fugitive slaves hid behind a secret door in this Indiana house on the Underground Railroad.

Free states   Slave states

Routes of the Underground Railroad

0   75   150 Miles
0   75   150 Kilometers

This painting, *A Ride for Liberty—The Fugitive Slaves* by Eastman Johnson, shows an African American family riding toward freedom.

GEOGRAPHY SKILLS **INTERPRETING MAPS**

1. **Place** Which northern cities were destinations for escaped slaves?
2. **Movement** Which rivers were routes for the Underground Railroad?

NEW MOVEMENTS IN AMERICA **457**

Main Idea

❸ Opposition to Ending Slavery

Despite efforts of abolitionists, many Americans remained opposed to ending slavery.

Explain What was the purpose of the gag rule in Congress? *to prevent members of Congress from discussing the many anti-slavery petitions they received*

Make Inferences How did John Quincy Adams contribute to the abolitionist movement? *He was able to get the gag rule overturned.*

Identify Cause and Effect What effect did Nat Turner's Rebellion have on southern attitudes about slavery? *Open talk about slavery ended for fear of future slave revolts.*

Did you know . . .

Most fugitives traveled by foot or in wagons with hidden compartments, but some used other means of escape. In 1849, Henry "Box" Brown escaped slavery by shipping himself in a box from Richmond, Virginia, to an antislavery office in Philadelphia, Pennsylvania. After some 27 hours in a 3-by-2-foot crate, Brown gained his freedom.

Answers

Analyzing Primary Sources
language charged with fear and anger—"Outrage," "revolting character," "seditious Lecture," and "tool of evil and fanaticism"

Reading Check *to make it difficult for fugitives, conductors, and station masters to be followed or captured*

458

Primary Source

HANDBILL
Anti-Abolitionist Rally

Members of an anti-abolitionist group used this flyer to call people together in order to disrupt a meeting of abolitionists in 1837.

Seditious means "guilty of rebelling against lawful authority."

The group believes abolition violates the Constitution.

OUTRAGE.

Fellow Citizens,

AN
ABOLITIONIST,

of the most revolting character is among you, exciting the feelings of the North against the South. A seditious Lecture is to be delivered

THIS EVENING,

at 7 o'clock, at the Presbyterian Church in Cannon-street. You are requested to attend and unite in putting down and silencing by peaceable means this tool of evil and fanaticism. Let the rights of the States guaranteed by the Constitution be protected.

Feb. 27, 1837. *The Union forever!*

ANALYSIS SKILL **ANALYZING PRIMARY SOURCES**

What emotional language does this handbill use to get its message across?

The most famous and daring conductor on the Underground Railroad was **Harriet Tubman**. When Tubman escaped slavery in 1849, she left behind her family. She swore that she would return and lead her whole family to freedom in the North. Tubman returned to the South 19 times, successfully leading her family and more than 300 other slaves to freedom. At one time the reward for Tubman's capture reportedly climbed to $40,000, a huge amount of money at that time.

READING CHECK **Drawing Inferences** Why were the operations of the Underground Railroad kept secret?

Opposition to Ending Slavery

Although the North was the center of the abolitionist movement, many white northerners agreed with the South and supported slavery. Others disliked slavery but opposed equality for African Americans.

Newspaper editors and politicians warned that freed slaves would move north and take jobs from white workers. Some workers feared losing jobs to newly freed African Americans, whom they believed would accept lower wages. Abolitionist leaders were threatened with violence as some northerners joined mobs. Such a mob killed abolitionist Elijah Lovejoy in 1837 in Alton, Illinois.

The federal government also obstructed abolitionists. Between 1836 and 1844, the U.S. House of Representatives used what was called a gag rule. Congress had received thousands of antislavery petitions. Yet the gag rule forbade members of Congress from discussing them. This rule violated the First Amendment right of citizens to petition the government. But southern members of Congress did not want to debate slavery. Many northern Congressmembers preferred to avoid the issue.

Eventually, representative and former president John Quincy Adams was able to get the gag rule overturned. His resolution to enact a constitutional amendment halting the expansion of slavery never passed, however.

Many white southerners saw slavery as vital to the South's economy and culture. They also felt that outsiders should not

---

Critical Thinking: Identifying Points of View | **At Level**

Report on Opposition to Abolition

1. Ask students to imagine that they are members of an antislavery society. The head of the society wants to know more about the views of people who oppose abolition and the students have been selected to gather the information and report back.

2. Have each student create a large graphic or chart that identifies and explains both the views of northerners who oppose abolition and the views of southerners toward abolitionists and slavery.

3. In addition, each student should suggest ways that the antislavery society can address some of these views in its fight to end slavery.

4. Ask for volunteers to present their "reports" to the class. **LS Visual/Spatial**

📝 Alternative Assessment Handbook, Rubrics 7: Charts; and 13: Graphic Organizers

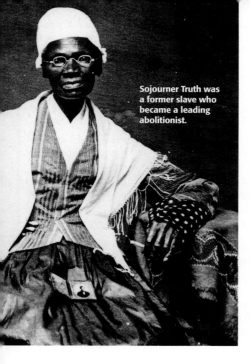

Sojourner Truth was a former slave who became a leading abolitionist.

interfere with their way of life. After Nat Turner's Rebellion in 1831, when Turner led some slaves to kill slaveholders, open talk about slavery diappeared in the South. It became dangerous to voice antislavery sentiments in southern states. Abolitionists like the Grimké sisters left rather than air unpopular views to hostile neighbors. Racism, fear, and economic dependence on slavery made emancipation all but impossible in the South.

READING CHECK Drawing Conclusions

Why did many northern workers oppose the abolition movement?

SUMMARY AND PREVIEW The issue of slavery grew more controversial in the United States during the first half of the nineteenth century. In the next section you will learn about women's rights.

Section 4 Assessment

go.hrw.com
Online Quiz
KEYWORD: SR8 HP14

Reviewing Ideas, Terms, and People

1. **a. Identify** What contributions did **William Lloyd Garrison** make to the abolition movement?
   b. Draw Conclusions In what ways did contributions from African Americans aid the struggle for abolition?
   c. Elaborate What do you think about the American Colonization Society's plan to return free African Americans to Liberia?
2. **a. Describe** How did the **Underground Railroad** work?
   b. Explain Why did **Harriet Tubman** first become involved with the Underground Railroad?
   c. Evaluate Do you think the Underground Railroad was a success? Why or why not?
3. **a. Describe** What action did Congress take to block abolitionists?
   b. Analyze Why did some Americans oppose equality for African Americans?
   c. Predict How might the debate over slavery lead to conflict in the future?

Critical Thinking

4. **Identifying Cause and Effect** Review your notes on the abolitionist movement. Then use a graphic organizer like the one below to show the reasons for opposition to the movement and the effects of that opposition.

Reasons for Opposing the End of Slavery		Effects of Opposition to the Movement

FOCUS ON WRITING

5. **Describing Abolition** Add notes about the abolitionist movement and its leaders to your chart. Be sure to note how abolitionists influenced life in the United States. What were they fighting for? Who opposed them, and why?

NEW MOVEMENTS IN AMERICA **459**

Frederick Douglass

As a freed slave, how would you help people still enslaved?

When did he live? 1817–1895

Where did he live? Frederick Douglass was born in rural Maryland. At age six he was sent to live in Baltimore, and at age 20 he escaped to New York City. For most of his life, Douglass lived in Rochester, New York, making his home into a stop along the Underground Railroad. He travelled often, giving powerful antislavery speeches to audiences throughout the North and in Europe.

What did he do? After hearing the abolitionist William Lloyd Garrison speak in 1841, Douglass began his own speaking tours about his experiences as a slave. In mid-life he wrote an autobiography and started an abolitionist newspaper called the *North Star*. During the Civil War, Douglass persuaded black soldiers to fight for the North.

Why is he important? Douglass was the most famous African American in the 1800s. His personal stories and elegant speaking style helped the abolitionist movement to grow. His words remain an inspiration to this day.

Drawing Conclusions What made Frederick Douglass's speeches and writings so powerful?

Frederick Douglass began publishing the *North Star*, an abolitionist newspaper, in 1847.

THE NORTH STAR.

KEY EVENTS

- **1817** Born a slave in Maryland
- **1837** Escapes slavery disguised as a sailor
- **1841** Begins his career as a speaker on abolition
- **1845** Writes *Narrative of the Life of Frederick Douglass*, his first autobiography
- **1847** Publishes first issue of the *North Star*
- **1863** Meets President Lincoln and becomes an adviser
- **1889** Named American consul general to Haiti
- **1895** Dies in Washington, D.C.

Collaborative Learning

At Level

Legacy of Frederick Douglass Mural

Materials: butcher paper, art supplies

1. Have students list Frederick Douglass's many contributions. Write the list for students to see. Use the list to lead a discussion on Douglass's significance in his time and the lasting effects of his actions on society.

2. Then have students, working as a class or in small groups, create a mural about Frederick Douglass to display in the school. The mural should use text and images to highlight Douglass's actions and contributions in the fight against slavery. If time allows, have students conduct research to find quotations from Douglass to add to the mural. Display the completed mural in the school.

🔑 **Interpersonal, Visual/Spatial**

📰 Alternative Assessment Handbook, Rubrics 3: Artwork; and 14: Group Activity

Women's Rights

If YOU were there...

You are a schoolteacher in New York State in 1848. Although you earn a small salary, you still live at home. Your father does not believe that unmarried women should live alone or look after their own money. One day in a shop, you see a poster about a public meeting to discuss women's rights. You know your father will be angry if you go to the meeting. But you are very curious.

Would you attend the meeting? Why?

> **BUILDING BACKGROUND** Women were active in the movements to reform prisons and schools. They fought for temperance and worked for abolition. But with all their work for social change, women still lacked many rights and opportunities of their own. Throughout the 1800s, the women's rights movement gradually became stronger and more organized.

Women's Struggle for Equal Rights

Fighting for the rights of African Americans led many female abolitionists to fight for women's rights. In the mid-1800s, these women found that they had to defend their right to speak in public, particularly when a woman addressed both men and women. For example, members of the press, the clergy, and even some male abolitionists criticized the Grimké sisters. These critics thought that the sisters should not give public speeches. They did not want women to leave their traditional female roles. The Grimkés protested that women had a moral duty to lead the antislavery movement.

Early Writings for Women's Rights

In 1838 Sarah Grimké published a pamphlet arguing for equal rights for women. She titled it *Letters on the Equality of the Sexes and the Condition of Women.*

> "I ask no favors for my sex ... All I ask our brethren [brothers] is that they will take their feet from off our necks, and permit us to stand upright on that ground which God designed us to occupy."
>
> —Sarah Grimké, quoted in *The Grimké Sisters from South Carolina,* edited by Gerda Lerner

What You Will Learn...

Main Ideas

1. Influenced by the abolition movement, many women struggled to gain equal rights for themselves.
2. Calls for women's rights met opposition from men and women.
3. The Seneca Falls Convention launched the first organized women's rights movement in the United States.

The Big Idea

Reformers sought to improve women's rights in American society.

Key Terms and People

Elizabeth Cady Stanton, *p. 464*
Lucretia Mott, *p. 464*
Seneca Falls Convention, *p. 464*
Declaration of Sentiments, *p. 464*
Lucy Stone, *p. 465*
Susan B. Anthony, *p. 465*

TAKING NOTES Create a graphic organizer like the one shown below. Use it to show some of the significant events in the struggle for women's rights.

Date	Events
1838	
1848	
1851	
1860	

❶ Women's Struggle for Equal Rights

Influenced by the abolition movement, many women struggled to gain equal rights for themselves.

Identify Who were some leaders in the early struggle for women's rights? *Sarah and Angelina Grimké, Margaret Fuller, Sojourner Truth*

Analyze How did the Grimké sisters' actions regarding marriage reflect their views on women's rights? *Both women disliked traditional views of marriage. Sarah chose not to marry because she thought it made her more of a slave than a wife. Angelina's marriage vows did not include the word* obey, *and her husband gave up his legal right to control her property.*

Draw Conclusions In the quotation, what message does Sojourner Truth express? *possible answer—that women are more capable than men give them credit for*

Linking to Today

Activity Changing Attitudes Toward Women During this section, discuss with students the ways in which attitudes toward women have changed—and continue to change—in American society. Remind students to keep these changes in mind in particular as they study opposition to women's rights.

Answers

Reading Check *Female abolitionists discovered that they often had to defend their right to speak in public, and fighting for others' rights led women to want to fight for their own.*

Sarah Grimké also argued for equal educational opportunities. She pointed out laws that negatively affected women. In addition, she demanded equal pay for equal work.

Sarah Grimké never married. She explained that the laws of the day gave a husband complete control of his wife's property. Therefore, she feared that by marrying, she would become more like a slave than a wife. Her sister, Angelina, did marry, but she refused to promise to obey her husband during their marriage ceremony. She married Theodore Weld, an abolitionist. Weld agreed to give up his legal right to control her property after they married. For the Grimkés, the abolitionist principles and women's rights principles were identical.

In 1845 the famous transcendentalist Margaret Fuller published *Woman in the Nineteenth Century.* This book used well-known sayings to explain the role of women in American society. Fuller used democratic and transcendentalist principles to stress the importance of individualism to all people, especially women. The book influenced many leaders of the women's rights movement.

Sojourner Truth

Sojourner Truth was another powerful supporter of both abolition and women's rights.

She had been born into slavery in about 1797. Her birth name was Isabella Baumfree. She took the name Sojourner Truth because she felt that her mission was to be a sojourner, or traveler, and spread the truth. Though she never learned to read or write, she impressed many well-educated people. One person who thought highly of her was the author Harriet Beecher Stowe. Stowe said that she had never spoken "with anyone who had more . . . personal presence than this woman." Truth stood six feet tall and was a confident speaker.

In 1851 Truth gave a speech that is often quoted to this day.

❝That man over here says that women need to be helped into carriages and lifted over ditches, and to have the best place everywhere. Nobody ever helps me into carriages or over mud puddles, or gives me any best place …Look at me! I have ploughed and planted and …no man could head [outwork] me. And ain't I a woman?❞

—Sojourner Truth, quoted in *A History of Women in America* by Carol Hymowitz and Michaele Weissman

Truth, the Grimké sisters, and other supporters of the women's movement were determined to be heard.

READING CHECK Drawing Inferences
Why would reformers link the issues of abolition and women's rights?

Women's Voting Rights

1776 Abigail Adams asks her husband, John Adams, to "remember the ladies" and their rights in the Declaration of Independence.

1848 The Seneca Falls Convention is held and the Declaration of Sentiments is written.

462 CHAPTER 14

Differentiating Instruction

Below Level

Struggling Readers

1. Draw the graphic organizer for students to see. Omit the blue, italicized answers.

2. Have each student copy the chart and complete it by explaining how the abolitionist movement influenced the women's rights movement.

LS Visual/Spatial

Alternative Assessment Handbook, Rubric 13: Graphic Organizers

Abolitionist Movement

Female abolitionists found they often had to defend their right to speak in public, particularly when addressing men; Fighting for others' rights led women to want to fight for their own.

Women's Rights Movement

Opposing the Call for Women's Rights

Publications about women's rights first appeared in the United States shortly after the American Revolution. However, women's concerns did not become a national issue with strong opposition for many more years.

The Movement Grows

The change took place when women took a more active and leading role in reform and abolition. Other social changes also led to the rise of the women's movement. Women took advantage of better educational opportunities in the early 1800s. Their efforts on behalf of reform groups helped them learn how to organize more effectively and to work together.

Another benefit of reform-group work was that some men began to fight for women's rights. Many activists, both men and women, found it unacceptable that women were not allowed to vote or sit on juries. They were also upset that married women in many states had little or no control over their own property.

Opposition to Women's Rights

Like the abolitionist movement, the struggle for women's rights faced opposition. Many people did not agree with some of the goals of the women's rights movement. Some women believed that they did not need new rights. They said that women were not unequal to men, only different. Some critics believed that women should not try to work in public for social changes. Women were welcome to work for social change, but only from within their homes. "Let her not look away from her own little family circle for the means of producing moral and social reforms," wrote T. S. Arthur. His advice appeared in a popular women's magazine called *The Lady at Home*.

Some people also thought that women lacked the physical or mental strength to survive without men's protection. They believed that a woman should go from the protection of her father's home to that of her husband's. They also thought that women could not cope with the outside world; therefore, a husband should control his wife's property. Despite opposition, women continued to pursue their goal of greater rights.

READING CHECK ▸ **Drawing Conclusions**
Why did some men and women think that the women's rights movement was misguided?

1872 Susan B. Anthony is arrested while trying to vote in New York.

1890 Wyoming's new state constitution includes women's suffrage.

"There never will be complete equality until women themselves help to make laws and elect lawmakers."
Susan B. Anthony

1911 The National Association Opposed to Woman Suffrage is formed.

1920 On August 26, the Nineteenth Amendment is declared ratified by Congress, giving women the right to vote.

ANALYSIS SKILL | **READING TIME LINES**
Women in Wyoming could vote how many years before women in the rest of the country could?

NEW MOVEMENTS IN AMERICA **463**

Critical Thinking: Identifying Points of View
Above Level

Addressing the Opposition

1. Review with students the reasons some Americans opposed the women's rights movement.

2. Ask students to imagine that they are supporters of the women's rights movement in the mid-1800s. Have each student write an editorial responding to the criticisms of the women's rights movement.

3. Students' editorials should address each of the reasons Americans opposed the movement. Remind students to provide reasons to support their positions and to back up their reasons with facts and examples.

4. Have volunteers read their essays to the class.
   LS **Verbal/Linguistic**

   📝 Alternative Assessment Handbook, Rubric 43: Writing to Persuade

---

• Direct Teach •

Main Idea

❷ Opposing the Call for Women's Rights

Calls for women's rights met opposition from men and women.

Recall What social changes led women to become more interested in women's rights? *women's growing involvement in reform and abolition, improved educational opportunities for women, and the knowledge women gained from reform work about how to work together and organize more effectively*

Identify Points of View Why did some women oppose the call for women's rights? *did not believe they needed new rights, thought they were equal to men and just had different roles, and thought women should focus on their families*

Info to Know

Dress Reform Female reformers also fought for what most women today consider a personal right—freedom of dress. During the mid-1800s, women were expected to wear long skirts that weighed about 20 pounds and corsets that put extreme pressure on the abdominal area. These corsets often broke ribs and damaged internal organs. Some women's rights activists began wearing bloomers—baggy pants worn under a short skirt. People would follow these women and jeer, however. As a result, many women's rights activists stopped wearing them because they distracted people from the more important demand for women's suffrage.

Answers

Reading Time Lines *30 years*
Reading Check *thought that women were equal to men and just had different roles, women should not work for change in public, women's responsibilities were in the home, women lacked the physical and mental strength to survive, women could not cope with the outside world*

463

Main Idea

❸ Seneca Falls Convention

The Seneca Falls Convention launched the first organized women's rights movement in the United States.

Recall Why did Elizabeth Cady Stanton and Lucretia Mott decide to hold the Seneca Falls Convention? *because they were not allowed to participate in the World's Anti-Slavery Convention in 1840 and made to sit behind a curtain*

Summarize Why was the Seneca Falls Convention important? *It brought together many reformers and was the first public meeting on women's rights in the United States.*

- **CRF:** Biography Activity: Suffragettes
- **CRF:** Primary Source Activity: Elizabeth Cady Stanton, Letter to Lucretia Mott, 1876

Primary Source

Reading Like a Historian

Declaration of Sentiments Help students practice reading the document like historians. Ask:

- What political views of the period shaped the document?
- What did the authors hope to gain by writing the document?
- How did patterning the document after the Declaration of Independence give it more power?

Answers

Analyzing Primary Sources *because it stated the inalienable rights people should have, but it failed to extend those rights to women*

464

HISTORIC DOCUMENT
Declaration of Sentiments

At the 1848 Seneca Falls Convention, 100 people signed the Declaration of Sentiments, a document declaring the rights of women. The wording of the document purposely echoed the Declaration of Independence.

> The authors use the same words that are in the Declaration of Independence, but include women.

> Here the women demand that they become a part of government.

We hold these truths to be self-evident: that all men and women are created equal; that they are endowed by their Creator with certain inalienable[1] rights; that among these are life, liberty, and the pursuit of happiness; that to secure these rights governments are instituted, deriving their just powers from the consent of the governed. Whenever any form of government becomes destructive of these ends, it is the right of those who suffer from it to refuse allegiance[2] to it, and to insist upon the institution of a new government, laying its foundation on such principles, and organizing its powers in such form, as to them shall seem most likely to effect their safety and happiness.

1. **inalienable** not able to be taken away 2. **allegiance** loyalty

ANALYSIS SKILL | **ANALYZING PRIMARY SOURCES**

Why would women want to use the Declaration of Independence as a source for their own declaration?

Seneca Falls Convention

In 1840 **Elizabeth Cady Stanton** attended the World's Anti-Slavery Convention in London, England, while on her honeymoon. She discovered that, unlike her husband, she was not allowed to participate. All women in attendance had to sit behind a curtain in a separate gallery of the convention hall. William Lloyd Garrison, who had helped found the American Anti-Slavery Society, sat with them in protest.

The treatment of women abolitionists at the convention angered Stanton and her new friend, **Lucretia Mott**. Apparently, even many abolitionists did not think that women were equal to men. Stanton and Mott wanted to change this, so they planned to "form a society to advance the rights of women." Eight years passed before Stanton and Mott finally announced the **Seneca Falls Convention**, the first public meeting about women's rights held in the United States. It opened on July 19, 1848, in Seneca Falls, New York.

Declaration of Sentiments

The convention organizers wrote a **Declaration of Sentiments**. This document detailed beliefs about social injustice toward women. They used the Declaration of Independence as the basis for the language for their Declaration of Sentiments. The authors included 18 charges against men—the same number that had been charged against King George III. The Declaration of Sentiments was signed by some 100 people.

About 240 people attended the Seneca Falls Convention, including men such as abolitionist Frederick Douglass. Many other reformers who also worked in the temperance and abolitionist movements were present. Several women who participated in the convention worked in nearby factories. One of them, 19-year-old Charlotte Woodward, signed the Declaration of Sentiments. She worked long hours in a factory, making gloves. Her wages were very low, and she could not even keep her earnings. She had to turn her wages over to her father.

464 CHAPTER 14

Collaborative Learning

At Level

Seneca Falls Convention Promotional Piece

Materials: art supplies

1. Organize students into small groups. Have half the groups create promotional pieces to encourage attendance at the Seneca Falls Convention. Have the other half of the groups create similar items discouraging attendance. Promotional items might include fliers, posters, and buttons. To modernize the activity, have students create radio and television spots instead.

2. Students should focus on the purpose of the convention and what the people holding it hoped to achieve. Remind students to use messages that would appeal to Americans in the mid-1800s.

3. Have each group present its work to the class.
   LS Interpersonal, Verbal/Linguistic

Alternative Assessment Handbook, Rubrics 14: Group Activity; and 29: Presentations

Women's Rights Leaders

After the convention, the struggle continued. Women's rights activists battled many difficulties and much opposition. Still, they kept working to obtain greater equality for women. Among the many women working for women's rights, three became important leaders: Lucy Stone, Susan B. Anthony, and Elizabeth Cady Stanton. Each brought different strengths to the fight for women's rights.

Lucy Stone was a well-known spokesperson for the Anti-Slavery Society. In the early years of the women's rights movement, Stone became known as a gifted speaker. Elizabeth Cady Stanton called her "the first who really stirred the nation's heart on the subject of women's wrongs."

Susan B. Anthony brought strong organizational skills to the women's rights movement. She did much to turn the fight for women's rights into a political movement. Anthony argued that women and men should receive equal pay for equal work. She also believed that women should be allowed to enter traditionally male professions, such as religion and law. Anthony was especially concerned with laws that affected women's control of money and property.

Anthony led a campaign to change laws regarding the property rights of women. She wrote in her diary that no woman could ever be free without "a purse of her own." After forming a network to cover the entire state of New York, she collected more than 6,000 signatures to petition for a new property-rights law. In 1860, due largely to the efforts of Anthony, New York finally gave married women ownership of their wages and property. Other states in the Northeast and Midwest soon created similar laws.

THE IMPACT TODAY

As of the year 2000, women earned about 75 percent as much as men in the United States did.

The Antisuffragists

As the suffrage movement picked up speed, opponents to women's suffrage also began to organize. The antisuffragists, or "antis," formed statewide groups opposing the suffrage movement during the late 1800s. In 1911, Josephine Dodge united many of these groups' efforts by creating the National Association Opposed to Woman Suffrage in New York City. Dodge and other antisuffragists argued that women's suffrage would distract women from building strong families and improving communities.

HEADQUARTERS NATIONAL ASSOCIATION OPPOSED TO WOMAN SUFFRAGE

NEW MOVEMENTS IN AMERICA **465**

Critical Thinking: Comparing and Contrasting [Below Level]

Women's Rights Collage

Materials: magazines, newspapers, paper, glue

1. Review with students the limited opportunities and rights that women in the mid-1800s had in the categories of education, politics, and employment.

2. Have students, working individually or in small groups, create collages illustrating the gains women have made in each of the above categories. Students should write short captions explaining their collages.

3. Display the collages in the classroom.
LS Visual/Spatial

📝 Alternative Assessment Handbook, Rubric 8: Collages

Linking to Today

Women's Rights National Historical Park The National Park Service has designated certain areas and homes in Seneca Falls, New York, as the Women's Rights National Historical Park. The park includes the building where the Seneca Falls Convention took place and the home of Elizabeth Cady Stanton.

Close

Have students review the early women's rights movement, including the significant leaders and events.

Review

Online Quiz, Section 5

Assess

SE Section 5 Assessment

PASS: Section 5 Quiz

Alternative Assessment Handbook

Reteach/Classroom Intervention

Interactive Reader and Study Guide, Section 5

Interactive Skills Tutor CD-ROM

Answers

Reading Check *Anthony meant that without any financial independence or economic power, women would never have true political or social equality.*

466

Elizabeth Cady Stanton wrote many of the documents and speeches of the movement, which were often delivered by Anthony. Stanton was a founder and important leader of the National Woman Suffrage Association. This organization was considered one of the more radical groups because of its position that abolition was not a more important cause than women's rights.

Not every battle was won. Other major reforms, such as women's right to vote, were not achieved at this time. Still, more women than ever before became actively involved in women's rights issues. This increased activity was one of the movement's greatest accomplishments.

Lucy Stone worked for equal rights for women and African Americans.

READING CHECK **Identifying Points of View** What did Susan B. Anthony mean when she said that no woman could be free without "a purse of her own"?

SUMMARY AND PREVIEW Women's rights became a major issue in the mid-1800s, as women began to demand a greater degree of equality. In the next chapter you will read about western expansion.

---

go.hrw.com
Online Quiz
KEYWORD: SR8 HP14

Section 5 Assessment

Reviewing Ideas, Terms, and People

1. **a. Identify** What role did Sojourner Truth play in both the abolition and women's rights movements?
   b. Analyze How did the abolition movement influence women to demand equal rights?

2. **a. Identify** What limitations on women's rights did many activists find unacceptable?
   b. Summarize Why did many Americans oppose equal rights for women?
   c. Elaborate What arguments might you use to counter the arguments of men and women who opposed equal rights for women?

3. **a. Recall** Who were the three main leaders of the women's rights movement, and how did they each contribute to the movement?
   b. Draw Conclusions Why might working-class women like Charlotte Woodward have supported the **Seneca Falls Convention** and the **Declaration of Sentiments**?
   c. Evaluate Do you agree with **Susan B. Anthony** that women should receive equal pay for equal work? Explain your answer.

Critical Thinking

4. **Analyzing** Review your notes on events in the women's rights movement. Then copy the graphic organizer shown below and use it to show the goals of the movement, as well as the arguments against it.

Goals	Opponents' Arguments

FOCUS ON WRITING

5. **Describing Women's Suffrage** Add notes about the women's suffrage movement to your chart. Note important leaders and describe what they were fighting for. Ask yourself, "How did the women's suffrage movement change life in the United States?"

466 CHAPTER 14

Section 5 Assessment Answers

1. **a.** as a public speaker and supporter
   b. Female abolitionists found they were denied some rights.

2. **a.** lacked the right to vote, married women lost control of money and property, limited educational opportunities, pay inequalities
   b. thought women and men were equal just different; women should focus on the home; women lacked the physical and mental strength to cope with some things
   c. Answers will vary, but arguments should address the issues in the previous answer.

3. **a.** Lucy Stone—spokesperson; Susan B. Anthony—strong organizer; Elizabeth Cady Stanton—wrote documents and speeches
   b. wanted control of her own money
   c. possible answers—Yes, women and men are equal and should be paid the same; no, men need to earn more to support families.

4. sample answer—goals: vote; opponents' arguments: lacked strength

5. See Answers 3a and 4 above.

Elizabeth Cady Stanton

What steps would you take to bring about nationwide change?

When did she live? 1815–1902

Where did she live? Elizabeth Cady Stanton was born in Johnstown, New York. She married a prominent abolitionist and settled in Seneca Falls, New York, where she had seven children. Later in life she traveled widely, giving lectures and speeches across the country.

What did she do? Stanton and fellow activist Lucretia Mott organized the nation's first women's rights convention, at Seneca Falls in 1848. She and Susan B. Anthony founded the National Woman Suffrage Association in 1869. For nearly six decades, she spoke and wrote passionately about women's rights.

Why is she important? Stanton helped author the Declaration of Sentiments, which demanded equal rights for women, including the right to vote. A brilliant speaker and debater, Stanton spoke out against laws that kept married women from owning property, earning wages, and keeping custody of their children.

Finding Main Ideas What problems did Stanton try to correct? What problems did she face in accomplishing her goals?

Elizabeth Cady Stanton helped author the Declaration of Sentiments at the Seneca Falls Convention.

KEY EVENTS

- **1815** Born in Johnstown, New York

- **1840** Meets Lucretia Mott at the World's Anti-Slavery Convention, where they are barred from participating

- **1848** Helps organize the first national meeting of women's suffrage reformers at Seneca Falls, New York

- **1851** Meets Susan B. Anthony, with whom she will later lead the National Woman Suffrage Association

- **1895** Publishes the Woman's Bible

- **1902** Dies in New York City

A WOMAN'S DECLARATION OF INDEPENDENCE 1848

NEW MOVEMENTS IN AMERICA **467**

Reading Focus Question

Have students discuss the introductory question before reading the biography. Ask students what actions they might take to effect change and what issues they might address. Then instruct students as they read the biography to note the actions Stanton took to bring about nationwide change, even though she lacked many legal and political rights.

CRF: Biography Activity: Suffragettes

CRF: Primary Source Activity: Elizabeth Cady Stanton, Letter to Lucretia Mott, 1876

Info to Know

Stanton's Education As a young girl, Stanton went to a coed school, but she later wrote that she was "the only girl in the higher classes of mathematics and the languages." Because she was female, she was not allowed to attend college. Stanton had studied law with her father, a judge, but as a woman, she was not allowed to practice law.

A Strong Woman Stanton never shied away from controversy. She urged reforms in divorce laws and in women's styles of dress. Her support of women's suffrage went against the beliefs of many of her fellow reformers. Still, Stanton did not bend. Seventeen years after her death, her goal of suffrage for women became a reality.

Critical Thinking: Finding Main Ideas | At Level

Persuasive Letter about Stanton

1. Ask students to imagine the following scenario: The school library has displayed posters of several famous Americans. None of the posters is of a woman, however.

2. Have each student write a letter to the school librarian asking him or her to display a poster of Elizabeth Cady Stanton in the library.

3. Students' letters should explain why Stanton should be included by listing her significant achievements and contributions in gaining rights for women. **LS Verbal/Linguistic**

4. **Extend** Have each student create a sketch of the Stanton poster to display in the library. The poster should highlight Stanton's legacy.
   LS Visual/Spatial

   Alternative Assessment Handbook, Rubrics 28: Posters; and 43: Writing to Persuade

Answers

Finding Main Ideas *problems tried to correct—ending slavery; gaining equal rights for women; changing laws that prevented women from owning property, earning wages, and keeping custody of their children; problems faced—opposition of those who opposed women's rights*

Accepting Social Responsibility

Activity Getting Involved Lead students in a discussion about the need for all members of society to behave in socially responsible ways. Ask students to identify the socially responsible behaviors mentioned in the lesson *(obligation to not do anything that harms society; duty to participate in society by exercising the rights and responsibilities of membership, such as keeping informed about issues; and supporting change to benefit society).* Write the list for students to see.

Then have students discuss ways in which they can get involved to bring about change to benefit society. Help students consider means of protest as well as other means. Then give students 15 minutes to free-write about why Americans should get involved and take action to improve society. Have volunteers read their responses to the class. Encourage discussion and feedback.

LS Verbal/Linguistic

Alternative Assessment Handbook, Rubric 37: Writing Assignments

Answers

Practice the Skill 1. *possible answer—yes, because slavery is morally wrong, corrupts a society that supports it, and harms all members of society who are enslaved;* **2.** *possible answers—yes, because I want to act on my beliefs; no, because I am afraid I will put the rest of my family at harm;* **3.** *possible answers—yes, I would be willing to help, but I am not willing to break the law; no, I believe that the law is wrong and that my actions will not hurt anyone but rather help people.* **4.** *possible answer—yes, because I would be acting to help others in society, and my actions might help bring about changes that will improve society.*

468

Accepting Social Responsibility

Define the Skill

A *society* is an organized group of people who share a common set of activities, traditions, and goals. You are part of many societies—your school, community, and nation are just three. Every society's strength depends on the support and contributions of its members. *Social responsibility* is the obligation that every person has to the societies in which he or she is a member.

Learn the Skill

As a part of your school, community, and nation, you have obligations to the people around you. The most obvious is to do nothing to harm your society. You also have a duty to be part of it. At the very least, this means exercising the rights and responsibilities of membership. These include being informed about issues in your society.

Another level of social responsibility is support of change to benefit society. This level of involvement goes beyond being informed about issues to trying to do something about them. If you take this important step, here are some points to consider.

1 Few efforts to change society have everyone's support. Some people will want things to stay the same. They may treat you badly if you work for change. You must be prepared for this possibility if you decide to take action.

2 Sometimes efforts to improve things involve opposing laws or rules that need to be changed. No matter how just your cause is, if you break law or rules, you must be willing to accept the consequences of your behavior.

3 Remember that violence is *never* an acceptable method for change. People who use force in seeking change are not behaving in a socially responsible manner, even if their cause is good.

This chapter was filled with the stories of socially responsible people. Many of them devoted their lives to changing society for the better. Some did so at great personal risk. Boston abolitionist William Lloyd Garrison barely escaped with his life from a local mob that tried to lynch him because of his views.

Garrison and the other reformers you read about demonstrated the highest level of social responsibility. They saw an issue they believed to be a problem in society, and they worked tirelessly to change it and make society better.

Practice the Skill

Review the "If you were there" scene on page 454. Imagine yourself as that Ohioan. You believe slavery to be wrong. However, you also respect the law, and it is illegal to help an escaped slave. In addition, you know that most of your neighbors do not feel as you do about slavery. They might harm you or your property if you take this stand against it.

1. Would agreeing to your friend's request help benefit society? Explain why or why not.

2. Are you willing to risk the anger of your neighbors? Why or why not?

3. Is the idea of breaking the law or possibly going to jail a factor in your decision? Explain.

4. Would agreeing to your friend's request be a socially responsible thing to do? Explain why or why not?

Social Studies Skills Activity: Accepting Social Responsibility

Posters Promoting Social Responsibility `At Level`

Materials: art supplies, colored markers, poster board

1. Have students create posters urging their fellow students to get involved in change to benefit society. Students might focus the theme of their posters on a specific type of involvement or cause, or instead focus on social action and involvement in general.

2. Students' posters should include a slogan and one or more images. Students might also include additional text to explain the meaning of their message. Remind students that when creating posters one or two large, emotionally charged images often are more powerful than many smaller images.

3. Display students' posters in public areas of the school. **LS Visual/Spatial**

Alternative Assessment Handbook, Rubric 28: Posters

Visual Summary

Use the visual summary below to help you review the main ideas of the chapter.

QUICK FACTS

IMMIGRATION · ABOLITION · EDUCATION AND PRISON REFORM · WOMEN'S RIGHTS · AMERICAN LITERATURE AND ART

Reviewing Vocabulary, Terms, and People

1. Which of the following authors wrote about Puritan life in *The Scarlet Letter*?
 a. Emily Dickinson **c.** Thomas Gallaudet
 b. Herman Melville **d.** Nathaniel Hawthorne

2. Which document expressed the complaints of supporters of women's rights?
 a. Declaration of the   **c.** Letters on
 Rights of Women   Women's Rights
 b. Declaration of   **d.** Seneca Falls
 Sentiments   Convention

3. As leader of the common-school movement, who worked to improve free public education?
 a. Walt Whitman **c.** Lyman Beecher
 b. Horace Mann **d.** Sojourner Truth

Comprehension and Critical Thinking

SECTION 1 *(Pages 438–442)*

4. a. Identify What political party was founded by nativists, and what policies did it support?
 b. Analyze What factors caused U.S. cities to grow so fast?
 c. Evaluate Do you think that the benefits of city life outweighed its drawbacks? Explain.

SECTION 2 *(Pages 443–445)*

5. a. Describe Who were some important transcendentalists, and what ideas did they promote?
 b. Compare and Contrast In what ways were transcendentalists and Romantics similar and different?
 c. Elaborate Which movement appeals to you more—American transcendentalism or Romanticism? Why?

Answers

Visual Summary

Review and Inquiry Have students list key events and people for each sign. Then have students write a brief paragraph describing how the visual summary captures the spirit of the reform movements of the 1800s.

 Quick Facts Transparency: New Movements in America Visual Summary

Reviewing Vocabulary, Terms, and People

 1. d
 2. b
 3. b

Comprehension and Critical Thinking

4. a. Know-Nothing Party, policies to keep Catholics and immigrants out of public office
 b. Transportation improvements and new jobs created by the Industrial Revolution led many people to move to urban areas.
 c. Students' answers will vary but should describe the benefits and drawbacks of living in a city.

5. a. Emerson, Fuller, Thoreau; belief that people could rise above material things, should be self-reliant, and live simply in tune with nature
 b. similar—focus on nature and simple life, individualism, personal insight; different—transcendentalism: a philosophy; Romantics: focused more on emotion and history
 c. Answers should show an understanding of both movements.

Review and Assessment Resources

Review and Reinforce

SE Chapter Review

 CRF: Chapter Review Activity

 Quick Facts Transparency: New Movements in America Visual Summary

 Spanish Chapter Summaries Audio CD Program

 Online Chapter Summaries in Six Languages

OSP Holt PuzzlePro; GameTool for ExamView

 Quiz Game CD-ROM

Assess

SE Standardized Test Practice

 PASS: Chapter Test, Forms A and B

 Alternative Assessment Handbook

OSP Examview Test Generator, Chapter Test

 Differentiated Instruction Modified Worksheets and Tests CD-ROM: Chapter Test

 Holt Online Assessment Program (in the Premier Online Edition)

Reteach/Intervene

 Interactive Reader and Study Guide

 Differentiated Instruction Teacher Management System: Lesson Plans for Differentiated Instruction

 Differentiated Instruction Modified Worksheets and Tests CD-ROM

 Interactive Skills Tutor CD-ROM

go.hrw.com

Online Resources

Chapter Resources:
KEYWORD: SR8 US14

6. a. alcohol abuse, prison reform, and education reform

b. Reformers believed that education made children responsible citizens.

c. Answers will vary but should demonstrate an understanding of the reform movements of the period and their effects.

7. a. religious reasons, thought slavery was morally wrong, thought slavery went against the right to liberty for which the American Revolution had been fought

b. northerners—feared that freed African Americans would work for lower wages and take away jobs; southerners—thought slavery was vital to the Southern economy

c. Answers will vary but should reflect an understanding of the methods used, such as speeches, publications, literature, antislavery societies, and petitions to Congress.

8. a. women's involvement in the abolitionist movement and the discrimination they faced; improved educational opportunities for women, and the knowledge women gained from reform work

b. possible answer—They wanted control over their wages.

c. Answers will vary but should reflect that the movement had achieved some success but that women still could not vote.

Using the Internet

9. Go to the HRW Web site and enter the keyword shown to access a rubric for this activity.

> KEYWORD: SR8 TEACHER

Reading Skills

10. d

SECTION 3 *(Pages 448–453)*

6. a. Identify What important reform movements became popular in the early 1800s?

b. Analyze Why did education become an important topic for reformers in the 1800s?

c. Evaluate Which reform movement do you think had the greatest effect on the United States? Why?

SECTION 4 *(Pages 454–459)*

7. a. Recall What are the different reasons why people supported abolition?

b. Make Inferences How did northerners and southerners differ in their opposition to abolition?

c. Evaluate Which of the methods used by abolitionists to oppose slavery do you think was most successful? Why?

SECTION 5 *(Pages 461–466)*

8. a. Recall What led many women to question their place in American society?

b. Make Inferences Why did female factory workers like Charlotte Woodward support the women's rights movement?

c. Evaluate By 1860 do you think the women's movement had been successful? Explain your answer.

Using the Internet

go.hrw.com
KEYWORD: SR8 US14

9. Activity: Creating Visuals The *Liberator* and *North Star* were two newspapers that encouraged the end of slavery. Enter the activity keyword and research the influence of abolitionist newspapers, such as those written by William Lloyd Garrison and Frederick Douglass. Then create a visual display that illustrates how each newspaper represented the abolitionist point of view.

Reviewing Themes

11. Immigration increased; cities grew rapidly, and urban problems developed; transcendentalists and American Romantics enriched the culture; Second Great Awakening increased church membership and religious faith; reformers worked to improve education, care for the mentally ill, prisons, and women's rights and to fight alcohol abuse and slavery.

Social Studies Skills

12. Students should note that the first three are socially responsible and that the last is not and explain why.

Reading Skills

Information and Propaganda *Use the Reading Skills taught in this chapter to answer the question below.*

10. Which of the following is *not* an example of propaganda?

a. a flyer protesting new tax laws

b. an ad about a political candidate

c. a radio announcement sponsored by an interest group

d. a list of camping rules from a park

Reviewing Themes

11. Society and Culture What social and cultural changes took place from 1800 to the mid-1800s?

Social Studies Skills

Accepting Social Responsibility *Use the Social Studies Skills taught in this chapter to fill in the chart below.*

12.

Action	Is it socially responsible?	Why or why not?
Removing litter from a park		
Voting		
Reading a political magazine		
Running a red light		

FOCUS ON WRITING

13. Writing Your Persuasive Letter You've described a number of important events and political, religious, and artistic movements in your notebook. Now, it's time to choose the one you consider most important. Think about how it changed life for people in the United States. Then write a two-paragraph persuasive letter to the newspaper, arguing for the event or movement you chose. In the first paragraph, identify the event or movement you chose as well as a thesis explaining why it is important. In the second paragraph, include details about the event or movement that support your thesis. Close with one or two sentences that sum up your points.

Focus on Writing

13. Rubric Students' letters should:

• provide a thesis explaining why the event or movement chosen is the most important

• provide details that support the thesis

• end with a summary

• include a salutation and a closing

CRF: Focus on Writing Activity: Persuasive Letter

Standardized Test Practice

DIRECTIONS: Read each question and write the letter of the best response.

1 A potato blight in Europe brought a large number of immigrants to the United States who were
  A Jewish.
  B German.
  C Irish.
  D Protestant.

2 All of these American writers of the mid-1800s are famous poets *except*
  A James Fenimore Cooper.
  B Edgar Allan Poe.
  C Walt Whitman.
  D Emily Dickinson.

3 The most famous leader of the Underground Railroad was
  A Frederick Douglass.
  B Harriet Tubman.
  C William Lloyd Garrison.
  D Harriet Beecher Stowe.

4 Which of these statements about the education of African Americans in the mid-1800s is *not* true?
  A Educational opportunities generally were greater in the North than in the South.
  B African American students often went to separate schools from white students.
  C Opportunities for college were rare until black colleges were founded in the 1840s.
  D Southern African Americans benefited from the educational reforms of Horace Mann.

5 The temperance movement, efforts at prison reform, and the abolition movement were all elements of
  A social reforms of the mid-1800s.
  B the Second Great Awakening.
  C transcendentalism.
  D the women's rights movement.

6 Which of the following people would *most likely* have supported a law prohibiting foreigners from holding public office?
  A an antisuffragist
  B a nativist
  C an abolitionist
  D a transcendentalist

7 Examine the following cartoon about women breaking kegs of liquor and then use it to answer the question below.

What does the shield of the woman on horseback represent? How can you tell?

Answers

1. C
Break Down the Question This question requires students to recall factual information. Refer students who have trouble to the text titled "Fleeing the Irish Potato Famine" in Section 1.

2. A
Break Down the Question This question requires students to recall factual information. Point out that the word *except* means students should select the person who was *not* a poet.

3. B
Break Down the Question This question requires students to recall factual information. Refer students who have trouble to the text titled "The Underground Railroad" in Section 4.

4. D
Break Down the Question Remind students to choose the answer that is not true. Refer students who have trouble to the text titled "African American Communities" in Section 3.

5. A
Break Down the Question This question requires students to recall factual information. Encourage students to use process of elimination to answer this question.

6. B
Break Down the Question This question requires students to recall factual information. Encourage students to use process of elimination to answer this question.

7. Answers should reflect an understanding of the temperance movement and be supported.

Intervention Resources

Reproducible
- Interactive Reader and Study Guide
- Differentiated Instruction Teacher Management System: Lesson Plans for Differentiated Instruction

Technology
- Quick Facts Transparency: New Movements in America Visual Summary
- Differentiated Instruction Modified Worksheets and Tests CD-ROM
- Interactive Skills Tutor CD-ROM

Tips for Test Taking

Spot Those Numbers Have students ever said, "I got off by one number and spent most of my time fixing my answer sheet"? To help students avoid this problem, tell them to do the following:
- Each time you answer a question, match the number of the question to the numbered space on the answer sheet.
- If you skip a question, leave the answer space blank.
- Keep a list of the questions you have skipped, but not on your answer sheet. You do not want to erase any more than necessary.

Chapter 15 Planning Guide

A Divided Nation

Chapter Overview	Reproducible Resources	Technology Resources
CHAPTER 15 pp. 472–501 **Overview: In this chapter, students will study the events leading up to the Civil War.**	**Differentiated Instruction Teacher Management System:*** • Instructional Benchmarking Guides • Lesson Plans for Differentiated Instruction **Interactive Reader and Study Guide:** Chapter Graphic Organizer* **Chapter Resource File:*** • Focus on Writing Activity: Writing an Autobiographical Sketch • Social Studies Skills Activity: Assessing Primary and Secondary Sources • Chapter Review Activity	**Power Presentations with Video CD-ROM** **Differentiated Instruction Modified Worksheets and Tests CD-ROM** **Primary Source Library CD-ROM for United States History** **Interactive Skills Tutor CD-ROM** **Student Edition on Audio CD Program** **History's Impact: United States History Video Program (VHS/DVD):** A Divided Nation*
Section 1: **The Debate over Slavery** **The Big Idea:** Antislavery literature and the annexation of new lands intensified the debate over slavery.	**Differentiated Instruction Teacher Management System:** Section 1 Lesson Plan* **Interactive Reader and Study Guide:** Section 1 Summary* **Chapter Resource File:*** • Vocabulary Builder Activity, Section 1 • Economics and History Activity: Economic Rivalry • History and Geography Activity: Free and Slave States • Primary Source Activity: William P. Newman • Biography Activity: Sojourner Truth **Political Cartoons Activities for United States History,** Cartoon 16: Antislavery Poster*	**Daily Bellringer Transparency:** Section 1* **Quick Facts Transparency:** Upsetting the Balance* **Internet Activity:** Slave Narratives
Section 2: **Trouble in Kansas** **The Big Idea:** The Kansas-Nebraska Act heightened tensions in the conflict over slavery.	**Differentiated Instruction Teacher Management System:** Section 2 Lesson Plan* **Interactive Reader and Study Guide:** Section 2 Summary* **Chapter Resource File:*** • Vocabulary Builder Activity, Section 2 • Biography Activity: Stephen Douglas • Primary Source Activity: Charles Sumner	**Daily Bellringer Transparency:** Section 2* **Map Transparency:** From Compromise to Conflict*
Section 3: **Political Divisions** **The Big Idea:** The split over the issue of slavery intensified due to political division and judicial decisions.	**Differentiated Instruction Teacher Management System:** Section 3 Lesson Plan* **Interactive Reader and Study Guide:** Section 3 Summary* **Chapter Resource File:*** • Vocabulary Builder Activity, Section 3 • Biography Activities: Dred Scott; Stephen Douglas • Literature Activity: Chicago Speech of 1858 **U.S. Supreme Court Case Studies:** *Dred Scott* v. *Sandford* (1857)*	**Daily Bellringer Transparency:** Section 3* **Quick Facts Transparency:** A Growing Conflict* **Internet Activity:** Lincoln-Douglas Debates Graphic Organizer
Section 4: **The Nation Divides** **The Big Idea:** The United States broke apart due to the growing conflict over slavery.	**Differentiated Instruction Teacher Management System:** Section 4 Lesson Plan* **Interactive Reader and Study Guide:** Section 4 Summary* **Chapter Resource File:*** • Vocabulary Builder Activity, Section 4 • Primary Source Activity: John Brown • Biography Activity: Jefferson Davis	**Daily Bellringer Transparency:** Section 4* **Map Transparency:** Election of 1860*

SE Student Edition
TE Teacher's Edition
go.hrw.com go.hrw.com
OSP One-Stop Planner CD-ROM

Print Resource
Transparency
LS Learning Styles

Audio CD
CD-ROM
Video

* also on One-Stop Planner CD

HOLT
History's Impact
United States History Video Program (VHS/DVD)
A Divided Nation
Suggested use: as a chapter introduction

Review, Assessment, Intervention

- **Quick Facts Transparency:** A Divided Nation Visual Summary*
- **Spanish Chapter Summaries Audio CD Program**
- **Progress Assessment Support System (PASS):** Chapter Test*
- **Differentiated Instruction Modified Worksheets and Tests CD-ROM:** Modified Chapter Test
- **One-Stop Planner CD-ROM:** ExamView Test Generator (English/Spanish)
- **Holt Online Assessment Program (HOAP),** in the Holt Premier Online Student Edition

- **PASS:** Section 1 Quiz*
- **Online Quiz:** Section 1
- **Alternative Assessment Handbook**

- **PASS:** Section 2 Quiz*
- **Online Quiz:** Section 2
- **Alternative Assessment Handbook**

- **PASS:** Section 3 Quiz*
- **Online Quiz:** Section 3
- **Alternative Assessment Handbook**

- **PASS:** Section 4 Quiz*
- **Online Quiz:** Section 4
- **Alternative Assessment Handbook**

Power Presentations with Video CD-ROM

Power Presentations with Video are visual presentations of each chapter's main ideas. Presentations can be customized by including Quick Facts charts, images from the text, and video clips.

Power Presentations with Video CD-ROM
HOLT
United States History
Beginnings to 1877
HOLT, RINEHART AND WINSTON
A Harcourt Education Company

DIVISION FOR **PUBLIC EDUCATION**
AMERICAN BAR ASSOCIATION

Developed by the Division for Public Education of the American Bar Association, these materials are part of the **Democracy and Civic Education Resources.**

- **Constitution Study Guide**
- **Supreme Court Case Studies**

Holt Online Learning

Teacher Resources
KEYWORD: SR8 TEACHER

Student Resources
KEYWORD: SR8 US15

- Document-Based Questions
- Interactive Multimedia Activities

- Current Events
- Chapter-based Internet Activities
- and more!

Holt Premier
Online Student Edition
Complete online support for interactivity, assessment, and reporting

- Interactive Maps and Notebook
- Standardized Test Prep
- Homework Practice and Research Activities Online

Differentiating Instruction

ENGLISH-LANGUAGE LEARNERS & STRUGGLING READERS

TARGET RESOURCE

Live Ink® Online Reading Help

Spanish Resources
Spanish Chapter Summaries Audio CD Program
One-Stop Planner CD-ROM:
- ExamView Test Generator, Spanish
- PuzzlePro, Spanish

Additional Resources
Differentiated Instruction Teacher Management System: Lesson Plans for Differentiated Instruction

Chapter Resource File:
- Vocabulary Builder Activities
- Social Studies Skills Activity: Assessing Primary and Secondary Sources

Quick Facts Transparencies:
- Upsetting the Balance
- A Growing Conflict
- A Divided Nation Visual Summary

Student Edition on Audio CD Program
Online Chapter Summaries in Six Languages
Interactive Skills Tutor CD-ROM

SPECIAL NEEDS LEARNERS

TARGET RESOURCE

Differentiated Instruction Modified Worksheets and Tests CD-ROM
- Vocabulary Flash Cards
- Modified Vocabulary Builder Activities
- Modified Chapter Review Activity
- Modified Chapter Test

Additional Resources
Differentiated Instruction Teacher Management System: Lesson Plans for Differentiated Instruction

Interactive Reader and Study Guide

Social Studies Skills Activity: Assessing Primary and Secondary Sources

Student Edition on Audio CD Program

Interactive Skills Tutor CD-ROM

Live Ink® Online Reading Help

ADVANCED/GIFTED AND TALENTED STUDENTS

TARGET RESOURCE

Primary Source Library CD-ROM for United States History

The Library contains longer versions of quotations in the text, extra sources, and images. Included are point-of-view articles, journals, diaries, historical fiction, and political documents.

Additional Resources
Political Cartoons Activities for United States History: Cartoon 16: Antislavery Poster

United States History Document-Based Questions Activities

Differentiated Instruction Teacher Management System: Lesson Plans for Differentiated Instruction

Chapter Resource File:
- Focus on Writing Activity: Writing an Autobiographical Sketch
- Literature Activity: Chicago Speech of 1858
- Primary Source Activity: William P. Newman, A Response to the Fugitive Slave Act
- Primary Source Activity: Charles Sumner on the Crime against Kansas
- Primary Source: John Brown, Address to the Court

One-Stop Planner® CD-ROM for Differentiated Instruction

Your differentiated instruction lesson plans are available at your fingertips. Holt's Teacher Management System links teaching support tools to pages in the Interactive Teacher's Edition.

The One-Stop Planner features:
- Interactive Teacher's Edition
- Calendar Planner and pacing guides
- Editable lesson plans
- All reproducible ancillaries in Adobe Acrobat (PDF) format
- ExamView Test Generator (English and Spanish)
- Transparency and video previews

Professional Development

- **In-service and staff development** as part of your Holt Social Studies product purchase
- **Quick Teacher Tutorial Lesson Presentation CD-ROM**
- Intensive tuition-based **Teacher Development Institute**
- **Teaching American History Online**—2 Module Professional Development Course
- **Convenient Holt Speaker Bureau**—face-to-face workshop options
- **PRAXIS™ Test Prep** interactive Web-based content refreshers*
- **24/7 Ask A Professional Development Expert** at http://www.hrw.com/prodev/

* PRAXIS is a trademark of Educational Testing Service (ETS). This publication is not endorsed or approved by ETS.

Chapter Big Ideas

Section 1 Antislavery literature and the annexation of new lands intensified the debate over slavery.

Section 2 The Kansas-Nebraska Act heightened tensions in the conflict over slavery.

Section 3 The split over the issue of slavery intensified due to political division and judicial decisions.

Section 4 The United States broke apart due to the growing conflict over slavery.

Focus on Writing

The **Chapter Resource File** provides a Focus on Writing worksheet to help students organize and write their autobiographical sketches.

CRF: Focus on Writing Activity: Writing an Autobiographical Sketch

A Divided Nation

FOCUS ON WRITING

Writing an Autobiographical Sketch When you read about history, it can be difficult to imagine how the events you read about affected ordinary people. In this chapter you will read about slavery in the United States. Then you will write an autobiography of a fictional character, telling how these events affected him or her. Your fictional character can live in any part of the United States. He or she might be an enslaved African, a southern plantation owner, a northern abolitionist, or a settler in one of the new territories. Your classmates are your audience.

UNITED STATES

1848
The Free-Soil Party is formed on August 9.

1848

WORLD

1848
Revolutionary movements sweep across Europe.

Key to Differentiating Instruction

Below Level

Basic-level activities designed for all students encountering new material

At Level

Intermediate-level activities designed for average students

Above Level

Challenging activities designed for honors and gifted and talented students

Standard English Mastery

Activities designed to improve standard English usage

Introduce the Chapter
At Level

Resolving Differences and Compromise

1. Ask students to imagine an issue that might divide their school. For example, suppose one group wants to eliminate the lunch break so that students can go home earlier. A second group wants to keep the lunch break and current school hours. Have students consider the pros and cons of each side.

2. Next, focus students' attention on how they might resolve such a dispute. Would they compromise? Would they vote and make all

students abide by the majority decision? Have students explore several resolution options.

3. Then have students consider the pros and cons of each choice. For example, what might be positive and negative results of compromising?

4. Explain to students that they are going to learn about how the issue of slavery increasingly divided the nation, sometimes with violent results, and how the nation's leaders tried to resolve the problem. **LS** **Verbal/Linguistic**

...for no man should take me

Harriet Tubman, who returned to the South 19 times, helping more than three hundred enslaved

HOLT

History's Impact
▶ video series
Watch the video to understand the impact of the states' rights debate on national unity.

What You Will Learn...
Two women look at a display called "Survival of Spirit" at the Museum of African American History in Detroit, Michigan. The display shows a history of resistance to slavery. In this chapter you will learn about how the debate over slavery increasingly divided Americans during the mid-1800s.

CHARLESTON
MERCURY
EXTRA:

UNION
IS
DISSOLVED!

• **Chapter Preview** •

HOLT

History's Impact
▶ video series
See the Video Teacher's Guide for strategies for using the chapter video **A Divided Nation**.

Explore the Picture
Survival of Spirit The Charles H. Wright Museum of African American History in Detroit, Michigan, is the world's largest African American history museum. Dr. Charles Wright, the museum's founder, started the museum to enrich the spirits of African Americans by giving them a sense of where they came from.

Analyzing Visuals Why do you think the exhibit shown in the photograph is called Survival of Spirit? *possible answer—because the exhibit highlights how African Americans endured, fought, escaped, and overcame slavery*

go.hrw.com
Online Resources
Chapter Resources:
KEYWORD: SR8 US15
Teacher Resources:
KEYWORD: SR8 TEACHER

1850 Congress passes the Fugitive Slave Act on September 18.

1852 *Uncle Tom's Cabin* is published by Harriet Beecher Stowe.

1856 In the Sack of Lawrence, pro-slavery forces attack the town of Lawrence, Kansas, on May 21.

1859 John Brown takes control of the federal arsenal at Harpers Ferry, Virginia.

1860 On December 20, South Carolina votes to secede from the United States.

1850

1855

1860

1852 Louis-Napoléon declares himself Emperor Napoléon III of France.

1856 British and French forces defeat Russia in the Crimean War.

1857 Indian soldiers in the British army begin the Sepoy Mutiny against British control of India.

473

Explore the Time Line
1. When did John Brown attack the federal arsenal at Harpers Ferry, Virginia? *1859*
2. What happened in South Carolina the year after the incident at Harpers Ferry? *South Carolina seceded from the United States.*
3. Slave narratives and books, such as Harriet Beecher Stowe's *Uncle Tom's Cabin*, helped people in the United States and Europe learn about the harsh realities of slavery. When was *Uncle Tom's Cabin* published? *1852*

Info to Know
Shifts in U.S. Political Parties Increasingly divided over slavery, Americans saw the rise and fall of political parties during the mid-1800s. The Free-Soil Party formed in 1848 to support free labor and to oppose the spread of slavery. By 1854 the party was gone, as was the Whig Party. That same year, some members of both parties joined with some abolitionists and Democrats to form the Republican Party. In 1860 this party would nominate an Illinois politician named Abraham Lincoln for president.

Reading Social Studies

Understanding Themes

Remind students about the debate that existed in the United States over the issue of slavery. Ask students how that debate might have had political ramifications for the United States. Ask students to predict some of those effects. Then ask students how the society and culture of the United States might have been affected by this growing division over slavery, and the resulting political effects. Help students to understand that the issue of slavery was the subject of much controversy.

Facts, Opinions, and the Past

Focus on Reading Bring in copies of the local newspaper or pages from different types of magazines. Organize the class into small groups and give each group different pages. Ask each group to find examples of facts and opinions in the pages it was given. Remind students that even in reputable newspapers or magazines, authors express opinions. Have each group present the facts and the opinions it found. Review these as a class and evaluate them.

Reading Social Studies

by Kylene Beers

| Economics | Geography | Politics | Society and Culture | Science and Technology |

Focus on Themes This chapter describes the growing tension between the North and the South over the slavery issue. You will read what happened as more states were admitted to the Union and people argued if they should be slave states or not. You will read about events that widened the division between the North and South so that the South finally chose to secede from the Union. Throughout the chapter you will see that **cultural** differences influenced **political** decisions.

Facts, Opinions, and the Past

Focus on Reading When you are trying to learn about history, separating facts from opinions helps you know what really happened.

Identifying Facts and Opinions Something is a **fact** if there is a way to prove it. For example, research can prove or disprove the following statement: "Abraham Lincoln belonged to the Republican Party." But research can't prove the following statement because it is just an **opinion**, or someone's belief: "Lincoln was the greatest president in American history."

Use the process below to decide whether a statement is fact or opinion.

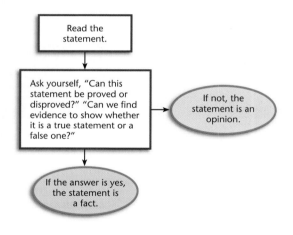

Read the statement.

Ask yourself, "Can this statement be proved or disproved?" "Can we find evidence to show whether it is a true statement or a false one?"

If not, the statement is an opinion.

If the answer is yes, the statement is a fact.

Reading and Skills Resources

Reading Support
- Interactive Reader and Study Guide
- Student Edition on Audio CD Program
- Spanish Chapter Summaries Audio CD Program

Social Studies Skills Support
- Interactive Skills Tutor CD-ROM

Vocabulary Support
- **CRF:** Vocabulary Builder Activities
- **CRF:** Chapter Review Activity
- Differentiated Instruction Modified Worksheets and Tests CD-ROM:
  - Vocabulary Flash Cards
  - Vocabulary Builder Activity
  - Chapter Review Activity

OSP Holt PuzzlePro

You Try It!

The following passage tells about the debates that Abraham Lincoln had with Stephen Douglas. All the statements in this passage are facts. What makes them facts and not opinions?

The Lincoln-Douglas Debates

In 1858 Illinois Republicans nominated Abraham Lincoln for the U.S. Senate. His opponent was Democrat Stephen Douglas, who had represented Illinois in the Senate since 1847. Lincoln challenged Douglas in what became the historic Lincoln-Douglas debates.

In each debate, Lincoln stressed that the central issue of the campaign was the spread of slavery in the West. He said that the Democrats were trying to spread slavery across the nation.

Lincoln talked about the *Dred Scott* decision. He said that African Americans were "entitled to all the natural rights" listed in the Declaration of Independence, specifically mentioning "the right to life, liberty, and the pursuit of happiness."

From Chapter 15, p. 491

Identify each of the following as a fact or an opinion and then explain your choice.

1. Lincoln accused the Democrats of trying to spread slavery across the nation.

2. The Lincoln-Douglas debates were the most important debates in the history of the nation.

3. Stephen Douglas was a U.S. Senator from Illinois.

4. Abraham Lincoln ran against Douglas in the 1858 Senate election.

5. Most Americans believed that the *Dred Scott* decision was a good one.

6. Lincoln was the best debater people from Illinois had ever heard.

As you read Chapter 15, look closely at quotes from historical figures. Are these quotes showing you facts or opinions?

Reading Social Studies

Key Terms and People

Preteach the key terms and people from this chapter by reviewing each term or person with the class. Then have each student create a set of flashcards using the key terms and people. Have students write the term or name on one side of the card and the definition or description of that term on the other side. Encourage students to use their flashcards regularly to study these people and terms. **LS** **Verbal/Linguistic, Kinesthetic**

Focus on Reading

See the **Focus on Reading** questions in this chapter for more practice on this reading social studies skill.

Reading Social Studies Assessment

See the **Chapter Review** at the end of this chapter for student assessment questions related to this reading skill.

Teaching Tip

Remind students of the sources they should use when checking facts. These include reliable sources such as encyclopedias, almanacs, dictionaries, public documents, and scientific journals. Remind students that even when they use verifiable sources, they should be able to find the same information in more than one source. Finally, remind students to evaluate sources from the Internet carefully.

Answers

You Try It! 1. *fact; it is supported by information in the passage;* **2.** *opinion; this cannot be proved;* **3.** *fact; this is supported by the passage;* **4.** *fact; this is stated in the passage;* **5.** *opinion; this cannot be verified or proved;* **6.** *opinion; there is no evidence to prove this*

Bellringer

If YOU were there . . . Use the **Daily Bellringer Transparency** to help students answer the question.

📠 Daily Bellringer Transparency, Section 1

Building Vocabulary

Preteach or review the following terms:

abolitionists people working to end slavery (p. 480)

proviso a condition, as part of an agreement (p. 476)

secession formally withdrawing (p. 478)

sovereignty supreme authority (p. 476)

📝 **CRF:** Vocabulary Builder Activity, Section 1

Taking Notes

Have students copy the graphic organizer onto their own paper and then use it to take notes on the section. This activity will prepare students for the Section Assessment, in which they will complete a graphic organizer that builds on the information using a critical thinking skill.

The Debate over Slavery

What You Will Learn...

Main Ideas

1. The addition of new land in the West renewed disputes over the expansion of slavery.
2. The Compromise of 1850 tried to solve the disputes over slavery.
3. The Fugitive Slave Act caused more controversy.
4. Abolitionists used antislavery literature to promote opposition.

The Big Idea

Antislavery literature and the annexation of new lands intensified the debate over slavery.

Key Terms and People

popular sovereignty, *p. 476*
Wilmot Proviso, *p. 476*
sectionalism, *p. 477*
Free-Soil Party, *p. 477*
Compromise of 1850, *p. 479*
Fugitive Slave Act, *p. 479*
Anthony Burns, *p. 480*
Uncle Tom's Cabin, p. 481
Harriet Beecher Stowe, *p. 481*

 TAKING NOTES Copy the graphic organizer below. As you read, take notes on the sequence of events in the debate over slavery. Be sure to describe the effects of each event.

Significant Events in the Slavery Debate	
Event	Effect
1.	
2.	
3.	
4.	
5.	
6.	

If YOU were there...

You live in a crowded neighborhood in New York City in 1854. Your apartment building is home to a variety of people—long-time residents, Irish immigrants, free African Americans. One day federal marshals knock on your door. They claim that one of your neighbors is a fugitive slave. The marshals say you must help them find her. If you don't, you will be fined or even sent to jail.

What would you tell the federal marshals?

> **BUILDING BACKGROUND** Some reform movements of the 1800s drew stubborn and often violent opposition. This was especially true of the abolitionist movement. Pro-slavery supporters fought for laws to protect slavery and extend the slave system. These laws were a threat to African Americans in the North.

New Land Renews Slavery Disputes

The United States added more than 500,000 square miles of land as a result of winning the Mexican-American War in 1848. The additional land caused bitter debate about slavery. The Missouri Compromise of 1820 had divided the Louisiana Purchase into either free or slave regions. It prohibited slavery north of latitude 36°30' but let Missouri become a slave state. In the 1840s President James K. Polk wanted to extend the 36°30' line to the West coast, dividing the Mexican Cession into two parts—one free and one enslaved. Some leaders, including Senator Lewis Cass of Michigan, encouraged **popular sovereignty**, the idea that political power belongs to the people, who should decide on banning or allowing slavery.

Regional Differences about Slavery

Some northerners wanted to outlaw slavery in all parts of the Mexican Cession. During the war, Representative David Wilmot offered the **Wilmot Proviso**, a document stating that "neither slavery nor involuntary servitude shall ever exist in any part of [the] territory."

Teach the Big Idea

The Debate over Slavery

1. **Teach** Ask students the questions in the Main Idea boxes to teach this section.

2. **Apply** Draw a two-column chart and label the columns *Cause* and *Effect*. Have students copy the chart and complete it by listing the major cause-and-effect relationships between events in the section. Model the activity for students by listing the following: *cause—gain of Mexican Cession; effect—renewed bitter debate over slavery.*
   LS **Verbal/Linguistic**

3. **Review** As you review the section's main ideas, have students share the cause-and-effect relationships they listed.

4. **Practice/Homework** Have each student create either a letter to the editor or a political cartoon opposing the Fugitive Slave Act.
   LS **Verbal/Linguistic, Visual/Spatial**

   📝 Alternative Assessment Handbook, Rubrics 7: Charts; 27: Political Cartoons; and 37: Writing Assignments

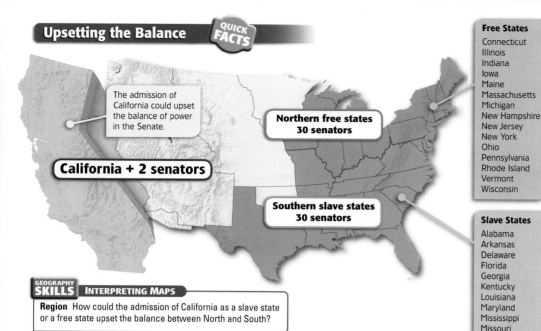

Upsetting the Balance — QUICK FACTS

The admission of California could upset the balance of power in the Senate.

California + 2 senators

Northern free states
30 senators

Southern slave states
30 senators

Free States
Connecticut
Illinois
Indiana
Iowa
Maine
Massachusetts
Michigan
New Hampshire
New Jersey
New York
Ohio
Pennsylvania
Rhode Island
Vermont
Wisconsin

Slave States
Alabama
Arkansas
Delaware
Florida
Georgia
Kentucky
Louisiana
Maryland
Mississippi
Missouri
North Carolina
South Carolina
Tennessee
Texas
Virginia

GEOGRAPHY SKILLS | **INTERPRETING MAPS**

Region How could the admission of California as a slave state or a free state upset the balance between North and South?

The northern-controlled House passed the document, but in the Senate, the South had more power. The Wilmot Proviso did not pass. Before this time, politicians had usually supported the ideas of their political parties. However, the Wilmot Proviso spurred a debate that showed growing **sectionalism**, or favoring the interests of one section or region over the interests of the entire country.

To attract voters, the Democrats and the Whigs did not take a clear position on slavery in the presidential campaign of 1848. In response, antislavery northerners formed a new party, the **Free-Soil Party**, which supported the Wilmot Proviso. They worried that slave labor would mean fewer jobs for white workers. Party members chose former president Martin Van Buren as their candidate. The new party won 10 percent of the popular vote, drawing away votes from Democrat Lewis Cass. Whig candidate Zachary Taylor won a narrow victory.

The California Question

The California gold rush caused such rapid population growth that California applied to join the Union as a state instead of as a territory. But would California enter the Union as a free state or a slave state?

Most Californians opposed slavery, which had been illegal when the state was part of Mexico. Also, many forty-niners had come from free states. But if California became a free state, the balance between free and slave states would change, favoring the free states.

In the South, an imbalance was unacceptable. "We are about permanently to destroy the balance of power between the sections," said Senator Jefferson Davis of Mississippi. He and many other southerners did not want California to enter the Union as a free state.

READING CHECK Drawing Inferences
Why did sectionalism in the United States increase in the late 1840s?

THE IMPACT TODAY
Small parties still affect presidential elections in a similar way today.

A DIVIDED NATION **477**

❷ Compromise of 1850

The Compromise of 1850 tried to solve the disputes over slavery.

Recall What were the five key points of Henry Clay's Compromise of 1850? *See the list at right.*

Summarize In their response to the Compromise of 1850, what views did senators Seward, Calhoun, and Webster represent? *Seward— antislavery view: opposed compromise because wanted California admitted without qualifications; Calhoun— southern view: opposed compromise because did not want balance of power upset; Webster—supported compromise as a way to preserve the Union*

Predict Do you think the Compromise of 1850 settled the question of slavery in the United States? Why or why not? *possible answer— no, because the issue would continue to arise as new territories requested statehood, the nation remained sectionally divided, and enslaved African Americans and abolitionists would continue to fight the injustice of slavery*

Primary Source
Reading Like a Historian
Comparing Documents Help students practice reading the documents like historians. Ask:

- What major issues do the two passages address?

- How do the two passages differ in tone?

- What assumptions does each speaker make?

Answers

Analyzing Primary Sources *He thought secession would lead to war and wanted to preserve the Union.*

478

Compromise of 1850

Senator Henry Clay of Kentucky had helped to settle the Missouri crisis of 1819–20 and the nullification crisis of 1832–33 by proposing compromises. He now had another plan to help the nation maintain peace. His ideas were designed to give both sides things that they wanted:

Primary Source

SPEECH
The Seventh of March Speech

On March 7, 1850, Daniel Webster spoke on the floor of the Senate in favor of the Compromise of 1850.

I hear with distress and anguish the word "secession." Secession! Peaceable secession! Sir, your eyes and mine are never destined to see the miracle. The dismemberment [taking apart] of this vast country without convulsion! The breaking up of the fountains of the great deep without ruffing the surface! Who is so foolish, I beg everybody's pardon, as to expect to see any such thing? . . . There can be no such thing as peaceable secession.

—quoted in *Daniel Webster: The Completest Man*, edited by Kenneth Shewmaker

> Webster is upset by talk of secession.

> Webster is saying that just as it is impossible to move water in the ocean without making waves, it is impossible for states to peacefully secede.

ANALYSIS SKILL | **ANALYZING PRIMARY SOURCES**
Why did Webster support the Compromise of 1850?

Henry Clay introduced the Compromise of 1850 on the Senate floor.

Daniel Webster spoke eloquently in support of the compromise.

478 CHAPTER 15

1. California would enter the Union as a free state.
2. The rest of the Mexican Cession would be federal land. In this territory, popular sovereignty would decide on slavery.
3. Texas would give up land east of the upper Rio Grande. In return, the government would pay Texas's debts from when it was an independent republic.
4. The slave trade—but not slavery— would end in the nation's capital.
5. A more effective fugitive slave law would be passed.

Clay's plan drew attack, especially regarding California. Senator William Seward of New York defended antislavery views and wanted California admitted "directly, without conditions, without qualifications, and without compromise." However, Senator John C. Calhoun of South Carolina argued that letting California enter as a free state would destroy the nation's balance. He warned people of issues that would later start the Civil War. Calhoun asked that the slave states be allowed "to separate and part in peace."

Differentiating Instruction

Below Level

Struggling Readers

Standard English Mastery

1. List the section's Key Terms and People for students to see. Help students define them.

2. Next, ask students to write eight sentences that summarize the section and use all the key terms and people. Students should write two sentences for each subsection, indicated by the blue headings.

3. Ask students who have trouble putting thoughts into words to summarize each part of the section aloud. Then help students get their ideas on paper.

4. As a class, students should share their sentences for each subsection. Write them for students to see. Correct any errors and improve students' use of standard English. Have the students help you work on the sentences until you have a model summary of the section. **LS Verbal/Linguistic**

📄 Alternative Assessment Handbook, Rubric 37: Writing Assignments

In contrast, Senator Daniel Webster of Massachusetts favored Clay's plan:

"I wish to speak today, not as a Massachusetts man, nor as a Northern man, but as an American ... I speak today for the preservation of the Union. Hear me for my cause."
—Daniel Webster, quoted in *Battle Cry of Freedom* by James M. McPherson

Webster criticized northern abolitionists and southerners who talked of secession.

A compromise was enacted that year and seemed to settle most disputes between free and slave states. It achieved the majority of Clay's proposals. With the **Compromise of 1850**, California was able to enter the Union as a free state. The rest of the Mexican Cession was divided into two territories—Utah and New Mexico—where the question of whether to allow slavery would be decided by popular sovereignty.

Texas agreed to give up its land claims in New Mexico in exchange for financial aid from the federal government. The compromise outlawed the slave trade in the District of Columbia and established a new fugitive slave law.

READING CHECK Analyzing How was Texas affected by the Compromise of 1850?

Fugitive Slave Act

The newly passed **Fugitive Slave Act** made it a crime to help runaway slaves and allowed officials to arrest those slaves in free areas. Slaveholders were permitted to take suspected fugitives to U.S. commissioners, who decided their fate.

Details of the Fugitive Slave Act

Slaveholders could use testimony from white witnesses, but enslaved African Americans accused of being fugitives could not testify. Nor could people who hid or helped a runaway slave—they faced six months in jail and a $1,000 fine. Commissioners who rejected a slaveholder's claim earned $5 while those who returned suspected fugitives to slaveholders earned $10. Clearly, the commissioners benefited from helping slaveholders.

Reactions to the Fugitive Slave Act

Enforcement of the Fugitive Slave Act began immediately. In September 1850—the same month the law was passed—federal marshals arrested African American James Hamlet. They returned him to a slaveholder in

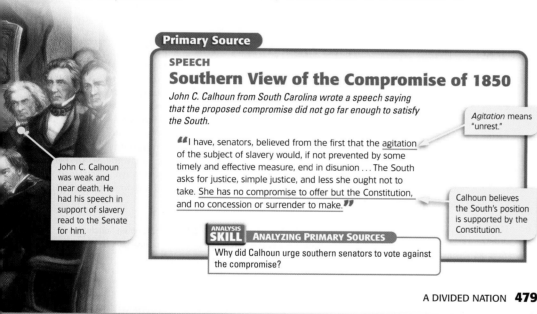

SPEECH
Southern View of the Compromise of 1850

John C. Calhoun from South Carolina wrote a speech saying that the proposed compromise did not go far enough to satisfy the South.

"I have, senators, believed from the first that the agitation of the subject of slavery would, if not prevented by some timely and effective measure, end in disunion ... The South asks for justice, simple justice, and less she ought not to take. She has no compromise to offer but the Constitution, and no concession or surrender to make."

Agitation means "unrest."

Calhoun believes the South's position is supported by the Constitution.

John C. Calhoun was weak and near death. He had his speech in support of slavery read to the Senate for him.

ANALYSIS SKILL ANALYZING PRIMARY SOURCES
Why did Calhoun urge southern senators to vote against the compromise?

A DIVIDED NATION **479**

Direct Teach

Main Idea

❸ Fugitive Slave Act

The Fugitive Slave Act caused more controversy.

Define What was the purpose of the Fugitive Slave Act? *made it a crime to help runaway slaves and allowed officials to arrest those slaves in free areas*

Summarize How was the Fugitive Slave Act biased in favor of slaveholders? *prevented fugitive slaves and those who helped them from testifying, used monetary rewards to encourage commissioners to decide in favor of slaveholders*

Draw Conclusions Why do you think that of 343 fugitive slave cases, fugitive slaves were declared free only 11 times? *Students should mention the bias of the law, such as restrictions on who could testify.*

📖 **CRF:** Primary Source Activity: William P. Newman, A Response to the Fugitive Slave Act

Info to Know

Approving the Compromise Henry Clay was unable to get his compromise approved as a whole. On the advice of fellow legislator Stephen Douglas, Clay divided the bill into separate parts. The plan worked. Each of the separate measures passed, usually by votes that revealed sectional biases.

Critical Thinking: Identifying Points of View   **At Level**

Debate over Slavery Chart

Materials: construction paper or poster board

1. As students read the section, have them make a list of the key leaders connected to the slavery issue. Lists should include David Wilmot, Lewis Cass, Jefferson Davis, Henry Clay, Daniel Webster, and John C. Calhoun.

2. Then ask each student to create a large chart of the leaders on construction paper or poster board. For each leader, students should provide a short caption identifying the person and his view on the slavery issue. To illustrate each

person's views students might also include short quotes where available. Tell students to group the leaders according to the leaders' views.

3. Have students share the information they listed to help you create a large master chart. Display the master chart in the classroom and add to it during the study of the chapter.

🔲 **Verbal/Linguistic, Visual/Spatial**

📋 Alternative Assessment Handbook, Rubric 7: Charts

Answers

Analyzing Primary Sources *Calhoun thought the proposed compromise did not satisfy the South and provide justice.*

Reading Check *Texas gave up land claims in New Mexico in exchange for financial help from the government.*

Direct Teach

Connect to Literature

Slave Narratives Frederick Douglass's autobiography is only one of a number of slave narratives. One historian has estimated that more than 6,000 such narratives exist. The earliest known narrative—the story of Adam, the "servant of John Saffin, Esquire"—was published in 1703. Douglass's work, however, is probably the best known.

Checking for Understanding

Select the best answer for each of the following.

1. The debate over California's admission as a free state revealed increased
   a. popular sovereignty.
   b. *sectionalism.*
   c. slavery.
   d. unity.
2. What did Henry Clay propose to solve the debate over California?
   a. *Compromise of 1850*
   b. Free-Soil Party
   c. popular sovereignty
   d. Wilmot Proviso
3. Why did many northerners dislike the Fugitive Slave Act?
   a. too soft on the North
   b. ineffective
   c. *unfair*
   d. too hard on the South

Answers

Analyzing Primary Sources *possible answers—a symbol of pride; showed support for their cause*

Reading Check *Northerners worried that accused fugitives were not granted due process and that commissioners would be biased because of differences in fees.*

480

PHOTOGRAPH
A Fugitive Slave Convention

The Fugitive Slave Act enraged abolitionists. To protest the new law, they held many meetings to publicly denounce it. One such meeting was held in 1850 in the small town of Cazenovia in central New York, a center for abolitionist activity. About 2,000 people—including many former slaves—attended the convention. They listened to speeches, made plans, and raised their voices for freedom. This photo was a point of pride for the delegates, but it also was used by opponents of the movement as a symbol of the poor morals of abolitionists: Not only were whites allowed to mix with African Americans, women and men were allowed to mix as well. This angered many people.

Gerrit Smith organized the convention.

Frederick Douglass spoke to the crowd.

The Edmonson sisters, Mary (left) and Emily, tried to escape from slavery but were captured. Abolitionists later purchased their freedom.

ANALYSIS SKILL **ANALYZING PRIMARY SOURCES**
Why would the abolitionists want a photograph of their convention?

Maryland, although he had lived in New York City for three years.

Thousands of northern African Americans fled to Canada in fear. In the 10 years after Congress passed the Fugitive Slave Act, some 343 fugitive slave cases were reviewed. The accused fugitives were declared free in only 11 cases.

The Fugitive Slave Act upset northerners, who were uncomfortable with the commissioners' power. Northerners disliked the idea of a trial without a jury. They also disapproved of commissioners' higher fees for returning slaves. Most were horrified that some free African Americans had been captured and sent to the South.

Most northerners opposed to the Act peacefully resisted, but violence did erupt. In 1854 **Anthony Burns**, a Virginia fugitive slave, was arrested in Boston. Abolitionists used force while trying to rescue him from jail, killing a deputy marshal. A federal ship was ordered to return Burns to Virginia after his trial. Many people in the North, particularly in Massachusetts, were outraged. The event persuaded many to join the abolitionist cause.

READING CHECK **Drawing Conclusions**
What concerns did northerners have about the Fugitive Slave Act?

Cross-Discipline Activity: Literature

At Level

Harriet Beecher Stowe Book Signing

Materials: *Uncle Tom's Cabin* (optional)

1. Ask students to imagine that they belong to an abolitionist group sponsoring an event at which Harriet Beecher Stowe will be signing copies of *Uncle Tom's Cabin*. Have each student create a newspaper piece promoting the event.
2. The promotional piece should briefly describe who Harriet Beecher Stowe is, explain what *Uncle Tom's Cabin* is about, and promote the

sale of the book. At the same time, the piece should subtly promote the views of Stowe and other abolitionists regarding slavery and the Fugitive Slave Act.

3. If possible, provide copies of *Uncle Tom's Cabin* and have students select excerpts from the book to include in their promotional pieces. **LS** **Verbal/Linguistic**

Alternative Assessment Handbook, Rubrics 2: Advertisements; and 43: Writing to Persuade

Antislavery Literature

Abolitionists in the North used the stories of fugitive slaves like James Hamlet and Anthony Burns to gain sympathy for their cause. Slave narratives also educated people about their hardships.

Fiction also informed people about the evils of slavery. **Uncle Tom's Cabin**, the antislavery novel written by **Harriet Beecher Stowe**, spoke out powerfully against slavery. Stowe, the daughter of Connecticut minister Lyman Beecher, moved to Ohio when she was 21. There she met fugitive slaves and learned about the cruelties of slavery. The Fugitive Slave Act greatly angered Stowe. She decided to write a book that would educate northerners about the realities of slavery.

Uncle Tom's Cabin was published in 1852. The main character, a kindly enslaved African American named Tom, is taken from his wife and sold "down the river" in Louisiana. Tom becomes the slave of cruel Simon Legree. In a rage, Legree has Tom beaten to death.

The novel electrified the nation and sparked outrage in the South. Louisa McCord, a famous southern writer, questioned the "foul imagination which could invent such scenes."

Within a decade, more than 2 million copies of *Uncle Tom's Cabin* had been sold in the United States. The book's popularity caused one northerner to remark that Stowe and her book had created "two millions of abolitionists." Stowe later wrote *A Key to Uncle Tom's Cabin* to answer those who had criticized her book.

The impact of Stowe's book is suggested by her reported meeting with Abraham Lincoln in 1862, a year after the start of the Civil War. Lincoln supposedly said to Stowe that she was "the little lady who made this big war." Her book is still widely read today as a source of information about the harsh realities of slavery.

READING CHECK Identifying Cause and Effect Why did abolitionists use antislavery literature to promote their cause, and what effect did it have on the slavery debate?

SUMMARY AND PREVIEW The United States experienced increasing disagreement over the issue of slavery. The Compromise of 1850 and the Fugitive Slave Act tried to address these disagreements with legislation. In the next section you will read about another disputed law concerning slavery, the Kansas-Nebraska Act, and the violence it sparked.

Section 1 Assessment

go.hrw.com
Online Quiz
KEYWORD: SR8 HP15

Reviewing Ideas, Terms, and People

1. **a. Describe** What ideas did the **Free-Soil Party** promote?
   b. Predict What are some possible results of the growing sectional debate over slavery?
2. **a. Describe** What were the major points of the **Compromise of 1850**?
   b. Contrast What differing opinions emerged toward Henry Clay's proposed compromise?
3. **a. Identify** What were the effects of the **Fugitive Slave Act**?
   b. Draw Conclusions Why did some Americans believe the Fugitive Slave Act was unfair?
4. **a. Identify** What are three examples of antislavery literature?
   b. Elaborate Do you think literature was an effective tool against slavery? Why or why not?

Critical Thinking

5. **Evaluating** Review your notes on the debate over slavery. Then evaluate how the Compromise of 1850, the Fugitive Slave Act, and antislavery literature affected the slavery debate. Use a graphic organizer like the one below.

FOCUS ON WRITING

6. **Taking Notes on the Debate over Slavery** Make some notes on the Wilmot Proviso, the Free-Soil Party, the Compromise of 1850, and the Fugitive Slave Act. Decide how your character feels about each of these. How do the Compromise of 1850 and the Fugitive Slave Act affect your character?

A DIVIDED NATION **481**

• **Direct Teach** •

Main Idea

4 Antislavery Literature

Abolitionists used antislavery literature to promote opposition.

Identify What important antislavery novel was published in 1852, and who was its author? *Uncle Tom's Cabin, by Harriet Beecher Stowe*

Identify Cause and Effect What effect did *Uncle Tom's Cabin* have? *electrified the nation, sparked outrage in the South, and increased abolitionist support*

📄 **CRF:** Biography Activity: Sojourner Truth

📄 Political Cartoons Activities for United States History, Cartoon 16: Antislavery Poster

• Review & Assess •

Close

Have students summarize the ways in which the nation tried to deal with increasing tensions and sectionalism over the issue of slavery.

Review

📄 Online Quiz, Section 1

Assess

SE Section 1 Assessment

📄 PASS: Section 1 Quiz

📄 Alternative Assessment Handbook

Reteach/Classroom Intervention

📄 Interactive Reader and Study Guide, Section 1

💿 Interactive Skills Tutor CD-ROM

Section 1 Assessment Answers

1. **a.** supported the Wilmot Proviso
   b. possible answers—continued conflicts in Congress; secession of slave states; civil war

2. **a.** See the list on p. 478.
   b. Calhoun—against, destroys balance of power between free and slave states; slave states should leave the Union; Webster—for, preserves the Union

3. **a.** upset many northerners; many fugitive slaves returned; some violent opposition
   b. restrictions on who could testify, trial without a jury, biased fee structure

4. **a.** slave narratives, Uncle Tom's Cabin, A Key to Uncle Tom's Cabin
   b. possible answers—yes, helped people realize the cruelty of slavery; no, read only by those who opposed slavery

5. Compromise of 1850—sparked debate between leaders and increased sectionalism; Fugitive Slave Act—upset many northerners and angered abolitionists; Antislavery Literature—educated and persuaded people

6. Students should show an understanding of Americans' different views toward slavery.

Answers

Reading Check *helped educate people about the hardships of enslaved African Americans; increased sympathy and support for the abolitionist movement*

481

Literature in History

Uncle Tom's Cabin

As You Read As students read, have them list words and phrases that appeal to their emotions. Next, ask volunteers to share some of the words and phrases they listed. What feelings and sentiments does each one provoke? Why? Have students discuss the sentiments that Stowe hoped to evoke in her readers and why. Close by having students discuss how Stowe's ability to provoke certain feelings contributed to her novel's lasting influence.

Meet the Writer

Harriet Beecher Stowe (1811–1896)
Born in Litchfield, Connecticut, Stowe was the seventh of nine children. Her father was a prominent Presbyterian minister, and her strong religious upbringing and faith shaped her life. After marrying, Stowe began writing stories and essays to supplement her husband's small income. The success of *Uncle Tom's Cabin* made her an instant celebrity. Her later novels include *Minister's Wooing* (1859), *The Pearl of Orr's Island* (1862), and *Oldtown Folks* (1869). She was elected to the National Women's Hall of Fame in 1910.

Antislavery Literature
from Uncle Tom's Cabin

by Harriet Beecher Stowe (1811–1896)

About the Reading *Published nine years before the outbreak of the Civil War,* Uncle Tom's Cabin *focused the nation's attention on the cruelties of slavery. In the following section, Stowe describes how a slave named Eliza is trying to escape to save her son from being sold.*

AS YOU READ Look for details that appeal to your feelings.

It is impossible to conceive of a human creature more wholly desolate and forlorn than Eliza when she turned her footsteps from Uncle Tom's cabin . . .

The boundaries of the farm, the grove, the wood lot passed by her dizzily as she walked on; and still she went, leaving one familiar object after another, slacking not, pausing not, till reddening daylight found her many a long mile from all traces of any familiar objects upon the open highway. ❶

She had often been, with her mistress, to visit some connections in the little town of T—, not far from the Ohio River, and knew the road well. ❷ To go thither, to escape across the Ohio River, were the first hurried outlines of her plan of escape; beyond that she could only hope in God . . .

GUIDED READING

WORD HELP

conceive imagine
desolate alone
forlorn unhappy
slacking slowing down
thither there
constrained forced
composedly calmly

❶ What detail tells you how long Eliza has walked up to this point?

❷ Why do you think she chooses that escape route?

CONNECTING LITERATURE TO HISTORY

1. Slaves had no legal rights. They were considered to be property, not human beings. How do the actions and dialogue in this passage contradict these ideas about slaves?

2. Frederick Douglass, Sojourner Truth, and other former slaves wrote narratives about their experiences. Yet these true stories did not have as much impact as Stowe's novel. Why do you think this fictional story about slavery had more impact than true slave narratives?

482 CHAPTER 15

Answers

Guided Reading 1. *mentions of having gone many a mile, of leaving familiar sights behind, of the day ending;* **2.** *because she has been there once before so she is slightly familiar with it*

Connecting Literature to History
1. *The passage shows that slaves have feelings for others and themselves, just like all human beings.* **2.** *Fiction can be made more dramatic and interesting than real-life accounts.*

482

Cross-Discipline Activity: Literature

At Level

Uncle Tom's Cabin Book Jacket

Materials: sample book jacket or book jacket template, heavy white paper, colored markers

1. Have each student create a book jacket for *Uncle Tom's Cabin*. Provide either a model book jacket or a book jacket template for students to use.

2. Students should fold a piece of paper to create front and back covers, a spine, and end flaps.

3. On the front cover, students should provide the title and author of the novel, a promotional tag line, and a strong image. On the end flaps, students should provide a brief summary of the book, followed by a brief biography of the author. On the spine, students should list the title and author. On the back cover, students should provide comments about the book's influence. **LS** Verbal/Linguistic, Visual/Spatial

Alternative Assessment Handbook, Rubrics 3: Artwork; and 42: Writing to Inform

Trouble in Kansas

If YOU were there...

You live on a New England farm in 1855. You often think about moving West. But the last few harvests have been bad, and you can't afford it. Now the Emigrant Aid Society offers to help you get to Kansas. To bring in antislavery voters like you, they'll give you a wagon, livestock, and farm machines. Still, you know that Kansas might be dangerous.

Would you decide to risk settling in Kansas?

> **BUILDING BACKGROUND** The argument over the extension of slavery grew stronger and more bitter. It dominated American politics in the mid-1800s. Laws that tried to find compromises ended by causing more violence. The bloodiest battleground of this period was in Kansas.

Election of 1852

Four leading candidates for the Democratic presidential nomination emerged in 1852. It became clear that none of them would win a majority of votes. Frustrated delegates at the Democratic National Convention turned to **Franklin Pierce**, a little-known politician from New Hampshire. Pierce promised to honor the Compromise

MURDER !!! help— neighbors help. O my poor Wife and Children.

CENTRAL AMERICA

CUBA

KANSAS

DEMOCRATIC PLATFORM

FORCING SLAVERY DOWN THE THROAT OF A FREESOILER

This political cartoon shows pro–slavery politicians forcing slavery on a settler in Kansas who is a member of the antislavery Free-Soil political party.

What You Will Learn...

Main Ideas

1. The debate over the expansion of slavery influenced the election of 1852.
2. The Kansas-Nebraska Act allowed voters to allow or prohibit slavery.
3. Pro-slavery and antislavery groups clashed violently in what became known as "Bleeding Kansas."

The Big Idea

The Kansas-Nebraska Act heightened tensions in the conflict over slavery.

Key Terms and People

Franklin Pierce, *p. 483*
Stephen Douglas, *p. 484*
Kansas-Nebraska Act, *p. 485*
Pottawatomie Massacre, *p. 487*
Charles Sumner, *p. 487*
Preston Brooks, *p. 487*

TAKING NOTES As you read, take notes on Stephen Douglas's plan for a railroad to the Pacific Ocean, southern congressmembers' views of his plan, and the resulting Kansas-Nebraska Act. Write details about each in a graphic organizer like the one shown below.

Douglas's plan	
Southern congress-members' reaction	

→

Kansas-Nebraska Act

A DIVIDED NATION **483**

Academic Vocabulary

Review with students the high-use academic term in this section.

implications things that are inferred or deduced (p. 485)

📋 **CRF:** Vocabulary Builder Activity, Section 2

Taking Notes

Have students copy the graphic organizer onto their own paper and then use it to take notes on the section. This activity will prepare students for the Section Assessment, in which they will complete a graphic organizer that builds on the information using a critical thinking skill.

Teach the Big Idea

At Level

Trouble in Kansas

1. **Teach** Ask students the questions in the Main Idea boxes to teach this section.
2. **Apply** Have each student list the section's blue and red headings on a piece of paper and leave room below each heading. Then instruct students to make short entries under each heading that detail the significant people, places, and events that contributed to violence in Kansas and in the Senate.
   LS Verbal/Linguistic
3. **Review** As you review the section's main ideas, have students share their notes on the issues and events that led to violence.
4. **Practice/Homework** Have each student write a one-paragraph radio news report for each of the blue headings in the section. Have volunteers present their reports to the class.
   📋 Alternative Assessment Handbook, Rubrics 37: Writing Assignments; and 42: Writing to Inform

❶ Election of 1852

The debate over the expansion of slavery influenced the election of 1852.

Explain Whom did the Democrats choose as their presidential candidate in 1852, and why? *Franklin Pierce; because none of the other nominees could win a majority of votes, and southerners trusted Pierce on the issue of slavery because he promised to honor the Compromise of 1850 and enforce the Fugitive Slave Act*

Analyze How did the Whigs' decision to nominate Winfield Scott as their candidate in 1852 backfire? *Scott's limited support of the Compromise of 1850 led southern voters to distrust him, and he lost.*

🗝 Map Transparency: From Compromise to Conflict

Answers

Focus on Reading *Everything is a fact except for the following phrase, which is an opinion—"this had been a good strategy."*

Reading Check *The debate over the expansion of slavery was the main issue, and Pierce's support of the Compromise of 1850 and Fugitive Slave Act helped him win the election.*

From Compromise to Conflict

The Missouri Compromise, 1820
Under the Missouri Compromise of 1820, there are an equal number of free states (orange) and slave states (green).

☐ Free state
☐ Free territory
☐ Slave state
☐ Slave territory

The Compromise of 1850
The Compromise of 1850 allowed for one more free state than slave state, but also passed a strict fugitive slave law.

What facts and what opinions are mentioned in this paragraph?

of 1850 and the Fugitive Slave Act. Therefore, southerners trusted Pierce on the issue of slavery.

The opposing Whigs also held their convention in 1852. In other presidential elections, they had nominated well-known former generals such as William Henry Harrison and Zachary Taylor. This had been a good strategy, as both men had won. The Whigs decided to choose another war hero. They passed over the current president, Millard Fillmore, because they believed that his strict enforcement of the Fugitive Slave Act would cost votes. Instead, they chose Winfield Scott, a Mexican War hero. Southerners did not trust Scott, however, because he had not fully supported the Compromise of 1850.

Pierce won the election of 1852 by a large margin. Many Whigs viewed the election as a painful defeat, not just for their candidate, but for their party.

READING CHECK Drawing Conclusions
What issues determined the outcome of the presidential election of 1852?

The Kansas-Nebraska Act

In his inaugural address, President Pierce expressed his hope that the slavery issue had been put to rest "and that no sectional . . . excitement may again threaten the durability [stability] of our institutions." Less than a year later, however, a proposal to build a railroad to the West coast helped revive the slavery controversy and opened a new period of sectional conflict.

Douglas and the Railroad

Ever since entering Congress in the mid-1840s, **Stephen Douglas** had supported the idea of building a railroad to the Pacific Ocean. Douglas favored a line running from Chicago. The first step toward building such a railroad would be organizing what remained of the Louisiana Purchase into a federal territory. The Missouri Compromise required that this land be free territory and eventually free states.

Southerners in Congress did not support Douglas's plan, recommending a southern route for the railroad. Their preferred line

---

Struggling Readers

1. Draw the graphic organizer for students to see. Omit the blue, italicized answers.

2. Have each student copy the graphic organizer and complete it by describing the Kansas-Nebraska Act and the events that resulted.
LS Visual/Spatial

📖 Alternative Assessment Handbook, Rubric 13: Graphic Organizers

Kansas-Nebraska Act
- **When passed:** *1854*
- **What it did:**
  divided rest of Louisiana Purchase into Kansas and Nebraska territories
- **How it dealt with slavery:**
  removed Missouri Compromise's limit on slavery north of 36°30' latitude; let residents vote whether to allow slavery

➡ **Effect:** *Both antislavery and pro-slavery groups send supporters to Kansas to vote.*

➡ **Effect:** *With help from Missouri voters, pro-slavery forces gain control of legislature. Antislavery forces form own legislature in response.*

➡ **Effect:** *Pro-slavery forces try to arrest antislavery government, leading to the Sack of Lawrence and one death.*

➡ **Effect:** *Abolitionist John Brown leads Pottawatomie Massacre, in which five pro-slavery men are killed.*

The Kansas-Nebraska Act
As a result of the Kansas-Nebraska Act, the question of slavery is to be decided by popular sovereignty—by the people who vote in the elections there—in the newly organized territories of Kansas and Nebraska. The act sparked violent conflict between pro-slavery and antislavery groups.

Free state
Free territory
Slave state
Slave territory
Popular sovereignty

GEOGRAPHY SKILLS INTERPRETING MAPS

1. **Region** In what part of the United States were the slave states located?
2. **Place** What free state was added with the Compromise of 1850?

ran from New Orleans, across Texas and New Mexico Territory, to southern California. Determined to have the railroad start in Chicago, Douglas asked a few key southern senators to support his plan. They agreed to do so if the new territory west of Missouri was opened to slavery.

Two New Territories

In January 1854, Douglas introduced what became the **Kansas-Nebraska Act**, a plan that would divide the remainder of the Louisiana Purchase into two territories—Kansas and Nebraska—and allow the people in each territory to decide on the question of slavery. The act would eliminate the Missouri Compromise's restriction on slavery north of the 36° 30′ line.

Antislavery northerners were outraged by the **implications**. Some believed the proposal was part of a terrible plot to turn free territory into a "dreary region . . . inhabited by masters and slaves." All across the North, citizens attended protest meetings and sent anti-Nebraska petitions to Congress.

Even so, with strong southern support—and with Douglas and President Pierce pressuring their fellow Democrats to vote for it—the measure passed both houses of Congress and was signed into law on May 30, 1854. Lost amid all the controversy over the territorial bill was Douglas's proposed railroad to the Pacific Ocean. Congress would not approve the construction of such a railroad until 1862.

Kansas Divided

Antislavery and pro-slavery groups rushed their supporters to Kansas. One of the people who spoke out strongly against slavery in Kansas was Senator Seward.

"Gentlemen of the Slave States . . . I accept [your challenge] in . . . the cause of freedom. We will engage in competition for . . . Kansas, and God give the victory to the side which is stronger in numbers as it is in right."
—William Henry Seward, quoted in *The Impending Crisis, 1848–1861* by David M. Potter

Elections for the Kansas territorial legislature were held in March 1855. Almost 5,000

ACADEMIC VOCABULARY
implications
things that are inferred or deduced

A DIVIDED NATION **485**

Main Idea

❸ Bleeding Kansas

Pro-slavery and antislavery groups clashed violently in what became known as "Bleeding Kansas."

Describe What was the situation in Kansas in early 1856? *two opposing governments and an angry and armed populace*

Summarize What occurred during the Sack of Lawrence? *A pro-slavery posse came to arrest leaders of the antislavery government and, not finding them, took out their anger by burning and looting the city.*

Identify Cause and Effect How did the Sack of Lawrence lead to further violence? *It angered abolitionist John Brown, who led an attack that became known as the Pottawatomie Massacre, during which he and his men killed five pro-slavery men.*

Evaluate Why do you think the situation in Kansas led to violence in the Senate chambers? *The violence and the slavery issue so inflamed people that they lost control of themselves.*

📝 **CRF:** Primary Source Activity: Charles Sumner on the Crime against Kansas

---

pro-slavery voters crossed the border from Missouri, voted in Kansas, and then returned home. As a result, the new legislature had a huge pro-slavery majority. The members of the legislature passed strict laws that made it a crime to question slaveholders' rights and said that those who helped fugitive slaves could be put to death. In protest, antislavery Kansans formed their own legislature 25 miles away in Topeka. President Pierce, however, only recognized the pro-slavery legislature.

READING CHECK **Analyzing** Why did northerners dislike the Kansas-Nebraska Act?

Bleeding Kansas

By early 1856 Kansas had two opposing governments, and the population was angry. Settlers had moved to Kansas to homestead in peace, but the controversy over slavery began to affect everyone.

"Bleeding Kansas"

Abolitionists and pro-slavery forces clashed in Kansas, killing many people. Shown here is a group of abolitionists who took the law into their own hands to free one of their group from prison.

Why might these men have fought against slavery?

John Noy was imprisoned for his abolitionist activities but was freed by other abolitionists.

In April 1856, a congressional committee arrived in Kansas to decide which government was legitimate. Although committee members declared the election of the pro-slavery legislature to be unfair, the federal government did not agree.

Attack on Lawrence

The new pro-slavery settlers owned guns, and antislavery settlers received weapons shipments from friends in the East. Then, violence broke out. In May 1856 a pro-slavery grand jury in Kansas charged leaders of the antislavery government with treason. About 800 men rode to the city of Lawrence to arrest the antislavery leaders, but they had fled. The posse took its anger out on Lawrence by setting fires, looting buildings, and destroying presses used to print antislavery newspapers. One man was killed in the pro-slavery attack that became known as the Sack of Lawrence.

John Brown's Response

Abolitionist John Brown was from New England, but he and some of his sons had moved to Kansas in 1855. The Sack of Lawrence made him determined to "fight fire with fire" and to "strike terror in the hearts of the pro-slavery people." On the night of May 24, 1856, along Pottawatomie Creek,

---

Collaborative Learning

At Level

The Nightly News from Kansas

1. Organize students into five groups and have each group create a TV newscast about one of the following: Kansas-Nebraska Act, formation of two Kansas governments, Sack of Lawrence, Pottawatomie Massacre, or the caning of Charles Sumner.

2. Each group should assign members roles, such as anchors, on-the-spot reporters, interviewees, writers, and so on. The TV report should provide coverage of the assigned event as well

as interviews with key figures and others. Encourage the groups to include visual aids in their reports.

3. Have each group perform its newscast for the class. After each newscast, point out any missing information or inaccuracies.

LS **Interpersonal, Kinesthetic**

📝 Alternative Assessment Handbook, Rubrics 14: Group Activity; and 33: Skits and Reader's Theater

---

Answers

"Bleeding Kansas" *felt it was unfair, cruel, unjust, and immoral*

Reading Check *It eliminated the Missouri Compromise's restriction on slavery north of 36°30'.*

Brown and his men killed five pro-slavery men in Kansas in what became known as the **Pottawatomie Massacre**. Brown and his men dragged the pro-slavery men out of their cabins and killed them with swords. The abolitionist band managed to escape capture. Brown declared that his actions had been ordered by God.

Kansas collapsed into civil war, and about 200 people were killed. The events in "Bleeding Kansas" became national front-page stories. In September 1856, a new territorial governor arrived and began to restore order.

Brooks Attacks Sumner

Congress also reacted to the violence of the Sack of Lawrence. Senator **Charles Sumner** of Massachusetts criticized pro-slavery people in Kansas and personally insulted Andrew Pickens Butler, a pro-slavery senator from South Carolina. Representative **Preston Brooks**, a relative of Butler's, responded strongly. On May 22, 1856, Brooks used a walking cane to beat Sumner unconscious in the Senate chambers.

Dozens of southerners sent Brooks new canes, but northerners were outraged and called the attacker "Bully Brooks". Brooks only had to pay a $300 fine to the federal court. It took Sumner three years before he was well enough to return to the Senate.

READING CHECK **Summarizing** What were some of the results of the intense division in Kansas?

SUMMARY AND PREVIEW The Kansas-Nebraska Act produced a national uproar. In the next section you will read about divisions in political parties.

> The cartoon above shows Preston Brooks beating Charles Sumner with his cane. Sumner's only protection is a quill pen symbolically representing the law.

Section 2 Assessment

go.hrw.com
Online Quiz
KEYWORD: SR8 HP15

Reviewing Ideas, Terms, and People

1. **a. Identify** What issues influenced the outcome of the election of 1852?
   b. Draw Conclusions Why did northern and southern Democrats support **Franklin Pierce**?
2. **a. Recall** What did the **Kansas-Nebraska Act** do?
   b. Explain Why did antislavery and pro-slavery groups encourage people to move to Kansas?
   c. Evaluate Would you have supported or opposed the Kansas-Nebraska Act? Why?
3. **a. Describe** What was the **Pottawatomie Massacre**?
   b. Analyze How did **Charles Sumner**'s views on "Bleeding Kansas" create conflict?
   c. Elaborate Do you think **Preston Brooks**'s punishment was reasonable? Why or why not?

Critical Thinking

4. **Sequencing** Review your notes on the Kansas-Nebraska Act. Then copy the graphic organizer shown below and use it to show how the act and later events led to violence in Kansas.

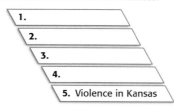

1.
2.
3.
4.
5. Violence in Kansas

FOCUS ON WRITING

5. **Taking Notes on the Trouble in Kansas** Make some notes on the election of 1852, the Kansas-Nebraska Act, and the events in Kansas. Decide how your character feels about each of these. How do these events affect your character?

A DIVIDED NATION **487**

487

Section 2 Assessment Answers

1. **a.** Fugitive Slave Act, Compromise of 1850
   b. He promised to honor the Compromise of 1850 and the Fugitive Slave Act.

2. **a.** created two new territories, in which popular sovereignty would decide the slavery issue; eliminated the Missouri Compromise's restriction on slavery north of 36°30′ latitude
   b. to try to make Kansas a free or slave state
   c. possible answers—yes, gave the people the power; no, allowed the expansion of slavery

3. **a.** 1856 incident in which John Brown led a group that killed five pro-slavery men
   b. His criticisms of pro-slavery Kansans and of a pro-slavery senator led a legislator to cane him senseless in the Senate chambers.
   c. possible answer—unreasonable, because Sumner could not work for three years

4. (1) election of Democrat Franklin Pierce as president; (2) Kansas-Nebraska Act; (3) rush of antislavery and pro-slavery activists to Kansas; (4) Kansas divided, with two opposing governments and angry, armed populace

5. Students should address each of the major events in this section.

Political Divisions

Bellringer

If YOU were there . . . Use the **Daily Bellringer Transparency** to help students answer the question.

🖶 Daily Bellringer Transparency, Section 3

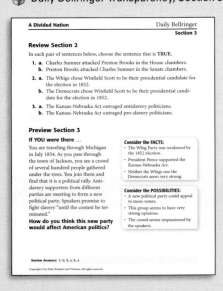

A Divided Nation | Daily Bellringer
Section 3

Review Section 2

In each pair of sentences below, choose the sentence that is TRUE.

1. **a.** Charles Sumner attacked Preston Brooks in the House chambers.
   b. Preston Brooks attacked Charles Sumner in the Senate chambers.
2. **a.** The Whigs chose Winfield Scott to be their presidential candidate for the election in 1852.
   b. The Democrats chose Winfield Scott to be their presidential candidate for the election in 1852.
3. **a.** The Kansas-Nebraska Act outraged antislavery politicians.
   b. The Kansas-Nebraska Act outraged pro-slavery politicians.

Preview Section 3

If YOU were there ...
You are traveling through Michigan in July 1854. As you pass through the town of Jackson, you see a crowd of several hundred people gathered under the trees. You join them and find that it is a political rally. Antislavery supporters from different parties are meeting to form a new political party. Speakers promise to fight slavery "until the contest be terminated."

How do you think this new party would affect American politics?

Consider the FACTS:
• The Whig Party was weakened by the 1852 election.
• President Pierce supported the Kansas-Nebraska Act.
• Neither the Whigs nor the Democrats seem very strong.

Consider the POSSIBILITIES:
• A new political party could appeal to more voters.
• This group seems to have very strong opinions.
• The crowd seems impassioned by the speakers.

Review Answers: 1. b; 2. a; 3. a

Copyright © by Holt, Rinehart and Winston. All rights reserved.

Academic Vocabulary

Review with students the high-use academic term in this section.

complex difficult, not simple (p. 489)

🖹 **CRF:** Vocabulary Builder Activity, Section 3

Taking Notes

Have students copy the graphic organizer onto their own paper and then use it to take notes on the section. This activity will prepare students for the Section Assessment, in which they will complete a graphic organizer that builds on the information using a critical thinking skill.

What You Will Learn...

Main Ideas

1. Political parties in the United States underwent change due to the movement to expand slavery.
2. The *Dred Scott* decision created further division over the issue of slavery.
3. The Lincoln-Douglas debates brought much attention to the conflict over slavery.

The Big Idea

The split over the issue of slavery intensified due to political division and judicial decisions.

Key Terms and People

Republican Party, *p. 488*
James Buchanan, *p. 488*
John C. Frémont, *p. 489*
Dred Scott, *p. 489*
Roger B. Taney, *p. 490*
Abraham Lincoln, *p. 490*
Lincoln-Douglas debates, *p. 491*
Freeport Doctrine, *p. 492*

TAKING NOTES As you read, take notes on the effects of political divisions and the *Dred Scott* case on the debate over slavery. Write your notes in a graphic organizer like the one below.

Political divisions ⟹ Debate over Slavery

Dred Scott case ⟹

If **YOU** were there...

You are traveling through Michigan in July 1854. As you pass through the town of Jackson, you see a crowd of several hundred people gathered under the trees. You join them and find that it is a political rally. Antislavery supporters from different parties are meeting to form a new political party. Speakers promise to fight slavery "until the contest be terminated."

How do you think this new party will affect American politics?

> **BUILDING BACKGROUND** The slavery question continued to divide the country and lead to violence. The issue not only dominated American politics in the mid-1800s but also brought changes in the makeup of American political parties.

Political Parties Undergo Change

Democrat Stephen Douglas had predicted that the Kansas-Nebraska Act would "raise a . . . storm." He was right. The Kansas-Nebraska Act brought the slavery issue back into the national spotlight. Some Whigs, Democrats, Free-Soilers, and abolitionists joined in 1854 to form the **Republican Party**, a political party united against the spread of slavery in the West.

Democrats were in trouble. Those who supported the Kansas-Nebraska Act were not re-elected. The Whig Party also fell apart when northern and southern Whigs refused to work together. A senator from Connecticut complained, "The Whig Party has been killed off . . . by that miserable Nebraska business." Some Whigs and Democrats joined the American Party, also known as the Know-Nothing Party. At the party's convention, delegates argued over slavery, then chose former president Millard Fillmore as their candidate for the election of 1856.

The Democrats knew they could not choose a strong supporter of the Kansas-Nebraska Act, such as President Pierce or Senator Douglas. They nominated **James Buchanan** of Pennsylvania. Buchanan had a great deal of political experience as Polk's secretary of state. Most

Political Divisions

Standard English Mastery

1. **Teach** Ask students the questions in the Main Idea boxes to teach this section.

2. **Apply** Ask students to imagine that they are abolitionists in the 1850s. Have each student write three short letters to a fellow abolitionist in Great Britain. The letters should describe the changes in U.S. political parties, the *Dred Scott* decision, and the Lincoln-Douglas debates. Tell students to describe the events and to identify various groups' views of them. **LS Verbal/Linguistic**

3. **Review** As you review the section's main ideas, have volunteers read their letters aloud. Correct errors to improve students' use of standard English.

4. **Practice/Homework** Have each student write a fourth letter predicting how these events might affect the nation's future.

🖹 Alternative Assessment Handbook, Rubrics 25: Personal Letters; and 41: Writing to Express importantly, he had been in Great Britain as ambassador during the Kansas-Nebraska Act dispute and had not been involved in the debate.

At their first nominating convention, the Republicans chose explorer **John C. Frémont** as their candidate. He had little political experience, but he stood against the spread of slavery. The public saw Republicans as a single-issue party. They had almost no supporters outside of the free states.

On election day, Buchanan won 14 of the 15 slave states and became the new president. Frémont won 11 of the 16 free states. Fillmore won only one state—Maryland. Buchanan had won the election.

> **READING CHECK** **Summarizing** What were the major political parties in the election of 1856, and who was the candidate for each party?

Dred Scott Decision

Just two days after Buchanan became president, the Supreme Court issued a historic ruling about slavery. News of the decision threw the country back into crisis. The Court reviewed and decided the **complex** case involving an enslaved man named **Dred Scott**.

Dred Scott Sues for Freedom

Dred Scott was the slave of Dr. John Emerson, an army surgeon who lived in St. Louis, Missouri. In the 1830s, Emerson had taken Scott on tours of duty in Illinois and the Wisconsin Territory. After they returned to Missouri, the doctor died, and Scott became the slave of Emerson's widow. In 1846 Scott sued for his freedom in the Missouri state courts, arguing that he had become free when he lived in free territory. Though a lower court ruled in

ACADEMIC VOCABULARY

complex difficult, not simple

SUPREME COURT DECISIONS

Dred Scott v. Sandford (1857)

Background of the Case Born a slave in Virginia, Dred Scott moved with his slaveholder to the free state of Illinois and then to the Wisconsin Territory. After returning to the South, Scott sued for his freedom. He claimed that because he had lived in a state that banned slavery, he was no longer a slave.

The Court's Ruling
The Court ruled that African Americans, whether free or slave, were not considered citizens of the United States, and therefore had no right to sue in federal court. It also decided that the Missouri Compromise was unconstitutional.

The Court's Reasoning
Chief Justice Roger B. Taney wrote in the majority opinion that the Court did not believe that African Americans were included in the Constitution's definition of citizens and that they "had no rights which the white man was bound to respect." Addressing a side issue in the case, the opinion also stated

that Congress could not outlaw slavery in the territories. This struck down the Missouri Compromise, which had made slavery illegal in territories north of the 36°30′ dividing line.

Why It Matters
The *Dred Scott* case was seen as a setback to abolitionist ideas against slavery. It reduced the status of free African Americans and upheld the view of slaves as property without rights or protection under the Constitution. It also took from Congress the power to ban slavery in its territories, which would aid the spread of slavery in new states. Because of its pro-slavery decision, the reputation of the Court suffered greatly in parts of the North.

ANALYSIS SKILL **ANALYZING INFORMATION**
1. Why do you think the Court ruled that African Americans had no access to federal courts?
2. How did this case affect abolitionist efforts?

A DIVIDED NATION **489**

A DIVIDED NATION **489**

Main Idea

❶ Political Parties Undergo Change

Political parties in the United States underwent change due to the movement to expand slavery.

Identify Members of which groups united to form the new Republican Party? *Whigs, Democrats, Free-Soilers, abolitionists*

Elaborate Who won the election of 1856, and what advantages did he have over the other candidates? *James Buchanan of Pennsylvania; He was experienced in politics and was overseas during the heat of the Kansas-Nebraska Act debate, so he was not connected to one side or the other in people's minds.*

Answers

Analyzing Information 1. *because the Court did not believe that African Americans, free or enslaved, were included in the Constitution's definition of citizens;* **2.** *was a setback to abolitionist efforts, particularly in stopping the expansion of slavery*

Reading Check *Republicans, John C. Frémont; Democrats, James Buchanan; Know-Nothing Party, Millard Fillmore*

Differentiating Instruction

Below Level

Struggling Readers

1. Explain to students that the Kansas-Nebraska Act caused changes in the makeup of U.S. political parties.

2. Draw the graphic organizer for students to see. Omit the blue, italicized answers. Have students copy the graphic organizer and complete it by listing changes that occurred in U.S. political parties as a result of the Kansas-Nebraska Act. **LS Visual/Spatial**

Alternative Assessment Handbook, Rubric 13: Graphic Organizers

Kansas-Nebraska Act

Republican Party	Democratic Party	Whig Party	Know-Nothing Party
Some members of the Whig, Democratic, and Free-Soil parties formed this party to oppose the spread of slavery.	*Most of those who voted for the act suffered politically; Buchanan, who had no connection to the act, was nominated in 1856.*	*Party fell apart when it became divided between northern and southern Whigs.*	*Some Whigs and Democrats joined this secretive party, which nominated former president Fillmore in 1856.*

Main Idea

❷ *Dred Scott* Decision

The *Dred Scott* decision created further division over the issue of slavery.

Recall Who was Dred Scott, and why did he sue? *an enslaved man who sued for his freedom after his slaveholder died*

Summarize Why was the *Dred Scott* decision significant? *It increased sectional tensions, overturned the Missouri Compromise, increased the chance of the spread of slavery, and declared that African Americans were not citizens.*

Develop Briefly defend Dred Scott's right to freedom. *possible answers— All people born in the United States should be citizens; human beings have a right to freedom, and slavery is wrong; he had lived on free soil, and his slaveholder was dead.*

📋 **CRF:** Biography Activity: Dred Scott

📋 **U.S. Supreme Court Case Studies:** *Dred Scott* v. *Sandford* (1857)

🗄 **Quick Facts Transparency:** A Growing Conflict

Biography

Dred Scott (c. 1795–1858) Following the Supreme Court ruling in his case, Scott and his family were bought by Henry Blow, who freed them. Scott worked as a hotel porter in St. Louis until his death in 1858.

A Growing Conflict — QUICK FACTS

Causes of Conflict
- Failure of Missouri Compromise
- Failure of Compromise of 1850
- Kansas-Nebraska Act
- *Dred Scott* decision

Short-Term Effects
- Political battles
- Sectional differences
- "Bleeding Kansas"
- Lincoln-Douglas debates

Long-Term Effect
- Civil War

his favor, the Missouri Supreme Court overturned this ruling.

Scott's case reached the U.S. Supreme Court 11 years later, in 1857. The justices—a majority of whom were from the South— had three key issues before them. First, the Court had to rule on whether Scott was a citizen. Only citizens could sue in federal court. Second, the Court had to decide if his time living on free soil made him free. Third, the Court had to determine the constitutionality of prohibiting slavery in parts of the Louisiana Purchase.

The Supreme Court's Ruling

Chief Justice **Roger B. Taney** (TAW-nee), himself from a slaveholding family in Maryland, wrote the majority opinion in the *Dred Scott* decision in March 1857. First, he addressed the issue of Dred Scott's citizenship. Taney

said the nation's founders believed that African Americans "had no rights which a white man was bound to respect." He therefore concluded that all African Americans, whether slave or free, were not citizens under the U.S. Constitution. Thus, Dred Scott did not have the right to file suit in federal court.

Taney also ruled on the other issues before the Court. As to whether Scott's residence on free soil made him free, Taney flatly said it did not. Because Scott had returned to the slave state of Missouri, the chief justice said, "his *status,* as free or slave, depended on the laws of Missouri."

Finally, Taney declared the Missouri Compromise restriction on slavery north of 36°30′ to be unconstitutional. He pointed out that the Fifth Amendment said no one could "be deprived of life, liberty, or property without due process of law." Because slaves were considered property, Congress could not prohibit someone from taking slaves into a federal territory. Under this ruling, Congress had no right to ban slavery in any federal territory.

Most white southerners cheered this decision. It "covers every question regarding slavery and settles it in favor of the South," reported a Georgia newspaper. Another newspaper, the New Orleans *Picayune,* assured its readers that the ruling put "the whole basis of the . . . Republican organization under the ban of law."

The ruling stunned many northerners. The Republicans were particularly upset because their platform in 1856 had argued that Congress held the right to ban slavery in the federal territories. Now the nation's highest court had ruled that Congress did not have this right.

Indeed, some northerners feared that the spread of slavery would not stop with the federal territories. Illinois lawyer **Abraham Lincoln** warned that a future Court ruling, or what he called "the next *Dred Scott* decision," would prohibit states from banning slavery.

Critical Thinking: Drawing Conclusions `Above Level`

Interview with Dred Scott

1. Ask students to imagine that they are abolitionist reporters covering Dred Scott's case. They have been granted an exclusive interview with Dred Scott following the Supreme Court's ruling in the case.

2. Have each student use the information in the text to write a fictional interview with Scott. Students should ask Scott why he sued for his freedom, how the Supreme Court ruled on his case, and what his reaction to the decision was.

Students should write both their questions and Scott's answers.

3. Have volunteers share their interviews with the class. **LS Verbal/Linguistic**

4. **Extend** Have students use the Declaration of Independence and the Fifth Amendment as a basis for a defense of Scott's freedom. **LS Logical/Mathematical, Verbal/Linguistic**

📋 Alternative Assessment Handbook, Rubrics 11: Discussions; and 37: Writing Assignments

SPEECH
A House Divided

In 1858 Abraham Lincoln gave a passionate speech to Illinois Republicans about the dangers of the disagreement over slavery. Some considered it a call for war.

> **"** In my opinion, it [disagreement over slavery] will not cease [stop], until a crisis shall have been reached and passed. "A house divided against itself cannot stand." I believe this government cannot endure permanently half slave and half free. I do not expect the Union to be dissolved—I do not expect the house to fall—but I do expect it will cease to be divided. **"**

—**Abraham Lincoln,**
quoted in *Abraham Lincoln: Speeches and Writings 1832–1858*
edited by Don E. Fehrenbacher

This line is a paraphrase of a line in the Bible.

Lincoln expresses confidence that the Union will survive.

ANALYSIS SKILL **ANALYZING PRIMARY SOURCES**

What do you think Lincoln meant by "crisis"?

> **"** We shall *lie down* pleasantly dreaming that the people of *Missouri* are on the verge of [close to] making their state *free;* and we shall *awake* to the *reality,* instead, that the 90 Supreme Court has made *Illinois* a *slave state.* **"**
>
> —Abraham Lincoln, quoted in *The Collected Works of Abraham Lincoln,* edited by Roy P. Basler

READING CHECK **Summarizing** What were the major rulings of the *Dred Scott* decision?

Lincoln-Douglas Debates

In 1858 Illinois Republicans nominated Abraham Lincoln for the U.S. Senate. His opponent was Democrat Stephen Douglas, who had represented Illinois in the Senate since 1847. Lincoln challenged Douglas in what became the historic **Lincoln-Douglas debates**.

In each debate, Lincoln stressed that the central issue of the campaign was the spread of slavery in the West. He said that the Democrats were trying to spread slavery across the nation.

Lincoln talked about the *Dred Scott* decision. He said that African Americans were "entitled to all the natural rights" listed in the Declaration of Independence, specifically mentioning "the right to life, liberty, and the pursuit of happiness." However, Lincoln believed that African Americans were not necessarily the social or political equals of whites. Hoping to cost Lincoln votes, Douglas charged that Lincoln "thinks that the Negro is his brother . . ."

Douglas also criticized Lincoln for saying that the nation could not remain "half slave and half free." Douglas said that the statement revealed a Republican desire to make every state a free state. This, he warned, would only lead to "a dissolution [destruction] of the Union" and "warfare between the North and the South."

At the second debate, in the northern Illinois town of Freeport, Illinois, Lincoln pressed Douglas on the apparent contradiction between the Democrats' belief in popu-

THE IMPACT TODAY
Today political debates are televised and can be seen around the world.

A DIVIDED NATION **491**

Info to Know

The Lincoln-Douglas Debates The fact that Lincoln lost the Illinois race for U.S. Senate to Douglas did not necessarily indicate that his views were not popular with Illinois voters. At that time, state legislatures, and not the people, elected senators. Although Republicans held some seats in the Illinois legislature, Democrats had done well in the 1856 elections and were able to ensure that Douglas won the Senate seat.

go.hrw.com
Online Resources

KEYWORD: SR8 US15
ACTIVITY: Lincoln-Douglas Debates Graphic Organizer

Close

Discuss the ways that the political parties chose to deal with the issue of slavery. Include views on popular sovereignty as well as state versus federal control in the territories.

Review

Online Quiz, Section 3

Assess

SE   Section 3 Assessment

PASS: Section 3 Quiz

Alternative Assessment Handbook

Reteach/Classroom Intervention

Interactive Reader and Study Guide, Section 3

Interactive Skills Tutor CD-ROM

Answers

Reading Check *He wanted to show Douglas's role in the Kansas-Nebraska Act and emphasize the Democrats' support of the spread of slavery*

492

Lincoln-Douglas Debates

Lincoln ran for the U.S. Senate in Illinois against Douglas in 1858. The two men debated seven times at various locations around the state. Lincoln lost the election but gained national recognition.

Abraham Lincoln

Stephen Douglas

lar sovereignty and the *Dred Scott* decision. Lincoln asked Douglas to explain how, if Congress could not ban slavery from a federal territory, Congress could allow the citizens of that territory to ban it.

Douglas responded that it did not matter what the Supreme Court decided about slavery. He argued that "the people have the lawful means to introduce it or exclude it as they please, for the reason that slavery cannot exist a day or an hour anywhere, unless it is supported by local police regulations."

This notion that the police would enforce the voters' decision if it contradicted the Supreme Court's decision in the Dred Scott case became known as the **Freeport Doctrine**.

The Freeport Doctrine put the slavery question back in the hands of American citizens. It helped Douglas win the Senate seat. Lincoln, while not victorious, made a strong important leader of the Republican Party.

READING CHECK **Drawing Inferences** Why did Abraham Lincoln make slavery's expansion the central issue of the Lincoln-Douglas debates?

SUMMARY AND PREVIEW The *Dred Scott* decision and the Lincoln-Douglas debates dealt with the conflict over slavery in the western territories. In the next section you will read about how the conflict broke apart the Union.

Section 3 Assessment

go.hrw.com
Online Quiz
KEYWORD: SR8 HP15

Reviewing Ideas, Terms, and People

1. **a. Identify** What was the major issue of the newly formed **Republican Party**?
   b. Draw Conclusions How did the Kansas-Nebraska Act affect political parties?
   c. Elaborate Why do you think **James Buchanan** won the election of 1856?
2. **a. Identify** Who was **Roger B. Taney**, and why was he important?
   b. Draw Conclusions How did the ***Dred Scott* decision** affect the Missouri Compromise and the expansion of slavery?
   c. Predict What problems might result from the Supreme Court's ruling in the *Dred Scott* case?
3. **a. Recall** What was the major issue of the **Lincoln-Douglas debates**?
   b. Make Inferences Despite his loss in the election, how did Lincoln become the leader of the Republican Party?

Critical Thinking

4. **Identifying Points of View** Review your notes on political divisions and the Dred Scott decision. Then copy the graphic organizer below and use it to identify the views of Abraham Lincoln and Stephen Douglas on slavery.

Lincoln		Douglas
	vs.	

FOCUS ON WRITING

5. **Taking Notes on the Political Divisions** Make some notes on the Republican Party, the *Dred Scott* decision, and the Lincoln-Douglas debates. Decide how your character feels about each of these. How do these events affect your character?

492   CHAPTER 15

Section 3 Assessment Answers

1. **a.** opposition to the spread of slavery
   b. led some to form the Republican Party; hurt northern Democrats who voted for the act; divided and then led to the end of the Whig Party; led some to join the Know-Nothing Party
   c. He had political experience but was not involved in the Kansas-Nebraska Act.
2. **a.** chief justice of the United States who wrote the majority opinion in the Dred Scott case
   b. overturned the Missouri Compromise, which opened all the territories to slavery
   c. more sectional tensions and conflict

3. **a.** spread of slavery in the West
   b. His strong showing in the debate gained him national prominence.

4. Lincoln: opposed slavery; believed African Americans entitled to rights listed in the Declaration of Independence; Douglas: opposed Lincoln's views; said making states free states would lead to war; believed citizens should decide slavery question

5. Students should describe how the *Dred Scott* decision and the discussions in the Lincoln-Douglas debates would affect their characters.

The Nation Divides

If YOU were there...

You work for the weekly newspaper in Harpers Ferry, Virginia. You strongly oppose slavery, but you think the question ought to be resolved by laws, not bloodshed. Now your paper has sent you to interview the famous abolitionist John Brown in prison. His raids in "Bleeding Kansas" killed several people. Now he is in jail for attacking a federal arsenal and taking weapons.

What questions would you ask John Brown?

BUILDING BACKGROUND Unpopular compromises and court decisions deepened the divisions between pro-slavery and antislavery advocates. The Lincoln-Douglas debates attracted more attention to the issue. As the disagreements grew, violence increased, though many Americans hoped to avoid it. But it was too late to keep the nation unified.

Raid on Harpers Ferry

In 1858 John Brown tried to start an uprising. He wanted to attack the federal arsenal in Virginia and seize weapons there. He planned to arm local slaves. Brown expected to kill or take hostage white southerners who stood in his way. He urged abolitionists to give him money so that he could support a small army. But after nearly two years, Brown's army had only about 20 men.

On the night of October 16, 1859, **John Brown's raid** began when he and his men took over the arsenal in Harpers Ferry, Virginia, in hopes of starting a slave rebellion. He sent several of his men into the countryside to get slaves to join him. However, enslaved African Americans did not come to Harpers Ferry, fearing punishment if they took part. Instead, local white southerners attacked Brown. Eight of his men and three local men were killed. Brown and some followers retreated to a firehouse.

Federal troops arrived in Harpers Ferry the following night. The next morning, Colonel Robert E. Lee ordered a squad of marines to storm the firehouse. In a matter of seconds, the marines killed two more of Brown's men and captured the rest—including Brown.

What You Will Learn...

Main Ideas

1. John Brown's raid on Harpers Ferry intensified the disagreement between free states and slave states.
2. The outcome of the election of 1860 divided the United States.
3. The dispute over slavery led the South to secede.

The Big Idea

The United States broke apart due to the growing conflict over slavery.

Key Terms and People

John Brown's raid, *p. 493*
John C. Breckinridge, *p. 495*
Constitutional Union Party, *p. 495*
John Bell, *p. 495*
secession, *p. 496*
Confederate States of America, *p. 496*
Jefferson Davis, *p. 496*
John J. Crittenden, *p. 497*

TAKING NOTES Create a chart like the one below. As you read, take notes on the significance of each of the people listed in the chart and his relationship to the events of the section.

Person	Significance
John Brown	
John C. Breckinridge	
John Bell	
Abraham Lincoln	
Jefferson Davis	
John J. Crittenden	

A DIVIDED NATION **493**

---

❶ Raid on Harpers Ferry

John Brown's raid on Harpers Ferry intensified the disagreement between free states and slave states.

Describe What was the result of John Brown's raid on Harpers Ferry? *Some of Brown's men were killed, some local white southerners were killed, and Brown and some of his men were captured. Brown was hanged. Many southerners felt scared and began talking about leaving the Union.*

Compare and Contrast How were Lincoln's views similar to and different from John Brown's? *similar—Lincoln agreed with Brown that slavery was wrong; different—Lincoln opposed the use of violence and treason.*

📄 **CRF:** Primary Source Activity: John Brown, Address to the Court

Primary Source

Reading Like a Historian

John Brown's Last Speech Help students practice reading the selection like historians. Ask:

• When did John Brown deliver this speech?

• What is his purpose?

• What personal biases shaped Brown's defense of his actions?

Answers

Analyzing Primary Sources
Whereas the court ruled that John Brown should be punished, he stated that his actions were right.

Reading Check *Southerners worried that other opponents of slavery would attack them or incite slave rebellions and that leaving the Union was the only way to protect their safety.*

494

SPEECH
John Brown's Last Speech

At his trial, after being pronounced guilty, John Brown spoke in his own defense about his plan to free slaves.

Brown says he never meant to start a rebellion.

❝I intended certainly to have made a clean thing of that matter [freeing slaves] . . . I never did intend murder or treason, or the destruction of property, or to excite or incite the slaves to rebellion, or to make insurrection [revolt] . . . Had I interfered in the manner which I admit . . . in behalf of the rich, the powerful, the intelligent, the so-called great . . . it would have been all right, and every man in this Court would have deemed it an act worthy of reward rather than punishment . . . I believe that to have interfered as I have done . . . in behalf of His despised poor, is no wrong, but right.❞

—**John Brown,**
quoted in *The Life, Trial and Execution of Captain John Brown*

By *His*, Brown means God's.

ANALYSIS SKILL **ANALYZING PRIMARY SOURCES**

How does Brown contrast his ideas with the Court's ideas?

Brown was quickly convicted of treason, murder, and conspiracy. Some of his men received death sentences. John A. Copeland, a fugitive slave, defended his actions. "If I am dying for freedom, I could not die for a better cause." Convinced that he also would be sentenced to death, Brown delivered a memorable speech.

❝Now, if it is deemed [thought] necessary that I should forfeit [give up] my life for the furtherance of the ends of justice, and mingle [mix] my blood . . . with the blood of millions in this slave country whose rights are disregarded by wicked, cruel, and unjust enactments, I say, let it be done.❞

—John Brown, quoted in *John Brown, 1800–1859* by Oswald Garrison Villard

As expected, the judge ordered Brown to be hanged. The sentence was carried out one month later on December 2, 1859.

Many northerners mourned John Brown's death, but some abolitionists criticized his extreme actions. Abraham Lincoln said Brown "agreed with us in thinking slavery wrong." However, Lincoln continued, "That cannot excuse violence, bloodshed, and treason."

Most southern whites—both slaveholders and non-slaveholders—felt threatened by the actions of John Brown. They worried that a "John Brown the Second" might attack. One South Carolina newspaper voiced these fears: "We are convinced the safety of the South lies only outside the present Union." Another newspaper stated that "the sooner we get out of the Union, the better."

READING CHECK **Drawing Conclusions** Why did John Brown's raid lead some southerners to talk about leaving the Union?

Differentiating Instruction

Below Level

English-Language Learners

Standard English Mastery

1. Write the following terms for the class to see:
   - **arm**
   - **arsenal**
   - **conspiracy**
   - **ferry**
   - **marines**
   - **mourned**
   - **raid**
   - **squad**
   - **treason**
   - **uprising**

2. Work with students as a class to locate each term and define it as used in the text.

3. Then have students work in pairs or small groups to create a sequential flow chart listing the events connected to John Brown's raid.

4. Have students share the events they listed with the class. List events for students to see. Then help students use the list to write a summary of John Brown's raid. Model for students the use of standard English and correct grammar. **LS Verbal/Linguistic**

📄 Alternative Assessment Handbook, Rubrics 36: Time Lines; and 37: Writing Assignments

Election of 1860

In this climate of distrust, Americans prepared for another presidential election in 1860. The northern and southern Democrats could not agree on a candidate. Northern Democrats chose Senator Stephen Douglas. Southern Democrats backed the current vice president, **John C. Breckinridge** of Kentucky, who supported slavery in the territories.

Meanwhile, a new political party emerged. The **Constitutional Union Party** recognized "no political principles other than the Constitution of the country, the Union of the states, and the enforcement of the laws." Members of this new party met in Baltimore, Maryland, and selected **John Bell** of Tennessee as their candidate. Bell was a slaveholder, but he had opposed the Kansas-Nebraska Act in 1854.

Senator William Seward of New York was the Republican's leading candidate at the start of their convention. But it turned out that Lincoln appealed to more party members. A moderate who was against the spread of slavery, Lincoln promised not to abolish slavery where it already existed.

Douglas, Breckinridge, and Bell each knew he might not win the election. They hoped to win enough electoral votes to prevent Lincoln from winning in the electoral college. But with a unified Republican Party behind him, Lincoln won. Although he received the highest number of votes, he won only about 40 percent of the overall popular vote.

Lincoln won 180 of 183 electoral votes in free states. Douglas had the second-highest number of popular votes, but he won only one state. He earned just 12 electoral votes. Breckinridge and Bell split electoral votes in other slave states.

The election results angered southerners. Lincoln did not campaign in their region and did not carry any southern states, but he became the next president. The election signaled that the South was losing its national political power.

READING CHECK **Analyzing** Why was Lincoln viewed by many as a moderate candidate during his campaign for the presidency?

Election of 1860

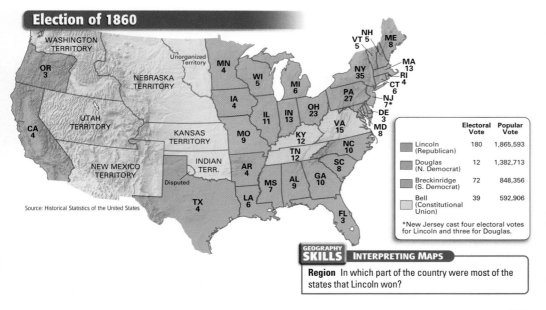

Source: Historical Statistics of the United States

	Electoral Vote	Popular Vote
Lincoln (Republican)	180	1,865,593
Douglas (N. Democrat)	12	1,382,713
Breckinridge (S. Democrat)	72	848,356
Bell (Constitutional Union)	39	592,906

*New Jersey cast four electoral votes for Lincoln and three for Douglas.

GEOGRAPHY SKILLS **INTERPRETING MAPS**

Region In which part of the country were most of the states that Lincoln won?

A DIVIDED NATION **495**

Main Idea

❸ The South Secedes

The dispute over slavery led the South to secede.

Explain How did the southern states respond to the election of 1860, and why? *Several seceded, starting with South Carolina, and formed the Confederate States of America. They believed their economy and way of life were at stake and that slavery was threatened.*

Analyze Why did southerners who supported secession believe the action was constitutional? *The states had voluntarily joined the Union, so they should be free to leave.*

▤ CRF: Biography Activity: Jefferson Davis

Did you know . . .

On January 9, 1861, the mayor of New York City, Democrat Fernando Wood, proposed to the city council that the city join the southern states in seceding. Wood wanted to form a new city made up of Manhattan, Staten Island, and Long Island. The proposal did not pass.

The South Secedes

Lincoln insisted that he would not change slavery in the South. However, he said that slavery could not expand and thus would eventually die out completely. That idea angered many southerners.

Southerners' Reactions

People in the South believed their economy and way of life would be destroyed without slave labor. They reacted immediately. Within a week of Lincoln's election, South Carolina's legislature called for a special convention. The delegates considered **secession**, or formally withdrawing from the Union. South Carolina elected to dissolve "the union now subsisting [existing] between South Carolina and other States." Southern secessionists believed that they had a right to leave the Union. They pointed out that each of the original states had voluntarily joined the Union by holding a special convention that had ratified the Constitution. Surely, they reasoned, states could leave the Union by the same process.

Critics of secession thought this argument was ridiculous. President Buchanan said the Union was not "a mere voluntary association of States, to be dissolved at pleasure by any one of the contracting parties." President-elect Abraham Lincoln agreed, saying, "No State, upon its own mere motion, can lawfully get out of the Union." Lincoln added, "They can only do so against [the] law, and by revolution."

The Confederate States of America

Mississippi, Florida, Alabama, Georgia, Louisiana, and Texas also seceded to form the **Confederate States of America**, also called the Confederacy. Its new constitution guaranteed citizens the right to own slaves.

Delegates from seceded states elected **Jefferson Davis** of Mississippi as president of the Confederacy. Davis had hoped to be the commanding general of Mississippi's troops. He responded to the news of his election with reluctance.

While the South Carolina representatives were meeting to discuss secession, Congress

Jefferson Davis takes the oath of office for president of the Confederate States of America.

Rebel Government

This photograph is of the inauguration of Jefferson Davis as the president of the Confederate States of America. A former U.S. secretary of war, Davis was elected president of the confederacy in 1861.

How does this photo show the state of the southern government?

496 CHAPTER 15

Collaborative Learning

At Level

Issue of Secession

1. Organize students into groups and ask them to imagine that they are members of the South Carolina secession convention.

2. Have each group draft a formal letter to President Lincoln informing him that South Carolina is officially seceding from the Union. The letter should list and explain the events and other causes that led to the decision.

3. Have group representatives read the letters to the class. Then have students discuss—first in their groups and then as a class—whether states have the right to secede and, if so, under what circumstances. ▰ **Verbal/Linguistic**

▤ Alternative Assessment Handbook, Rubrics 11: Discussions; and 37: Writing Assignments

Answers

Rebel Government *depicts it as having broken away from the Union and having chosen its own president*

examined a plan to save the Union. Senator **John J. Crittenden** of Kentucky proposed a series of constitutional amendments that he believed would satisfy the South by protecting slavery. Crittenden hoped the country could avoid secession and a civil war.

Lincoln disagreed with Crittenden's plan. He believed there could be no compromise about the extension of slavery. Lincoln wrote, "The tug has to come and better now than later." A Senate committee voted on Crittenden's plan, and every Republican rejected it, as Lincoln had requested.

When the southern states seceded, the question of who owned federal property in the South arose. For instance, the forts in the harbor of Charleston, South Carolina, were federal property. However, Confederate president Davis and the Confederacy were ready to prevent the federal army from controlling the property.

Lincoln Takes Office

President Lincoln was inaugurated on March 4, 1861. In writing his inaugural address, Lincoln looked to many of the nation's founding documents. Referring to the idea that governments receive "their just powers from the consent of the governed," a line from the Declaration of Independence, Lincoln stated, "This country, with its institutions, belongs to the people who inhabit it. Whenever they grow weary of the existing Government, they can exercise their *constitutional* right of amending it or their *revolutionary* right to dismember [take apart] or overthrow it. I can not be ignorant of the fact that many worthy and patriotic citizens are desirous [wanting] of having the National Constitution amended . . ."

While he believed that U.S. citizens had the power to change their government through majority consent, he opposed the idea that southern states could leave the Union because they were unhappy with the government's position on slavery.

He announced in his inaugural address that he would keep all government property in the seceding states. However, he also tried to convince southerners that his government would not provoke a war. He hoped that, given time, southern states would return to the Union.

READING CHECK Drawing Conclusions Why did some southern states secede from the Union?

SUMMARY AND PREVIEW The secession of the southern states hinted at the violence to come. In the next chapter you will read about the Civil War.

Section 4 Assessment

go.hrw.com
Online Quiz
KEYWORD: SR8 HP15

Reviewing Ideas, Terms, and People

1. **a. Recall** Why did John Brown want to seize the federal arsenal at Harpers Ferry?
   b. Explain Why did some abolitionists disagree with Brown's actions?
2. **a. Identify** List the candidates in the presidential election of 1860, and what party each supported.
   b. Predict How might Abraham Lincoln's victory in the election of 1860 lead to future problems?
3. **a. Identify** What states made up the **Confederate States of America**?
   b. Explain Why did Lincoln disagree with **John J. Crittenden**'s plan to keep the Union together?
   c. Elaborate Do you believe that the southern states had the right to secede? Why or why not?

Critical Thinking

4. **Summarizing** Review your notes on the significant people in the section. Then copy the graphic organizer below and use it to summarize the causes of secession.

FOCUS ON WRITING

5. **Taking Notes on Secession** Make some notes on the raid on Harpers Ferry, the election of 1860, and the secession of the South. Decide how your character feels about each of these. How do these events affect your character?

A DIVIDED NATION **497**

Direct Teach

Main Idea

❸ The South Secedes

The dispute over slavery led the South to secede.

Describe What was the plan that John J. Crittenden proposed to preserve the Union? *a series of constitutional amendments related to slavery issues that were meant to pacify the South and thereby avoid secession*

Identify Points of View In his inaugural address, what view did Lincoln express regarding secession? *He stated that the government receives its power from the people and that Americans have the right to change the government through either constitutional amendments or revolution, but he opposed secession.*

Review & Assess

Close

Have students review the causes of secession and then discuss whether it was inevitable.

Review

Online Quiz, Section 4

Assess

SE Section 4 Assessment

PASS: Section 4 Quiz

Alternative Assessment Handbook

Reteach/Classroom Intervention

Interactive Reader and Study Guide, Section 4

Interactive Skills Tutor CD-ROM

Answers

Reading Check *They believed the election of 1860 showed that they had lost power and that Abraham Lincoln's views on slavery would lead to its end.*

497

Section 4 Assessment Answers

1. **a.** wanted to start and arm a slave uprising
   b. believed violence was not the answer to the slavery issue
2. **a.** Stephen Douglas, Northern Democrats; John Breckinridge, Southern Democrats; Abraham Lincoln, Republicans; John Bell, Constitutional Union Party
   b. possible answer—Southerners might feel they had lost political power and that slavery was threatened and so choose to secede.
3. **a.** South Carolina, Mississippi, Florida, Alabama, Georgia, Louisiana, Texas

b. Lincoln believed there could be no compromise over the spread of slavery.
c. possible answers—Yes, states have a right to leave the Union if people feel the government is denying their rights; no, secession harms the strength of the nation; if states can leave whenever people are unhappy, the federal government loses its authority.
4. Causes—fear resulting from John Brown's raid and similar events; Lincoln's election
5. Students should describe how their character feels about how these events led to secession.

Social Studies Skills

Assessing Primary and Secondary Sources

Activity Graphic Organizer Have students discuss the importance of using both primary and secondary sources in the study of history. Then have each student create a graphic organizer of his or her choosing that illustrates what primary and secondary sources are, the problems with each (such as bias), and how they combine to provide a better picture of history. **LS Verbal/Linguistic, Visual/Spatial**

Alternative Assessment Handbook, Rubric 13: Graphic Organizers

Interactive Skills Tutor CD-ROM, Lesson 2: Identify Primary and Secondary Sources; Lesson 17: Interpret Primary Sources

Social Studies Skills

| Analysis | Critical Thinking | Civic Participation | Study |

Assessing Primary and Secondary Sources

Define the Skill

All historical information comes from primary and secondary sources. *Primary sources* are documents written by someone who witnessed or took part in an event. They include diaries, letters, autobiographies, and newspaper reports. *Secondary sources* are accounts of events written after the events have occurred by someone who did not witness or take part in them. They retell, interpret, and summarize information from primary sources History books and biographies are examples of secondary sources.

Historical sources often disagree. One writer's version of an event may be different from another writer's version. You must assess the reliability of a primary or secondary source in order to weigh its value to you as a source of accurate information.

Learn the Skill

Use these guidelines to analyze and evaluate primary and secondary sources.

1. Identify the nature of the material. Is it a first-hand, eye-witness account or is it based on information provided by others?

2. Evaluate the author. If the material is a secondary source, what qualifications does the author have to interpret the sources from which it came? If the material is a primary source, what was the author's connection to the event he or she is writing about?

3. Determine the audience. Was the source meant to be seen by the public? Was it meant for a friend, or for the writer alone? The intended audience can influence a source's content.

4. Determine the purpose. Even authors of primary sources can have reasons to distort the truth to suit their own purposes. Look for evidence of emotion, exaggeration, opinion, or bias that may have influenced the account.

5. Look for documentation. Look for other information or evidence that supports the source's account. Compare sources whenever possible.

Practice the Skill

The passage below concerns the attack on Lawrence, Kansas, that you read about in this chapter. The passage contains both a primary and a secondary source. The secondary account was written by John A. Garraty, a well-known historian. Review the information on page 486, analyze the passage, and answer the questions that follow.

"Sheriff Jones, at the head of an army of Missourians, marched into Lawrence. In broad daylight they threw the printing presses of two newspapers into a river. They burned down the Free State Hotel and other buildings. Antislavery Kansans seethed with rage. One eyewitness described the attack."

Sheriff Jones, after looking at the flames rising from the hotel and saying that it was 'the happiest day of his life,' dismissed the troops and they began their lawless destruction."

1. Did the author of the primary source likely support the attackers or the people of Lawrence? What clues in the passage suggest this?

2. For whom was the primary source likely written?

3. Which source is more reliable for information about this incident? Explain why.

498 CHAPTER 15

Social Studies Skills Activity: Assessing Primary and Secondary Sources

Evaluating Sources   At Level

1. Have students review the text in Section 2 under the heading "Brooks Attacks Sumner." Ask students to closely examine the image. Lead students through the five steps under "Learn the Skill" to evaluate the image.

2. Then have students examine the textbook coverage of the event. Again, lead students through the five steps under "Learn the Skill" to evaluate this source.

3. Then have students discuss why the two sources combine to provide a more complete account of the event than any one alone. **LS Verbal/Linguistic, Visual Spatial**

Alternative Assessment Handbook, Rubric 11: Discussions

Answers

Practice the Skill 1. *people of Lawrence; phrase "lawless destruction";* **2.** *possible answers—not enough information provided to tell;* **3.** *secondary source, because historians try to report events objectively, while eyewitness accounts usually present a view shaped by their personal opinions and biases*

Visual Summary

Use the visual summary below to help you review the main ideas of the chapter.

QUICK FACTS

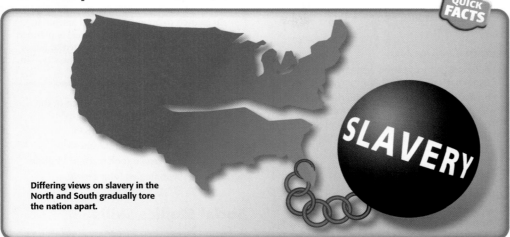

SLAVERY

Differing views on slavery in the North and South gradually tore the nation apart.

Reviewing Vocabulary, Terms, and People

Identify the correct term or person from the chapter that best fits each of the following descriptions.

1. belief that voters should be given the right to decide if slavery would be permitted or banned

2. chief justice of the Supreme Court who wrote the majority opinion for the *Dred Scott* decision

3. Democratic candidate for president in 1852 who promised to enforce the Compromise of 1850 and the Fugitive Slave Act

4. a fugitive slave whose arrest led to violence between government officials and abolitionists

5. Republican candidate for the presidency in 1856 who opposed the spread of slavery in the West

6. slave who sued for freedom, claiming that by living in free territory, he had earned his freedom

7. Stephen Douglas's claim that states and territories should determine the issue of slavery through popular sovereignty

Comprehension and Critical Thinking

SECTION 1 *(Pages 476–481)*

8. a. Describe How did literature aid the antislavery movement?

b. Draw Conclusions How did the issue of slavery promote sectionalism?

c. Evaluate Do you think the Compromise of 1850 was a good solution? Explain your answer.

SECTION 2 *(Pages 483–487)*

9. a. Identify Who were the candidates in the presidential election of 1852, and what issues did each support?

b. Analyze How did the Kansas-Nebraska Act lead to growing hostility between pro-slavery and antislavery supporters?

c. Elaborate Why do you think "Bleeding Kansas" produced intense controversy between many Americans?

A DIVIDED NATION **499**

Answers

Visual Summary

Review and Inquiry The ball and chain (marked "Slavery") attached to the lower half of the United States seems to be pulling the country apart. Have students write a paragraph about how the slavery issue gradually divided the nation until it broke apart in secession. Students should include how geographic and economic differences between the North and the South contributed to sectionalism.

📖 Quick Facts Transparency: A Divided Nation Visual Summary

Reviewing Vocabulary, Terms, and People

1. popular sovereignty
2. Roger B. Taney
3. Franklin Pierce
4. Anthony Burns
5. John C. Frémont
6. Dred Scott
7. Kansas-Nebraska Act

Comprehension and Critical Thinking

8. a. educated people about the hardships of slavery and gained sympathy for abolitionism

b. Because the South's economy was dependent on slave labor and the North's was not, the regions became divided over the slavery issue, which encouraged leaders to promote sectional interests.

Review and Assessment Resources

Review and Reinforce

SE Chapter Review

📄 **CRF:** Chapter Review Activity

📖 Quick Facts Transparency: A Divided Nation Visual Summary

🔊 Spanish Chapter Summaries Audio CD Program

🌐 Online Chapter Summaries in Six Languages

OSP Holt PuzzlePro; GameTool for ExamView

💿 Quiz Game CD-ROM

Assess

SE Standardized Test Practice

📄 PASS: Chapter Test, Forms A and B

📄 Alternative Assessment Handbook

OSP ExamView Test Generator, Chapter Test

💿 Differentiated Instruction Modified Worksheets and Tests CD-ROM: Chapter Test

🌐 Holt Online Assessment Program (in the Premier Online Edition)

Reteach/Intervene

📄 Interactive Reader and Study Guide

📄 Differentiated Instruction Teacher Management System: Lesson Plans for Differentiated Instruction

💿 Differentiated Instruction Modified Worksheets and Tests CD-ROM

💿 Interactive Skills Tutor CD-ROM

go.hrw.com
Online Resources

Chapter Resources:
KEYWORD: SR8 US15

c. possible answers—Yes, it prevented secession for the moment and appeased both the North and the South; no, it only postponed the resolution of the slavery issue.

9. a. Franklin Pierce—promised to honor the Compromise of 1850 and the Fugitive Slave Act; Winfield Scott—limited support of the Compromise of 1850
b. It removed the Missouri Compromise's restriction on slavery in the Kansas and Nebraska territories and let popular sovereignty decide the slavery issue.
c. because of the violence and tensions over the issue of slavery

10. a. a slave who sued for his freedom; the case declared that African Americans were not citizens and ruled that the Missouri Compromise was unconstitutional
b. The issue led to the formation of new parties and to the end of some existing parties.
c. hoped his support for the Kansas-Nebraska Act had weakened his chance for re-election

11. a. They feared more attacks like John Brown's raid, were angry over the election of 1860, and felt their economy and way of life were threatened. Lincoln tried to convince southern states to return.
b. because Lincoln had won without carrying one southern state
c. possible answers—Yes, he was fighting for justice and to free people from bondage; no, violence is never right.

Reviewing Themes
12. changed the makeup of political parties and created new ones aligned with sectional pro-slavery and antislavery views
13. electrified the nation, sparked outrage in the South, increased sectional tensions and support for abolitionism

SECTION 3 *(Pages 488–492)*

10. a. Identify Who was Dred Scott, and why was his case important?
  b. Analyze How were political parties affected by the debate over slavery?
  c. Elaborate Why do you think Republicans challenged Stephen Douglas's run for the Senate?

SECTION 4 *(Pages 493–497)*

11. a. Recall Why did the southern states secede, and what was the North's response?
  b. Draw Conclusions Why did the results of the election of 1860 anger southerners?
  c. Evaluate Do you think John Brown was right to use violence to protest slavery? Explain.

Reviewing Themes
12. Politics How did sectionalism affect American politics?
13. Society and Culture What effect did Harriet Beecher Stowe's book *Uncle Tom's Cabin* have on the debate over slavery?

Using the Internet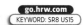
14. Activity: Creating a Newspaper Harriet Beecher Stowe's novel and John Brown's raids were two important events that created more debate over slavery and heightened tension between sides. Enter the activity keyword and learn more about antislavery actions. Then create a newspaper with which to display your research. Remember to write from the point of view of someone from the mid-1800s.

Reading Skills
Facts, Opinions, and the Past *Use the Reading Skills taught in this chapter to answer the question about the reading selection below.*

> In 1858 John Brown tried to start an uprising. He wanted to attack the federal arsenal in Virginia and seize weapons there. He planned to arm local slaves. Brown expected to kill or take hostage white southerners who stood in his way. *(p. 493)*

15. Based on the reading above, which of the following statements is an opinion?
  a. John Brown's raid was in 1858.
  b. John Brown hated all slaveholders.
  c. John Brown's raid took place in Virginia.
  d. Local slaves helped John Brown.

Social Studies Skills
Assessing Primary and Secondary Sources *Use the Social Studies Skills taught in this chapter to answer the question below.*

16. Which of the following is *not* an example of a primary source used in this chapter?
  a. *A People's History of the United States* by Howard Zinn
  b. The Seventh of March speech by Daniel Webster
  c. A House Divided speech by Abraham Lincoln
  d. John Brown's last speech

FOCUS ON WRITING

17. Writing Your Autobiography Review your notes. Then write your autobiography, being sure to mention each of the events from your notes. Tell how your character heard about each event, what he or she was doing at the time, how he or she felt about the event, and how it affected him or her. What are your character's hopes and fears for the future?

Using the Internet
14. Go to the HRW Web site and enter the keyword shown to access a rubric for this activity.

KEYWORD: SR8 US15

Reading Skills
15. b

Social Studies Skills
16. a

Focus on Writing
17. Rubric Students' autobiographies should:
  • explain how each of the chapter's key events affected the character
  • describe how the character learned and felt about each key event
  • describe the character's hopes and fears for the future

  CRF: Focus on Writing Activity: Writing an Autobiographical Sketch

Standardized Test Practice

DIRECTIONS: Read each question and write the letter of the best response.

1 Use the map below to answer the following question.

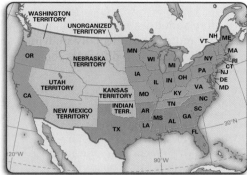

From the information in this map, you can conclude that it shows

A the provisions of the Compromise of 1850.

B the results of the election of 1860.

C the formation of the Confederacy.

D the results of the *Dred Scott* decision.

2 Which leader was responsible for settling the dispute over the expansion of slavery that arose after the Mexican War?

A David Wilmot

B Henry Clay

C Abraham Lincoln

D Jefferson Davis

3 California's admission as a free state after the Mexican War aroused controversy because

A many Californians already held slaves.

B it would upset the balance between free states and slave states.

C Mexico still claimed that California was part of Mexico's territory.

D most Californians wanted independence.

4 Widespread violence erupted in Kansas over slavery in the mid-1850s *mainly* due to

A the practice of popular sovereignty.

B the Pottawatomie Massacre.

C the Missouri Compromise.

D the threat of secession.

5 The Kansas-Nebraska Act of 1854 directly or indirectly led to all of the following *except*

A the rise of the Republican Party.

B the collapse of the Whig Party.

C Abraham Lincoln's election as president.

D The Missouri Compromise.

6 The Compromise of 1850 was *most* similar to what earlier compromise between free states and slave states?

A the Great Compromise

B the Rush-Bagot Agreement

C the Northwest Ordinance

D the Missouri Compromise

7 Examine the following passage written by a southerner before secession and then use it to answer the question below.

> " As we sat around the long table today the talk turned to the [secession] convention, so soon to meet in Tallahassee [Florida]. Father said he considered this the most important year in the history of the South. He is for secession, and he does not think that war will necessarily [certainly] follow. Brother Junius is a strong Union man, and he thinks we will certainly have war. If the South secedes, the North will fight to keep us. If we do not secede, all property rights will be taken from us and we will be forced to fight to hold our own. "
>
> –Susan Bradford, adapted from *Heroines of Dixie,* edited by Katharine Jones

What do you think will be the outcome of the convention discussed in this passage? Why?

A DIVIDED NATION **501**

Tips for Test Taking

Rely on 50/50 When students have no idea what an answer is, tell them to do the following to make an educated guess:

- Read every choice carefully.
- Eliminate the least likely choice, then the next, and so on until one answer is left.
- Watch out for distracters—choices that are true but either too broad, too narrow, or not relevant.
- If more than one choice seems correct, see if "All of the above" is an option. If none of the choices seems correct, look for "None of the above."

1. A

Break Down the Question: Option B is not correct because the map does not include numbers of state electors. Option D does not make sense for a map, and Option C is incorrect because the map does not identify the seceding states.

2. B

Break Down the Question: This question requires students to recall factual information. Refer students who have trouble to the text titled "Compromise of 1850" in Section 1.

3. B

Break Down the Question: Explain that a question sometimes provides clues to its answer. For example, point out the phrase "admission as a free state" in this question.

4 A

Break Down the Question: This question requires students to identify cause and effect. Explain that Option B is incorrect because it is an example of the violence, not a cause. Option D is an effect of the violence.

5. D

Break Down the Question: This question also requires students to identify cause and effect. Point out that the word *except* means students should select the answer that was *not* an effect.

6. B

Break Down the Question: This question requires students to recall factual information from Section 1.

7. D

Break Down the Question: This question requires students to look for facts and opinions within the passage to help frame an answer.

Preteach

Preteach

Bellringer

Motivate Write the words *cat* and *dog* for students to see. Ask students how the two animals are similar. Then ask students how they are different. Explain that comparing (showing how things are similar) and contrasting (showing how things are different) is one way to learn about events and people in history. Tell students that they will write a paper comparing and contrasting a historical topic.

- Interactive Skills Tutor CD-ROM, Lesson 1: Compare and Contrast

Direct Teach

Writing a Thesis

Make a Point After students have selected the topic of their paper and made lists of similarities and differences, have them examine the lists. Were the two groups or events they compared mainly alike or mainly different? Did certain similarities or differences stand out as significant or influential? Have students write one sentence in answer to each question. Tell students to use the sentences as a starting point for selecting and writing a thesis.

Organizing

Once Around the Block Students who use the block style to organize their papers should check that they address the same points in the same order for each topic. Have students use a different color of ink to underline each point they made about the first topic. Then have students use the same colors to underline the points they made about the second topic. The colors and order should match.

Assignment

Write a paper comparing and contrasting one of the following: (1) America before and after the Industrial Revolution, (2) the lives of free blacks in the North with the lives of free blacks in the South.

TIP Using Graphic Organizers
Venn diagrams help you focus on similarities and differences. Write details the subjects have in common in the overlapping area. Write details that make each subject different in the sections that do not overlap.

Comparing People and Events

One way to learn more about historical figures and events is to compare and contrast them. By studying how the figures or events are alike and different, you can begin to see each one more clearly.

1. Prewrite

Getting Started

"How are they alike?" "How are they different?" Jot down answers to these questions as you research the presidents or the Industrial Revolution. Group your answers into points of comparison. For example, points of comparison for the lives of free blacks might be work, education, etc. Points of comparison for the Industrial Revolution might be factories or farming.

Organizing Your Information

There are two ways to organize a compare-and-contrast paper.

- **Block Style** Say everything you have to say about one subject. Then say everything you have to say about the second subject. Discuss the points of comparison in the same order for each subject.
- **Point-by-Point Style** Discuss the points of comparison one at a time. Explain how the subjects are alike and different on one point of comparison, then another, and so on. Discuss the subjects in the same order for each point of comparison.

2. Write

You can use this framework with your notes to help you write your first draft.

A Writer's Framework

Introduction	Body	Conclusion
■ Identify the two subjects and give background information to help readers understand your comparisons. ■ State your big idea, or main purpose, in comparing and contrasting them.	■ Use block or point-by-point organization. ■ Use three points of comparison. ■ Support your points with specific historical facts, details, and examples.	■ Restate your big idea. ■ Summarize the points you made. ■ Expand on your big idea, perhaps by relating it to later historical events or other historical figures.

502 UNIT 4

Differentiating Instruction

Special Needs Learners   Below Level

1. Have special needs learners work in small groups to create Venn diagrams before writing.

2. Have an aide read a short part of the relevant portion of the textbook aloud. Then have the students add the information to their diagrams. Have the aide continue to read the text aloud, stopping frequently to allow students to add to their Venn diagrams. **LS** Visual/Spatial

English-Language Learners   Below Level
                                Standard English Mastery

1. Have English learners write the drafts for their papers in their primary language.

2. Students should then refer back to these drafts as they write their final papers in English.

3. Before students write in English, review the rules for forming comparative and superlative adjectives and adverbs. Provide guided practice as needed. **LS** Verbal/Linguistic

3. Evaluate and Revise

Evaluating

Use these questions to discover ways to improve your paper.

Evaluation Questions for a Comparison/Contrast Paper

- Do you introduce both subjects in the first paragraph?
- Do you provide relevant background information in a clear and concise manner?
- Do you state your big idea in the introduction?
- Do you include three points of comparison between the subjects?

- Do you use either the block style or point-by-point style to organize your points of comparison?
- Do you support your points of comparison with appropriate historical facts, details, and examples?
- Do you restate your big idea and summarize your points?

Revising

As you reread your paper, look for sentences that start with *There was* or *There were*. Sentences beginning with *There was/There were* tend to be weak: The verbs *was* and *were* do not convey any action.

Weak

There was a decline in southern agriculture after the American Revolution.

Stronger

Southern agriculture declined after the American Revolution.

4. Proofread and Publish

Proofreading

In a research report, you may be referring to the titles of your sources of information. Check to see whether you have punctuated any titles according to these guidelines.

- Underlining (if you are writing) or italics (if you are using a computer) for books, movies, TV programs, Internet sites, and magazines or newspapers
- Quotation marks for magazine articles, newspaper articles, chapters in a book

Publishing

Share your paper with one or more classmates. After reading each other's papers, you can compare and contrast them.

5. Practice and Apply

Use the steps and strategies outlined in this workshop to write your paper comparing and contrasting two people or events.

TIP   **Making Meaning Clear**

One way to make relationships between ideas clear is to repeat key or similar words and phrases in your writing. For example, you can use similar wording when comparing two historical figures on the same point of comparison.

EXAMPLE

Samuel Slater filled his labor needs by hiring entire families to work in the mills. Frances Lowell filled his labor needs by hiring young, unmarried women to work in the mills.

Introduce the Unit

Share the information in the chapter overviews with students.

Chapter 16 Soon after Lincoln's inauguration, the Civil War began, dividing the country between the North and the South. Initially, the South won several major battles. The North then turned the tide of the war with victories in both the West and the East. In April 1865 the Confederates surrendered, and the North won the war. The war resulted in terrible death and destruction but also led to the long-sought freedom of enslaved Africans.

Chapter 17 After the war, the period of rebuilding, known as Reconstruction, was a difficult and long process. The United States faced two major challenges—to reunite the country and to define the rights of African Americans. In 1865 the Thirteenth Amendment ended slavery in the United States. Additional amendments extended citizenship and other rights to African Americans. In time, however, politicians who opposed Reconstruction gained power. Southern states began passing laws limiting African Americans' civil rights. Many former slaves continued to work on plantations. Meanwhile, the South began to rebuild and develop its industry.

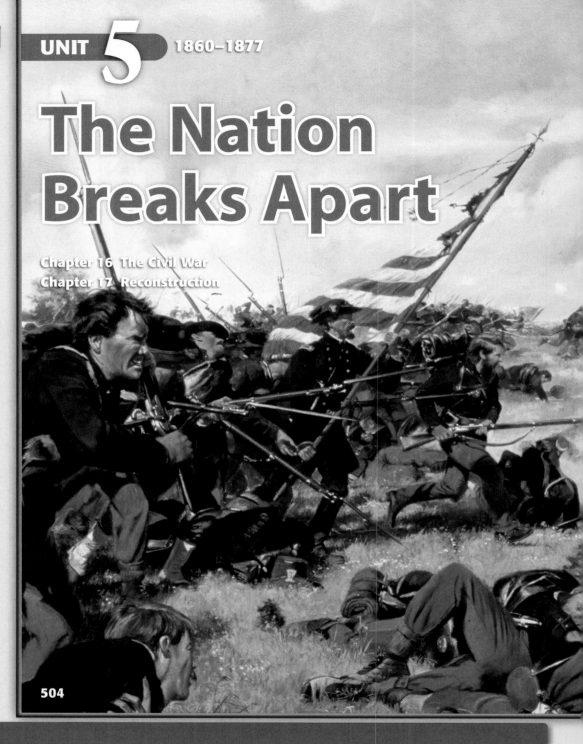

UNIT 5 1860–1877

The Nation Breaks Apart

Chapter 16 The Civil War
Chapter 17 Reconstruction

504

Unit Resources

Planning

- Teacher Management System: Unit Instructional Benchmarking Guides
- One-Stop Planner CD-ROM with Test Generator: Calendar Planner
- Power Presentations with Video CD-ROM
- A Teacher's Guide to Religion in the Public Schools

Differentiating Instruction

- Differentiated Instruction Teacher Management System: Lesson Plans for Differentiated Instruction
- Pre-AP Activities Guide for United States History
- Differentiated Instruction Modified Worksheets and Tests CD-ROM

Enrichment

- **CRF 16:** Interdisciplinary Project: The Ironclads: The *Monitor* and the *Virginia*
- **CRF 17:** Economics and History: The Devastation of War
- Civic Participation Activities
- Primary Source Library CD-ROM

Assessment

- Progress Assessment System Solution: Unit Test
- OSP ExamView Test Generator: Unit Test
- Holt Online Assessment Program, in the Premier Online Student Edition
- Alternative Assessment Handbook

505

What You Will Learn...

When compromise after compromise failed, the United States was divided by war. The American Civil War tested the strength of the bond between the states. During the Civil War, Americans fought each other on battlefields and in government. Ideas about slavery and sovereignty led many soldiers to fight. Eventually the nation was reunited, but deep scars remained. In the next two chapters, you will learn about the war and the period after when rebuilding the South became a priority.

Explore the Art

This painting is titled *Fight for the Colors*. It shows Union and Confederate troops at the Battle of Gettysburg, which began in Pennsylvania on July 1, 1863. This 3-day battle was the largest and bloodiest in the Civil War.

What aspects of the Civil War does this picture show?

Connect to the Unit

Activity **Analyzing the Costs and Benefits of War** Create a cause-and-effect chart for students to see. Ask students to consider warfare in general and to discuss some of the causes of war. Write students' ideas in the chart. Next, ask students to discuss some of the effects of war. Challenge students to consider both positive and negative effects. Add students' responses to the chart. Then have students discuss the costs and benefits of warfare. When do students think war is justified? In what situations do they think the benefits of war outweigh the costs?

Save the cause-and-effect chart. At the end of the unit, have students review the chart and then create a second chart listing the causes and effects of the Civil War, including long-term effects. Conclude by having students examine the costs and benefits of the Civil War and Reconstruction.

LS **Logical/Mathematical, Visual/Spatial**

Explore the Art

Not only did the Civil War have a profound effect on those who lived through it, but it shaped our nation's history as well. This painting depicts a scene from one of the war's many brutal battles involving hand-to-hand combat between Union and Confederate soldiers. The sacrifices made by the soldiers depicted here and hundreds of thousands of others like them would leave a deep mark on the country for years to come.

About the Illustration

This illustration is an artist's conception based on available sources. However, historians are uncertain exactly what this scene looked like.

Democracy and Civic Education

At Level

Justice: Equal Protection of the Laws

Research Required

Background Explain to students that the Fourteenth Amendment (1868) ensures the equal protection of laws. This protection guarantees that no person or group will be treated differently under the law from any other person or group in a similar situation unless a just and good reason exists for doing so.

1. Have students work in small groups to conduct research on how effective the equal protection clause has been over time. How have various groups used the clause to extend civil rights and to fight segregation, particularly during the 1950s and 1960s?

2. Have each group use its research to create a brochure for immigrants to inform them about their right to equal protection of the laws. The brochure should explain the concept and provide examples of how it has been used.
LS **Interpersonal, Verbal/Linguistic**

📋 Alternative Assessment Handbook, Rubrics 14: Group Activity; and 37: Writing Assignments

📋 Civic Participation

Answers

Explore the Art *possible answers— intense fighting and emotions; close- range, hand-to-hand combat*

Chapter 16 Planning Guide

The Civil War

Chapter Overview	Reproducible Resources	Technology Resources
CHAPTER 16 pp. 506–547 **Overview:** In this chapter, students will analyze the events of the Civil War along with the effect these events had on the lives of Americans.	**Differentiated Instruction Teacher Management System:*** • Instructional Benchmarking Guides • Lesson Plans for Differentiated Instruction **Interactive Reader and Study Guide:** Chapter Graphic Organizer* **Chapter Resource File:*** • Focus on Writing: Newspaper Article • Social Studies Skills: Political Cartoons • Chapter Review Activity	**Power Presentations with Video CD-ROM** **Differentiated Instruction Modified Worksheets and Tests CD-ROM** **Primary Source Library CD-ROM for United States History** **Student Edition on Audio CD Program** **History's Impact: United States History Video Program (VHS/DVD):** The Civil War*
Section 1: **The War Begins** **The Big Idea:** Civil War broke out between the North and the South in 1861.	**Differentiated Instruction Teacher Management System:** Section 1 Lesson Plan* **Interactive Reader and Study Guide:** Section 1 Summary* **Chapter Resource File:*** • Vocabulary Builder Activity, Section 1 • History and Geography Activity: Choosing Sides **Political Cartoons Activities for United States History,** Cartoon 17: The Folly of Secession	**Daily Bellringer Transparency:** Section 1* **Map Transparency:** Fort Sumter and Charleston* **Quick Facts Transparencies:** North Versus South; Resources of the North and South*
Section 2: **The War in the East** **The Big Idea:** Confederate and Union forces faced off in Virginia and at sea.	**Differentiated Instruction Teacher Management System:** Section 2 Lesson Plan* **Interactive Reader and Study Guide:** Section 2 Summary* **Chapter Resource File:*** • Vocabulary Builder Activity, Section 2 • Interdisciplinary Project: The Ironclads	**Daily Bellringer Transparency:** Section 2* **Map Transparency:** Battles in the East* **Map Transparency:** Union Blockade*
Section 3: **The War in the West** **The Big Idea:** Fighting in the Civil War spread to the western United States.	**Differentiated Instruction Teacher Management System:** Section 3 Lesson Plan* **Interactive Reader and Study Guide:** Section 3 Summary* **Chapter Resource File:*** • Vocabulary Builder Activity, Section 3 • Primary Source: The Battle of Shiloh, April 1862	**Daily Bellringer Transparency:** Section 3* **Map Transparency:** The War in the West*
Section 4: **Daily Life during War** **The Big Idea:** The lives of many Americans were affected by the Civil War.	**Differentiated Instruction Teacher Management System:** Section 4 Lesson Plan* **Interactive Reader and Study Guide:** Section 4 Summary* **Chapter Resource File:*** • Vocabulary Builder Activity, Section 4 • Biography Activities: William Carney; Clara Barton • Primary Source Activity: Civil War Era Diary	**Daily Bellringer Transparency:** Section 4* **Map Transparency:** Emancipation Proclamation* **Internet Activity:** Civil War Authors
Section 5: **The Tide of War Turns** **The Big Idea:** Union victories in 1863, 1864, and 1865 brought the Civil War to an end.	**Differentiated Instruction Teacher Management System:** Section 5 Lesson Plan* **Interactive Reader and Study Guide:** Section 5 Summary* **Chapter Resource File:*** • Vocabulary Builder Activity, Section 5 • Biography Activity: William Tecumseh Sherman	**Daily Bellringer Transparency:** Section 5* **Map Transparencies:** Pickett's Charge, July 3, 1863; Final Campaigns* **Quick Facts Transparency:** Causes and Effects of the Civil War* **Internet Activity:** 3-D Model of Gettysburg and Other Battles

HOLT

History's Impact
United States History Video Program (VHS/DVD)
The Civil War
Suggested use: as a chapter introduction

Review, Assessment, Intervention

Quick Facts Transparency: The Civil War Visual Summary*

Progress Assessment Support System (PASS): Chapter Test*

Differentiated Instruction Modified Worksheets and Tests CD-ROM: Modified Chapter Test

One-Stop Planner CD-ROM: ExamView Test Generator (English/Spanish)

Alternative Assessment Handbook

PASS: Section 1 Quiz*

Online Quiz: Section 1

Alternative Assessment Handbook

PASS: Section 2 Quiz*

Online Quiz: Section 2

Alternative Assessment Handbook

PASS: Section 3 Quiz*

Online Quiz: Section 3

Alternative Assessment Handbook

PASS: Section 4 Quiz*

Online Quiz: Section 4

Alternative Assessment Handbook

PASS: Section 5 Quiz*

Online Quiz: Section 5

Alternative Assessment Handbook

Power Presentations with Video CD-ROM

Power Presentations with Video are visual presentations of each chapter's main ideas. Presentations can be customized by including Quick Facts charts, images from the text, and video clips.

Power Presentations with Video CD-ROM

HOLT
United States History
Beginnings to 1877

DIVISION FOR PUBLIC EDUCATION
AMERICAN BAR ASSOCIATION

Developed by the Division for Public Education of the American Bar Association, these materials are part of the **Democracy and Civic Education Resources.**

• **Constitution Study Guide**

• **Supreme Court Case Studies**

Holt Online Learning

Teacher Resources

KEYWORD: SR8 TEACHER

Student Resources

KEYWORD: SR8 US16

• Document-Based Questions

• Interactive Multimedia Activities

• Current Events

• Chapter-based Internet Activities

• and more!

Holt Premier
Online Student Edition

Complete online support for interactivity, assessment, and reporting

• Interactive Maps and Notebook

• Standardized Test Prep

• Homework Practice and Research Activities Online

CHAPTER 16 PLANNING GUIDE

Differentiating Instruction

ENGLISH-LANGUAGE LEARNERS & STRUGGLING READERS

 TARGET RESOURCE

Live Ink® Online Reading Help

Spanish Resources

Spanish Chapter Summaries Audio CD Program

One-Stop Planner CD-ROM:
- ExamView Test Generator, Spanish
- PuzzlePro, Spanish

Additional Resources

Differentiated Instruction Teacher Management System: Lesson Plans for Differentiated Instruction

Chapter Resources:
- Vocabulary Builder Activities
- Social Studies Skills Activity: Interpreting Political Cartoons

Quick Facts Transparencies:
- North Versus South
- Resources of the North and South
- Causes and Effects of the Civil War
- The Civil War Visual Summary

Student Edition on Audio CD Program

Online Chapter Summaries in Six Languages

Interactive Skills Tutor CD-ROM

SPECIAL NEEDS LEARNERS

 TARGET RESOURCE

Differentiated Instruction Modified Worksheets and Tests CD-ROM

- Vocabulary Flash Cards
- Modified Vocabulary Builder Activities
- Modified Chapter Review Activity
- Modified Chapter Test

Additional Resources

Differentiated Instruction Teacher Management System: Lesson Plans for Differentiated Instruction

Interactive Reader and Study Guide

Social Studies Skills Activity: Interpreting Political Cartoons

Student Edition on Audio CD Program

Interactive Skills Tutor CD-ROM

Live Ink® Online Reading Help

ADVANCED/GIFTED AND TALENTED STUDENTS

 TARGET RESOURCE

Primary Source Library CD-ROM for United States History

The Library contains longer versions of quotations in the text, extra sources, and images. Included are point-of-view articles, journals, diaries, historical fiction, and political documents.

Additional Resources

Political Cartoons Activities for United States History: Cartoon 17: The Folly of Secession

United States History Document-Based Questions Activities

Differentiated Instruction Teacher Management System: Lesson Plans for Differentiated Instruction

Pre-AP Activities Guide for United States History: Supporting Arguments

Chapter Resource File:
- Focus on Writing Activity: Writing a Newspaper Article
- Primary Source Activity: The Battle of Shiloh, April 1862
- Primary Source Activity: John L. Ranson, *Andersonville Diary*

One-Stop Planner® CD-ROM
for Differentiated Instruction

Your differentiated instruction lesson plans are available at your fingertips. Holt's Teacher Management System links teaching support tools to pages in the Interactive Teacher's Edition.

The One-Stop Planner features:
- Interactive Teacher's Edition
- Calendar Planner and pacing guides
- Editable lesson plans
- All reproducible ancillaries in Adobe Acrobat (PDF) format
- ExamView Test Generator (English and Spanish)
- Transparency and video previews

Professional Development

- **In-service and staff development** as part of your Holt Social Studies product purchase
- **Quick Teacher Tutorial Lesson Presentation CD-ROM**
- Intensive tuition-based **Teacher Development Institute**
- **Teaching American History Online**—2 Module Professional Development Course
- **Convenient Holt Speaker Bureau**—face-to-face workshop options
- **PRAXIS™ Test Prep** interactive Web-based content refreshers*
- **24/7 Ask A Professional Development Expert** at http://www.hrw.com/prodev/

* PRAXIS is a trademark of Educational Testing Service (ETS). This publication is not endorsed or approved by ETS.

DIFFERENTIATED INSTRUCTION PLANNING GUIDE

Chapter Big Ideas

Section 1 Civil War broke out between the North and the South in 1861.

Section 2 Confederate and Union forces faced off in Virginia and at sea.

Section 3 Fighting in the Civil War spread to the western United States.

Section 4 The lives of many Americans were affected by the Civil War.

Section 5 Union victories in 1863, 1864, and 1865 brought the Civil War to an end.

Focus on Writing

The **Chapter Resource File** provides a Focus on Writing worksheet to help students organize and write their newspaper articles.

CRF: Focus on Writing Activity: Writing a Newspaper Article

CHAPTER 16 1861–1865

The Civil War

FOCUS ON WRITING

Writing a Newspaper Article For most of this nation's history, newspapers have been an important way for citizens to learn about what is happening in the United States. In this chapter you will read about the main events of the Civil War. Then you will choose one of these events and write a newspaper article about it.

UNITED STATES **1861** Confederate guns open fire on Fort Sumter on April 12. Confederates win the first battle of the Civil War on July 21 at Bull Run in Virginia.

1861

WORLD **1861** Great Britain and France decide to buy cotton from Egypt instead of from the Confederacy.

506 CHAPTER 16

Key to Differentiating Instruction

Below Level

Basic-level activities designed for all students encountering new material

At Level

Intermediate-level activities designed for average students

Above Level

Challenging activities designed for honors and gifted and talented students

Standard English Mastery

Activities designed to improve standard English usage

Introduce the Chapter

At Level

Focus on the Effects of War

1. Ask students to imagine that the people in part of their state have risen up against the U.S. government, which they claim is abusing its power and denying their rights. Tell students to imagine that some of their friends and even members of their family have decided to fight with the rebels.

2. Have students discuss the results of such a situation. How would they feel if they had to fight against family members and friends in battle? What would it be like if battles were

taking place in their local community? What would be some of the effects on the people and local environment?

3. Explain to students that the Civil War divided Americans and resulted in extreme death and destruction across large parts of the nation. Tell students as they study the chapter to note how the war affected soldiers, civilians, and the environment. **LS Verbal/Linguistic**

HOLT
History's Impact
► **video series**
Watch the video to
understand the impact of
the Civil War.

What You Will Learn...

In this chapter you will learn how the resources
of the North enabled it to defeat the South in the
Civil War. Among those who marched off to war
were these drummer boys of the Union army.

• **Chapter Preview** •

HOLT
History's Impact
► **video series**
See the Video Teacher's Guide
for strategies for using the
chapter video **The Civil War**.

Explore the Picture

Young Soldiers Thousands of boys
and teenagers fought in the Civil War.
Many boys who joined the army served
as drummers, such as the ones shown in
the picture at left. The beat of the drum
was an important way to communicate
orders to soldiers. As a result, drummers
often found themselves in the target of
enemy fire.

Analyzing Visuals What do the
expressions on the drummers' faces suggest about what they might be feeling
and thinking? *possible answers—They
seem to look determined and focused on
their work ahead. Some look like they
might be nervous or afraid.*

go.hrw.com
Online Resources
Chapter Resources:
KEYWORD: SR8 US16
Teacher Resources:
KEYWORD: SR8 TEACHER

1862 The *Monitor*
fights the *Virginia* on
March 9.

1863 The
Emancipation
Proclamation
is issued on
January 1.

1865 General Robert
E. Lee surrenders to
General Ulysses
S. Grant on April 9.

1862   1863   1864   1865

1862 An
imperial decree
expels foreigners
from Japan.

1864 With the support
of French troops, Archduke
Maximilian of Austria
becomes emperor of Mexico.

1864 The Taiping
Rebellion in China ends
after the capture of
Nanjing in July.

THE CIVIL WAR **507**

Explore the Time Line

1. When was the first battle of the Civil War, and
   where did it occur? *July 21, 1861; at Bull Run
   in Virginia*

2. In what year did a sea battle take place
   between the *Monitor* and the *Virginia*? *1862*

3. When was the Emancipation Proclamation
   issued? *January 1, 1863*

4. How long was the Civil War? *about four years*

Info to Know

Response to the Fall of Fort Sumter The
Confederate attack on Fort Sumter in April 1861
began the Civil War. News of the attack spread
quickly by telegraph throughout the North and
the South. In the North, people were stunned
by the news. In Boston, sorrowful bells tolled
all day. In much of the South, people rushed
into the streets to celebrate. The secretary of
war for the Confederacy proclaimed that the
Confederate flag would "float over the dome of
the old Capitol in Washington" by May.

Reading Social Studies

Understanding Themes

Two themes—politics, and society and culture—are presented in this chapter. Ask students to think about some of the effects that a civil war might have on a nation. Guide students in a discussion of the challenges that individuals and governments might face. Tell students that as they study this chapter, they will learn about the problems Americans faced during the Civil War, and how they worked to overcome those social and political problems.

Supporting Facts and Details

Focus on Reading Explain to students that writers are more effective when they provide credible statements that explain or prove their points. To illustrate this to students, ask each student to write a short paragraph explaining what they know about their local government. Ask students to evaluate their paragraphs. Ask them what is missing that could make their writing more effective. Help students to see that by adding anecdotes, facts and statistics, quotes, and examples, their paragraph would be more interesting and informative.

Focus on Themes As you read this chapter about the Civil War, you will see that this was a time in our history dominated by two major concerns: **politics** and **society and culture**. You will not only read about the political decisions made during this war, but also you will see how the war affected all of American society. You will read about the causes and the key events during the war and the many consequences of this war. This chapter tells of one of the most important events in our history.

Supporting Facts and Details

Focus on Reading Main ideas and big ideas are just that, ideas. How do we know what those ideas really mean?

Understanding Ideas and Their Support A main idea or big idea may be a kind of summary statement, or it may be a statement of the author's opinion. Either way, a good reader looks to see what support— facts and various kinds of details—the writer provides. If the writer doesn't provide good support, the ideas may not be trustworthy.

Notice how the passage below uses facts and details to support the main idea.

> Civil War armies fought in the ancient battlefield formation that produced massive casualties. Endless rows of troops fired directly at one another, with cannonballs landing amid them. When the order was given, soldiers would attach bayonets to their guns and rush toward their enemy. Men died to gain every inch of ground.
>
> Despite the huge battlefield losses, the biggest killer in the Civil War was not the fighting. It was diseases such as typhoid, pneumonia, and tuberculosis. Nearly twice as many soldiers died of illnesses as died in combat.
>
> *From Chapter 16, p. 533*

The main idea is stated first.

These sentences provide details about the challenges soldiers faced.

The writer concludes with some facts as support.

Writers support propositions with . . .

1. **Facts and statistics**—statements that can be proved; facts in number form
2. **Examples**—specific instances that illustrate the facts
3. **Anecdotes**—brief stories that help explain the facts
4. **Definitions**—explanation of unusual terms or words
5. **Comments from the experts or eyewitnesses**—statements from reliable sources

Reading and Skills Resources

Reading Support
- Interactive Reader and Study Guide
- Student Edition on Audio CD
- Spanish Chapter Summaries Audio CD Program

Social Studies Skills Support
- Interactive Skills Tutor CD-ROM

Vocabulary Support
- **CRF:** Vocabulary Builder Activities
- **CRF:** Chapter Review Activity
- Differentiated Instruction Modified Worksheets and Tests CD-ROM:
  - Vocabulary Flash Cards
  - Vocabulary Builder Activity
  - Chapter Review Activity

OSP Holt PuzzlePro

You Try It!

The following passage is from the chapter you are about to read. As you read it, look for the writer's main idea and support.

> In February 1862, Grant led an assault force into Tennessee. With help from navy gunboats, Grant's Army of Tennessee took two outposts on key rivers in the west. On February 6, he captured Fort Henry on the Tennessee River. Several days later he took Fort Donelson on the Cumberland River.
>
> Fort Donelson's commander asked for the terms of surrender. Grant replied, "No terms except an unconditional and immediate surrender can be accepted." The fort surrendered. The North gave a new name to Grant's initials: "Unconditional Surrender" Grant.

From Chapter 16, pp. 522–523

After you read the passage, answer the following questions.

1. Which sentence best states the writer's main idea?
   a. The fort surrendered.
   b. In February 1862, Grant led an assault force into Tennessee.
   c. Fort Donelson's commander asked for the terms of surrender.

2. Which method of support is not used to support the main idea?
   a. facts
   b. comments from experts or eyewitnesses
   c. anecdotes

3. Which sentence in this passage provides a comment from an expert or eyewitness?

As you read Chapter 16, pay attention to the details that the writers have chosen to support their main ideas.

Key Terms and People

Chapter 16

Section 1
Fort Sumter *(p. 511)*
border states *(p. 512)*
Winfield Scott *(p. 513)*
cotton diplomacy *(p. 513)*

Section 2
Thomas "Stonewall" Jackson *(p. 517)*
First Battle of Bull Run *(p. 517)*
George B. McClellan *(p. 517)*
Robert E. Lee *(p. 517)*
Seven Days' Battle *(p. 518)*
Second Battle of Bull Run *(p. 518)*
Battle of Antietam *(p. 519)*
ironclads *(p. 520)*

Section 3
Ulysses S. Grant *(p. 522)*
Battle of Shiloh *(p. 523)*
David Farragut *(p. 524)*
Siege of Vicksburg *(p. 524)*

Section 4
emancipation *(p. 529)*
Emancipation Proclamation *(p. 529)*
contrabands *(p. 531)*
54th Massachusetts Infantry *(p. 531)*
Copperheads *(p. 532)*
habeas corpus *(p. 532)*
Clara Barton *(p.534)*

Section 5
George G. Meade *(p. 537)*
Battle of Gettysburg *(p. 537)*
George Pickett *(p. 538)*
Pickett's Charge *(p. 538)*
Gettysburg Address *(p. 540)*
Wilderness Campaign *(p. 540)*
William Tecumseh Sherman *(p. 541)*
total war *(p. 542)*
Appomattox Courthouse *(p. 542)*

Academic Vocabulary

In this chapter, you will learn the following academic words:

innovation *(p. 520)*
execute *(p. 540)*

Reading Social Studies

Key Terms and People

Assign each student a key term or person from the list at left. Have students define or identify their assigned term or name, then have students explain the importance of that term during the Civil War. Ask students to imagine that they are creating a series of bumper stickers with historical themes. Have each student create a slogan for a bumper sticker that relates the importance of the term or person they were assigned. Remind students to keep their slogan short, interesting, and to the point. One example might be, "Ironclads—Try as you might, you can't sink 'em!"

LS Verbal/Linguistic, Visual/Spatial

Focus on Reading

See the **Focus on Reading** questions in this chapter for more practice on this reading social studies skill.

Reading Social Studies Assessment

See the **Chapter Review** at the end of this chapter for student assessment questions related to this reading skill.

Teaching Tip

To help reinforce the importance of supporting details, select a paragraph or two from the textbook. Then rewrite each paragraph, omitting facts, examples, anecdotes, and quotes. Have students read what little of the paragraph remains. Then ask students what types of information they might add to the paragraph to provide support for the main idea.

Answers

You Try It! 1. *b;* **2.** *c;* **3.** *second sentence in second paragraph; "Grant replied, 'No terms except an unconditional and immediate surrender can be accepted.'"*

Bellringer

If YOU were there . . . Use the **Daily Bellringer Transparency** to help students answer the question.

🖎 Daily Bellringer Transparency, Section 1

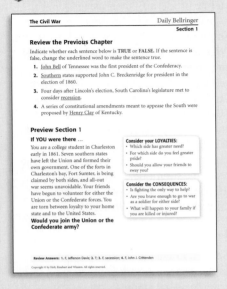

Building Vocabulary

Preteach or review the following terms:

mint place to make coins (p. 510)

secede to separate from the Union (p. 510)

📝 **CRF:** Vocabulary Builder Activity, Section 1

Taking Notes

Have students copy the graphic organizer onto their own paper and then use it to take notes on the section. This activity will prepare students for the Section Assessment, in which they will complete a graphic organizer that builds on the information using a critical thinking skill.

What You Will Learn...

Main Ideas

1. Following the outbreak of war at Fort Sumter, Americans chose sides.
2. The Union and the Confederacy prepared for war.

The Big Idea

Civil war broke out between the North and the South in 1861.

Key Terms and People

Fort Sumter, *p. 511*
border states, *p. 512*
Winfield Scott, *p. 513*
cotton diplomacy, *p. 513*

TAKING NOTES As you read, take notes on the Civil War and how Americans chose sides and how each side prepared for the war.

	Choosing Sides	Preparing for War
North		
South		

510 CHAPTER 16

If YOU were there...

You are a college student in Charleston in early 1861. Seven southern states have left the Union and formed their own government. One of the forts in Charleston's bay, Fort Sumter, is being claimed by both sides, and all-out war seems unavoidable. Your friends have begun to volunteer for either the Union or the Confederate forces. You are torn between loyalty to your home state and to the United States.

Would you join the Union or the Confederate army?

BUILDING BACKGROUND The divisions within the United States reached a breaking point with the election of Abraham Lincoln in 1860. Several southern states angrily left the Union to form a new confederation. In border states such as Virginia and Kentucky, people were divided. The question now was whether the United States could survive as a disunified country.

Americans Choose Sides

Abraham Lincoln became president on the eve of a four-year national nightmare. Furious at Lincoln's election and fearing a federal invasion, seven southern states had seceded. The new commander in chief tried desperately to save the Union.

In his inaugural address, Lincoln promised not to end slavery where it existed. The federal government "will not assail [attack] you. You can have no conflict without being yourselves the aggressors," he said, trying to calm southerners' fears. However, Lincoln also stated his intention to preserve the Union. He believed that saving the Union would help to save democracy. If the Union and its government failed, then monarchs could say that people were unable to rule themselves. As a result, Lincoln refused to recognize secession, declaring the Union to be "unbroken."

In fact, after decades of painful compromises, the Union was badly broken. From the lower South, a battle cry was arising, born out of fear, rage—and excitement. Confederate officials began seizing branches of the federal mint, arsenals, and military outposts. In the highly charged atmosphere, it would take only a spark to unleash the heat of war.

Teach the Big Idea

At Level

The War Begins

1. **Teach** Ask students the questions in the Main Idea boxes to teach this section.

2. **Apply** Discuss with students the crisis Lincoln faced upon becoming president, including his views on secession. Then discuss how the attack on Fort Sumter triggered the outbreak of the Civil War. Draw a jagged circle for students to see and label it *Fort Sumter*. Below the circle, draw three large boxes and label them *Americans Choose Sides, The North Versus the South,* and *Preparing for War.* **LS Visual/Spatial**

3. **Review** Have students help you complete each box by listing main ideas for that topic. Have students copy the completed chart.

4. **Practice/Homework** Have each student write a journal entry from the point of view of someone in the North or the South expressing his or her views on the outbreak of war. **LS Verbal/Linguistic**

📝 Alternative Assessment Handbook, Rubrics 7: Charts; and 15: Journals

Fort Sumter

Charleston

Castle Pinckney

In Charleston, all activity came to a complete stop. Citizens crowded rooftops to watch the battle.

Charleston Harbor

Shots fired at the ironclad battery did little damage.

Charleston

The first shot fired on Fort Sumter was fired from Fort Johnson.

Fort Johnson

Fort Sumter

Fort Moultrie

Fort Sumter was strategically placed to control Charleston Harbor.

Cummings Point

Atlantic Ocean

The first shots of the Civil War were fired at Fort Sumter, South Carolina. Although no one was killed there, the bloodiest war in the country's history had begun.

GEOGRAPHY SKILLS INTERPRETING MAPS

1. Why would the Union Army need to resupply Fort Sumter?
2. What advantages would a floating battery have?

In 1861, that spark occurred at **Fort Sumter**, a federal outpost in Charleston, South Carolina, that was attacked by Confederate troops, beginning the Civil War. Determined to seize the fortress—which controlled the entrance to Charleston harbor—the Confederates ringed the harbor with heavy guns. Instead of surrendering the fort, Lincoln decided to send in ships to provide badly needed supplies to defend the fort. Confederate officials demanded that the federal troops evacuate. The fort's commander, Major Robert Anderson, refused.

Before sunrise on April 12, 1861, Confederate guns opened fire on Fort Sumter. A witness wrote that the first shots brought "every soldier in the harbor to his feet, and every man, woman, and child in the city of Charleston from their beds." The Civil War had begun.

The fort, although massive, stood little chance. Its heavy guns faced the Atlantic Ocean, not the shore. After 34 hours of cannon blasts, Fort Sumter surrendered. "The last ray of hope for preserving the Union has expired at the assault upon Fort Sumter . . ." Lincoln wrote.

Reaction to Lincoln's Call

The fall of Fort Sumter stunned the North. Lincoln declared the South to be in a state of rebellion and asked state governors for 75,000 militiamen to put down the rebellion. States now had to choose: Would they secede, or would they stay in the Union? Democratic Senator Stephen Douglas, speaking in support of Lincoln's call for troops, declared, "There can be no neutrals in this war, *only patriots—or traitors.*"

Collaborative Learning

At Level

Front Page News: Fort Sumter

1. Organize the class into small groups and have each group create the front page of a newspaper covering the attack on Fort Sumter. Half of the groups should create their pages from the point of view of a southern newspaper. The other half of the groups should create pages for a northern newspaper.

2. Each group should create a masthead, two articles with headlines, an editorial, and a political cartoon explaining what happened and why the event was significant.

3. To ensure that all students participate, have groups assign each member specific tasks. Students might use poster board or computer software to produce their news pages.

4. Have each group present its front page to the class. **LS Interpersonal, Verbal/Linguistic, Visual/Spatial**

   Alternative Assessment Handbook, Rubric 23: Newspapers

Main Idea

❶ Americans Choose Sides

Following the outbreak of war at Fort Sumter, Americans chose sides.

Recall What event led to the start of the Civil War, and when did it occur? *Confederate attack on Fort Sumter on April 12, 1861*

Draw Conclusions How did the issue of secession contribute to the attack on Fort Sumter? *possible answer—Because South Carolina had seceded, its leaders believed they had the right to take Fort Sumter, which they considered to no longer be in federally controlled territory.*

Evaluate Do you think war could have been avoided? Why or why not? *possible answers—Yes, Lincoln had stated in his Inaugural Address that he would respect southerners' concerns; no, war was inevitable once southern states seceded.*

📰 Political Cartoons Activities for United States History, Cartoon 17: The Folly of Secession

🗺 Map Transparency: Charleston, South Carolina, Area Forts

Info to Know

Meanwhile, in Florida While events were unfolding at Fort Sumter, a similar situation was taking place at Fort Pickens near Pensacola, Florida. The Union forces at the fort were running low on supplies, and the Confederates were preparing to attack. Then news arrived of the fighting at Fort Sumter. The Confederates withdrew from the area to focus their efforts elsewhere.

Answers

Interpreting Maps 1. *it was surrounded by Confederate forces and badly needed supplies;* **2.** *it could move to avoid fire and find the fort's weakest point*

Main Idea

❶ Americans Choose Sides

Following the outbreak of war at Fort Sumter, Americans chose sides.

Explain Why were the border states significant? *Kentucky and Missouri controlled parts of important rivers; Maryland separated Washington, D.C. from the rest of the North.*

Summarize Describe the strategy of the North. *destroy the South's economy by blockading southern ports, gain control of the Mississippi River to divide the South; capture Richmond, the Confederate capital*

Identify Points of View How did the war affect family loyalties and friendships on each side? *deeply divided families and friends as people chose different sides*

📝 **CRF:** History and Geography Activity: Choosing Sides

📦 Quick Facts Transparency: North Versus South

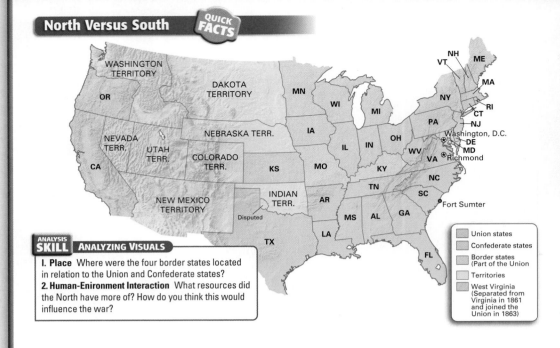

North Versus South — QUICK FACTS

ANALYSIS SKILL — ANALYZING VISUALS

1. Place Where were the four border states located in relation to the Union and Confederate states?

2. Human-Enironment Interaction What resources did the North have more of? How do you think this would influence the war?

Legend:
- Union states
- Confederate states
- Border states (Part of the Union)
- Territories
- West Virginia (Separated from Virginia in 1861 and joined the Union in 1863)

Pennsylvania, New Jersey, and the states north of them rallied to the president's call. The crucial slave states of the Upper South—North Carolina, Tennessee, Virginia, and Arkansas—seceded. They provided soldiers and supplies to the South. Mary Boykin Chesnut, whose husband became a Confederate congressman, wrote in her diary during this time:

❝I did not know that one could live in such days of excitement…Everybody tells you half of something, and then rushes off…to hear the last news.❞

Wedged between the North and the South were the key **border states** of Delaware, Kentucky, Maryland, and Missouri—slave states that did not join the Confederacy. Kentucky and Missouri controlled parts of important rivers. Maryland separated the Union capital, Washington, D.C., from the North.

People in the border states were deeply divided on the war. The president's own wife,

Mary Todd Lincoln, had four brothers from Kentucky who fought for the Confederacy. Lincoln sent federal troops into the border states to help keep them in the Union. He also sent soldiers into western Virginia, where Union loyalties were strong. West Virginia set up its own state government in 1863.

Northern Resources

Numbers tell an important story about the Civil War. Consider the North's advantages. It could draw soldiers and workers from a population of 22 million, compared with the South's 5.5 million. One of its greatest advantages was its network of roads, canals, and railroads. Some 22,000 miles of railroad track could move soldiers and supplies throughout the North. The South had only about 9,000 miles of track.

In the North, the Civil War stimulated economic growth. To supply the military, the production of coal, iron, wheat, and wool increased. Also, the export of corn, wheat, beef,

512 CHAPTER 16

Critical Thinking: Evaluating Information   **At Level**

The North Versus the South

1. Organize the class into small groups. Assign the North to half the groups and the South to the other half. Ask students to imagine that they are military advisers for their side at the start of the Civil War.

2. Each group should prepare a report for its president that analyzes the strengths and weaknesses of the other side at the start of the war. Students should address both available resources and military strategies. Encourage

students to incorporate maps, charts, and graphs as visual aids. Students might use presentation software as well.

3. Have volunteer groups share their reports with the class. Conclude with a discussion about the strengths and weaknesses of each side at the start of the war. **LS Interpersonal, Logical/Mathematical**

📝 Alternative Assessment Handbook, Rubrics 29: Presentations; and 42: Writing to Inform

---

Answers

Analyzing Visuals 1. *between the Union and Confederate states;* **2.** *population, railroad miles, industrial establishments; give the North an advantage over the South*

and pork to Europe doubled. In the South, the export of resources decreased because of the Union blockade.

Finally, the Union had money. It had a more developed economy, banking system, and currency. The South had to start printing its own Confederate dollars. Some states printed their own money, too. This led to financial chaos.

Taking advantage of the Union's strengths, General **Winfield Scott** developed a two-part strategy: (1) destroy the South's economy with a naval blockade of southern ports; (2) gain control of the Mississippi River to divide the South. Other leaders urged an attack on Richmond, Virginia, the Confederate capital.

Southern Resources

The Confederacy had advantages as well. With its strong military tradition, the South put many brilliant officers into battle. Southern farms provided food for its armies. The South's best advantage, however, was strategic. It needed only to defend itself until the North grew tired of fighting.

The North had to invade and control the South. To accomplish this, the Union army had to travel huge distances. For example, the distance from northern Virginia to central Georgia is about the length of Scotland and England combined. Because of distances such as this, the North had to maintain long supply lines.

In addition, wilderness covered much of the South. Armies found this land difficult to cross. Also, in Virginia, many of the rivers ran from east to west. Because of this, they formed a natural defense against an army that attacked from the north to the south. As a result, Northern generals were often forced to attack Confederate troops from the side rather than from the front. Furthermore, because Southerners fought mostly on their home soil, they were often familiar with the area.

The South hoped to wear down the North and to capture Washington, D.C. Confederate president Jefferson Davis also tried to win foreign allies through **cotton diplomacy**. This was the idea that Great Britain would support the Confederacy because it needed the South's raw cotton to supply its booming textile industry. Cotton diplomacy did not work as the South had hoped. Britain had large supplies of cotton, and it got more from India and Egypt.

READING CHECK **Comparing** What advantages did the North and South have leading up to the war?

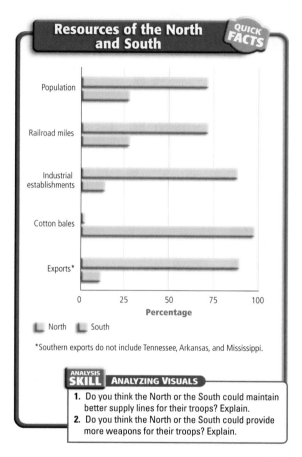

Resources of the North and South QUICK FACTS

*Southern exports do not include Tennessee, Arkansas, and Mississippi.

ANALYSIS SKILL **ANALYZING VISUALS**

1. Do you think the North or the South could maintain better supply lines for their troops? Explain.
2. Do you think the North or the South could provide more weapons for their troops? Explain.

THE CIVIL WAR **513**

513

Main Idea

❷ Preparing for War

The Union and the Confederacy prepared for war.

Describe In what ways did civilians support the troops? *raised money, provided aid for soldiers and their families, ran emergency hospitals*

Explain What was the purpose of the U.S. Sanitary Commission? *to send bandages, medicine, and food to Union army camps and hospitals*

Summarize What problems did both armies face at the start of the war? *shortages of clothing, food, and rifles; inexperienced volunteers who needed to be trained for combat*

Info to Know

The Blue and the Gray Towns formed volunteer militia units, which were then combined to form regiments. As a result, the variety of uniforms within regiments varied greatly, from elaborate homemade uniforms to uniforms dating back to the Revolutionary War. Soldiers soon learned the importance of consistent uniforms, however, particularly regarding color. For example, at the Battle of Bull Run, Confederate soldiers learned this lesson when their blue uniforms created confusion about which side they were on.

Answers

Analyzing Visuals *similar equipment and uniforms, different details and colors*

514

Union and Confederate Soldiers

Early in the war, uniforms differed greatly, especially in the Confederate army. Uniforms became simpler and more standard as the war dragged on.

The soldiers carried food, extra ammunition, and other items in their haversacks.

Each soldier was armed with a bayonet, a knife that can be attached to the barrel of a rifle. The bayonets were stored in scabbards on their belts.

Confederate Soldier

Both soldiers were also armed with single-shot, muzzle-loading rifles.

Union Soldier

ANALYSIS SKILL **ANALYZING VISUALS**

How are the Union and Confederate uniforms and equipment similar and different?

Preparing for War

The North and the South now rushed to war. Neither side was prepared for the tragedy to come.

Volunteer Armies

Volunteer militias had sparked the revolution that created the United States. Now they would battle for its future. At the start of the war, the Union army had only 16,000 soldiers. Within months that number had swelled to a half million. Southern men rose up to defend their land and their ways of life. Virginian Thomas Webber came to fight "against the invading foe [enemy] who now pollute the sacred soil of my beloved native state." When Union soldiers asked one captured rebel why he was fighting, he replied, "I'm fighting because you're down here."

Helping the Troops

Civilians on both sides helped those in uniform. They raised money, provided aid for soldiers and their families, and ran emergency hospitals. Dr. Elizabeth Blackwell, the first woman to receive a license to practice medicine, organized a group that pressured President Lincoln to form the U.S. Sanitary Commission in June 1861. The Sanitary, as it was called, was run by clergyman Henry Bellows. Tens of thousands of volunteers worked with the U.S. Sanitary Commission to send bandages, medicines, and food to Union army camps and hospitals. Some 3,000 women served as nurses in the Union army.

Training the Soldiers

Both the Union and Confederate armies faced shortages of clothing, food, and even rifles. Most troops lacked standard uniforms and simply wore their own clothes. Eventually, each side chose a color for their uniforms. The Union chose blue. The Confederates wore gray.

Critical Thinking: Analyzing Primary Sources

At Level

Union Army Fact Chart

1. Have students read the quote by David R. P. Shoemaker on page 515.

2. Create a two-column chart for students to see. Title the first column, *What We Know,* and the second column, *What We Infer.*

3. Discuss with the class what specific details about the Union army they can learn about from this source. List students' responses in the chart. Ask students what they can infer from the source, using prior knowledge and

information from the textbook. *Inferences may include why the army conducted so many drills, how soldiers felt about the drills, and if the drills were helpful.*

4. Have each student write an informative paragraph about the purpose and type of training soldiers received. **LS** **Verbal/Linguistic**

   📝 Alternative Assessment Handbook, Rubric 37: Writing Assignments

The problem with volunteers was that many of them had no idea how to fight. Schoolteachers, farmers, and laborers all had to learn the combat basics of marching, shooting, and using bayonets.

In a letter to a friend, a Union soldier described life in the training camp.

"We have been wading through mud knee deep all winter … For the last two weeks we have been drilled almost to death. Squad drill from 6 to 7 A.M. Company drill from 9 to 11 A.M. Batallion Drill from 2 to 4 1/2 P.M. Dress Parade from 5 to 5 1/2 P.M. and non-commissioned officers' school from 7 to 8 in the evening. If we don't soon become a well drilled Regiment, we ought to."

—David R. P. Shoemaker, 1862

With visions of glory and action, many young soldiers were eager to fight. They would not have to wait long.

Discipline and drill were used to turn raw volunteers into an efficient fighting machine. During a battle, the success or failure of a regiment often depended on its discipline—how well it responded to orders.

Volunteers also learned how to use rifles. Eventually, soldiers were expected to be able to load, aim, and fire their rifles three times in one minute. The quality of the weapons provided varied greatly. Most soldiers favored the Springfield and Enfield rifles for their accuracy. On the other hand, soldiers often complained about their Austrian and Belgian rifles. A soldier remarked, "I don't believe one could hit the broadside of a barn with them."

The Union army provided the infantry with two-person tents. However, soldiers often discarded these tents in favor of more portable ones. The Confederate army did not usually issue tents. Instead, Confederates often used tents that were captured from the Union army.

READING CHECK **Summarizing** How did soldiers and civilians prepare for war?

SUMMARY AND PREVIEW As citizens chose sides in the Civil War, civilians became involved in the war effort. In the next section you will learn about some early battles in the war.

Section 1 Assessment

go.hrw.com
Online Quiz
KEYWORD: SR8 HP16

Reviewing Ideas, Terms, and People

1. **a. Identify** What event triggered the war between the Union and the Confederacy?
   b. Contrast How did the Union's strategy differ from that of the Confederacy?
   c. Evaluate Which side do you believe was best prepared for war? Explain your answer.
2. **a. Describe** How did women take part in the war?
   b. Summarize In what ways were the armies of the North and South unprepared for war?
   c. Elaborate Why did men volunteer to fight in the war?

Critical Thinking

3. **Comparing and Contrasting** Review your notes on the preparations for war by the North and the South.

Then copy the graphic organizer shown below and use it to show the strengths and weaknesses of each side in the war.

	Union	Confederacy
Strengths		
Weaknesses		

FOCUS ON WRITING

4. **Taking Notes on the War's Beginning** As you read this section, take notes on the crisis at Fort Sumter and on the recruiting and training of the armies. Be sure to answer the following questions: Who? Where? When? Why? and How?

THE CIVIL WAR **515**

Section 1 Assessment Answers

1. **a.** Confederate attack on Fort Sumter
   b. North—blockade southern ports to destroy the South's economy, control the Mississippi River to divide the South; South—fight until the North was worn down, win foreign allies through cotton diplomacy
   c. Answers should reflect an understanding of each side's strengths and weaknesses.

2. **a.** raised money, served in the U.S. Sanitary Commission, served as nurses
   b. shortages of supplies, inexperienced troops who needed training in basic combat

   c. for glory and action, out of loyalty and patriotism; in the South, to defend their land and ways of life

3. Strengths—Union: larger population, better transportation network, stronger economy; Confederacy: military tradition, strategic advantage of fighting on home soil; Weaknesses—Union: fighting in enemy territory; Confederacy: lack of developed economy and banking system

4. Students' notes should be categorized to address each of the questions listed.

• **Direct Teach** •

Main Idea

❷ Preparing for War

The Union and the Confederacy prepared for war.

Recall What types of supplies were issued to soldiers? *rifles, bayonets, tents*

Make Judgments Which do you think soldiers preferred, the training they received or the supplies they received? Why? *possible answer— Soldiers preferred supplies, especially weapons and food, to training because training was hard work.*

• **Review & Assess** •

Close

Have students discuss how Americans on each side viewed the Civil War at its start and how these views probably changed over time.

Review

Online Quiz, Section 1

Assess

SE Section 1 Assessment
PASS: Section 1 Quiz
Alternative Assessment Handbook

Reteach/Classroom Intervention

Review Workbook
Interactive Reader and Study Guide, Section 1
Interactive Skills Tutor CD-ROM

Answers

Reading Check *soldiers— volunteered, trained to learn combat basics; civilians—raised money, provided aid, served as nurses*

515

Bellringer

If YOU were there . . . Use the **Daily Bellringer Transparency** to help students answer the question.

🗝 Daily Bellringer Transparency, Section 2

Academic Vocabulary

Review with students the high-use academic term in this section.

innovation a new idea or way of doing something (p. 520)

Building Vocabulary

Preteach or review the following terms:

casualties people who are killed, wounded, captured, or missing in a military conflict (p. 518)

peninsula land mass surrounded on three sides by water (p. 517)

🗒 CRF: Vocabulary Builder Activity, Section 2

Taking Notes

Have students copy the graphic organizer onto their own paper and then use it to take notes on the section. This activity will prepare students for the Section Assessment, in which they will complete a graphic organizer that builds on the information using a critical thinking skill.

The War in the East

What You Will Learn...

Main Ideas
1. Union and Confederate forces fought for control of the war in Virginia.
2. The Battle of Antietam gave the North a slight advantage.
3. The Confederacy attempted to break the Union naval blockade.

The Big Idea
Confederate and Union forces faced off in Virginia and at sea.

Key Terms and People
Thomas "Stonewall" Jackson, p. 517
First Battle of Bull Run, p. 517
George B. McClellan, p. 517
Robert E. Lee, p. 517
Seven Days' Battles, p. 518
Second Battle of Bull Run, p. 518
Battle of Antietam, p. 519
ironclads, p. 520

TAKING NOTES As you read, take notes on the battles in the east and at sea and the winners of each. Write your notes in a chart like the one below.

Battle	Winner

If YOU were there...

You live in Washington, D.C., in July 1861. You and your friends are on your way to Manassas, near Washington, to watch the battle there. Everyone expects a quick Union victory. Your wagon is loaded with food for a picnic, and people are in a holiday mood. You see some members of Congress riding toward Manassas, too. Maybe this battle will end the war!

Why would you want to watch this battle?

BUILDING BACKGROUND The shots fired at Fort Sumter made the war a reality. Neither the North nor the South was really prepared. Each side had some advantages—more industry and railroads in the North, a military tradition in the South. The war in the East centered in the region around the two capitals: Washington, D.C., and Richmond, Virginia.

War in Virginia

The troops that met in the first major battle of the Civil War found that it was no picnic. In July 1861, Lincoln ordered General Irvin McDowell to lead his 35,000-man army from the Union capital, Washington, to the Confederate capital, Richmond. The soldiers were barely trained. McDowell complained that they "stopped every moment to pick blackberries or get water; they would not keep in the ranks." The first day's march covered only five miles.

Bull Run/Manassas

McDowell's army was headed to Manassas, Virginia, an important railroad junction. If McDowell could seize Manassas, he would control the best route to the Confederate capital. Some 22,000 Confederate troops under the command of General Pierre G. T. Beauregard were waiting for McDowell and his troops along a creek called Bull Run. For two days, Union troops tried to find a way around the Confederates. During that time, Beauregard requested assistance, and

---

Teach the Big Idea

At Level

The War in the East

1. **Teach** Ask students the questions in the Main Idea boxes to teach this section.

2. **Apply** As students read this section, have them make lists of the key people and battles discussed. Have students write two facts about each person, two details about each battle, and one detail about each battle's outcome and significance or consequence.

3. **Review** As you review the section's main ideas, have volunteers share the information they listed about each person or battle.

4. **Practice/Homework** Ask students to imagine that they are southern or northern journalists covering the early battles of the Civil War. Have each student choose one battle and write an eyewitness account of it. Ask volunteers to read their accounts to the class. 🄻🅂 **Verbal/Linguistic**

🗒 Alternative Assessment Handbook, Rubric 40: Writing to Describe

General Joseph E. Johnston headed toward Manassas with another 10,000 Confederate troops. By July 21, 1861, they had all arrived.

That morning, Union troops managed to cross the creek and drive back the left side of the Confederate line. Yet one unit held firmly in place.

"There is Jackson standing like a stone wall!" cried one southern officer. "Rally behind the Virginians!" At that moment, General **Thomas "Stonewall" Jackson** earned his famous nickname.

A steady stream of Virginia volunteers arrived to counter the attack. The Confederates surged forward, letting out their terrifying "rebel yell." One eyewitness described the awful scene.

" There is smoke, dust, wild talking, shouting; hissings, howlings, explosions. It is a new, strange, unanticipated experience to the soldiers of both armies, far different from what they thought it would be. "

—Charles Coffin,
quoted in *Voices of the Civil War* by Richard Wheeler

The battle raged through the day, with rebel soldiers still arriving. Finally, the weary Union troops gave out. They tried to make an orderly retreat back across the creek, but the roads were clogged with the fancy carriages of panicked spectators. The Union army scattered in the chaos.

The Confederates lacked the strength to push north and capture Washington, D.C. But clearly, the rebels had won the day. The **First Battle of Bull Run** was the first major battle of the Civil War, and the Confederates' victory. The battle is also known as the first Battle of Manassas. It shattered the North's hopes of winning the war quickly.

More Battles in Virginia

The shock at Bull Run persuaded Lincoln of the need for a better trained army. He put his hopes in General **George B. McClellan**. The general assembled a highly disciplined force of 100,000 soldiers called the Army of the Potomac. The careful McClellan spent months training. However, because

Battles in the East

GEOGRAPHY SKILLS | **INTERPRETING MAPS**

1. **Location** Which battle was fought in Maryland?
2. **Human-Environment Interaction** How did geography influence the movement of forces?

he overestimated the size of the Confederate army, McClellan hesitated to attack. Lincoln grew impatient. Finally, in the spring of 1862, McClellan launched an effort to capture Richmond called the "Peninsular Campaign." Instead of marching south for a direct assault, McClellan slowly brought his force through the peninsula between the James and York rivers. More time slipped away.

The South feared that McClellan would receive reinforcements from Washington. To prevent this, Stonewall Jackson launched an attack toward Washington. Although the attack was pushed back, it prevented the Union from sending reinforcements to McClellan.

THE IMPACT TODAY

Many Americans continue to be fascinated by the Civil War. Some history buffs regularly stage re-enactments of famous battles, complete with uniforms, guns, and bayonets.

THE CIVIL WAR **517**

❶ War in Virginia

Union and Confederate forces fought for control of the war in Virginia.

Recall Who became the leader of the main Union army, and what was this army called? *General George B. McClellan; Army of the Potomac*

Identify Who became the new leader of the Confederate Army, and what skills did he bring to the job? *Robert E. Lee, experienced soldier, skilled strategist, risk-taker*

Summarize Describe the Seven Days' Battles and the outcome. *series of clashes in the summer of 1862 between McClellan's and Lee's forces in Virginia; Confederate victory; Lee protected Richmond and forced McClellan to retreat.*

Elaborate How did Jackson's defeat of General Pope's Union forces at the Second Battle of Bull Run affect Lee's plans? *Lee decided to take the war to the North.*

Info to Know

McClellan Union general George B. McClellan's strengths included his abilities to organize and plan. After the first defeat at Bull Run, he helped restore order and morale to the Army of the Potomac. McClellan's unwillingness to take action against the Confederate army led to criticism, however. Leaders in Washington began to accuse him of not wanting to fight or of being pro-South. One 1862 political cartoon showed Lincoln having to carry McClellan to get him to Richmond.

Answers

Reading Check *Lee led a series of attacks known as the Seven Days' Battles, which forced the Army of the Potomac to retreat; Lincoln then ordered General John Pope to march on Richmond; Jackson wanted to defeat Pope's army before it could join the Army of the Potomac. After 3 days of fighting, Jackson defeated Pope.*

In June 1862, with McClellan's force poised outside Richmond, the Confederate army in Virginia came under the command of General **Robert E. Lee**. A graduate of the U.S. Military Academy at West Point, Lee had served in the Mexican War and had led federal troops at Harpers Ferry. Lee was willing to take risks and make unpredictable moves to throw Union forces off balance.

During the summer of 1862, Lee strengthened his positions. On June 26, he attacked, launching a series of clashes known as the **Seven Days' Battles** that forced the Union army to retreat from near Richmond. Confederate General D. H. Hill described one failed attack. "It was not war—it was murder," he said. Lee saved Richmond and forced McClellan to retreat.

A frustrated Lincoln ordered General John Pope to march directly on Richmond from Washington. Pope told his soldiers, "Let us look before us and not behind. Success and glory are in the advance."

Jackson wanted to defeat Pope's army before it could join up with McClellan's larger Army of the Potomac. Jackson's troops met Pope's Union forces on the battlefield in August in 1862. The three-day battle became known as the **Second Battle of Bull Run**, or the Second Battle of Manassas.

The first day's fighting was savage. Captain George Fairfield of the 7th Wisconsin regiment later recalled, "What a slaughter! No one appeared to know the object of the fight, and there we stood for one hour, the men falling all around." The fighting ended in a stalemate.

On the second day, Pope found Jackson's troops along an unfinished railroad grade. Pope hurled his men against the Confederates. But the attacks were pushed back with heavy casualties on both sides.

On the third day, the Confederates crushed the Union army's assault and forced it to retreat in defeat. The Confederates had won a major victory, and General Robert E. Lee decided it was time to take the war to the North.

READING CHECK **Sequencing** List in order the events that forced Union troops out of Virginia.

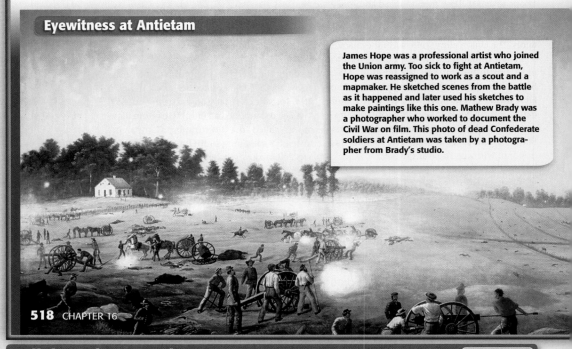

Eyewitness at Antietam

James Hope was a professional artist who joined the Union army. Too sick to fight at Antietam, Hope was reassigned to work as a scout and a mapmaker. He sketched scenes from the battle as it happened and later used his sketches to make paintings like this one. Mathew Brady was a photographer who worked to document the Civil War on film. This photo of dead Confederate soldiers at Antietam was taken by a photographer from Brady's studio.

518 CHAPTER 16

Early Battles Illustrated Articles

1. Organize the class into eight groups. Assign each group one of the four key battles in this section—First Battle of Bull Run, Seven Days' Battles, Second Battle of Bull Run, or the Battle of Antietam. Two groups will have each battle. Have one of the groups adopt the perspective of a northern newspaper and the other adopt that of a southern newspaper.

2. Have each group create a newspaper article, with a headline, about the significance of its assigned battle. In addition, students should provide a map or illustration showing the location of the battle and troop movements. Encourage groups to use computer software to lay out their articles and visuals.

3. Display students' illustrated articles around the classroom. **LS** **Interpersonal, Verbal/Linguistic, Visual/Spatial**

📝 Alternative Assessment Handbook, Rubrics 14: Group Activity; and 29: Presentations

Battle of Antietam

Confederate leaders hoped to follow up Lee's successes in Virginia with a major victory on northern soil. On September 4, 1862, some 40,000 Confederate soldiers began crossing into Maryland. General Robert E. Lee decided to divide his army. He sent about half of his troops, under the command of Stonewall Jackson, to Harpers Ferry. There they defeated a Union force and captured the town. Meanwhile, Lee arrived in the town of Frederick and issued a Proclamation to the People of Maryland, urging them to join the Confederates. However, his words would not be enough to convince Marylanders to abandon the Union. Union soldiers, however, found a copy of Lee's battle plan, which had been left at an abandoned Confederate camp. General McClellan learned that Lee had divided his army in order to attack Harpers Ferry. However, McClellan hesitated to attack. As a result, the Confederates had time to reunite.

The two armies met along Antietam Creek in Maryland on September 17, 1862. The battle lasted for hours. By the end of the day, the Union had suffered more than 12,000 casualties. The Confederates endured more than 13,000 casualties. Union officer A. H. Nickerson later recalled, "It seemed that everybody near me was killed." The **Battle of Antietam,** also known as the Battle of Sharpsburg, was the bloodiest single-day battle of the Civil War—and of U.S. history. More soldiers were killed and wounded at the Battle of Antietam than the deaths of all Americans in the American Revolution, War of 1812, and Mexican-American War combined.

During the battle, McClellan kept four divisions of soldiers in reserve and refused to use them to attack Lee's devastated army. McClellan was convinced that Lee was massing reserves for a counterattack. Those reserves did not exist. Despite this blunder, Antietam was an important victory. Lee's northward advance had been stopped.

READING CHECK Analyzing Why was the Battle of Antietam significant?

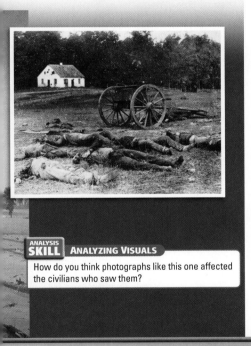

ANALYSIS SKILL **ANALYZING VISUALS**
How do you think photographs like this one affected the civilians who saw them?

❸ Breaking the Union's Blockade

The Confederacy attempted to break the Union naval blockade.

Recall Which side held the naval advantage in the war, and why? *Union; had most of the U.S. Navy's small fleet, many experienced naval officers, and enough industry to build more ships*

Make Inferences Why might control of the seas benefit a power at war? *provide the ability to ship goods and supplies to troops and to prevent enemies from receiving supplies*

Elaborate How did the ironclads signal a revolution in naval warfare? *They introduced new materials and features—such as heavy iron armor and revolving gun towers—that were major advances over wooden ships powered by wind and sails.*

📄 **CRF:** Interdisciplinary Project: The Ironclads: The *Monitor* and the *Virginia*

📦 Map Transparency: Union Blockade

Primary Source
Anaconda Plan
Have students examine the images in the political cartoon. Ask them to describe how the cartoonist uses the images to present a negative view of the South. *He shows enslaved Africans being mistreated or shot and Union supporters being hanged.*

Answers
Analyzing Primary Sources
Anacondas are constricting, water-loving snakes. Like an anaconda, the strategy was water-based and constrictive. The blockade was meant to snake along the South's coast, squeeze the South's economy, and thereby strike at the South's heart.

520

POLITICAL CARTOON
Anaconda Plan

This cartoon shows visually the North's plan to cut off supplies to the South through naval blockades, a strategy called the Anaconda Plan.

> Why is the snake's head red, white, and blue?

> How does the cartoonist show what the snake represents?

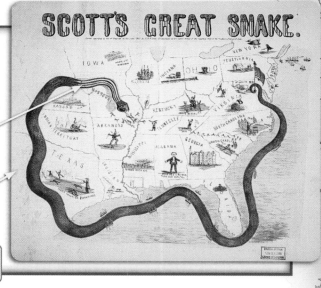

ANALYSIS SKILL **ANALYZING PRIMARY SOURCES**
Why do you think the plan was called the Anaconda Plan?

Breaking the Union's Blockade

While the two armies fought for control of the land, the Union navy controlled the sea. The North had most of the U.S. Navy's small fleet, and many experienced naval officers had remained loyal to the Union. The North also had enough industry to build more ships.

The Union's Naval Strategy

ACADEMIC VOCABULARY
innovation a new idea or way of doing something

The Union navy quickly mobilized to set up a blockade of southern ports. The blockade largely prevented the South from selling or receiving goods, and it seriously damaged the southern economy.

The blockade was hard to maintain because the Union navy had to patrol thousands of miles of coastline from Virginia to Texas. The South used small, fast ships to outrun the larger Union warships. Most of these blockade runners traveled to the Bahamas or Nassau to buy supplies for the Confederacy. These ships, however, could not make up for

the South's loss of trade. The Union blockade reduced the number of ships entering southern ports from 6,000 to 800 per year.

Clash of the Ironclads

Hoping to take away the Union's advantage at sea, the Confederacy turned to a new type of warship—**ironclads**, or ships heavily armored with iron. The Confederates had captured a Union steamship, the *Merrimack*, and turned it into an ironclad, renamed the *Virginia*. One Union sailor described the **innovation** as "a huge half-submerged crocodile." In early March 1862, the ironclad sailed into Hampton Roads, Virginia, an important waterway guarded by Union ships. Before nightfall, the *Virginia* easily sank two of the Union's wooden warships, while it received minor damage. A Baltimore reporter predicted doom the next day.

> "There appeared no reason why the iron monster might not clear [Hampton] Roads of our fleet, [and] destroy all the stores [supplies] and warehouses on the beach."
> —quoted in *The Rebellion Record, Vol. 4*

Differentiating Instruction

English-Language Learners

Materials: pictures of ironclads (optional)

1. Pair students and have each pair create a storyboard or historical cartoon strip that illustrates the sequence of events in the clash of the ironclads the *Monitor* and the *Virginia*.

2. Have students use the information in the section to list the sequence of events for their storyboards or cartoon strips. In addition, encourage students to conduct research on the way the ironclads looked to make the illustrations more realistic.

3. Students should provide captions for each panel in their storyboards or cartoon strips.

4. Display students' storyboards or cartoon strips in the classroom. **LS Interpersonal, Visual/Spatial**

📄 Alternative Assessment Handbook, Rubrics 3: Artwork; and 29: Presentations

Union Blockade

Legend:
- Union states
- Confederate states
- Union blockade

0   100   200 Miles
0   100   200 Kilometers

Ohio

Mississippi River

Washington, D.C.

Richmond

Hampton Roads

Monitor battles *Virginia* at Hampton Roads.

Charleston

80°W   30°N

ATLANTIC OCEAN

New Orleans

Gulf of Mexico

90°W

Tropic of Cancer

GEOGRAPHY SKILLS INTERPRETING MAPS

Location What major port cities in the South were affected by the blockade?

The Union navy had already built its own ironclad, the *Monitor*, designed by Swedish-born engineer John Ericsson. Ericsson's ship had unusual new features, such as a revolving gun tower. One Confederate soldier called the *Monitor* "a tin can on a shingle!" Although small, the *Monitor* carried powerful guns and had thick plating.

When the *Virginia* returned to Hampton Roads later that month, the *Monitor* was waiting. After several hours of fighting, neither ship was seriously damaged, but the *Monitor* forced the *Virginia* to withdraw. This success saved the Union fleet and continued the blockade. The clash of the ironclads also signaled a revolution in naval warfare. The days of wooden warships powered by wind and sails were drawing to a close.

THE IMPACT TODAY The *Monitor* sank in North Carolina in the winter of 1862. The shipwreck was located by scientists in 1973, and efforts to save it for further study continue today.

READING CHECK **Evaluating** How effective was the Union blockade?

SUMMARY AND PREVIEW The early battles of the Civil War were centered in the East. In the next section you will read about battles in the West.

Section 2 Assessment

go.hrw.com
Online Quiz
KEYWORD: SR8 HP16

Reviewing Ideas, Terms, and People

1. a. Identify List the early battles in the East and the outcome of each battle.
b. Elaborate Why do you think the Union lost the **First Battle of Bull Run?**

2. a. Describe What costly mistake did the Confederacy make before the **Battle of Antietam?**
b. Analyze What was the outcome of the **Battle of Antietam,** and what effect did it have on both the North and the South?
c. Elaborate Why do you think General **George B. McClellan** did not finish off General **Robert E. Lee's** troops when he had the chance?

3. a. Describe What was the Union's strategy in the war at sea?
b. Draw Conclusions Why were **ironclads** more successful than older, wooden ships?

Critical Thinking

4. Supporting a Point of View Review your notes on the battles in the east and at sea. Then copy the graphic organizer below and use it to show which three conflicts you think were the most signficant and why.

Most Significant	Why

FOCUS ON WRITING

5. Taking Notes on the War in the East As you read this section, take notes on the First Battle of Bull Run, the Seven Days' Battles, the Second Battle of Bull Run, and the Battle of Antietam. Be sure to answer the following questions: Who? Where? When? Why? and How?

THE CIVIL WAR **521**

Section 2 Assessment Answers

1. a. First Battle of Bull Run—Confederacy, shattered Union hopes of a quick war; Seven Day's Battles—Confederacy, forced a Union retreat; Second Battle of Bull Run—Confederacy, pushed most Union forces out of Virginia; Antietam—Union, stopped Confederates' northward advance
b. Union soldiers were untrained and did not take the battle seriously.

2. a. left behind a copy of Lee's battle plan
b. tremendous losses on both sides; stopped the Confederates' northward advance

c. possible answers—He was overly cautious; he was convinced that Lee was massing reserves for a counterattack.

3. a. to blockade southern ports and thereby squeeze the South's trade and economy
b. protected with iron plating; more powerful features, such as revolving gun towers

4. Students will select three battles and explain their significance

5. Students should provide information similar to Questions 1 and 4.

Direct Teach

Connect to Economics

Blockade Runners The blockade-running business was quite profitable for those willing to risk being targets of northern ships. For example, salt, which sold for $6.50 a ton in the Bahamas, sold for $1,700 a ton in the South. Coffee, which sold for $249 in the Bahamas, brought $5,500 in the South. A successful blockade captain could earn $5,000 on one run, while a captain in the merchant service would only earn about $150 for equivalent work.

Review & Assess

Close

Have students discuss which side they think was winning the war at this point. Encourage students to identify specific battles and outcomes to support their positions.

Review

Online Quiz, Section 2

Assess

SE Section 2 Assessment
PASS: Section 2 Quiz
Alternative Assessment Handbook

Reteach/Classroom Intervention

Review Workbook
Interactive Reader and Study Guide, Section 2
Interactive Skills Tutor CD-ROM

Answers

Interpreting Maps *Charleston, South Carolina; New Orleans, Louisiana*
Reading Check *Although hard to maintain, the blockade effectively limited southern trade and seriously damaged the southern economy.*

521

Bellringer

If YOU were there . . . Use the **Daily Bellringer Transparency** to help students answer the question.

📖 Daily Bellringer Transparency, Section 3

Building Vocabulary

Preteach or review the following terms:

campaign series of related military operations in a war (p. 522)

maneuvers strategic movement of troops, ships, or firepower (p. 522)

📝 **CRF:** Vocabulary Builder Activity, Section 3

Taking Notes

Have students copy the graphic organizer onto their own paper and then use it to take notes on the section. This activity will prepare students for the Section Assessment, in which they will complete a graphic organizer that builds on the information using a critical thinking skill.

The War in the West

What You Will Learn...

Main Ideas

1. Union strategy in the West centered on control of the Mississippi River.
2. Confederate and Union troops struggled for dominance in the Far West.

The Big Idea

Fighting in the Civil War spread to the western United States.

Key Terms and People

Ulysses S. Grant, *p. 522*
Battle of Shiloh, *p. 523*
David Farragut, *p. 524*
Siege of Vicksburg, *p. 524*

TAKING NOTES As you read, take notes on Civil War battles in the West. Write your notes in a graphic organizer like the one below.

Battles in the West
1.
2.
3.
4.
5.
6.

522 CHAPTER 16

If YOU were there...

You live in the city of Vicksburg, set on high bluffs above the Mississippi River. Vicksburg is vital to the control of the river, and Confederate defenses are strong. But the Union general is determined to take the town. For weeks, you have been surrounded and besieged. Cannon shells burst overhead, day and night. Some have fallen on nearby homes. Supplies of food are running low.

How would you survive this siege?

BUILDING BACKGROUND The Civil War was fought on many fronts, all across the continent and even at sea. In the East, fighting was at first concentrated in Virginia. In the West, cities and forts along the Mississippi River were the main target of Union forces. Northern control of the river would cut off the western states of the Confederacy.

Union Strategy in the West

While Lincoln fumed over the cautious, hesitant General McClellan, he had no such problems with **Ulysses S. Grant**. Bold and restless, Grant grew impatient when he was asked to lead defensive maneuvers. He wanted to be on the attack. As a commander of forces in the Union's western campaign, he would get his wish.

The western campaign focused on taking control of the Mississippi River. This strategy would cut off the eastern part of the Confederacy from sources of food production in Arkansas, Louisiana, and Texas. From bases on the Mississippi, the Union army could attack southern communication and transportation networks.

In February 1862, Grant led an assault force into Tennessee. With help from navy gunboats, Grant's Army of Tennessee took two outposts on key rivers in the west. On February 6, he captured Fort Henry on the Tennessee River. Several days later he took Fort Donelson on the Cumberland River.

Fort Donelson's commander asked for the terms of surrender. Grant replied, "No terms except an unconditional and immediate

---

Teach the Big Idea

The War in the West

1. **Teach** Ask students the questions in the Main Idea boxes to teach this section.

2. **Apply** Have each student list the section's Key Terms and People. Under each name, have students write the following questions: *Why is this person significant? What did this person accomplish? When? Where?* Under each event, have students write the following questions: *Why is this event significant? When and where did this event occur? What happened during this event?* As students

read the section, have them write the answer to each question. **LS** **Verbal/Linguistic**

3. **Review** As you review the section, have volunteers share their answers.

4. **Practice/Homework** Have each student create a five-question quiz for the section as well as an answer key. Have students exchange quizzes, complete them, and then return them for grading. **LS** **Verbal/Linguistic**

The War In the West

INDIAN TERRITORY

AR

Memphis

Corinth

Vicksburg
May–July 1863

Jackson

LA

Natchez

Port Hudson
May–July 1863

Baton Rouge

New Orleans
April 1862

Louisville

Ohio River

Paducah

Ft. Donelson
Feb. 1862

Nashville

Ft. Henry
Feb. 1862

Murfreesboro
Dec. 1862–Jan. 1863

Shiloh
April 1862

TN

Chattanooga
Nov. 1863

Chickamauga
Sept. 1863

Birmingham

Atlanta

SC

GA

MS

AL

VA

KY

NC

FL

Gulf of Mexico

UNION BLOCKADE

Legend:
- Union state or territory
- Union occupied 1863
- Confederate state
- Union forces
- Union blockade
- Union victory
- Confederate forces
- Confederate victory

0   100   200 Miles
0   100   200 Kilometers

GEOGRAPHY SKILLS · INTERPRETING MAPS

1. **Location** What river did Union forces fight to control?
2. **Human-Environment Interaction** Why do you think so many battles took place along rivers?

---

surrender can be accepted." The fort surrendered. The North gave a new name to Grant's initials: "Unconditional Surrender" Grant.

Advancing south in Tennessee, General Grant paused near Shiloh Church to await the arrival of the Army of Ohio. Grant knew that the large rebel army of General A. S. Johnston was nearby in Corinth, Mississippi, but he did not expect an attack. Instead of setting up defenses, he worked on drilling his new recruits.

In the early morning of April 6, 1862, the rebels sprang on Grant's sleepy camp. This began the **Battle of Shiloh**, in which the Union army gained greater control of the Mississippi River valley.

During the bloody two-day battle, each side gained and lost ground. Johnston was killed on the first day. The arrival of the Ohio force helped Grant regain territory and push the enemy back into Mississippi. The armies finally gave out, each with about 10,000 casualties. Both sides claimed victory, but, in fact, the victor was Grant.

The Fall of New Orleans

As Grant battled his way down the Mississippi, the Union navy prepared to blast its way upriver to meet him. The first obstacle was the port of New Orleans, the largest city in the Confederacy and the gateway to the Mississippi River.

BIOGRAPHY

David Farragut
(1801–1870)

David Farragut was born in Tennessee to a Spanish father and an American mother. At age seven Farragut was adopted by a family friend who agreed to train the young boy for the navy. Farragut received his first navy position—midshipman at large—at age nine and commanded his first vessel at 12. He spent the rest of his life in the U.S. Navy. Farragut led key attacks on the southern ports of Vicksburg and New Orleans.

Drawing Inferences How did Farragut help the war effort of the North?

THE CIVIL WAR **523**

Critical Thinking: Summarizing

At Level

Interviews with Grant and Farragut

1. Discuss with students the main events of the war in the West. Then ask students to imagine that they are roving correspondents for a newspaper during the Civil War. Vicksburg has just surrendered, and their editor has assigned them to interview either Ulysses S. Grant or Admiral David Farragut.

2. Pair students and assign each pair either Grant or Farragut. Have each pair write at least 10 questions and answers for the interview.

Questions should address the goals of the campaign in the West, the fighting in which the assigned leader has been involved, the significance of this action, and the leader's views on the progress of the war in the West.

3. Have volunteer pairs act out their interviews.
LS Interpersonal, Verbal/Linguistic

📝 Alternative Assessment Handbook, Rubric 37: Writing Assignments

523

Main Idea

❶ Union Strategy in the West

Union strategy in the West centered on control of the Mississippi River.

Explain How was Admiral Farragut able to capture New Orleans? *Unable to destroy the two forts protecting the city, he camouflaged his fleet and led a daring and successful pre-dawn dash past the forts, after which he easily took New Orleans.*

Identify Cause and Effect Why did Grant decide to starve Vicksburg into surrender? *The city's strategic geographic location on a high cliff above the Mississippi River made invasion all but impossible, and Farragut's cannons could not reach the city.*

Info to Know

The War in Indian Territory The Civil War divided Native Americans in Indian Territory. The Choctaw, Chickasaw, Cherokee, Creek, and Seminole nations split, with some supporting the Confederacy and others the Union. Some 10,000 Native Americans served with the Confederates during the war. By the war's end in 1865, an estimated 6,000 to 10,000 Native Americans had died as a result of the fighting.

Answers

Analyzing Primary Sources *shows that although he is surrendering he remains loyal to the South*

524

With 18 ships and 700 men, Admiral **David Farragut** approached the two forts that guarded the entrance to New Orleans from the Gulf of Mexico. Unable to destroy the forts, Farragut decided to race past them.

The risky operation would take place at night. Farragut had his wooden ships wrapped in heavy chains to protect them like ironclads. Sailors slapped Mississippi mud on the ships' hulls to make them hard to see. Trees were tied to the masts to make the ships look like the forested shore.

Before dawn on April 24, 1862, the warships made their daring dash. The Confederates fired at Farragut's ships from the shore and from gunboats. They launched burning rafts, one of which scorched Farragut's own ship. But his fleet slipped by the twin forts and made it to New Orleans. The city fell on April 29.

Farragut sailed up the Mississippi River, taking Baton Rouge, Louisiana, and Natchez,

524 CHAPTER 16

Mississippi. He then approached the city of Vicksburg, Mississippi.

The Siege of Vicksburg

Vicksburg's geography made invasion all but impossible. Perched on 200-foot-high cliffs above the Mississippi River, the city could rain down firepower on enemy ships or on soldiers trying to scale the cliffs. Deep gorges surrounded the city, turning back land assaults. Nevertheless, Farragut ordered Vicksburg to surrender.

❝Mississippians don't know, and refuse to learn, how to surrender … If Commodore Farragut … can teach them, let [him] come and try.❞
—Colonel James L. Autry, military commander of Vicksburg

Farragut's guns had trouble reaching the city above. It was up to General Grant. His solution was to starve the city into surrender.

General Grant's troops began the **Siege of Vicksburg** in mid-May, 1863, cutting off the city and shelling it repeatedly. As food ran out, residents and soldiers survived by eating horses, dogs, and rats. "We are utterly cut off from the world, surrounded by a circle of fire," wrote one woman. "People do nothing

The Union navy played an important part in the Civil War. Besides blockading and raiding southern ports, the navy joined battles along the Mississippi River, as in this painting of Vicksburg.

Critical Thinking: Identifying Points of View   At Level

Letter from Vicksburg

1. Review with students the events of the Siege of Vicksburg. Then have students examine the History and Geography feature "The Vicksburg Strategy" that follows this section.

2. Ask students to imagine that they are either Confederate soldiers or civilians in Vicksburg during the Union siege of the city. Have each student write a letter to an imaginary friend or family member living elsewhere in the South telling them about the experience.

3. Students' letters should describe the siege, such as the constant shelling and the lack of food and supplies, their feelings about it, whether they think the city should surrender, and what the consequences of surrendering might be.

4. Have volunteers read their letters to the class.
LS Verbal/Linguistic

Alternative Assessment Handbook, Rubric 25: Personal Letters but eat what they can get, sleep when they can, and dodge the shells."

The Confederate soldiers were also sick and hungry. In late June a group of soldiers sent their commander a warning.

"The army is now ripe for mutiny [rebellion], unless it can be fed. If you can't feed us, you'd better surrender us, horrible as the idea is."

—Confederate soldiers at Vicksburg to General John C. Pemberton, 1863

On July 4, Pemberton surrendered. Grant immediately sent food to the soldiers and civilians. He later claimed that "the fate of the Confederacy was sealed when Vicksburg fell."

READING CHECK **Summarizing** How did the Union gain control of the Mississippi River?

Struggle for the Far West

Early on in the war, the Union halted several attempts by Confederate armies to control lands west of the Mississippi. In August 1861, a Union detachment from Colorado turned back a Confederate force at Glorieta Pass. Union volunteers also defeated rebel forces at Arizona's Pichaco Pass.

Confederate attempts to take the border state of Missouri also collapsed. Failing to seize the federal arsenal at St. Louis mid-1861, the rebels fell back to Pea Ridge in northwestern Arkansas. There, in March 1862, they attacked again, aided by some 800 Cherokee. The Indians hoped the Confederates would give them greater freedom. In addition, slavery was legal in Indian Territory, and some Native Americans who were slaveholders supported the Confederacy. Despite being outnumbered, Union forces won the Battle of Pea Ridge. The Union defense of Missouri held.

Pro-Confederate forces remained active in the region throughout the war. They attacked Union forts and raided towns in Missouri and Kansas, forcing Union commanders to keep valuable troops stationed in the area.

READING CHECK **Analyzing** What was the importance of the fighting in the Far West?

SUMMARY AND PREVIEW The North and the South continued their struggle with battles in the West. A number of key battles took place in the Western theatre, and several important Union leaders emerged from these battles. One, Ulysses S. Grant, would soon become even more important to the Union army. In the next section you will learn about the lives of civilians, enslaved Africans, and soldiers during the war.

Section 3 Assessment

go.hrw.com
Online Quiz
KEYWORD: SR8 HP16

Reviewing Ideas, Terms, and People

1. **a. Identify** What role did **Ulysses S. Grant** play in the war in the West?
   b. Explain Why was the **Battle of Shiloh** important?
   c. Elaborate Do you think President Lincoln would have approved of Grant's actions in the West? Why or why not?
2. **a. Describe** How did the Union take New Orleans, and why was it an important victory?
   b. Draw Conclusions How were civilians affected by the **Siege of Vicksburg**?
   c. Predict What might be some possible results of the Union victory at Vicksburg?

Critical Thinking

3. **Identifying Cause and Effect** Review your notes on Union strategy in the West. Then copy this graphic organizer and use it to show the causes and effects of each battle.

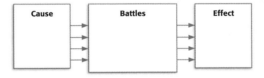

| Cause | Battles | Effect |

FOCUS ON WRITING

4. **Taking Notes on the War in the West** As you read this section, take notes on the fight for the Mississippi River and the Siege of Vicksburg. Be sure to answer the following questions: Who? Where? When? Why? and How?

THE CIVIL WAR **525**

Activity Vicksburg Strategy

Headlines Have students read the feature. Ask a volunteer to explain why Lincoln thought Vicksburg was such an important Union target. Next, have students trace the stages in the Vicksburg strategy. Ask students to identify the geographic factors that affected Grant's decisions and actions at various points along his march. Then have students write at least one newspaper headline for each stage numbered on the map at right. Ask volunteers to read their headlines to the class. **LS Verbal/Linguistic, Visual/Spatial**

Info to Know

Grant's Supply Strategy Instead of waiting for supply wagons, Union general Ulysses S. Grant had his troops live off the land. The soldiers combed the southern countryside taking horses, oxen, farm wagons, and even carriages from area farms and plantations. Grant knew from earlier campaigns that the farms in Mississippi had plenty of food as well, and his troops raided for cattle, pigs, and other goods.

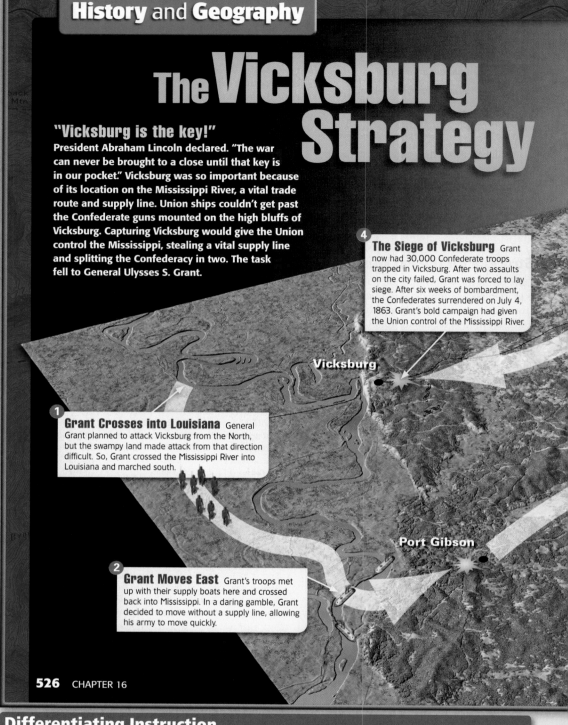

History and Geography

The Vicksburg Strategy

"Vicksburg is the key!"

President Abraham Lincoln declared. "The war can never be brought to a close until that key is in our pocket." Vicksburg was so important because of its location on the Mississippi River, a vital trade route and supply line. Union ships couldn't get past the Confederate guns mounted on the high bluffs of Vicksburg. Capturing Vicksburg would give the Union control the Mississippi, stealing a vital supply line and splitting the Confederacy in two. The task fell to General Ulysses S. Grant.

4 The Siege of Vicksburg Grant now had 30,000 Confederate troops trapped in Vicksburg. After two assaults on the city failed, Grant was forced to lay siege. After six weeks of bombardment, the Confederates surrendered on July 4, 1863. Grant's bold campaign had given the Union control of the Mississippi River.

Vicksburg

1 Grant Crosses into Louisiana General Grant planned to attack Vicksburg from the North, but the swampy land made attack from that direction difficult. So, Grant crossed the Mississippi River into Louisiana and marched south.

Port Gibson

2 Grant Moves East Grant's troops met up with their supply boats here and crossed back into Mississippi. In a daring gamble, Grant decided to move without a supply line, allowing his army to move quickly.

Differentiating Instruction

Special Needs Learners   Below Level

1. Discuss the feature with students.

2. Have students work in pairs to create time lines of the events in the Vicksburg campaign shown above. Students should note one detail about each event. **LS Visual/Spatial**

   Alternative Assessment Handbook, Rubric 36: Time Lines

English-Language Learners   Below Level

1. Have students write down each word or phrase in the feature they do not understand.

2. Organize students into mixed-ability pairs. Have partners look up the definitions of the words on their lists. Then have partners quiz each other on the words' meanings. **LS Interpersonal, Verbal/Linguistic**

UNION CONTROL

CONFEDERATE CONTROL

GULF OF MEXICO

Ironclads

Union ironclads were vital to the Vicksburg campaign. These gunboats protected Grant's troops when they crossed the Mississippi. Later, they bombarded Vicksburg during the siege of the city.

The Battle of Jackson Grant defeated a Confederate army at Jackson and then moved on to Vicksburg. This prevented Confederate forces from reinforcing Vicksburg.

BIOGRAPHY

Ulysses S. Grant
(1822–1885)

Ulysses S. Grant was born in April 1822 in New York. Grant attended West Point and fought in the Mexican-American War. He resigned in 1854 and worked at various jobs in farming, real estate, and retail. When the Civil War started, he joined the Union army and was quickly promoted to general. After the Civil War, Grant rode a wave of popularity to become president of the United States.

GEOGRAPHY
SKILLS INTERPRETING MAPS

1. **Location** Why was Vicksburg's location so important?
2. **Place** What natural features made Vicksburg difficult to attack?

THE CIVIL WAR **527**

Info to Know

Vicksburg Cave Homes The city of Vicksburg was built on a hill. During the Siege of Vicksburg, the city's residents burrowed a system of more than 500 caves in the side of the hill in which to take cover from the Union artillery attacks. Caves for a single family usually had one or two chambers. Some large caves could hold as many as 200 people. People furnished their caves with carpets, furniture, cook stoves, and mirrors. They also built shelves into the walls to hold candles and other belongings.

Info to Know

Terms of Surrender Although General Grant originally demanded an unconditional surrender from the Confederates at Vicksburg, his final terms were more lenient. Grant decided it would be too costly and time-consuming to take the Confederate prisoners to Union prison camps. Instead, he allowed most of the defeated soldiers to surrender their weapons and leave as prisoners on parole.

Did you know . . .

The Confederate surrender ended the Siege of Vicksburg on July 4, 1863. As a result, the city's residents did not celebrate Independence Day for more than 80 years.

Critical Thinking: Analyzing Primary Sources
At Level

The Mighty Mississippi

Background After the fall of Vicksburg, President Abraham Lincoln summed up the event's significance: "The father of waters rolls unvexed to the sea."

1. Write the above quotation from Lincoln for student to see. Discuss the expression "the father of waters" with students so that they understand that Lincoln was talking about the Mississippi River.

2. Organize the class into small groups. Have each group discuss this quotation and the importance of the Mississippi River to both the North and the South during the Civil War.

3. Then have each student write a brief essay explaining the quotation and the significance of the Siege of Vicksburg to the Civil War.

Alternative Assessment Handbook, Rubrics 14: Group Activity; and 37: Writing Assignments

Answers

Interpreting Maps 1. *Capturing Vicksburg would give the Union control of the Mississippi River, which would cut off a vital supply line for the South and cut the Confederacy in two.* **2.** *It was located on high bluffs directly above the Mississippi and the land to the north was swampy, which made attack from that approach difficult.*

527

Bellringer

If YOU were there . . . Use the **Daily Bellringer Transparency** to help students answer the question.

Daily Bellringer Transparency, Section 4

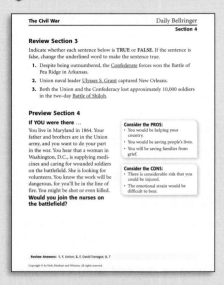

The Civil War — Daily Bellringer — Section 4

Review Section 3
Indicate whether each sentence below is **TRUE** or **FALSE**. If the sentence is false, change the underlined word to make the sentence true.

1. Despite being outnumbered, the <u>Confederate</u> forces won the Battle of Pea Ridge in Arkansas.
2. Union naval leader <u>Ulysses S. Grant</u> captured New Orleans.
3. Both the Union and the Confederacy lost approximately 10,000 soldiers in the two-day <u>Battle of Shiloh</u>.

Preview Section 4
If YOU were there ...
You live in Maryland in 1864. Your father and brothers are in the Union army, and you want to do your part in the war. You hear that a woman in Washington, D.C., is supplying medicines and caring for wounded soldiers on the battlefield. She is looking for volunteers. You know the work will be dangerous, for you'll be in the line of fire. You might be shot or even killed. **Would you join the nurses on the battlefield?**

Consider the PROS:
• You would be helping your country.
• You would be saving people's lives.
• You will be saving families from grief.

Consider the CONS:
• There is considerable risk that you could be injured.
• The emotional strain would be difficult to bear.

Review Answers: 1. F, Union; 2. F, David Farragut; 3. T

Copyright © by Holt, Rinehart and Winston. All rights reserved.

Building Vocabulary

Preteach or review the following term:

abolitionist supporter of the movement to end slavery (p. 529)

CRF: Vocabulary Builder Activity, Section 4

Taking Notes

Have students copy the graphic organizer onto their own paper and then use it to take notes on the section. This activity will prepare students for the Section Assessment, in which they will complete a graphic organizer that builds on the information using a critical thinking skill.

Daily Life during the War

What You Will Learn...

Main Ideas

1. The Emancipation Proclamation freed slaves in Confederate states.
2. African Americans participated in the war in a variety of ways.
3. President Lincoln faced opposition to the war.
4. Life was difficult for soldiers and civilians alike.

The Big Idea

The lives of many Americans were affected by the Civil War.

Key Terms and People

emancipation, *p. 529*
Emancipation Proclamation, *p. 529*
contrabands, *p. 531*
54th Massachusetts Infantry, *p. 531*
Copperheads, *p. 532*
habeas corpus, *p. 532*
Clara Barton, *p. 534*

TAKING NOTES As you read, take notes on the effects of the Civil War on the lives of African Americans, soldiers, and women and children. Write your notes in a graphic organizer like the one below.

How the Civil War affected:	
African Americans	
Soldiers	
Women and children	

528 CHAPTER 16

If YOU were there...

You live in Maryland in 1864. Your father and brothers are in the Union army, and you want to do your part in the war. You hear that a woman in Washington, D.C., is supplying medicines and caring for wounded soldiers on the battlefield. She is looking for volunteers. You know the work will be dangerous, for you'll be in the line of fire. You might be shot or even killed.

Would you join the nurses on the battlefield?

BUILDING BACKGROUND The Civil War touched almost all Americans. Some 3 million men fought in the two armies. Thousands of other men and women worked behind the lines, providing food, supplies, medical care, and other necessary services. Civilians could not escape the effects of war, as the fighting destroyed farms, homes, and cities.

Emancipation Proclamation

Teach the Big Idea

Daily Life during the War

Materials: paper, stapler

1. **Teach** Ask students the questions in the Main Idea boxes to teach this section.
2. **Apply** Have each student take four sheets of paper and fold and staple them to create an eight-page booklet. On each left-hand page, have students write one of the section's blue headings. Below the heading, students should list the key people, events, and issues in that part of the text. Students should use the right-hand page to provide drawings, phrases, and charts that relate to the information on the left-hand page. **Verbal/Linguistic, Visual/Spatial**
3. **Review** As you review the section, have volunteers share the information they listed.
4. **Practice/Homework** Have students write a short summary for each part of their booklets. **Verbal/Linguistic**

Alternative Assessment Handbook, Rubrics 3: Artwork; and 37: Writing Assignments

---

Emancipation Proclamation

At the heart of the nation's bloody struggle were millions of enslaved African Americans. Abolitionists urged President Lincoln to free them.

"You know I dislike slavery," Lincoln had written to a friend in 1855. In an 1858 speech, he declared, "There is no reason in the world why the negro is not entitled to all the natural rights numerated in the Declaration of Independence—the right to life, liberty, and the pursuit of happiness." Yet as president, Lincoln found **emancipation**, or the freeing of slaves, to be a difficult issue. He did not believe he had the constitutional power. He also worried about the effects of emancipation.

Lincoln Issues the Proclamation

Northerners had a range of opinions about abolishing slavery.

- The Democratic Party, which included many laborers, opposed emancipation. Laborers feared that freed slaves would come north and take their jobs at lower wages.
- Abolitionists argued that the war was pointless if it did not win freedom for African Americans. They warned that the Union

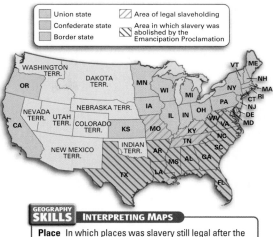

Emancipation Proclamation

	Union state		Area of legal slaveholding
	Confederate state		Area in which slavery was abolished by the Emancipation Proclamation
	Border state		

GEOGRAPHY SKILLS INTERPRETING MAPS

Place In which places was slavery still legal after the Emancipation Proclamation?

The painting at left shows Lincoln and his cabinet after the signing of the Emancipation Proclamation. Above is a photo of former slaves that were freed by the proclamation.

How do you think the Emancipation Proclamation would affect the Civil War?

would remain divided until the problem was resolved.

- Some in Lincoln's government predicted that emancipation would anger voters, causing Republicans to be defeated in the 1862 midterm elections. Lincoln worried about losing support for the war.
- Others, including Secretary of War Edwin Stanton, agreed with Lincoln's reasoning. The use of slave labor was helping the Confederacy make war. Therefore, as commander in chief, the president could free the slaves in all rebellious states. Freed African Americans could then be recruited into the Union army.

For several weeks in 1862, Lincoln worked intensely, thinking, writing, and rewriting. He finally wrote the **Emancipation Proclamation**, the order to free the Confederate slaves. The proclamation declared that:

" …all persons held as slaves within any State or designated part of a State the people whereof shall then be in rebellion against the United States shall be then, thenceforward, and forever free. "
—Emancipation Proclamation, 1862

THE CIVIL WAR **529**

Main Idea

❶ Emancipation Proclamation

The Emancipation Proclamation freed slaves in Confederate states.

Identify What issue lay at the heart of the Civil War? *slavery and the millions of African Americans living in bondage*

Identify Points of View Why did some northerners oppose abolishing slavery? *feared that freed slaves would work for lower wages and take jobs; feared that emancipation would weaken support for the war*

Evaluate How did Lincoln address the difficult issue of emancipation, and why did he make this choice? *He issued a military proclamation freeing all enslaved Africans in rebellious states. He did not believe he had the constitutional power to end slavery but as commander-in-chief he believed he could take action to stop slave labor from being used to help the southern war effort.*

📖 Map Transparency: Emancipation Proclamation

Info to Know

Support for Lincoln After the Emancipation Proclamation was issued, an African American congregation in Baltimore raised about $580 to buy Lincoln a Bible. The cover had a picture of Lincoln breaking off the chains of a slave working in a cotton field.

Critical Thinking: Identifying Points of View   At Level

Emancipation Proclamation

1. Have students read the Emancipation Proclamation (provided in the back of the textbook) as a class and summarize its main points. Guide the class in a discussion of the importance of the proclamation and its impact on the North and the South.

2. Ask students to identify how different groups in the North reacted to the proclamation. Encourage students to elaborate on why some northerners might have opposed it.

3. Then ask students to imagine that they live during the time of the Civil War and Lincoln has just issued the Emancipation Proclamation. Have each student write a letter to Lincoln expressing support for the proclamation and explaining how he or she thinks it will affect the war. Have volunteers read their letters to the class. **LS Verbal/Linguistic**

📝 Alternative Assessment Handbook, Rubric 41: Writing to Express

Answers

Interpreting Maps *Missouri, Kentucky, Maryland, Delaware, Tennessee, and the southern tip of Louisiana*

Emancipation Proclamation *possible answer—might hurt the South's ability to wage war as slaves escape to Union camps; might help the northern war effort as freed slaves join the Union ranks*

529

Main Idea

❶ Emancipation Proclamation

The Emancipation Proclamation freed slaves in Confederate states.

Identify Points of View Why did some abolitionists criticize the Emancipation Proclamation? *because it did not end slavery completely or free all slaves*

Make Judgments Do you think Lincoln should have expanded the Emancipation Proclamation to free all slaves? Why or why not? *possible answers—no, because he might have lost political support and the border states might have left the Union, thereby risking the war and any chance for helping slaves; yes, because slavery is morally wrong*

Activity **Celebrating Emancipation** Have each student create a poem from the point of view of a freed slave celebrating the Emancipation Proclamation.

📓 Alternative Assessment Handbook, Rubric 26: Poems and Songs

World Events

European Reactions to Emancipation
The Emancipation Proclamation drew the attention of many Europeans. Some workers from Manchester, England, wrote to President Lincoln, "We joyfully honor you . . . [for] your belief in the words of your great founders: 'All men are created free and equal.'"

Answers

Reading Check *possible answers—Abolitionists supported it, although some thought it did not go far enough; some laborers feared they would lose their jobs to freed slaves who might work for less.*

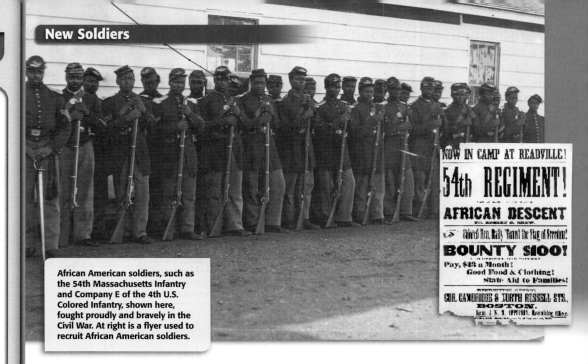

New Soldiers

African American soldiers, such as the 54th Massachusetts Infantry and Company E of the 4th U.S. Colored Infantry, shown here, fought proudly and bravely in the Civil War. At right is a flyer used to recruit African American soldiers.

NOW IN CAMP AT READVILLE!
54th REGIMENT!
AFRICAN DESCENT
COL. ROBERT G. SHAW.
Colored Men, Rally 'Round the Flag of Freedom!
BOUNTY $100!
Pay, $13 a Month!
Good Food & Clothing!
State Aid to Families!
COR. CAMBRIDGE & NORTH RUSSELL STS.,
BOSTON.
Lieut. J. W. M. APPLETON, Recruiting Officer.

The Emancipation Proclamation was a military order that freed slaves only in areas controlled by the Confederacy. In fact, the proclamation had little immediate effect. It was impossible for the federal government to enforce the proclamation in the areas where it actually applied—the states in rebellion that were not under federal control. The proclamation did not stop slavery in the border states, where the federal government would have had the power to enforce it. The words written in the Emancipation Proclamation were powerful, but the impact of the document was more symbolic than real.

Lincoln wanted to be in a strong position in the war before announcing his plan. The Battle of Antietam gave him the victory he needed. He issued the Emancipation Proclamation on September 22, 1862. The proclamation went into effect on January 1, 1863.

Reaction to the Proclamation

New Year's Eve, December 31, 1862: In "night watch" meetings at many African American churches, worshippers prayed, sang, and gave thanks. When the clocks struck midnight, millions were free. Abolitionists rejoiced. Frederick Douglass called January 1, 1863, "the great day which is to determine the destiny not only of the American Republic, but that of the American Continent."

William Lloyd Garrison was quick to note, however, that "slavery, as a system" continued to exist in the loyal slave states. Yet where slavery remained, the proclamation encouraged many enslaved Africans to escape when the Union troops came near. They flocked to the Union camps and followed them for protection. The loss of slaves crippled the South's ability to wage war.

READING CHECK **Finding Main Ideas** How did northerners view the Emancipation Proclamation?

Differentiating Instruction

Below Level

Struggling Readers

1. Review the information about African American soldiers in this section. Then draw the chart for students to see. Omit the blue, italicized answers.

2. Have each student copy the chart and complete it by listing reasons why African Americans joined the Union and some of the hardships they faced. **LS** **Visual/Spatial**

📓 Alternative Assessment Handbook, Rubric 7: Charts

African American Union Soldiers	
Reasons Joined	**Hardships Faced**
• *freedom*	• *if captured, often killed or sold into slavery*
• *citizenship*	• *received less pay than white soldiers*
• *honor*	• *no guarantee of gaining the rights of citizenship*
• *respect*	
• *pay*	

African Americans Participate in the War

As the war casualties climbed, the Union needed even more troops. African Americans were ready to volunteer. Not all white northerners were ready to accept them, but eventually they had to. Frederick Douglass believed that military service would help African Americans gain rights.

"Once let the black man get upon his person the brass letters, U.S.; … and a musket on his shoulder and bullets in his pocket, and there is no power on earth which can deny that he has earned the right to citizenship."

—Frederick Douglass

Congress began allowing the army to sign up African American volunteers as laborers in July 1862. The War Department also gave **contrabands**, or escaped slaves, the right to join the Union army in South Carolina. Free African Americans in Louisiana and Kansas also formed their own units in the Union army. By the spring of 1863, African American army units were proving themselves in combat. They took part in a Union attack on Port Hudson, Louisiana, in May.

One unit stood out above the others. The **54th Massachusetts Infantry** consisted mostly of free African Americans. In July 1863 this regiment led a heroic charge on South Carolina's Fort Wagner. The 54th took heavy fire and suffered huge casualties in the failed operation. About half the regiment was killed, wounded, or captured. Edward L. Pierce, a correspondent for the *New York Tribune*, wrote, "The Fifty-fourth did well and nobly…They moved up as gallantly as any troops could, and with their enthusiasm they deserved a better fate." The bravery of the 54th regiment made it the most celebrated African American unit of the war.

About 180,000 African Americans served with the Union army. They received $10 a month, while white soldiers got $13. They were usually led by white officers, some from abolitionist families.

African Americans faced special horrors on the battlefield. Confederates often killed their black captives or sold them into slavery. In the 1864 election, Lincoln suggested rewarding African American soldiers by giving them the right to vote.

READING CHECK **Analyzing Information**
How did African Americans support the Union?

---

❸ Growing Opposition

President Lincoln faced opposition to the war.

Define What is a military draft? *forced military service*

Identify Points of View Why did the Copperheads oppose the war? *They sympathized with the South, opposed abolition, and believed the war was unnecessary and that too many Americans were being killed.*

Analyze Why did some people call the Civil War "a rich man's war and a poor man's fight"? *While rich men bought their way out of military service, poor men were being drafted to fight the war.*

Activity **Northern Draft Political Cartoons** Have students draw two political cartoons, one supporting and one opposing the northern draft.

📖 Alternative Assessment Handbook, Rubric 27: Political Cartoons

Info to Know

Civil War Armies The Union and Confederate armies followed similar paths when it came to filling their ranks. Both started with short enlistment terms that were lengthened to three years or the duration of the war. Both armies eventually had difficulties filling their quotas with volunteers and had to resort to drafting men. When Union army volunteers re-enlisted after their three-year terms, they received a 30-day leave, transportation home, and a $400 bonus.

Answers

Infantry Family *possible answers—to prepare food, mend clothes, make life easier for the soldiers and their families*

Growing Opposition

The deepening shadows in Lincoln's face reflected the huge responsibilities he carried. Besides running the war, he had to deal with growing tensions in the North.

Copperheads

As the months rolled on and the number of dead continued to increase, a group of northern Democrats began speaking out against the war. Led by U.S. Representative Clement L. Vallandigham of Ohio, they called themselves Peace Democrats. Their enemies called them Copperheads, comparing them to a poisonous snake. The name stuck.

Many **Copperheads** were midwesterners that sympathized with the South and opposed abolition. They believed the war was not necessary and called for its end. Vallandigham asked what the war had gained, and then said, "Let the dead at Fredericksburg and Vicksburg answer."

Lincoln saw the Copperheads as a threat to the war effort. To silence them, he suspended the right of habeas corpus. **Habeas corpus** is a constitutional protection against unlawful imprisonment. Ignoring this protection, Union officials jailed their enemies, including some Copperheads, without evidence or trial. Lincoln's action greatly angered Democrats and some Republicans.

Northern Draft

In March 1863, war critics erupted again when Congress approved a draft, or forced military service. For $300, men were allowed to buy their way out of military service. For an unskilled laborer, however, that was nearly a year's wages. Critics of the draft called the Civil War a "rich man's war and a poor man's fight."

In July 1863, riots broke out when African Americans were brought into New York City to replace striking Irish dock workers. The city happened to be holding a war draft at the same time. The two events enraged rioters, who attacked African Americans and draft offices. More than 100 people died.

In this tense situation, the northern Democrats nominated former General George McClellan for president in 1864. They called

Infantry Family

While wealthy civilians could avoid military service, poorer men were drafted to serve in the Union army. This member of the 31st Pennsylvania Infantry brought his family along with him. His wife probably helped the soldier with many daily chores such as cooking and laundry.

Why would soldiers bring their families to live with them in camp?

Differentiating Instruction

Above Level

Advanced/Gifted and Talented

1. Explain that the U.S. Constitution gives Congress the power to raise and support armies but does not mention conscription or a military draft. During the Civil War, both the North and the South resorted to using drafts.

2. Organize students into two groups. Have one group support a military draft, and have the other group oppose it. Have students work independently to jot down their ideas and arguments. Then give the groups time to prepare defenses and arguments supporting their assigned positions. If time allows, have students conduct research on the topic.

3. Hold a debate between the two sides and serve as the moderator. Afterward, discuss the reasons for the drafts in the Civil War.

LS Interpersonal, Logical/Mathematical

📖 Alternative Assessment Handbook, Rubric 10: Debates

for an immediate end to the war. Lincoln defeated McClellan in the popular vote, winning by about 400,000 votes out of 4 million cast. The electoral vote was not even close. Lincoln won 212 to 21.

READING CHECK Identifying Cause and Effect Who opposed the war, and how did Lincoln respond to the conflict?

Life for Soldiers and Civilians

Young, fresh recruits in both armies were generally eager to fight. Experienced troops, however, knew better.

On the Battlefield

Civil War armies fought in the ancient battlefield formation that produced massive casualties. Endless rows of troops fired directly at one another, with cannonballs landing amid them. When the order was given, soldiers would attach bayonets to their guns and rush toward their enemy. Men died to gain every inch of ground.

Doctors and nurses in the field saved many lives. Yet they had no medicines to stop infections that developed after soldiers were wounded. Many soldiers endured the horror of having infected legs and arms amputated without painkillers. Infections from minor injuries caused many deaths.

Despite the huge battlefield losses, the biggest killer in the Civil War was not the fighting. It was diseases such as typhoid, pneumonia, and tuberculosis. Nearly twice as many soldiers died of illnesses as died in combat.

Prisoners of War

Military prisoners on both sides lived in unimaginable misery. In prison camps, such as Andersonville, Georgia, and Elmira, New York, soldiers were packed into camps designed to hold only a fraction of their number. Soldiers had little shelter, food, or clothing. Starvation and disease killed thousands of prisoners.

LINKING TO TODAY

Battlefield Communications

The drummer was an essential member of every Civil War unit. Drummers served army commanders by drumming specific beats that directed troop movements during battle. Different beats were used to order troops to prepare to attack, to fire, to cease fire, and to signal a truce. Drummers had to stay near their commanders to hear orders. This meant that the drummers—some as young as nine years old—often saw deadly combat conditions.

The Civil War gave birth to the Signal Corps, the army unit devoted to communications. Today battlefield communications are primarily electronic. Radio, e-mail, facsimile, and telephone messages, often relayed by satellites, enable orders and other information to be transmitted nearly instantaneously all over the globe.

Union Signal Corps

Modern battlefield communications

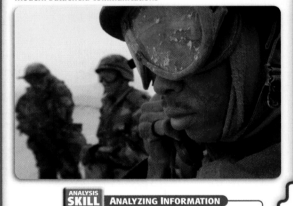

ANALYSIS SKILL ANALYZING INFORMATION
Why is communication so important on the battlefield?

THE CIVIL WAR **533**

• **Direct Teach** •

Main Idea

❹ Life for Soldiers and Civilians

Life was difficult for soldiers and civilians alike.

Explain Why was the Civil War death toll so high? *firing at close range, bayoneting, lack of medicine and medical treatment*

Make Generalizations How did life for women, the elderly, and children change during the war? *They had to take over work, such as farm work and factory jobs, formerly done by men who were fighting.*

📖 **CRF:** Primary Source Activity: John L. Ranson, *Andersonville Diary*

Biography

Johnny Clem One of the most famous Civil War drummers was Johnny Clem. At the age of nine, Clem ran away from his home in Ohio to join the Union army. Clem went from drummer boy to soldier during the Battle of Shiloh. After his drum was shattered, young Clem picked up a gun and began firing. Within two years, he was promoted to sergeant to become the youngest noncommissioned officer in the Union army. After the Civil War, Clem attended West Point and made the military his career.

go.hrw.com
Online Resources
KEYWORD: SR8 US16
ACTIVITY: Civil War Authors

Critical Thinking: Finding Main Ideas

At Level

Civil War Letters

1. Review with students the experiences of soldiers and civilians in the Civil War and the ways in which civilians aided the war effort.

2. Then have each student write a series of letters between an imaginary Civil War soldier and his wife or sister back on the home front.

3. Students' letters should describe the different experiences of soldiers and civilians, the hardships each faced, and some of the ways

in which women supported the war effort. Encourage students to make their letters expressive and descriptive while remaining true to the history.

4. Have volunteers read some of their letters to the class. **LS Verbal/Linguistic**

📖 Alternative Assessment Handbook, Rubric 25: Personal Letters

Answers

Analyzing Information *enables leaders to control troop movements*

Reading Check *Copperheads; Lincoln suspended the right of habeas corpus, which enabled Union officials to jail their enemies without evidence or trial.*

Direct Teach

Main Idea

4 Life for Soldiers and Civilians

Life was difficult for soldiers and civilians alike.

Identify Who was Clara Barton? *"Angel of the battlefield" who worked at field hospitals. Her work formed the basis for the future American Red Cross.*

Identify Cause and Effect How did the Civil War affect the North's economy? *The lack of workers caused wages to rise, and the northern economy boomed as production and prices soared.*

📋 **CRF:** Biography Activity: Clara Barton

📋 **CRF:** Primary Source Activity: Civil War Era Diary

Review & Assess

Close

Have students describe in their own words life during the Civil War.

Review

🖥 Online Quiz, Section 4

Assess

SE Section 4 Assessment

📋 PASS: Section 4 Quiz

📋 Alternative Assessment Handbook

Reteach/Classroom Intervention

📋 Review Workbook

📋 Interactive Reader and Study Guide, Section 4

💿 Interactive Skills Tutor CD-ROM

Answers

Reading Check *Women worked in factories and on farms, cared for wounded soldiers, organized collections of medicine and supplies, worked in field hospitals, and established hospitals.*

534

Life as a Civilian

The war effort involved all levels of society. Women as well as people too young or too old for military service worked in factories and on farms. Economy in the North boomed as production and prices soared. The lack of workers caused wages to rise by 43 percent between 1860 and 1865.

THE IMPACT TODAY
The American Red Cross today supplies victims of natural disasters with relief aid.

Women were the backbone of civilian life. On the farms, women and children performed the daily chores usually done by men. One visitor to Iowa in 1862 reported that he "met more women . . . at work in the fields than men." Southern women also managed farms and plantations.

One woman brought strength and comfort to countless wounded Union soldiers. Volunteer **Clara Barton** organized the collection of medicine and supplies for delivery to the battlefield. At the field hospitals,

Clara Barton
founded the American Red Cross.

the "angel of the battlefield" soothed the wounded and dying and assisted doctors as bullets flew around her. Barton's work formed the basis for the future American Red Cross.

In the South, Sally Louisa Tompkins established a small hospital in Richmond, Virginia. By the end of the war, it had grown into a major army hospital. Jefferson Davis recognized her value to the war effort by making her a captain in the Confederate army.

READING CHECK **Analyzing** How did women help the war effort on both sides?

SUMMARY AND PREVIEW Many lives were changed by the war. In the next section you will learn about the end of the war.

Section 4 Assessment

go.hrw.com
Online Quiz
KEYWORD: SR8 HP16

Reviewing Ideas, Terms, and People

1. **a. Recall** Why did some Americans want to end slavery?
   b. Contrast How did reactions to the **Emancipation Proclamation** differ?
   c. Elaborate Do you think that the **emancipation** of slaves should have extended to the border states? Explain your answer.
2. **a. Recall** Why did some northerners want to recruit African Americans into the Union army?
   b. Contrast In what ways did African American soldiers face more difficulties than white soldiers did?
3. **a. Identify** Who were **Copperheads**, and why did they oppose the war?
   b. Evaluate Should President Lincoln have suspended the right to **habeas corpus**? Why?
4. **a. Describe** What were conditions like in military camps?
   b. Draw Conclusions How did the war change life on the home front?

Critical Thinking

5. **Identifying Effects** Review your notes. Then copy the graphic organizer below. Use it to summarize the reasons for the Emancipation Proclamation, its main points, and its effects on different people.

Reasons for the Emancipation Proclamation
Main points of the Proclamation
Effect on People's Lives

FOCUS ON WRITING

6. **Taking Notes on Life During the War** As you read this section, take notes on the emancipation of the slaves, African American soldiers, and women who provided medical care for soldiers. Answer the following questions: Who? Where? When? Why? and How?

534 CHAPTER 16

Section 4 Assessment Answers

1. **a.** possible answers—all deserve natural rights; Union would be divided until ended
   b. Democrats opposed it; some abolitionists thought it should end all slavery; African Americans rejoiced; many slaves escaped
   c. possible answers—yes, slavery is wrong; no, border states might have left the Union and cost the North the war

2. **a.** The Union needed more troops.
   b. often killed or sold into slavery when captured; paid less than white soldiers

3. **a.** northern Democrats who opposed the war; sympathized with South, opposed abolition
   b. possible answers—yes, the war effort was threatened; no, violated people's rights

4. **a.** unsanitary, with many illnesses; deadly
   b. All levels of society took on farm and factory work; North's economy boomed.

5. See Questions 1a., b. It freed slaves in Confederate areas.

6. Notes should include key people and issues.

Abraham Lincoln

What would you do to save the struggling Union?

When did he live? 1809–1865

Where did he live? Abraham Lincoln was born in a log cabin to a poor family in Kentucky. Growing up in Kentucky and Illinois, Lincoln went to school for less than a year. He taught himself law and settled in Springfield, where he practiced law and politics. As president he lived in Washington, D.C. There, at age 56, his life was cut short by an assassin, John Wilkes Booth.

What did he do? The issue of slavery defined Lincoln's political career. He was not an abolitionist, but he strongly opposed extending slavery into the territories. In a series of famous debates against Senator Stephen Douglas of Illinois, Lincoln championed his views on slavery and made a brilliant defense of democracy and the Union. As president, Lincoln led the nation through the Civil War.

Why is he important? Lincoln is one of the great symbols of American democracy. "A house divided against itself cannot stand," he declared in a debate with Douglas. In 1863 Lincoln issued the Emancipation Proclamation. His address to commemorate the bloody battlefield at Gettysburg is widely considered to be one of the best political speeches in American history.

Summarizing Why is Lincoln such an important figure in American history?

Abraham Lincoln led the United States during the Civil War.

THE CIVIL WAR **535**

KEY EVENTS

- **1834** Elected to the Illinois legislature
- **1842** Marries Mary Todd
- **1858** Holds series of famous debates with U.S. Senator Stephen Douglas
- **1860** Elected president on November 6
- **1863** Issues the Emancipation Proclamation on January 1
- **1863** Gives the Gettysburg Address on November 19
- **1865** Gives second inaugural address on March 4
- **1865** Shot on April 14; dies the next day

Critical Thinking: Summarizing

At Level

Abraham Lincoln Acrostic

1. Have students discuss Lincoln's achievements and his importance in American history.

2. Ask students to suggest words and short phrases that describe Lincoln, his accomplishments, and his legacy. Create a list for students to see.

3. Then have students create an acrostic out of Lincoln's name. First, write *Abraham Lincoln* vertically in all capital letters. Second, model the activity by selecting a word from the list that includes an *A* (or use *Gettysburg Address*). Write the word vertically so that it uses the *A* in *Abraham*.

4. Then have students work individually or in mixed-ability pairs to complete the acrostic.

5. Have volunteers share some of their answers with the class. **LS Verbal/Linguistic**

📋 Alternative Assessment Handbook, Rubric 13: Graphic Organizers

---

Reading Focus Question

Have students discuss the introductory question before reading the biography. Remind students of the crisis that Abraham Lincoln faced when he took office as president. Ask students how they might have acted in his place to preserve the Union. Encourage discussion. Then have students note as they read the biography the ways in which Lincoln supported the preservation of the Union during his lifetime.

MISCONCEPTION ///ALERT\\\

Gettysburg Address Despite what is commonly stated, Abraham Lincoln did not hastily write the Gettysburg Address during the train trip to the battlefield. Two copies of the speech exist, the earliest of which was written on White House stationery and the other on lined paper. Most scholars believe the stationery version to be the one that Lincoln read from at Gettysburg. However, based on actual accounts of the speech, small differences exist between this written copy and Lincoln's actual speech. As a result, some scholars believe that the version of the speech that Lincoln actually used is now lost, because Lincoln usually did not vary much from his written speeches.

Info to Know

Lincoln and Booth Abraham Lincoln and John Wilkes Booth had crossed paths several times before the fatal assassination. Lincoln had previously attended a production of a play at Ford's Theatre in which Booth was one of the stars. At Lincoln's second inauguration, Booth was an invited guest and can even be seen in several photos of the event.

Answers

Summarizing *He symbolized American democracy and the vision of a unified nation, and he acted to preserve those ideals.*

535

Bellringer

If YOU were there . . . Use the **Daily Bellringer Transparency** to help students answer the question.

🖨 Daily Bellringer Transparency, Section 5

Academic Vocabulary

Review with students the high-use academic term in this section.

execute to perform, carry out (p. 540)

📝 **CRF:** Vocabulary Builder Activity, Section 5

Taking Notes

Have students copy the graphic organizer onto their own paper and then use it to take notes on the section. This activity will prepare students for the Section Assessment, in which they will complete a graphic organizer that builds on the information using a critical thinking skill.

What You Will Learn...

Main Ideas

1. The Union tried to divide the Confederate Army at Federicksberg, but the attempt failed.
2. The Battle of Gettysburg in 1863 was a major turning point in the war.
3. During 1864, Union campaigns in the East and South dealt crippling blows to the Confederacy.
4. Union troops forced the South to surrender in 1865, ending the Civil War.

The Big Idea

Union victories in 1863, 1864, and 1865 ended the Civil War.

Key Terms and People

Battle of Gettysburg, *p. 537*
George Pickett, *p. 538*
Pickett's Charge, *p. 538*
Gettysburg Address, *p. 540*
Wilderness Campaign, *p. 540*
William Tecumseh Sherman, *p. 541*
total war, *p. 542*
Appomattox Courthouse, *p. 542*

TAKING NOTES Copy the graphic organizer. Use it to recall the events that led to the end of the Civil War.

| July 1–3, 1863 |
| May–June, 1864 |
| September 2, 1864 |
| December 10, 1864 |
| April 2, 1865 |
| April 9, 1865 |

The Tide of War Turns

If YOU were there...

You live in southern Pennsylvania in 1863, near a battlefield where thousands died. Now people have come from miles around to dedicate a cemetery here. You are near the front of the crowd. The first speaker impresses everyone with two hours of dramatic words and gestures. Then President Lincoln speaks—just a few minutes of simple words. Many people are disappointed.

Why do you think the president's speech was so short?

BUILDING BACKGROUND Many people, especially in the North, had expected a quick victory, but the war dragged on for years. The balance of victories seemed to seesaw between North and South, and both sides suffered terrible casualties. The last Confederate push into the North ended at Gettysburg in one of the bloodiest battles of the war.

Fredericksburg and Chancellorsville

Frustrated by McClellan's lack of aggression, Lincoln replaced him with General Ambrose E. Burnside as leader of the Army of the Potomac. Burnside favored a swift, decisive attack on Richmond by way of Fredericksburg. In November 1862, he set out with 120,000 troops.

Burnside's tactics surprised General Lee. The Confederate commander had divided his force of 78,000 men. Neither section of the Confederate army was in a good position to defend Fredericksburg. However, Burnside's army experienced delays in crossing the Rappahannock River. These delays allowed Lee's army to reunite and entrench themselves around Fredericksburg. Finally, the Union army crossed the Rappahannock and launched a series of charges. These attacks had heavy casualties and failed to break the Confederate line. Eventually, after suffering about 12,600 casualties, Burnside ordered a retreat. The Confederates had about 5,300 casualties.

Soon Burnside stepped down from his position. Then Lincoln made General Joseph Hooker the commander of the Army of the Potomac. At the end of April 1863, Hooker and his army of about 138,000 men launched a frontal attack on Fredericksburg. Then

---

Teach the Big Idea

The Tide of War Turns

1. **Teach** Ask students the questions in the Main Idea boxes to teach this section.

2. **Apply** Discuss the events that led to the end of the war. Then have each student create a visual diagram titled *The Road to Surrender*. The diagram should use one or more images to show the key events from the Battle of Gettysburg and after that led to Lee's surrender at Appomattox Courthouse. Students should incorporate dates. **LS Visual/Spatial**

3. **Review** As you review the section, have volunteers share their visual diagrams.

4. **Practice/Homework** Have each student write a newspaper editorial about Lee's surrender at Appomattox Courthouse. Students should decide whether to write the editorial from the perspective of a northerner or a southerner. **LS Verbal/Linguistic**

📝 Alternative Assessment Handbook, Rubrics 3: Artwork; and 41: Writing to Express

Hooker ordered about 115,000 of his troops to split off and approach the Confederate's flank, or side. Hooker's strategy seemed about to work. But for some reason he hesitated and had his flanking troops take a defensive position at Chancellorsville. This town was located a few miles west of Fredericksburg.

The following day, Lee used most of his army (about 60,000 men) to attack Hooker's troops at Chancellorsville. Stonewall Jackson led an attack on Hooker's flank while Lee commanded an assault on the Union front. The Union army was almost cut in two. They managed to form a defensive line, which they held for three days. Then Hooker ordered a retreat.

Lee's army won a major victory. But this victory had severe casualties. During the battle, Lee's trusted general, Stonewall Jackson, was accidentally shot by his own troops. He died a few days later.

READING CHECK Comparing What did generals McClellan, Burnside, and Hooker have in common?

Battle of Gettysburg

General Lee launched more attacks within Union territory. As before, his goal was to break the North's will to fight. He also hoped that a victory would convince other nations to recognize the Confederacy.

First Day

In early June 1863, Lee cut across northern Maryland into southern Pennsylvania. His forces gathered west of a small town called Gettysburg. Lee was unaware that Union soldiers were encamped closer to town. He had been suffering from lack of enemy information for three days because his cavalry chief "Jeb" Stuart was not performing his duties. Stuart and his cavalry had gone off on their own raiding party, disobeying Lee's orders.

Another Confederate raiding party went to Gettysburg for boots and other supplies. There, Lee's troops ran right into Union general George G. Meade's cavalry, triggering the **Battle of Gettysburg**, a key battle that finally turned the tide against the Confederates. The battle began on July 1, 1863, when the

Three Days at Gettysburg

Gettysburg was the largest and bloodiest battle of the Civil War. In three days, more than 51,000 soldiers were killed, wounded, captured, or went missing. It was an important victory for the Union, and it stopped Lee's plan of invading the North.

Artillery played a key role in the Battle of Gettysburg on July 1, 1863.

Day One: July 1, 1863

THE CIVIL WAR **537**

Direct Teach

Main Idea

❶ Fredericksburg and Chancellorsville

The Union tried to divide the Confederate Army at Fredericksburg, but the attempt failed.

Identify Who replaced McClellan as head of the Army of the Potomac? *General Ambrose E. Burnside*

Compare How did Burnside's tactics differ from McClellan's? *Burnside began with a swift, decisive attack.*

Make Inferences Why do you think Burnside stepped down from his position as leader of the Potomac? *to allow Lincoln to appoint another general since Burnside had not had success*

Did you know . . .

General Burnside had a unique way of growing his whiskers on the "sides" of his face along his jaw line. This style became popular during the Civil War and was known as "sideburns" after General Burnside.

Critical Thinking: Cause and Effect

At Level

Decisions and Consequences Flow Chart

1. Create a flow chart for students to see. Label the box on the left *Decision*, and the box on the right *Consequence*.

2. In the box labeled *Decision* write the phrase "Lincoln replaces McClellan." Ask students: What was the consequence of that decision? Write students' responses in the box labeled *Consequence*.

3. Continue to create and fill in *Decision* and *Consequence* boxes for the rest of the section content under the heading "Fredericksburg and Chancellorsville."

4. Ask students to predict if General Hooker will retain his position as leader of the Army of the Potomac. **LS** Visual/Spatial

📃 Alternative Assessment Handbook, Rubric 13: Graphic Organizers

Answers

Reading Check *They were defeated by Confederate forces.*

537

Main Idea

❷ Battle of Gettysburg

The Battle of Gettysburg in 1863 was a major turning point in the war.

Explain Why did Lee again launch attacks within Union territory? *He hoped that a victory on northern soil would break the North's will to fight and convince other nations to recognize the Confederacy.*

Recall When did the Battle of Gettysburg begin, and what event triggered the start of the battle? *July 1, 1863; A Confederate raiding party ran into Union general George G. Meade's cavalry near the small town of Gettysburg, Pennsylvania.*

Evaluate Who had the best military position at the start of the battle, and why was the position a good one? *the Union troops, who had dug in atop Cemetery Ridge and Culp's Hill; provided strong defensive positions*

Linking to Today

Reunion at Gettysburg Fifty years after the decisive Battle of Gettysburg, Civil War veterans from both the North and the South returned to the battleground for a three-day reunion. Thousands of tourists came as well. According to one attendee, the high point of the gathering was a re-enactment of Pickett's Charge.

go.hrw.com
Online Resources

KEYWORD: SR8 US16
ACTIVITY: 3-D Model of Gettysburg and Other Battles

Confederate raiding party and the Union forces began exchanging fire. The larger Confederate forces began to push the Union troops back through Gettysburg.

The Union soldiers regrouped along the high ground of Cemetery Ridge and Culp's Hill. General Lee wanted to prevent the Union forces from entrenching themselves. He therefore ordered General Ewell to attack immediately. However, Ewell hesitated and thereby gave the Federals time to establish an excellent defensive position.

In fact, Confederate General James Longstreet thought that the Union position was almost impossible to overrun. Instead of attacking, he felt that the Confederate army should move east, take a strong defensive position themselves, and wait for the Union forces to attack them. However, General Lee was not convinced. He believed that his troops were invincible.

The Confederates camped at Cemetery Ridge, which ran parallel to the Union forces. Both camps called for their main forces to reinforce them and prepare for combat the next day.

Second Day

On July 2, Lee ordered an attack on the left side of the Union line. Lee knew that he could win the battle if his troops captured Little Round Top from the Union forces. From this hill, Lee's troops could easily fire down on the line of Union forces. Union forces and Confederate troops fought viciously for control of Little Round Top. The fighting was particularly fierce on the south side of the hill. There the 20th Maine led by Colonel Joshua Chamberlain battled the 15th Alabama led by Colonel William Oates. Later, when describing the conflict, Oates said, "The blood stood in puddles in some places in the rocks." Eventually, the Union forced the Confederates to pull back from Little Round Top.

Then the Confederates attacked Cemetery Hill and Culp's Hill. The fighting lasted until nightfall. The assault on Cemetery Hill was unsuccessful. The Confederates did manage to take a few trenches on Culp's Hill. Even so, the Union forces still held a strong defensive position by the day's end.

Three Days at Gettysburg (continued)

Day Two: July 2, 1863, 10 a.m.

Union soldiers desperately defended Little Round Top from a fierce Confederate charge.

538 CHAPTER 16

Collaborative Learning

At Level

Battle of Gettysburg Storyboards

1. Have students work in pairs or in small groups to create storyboards that depict through illustrations and an easy-to-understand narrative the main events in the Battle of Gettysburg. Students should break down the storyboards into three main parts to represent each day of the battle.

2. Partners or group members might work together to create the illustrations and narrative or divide up the work. Storyboards might include maps, chart, and photographs as well as illustrations.

3. Display students' storyboards around the classroom. Then have students discuss the importance of geography in the Union's victory in the Battle of Gettysburg.

LS Interpersonal, Visual/Spatial

📑 Alternative Assessment Handbook, Rubrics 3: Artwork; and 14: Group Activity

Pickett's Charge

On the third day of battle, Longstreet again tried to convince Lee not to attack. But Lee thought that the Union forces were severely battered and ready to break. Because of this, he planned to attack the center of the Union line on Cemetery Ridge. Such a tactic, he felt, would not be expected. Indeed, General Meade left only about 5,750 troops to defend the center.

For over an hour, the Confederates shelled Cemetery Ridge with cannon fire. For a while, the Union cannons fired back. Then they slacked off. The Confederates assumed that they had seriously damaged the Union artillery. In reality, the Confederate barrage did little damage.

The task of charging the Union center fell to three divisions of Confederate soldiers. General **George Pickett** commanded the largest unit. In late afternoon, nearly 15,000 men took part in **Pickett's Charge**. For one mile, the Confederates marched slowly up toward Cemetery Ridge. Showered with cannon and rifle fire, they suffered severe losses. But eventually, some of them almost reached their destination. Then Union reinforcements added to the barrage on the rebels. Soon the

Pickett's Charge, July 3, 1863

General George Pickett led his troops across Emmitsburg Road to attack the Union position. He lost more than half of his men in the 50-minute battle.

Map key:
— Union positions
→ Confederate troop movements
▬ Confederate positions
— Roads

0   0.5   1 Mile
0   0.5   1 Kilometer

GEOGRAPHY SKILLS | **INTERPRETING MAPS**

1. **Human-Environment Interaction** How do you think geography affected Pickett's Charge?
2. **Movement** In which direction did Pickett's soldiers charge?

Pickett's Charge

Pickett's Charge proved a disaster for the Confederate attackers. Fewer than half of them survived.

Day Three: July 3, 1863, 3 p.m.

THE CIVIL WAR **539**

Main Idea

❷ Battle of Gettysburg

The Battle of Gettysburg in 1863 was a major turning point in the war.

Recall At what event did Lincoln deliver the Gettysburg Address? *at the dedication of the Gettysburg battlefield cemetery*

Elaborate In the Gettysburg Address, how did Lincoln express the reasons for which the war was being fought? *He referenced the ideals of liberty, equality, democracy, and unity.*

Draw Conclusions Why do you think the short Gettysburg Address is one of the most famous speeches in American history? *because of the important ideals expressed and the power and emotion of the language*

Connect to Science and Technology

Photos of the Gettysburg Address?
No photographs captured President Abraham Lincoln's image as he delivered the Gettysburg Address. The speech lasted only about two minutes—much shorter than the average speech of the era—and the photographer was still setting up his camera when Lincoln finished the speech and sat down. One historian has pointed out that Lincoln spoke so briefly that the photographer probably did not even have time to get his camera's shutter open.

Answers

Reading Check *weakened the South; was the last Confederate attack on Union soil; ended the South's hopes of gaining foreign support and allies*

540

Confederates retreated, leaving about 7,500 casualties on the field of battle. Distressed by this defeat, General Lee rode among the survivors and told them, "It is all my fault."

On the fourth day, Lee began to retreat to Virginia. In all, nearly 75,000 Confederate soldiers and 90,000 Union troops had fought during the Battle of Gettysburg.

General Meade decided not to follow Lee's army. This decision angered Lincoln. He felt that Meade had missed an opportunity to crush the Confederates and possibly end the war.

Aftermath of Gettysburg

Gettysburg was a turning point in the war. Lee's troops would never again launch an attack in the North. The Union victory at Gettysburg also took place on the same day as Grant's capture of Vicksburg, Mississippi. These victories made northerners believe that the war could be won.

In addition, the Union win at Gettysburg helped to end the South's search for foreign influence in the war. After Gettysburg, Great Britain and France refused to provide aid to the Confederacy. The South's attempt at cotton diplomacy failed.

The Gettysburg Address

On November 19, 1863, at the dedicating ceremony of the Gettysburg battlefield cemetery, President Lincoln gave a speech called the **Gettysburg Address**, in which he praised the bravery of Union soldiers and renewed his commitment to winning the Civil War. This short but moving speech is one of the most famous in American history. In one of its frequently quoted lines, Lincoln referenced the Declaration of Independence and its ideals of liberty, equality, and democracy. He reminded listeners that the war was being fought for those reasons.

Lincoln rededicated himself to winning the war and preserving the Union. A difficult road still lay ahead.

READING CHECK Analyzing Why was Gettysburg a turning point?

FOCUS ON READING
The first sentence of the paragraph to the right is a main idea. The rest of this paragraph supports the idea.

ACADEMIC VOCABULARY
execute to perform, carry out

540 CHAPTER 16

Union Campaigns Cripple the Confederacy

Lincoln had been impressed with General Grant's successes in capturing Vicksburg. He transferred Grant to the East and gave him command of the Union army. In early 1864, Grant forced Lee to fight a series of battles in Virginia that stretched Confederate soldiers and supplies to their limits.

Wilderness Campaign in the East

From May through June, the armies fought in northern and central Virginia. Union troops launched the **Wilderness Campaign**—a series of battles designed to capture the Confederate capital at Richmond, Virginia. The first battle took place in early May, in woods about 50 miles outside of Richmond. Grant then ordered General Meade to Spotsylvania, where the fighting raged for 10 days.

Over the next month, Union soldiers moved the Confederate troops back toward Richmond. However, Grant experienced his worst defeat at the Battle of Cold Harbor in early June, just 10 miles northeast of Richmond. In only a few hours the Union army suffered 7,000 casualties. The battle delayed Grant's plans to take the Confederate capital.

Union forces had suffered twice as many casualties as the Confederates had, yet Grant continued his strategy. He knew he would be getting additional soldiers, and Lee could not. Grant slowly but surely advanced his troops through Virginia. He told another officer, "I propose to fight it out on this line if it takes all summer."

After Cold Harbor, General Grant moved south of Richmond. He had hoped to take control of the key railroad junction at Petersburg, Virginia. Lee's army, however, formed a solid defense, and Grant could not **execute** his attack. Grant was winning the war, but he still had not captured Richmond. Facing re-election, Lincoln was especially discouraged by this failure.

Critical Thinking: Analyzing Primary Sources

At Level

The Gettysburg Address

1. Have students read the Gettysburg Address as a class. The speech is located in the textbook's Historical Documents section.

2. Work through the speech a few sentences at a time to help students understand the language. Have students paraphrase the speech in modern language as you go.

3. Ask students to discuss the reasons for which Lincoln stated the war was being fought—such as the ideals of liberty, equality, and democracy—and why these reasons still resonate so powerfully with Americans.

4. Then ask students to imagine that they are newspaper reporters covering the dedication of the Gettysburg battlefield cemetery. Have each student write an article describing Lincoln's speech and its significance. Students should include excerpts from the speech in their articles. **LS Verbal/Linguistic**

📖 Alternative Assessment Handbook, Rubric 42: Writing to Inform

Final Campaigns

Union state
Union occupied, 1865
Confederate state
➜ Union forces
✹ Union victory
➜ Confederate forces
✹ Confederate victory

0   100   200 Miles
0   100   200 Kilometers

GEOGRAPHY SKILLS **INTERPRETING MAPS**

1. **Movement** About how long was Sherman's March to the Sea from Atlanta to Savannah?
2. **Movement** What challenges do you think Sherman faced on his southern attacks?

Sherman Strikes the South

Lincoln needed a victory for the Union army to help him win re-election in 1864. The bold campaign of General **William Tecumseh Sherman** provided this key victory. Sherman carried out the Union plan to destroy southern railroads and industries.

In the spring of 1864, Sherman marched south from Tennessee with 100,000 troops. His goal was to take Atlanta, Georgia, and knock out an important railroad link. From May through August, Sherman's army moved steadily through the Appalachian Mountains toward Atlanta. Several times, Sherman avoided defenses set up by Confederate general Joseph Johnston.

In July, Sherman was within sight of Atlanta. Confederate president Jefferson Davis gave General John Hood command of Confederate forces in the region. Hood repeatedly attacked Sherman in a final attempt to

save Atlanta, but the Union troops proved stronger. The Confederate troops retreated as Sherman held Atlanta under siege.

Atlanta fell to Sherman's troops on September 2, 1864. Much of the city was destroyed by artillery and fire. Sherman ordered the residents who still remained to leave. Responding to his critics, Sherman later wrote, "War is war, and not popularity-seeking." The loss of Atlanta cost the South an important railroad link and its center of industry.

Many people in the North had been upset with the length of the war. However, the capture of Atlanta showed that progress was being made in defeating the South. This success helped to convince Union voters to re-elect Lincoln in a landslide.

Sherman did not wait long to begin his next campaign. His goal was the port city of Savannah, Georgia. In mid-November 1864,

THE CIVIL WAR **541**

Main Idea

❹ The South Surrenders

Union troops forced the South to surrender in 1865, ending the Civil War.

Describe How did Grant cut off Lee's escape to North Carolina? *He surrounded Lee's army just west of Richmond.*

Summarize What was the condition of Lee's Confederate troops at this point? *They were tired and hungry and lacked weapons and supplies.*

Recall When and where did Lee surrender to Grant? *Appomattox Courthouse, April 9, 1865*

Analyze What do the terms of the surrender reveal about Grant's character and his feelings for Lee? *The terms reveal Grant's fairness and civility as well as his tremendous respect for Lee and his soldiers.*

🎴 Quick Facts Transparency: Causes and Effects of the Civil War

MISCONCEPTION ///ALERT\\\

Appomattox Courthouse Make certain that students understand that Appomattox Courthouse is not the name of a courthouse but of the town where Lee and Grant met to discuss the terms of surrender. The two men met to discuss the surrender at the McLean home, not a courthouse.

Answers

Interpreting Charts *It was an integral and central issue.*

Reading Check *He hoped to ruin the South's economy and its ability to fight.*

542

Sherman left Atlanta with a force of about 60,000 men. He said he would "make Georgia howl!"

During his March to the Sea, Sherman practiced **total war**—destroying civilian and economic resources. Sherman believed that total war would ruin the South's economy and its ability to fight. He ordered his troops to destroy railways, bridges, crops, livestock, and other resources. They burned plantations and freed slaves.

Sherman's army reached Savannah on December 10, 1864. They left behind a path of destruction 60 miles wide. Sherman believed that this march would speed the end of the war. He wanted to break the South's will to fight by marching Union troops through the heart of the Confederacy. In the end, Sherman's destruction of the South led to anger and resentment toward the people of the North that would last for generations.

READING CHECK Drawing Conclusions
How did Sherman hope to help the Union with his total-war strategy?

Causes and Effects of the Civil War — QUICK FACTS

Causes
- Disagreement over the institution of slavery
- Economic differences
- Political differences

⬇

Effects
- Slavery ends
- 620,000 Americans killed
- Military districts created
- Southern economy in ruins

ANALYSIS SKILL **INTERPRETING CHARTS**
How important was slavery to the Civil War?

The South Surrenders

In early April, Sherman closed in on the last Confederate defenders in North Carolina. At the same time, Grant finally broke through the Confederate defenses at Petersburg. On April 2, Lee was forced to retreat from Richmond.

Fighting Ends

By the second week of April 1865, Grant had surrounded Lee's army and demanded the soldiers' surrender. Lee hoped to join other Confederates in fighting in North Carolina, but Grant cut off his escape just west of Richmond. Lee tried some last minute attacks but could not break the Union line. Lee's forces were running low on supplies. General James Longstreet told about the condition of Confederate troops. "Many weary soldiers were picked up . . . some with, many without, arms [weapons],—all asking for food."

Trapped by the Union army, Lee recognized that the situation was hopeless. "There is nothing left for me to do but go and see General Grant," Lee said, "and I would rather die a thousand deaths."

On April 9, 1865, the Union and Confederate leaders met at a home in the small town of **Appomattox Courthouse** where Lee surrendered to Grant, thus ending the Civil War.

During the meeting, Grant assured Lee that his troops would be fed and allowed to keep their horses, and they would not be tried for treason. Then Lee signed the surrender documents. The long, bloody war had finally ended. Grant later wrote that he found the scene at Appomattox Courthouse more tragic than joyful.

❝ I felt . . . sad and depressed at the downfall of a foe [enemy] who had fought so long and valiantly [bravely], and had suffered so much for a cause, though that cause was, I believe, one of the worst for which a people ever fought. ❞
—Ulysses S. Grant

Critical Thinking: Analyzing and Predicting — At Level

Letter about Lee's Surrender

1. Discuss with students the events leading up to Lee's surrender and what it meant for the future of the Union. Have students consider how the war had affected the people, economies, property, and land on both sides. Then have students predict how the surrender will affect the nation.

2. Ask students to imagine that they were one of the soldiers who witnessed Lee's surrender at Appomattox Courthouse. Have each student adopt the point of view of either a southern or northern soldier and write a letter to a friend or family member about the surrender. Students' letters should describe the events that led to the surrender as well as the surrender itself and then speculate about the effects of the surrender.

3. Ask for volunteers to read their letters to the class. 🅛🅢 **Verbal/Linguistic**

📓 Alternative Assessment Handbook, Rubric 25: Personal Letters

Surrender at Appomattox

Union general Grant rose to shake hands with Confederate general Lee after the surrender. Grant allowed Lee to keep his sword and Lee's men to keep their horses.

Why was it important for Grant and Lee to shake hands? Why or why not?

As General Lee returned to his troops, General Grant stopped Union forces from cheering their victory. "The war is over," Grant said with relief. "The rebels are our countrymen again."

The Effects of the War

The Civil War had deep and long-lasting effects. Almost 620,000 Americans lost their lives during the four years of fighting.

The defeat of the South ended slavery there. The majority of former slaves, however, had no homes or jobs. The southern economy was in ruins.

A tremendous amount of hostility remained, even after the fighting had ceased. The war was over, but the question remained: How could the United States be united once more?

READING CHECK **Predicting** What problems might the Union face following the Civil War?

SUMMARY AND PREVIEW After four long years of battles, the Civil War ended with General Lee's surrender at Appomattox Courthouse. In the next chapter you will read about the consequences of the war in the South.

Section 5 Assessment

Online Quiz
KEYWORD: SR8 HP16
go.hrw.com

Reviewing Ideas, Terms, and People

1. a. Identify What was the **Gettysburg Address**?
b. Analyze Why was geography important to the outcome of the **Battle of Gettysburg**?
c. Predict How might the war have been different if Confederate forces had won the Battle of Gettysburg?
2. a. Recall What was the purpose of the **Wilderness Campaign**?
b. Draw Conclusions In what way was the capture of Atlanta an important victory for President Lincoln?
3. a. Identify What events led to Lee's surrender at **Appomattox Courthouse**?
b. Summarize What problems did the South face at the end of the war?

Critical Thinking

4. Supporting a Point of View Review your notes on the end of the Civil War. Then copy the graphic organizer below. Use it to show the three events in this section that you think contributed most to the end of the Civil War and explain why.

FOCUS ON WRITING

5. Taking Notes on the End of the War As you read this section, take notes on the Battle of Gettysburg, the Wilderness Campaign, the fall of Atlanta, and the South's surrender. Be sure to answer the following questions: Who? Where? When? Why? and How?

THE CIVIL WAR **543**

Section 5 Assessment Answers

1. a. short but moving speech that Lincoln gave at the dedication of the Gettysburg battlefield cemetery; famous in American history
b. Hills provided Union forces with strong defensive positions that helped them win.
c. possible answers—France and Great Britain might have aided the Confederacy, the South might have gone on to win the war.

2. a. to stretch Lee's forces; to reach Richmond
b. showed that progress was being made in defeating the South, which helped convince Union voters to re-elect Lincoln as president

3. a. Wilderness Campaign; break in Confederate defenses at Petersburg; Lee's army forced to retreat from Richmond and then surrounded
b. possible answers—an uncertain future, a ruined economy, enormous task of rebuilding

4. possible answers—Gettysburg, Sherman in the South, Wilderness Campaign; Students' responses should contain explanations.

5. Students should mention the key battles and the roles of Grant, Sherman, and Lee.

Direct Teach

Checking for Understanding

True or False Answer each statement *T* if it is true or *F* if it is false. If false, explain why.

1. The Wilderness Campaign was a major turning point in the Civil War. *F; Battle of Gettysburg*
2. In his inaugural address, Lincoln reminded Americans of the ideals for which the war was being fought. *F; Gettysburg Address*
3. General William Tecumseh Sherman practiced total war during his March to the Sea. *T*

Review & Assess

Close

Review with students the major battles that led to the South's defeat, beginning with Gettysburg and ending with Lee's surrender.

Review

Online Quiz, Section 5

Assess

SE Section 5 Assessment
PASS: Section 5 Quiz
Alternative Assessment Handbook

Reteach/Classroom Intervention

Review Workbook
Interactive Reader and Study Guide, Section 5
Interactive Skills Tutor CD-ROM

Answers

Surrender at Appomattox *to show respect and a desire for the Union to be restored*

Reading Check *possible answers—helping the South recover from the devastation and destruction of the war; bringing the South back into the Union; overcoming remaining animosity between northerners and southerners*

543

Social Studies Skills

Analysis | Critical Thinking | Civic Participation | Study

Interpreting Political Cartoons

Define the Skill

Political cartoons are drawings that express views on important issues. They have been used throughout history to influence public opinion. The ability to interpret political cartoons will help you understand issues and people's attitudes about them.

Learn the Skill

Political cartoons use both words and images to convey their message. They often contain caricatures or symbolism. A caricature is a drawing that exaggerates the features of a person or object. Symbolism is the use of one thing to represent something else. Cartoonists use these techniques to help make their point clear. They also use titles, labels, and captions to get their message across.

Use these steps to interpret political cartoons.

1 Read any title, labels, and caption to identify the cartoon's general topic.

2 Identify the people and objects. Determine if they are exaggerated and, if so, why. Identify any symbols and analyze their meaning.

3 Draw conclusions about the message the cartoonist is trying to convey.

The following cartoon was published in the North in 1863. The cartoonist has used symbols to make his point. Lady Liberty, representing the Union, is being threatened by the Copperheads. The cartoonist has expressed his opinion of these people by drawing them as the poisonous snake for which they were named. This cartoon clearly supports the Union's continuing to fight the war.

Practice the Skill

Apply the guidelines to interpret the cartoon below and answer the questions that follow.

1. What do the tree and the man in it symbolize?

2. What policy or action of President Lincoln is this cartoon supporting?

LINCOLN'S LAST WARNING.
"Now, if you don't come down, I'll cut the Tree from under you."

544 CHAPTER 16

Visual Summary

Use the visual summary below to help you review the main ideas of the chapter.

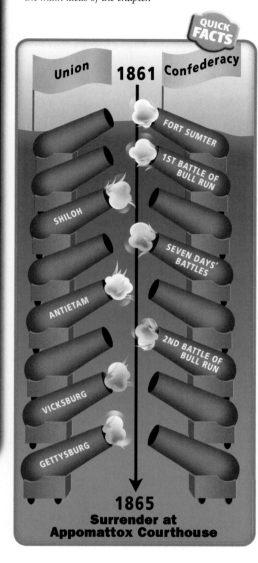

QUICK FACTS

Union 1861 Confederacy

FORT SUMTER

1ST BATTLE OF BULL RUN

SHILOH

SEVEN DAYS' BATTLES

ANTIETAM

2ND BATTLE OF BULL RUN

VICKSBURG

GETTYSBURG

1865
Surrender at Appomattox Courthouse

Reviewing Vocabulary, Terms, and People

Match the numbered definitions with the correct terms from the list below.

- **a.** contrabands
- **b.** cotton diplomacy
- **c.** Second Battle of Bull Run
- **d.** Siege of Vicksburg
- **e.** Thomas "Stonewall" Jackson

1. Attack by Union general Ulysses S. Grant that gave the North control of the Mississippi River
2. Confederate general who held off Union attacks and helped the South win the First Battle of Bull Run
3. Important Confederate victory in which General Robert E. Lee defeated Union troops and pushed into Union territory for the first time
4. Southern strategy of using cotton exports to gain Britain's support in the Civil War
5. Term given to escaped slaves from the South

Comprehension and Critical Thinking

SECTION 1 *(Pages 510–515)*

6. **a. Identify** When and where did fighting in the U.S. Civil War begin?

    b. Analyze How did civilians help the war effort in both the North and the South?

    c. Elaborate Why do you think the border states chose to remain in the Union despite their support of slavery?

SECTION 2 *(Pages 516–521)*

7. **a. Identify** What was the first major battle of the war? What was the outcome of the battle?

    b. Analyze What was the Union army hoping to accomplish when it marched into Virginia at the start of the war?

    c. Evaluate Was the Union's naval blockade of the South successful? Why or why not?

THE CIVIL WAR **545**

Review and Assessment Resources

Review and Reinforce

SE Chapter Review

📋 **CRF:** Chapter Review Activity

📖 Quick Facts Transparency: The Civil War Visual Summary

🔊 Spanish Chapter Summaries Audio CD Program

💻 Online Chapter Summaries in Six Languages

OSP Holt PuzzlePro; GameTool for ExamView

💿 Quiz Game CD-ROM

Assess

SE Standardized Test Practice

📋 PASS: Chapter Test, Forms A and B

📋 Alternative Assessment Handbook

OSP ExamView Test Generator, Chapter Test

💿 Differentiated Instruction Modified Worksheets and Tests CD-ROM: Chapter Test

💻 Holt Online Assessment Program (in the Premier Online Edition)

Reteach/Intervene

📋 Interactive Reader and Study Guide

📋 Differentiated Instruction Teacher Management System: Lesson Plans for Differentiated Instruction

💿 Differentiated Instruction Modified Worksheets and Tests CD-ROM

💿 Interactive Skills Tutor CD-ROM

go.hrw.com

Chapter Resources:
KEYWORD: SR8 US16

8. a. Many supported the South because they hoped the Confederacy would give them greater freedom and because some Native Americans were slaveholders.

b. gained control of the Mississippi River, which divided the South; held Union territory in the Far West

c. possible answers—victory at Vicksburg, because its fall gave the Union control of the entire Mississippi Valley; victory at New Orleans, because it opened the way for the Union to gain control of the Mississippi River

9. a. worked on farms and in factories; provided medical support and aid, established and worked at hospitals

b. Copperheads opposed the war; Lincoln suspended the right of habeas corpus.

c. possible answers—lack of basic necessities, such as housing, clothing, food; lack of work; risk of capture

10. a. April 9, 1865; Appomattox Courthouse, Virginia

b. similar—waged campaigns to wear down the Confederate forces; different—Sherman waged total war and captured major southern cities; Grant pressed Lee's army.

c. possible answer—Their smaller population and limited manufacturing led to their being outnumbered in battle and resulted in serious shortages.

Social Studies Skills

11. that they are threatening the Union's survival and war effort

Reading Skills

12. d

Reviewing Themes

13. possible answers—resulted in many deaths and much destruction of property and land, led to freedom for enslaved Africans, led to new roles for women, improved northern economy, destroyed southern economy, created lingering anger and resentment in the South

---

SECTION 3 *(Pages 522–525)*

8. a. Identify Which side did the Cherokee support in the fighting at Pea Ridge? Why?

b. Draw Conclusions What progress did Union leaders make in the war in the West?

c. Evaluate Which victory in the West was most valuable to the Union? Why?

SECTION 4 *(Pages 528–534)*

9. a. Describe What responsibilities did women take on during the war?

b. Analyze What opposition to the war did President Lincoln face, and how did he deal with that opposition?

c. Predict What might be some possible problems that the newly freed slaves in the South might face?

SECTION 5 *(Pages 536–543)*

10. a. Recall When and where did the war finally end?

b. Compare and Contrast How were the efforts of Generals Grant and Sherman at the end of the war similar and different?

c. Elaborate What do you think led to the South's defeat in the Civil War? Explain.

Social Studies Skills

Interpreting Political Cartoons *Use the Social Studies Skills taught in this chapter to answer the question about the political cartoon below.*

11. What do you think the artist is saying about politicians with this cartoon?

Reading Skills

Understanding Ideas and Their Support *Use the Reading Skills taught in this chapter to answer the question about the reading selection below.*

> Lee was unaware that Union soldiers were encamped closer to town. He had been suffering from lack of enemy information for three days because his cavalry chief "Jeb" Stuart was not performing his duties. Stuart and his cavalry had gone off on their own raiding party, disobeying Lee's orders. *(p. 537)*

12. What is the main idea of the above reading section?

a. "Jeb" Stuart was not performing his duties.

b. Stuart and his cavalry had gone off on their own.

c. Stuart and his cavalry disobeyed Lee's orders.

d. Lee was suffering from a lack of enemy information.

Reviewing Themes

13. Society and Culture What effects did the Civil War have on American society?

14. Politics What political difficulties did the Emancipation Proclamation cause for President Lincoln?

Using the Internet

15. Activity: Writing a Poem Soldiers in the Civil War came from all walks of life. Despite the hope for glory and adventure, many encountered dangerous and uncomfortable conditions. Enter the activity keyword to learn more about Civil War soldiers. After viewing photographs and reading letters, write a poem describing the life of a soldier. Your poem should reflect on the soldier's emotions and experiences.

FOCUS ON WRITING

16. Write Your Newspaper Article Review your notes. Then choose the subject you think would make the best newspaper article. Write an attention-grabbing headline. Then write your article, giving as many facts as possible.

---

14. If he emancipated all the slaves, he risked going against the Constitution and losing political support in the strategic border states; if he emancipated only some of the slaves, he risked angering some abolitionists.

Using the Internet

15. Go to the HRW Web site and enter the keyword shown to access a rubric for this activity.

KEYWORD: SR8 TEACHER

Focus on Writing

16. Rubric Students' newspaper articles should

- have an attention-grabbing headline.
- describe one of the events in the chapter.
- answer the questions Who? Where? When? Why? and How?
- included as many facts as possible about the selected event.
- use proper grammar, punctuation, spelling, and capitalization.

CRF: Focus on Writing Activity: Writing a Newspaper Article

Standardized Test Practice

DIRECTIONS: *Read each question and write the letter of the best response.*

1 Use the map below to answer the following question.

The place where two major battles of the Civil War were fought is indicated on the map by what letter?

A W
B X
C Y
D Z

2 The Battle of Gettysburg was an important battle of the Civil War because

A it was an overwhelming Confederate victory.
B the Union army's advance on the Confederate capital was stopped.
C it ended Lee's hopes of advancing into northern territory.
D it enabled the Union to control the Mississippi River.

3 Overall command of Confederate forces in Virginia during most of the Civil War was held by

A Jefferson Davis.
B William Tecumseh Sherman.
C Thomas "Stonewall" Jackson.
D Robert E. Lee.

4 Which of Lincoln's speeches and writings reflected the statement of the Declaration of Independence that "all men are created equal"?

A the Emancipation Proclamation
B the first inaugural address (1861)
C the second inaugural address (1865)
D the Gettysburg Address

5 The tactics that Sherman used against Confederate armies in the South were based on what strategy?

A cutting off troops from their officers
B a naval blockade of southern ports
C destroying the South's resources and economy
D hit-and-run attacks on major southern cities

6 In the War of 1812 the British navy blockaded American seaports in the hope that the U.S. economy would suffer and the United States would surrender. Which Civil War strategy was similar?

A General Winfield Scott's plan to destroy the southern economy
B General William Tecumseh Sherman's March to the Sea
C General Ulysses S. Grant's capture of Vicksburg
D Admiral David Farragut's defeat of New Orleans

7

> *"*What General Lee's feelings were I do not know. He was a man of much dignity, without expression on his face. It was impossible to say whether he felt inwardly glad that the end had finally come, or felt sad over the result, and was too manly to show it. Whatever his feelings, they were entirely hidden from me.*"*
>
> –Ulysses S. Grant, adapted from *Personal Memoirs of U.S. Grant*, Vol. II

What is your opinion about what Lee might have been feeling during his surrender?

Answers

1. D
Break Down the Question This question requires students to interpret the map and then recall factual information. Have students first try to identify the location where two battles were fought and then find the location on the map.

2. C
Break Down the Question This question requires students to identify cause and effect. Refer students who miss the question to Section 5.

3. D
Break Down the Question This question requires students to recall factual information. Suggest that students first eliminate all non-Confederate leaders (B) to narrow their choices.

4 D
Break Down the Question This question requires students to recall the main points expressed in the Gettysburg Address. Refer students who have trouble to the text in Section 5 titled "The Gettysburg Address."

5. C
Break Down the Question This question requires students to identify the main idea. Refer students who have trouble to the text in Section 5 titled "Sherman Strikes the South."

6. A
Break Down the Question This question connects to information covered in Chapter 7.

7.
Break Down the Question This question requires students to reflect on General Lee's role in the war and then, based on this assessment, to imagine what his reaction might have been to having to surrender.

Intervention Resources

Reproducible
- Interactive Reader and Study Guide
- Differentiated Instruction Teacher Management System: Lesson Plans for Differentiated Instruction

Technology
- Quick Facts Transparency: The Civil War Visual Summary
- Differentiated Instruction Modified Worksheets and Tests CD-ROM
- Interactive Skills Tutor CD-ROM

Tips for Test Taking

Try, Try, Try Read the following to students: Keep at it. Don't give up. This sounds obvious, so why say it? You might be surprised by how many students do give up. Remember, the last question is worth just as much as the first question, and the questions do not get harder as you go. If the question you just finished was really hard, an easier one is probably coming up soon. Take a deep breath and keep on slogging. Give it your all, all the way to the end.

Chapter 17 Planning Guide

Reconstruction

Chapter Overview	Reproducible Resources	Technology Resources
CHAPTER 17 pp. 548–575 **Overview:** In this chapter, students will learn about the challenges that faced the nation after the Civil War and the efforts made to meet those challenges.	**Differentiated Instruction Teacher Management System:*** • Instructional Benchmarking Guides • Lesson Plans for Differentiated Instruction **Interactive Reader and Study Guide:** Chapter Graphic Organizer* **Chapter Resource File:*** • Focus on Writing Activity: Job History • Social Studies Skills Activity: Chance, Oversight, and Error in History • Chapter Review Activity **Pre-AP Activities Guide for United States History:** Evaluating Information* **A Teacher's Guide to Religion in the Public Schools***	**Power Presentations with Video CD-ROM** **Differentiated Instruction Modified Worksheets and Tests CD-ROM** **Primary Source Library CD-ROM for United States History** **Interactive Skills Tutor CD-ROM** **Student Edition on Audio CD Program** **History's Impact: United States History Video Program (VHS/DVD):** Reconstruction*
Section 1: **Rebuilding the South** **The Big Idea:** The nation faced many problems in rebuilding the Union.	**Differentiated Instruction Teacher Management System:** Section 1 Lesson Plan* **Interactive Reader and Study Guide:** Section 1 Summary* **Chapter Resource File:*** • Vocabulary Builder Activity, Section 1 • Economics and History Activity: The Devastation of War • Biography Activity: Andrew Johnson **Political Cartoons Activities for United States History,** Cartoon 18: Lincoln Repairing the Union*	**Daily Bellringer Transparency:** Section 1* **Internet Activity:** Population Chart
Section 2: **The Fight over Reconstruction** **The Big Idea:** The return to power of the pre-war southern leadership led Republicans in Congress to take control of Reconstruction.	**Differentiated Instruction Teacher Management System:** Section 2 Lesson Plan* **Interactive Reader and Study Guide:** Section 2 Summary* **Chapter Resource File:*** • Vocabulary Builder Activity, Section 2 • Biography Activity: Thaddeus Stevens • History and Geography Activity: The Reconstruction Acts	**Daily Bellringer Transparency:** Section 2* **Map Transparency:** Reconstruction Military Districts* **Quick Facts Transparency:** The Reconstruction Amendments* **Internet Activity:** Writing Editorials for a Newspaper
Section 3: **Reconstruction in the South** **The Big Idea:** As Reconstruction ended, African Americans faced new hurdles and the South attempted to rebuild.	**Differentiated Instruction Teacher Management System:** Section 3 Lesson Plan* **Interactive Reader and Study Guide:** Section 3 Summary* **Chapter Resource File:*** • Vocabulary Builder Activity, Section 3 • Biography Activity: Blanche K. Bruce • Primary Source Activity: Reconstruction and the Ku Klux Klan • Primary Source Activity: *Plessy* v. *Ferguson* • Literature Activity: The Jim Crow Laws **U.S. Supreme Court Case Studies:** *Plessy* v. *Ferguson* (1896)*	**Daily Bellringer Transparency:** Section 3* **Map Transparency:** African American Representation in the South, 1870* **Quick Facts Transparency:** Hopes Raised and Denied*

SE	Student Edition		Print Resource		Audio CD
TE	Teacher's Edition		Transparency		CD-ROM
go.hrw.com			Learning Styles		Video
OSP	One-Stop Planner CD-ROM		* also on One-Stop Planner CD

HOLT

History's Impact
United States History Video Program (VHS/DVD)
Reconstruction
Suggested use: as a chapter introduction

Review, Assessment, Intervention

 Quick Facts Transparency: Reconstruction Visual Summary*

 Spanish Chapter Summaries Audio CD Program

 Progress Assessment Support System (PASS): Chapter Test*

 Differentiated Instruction Modified Worksheets and Tests CD-ROM: Modified Chapter Test

 Online Chapter Summaries in Six Languages

 Quiz Game CD-ROM

One-Stop Planner CD-ROM: ExamView Test Generator (English/Spanish)

Alternative Assessment Handbook

Holt Online Assessment Program (HOAP), in the Holt Premier Online Student Edition

 PASS: Section 1 Quiz*

 Online Quiz: Section 1

Alternative Assessment Handbook

 PASS: Section 2 Quiz*

 Online Quiz: Section 2

 Alternative Assessment Handbook

 PASS: Section 3 Quiz*

 Online Quiz: Section 3

Alternative Assessment Handbook

Power Presentations with Video CD-ROM

Power Presentations with Video are visual presentations of each chapter's main ideas. Presentations can be customized by including Quick Facts charts, images from the text, and video clips.

Power Presentations with Video CD-ROM

HOLT
United States History
Beginnings to 1877

HOLT, RINEHART and WINSTON
A Harcourt Education Company

Developed by the Division for Public Education of the American Bar Association, these materials are part of the **Democracy and Civic Education Resources.**

DIVISION FOR PUBLIC EDUCATION
AMERICAN BAR ASSOCIATION

• **Constitution Study Guide**

• **Supreme Court Case Studies**

Holt Online Learning

| **Teacher Resources** |
| KEYWORD: SR8 TEACHER |

| **Student Resources** |
| KEYWORD: SR8 US17 |

• Document-Based Questions
• Interactive Multimedia Activities

• Current Events
• Chapter-based Internet Activities
• and more!

Holt Premier
Online Student Edition

Complete online support for interactivity, assessment, and reporting

• Interactive Maps and Notebook
• Standardized Test Prep
• Homework Practice and Research Activities Online

CHAPTER 17 PLANNING GUIDE

Differentiating Instruction

ENGLISH-LANGUAGE LEARNERS & STRUGGLING READERS

TARGET RESOURCE

Live Ink® Online Reading Help

Spanish Resources

Spanish Chapter Summaries Audio CD Program

One-Stop Planner CD-ROM:
- ExamView Test Generator, Spanish
- PuzzlePro, Spanish

Additional Resources

Differentiated Instruction Teacher Management System: Lesson Plans for Differentiated Instruction

Chapter Resources:
- Vocabulary Builder Activities
- Social Studies Skills Activity: Chance, Oversight, and Error in History

Quick Facts Transparencies:
- The Reconstruction Amendments
- Hopes Raised and Denied
- Reconstruction Visual Summary

Student Edition on Audio CD Program

Online Chapter Summaries in Six Languages

Interactive Skills Tutor CD-ROM

SPECIAL NEEDS LEARNERS

TARGET RESOURCE

Differentiated Instruction Modified Worksheets and Tests CD-ROM

- Vocabulary Flash Cards
- Modified Vocabulary Builder Activities
- Modified Chapter Review Activity
- Modified Chapter Test

Additional Resources

Differentiated Instruction Teacher Management System: Lesson Plans for Differentiated Instruction

Interactive Reader and Study Guide

Social Studies Skills Activity: Chance, Oversight, and Error in History

Student Edition on Audio CD Program

Interactive Skills Tutor CD-ROM

Live Ink® Online Reading Help

ADVANCED/GIFTED AND TALENTED STUDENTS

TARGET RESOURCE

Primary Source Library CD-ROM for United States History

The Library contains longer versions of quotations in the text, extra sources, and images. Included are point-of-view articles, journals, diaries, historical fiction, and political documents.

Additional Resources

Political Cartoons Activities for United States History: Cartoon 18: Lincoln Repairing the Union

United States History Document-Based Questions Activities

Differentiated Instruction Teacher Management System: Lesson Plans for Differentiated Instruction

Pre-AP Activities Guide for United States History: Evaluating Information

Chapter Resource File:
- Focus on Writing Activity: Job History
- Literature Activity: The Jim Crow Laws
- Primary Source Activity: Reconstruction and the Ku Klux Klan
- Primary Source Activity: *Plessy* v. *Ferguson*

Differentiated Activities in the Teacher's Edition

- Reconstruction Acrostic, p. 559
- Letter to a Northern Newspaper, p. 569
- Southern African American Political Cartoon, p. 569

Differentiated Activities in the Teacher's Edition

- Reconstruction Plans Chart, p. 553
- Making Political Slogans, p. 565
- Cause-and-Effect Graphic Organizer, p. 566

Differentiated Activities in the Teacher's Edition

- Summary of Lincoln's 2nd Inaugural Address, p. 553
- Conducting an Impeachment Trial, p. 562
- End of Reconstruction Debate, p. 567
- Supreme Court Decisions, p. 568
- Paper on the word *Revolutionary,* p. 570

One-Stop Planner® CD-ROM
for Differentiated Instruction

Your differentiated instruction lesson plans are available at your fingertips. Holt's Teacher Management System links teaching support tools to pages in the Interactive Teacher's Edition.

The One-Stop Planner features:
- Interactive Teacher's Edition
- Calendar Planner and pacing guides
- Editable lesson plans
- All reproducible ancillaries in Adobe Acrobat (PDF) format
- ExamView Test Generator (English and Spanish)
- Transparency and video previews

Professional Development

- **In-service and staff development** as part of your Holt Social Studies product purchase
- **Quick Teacher Tutorial Lesson Presentation CD-ROM**
- Intensive tuition-based **Teacher Development Institute**
- **Teaching American History Online**—2 Module Professional Development Course
- **Convenient Holt Speaker Bureau**—face-to-face workshop options
- **PRAXIS™ Test Prep** interactive Web-based content refreshers*
- **24/7 Ask A Professional Development Expert** at http://www.hrw.com/prodev/

* PRAXIS is a trademark of Educational Testing Service (ETS). This publication is not endorsed or approved by ETS.

Chapter Big Ideas

Section 1 The nation faced many problems in rebuilding the Union.

Section 2 The return to power of the pre-war southern leadership led Republicans in Congress to take control of Reconstruction.

Section 3 As Reconstruction ended, African Americans faced new hurdles and the South attempted to rebuild.

Focus on Writing

The **Chapter Resource File** provides a Focus on Writing worksheet to help students organize and write their job histories.

📝 **CRF:** Focus on Writing Activity: Job History

CHAPTER 17   1865–1877

Reconstruction

FOCUS ON WRITING

Job History When the Civil War ended, it was time to rebuild. People were ready to get back to work. But life had changed for many people and would continue to change. As you read this chapter, think about jobs people may have had during Reconstruction.

UNITED STATES
1865
Abraham Lincoln is assassinated.

1865

WORLD
1865
Black Jamaicans rebel against the wealthy planter class.

Below Level

Basic-level activities designed for all students encountering new material

At Level

Intermediate-level activities designed for average students

Above Level

Challenging activities designed for honors and gifted and talented students

Standard English Mastery

Activities designed to improve standard English usage

Introduce the Chapter

At Level

Focus on Rebuilding

1. Have students imagine that their town or city has been devastated by a natural disaster. For example, traffic signals do not work, hospitals and schools are closed, grocery stores have been stripped of food, and power and water plants have been destroyed.

2. Ask students to list, in order of importance, what the town should focus on rebuilding or replacing first. Ask for volunteers to share their lists with the class.

3. Explain to students that they will be learning about the efforts to rebuild and reunite the United States following the Civil War. Inform students that not only were cities and farmland destroyed but the nation had to be put back together. Ask students to use their prior knowledge to predict what social, economic, and political issues might cause the North and South to disagree over priorities in rebuilding the nation. **LS Verbal/Linguistic**

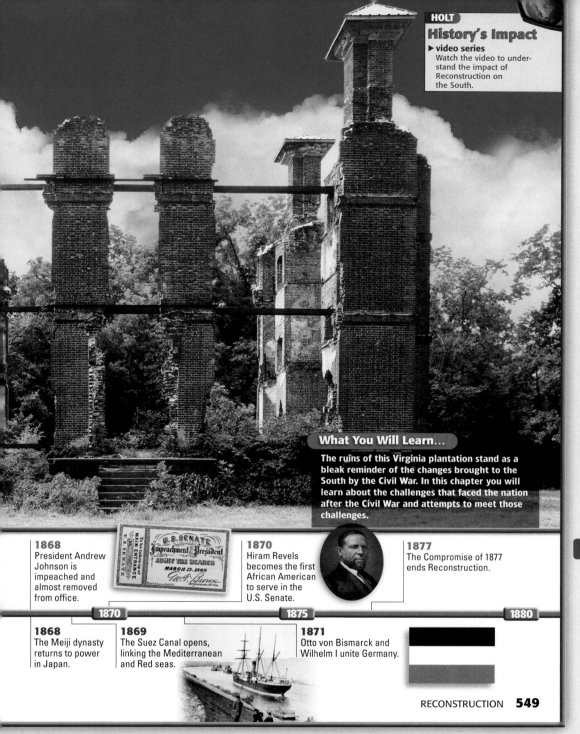

What You Will Learn...

The ruins of this Virginia plantation stand as a bleak reminder of the changes brought to the South by the Civil War. In this chapter you will learn about the challenges that faced the nation after the Civil War and attempts to meet those challenges.

1868
President Andrew Johnson is impeached and almost removed from office.

1870
Hiram Revels becomes the first African American to serve in the U.S. Senate.

1877
The Compromise of 1877 ends Reconstruction.

1870   1875   1880

1868
The Meiji dynasty returns to power in Japan.

1869
The Suez Canal opens, linking the Mediterranean and Red seas.

1871
Otto von Bismarck and Wilhelm I unite Germany.

RECONSTRUCTION   **549**

• Chapter Preview •

HOLT
History's Impact
▶ video series
See the Video Teacher's Guide for strategies for using the chapter video **Reconstruction**.

Explore the Picture

Aftermath of War There are many ruins of plantations across the South today. Many plantations were damaged during the fighting that took place during the Civil War. Others were abandoned by their owners, who could no longer afford to run their plantations. The ruin reflected by this image shows the great challenges that faced the nation as it attempted to rebuild in the aftermath of the Civil War.

Analyzing Visuals How might the sight of abandoned or damaged plantations have affected people after the Civil War? *Wealthy southerners might have been angered or saddened by such sights. Former slaves might have felt justice had been served and seen the ruins as a symbol of the end of slavery.*

go.hrw.com
Online Resources

Chapter Resources:
KEYWORD: SR8 US17
Teacher Resources:
KEYWORD: SR8 TEACHER

Explore the Time Line

1. In what year was President Abraham Lincoln assassinated? *1865*

2. What event occurred in Jamaica in the same year that Abraham Lincoln was assassinated? *Black Jamaicans rebelled against the planters.*

3. How many years passed between the assassination of Abraham Lincoln and the end of Reconstruction? *12 years*

4. Which president was impeached in 1868? *Andrew Johnson*

World Events

Connecting Two Seas In 1869 the Suez Canal opened, connecting the Mediterranean and Red seas. This artificial channel is just over 100 miles in length. Because the levels of both seas are relatively equal, the builders did not need to construct locks to raise or lower ships. The creation of the Suez Canal reduced the voyage from Europe to the Indian Ocean by about 5,000 miles. By 1945 the number of annual shipments through the canal peaked at 984,000. In recent years, however, traffic has dropped, as more cargo is sent by other means.

Understanding Themes

Point out to students that during Reconstruction, many political changes took place in an effort to mend the damage done by war and to grant rights to the newly-freed slaves. Ask students what political changes might have been necessary and how each change would have affected both the North and the South. What social and cultural changes might have taken place during Reconstruction? What different groups might have been affected by these changes? Help students understand the importance of these two themes.

Analyzing Historical Information

Focus on Reading Read students an article from a current, popular magazine or a short article from the local newspaper. Have students take notes as you read. Tell them to record only the relevant information from your reading. When finished, have several volunteers read their notes. Compile a list of the relevant information for all to see. Then guide students in a discussion of what was important, and what was not. Tell students that when they analyze historical information, they are using this same skill, figuring out what is important or relevant, and what is not.

Reading Social Studies
by Kylene Beers

| Economics | Geography | **Politics** | **Society and Culture** | Science and Technology |

Focus on Themes In this chapter you will read about the time immediately after the Civil War. You will see how the government tried to help the South rebuild itself and will learn about how life changed for African Americans after slavery was declared illegal. You will read about the **political** conflicts that emerged as southern leadership worked to gain control of Reconstruction efforts. Throughout the chapter, you will read how the **culture** of the South changed after the War.

Analyzing Historical Information

Focus on Reading History books are full of information. As you read, you are confronted with names, dates, places, terms, and descriptions on every page. You don't want to have to deal with anything unimportant or untrue.

Identifying Relevant and Essential Information Information in a history book should be relevant to the topic you're studying. It should also be essential to understanding that topic and verifiable. Anything else distracts from the material you are studying.

The first passage below includes several pieces of irrelevant and nonessential information. In the second, this information has been removed. Note how much easier the revised passage is to comprehend.

First Passage

President Abraham Lincoln, <u>who was very tall</u>, wanted to reunite the nation as quickly and painlessly as possible. He had proposed a plan for readmitting the southern states even before the war ended, <u>which happened on a Sunday</u>. Called the Ten Percent Plan, it offered southerners amnesty, or official pardon for all illegal acts supporting the rebellion. <u>Today a group called Amnesty International works to protect the rights of prisoners. Lincoln's plan certainly would have worked if it would have been implemented.</u>

> Lincoln's appearance and the day on which the war ended are not essential facts.

> Amnesty International is not relevant to this topic.

> There is no way to prove the accuracy of the last sentence.

Revised Passage

President Abraham Lincoln wanted to reunite the nation as quickly and painlessly as possible. He had proposed a plan for readmitting the southern states even before the war ended. Called the Ten Percent Plan, it offered southerners amnesty, or official pardon for all illegal acts supporting the rebellion.

From Chapter 17, p. 553

Reading and Skills Resources

Reading Support

📖 Interactive Reader and Study Guide

🔊 Student Edition on Audio CD Program

🔊 Spanish Chapter Summaries Audio CD Program

Social Studies Skills Support

💿 Interactive Skills Tutor CD-ROM

Vocabulary Support

📖 **CRF:** Vocabulary Builder Activities

📖 **CRF:** Chapter Review Activity

💿 Differentiated Instruction Modified Worksheets and Tests CD-ROM:
- Vocabulary Flash Cards
- Vocabulary Builder Activity
- Chapter Review Activity

OSP Holt PuzzlePro

You Try It!

The following passage is adapted from the chapter you are about to read. As you read, look for irrelevant, nonessential, or unverifiable information.

The Freedman's Bureau

From Chapter 17, p. 530

In 1865 Congress established the Freedmen's Bureau, an agency providing relief for freed people and certain poor people in the South. The Bureau had a difficult job. It may have been one of the most difficult jobs ever. At its high point, about 900 agents served the entire South. All 900 people could fit into one hotel ballroom today. Bureau commissioner Oliver O. Howard eventually decided to use the Bureau's limited budget to distribute food to the poor and to provide education and legal help for freedpeople. One common food in the south at that time was salted meat. The Bureau also helped African American war veterans. Today the Department of Veterans' Affairs assists American war veterans.

After you read the passage, answer the following questions.

1. Which sentence in this passage is unverifiable and should be cut?

2. Find two sentences in this passage that are irrelevant to the discussion of the Freedmen's Bureau. What makes those sentences irrelevant?

3. Look at the last sentence of the passage. Do you think this sentence is essential to the discussion? Why or why not?

As you read Chapter 17, ask yourself what makes the information you are reading essential to a study of Reconstruction.

Key Terms and People

Chapter 17

Section 1
Reconstruction *(p. 552)*
Ten Percent Plan *(p. 553)*
Thirteenth Amendment *(p. 554)*
Freedmen's Bureau *(p. 556)*
Andrew Johnson *(p. 557)*

Section 2
Black Codes *(p. 558)*
Radical Republicans *(p. 559)*
Civil Rights Act of 1866 *(p. 560)*
Fourteenth Amendment *(p. 561)*
Reconstruction Acts *(p. 561)*
impeachment *(p. 562)*
Fifteenth Amendment *(p. 563)*

Section 3
Hiram Revels *(p. 565)*
Ku Klux Klan *(p. 566)*
Compromise of 1877 *(p. 567)*
poll tax *(p. 568)*
segregation *(p. 568)*
Jim Crow laws *(p. 568)*
Plessy v. *Ferguson* *(p. 569)*
sharecropping *(p. 569)*

Academic Vocabulary

Success in school is related to knowing academic vocabulary—the words that are frequently used in school assignments an discussions. In this chapter, you will learn the following academic words:

procedure *(p. 553)*
principle *(p. 560)*

Reading Social Studies

Key Terms and People

Introduce the key terms and people from this chapter by reviewing with the class each term and its description. Check to see that students understand the meaning of each term. Then have each student write three multiple-choice questions over terms or people from the list. Have students exchange questions with a partner and answer the questions. Have each pair review the correct answers together. **LS** **Verbal/Linguistic, Interpersonal**

Focus on Reading

See the **Focus on Reading** questions in this chapter for more practice on this reading social studies skill.

Reading Social Studies Assessment

See the **Chapter Review** at the end of this chapter for student assessment questions related to this reading skill.

Teaching Tip

Remind students that when there are quotes included in the text, it is important to read them and understand what the author is saying. Quotes may not necessarily include essential information; they may be reinforcing material that has already been discussed in the text. Sometimes, however, quotes by a well-known individual whose statements and beliefs were influential can be essential in analyzing historical information.

Answers

You Try It! 1. It may have been one of the most difficult jobs ever **2.** All 900 people could fit into one hotel ballroom today; One common food in the South at that time was salted meat; Today the Department of Veterans' Affairs assists American war veterans. *They do not pertain to the Freedmen's Bureau.*
3. *not essential; the paragraph is about the Freedmen's Bureau, not about current affairs*

Bellringer

If YOU were there . . . Use the **Daily Bellringer Transparency** to help students answer the question.

 Daily Bellringer Transparency, Section 1

Academic Vocabulary

Review with students the high-use academic term in this section.

procedure a series of steps taken to accomplish a task (p. 553)

CRF: Vocabulary Builder Activity, Section 1

Taking Notes

Have students copy the graphic organizer onto their own paper and then use it to take notes on the section. This activity will prepare students for the Section Assessment, in which they will complete a graphic organizer that builds on the information using a critical thinking skill.

SECTION 1

Rebuilding the South

What You Will Learn...

Main Ideas

1. President Lincoln and Congress differed in their views as Reconstruction began.
2. The end of the Civil War meant freedom for African Americans in the South.
3. President Johnson's plan began the process of Reconstruction.

The Big Idea

The nation faced many problems in rebuilding the Union.

Key Terms and People

Reconstruction, *p. 552*
Ten Percent Plan, *p. 553*
Thirteenth Amendment, *p. 554*
Freedmen's Bureau, *p. 556*
Andrew Johnson, *p. 557*

 TAKING NOTES As you read, take notes on the different ways the U.S. government attempted to reconstruct the south after the Civil War. Write your notes in a graphic organizer like the one below.

Rebuilding and Reconstruction
1.
2.
3.
4.
5.
6.
7.

If YOU were there...

You are a young soldier who has been fighting in the Civil War for many months. Now that the war is over, you are on your way home. During your journey, you pass plantation manor homes, houses, and barns that have been burned down. No one is doing spring planting in the fields. As you near your family's farm, you see that fences and sheds have been destroyed.

What would you think your future on the farm would be like?

BUILDING BACKGROUND When the Civil War ended, much of the South lay in ruins. Like the young soldier above, many people returned to destroyed homes and farms. Harvests of corn, cotton, rice, and other crops fell far below normal. Many farm animals had been killed or were roaming free. These were some of the challenges in restoring the nation.

Reconstruction Begins

After the Civil War ended in 1865, the U.S. government faced the problem of dealing with the defeated southern states. The nation dealt with the challenges of **Reconstruction**, the process of readmitting the former Confederate states to the Union. It lasted from 1865 to 1877.

Teach the Big Idea

At Level

Rebuilding the South

1. **Teach** Ask students the questions in the Main Idea boxes to teach this section.

2. **Apply** Have each student examine the main ideas for this section. Then have students create as many questions for each main idea as they can. For example, for the first main idea, students might ask why President Lincoln and Congress differed in their views about Reconstruction. **LS** **Verbal/Linguistic**

3. **Review** Have students review the section and provide answers for each of the questions they created.

4. **Practice/Homework** Have students use their questions and answers to write a one-page summary about the effect that rebuilding the South had on American society. **LS** **Verbal/Linguistic**

   Alternative Assessment Handbook, Rubric 1: Acquiring Information

Damaged South

Tired southern soldiers returned home to find that the world they had known before the war was gone. Cities, towns, and farms had been ruined. Because of high food prices and widespread crop failures, many southerners faced starvation. The Confederate money held by most southerners was now worthless. Banks failed, and merchants had gone bankrupt because people could not pay their debts.

Former Confederate general Braxton Bragg was one of many southerners who faced economic hardship. He found that "*all, all* was lost, except my debts." In South Carolina, Mary Boykin Chesnut wrote in her diary about the isolation she experienced after the war. "We are shut in here. . . . All RR's [railroads] destroyed—bridges gone. We are cut off from the world."

Lincoln's Plan

President Abraham Lincoln wanted to reunite the nation as quickly and painlessly as possible. He had proposed a plan for readmitting the southern states even before the war ended. Called the **Ten Percent Plan**, it offered southerners amnesty, or official pardon, for all illegal acts supporting the rebellion. To receive amnesty, southerners had to do two things. They had to swear an oath of loyalty to the United States. They also had to agree that slavery was illegal. Once 10 percent of voters in

a state made these pledges, they could form a new government. The state then could be readmitted to the Union.

Louisiana quickly elected a new state legislature under the Ten Percent Plan. Other southern states that had been occupied by Union troops soon followed Louisiana back into the United States.

Wade-Davis Bill

Some politicians argued that Congress, not the president, should control the southern states' return to the Union. They believed that Congress had the power to admit new states. Also, many Republican members of Congress thought the Ten Percent Plan did not go far enough. A senator from Michigan expressed their views.

" The people of the North are not such fools as to ... turn around and say to the traitors, 'all you have to do [to return] is ... take an oath that henceforth you will be true to the Government.' "
–Senator Jacob Howard, quoted in *Reconstruction: America's Unfinished Revolution, 1863–1877*, by Eric Foner

Two Republicans—Senator Benjamin Wade and Representative Henry Davis—had an alternative to Lincoln's plan. Under the **procedure** of the Wade-Davis bill, a state had to meet two conditions before it could rejoin the Union. First, it had to ban slavery. Second, a majority of adult males in the state had to take the loyalty oath.

ACADEMIC VOCABULARY

procedure
a series of steps taken to accomplish a task

War destroyed Richmond, Virginia, once the proud capital of the Confederacy.

RECONSTRUCTION **553**

Primary Source

Reading Like a Historian

Help students practice reading the documents like historians. Ask:

- Who placed the advertisement? Why? *Saml. [Samuel] Dove; looking for family members who were separated and sold to different slaveholders.*

- Why might the people on the boat be leaving Richmond? *possible answers—The city has been damaged in the war; African Americans are leaving the South now that they are free.*

Info to Know

Pocket Veto The U.S. Congress approved the Wade-Davis Bill just before adjourning in 1864. The end of the congressional session made it possible for President Lincoln to use a pocket veto to kill the measure. Usually, if a president does not sign a bill within 10 days while Congress is in session, the bill automatically becomes a law. However, if Congress is adjourned, a bill dies if the president does not sign it. A pocket veto cannot be overturned by a congressional vote.

Answers

Reading Check *Ten Percent Plan—Ten percent of all voters in Confederate states had to pledge loyalty to the Union and accept slavery as illegal; Wade-Davis Bill—A majority of voters in Confederate states had to pledge loyalty to the Union, and only southerners who had never supported the Confederacy could vote or hold office.*

554

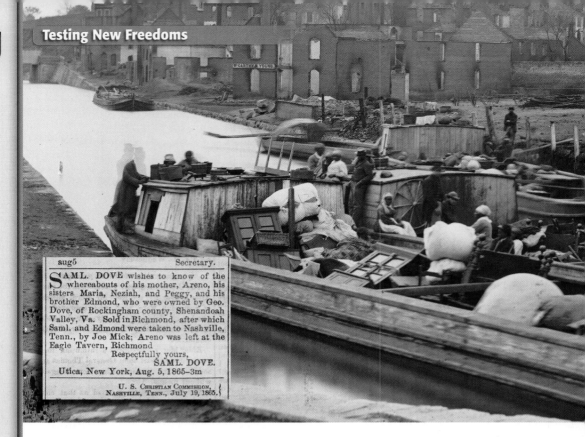

Testing New Freedoms

aug5   Secretary.

SAML. DOVE wishes to know of the whereabouts of his mother, Areno, his sisters Maria, Neziah, and Peggy, and his brother Edmond, who were owned by Geo. Dove, of Rockingham county, Shenandoah Valley, Va. Sold in Richmond, after which Saml. and Edmond were taken to Nashville, Tenn., by Joe Mick; Areno was left at the Eagle Tavern, Richmond
Respectfully yours,
SAML. DOVE.
Utica, New York, Aug. 5, 1865—3m

U. S. CHRISTIAN COMMISSION,
NASHVILLE, TENN., July 19, 1865.

Under the Wade-Davis bill, only southerners who swore that they had never supported the Confederacy could vote or hold office. In general, the bill was much stricter than the Ten Percent Plan. Its provisions would make it harder for southern states to rejoin the Union quickly.

President Lincoln therefore refused to sign the bill into law. He thought that few southern states would agree to meet its requirements. He believed that his plan would help restore order more quickly.

READING CHECK **Contrasting** How was the Ten Percent Plan different from the Wade-Davis Bill?

Freedom for African Americans

One thing Republicans agreed on was abolishing slavery. The Emancipation Proclamation had freed slaves only in areas that had not been occupied by Union forces, not in the border states. Many people feared that the federal courts might someday declare it unconstitutional.

Slavery Ends

On January 31, 1865, at President Lincoln's urging, Congress proposed the **Thirteenth Amendment**. This amendment made slavery illegal throughout the United States.

554 CHAPTER 17

Collaborative Learning   At Level

Congressional Committees

1. Review with students the Reconstruction plans of Congress and President Lincoln. Ask students why Congress might have opposed the Ten Percent Plan and what Lincoln disliked about the Wade-Davis Bill.

2. Organize students into small groups. Ask them to imagine that they are members of Congress in 1864. Have them work in committees to write a plan that they think Lincoln would have accepted for readmitting the states. Encourage students to consider

what rules they would set to ensure that ex-Confederates would support the Union and end slavery. Remind students to use standard grammar, spelling, sentence structure, and punctuation in their plans.

3. Ask groups to present their plans to the class. After all groups have presented their proposals, lead a class discussion of the pros and cons of each plan. **LS Interpersonal, Verbal/Linguistic**

📖 Alternative Assessment Handbook, Rubrics 14: Group Activity; and 24: Oral Presentations

The freedpeople at left have packed their household belongings and are leaving Richmond. Many people traveled in search of relatives. Others placed newspaper advertisements looking for long-lost relatives. For other freedpeople, like the couple above, freedom brought the right to marry.

In what ways did former slaves react to freedom?

The amendment was ratified and took effect on December 18, 1865. When abolitionist William Lloyd Garrison heard the news, he declared that his work was now finished. He called for the American Anti-Slavery Society to break up. Not all abolitionists agreed that their work was done, however. Frederick Douglass insisted that "slavery is not abolished until the black man has the ballot [vote]."

Freedom brought important changes to newly freed slaves. Many couples held ceremonies to legalize marriages that had not been recognized under slavery. Many freedpeople searched for relatives who had been sold away from their families years earlier. Others placed newspaper ads seeking information about their children. Many women began to work at home instead of in the fields. Still others adopted children of dead relatives to keep families together. Church members established voluntary associations and mutual-aid societies to help those in need.

Now that they could travel without a pass, many freedpeople moved from mostly white counties to places with more African Americans. Other freedpeople traveled simply to test their new freedom of movement. A South Carolina woman explained this need. "I must go, if I stay here I'll never know I'm free."

For most former slaves, freedom to travel was just the first step on a long road toward equal rights and new ways of life. Adults took new last names and began to insist on being called Mr. or Mrs. as a sign of respect, rather than by their first names or by nicknames. Freedpeople began to demand the same economic and political rights as white citizens. Henry Adams, a former slave, argued that "if I cannot do like a white man I am not free."

Forty Acres to Farm?

Many former slaves wanted their own land to farm. Near the end of the Civil War, Union general William Tecumseh Sherman had issued an order to break up plantations in coastal South Carolina and Georgia. He wanted to divide the land into 40-acre plots and give them to former slaves as compensation for their forced labor before the war.

Many white planters refused to surrender their land. Some freedpeople pointed out that it was only fair that they receive some of this land because their labor had made the plantations prosper. In the end, the U.S. government returned the land to its original owners. At this time, many freedpeople were unsure about where they would live, what kind of work they would do, and what rights they had. Many freedoms that were theirs by law were difficult to enforce.

RECONSTRUCTION **555**

555

Main Idea

❷ Freedom for African Americans

The end of the Civil War meant freedom for African Americans in the South.

Recall What were the goals of the Freedmen's Bureau? *to distribute food to poor people, provide education and legal help for freedpeople, and assist African American war veterans*

Describe Who taught at the schools for African Americans? *mostly women who were committed to helping freedpeople*

Make Inferences How did education for African Americans benefit both black and white southerners? *possible answers—created access to better education, provided more educated workers*

Linking to Today

Howard University Howard University was named for Oliver O. Howard, the head of the Freedmen's Bureau. The university opened in May 1867 in response to the move to provide more educational opportunities for freedpeople. The original goal of the school was "training for preachers and teachers." From the beginning, Howard University was open to men and women of all races. Today Howard University has expanded to include schools of law, dentistry, medicine, education, social work, business, and more.

Answers

Helping the Freedpeople *See the bulleted list above the question.*

Reading Check *It helped establish schools and several colleges in the South.*

556

Freedmen's Bureau

In 1865 Congress established the **Freedmen's Bureau**, an agency providing relief for freedpeople and certain poor people in the South. The Bureau had a difficult job. At its high point, about 900 agents served the entire South. Bureau commissioner Oliver O. Howard eventually decided to use the Bureau's limited budget to distribute food to the poor and to provide education and legal help for freedpeople. The Bureau also helped African American war veterans.

The Freedmen's Bureau played an important role in establishing more schools in the South. Laws against educating slaves meant that most freedpeople had never learned to read or write. Before the war ended, however, northern groups, such as the American Missionary Association, began providing books and teachers to African Americans. The teachers were mostly women who were committed to helping freedpeople. One teacher said of her students, "I never before saw children so eager to learn . . . It is wonderful how [they] . . . can have so great a desire for knowledge, and such a capacity for attaining [reaching] it."

After the war, some freedpeople organized their own education efforts. For example, Freedmen's Bureau agents found that some African Americans had opened schools in abandoned buildings. Many white southerners continued to believe that African Americans should not be educated. Despite opposition, by 1869 more than 150,000 African American students were attending more than 3,000 schools. The Freedmen's Bureau also helped establish several universities for African Americans, including Howard and Fisk universities.

Students quickly filled the new classrooms. Working adults attended classes in the evening. African Americans hoped that education would help them to understand and protect their rights and to enable them to find better jobs. Both black and white southerners benefited from the effort to provide greater access to education in the South.

READING CHECK Analyzing How did the Freedmen's Bureau help reform education in the South?

Helping the Freedpeople

Congress created the Freedmen's Bureau to help freedpeople and poor southerners recover from the Civil War. The Bureau assisted people by:

- providing supplies and medical services
- establishing schools
- supervising contracts between freedpeople and employers
- taking care of lands abandoned or captured during the war.

What role did the Freedmen's Bureau play during Reconstruction?

556 CHAPTER 17

Critical Thinking: Supporting a Point of View   At Level

Writing a Proposal

1. Review with students the goals and accomplishments of the Freedmen's Bureau. Then ask students to imagine that they are serving on a committee working to promote the contributions of the Freedmen's Bureau.

2. Organize students into pairs. Ask each pair to select some method of honoring and promoting the accomplishments of the Freedmen's Bureau. Examples might include a commemorative postage stamp, a statue or historical marker, or even a national holiday. Have students develop the specifics for their plans.

3. Have each pair of students write a proposal that explains why the Freedmen's Bureau deserves an honor and what the memorial would be like. Encourage students to create an image of the memorial, if applicable.

4. Have volunteers share their proposals with the class. **LS** **Interpersonal, Visual/Spatial**

📖 Alternative Assessment Handbook, Rubric 43: Writing to Persuade

President Johnson's Reconstruction Plan

While the Freedmen's Bureau was helping African Americans, the issue of how the South would politically rejoin the Union remained unresolved. Soon, however, a tragic event ended Lincoln's dream of peacefully reuniting the country.

A New President

On the evening of April 14, 1865, President Lincoln and his wife attended a play at Ford's Theater in Washington, D.C. During the play, John Wilkes Booth, a southerner who opposed Lincoln's policies, sneaked into the president's theater box and shot him. Lincoln was rushed to a boardinghouse across the street, where he died at about 7:30 the next morning. Vice President **Andrew Johnson** was sworn into office quickly. Reconstruction had now become his responsibility. He would have to win the trust of a nation shocked at their leader's death.

Johnson's plan for bringing southern states back into the Union was similar to Lincoln's plan. However, he decided that wealthy southerners and former Confederate officials would need a presidential pardon to receive amnesty. Johnson shocked Radical Republicans by eventually pardoning more than 7,000 people by 1866.

New State Governments

Johnson was a Democrat whom Republicans had put on the ticket in 1864 to appeal to the border states. A former slaveholder, he was a stubborn man who would soon face a hostile Congress.

Johnson offered a mild program for setting up new southern state governments. First, he appointed a temporary governor for each state. Then he required that the states revise their constitutions. Next, voters elected state and federal representatives. The new state government had to declare that secession was illegal. It also had to ratify the Thirteenth Amendment and refuse to pay Confederate debts.

By the end of 1865, all the southern states except Texas had created new governments. Johnson approved them all and declared that the United States was restored. Newly elected representatives came to Washington from each reconstructed southern state. However, Republicans complained that many new representatives had been leaders of the Confederacy. Congress therefore refused to readmit the southern states into the Union. Clearly, the nation was still divided.

READING CHECK **Summarizing** What was President Johnson's plan for Reconstruction?

SUMMARY AND PREVIEW In this section you learned about early plans for Reconstruction. In the next section, you will learn that disagreements about Reconstruction became so serious that the president was almost removed from office.

go.hrw.com
Online Quiz
KEYWORD: SR8 HP17

Section 1 Assessment

Reviewing Ideas, Terms, and People

1. **a. Identify** What does **Reconstruction** mean?
   b. Summarize What was President Lincoln's plan for Reconstruction?
2. **a. Recall** What is the **Thirteenth Amendment**?
   b. Elaborate In your opinion, what was the most important accomplishment of the **Freedmen's Bureau**? Explain.
3. **a. Recall** Why was President Lincoln killed?
   b. Analyze Why did some Americans oppose President Johnson's Reconstruction plan?

Critical Thinking

4. **Summarizing** Review your notes on Reconstruction. Then copy the graphic organizer below and use it to show how African Americans were affected by the end of the war and Reconstruction. Add lines to the diagram as necessary.

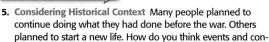

African Americans and Reconstruction — Marriages are legalized.

FOCUS ON WRITING

5. **Considering Historical Context** Many people planned to continue doing what they had done before the war. Others planned to start a new life. How do you think events and conditions you just read about might have affected their plans?

RECONSTRUCTION **557**

Main Idea

❸ **President Johnson's Reconstruction Plan**

President Johnson's plan began the process of Reconstruction.

Explain After President Johnson approved the new governments of the southern states, Republicans complained. Why? *complained that many of the new southern representatives had been Confederate leaders and that Johnson's plan was too lenient on the South*

📖 **CRF:** Biography Activity: Andrew Johnson

• **Review & Assess** •

Close

Have students write a short paragraph that summarizes the section.

Review

📄 Online Quiz, Section 1

Assess

SE Section 1 Assessment

📄 PASS: Section 1 Quiz

📄 Alternative Assessment Handbook

Reteach/Classroom Intervention

📄 Interactive Reader and Study Guide, Section 1

💿 Interactive Skills Tutor CD-ROM

Section 1 Assessment Answers

1. **a.** the process of reuniting and rebuilding the nation after the Civil War
   b. offer amnesty if people swore loyalty to the U.S. and agreed that slavery was illegal; a state could be readmitted once 10 percent of the state's voters had done this

2. **a.** a constitutional amendment that made slavery illegal in the United States
   b. possible answer—creating more educational opportunities in the South; creating a better educated workforce

3. **a.** Booth opposed Lincoln's policies.
   b. New representatives from the South had been Confederate leaders.

4. family members could search for each other; women worked in the home; families could stay together; traveled; took new names; began demanding same rights as white people

5. Aftermath of war made it impossible for some to resume former life; others gained new opportunities.

Answers

Reading Check *Johnson wanted southern states to revise their constitutions, elect new representatives, declare secession illegal, and ratify the Thirteenth Amendment.*

557

The Fight over Reconstruction

Preteach

Bellringer

If YOU were there . . . Use the **Daily Bellringer Transparency** to help students answer the question.

🖨 Daily Bellringer Transparency, Section 2

Academic Vocabulary

Review with students the high-use academic term in this section.

principle basic belief, rule, or law (p. 560)

Building Vocabulary

Preteach or review the following term:

moderate one who holds views that are not extreme or excessive (p. 559)

🖨 **CRF:** Vocabulary Builder Activity, Section 2

Taking Notes

Have students copy the graphic organizer onto their own paper and then use it to take notes on the section. This activity will prepare students for the Section Assessment, in which they will complete a graphic organizer that builds on the information using a critical thinking skill.

What You Will Learn...

Main Ideas

1. Black Codes led to opposition to President Johnson's plan for Reconstruction.
2. The Fourteenth Amendment ensured citizenship for African Americans.
3. Radical Republicans in Congress took charge of Reconstruction.
4. The Fifteenth Amendment gave African Americans the right to vote.

The Big Idea

The return to power of the pre-war southern leadership led Republicans in Congress to take control of Reconstruction.

Key Terms and People

Black Codes, *p. 558*
Radical Republicans, *p. 559*
Civil Rights Act of 1866, *p. 560*
Fourteenth Amendment, *p. 561*
Reconstruction Acts, *p. 561*
impeachment, *p. 562*
Fifteenth Amendment, *p. 563*

 TAKING NOTES As you read, take notes on the issues that led Republicans in Congress to take over Reconstruction and the steps they took to change Reconstruction policies. Write your notes in a graphic organizer like the one below.

Issues that Concerned Republicans	Changes by the Republican Congress

If YOU were there...

A member of Congress, you belong to the same political party as the president. But you strongly disagree with his ideas about Reconstruction and civil rights for African Americans. Now some of the president's opponents are trying to remove him from office. You do not think he is a good president. On the other hand, you think removing him would be bad for the unity of the country.

Will you vote to remove the president?

BUILDING BACKGROUND Americans were bitterly divided about what should happen in the South during Reconstruction. They disagreed about ending racial inequality and guaranteeing civil rights for African Americans. These conflicts split political parties. They led to showdowns between Congress and the president. Political fights even threatened the president's job.

Opposition to President Johnson

In 1866 Congress continued to debate the rules for restoring the Union. Meanwhile, new state legislatures approved by President Johnson had already begun passing laws to deny African Americans' civil rights. "This is a white man's government, and intended for white men only," declared Governor Benjamin F. Perry of South Carolina.

Black Codes

Soon, every southern state passed **Black Codes**, or laws that greatly limited the freedom of African Americans. They required African Americans to sign work contracts, creating working conditions similar to those under slavery. In most southern states, any African Americans who could not prove they were employed could be arrested. Their punishment might be one year of work without pay. African Americans were also prevented from owning guns. In addition, they were not allowed to rent property except in cities.

The Black Codes alarmed many Americans. As one Civil War veteran asked, "If you call this freedom, what do you call slavery?"

Teach the Big Idea

At Level

The Fight over Reconstruction

1. **Teach** Ask students the questions in the Main Idea boxes to teach this section.

2. **Apply** Draw a four-column chart for students to see. Label the columns *Opposition to President Johnson, Fourteenth Amendment, Congress Takes Control,* and *Fifteenth Amendment.* Have each student make a copy of the chart and complete it by listing the section's main ideas and events in the appropriate column. **LS Verbal/Linguistic**

3. **Review** To review the section's main ideas, have students help you complete the master copy of the chart.

4. **Practice/Homework** For each column in the chart, have students write one to three sentences summarizing the information they identified. **LS Verbal/Linguistic**

🖨 Alternative Assessment Handbook, Rubric 7: Charts

African Americans organized to oppose the codes. One group sent a petition to officials in South Carolina.

" We simply ask ... that the same laws which govern *white men* shall govern *black men* ... that, in short, we be dealt with as others are—in equity [equality] and justice. "

—Petition from an African American convention held in South Carolina, quoted in *There is a River: The Black Struggle for Freedom in America* by Vincent Harding

Radical Republicans

The Black Codes angered many Republicans who felt the South was returning to its old ways. Most Republicans were moderates who wanted the South to have loyal state governments. They also believed that African Americans should have rights as citizens. They hoped that the national government would not have to force the South to follow federal laws.

Radical Republicans on the other hand, took a harsher stance. They wanted the federal government to force change in the South. Like the moderates, they thought the Black Codes were cruel and unjust. The radicals, however, wanted the federal government to be much more involved in Reconstruction. They feared that too many southern leaders remained loyal to the former Confederacy and would not enforce the new laws. Thaddeus Stevens

POLITICAL CARTOON
Supporting Radical Republican Ideas

Republicans were outraged to see former Confederates return to power as leaders of the Democratic Party. This 1868 political cartoon shows former Confederates Raphael Semmes and Nathan Bedford Forrest. Semmes was a Confederate admiral who had captured 62 Union merchant ships during the Civil War. Forrest was a cavalry officer known for brutality who later founded the Ku Klux Klan.

How do the actions of the people in these illustrations support the artist's point of view?

How do events in the background of these illustrations support the artist's point of view?

ANALYSIS SKILL **ANALYZING PRIMARY SOURCES**

Why do you think that the men are shown in their Confederate uniforms?

RECONSTRUCTION **559**

559

560

Direct Teach

Main Idea

② Fourteenth Amendment

The Fourteenth Amendment ensured citizenship for African Americans.

Recall What was the purpose of the proposed Freedmen's Bureau Bill, and why did Johnson veto it? *It was supposed to give the Freedmen's Bureau more powers; he did not want Congress to pass any laws until southern states were represented.*

Explain Why was the Civil Rights Act of 1866 created? *When Johnson vetoed the Freedmen's Bureau Bill, Congress countered by passing the Civil Rights Act of 1866.*

Generalize What rights did the Fourteenth Amendment protect? *defined citizens and guaranteed citizens equal protection*

📄 **CRF:** Biography Activity: Thaddeus Stevens

📦 Map Transparency: Reconstruction Military Districts

go.hrw.com
Online Resources

KEYWORD: SR8 US17
ACTIVITY: Writing Editorials for a Newspaper

Answers

Identifying Points of View *Johnson felt that the military government would cause the South to resent the federal government, but Stevens believed that the federal government should control the South.*

Reading Check *similar—Both wanted loyalty to the Union and rights for African Americans; different—Moderates wanted little federal involvement, but radicals wanted more rights for African Americans and more federal involvement.*

Primary Source

POINTS OF VIEW
Johnson vs. Stevens

President Andrew Johnson argued that the South should not be placed under military control.

❝Military governments . . . established for an indefinite period, would have divided the people into the vanquishers and the vanquished, and would have envenomed [made poisonous] hatred rather than have restored affection.❞

—**Andrew Johnson**

Thaddeus Stevens believed that Congress had the power to treat the South as conquered territory.

❝The future condition of the conquered power depends on the will of the conqueror. They must come in as new states or remain as conquered provinces. Congress . . . is the only power that can act in the matter.❞

—**Thaddeus Stevens**

ANALYSIS SKILL IDENTIFYING POINTS OF VIEW

How did Johnson's and Stevens's views on the South differ?

---

of Pennsylvania and Charles Sumner of Massachusetts were the leaders of the Radical Republicans.

A harsh critic of President Johnson, Stevens was known for his honesty and sharp tongue. He wanted economic and political justice for both African Americans and poor white southerners. Sumner had been a strong opponent of slavery before the Civil War. He continued to argue tirelessly for African Americans' civil rights, including the right to vote and the right to fair laws.

Both Stevens and Sumner believed that President Johnson's Reconstruction plan was a failure. Although the Radicals did not control Congress, they began to gain support among moderates when President Johnson ignored criticism of the Black Codes. Stevens believed the federal government could not allow racial inequality to survive.

ACADEMIC VOCABULARY
principle basic belief, rule, or law

READING CHECK Comparing and Contrasting How were Radical Republicans and moderate Republicans similar and different?

Fourteenth Amendment

Urged on by the Radicals in 1866, Congress proposed a new bill. It would give the Freedmen's Bureau more powers. The law would allow the Freedmen's Bureau to use military courts to try people accused of violating African Americans' rights. The bill's supporters hoped that these courts would be fairer than local courts in the South.

Johnson versus Congress

To the surprise of many in Congress, Johnson vetoed the Freedmen's Bureau Bill. He insisted that Congress could not pass any new laws until the southern states were represented in Congress. Johnson also argued that the Freedmen's Bureau was unconstitutional.

Republicans responded with the **Civil Rights Act of 1866**. This act provided African Americans with the same legal rights as white Americans. President Johnson once again used his veto power. He argued that the act gave too much power to the federal government. He also rejected the **principle** of equal

560 CHAPTER 17

Collaborative Learning

At Level

Breaking News on the Fourteenth Amendment

Research Required

1. Organize students into groups. Students will research, write, and enact a newscast featuring the lead story of the day, "Fourteenth Amendment Is Ratified." Have students use the library, Internet, or other resources to gather information.

2. Have each group create a news skit summarizing events leading up to the ratification of the amendment. Remind groups to provide information regarding the provisions of the Fourteenth Amendment as well as voting

information from Congress and from some of the states.

3. Encourage students to act out dialogue between anchors or have students cut to a reporter standing by "on the scene."

4. Have each group perform its broadcast.
   LS Interpersonal, Verbal/Linguistic

📄 Alternative Assessment Handbook, Rubrics 14: Group Activity; and 33: Skits and Reader's Theater rights for African Americans. Congress, however, overrode Johnson's veto.

Many Republicans worried about what would happen when the southern states were readmitted. Fearing that the Civil Rights Act might be overturned, the Republicans proposed the **Fourteenth Amendment** in the summer of 1866. The Fourteenth Amendment included the following provisions.

1. It defined all people born or naturalized within the United States, except Native Americans, as citizens.
2. It guaranteed citizens the equal protection of the laws.
3. It said that states could not "deprive any person of life, liberty, or property, without due process of law."
4. It banned many former Confederate officials from holding state or federal offices.
5. It made state laws subject to federal court review.
6. It gave Congress the power to pass any laws needed to enforce it.

1866 Elections

President Johnson and most Democrats opposed the Fourteenth Amendment. As a result, civil rights for African Americans became a key issue in the 1866 congressional elections. To help the Democrats, Johnson traveled around the country defending his Reconstruction plan. Johnson's speaking tour was a disaster. It did little to win votes for the Democratic Party. Johnson even got into arguments with people in the audiences of some of his speaking engagements.

Two major riots in the South also hurt Johnson's campaign. On May 1, 1866, a dispute in Memphis, Tennessee, took place between local police and black Union soldiers. The dispute turned into a three-day wave of violence against African Americans. About three months later, another riot took place during a political demonstration in New Orleans. During that dispute, 34 African Americans and three white Republicans were killed.

READING CHECK **Summarizing** What issue did the Fourteenth Amendment address, and how did it affect the congressional elections of 1866?

Congress Takes Control of Reconstruction

The 1866 elections gave the Republican Party a commanding two-thirds majority in both the House and the Senate. This majority gave the Republicans the power to override any presidential veto. In addition, the Republicans became united as the moderates joined with the Radicals. Together, they called for a new form of Reconstruction.

Reconstruction Acts

In March 1867, Congress passed the first of several **Reconstruction Acts**. These laws divided the South into five districts. A U.S. military commander controlled each district. The

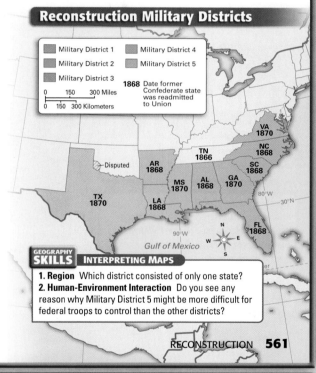

Reconstruction Military Districts

- Military District 1
- Military District 2
- Military District 3
- Military District 4
- Military District 5

0   150   300 Miles
0   150   300 Kilometers

1868 Date former Confederate state was readmitted to Union

VA 1870
TN 1866
NC 1868
SC 1868
AR 1868
AL 1868
GA 1870
MS 1870
TX 1870
LA 1868
FL 1868

Disputed

Gulf of Mexico

GEOGRAPHY SKILLS **INTERPRETING MAPS**

1. **Region** Which district consisted of only one state?
2. **Human-Environment Interaction** Do you see any reason why Military District 5 might be more difficult for federal troops to control than the other districts?

RECONSTRUCTION **561**

Answers

Interpreting Maps 1. *District 1, Virginia;* **2.** *larger, farther away from Washington, D.C.*

Reading Check *equal protection under the law for all citizens; led to civil rights becoming the key issue in the 1866 elections and to violence over the dispute*

561

❸ Congress Takes Control of Reconstruction

Radical Republicans in Congress took charge of Reconstruction.

Describe How were states to be readmitted under the Reconstruction Acts? *States had to write a new constitution supporting the Fourteenth Amendment and give African American men the right to vote.*

Identify Cause and Effect What led Congress to call for the impeachment of President Johnson, and what was the result of the impeachment trial? *Johnson removed a cabinet official, which Congress had to approve; Johnson was not convicted.*

Recall Who won the election of 1868? *Ulysses S. Grant*

📑 **CRF:** History and Geography Activity: The Reconstruction Acts

📖 Quick Facts Transparency: The Reconstruction Amendments

MISCONCEPTION ///ALERT\\\

Impeachment People often misunderstand the meaning of the word *impeachment*. The term does not mean "removal from office." It means only that a public official has been charged with improper conduct of some sort.

Did you know . . .

In the history of the United States, two presidents have faced impeachment proceedings—Andrew Johnson in 1868 and Bill Clinton in 1998. Both presidents were acquitted of the charges.

Answers

The Reconstruction Amendments
the right of African American men to vote

---

military would remain in control of the South until the southern states rejoined the Union. To be readmitted, a state had to write a new state constitution supporting the Fourteenth Amendment. Finally, the state had to give African American men the right to vote.

Thaddeus Stevens was one of the new Reconstruction Acts' most enthusiastic supporters. He spoke in Congress to defend the acts.

❝Have not loyal blacks quite as good a right to choose rulers and make laws as rebel whites? Every man, no matter what his race or color . . .

has an equal right to justice, honesty, and fair play with every other man; and the law should secure him those rights.❞

–Thaddeus Stevens, quoted in *Sources of the American Republic*, edited by Marvin Meyers et al.

The Reconstruction Amendments QUICK FACTS

Thirteenth Amendment (1865)
Banned slavery throughout the United States

Fourteenth Amendment (1868)
Overturned the *Dred Scott* case by granting citizenship to all people born in the United States (except for Native Americans)

Fifteenth Amendment (1870)
Gave African American men the right to vote

This Reconstruction-era painting shows African Americans voting after passage of the Fifteenth Amendment.

What right did the Fifteenth Amendment protect?

President on Trial

President Johnson strongly disagreed with Stevens. He argued that African Americans did not deserve the same treatment as white people. The Reconstruction Acts, he said, used "powers not granted to the federal government or any one of its branches." Knowing that Johnson did not support its Reconstruction policies, Congress passed a law limiting his power. This law prevented the president from removing cabinet officials without Senate approval. Johnson quickly broke the law by firing Edwin Stanton, the secretary of war.

For the first time in United States history, the House of Representatives responded by voting to impeach the president. **Impeachment** is the process used by a legislative body to bring charges of wrongdoing against a public official. The next step, under Article I of the Constitution, was a trial in the Senate. A two-thirds majority was required to find Johnson guilty and remove him from office.

Although Johnson was unpopular with Republicans, some of them believed he was being judged unfairly. Others did not trust the president pro tempore of the Senate, Benjamin Wade. He would become president if Johnson were removed from office. By a single vote, Senate Republicans failed to convict Johnson. Even so, the trial broke his power as president.

Election of 1868

Johnson did not run for another term in 1868. Instead, the Demo-

---

Collaborative Learning

Above Level

Conducting an Impeachment Trial

1. As a class, conduct a mock impeachment trial for President Andrew Johnson.

2. Organize the class into four groups. Assign one group to act as impeachment managers for the House of Representatives and to present the case against the president. Have the second group prepare a defense of the president. Assign a third group to prepare and ask questions of witnesses. The fourth group will listen to testimony and vote on the charges presented.

3. Have each group use the library, Internet, or other resources to gather information about the impeachment proceedings against Andrew Johnson. Then have the class stage the mock trial.

4. After the trial, discuss with students what happened during each aspect of the actual case and how it affected Reconstruction.

🗝 **Interpersonal, Verbal/Linguistic**

📋 Alternative Assessment Handbook, Rubric 10: Debates

crats chose former New York governor Horatio Seymour as their presidential candidate. The Republicans chose Ulysses S. Grant. As a war hero, Grant appealed to many northern voters. He had no political experience but supported the congressional Reconstruction plan. He ran under the slogan "Let Us Have Peace."

Shortly after Grant was nominated, Congress readmitted seven southern states—Alabama, Arkansas, Florida, Georgia, Louisiana, North Carolina, and South Carolina. (Tennessee had already been readmitted in 1866.) Under the terms of readmission, these seven states approved the Fourteenth Amendment. They also agreed to let African American men vote. However, white southerners used violence to try to keep African Americans away from the polls.

Despite such tactics, hundreds of thousands of African Americans voted for Grant and the "party of Lincoln." The *New Orleans Tribune* reported that many former slaves "see clearly enough that the Republican party [is] their political life boat." African American votes helped Grant to win a narrow victory.

READING CHECK **Analyzing** To what voters did Grant appeal in the presidential election of 1868?

Fifteenth Amendment

After Grant's victory, Congressional Republicans wanted to protect their Reconstruction plan. They worried that the southern states might try to keep black voters from the polls in future elections. Also, some Radical Republicans argued that it was not fair that many northern states still had laws preventing African Americans from voting. After all, every southern state was required to grant suffrage to African American men.

In 1869 Congress proposed the **Fifteenth Amendment**, which gave African American men the right to vote. Abolitionist William Lloyd Garrison praised "this wonderful, quiet, sudden transformation of four millions of human beings from . . . the auction block to the ballot-box." The amendment went into effect in

1870. It was one of the last important Reconstruction laws passed at the federal level.

The Fifteenth Amendment did not please every reformer, however. Many women were angry because the amendment did not also grant them the right to vote.

READING CHECK **Finding Main Ideas** How did Radical Republicans take control of Reconstruction?

SUMMARY AND PREVIEW In this section you learned that Congress took control of Reconstruction away from President Johnson and took steps to protect the rights of African Americans. In the next section you will learn about increasing opposition to Reconstruction.

go.hrw.com
Online Quiz
KEYWORD: SR8 HP17

Section 2 Assessment

Reviewing Ideas, Terms, and People
1. **a. Describe** What were **Black Codes**?
   b. Make Inferences Why did Republicans think Johnson's Reconstruction plan was a failure?
2. **a. Recall** What was the **Civil Rights Act of 1866**?
   b. Summarize Why was the **Fourteenth Amendment** important?
3. **a. Recall** Why was President Johnson impeached?
   b. Evaluate Which element of the **Reconstruction Acts** do you believe was most important? Why?
4. **a. Recall** What does the **Fifteenth Amendment** state?
   b. Elaborate Do you think that women should have been included in the Fifteenth Amendment? Explain.

Critical Thinking
5. **Identify** Review your notes on the issues that led Republicans to take over Reconstruction. Then copy the graphic organizer below and use it to identify the main provisions of the Fourteenth Amendment and their effects.

Provisions	Effects

FOCUS ON WRITING
6. **Recognizing Cause-and-Effect Relationships** As you have read in this section, social and political unrest continued long after the war ended. How could this unrest cause people to leave their jobs? What new jobs might they find?

RECONSTRUCTION **563**

THE IMPACT
TODAY
Today the Voting Rights Act of 1965 enforces and expands the voting protections of the Fifteenth Amendment.

Direct Teach

Main Idea

➍ Fifteenth Amendment

The Fifteenth Amendment gave African Americans the right to vote.

Identify When did the Fifteenth Amendment go into effect? *1870*

Make Predictions What effect might the Fifteenth Amendment have on women in the United States? *possible answers—They might be angry that they did not gain the right to vote; they might demand voting rights.*

Activity **Illustrated Amendments** Have students create a drawing for each of the three Reconstruction amendments. **LS** **Visual/Spatial**

Review & Assess

Close
Discuss with the class how Congress changed Reconstruction.

Review
Online Quiz, Section 2

Assess
SE Section 2 Assessment
PASS: Section 2 Quiz
Alternative Assessment Handbook

Reteach/Classroom Intervention
Interactive Reader and Study Guide, Section 2
Interactive Skills Tutor CD-ROM

Section 2 Assessment Answers

1. **a.** laws that limited rights and opportunities for African Americans
   b. It allowed Black Codes and returned Confederate leaders to power.
2. **a.** It provided African Americans the same rights as white Americans.
   b. See the numbered list on p. 561.
3. **a.** He removed a cabinet official without the approval of Congress.
   b. possible answer—giving African Americans the right to vote; because that allowed them a say in government

4. **a.** It gave African American citizens the right to vote in all states.
   b. Answers will vary, but students should provide a rationale for their answers.
5. Provisions—see list on p. 561; effects—former slaves granted citizenship, protected from restrictions of Black Codes, removed Confederate leaders from power in the South, and gave Congress more control over enforcing these laws.
6. possible answer—Riots might cause people to flee jobs in the South.

Answers

Reading Check (left) *northern voters and African Americans;* **(right)** *The 1866 elections gave them a majority in both houses of Congress; they overrode presidential vetoes and took power from Johnson.*

563

Bellringer

If YOU were there . . . Use the **Daily Bellringer Transparency** to help students answer the question.

📖 Daily Bellringer Transparency, Section 3

Building Vocabulary

Preteach or review the following term:

carpetbaggers northerners who moved to the South during Reconstruction (p. 564)

📖 **CRF:** Vocabulary Builder Activity, Section 3

Taking Notes

Have students copy the graphic organizer onto their own paper and then use it to take notes on the section. This activity will prepare students for the Section Assessment, in which they will complete a graphic organizer that builds on the information using a critical thinking skill.

Reconstruction in the South

What You Will Learn...

Main Ideas

1. Reconstruction governments helped reform the South.
2. The Ku Klux Klan was organized as African Americans moved into positions of power.
3. As Reconstruction ended, the rights of African Americans were restricted.
4. Southern business leaders relied on industry to rebuild the South.

The Big Idea

As Reconstruction ended, African Americans faced new hurdles and the South attempted to rebuild.

Key Terms and People

Hiram Revels, *p. 565*
Ku Klux Klan, *p. 566*
Compromise of 1877, *p. 567*
poll tax, *p. 568*
segregation, *p. 568*
Jim Crow laws, *p. 568*
Plessy v. *Ferguson, p. 569*
sharecropping, *p. 569*

 TAKING NOTES As you read, look for information related to the South's efforts to rebuild and the effects on African Americans.

Rebuilding the South → Effects on African Americans

If YOU were there...

You live on a farm in the South in the 1870s. Times are hard because you do not own your farm. Instead, you and your family work in a landowner's cotton fields. You never seem to earn enough to buy land of your own. Some of your neighbors have decided to give up farming and move to the city. Others are going to work in the textile mills. But you have always been a farmer.

Will you decide to change your way of life?

BUILDING BACKGROUND Reconstruction affected politics and economics in the South. Republican and Democratic politicians fought over policies and programs. New state governments began reforms, but later leaders ended many of them. Some parts of the southern economy improved. However, many farmers, like the family above, went through hard times.

Reconstruction Governments

After Grant became president in 1869, the Republicans seemed stronger than ever. They controlled most southern governments, partly because of the support of African American voters. However, most of the Republican officeholders were unpopular with white southerners.

Carpetbaggers and Scalawags

Some of these office-holders were northern-born Republicans who had moved South after the war. Many white southerners called them carpetbaggers. Supposedly, they had rushed South carrying all their possessions in bags made from carpeting. Many southerners resented these northerners, accusing them—often unfairly—of trying to profit from Reconstruction.

Southern Democrats cared even less for white southern Republicans. They referred to them as scalawags, or greedy rascals. Democrats believed that these southerners had betrayed the South by

---

Teach the Big Idea

Reconstruction in the South

1. **Teach** Ask students the questions in the Main Idea boxes to teach this section.

2. **Apply** Help students list the main people, events, and issues in the section. Then ask students to imagine that they are news reporters. Have each student write one news headline for each of the section's main events and issues. Model the activity for students by doing the first headline as a class. **LS Verbal/Linguistic**

3. **Review** As you review the section's main ideas, have students share their related headlines with the class.

4. **Practice/Homework** Select one headline and have each student write a news article or draw a political cartoon to accompany the headline. **LS Verbal/Linguistic, Visual/Spatial**

📖 Alternative Assessment Handbook, Rubrics 27: Political Cartoons; and 42: Writing to Inform

African American Representation in the South, 1870

Hiram Revels was the son of former slaves and helped organize African American regiments in the Civil War. Revels was selected to fill the U.S. Senate seat formerly held by Jefferson Davis, president of the Confederacy.

Blanche K. Bruce escaped from slavery and began a school for African Americans before the Civil War. Bruce was the first African American elected to a full six-year term in the U.S. Senate.

● Member of U.S. Congress
○ State legislator

0   150   300 Miles
0   150   300 Kilometers

Washington, DC
VA
TN
NC
AR
SC
TX
AL
MS
GA
LA
ATLANTIC OCEAN
FL
Gulf of Mexico

GEOGRAPHY SKILLS **INTERPRETING MAPS**

1. **Location** Which state had the most African American state legislators?
2. **Region** Which southern states had the fewest African American representatives?

voting for the Republican Party. Many southern Republicans were small farmers who had supported the Union during the war. Others, like Mississippi governor James Alcorn, were former members of the Whig Party. They preferred to become Republicans rather than join the Democrats.

African American Leaders

African Americans were the largest group of southern Republican voters. During Reconstruction, more than 600 African Americans won election to state legislatures. Some 16 of these politicians were elected to Congress. Other African Americans held local offices in counties throughout the South.

African American politicians came from many backgrounds. **Hiram Revels** was born free in North Carolina and went to college in Illinois. He became a Methodist minister and served as a chaplain in the Union army. In 1870 Revels became the first African American in the U.S. Senate. He took over the seat previously held by Confederate president

Jefferson Davis. Unlike Revels, Blanche K. Bruce grew up in slavery in Virginia. Bruce became an important Republican in Mississippi and served one term as a U.S. senator.

State Governments Change Direction

Reconstruction governments provided money for many new programs and organizations in the South. They helped to establish some of the first state-funded public school systems in the South. They also built new hospitals, prisons, and orphanages and passed laws prohibiting discrimination against African Americans.

Southern states under Republican control spent large amounts of money. They aided the construction of railroads, bridges, and public buildings. These improvements were intended to help the southern economy recover from the war. To get the money for these projects, the Reconstruction governments raised taxes and issued bonds.

FOCUS ON READING

How does the heading of this section tell you about what you will learn?

READING CHECK **Summarizing** What reforms did Reconstruction state governments carry out?

RECONSTRUCTION **565**

Main Idea

❷ Ku Klux Klan

The Ku Klux Klan was organized as African Americans moved into positions of power.

Explain Why did resistance to Reconstruction increase? *Some southerners claimed the new governments were corrupt, illegal, and unjust; disapproved of African American officeholders; and disliked having federal troops in their states.*

Summarize How did the federal government address the activities of the Ku Klux Klan? *Congress passed laws that made it a federal crime to interfere with elections or to deny citizens equal protection under the law.*

📄 **CRF:** Primary Source Activity: Reconstruction and the Ku Klux Klan

Info to Know

Stopping the Klan As violence against African Americans mounted, many Americans demanded that the government take action. Congress responded to this call in 1870 and 1871 by passing legislation designed to stop violence and discrimination against African Americans. Known as the Enforcement Acts, these laws were designed to enforce the Fifteenth Amendment and to stop the Ku Klux Klan. The Enforcement Acts authorized President Grant to send federal troops to restore order. In 1871 nine counties in South Carolina were placed under martial law after an outbreak of Klan violence. Due to the Enforcement Acts, hundreds of Klan members were tried and imprisoned, leading to the Klan's decline.

Answers

The Ku Klux Klan *because their actions were illegal*

Reading Check *They were unhappy with changes introduced by Reconstruction governments.*

Ku Klux Klan

As more African Americans took office, resistance to Reconstruction increased among white southerners. Democrats claimed that the Reconstruction governments were corrupt, illegal, and unjust. They also disliked having federal soldiers stationed in their states. Many white southerners disapproved of African American officeholders. One Democrat noted, "'A white man's government' [is] the most popular rallying cry we have." In 1866 a group of white southerners in Tennessee created the **Ku Klux Klan**. This secret society opposed civil rights, particularly suffrage, for African Americans. The Klan used violence and terror against African Americans. The group's membership grew rapidly as it spread throughout the South.

Klan members wore robes and disguises to hide their identities. They attacked—and even murdered—African Americans, white Republican voters, and public officials, usually at night.

Local governments did little to stop the violence. Many officials feared the Klan or were sympathetic to its activities. In 1870 and 1871 the federal government took action. Congress passed laws that made it a federal crime to interfere with elections or to deny citizens equal protection under the law.

Within a few years, the Klan was no longer an organized threat. But groups of whites continued to assault African Americans and Republicans throughout the 1870s.

READING CHECK **Drawing Conclusions** Why did southerners join the Ku Klux Klan?

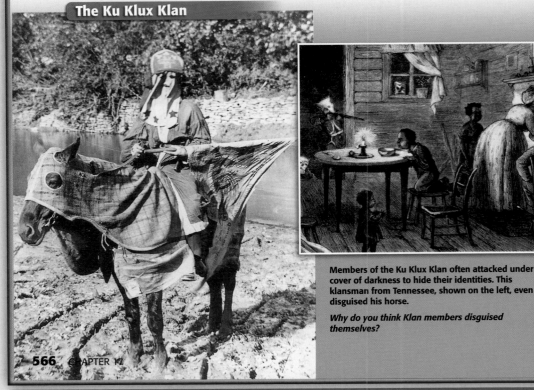

The Ku Klux Klan

Members of the Ku Klux Klan often attacked under cover of darkness to hide their identities. This klansman from Tennessee, shown on the left, even disguised his horse.

Why do you think Klan members disguised themselves?

566 CHAPTER 17

Critical Thinking: Identifying Cause and Effect   Below Level

Cause-and-Effect Graphic Organizer

1. Discuss with students the details of the rise of the Ku Klux Klan and the effects the Klan had on the South during Reconstruction.

2. To help students understand the causes and effects of the rise of the Ku Klux Klan, draw the graphic organizer for students to see. Omit the blue, italicized answers.

3. Have students copy the graphic organizer and complete it by identifying the causes and effects of the rise of the Klan.

LS Verbal/Linguistic, Visual/Spatial

Rise of the Ku Klux Klan	
Causes	**Effects**
• *opposition to African American leaders* • *unhappy with federal troops in South* • *dislike of Reconstruction governments*	• *violence against African Americans and white Republicans* • *Local leaders do little to stop them.* • *Federal government stops them.*

Reconstruction Ends

The violence of the Ku Klux Klan was not the only challenge to Reconstruction. Republicans slowly lost control of southern state governments to the Democratic Party. The General Amnesty Act of 1872 allowed former Confederates, except those who had held high ranks, to serve in public office. Many of these former Confederates, most of whom were Democrats, were soon elected to southern governments.

The Republican Party also began losing its power in the North. Although President Grant was re-elected in 1872, financial and political scandals in his administration upset voters. In his first term, a gold-buying scheme in which Grant's cousin took a leading role led to a brief crisis on the stock market called Black Friday. During his second term, his personal secretary was involved in the Whiskey Ring scandal, in which whiskey distillers and public officials worked together to steal liquor taxes from the federal government. Furthermore, people blamed Republican policies for the Panic of 1873.

Panic of 1873

This severe economic downturn began in September 1873 when Jay Cooke and Company, a major investor in railroads and the largest financier of the Union's Civil War effort, declared bankruptcy. The company had lied about the value of land along the side of the Northern Pacific Railroad that it owned and was trying to sell. When the truth leaked out, the company failed.

The failure of such an important business sent panic through the stock market, and investors began selling shares of stock more rapidly than people wanted to buy them. Companies had to buy their shares back from the investors. Soon, 89 of the nations 364 railroads had failed as well. The failure of almost 18,000 other businesses followed within two years, leaving the nation in an economic crisis. By 1876 unemployment had risen to 14 percent, with an estimated 2 million people

out of work. The high unemployment rate set off numerous strikes and protests around the nation, many involving railroad workers. In 1874 the Democrats gained control of the House of Representatives. Northerners were becoming less concerned about southern racism and more concerned about their financial well-being.

Election of 1876

Republicans could tell that northern support for Reconstruction was fading. Voters' attention was shifting to economic problems. In 1874 the Republican Party lost control of the House of Representatives to the Democrats. The Republicans in Congress managed to pass one last civil rights law. The Civil Rights Act of 1875 guaranteed African Americans equal rights in public places, such as theaters and public transportation. But as Americans became increasingly worried about economic problems and government corruption, the Republican Party began to abandon Reconstruction.

Republicans selected Ohio governor Rutherford B. Hayes as their 1876 presidential candidate. He believed in ending federal support of the Reconstruction governments. The Democrats nominated New York governor Samuel J. Tilden. During the election, Democrats in the South again used violence at the polls to keep Republican voters away.

The election between Hayes and Tilden was close. Tilden appeared to have won. Republicans challenged the electoral votes in Oregon and three southern states. A special commission of members of Congress and Supreme Court justices was appointed to settle the issue.

The commission narrowly decided to give all the disputed votes to Hayes. Hayes thus won the presidency by one electoral vote. In the **Compromise of 1877**, the Democrats agreed to accept Hayes's victory. In return, they wanted all remaining federal troops removed from the South. They also asked for funding for internal improvements in the South and

Main Idea

❸ Reconstruction Ends

As Reconstruction ended, the rights of African Americans were restricted.

Explain How was the United States affected by the Panic of 1873? *People blamed Republicans for the panic, almost 18,000 businesses declared bankruptcy, and unemployment rose, leading to protests.*

Analyze What issues caused the Republican Party to abandon Reconstruction? *Americans became increasingly worried about economic problems and corruption, and Republicans lost control of the House of Representatives.*

Info to Know

Disputed Election The election of 1876 was the subject of much debate and investigation. The popular election, held in November 1876, favored Samuel J. Tilden by 250,000 votes over Rutherford B. Hayes. Election results in Florida, Louisiana, South Carolina, and Oregon, however, were disputed. After investigation by an electoral commission, Hayes was declared the winner of the election in March 1877—almost four months after the election.

Differentiating Instruction

Advanced/Gifted and Talented

1. Have students use their textbooks or class notes to determine the main factors that led to the end of Reconstruction. Then ask students to decide which factor they believe was the most important in ending Reconstruction.

2. Have students prepare to debate the factor they feel was most important. Remind students to support their stance with specific details and to be prepared to counter opposing arguments.

3. Have several different students engage in a debate over the issue. Moderate the debate. When students have finished the debate, ask all students to vote on which factor they believe was the most important in leading to the end of Reconstruction. **LS Interpersonal, Verbal/Linguistic**

📝 Alternative Assessment Handbook, Rubric 10: Debates

Main Idea

❸ Reconstruction Ends

As Reconstruction ended, the rights of African Americans were restricted.

Identify Who were the Redeemers? *Democrats who brought their party back in control of southern state governments*

Analyze In what ways were African American men restricted from voting? *Being forced to pay a poll tax or pass a literacy test denied voting rights because many African American men had not been to school or did not have the extra money for the tax.*

Evaluate How did segregation become the key issue in the *Plessy* v. *Ferguson* case? *because Plessy, an African American, refused to leave a restricted whites-only part of a train*

📑 **CRF:** Primary Source Activity: *Plessy* v. *Ferguson*

📑 **CRF:** Literature, Activity: The Jim Crow Laws

📑 **U.S. Supreme Court Case Studies:** *Plessy* v. *Ferguson* (1896)

Did you know . . .

The *Plessy* v. *Ferguson* decision stood for 58 years. In 1954 the Supreme Court reversed the *Plessy* v. *Ferguson* decision with the landmark case *Brown* v. *Board of Education*. In that decision the Supreme Court ruled that segregation in public education was a denial of equal protection of the law.

Answers

Analyzing Information 1. *The Court stated that the Thirteenth Amendment did not apply and that the Fourteenth Amendment protected against only political barriers, not social ones.*
2. *It legalized segregation by saying "separate but equal" facilities were acceptable.*

SUPREME COURT DECISIONS

Plessy v. *Ferguson* (1896)

Background of the Case In 1892, Homer Plessy took a seat in the "whites only" car of a train in Louisiana. He was arrested, put on trial, and convicted of violating Louisiana's segregation law. Plessy argued that the Louisiana law violated the Thirteenth Amendment and denied him the equal protection of the law as guaranteed.

The Court's Ruling
The Court ruled that the Louisiana "separate-but-equal" law was constitutional.

The Court's Reasoning
The Court stated that the Thirteenth and Fourteenth Amendments did not apply. The Court decided that the case had nothing to do with the abolition of slavery mentioned in the Thirteenth Amendment. The justices also ruled that the Fourteenth Amendment was not designed to eliminate social barriers to equality between the races, only political barriers.

Justice John Marshall Harlan disagreed with the Court's ruling. In a dissenting opinion, he wrote that "in respect of civil rights, all citizens are equal before the law."

Why It Matters
Plessy was important because it approved the idea of separate but equal facilities for people based on race. The doctrine of separate but equal led to segregation in trains, buses, schools, restaurants, and many other social institutions.

The separate-but-equal doctrine led to unequal treatment of minority groups for decades. It was finally struck down by another Supreme Court ruling, *Brown* v. *Board of Education*, in 1954.

ANALYSIS SKILL | ANALYZING INFORMATION
1. Why did the Court reject Plessy's arguments?
2. Why was *Plessy* v. *Ferguson* an important Supreme Court case?

the appointment of a southern Democrat to the president's cabinet. Shortly after he took office in 1877, President Hayes removed the last of the federal troops from the South.

Redeemers

Gradually, Democrats regained control of state governments in the South. In each state, they moved quickly to get rid of the Reconstruction reforms.

Democrats who brought their party back to power in the South were called Redeemers. They came from a variety of backgrounds. For instance, U.S. senator John T. Morgan of Alabama was a former general in the Confederate army. Newspaper editor Henry Grady of Georgia was interested in promoting southern industry.

Redeemers wanted to reduce the size of state government and limit the rights of African Americans. They lowered state budgets and got rid of a variety of social programs. The Redeemers cut property taxes and reduced public funding for schools. They also succeeded in limiting African Americans' civil rights.

African Americans' Rights Restricted

Redeemers set up the poll tax in an effort to deny the vote to African Americans. The **poll tax** was a special tax people had to pay before they could vote.

Some states also targeted African American voters by requiring them to pass a literacy test. A so-called grandfather clause written into law affected men whose fathers or grandfathers could vote before 1867. In those cases, a voter did not have to pay a poll tax or pass a literacy test. As a result, almost every white man could escape the voting restrictions.

Redeemer governments also introduced legal **segregation**, the forced separation of whites and African Americans in public places. **Jim Crow laws** —laws that enforced segregation—became common in southern states in the 1880s.

African Americans challenged Jim Crow laws in court. In 1883, however, the U.S. Supreme Court ruled that the Civil Rights Act of 1875 was unconstitutional. The Court

Cross-Discipline Activity: Government

Above Level

Supreme Court Decisions

Research Required

1. Review with students the details of the *Plessy* v. *Ferguson* ruling. Then discuss with the class the 1954 Supreme Court ruling *Brown* v. *Board of Education*, which reversed the *Plessy* decision.

2. Organize the class into small groups. Have each group use the library, the Internet, or other resources to conduct research on both Supreme Court rulings.

3. Have each group create a poster that compares and contrasts the two Supreme Court decisions, including the effect of each on African Americans and other minorities. Ask students to make their posters visually appealing. Then have each group write a short paragraph that draws conclusions about why the Supreme Court reversed its earlier conclusion.

📑 Alternative Assessment Handbook, Rubrics 28: Posters; and 37: Writing Assignments also ruled that the Fourteenth Amendment applied only to the actions of state governments. This ruling allowed private individuals and businesses to practice segregation.

Plessy v. Ferguson

In 1896, the U.S. Supreme Court returned to the issue of segregation. When Homer Plessy, an African American, refused to leave the whites-only Louisiana train car he was riding on, he was arrested and accused of breaking a state law requiring separate cars for blacks and whites. Plessy sued the railroad company and lost. His lawyers argued that the law violated his right to equal treatment under the Fourteenth Amendment. He then appealed to the U.S. Supreme Court. The Supreme Court ruled against Plessy in **Plessy v. Ferguson**. Segregation was allowed, said the Court, if "separate-but-equal" facilities were provided. Among the justices, only John Marshall Harlan disagreed with the Court's decision. He explained his disagreement in a dissenting opinion:

> "In the eye of the law, there is in the country no superior, dominant [controlling], ruling class of citizens.... Our constitution is color-blind, and neither knows nor tolerates classes among citizens. In respect of civil rights, all citizens are equal before the law."

Despite Harlan's view, segregation became widespread across the country. African Americans were forced to use separate public schools, libraries, and parks. When they existed, these facilities were usually of poorer quality than those created for whites. In practice, these so-called separate but equal facilities were separate and unequal.

Farming in the South

Few African Americans in the South could afford to buy or even rent farms. Moving West also was costly. Many African Americans therefore remained on plantations. Others tried to make a living in the cities.

African Americans who stayed on plantations often became part of a system known as **sharecropping**, or sharing the crop. Land-owners provided the land, tools, and supplies, and sharecroppers provided the labor. At harvest time, the sharecropper usually had to give most of the crop to the land-owner. Whatever remained belonged to the sharecropper. Many sharecroppers hoped to save enough money from selling their share of the crops to one day be able to buy a farm. Unfortunately, only a few ever achieved this dream.

Instead, most sharecroppers lived in a cycle of debt. When they needed food, clothing, or supplies, most families had to buy goods on credit because they had little cash.

Hopes Raised and Denied QUICK FACTS

Slavery
- No rights
- Forced labor
- No freedom of movement without permission
- Family members sold away from one another
- No representation in government

Freedom
- Slavery banned
- Free to work for wages
- Could move and live anywhere
- Many families reunited
- Could serve in political office

Rights Denied
- Sharecropping system put in place
- Ability to vote and hold office restricted
- White leadership regained control of southern state governments

Direct Teach

Main Idea

❸ Reconstruction Ends

As Reconstruction ended, the rights of African Americans were restricted.

Analyze Why did many African Americans stay on plantations? *too costly to buy or rent farms or to move west*

Predict Why would the cycle of debt continue for sharecroppers? *There would be continuing problems with weather, poor harvests, and low crop prices, making it nearly impossible for sharecroppers to escape debt.*

📦 Quick Facts Transparency: Hopes Raised and Denied

Linking to Today
African American Civil Rights
When Reconstruction ended, African Americans lost many of the rights they had gained. Over time, however, African Americans have fought to regain access to all the rights of citizenship. By the 1960s, the push for greater civil rights for African Americans had become a true social movement in America. African Americans were joined in these efforts by Americans from all walks of life. Their efforts changed people's attitudes and led to greater civil rights for African Americans as well as other minorities.

Differentiating Instruction

Struggling Readers Below Level

1. Ask students to explain how poll taxes, Jim Crow laws, and the *Plessy* v. *Ferguson* decision affected African Americans. Write student comments for everyone to see.

2. Have each student write a one-page letter to a northern newspaper from the perspective of a southern African American. The letter should describe how the person's life has changed since the end of Reconstruction.

3. Ask volunteers to read their letters to the class. **LS Verbal/Linguistic**

📝 Alternative Assessment Handbook, Rubric 17: Letters to Editors

English-Language Learners Below Level

1. Ask students to explain how poll taxes, Jim Crow laws, and the *Plessy* v. *Ferguson* decision affected African Americans. Write student comments for everyone to see.

2. Have students create a political cartoon that expresses the point of view of a southern African American. Explain to students that political cartoons often try to draw attention to a problem or issue by using satire.

3. Ask volunteers to share their cartoons with the class. **LS Visual/Spatial**

📝 Alternative Assessment Handbook, Rubric 27: Political Cartoons

Direct Teach

Main Idea

❹ Rebuilding Southern Industry

Southern business leaders relied on industry to rebuild the South.

Identify What was the most successful industrial development in the South after Reconstruction? *textile production*

Summarize What were the benefits and drawbacks of mill work? *benefits— Entire families were employed, women were valued workers, and it was an alternative to farming; drawbacks— tedious work and long hours, asthma, brown-lung disease, injuries, death, few advancement opportunities for women*

Info to Know

Railroads Another way the South modernized its economy was by building railroads. From 1877 to 1900, the South built railroad lines at a faster rate than did the nation as a whole. Railroad building had an immediate effect on the southern economy. Landowners profited by selling lumber to railroad companies, who could use it as railroad ties. Farm families also made money by selling chickens, eggs, meat, and other farm products to railroad workers. Once the railroads were complete, southern towns and cities were connected to the rest of the nation.

When sharecroppers sold their crops, they hoped to be able to pay off these debts. However, bad weather, poor harvests, or low crop prices often made this dream impossible.

Sharecroppers usually grew cotton, one of the South's most important cash crops. When too many farmers planted cotton, however, the supply became excessive. As a result, the price per bale of cotton dropped. Many farmers understood the drawbacks of planting cotton. However, farmers felt pressure from banks and others to keep raising cotton. A southern farmer explained why so many sharecroppers depended on cotton:

> "Cotton is the thing to get credit on in this country ... You can always sell cotton ... [Y]ou load up your wagon with wheat or corn ...and I doubt some days whether you could sell it."
>
> –Farmer quoted in *The Promise of the New South*, by Edward L. Ayers

READING CHECK **Finding Main Ideas** How were African Americans' rights restricted?

Rebuilding Southern Industry

The southern economy suffered through cycles of good and bad years as cotton prices went up and down. Some business leaders hoped industry would strengthen the southern economy and create a New South.

Southern Industry

Henry Grady, an Atlanta newspaper editor, was a leader of the New South movement. "The new South presents . . . a diversified [varied] industry that meets the complex needs of this complex age," he wrote. Grady and his supporters felt that with its cheap and abundant labor, the South could build factories and provide a workforce for them.

The most successful industrial development in the South involved textile production. Businesspeople built textile mills in many small towns to produce cotton fabric. Many people from rural areas came to work in the mills, but African Americans were not allowed to work in most of them.

Differentiating Instruction

Above Level

Advanced/Gifted and Talented

1. Write the following statement for students to see: *The effects of Reconstruction were revolutionary.* Discuss with students the meaning of the word *revolutionary.*

2. Ask students whether they agree with the statement. Then have students write one-page papers explaining their views and supporting their positions.

3. Remind students that to support their points of view, they need to consider political, social, and economic effects of Reconstruction.

4. Encourage students to support their conclusion with specific examples, quotations, or comparisons. **LS** **Verbal/Linguistic**

   📝 Alternative Assessment Handbook , Rubric 37: Writing Assignments

Answers

Reading Check *legally segregated from white Americans, forced to pay poll taxes, and discriminated against*

"The New South...is stirred with the breath of a new life."

—Henry Grady

Atlanta rebuilt quickly after the war, becoming a leading railroad and industrial center. Newspaper editor Henry Grady gave stirring speeches about the need for industry in the South. He became one of the best-known spokesmen of the "New South."

Why might Grady point to Atlanta as a model for economic change?

Southern Mill Life

Work in the cotton mills appealed to farm families who had trouble making ends meet. As one mill worker explained, "It was a necessity to move and get a job, rather than depend on the farm." Recruiters sent out by the mills promised good wages and steady work.

Entire families often worked in the same cotton mill. Mills employed large numbers of women and children. Many children started working at about the age of 12. Some children started working at an even earlier age. Women did most of the spinning and were valued workers. However, few women had the opportunity to advance within the company.

Many mill workers were proud of the skills they used, but they did not enjoy their work. One unhappy worker described it as "the same thing over and over again . . . The more you do, the more they want done." Workers often labored 12 hours a day, six days a week. Cotton dust and lint filled the air, causing asthma and an illness known as brown-lung disease. Fast-moving machinery caused

injuries and even deaths. Despite the long hours and dangerous working conditions, wages remained low. However, mill work did offer an alternative to farming.

READING CHECK **Finding Main Ideas** What did southern business leaders hope industry would do?

SUMMARY AND PREVIEW In this section you learned about the end of Reconstruction. In the next chapter you will learn about America's continued westward expansion.

go.hrw.com
Online Quiz
KEYWORD: SR8 HP17

Section 3 Assessment

Reviewing Ideas, Terms, and People

1. **a. Identify** Who were some prominent African American leaders during Reconstruction?
   b. Evaluate What do you think was the most important change made by Reconstruction state governments? Explain your answer.
2. **a. Recall** Why didn't some local governments stop the **Ku Klux Klan**?
   b. Draw Conclusions How did the Ku Klux Klan's use of terror interfere with elections in the South?
3. **a. Recall** How did Reconstruction come to an end?
   b. Explain What was the relationship between **Jim Crow laws** and **segregation**?
4. **a. Identify** Who was **Henry Grady**, and why was he important?
   b. Predict What are some possible results of the rise of the "New South"?

Critical Thinking

5. **Identifying Causes and Effects** Review your notes on Reconstruction governments. Then copy the graphic organizer below and use it to show why Reconstruction ended, as well as the results of its end.

```
┌─────────┐     ┌──────────────┐     ┌─────────┐
│ Causes  │ ──▶ │ Effect/Cause │ ──▶ │ Effects │
│         │     │   End of     │     │         │
│         │     │Reconstruction│     │         │
└─────────┘     └──────────────┘     └─────────┘
```

WRITING JOURNAL

6. **Relating Historical Change to Individual Choice** Despite the difficulties of Reconstruction, the Freedmen's Bureau and plans to bring industry to the "New South" did create new jobs. What might have led people to leave their jobs for new ones?

RECONSTRUCTION **571**

571

Chance, Oversight, and Error in History

Activity **Make it Personal** Ask students if they think differently about chance, oversight, and error after learning about the critical ways in which they can shape history. After a brief discussion, ask volunteers to share examples of when chance, oversight, or error shaped events in their lives. Then challenge students to identify examples in which chance, oversight, or error have shaped recent national or world events. Correct students' interpretations where necessary. Use the discussion to make certain that students understand the difference among error, chance, and oversight and how they can affect historical events. **LS Intrapersonal, Verbal/Linguistic**

Alternative Assessment Handbook, Rubric 11: Discussions

Social Studies Skills

| Analysis | Critical Thinking | Civic Participation | Study |

Chance, Oversight, and Error in History

Understand the Skill

Sometimes, history can seem very routine. One event leads to others which, in turn, lead to still others. You learn to look for cause-and-effect relationships among events. You learn how point of view and bias can influence decisions and actions. These approaches to the study of history imply that the events of the past are orderly and predictable.

In fact, many of the events of the past *are* orderly and predictable! They may seem even more so since they're over and done with, and we know how things turned out. Yet, predictable patterns of behavior *do* exist throughout history. Recognizing them is one of the great values and rewards of studying the past. As the philosopher George Santayana once famously said, Those who cannot remember the past are condemned to repeat it."

At its most basic level, however, history is people, and people are "human." They make mistakes. Unexpected things happen to them, both good things and bad. This is the unpredictable element of history. The current phrase "stuff happens" is just as true of the past as it is today. Mistakes, oversights, and just plain "dumb luck" have shaped the course of history—and have helped to make the study of it so exciting!

Learn the Skill

California merchant John Sutter decided to build a sawmill along the nearby American River in 1848. He planned to sell the lumber it produced to settlers who were moving into the area. Sutter put James W. Marshall to work building the mill. To install the large water wheel that would power the saw,

Marshall first had to deepen the river bed next to the mill. During his digging, he noticed some shiny bits of yellow metal in the water. The result of this accidental find was the California Gold Rush, which sent thousands of Americans to California, and speeded settlement of the West.

In 1863 the army of Confederate General Robert E. Lee invaded Maryland. The Civil War had been going well for the South. Lee hoped a southern victory on Union soil would convince the British to aid the South in the war. However, a Confederate officer forgot his cigars as his unit left its camp in the Maryland countryside. Wrapped around the cigars was a copy of Lee's battle plans. When a Union soldier came upon the abandoned camp, he spotted the cigars. This chance discovery enabled the Union army to defeat Lee at the Battle of Antietam. The Union victory helped keep the British out of the war. More importantly, it allowed President Lincoln to issue the Emancipation Proclamation and begin the process of ending slavery in the United States.

Practice the Skill

In April 1865 President Lincoln was assassinated while attending the theater in Washington, D.C. Bodyguard John Parker was stationed outside the door of the President's box. However, Parker left his post to find a seat from which he could watch the play. This allowed the killer to enter the box and shoot the unprotected President.

Write an essay about how this chance event altered the course of history. How might Reconstruction, North–South relations, and African Americans' struggle for equality have be different had Lincoln lived?

Answers

Practice and Apply the Skill *Essays will vary, but students may speculate that Reconstruction might have been less bitter had Lincoln lived. His strength, experience, and popularity—particularly as compared to that of Andrew Johnson—might have kept the Radical Republicans from gaining control over Reconstruction. This change might have resulted in a Reconstruction plan that stressed unity and forgiveness more and, thus, might have resulted in less bitterness and resentment on the part of the South toward the North.*

572

Social Studies Skills Activity: Chance, Oversight, and Error in History

Analyzing Previous Chapters   **At Level**

1. Organize students into small groups and assign each group a chapter that they have studied recently.

2. Have each group scan the chapter and look for events where chance, oversight, or error played a role in influencing the course of history.

3. Each group should make a list of the instances it finds and write a brief explanation of the way in which chance, oversight, or error shaped history in that instance.

4. Have each group share its findings with the class. Correct students' interpretations where necessary. Then conclude by having students predict how the course of history might have changed if some of the instances they mentioned had turned out differently.
LS Interpersonal, Verbal/Linguistic

Alternative Assessment Handbook, Rubric 14: Group Activity

Chapter Review

Visual Summary

Use the visual summary below to help you review the main ideas of the chapter.

QUICK FACTS

Reform During Reconstruction, the Freedmen's Bureau opened schools for former slaves and performed other services to help the poorest southerners.

Dispute Differing ideas about how to govern the South led to conflicts between African Americans and white southerners, as well as between Republicans and Democrats.

Division After the Compromise of 1877 ended Reconstruction, segregation laws were enacted by southern governments and upheld by the U.S. Supreme Court.

Reviewing Vocabulary, Terms, and People

Complete each sentence by filling in the blank with the correct term or person from the chapter.

1. _____ were laws that allowed racial segregation in public places.

2. The Radical Republicans were led by _____, a member of Congress from Pennsylvania.

3. The period from 1865 to 1877 that focused on reuniting the nation is known as _____.

4. Following the Civil War, many African Americans in the South made a living by participating in the _____ system.

5. After opposing Congress, Andrew Johnson became the first president to face _____ proceedings.

6. The _____ Amendment made slavery in the United States illegal.

7. In 1870, _____ became the first African American to serve in the U.S. Senate.

Comprehension and Critical Thinking

SECTION 1 *(Pages 552–557)*

8. **a. Describe** How did the lives of African Americans change after the Civil War?

   b. Compare and Contrast How was President Johnson's Reconstruction plan similar and different from President Lincoln's Ten Percent Plan?

   c. Evaluate Which of the three Reconstruction plans that were originally proposed do you think would have been the most successful? Why?

SECTION 2 *(Pages 558–563)*

9. **a. Identify** Who were the Radical Republicans, and how did they change Reconstruction?

   b. Analyze How did the debate over the Fourteenth Amendment affect the election of 1866?

   c. Elaborate Do you think Congress was right to impeach President Andrew Johnson? Explain.

RECONSTRUCTION **573**

Review and Assessment Resources

Review and Reinforce

SE Chapter Review

📋 **CRF:** Chapter Review Activity

🗄 Quick Facts Transparency: Reconstruction Visual Summary

🔊 Spanish Chapter Summaries Audio CD Program

📲 Online Chapter Summaries in Six Languages

OSP Holt PuzzlePro; GameTool for ExamView

💿 Quiz Game CD-ROM

Assess

SE Standardized Test Practice

📋 PASS: Chapter Test, Forms A and B

📋 Alternative Assessment Handbook

OSP ExamView Test Generator, Chapter Test

💿 Differentiated Instruction Modified Worksheets and Tests CD-ROM: Chapter Test

📲 Holt Online Assessment Program (in the Premier Online Edition)

Reteach/Intervene

📋 Interactive Reader and Study Guide

📋 Differentiated Instruction Teacher Management System: Lesson Plans for Differentiated Instruction

💿 Differentiated Instruction Modified Worksheets and Tests CD-ROM

💿 Interactive Skills Tutor CD-ROM

go.hrw.com
Online Resources
Chapter Resources:
KEYWORD: SR8 US17

9. a. Republicans who wanted the federal government to be much more involved in Reconstruction; they took control of Reconstruction away from President Johnson
b. Debate over civil rights for African Americans became the key issue of the election of 1866 and even led to riots.
c. possible answers: yes—He defied the law by firing Edwin Stanton without their approval; no—Congress did not have the power to limit the president.

10. a. They tried to help the South recover from the war by establishing public schools, hospitals, and prisons; passing laws prohibiting discrimination against African Americans; and aiding the construction of railroads, bridges, and public buildings.
b. They worked to limit the rights of African Americans, reduce the size of state governments, eliminate social programs, and prevent African Americans from voting.
c. Answers will vary, but students should support their answers with specific examples.

Reviewing Themes

11. The key political struggle was between Republicans, who supported rights for African Americans and strict guidelines for readmitting southern states, and Democrats, who favored leniency toward southern states and limited freedoms for African Americans.

12. The rights of African Americans were severely limited by poll taxes, Jim Crow laws, and the separate-but-equal doctrine. Many southerners were negatively affected by the sharecropping system and poor working conditions in mills.

SECTION 3 *(Pages 564–571)*

10. a. Describe What reforms did Reconstruction governments in the South support?
  b. Draw Conclusions In what ways did southern governments attempt to reverse the accomplishments of Reconstruction?
  c. Evaluate Do you think the South was successful or unsuccessful in its rebuilding efforts? Explain your answer.

Reviewing Themes

11. Politics Explain the political struggles that took place during Reconstruction.

12. Society and Culture How were the lives of ordinary southerners affected in the years after Reconstruction?

Using the Internet

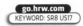
go.hrw.com
KEYWORD: SR8 US17

13. Activity: Drawing conclusions A challenge for anyone trying to understand Reconstruction is drawing conclusions from primary and secondary sources from the time period. This activity will help you see how complex this can be. Enter the activity keyword, and then rate the credibility of the sources provided. Make sure you explain whether the source is a primary or secondary source, whether or not you think the source is credible, and the reasons for your thoughts.

Reading Skills

Analyzing Historical Information *Use the Reading Skills taught in this chapter to answer the question about the reading selection below.*

> Radical Republicans wanted the South to change much more than it already had before it could return to the Union. Like the moderates, they thought the Black Codes were cruel and unjust. The radicals, however, wanted the federal government to be much more involved in Reconstruction. *(p. 559)*

---

14. Which of the following is relevant information for the passage above?
  a. Thaddeus Stevens was a Radical Republican.
  b. Andrew Johnson was a Democrat.
  c. Radical Republicans wanted the federal government to make major changes in the South.
  d. Radical Republicans were eventually removed from power.

Social Studies Skills

Chance, Oversight, and Error in History *Use the Social Studies Skills taught in this chapter to answer the question about the reading selection below.*

> Johnson's speaking tour was a disaster. It did little to win votes for the Democratic Party. He even got into arguments with people in the audience. *(p. 561)*

15. Which of the following is an example of chance, oversight, or error that affected history?
  a. Johnson got into arguments with audiences.
  b. The tour was a disaster.
  c. The tour didn't win votes.
  d. Johnson spoke for the Democratic Party.

FOCUS ON WRITING

16. Writing A Job History Review your notes about the changing job scene during Reconstruction. Put yourself in the shoes of a person living then. It could be anyone—a returning soldier, a shopkeeper, a schoolteacher, or a politician. What jobs would that person seek? Why would he or she leave one job for another?

  Write a brief job history for that person during Reconstruction. Include at least four jobs. Make each job description 2 to 4 sentences long. End each one with a sentence or two about why the person left that job. Add one sentence explaining why they took the next job. Be sure to include specific historical details.

Using the Internet

13. Go to the HRW Web site and enter the keyword shown to access a rubric for this activity.

KEYWORD: SR8 TEACHER

Reading Skills

14. c

Social Studies Skills

15. d

Focus on Writing

16. Rubric Students' job histories should:
  • include at least four job descriptions.
  • end each description with an explanation of why the person left.
  • explain why the person took each job.
  • include specific historical details.

📃 **CRF:** Focus on Writing Activity: Job History

Standardized Test Practice

DIRECTIONS: Read each question and write the letter of the best response.

1 Use the map below to answer the following question.

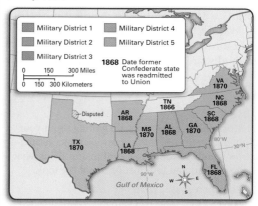

Military District 1
Military District 2
Military District 3
Military District 4
Military District 5
1868 Date former Confederate state was readmitted to Union

0   150   300 Miles
0   150   300 Kilometers

VA 1870
NC 1868
TN 1866
Disputed
AR 1868
SC 1868
MS 1870
AL 1868
GA 1870
TX 1870
LA 1868
FL 1868
Gulf of Mexico
80°W
30°N
90°W

Which military district contained the largest number of states?

A Military District 2
B Military District 3
C Military District 4
D Military District 5

2 What can you infer from the map information?

A South Carolina was difficult to reconstruct.
B The largest number of troops was in Military District 1.
C Military District 5 was the last district to end Reconstruction.
D Tennessee was readmitted to the Union before the other southern states.

3 The quickest approach to reuniting the nation was proposed by the

A Ten Percent Plan.
B Wade-Davis Bill.
C Civil Rights Act of 1866.
D Compromise of 1877.

4 What development convinced Republicans in Congress to take control of Reconstruction from the president?

A President Abraham Lincoln was assassinated by a southern sympathizer.
B President Andrew Johnson vetoed the Wade-Davis bill.
C Southern states began passing Black Codes to deprive African Americans of their freedoms.
D White southern women refused to support the Fifteenth Amendment.

5 All of the following limited opportunities for African Americans in the South after Reconstruction ended *except*

A sharecropping.
B the Redeemers.
C Jim Crow laws.
D carpetbaggers.

6 Examine the following passage from a northern schoolteacher's letter home and then use it to answer the question.

> "Wishing to work where there was the most need—there are so many places where nothing has been done for the freedmen, and where they are sorely persecuted—we came here. A schoolhouse built by the soldiers had just been destroyed by the citizens. The feeling is intensely bitter against anything northern. The affairs of the [Freedmen's] Bureau have been very much mismanaged in Columbus, and our government has been disgraced by the troops who were staioned here."
>
> –Sarah Chase, from *Dear Ones at Home*

What were some of the problems facing the Freedmen's Bureau in the South?

1. B
Break Down the Question: Students should note that District 3 has three states, more than any other district.

2. D
Break Down the Question: Point out to students that answer choices A, B, and C cannot be inferred from the map, but D can.

3. A
Break Down the Question: This question requires students to recall factual information from Section 1.

4. C
Break Down the Question: This question requires students to recall factual information from Section 2.

5. D
Break Down the Question: Remind students that the word *except* in the question means that they should identify the answer choice that is *not* true.

6. They faced persecution, violence from southern citizens, intense anti-northern sentiments, and mismanagement of the bureau.

Intervention Resources

Reproducible

- Interactive Reader and Study Guide
- Differentiated Instruction Teacher Management System: Differentiated Instruction Lesson Plans

Technology

- Quick Facts Transparency: Reconstruction Visual Summary
- Differentiated Instruction Modified Worksheets and Tests CD-ROM
- Interactive Skills Tutor CD-ROM

Tips for Test Taking

Find the Main Idea Tell students that the main goal of a reading comprehension section is to test their understanding of a reading passage. Have students keep these suggestions in mind when they read a selection on a test:

- Read the passage once to get a general overview of the topic.
- If you don't understand the passage at first, keep reading. Try to find the main idea.
- Then read the questions so that you know what to look for when you reread the passage.

Preteach

Bellringer

Motivate Ask students to think about topics related to the Civil War that interested them. What Civil War topics would students like to know more about? What questions do students have about these topics? Write the questions for students to see. Then tell students that in this workshop they will answer a similar question by conducting research and writing an informative report.

Direct Teach

Finding Historical Information

Ask an Expert Another source students might consult is an expert on their topic. Students might arrange an interview with an expert or attend a presentation that he or she is giving. If students plan to interview a person, they should write out several questions in advance and leave space after each question for taking notes. If students wish to record an interview, remind them to ask the person's permission in advance.

Taking Notes

Keep It Relevant Tell students that when they are not sure whether to take notes on a piece of information, they should ask themselves, "Does this information help answer my research question?" If the answer is yes, they should include the information in their notes. If the answer is no, they should not.

Assignment

Collect information and write an informative report on a topic related to the Civil War.

TIP **Narrowing the Task** The key to a successful research report is picking a topic that is broad enough that you can find information, but narrow enough that you can cover it in detail. To narrow a subject, focus on one aspect of the larger subject. Then think about whether that one aspect can be broken down into smaller parts. Here's an example of how to narrow a topic:

Too Broad: Civil War Leaders
Less Broad: Civil War Generals
Narrower: Robert E. Lee's Role in the Civil War

A Social Studies Report

All research begins with a question. Why did the North win the Civil War? Why did Abraham Lincoln choose Ulysses S. Grant? In a research report, you find answers to questions like these and share what you learn with your reader.

1. Prewrite

Choosing a Subject

Since you will spend a lot of time researching and writing about your topic, pick one that interests you. First, think of several topics related to the Civil War. Narrow your list to one topic by thinking about what interests you and where you can find information about the topic.

Developing a Research Question

A guiding question related to your topic will help focus your research. For example, here is a research question for the topic "Robert E. Lee's Role in the Civil War": *How did Lee's decision to turn down the leadership of the Union Army affect the Civil War?* The answer to this question becomes the thesis, or the big idea of your report.

Finding Historical Information

Use at least three sources of historical information besides your textbook. Good sources include

- books, maps, magazines, newspapers
- television programs, movies, Internet sites, CD-ROMs.

For each source, write down the kinds of information shown below. When taking notes, put a circled number next to each source.

Encyclopedia article
① "Title of Article." <u>Name of Encyclopedia</u>. Edition or year published.
Book
② Author. <u>Title</u>. City of Publication: Publisher, Year published.
Magazine or newspaper article
③ Author. "Title of Article." <u>Publication name</u>. Date: page number(s).
Internet site
④ Author (if known). "Document title." <u>Web Site</u>. Date of electronic publication. Date information was accessed <url>.

Differentiating Instruction

Struggling Readers   Below Level

1. When doing research, students need to learn to evaluate each source quickly to determine its usefulness. As guided practice, write the list of fictional sources at right for students to see. Have students identify which of the sources they think would be most helpful for an informative report on Ulysses S. Grant.

2. Have students use the following scale to rate each source: 4 = extremely useful; 3 = useful; 2 = might be useful; 1 = not useful.

- *Ulysses S. Grant: A Biography* (book)
- *The Life and Times of Lincoln* (book)
- "Grant's Military Campaigns" (historical journal article)
- "Interactive History of the Civil War" (university Web site)
- "My General Grant Page" (personal Web site)
LS **Verbal/Linguistic**

Taking Notes

As you read the source material, take thorough notes on facts, statistics, comparisons, and quotations. Take special care to spell names correctly and to record dates and facts accurately. If you use a direct quotation from a source, copy it word for word and enclose it in quotation marks. Along with each note, include the number of its source and its page number.

Organizing Your Ideas and Information

Informative research reports are usually organized in one of these ways:

- Chronological order (the order in which events occurred)
- Order of importance
- Causes (actions or situations that make something else happen) and effects (what happened as a result of something else).

Use one of these orders to organize your notes in an outline. Here is a partial outline for a paper on Robert E. Lee.

The Thesis/Big Idea: Robert E. Lee's decision to decline the leadership of the Union Army had serious consequences for the path of the Civil War.

I. Lee's Military Expertise
   A. Achievements at the U.S. Military Academy
   B. Achievements during the Mexican War
II. Lee's Personality and Character
   A. Intelligence and strength
   B. Honesty and fairness
   C. Daring and courage
III. Lee's Military Victories
   A. Battle of Fredericksburg
   B. Battle of Chancellorsville

2. Write

You can use this framework to help you write your first draft.

A Writer's Framework

Introduction	Body	Conclusion
■ Start with a quote or an interesting historical detail to grab your reader's attention. ■ State the main idea of your report. ■ Provide any historical background readers need to understand your main idea.	■ Present your information under at least three main ideas, using logical order. ■ Write at least one paragraph for each of these main ideas. ■ Add supporting details, facts, or examples to each paragraph.	■ Restate your main idea, using slightly different words. ■ Include a general comment about your topic. ■ You might comment on how the historical information in your report relates to later historical events.

TIP **Seeing Different Viewpoints**
Consult a variety of sources, including those with different points of view on the topic. Reading sources with different opinions will give you a more complete picture of your subject. For example, reading articles about Robert E. Lee written by a southern writer as well as a northern writer may give you a more balanced view of Lee.

TIP **Recording Others' Ideas** You will be taking three types of notes.
Paraphrases Restatements of all the ideas in your own words.
Summaries Brief restatements of only the most important parts.
Direct quotations The writer's exact words inside quotation marks.

Writing Introductions

First Things Last Tell students that they will probably be able to write a stronger introduction after they have drafted the body of the paper. Have students begin by writing their thesis statement. They should then start a new paragraph to begin the body of the report. After they have drafted the body, have students reread the report and then write the introduction. Have students ask themselves the following questions before they write the introduction:

- How can I grab my readers' attention?
- How can I set the scene for what I am about to discuss in the rest of my report?
- How can I make my readers want to read more?

Writing the Body

The Right Fit Explain to students that if they are having trouble making their reports flow, they may need to reconsider the kind of organization they chose. Tell students to scan their papers for transitions and other words that determine the logical relationship of the information. For instance, words such as *because, therefore,* and *so* indicate a cause-and-effect relationship. Words such as *first, next, then,* and *after* indicate a chronological relationship. Words such as *primarily, main,* and *major* indicate a relationship based on importance. Students should make sure they are using the organization that best matches what they are trying to say. If not, students should create a new outline with a different organization and then use the outline to revise their drafts.

Advanced/Gifted and Talented   **Above Level**

1. Challenge students to choose a research topic about which there is some disagreement or controversy. Students should then address in their reports the complexity of their topics, the reasons for controversy, and the discrepancies in the available information.

2. Check students' topics to make sure you approve before students begin their research. **LS** **Verbal/Linguistic**

Special Needs Learners   **Below Level**

1. Assign all special education students one topic.

2. Have an aide take the students as a group to the library to assist with research. The aide should instruct students in the use of card catalogs, computer catalogs, and library media centers.

3. The aide should then help the students select and find sources. **LS** **Verbal/Linguistic**

Studying a Model

Identify Organization Lead a class discussion to identify the type of organization used in the model research paper. Write the three types of organization for students to see. Have students consider each type of organization in turn.

- **Chronological order:** Point out that although the first body paragraph describes Lee's education and the last discusses his actions during the war, the middle body paragraph discusses his personality, which does not fit a chronological scheme.

- **Cause and effect:** Point out that while the thesis states a cause and effect (Lee's decision strengthened the South and likely lengthened the war), the supporting points are not related by cause and effect.

- **Order of importance:** Students should conclude that the model is organized by order of importance.

Then discuss whether the most important main ideas are provided first or last *(last, because Lee's actual performance in the field is the strongest evidence).*

Technology Tip

Using Technology to Provide Visual Aids Students may want to include maps, charts, diagrams, or illustrations in their papers. Explain that many word-processing programs include drawing tools or provide ways to import graphics from other computer programs. Encourage students who want to include visual aids to find out more about the graphic tools available.

Studying a Model

Here is a model of a research report. Study it to see how one student developed a paper. The first and the concluding paragraphs are shown in full. The paragraphs in the body of the paper are summarized.

INTRODUCTORY PARAGRAPH
Attention grabber

"I cannot raise my hand against my birthplace, my home, my children." With these words, Robert E. Lee changed the course of the Civil War. Abraham Lincoln had turned to Lee as his first choice for commander of the Union Army. However, Lee turned Lincoln down, choosing instead to side with his home state of Virginia and take command of the Confederate Army. Lee's decision to turn Lincoln down weakened the North and strengthened the Confederates, turning what might have been an easy victory for the North into a long, costly war.

Statement of thesis

BODY PARAGRAPHS

In the first part of the body, the student points out that Lee graduated from the U.S. Military Academy at West Point, served in the Mexican War, and was a member of the Union Army. She goes on to explain that he would have been a strong leader for the North, and his absence made the North weaker.

In the middle of the report, the writer discusses Lee's personality and character. She includes information about the strength of character he showed while in the military academy and while leading the Confederate Army. She discusses and gives examples of his intelligence, his daring, his courage, and his honesty.

In the last part of the body of the report, the student provides examples of Lee leading the outnumbered Confederate Army to a series of victories. The student provides details of the battles of Fredericksburg and Chancellorsville and explains how a lesser general than Lee may have lost both battles.

CONCLUDING PARAGRAPH
Summary of main points
Restatement of big idea

Lee's brilliant and resourceful leadership bedeviled a series of Union generals. He won battles that most generals would have lost. If Lee had used these skills to lead the larger and more powerful Union Army, the Civil War might have ended in months instead of years.

Cross-Discipline Activity: Math

At Level

Research Guided Practice

1. Send students to the library on an information scavenger hunt. Tell them their task is to find out how much the Civil War cost in lives and money. The monetary cost might include both the costs of maintaining the armies and the property losses suffered by civilians. The first student to find the information from a credible source wins.

2. Ask students to use their textbooks to calculate how many months, weeks, and days the Civil War lasted.

3. As a class, divide the monetary and human costs of the war by its length to determine the costs per month, week, and day. Explain to students that the actual costs were not incurred evenly throughout the period, so the numbers produced by the class are averages, not actual figures.

4. Use the findings to discuss the effects of war on soldiers, civilians, property, economies, and the environment. **LS Logical/Mathematical, Verbal/Linguistic**

3. Evaluate and Revise

Evaluating and Revising Your Draft

Evaluate your first draft by carefully reading it twice. Ask the questions below to decide which parts of your first draft should be revised.

Evaluation Questions for an Informative Report

- Does the introduction attract the readers' interest and state the big idea/thesis of your report?
- Does the body of your report have at least three paragraphs that develop your big idea? Is the main idea in each paragraph clearly stated?
- Have you included enough information to support each of your main ideas? Are all facts, details, and examples accurate? Are all of them clearly related to the main ideas they support?

- Is the report clearly organized? Does it use chronological order, order of importance, or cause and effect?
- Does the conclusion restate the big idea of your report? Does it end with a general comment about the importance or significance of your topic?
- Have you included at least three sources in your bibliography? Have you included all the sources you used and not any you did not use?

4. Proofread and Publish

Proofreading

To improve your report before sharing it, check the following:
- The spelling and capitalization of all proper names for people, places, things, and events.
- Punctuation marks around any direct quotation.
- Your list of sources (Works Cited or Bibliography) against a guide to writing research papers. Make sure you follow the examples in the guide when punctuating and capitalizing your source listings.

Publishing

Choose one or more of these ideas to publish your report.
- Share your report with your classmates by turning it into an informative speech.
- Submit your report to an online discussion group that focuses on the Civil War and ask for feedback.
- With your classmates, create a magazine that includes reports on several different topics or post the reports on your school Web site.

5. Practice and Apply

Use the steps and strategies outlined in this workshop to research and write an informative report on the Civil War.

TIP **Organizing Your Time** By creating a schedule and following it, you can avoid that panicky moment when the due date is near and you haven't even started your research. To create your schedule and manage your time, include these six steps.

1. Develop a question and research your topic (10% of your total time).
2. Research and take notes (25%).
3. Write your main idea statement and create an outline (15%).
4. Write a first draft (25%).
5. Evaluate and revise your first draft (15%).
6. Proofread and publish your report (10%).

Linking Past to Present

America became a global power in the 1900s as U.S. troops fought in two world wars.

America Since 1877

The United States of America is a very different place today than it was in 1877. The nation is now bigger, more powerful, and more involved in world affairs. It has changed from a nation where most people lived in small towns to one in which most people live in cities, many with populations of more than 1 million people. The nation is also a more democratic place today—more Americans have access to the privileges and responsibilities of citizenship than at any other time in the country's history.

Despite these differences, America faces some of the same challenges that it faced in 1877. For example, Americans still debate questions about civil rights, religion, taxes, and the role of government in their lives. They also worry about the health of the environment, children, and the poor.

Americans do not always agree on these issues. But they do believe strongly in their right to debate and to disagree. The freedom to do so—in peaceful and productive ways—is a testament of the strength of the founding fathers' plan for government.

America as a Global Power

After the Civil War, the conflict between the United States and Native Americans increased. With the last major battle at Wounded Knee in 1890, American settlers began moving west in even greater numbers. In 1898, U.S. troops were sent to Cuba to combat Spanish forces. Eventually, the United States and Spain clashed over the Philippines. The Spanish-American War began a period of American imperialism during which U.S. influence spread throughout Latin America.

In 1914 World War I began in Europe. By 1917 the United States had entered the war, and American soldiers fought and died on the battlefields of Europe. That experience forever changed the United States. America had stepped onto the world stage with its military and industrial might.

War tore Europe apart again in the 1930s and 1940s during World War II. When Japan attacked the United States at Pearl Harbor in late 1941, the United States entered the global struggle.

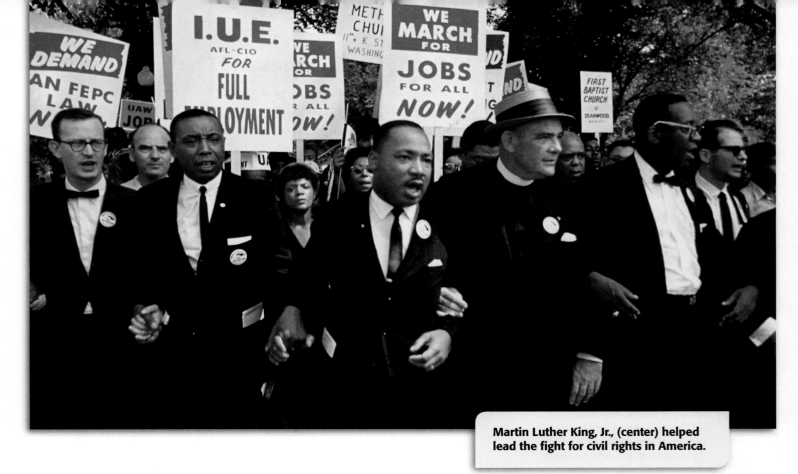

Martin Luther King, Jr., (center) helped lead the fight for civil rights in America.

The Civil Rights Era

The U.S. victory in World War II had other consequences as well. Millions of World War II veterans returned home ready to start new lives in peacetime. These veterans enrolled in college in record numbers, settled into the nation's cities and new suburbs, and started families.

Soldiers who had fought on the side of democracy abroad also fought for democracy at home. This was especially true of the nation's African American and Mexican American soldiers. Their efforts to seek greater access to the rights of citizenship helped invigorate the civil rights movement. They were joined in these efforts by Americans from all walks of life—people who believed that America worked best when the promises of freedom were open to all.

By the 1960s, the push for greater civil rights had become a true social movement in America. It was a grassroots effort on the part of ordinary Americans to change both people's attitudes and federal laws. This movement for greater civil, educational, and political rights among racial and ethnic groups helped spur the women's rights movement of the 1960s and 1970s as well.

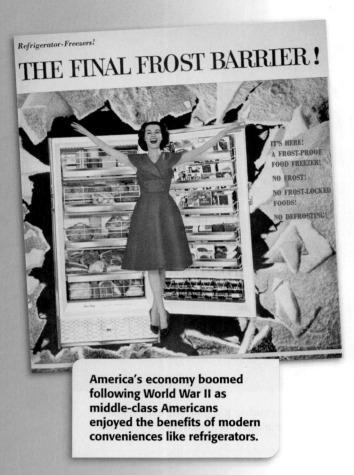

Refrigerator-Freezers!

THE FINAL FROST BARRIER!

IT'S HERE!
A FROST-PROOF
FOOD FREEZER!
NO FROST!
NO FROST-LOCKED
FOODS!
NO DEFROSTING!

America's economy boomed following World War II as middle-class Americans enjoyed the benefits of modern conveniences like refrigerators.

Economic Changes and Challenges

The U.S. economy has also changed dramatically since 1877. After 1877, dramatic changes in technology led to a second industrial revolution in which manufacturing processes became more focused on machinery than on workers. In the 1930s, millions of Americans were affected by the huge economic collapse known as the Great Depression. After World War II, the U.S. economy recovered and the nation enjoyed a long period of prosperity. Many Americans joined the middle class for the first time. During the 1950s and 1960s they bought homes, televisions and appliances, and cars in record numbers.

Since the 1970s, the economy has had more ups and downs. Industrial jobs, which were once so plentiful in America, have become far less important in recent decades. Many American companies have moved their factories overseas to take advantage of lower wages in other countries. As a result, the U.S. economy is now becoming more of a service economy—one in which workers provide services (like banking or law) instead of actually making products.

Immigration

Immigration has been an important feature of the United States ever since the country first began. Since 1877, this strong tradition of immigration has continued. Between 1880 and 1920, in fact, almost 24 million people immigrated to the United States. In 1882, Congress began passing legislation that limited who could enter the United States. During the early 1900s, however, people from every corner of the world came to America to settle. These new immigrants were Buddhists, Christians, Muslims, and Sikhs. They came from Latin America, Africa, Asia, and Europe. They

With its long history of immigration, America is one of the most ethnically diverse places in the world. Here, Sikhs celebrate their culture at a parade in New York.

came in search of a brighter future, greater freedom, and a chance to start their lives over again.

America Then and Now

In the years since 1877, the United States has faced many difficult challenges that have drawn citizens together. The terrorist attacks of September 11, 2001, are the latest of these challenges. Since 2001, a War on Terror has been ongoing as the United States tries to effectively end the threat of terrorism around the world. Part of this War on Terror has been a military action in Afghanistan. Alleged links were also found between Iraq and terrorist suspects, encouraging President George W. Bush to begin Operation Iraqi Freedom. The links between Iraq and terrorism have since been disproved.

Terrorism in Iraq and other foreign countries continues to be a danger to citizens of the United States and other countries. Kidnappings and bombings threaten peace efforts in all parts of the world.

In order to confront the growing threat of terrorism within the United States, President Bush created the Department of Homeland Security and a corresponding new cabinet position. The department oversees 22 agencies responsible for protecting America from terrorism. In addition, the department maintains a system for notifying the public of terrorist threats.

More than 200 years ago, the Founding Fathers insisted that the United States of America was an experiment—a new nation devoted to the possibility that principles of virtue and ideals of freedom could be supported by democracy, justice, and the rule of law. Today, just as then, this experiment works best when American citizens exercise their rights carefully and seriously.

The terrorist attacks of September 11, 2001, marked the beginning of a new challenge in American history—the war against terrorism.

Cities such as St. Louis, shown here, are part of America's past, present, and future. Once a small town known as the Gateway to the West, St. Louis has grown into a large and modern American city.

References

The United States of America: Political

CANADA

WASHINGTON
- Seattle
- Tacoma
- Olympia ★
- Spokane
- Portland
- Puget Sound
- Franklin D. Roosevelt Lake
- Pend Oreille
- Columbia River

OREGON
- Salem ★
- Eugene
- Goose Lake

IDAHO
- Boise ★
- Sun Valley
- Pocatello
- Snake River

MONTANA
- Great Falls
- Helena ★
- Billings
- Flathead Lake
- Fort Peck Lake
- Missouri River
- Yellowstone River

NORTH DAKOT
- Bismarck
- Lake Sakakawea

SOUTH DAKOTA
- Rapid City
- Pierre ★
- Lake Oahe

WYOMING
- Yellowstone Lake
- Cheyenne ★

NEBRASKA
- Platte Riv

NEVADA
- Reno
- Carson City ★
- Lake Tahoe
- Pyramid Lake

UTAH
- Ogden
- Salt Lake City ★
- Provo
- Great Salt Lake
- Utah Lake
- Green River
- Lake Powell

COLORADO
- Boulder
- Vail
- Denver ★
- Aspen
- Colorado Springs
- Pueblo
- Arkansas River

KANSAS

CALIFORNIA
- Berkeley
- Oakland
- San Francisco
- San Jose
- Sacramento ★
- Fresno
- San Francisco Bay
- Monterey Bay
- Cape Mendocino
- Shasta Lake
- Sacramento River
- San Joaquin River
- Santa Barbara
- Ventura
- Los Angeles
- Long Beach
- Anaheim
- Santa Ana
- Riverside
- Palm Springs
- San Diego
- Channel Islands
- Salton Sea
- Las Vegas

ARIZONA
- Flagstaff
- Phoenix ★
- Casa Grande
- Tucson
- Lake Mead
- Colorado River
- Gila River

NEW MEXICO
- Taos
- Santa Fe ★
- Albuquerque
- Las Cruces
- El Paso

OKLAHOM
- Oklahoma
- Law
- Canadian River

TEXAS
- Amarillo
- Lubbock
- Abilene
- Fort Wo
- Midland
- Odessa
- Brazos River
- Pecos River
- Colorado Rive
- San Antonio
- Austi
- Corpus Christ
- Laredo
- Pa
- Isla
- Rio Grande
- Amistad Reservoir

PACIFIC OCEAN

MEXICO
- Gulf of California

To understand the relative locations of Alaska and Hawaii, as well as the vast distances separating them from the rest of the United States, see the world map.

HAWAII
- Kauai
- Niihau
- Oahu
- Honolulu
- Molokai
- Lanai
- Maui
- Kahoolawe
- Hilo
- Hawaii
- PACIFIC OCEAN
- 22°N
- 155°W
- 160°W
- 19°N

```
0        75      150 Miles
0        75      150 Kilometers
Projection: Mercator
```

ALASKA
- ARCTIC OCEAN
- Arctic Circle
- Bering Strait
- RUSSIA
- Nome
- Yukon River
- St. Lawrence Island
- St. Matthew Island
- Nunivak Island
- Fairbanks
- CANADA
- Anchorage
- Valdez
- Skagway
- Juneau ★
- Gulf of Alaska
- Kodiak Island
- Alexander Archipelago
- Bering Sea
- Attu Island
- PACIFIC OCEAN
- 55°N
- 50°N
- 170°E
- 180°
- 170°W
- 160°W
- 150°W
- 140°W
- 55°N

```
0        250      500 Miles
0        250      500 Kilometers
Projection: Albers Equal Area
```

45°N
40°N
35°N
30°N
125°W
120°W
125°W

CANADA

MINNESOTA

Grand Forks
Fargo
Red River
Minnesota River
Duluth
Superior
Marquette
Sault Ste. Marie
Lake Superior

MICHIGAN

WISCONSIN

Minneapolis
★ St. Paul
Green Bay
Madison ★
Milwaukee
Lake Michigan
Grand Rapids
Lansing ★
Saginaw
Lake Huron

Sioux Falls
Sioux City
IOWA
Cedar Rapids
Davenport
Des Moines ★
Rockford
Chicago
Gary
Fort Wayne
South Bend
Detroit
Ann Arbor
Toledo
Cleveland
Lake Erie
Erie
Youngstown
Akron

maha
ncoln
Missouri River
MISSOURI
Peoria
Springfield ★
ILLINOIS
Illinois River
INDIANA
Indianapolis ★
Dayton
Cincinnati
OHIO
Columbus ★

Topeka ★
Kansas City
Kansas City
Wichita
St. Louis
East St. Louis
Jefferson City ★
Lake of the Ozarks
Louisville
Evansville
Frankfort ★
Lexington
Ohio River
KENTUCKY
Lake Barkley

Keystone Lake
Tulsa
ufaula Lake
Springfield
Fayetteville
Kentucky River
Kentucky Lake
Nashville ★
Knoxville
Chattanooga
Asheville

ARKANSAS
Lake Texoma
Little Rock ★
Pine Bluff
Memphis
Mississippi River
TENNESSEE
Huntsville

Dallas
Waco
Shreveport
Red River
Toledo Bend Reservoir
Vicksburg
Jackson ★
Meridian
Montgomery ★
MISSISSIPPI
ALABAMA
Birmingham
GEORGIA
Columbus
Macon
Atlanta

LOUISIANA
Beaumont
Houston
Galveston
Baton Rouge ★
New Orleans
Biloxi
Chandeleur Islands
Mobile
Pensacola
Gulf of Mexico

NEW YORK
Rochester
Buffalo
Syracuse
Albany ★
Lake Ontario

St. Lawrence River
MAINE
Augusta ★
Burlington
Montpelier ★
Lake Champlain
VT
NH
Concord ★
Manchester
Portland
Boston ★
Worcester
Providence ★
Cape Cod
MA
Springfield
Hartford ★
CT **RI**
New Haven
Bridgeport
Jersey City
Newark
Yonkers
New York City
Long Island
Long Island Sound
Hudson R.
Connecticut R.

PENNSYLVANIA
Allentown
Harrisburg ★
Pittsburgh
Philadelphia
Trenton ★
Camden
NJ
Atlantic City
Susquehanna River
40°N
70°W

WEST VIRGINIA
Charleston ★
Washington, D.C. ⊛
Baltimore
MD
Annapolis ★
Dover ★
DE
Delaware Bay

VIRGINIA
Richmond ★
Newport News
Norfolk
Virginia Beach
Chesapeake Bay

ATLANTIC OCEAN

Winston-Salem
Greensboro
Durham
Raleigh ★
Cape Hatteras
35°N

NORTH CAROLINA
Charlotte
Greenville
SOUTH CAROLINA
Columbia ★
Charleston
Savannah
Savannah River
Sea Islands
30°N

Jacksonville
Tallahassee ★
Gainesville
FLORIDA
Orlando
Tampa
St. Petersburg
Lake Okeechobee
Cape Canaveral
Fort Myers
Fort Lauderdale
Miami
80°W
Cape Sable
Florida Keys
Straits of Florida
25°N

THE BAHAMAS
75°W

Chattahoochee R.

Legend	
⊛	National capital
★	State capitals
•	Other cities

Scale:
0 — 100 — 200 Miles
0 — 100 — 200 Kilometers
Projection: Albers Equal Area

95°W
90°W
85°W
25°N

The United States of America: Physical

CANADA

MEXICO

PACIFIC OCEAN

COAST RANGES

CASCADE RANGE

SIERRA NEVADA

Coast Ranges

ROCKY MOUNTAINS

GREAT BASIN

COLORADO PLATEAU

GREAT PLAINS

Cape Mendocino

Mount Rainier
14,410 ft.
(4,392 m)

Puget Sound

Columbia River

Willamette River

Klamath River

Goose Lake

Shasta Lake

Pyramid Lake

Central Valley

Sacramento River

San Joaquin River

Lake Tahoe

Monterey Bay

San Francisco Bay

Channel Islands

Mount Whitney
14,494 ft.
(4,419 m)

Death Valley

Mojave Desert

Salton Sea

Imperial Valley

Columbia River

Columbia Plateau

Snake River

Franklin D. Roosevelt Lake

Pend Oreille

Clark Fork

Flathead River

Flathead Lake

Bitterroot Range

Salmon River

Salmon River Mts.

Sawtooth Mts.

Lewis Range

CONTINENTAL

Grand Tetons

Gannett Peak
13,804 ft.
(4,207 m)

Wind River Range

Yellowstone Lake

Bighorn Mts.

Bighorn River

Wind River

Powder River

Milk River

Missouri River

Yellowstone River

Fort Peck Lake

Lake Sakakawea

Lake Oahe

Black Hills

Cheyenne River

White River

Niobrara River

James River

Wasatch Range

Great Salt Lake

Utah Lake

Uinta Mts.

Green River

Colorado River

Mount Elbert
14,433 ft.
(4,400 m)

DIVIDE

Front Range

Lake Powell

San Juan River

Grand Canyon

Lake Mead

Colorado River

Painted Desert

Sangre De Cristo Mts.

San Luis Valley

Pikes Peak
14,110 ft.
(4,301 m)

South Platte River

North Platte River

Platte River

Republican River

Smoky Hill River

Gila River

Sonoran Desert

CONTINENTAL DIVIDE

Rio Grande

Pecos River

Canadian River

Gulf of California

Nueces River

Amistad Reservoir

Rio Grande

Colorado River

Pad Islar

45°N

40°N

35°N

30°N

125°W

120°W

125°W

To understand the relative locations of Alaska and Hawaii, as well as the vast distances separating them from the rest of the United States, see the world map.

HAWAII

Kauai

Niihau

Oahu

Molokai

Lanai

Kahoolawe

Maui

Mauna Kea
13,796 ft.
(4,206 m)

Hawaii

PACIFIC OCEAN

22°N

19°N

160°W

155°W

0   75   150 Miles

0   75   150 Kilometers

Projection: Mercator

ARCTIC OCEAN

RUSSIA

Bering Strait

Arctic Circle

BROOKS RANGE

Yukon River

Tanana River

Kuskokwim River

ALASKA RANGE

Mount McKinley
20,320 ft.
(6,194 m)

CANADA

St. Lawrence Island

St. Matthew Island

Nunivak Island

Gulf of Alaska

Kodiak Island

Alexander Archipelago

Bering Sea

Attu Island

PACIFIC OCEAN

55°N

50°N

55°N

170°E

180°

170°W

160°W

150°W

140°W

0   250   500 Miles

0   250   500 Kilometers

Projection: Albers Equal Area

CANADA

Isle Royale
Mesabi Range
Lake Superior

Bad River
Minnesota River
Mississippi River
Wisconsin River
Lake Michigan
Lake Huron
Lake Erie
Lake Ontario

St. Lawrence Seaway
St. Lawrence River
St. John River
Longfellow Mts.
Penobscot River

Lake Champlain
Green Mts.
White Mts.
Adirondack Mts.
Hudson River
Connecticut River
Cape Cod

Long Island Sound
Long Island

PLATEAU
MOUNTAINS

Catskill Mts.
Allegheny R.
Susquehanna River
Delaware River

40°N

ALLEGHENY

APPALACHIAN MOUNTAINS

Delaware Bay
Chesapeake Bay

ATLANTIC OCEAN

70°W

P L A I N S

Missouri River
Des Moines River
Illinois River
Wabash River
Scioto River
Ohio River
Monongahela R.
Potomac River

Kansas R.

Lake of the Ozarks
OZARK PLATEAU

Keystone Lake

Lake Barkley
Cumberland River
Cumberland Plateau
Kentucky Lake
Kanawha River
BLUE RIDGE MOUNTAINS
James River

Roanoke River

35°N

Pamlico Sound
Cape Hatteras

Eufaula Lake
Arkansas River
White River
Ouachita Mts.
Lake Texoma

Kentucky
Tennessee River
Great Smoky Mts.
PIEDMONT

Oconee River
Savannah River

Trinity River
Red River
Sabine River
Mississippi River
Pearl River
Tombigbee River
Alabama R.
Coosa River
Chattahoochee River
Altamaha River
Sea Islands

COASTAL
PLAIN

GULF

Toledo Bend Reservoir

Chandeleur Islands
Mississippi Delta

Okefenokee Swamp

Brazos River

N
W   E
S

FLORIDA PENINSULA

Cape Canaveral

Gulf of Mexico

Lake Okeechobee

THE BAHAMAS

25°N

The Everglades
Cape Sable
Florida Keys
Straits of Florida

85°W
90°W
95°W
80°W
75°W

ELEVATION

Feet	Meters
13,120	4,000
6,560	2,000
1,640	500
656	200
(Sea level) 0	0 (Sea level)
Below sea level	Below sea level

0   100   200 Miles
0   100   200 Kilometers
Projection: Albers Equal Area

ATLAS

ARCTIC OCEAN

Greenland
(DENMARK)

ALASKA
(U.S.)

ICELAN

Godthåb

60°N

CANADA

Aleutian Islands

Winnipeg

Vancouver

Ottawa   Montreal

NORTH
AMERICA

Chicago   Toronto

40°N

UNITED
STATES

New York City

ATLANTIC
OCEAN

Washington,
D.C.

Rabat

Los Angeles

Casablanca

MOROCCO

Houston

Bermuda
(U.K.)

WESTERN
SAHARA
(Sovereignty
Disputed)

Tropic of Cancer

MEXICO

20°N

Mexico
City

MAURITANIA

HAWAII
(U.S.)

Nouakchott

CAPE VERDE   SENEGAL

Dakar

Caracas

Bama
BU

GAMBIA

GUINEA-BISSAU

GUINEA

VENEZUELA   GUYANA

SIERRA
LEONE

G
D'IVO

COLOMBIA

Bogotá

Georgetown

SURINAME

FRENCH GUIANA
(FRANCE)

LIBERIA

Paramaribo

0°   Equator

Quito

KIRIBATI

ECUADOR

N

Galápagos
Islands
(ECUADOR)

PACIFIC
OCEAN

W   E

S

PERU

SOUTH
AMERICA

SAMOA

American
Samoa

BRAZIL

Lima

Brasília

BOLIVIA

20°S

La Paz

TONGA

Sucre

Tropic of Capricorn

Rio de Janeiro

PARAGUAY

São Paulo

ATLANTIC

Asunción

CHILE

OCEAN

Buenos
Aires

URUGUAY

Santiago

Montevideo

40°S

ARGENTINA

Boundaries

National capitals

Other cities

Falkland
Islands
(U.K.)

South
Georgia
(U.K.)

South Sandwich
Islands

0   500   1,000 Miles

0   500 1,000 Kilometers

Projection: Mollweide

60°S

Antarctic Circle

160°W   140°W   120°W   100°W   80°W   60°W   40°W   20°W

90°W

80°W

0   200   400 Miles

FLORIDA
(U.S.)

70°W

Tropic of Cancer

0   200 400 Kilometers

Nassau

Projection: Mercator

BAHAMAS

Havana

Turks and Caicos Is.
(U.K.)

60°W

ATLANTIC   OCEAN

20°N

GULF OF
MEXICO

CUBA

Cayman Is.
(U.K.)

HAITI

DOMINICAN
REPUBLIC

Virgin Islands
(U.S. and U.K.)

1

MEXICO

BELIZE

JAMAICA

Port-au-Prince

Santo
Domingo

2

Belmopan

Kingston

Puerto Rico
(U.S.)

Guadeloupe (FRANCE)

GUATEMALA

HONDURAS

CARIBBEAN   SEA

3

Martinique (FRANCE)

Guatemala City

Tegucigalpa

Netherlands
Antilles
(NETHERLANDS)

4

San Salvador

NICARAGUA

Aruba
(NETHERLANDS)

5   6

EL SALVADOR

N

Managua

7

W   E

COSTA RICA

Panama
City

Port-of-
Spain

TRINIDAD AND
TOBAGO

S

San José

10°N

PANAMA

VENEZUELA

PACIFIC
OCEAN

COLOMBIA

GUYANA

90°W

COUNTRY	CAPITAL
1 Antigua and Barbuda	St. Johns
2 St. Kitts and Nevis	Basseterre
3 Dominica	Roseau
4 St. Lucia	Castries
5 St. Vincent and the Grenadines	Kingstown
6 Barbados	Bridgetown
7 Grenada	St. George's

ARCTIC OCEAN

RUSSIA

Moscow

EUROPE

KAZAKHSTAN

ASIA

MONGOLIA

Astana

Ulaanbaatar

Harbin

60°N

GEORGIA

UZBEKISTAN

Almaty

KYRGYZSTAN

Beijing

NORTH
KOREA

JAPAN

40°N

Istanbul

Ankara

ARMENIA

Baku

Tashkent

Tianjin

P'yŏngyang

Seoul

Tokyo

TURKEY

AZERBAIJAN

TURKMENISTAN

TAJIKISTAN

CHINA

SOUTH
KOREA

Nagoya

Yokohama

Nicosia

Tehran

CYPRUS

SYRIA

Ashgabat

Osaka

rs

Beirut

Damascus

Kabul

Wuhan

TUNISIA

Tripoli

LEBANON

IRAQ

Baghdad

IRAN

AFGHANISTAN

Islamabad

Shanghai

Jerusalem

Amman

Delhi

NEPAL

Chongqing

Cairo

JORDAN

ISRAEL

KUWAIT

BAHRAIN

PAKISTAN

Kathmandu

BHUTAN

Taipei

TAIWAN

Tropic of Cancer

LIBYA

EGYPT

SAUDI
ARABIA

QATAR

Karachi

New
Delhi

BANGLADESH

Guangzhou

Hong
Kong

20°N

ERIA

Riyadh

UNITED ARAB
EMIRATES

OMAN

Muscat

INDIA

Dhaka

Calcutta

MYANMAR
(BURMA)

LAOS

Hanoi

Northern
Mariana
(U.S.)

PACIFIC
OCEAN

AFRICA

Mumbai
(Bombay)

Chennai
(Madras)

Yangon
(Rangoon)

THAILAND

VIETNAM

Manila

Guam (U.S.)

MARSHALL
ISLANDS

NIGER

CHAD

Khartoum

ERITREA

YEMEN

Asmara

Sanaa

OMAN

Bangkok

CAMBODIA

Phnom Penh

PHILIPPINES

iamey

N'Djamena

NIGERIA

Abuja

SUDAN

DJIBOUTI

Ho Chi
Minh City

BRUNEI

PALAU

FEDERATED STATES
OF MICRONESIA

IN

Lagos

CENTRAL
AFRICAN
REPUBLIC

ETHIOPIA

Addis Ababa

SOMALIA

SRI
LANKA

Colombo

Kuala
Lumpur

MALAYSIA

O

CAMEROON

UGANDA

KENYA

MALDIVES

Singapore

SINGAPORE

Equator

NAURU

0°

UA-
RIAL
NEA

DEMOCRATIC
REPUBLIC
OF THE
CONGO

INDONESIA

KIRIBATI

GABON

RWANDA

BURUNDI

Nairobi

PAPUA
NEW
GUINEA

OMÉ
CIPE

Kinshasa

TANZANIA

SEYCHELLES

Jakarta

Surabaya

EAST TIMOR

Port Moresby

SOLOMON
ISLANDS

TUVALU

CABINDA
ANGOLA)

Luanda

Dodoma

Dar es Salaam

ANGOLA

MALAWI

COMOROS

INDIAN OCEAN

VANUATU

FIJI

ZAMBIA

MOZAMBIQUE

Lusaka

MADAGASCAR

New Caledonia
(FRANCE)

20°S

NAMIBIA

ZIMBABWE

Harare

Antananarivo

AUSTRALIA

Windhoek

BOTSWANA

MAURITIUS

Réunion
(FRANCE)

Tropic of Capricorn

Gaborone

Pretoria

Johannesburg

Maputo

SWAZILAND

Bloemfontein

LESOTHO

SOUTH
AFRICA

Cape Town

Sydney

Canberra

NEW
ZEALAND

Melbourne

Wellington

Tasmania

60°S

ANTARCTICA

20°E

40°E

60°E

80°E

100°E

120°E

140°E

160°E

COUNTRY	CAPITAL
1 Czech Republic	Prague
2 Slovakia	Bratislava
3 Slovenia	Ljubljana
4 Croatia	Zagreb
5 Bosnia and Herzegovina	Sarajevo
6 Macedonia	Skopje
7 Serbia and Montenegro	Belgrade
8 Lithuania	Vilnius
9 Latvia	Riga
10 Estonia	Tallinn

0 250 500 Miles
0 250 500 Kilometers
Projection: Mollweide

ICELAND

Reykjavik

SWEDEN

FINLAND

Arctic
Circle

NORWAY

Helsinki

St. Petersburg

RUSSIA

Oslo

Stockholm

10

60°N

UNITED
KINGDOM

NORTH
SEA

DENMARK

Copenhagen

9

8

Minsk

Moscow

Dublin

NETHERLANDS

Amsterdam

Berlin

Warsaw

BELARUS

IRELAND

London

The Hague

GERMANY

POLAND

Kiev

ATLANTIC

Brussels

BELGIUM

1

2

UKRAINE

OCEAN

Paris

LUXEMBOURG

Vienna

Budapest

MOLDOVA

Chişinău

50°N

FRANCE

Bern

SWITZERLAND

AUSTRIA

HUNGARY

ROMANIA

LIECHTENSTEIN

3

4

5

7

Bucharest

MONACO

ITALY

SAN MARINO

BULGARIA

BLACK SEA

PORTUGAL

ANDORRA

Corsica
(FRANCE)

VATICAN CITY

Rome

Tiranë

6

Sofia

ALBANIA

Lisbon

SPAIN

Madrid

Balearic
Is. (SPAIN)

Sardinia
(ITALY)

GREECE

40°N

MEDITERRANEAN

Sicily

Athens

Gibraltar (U.K.)

SEA

MALTA

Crete

North America: Political

ASIA

ARCTIC OCEAN

EUROPE

+ North Pole

Bering Strait

St. Lawrence Island

Bering Sea

Nunivak Island

Point Barrow

Beaufort Sea

Banks Island

Queen Elizabeth Islands

ICELAND

Greenland (DENMARK)

Denmark Strait

Arctic Circle

Victoria Island

Yukon River

ALASKA (U.S.)

Anchorage

Kodiak Island

Gulf of Alaska

Mackenzie River

Great Bear Lake

Baffin Island

Baffin Bay

Davis Strait

Cape Farewell

Labrador Sea

Alexander Archipelago

Juneau

Queen Charlotte Islands

Peace River

Great Slave Lake

Southampton Island

Coats Island

Mansel Island

Hudson Strait

PACIFIC OCEAN

Vancouver Island

Edmonton

CANADA

Hudson Bay

Anticosti Island

Newfoundland

Vancouver

Seattle

Portland

Columbia River

Calgary

Lake Winnipeg

Winnipeg

St. Lawrence R.

Prince Edward Island

Gulf of St. Lawrence

Cape Breton Island

St. Pierre and Miquelon (FRANCE)

Quebec

Montreal

Lake Superior

Lake Huron

Ottawa

Toronto

Lake Ontario

Lake Erie

Boston

Cape Cod

San Francisco

San Jose

Snake River

Salt Lake City

Great Salt Lake

Denver

Platte River

Missouri River

Minneapolis

Milwaukee

Chicago

Lake Michigan

Detroit

Cleveland

Columbus

New York City

Philadelphia

Baltimore

Washington, D.C.

Norfolk

ATLANTIC OCEAN

Kansas City

Indianapolis

St. Louis

Ohio R.

Colorado River

UNITED STATES

Memphis

Cape Hatteras

Bermuda (U.K.)

Los Angeles

San Diego

Tijuana

Phoenix

Red River

Atlanta

Birmingham

Dallas

Rio Grande

Mississippi River

Jacksonville

Cape Canaveral

Tropic of Cancer

Austin

San Antonio

Houston

New Orleans

Miami

Florida Keys

THE BAHAMAS

Nassau

Turks and Caicos Islands (U.K.)

DOMINICAN REPUBLIC

Puerto Rico (U.S.)

San Juan

ST. KITTS & NEVIS

ANTIGUA & BARBUDA

Guadeloupe (FRANCE)

DOMINICA

Monterrey

Gulf of Mexico

Havana

CUBA

HAITI

Santo Domingo

Virgin Is. (U.S. & U.K.)

Martinique (FRANCE)

BARBADOS

MEXICO

Guadalajara

Mexico City

Puebla

Mérida

Balsas R.

Cayman Is. (U.K.)

Kingston

JAMAICA

Port-au-Prince

Caribbean Sea

ST. LUCIA

ST. VINCENT AND THE GRENADINES

Netherlands Antilles (NETHERLANDS)

GRENADA

Belmopan

BELIZE

GUATEMALA

Guatemala City

HONDURAS

Tegucigalpa

NICARAGUA

Aruba (NETHERLANDS)

TRINIDAD AND TOBAGO

San Salvador

EL SALVADOR

Managua

Panama Canal

COSTA RICA

San José

PANAMA

Panama City

SOUTH AMERICA

Boundaries

⊛ National capitals

• Other cities

0   300   600 Miles

0   300   600 Kilometers

Projection: Azimuthal Equal Area

N W E S

0° Equator

ATLAS

South America: Political

CENTRAL
AMERICA

Caribbean Sea

ATLANTIC
OCEAN

Barranquilla
Cartagena
Caracas

Lake
Maracaibo

VENEZUELA

Medellín

Georgetown
Paramaribo

GUYANA

Cayenne

Bogotá

Orinoco River

SURINAME FRENCH
GUIANA
(FRANCE)

COLOMBIA

Cali

*Malpelo
Island*
(COLOMBIA)

Río Negro

Amazon River

Equator

Quito

ECUADOR

Belém

Guayaquil

0° Equator

*Galápagos
Islands*
(ECUADOR)

Amazon River

Marañón River

PERU

BRAZIL

Ucayali River

Recife

Trujillo

São Francisco River

Callao Lima

Brasília

Salvado

PACIFIC
OCEAN

*Lake
Titicaca*

Arequipa

La Paz

BOLIVIA

Belo Horizonte

*Lake
Poopó*

Sucre

Campinas

São Paulo

PARAGUAY

Rio de Janeiro

Paraguay River

Asunción

Curitiba

Tropic of Capricorn

*San Ambrosio
Island*
(CHILE)

San Félix Island
(CHILE)

Pôrto Alegre

CHILE

*Paraná
River*

Uruguay River

ATLANTIC
OCEAN

Córdoba

*Juan Fernández
Islands*
(CHILE)

Rosario

URUGUAY

Valparaíso
Santiago

Buenos Aires
Montevideo

Rio de la Plata

ARGENTINA

Boundaries

National capitals

Other cities

```
0       250    500 Miles
0       250    500 Kilometers
```
Projection: Azimuthal Equal Area

*Strait of
Magellan*

*Falkland
Islands* (U.K.)

*South Georgia
Island*
(U.K.)

*Tierra del
Fuego*

Europe: Political

Boundaries
⊛ National capitals
• Other cities

| 0 | 150 | 300 Miles |
| 0 | 150 | 300 Kilometers |

Projection: Azimuthal Equal Area

Asia: Political

Boundaries
⊛ National capitals
• Other cities

750 Miles
500
250
0
0 250 500 750 Kilometers
Projection: Two-Point Equidistant

ATLAS

Bodies of Water and Regions

PACIFIC OCEAN
INDIAN OCEAN
Bering Sea
Sea of Okhotsk
Barents Sea
Kara Sea
Laptev Sea
Yellow Sea
East China Sea
South China Sea
Celebes Sea
Java Sea
Arafura Sea
Bay of Bengal
Arabian Sea
Caspian Sea
Black Sea
Mediterranean Sea
Red Sea
Persian Gulf
Gulf of Aden
Gulf of Oman
Gulf of Thailand
Lake Baykal
Lake Balkhash
Aral Sea
Arctic Circle
Tropic of Cancer
Equator
North Pole

EUROPE
AFRICA
AUSTRALIA
New Guinea

Countries and Cities

RUSSIA — Moscow, Yekaterinburg, Chelyabinsk, Omsk, Novosibirsk, Irkutsk, Yakutsk, Vladivostok

MONGOLIA — Ulaanbaatar

CHINA — Beijing, Harbin, Changchun, Fushun, Dalian, Shenyang, Qingdao, Nanjing, Shanghai, Wuhan, Xi'an, Chengdu, Chongqing, Guangzhou, Hong Kong, Macao

KAZAKHSTAN — Astana, Almaty
UZBEKISTAN — Tashkent
KYRGYZSTAN — Bishkek
TAJIKISTAN — Dushanbe
TURKMENISTAN — Ashgabat
AFGHANISTAN — Kabul
PAKISTAN — Islamabad, Lahore, Faisalabad, Karachi

INDIA — New Delhi, Delhi, Jaipur, Ahmadabad, Bhopal, Nagpur, Mumbai (Bombay), Bangalore, Hyderabad, Chennai (Madras), Kolkata (Calcutta)

NEPAL — Kathmandu
BHUTAN — Thimphu
BANGLADESH — Dhaka, Chittagong
SRI LANKA — Colombo
MALDIVES — Male

MYANMAR (BURMA) — Yangon (Rangoon), Mandalay
THAILAND — Bangkok
LAOS — Vientiane
VIETNAM — Hanoi, Ho Chi Minh City
CAMBODIA — Phnom Penh
MALAYSIA — Kuala Lumpur
SINGAPORE — Singapore
BRUNEI — Bandar Seri Begawan
INDONESIA — Jakarta, Bandung, Semarang, Surabaya, Ujung Pandang, Medan
PHILIPPINES — Manila
EAST TIMOR

JAPAN — Tokyo, Yokohama, Nagoya, Osaka, Kyoto, Hiroshima, Nagasaki, Sapporo
NORTH KOREA — Pyongyang
SOUTH KOREA — Seoul
TAIWAN — Taipei

IRAN — Tehran, Mashhad, Isfahan, Shiraz, Tabriz
IRAQ — Baghdad, Mosul, Basra
SAUDI ARABIA — Riyadh, Mecca, Jidda
YEMEN — Sanaa
OMAN — Masqat (Muscat)
UNITED ARAB EMIRATES — Abu Dhabi
QATAR — Doha
BAHRAIN — Manama
KUWAIT — Kuwait City
JORDAN — Amman
SYRIA — Damascus, Aleppo
LEBANON — Beirut
ISRAEL — Tel Aviv, Jerusalem
CYPRUS — Nicosia
TURKEY — Ankara, Istanbul, Izmir
GEORGIA — T'bilisi
ARMENIA — Yerevan
AZERBAIJAN — Baku

Socotra (YEMEN)
Aleutian Islands
Kuril Islands (RUSSIA)
Sakhalin Island
Ryukyu Islands (JAPAN)
Hainan (CHINA)
Andaman Islands (INDIA)
Nicobar Islands (INDIA)
Lakshadweep Islands (INDIA)

Ob River, Irtysh River, Yenisey River, Angara River, Lena River, Amur River, Ural River, Syr Darya, Amu Darya, Indus River, Ganges River, Brahmaputra River, Yellow He (Huang He), Yangtze (Chang Jiang), Mekong River, Nu River, Tigris River, Euphrates River, Great Wall of China, Ural Mountains

Africa: Political

EUROPE

SOUTHWEST ASIA

Mediterranean Sea

Strait of Gibraltar

Azores (PORTUGAL)

Madeira (PORTUGAL)

Algiers • Tunis
Casablanca • Rabat

TUNISIA

Tripoli

MOROCCO

Canary Islands (SPAIN)

El Aaiún

WESTERN SAHARA (Claimed by Morocco)

Tropic of Cancer

ALGERIA

LIBYA

Alexandria
Giza • Cairo

Suez Canal

EGYPT

Lake Nasser

Nile River

Red Sea

MAURITANIA

Nouakchott

CAPE VERDE

Praia

MALI

NIGER

Niamey

CHAD

N'Djamena

Lake Chad

Khartoum

SUDAN

Blue Nile

White Nile

ERITREA

Asmara

Gulf of Aden

DJIBOUTI

Djibouti

SENEGAL

Dakar
GAMBIA
Banjul
Bissau
GUINEA-BISSAU

Bamako

BURKINA FASO

Ouagadougou

GUINEA

Conakry
Freetown
SIERRA LEONE
Monrovia
LIBERIA

CÔTE D'IVOIRE

Yamoussoukro
Abidjan

GHANA

Accra

TOGO
BENIN
Lomé
Porto-Novo

NIGERIA

Abuja

Lagos

CENTRAL AFRICAN REPUBLIC

Bangui

ETHIOPIA

Addis Ababa

SOMALIA

Mogadishu

Gulf of Guinea

Malabo

EQUATORIAL GUINEA

SÃO TOMÉ AND PRÍNCIPE

São Tomé

CAMEROON

Yaoundé

Libreville

GABON

REPUBLIC OF THE CONGO

Congo River

Kisangani

DEMOCRATIC REPUBLIC OF THE CONGO

Brazzaville
Kinshasa

Equator

UGANDA

Kampala

RWANDA
Kigali
BURUNDI
Bujumbura

Lake Victoria

KENYA

Nairobi

INDIAN OCEAN

Victoria

SEYCHELLES

TANZANIA

Dodoma

Mombasa
Pemba
Zanzibar
Dar es Salaam

Lake Tanganyika

CABINDA (ANGOLA)

Luanda

ATLANTIC OCEAN

St. Helena (U.K.)

ANGOLA

Lubumbashi

Lake Malawi (Nyasa)

COMOROS

Moroni

MALAWI

Lilongwe

ZAMBIA

Lusaka

Zambezi River

MOZAMBIQUE

Harare
ZIMBABWE
Bulawayo

Antananarivo

MADAGASCAR

MAURITIUS

Port Louis
Réunion (FRANCE)

Tropic of Capricorn

NAMIBIA

Windhoek

BOTSWANA

Gaborone

Pretoria

Johannesburg
Bloemfontein

Maputo
Mbabane

SWAZILAND

Maseru

LESOTHO

SOUTH AFRICA

Orange River

Cape Town

N
W E
S

Boundaries

⊛ National capitals

• Other cities

0   250   500 Miles

0   250   500 Kilometers

Projection: Azimuthal Equal Area

ATLAS

ATLAS

NORTH AMERICA

ASIA

NORTH PACIFIC OCEAN

SOUTH PACIFIC OCEAN

INDIAN OCEAN

Equator

Tropic of Cancer

Tropic of Capricorn

International Date Line

AUSTRALIA

NEW ZEALAND

North Island

South Island

Auckland

Wellington

Christchurch

MICRONESIA

MELANESIA

POLYNESIA

KIRIBATI

MARSHALL ISLANDS

FEDERATED STATES OF MICRONESIA

PALAU

NAURU

SOLOMON ISLANDS

TUVALU

PAPUA NEW GUINEA

VANUATU

FIJI

SAMOA

TONGA

Hawaiian Islands

Hawaii (U.S.)

Midway Island (U.S.)

Johnston Island (U.S.)

Wake Island (U.S.)

Bonin Islands (JAPAN)

Volcano Islands (JAPAN)

Northern Marianas (U.S.)

Guam (U.S.)

Agana

Koror

Palikir

Eniwetok I.

Kwajalein Island

Majuro

Tarawa

Gilbert Islands

Yaren

Funafuti

Kingman Reef (U.S.)

Palmyra Island (U.S.)

Washington Island

Fanning Island

Howland I. (U.S.)

Baker I. (U.S.)

Jarvis I. (U.S.)

Phoenix Islands

McKean I.

Gardner

Starbuck Island

Manihiki Island

Tokelau (N.Z.)

American Samoa

Pago Pago

Apia

Niue (N.Z.)

Nuku'alofa

Wallis & Futuna (FR.)

Suva

Port-Vila

Espiritu Santo I.

Malekula I.

Guadalcanal I.

Honiara

Port Moresby

New Guinea

Bismarck Archipelago

Truk Is.

Cook Islands (NEW ZEALAND)

Rarotonga Island

Society Islands (FRANCE)

French Polynesia

Tahiti (FRANCE)

Papeete

Tubuai Islands (FRANCE)

Rapa Island (FRANCE)

Tuamotu Archipelago (FRANCE)

Marquesas Islands (FRANCE)

Pitcairn Island

Pitcairn (U.K.)

Ducie Island

Easter Island (CHILE)

Kermadec Islands (N.Z.)

Norfolk Island (AUSTRALIA)

Chatham Islands (N.Z.)

Bounty Islands (N.Z.)

Auckland Islands (NEW ZEALAND)

New Caledonia (FRANCE)

Loyalty Islands (FRANCE)

Noumea

Darwin

Brisbane

Sydney

Canberra

Melbourne

Hobart

Adelaide

Perth

Arafura Sea

Timor Sea

Coral Sea

Tasman Sea

Flinders R.

Darling R.

Lachlan R.

Murray R.

South China Sea

Philippine Sea

Christmas Island (AUSTRALIA)

Projection: Mercator

Boundaries

⊛ National capitals

• Other cities

1,000 Miles

1,000 Kilometers

500

500

0

0

N E S W

30°N

15°N

0°

15°S

30°S

45°S

135°E

150°E

165°E

180°

165°W

150°W

135°W

120°W

Gazetteer

A

Africa Second-largest continent. Lies in both the Northern and the Southern Hemispheres. p. 13

Alabama (AL) State in the southern United States. Admitted as a state in 1819. Capital: Montgomery. (33°N 87°W) p. 286

Alaska (AK) U.S. state in northwestern North America. Purchased from Russia in 1867. Became a territory in 1912. Admitted as a state in 1959. Capital: Juneau. (64°N 150°W) p. 8

Albany Capital of New York. (42°N 74°W). p. 92

Andes Mountains a mountain range along the west coast of South America p. 47

Appalachian Mountains Mountain system in eastern North America that extends from Canada to central Alabama. p. 59

Arctic Region around the North Pole including Arctic Ocean, parts of Alaska, Canada, Russia and Scandinavian countries. (90°N 0°E) p. 8

Arizona (AZ) State in the southwestern United States. Organized into a territory in 1863. Admitted as a state in 1912. Capital: Phoenix. (34°N 113°W) p. 8

Arkansas (AR) State in the south-central United States. Admitted as a state in 1836. Capital: Little Rock. (35°N 93°W) p. 26

Asia Largest continent. Occupies the same land mass as Europe. p. 13

Athens an ancient city and modern capital of Greece; the world's first democracy developed in Athens around 500 BC (38°N 24°E) p. 23

Atlanta Capital of Georgia. (33°N 84°W) p. 539

Atlantic Ocean Vast body of water separating North and South America from Europe and Africa. p. 7

B

Baltimore Maryland city northeast of Washington, D.C., on the Chesapeake Bay. (39°N 76°W) p. 286

Bering Land Bridge Land bridge that once connected what is now Alaska with Siberia. p. 6

Boston Capital of Massachusetts. (42°N 71°W) p. 44

Buena Vista City in northeastern Mexico. (33°N 117°W) p. 360

Bull Run Creek in northeastern Virginia where the Confederates won two major battles during the Civil War. p. 517

Bunker Hill Hill in Boston, Massachusetts. Site of an early Revolutionary War battle. p. 79

C

Cahokia a site in modern Missouri where the Mississippian culture built large settlements (38°N 90°W) p. 11

California (CA) State in the western United States. Admitted as a state in 1850. Capital: Sacramento. (38°N 121°W) p. 10

Canada Country in northern North America. Capital: Ottawa. (50°N 100°W) p. 8

Cape of Good Hope Southern tip of Africa. p. 15

Caribbean Sea Arm of the Atlantic Ocean between North and South America. p. 55

Central America Region of land connecting North and South America. p. 22

Charleston Port city in southeastern South Carolina. Originally called Charles Town. (33°N 80°W) p. 97

Chesapeake Bay Inlet of the Atlantic Ocean in Virginia and Maryland. p. 37

Chicago Large U.S. City in northeastern Illinois on Lake Michigan. Major port (41°N 87°W) p. 396

Chile a country in western South America; the Inca Empire stretched into central Chile p. 47

China Country in East Asia with the world's largest population. Capital: Beijing. (Official name: People's Republic of China) p. 13

Colombia Republic in northwest South America. Capital: Bogotá. (4°N 72°W) p. 21

Columbia River River in northwestern United States and southwestern Canada. Forms part of boundary between Oregon and Washington. p. 276

Colorado (CO) State in the southwestern United States. Admitted as a state in 1876. Capital: Denver. (39°N 107°W) p. 8

Concord One of two northeastern Massachusetts towns (along with Lexington) where the first fighting of the American Revolution took place in 1775. (42°N 71°W) p. 77

Connecticut (CT) State in the northeastern United States. One of the original thirteen colonies. Admitted as a state in 1788. Capital: Hartford. (41°N 73°W) p. 46

Cuzco a city in Peru; it was the capital of the Inca Empire (14°S 72°W) p. 47

D

Delaware (DE) State in the eastern United States. One of the original thirteen colonies. Capital: Dover. (38°N 75°W) p. 76

District of Columbia Federal district between Maryland and Virginia where the capital of the United States is located. (39°N 77°W) p. 240

Ecuador Republic in northwest South America. Capital: Quito. (2°S 78°W) p. 8

England Region of the United Kingdom that makes up most of the southern part of the island of Great Britain. Capital: London. (51°N 1°W) p. 25

Erie Canal An early 1800s building project created a waterway between New York cities of Albany, the capital, and Buffalo, on Lake Erie. p. 295

Europe Continent occupying the same land mass as Asia. p. 12

Florence a city in Italy; ruled by the Medici family in the 1400s, it was a major center for culture and trade (44°N 11°E) p. 27

Florida (FL) State in the southeastern United States. Organized as a territory in 1822. Admitted as a state in 1845. Capital: Tallahassee. (30°N 84°W) p. 22

Fort McHenry U.S. fort that guarded Baltimore, Maryland. The British attacked the fort in the War of 1812. p. 286

Fort Necessity Site where the French defeated British colonists in 1754, in what was the first battle of the French and Indian War. p. 58

Fort Sumter Fort on Charleston Harbor, South Carolina. Attack by Confederate forces here began the Civil War. p. 511

France Country in Western Europe. Capital: Paris. (46°N 0°W) p. 18

Georgia (GA) State in the southeastern United States. Admitted as a state in 1788. One of the original thirteen colonies. Capital: Atlanta. (32°N 84°W) p. 40

Germany Country in Western Europe. Capital: Berlin. (51°N 8°E) p. 24

Gettysburg Town in southern Pennsylvania. (40°N 77°W) p. 536

Ghana a West African country located between the Niger and Senegal Rivers; it was the site of a powerful empire established around 300 p. 16

Great Basin Elevated region made up of parts of California, Idaho, Nevada, Oregon, Utah, and Wyoming that was home to many American Indian nations. p. 10

Great Britain Kingdom in western Europe that includes England, Scotland, and Wales. p. 54

Great Lakes Chain of lakes located in central North America and that extends across the U.S.-Canada border. Includes Lake Superior, Lake Michigan, Lake Huron, Lake Erie, and Lake Ontario. p. 18

Great Plains Region of central North America that lies between the Mississippi River and the Rocky Mountains p. 10

Greece a country in southern Europe with mountains, rugged coastlines and scenic islands; the country is called the birthplace of democracy p. 22

Greenland an island in the North Atlantic that was settled by the Vikings p. 38

Gulf of Mexico Gulf on the southeastern coast of North America, bordered by the United States, Mexico, and Cuba. p. 7

Hartford Capital of Connecticut. (41°N 72°W) p. 287

Hispaniola Island that includes the countries of Haiti and the Dominican Republic. p. 17

Hudson Bay Inland sea in east-central Canada. Explored by Henry Hudson in 1610. p. 9

Hudson River River flowing from northeastern to southern New York. p. 27

Idaho (ID) State in the northwestern United States. Admitted as a state in 1890. Capital: Boise. (44°N 115°W) p. 324

Illinois (IL) State in the north-central United States. Admitted as a state in 1819. Capital: Springfield. (40°N 90°W) p. 95

India Large republic in southern Asia. Capital: New Delhi. (28°N 77°E) p. 14

Indiana (IN) State in the north-central United States. Admitted as a state in 1816 Capital: Indianapolis. (40°N 86°W) p. 155

Indian Ocean Vast body of water east of Africa, south of Asia, west of Australia, and north of Antarctica. p. 14

Iowa (IA) State in the north-central United States. Admitted as a state in 1846. Capital: Des Moines. (42°N 94°W) p. 239

Ireland Island in the British Isles. Divided into Northern Ireland (Capital: Belfast), and the Republic of Ireland (Capital: Dublin). (54°N 8°W) p. 438

Italy Country in southern Europe. Capital: Rome. (44°N 11°E) p. 12

Jamestown First successful English colony in America. Established in eastern Virginia in 1607. p. 36

Kansas (KS) State in the central United States. Organized as a territory in 1854. Admitted as a state in 1861. Capital: Topeka. (38°N 99°W) p. 277

Kentucky (KY) State in the east-central United States. Admitted as a state in 1792. Capital: Frankfort. (37°N 87°W) p. 210

Lake Erie One of the Great Lakes. Located in the United States and Canada. p. 285

Latin America Spanish-speaking countries of North and South America that were once claimed by Spain and Portugal. p. 300

Lexington One of two northeastern Massachusetts towns (along with Concord) where the first fighting of the American Revolution took place in 1775. (42°N 71°W) p. 77

Liberia Country on the west coast of Africa. (6°N 10°W) p. 455

London Capital of the United Kingdom, in England. (52°N 0°W) p. 42

Los Angeles Large city in southern California. (34°N 118°W) p. 358

Louisiana (LA) State in the southeastern United States carved out of the Louisiana Territory. Admitted as a state in 1812. Capital: Baton Rouge. (31°N 92°W) p. 26

Maine (ME) State in the northeastern United States. Admitted as a state in 1820. Capital: Augusta. (45°N 70°W) p. 18

Mali a West African country located on the Niger River; it was the location of an empire that reached its height around 1300 p. 16

Manhattan Island Island at the north end of New York Bay. One of the five boroughs that make up New York City. p. 27

Maryland (MD) State in the east-central United States. One of the original thirteen colonies. Admitted as a state in 1788. Capital: Annapolis. (39°N 76°W) p. 39

Massachusetts (MA) State in the northeastern United States. One of the original thirteen colonies. Admitted as a state in 1788. Capital: Boston. (42°N 72°W) p. 44

Mecca an ancient city in Arabia and the birthplace of Muhammad (21°N 40°E) p. 18

Mediterranean Sea Large sea bordered by southern Europe, Southwest Asia, and northern Africa. p. 14

Mesoamerica Area from Mexico to North Central American during pre-Spanish culture. p. 8

Mexico Country in southern North America. Capital: Mexico City. (23°N 104°W) p. 8

Michigan (MI) State in the north-central United States. Admitted as a state in 1837. Capital: Lansing. (46°N 87°W) p. 155

Minnesota (MN) State in the north-central United States. Admitted as a state in 1858. Capital: St. Paul. (46°N 90°W) p. 277

Mississippi (MS) State in the southeastern United States. Admitted as a state in 1817. Capital: Jackson. (32°N 89°W) p. 332

Mississippi River River that flows from Minnesota south to the Gulf of Mexico. p. 8

Missouri (MO) State in the central United States. Admitted as a state in 1821. Capital: Jefferson City. (38°N 93°W) p. 277

Missouri River River that flows from southern Montana and joins the Mississippi River. p. 8

Montana (MT) State in the northwestern United States. Admitted as a state in 1889. Capital: Helena. (47°N 112°W) p. 277

Montreal City in southeastern Canada founded by the French in 1642. (46°N 74°W) p. 18

Nebraska (NE) State in the central United States. Admitted as a state in 1867. Capital: Lincoln. (41°N 101°W) p. 277

Netherlands Country in northwestern Europe. Capital: Amsterdam. (52°N 5°E) p. 27

Nevada (NV) State in the western United States. Organized as a territory in 1861. Admitted as a state in 1864. Capital: Carson City. (39°N 117°W) p. 356

New Amsterdam Dutch settlement on the island of Manhattan. Founded in 1626. p. 24

New England Northeastern section of the United States. Made up of Connecticut, Maine, Massachusetts, New Hampshire, Rhode Island, and Vermont. p. 42

New Hampshire (NH) State in the northeastern United States. One of the original thirteen colonies. Admitted as a state in 1788. Capital: Concord. (44°N 71°W) p. 44

New Jersey (NJ) State in the northeastern United States. One of the original thirteen colonies. Admitted as a state in 1787. Capital: Trenton. (40°N 75°W) p. 49

New Mexico (NM) State in the southwestern United States. Admitted as a state in 1912. Capital: Santa Fe. (34°N 107°W) p. 8

New Orleans Port city in southeastern Louisiana. (30°N 90°W) p. 26

New Spain Vast area of North America controlled by Spain. p. 22

New Sweden Swedish colony in North America that was located along the Delaware River. p. 27

New York (NY) State in the northeastern United States. One of the original thirteen colonies. Admitted as a state in 1788. Capital: Albany. (42°N 78°W) p. 18

New York City Largest city in the United States. (41°N 74°W) p. 51

Niger River a major river in West Africa p. 18

North America Continent in the northern Western Hemisphere. p. 8

North Carolina (NC) State in the southeastern United States. One of the original thirteen colonies. Admitted as a state in 1789. Capital: Raleigh. (35°N 81°W) p. 18

North Dakota (ND) State in the north-central United States. Admitted as a state in 1889. Capital: Bismarck. (47°N 102°W) p. 277

Ohio (OH) State in the north-central United States. Originally part of the Northwest Territory. Admitted as a state in 1803. Capital: Columbus. (40°N 83°W) p. 59

Ohio River River that flows through Pennsylvania, Ohio, Indiana, and Illinois. p. 8

Oklahoma (OK) State in the south-central United States. Organized as a territory in 1890. Admitted as a state in 1907. Capital: Oklahoma City. (36°N 98°W) p. 277

Oregon (OR) State in the northwestern United States. Admitted as a state in 1859. Capital: Salem. (43°N 122°W) p. 355

Pacific Ocean Body of water extending from the Arctic Circle to Antarctica and from western North and South America to Australia, the Malay Archipelago, and East Asia. p. 7

Panama Country in southern Central America. Location of the Panama Canal. Capital: Panama City. (8°N 81°W) p. 652

Pennsylvania (PA) State in the eastern United States. One of the original thirteen colonies. Admitted as a state in 1787. Capital: Harrisburg. (41°N 78°W) p. 50

Peru Country in western South America. Capital: Lima (10°S 75°W) p. 22

Philadelphia City in southeastern Pennsylvania. Capital of the United States from 1790 to 1800. (40°N 75°W) p. 50

Philippines Country in the western Pacific Ocean. Made up of about 7,100 islands. Capital: Manila. (14°N 125°E) p. 647

Plymouth Site in Massachusetts where the Pilgrims first landed in North America in 1620. (42°N 70°W) p. 43

Portugal Country in southwestern Europe on the western Iberian Peninsula. (38°N 8°W) p. 14

Providence Capital of Rhode Island. (42°N 71°W) p. 46

Rhode Island (RI) State in the northeastern United States. One of the original thirteen colonies. Admitted as a state in 1790. Capital: Providence. (41°N 71°W) p. 46

Richmond Capital of Virginia. Capital of the Confederate States of America during the Civil War. (37°N 7°W) p. 419

Rio Grande Spanish for Great River. Forms the border between Texas and Mexico. p. 358

Roanoke Island Island off the coast of North Carolina. Site of Britain's first settlement in North America. p. 27

Rocky Mountains Mountain range in western North America that extends from Alaska south to New Mexico. p. 11

Rome a city in Italy near the Mediterranean Sea; it was the capital of the Roman Empire (42°N 13°E) p. 23

Russia Vast country that extends from Eastern Europe through northwestern Asia. Capital: Moscow. (61°N 60°E) p. 300

S

Sacramento River River in northwest California. Sacramento, capital of California sits at its head. (38°N 121°W) p. 365

Sahara the world's largest desert, located in northern Africa p. 17

San Antonio City in southern Texas. Site of the Mexican victory over Texas forces at the Alamo during the Texas Revolution. (29°N 99°W) p. 352

San Diego City in southern California. Located on San Diego Bay. (33°N 117°W) p. 358

San Francisco City in western California on a peninsula between the Pacific Ocean and San Francisco Bay. (37°N 122°W) p. 23

Santa Fe Capital of New Mexico. (35°N 106°W) p. 347

Saratoga Site in eastern New York of the Revolutionary War's Battle of Saratoga, the turning point of the war. p. 92

Savannah Port city in southeastern Georgia. Founded by James Oglethorpe in 1733. (32°N 81°W) p. 40

Scandinavia a large peninsula in northern Europe p. 38

Seneca Falls Village in west-central New York State. Site of the first women's rights convention in the United States in 1848. (43°N 77°W) p. 464

Sierra Nevada Large mountain range in eastern California. p. 347

Songhai a large and powerful empire in West Africa during the 1400s and 1500s. p. 16

South America Continent in the southern Western Hemisphere. p. 6

South Carolina (SC) State in the southeastern United States. One of the original thirteen colonies. Admitted as a state in 1788. Capital: Columbia. (34°N 81°W) p. 40

South Dakota (SD) State in the north-central United States. Organized as part of the Dakota Territory in 1861. Admitted as a state in 1889. Capital: Pierre. (44°N 102°W) p. 277

Spain Country in southwestern Europe that occupies the greater part of the Iberian Peninsula. Capital: Madrid. (40°N 4°W) p. 12

T

Tennessee (TN) State in the south-central United States. Admitted as a state in 1796. Capital: Nashville. (36°N 88°W) p. 272

Tenochtitlán Aztec island-city that was located on the site what is now Mexico City. p. 20

Texas (TX) State in the south-central United States. Independent republic from 1836 to 1845. Admitted as a state in 1845. Capital: Austin. (31°N 101°W) p. 10

Timbuktu a city in West Africa that began as a camp for traders around AD 1100 and became a major center of culture and learning (17°N 3°W) p. 18

U

United States of America Country in central North America. Capital: Washington, D.C. (38°N 110°W) p. 7

Utah (UT) State in the western United States. Admitted as a state in 1896. Capital: Salt Lake City. (39°N 112°W) p. 8

V

Valley Forge Site in southeastern Pennsylvania where General George Washington and his troops spent the harsh winter of 1777–78. p. 94

Vermont (VT) State in the northeastern United States. Admitted as a state in 1791. Capital: Montpelier. (44°N 73°W) p. 299

Vicksburg City in western Mississippi on the bluffs above the Mississippi River. (42°N 85°W) p. 522

Virginia (VA) State in the eastern United States. One of the original thirteen colonies. Admitted as a state in 1788. Capital: Richmond. (37°N 80°W) p. 27

W

Washington (WA) State in the northwestern United States. Admitted as a state in 1889. Capital: Olympia. (47°N 121°W) p. 362

Washington, D.C. Capital of the United States. Located on the Potomac River between Virginia and Maryland. (39°N 77°W) p. 240

West Virginia (WV) State in the east-central United States. Part of Virginia until the area refused to join the Confederacy in 1861. Admitted as a state in 1863. Capital: Charleston. (39°N 81°W) p. 512

Wisconsin (WI) State in the north-central United States. Became part of the Northwest Territory in 1787. Admitted as a state in 1848. Capital: Madison. (44°N 91°W) p. 154

Wyoming (WY) State in the northwestern United States. Admitted as a state in 1890. Capital: Cheyenne. (43°N 108°W) p. 361

Presidents

1 **GEORGE WASHINGTON**
Born: 1732 **Died:** 1799
Years in Office: 1789–97
Political Party: None
Home State: Virginia
Vice President:

2 **JOHN ADAMS**
Born: 1735 **Died:** 1826
Years in Office: 1797–1801
Political Party: Federalist
Home State: Massachusetts
Vice President: Thomas Jefferson

3 **THOMAS JEFFERSON**
Born: 1743 **Died:** 1826
Years in Office: 1801–09
Political Party: Republican*
Home State: Virginia
Vice Presidents: Aaron Burr,
George Clinton

4 **JAMES MADISON**
Born: 1751 **Died:** 1836
Years in Office: 1809–17
Political Party: Republican
Home State: Virginia
Vice Presidents: George Clinton,
Elbridge Gerry

5 **JAMES MONROE**
Born: 1758 **Died:** 1831
Years in Office: 1817–25
Political Party: Republican
Home State: Virginia
Vice President: Daniel D. Tompkins

6 **JOHN QUINCY ADAMS**
Born: 1767 **Died:** 1848
Years in Office: 1825–29
Political Party: Republican
Home State: Massachusetts
Vice President: John C. Calhoun

7 **ANDREW JACKSON**
Born: 1767 **Died:** 1845
Years in Office: 1829–37
Political Party: Democratic
Home State: Tennessee
Vice Presidents: John C. Calhoun,
Martin Van Buren

8 **MARTIN VAN BUREN**
Born: 1782 **Died:** 1862
Years in Office: 1837–41
Political Party: Democratic
Home State: New York
Vice President: Richard M. Johnson

* The Republican Party of the third through sixth presidents is not the party of Abraham Lincoln, which was founded in 1854.

9 WILLIAM HENRY HARRISON
Born: 1773 **Died:** 1841
Years in Office: 1841
Political Party: Whig
Home State: Ohio
Vice President: John Tyler

10 JOHN TYLER
Born: 1790 **Died:** 1862
Years in Office: 1841–45
Political Party: Whig
Home State: Virginia
Vice President: None

11 JAMES K. POLK
Born: 1795 **Died:** 1849
Years in Office: 1845–49
Political Party: Democratic
Home State: Tennessee
Vice President: George M. Dallas

12 ZACHARY TAYLOR
Born: 1784 **Died:** 1850
Years in Office: 1849–50
Political Party: Whig
Home State: Louisiana
Vice President: Millard Fillmore

13 MILLARD FILLMORE
Born: 1800 **Died:** 1874
Years in Office: 1850–53
Political Party: Whig
Home State: New York
Vice President: None

14 FRANKLIN PIERCE
Born: 1804 **Died:** 1869
Years in Office: 1853–57
Political Party: Democratic
Home State: New Hampshire
Vice President: William R. King

15 JAMES BUCHANAN
Born: 1791 **Died:** 1868
Years in Office: 1857–61
Political Party: Democratic
Home State: Pennsylvania
Vice President: John C. Breckinridge

16 ABRAHAM LINCOLN
Born: 1809 **Died:** 1865
Years in Office: 1861–65
Political Party: Republican
Home State: Illinois
Vice Presidents: Hannibal Hamlin,
Andrew Johnson

17 ANDREW JOHNSON
Born: 1808 **Died:** 1875
Years in Office: 1865–69
Political Party: Republican
Home State: Tennessee
Vice President: None

18 ULYSSES S. GRANT
Born: 1822 **Died:** 1885
Years in Office: 1869–77
Political Party: Republican
Home State: Illinois
Vice Presidents: Schuyler Colfax, Henry Wilson

19 RUTHERFORD B. HAYES
Born: 1822 **Died:** 1893
Years in Office: 1877–81
Political Party: Republican
Home State: Ohio
Vice President: William A. Wheeler

20 JAMES A. GARFIELD
Born: 1831 **Died:** 1881
Years in Office: 1881
Political Party: Republican
Home State: Ohio
Vice President: Chester A. Arthur

21 CHESTER A. ARTHUR
Born: 1829 **Died:** 1886
Years in Office: 1881–85
Political Party: Republican
Home State: New York
Vice President: None

22 GROVER CLEVELAND
Born: 1837 **Died:** 1908
Years in Office: 1885–89
Political Party: Democratic
Home State: New York
Vice President: Thomas A. Hendricks

23 BENJAMIN HARRISON
Born: 1833 **Died:** 1901
Years in Office: 1889–93
Political Party: Republican
Home State: Indiana
Vice President: Levi P. Morton

24 GROVER CLEVELAND
Born: 1837 **Died:** 1908
Years in Office: 1893–97
Political Party: Democratic
Home State: New York
Vice President: Adlai E. Stevenson

25 WILLIAM McKINLEY
Born: 1843 **Died:** 1901
Years in Office: 1897–1901
Political Party: Republican
Home State: Ohio
Vice Presidents: Garret A. Hobart, Theodore Roosevelt

26 THEODORE ROOSEVELT
Born: 1858 **Died:** 1919
Years in Office: 1901–09
Political Party: Republican
Home State: New York
Vice President: Charles W. Fairbanks

27 WILLIAM HOWARD TAFT
Born: 1857 **Died:** 1930
Years in Office: 1909–13
Political Party: Republican
Home State: Ohio
Vice President: James S. Sherman

28 WOODROW WILSON
Born: 1856 **Died:** 1924
Years in Office: 1913–21
Political Party: Democratic
Home State: New Jersey
Vice President: Thomas R. Marshall

29 WARREN G. HARDING
Born: 1865 **Died:** 1923
Years in Office: 1921–23
Political Party: Republican
Home State: Ohio
Vice President: Calvin Coolidge

30 CALVIN COOLIDGE
Born: 1872 **Died:** 1933
Years in Office: 1923–29
Political Party: Republican
Home State: Massachusetts
Vice President: Charles G. Dawes

31 HERBERT HOOVER
Born: 1874 **Died:** 1964
Years in Office: 1929–33
Political Party: Republican
Home State: California
Vice President: Charles Curtis

32 FRANKLIN D. ROOSEVELT
Born: 1882 **Died:** 1945
Years in Office: 1933–45
Political Party: Democratic
Home State: New York
Vice Presidents: John Nance Garner,
Henry Wallace, Harry S Truman

33 HARRY S TRUMAN
Born: 1884 **Died:** 1972
Years in Office: 1945–53
Political Party: Democratic
Home State: Missouri
Vice President: Alben W. Barkley

34 DWIGHT D. EISENHOWER
Born: 1890 **Died:** 1969
Years in Office: 1953–61
Political Party: Republican
Home State: Kansas
Vice President: Richard M. Nixon

35 JOHN F. KENNEDY
Born: 1917 **Died:** 1963
Years in Office: 1961–63
Political Party: Democratic
Home State: Massachusetts
Vice President: Lyndon B. Johnson

36 LYNDON B. JOHNSON
Born: 1908   **Died:** 1973
Years in Office: 1963–69
Political Party: Democratic
Home State: Texas
Vice President: Hubert H. Humphrey

37 RICHARD M. NIXON
Born: 1913   **Died:** 1994
Years in Office: 1969–74
Political Party: Republican
Home State: California
Vice Presidents: Spiro T. Agnew,
Gerald R. Ford

38 GERALD R. FORD
Born: 1913
Years in Office: 1974–77
Political Party: Republican
Home State: Michigan
Vice President: Nelson A. Rockefeller

39 JIMMY CARTER
Born: 1924
Years in Office: 1977–81
Political Party: Democratic
Home State: Georgia
Vice President: Walter F. Mondale

40 RONALD REAGAN
Born: 1911   **Died:** 2004
Years in Office: 1981–89
Political Party: Republican
Home State: California
Vice President: George Bush

41 GEORGE BUSH
Born: 1924
Years in Office: 1989–93
Political Party: Republican
Home State: Texas
Vice President: J. Danforth Quayle

42 BILL CLINTON
Born: 1946
Years in Office: 1993–2001
Political Party: Democratic
Home State: Arkansas
Vice President: Albert Gore Jr.

43 GEORGE W. BUSH
Born: 1946
Years in Office: 2001–
Political Party: Republican
Home State: Texas
Vice President: Richard B. Cheney

Facts About the States

State	Year of Statehood	2003 Population	Area (Sq. Mi.)	Population Density (Sq Mi.)	Capital
Alabama	1819	4,500,752	50,744	88.7	Montgomery
Alaska	1959	648,818	571,951	1.1	Juneau
Arizona	1912	5,580,811	113,635	49.1	Phoenix
Arkansas	1836	2,725,714	52,068	52.3	Little Rock
California	1850	35,484,453	155,959	227.5	Sacramento
Colorado	1876	4,550,688	103,718	43.9	Denver
Connecticut	1788	3,483,372	4,845	719.0	Hartford
Delaware	1787	817,491	1,954	418.4	Dover
District of Columbia	—	563,384	61	9,235.8	—
Florida	1845	17,019,068	53,927	315.6	Tallahassee
Georgia	1788	8,684,715	57,906	150.0	Atlanta
Hawaii	1959	1,257,608	6,423	195.8	Honolulu
Idaho	1890	1,366,332	82,747	16.5	Boise
Illinois	1818	12,653,544	55,584	227.6	Springfield
Indiana	1816	6,195,643	35,867	172.7	Indianapolis
Iowa	1846	2,944,062	55,869	52.7	Des Moines
Kansas	1861	2,723,507	81,815	33.3	Topeka
Kentucky	1792	4,117,827	39,728	103.7	Frankfort
Louisiana	1812	4,496,334	43,562	103.2	Baton Rouge
Maine	1820	1,305,728	30,862	42.3	Augusta
Maryland	1788	5,508,909	9,774	563.6	Annapolis
Massachusetts	1788	6,433,422	7,840	820.6	Boston
Michigan	1837	10,079,985	56,804	177.5	Lansing
Minnesota	1858	5,059,375	79,610	63.6	St. Paul

State	Year of Statehood	2003 Population	Area (Sq. Mi.)	Population Density (Sq Mi.)	Capital
Mississippi	1817	2,881,281	46,907	61.4	Jackson
Missouri	1821	5,704,484	68,886	82.8	Jefferson City
Montana	1889	917,621	145,552	6.3	Helena
Nebraska	1867	1,739,291	76,872	22.6	Lincoln
Nevada	1864	2,241,154	109,826	20.4	Carson City
New Hampshire	1788	1,287,687	8,968	143.6	Concord
New Jersey	1787	8,638,396	7,417	1,164.7	Trenton
New Mexico	1912	1,874,614	121,356	15.4	Santa Fe
New York	1788	19,190,115	47,214	406.4	Albany
North Carolina	1789	8,407,248	48,711	172.6	Raleigh
North Dakota	1889	633,837	68,976	9.2	Bismarck
Ohio	1803	11,435,798	40,948	279.3	Columbus
Oklahoma	1907	3,511,532	68,667	51.1	Oklahoma City
Oregon	1859	3,559,596	95,997	37.1	Salem
Pennsylvania	1787	12,365,455	44,817	275.9	Harrisburg
Rhode Island	1790	1,076,164	1,045	1,029.8	Providence
South Carolina	1788	4,147,152	30,109	137.7	Columbia
South Dakota	1889	764,309	75,885	10.1	Pierre
Tennessee	1796	5,841,748	41,217	141.7	Nashville
Texas	1845	22,118,509	261,797	84.5	Austin
Utah	1896	2,351,467	82,144	28.6	Salt Lake City
Vermont	1791	619,107	9,250	66.9	Montpelier
Virginia	1788	7,386,330	39,594	186.6	Richmond
Washington	1889	6,131,445	66,544	92.1	Olympia
West Virginia	1863	1,810,354	24,078	75.2	Charleston
Wisconsin	1848	5,472,299	54,310	100.8	Madison
Wyoming	1890	501,242	97,100	5.2	Cheyenne

American Flag

The American flag is a symbol of the nation. It is recognized instantly, whether as a big banner waving in the wind or a tiny emblem worn on a lapel. The flag is so important that it is a major theme of the national anthem, "The Star-Spangled Banner." One of the most popular names for the flag is the Stars and Stripes. It is also known as Old Glory.

THE MEANING OF THE FLAG

The American flag has 13 stripes—7 red and 6 white. In the upper-left corner of the flag is the union—50 white five-pointed stars against a blue background.

The 13 stripes stand for the original 13 American states, and the 50 stars represent the states of the nation today. According to the U.S. Department of State, the colors of the flag also are symbolic:

Red stands for courage.

White symbolizes purity.

Blue is the color of vigilance, perseverance, and justice.

DISPLAYING THE FLAG

It is customary not to display the American flag in bad weather. It is also customary for the flag to be displayed outdoors only from sunrise to sunset, except on certain occasions. In a few special places, however, the flag is always flown day and night. When flown at night, the flag should be illuminated.

Near a speaker's platform, the flag should occupy the place of honor at the speaker's right. When carried in a parade with other flags, the American flag should be on the marching right or in front at the center. When flying with the flags of the 50 states, the national flag must be at the center and the highest point. In a group of national flags, all should be of equal size and all should be flown from staffs, or flagpoles, of equal height.

The flag should never touch the ground or the floor. It should not be marked with any insignia, pictures, or words. Nor should it be used in any disrespectful way—as an advertising decoration, for instance. The flag should never be dipped to honor any person or thing.

SALUTING THE FLAG

The United States, like other countries, has a flag code, or rules for displaying and honoring the flag. For example, all those present should stand at attention facing the flag and salute it when it is being raised or lowered or when it is carried past them in a parade or procession. A man wearing a hat should take it off and hold it with his right hand over his heart. All women and hatless men should stand with their right hands over their hearts to show their respect for the flag. The flag should also receive these honors during the playing of the national anthem and the reciting of the Pledge of Allegiance.

THE PLEDGE OF ALLEGIANCE

The Pledge of Allegiance was written in 1892 by Massachusetts magazine (*Youth's Companion*) editor Francis Bellamy. (Congress added the words "under God" in 1954.)

I pledge allegiance to the flag of the United States of America and to the republic for which it stands, one nation under God, indivisible, with liberty and justice for all.

Civilians should say the Pledge of Allegiance with their right hands placed over their hearts. People in the armed forces give the military salute. By saying the Pledge of Allegiance, we promise loyalty ("pledge allegiance") to the United States and its ideals.

"THE STAR-SPANGLED BANNER"

"The Star-Spangled Banner" is the national anthem of the United States. It was written by Francis Scott Key during the War of 1812. While being detained by the British aboard a ship on September 13–14, 1814, Key watched the British bombardment of Fort McHenry at Baltimore. The attack lasted 25 hours. The smoke was so thick that Key could not tell who had won. When the air cleared, Key saw the American flag that was still flying over the fort. "The Star-Spangled Banner" is sung to music written by British composer John Stafford Smith. In 1931 Congress designated "The Star-Spangled Banner" as the national anthem.

I

Oh, say, can you see, by the dawn's early light,
What so proudly we hailed at the twilight's last gleaming,
Whose broad stripes and bright stars through the perilous fight,
O'er the ramparts we watched were so gallantly streaming?
And the rockets' red glare, the bombs bursting in air,
Gave proof through the night that our flag was still there.
Oh, say, does that star-spangled banner yet wave
O'er the land of the free, and the home of the brave?

II

On the shore, dimly seen through the mists of the deep,
Where the foe's haughty host in dread silence reposes,
What is that which the breeze, o'er the towering steep,
As it fitfully blows, half conceals, half discloses?
Now it catches the gleam of the morning's first beam,
In full glory reflected, now shines on the stream.
'Tis the star-spangled banner; oh, long may it wave
O'er the land of the free, and the home of the brave!

III

And where is that band who so vauntingly swore
That the havoc of war and the battle's confusion
A home and a country should leave us no more?
Their blood has washed out their foul footsteps' pollution.
No refuge could save the hireling and slave
From the terror of flight, or the gloom of the grave:
And the star-spangled banner in triumph doth wave
O'er the land of the free, and the home of the brave!

IV

Oh! thus be it ever when freemen shall stand
Between their loved homes and the war's desolation!
Blest with victory and peace, may the heaven-rescued land
Praise the Power that hath made and preserved us a nation!
Then conquer we must, for our cause it is just,
And this be our motto: "In God is our trust!"
And the star-spangled banner in triumph shall wave,
O'er the land of the free, and the home of the brave!

Sheet music to the national anthem

"AMERICA, THE BEAUTIFUL"

One of the most beloved songs celebrating our nation is "America, the Beautiful." Katharine Lee Bates first wrote the lyrics to the song in 1893 after visiting Colorado. The version of the song we know today is set to music by Samuel A. Ward. The first and last stanzas of "America, the Beautiful" are shown below.

O beautiful for spacious skies,
For amber waves of grain,
For purple mountain majesties
Above the fruited plain!
America! America!
God shed his grace on thee
And crown thy good with brotherhood
From sea to shining sea!

O beautiful for patriot dream
That sees beyond the years
Thine alabaster cities gleam
Undimmed by human tears!
America! America!
God shed his grace on thee
And crown thy good with brotherhood
From sea to shining sea!

Supreme Court Decisions

Marbury v. Madison, (1803)

Significance: This ruling established the Supreme Court's power of judicial review, by which the Court decides whether laws passed by Congress are constitutional. This decision greatly increased the prestige of the Court and gave the judiciary branch a powerful check against the legislative and executive branches.

Background: William Marbury and several others were commissioned as judges by Federalist president John Adams during his last days in office. This act angered the new Democratic-Republican president, Thomas Jefferson. Jefferson ordered his secretary of state, James Madison, not to deliver the commissions. Marbury took advantage of a section in the Judiciary Act of 1789 that allowed him to take his case directly to the Supreme Court. He sued Madison, demanding the commission and the judgeship.

Decision: This case was decided on February 24, 1803, by a vote of 5 to 0. Chief Justice John Marshall spoke for the Court, which decided against Marbury. The court ruled that although Marbury's commission had been unfairly withheld, he could not lawfully take his case to the Supreme Court without first trying it in a lower court. Marshall said that the section of the Judiciary Act that Marbury had used was actually unconstitutional, and that the Constitution must take priority over laws passed by Congress.

McCulloch v. Maryland, (1819)

Significance: This ruling established that Congress had the constitutional power to charter a national bank. The case also established the principle of national supremacy, which states that the Constitution and other laws of the federal government take priority over state laws. In addition, the ruling reinforced the loose construction interpretation of the Constitution favored by many Federalists.

Background: In 1816 the federal government set up the Second Bank of the United States to stabilize the economy following the War of 1812. Many states were opposed to the competition provided by the new national bank. Some of these states passed heavy taxes on the Bank. The national bank refused to pay the taxes. This led the state of Maryland to sue James McCulloch, the cashier of the Baltimore, Maryland, branch of the national bank.

Decision: This case was decided on March 6, 1819, by a vote of 7 to 0. Chief Justice John Marshall spoke for the unanimous Court, which ruled that the national bank was constitutional because it helped the federal government carry out other powers granted to it by the Constitution. The Court declared that any attempt by the states to interfere with the duties of the federal government could not be permitted.

Gibbons v. Ogden, (1824)

Significance: This ruling was the first case to deal with the clause of the Constitution that allows Congress to regulate interstate and foreign commerce. This case was important because it reinforced both the authority of the federal government over the states and the division of powers between the federal government and the state governments.

Background: Steamboat operators who wanted to travel on New York waters had to obtain a state license. Thomas Gibbons had a federal license to travel along the coast, but not a state license for New York. He wanted the freedom to compete with state-licensed Aaron Ogden for steam travel between New Jersey and the New York island of Manhattan.

Decision: This case was decided on March 2, 1824, by a vote of 6 to 0. Chief Justice John Marshall spoke for the Court, which ruled in favor of Gibbons. The Court stated that the congressional statute (Gibbons's federal license) took priority over the state statute (Ogden's state-monopoly license). The ruling also defined commerce as more than simply the exchange of goods, broadening it to include the transportation of people and the use of new inventions (such as the steamboat).

Scott v. Sandford, (1857)

Significance: This ruling denied enslaved African Americans U.S. citizenship and the right to sue in federal court. The decision also invalidated the Missouri Compromise, which had prevented slavery in territories north of the 36° 30' line of latitude. The ruling increased the controversy over the expansion of slavery in new states and territories.

Supreme Court Building, Washington, D. C.

Background: John Emerson, an army doctor, took his slave Dred Scott with him to live in Illinois and then Wisconsin Territory, both of which had banned slavery. In 1842 the two moved to Missouri, a slave state. Four years later, Scott sued for his freedom according to a Missouri legal principle of "once free, always free." The principle meant that a slave was entitled to freedom if he or she had once lived in a free state or territory.

Decision: This case was decided March 6–7, 1857, by a vote of 7 to 2. Chief Justice Roger B. Taney spoke for the Court, which ruled that slaves did not have the right to sue in federal courts because they were considered property, not citizens. In addition, the Court ruled that Congress did not have the power to abolish slavery in territories because that power was not strictly defined in the Constitution. Furthermore, the Court overturned the once-free, always-free principle.

Plessy v. Ferguson, (1896)

Significance: This case upheld the constitutionality of racial segregation by ruling that separate facilities for different races were legal as long as those facilities were equal to one another. This case provided a legal justification for racial segregation for nearly 60 years until it was overturned by *Brown* v. *Board of Education* in 1954.

Background: An 1890 Louisiana law required that all railway companies in the state use "separate-but-equal" railcars for white and African American passengers. A group of citizens in New Orleans banded together to challenge the law and chose Homer Plessy to test the law in 1892. Plessy took a seat in a whites-only coach, and when he refused to move, he was arrested. Plessy eventually sought review by the U.S. Supreme Court, claiming that the Louisiana law violated his Fourteenth Amendment right to equal protection.

Decision: This case was decided on May 18, 1896, by a vote of 7 to 1. Justice Henry Billings Brown spoke for the Court, which upheld the constitutionality of the Louisiana law that segregated railcars. Justice John M. Harlan dissented, arguing that the Constitution should not be interpreted in ways that recognize class or racial distinctions.

Historical Documents

Magna Carta

England's King John angered many people with high taxes. In 1215 a group of English nobles joined the archbishop of Canterbury to force the king to agree to sign Magna Carta. This document stated that the king was subject to the rule of law, just as other citizens of England were. It also presented the ideas of a fair and speedy trial and due process of law. These principles are still a part of the U.S. Bill of Rights.

1. In the first place have granted to God, and by this our present charter confirmed for us and our heirs for ever that the English church shall be free, and shall have its rights undiminished and its liberties unimpaired . . . We have also granted to all free men of our kingdom, for ourselves and our heirs for ever, all the liberties written below, to be had and held by them and their heirs of us and our heirs.

2. If any of our earls or barons or others holding of us in chief by knight service dies, and at his death his heir be of full age and owe relief he shall have his inheritance on payment of the old relief, namely the heir or heirs of an earl 100 for a whole earl's barony, the heir or heirs of a baron 100 for a whole barony, the heir or heirs of a knight 100s, at most, for a whole knight's fee; and he who owes less shall give less according to the ancient usage of fiefs.

3. If, however, the heir of any such be under age and a ward, he shall have his inheritance when he comes of age without paying relief and without making fine.

40. To no one will we sell, to no one will we refuse or delay right or justice.

41. All merchants shall be able to go out of and come into England safely and securely and stay and travel throughout England, as well by land as by water, for buying and selling by the ancient and right customs free from all evil tolls, except in time of war and if they are of the land that is at war with us . . .

42. It shall be lawful in future for anyone, without prejudicing the allegiance due to us, to leave our kingdom and return safely and securely by land and water, save, in the public interest, for a short period in time of war—except for those imprisoned or outlawed in accordance with the law of the kingdom and natives of a land that is at war with us and merchants (who shall be treated as aforesaid).

62. And we have fully remitted and pardoned to everyone all the ill–will, indignation and rancour that have arisen between us and our men, clergy and laity, from the time of the quarrel. Furthermore, we have fully remitted to all, clergy and laity, and as far as pertains to us have completely forgiven, all trespasses occasioned by the same quarrel between Easter in the sixteenth year of our reign and the restoration of peace. And, besides, we have caused to be made for them letters testimonial patent of the lord Stephen archbishop of Canterbury, of the lord Henry archbishop of Dublin and of the aforementioned bishops and of master Pandulf about this security and the aforementioned concessions.

63. An oath, moreover, has been taken, as well on our part as on the part of the barons, that all these things aforesaid shall be observed in good faith and without evil disposition. Witness the above–mentioned and many others. Given by our hand in the meadow which is called Runnymede between Windsor and Staines on the fifteenth day of June, in the seventeenth year of our reign.

From "English Bill of Rights." Britannica Online. Vers. 99.1. 1994–1999. Encyclopedia Britannica. Copyright © 1994–1999 Encyclopedia Britannica, Inc.

The Mayflower Compact

In November 1620, the Pilgrim leaders aboard the Mayflower *drafted the Mayflower Compact. This was the first document in the English colonies to establish guidelines for self-government. This excerpt from the Mayflower Compact describes the principles of the Pilgrim colony's government.*

The Mayflower Compact

We whose names are underwritten, the loyal subjects of our dread Sovereign Lord King James, by the Grace of God of Great Britain, France and Ireland, King, Defender of the Faith, etc.

Having undertaken, for the Glory of God and advancement of the Christian Faith and Honour of our King and Country, a Voyage to plant the First Colony in the Northern Parts of Virginia, do by these presents solemnly and mutually in the presence of God and one of another, Covenant and Combine ourselves together into a Civil Body Politic, for our better ordering and preservation and furtherance of the ends aforesaid; and by virtue hereof to enact, constitute and frame such just and equal Laws, Ordinances, Acts, Constitutions and Offices, from time to time, as shall be thought most meet and convenient for the general good of the Colony, unto which we promise all due submission and obedience. In witness whereof we have hereunder subscribed our names at Cape Cod, the 11th of November, in the year of the reign of our Sovereign Lord King James, of England, France and Ireland the eighteenth, and of Scotland the fifty-fourth. Anno Domini 1620.

Source: *William Bradford, Of Plymouth Plantation, 1620–1647 (Samuel Eliot Morison, ed., 1952), 75–76*

Fundamental Orders of Connecticut

In January 1639, settlers in Connecticut led by Thomas Hooker drew up the Fundamental Orders of Connecticut—America's first written Constitution. It is essentially a compact among the settlers and a body of laws.

Forasmuch as it hath pleased the All-mighty God by the wise disposition of his divyne pruvidence so to Order and dispose of things that we the Inhabitants and Residents of Windsor, Harteford and Wethersfield are now cohabiting and dwelling in and uppon the River of Conectecotte and the Lands thereunto adioyneing; As also in our Civell Affaires to be guided and governed according to such Lawes, Rules, Orders and decrees as shall be made, ordered & decreed, as followeth:—

1. It is Ordered . . . that there shall be yerely two generall Assemblies or Courts, the one the second thursday in Aprill, the other the second thursday in September, following; the first shall be called the Courte of Election, wherein shall be yerely Chosen . . . soe many Magestrats and other publike Officers as shall be found requisitte: which choise shall be made by all that are admitted freemen and have taken the Oath of Fidelity, and doe cohabitte within this Jurisdiction, (having beene admitted Inhabitants by the major part of the Towne wherein they live,) or the major parte of such as shall be then present . . .

Source: *F. N. Thorpe, ed., Federal and State Constitutions, vol.1 (1909), 519.*

The English Bill of Rights

In 1689, after the Glorious Revolution, Parliament passed the English Bill of Rights, which ensured that Parliament would have supreme power over the monarchy. The bill also protected the rights of English citizens.

By assuming and exercising a power of dispensing with and suspending of laws and the execution of laws without consent of Parliament; . . .

By levying money for and to the use of the Crown by pretence of prerogative for other time and in other manner than the same was granted by Parliament;

By raising and keeping a standing army within this kingdom in time of peace without consent of Parliament, and quartering soldiers contrary to law; . . .

And excessive bail hath been required of persons committed in criminal cases to elude the benefit of the laws made for the liberty of the subjects;

And excessive fines have been imposed;

And illegal and cruel punishments inflicted;

And several grants and promises made of fines and forfeitures before any conviction or judgment against the persons upon whom the same were to be levied;

All which are utterly and directly contrary to the known laws and statutes and freedom of this realm . . .

From "English Bill of Rights." Britannica Online. Vers. 99.1. 1994–1999. Encyclopedia Britannica. Copyright © 1994–1999 Encyclopedia Britannica, Inc.

Virginia Statute for Religious Freedom

In 1777 Thomas Jefferson wrote the Virginia Statute for Religious Freedom. Jefferson hoped that by separating church and state, Virginians could practice their religion—whatever it might be—freely.

. . . to compel a man to furnish contributions of money for the propagation of opinions which he disbelieves, is sinful and tyrannical; that even the forcing him to support this or that teacher of his own religious persuasion, is depriving him of the comfortable liberty of giving his contributions to the particular pastor . . . that our civil rights have no dependence on our religious opinions, any more than our opinions in physics or geometry; that therefore the proscribing any citizen as unworthy the public confidence by laying upon him an incapacity of being called to offices of trust and emolument, unless he profess or renounce this or that religious opinion, is depriving him injuriously of those privileges and advantages to which in common with his fellow-citizens he has a natural right . . .

Be it enacted by the General Assembly, That no man shall be compelled to frequent or support any religious worship, place, or ministry whatsoever, nor shall be enforced, restrained, molested, or burthened in his body or goods, nor shall otherwise suffer on account of his religious opinions or belief; but that all men shall be free to profess, and by argument to maintain, their opinion in matters of religion, and that the same shall in no wise diminish enlarge, or affect their civil capacities.

. . . yet we are free to declare, and do declare, that the rights hereby asserted are of the natural rights of mankind, and that if any act shall be hereafter passed to repeal the present, or to narrow its operation, such act shall be an infringement of natural right.

Source: *W.W. Hening, ed., Statutes at Large of Virginia, vol. 12 (1823): 84–86.*

Objections to This Constitution of Government

George Mason played a behind-the-scenes role in the Revolutionary War and wrote Virginia's Declaration of Rights. He attended the Constitutional Convention in 1787. Mason criticized the proposed Constitution for allowing slavery, creating a strong central government, and lacking a bill of rights. As a result, he refused to sign the Constitution. In the following excerpt, Mason explains why he would not sign the Constitution.

There is no Declaration of Rights, and the laws of the general government being paramount to the laws and constitution of the several States, the Declarations of Rights in the separate States are no security. Nor are the people secured even in the enjoyment of the benefit of the common law.

In the House of Representatives there is not the substance but the shadow only of representation . . .

The Senate have the power of altering all money bills, and of originating appropriations of money, and the salaries of the officers of their own appointment, in conjunction with the president of the United States, although they are not the representatives of the people or amenable to them. . . .

The Judiciary of the United States is so constructed and extended, as to absorb and destroy the judiciaries of the several States; thereby rendering law as tedious, intricate and expensive, and justice as unattainable, by a great part of the community, as in England, and enabling the rich to oppress and ruin the poor.

The President of the United States has no Constitutional Council, a thing unknown in any safe and regular government. He will therefore be unsupported by proper information and advice, and will generally be directed by minions and favorites; or he will become a tool to the Senate . . .

The President of the United States has the unrestrained power of granting pardons for treason, which may be sometimes exercised to screen from punishment those whom he had secretly instigated to commit the crime, and thereby prevent a discovery of his own guilt. . . .

Washington's Farewell Address

In 1796 at the end of his second term as president, George Washington wrote his farewell address with the help of Alexander Hamilton and James Madison. In it he spoke of the dangers facing the young nation. He warned against the dangers of political parties and sectionalism, and he advised the nation against permanent alliances with other nations.

In contemplating the causes, which may disturb our Union, it occurs as matter of serious concern, that any ground should have been furnished for characterizing parties by geographical discriminations-Northern and Southern-Atlantic and Western . . .

No alliances, however strict, between the parts can be an adequate substitute; they must inevitably experience the infractions and interruptions which all alliances in all times have experienced . . .

The great rule of conduct for us, in regard to foreign nations, is, in extending our commercial relations, to have with them as little political connexion as possible. So far as we have already formed engagements, let them be fulfilled with perfect good faith. Here let us stop.

From Annals of Congress, 4th Congress, pp. 2869–2880. American Memory Library of Congress. 1999. Address

Jefferson's 1801 Inaugural Address

In 1800 Thomas Jefferson, representing the Democratic-Republican Party, ran against the Federalist candidate, President John Adams. Jefferson won the election and used his inaugural address to try to bridge the gap between the new political parties and to reach out to the Federalists.

March 4, 1801

Friends and Fellow–Citizens:

Called upon to undertake the duties of the first executive office of our country, I avail myself of the presence of that portion of my fellow–citizens which is here assembled to express my grateful thanks for the favor with which they have been pleased to look toward me, to declare a sincere consciousness that the task is above my talents, and that I approach it with those anxious and awful presentiments which the greatness of the charge and the weakness of my powers so justly inspire. A rising nation, spread over a wide and fruitful land, traversing all the seas with the rich productions of their industry, engaged in commerce with nations who feel power and forget right, advancing rapidly to destinies beyond the reach of mortal eye when I contemplate these transcendent objects, and see the honor, the happiness, and the hopes of this beloved country committed to the issue, and the auspices of this day, I shrink from the contemplation, and humble myself before the magnitude of the undertaking. . . .

I repair, then, fellow–citizens, to the post you have assigned me. With experience enough in subordinate offices to have seen the difficulties of this the greatest of all, I have learnt to expect that it will rarely fall to the lot of imperfect man to retire from this station with the reputation and the favor which bring him into it. Without pretensions to that high confidence you reposed in our first and greatest revolutionary character, whose preeminent services had entitled him to the first place in his country's love and destined for him the fairest page in the volume of faithful history, I ask so much confidence only as may give firmness and effect to the legal administration of your affairs.

From Inaugural Addresses of the Presidents of the United States. 1989. Bartleby Library.

John Quincy Adams's Fourth of July 1821 Address

John Quincy Adams made the following Fourth of July speech in 1821.

And now, friends and countrymen, if the wise and learned philosophers of the elder world, the first observers of nutation and aberration, the discoverers of maddening ether and invisible planets, the inventors of Congreve rockets and Shrapnel shells, should find their hearts disposed to enquire what has America done for the benefit of mankind?

Let our answer be this: America, with the same voice which spoke herself into existence as a nation, proclaimed to mankind the inextinguishable rights of human nature, and the only lawful foundations of government.

She has abstained from interference in the concerns of others, even when conflict has been for principles to which she clings, as to the last vital drop that visits the heart. . . .

[America's] glory is not *dominion*, but *liberty*. Her march is the march of the mind. She has a spear and a shield: but the motto upon her shield is, *Freedom, Independence, Peace*. This has been her Declaration: this has been, as far as her necessary intercourse with the rest of mankind would permit, her practice.

Monroe Doctrine

In 1823 President James Monroe proclaimed the Monroe Doctrine. Designed to end European influence in the Western Hemisphere, it became a cornerstone of U.S. foreign policy.

With the existing colonies or dependencies of any European power we have not interfered and shall not interfere. But with the governments who have declared their independence and maintained it, and whose independence we have, on great consideration and on just principles, acknowledged, we could not view any interposition for the purpose of oppressing them, or controlling in any other manner their destiny, by any European power in any other light than as the manifestation of an unfriendly disposition toward the United States. . . .

Our policy in regard to Europe, which was adopted at an early stage of the wars which have so long agitated that quarter of the globe, nevertheless remains the same, which is not to interfere in the internal concerns of any of its powers; to consider the government de facto as the legitimate government for us; to cultivate friendly relations with it, and to preserve those relations by a frank, firm, and manly policy, meeting in all instances the just claims of every power, submitting to injuries from none.

From "The Monroe Doctrine" by James Monroe reprinted in The Annals of America: Volume 5, 1821–1832. Copyright © 1976 by Encyclopedia Britannica.

Seneca Falls Declaration of Sentiments

One of the first documents to express the desire for equal rights for women is the Declaration of Sentiments, issued in 1848 at the Seneca Falls Convention in Seneca Falls, New York. Led by Elizabeth Cady Stanton and Lucretia Mott, the delegates adopted a set of resolutions modeled on the Declaration of Independence.

When, in the course of human events, it becomes necessary for one portion of the family of man to assume among the people of the earth a position different from that which they have hitherto occupied, but one to which the laws of nature and of nature's God entitle them, a decent respect to the opinions of mankind requires that they should declare the causes that impel them to such a course.

We hold these truths to be self–evident: that all men and women are created equal; that they are endowed by their Creator with certain inalienable rights; that among these are life, liberty, and the pursuit of happiness; that to secure these rights governments are instituted, deriving their just powers from the consent of the governed. Whenever any form of government becomes destructive of these ends, it is the right of those who suffer from it to refuse allegiance to it, and to insist upon the institution of a new government, laying its foundation on such principles, and organizing its powers in such form, as to them shall seem most likely to effect their safety and happiness.

From "Seneca Falls Declaration on Women's Rights" reprinted in The Annals of America: Volume 7, 1841–1849. Copyright © 1976 by Encyclopedia Britannica.

Denmark Vesey Document

Some enslaved African Americans struck back against the slave system in the South by using violence. Denmark Vesey, a free African American, planned a revolt in 1822. He was betrayed before the revolt began, and he and other people were executed. Included below is an excerpt from A Narrative of the Conspiracy and Intended Insurrection *by Denmark Vesey.*

Excerpts from A NARRATIVE OF THE Conspiracy and Intended Insurrection, AMONGST A PORTION OF THE Negroes in the State of South-Carolina, *In the Year 1822.*

At the head of this conspiracy stood Denmark Vesey, a free negro; with him the idea undoubtedly originated. For several years before he disclosed his intentions to any one, he appears to have been constantly and assiduously engaged in endeavoring to embitter the minds of the colored population against the white. He rendered himself perfectly familiar with all those parts of the Scriptures, which he thought he could pervert to his purpose; and would readily quote them, to prove that slavery was contrary to the laws of God; that slaves were bound to attempt their emancipation, however shocking and bloody might be the consequences, and that such efforts would not only be pleasing to the Almighty, but were absolutely enjoined, and their success predicted in the Scriptures. . . .

In the selection of his leaders, Vesey shewed great penetration and sound judgment. Rolla was plausible, and possessed uncommon self-possession; bold and ardent, he was not to be deterred from his purpose by danger. Ned's appearance indicated, that he was a man of firm nerves, and desperate courage. Peter was intrepid and resolute, true to his engagements, and cautious in observing secrecy where it was necessary; he was not to be daunted nor impeded by difficulties, and though confident of success, was careful in providing against any obstacles or casualties which might arise, and intent upon discovering every means which might be in their power if thought of before hand. Gullah Jack was regarded as a Sorcerer, and as such feared by the natives of Africa, who believe in witchcraft. He was not only considered invulnerable, but that he could make others so by his charms; and that he could and certainly would provide all his followers with arms. He was artful, cruel, bloody; his disposition in short was diabolical. His influence amongst the Africans was inconceiveable. Monday was firm, resolute, discreet and intelligent. . . .

As Vesey, from whom all orders emanated, and perhaps to whom only all important information was conveyed, died without confessing any thing, any opinion formed as to the numbers actually engaged in the plot, must be altogether conjectural; but enough has been disclosed to satisfy every reasonable mind, that considerable numbers were concerned. Indeed the plan of attack, which embraced so many points to be assailed at the same instant, affords sufficient evidence of the fact.

Lincoln's First Inaugural Address

After his election as president of the United States in 1860, Abraham Lincoln pledged that there would be no war unless the South started it. He discusses the disagreements that led to the nation's greatest crisis in the excerpt below from his first inaugural address.

March 4, 1861

Fellow–Citizens of the United States:

In compliance with a custom as old as the Government itself, I appear before you to address you briefly and to take in your presence the oath prescribed by the Constitution of the United States to be taken by the President "before he enters on the execution of this office." . . .

I have no purpose, directly or indirectly, to interfere with the institution of slavery in the States where it exists. I believe I have no lawful right to do so, and I have no inclination to do so.

Those who nominated and elected me did so with full knowledge that I had made this and many similar declarations and had never recanted them; and more than this, they placed in the platform for my acceptance, and as a law to themselves and to me, the clear and emphatic resolution which I now read:

. . . In any law upon this subject ought not all the safeguards of liberty known in civilized and humane jurisprudence to be introduced, so that a free man be not in any case surrendered as a slave? And might it not be well at the same time to provide by law for the enforcement of that clause in the Constitution which guarantees that "the citizens of each State shall be entitled to all privileges and immunities of citizens in the several States?" . . .

It follows from these views that no State upon its own mere motion can lawfully get out of the Union; that resolves and ordinances to that effect are legally void, and that acts of violence within any State or States against the authority of the United States are insurrectionary or revolutionary, according to circumstances.

I therefore consider that in view of the Constitution and the laws the Union is unbroken, and to the extent of my ability, I shall take care, as the Constitution itself expressly enjoins upon me, that the laws of the Union be faithfully executed in all the States. . . .

One section of our country believes slavery is right and ought to be extended, while the other believes it is wrong and ought not to be extended. This is the only substantial dispute.

Physically speaking, we can not separate. We can not remove our respective sections from each other nor build an impassable wall between them. A husband and wife may be divorced and go out of the presence and beyond the reach of each other, but the different parts of our country can not do this.

This country, with its institutions, belongs to the people who inhabit it. Whenever they shall grow weary of the existing Government, they can exercise their constitutional right of amending it or their revolutionary right to dismember or overthrow it. . . .

In your hands, my dissatisfied fellow–countrymen, and not in mine, is the momentous issue of civil war. The Government will not assail you. You can have no conflict without being yourselves the aggressors. You have no oath registered in heaven to destroy the Government, while I shall have the most solemn one to "preserve, protect, and defend it."

I am loath to close. We are not enemies, but friends. We must not be enemies. Though passion may have strained it must not break our bonds of affection. The mystic chords of memory, stretching from every battlefield and patriot grave to every living heart and hearthstone all over this broad land, will yet swell the chorus of the Union, when again touched, as surely they will be, by the better angels of our nature.

From Inaugural Addresses of the Presidents of the United States. 1989. Bartleby Library.

The Emancipation Proclamation

When the Union army won the Battle of Antietam, President Abraham Lincoln decided to issue the Emancipation Proclamation, which freed all enslaved people in states under Confederate control. The proclamation, which went into effect on January 1, 1863, was a step toward the Thirteenth Amendment (1865), which ended slavery in all of the United States.

That on the 1st day of January, in the year of our Lord 1863, all persons held as slaves within any state or designated part of a state, the people whereof shall then be in rebellion against the United States, shall be then, thenceforward, and forever free; and the executive government of the United States, including the military and naval authority thereof, will recognize and maintain the freedom of such persons and will do no act or acts to repress such persons, or any of them, in any efforts they may make for their actual freedom. . . .

And I further declare and make known that such persons of suitable condition will be received into the armed service of the United States to garrison forts, positions, stations, and other places, and to man vessels of all sorts in said service.

And upon this act, sincerely believed to be an act of justice, warranted by the Constitution upon military necessity, I invoke the considerate judgment of mankind and the gracious favor of Almighty God.

From "Emancipation Proclamation" by Abraham Lincoln. Reprinted in The Annals of America: Volume 9, 1858–1865. Copyright © 1976 by Encyclopedia Britannica, Inc.

Lincoln's Gettysburg Address

On November 19, 1863, Abraham Lincoln addressed a crowd gathered to dedicate a cemetery at the Gettysburg battlefield. His short speech, which is excerpted below, reminded Americans of the ideals on which the Republic was founded.

FOUR SCORE AND SEVEN YEARS ago our fathers brought forth on this continent a new nation, conceived in liberty and dedicated to the proposition that all men are created equal.

Now we are engaged in a great civil war, testing whether that nation or any nation so conceived and so dedicated can long endure. We are met on a great battlefield of that war. We have come to dedicate a portion of that field as a final resting–place for those who here gave their lives that that nation might live. It is altogether fitting and proper that we should do this.

But in a larger sense, we cannot dedicate—we cannot consecrate—we cannot hallow—this ground. The brave men, living and dead, who struggled here have consecrated it far above our poor power to add or detract. The world will little note nor long remember what we say here, but it can never forget what they did here. It is for us, the living, rather, to be dedicated here to the unfinished work which they who fought here have thus far so nobly advanced.

It is rather for us to be here dedicated to the great task remaining before us—that from these honored dead we take increased devotion to that cause for which they gave the last full measure of devotion; that we here highly resolve that these dead shall not have died in vain; that this nation, under God, shall have a new birth of freedom; and that government of the people, by the people, for the people shall not perish from the earth.

From "The Gettysburg Address" by Abraham Lincoln. Reprinted in The Annals of America: Volume 9, 1858–1865. Copyright ©1976 by Encyclopedia Britannica, Inc.

Lincoln's Second Inaugural Address

On March 4, 1865, President Lincoln laid out his approach to Reconstruction in his second inaugural address. As the excerpt below shows, Lincoln hoped to peacefully reunite the nation and its people.

At this second appearing to take the oath of the Presidential office there is less occasion for an extended address than there was at the first. Then a statement somewhat in detail of a course to be pursued seemed fitting and proper. Now, at the expiration of four years, during which public declarations have been constantly called forth on every point and phase of the great contest which still absorbs the attention and engrosses the energies of the nation, little that is new could be presented. The progress of our arms, upon which all else chiefly depends, is as well known to the public as to myself, and it is, I trust, reasonably satisfactory and encouraging to all. With high hope for the future, no prediction in regard to it is ventured.

On the occasion corresponding to this four years ago all thoughts were anxiously directed to an impending civil war. All dreaded it, all sought to avert it. While the inaugural address was being delivered from this place, devoted altogether to saving the Union without war, urgent agents were in the city seeking to destroy it without war—seeking to dissolve the Union and divide effects by negotiation. Both parties deprecated war, but one of them would make war rather than let the nation survive, and the other would accept war rather than let it perish, and the war came. . . .

With malice toward none, with charity for all, with firmness in the right as God gives us to see the right, let us strive on to finish the work we are in, to bind up the nation's wounds, to care for him who shall have borne the battle and for his widow and his orphan, to do all which may achieve and cherish a just and lasting peace among ourselves and with all nations.

From Inaugural Addresses of the Presidents of the United States. 1989. Bartleby Library.

Declaration of the Rights of Women

Included below are excerpts from a speech made on July 4, 1876, by Susan B. Anthony in support of rights for women.

Susan B. Anthony, July 4, 1876

While the nation is buoyant with patriotism, and all hearts are attuned to praise, it is with sorrow we come to strike the one discordant note, on this one-hundredth anniversary of our country's birth. When subjects of kings, emperors, and czars from the old world join in our national jubilee, shall the women of the republic refuse to lay their hands with benedictions on the nation's head? . . . Yet we cannot forget, even in this glad hour, that while all men of every race, and clime, and condition, have been invested with the full rights of citizenship under our hospitable flag, all women still suffer the degradation of disfranchisement.

The history of our country the past one hundred years has been a series of assumptions and usurpations of power over woman, in direct opposition to the principles of just government, acknowledged by the United States as its foundations, which are:

First - the natural rights of each individual
Second - the equality of these rights
Third - that rights not delegated are retained by the individual
Fourth - that no person can exercise the rights of others without delegated authority
Fifth - that the non-use of rights does not destroy them

And for the violation of these fundamental principles of our government, we arraign our rulers on this Fourth day of July, 1876 . . .

These articles of impeachment against our rulers we now submit to the impartial judgment of the people. To all these wrongs and oppressions woman has not submitted in silence and resignation. From the beginning of the century, when Abigail Adams, the wife of one president and the mother of another, said, "We will not hold ourselves bound to obey laws in which we have no voice or representation," until now, woman's discontent has been steadily increasing, culminating nearly thirty years ago in a simultaneous movement among the women of the nation, demanding the right of suffrage. . . .

And now, at the close of a hundred years, as the hour hand of the great clock that marks the centuries points to 1876, we declare our faith in the principles of self-government; our full equality with man in natural rights . . . We ask of our rulers, at this hour, no special favors, no special privileges, no special legislation. We ask justice, we ask equality, we ask that all the civil and political rights that belong to citizens of the United States, be guaranteed to us and our daughters forever.

Biographical Dictionary

A

Adams, John (1735–1826) American statesman, he was a delegate to the Continental Congress, a member of the committee that drafted the Declaration of Independence, vice president to George Washington, and was the second president of the United States. (p. 266)

Adams, John Quincy (1767–1848) Son of President John Adams and the secretary of state to James Monroe, he largely formulated the Monroe Doctrine. He was the sixth president of the United States and later became a representative in Congress. (p. 305)

Adams, Samuel (1722–1803) American revolutionary who led the agitation that led to the Boston Tea Party; he signed the Declaration of Independence. (p. 99)

Alcott, Louisa May (1832–1888) American novelist, her revised letters written as a Civil War nurse were published as *Hospital Sketches*. She is famed for the novel, *Little Women,* and its sequels. (p. 447)

Anthony, Susan B. (1820–1906) American social reformer, she was active in the temperance, abolitionist, and women's suffrage movements and was co-organizer and president of the National Woman Suffrage Association. (p. 465)

Aristotle (384–322 BC) Greek philosopher, he thought that people should live in moderation and use reason. (p. 22)

Arkwright, Richard (1732–1792) English inventor, he patented the water-powered spinning frame, improving the production of cotton thread. (p. 385)

Askia the Great (c. 1443–1538) Songhai ruler, he overthrew Sunni Baru. Originally named Muhammad Ture, he took the military title askia and became known as Askia the Great. (p. 19)

Astor, John Jacob (1763–1848) American fur trader and financier, he founded the fur-trading post of Astoria and the American Fur Company. (p. 346)

Austin, Stephen F. (1793–1836) American colonizer in Texas, he was imprisoned for urging Texas statehood after Santa Anna suspended Mexico's constitution. After helping Texas win independence from Mexico, he became secretary of state for the Texas Republic. (p. 351)

B

Bagley, Sarah G. (d. 1847?) American mill worker and union activist, she advocated the 10-hour workday for private industry. She was elected vice president of the New England Working Men's Association, becoming the first woman to hold such high rank in the American labor movement. (p. 395)

Banneker, Benjamin (1731–1806) African American mathematician and astronomer, he was hired by Thomas Jefferson to help survey land for the new capital in Washington, D.C. (p. 240)

Barton, Clara (1821–1912) Founder of the American Red Cross, she obtained and administered supplies and care to the Union soldiers during the American Civil War. (p. 534)

Beecher, Catharine (1800–1878) American educator and the daughter of Lyman Beecher, she promoted education for women in such writings as *An Essay on the Education of Female Teachers*. She founded the first all-female academy. (p. 451)

Beecher, Lyman (1775–1863) American clergyman, he disapproved of the style of preaching of the Great Awakening ministers. He served as president of the Lane Theological Seminary and supported female higher education. (p. 448)

Black Hawk (1767–1838) Native American leader of Fox and Sauk Indians, he resisted the U.S.-ordered removal of Indian nations from Illinois and raided settlements and fought the U.S. Army. (p. 335)

Bolívar, Simon (1783–1830) South American revolutionary leader who was nicknamed the Liberator, he fought many battles for independence, winning the support of many U.S. leaders. (p. 300)

Brooks, Preston (1819–1857) American congressman, he assaulted and beat Senator Charles Sumner for his antislavery speeches and for insulting a pro-slavery relative. He was nicknamed Bully Brooks by northerners. (p. 487)

Brown, John (1800–1859) American abolitionist, he started the Pottawatomie Massacre in Kansas to revenge killings of abolitionists; he later seized the federal arsenal at Harpers Ferry, Virginia, to encourage a slave revolt. He was later tried and executed. (p. 493)

Buchanan, James (1791–1868) American politician and fifteenth president of the United States, he was chosen as the Democratic nominee for president in 1854 for being politically experienced and not offensive to slave states. (p. 488)

Burns, Anthony (1834–1862) American enslaved African, he ran away and was arrested in Boston. His arrest became the center of violent protests by northern opponents of the Fugitive Slave Act. (p. 480)

C

Calhoun, John C. (1782–1850) American politician and supporter of slavery and states' rights, he served as vice president to Andrew Jackson and was instrumental in the South Carolina nullification crisis. (p. 323)

Cartier, Jacques (1491–1557) French sailor and explorer, he made three voyages to Canada for Francis I. (p. 54)

Clark, George Rogers (1752–1818) American Revolutionary soldier and frontier leader, he captured the British trading village of Kaskaskia during the Revolution and encouraged Indian leaders to remain neutral. (p. 133)

Clark, William (1770–1838) American soldier and friend of Meriwether Lewis, he was invited to explore the Louisiana Purchase and joined what became known as the Lewis and Clark expedition. (p. 275)

Clay, Henry (1777–1852) American politician from Kentucky, he was known as the Great Pacificator because of his support of the Missouri Compromise. He developed the Compromise of 1850 to try to avoid civil war. (p. 302)

Cole, Thomas (1801–1848) American painter, he was the founder of the Hudson River school, a group of artists who emphasized the beauty of the American landscape, especially the Hudson River valley. (p. 310)

Columbus, Christopher (1451–1506) Italian explorer, he was convinced that he could reach Asia by sailing westward across the Atlantic Ocean. He gained the support of Spain's monarchs and commanded a small fleet that reached the so-called New World, setting off a tide of European exploration of the area. (p. 42)

Cooper, James Fenimore (1789–1851) Well-known Early American novelist, he wrote the *Last of the Mohicans* and many stories about the West. (p. 309)

Cooper, Peter (1791–1883) American ironworks manufacturer who designed and built *Tom Thumb,* the first American locomotive. (p. 398)

Cortés, Hernán (1485–1547) Spanish conquistador, he conquered Mexico and brought about the fall of the Aztec Empire. (p. 46)

Crittenden, John J. (1787–1863) Kentucky senator, he attempted to save the Union by reconciling differences between northern and southern states in the Senate proposal known as Crittenden's Compromise. (p. 497)

D

da Vinci, Leonardo (1452–1519) Italian painter, sculptor, architect, engineer, scientist, and inventor. (p. 26)

Davis, Jefferson (1808–1889) First and only president of the Confederate States of America after the election of President Abraham Lincoln in 1860 led to the secession of many southern states. (p. 496)

Deere, John (1804–1886) American industrialist; he developed a steel plow to ease difficulty of turning thick soil on the Great Plains. (p. 404)

Dickinson, Emily (1830–1886) American poet, she lived a reclusive life, and her poems were not widely acclaimed until after her death. (p. 445)

Dix, Dorothea (1802–1887) American philanthropist and social reformer, she helped change the prison system nationwide by advocating the development of state hospitals for treatment for the mentally ill instead of imprisonment. (p. 450)

Douglas, Stephen (1813–1861) American politician and pro-slavery nominee for president, he debated Abraham Lincoln about slavery during the Illinois senatorial race. He proposed the unpopular Kansas-Nebraska Act, and he established the Freeport Doctrine, upholding the idea of popular sovereignty. (p. 484)

Douglass, Frederick (1817–1895) American abolitionist and writer, he escaped slavery and became a leading African American spokesman and writer. He published his biography, *The Narrative of the Life of Frederick Douglass,* and founded the abolitionist newspaper, the *North Star.* (pp. 456, 458)

E

Edwards, Jonathan (1703–1758) Important and influential revivalist leader in the Great Awakening religious movement, he delivered dramatic sermons on the choice between salvation and damnation. (p. 94)

Emerson, Ralph Waldo (1803–1882) American essayist and poet, he was a supporter of the transcendentalist philosophy of self-reliance. (p. 443)

Equiano, Olaudah (c.1750–1797) African American abolitionist, he was an enslaved African who was eventually freed and became a leader of the abolitionist meovement and writer of *The Interesting Narrative of the Life of Olaudah Equiano.* (p. 77)

Eriksson, Lief (c. 1000) Norwegian explorer, son of Erik the Red, was first European to explore the Americas. (p. 38)

F

Farragut, David (1801–1870) American soldier, he was the first commissioned American admiral, and in the Civil War he captured New Orleans and maintained a blockade along the Gulf Coast against Confederate forces. (pp. 523, 524)

Finney, Charles Grandison (1792–1875) American clergyman and educator, he became influential in the Second Great Awakening after a dramatic religious experience and conversion. He led long revivals that annoyed conventional ministers. (p. 448)

Franklin, Benjamin (1706–1790) American statesman, he was a philosopher, scientist, inventor, writer, publisher, first U.S. postmaster, and member of the committee to draft the Constitution. He invented bifocals and the lightning rod and wrote *Poor Richard's Almanack.* (p. 169)

Frémont, John C. (1813–1890) American explorer, army officer, and politician, he was chosen as the first Republican candidate for president. He was against the spread of slavery, and he was rejected by all but the free states as a "single issue" candidate in the election of 1856. (p. 489)

Fulton, Robert (1765–1815) American engineer and inventor, he built the first commercially successful full-sized steamboat, the *Clermont,* which lead to the development of commercial steamboat ferry services for goods and people. (p. 397)

G

Gallaudet, Thomas (1787–1851) American educator, he studied techniques for instructing hearing-impaired people and established the first American school for the hearing impaired. (p. 451)

Gálvez, Bernardo de (1746–1786) Governor of Spanish Louisiana, he captured key cities from the British, greatly aiding the American Patriot movement and enabling the Spanish acquisition of Florida. (p. 131)

Garrison, William Lloyd (1805–1879) American journalist and reformer; he published the famous antislavery newspaper, the *Liberator,* and helped found the American Anti–Slavery Society, promoting immediate emancipation and racial equality. (p. 455)

Grant, Ulysses S. (1822–1885) Eighteenth president of the United States, he received a field promotion to lieutenant general in charge of all Union forces after leading a successful battle. He accepted General Lee's surrender of Confederate forces at Appomattox Courthouse, ending the Civil War. (p. 522)

Grimké, Angelina (1805–1879) and **Sarah** (1792–1873) American sisters and reformers, they were the daughters of a slaveholding family from South Carolina who became antislavery supporters and lecturers for the American Anti-Slavery Society. They also took up the women's rights campaign. (p. 455)

Hamilton, Alexander (1755–1804) American statesman and member of the Continental Congress and the Constitutional Convention, he was an author of the *Federalist Papers,* which supported ratification of the Constitution. He was the first secretary of treasury under George Washington and developed the Bank of the United States. (p. 238)

Harrison, William Henry (1773–1841) American politician, he served as the governor of Indian Territory and fought Tecumseh in the Battle of Tippecanoe. He was the ninth president of the United States. (p. 331)

Hawthorne, Nathaniel (1804–1864) American writer, he is famous for his many stories and books, including *The Scarlet Letter,* and he is recognized as one of the first authors to write in a unique American style. (p. 444)

Henry the Navigator (1394–1460) King of Portugal who established a school of navigation and financed trips of exploration. (p. 39)

Hidalgo y Costilla, Father Miguel (1753–1811) Mexican priest and revolutionist, he led a rebellion of about 80,000 impoverished Indians and *mestizos* against Spain in the hope of improving living conditions; though defeated, the rebellion eventually grew and helped lead to Mexican independence. (p. 350)

Hutchinson, Anne (1591–1643) Puritan leader who angered other Puritans by claiming that people's relationship to God did not need guidance from ministers; she was tried and convicted of undermining church authorities and was banished from Massachusetts colony; she later established the colony of Portsmouth in present-day Rhode Island. (p. 82)

Irving, Washington (1783–1859) Early American satirical writer, he was the first American writer to gain international acclaim. His works include *Rip Van Winkle* and *The Legend of Sleepy Hollow.* He often used American history and authentic American settings and characters. (p. 308)

Jackson, Andrew (1767–1845) Nicknamed Old Hickory, he was an American hero in the Battle of New Orleans. As commander of the Tennessee militia, he defeated the Creek Indians, securing 23 million acres of land. His election as the seventh president of the United States marked an era of democracy called Jeffersonian Democracy. (pp. 286, 323)

Jackson, Thomas "Stonewall" (1824–1863) American Confederate general, he led the Shenandoah Valley campaign and fought with Lee in the Seven Days' Battles and the First and Second Battles of Bull Run. (p. 317)

Jay, John (1745–1829) American statesman and member of the Continental Congress, he authored some of the *Federalist Papers* and negotiated Jay's Treaty with Great Britain to settle outstanding disputes. (p. 245)

Jefferson, Thomas (1743–1826) American statesman, and member of two Continental Congresses, chairman of the committee to draft the Declaration of Independence, the Declaration's main author and one of its signers, and the third president of the United States. (p. 119)

Johnson, Andrew (1808–1875) American politician and the seventeenth president of the United States upon the assassination of Lincoln, he was impeached for his unpopular ideas about Reconstruction. He held onto the office by a one-vote margin. (p. 555)

Jones, John Paul (1747–1792) American naval officer famed for bravery, his most famous victory was the defeat of the British warship *Serapis,* during which he declared, "I have not yet begun to fight!" (p. 133)

Lafayette, Marquis de (1757–1834) French statesman and officer who viewed the American Revolution as important to the world, he helped finance the Revolution and served as major general. (p. 131)

Las Casas, Bartolomé de (1474–1566) Spanish missionary and historian, he became the first ordained Catholic priest in the New World and advocated for the welfare and protection of Native Americans as well as preached against the slavery system. (p. 51)

Lee, Robert E. (1807–1870) American soldier, he refused Lincoln's offer to head the Union Army and agreed to lead Confederate forces. He successfully led several major battles until his defeat at Gettysburg, and he surrendered to the Union's commander General Grant at Appomattox Courthouse. (pp. 517, 519)

Lewis, Meriwether (1774–1809) Former army captain selected by President Jefferson to explore the Louisiana Purchase, he lead the expedition that became known as the Lewis and Clark expedition. (p. 275)

Lincoln, Abraham (1809–1865) Sixteenth president of the United States, he promoted equal rights for African Americans in the famed Lincoln-Douglas debates. He issued the Emancipation Proclamation and set in motion the Civil War, but he was determined to preserve the Union. He was assassinated in 1865. (pp. 490, 535)

Little Turtle (c. 1752–1812) Miami chief who led a Native American alliance that raided settlements in the Northwest Territory, he was defeated and forced to sign the Treaty of Greenville, and he later became an advocate for peace. (p. 246)

Longfellow, Henry Wadsworth (1807–1882) American poet in the mid-nineteenth century, he is best known for his story-poems, such as "Paul Revere's Ride" in *Tales of a Wayside Inn* and *The Song of Hiawatha.* (p. 445)

Lowell, Francis Cabot (1775–1817) American industrialist who developed the Lowell system, a mill system that included looms that could both weave thread and spin cloth. He hired young women to live and work in his mill. (p. 392)

McClellan, George B. (1826–1885) American army general put in charge of Union troops and later removed by Lincoln for failure to press Lee's Confederate troops in Richmond. (p. 517)

McCormick, Cyrus (1809–1884) American inventor and industrialist, he invented the mechanical reaper and harvesting machine that quickly cut down wheat. (p. 404)

Madison, James (1751–1836) American statesman, he was a delegate to the Constitutional Convention, the fourth president of the United States, the author of some of the *Federalist Papers,* and is called the father of the Constitution for his proposals at the Constitutional Convention. He led the United States through the War of 1812. (pp. 164, 187)

Magellan (muh–jel–uhn), **Ferdinand** (1480–1521) Portuguese captain of a Spanish fleet that sought a western route to Asia via the "Southern Ocean", he found a passage through South America, now known as the Strait of Magellan, but died during the expedition. His crew of 18 people with one remaining ship successfully circumnavigated the world. (p. 44)

Mann, Horace (1796–1859) American educator, he is considered the father of American public education. He was a leader of the common-school movement, advocating education for all children. (pp. 450, 451)

Mansa Musa (d. 1332?) Emperor of Mali, grandson or grandnephew of Sundiata, made pilgrimage to Mecca in 1324. (p. 18)

Marion, Francis (1732?–1795) Revolutionary War commander of Marion's Brigade, a group of guerrilla soldiers in South Carolina that used surprise raids against British communications and supply lines. (p. 136)

Marshall, John (1755–1835) Federalist leader who served in the House of Representatives and as U.S. Secretary of State, he later became the Chief Justice of the U.S. Supreme Court, establishing in *Marbury* v. *Madison* the Supreme Court's power of judicial review. (p. 270)

Marshall, Thurgood (1908–1993) First African American U.S. Supreme Court Justice, he represented as a lawyer the National Association for the Advancement of Colored People and fought racial segregation. (p. 186)

Meade, George G. (1815–1872) American army officer, he served as a Union general at major Civil War battles. He forced back General Lee's Confederate army at Gettysburg but failed to obtain a decisive victory. (p. 536)

Melville, Herman (1819–1891) American writer, he based his books on his own sailing experiences and is famous for *Moby-Dick*. (p. 445)

Michelangelo (1475–1564) Italian sculptor, painter, architect, and poet. (p. 26)

Moctezuma II (1466–1520) Emperor of Mexico's Aztec Empire, he welcomed explorer Cortés as a god but was taken prisoner by him. He was later killed, and the Aztec capital was destroyed during the following Aztec uprising. (p. 46)

Monroe, James (1758–1831) Leading Revolutionary figure and negotiator of the Louisiana Purchase, he was the fifth president of the United States. He put forth the Monroe Doctrine establishing the U.S. sphere of influence in the Western Hemisphere that became the foundation of U.S. foreign policy. (p. 299)

Morse, Samuel F. B. (1791–1872) American artist and inventor, he applied scientists' discoveries of electricity and magnetism to develop the telegraph, which soon sent messages all across the country. (pp. 402, 403)

Mott, Lucretia (1793–1880) American reformer, she planned the Seneca Falls Convention with Elizabeth Cady Stanton, the first organized meeting for women's rights in the United States. (p. 464)

O'Connor, Sandra Day (1930–) Associate justice of the U.S. Supreme Court, she was the first woman appointed to the Court. (p. 186)

Osceola (c.1804–1838) Florida Seminole leader, he resisted removal by the U.S. government despite an earlier treaty that Seminole leaders had been forced to sign. He was eventually captured and died in prison. (p. 335)

P

Paine, Thomas (1737–1809) American political philosopher and author, he urged an immediate declaration of independence from England in his anonymously and simply written pamphlet, *Common Sense*. (p. 118)

Penn, William (1644–1718) Quaker leader who founded a colony for Quakers in Pennsylvania; the colony provided an important example of representative self-government and became a model of freedom and tolerance. (p. 86)

Perry, Oliver Hazard (1785–1819) American naval captain who put together the fleet that defeated the British at the Battle of Lake Erie in the War of 1812. (p. 285)

Pickett, George (1825–1875) American general in the Confederate army, he was famed for Pickett's Charge, a failed but heroic effort at Cemetery Ridge in the Battle of Gettysburg, often considered a turning point of the Civil War. (p. 538)

Pierce, Franklin (1804–1869) Democratic candidate for president in 1852 and the fourteenth president of the United States, he made the Gadsden Purchase, which opened the Northwest for settlement, and passed the unpopular Kansas-Nebraska Act. (p. 483)

Pike, Zebulon (1779–1813) Army officer sent on a mission to explore the West, he was ordered to find the headwaters of the Red River. He attempted to climb what is now known as Pikes Peak in Colorado. (p. 276)

Pizarro (puh–ZAHR–oh), **Francisco** (c. 1475–1541) Spanish conquistador who sailed with Balboa on the discovery of the Pacific Ocean, he later pursued rumors of golden cities in the Andes Mountains of South America and conquered the Inca Empire. (p. 47)

Plato (c. 428-348 BC) Greek philosopher, student of Plato and teacher of Aristotle, wrote The Republic. (p. 22)

Pocahontas (c.1595–1617) American Indian princess, she saved the life of John Smith when he was captured and sentenced to death by the Powhatan. She was later taken prisoner by the English, converted to Christianity, and married colonist John Rolfe. (p. 73)

Poe, Edgar Allan (1809–1849) American writer, he is famed for his haunting poem, "The Raven," as well as many other chilling or romantic stories and poems. He is credited with creating the first detective story, *The Gold Bug*. (p. 445)

Polk, James K. (1795–1849) Eleventh president of the United States, he settled the Oregon boundary with Great Britain and successfully conducted the Mexican-American War. (p. 355)

Pontiac (c.1720–1769) Ottawa chief who united the Great Lakes' Indians to try to halt the advance of European settlements, he attacked British forts in a rebellion known as Pontiac's Rebellion; he eventually surrendered in 1766. (p. 97)

Revels, Hiram (1822–1901) American clergyman, educator, and politician, he became the first African American in the U.S. Senate. (p. 565)

Sacagawea (sak–uh–juh–WEE–uh) (1786?–1812) Shoshone woman who, along with French fur trapper husband, accompanied and aided Lewis and Clark on their expedition. (p. 276)

Santa Anna, Antonio López de (1794–1876) Mexican general and politician, he was president of Mexico and became a dictator. He fought in the Texas Revolution and seized the Alamo but was defeated and captured by Sam Houston at San Jacinto. (p. 351)

Scott, Dred (1795?–1858) Enslaved African who filed suit for his freedom stating that his time living in a free state made him a free man; the Supreme Court ruling known as the *Dred Scott* decision upheld slavery and found the Missouri Compromise unconstitutional. (p. 489)

Scott, Winfield (1786–1866) American general, he served as commander in the Mexican War and used a two-part strategy against the South in the Civil War; he wanted to destroy the South's economy with a naval blockade and gain control of the Mississippi River. (p. 513)

Sequoya (between 1760 and 1770–1843) American Indian scholar and craftsman, he created a writing system for the Cherokee language and taught literacy to many Cherokee. (p. 333)

Serra (ser–rah), **Junípero** (hoo–nee–pay–roh) (1713–1784) Spanish Franciscan missionary to California, he planned or founded numerous missions all along the Pacific coast and founded San Francisco in an effort to spread Christianity. (p. 23)

Shays, Daniel (1747?–1825) Revolutionary War officer who led Shays's Rebellion, an uprising of farmers in western Massachusetts that shut down the courts so that farmers would not lose their farms for tax debts. He was defeated and condemned to death, but pardoned. (p. 161)

Sherman, William Tecumseh (1820–1891) American Union army officer, his famous March to the Sea captured Atlanta, Georgia, marking an important turning point in the war. (p. 541)

Singer, Isaac (1811–1875) American inventor; he patented an improved sewing machine and by

1860, was the largest manufacturer of sewing machines in the country. (p. 405)

Slater, Samuel (1768–1835) English industrialist who brought a design for a textile mill to America, he is considered the founder of the American cotton industry. (p. 386)

Smith, John (c.1580–1631) English colonist to the Americas who helped found Jamestown Colony and encouraged settlers to work harder and build better housing. (p. 73)

Socrates (c. 470–399 BC) Greek philosopher and teacher who wanted to make people question their own beliefs and think for themselves. (p. 22)

Squanto (?–1622) Patuxet Indian who was captured and enslaved in Spain but later escaped to England and then America; he taught the Pilgrims native farming methods and helped them establish relations with the Wampanoag, the Indians at the feast later known as Thanksgiving. (p. 79)

Stanton, Elizabeth Cady (1815–1902) American woman suffrage leader, she organized the Seneca Falls Convention with Lucretia Mott. The convention was the first organized meeting for women's rights in the United States, which launched the suffrage movement. (pp. 464, 467)

Stevens, Thaddeus (1792–1868) American lawyer and politician, he was the leader of the Radical Republicans in the Reconstruction effort and was an opponent and critic of Andrew Johnson's policies. He sought economic justice for freedmen and poor southerners. (p. 560)

Stone, Lucy (1818–1893) American woman suffragist, she was a well–known and accomplished antislavery speaker who supported the women's rights movement. (p. 465)

Stowe, Harriet Beecher (1811–1896) American author and daughter of Lyman Beecher, she was an abolitionist and author of the famous antislavery novel, *Uncle Tom's Cabin*. (p. 481)

Stuyvesant (STY–vuh–suhnt), **Peter** (c.1610–1672) Director general of the Dutch New Netherland colony, he was forced to surrender New Netherland to the English. (p. 85)

Sutter, John (1803–1880) American pioneer who built Sutter's Fort, a trading post on the California frontier; gold was discovered leading to the California gold rush. (p. 365)

Taney (TAW–nee), **Roger B.** (1777–1864) U.S. Supreme Court Chief Justice he wrote the majority opinion in the *Dred Scott* decision, stating that African Americans were not citizens and that the Missouri Compromise was unconstitutional. (p. 490)

Tecumseh (1768–1813) Shawnee chief who attempted to form an Indian confederation to resist white settlement in the Northwest Territory. (p. 280)

Thoreau, Henry David (1817–1862) American writer and transcendentalist philosopher, he studied nature and published a magazine article, "Civil Disobedience," as well as his famous book, *Walden Pond*. (p. 443)

Truth, Sojourner (c.1797–1883) American evangelist and reformer, she was born an enslaved African but was later freed and became a speaker for abolition and women's suffrage. (p. 456)

Tubman, Harriet (c.1820–1913) American abolitionist who escaped slavery and assisted other enslaved Africans to escape; she is the most famous Underground Railroad conductor and is known as the Moses of her people. (p. 458)

Turner, Nat (1800–1831) American slave leader, he claimed that divine inspiration had led him to end the slavery system. Called Nat Turner's Rebellion, the slave revolt was the most violent one in U.S. history; he was tried, convicted, and executed. (p. 428)

Vallejo, Mariano Guadalupe (1808–1890)

American soldier and politician, he increased settlement in northern California and became a rich cattleman. He helped in the effort to get statehood for California. (p. 357)

Van Buren, Martin (1782–1862) American politician and secretary of state under Andrew Jackson, he later became the eighth president of the United States. (p. 320)

Vesey, Denmark (c.1767–1822) American insurrectionist, he was brought to America as a slave but purchased his own freedom. He planned a large slave uprising in South Carolina and was tried and hanged along with 36 others accused of plotting the rebellion. (p. 428)

W

Washington, George (1732–1799) Revolutionary War hero and Patriot leader, he served as a representative to the Continental Congresses, commanded the Continental Army, and was unanimously elected to two terms as president of the United States. (pp. 112)

Webster, Daniel (1782–1852) American lawyer and statesman, he spoke out against nullification and states' rights, believing that the country should stay unified. (p. 328)

Whitman, Walt (1819–1892) American poet, he gained recognition abroad and later at home for unrhymed works of poetry praising the United States, Americans, democracy, and individualism.(p. 445)

Whitney, Eli (1765–1825) American inventor whose cotton gin changed cotton harvesting procedures and enabled large increases in cotton production; he introduced the technology of mass production through the development of interchangeable parts in gun-making. (p. 387)

Winthrop, John (1588–1649) Leader of the Massachusetts Bay Colony who led Puritan colonists to Massachusetts to establish an ideal Christian community; he later became the colony's first governor. (p. 80)

Y

Young, Brigham (1801–1877) American religious leader who headed the Mormon Church after the murder of Joseph Smith, he moved the community to Utah, leading thousands along what came to be known as the Mormon Trail to the main settlement at Salt Lake City. (p. 349)

English and Spanish Glossary

MARK	AS IN	RESPELLING	EXAMPLE
a	alphabet	a	*AL-fuh-bet
ā	Asia	ay	AY-zhuh
ä	cart, top	ah	KAHRT, TAHP
e	let, ten	e	LET, TEN
ē	even, leaf	ee	EE-vuhn, LEEF
i	it, tip, British	i	IT, TIP, BRIT-ish
ī	site, buy, Ohio	y	SYT, BY, oh-HY-oh
	iris	eye	EYE-ris
k	card	k	KAHRD
ō	over, rainbow	oh	OH-vuhr, RAYN-boh
ů	book, wood	ooh	BOOHK, WOOHD
ò	all, orchid	aw	AWL, AWR-kid
òi	foil, coin	oy	FOYL, KOYN
àu	out	ow	OWT
ə	cup, butter	uh	KUHP, BUHT-uhr
ü	rule, food	oo	ROOL, FOOD
yü	few	yoo	FYOO
zh	vision	zh	VIZH-uhn

*A syllable printed in small capital letters receives heavier emphasis than the other syllable(s) in a word.

Phonetic Respelling and Pronunciation Guide

Many of the key terms in this textbook have been respelled to help you pronounce them. The letter combinations used in the respelling throughout the narrative are explained in the following phonetic respelling and pronunciation guide. The guide is adapted from *Webster's Tenth New College Dictionary, Merriam-Webster's New Geographical Dictionary,* and *Merriam-Webster's New Biographical Dictionary.*

A

abolition an end to slavery (p. 454)
abolición fin de la esclavitud (pág. 454)

Adams-Onís Treaty (1819) an agreement in which Spain gave East Florida to the United States (p. 299)
tratado de Adams y Onís (1819) acuerdo en el que España cedió el territorio del este de Florida a Estados Unidos (pág. 299)

Alamo Spanish mission in San Antonio, Texas, that was the site of a famous battle of the Texas Revolution in 1836 (p. 352)
El Álamo misión española en San Antonio, Texas; escenario de una famosa batalla durante la Revolución texana de 1836 (pág. 352)

Alien and Sedition Acts (1798) laws passed by a Federalist-dominated Congress aimed at protecting the government from treasonous ideas, actions, and people (p. 253)
Leyes de No Intervención Extranjera (1798) leyes aprobadas por un Congreso mayormente federalista con el fin de proteger al gobierno de la influencia de ideas, acciones y personas desleales (pág. 253)

amendment official change, correction, or addition to a law or constitution (p. 173)
enmienda cambio, corrección o adición realizado de manera oficial a una ley o constitución (pág. 173)

American System Henry Clay's plan for raising tariffs to pay for internal improvements such as better roads and canals (p. 302)
Sistema estadounidense plan de alza de impuestos creado por Henry Clay para realizar mejoras internas como la reparación de caminos y canales (pág. 302)

Antifederalists people who opposed ratification of the Constitution (p. 170)
antifederalistas personas que se oponían a la aprobación de la Constitución (pág. 170)

American Anti-Slavery Society an organization started by William Lloyd Garrison whose members wanted immediate emancipation and racial equality for African Americans (p. 454)
Sociedad Americana contra la Esclavitud organización fundada por William Lloyd Garrison cuyos miembros pedían la emancipación inmediata y la igualdad racial de los afroamericanos (pág. 454)

Appomattox Courthouse Virginia town where General Robert E. Lee was forced to surrender, thus ending the Civil War (p. 541)

Appomattox Courthouse poblado de Virginia donde el general Robert E. Lee fue obligado a rendirse, dando fin a la Guerra Civil (pág. 541)

Articles of Confederation (1777) the document that created the first central government for the United States; was replaced by the Constitution in 1789 (p. 154)

Artículos de la Confederación (1777) documento que creó el primer gobierno central en Estados Unidos; fue reemplazado por la Constitución en 1789 (pág. 154)

astrolabe a device that enabled navigators to learn their ship's location by charting the position of the stars (p. 40)

astrolabio instrumento que permitía a los navegantes determinar la posición de una embarcación según la posición de las estrellas (pág. 40)

B

Bacon's Rebellion (1676) an atttack led by Nathaniel Bacon against American Indians and the colonial government in Virginia (p. 74)

Rebelión de Bacon (1676) ataque encabezado por Nathaniel Bacon contra los indígenas norteamericanos y el gobierno colonial en Virginia (pág. 74)

Bank of the United States a national bank chartered by Congress in 1791 to provide security for the U.S. economy (p. 242)

Banco de Estados Unidos banco nacional constituido por el Congreso en 1791 para dar establidad a la economía de Estados Unidos (pág. 242)

Battle of Antietam (1862) a Union victory in the Civil War that marked the bloodiest single-day battle in U.S. military history (p. 516)

batalla de Antietam (1862) victoria del ejército de la Unión durante la Guerra Civil en la batalla de un solo día más sangrienta en la historia militar de Estados Unidos (pág. 516)

Battle of Bunker Hill (1775) a Revolutionary War battle in Boston that demonstrated that the colonists could fight well against the British army (p. 115)

batalla de Bunker Hill (1775) batalla de la Guerra de Independencia estadounidense que tuvo lugar en Boston; en ésta se demostró que los colonos podían luchar bien contra el ejército británico (pág. 115)

Battle of Fallen Timbers (1794) a battle between U.S. troops and an American Indian confederation that ended Indian efforts to halt white settlement in the Northwest Territory (p. 247)

batalla de Fallen Timbers (1794) batalla entre las tropas estadounidenses y una confederación de indígenas norteamericanos que puso fin a los intentos de los indígenas para detener la emigración de personas de raza blanca al Territorio del Noroeste (pág. 247)

Battle of Gettysburg (1863) a Union Civil War victory that turned the tide against the Confederates at Gettysburg, Pennsylvania (p. 537)

batalla de Gettysburg (1863) victoria del ejército de la Unión durante la Guerra Civil que cambió el curso de la guerra en contra de los confederados en Gettysburg, Pensilvania (pág. 537)

Battle of Lake Erie (1813) U.S. victory in the War of 1812, led by Oliver Hazard Perry; broke Britain's control of Lake Erie (p. 285)

batalla del lago Erie (1813) victoria en la Guerra de 1812 en la que el ejército estadounidense, comandado por Oliver Hazard Perry, puso fin al control británico del lago Erie (pág. 285)

Battle of New Orleans (1815) the greatest U.S. victory in the War of 1812; actually took place two weeks after a peace treaty had been signed ending the war (p. 286)

batalla de Nueva Orleáns (1815) la mayor victoria del ejército estadounidense en la Guerra de 1812; tuvo lugar dos semanas después de la firma de un tratado de paz en el que se declaraba el final de la guerra (pág. 286)

Battle of San Jacinto (1836) the final battle of the Texas Revolution; resulted in the defeat of the Mexican army and independence for Texas (p. 352)

batalla de San Jacinto (1836) batalla final de la Revolución texana en la que fue derrotado el ejército mexicano y Texas obtuvo su independencia (pág. 352)

Battle of Saratoga (1777) a Revolutionary War battle in New York that resulted in a major defeat of British troops; marked the Patriots' greatest victory up to that point in the war (p. 130)

batalla de Saratoga (1777) batalla de la Guerra de Independencia estadounidense que tuvo lugar en Nueva York y en la que las fuerzas británicas sufrieron una de sus mayores derrotas; los patriotas obtuvieron su mayor victoria hasta ese momento (pág. 130)

Battle of Shiloh (1862) a Civil War battle in Tennessee in which the Union army gained greater control over the Mississippi River valley (p. 523)

batalla de Shiloh (1862) batalla de la Guerra Civil en Tennessee en la que el ejército de la Unión adquirió mayor control sobre el valle del río Mississippi (pág. 523)

Battle of Tippecanoe (1811) U.S. victory over an Indian confederation that wanted to stop white settlement in the Northwest Territory; increased tensions between Great Britain and the United States (p. 282)

batalla de Tippecanoe (1811) victoria del ejército estadounidense sobre la confederación indígena que intentaba evitar el establecimiento de poblaciones de blancos en el Territorio del Noroeste; esta batalla aumentó las hostilidades entre Gran Bretaña y Estados Unidos (pág. 282)

Battle of Trenton (1776) a Revolutionary War battle in New Jersey in which Patriot forces captured more than 900 Hessian troops (p. 129)

batalla de Trenton (1776) batalla de la Guerra de Independencia estadounidense que tuvo lugar en Nueva Jersey; en esta batalla las fuerzas de los patriotas capturaron a más de 900 soldados mercenarios hessianos (pág. 129)

Battle of Yorktown (1781) the last major battle of the Revolutionary War; site of British general Charles Cornwallis's surrender to the Patriots in Virginia (p. 137)
batalla de Yorktown (1781) la última batalla importante de la Guerra de Independencia estadounidense; lugar donde se rindió el general británico Charles Cornwallis ante las tropas de los patriotas en Virginia (pág. 137)

Bear Flag Revolt (1846) a revolt against Mexico by American settlers in California who declared the territory an independent republic (p. 358)
Revuelta de Bear Flag (1846) rebelión iniciada por colonos estadounidenses en contra de México para declarar al territorio de California una república independiente (pág. 358)

Berbers a group of people from northern Africa (p. 16)
bereberes grupo de pueblos que habitaban en el norte de África (pág. 16)

Bill of Rights the first 10 amendments to the Constitution; ratified in 1791 (p. 173)
Declaración de Derechos primeras 10 enmiendas hechas a la Constitución; aprobada en 1791 (pág. 173)

Black Codes laws passed in the southern states during Reconstruction that greatly limited the freedom and rights of African Americans (p. 558)
códigos para negros decretos aprobados en los estados sureños en la época de la Reconstrucción que limitaron en gran medida la libertad y los derechos de los afroamericanos (pág. 558)

Black Death a series of plagues that killed about 25 million people in Europe starting in 1347 (p. 25)
Peste Negra serie de plagas que asolaron Europa, causando la muerte a casi 25 millones de personas; comenzaron en 1347 (pág. 25)

bond a certificate that represents money the government has borrowed from private citizens (p. 238)
bono certificado que representa dinero que el gobierno toma prestado de los ciudadanos (pág. 238)

border states Delaware, Kentucky, Maryland, and Missouri; slave states that lay between the North and the South and did not join the Confederacy during the Civil War (p. 512)
estados fronterizos Delaware, Kentucky, Maryland y Missouri; estados ubicados entre el Norte y el Sur, que practicaban la esclavitud y que no se unieron a la Confederación durante la Guerra Civil (pág. 512)

Boston Massacre (1770) an incident in which British soldiers fired into a crowd of colonists, killing five people (p. 101)

matanza de Boston (1770) incidente en el que los soldados británicos dispararon entre una multitud de colonos, ocasionando la muerte a cinco personas (pág. 101)

Boston Tea Party (1773) a protest against the Tea Act in which a group of colonists boarded British tea ships and dumped more than 340 chests of tea into Boston Harbor (p. 102)
Motín del Té de Boston (1773) protesta en contra de la Ley del Té en la que un grupo de colonos abordó barcos británicos que transportaban té y arrojó al mar alrededor de 340 baúles con este producto en el puerto de Boston (pág. 102)

Bureau of Indian Affairs a government agency created in the 1800s to oversee federal policy toward Native Americans (p. 332)
Oficina de Asuntos Indígenas agencia creada por el gobierno en el siglo XIX para encargarse de las políticas federales sobre los indígenas norteamericanos (pág. 332)

C

Californios Spanish colonists in California in the 1800s (p. 357)
californios colonos españoles que vivían en California en el siglo XIX (pág. 357)

caravels ships that used triangular sails to sail against the wind, and had rudders to improve steering (p. 40)
carabelas barcos que usaban velas triangulares para navegar contra el viento y que tenían timones para mejorar la dirección (pág. 40)

charter an official document that gives a person the right to establish a colony (p. 54)
carta de constitución documento real que da a una persona el derecho a establecer una colonia (pág. 54)

checks and balances a system established by the Constitution that prevents any branch of government from becoming too powerful (p. 167)
pesos y contrapesos sistema establecido por la Constitución para evitar que cualquier poder del gobierno adquiera demasiada autoridad en relación con los demás (pág. 167)

circumnavigate to travel all the way around the globe (p. 44)
circunnavegar viajar rodeando por completo la Tierra (pág. 44)

Civil Rights Act of 1866 a law that gave African Americans legal rights equal to those of white Americans (p. 560)
Ley de Derechos Civiles de 1866 ley que daba a los afroamericanos derechos legales similares a los que tenían los ciudadanos de raza blanca (pág. 560)

Clermont the first full-sized U.S. commercial steamboat; developed by Robert Fulton and tested in 1807 (p. 397)
Clermont primer barco comercial de vapor de grandes dimensiones, diseñado por Robert Fulton y probado en 1807 (pág. 397)

Columbian Exchange the transfer of plants, animals, and diseases between the Americas and Europe, Asia, and Africa (p. 45)
intercambio colombino intercambio de plantas y animales entre el Nuevo Mundo y el Viejo Mundo que tuvo lugar tras el viaje de Colón (pág. 45)

Committees of Correspondence committees created by the Massachusetts House of Representatives in the 1760s to help towns and colonies share information about resisting British laws (p. 99)
comités de correspondencia comités creados por la Cámara de Representantes de Massachusetts en la década de 1760 para que poblados y colonias compartieran información que los ayudara a resistirse a las leyes británicas (pág. 99)

common-school movement a social reform effort that began in the mid-1800s and promoted the idea of having all children educated in a common place regardless of social class or background (p. 450)
movimiento de escuelas comunes reforma social iniciada a mediados del siglo XIX para fomentar la idea de que todos los niños debían recibir educación en un mismo lugar sin importar su origen o clase social (pág. 450)

Common Sense (1776) a pamphlet written by Thomas Paine that criticized monarchies and convinced many American colonists of the need to break away from Britain (p. 118)
Sentido común (1776) folleto escrito por Thomas Paine en el que criticaba a las monarquías con el fin de convencer a los colonos estadounidenses de la necesidad de independizarse de Gran Bretaña (pág. 118)

Compromise of 1850 Henry Clay's proposed agreement that allowed California to enter the Union as a free state and divided the rest of the Mexican Cession into two territories where slavery would be decided by popular sovereignty (p. 479)
Acuerdo de 1850 acuerdo redactado por Henry Clay en que se permitía a California ingresar en la Unión como estado libre y se proponía la división del resto del territorio cedido por México en dos partes donde la esclavitud sería reglamentada por soberanía popular (pág. 479)

Compromise of 1877 an agreement to settle the disputed presidential election of 1876; Democrats agreed to accept Republican Rutherford B. Hayes as president in return for the removal of federal troops from the South (p. 567)

Acuerdo de 1877 acuerdo en el que se resolvió la disputa de las elecciones presidenciales de 1876; los demócratas aceptaron al republicano Rutherford B. Hayes como presidente a cambio del retiro de las tropas federales del Sur (pág. 567)

Confederate States of America the nation formed by the southern states when they seceded from the Union; also known as the Confederacy (p. 496)
Estados Confederados de América nación formada por los estados del Sur cuando se separaron de la Unión; también conocida como Confederación (pág. 496)

conquistador a Spanish soldier and explorer who led military expeditions in the Americas and captured land for Spain (p. 46)
conquistador soldado y explorador español que encabezó expediciones militares en América y capturó territorios en nombre de España (pág. 46)

constitution a set of basic principles that determines the powers and duties of a government (p. 153)
constitución conjunto de principios básicos que determina los poderes y las obligaciones de un gobierno (pág. 153)

Constitutional Convention (1787) a meeting held in Philadelphia at which delegates from the states wrote the Constitution (p. 164)
Convención Constitucional (1787) encuentro realizado en Filadelfia en el que delegados de los estados redactaron la Constitución (pág. 164)

Constitutional Union Party a political party formed in 1860 by a group of northerners and southerners who supported the Union, its laws, and the Constitution (p. 495)
Partido Constitucional por la Unión partido político formado en 1860 por habitantes del Norte y del Sur en apoyo de la Unión, sus leyes y la Constitución (pág. 495)

Continental Army the army created by the Second Continental Congress in 1775 to defend the American colonies from Britain (p. 114)
Ejército Continental ejército creado por el Segundo Congreso Continental en 1775 para defender las colonias estadounidenses del dominio británico (pág. 114)

contraband an escaped slave who joined the Union army during the Civil War (p. 531)
contrabando bienes introducidos en un país de forma ilegal; esclavo que escapó y que se unió al ejército de la Unión durante la Guerra Civil (pág. 531)

Convention of 1818 an agreement between the United States and Great Britain that settled fishing rights and established new North American borders (p. 298)
Convención de 1818 acuerdo entre Estados Unidos y Gran Bretaña para definir los derechos de pesca y establecer las nuevas fronteras norteamericanas (pág. 298)

ENGLISH AND SPANISH GLOSSARY

Copperheads a group of northern Democrats who opposed abolition and sympathized with the South during the Civil War (p. 532)
copperheads grupo de demócratas del Norte que se oponían a la abolición de la esclavitud y simpatizaban con las creencias sureñas durante la Guerra Civil (pág. 532)

cotton belt a region stretching from South Carolina to east Texas where most U.S. cotton was produced during the mid-1800s (p. 417)
región algodonera zona que se extendía desde Carolina del Sur hasta el este de Texas, en la que se producía la mayor parte del algodón cosechado en Estados Unidos a mediados del siglo XIX (pág. 417)

cotton diplomacy Confederate efforts to use the importance of southern cotton to Britain's textile industry to persuade the British to support the Confederacy in the Civil War (p. 513)
diplomacia del algodón esfuerzos de la Confederación por aprovechar la influencia del algodón del Sur en la industria textil británica para convencer a Gran Bretaña de apoyar su causa durante la Guerra Civil (pág. 513)

cotton gin a machine invented by Eli Whitney in 1793 to remove seeds from short-staple cotton; revolutionized the cotton industry (p. 415)
desmotadora de algodón máquina inventada por Eli Whitney en 1793 para separar las fibras de algodón de las semillas; revolucionó la industria del algodón (pág. 415)

culture the common values and traditions of a society, such as language, government, and family relationships (p. 7)
cultura valores y tradiciones comunes de una sociedad, como el lenguaje, la forma de gobierno y las relaciones familiares (pág. 7)

Cumberland Road the first federal road project, construction of which began in 1815; ran from Cumberland, Maryland, to present-day Wheeling, West Virginia (p. 303)
camino de Cumberland primer proyecto federal de construcción de carreteras, iniciado en 1815 para crear un camino entre Cumberland, Maryland y el poblado que actualmente lleva el nombre de Wheeling, en Virginia Occidental (pág. 303)

Declaration of Independence (1776) the document written to declare the colonies free from British rule (p. 119)
Declaración de Independencia (1776) documento redactado para declarar la independencia de las colonias del dominio británico (pág. 119)

Declaration of Sentiments (1848) a statement written and signed by women's rights supporters at the Seneca Falls Convention; detailed their beliefs about social injustice against women (p. 464)
Declaración de Sentimientos (1848) declaración redactada y firmada por una serie de personas en apoyo de los derechos de la mujer durante la Convención de Seneca Falls, en la que se describía con detalle su punto de vista sobre las injusticias sociales que afectaban a las mujeres (pág. 464)

democracy a government in which people rule themselves (p. 23)
democracia gobierno en el que el pueblo se gobierna a sí mismo (pág. 23)

Democratic Party a political party formed by supporters of Andrew Jackson after the presidential election of 1824 (p. 323)
Partido Demócrata partido político formado por partidarios de Andrew Jackson después de las elecciones presidenciales de 1824 (pág. 323)

Democratic-Republican Party a political party founded in the 1790s by Thomas Jefferson, James Madison, and other leaders who wanted to preserve the power of the state governments and promote agriculture (p. 250)
Partido Demócrata Republicano partido político formado en la década de 1790 por Thomas Jefferson, James Madison y otros líderes políticos con el fin de preservar el poder de los gobiernos estatales y promover la agricultura (pág. 250)

deport to send an immigrant back to his or her country of origin (p. 222)
deportar enviar a un inmigrante de regreso a su país de origen (pág. 222)

depression a steep drop in economic activity combined with rising unemployment (p. 161)
depresión descenso considerable en la actividad económica, combinado con un alza en el desempleo (pág. 161)

Donner party a group of western travelers who were stranded in the Sierra Nevada during the winter of 1846–47; only 45 of the party's 87 members survived (p. 365)
grupo Donner grupo de viajeros del Oeste extraviados en la Sierra Nevada durante el invierno de 1846–47; sólo 45 de los 87 viajeros sobrevivieron (pág. 365)

double jeopardy the act of trying a person twice for the same crime (p. 218)
doble proceso acto de juzgar a una persona dos veces por el mismo delito (pág. 218)

draft a system of required service in the armed forces (p. 223)
conscripción sistema de servicio obligatorio en las fuerzas armadas (pág. 223)

Dred Scott (1857) a slave whose courtcase led to a U.S. Supreme Court ruling that declared African Americans were not U.S. citizens, that the Missouri Compromise's restriction on slavery was unconstitutional, and that Congress did not have the right to ban slavery in any federal territory (p. 489)
Dred Scott (1857) esclavo que fue encausado y cuyo juicio concluyó con una decisión de la Corte Suprema; en la que se declaraba que los afroamericanos no podían ser ciudadanos de Estados Unidos, que las restricciones de la esclavitud impuestas en el Acuerdo de Missouri eran inconstitucionales y que el Congreso no tenía derecho de abolir la esclavitud en ninguna parte del territorio federal (pág. 489)

due process the fair application of the law (p. 218)
debido proceso aplicación justa de la ley (pág. 218)

electoral college a group of people selected from each of the states to cast votes in presidential elections (p. 234)
colegio electoral grupo de personas elegido en cada estado para votar en las elecciones presidenciales (pág. 234)

emancipation freeing of the slaves (p. 529)
emancipación liberación de los esclavos (pág. 529)

Emancipation Proclamation (1862) an order issued by President Abraham Lincoln freeing the slaves in areas rebelling against the Union; took effect January 1, 1863 (p. 529)
Proclamación de Emancipación (1862) decreto emitido por el presidente Abraham Lincoln para liberar a los esclavos en las áreas que luchaban contra la Unión; entró en vigor el primero de enero de 1863 (pág. 529)

embargo the banning of trade with a country (p. 279)
embargo prohibición del comercio con un país (pág. 279)

Embargo Act (1807) a law that prohibited American merchants from trading with other countries (p. 279)
Ley de Embargo (1807) ley que prohibía a los comerciantes estadounidenses comerciar con otros países (pág. 279)

eminent domain the government's power to take personal property to benefit the public (p. 218)
derecho de expropiación poder otorgado al gobierno para tomar propiedades particulares por el bien común (pág. 218)

empresarios agents who were contracted by the Mexican republic to bring settlers to Texas in the early l800s (p. 350)
empresarios personas contratadas por la República Mexicana para reclutar personas que desearan establecer poblaciones en Texas a principios del siglo XIX (pág. 350)

encomienda system a system in Spanish America that gave settlers the right to tax local Indians or to demand their labor in exchange for protecting them and converting them to Christianity (p. 50)
sistema de encomienda sistema adoptado en la América española que permitía a los colonos cobrar impuestos a los indígenas o exigirles trabajo a cambio de su protección y de convertirlos al cristianismo (pág. 50)

English Bill of Rights (1689) a shift of political power from the British monarchy to Parliament (p. 91)
Declaración de Derechos inglesa (1689) cambio del poder político de la monarquía británica al Parlamento inglés (pág. 91)

Enlightenment the Age of Reason; movement that began in Europe in the 1700s as people began examining the natural world, society, and government (p. 95)
Ilustración Era de la Razón; movimiento iniciado en Europa en el siglo XVIII cuando las personas empezaron a adquirir más conocimientos sobre la naturaleza, la sociedad y el gobierno (pág. 95)

environment the climate and landscape that surrounds living things (p. 7)
medio ambiente el clima y paisaje donde habitan seres vivos (pág. 7)

Era of Good Feelings a period of peace, pride, and progress for the United States from 1815 to 1825 (p. 303)
Era de los buenos sentimientos período de paz, orgullo y progreso de los Estados Unidos de 1815 a 1825 (pág. 303)

Erie Canal the canal that runs from Albany to Buffalo, New York; completed in 1825 (p. 303)
canal de Erie canal que va de Albany a Búfalo, en el estado de Nueva York; completado en 1825 (pág. 303)

executive branch the division of the federal government that includes the president and the administrative departments; enforces the nation's laws (p. 167)
Poder Ejecutivo división del gobierno federal que incluye al presidente y a los departamentos administrativos; vigila el cumplimiento de las leyes de la nación (pág. 167)

executive orders nonlegislative directives issued by the U.S. president in certain circumstances; executive orders have the force of congressional law (p. 185)
órdenes ejecutivas órdenes no legislativas dictadas por el presidente de Estados Unidos en circunstancias específicas; tienen la misma validez que las leyes del Congreso (pág. 185)

factor a crop broker who managed the trade between southern planters and their customers (p. 417)

comisionado intermediario que administraba el intercambio comercial entre las plantaciones del Sur y sus clientes (pág. 417)

federal system a system that divided powers between the states and the federal government (p. 182)
sistema federal sistema en el que se distribuye el poder entre los estados y el gobierno federal (pág. 182)

federalism U.S. system of government in which power is distributed between a central government and individual states (p. 167)
federalismo sistema de gobierno de Estados Unidos en el que el poder está distribuido entre una autoridad centralizada y varios estados (pág. 167)

Federalist Papers a series of essays that defended and explained the Constitution and tried to reassure Americans that the states would not be overpowered by the proposed national government (p. 171)
Federalist Papers serie de ensayos que defienden y explican la Constitución con el propósito de que los ciudadanos quedaran convencidos de que el gobierno nacional propuesto no tendría supremacía sobre el gobierno de los estados (pág. 171)

Federalist Party a political party created in the 1790s and influenced by Alexander Hamilton that wanted to strengthen the federal government and promote industry and trade (p. 250)
Partido Federalista partido político creado en la década de 1790 siguiendo las ideas de Alexander Hamilton para fortalecer al gobierno federal y fomentar la industria y el intercambio comercial (pág. 250)

Federalists people who supported ratification of the Constitution (p. 170)
federalistas personas que apoyaban la ratificación de la Constitución (pág. 170)

Fifteenth Amendment (1870) a constitutional amendment that gave African American men the right to vote (p. 563)
Decimoquinta Enmienda (1870) enmienda constitucional que otorgaba a los hombres afroamericanos el derecho al voto (pág. 563)

54th Massachusetts Infantry African American Civil War regiment that captured Fort Wagner in South Carolina (p. 531)

54º Batallón de Infantería de Massachusetts regimiento de la Guerra Civil formado por soldados afroamericanos que tomó el fuerte Wagner en Carolina del Sur (pág. 531)

First Battle of Bull Run (1861) the first major battle of the Civil War, resulting in a Confederate victory; showed that the Civil War would not be won easily (p. 517)
primera batalla de Bull Run (1861) primera batalla importante de la Guerra Civil, en la cual el ejército confederado obtuvo la victoria; en esta batalla se demostró que ninguno de los bandos ganaría la guerra con facilidad (pág. 517)

First Continental Congress (1774) a meeting of colonial delegates in Philadelphia to decide how to respond to the closing of Boston Harbor, increased taxes, and abuses of authority by the British government; delegates petitioned King George III, listing the freedoms they believed colonists should enjoy (p. 112)
Primer Congreso Continental (1774) encuentro de delegados de las colonias en Filadelfia para decidir cómo responderían al cierre del puerto de Boston, al alza de impuestos y a los abusos de la autoridad británica; los delegados hicieron una serie de peticiones al rey Jorge III, incluyendo los derechos que consideraban justos para los colonos (pág. 112)

folktale a story that often provides a moral lesson (p. 427)
cuento popular narración que con frecuencia ofrece una moraleja (pág. 427)

Fort Sumter a federal outpost in Charleston, South Carolina, that was attacked by the Confederates in April 1861, sparking the Civil War (p. 511)
fuerte Sumter puesto de avanzada federal en Charleston, Carolina del Sur, cuyo ataque por parte de los confederados en abril de 1861 dio origen a la Guerra Civil (pág. 511)

forty-niner a gold-seeker who moved to California during the gold rush (p. 365)
gambusino buscador de oro que emigró a California durante la fiebre del oro (pág. 365)

Fourteenth Amendment (1866) a constitutional amendment giving full rights of citizenship to all people born or naturalized in the United States, except for American Indians (p. 561)
Decimocuarta Enmienda (1866) enmienda constitucional que otorgaba derechos totales de ciudadanía a todas las personas nacidas en Estados Unidos o naturalizadas estadounidenses, con excepción de los indígenas (pág. 561)

Freedmen's Bureau an agency established by Congress in 1865 to help poor people throughout the South (p. 556)
Oficina de Esclavos Libertos oficina creada por el Congreso en 1865 para ayudar a los pobres del Sur del país (pág. 556)

Freeport Doctrine (1858) a statement made by Stephen Douglas during the Lincoln-Douglas debates that pointed out how people could use popular sovereignty to determine if their state or territory should permit slavery (p. 492)
Doctrina de Freeport (1858) declaración hecha por Stephen Douglas durante los debates Lincoln-Douglas que señalaba que el pueblo podía usar la soberanía popular para decidir si su estado o territorio debía permitir la esclavitud (pág. 492)

Free-Soil Party a political party formed in 1848 by antislavery northerners who left the Whig and Democratic parties because neither addressed the slavery issue (p. 477)

Partido Tierra Libre partido político formado en 1848 por abolicionistas de los estados del Norte que habían abandonado al Partido Whig y al Partido Demócrata porque ninguno de los dos apoyaba esta causa (pág. 477)

French Revolution French rebellion that began in 1789 in which the French people overthrew the monarchy and made their country a republic (p. 243)
Revolución francesa rebelión francesa iniciada en 1789 en la que la población francesa derrocó la monarquía y convirtió el país en una república (pág. 243)

Fugitive Slave Act (1850) a law that made it a crime to help runaway slaves; allowed for the arrest of escaped slaves in areas where slavery was illegal and required their return to slaveholders (p. 479)
Ley de Esclavos Fugitivos (1850) ley que calificaba como delito el ayudar a un esclavo a escapar de su amo, además de permitir la captura de esclavos fugitivos en zonas donde la esclavitud era ilegal para devolverlos a sus dueños (pág. 479)

Gadsden Purchase (1853) U.S. purchase of land from Mexico that included the southern parts of present-day Arizona and New Mexico (p. 361)
Compra de Gadsden (1853) compra por parte del gobierno de Estados Unidos de territorio mexicano que incluía la región ocupada actualmente por el sur de Arizona y Nuevo México (pág. 361)

Gettysburg Address (1863) a speech given by Abraham Lincoln in which he praised the bravery of Union soldiers and renewed his commitment to winning the Civil War (p. 539)
Discurso de Gettysburg (1863) discurso presentado por Abraham Lincoln en el que alababa la valentía de las tropas de la Unión y renovaba su compromiso de triunfar en la Guerra Civil (pág. 539)

Gibbons v. *Ogden* (1824) a Supreme Court ruling that reinforced the federal government's authority over the states (p. 397)
Gibbons contra *Ogden* (1824) decreto de la Corte Suprema que reforzó la autoridad del gobierno federal sobre los estados (pág. 397)

Great Awakening a religious movement that became widespread in the American colonies in the 1730s and 1740s (p. 94)
Gran Despertar movimiento religioso que tuvo gran popularidad en las colonias estadounidenses en las décadas de 1730 y 1740 (pág. 94)

Great Compromise (1787) an agreement worked out at the Constitutional Convention establishing that a state's population would determine representation in the lower house of the legislature, while each state would have equal representation in the upper house of the legislature (p. 165)
Gran Acuerdo (1787) acuerdo redactado durante la Convención Constitucional en el que se establece que la población de un estado debe determinar su representación en la cámara baja de la asamblea legislativa y que cada estado debe tener igual representación en la cámara alta de ésta (pág. 165)

habeas corpus the constitutional protection against unlawful imprisonment (p. 532)
hábeas corpus protección constitucional contra el encarcelamiento ilegal (pág. 532)

hajj a pilgrimage to Mecca made by devout Muslims (p. 18)
hajj peregrinaje a la Meca que realizan los musulmanes devotos (pág. 18)

Hartford Convention (1815) a meeting of Federalists at Hartford, Connecticut, to protest the War of 1812 (p. 287)
Convención de Hartford (1815) encuentro de federalistas en Hartford, Connecticut, para protestar por la Guerra de 1812 (pág. 287)

Hudson River school a group of American artists in the mid-1800s whose paintings focused on the American landscape (p. 310)
Escuela del Río Hudson grupo de artistas norteamericanos a mediados del siglo XIX cuya obra muestra diversos paisajes del territorio estadounidense (pág. 310)

hunter-gatherer a person who hunts animals and gathers wild plants to provide for his or her needs (p. 6)
cazador y recolector persona que caza animales y recolecta plantas para satisfacer sus necesidades (pág. 6)

immigrant a person who moves to another country after leaving his or her homeland (p. 78)
inmigrante persona que abandona su país para establecerse en un país diferente (pág. 78)

impeach to bring charges against (p. 184)
someter a juicio político presentar cargos en contra de un funcionario (pág. 184)

impeachment the process used by a legislative body to bring charges of wrongdoing against a public official (p. 562)
juicio político proceso por el cual se presentan cargos en contra de un funcionario público (pág. 562)

impressment the practice of forcing people to serve in the army or navy; led to increased tensions between Great Britain and the United States in the early 1800s (p. 279)
leva práctica que obligaba a las personas a servir en el ejército o la marina; aumentó las fricciones entre Gran Bretaña y Estados Unidos a principios del siglo XIX (pág. 279)

indentured servant a colonist who received free passage to North America in exchange for working without pay for a certain number of years (p. 74)
sirviente por contrato colono que recibía un pasaje gratuito a Norteamérica a cambio de trabajar sin salario por varios años (pág. 74)

Indian Removal Act (1830) a congressional act that authorized the removal of Native Americans who lived east of the Mississippi River (p. 332)
Ley de Expulsión de Indígenas (1830) ley redactada por el Congreso que autorizaba la expulsión de los indígenas norteamericanos que habitaban al este del río Mississippi (pág. 332)

Indian Territory an area covering most of present-day Oklahoma to which most Native Americans in the Southeast were forced to move in the 1830s (p. 332)
Territorio Indígena área que abarcaba la mayor parte del actual estado de Oklahoma a la que la mayoría de las tribus indígenas del sureste fueron obligadas a trasladarse durante la década de 1830 (pág. 332)

indict to formally accuse (p. 218)
procesar acusar formalmente (pág. 218)

Industrial Revolution a period of rapid growth in the use of machines in manufacturing and production that began in the mid-1700s (p. 385)
revolución industrial período de rápido desarrollo debido al uso de maquinaria en la fabricación y producción; comenzó a mediados del siglo XVIII (pág. 385)

inflation increased prices for goods and services combined with the reduced value of money (p. 161)
inflación alza en los precios de los bienes al mismo tiempo que se produce una devaluación del dinero (pág. 161)

interchangeable parts a process developed by Eli Whitney in the 1790s that called for making each part of a machine exactly the same (p. 387)
piezas intercambiables proceso desarrollado por Eli Whitney en la década de 1790 para que las piezas de todas las máquinas similares fueran exactamente iguales (pág. 387)

interest group a group of people who share common interests for political action (p. 224)
grupo de interés grupo de personas que comparten intereses comunes en lo que respecta a iniciativas políticas (pág. 224)

interstate commerce trade between two or more states (p. 160)
comercio interestatal intercambio comercial entre dos o más estados (pág. 160)

Intolerable Acts (1774) laws passed by Parliament to punish the colonists for the Boston Tea Party and to tighten government control of the colonies (p. 102)
Ley de Asuntos Intolerables (1774) serie de decretos aprobados por el Parlamento para castigar a los colonos que participaron en el Motín del Té de Boston y para aumentar su control sobre las colonias (pág. 102)

ironclad a warship that is heavily armored with iron (p. 520)
acorazado buque de guerra fuertemente protegido con hierro (pág. 520)

Iroquois League a political confederation of five northeastern Native American nations of the Seneca, Oneida, Mohawk, Cayuga, and Onondaga that made decisions concerning war and peace (p. 14)
Liga de Iroqueses confederación política formada por cinco naciones indígenas del noreste de Estados Unidos (los senecas, los oneidas, los mohawks, los cayugas y los onondagas) para tomar decisiones relacionadas con asuntos de guerra y de paz (pág. 14)

Jacksonian Democracy an expansion of voting rights during the popular Andrew Jackson administration (p. 323)
democracia jacksoniana ampliación del derecho al voto durante el popular gobierno del presidente Andrew Jackson (pág. 323)

Jamestown the first colony in America; set up in 1607 along the James River in Virginia (p. 72)
Jamestown primera colonia estadounidense; fundada en 1607 a lo largo del río James en Virginia (pág. 72)

Jay's Treaty (1794) an agreement negotiated by John Jay to work out problems between Britain and the United States over northwestern lands, British seizure of U.S. ships, and U.S. debts owed to the British (p. 245)
Tratado de Jay (1794) acuerdo negociado por John Jay para resolver los problemas entre Gran Bretaña y Estados Unidos por los territorios del noroeste, por la incautación británica de barcos estadounidenses, y por las deudas estadounidenses con los británicos (pág. 245)

Jim Crow law a law that enforced segregation in the southern states (p. 568)
ley de Jim Crow ley que fomentaba la segregación en los estados del Sur (pág. 568)

John Brown's raid (1859) an incident in which abolitionist John Brown and 21 other men captured a federal arsenal in Harpers Ferry, Virginia, in hope of starting a slave rebellion (p. 493)

ataque de John Brown (1859) incidente en el que el abolicionista John Brown y otros 21 hombres se apropiaron de un arsenal federal en Harpers Ferry, Virginia, con la esperanza de iniciar una rebelión de esclavos (pág. 493)

joint-stock company a business formed by a group of people who jointly make an investment and share in the profits and losses (p. 27)

sociedad por acciones negocio formado por un grupo de personas que realizan una inversión conjuntamente y comparten las ganancias y las pérdidas (pág. 27)

judicial branch the division of the federal government that is made up of the national courts; interprets laws, punishes criminals, and settles disputes between states (p. 167)

Poder Judicial división del gobierno federal conformada por las cortes de justicia; interpreta las leyes, castiga a los delincuentes y resuelve las disputas entre estados (pág. 167)

judicial review the Supreme Court's power to declare acts of Congress unconstitutional (p. 270)

recurso de inconstitucionalidad poder de la Corte Suprema para declarar inconstitucionales las acciones del Congreso (pág. 270)

Judiciary Act of 1789 legislation passed by Congress that created the federal court system (p. 236)

Ley de Judicatura de 1789 decreto aprobado por el Congreso para crear el sistema federal de tribunales (pág. 236)

K

Kansas-Nebraska Act (1854) a law that allowed voters in Kansas and Nebraska to choose whether to allow slavery (p. 485)

Ley de Kansas y Nebraska (1854) ley que permitía a los votantes de Kansas y Nebraska decidir la aprobación o abolición de la esclavitud (pág. 485)

Kentucky and Virginia Resolutions (1798–99) Republican documents that argued that the Alien and Sedition Acts were unconstitutional (p. 253)

Resoluciones de Kentucky y Virginia (1798–99) documentos republicanos que argumentaban el carácter inconstitucional de las Leyes de No Intervención Extranjera (pág. 253)

Kitchen Cabinet President Andrew Jackson's group of informal advisers; so called because they often met in the White House kitchen (p. 324)

gabinete de la cocina grupo informal de consejeros del presidente Andrew Jackson; llamado así porque solían reunirse en la cocina de la Casa Blanca (pág. 324)

kivas underground ceremonial chambers at the center of Anasazi communities (p. 11)

kivas cámaras ceremoniales subterráneas en el centro de las comunidades anasazi (pág. 11)

knights warriors who fought on horseback in return for land from nobles (p. 24)

caballeros guerreros que luchaban a caballo a cambio de tierras que les proporcionaban los nobles (pág. 24)

Know-Nothing Party a political organization founded in 1849 by nativists who supported measures making it difficult for foreigners to become citizens and to hold office (p. 440)

Partido de los Ignorantes organización política fundada en 1849 por un grupo de nativistas; apoyaba medidas que dificultaban a los inmigrantes de otros países la adquisición de la ciudadanía estadounidense y su nombramiento en cargos públicos (pág. 440)

Ku Klux Klan a secret society created by white southerners in 1866 that used terror and violence to keep African Americans from obtaining their civil rights (p. 566)

Ku Klux Klan sociedad secreta creada en 1866 por personas de raza blanca del Sur que usaba el terror y la violencia para impedir que los afroamericanos obtuvieran derechos civiles (pág. 566)

L

Land Ordinance of 1785 legislation passed by Congress authorizing surveys and the division of public lands in the western region of the country (p. 155)

Ordenanza de Territorios de 1785 decreto aprobado por el Congreso en el que se autorizaban las mediciones de terreno y la división de territorios públicos en el oeste del país (pág. 155)

legislative branch the division of the government that proposes bills and passes them into laws (p. 167)

Poder Legislativo división del gobierno federal que propone proyectos de ley y los somete a aprobación para convertirlos en leyes (pág. 167)

Lewis and Clark expedition an expedition led by Meriwether Lewis and William Clark that began in 1804 to explore the Louisiana Purchase (p. 275)

expedición de Lewis y Clark expedición encabezada por Meriwether Lewis y William Clark que partió en 1804 para explorar el territorio adquirido en la Compra de Louisiana (pág. 275)

Lincoln-Douglas debates a series of debates between Republican Abraham Lincoln and Democrat Stephen Douglas during the 1858 U.S. Senate campaign in Illinois (p. 491)

debates Lincoln-Douglas serie de debates entre el republicano Abraham Lincoln y el demócrata Stephen Douglas durante la campaña de 1858 para el Senado estadounidense en Illinois (pág. 491)

loose construction a way of interpreting the Constitution that allows the federal government to take actions that the Constitution does not specifically forbid it from taking (p. 242)
interpretación flexible interpretación de la Constitución que permite al gobierno federal tomar acciones que el mismo documento no prohíbe de manera específica (pág. 242)

Louisiana Purchase (1803) the purchase of French land between the Mississippi River and the Rocky Mountains that doubled the size of the United States (p. 274)
Compra de Luisiana (1803) adquisición del territorio francés localizado entre el río Mississippi y las montañas Rocallosas, que duplicó el tamaño del territorio de Estados Unidos (pág. 274)

Lowell system the use of waterpowered textile mills that employed young, unmarried women in the 1800s (p. 392)
sistema de Lowell el uso de molinos de agua en la industria textil, medida que dio empleo a muchas mujeres jóvenes solteras en el siglo XIX (pág. 392)

Loyalists colonists who sided with Britain in the American Revolution (p. 119)
leales colonos que apoyaron la causa británica durante la Guerra de Independencia estadounidense (pág. 119)

M

Magna Carta (1215) a charter of liberties agreed to by King John of England, it made the king obey the same laws as citizens (p. 152)
Carta Magna (1215) carta de libertades, firmada por el rey Juan de Inglaterra, que establecía que el rey debía obedecer las mismas leyes que el resto de los ciudadanos (pág. 152)

majority rule the idea that policies are decided by the greatest number of people (p. 216)
principio de la mayoría idea de que las políticas se adoptan en función de lo que decida el mayor número de personas (pág. 216)

manifest destiny a belief shared by many Americans in the mid-1800s that the United States should expand across the continent to the Pacific Ocean (p. 354)
destino manifiesto creencia de muchos ciudadanos estadounidenses a mediados del siglo XIX de que Estados Unidos debía expandirse por todo el continente hasta el océano Pacífico (pág. 354)

Marbury v. Madison (1803) U.S. Supreme Court case that established the principle of judicial review (p. 270)
Marbury contra Madison (1803) caso de la Corte Suprema que dio origen al recurso de inconstitucionalidad (pág. 270)

mass production the efficient production of large numbers of identical goods (p. 387)
producción en masa producción eficiente de grandes cantidades de productos idénticos (pág. 387)

Mayflower Compact (1620) a document written by the Pilgrims establishing themselves as a political society and setting guidelines for self-government (p. 79)
Pacto del Mayflower (1620) documento redactado por los peregrinos en el que se constituían en una sociedad política y establecían los principios para gobernarse a sí mismos (pág. 79)

McCulloch v. Maryland (1819) U.S. Supreme Court case that declared the Second Bank of the United States was constitutional and that Maryland could not interfere with it (p. 330)
McCulloch contra Maryland (1819) caso de la Corte Suprema que declaraba que el Segundo Banco de la Nación era constitucional y que Maryland no podía intervenir en sus operaciones (pág. 330)

middle class the social and economic level between the wealthy and the poor (p. 440)
clase media nivel social y económico ubicado entre la clase rica y la clase pobre (pág. 440)

Middle Passage a voyage that brought enslaved Africans across the Atlantic Ocean to North America and the West Indies (p. 59)
Paso Central viaje a través del océano Atlántico para transportar esclavos africanos a Norteamérica y a las Antillas (pág. 59)

migration the movement of people from one region to another (p. 6)
migración desplazamiento de personas de una región a otra (pág. 6)

minutemen American colonial militia members ready to fight at a minute's notice (p. 114)
milicianos miembros de la milicia norteamericana en la época colonial que estaban preparados para combatir en cualquier momento si la situación lo requería (pág. 114)

Missouri Compromise (1820) an agreement proposed by Henry Clay that allowed Missouri to enter the Union as a slave state and Maine to enter as a free state and outlawed slavery in any territories or states north of 36°30′ latitude (p. 305)
Acuerdo de Missouri (1820) acuerdo redactado por Henry Clay en el que se aceptaba a Missouri en la Unión como estado esclavista y a Maine como estado libre, además de prohibir la esclavitud en los territorios o estados localizados al norte del paralelo 36°30′ (pág. 305)

Monroe Doctrine (1823) President James Monroe's statement forbidding further colonization in the Americas and declaring that any attempt by a foreign country to colonize would be considered an act of hostility (p. 300)

Doctrina Monroe (1823) declaración hecha por el presidente James Monroe en la que se prohibía la colonización adicional del continente americano a partir de entonces, considerando cualquier intento de colonización por parte de un país extranjero como inicio de hostilidades (pág. 300)

Mormon a member of the Church of Jesus Christ of Latter-day Saints (p. 349)

mormón miembro de la Iglesia de Jesucristo de los Santos de los Últimos Días (pág. 349)

Morse code a system developed by Alfred Lewis Vail for the telegraph that used a certain combination of dots and dashes to represent each letter of the alphabet (p. 403)

clave Morse sistema desarrollado por Alfred Lewis Vail para el telégrafo en el que una combinación de puntos y rayas representa cada letra del alfabeto (pág. 403)

mosques buildings used for Muslim prayer (p. 19)

mezquitas edificios musulmanes para la oración (pág. 19)

mountain men men hired by eastern companies to trap animals for fur in the Rocky Mountains and other western regions of the United States (p. 346)

montañeses hombres contratados por compañías del este para atrapar animales y obtener sus pieles en las montañas Rocallosas y en otras regiones del oeste de Estados Unidos (pág. 346)

N

national debt the total amount of money owed by a country to its lenders (p. 238)

deuda pública cantidad de dinero que un país debe a sus acreedores (pág. 238)

nationalism a sense of pride and devotion to a nation (p. 302)

nacionalismo sentimiento de orgullo y lealtad a una nación (pág. 302)

nativists U.S. citizens who opposed immigration because they were suspicious of immigrants and feared losing jobs to them (p. 440)

nativistas ciudadanos estadounidenses que se oponían a la aceptación de inmigrantes porque sospechaban de ellos y temían que se apropiaran de sus empleos (pág. 440)

Nat Turner's Rebellion (1831) a rebellion in which Nat Turner led a group of slaves in Virginia in an unsuccessful attempt to overthrow and kill planter families (p. 428)

Rebelión de Nat Turner (1831) rebelión de un grupo de esclavos encabezados por Nat Turner en Virginia en un intento frustrado de derrocar y asesinar a los dueños de plantaciones y a sus familias (pág. 428)

naturalized citizen a person born in another country who has been granted citizenship in the United States (p. 222)

ciudadano naturalizado persona nacida en otro país que ha obtenido la ciudadanía estadounidense (pág. 222)

Neutrality Proclamation (1793) a statement made by President George Washington that the United States would not side with any of the nations at war in Europe following the French Revolution (p. 244)

Proclamación de Neutralidad (1793) declaración en la que el presidente George Washington anunció que Estados Unidos no sería aliado de ninguna de las naciones europeas en guerra después de la Revolución francesa (pág. 244)

New Jersey Plan a proposal to create a unicameral legislature with equal representation of states rather than representation by population; rejected at the Constitutional Convention (p. 165)

Plan de Nueva Jersey propuesta para la creación de un gobierno con una sola cámara que contara con la misma representación por parte de cada estado, sin basarse en el tamaño de su población; la propuesta fue rechazada en la Convención Constitucional (pág. 165)

nominating conventions a meeting at which a political party selects its presidential and vice presidential candidate; first held in the 1820s (p. 323)

convenciones de nominación encuentro en el que un partido político elige a sus candidatos a la presidencia y la vicepresidencia; se realizaron por primera vez en la década de 1820 (pág. 323)

Non-Intercourse Act (1809) a law that replaced the Embargo Act and restored trade with all nations except Britain, France, and their colonies (p. 280)

Ley de No Interacción (1809) ley que reemplazaba a la Ley de Embargo, restableciendo el intercambio comercial con todas las naciones, excepto Gran Bretaña, Francia y sus colonias (pág. 280)

Northwest Ordinance of 1787 legislation passed by Congress to establish a political structure for the Northwest Territory and create a system for the admission of new states (p. 155)

Ordenanza del Noroeste de 1787 ley aprobada por el Congreso para establecer una estructura política en el Territorio del Noroeste y crear un proceso de admisión de nuevos estados (pág. 155)

Northwest Passage a nonexistent path through North America that early explorers searched for that would allow ships to sail from the Atlantic to the Pacific Ocean (p. 54)

Pasaje del Noroeste ruta a lo largo de Norteamérica para cruzar en barco del océano Atlántico al océano Pacífico (pág. 54)

Northwest Territory lands including present-day Illinois, Indiana, Michigan, Ohio, and Wisconsin; organized by the Northwest Ordinance of 1787 (p. 155)

Territorio del Noroeste organización del territorio que incluía los actuales estados de Illinois, Indiana, Michigan, Ohio y Wisconsin; creado por la Ordenanza del Noroeste de 1787 (pág. 155)

nullification crisis a dispute led by John C. Calhoun that said that states could ignore federal laws if they believed those laws violated the Constitution (p. 328)
crisis de anulación controversia iniciada por John C. Calhoun que argumentaba que los estados podían hacer caso omiso a las leyes federales si consideraban que dichas leyes violaban la Constitución (pág. 328)

Oregon Trail a 2,000-mile trail stretching through the Great Plains from western Missouri to the Oregon Territory (p. 348)
Camino de Oregón ruta de 2,000 millas que cruzaba las Grandes Planicies desde el oeste de Missouri hasta el Territorio de Oregón (pág. 348)

Paleo-Indians the first Americans who crossed from Asia into North America sometime between 38,000 and 10,000 BC (p. 6)
paleoindígenas primeros habitantes de América que cruzaron de Asia a Norteamérica entre el 38,000 y el 10,000 a. C. (pág. 6)

Panic of 1837 a financial crisis in the United States that led to an economic depression (p. 331)
Pánico de 1837 crisis financiera en Estados Unidos que provocó una depresión económica (pág. 331)

pardon freedom from punishment (p. 185)
indulto liberación de un castigo (pág. 185)

Patriots American colonists who fought for independence from Great Britain during the Revolutionary War (p. 113)
patriotas colonos estadounidenses que lucharon para independizarse de Gran Bretaña durante la Guerra de Independencia estadounidense (pág. 113)

petition to make a formal request of the government (p. 217)
petición hacer una solicitud formal al gobierno (pág. 217)

Pickett's Charge (1863) a failed Confederate attack during the Civil War led by General George Pickett at the Battle of Gettysburg (p. 538)
ataque de Pickett (1863) ataque fallido del ejército confederado, al mando del general George Pickett, en la batalla de Gettysburg durante la Guerra Civil (pág. 538)

Pilgrim a member of a Puritan Separatist sect that left England in the early 1600s to settle in the Americas (p. 78)
peregrino miembro de una secta separatista puritana que emigró de Inglaterra a principios del siglo XVII para establecerse en América (pág. 78)

Pinckney's Treaty (1795) an agreement between the United States and Spain that changed Florida's border and made it easier for American ships to use the port of New Orleans (p. 245)
tratado de Pinckney (1795) acuerdo entre Estados Unidos y España que modificó los límites de Florida y facilitó a los barcos estadounidenses el uso del puerto de Nueva Orleáns (pág. 245)

placer miner a person who mines for gold by using pans or other devices to wash gold nuggets out of loose rock and gravel (p. 366)
buscador de oro con batea persona que busca oro con bateas u otros dispositivos similares para lavar las pepitas de oro y separarlas de las piedras y la gravilla del lecho de un río (pág. 366)

plantation a large farm that usually specialized in growing one kind of crop for profit (p. 50)
plantación gran finca que por lo general se especializa en un cultivo específico para obtener ganancias (pág. 50)

planter a large-scale farmer who held more than 20 slaves (p. 416)
hacendado agricultor a gran escala que tenía más de 20 esclavos (pág. 416)

Plessy v. Ferguson (1896) U.S. Supreme Court case that established the separate-but-equal doctrine for public facilities (p. 569)
Plessy contra Ferguson (1896) caso en el que la Corte Suprema estableció la doctrina de "separados pero iguales" en los lugares públicos (pág. 569)

political action committee (PAC) an organization that collects money to distribute to candidates who support the same issues as the contributors (p. 224)
comité de acción política (PAC, por sus siglas en inglés) organización que recolecta dinero para distribuirlo entre los candidatos que apoyan los mismos asuntos que los contribuyentes (pág. 224)

political party a group of people who organize to help elect government officials and influence government policies (p. 250)
partido político grupo de personas que se organiza para facilitar la elección de los funcionarios del gobierno e influye en las políticas gubernamentales (pág. 250)

poll tax a special tax that a person had to pay in order to vote (p. 568)
impuesto electoral impuesto especial que debía pagar una persona para poder votar (pág. 568)

popular sovereignty the idea that political authority belongs to the people (pp. 167, 476)
soberanía popular idea de que la autoridad política pertenece al pueblo (págs. 167, 476)

Pottawatomie Massacre (1856) an incident in which abolitionist John Brown and seven other men murdered pro-slavery Kansans (p. 487)
matanza de Pottawatomie (1856) incidente en el que el abolicionista John Brown y siete hombres más asesinaron a habitantes de Kansas que apoyaban la esclavitud (pág. 487)

precedent an action or decision that later serves as an example (p. 235)
precedente acción o decisión que más tarde sirve de ejemplo (pág. 235)

privateer a private ship authorized by a nation to attack its enemies (p. 244)
corsario barco privado autorizado por una nación para atacar a sus enemigos (pág. 244)

prospect to search for gold (p. 366)
catear buscar oro (pág. 366)

Protestant Reformation a religious movement begun by Martin Luther and others in 1517 to reform the Catholic Church (p. 53)
Reforma protestante movimiento religioso iniciado por Martín Lutero y otros en 1517 para reformar la Iglesia católica (pág. 53)

Protestants reformers who protested certain practices of the Catholic Church (p. 53)
protestantes reformistas que protestaban por ciertas prácticas de la Iglesia católica (pág. 53)

pueblos aboveground houses made of a heavy clay called adobe that were built by Native Americans of the southwestern United States (p. 11)
pueblos casas elevadas por encima del suelo hechas con una arcilla fuerte llamada adobe que construían los indígenas norteamericanos del sudoeste de Estados Unidos (pág. 11)

Puritans Protestants who wanted to reform the Church of England (p. 78)
puritanos protestantes que querían reformar la Iglesia anglicana (pág. 78)

Q

Quakers Society of Friends; Protestant sect founded in 1640s in England whose members believed that salvation was available to all people (p. 86)
cuáqueros Sociedad de Amigos; secta protestante fundada en la década de 1640 en Inglaterra cuyos miembros creían que la salvación estaba al alcance de todos (pág. 86)

R

Radical Republicans members of Congress who felt that southern states needed to make great social changes before they could be readmitted to the Union (p. 559)
republicanos radicales integrantes del Congreso convencidos de que los estados del Sur necesitaban realizar grandes cambios sociales antes de volver a ser admitidos en la Unión (pág. 559)

ratification an official approval (p. 154)
ratificación aprobación formal (pág. 154)

reason clear and ordered thinking; Greek philosopher Aristotle believed it was the basis of a good life (p. 23)
razón pensamiento claro y ordenado; el filósofo griego Aristóteles creía que era la base para una buena vida (pág. 23)

Reconstruction (1865–77) the period following the Civil War during which the U.S. government worked to reunite the nation and to rebuild the southern states (p. 552)
Reconstrucción (1865–77) período posterior a la Guerra Civil en el que el gobierno de Estados Unidos trabajó por lograr la unificación de la nación y la reconstrucción de los estados del Sur (pág. 552)

Reconstruction Acts (1867–68) the laws that put the southern states under U.S. military control and required them to draft new constitutions upholding the Fourteenth Amendment (p. 541)
Leyes de Reconstrucción (1867–68) leyes que declaraban a los estados del Sur territorio sujeto a control militar estadounidense y los obligaban a reformar sus constituciones, de manera que defendieran la Decimocuarta Enmienda (pág. 541)

Redcoats British soldiers who fought against the colonists in the American Revolution; so called because of their bright red uniforms (p. 114)
casacas rojas soldados británicos que lucharon contra los colonos en la Guerra de Independencia estadounidense, llamados así por el color rojo brillante de sus uniformes (pág. 114)

Republican Party a political party formed in the 1850s to stop the spread of slavery in the West (p. 488)
Partido Republicano partido político formado en la década de 1850 para detener la expansión de la esclavitud en el Oeste (pág. 488)

Rhode Island system a system developed by Samuel Slater in the mid-1800s in which whole families were hired as textile workers and factory work was divided into simple tasks (p. 391)
Sistema de Rhode Island sistema desarrollado por Samuel Slater a mediados del siglo XIX mediante el cual se contrataba a familias completas para trabajar en la industria textil y en el que el trabajo de las fábricas estaba dividido en tareas sencillas (pág. 391)

Rush-Bagot Agreement (1817) an agreement that limited naval power on the Great Lakes for both the United States and British Canada (p. 298)
Acuerdo de Rush-Bagot (1817) acuerdo que limitaba el poder naval en los Grandes Lagos a embarcaciones de Estados Unidos y de la Canadá británica (pág. 298)

Santa Fe Trail an important trade trail west from Independence, Missouri, to Santa Fe, New Mexico (p. 349)
Camino de Santa Fe importante ruta comercial que va desde Independence, Missouri, hasta Santa Fe, Nuevo México (pág. 349)

search warrant a judge's order authorizing the search of a person's home or property to look for evidence of a crime (p. 218)
orden de cateo orden de un juez que permite registrar el hogar y las propiedades de una persona en busca de posibles pruebas de un delito (pág. 218)

secession the act of formally withdrawing from the Union (p. 496)
secesión acto de separarse formalmente de la Unión (pág. 496)

Second Battle of Bull Run (1862) a Civil War battle in which the Confederate army forced most of the Union army out of Virginia (p. 518)
segunda batalla de Bull Run (1862) batalla de la Guerra Civil en la que el ejército confederado obligó a gran parte de las tropas de la Unión a abandonar el territorio de Virginia (pág. 518)

Second Continental Congress (1775) a meeting of colonial delegates in Philadelphia to decide how to react to fighting at Lexington and Concord (p. 114)
Segundo Congreso Continental (1775) reunión de delegados coloniales realizada en Filadelfia para tomar decisiones acerca de la lucha en Lexington y Concord (pág. 114)

Second Great Awakening a period of religious evangelism that began in the 1790s and became widespread in the United States by the 1830s (p. 448)
Segundo Gran Despertar período de evangelización religiosa iniciado en la década de 1790 que se extendió por Estados Unidos para la década de 1830 (pág. 448)

sectionalism a devotion to the interests of one geographic region over the interests of the country as a whole (pp. 304, 477)
regionalismo dedicación a los intereses de una región geográfica y no a los de un país (págs. 304, 477)

segregation the forced separation of people of different races in public places (p. 568)
segregación separación obligada de personas de diferentes razas en lugares públicos (pág. 568)

Seneca Falls Convention (1848) the first national women's rights convention at which the Declaration of Sentiments was written (p. 464)
Convención de Seneca Falls (1848) primera convención nacional a favor de los derechos de la mujer, en la cual se redactó la Declaración de Sentimientos (pág. 464)

Seven Days' Battles (1862) a series of Civil War battles in which Confederate army successes forced the Union army to retreat from Richmond, Virginia, the Confederate capital (p. 518)
batallas de los Siete Días (1862) serie de batallas de la Guerra Civil en las que las victorias del ejército confederado obligaron a las tropas de la Unión a retirarse de Richmond, Virginia, la capital confederada (pág. 518)

sharecropping a system used on southern farms after the Civil War in which farmers worked land owned by someone else in return for a small portion of the crops (p. 569)
cultivo de aparceros sistema usado en las fincas sureñas después de la Guerra Civil en el que los agricultores trabajaban las tierras de otra persona a cambio de una pequeña porción de la cosecha (pág. 569)

Shays's Rebellion (1786–87) an uprising of Massachusetts's farmers, led by Daniel Shays, to protest high taxes, heavy debt, and farm foreclosures (p. 161)
Rebelión de Shays (1786–87) rebelión de los agricultores de Massachusetts, encabezados por Daniel Shays, para protestar por los altos impuestos, el aumento de sus deudas y la confiscación de las granjas (pág. 161)

Siege of Vicksburg (1863) the Union army's six-week blockade of Vicksburg that led the city to surrender during the Civil War (p. 524)
Sitio de Vicksburg (1863) bloqueo de seis semanas realizado por el ejército de la Unión en Vicksburg para forzar la rendición de esa ciudad durante la Guerra Civil (pág. 524)

slave codes laws passed in the colonies to control slaves (p. 77)
códigos de esclavos leyes aprobadas por las colonias para el control de los esclavos (pág. 77)

Spanish Armada a large Spanish fleet defeated by England in 1588 (p. 53)
Armada española gran flota de barcos de guerra que España reunió para protegerse de la piratería inglesa (pág. 53)

speculator an investor who buys items at low prices in hope that their values will rise (p. 239)
especulador inversionista que compra artículos a precios bajos con la esperanza de que aumente su valor (pág. 239)

ENGLISH AND SPANISH GLOSSARY

spirituals emotional Christian songs sung by enslaved people in the South that mixed African and European elements and usually expressed slaves' religious beliefs (p. 427)
espirituales canciones religiosas cantadas con gran emotividad por los esclavos del Sur que combinaban elementos de origen africano y europeo y solían expresar sus creencias religiosas (pág. 427)

spoils system a politicians' practice of giving government jobs to his or her supporters (p. 324)
tráfico de influencias práctica de los políticos de ofrecer empleos a las personas que los apoyan (pág. 324)

Stamp Act of 1765 a law passed by Parliament that raised tax money by requiring colonists to pay for an official stamp whenever they bought paper items such as newspapers, licenses, and legal documents (p. 100)
Ley del Timbre de 1765 ley aprobada por el Parlamento para recaudar impuestos en la que se obligaba a los colonos a pagar un timbre oficial cada vez que compraran artículos de papel, como periódicos, licencias y documentos legales (pág. 100)

staple crop a crop that is continuously in demand (p. 87)
cultivo básico producto de demanda constante (pág. 87)

states' rights doctrine the belief that the power of the states should be greater than the power of the federal government (p. 328)
doctrina de los derechos estatales creencia de que el poder de los estados debe ser mayor que el del gobierno federal (pág. 328)

strict construction a way of interpreting the Constitution that allows the federal government to take only those actions the Constitution specifically says it can take (p. 242)
interpretación estricta interpretación de la Constitución que sólo permite al gobierno federal realizar las acciones permitidas de manera específica en ella (pág. 242)

strike the refusal of workers to perform their jobs until employers meet their demands (p. 394)
huelga negativa de los empleados a trabajar hasta que sus empleadores satisfagan sus demandas (pág. 394)

suffrage voting rights (p. 153)
sufragio derecho al voto (pág. 153)

Tariff of Abominations (1828) the nickname given to a tariff by southerners who opposed it (p. 327)

Arancel de abominaciones (1828) sobrenombre dado a un nuevo impuesto por los habitantes del Sur que se oponían a éste (pág. 327)

tariff a tax on imports or exports (p. 159)
arancel impuestos pagados por los bienes importados o exportados (pág. 159)

Tea Act (1773) a law passed by Parliament allowing the British East India Company to sell its low-cost tea directly to the colonies, undermining colonial tea merchants; led to the Boston Tea Party (p. 102)
Tea Act/Ley del Té (1773) ley aprobada por el Parlamento británico que le permitía a la British East India Company vender té a bajo costo a las colonias sin intermediarios, afectando a los comerciantes locales de té; esta decisión dio origen al Motín del Té de Boston (pág. 102)

technology the tools used to produce goods or to do work (p. 387)
tecnología herramientas utilizadas para producir bienes o realizar un trabajo (pág. 387)

teepees cone-shaped shelters made of buffalo skins used by Native Americans in the Plains region (p. 14)
tipis tiendas de piel de búfalo de forma cónica que usaban como vivienda los indígenas norteamericanos en la región de las Planicies (pág. 14)

telegraph a machine perfected by Samuel F. B. Morse in 1832 that uses pulses of electric current to send messages across long distances through wires (p. 402)
telégrafo máquina perfeccionada por Samuel F. B. Morse en 1832 que emplea impulsos eléctricos transmitidos por cables para enviar mensajes a grandes distancias (pág. 402)

temperance movement a social reform effort begun in the mid-1800s to encourage people to drink less alcohol (p. 449)
movimiento de abstinencia movimiento de reforma social iniciado a mediados del siglo XIX para fomentar la disminución en el consumo de bebidas alcohólicas (pág. 449)

Ten Percent Plan President Abraham Lincoln's plan for Reconstruction; once 10 percent of voters in a former Confederate state took a U.S. loyalty oath, they could form a new state government and be readmitted to the Union (p. 553)
Plan del Diez por Ciento plan de Reconstrucción del presidente Abraham Lincoln; si el 10 por ciento de los votantes de un estado que había sido parte de la Confederación juraba lealtad a la nación, tenían derecho a formar un nuevo gobierno y ser readmitidos en la Unión (pág. 553)

tenements poorly built, overcrowded housing where many immigrants lived (p. 442)
barracas casas mal construidas donde vivían amontonados una gran cantidad de inmigrantes (pág. 442)

textile cloth (p. 385)
textil tela (pág. 385)

Thirteenth Amendment (1865) a constitutional amendment that outlawed slavery (p. 514)

Decimotercera Enmienda (1865) enmienda constitucional que abolió la esclavitud (pág. 514)

Three-Fifths Compromise (1787) an agreement worked out at the Constitutional Convention stating that enslaved people would be counted as three-fifths of a person when determining a state's population for representation in the lower house of Congress (p. 166)

Acuerdo de las Tres Quintas Partes (1787) acuerdo negociado durante la Convención Constitucional en el que se estableció que los esclavos contarían como tres quintas partes de una persona para determinar la representación de ese estado en el Congreso (pág. 166)

Toleration Act of 1649 a Maryland law that made restricting the religious rights of Christians a crime; the first law guaranteeing religious freedom to be passed in America (p. 75)

Ley de Tolerancia de 1649 ley de Maryland que calificaba como delito la restricción de los derechos religiosos de los cristianos; fue la primera ley que garantizó la libertad religiosa en América (pág. 75)

total war a type of war in which an army destroys its opponent's ability to fight by targeting civilian and economic as well as military resources (p. 541)

guerra total tipo de guerra en la que un ejército destruye la capacidad de lucha de su oponente mediante ataques a la población civil, la economía y los recursos militares (pág. 541)

totems images of ancestors or animal spirits; often carved onto tall, wooden poles by Native American peoples of the Pacific Northwest (p. 12)

tótems imágenes de antepasados o animales; a menudo talladas en troncos de árboles cortados por los indígenas de la costa noroeste del Pacífico (pág. 12)

town meeting a political meeting at which people make decisions on local issues; used primarily in New England (p. 91)

reunión del pueblo reunión política en la que los habitantes de una población toman decisiones sobre temas locales; se realizan principalmente en Nueva Inglaterra (pág. 91)

trade unions workers' organizations that try to improve working conditions (p. 394)

sindicatos organizaciones formadas por trabajadores para mejorar sus condiciones laborales (pág. 394)

Trail of Tears (1838–39) an 800-mile forced march made by the Cherokee from their homeland in Georgia to Indian Territory; resulted in the deaths of almost one-fourth of the Cherokee people (p. 334)

Ruta de las lágrimas (1838–39) marcha forzada de 800 millas que realizó la tribu cherokee desde su territorio natal en Georgia hasta el Territorio Indígena, y en la que perdió la vida casi una cuarta parte del pueblo cherokee (pág. 334)

transcendentalism the idea that people could rise above the material things in life; a popular movement among New England writers and thinkers in the mid-1800s (p. 443)

trascendentalismo creencia de que las personas podían prescindir de los objetos materiales en la vida; movimiento popular entre los escritores y pensadores de Nueva Inglaterra a mediados del siglo XIX (pág. 443)

Transportation Revolution the rapid growth in the speed and convenience of transportation (p. 396)

revolución del transporte rápido crecimiento de la velocidad y comodidad ofrecida por los medios de transporte (pág. 396)

Treaty of Fort Jackson a treaty signed after the U.S. victory at the Battle of Horseshoe Bend; the Creek was forced to give up 23 million acres of their land (p. 286)

tratado del fuerte Jackson tratado que se firmó tras la victoria de Estados Unidos en la batalla de Horseshoe Bend; los indígenas creek se vieron obligados a ceder 23 millones de acres de su territorio (pág. 286)

Treaty of Ghent (1814) a treaty signed by the United States and Britain ending the War of 1812 (p. 287)

tratado de Gante (1814) tratado firmado por Estados Unidos y Gran Bretaña para dar fin a la Guerra de 1812 (pág. 287)

Treaty of Greenville (1795) an agreement between Native American confederation leaders and the U.S. government that gave the United States Indian lands in the Northwest Territory and guaranteed that U.S. citizens could safely travel through the region (p. 247)

tratado de Greenville (1795) acuerdo entre los líderes de la confederación de indígenas norteamericanos y el gobierno estadounidense que otorgó a Estados Unidos parte del Territorio del Noroeste y garantizó la seguridad a los ciudadanos estadounidenses que viajaran por esas tierras (pág. 247)

Treaty of Guadalupe Hidalgo (1848) a treaty that ended the Mexican War and gave the United States much of Mexico's northern territory (p. 361)

tratado de Guadalupe Hidalgo (1848) tratado que daba por terminada la Guerra contra México y daba posesión a Estados Unidos de gran parte del norte del territorio mexicano (pág. 361)

Treaty of Paris of 1783 a peace agreement that officially ended the Revolutionary War and established British recognition of the independence of the United States (p. 139)

tratado de París de 1783 acuerdo de paz que oficialmente daba por terminada la Guerra de Independencia estadounidense y en el que Gran Bretaña reconocía la soberanía de Estados Unidos (pág. 139)

Tredegar Iron Works a large iron factory that operated in Richmond, Virginia, in the early to mid-1800s (p. 419)
Tredegar Iron Works gran fábrica de acero que operaba a mediados del siglo XIX en Richmond, Virginia (pág. 419)

triangular trade trading networks in which goods and slaves moved among England, the American colonies, and Africa (p. 93)
comercio triangular redes de intercambio de esclavos y bienes entre Inglaterra, las colonias americanas y África (pág. 93)

Uncle Tom's Cabin (1852) an antislavery novel written by Harriet Beecher Stowe that showed northerners the violent reality of slavery and drew many people to the abolitionists' cause (p. 481)
La cabaña del tío Tom (1852) novela abolicionista escrita por Harriet Beecher Stowe que mostró a los habitantes del norte del país la cruda realidad de la esclavitud e hizo que muchos de ellos se unieran a la causa abolicionista (pág. 481)

Underground Railroad a network of people who helped thousands of enslaved people escape to the North by providing transportation and hiding places (p. 456)
Tren Clandestino red de personas que ayudó a miles de esclavos a escapar al Norte ofreciéndoles transporte y lugares para ocultarse (pág. 456)

USS *Constitution* a large warship (p. 278)
USS *Constitution* gran buque de guerra (pág. 278)

utopian communities places where people worked to establish a perfect society; such communities were popular in the United States during the late 1700s and early to mid-1800s (p. 444)
comunidades utópicas lugares en los que un grupo de personas trabajaba para establecer una sociedad perfecta, como las que se popularizaron en Estados Unidos a finales del siglo XVIII y principios y mediados del XIX (pág. 444)

vaqueros Mexican cowboys in the West who tended cattle and horses (p. 357)
vaqueros arrieros mexicanos que vivían en el Oeste y se ganaban la vida arreando ganado y caballos (pág. 357)

veto to cancel (p. 184)
vetar cancelar (pág. 184)

Virginia Plan (1787) the plan for government proposed at the Constitutional Convention in which the national government would have supreme power and a legislative branch would have two houses with representation determined by state population (p. 164)
Plan de Virginia (1787) plan del gobierno propuesto en la Convención Constitucional por el que el gobierno nacional tendría poder supremo y habría un Poder Legislativo con dos cámaras en las que la representación de cada estado sería determinada por su población (pág. 164)

Virginia Statute for Religious Freedom (1786) a document that gave people in Virginia freedom of worship and prohibited tax money from being used to fund churches (p. 153)
Estatuto de Virginia por la Libertad Religiosa (1786) documento que reconocía a los habitantes de Virginia la libertad de culto y prohibía utilizar el dinero procedente de impuestos para financiar iglesias (pág. 153)

War Hawks members of Congress who wanted to declare war against Britain after the Battle of Tippecanoe (p. 282)
halcones de guerra integrantes del Congreso que tenían la intención de declarar la guerra a Gran Bretaña tras la batalla de Tippecanoe (pág. 282)

Whig Party a political party formed in 1834 by opponents of Andrew Jackson and who supported a strong legislature (p. 330)
Partido Whig partido político formado en 1834 por oponentes de Andrew Jackson que apoyaba una asamblea legislativa con mucha autoridad (pág. 330)

Whiskey Rebellion (1794) a protest of small farmers in Pennsylvania against new taxes on whiskey (p. 247)
Rebelión del Whisky (1794) protesta de pequeños agricultores de Pensilvania contra los nuevos impuestos sobre la producción de whisky (pág. 247)

Wilderness Campaign (1864) a series of battles between Union and Confederate forces in northern and central Virginia that delayed the Union capture of Richmond (p. 539)
Campaña Wilderness (1864) serie de batallas entre la Unión y los confederados en el norte y el centro de Virginia que retrasaron la captura de Richmond por parte de la Unión (pág. 539)

Wilmot Proviso (1846) a proposal to outlaw slavery in the territory added to the United States by the Mexican Cession; passed in the House of Representatives but was defeated in the Senate (p. 476)
Condición de Wilmot (1846) propuesta de prohibir la esclavitud en el territorio adherido a Estados Unidos por la Cesión mexicana; aprobada por la Cámara de Representantes, pero rechazada por el Senado (pág. 476)

Worcester v. Georgia (1832) the Supreme Court ruling that stated that the Cherokee nation was a distinct territory over which only the federal government had authority; ignored by both President Andrew Jackson and the state of Georgia (p. 334)
Worcester contra *Georgia* (1832) resolución de la Corte Suprema que establecía que la nación cherokee era un territorio distinto sobre el que sólo el gobierno federal tenía autoridad; fue ignorada por el presidente Andrew Jackson y por el estado de Georgia (pág. 334)

incidente XYZ (1797) incidente en el que funcionarios franceses intentaron obtener sobornos y préstamos de diplomáticos estadounidenses a cambio de un acuerdo por el cual sus barcos corsarios no atacarían más a los barcos estadounidenses; provocó una guerra no declarada entre las fuerzas navales de ambas naciones (pág. 252)

yeomen owners of small farms (p. 422)
pequeños terratenientes propietarios de granjas pequeñas (pág. 422)

XYZ affair (1797) an incident in which French agents attempted to get a bribe and loans from U.S. diplomats in exchange for an agreement that French privateers would no longer attack American ships; it led to an undeclared naval war between the two countries (p. 252)

Index

INDEX

D

E

factories, 385–88, 404, 411*p*; families and, 390–91, 391*p*, 571; immigrants and, 394; in the New South, 570–71, 570*p*; in the South, 418–19; steam power and, 404; trade unions and, 394–95

factors, 417

Fair Employment Act (1942), 179

Fallen Timbers, Battle of, 246*m*, 247

families: factories and, 390–91, 391*p*, 571; Pilgrim, 80; slavery and, 61, 426–27

farming, 7; equipment, 404; in the South, 569–70, 569*p*. See also agriculture

Farragut, David, 523–24

federal courts, 185, 236

federal government, 171, 182; branches of, 183; concurrent powers and, 182; delegated powers of, 182; functions of, 269; organizing the, 235–36; Tenth Amendment and, 221

Judiciary Act (1789), 185

federalism, 167, 182, 201*f*

Federalist Papers, 171, 172*f*

Federalist Party, 250; election of 1800, 266–67; Embargo Act and, 280

Federalists, 170–71, 266, 269

Ferdinand, King of Spain, 42

feudalism, 24

Few, William, 203

Fifteenth Amendment, 209, 562*f*, 563

Fifth Amendment, 204, 218, 219, 490

54th Massachusetts Infantry, 530*p*, 531

Fillmore, Millard, 484, 488

Finney, Charles Grandison, 448–49

fire protection, 442

First Amendment, 204, 216–17, 217*p*, 458

First Seminole War, 299

FitzSimons, Thomas, 203

Florida: exploration of, 48–49, 49*m*, 55, 56*m*; and French and Indian War, 96; Native Americans in, 299, 335, 335*m*; during Reconstruction, 561*m*; secedes from the Union, 496; Second Seminole War, 335, 335*m*; Spain and, 76, 245, 245*m*, 299, 299*m*

folk music, 310

folktales, 427

Ford's Theater, 557

foreign policy, 130; with Britain, 298, 299*m*, 300; with Canada, 298; of Jefferson, 272–73; Monroe Doctrine, 300–01; with Spain, 299, 299*m*

Fort Christina, 57

Fort Detroit, 97, 285, 285*m*

Fort Donelson, 522

Fort Greenville, 246

Fort Henry, 522

Fort McHenry, 286

Fort Mims, 285*m*, 286

Fort Necessity, 96

Fort Sackville, 133–134, 134*m*

Fort Sumter, 497, 506, 511, 516, 545

Fort Ticonderoga, 115, 116, 130

Fort Wagner, 531

Forty-niners, 365–68, 365*p*, 366*p*, 367*p*, 477

Fountain of Youth, 48

Four Corners, 10

Fourteenth Amendment, 208–09, 560–61, 562*f*, 563, 569

Fourth Amendment, 204, 218

France: American Revolution and, 130–131, 137; empire of, 96*m*; England and, 243, 243*p*, 244, 278; exploration by, 54, 55, 55*m*, 56*m*, 57; French and Indian War, 96; Louisiana and, 273–74; in Middle Ages, 24; Native Americans and, 57; revolution in, 243, 243*p*, 244; XYZ Affair, 252, 252*f*

Franklin, Benjamin, 84, 111, 119, 120, 120*p*, 131, 133, 169, 169*p*, 170, 203

Franklin, William, 119, 120

Franks, 24

Fredericksburg, Battle of, 536

Free Soil Party, 477, 488

free states, 304–05, 304*m*, 457*m*, 476–77, 477*m*, 512*m*

Freedmen's Bureau, 556, 556*p*, 560–61

freedpeople, 555, 555*p*–56*p*, 556

Freeport Doctrine, 491–92

Frémont, John C., 358, 489

French and Indian War, 96, 98, 130

French Revolution, 243, 243*p*, 244

French West Indies, 245

Fugitive Slave Act, 479–80, 481, 484

Fugitive Slave law, 478

Fuller, Margaret, 443

Fulton, Robert, 380*p*, 397

Fundamental Orders of Connecticut, 82

fur trade, 85, 86, 346

Futrell, Mary Hatwood, 221

Gadsden Purchase, 361

gag rule, 458

Gage, Thomas, 103, 113–114

Gallatin, Albert, 251*p*, 268, 269, 388

Gallaudet, Thomas, 451

Gálvez, Bernardo de, 131

gang-labor system, 424

Gao, 18, 20

Garrison, William Lloyd, 435, 455, 455*p*, 530, 555, 563

Gates, Horatio, 136

Gaul, 24

General Amnesty Act (1872), 567

General Court of Massachusetts, 81–82, 84

Genet, Edmond, 244

George II, King of England, 76

George III, King of England, 97, 112, 114, 119

Georgia, 48; Civil War in, 513, 533; colony of, 76, 76*m*; cotton in, 416*m*; Native Americans in, 334; ratification of the Constitution, 203; during Reconstruction, 563; Revolutionary War in, 135, 136; secedes from the Union, 496; slavery in, 426

German, Obadiah, 283

Germany: American Revolution and, 128, 129; immigrants from, 368, 439

Gettysburg, Battle of, 505*p*, 536–40, 537–38*p*, 541*m*, 545

Gettysburg Address, 540

Ghana, Kingdom of, 16–18, 17*p*, 18*m*

Gibbons, Thomas, 397

Gibbons v. *Ogden* **(1824),** 304, 397

Gilman, Nicholas, 203

gold, 17, 48, 334

Gold Rush, 364–69, 366*p*, 367*p*

Goliad, Texas, 352, 352*m*

Gorham, Nathaniel, 203

government: branches of, 167; colonial, 90–91, 91*f*, 100; federalism, 167; formation of, 153–54; General Court of Massachusetts, 81–82; of Greece, 22–23; influencing, 224; models of, 153; in Pennsylvania, 86; religion and, 82*f*; Roman, 23–24, 24*p*. See also federal government; state government

Grady, Henry, 568, 570, 570*p*

Grand Canyon, 49

Grant, Ulysses S., 507, 522, 542–43, 562–63

Great Awakening, 94–95, 94*p*; Second, 448–49, 450, 454

Great Britain: Declaration of Independence and, 119; Embargo Act and, 279–80; Industrial Revolution in, 384–85, 388; railroad in, 398; taxes and, 98–100, 101*p*; Treaty of Paris and, 111, 139, 139*m*. See also Britain; England

Timbuktu   **Washington**

Timbuktu, 18, 19, 20
Tippecanoe, Battle of, 281–82
tobacco, 45, 59, 73, 77, 327, 418
Tocqueville, Alexis de, 224, 405
Toleration Act (1649), 75
Tom Thumb (locomotive), 381*p*, 398
Tompkins, Sally Louisa, 534
Tories, 119–20
totems, 12
town meeting, 91, 91*f*, 152*f*, 153
Townshend Acts (1767), 100, 102, 103
Trade: barriers to, 159*m*; with Britain, 159, 159*m*, 160; with China, 355; closed markets, 160; cotton, 417, 419*p*; economics and, 27; in Middle Ages, 25; in Middle Colonies, 87; overland, 14*m*; with Spain, 159, 159*m*. *See also* free trade; triangular trade
trade laws, 92–93
trade unions, 394–95
Trail of Tears, 333*p*, 334
transcendentalism, 443–44
Transcontinental Railroad, 369
transportation, 302; canals, 303–04, 303*m*; railroad, 381*p*, 398–401; revolution in, 396; roads, 48, 303–04, 303*m*, 327, 417; ships, 73m; steamboat, 397, 397*p*; tariffs and, 302
Travis, Jim, 352
Treaty of Dancing Rabbit Creek, 333
Treaty of Fort Jackson (1814), 286
Treaty of Ghent (1814), 287, 298
Treaty of Greenville (1795), 247, 280
Treaty of Guadalupe Hidalgo (1848), 361, 362
Treaty of Paris (1763), 96, 111
Treaty of Paris (1783), 111, 139, 139*m*, 158
Treaty of Tordesillas (1494), 44
Tredegar Iron Works, 411*p*, 419
Trenton, Battle of, 129
trials, 219
triangular trade, 92*m*, 93–94, 93*p*
tricksters, 427
Truth, Sojourner, 456, 459*p*
Tubman, Harriet, 458, 456*p*
Ture, Muhammad, 19
Turner, Nat, 428–29, 428*m*, 428*p*
Twelfth Amendment, 206–07
Twentieth Amendment, 211–12
Twenty-fifth Amendment, 214–15
Twenty-first Amendment, 212
Twenty-fourth Amendment, 214
Twenty-second Amendment, 184, 213
Twenty-seventh Amendment, 215
Twenty-sixth Amendment, 179, 215
Twenty-third Amendment, 213

Two Years Before the Mast (Dana), 357
Tyler, John, 355
tyranny, 118

Uncle Tom's Cabin (Stowe), 481, 482*f*
Underground Railroad, 456–58, 457*m*
unicameral legislature, 165
Union Army, 529–31, 532*p*; *see also* Army of the Potomac
Utah: Compromise of 1850 and, 479; Mexican Cession and, 361; Mormons in, 349; Native Americans in, 11–12
Utah Territory, 347*m*, 349
Ute culture, 12, 13*m*
utopian communities, 444

Vail, Alfred Lewis, 403
Vallandingham, Clement L., 532
Vallejo, Mariano Guadalupe, 357, 357*p*, 359*m*
Valley Forge, 132, 132*p*
Van Buren, Martin, 319*p*, 324, 328, 477; election of 1836, 330, 331; labor and, 395
vaqueros, 356*p*, 357
vassal, 24
Veracruz, Mexico, 359*m*, 360
Verrazano, Giovanni da, 54, 55*m*
Vesey, Denmark, 428
Vespucci, Amerigo, 44
veto, 184
Vice President, 184; as president of the Senate, 183; term of office, 190*f*
Vicksburg, Battle of, 522–25, 526–27, 545
Vikings, 38–39
Vinland, 39
Virginia: Articles of Confederation and, 162; Civil War in, 507, 512, 516–17, 520–21, 534; education in, 84; government in, 91; House of Burgesses, 100, 153; Jamestown, 72–73, 73*m*, 74; ratification of the Constitution, 172, 203; Revolutionary War in, 131, 135, 136–37, 137*m*; slave revolts in, 493–94; slavery in, 74–75, 426; state debt of, 239; tax revolt in, 100; western frontier and, 97

Virginia, 507, 520
Virginia Company, 72–75, 73*m*, 91
Virginia Declaration of Rights, 173
Virginia Plan, 164–65
Virginia Statute for Religious Freedom, 153, 217
volunteer groups, 224–25, 225*p*
Von Steuben, Baron Friedrich, 131, 132
voting: age, 215; elections and, 224
voting rights, 153; of African Americans, 209, 423, 561, 561*m*, 562*p*, 563; poll taxes and, 568–69; in 1800s, 322–23; in Washington, D.C., 213; of women, 211, 211*p*, 563
Voting Rights Act (1970), 215

Wabash River, 282
Wade, Benjamin, 553, 562
Wade-Davis Bill, 553–54
wagon trains, 348, 348*p*
Walker, David, 455
Wall Street, 237
Waltham, Massachusetts, 392
Wampanoag culture, 95
war debts, 160–61
War Hawks, 282–83
War of 1812, 283; battles of, 284–86, 285*m*, 286*p*; causes and effects of, 287*f*; manufacturing and the, 389; Rush-Bagot Agreement and, 298
War of Independence. *See* Revolutionary War
Washington, D.C.: Civil War in, 512, 516; Compromise of 1850 and, 479; design of, 240; as nation's capital, 240, 240*p*, 268; voting rights in, 213; in War of 1812, 285*m*, 286, 286*p*
Washington, George: biography, 117, 117*p*; cabinet of, 235*p*; at Constitutional Convention, 164, 164*p*; court system and, 235–36; farewell address of, 248*f*, 249; as Federalist, 170; in French and Indian War, 96; inauguration of, 234–235; Jay's Treaty, 245; national bank and, 242; Neutrality Proclamation, 244–45; Northwest Territory and, 246–47, 246*m*; Pinckney's Treaty, 245–46, 245*m*; as president, 235–36, 235*p*; in Revolutionary War, 114, 116, 126, 128–29, 129*p*, 132, 139; Whiskey Rebellion and, 247
Washington, Martha, 235

R82   INDEX

INDEX

Credits and Acknowledgments

For permission to reproduce copyrighted material, grateful acknowledgment is made to the following sources:

Saint Martin's Press: Quote by Sarah G. Bagley from *The Belles of New England: The Women of the Textile Mills and the Families Whose Wealth They Wove* by William Moran. Copyright © 2002 by William Moran.

Sources Cited:

Quote by an Aztec messenger from *The Broken Spears: The Aztec Account of the Conquest of Mexico*, Expanded and Updated Edition, edited by Miguel León-Portilla. Published by Beacon Press, Boston, 1992.

Chapter Opener Timelines (tl) Photodisc Green/ Getty Images; (bl) © Stockbyte.

Unit One. Chapter 1: Pages 2-3 (t), © Rebecca Marvil/Index Stock Imagery, Inc. ; 2 (b), The Art Archive/National Anthropological Museum Mexico/Dagli Orti; 3 (both), Scala/Art Resource, NY; 7 (t), Smithsonian Institution, Washington, DC. Photograph by Chip Clark # 90-14563; 7 (b), Getty Images; 8 (t), The Field Museum of Natural History, Neg. A108557-c, Photo by Ron Testa 9 (tl), Ohio Historical Society; (tr), From the Collection of Gilcrease Museum, Tulsa; (bl), ©2000 The Art Institute of Chicago (detail); 10 (tl), ©Marilyn Wynn/Nativestock Pictures; (tr), The Granger Collection, New York; 13, Scala/Art Resource, NY; 17, Art Reference: AKG-Images; 21 ®, ©Robert Frerck/Woodfin Camp & Associates; 23, PRC Archive; 24 (l), Saint Bride Printing Library; 24-25, AKG-Images; 25 (r), Mary Evans Picture Library; 30, Sam Dudgeon/HRW. **Chapter 2:** Pages 32-33 (t), Ted Curtin for Plimoth Plantation; 32 (b), © David Ball/CORBIS; 33 (c), Courtesy of the Pilgrim Society, Plymouth, Massachusetts; 33 (bl), © SuperStock; 33 (br), © Culver Pictures, Inc.; 39 (b), Colonial Williamsburg Foundation; 46 (tl), Art Reference: PRC Archive; 49 (b), © SuperStock; 50 (bl), Art Reference: Historical Society of Pennsylvania; 57 (r), Art Reference: Royal Albert Memorial Museum, Exeter, Devon, UK/ Bridgeman Art Library; 57 (b), Private Collection/www.bridgeman.co.uk; 58 (t), National Portrait Library, London/Bridgeman Art Library; 61 (r), Art Reference: Courtesy of the Burton Historical Collection, Detroit Public Library; 64-65 (t), Virginia Historical Society; 67, Peter Newark's American Pictures; 68, Courtesy of the Massachusetts Historical Society; 69 (tl), © Bettmann/CORBIS; 69 (tr), American Antiquarian Society. **Chapter 3:** Pages 74-75 (t), © James Lemass/Index Stock Imagery; 75 (cl), The Granger Collection, New York; 75 (c), North Wind Picture Archives; 75 (br), © Christie's Images ; 79, © Concord Museum/ Photograph by Chip Fanelli; 82 (l), (art reference) Phoenix Museum of Art, Arizona/ Bridgeman Art Library; 82 (b), © Robert Llewellyn/SuperStock; 84, © Bettmann/CORBIS; 91 (l), #1921.101, ©Collection of The New-York Historical Society; 91 (r), ©Collection of The New-York Historical Society, neg. 31665; 93 (t), © SuperStock; 94 (l), Saratoga National Historic Park; 94 (r), Chateau de Versailles, France/Giraudon/ Bridgeman Art Library; 95 (l), Falmouth Art Gallery, Cornwall, UK/Bridgeman Art Library; 95 (r), Hotel Galvez, Galveston, Texas; 96, Superstock; 99, The Granger Collection, New York.

Unit Two. Chapter 4: Pages 110-111 (t), Joe Marquette/AP/Wide World Photos; 110, Library of Congress/PRC Archive; 111 (c), Collection of the American Numismatic Society, New York; 111 (bl), © Nik Wheeler/CORBIS; 111 (bc), © Andrea Jemolo/CORBIS; 111 (br), Tokyo National Museum; 115, The Granger Collection, New York; 122-123, The Granger Collection, New York; 125, © Dennis Degnan/CORBIS; 126 (t), Hall of Representatives, Washington, DC/ Bridgeman Art Library; 126 (bl), Independence National Historical Park ; 126 (bc), Stock Montage; 126 (br), Portrait by Robert S. Susan, Collection of the Supreme Court of the United States; 127, © Alex Wong/Getty Images; 128 (l), South Carolina Legal History Collection; 128 (r), City of Bristol Museum and Art Gallery/Bridgeman Art Library; 131 (l), (art reference) Historical Society of Pennsylvania; 131 (br), American Antiquarian Society; 133 (l), Stock Montage, Inc.; 133 (r), © Bettmann/CORBIS. **Chapter 5:** 140-141 (t), Sam Dudgeon/HRW Photo; 141 (cl), PRC Archive; 141 (cr), © Tony Freeman/PhotoEdit; 141 (b), © Bettmannn/CORBIS; 149 (both), National Archives (NARA); 152 (br), Dennis Cook/AP/Wide World Photos; 154-155 (bc), © Mark Wilson/ Getty Images; 154, © Royalty-Free/CORBIS; 155, © Brooks Kraft/CORBIS; 166 (bl), © Yang Liu/CORBIS; (bc), Norm Detlaff, Las Cruces Sun-News/AP/Wide World Photos; 167 (bl), ©Alex Webb/Magnum Photos; (bc), © David Young-Wolff/PhotoEdit; (br), © Bettmann/CORBIS; 171, Library of Congress/PRC Archive; 173, Library of Congress; 175 (l), © Bettmann/CORBIS; 175 (r), © Oscar White/CORBIS; 176 (tl), Dr. Hector P. Garcia Papers, Special Collections & Archives, Texas A&M University-Corpus Christi, Bell Library; 176 (tr), ©1978 Matt Herron/TakeStock; 176 (tc), Texas State Library & Archives Commission; 179, © Daily News Pix; 181, © Spencer Grant/PhotoEdit; 182-183 (b), © Ariel Skelley/CORBIS; 185, © David Butow/CORBIS; 186 (tl), ©James Pickerell/The Image Works; 186 (tr), © Brownie Harris/CORBIS; 187 (tl), © Ariel Skelly/CORBIS; (tc), Janet Knott/The Boston Globe. Republished with permission of The Globe Newspaper Company, Inc.; (tr), © Jeff Greenberg/ PhotoEdit. **Chapter 6:** Pages 192-193 (t), © Miles Ertman/Masterfile; 192, © Christie's Images; 193 (bl), Giraudon/Art Resource, NY; 193 (r), Art Resource, NY; 196-197 (b), ©SuperStock; 197, © The New York Public Library, Miriam and Ira D. Wallch Division of Art, Prints and Photographs, Astor, Lenox and Tilden Foundations / Art Resource, NY; 199, (inset) (#1907.32) © Collection of The New-York Historical Society; 202 (c), Photo ©2004 Roger Foley; 202 (b), © Joseph Sohm; Chromosohm, Inc./CORBIS; 203 (l), Stock Montage, Inc.; 203 (r), Stock Montage/Getty Images; 205, Réunion des Musées Nationaux/Art Resource, NY; 206 (l), Chicago Historical Society, #i35980aa; 206 (r), Library of Congress/PRC Archive; 207, HRW Photo Research Library; 208, Courtesy Ohio Historical Society; 210, © Museum of the City of New York/CORBIS ; 213 (tl), ©The New York Historical Society, New York, NY/ Bridgeman Art Library; 213 (tc), The Art Archive/Chateau de Blernacourt/Dagli Orti; 213 (tr), ©The New-York Historical Society, New York, NY/ Bridgeman Art Library; 213 (bl), Independence National Historical Park Collection; 213 (bc), The Henry Luce III Center for the Study of American Culture/ SuperStock; 213 (br), National Portrait Gallery, Smithsonian Institution, Washington, DC/Art Resource, NY; 214, Library of Congress/PRC Archive.

Unit Three. Pages 222-223 (Art Ref) ©Tom Bean/CORBIS. **Chapter 7:** Pages 224-225 (t), Superstock; 224, The Granger Collection, New York; 225 (bl), New Haven Colony Historical Society, Gift of George W. Crawford, 1973. #1973.20.C; 225 (cl), Benninghoff Collection of the American Revolution; 225 (cr), Portrait of the Founder, Munetada Kurozumi. Image courtesy of Kurozumikyo Shinto; 225 (cr), Library of Congress, LC-USZC4-6466; 229 (l), The Art Archive/Chateau de Blernacourt/Dagli Orti; 229 (r), © Bettmann/CORBIS; 229 bkgd © Alan Schein Photography/CORBIS; 231 (b), Getty Images; 232 (t), Washington and Lee University; 239, © Terry W. Eggers/CORBIS; 242 (l), The Mariners Museum; (r), North Wind Picture Archives; 243 (t), North Wind Picture Archives; 243 (bl), The Granger Collection, New York; 243 (br), © 1993 Mickey Osterreischer/Black Star; 244 (l), ©The Field Museum, Neg #A93851.1c, Chicago.; 244 (r), National Portrait Gallery, Smithsonian Institution, Washington, DC; gift of Mrs. Herbert Lee Pratt, Jr.; 248 (b), ©Bettmann/ CORBIS; 248(inset) © New-York Historical Society/Bridgeman Art Library. **Chapter 8:** Pages 256-257 (t), © Lee Snider/Photo Images/CORBIS ; 256, National Portrait Gallery, Smithsonian Institution, Washington, DC/Art Resource, NY; 257 (tl), The Granger Collection, New York; 257 (tr), Library of Congress #LC-USZC4-5801; 257 (bl), The Granger Collection, New York; 257 (br), Courtesy PRC Archive; 265 (t), © Bettmann/ CORBIS; 265 (b), Maryland Historical Society, Baltimore, Maryland; 266 (cl), (Art Reference) Chicago Historical Society; 270 (l), Hampton University Museum, Hampton, Virginia.; 271 (tl), Library of Congress; 271 (bl), © Andre Jenny/Alamy Photos; 271 (tr), © Bettmann/ CORBIS; 271 (br), American Antiquarian Society; 272 (b), Smithsonian American Art Museum, Washington DC/Art Resource, NY; 273, © Francis G. Mayer/CORBIS; **Chapter 9:** Pages 280-281, Detroit Publishing Company Collection, from *Birth of A Century*, KEA Publishing Services Ltd.; 280 (b), The Granger Collection, New York; 281 (tl), Janice L. and David J. Frent Collection of Political Americana; 281 (tr), National Portrait Gallery, Smithsonian Institution/Art Resource, NY; 281 (bl), The Stapleton Collection, UK/ Bridgeman Art Library; 281 (br), The Art Archive; 285 (t), R.W. Norton Art Gallery, Shreveport, LA. Used by permission; 285 (b), David Young-Wolff/PhotoEdit; 286-287 (bl), (Art Reference) © Board of Trustees, National Gallery of Art, Washington; 287 (br), The Hermitage, Home of Andrew Jackson; 289 (l), The Fine Arts Museum of San Francisco, Gift of Eleanor Martin, 37566; (c), Christie's Images/ Bridgeman Art Library; (r), American Museum of Textile History; 296, © Collection of The New-York Historical Society; 299, Superstock. **Chapter 10:** Pages 304-305 (t), Seaver Center for Western History Research, Natural History Museum of Los Angeles County; 305 (tl), Used by permission, Utah State Historical Society, all rights reserved; 305 (tr), © The Oakland Museum, The City of Oakland; 305 (bl), Peter Newark's Western Americana; 305 (br), Library of Congress, LC-USZC4-1307/PRC Archive; 309, © Bettmann/CORBIS; 313, (both), Courtesy of *Texas Highways* Magazine; 314, Jack Lewis/TxDOT; 315, Texas State Library and Archives Commission; 317 (t), Janice L. and David J. Frent Collection of Political Americana; 317 (b), American Antiquarian Society; 318-319 (b), James Walker, *Vaqueros in a Horse Corral*, 1877, #0126.1480, From the Collection of Gilcrease Museum, Tulsa, Oklahoma.; 319 (br), (Art Reference) Courtesy The Bancroft Library, University of California, Berkeley; 321 (t), Society of California Pioneers; 322-323, Texas State Library and Archives Commission; 324, J. Griffiths Smith/TxDOT; 327, (both)Collection of Matthew Isenburg; 328 (t), Courtesy of the California History Room, California State Library, Sacramento, California; 329 (tl), Seaver Center for Western History Research, Natural History Museum of Los Angeles County; 330, Library of Congress. #LC-USZC4-7421; 332-333, Courtesy Steve Pinkston; 333 (inset), Bob Burch/ Index Stock Imagery, Inc.

Unit Four. Chapter 11: Pages 342-343 (t), © Marilyn Root/Index Stock Imagery, Inc.; 342 (b), New York State Historical Association, Cooperstown; 343 (inset),George Eastman House; 343 (cl), PRC Archive; 343 (cr), © Southeast Museum; 343 (bl), NASA; 343 (br), © CORBIS; 348 (l), Samuel Finley

Breese Morse, Eli Whitney (1765-1825), Yale University Art Gallery. Gift of George Hoadley, B.A. 1801; 348 (r), Museum of Connecticut History; 349 (l), Museum of Connecticut History; 349 (r), New Haven Colony Historical Society; 350, © Bob Krist/CORBIS ; 353, Rhode Island Historical Society; 354, Jack Naylor Collection; 359, Library of Congress, Detroit Publishing Company Collection; 364, Museum of Connecticut History; 365 (t), (Art Ref) Stock Montage, Inc.; 365 (bl), Smithsonian Institution, Washington, DC (Photograph by Charles Phillips); 365 (br), Courtesy John Deere & Company Archives; 366 (l), National Museum of American History, Smithsonian Institution, Washington, DC (#89-6626); 366 (r), The Granger Collection, New York. **Chapter 12:** 372-373, Penn School Papers, Southern Historical Collection, University of North Carolina at Chapel Hill, Wilson Library, #P.3615/0824(A); 372, National Museum of American History, Smithsonian Institution, Washington, DC. Photo by Kim Neilson, #83-2953; 373 (bc), © Hulton-Deutsch Collection/ CORBIS; 373 (br), Library of Congress; 384 (tl), The Valentine Museum; 384 (tr), Collection of the American Numismatic Society, New York; 387 (b), The J. Paul Getty Museum, Los Angeles; 388-389 (t), *Hauling the Whole Week's Pickings* by William Henry Brown, The Historic New Orleans Collection; 389 (tr), South Carolina Historical Society; 390, North Wind Picture Archives. **Chapter 13:** Pages 396-397 (t), The Metropolitan Museum of Art, Gift of I.N. Phelps Stokes, Edward S. Hawes, Alice Mary Hawes, Marion Augusta Hawes, 1937.[37.14.22]. All rights reserved, The Metropolitan Museum of Art.; 397 (cl), Courtesy of the Massachusetts Historical Society; 397 (cr), PRC Archive; 397 (bl), Photo © David Modica, courtesy American Printing House for the Blind Museum; 397 (br), Peter Newark's American Pictures; 401 (c), Wiliam B. Becker Collection/ American Museum of Photography; 405, © Royalty-Free/CORBIS; 406-407, Brooklyn Museum of Art, Gift of the Brooklyn Institute of Arts and Sciences/ Bridgeman Art Library; 411 (r), The Metropolitan Museum of Art; 413 (t), (Art Reference) Library of Congress, #LC-USZC4-7396; 414-415, Courtesy of Oberlin Archives; 415 (inset) Museum of Art, Rhode Island School of Design. Gift of Lucy T. Aldrich; 417 (t), Trustees of the Boston Public Library; 418, Library of Congress; 419 (t), Courtesy of the Levi Coffin House Association and Waynet; 419 (b), Courtesy of The Brooklyn Museum of Art [40.59]; 420, Library of Congress; 421 (c), Courtesy of the Massachusetts Historical Society; 422 (l), (art reference) PRC Archive; 422 (r), Library of Congress, Manuscript Division; 424 (l), Courtesy of the Massachusetts Historical Society; 424 (r), The Granger Collection, New York; 425 (l), Courtesy of the Susan B. Anthony House, Rochester, NY; 425 (r), Library of Congress/PRC Archive; 427, Stock Montage, Inc.; 428, © Bettmann/CORBIS; 429 (bl), (Art Reference) Susan B. Anthony House; 429 (r), © 1973 Historical Documents Co. Harcourt Photo by Maria Paraskevas; 435 (bl), The Art Archive/ Private Collection/Dagli Orti; **Chapter 14:** Pages 434-453, (t), © Dave G. Houser; 435 (bl) The Art Archive/Private Collection/Dagli Orti; 435 (br), India Office Library & Records, The British Library; 435 (cr), Chicago Historical Society; 435 (cl), Nancy Gewitz/Antique Textile Resources; 440, PRC Archive; 442, The J. Paul Getty Museum, Los Angeles; 445, Library of Congress, LC-USZ62-92043; 448 (t), Kansas Museum of History; 448 (b), Kansas State Historical Society, Topeka, Kansas; 451, Getty Images; 452, Missouri Historical Society; 453, Library of Congress/PRC Archive; 454 (r), The Museum of American Political Life, University of Hartford, West Hartford, CT; 454 (tl), Picture History; 456 (t), Ohio Historical Society; 489, Naval Historical Center.

Unit Five. Chapter 15: Pages 466-467, Steve Stone w/special thanks to The American Civil War Society of the United Kingdom, 2nd

Wisconsin Volunteer Infantry (esp. 1st Lt. Tom Reed & Private James Reed), and the 18th Virginia Infantry, Company G (esp. Stuart Colquitt). 468-469 (t), Library of Congress, Brady Civil War Photo Collection; 468 (b), Confederate Museum, United Daughters of the Confederacy; 469 (cl), © SuperStock; 469 (cr), © SuperStock; 469 (b), Chicago Historical Society, # i26736aa; 479 (t), © Medford Historical Society Collection/ CORBIS; 480, National Park Service; 481 (b), Library of Congress; 482, Library of Congress/ PRC Archive; 485 (b), © 1989, The Greenwich Workshop, Inc., Reproduced with the permission of the Greenwich Workshop, Inc., Shelton, CT; 489, Naval Historical Center; 490, SuperStock; 491, South Carolina Historical Society; 492 (l), Courtesy of the Massachusetts Historical Society; (r) Library of Congress; 494, © Bettmann/ CORBIS; 495 (t), National Museum of American History, Smithsonian Institution, Washington, DC (ID#84-9312); 495 (b), © REUTERS/Kai Pfaffenbach/CORBIS; 496, American Antiquarian Society; 502, © SuperStock; 503, © Topham / The Image Works; 504, 506, The Granger Collection, New York; **Chapter 16:** Pages 508-509 (t), © Paul Rocheleau; 508 (b), © Kean Collection/Getty Images; 509 (cl), The Granger Collection, New York; 509 (cr), Herbert F. Johnson Museum of Art, Cornell University; 509 (bl), © Michael Maslan Historic Photographs/ CORBIS; 512-513 (b), National Archives (NARA); 514 (t), Library of Congress; 514 (inset), Chicago Historical Society; 515, University of Texas at El Paso Library, Special Collections Department, Ada Tharp Photograph Collection; 516, © William Gladstone Collection; 519, Library of Congress; 520 (l), Library of Congress; 520 (r), ©CORBIS; 522, North Wind Picture Archives; 525 (both), Library of Congress; 526, The Granger Collection, New York; 527, Tennessee State Museum Collection. Photography by June Dorman; 528, Getty Images; 529 (b), North Wind Picture Archives; 530, Courtesy of The Charleston Renaissance Gallery, Robert M. Hicklin, Jr. Inc., Charleston, South Carolina; 531, © Bettmann/CORBIS. **Chapter 17:** Pages 542-543 (t), © James L. Amos/CORBIS; 542 (b), Courtesy Wells Fargo Bank; 543 (cl), Southern Pacific Lines/PRC Archive; 543 (cr), © CORBIS; 543 (bl), The Art Archive /Musée d'Orsay Paris/ Dagli Orti; 543 (br), The Granger Collection, New York; 548 (l), Denver Public Library, Western History Collection; 548-549 (r), Nebraska State Historical Society, Photograph Collections; 549, Bob Boze Bell, *True West* Magazine; 550, © James L. Amos/CORBIS; 551, Library of Congress/PRC Archive; 552, The Granger Collection, New York; 553, SuperStock; 555, George Lane/AP/Wide World Photos; 556-557, © Bettmann/CORBIS; 557, Western History Division, National Museum of American History/Smithsonian Institution, Washington, DC; 558, The Granger Collection, New York; 559 (r) Janice & David Frent Collection of Political Americana; 561, Western History Collections, University of Oklahoma; 562 (t), Elias Carr Papers, East Carolina Manuscript Collection, J.Y. Joyner Library, East Carolina University, Greenville, NC. Photo by Dewane Frutiger; 562 (bl), Library of Congress; 562 (br), Courtesy of the Northern Indiana Center for History; 563 (l), Culver Pictures; 565, © CORBIS **Chapter 18:** Pages 570-571 (t), PRC Archive; 571 (c), George Meany Memorial Archives; 571 (bl), ©Bettmann/ CORBIS; 571 (br), Archives Larousse, Paris, France/Bridgeman Art Library; 574-575, Library of Congress; 576 (r), [neg. #40578] © Collection of The New York Historical Society; 577 (l), Property of AT&T Archives. Printed with permission of AT&T; (r), © Hulton Archive/ Getty Images; 578 (l), © CORBIS; (r), Library of Congress/PRC Archive; 579, Montgomery County Historical Society; 580, © CORBIS; 580 (inset), Courtesy of the Rockefeller Archive Center; 581, [#71880T] © Collection of The New-York Historical Society; 583 (l), (Art Ref) AP/Wide World Photos & © Bettmann/CORBIS; 583 (c), (Art Ref) AP/Wide World Photos; 583 (r), (Art Reference) Photo courtesy Union Pacific

Historical Collection; 585 (t), Brown Brothers; 585 (b), (Art Ref) © Bettmann/CORBIS; 589 (l), Copyright The New York Public Library/Art Resource, NY; (r), © Joseph Sohm, Chromosohm, Inc./CORBIS; 590 (l), National Archives, #90-G-152-2038; (r), Shades of L.A. Archives/Los Angeles Public Library; 591 (l), © CORBIS; 591 (r), Col. Ernest Swanson Papers, Swenson Swedish Immigration Research Center, Augustana College, Rock Island, IL; 592 (r), © A. Ramey/PhotoEdit; 595, Chicago Historical Society; 596 (l), Jane Addams Memorial Collection (JAMC neg 227), Special Collections, University Library, University of Illinois at Chicago; 596 (r), Curt Teich Postcard Archives, Lake County, IL Museum; 599, ©Bettmann/CORBIS. **Chapter 19:** Pages 602-603 (t), Elizabeth Cady Stanton Trust; 603 (cl, cr), Janice L. and David J. Frent Collection of Political Americana; 603 (b), The Granger Collection, New York; 608-609, PRC Archive; 609 (r), The Granger Collection, New York; 612, Museum of the City of New York, Jacob Riis Collection 502; 613, LifeCare Alliance/Ohio Historical Society; 615, National Archives; 616, Library of Congress; 618, Courtesy of Steve Latham; 623, © Bettmann/CORBIS; 625, Seaver Center for Western History Research, Natural History Museum of Los Angeles County; 626, Dr. Ching Collection/ PRC Archive; 628, Leroy Radanovich/Yosemite Museum; 628-629, © W. Perry Conway/CORBIS; 630, Stock Montage, Inc.; 635, Library of Congress. **Chapter 20:** Pages 636-637 (t), © Bettmann/CORBIS; 636 (b), © Charles Sleicher; 637 (c), Denver Public Library, Western History Collection; 637 (bl), Press Information Bureau of India; 641, Naval Parade, held in honor of commander George Dewey (1837-1917) 1898 (oil on canvas) by Fred Pansing (1854-1912) Museum of the City of New York, USA / Bridgeman Art Library; 642, © CORBIS; 643, National Portrait Gallery, Smithsonian Institution/ Art Resource, NY; 644, Trustees of the British Museum; 647 (t), PRC Archive; 647 (b), © Bettmann/CORBIS; 648, National Archives/PRC Archive; 649, Courtesy Frederic Remington Art Museum, Ogdensburg, New York; 650, Keystone-Mast Collection (KU58458)/University of California at Riverside/ California Museum of Photography; 654, © Danny Lehman/CORBIS; 656, The Granger Collection, New York; 659, 660, © Bettmann/ CORBIS; **Back Matter.** Pages R1-R5, White House Historical Association (White House Collection); R5 (last) The White House, photo by Eric Draper.

Staff Credits. The people who contributed to *Holt Middle School U.S. History* are listed below. They represent editorial, design, intellectual property resources, production, emedia, and permissions.

Lissa B. Anderson, Melanie Baccus, Charles Becker, Jessica Bega, Ed Blake, Gillian Brody, Shirley Cantrell, Erin Cornett, Rose Degollado, Chase Edmond, Mescal Evler, Rhonda Fariss, Marsh Flournoy, Leanna Ford, Bob Fullilove, Matthew Gierhart, Janet Harrington, Rhonda Haynes, Rob Hrechko, Wilonda Ieans, Cathy Jenevinein, Shannon Johnston, Kadonna Knape, Aylin Koker, Cathy Kuhles, Debbie Lofland, Bob McClellan, Joe Melomo, Richard Metzger, Cynthia Munoz, Karl Pallmeyer, Chanda Pearmon, Shelly Ramos, Désirée Reid, Curtis Riker, Marleis Roberts, Diana Rodriguez, Gene Rumann, Annette Saunders, Kay Selke, Ken Shepardson, Michele Shukers, Chris Smith, Elaine Tate, Jeannie Taylor, Joni Wackwitz, Ken Whiteside